The Cistercians in the
Early Middle Ages

Dedicated to

MADALINE STAPYLTON
(1899–1992)

whose hospitality in Cambridge for thirty-six years
enabled me to use the University Library

THE CISTERCIANS IN THE EARLY MIDDLE AGES

Written to Commemorate the Nine Hundredth Anniversary of
Foundation of the Order at Cîteaux in 1098

Under the Patronage of
Blessed Vincent Kadłubek
Bishop of Kraków (1208–18)
Monk of Jędrzejów (1218–1223)

David H. Williams

First published in 1998

Gracewing
Fowler Wright Books
2 Southern Avenue
Leominster
Herefordshire HR6 0QF

© David H. Williams 1998

ISBN 0 85244 350 1

Typesetting by
Action Typesetting Ltd, Gloucester, GL1 1SP

Printed by Cromwell Press
Trowbridge, Wiltshire BA14 0XB

CONTENTS

LIST OF MAPS

Maps:

1. Distribution and Growth of the Order
2. St Bernard's Journeys (1)
3. St Bernard's Journeys (2)
4. Expansion of the Order
5. Lineage within the Order
6. Approximate Routes taken to the General Chapter
7. Comparative Values
8. Origins of the Monks of Abbey Dore
9. Abbeys where Edward I stayed
10. Fortifications
11. Abbey Sites (1)
12. Abbey Sites (2)
13. Winter and Summer Dwellings
14. Land Expansion and Consolidation
15. Granges in the Netherlands
16. Llanfair Cilgoed Grange
17. Mill Sites
18. Delimitation of Pasture Rights
19. Transhumant Routes
20. Sources of Salt
21. Urban Property
22. Cistercian Nunneries

Plans

1. The Gate-House of Dargun Abbey
2. English Precinct Plans
3. The Twelfth and Thirteenth Century Churches of Tintern Abbey
4. Cloister Complex of Neath Abbey

Figures

1. Thirteenth Century Problems
2. Appropriation of Churches in SW France
3. French Cistercian Viticulture

LIST OF PLATES

Grace Dieu Abbey (Wales), mid-14th C: *Society of Antiquaries of London; plate – National Museum of Wales;* (4). Common Seal, Paradyż Abbey, Poland, by 1386: *KD III, 1857* – courtesy of Prof. A. Wyrwa, Collegium Historicum, Poznan: *plate – Piotr Namiota*; (5). Seal of the Abbot of Cîteaux, France, 1227: *by kind permission of Sir David Watkin Williams-Wynn; plate – National Library of Wales.* (6). Second Seal of St Bernard, 1151: *Service Photographique des Archives Nationales, Paris;* (7). Seal of Fra Diotallevi, *conversus* of Fossanova Abbey, Italy, mid-14th C: *courtesy of Bargello Museum.*

PREFACE

When I was a boy of about ten years old, and in the course of visiting family friends in Leeds during the Second World War, my late mother took me to Roundhay Park. It was my first contact, so far as I know, with what was once a Cistercian property, a manor of Kirkstall Abbey in Yorkshire. Years later, whilst reading historical geography at Cambridge, I came more fully into the field of Cistercian studies, preparing a short thesis on monastic economy in my native Monmouthshire. This present book, which has slowly emerged (due to the pressure of conflicting interests) over the last twenty-five years, happily coincides with the nine hundredth anniversary of the founding of the New Monastery at Cîteaux on March 21st, 1098. It deliberately covers the first two hundred and fifty years of the Order's existence, for after the Black Death its so-called 'Golden Age' had given way to an Order which was greatly changed.

I owe a special debt of gratitude to those who stimulated in me a liking for history and geography in my teenage years: Mr Edward Evans and Miss Gwyneth Meara of Bassaleg School, Gwent and to Mr Vaughan Lewis, on whose recommendation I was admitted to Trinity College, Cambridge, to read for the Geographical Tripos. Over the years, I have been greatly encouraged by several members of the Order, and not least Father Edmund Mikkers (for many years Editor of *Cîteaux*) and Frère Jean-François Holthof (formerly Prior of Cîteaux). Too many scholars to mention here have assisted in translating portions of texts in modern languages, the greatest burden falling on Mr Jack Roberts of Monmouth (from Italian) and Mr Louis Seigne of Wells (from German). Several other scholars in the field (again too numerous to record individually) have gladly answered enquiries, whilst, between them, Diane Drayson, Mr Martin Murphy and Dr David Robinson have cast a critical eye over much of the text. Most of the photographs result from my own photographic endeavour; others (and plans utilised) are acknowledged in their place. I have left to the last the person to whom this book owes most, and that is Mr Colin Williams, formerly Senior Assistant in the Department of Archaeology and Numismatics at the National Museum of Wales. It is his expertise as a draughtsman which has rendered my draft maps and plans into the fine finished form in which they are reproduced in these pages.

The precise number of male Cistercian abbeys is difficult to ascertain, perhaps in the region of six hundred and fifty or even more. I am happy to say that almost all of them find some mention in this book. They are listed (with an indication of their country) in the first section of the Index.

Last, but far from least, I express my thanks to Gracewing, and especially Mr Tom Longford its Managing Director, and Miss Jo Ashworth, its Publications Manager, for their kindness and interest in bringing this work into the published domain. We have been much encouraged by grants from the Catherine and Lady Grace James Foundation, from the Reverend Gerald Flood, and from the present-day Cistercian Abbeys of the Genesee, Piffard, St Joseph's, Spencer, the Holy Spirit, Conyers, and of Wettingen-Mehrerau.

Aberhafesp,   David H. Williams
St Bernard's Day, 1997

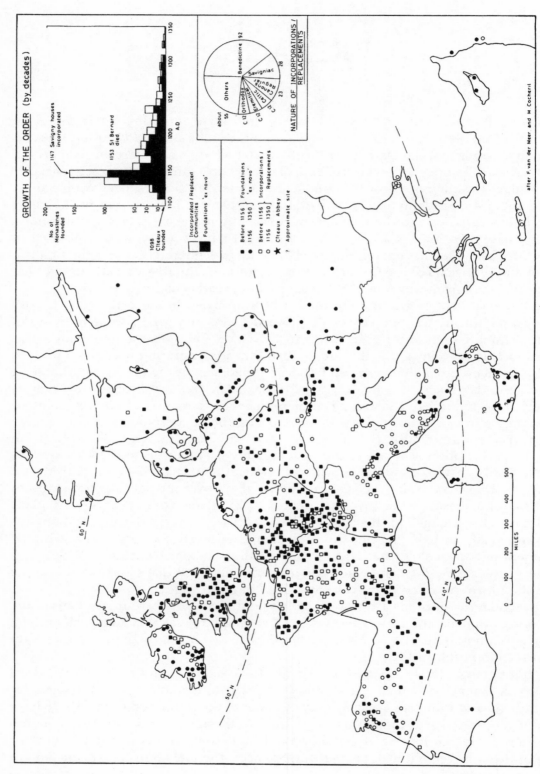

GROWTH OF THE ORDER (by decades)

NATURE OF INCORPORATIONS / REPLACEMENTS

Benedictine 92

Savigniac 28

C. 12 Augustinian Canons Regular 23

C. 12 Premonstratensian

C. 12 Celtic

C. 12 Orthodox

about 55 Others

No. of Monasteries founded

1147 Savigny houses incorporated

1153 St Bernard died

1098 Cîteaux founded

Incorporated / Replaced Communities

Foundations 'ex novo'

Before 1156 } Foundations 1156 1350 } 'ex novo'

Before 1156 } Incorporations / 1156 1350 } Replacements

★ Cîteaux Abbey

? Approximate site

50° N

40° N

50° N

50° N

MILES

0 100 200 300 400 500

after F. van der Meer and M. Cocheril

Map 1: Reproduced from the author's *Atlas of Cistercian Lands in Wales* (University of Wales Press, Cardiff; 1990). Drawn by Miss M. H. Bigwood

Chapter 1

ORIGINS AND EXPANSION

The Emergence of Cîteaux

In apostolic times Christians attempted to live in community with only transient success (Acts 2:44). The third century saw the emergence in the Egyptian desert of many solitaries who soon grouped into communities – especially under the influence of Pachomius (*c.* 290–346). Monastic life had started and evolved in the fourth century along quite severe lines following the work of Cassian (*c.* 360–435). His *Institutes* were superseded when Benedict of Nursia (*c.* 480–*c.* 530) wrote his *Rule*, a demanding yet moderated way of coenobitic life, which has inspired the régime of monasteries ever since[1]. In course of time Benedictine monasticism often departed from the simplicity of the *Rule*, and especially in the large congregation headed by the abbot of Cluny – with its lack of emphasis on manual labour, its absence of a proper period of novitiate, and its possession of tithes, serfs, and large landed estates. The reaction of many eleventh-century monks was to try to observe the Rule more closely. Amongst them were the reformers of Cîteaux[2]. Later, St Bernard of Clairvaux (1115–53) was to have a harsh dialogue with Peter the Venerable, abbot of Cluny (*c.* 1122–56)[3]. When, two centuries on, the Cistercians had lost much of their early 'simplicity', the two traditions were reconciled. In 1280 the Cistercians received the house of Cluny into spiritual fraternity, and from 1321 both Orders observed as major days the feasts of their famous pillars, St Bernard and St Hugh[4].

The Cistercian Order was not without antecedents[5]; many of its basic principles were but a synthesis of important notions suggested by other near-contemporaneous endeavours, and its development in parts of Europe walked hand-in-hand and along partly the same lines as other new ways of monasticism, notably the reforms of Tiron (1109)[6] and Prémontré (1121)[7], as well as (from 1084) the Carthusians – with whom there was a certain empathy[8]. The eleventh century was a time of renewal within the Church, and Cîteaux's origins owed much to this. Basic were the reforms advocated by Pope Gregory VII (1073–85) who urged clerical disengagement from worldly affairs[9]. Provincial assemblies also exhorted religious to live in simplicity, and stressed the importance of the component elements of Benedictine life (as silence and fasting); among them the Synods of Toulouse (1068) and of Rouen (1074). The Council of Poitiers (1078) discouraged monasteries from acquiring parish churches and their tithes, while the Council of Meaux (1082) emphasised that a religious community should not be less than ten in number[10]. Individual preachers, as Raymond of the Melinais (ob. 1103), favoured solitude by condemning the siting of monasteries in, or near, cities[11].

All these elements played a part in early Cistercian thinking, as did the contemporaneous *pauperes Christi* movement encouraged by Gregory VII[12]. The idea that the monks were 'the poor of Christ' (a term later used by St Bernard)[13] imitating 'Christ who Himself became poor' (*cf.* 2 Corinthians 8:9), was alluded to by benefactors in their charters, especially those granted to the abbeys of central and eastern Europe[14]. The eleventh century was also a period when the eremitical way of life was once again at a peak, stressing the virtues of withdrawal and silence[15]. A number of Cistercian houses were to evolve from hermitages or groups of hermits. Other reforms which gave spiritual seekers food for thought, included the congregation of Vallombrosa (fd 1039) whose religious kept strict silence and developed a system of visitation; the Carthusians (fd 1084) who wore white habits and practised manual labour; and the Grandmontines (all over France by 1100) whose policy of rejecting tithes made them feel 'no need to keep charters'[16]. There were not only antecedents, there were also precedents. Robert, who was to be the first abbot of Cîteaux, had twice left his monastery to lead a more austere life with groups of hermits[17]. It was out of one such foray that he founded the Burgundian abbey of Molesme (1075), basing it on traditional Cluniac usages[18], and it was against the background of all these several religious movements that the 'reform of Cîteaux' emerged.

The monastery at Molesme, despite a difficult start, grew to be economically flourishing, and the religious life there, while by no means decadent, left room for improvement in some eyes[19], with the consequence that certain dissatisfied monks left the abbey (about 1096) for its cell at Aulps, which was raised to abbey status and later itself became Cistercian (1136), possibly following a visit by St Bernard[20]. Severe tensions persisted at Molesme between those monks content with its territorial expansion and financial growth, and others disquieted and wishing to lead a simpler life. The upshot was that after Easter 1097, abbot Robert and twenty-one other monks (including prior Alberic and secretary Stephen Harding) left Molesme, and with the backing of the papal legate (Archbishop Hugh of Lyons) eventually settled ninety-six kilometres (60 miles) further south[21]. The new site was at Cîteaux (in later tradition a marshy, forested area), its Latin form – *Cistercium* – giving the adjectival 'Cistercian'[22]. The precise date of foundation is ascribed to 21 March, 1098 – both Palm Sunday and St Benedict's Day that year[23]. The monks remaining at Molesme complained bitterly that they needed abbot Robert back, although he was eighty years old, and (so ordered by the legate) he returned there in 1099, with perhaps a majority of the secessionists[24].

Robert may not have been the prime mover in the establishment of Cîteaux; he may have become involved simply because he was unable to control the differing factions at Molesme, as indeed he had once resigned the abbacy of St Benignus, Dijon (1068)[25]. His but brief stay at Cîteaux meant that many twelfth-century Cistercians did not regard him as truly its first abbot[26]; as late as 1190 Conrad of Eberbach berated him for 'desertion'[27], and it was not until 1222 that he was honoured liturgically in the Order[28]. Robert was succeeded at Cîteaux by prior Alberic (abbot, 1099–1109), to whose prudence must be ascribed much of the early stability of the 'New Monastery', as the founding fathers called it[29]. To counter still pressing demands from Molesme he obtained from Paschal II (1100) the bull *Desiderium quod*, commonly referred to as the 'Roman Privilege', intended to still opposition to the New Monastery[30]. Even more outstanding was the third abbot, Stephen Harding (1109–33). An Englishman, an erudite scholar educated at Sherborne, he is credited with much of the constitutional development of the Order[31], and was praised for contributing to its success by English, Danish and German chroniclers[32]. A trained scribe, he completed an illuminated bible, and oversaw the early development of the Cistercian chants, hymnal and breviary[33]. It was because of the flair of abbots Alberic and Stephen that Cîteaux became the 'first of many brethren'(*cf*. Romans 8:29), and (by 1113) a force to be reckoned with[34], of which the young St Bernard heard. It is well to remember that when the founding fathers settled at Cîteaux in 1098 it was to establish a 'New Monastery', where their community could live in simplicity; they could have had no idea that it would become the precursor and primate of a vast religious Order, penetrating the whole of the civilised world[35].

The Influence of St Bernard (1090–1153)

If SS. Robert, Alberic and Stephen laid firm foundations, it was Bernard, more than any other individual, who must be credited with facilitating the rapid expansion of the Cistercian Order. Born of noble descent, he was but twenty-three when he sought admission at Cîteaux, rather than at a Cluniac house, because, he said, his 'weak character needed strong medicine'[36]. He was accompanied by several relatives and friends (including three of his brothers), and later his father, Tescelin, and his youngest brother, Nivard, were also professed[37]. This large group of novices has been portrayed as proving to be the salvation of a declining and ageing community; nothing could be further from the truth. By the time Bernard entered Cîteaux (1113, not 1112 as previously supposed), the number of monks was more than sufficient to allow the foundation of its first two daughter-houses: La Ferté (May 1113) and Pontigny (a year later)[38]. Further, the numbers actually accompanying St Bernard may have been exaggerated in later hagiography[39]. What is significant is that Stephen Harding quickly appreciated the young Bernard's worth, sending him in 1115, after only two years of monastic formation, to lead a new community at Clairvaux over one hundred kilometres (63 miles) north. He remained abbot there for nearly forty years, until his death in 1153.

During Bernard's long abbacy at Clairvaux three hundred monasteries were established within the new Order, sixty-eight of them by Clairvaux, and without Bernard this would not have happened. He was a bundle of energy, a driving force and a dynamic personality – despite quite severe ill-health. He undertook very considerable journeys – though there is no record of his ever crossing the seas. His literary output was considerable, he was a famed and sought-after crusading preacher, and the frank adviser of popes and monarchs. He outstripped in esteem the founding fathers, so much so that the 'Cistercians' were sometimes called 'Bernardines'[40]. Under his tutelage at least seven monks rose to the episcopate – something which Bernard shrank from, declining election at both Langres and Rheims[41]. One of his monks was to become pope (Eugenius III, 1145–53). Bernard's was a household name, and his prestige as a colossus on the clerical scene could not do otherwise than help make the twelfth-century Cistercian Order a movement to which men of breeding and learning flocked. For the first ten years of his abbacy he perhaps only left Clairvaux on normal abbatial duties, but, early a protegé of Bishop William of Châlons-sur-Marne[42] and becoming a friend of Count Theobald of Blois[43], Bernard was not long in making his mark on French ecclesiastical affairs, backing (unsuccessfully) Alberic of Rheims for the see of Châlons (1126), helping to bring Archbishop Henry of Sens to a better realisation of his spiritual duties (1128), and urgently coming to the defence of the reforming Bishop Stephen of Paris at variance with his monarch, Louis VI (1129)[44].

It was a Church divided by rival claimants to the papacy that brought Bernard on to the European stage. Invited by King Louis to the Council of Étampes (1130), convoked to treat of the schism, it meant for Bernard, convinced that Innocent II was the rightfully-elected pontiff[45], eight years of travelling, debate and letter-writing[46], in order to establish his ascendancy over the anti-pope, Anacletus II[47]. At the Council of Liège (1131) Bernard stood up to Emperor Lothair (always something of a thorn in the flesh), and he preached that same year to the assembled prelates of the Council of Rheims[48]. In 1134, by journeying to south-west France, he persuaded the Duke of Aquitaine to end his opposition to Innocent, and in 1135 he attended the Diet of

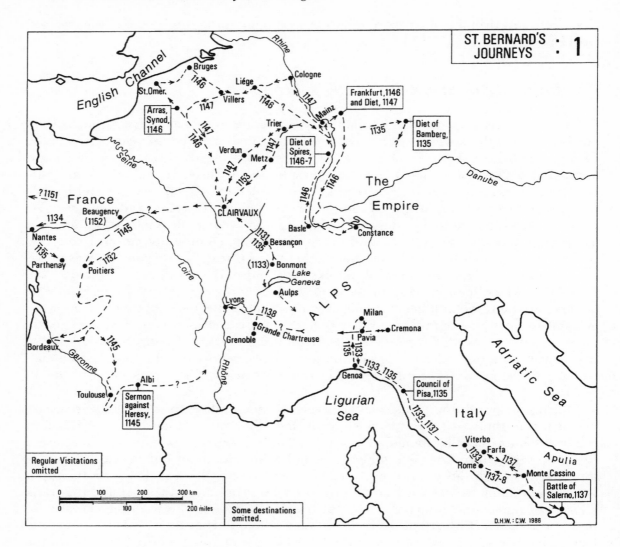

ST. BERNARD'S JOURNEYS : 1

Bamberg which finally brought Germany into line[49]. Thrice he visited Italy in the cause: in 1133, when perhaps he took in the Grand Chartreuse on the way[50]; in 1135, when he attended the Council of Pisa[51], and over the winter of 1137 to 1138, when he confronted King Roger of Sicily on the battlefield of Salerno, and finally in Rome reconciled the party of the now-dead Anacletus to Innocent[53], who, rightly grateful, praised Bernard's 'very great virtues'[54]. Bernard's part in the healing of the schism was for the lasting good of the Church, and assured him of very considerable influence in the remaining fifteen years of his life.

Bernard's reputation as a skilful and compelling preacher led to his involvement in the crusading movement. He was present at the foundation of the Knights Templar at Troyes (1128), he guided the drafting of their new *Rule*[55], and he wrote an appreciation of the new quasi-monastic Order (*De Laude Novae Militiae*)[56]. Having made a missionary journey to combat heresy in Languedoc (1145)[57], he turned his attention to the needs of the Second Crusade. This he fervently supported, seeing it as a just cause[58], by preaching in France, Belgium and Germany, encouraging King Louis VII in his endeavour, and persuading Emperor Conrad to take the Cross[59]. Further than Germany he did not go, but he wrote to the Duke of Bohemia advising him 'to put this business of Christ before everything else'[60]. The Crusade failed, but Bernard continued to be concerned for doctrinal orthodoxy on the home front, urging the crusade against the pagans of central Europe though forbidding any persecution of Jews, whom he called 'the living words of Scripture'[61]. He was himself invited (in 1149) to preach to the 'impious' Russians, Poles and Bohemians, but it was a journey he apparently did not make[62].

It is evident that Bernard spent much time away from his monastery[63]: his third Italian foray alone meant an absence of nine or so months. Often no sooner was he home than he set out again[64]. These great journeys, sometimes accompanied by healing miracles – as at Constance, Troyes and Milan[65] – were not without lasting benefit. His travels publicised the Cistercian Order and brought it new foundations such as Orval, Villers and Aulne, following his visits to Flanders[66]; Chiaravalle di Milano and Chiaravalle di Colomba after his trips to Italy[67]. He won many vocations from fighting men and young knights[68], and was especially successful with young people and students – as on his visits to Flanders (1131), Paris (1140), and Châlons-sur-Marne (1146)[69]. He personally made some notable conversions, comparing the decision of one Flanders lord to take the habit to the resurrection of Lazarus from the tomb[70]. Nor did he neglect the Order, being present, even in very busy years, at the consecration of Fontenay abbey church (1147) and attending the foundation of Cambron (1148)[71]. He continued to travel almost to his dying day[72]. So far as we can tell he never visited Britain, Iberia, or Scandinavia – where there were many houses of the lineage of Clairvaux – unless he did so without it being especially noted whilst on visitation in his early years. Several of his letters though, dealt with a disputed archiepiscopal election at York (1141–43)[73].

Another means by which Bernard publicised the Order was through the written word in which he did not hesitate to firmly address both pope and monarch[74]. Apart from major treatises, over three hundred of his sermons and nearly five hundred of his letters survive[75]. They helped him to be recognised as an oustanding spiritual teacher, they led him to be thought of as the 'last of the Fathers', and they earned him commendation from Innocent III as *Doctor Egregius* ('Excelling Doctor')[76]. His best known writings were: O*n the Degrees of Pride and Humility* – identifying pride as the chief obstacle to monastic progress; *On the Love of God* – an essay in mystical theology; and *On Consideration* – dealing with vital issues of the times. In his *Apology* he told why he became a Cistercian[76]. Not all Bernard's sermons were original, some were written by his notaries and corrected by him[77]. It was in those dwelling on the Song of Songs that he fully revealed and shared his own mystical experiences[78]. As for his letters, an edition of some of them was published by his secretary, Geoffrey, in his life-time[79]. In debate Bernard could be vitriolic[80], and his concern for doctrinal orthodoxy led him to denounce (at the Council of Sens in 1140) the intellectual independence of the fine Latin poet and theologian, Abelard[81].

Great a man as Bernard was, a question remains: how far was he a good monk and a good abbot? He once wrote: 'I have kept the habit of a monk, but I have long abandoned the life'[82]. What was the effect on his community of his frequent absences? The monks once clamoured for his return from Languedoc (1145)[83]. He realised his lack of stability – 'nothing is more remote from my calling?'[84] – but he saw his constant journeying as a necessary response to the needs of the Church[85]. What visitatorial care could he show for the many daughter-houses of Clairvaux – a duty he recognised[86] – busy otherwise as he often was and with some of them lying at a great distance? How far did bouts of acute illness keep him from the common life[87], and from the manual work of which he may not have been over-fond?[88] In his life-time he was criticised for his constant letter-writing, seen as contrary to the spirit of the *Rule*[89], and for the satire and venom (only rhetoric perhaps) that he often employed[90]. He was not always in tune with others of his Order, disagreeing with Isaac of Stella over the issue of soldier-monks[91], and at variance with the views to be expressed by Oger of Locedio on the newly evolving dogma of the Immaculate Conception. Bernard saw Our Lady as

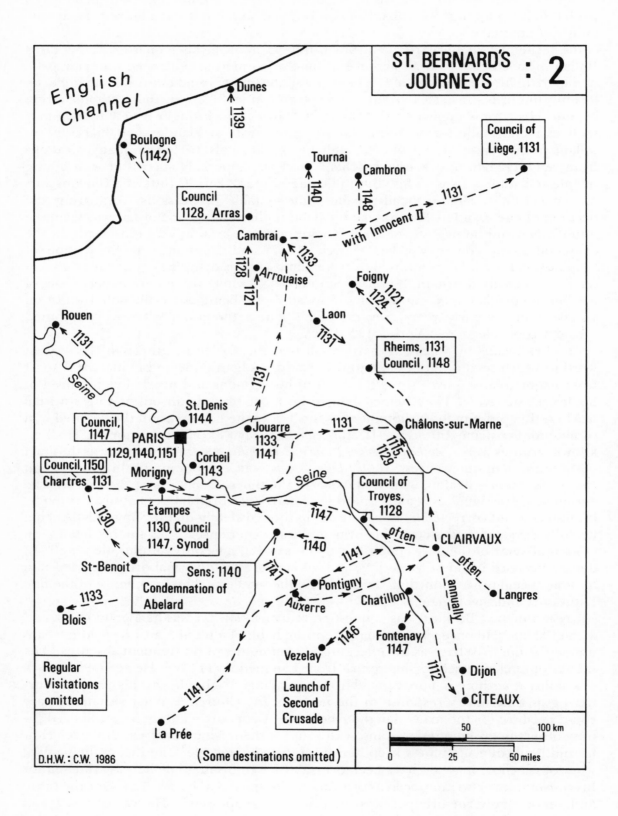

ST. BERNARD'S JOURNEYS : 2

English Channel

Dunes 1139

Boulogne (1142)

Tournai 1140

Cambron 1148

Council of Liège, 1131

Council 1128, Arras

1131 with Innocent II

Cambrai 1133

Arrouaise 1128 1121

Foigny 1121 1124

Laon 1137

Rheims, 1131 Council, 1148

Rouen 1131

Seine

St. Denis 1144

Council, 1147

PARIS 1129, 1140, 1151

Corbeil 1143

Jouarre 1133, 1141

1131

Châlons-sur-Marne

1115, 1129

Council, 1150

Chartres 1131

Morigny

Seine

1147

Council of Troyes, 1128

Étampes 1130, Council 1147, Synod

1130

1140

often

CLAIRVAUX

often annually

1141

St-Benoit

Sens; 1140 Condemnation of Abelard

1147

Pontigny

Chatillon

Langres

1133

Blois

Auxerre

1146

Fontenay 1147

1112

Dijon

Vezelay

CÎTEAUX

Regular Visitations omitted

1141

Launch of Second Crusade

La Prée

D.H.W.: C.W. 1986

(Some destinations omitted)

0   50   100 km
0   25   50 miles

'sanctified in the womb', but 'not conceived holy'[92]. He was especially criticised when the Second Crusade, which he did so much to propound, proved a failure. This troubled him deeply, and perhaps resulted in a degree of public disaffection for the Order[93].

It may have been some of these considerations that delayed Bernard's canonisation until 1174, twenty years after his death, at Clairvaux, on 20th August 1153. The first edition of his *Life* was written in five books, three of them by his former secretary, Geoffrey of Auxerre, one by abbot William of St Thierry, and the other by abbot Ernald of Bonnevaux[94]. The time-gap may have been due also to dissension arising from a revised edition of the *Life* issued by Geoffrey, himself later abbot of Clairvaux (1162–65)[95]. Honour within the Order also came slowly. In 1220 the General Chapter allowed a candle to burn before his shrine[96]; in 1250 the body of his mother, Aleth (ob. 1104) was translated to Clairvaux[97], and in 1260 his obit became a Feast of Sermon and the *conversi* were excused work[98]. In 1280 the new Cistercian colleges at Paris and Oxford were named after him[99]. Bernard had come of age. All great men have their weaknesses, and Bernard in especial had his detractors, but of his sanctity there is no doubt, and of his propelling the Order into a multi-national organisation there can be no question. His life and his standing can best be summed up in the words of a later Bohemian chronicler: 'Bernard was dear to God, and dear to man'[100].

The Backing of the Papacy

The Holy See was the ultimate court of appeal for the new Order when problems arose, and papal support had been vital in its early days[101], especially when Paschal II issued the 'Roman Privilege' (1100) and Calixtus II confirmed the earliest version of the *Charter of Charity* (1119)[102]. There followed a series of edicts in favour of the Cistercians, all of which promoted its autonomy and independence. Innocent II (1132) exempted them from attendance at diocesan synods; Eugenius III (1152) allowed them to hold services in time of interdict, and Lucius III (1184) freed them from the disciplinary authority of diocesan bishops (1184)[103]. For its part the General Chapter supported Alexander III (1159–81) against three successive anti-popes[104]. This policy placed the monasteries of Germany and the county of Burgundy in grave difficulty as Emperor Frederick I (Barbarossa) supported the anti-popes[105]. When opposition to Alexander had all but ceased (1177), after eighteen years, he singled out the abbots of Cîteaux and Clairvaux, together with the Cistercian bishop Bonce of Clermont and St Hugh of Bonnevaux, for their work for peace[106].

The loyalty of the Order may have been borne in mind by successive thirteenth-century popes. Innocent III (1198–1216) created new Cistercian cardinals (strengthening the Order in the Curia)[107], consecrated the abbey church of Fossanova and aided it financially[108], wrote the prayers for Mass on St Bernard's Day[109], and lauded abbot Arnauld I of Cîteaux (much involved in the Albigensian Crusade)[110]. He urged the white monks to undertake evangelical work in Livonia[111], and indeed delegated so many duties to Cistercian personnel that the General Chapter had humbly to ask him to desist[112]. He was succeeded by Honorius III (1216–27) who, only two days after his installation, addressed a letter of affection to the Order. He consecrated the new abbey church of Casamari, and sent white monks to reform other monasteries[113]. A monk of Rievaulx praised Honorius in verse: 'Because of him the Order of Cîteaux more than others shines'[114].

The Cistercians again supported a pontiff when Gregory IX (1227–41) excommunicated Frederick II. The Emperor consequently attacked a fleet carrying some of those summoned to a General Council in Rome (1241). The abbots of Cîteaux, Clairvaux, and L'Épau, after 'miseries at sea for a whole week', were taken 'naked and shoeless' to confinement at Pisa. Their imprisonment meant their absence from the General Chapters of 1240 and 1241, that body organising a relief fund for those who suffered[115]. Innocent IV (1243–54) maintained the privileges of the Order and backed the foundation of its college in Paris[116]. Clement IV (1265–68) issued an important bull in its favour, the 'Clementina'[117]. Much later, another dispute – between Boniface III and Philip the Fair of France – saw the abbot of Cîteaux imprisoned (1303) and forced to retire early because of his support for the pontiff[118].

The growing importance of the papacy and frequent criticism of the Order contributed to its decision to be permanently represented at the Curia (1220)[119]. At first stipendiary 'clerks ' or 'procurators' were employed[120], but from 1256 the representatives were abbots or monks[121]. Additional assistance was forthcoming from Cistercian cardinals[122], like John of Toledo (1256–61)[123], named as 'protectors' of the order. Their work, and that of the procurators, must have included representations which led to papal bulls confirming the rights of individual monasteries or of the Order as a whole. Apart from the preamble (naming the monastery concerned) and the sequel (detailing its possessions), the bulk of such bulls simply recounted, in almost identical wording, the privileges common to all houses of the Order at the time of issue[124]. These papal bulls were esteemed as vital, and so a difficult local situation, the accession of a new pope, or the granting of further possessions led many an abbey to seek (at a price) a new confirmatory bull, not once but several times. The cartulary of Fontmorigny (1177–1336) included transcriptions of no less than fifty-odd bulls[125]. An original bull attesting general privileges of the Order might be sent to chosen monasteries and there copied for other houses. Poblet (in 1157) gained a replica of a bull addressed to Cîteaux[126]. Four Czech abbots, meeting at Velehrad (in 1297), attested a copy of a bull of Alexander IV (1260) by 'imposing our seals'[127].

Founders, and their Motives

Cistercian monasteries were founded by people of substance, persons who had the necessary lands and wealth both to give a site and a fair endowment. Kings, barons, bishops, and other leading land-owners were to the fore, and it must be remembered that few benefactors restricted themselves to assisting the white monks at the expense of other Orders. The motives founders had for their generosity were varied. The early Middle Ages were a period of faith and hope in the eternal realities. Most foundation charters put in first place religious motives even if, in fact, there were other more pressing considerations in the mind of a benefactor[128]. King Mieszko III, establishing Ląd (1145) recalled the brevity of earthly life: 'just as a shadow passes and smoke disappears'[129]. Duke Buris Henriksem, founding Tvis (1163), intended 'to lay up for myself treasures in heaven' (*cf*. St Matthew 6:20)[130]. Margraves John and Otto, founding Chorin (1258), realised that one day 'we will stand before the judgement seat of Christ'[131]. Many founders hoped the monks would be their 'bedesmen'[132], expecting 'the prayers of the poor in Christ'[133]. Great magnates and ecclesiastics in establishing a monastery might have in mind not only personal blessings, but also the spiritual needs of their people. King Vladislas founded Plasy (1146) so that Bohemia might be 'enlightened'[134]. Other founders set up Cistercian houses in reparation for their sins – Boxley[135], Cercamp[136], and Sibton[137] among them. Fürstenfeld (1258) was endowed by Duke Leopold II of Bavaria in remorse for having beheaded his young wife, suspected of unfaithfulness[138].

Dreams and visions played their part: such led to the foundation of Beaulieu[139] and

Dieulacres[140]. It was after a troubled night that Prince Otto founded Lehnin (1183) as a spiritual castle in the onslaught against the Slavs[141]. Not a few abbeys resulted from vows made in perilous times[142], especially during storms at sea: amongst the latter were Grey[143], Hailes[144] and Vale Royal[145]. In each case a royal personage was involved, and the new monastery was an expression of gratitude for safe deliverance. For the same reasons, the official Latin name of both Le Valasse[146] and Tintern Minor[147] was *De Voto*, (the abbey 'of the Vow'). In the same spirit of thanksgiving, Maigue (1148) was founded by King Turloch of Thomond after victory in battle against the Norse[148]; Vitskøl (1185) by King Valdemar I after defeating his rival, Sven Grathe[149]; and Real Valle by Charles I of Anjou following success at the Battle of Benevento (1265)[150]. A special anniversary prompted Louis VI (1137) to transform the Benedictine priory at Chaâlis into a Cistercian abbey in memory of the assassination at Bruges, ten years previously, of his cousin Charles I of Flanders[151]. Contacts made on journeys (as those of St Bernard) might result in new monasteries. Ląd (1146) was founded by Prince Miezisław after a pilgrimage to Cologne, during which he visited Altenberg, which became its mother-house[152]. Other benefactors hoped for safety and success in taking up the Cross: Cherlieu[153] and Clairlieu[154] were both founded by nobles departing for the Crusades. Others found the endowment of a new monastery a convenient way of commuting their crusading vows, amongst them Ban Dominic Bors who founded the monastery which bears his name (Bors Monostor, 1197) with papal and royal approval, 'because I had received the Cross, and ought to have gone on the way to the sepulchre of the Lord'[155].

Some monasteries were founded with a burial place in mind, as Altzelle by Margave Otto[156] and Barbeaux by Louis VII[157]. Peter II of Aragon endowed Escarpe and expressed a wish to be buried there, but died in battle elsewhere[158]. Many founders were indeed interred in the abbeys they had established, including Queen Ermengarde at Balmerino[159], King Cathal of Connacht at Knockmoy[160], Madog ap Gruffydd at Valle Crucis[161], and Margrave Wladislas at Velehrad[162]. A few were heart-burials, as at Dieulacres (of Ralph de Blundeville)[163] and New Abbey (of John Balliol), giving the latter house its colloquial name, Sweet*heart* Abbey[164]. Founders were remembered by the insertion of their names in their abbey's necrology, as at La Cour-Dieu in its *Martyrology and Book of Benefactors*[165]; and by observing their annual obit with Mass and Office of the Dead. So many abbots wished to keep such anniversaries in their houses that (from 1250) the express permission of the General Chapter had to be sought[166].

In many an instance political considerations also played their part. Monarchs might set up Cistercian houses as visible testimonies to their temporal power[167]. Alfonso I may have founded Alcobaça (*c.* 1153) not so much in thanksgiving for victory over the Moors at Santarém, but because of the practical and political significance of a great Cistercian abbey in his emergent country of Portugal[168]. King Donal of Munster founded four abbeys (1170–79), three of them in areas where he was anxious to reinforce his authority at a time when his land was being over-run by Anglo-Norman settlers[169]. The foundation of Tamié (*c.* 1133) by Amadeus III of Savoy may have been intended as a peaceful influence during the War of the Two Burgundies[170]. Cistercian settlement east of the Oder meant assistance to the political process there of Teutonic colonisation. Valdemar I, during the conquest of West Pomerania, introduced Danish monks at Dargun and Kołbacz with a view to hindering infiltration by the German Church[171]. Where a kingdom was weak, one manifestation of the independence of other magnates was the sponsorship of monasteries. Barons rather than kings founded a number of Cistercian houses during the power vacuum in England during Stephen's reign (1135–54), in Germany where a parallel situation held good in the times of Lothair and Conrad II (1125–52), and in France – where royal power was for long limited to the Île-de-France[172]. All this at a most formative period for the Order.

Support from Kings and Bishops

Next to the papacy, the Cistercian Order derived much of its support from the temporal power – an authority usually more immediate and one to be reckoned with. Only a small minority of its monasteries were of royal foundation, but many received royal benefactions and confirmatory charters. In return, a monarch frequently expected diplomatic and fund-raising services from the abbots and substantial financial subsidies. The relations between the Order and a monarch might be uneasy (as with Frederick Barbarossa in Germany), but there were notable exceptions. The General Chapter (1191) showed its appreciation of what monarchs meant to it by ordering prayers at its annual meeting for Philip of France ('in whose reign Cîteaux was founded'), and Richard of England ('whose charity is assigned each year to the Chapter'), as well as for the Emperor and the king of Aragon[173].

All the thirteen Cistercian houses of Portugal were of royal foundation or backing, the most notable being Alcobaça (fd 1147)[174]. In Castile, Alfonso VII (1126–57) and Alfonso VIII (1158–1214) founded between them nearly twenty houses of the Order[175]. The first was Fitero (1141), but far better known was to be Poblet (1150)[176]. Alfonso VIII had for daughter Blanche of Castile who married Louis VIII of France and founded the convent of Maubuisson (1241), later being buried there[177]. (His second daughter became abbess of Las Huelgas.)[178] The Capetian dynasty was already closely involved in the Order's expansion[179], but when Blanche's son, St Louis (Louis IX), succeeded to the throne in 1226 few Cistercian houses of France were not touched by his patronage[180]. As a boy he attended the consecration of the church of Longpont with his mother, and later built Royaumont (1235) to the same model; it became the burial place of his family[181]. He frequently visited the monastery, and might even be seen serving the meals or tending the sick[182]. He visited the General Chapter in 1244[183], and was present at the translation of St Edmund at Pontigny in 1247[184]. After his canonisation (1297) his name was inserted in the Cistercian litany and his feast-day became a solemnity[185]. The Capetian dynasty extended in another direction when Béla III of Hungary (1172–96) took for his second wife Margaret Capet, daughter of Louis VII[186]. He received a delegation led by the abbot of Cîteaux (1183)[187], and he was responsible for the foundation or incorporation of five Cistercian abbeys[188]. His dynasty continued the tradition. His son, Imre (1196–1204), founded Cîrţa in Transylvania[189], and another son, Andrew II (1203–35), Toplica in Croatia[190]. Béla IV (1237–70) gave his name to *Béla*kút. Andrew II was buried at Egres[191], whilst his first two queens, Gertrude (1213) and Yolande (1233) were interred at Pilis[192].

English royal foundations were few. The future King Stephen (as lord of Lancaster) gave the site for Furness (1124)[193], in France (when count of Mortain) he founded Longvilliers (1135)[194], and as monarch jointly established Coggeshall (1140) with Queen Maud[195]. King John founded Beaulieu (1204)[196], Edward I – Vale Royal (1277–85)[197], and Edward III – St Mary Graces by the Tower of London (1350)[198]. The English monarch most closely associated with the Order was Richard I, who numbered abbot Elias of the Dunes amongst his advisers[199] and gave the Order the church of Scarborough[200]. His release from captivity in Bavaria (1193) was negotiated by the abbots of Boxley and Robertsbridge (conveniently placed to cross the Channel)[201]. His only foundation (as duke of Normandy) was Bonport (1200)[202]. King John, furious with the English abbeys for refusing him a subsidy and for observing the Interdict (1208–13), penalised many of them financially[203]. The Cistercians granted a subsidy of 1,000 marks to Henry III (paid over in 1226), but when later requests (1256–57) were refused he imposed tolls on those abbots crossing the Channel to the General Chapter[204].

Other countries which saw royal patronage extended to the Order included Ireland, where two-thirds of the abbeys had the backing of the native kings[205]. In Scotland, David I, much influenced by his friend St Aelred, founded Melrose (1136), Newbattle (1140) and Kinloss (1151)[206]. In Sweden, Alvastra and Varnhem (1143) were both of royal foundation[207]. In Austria, Leopold III (St Leopold) made several religious foundations, including Heiligenkreuz (1133), and numbered the Cistercian Otto of Freising amongst his eighteen children[208]. In Poland, whilst many of the abbots and monks were French or German throughout the Middle Ages, Polish princes were well to the fore in the early patronage of the Order[209]. Happy relations with the sovereign meant that the abbots of Zbraslav and Sedlec were numbered amongst the executors of King John of Bohemia (1340)[210].

Another major factor in Cistercian expansion was the goodwill or otherwise of the diocesan bishop. His permission was necessary before any new foundation could be made[211]. Although Cistercian abbeys became increasingly exempt from his jurisdiction, he normally retained the right to bless a newly-elected abbot, to ordain its priest-monks, and to institute the abbey's nominees as vicars of its appropriated parishes[212]. During the formative years of the Order, the Cistercians mostly received substantial backing from the episcopate – this was especially true during the archiepiscopates of St Malachy in Ireland and of Eskil in Sweden. In the thirteenth century there were increasing difficulties where Cistercian privileges encroached on the rights of the local see and cathedral chapter. During the 'Mellifont Conspiracy' in Ireland (1227–28) five bishops sided with the Irish rebel monks[213]. In France, a bishop of Soissons (1233) backed up, by physical attacks, his claim to have the right to examine, approve, and instal abbots-elect[214]. In Spain, the bishops of Vich and Tortosa sought to limit the lands and influence of Poblet (1203–36)[215]. In Denmark, Øm had a bitter dispute with Bishop Tyge of Århus (1263–67)[216], whilst Ryd described Bishop Jacob of Slesvig (d. 1287) as 'more of a tyrant than a bishop'[217]. These are a few examples of the sometimes less than happy Cistercian-episcopal relations in the thirteenth century.

Patronage

By the mid-ninth century royal power in the Holy Roman Empire was unable to offer effective protection, and for this Benedictine monasteries increasingly looked to the most powerful nobles at hand. These became their 'advocates' or 'patrons', took control of the house during a vacancy, and had an influential say in the election of abbots[218]. The term 'advocate' or 'patron' as applied to a Cistercian abbey should have meant a magnate and benefactor (perhaps the founder or his descendants) from whom the house could expect protection, goodwill, and the promotion of its interests[219]. As made clear in a bull of Innocent III for Margam (1203)[220] and a charter of Prince Llywelyn for Aberconwy (1204)[221], such 'patrons' were not expected to interefere in abbatial elections. The bond between patron and monastery was strongest when the 'advocate' resided nearby, as at Furness where William of Lancaster III (1240) could talk of 'my monks'[222]; weakest (so far as protection was concerned) when the patron lived more remotely – as for Margam and Neath in the instance of the earls of Gloucester[223]. In Germany, several Emperors insisted that they were the sole patrons of all Cistercian houses within the imperial domain, and whilst this may have restricted monastic independence, it may have been beneficial in restraining local interference[224].

Not only did founders and their dynasties come to be thought of as 'patrons', so too did later substantial benefactors. In France, bishop Vivien of Rodez (ob. 1274) amplified generously the possessions of Beaulieu-en-Rouergue founded by a predecessor, bishop Adema, and he gained himself thereby the title of 'second founder'[225]. Earl Roger of Norfolk (ob. 1306) who enabled Tintern abbey church to be completed and greatly enhanced its estates, was later thought of as 'founder', even though he lived nearly two centuries after its inception[226]. The need for a strong, defensive patron, saw the monks of Bindon (1272) elect King Edward I in this capacity, replacing Henry de Novo Burgo[227]. Borsmonostor (1353) sought King Louis I of Hungary as patron saying that the counts of Sopron had proved to be 'not their protectors but their oppressors'[228]. Good patrons were a great help, others could be a severe hindrance; this happened especially when there was a change of patronage – by inheritance, marriage or conquest. At Croxden, where relations with the de Verdun dynasty had been generally happy, when Thomas de Furnival (1319) acceded to the lordship matters became so bad that the monks erected a thorn-fence barring him access to the gate-house[229]. When the barony of Powys passed to an Englishman, John de Charlton (1309), he made life very difficult for the monks of Strata Marcella who hitherto had enjoyed close ties with the Welsh Gwenwynwyn dynasty[230]. In his day, Gregory IX (1234) spoke of widespread problems when he rebuked patrons who were a burden to their monasteries, demanding grain, hospitality and financial help[231]. Such papal stipulations had limited effect; for most monasteries Rome was far away, whereas their 'advocate' was close at hand[232].

The Spread Across Europe

The varied motives impelling founders to invite white monks to settle on their lands, the backing from popes, sovereigns and prelates, the reputation of the Order and of St Bernard, the many vocations which meant over-full monasteries, political movements (such as the Iberian Reconquest, the Baltic Crusades, and the establishment of the Latin Empire in the east), together with the acceptance of Cistercian life by numerous other religious houses, accounted not only for a rapid expansion in the total number of abbeys, but also for their widespread diffusion throughout Europe and into the Near East. The 'heartland' of the Order lay in Burgundy, but by 1130 white monks had founded, or incorporated, monasteries in Italy, Germany, Alsace, and England. In the next decade expansion took place in Austria, Belgium, Spain, Portugal, Switzerland, and Scotland. By the mid-twelfth century the Cistercians had more or less reached the bounds of the then 'civilised' world. As colonisation spread, a network of abbeys covered Europe from Portugal to Syria, and from Norway to Sicily[233]. By 1250, there were some 650 male monasteries of the Order, of which about 240 were in France and over 120 in the British Isles. This tremendous expansion was not without its inherent problems for the general organisation and unity of the Order.

The general thrust of Cistercian settlement was by means of a monastery with surplus monks sending out at least thirteen of their number (as representing Christ and the twelve apostles) to make a new foundation. 235 abbeys established daughter-houses in this way, the most significant numerically being Clairvaux (80), Cîteaux and Morimond (28 each), Pontigny (16), and Camp (13). The most productive houses were the pre-1150 abbeys of France[234]. Certain monasteries, strategically placed, had an important rôle in expansion beyond them: Foigny in the founding of monasteries in Flanders and further north; Camp as a stepping stone towards the east; Whitland opening the way to settlement in the heart of Wales; L'Escale-Dieu as a spring-board for colonisation in NE Spain. Cistercian settlement was concurrent with that of the

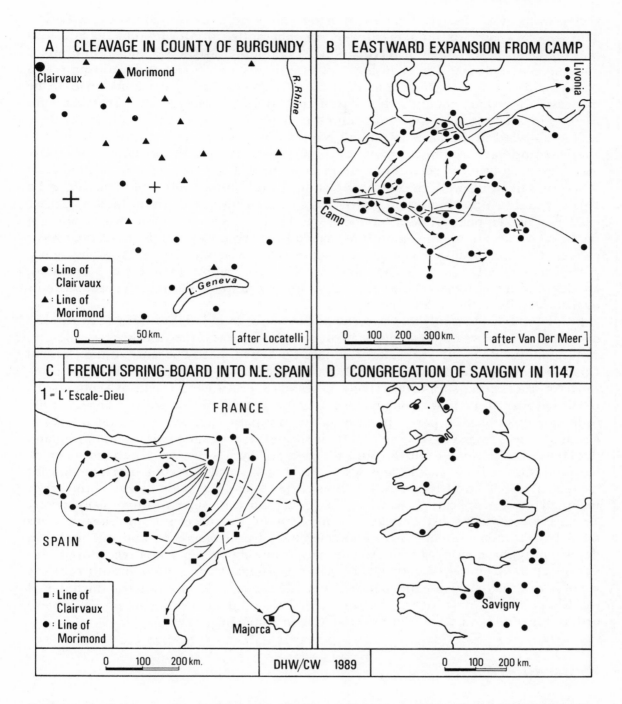

A	CLEAVAGE IN COUNTY OF BURGUNDY
B	EASTWARD EXPANSION FROM CAMP
C	FRENCH SPRING-BOARD INTO N.E. SPAIN
D	CONGREGATION OF SAVIGNY IN 1147

Premonstratensians – hence the friendly 'Peace' between them (in 1142) by which no abbey of either Order was to be founded within two leagues of an abbey of the other[235]. The 'Peace' was not always observed[236]. The first four Cistercian foundations were from Cîteaux itself, the 'proto-abbeys' or 'Elder Daughters': La Ferté (1113), Pontigny (1114), Clairvaux and Morimond (1115). The seniority of Morimond was slow to be recognised, despite its foundation in the same year (and some say on the same day) as Clairvaux[237]. It only became a reality after 1156, shortly after the death of St Bernard[238]. In 1159 the General Chapter may have met at Morimond[239]. The 'first four' abbots had a prestige next only to that of the abbot of Cîteaux, and had especial influence in those abbeys which had ultimately sprung from them.

All Cistercian abbeys derived from one of the five senior abbeys, directly or indirectly. In this way, distinct 'families' or 'generations' or 'lines' developed in the Order. The 'line' of Clairvaux numbered over 350 abbeys, that of Morimond over 200, and that of Cîteaux over 100, but the filiations of Pontigny were only some 40 in number and those of La Ferté less than 20[240]. These families were closely-knit groups: if a monk or abbot was promoted to the rule of another house, or monks had to be dispersed, it would generally be 'within the family'. 'Family ties' were taken into account in selecting arbitrators and definitors. The abbeys of the line of Clairvaux were well established in the Paris Basin and Normandy, in south and central Italy, in NW Iberia, Scandinavia, and the remoter parts of the British Isles[241]. The family of Cîteaux was present in other parts of France and in south and central England. A number of Pontigny's filiations were in central and south-west France, whilst the small line of La Ferté included nine houses in north Italy – a spring-board for influence further east[242]. The 'empire' of Morimond[243] was closely associated with two regions of medieval colonisation – the Spanish March and eastern Europe[244]. Its first abbot was a cousin of the archbishop of Cologne and a princely novice was Otto of Freising – hence perhaps its association with Germanic areas[245]. An important link for Morimond, looking eastwards, was its third daughter-house at Camp (Altenkamp, fd 1123) with its own sub-family of fifty monasteries[246].

From 1098 to 1124 only 26 Cistercian abbeys were founded, but from 1125 to 1151 over 300; certain years (*anni mirabiles*) were more important than others – 1131 and 1147 amongst them[247]. Thereafter the pace slackened, partly because of the General Chapter's deliberate policy (1152)[248], partly because of the deaths (in 1153) of St Bernard and strong supporters (Pope Eugenius III and King David of Scotland)[249], partly because of the now strong government in England and Germany – lessening the influence of nobles[250], partly because of the antipathy felt for the white monks in Germany (by Barbarossa – because of their support for Alexander III) and in England (by Henry II – because of the favours afforded St Thomas Becket)[251]. Added to which less land was readily available, and later there was the rival attraction of the mendicant Orders. By 1354 the Cistercian Tax Book listed some 690 male houses – though it included some duplicate entries[252]. The governance of such a numerically strong Order necessitated a list or *tabula* being kept by the precentor of Cîteaux. This recorded the official 'name, age, and calendar' of each house[253], and was useful in determining the seniority of abbots, checking taxation payments, and recording attendances at the General Chapter[254]. It was in existence by the mid-eleventh century, when it was customary for the names of new abbeys to be inserted on the third day of the Chapter[255]. A new list was drawn up in 1219, and further major revisions were ordered in 1239 and 1270[256]. Copies survive in whole or part[257].

Western Europe

In the county of Burgundy, despite the proximity of Cîteaux and La Ferté, Clairvaux and Morimond bore most fruit. The monasteries deriving from Clairvaux were mostly in the west and south (along the route St Bernard took to Italy) and were usually incorporated houses; those of the line of Morimond were chiefly in the north and east, and were nearly all new monastic settlements. Cistercian settlement in the county owed much to the helpful attitude of two archbishops of Besançon (Anseri [1117–34] and Humbert [1134–61]) – very important as the region was already well populated with religious houses – and to the prestige of great twelfth-century abbots, as Gaucher of Morimond, Lambert of Clairefontaine and Burchard of Balerne. Ponce of Bellevaux guided that house for nearly forty years, and, in like endeavour, Guy of Cherlieu underwent 'many labours, travels, and troubles for Christ'[258]. South-west France was

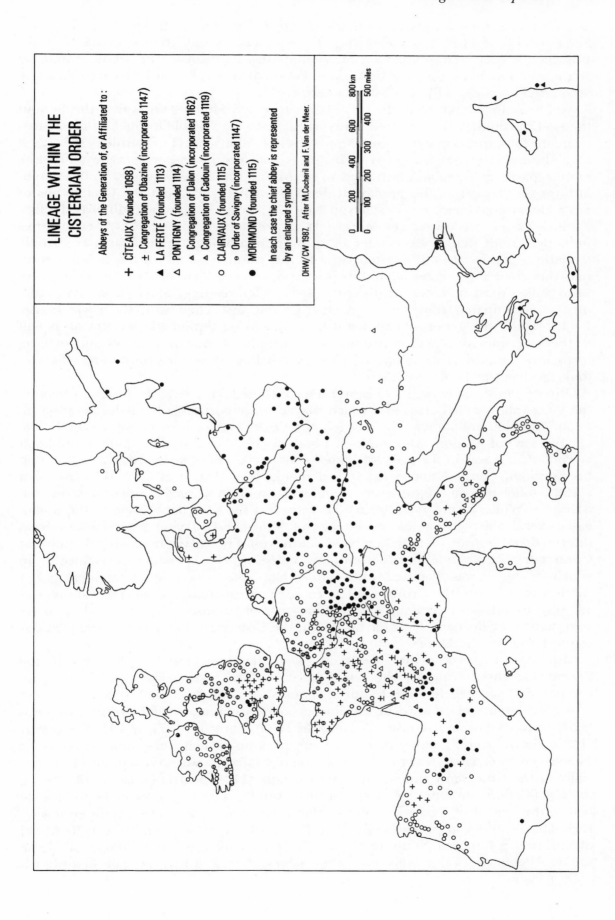

LINEAGE WITHIN THE
CISTERCIAN ORDER

Abbeys of the Generation of, or Affiliated to :

+ CÎTEAUX (founded 1098)
± Congregation of Obazine (incorporated 1147)
▲ LA FERTÉ (founded 1113)
△ PONTIGNY (founded 1114)
▲ Congregation of Dalon (incorporated 1162)
▲ Congregation of Cadouin (incorporated 1119)
○ CLAIRVAUX (founded 1115)
⊖ Order of Savigny (incorporated 1147)
● MORIMOND (founded 1115)

In each case the chief abbey is represented
by an enlarged symbol

DhW/CW 1987.   After M.Cocheril and F. Van der Meer.

also an area settled for centuries before Cistercian expansion there, the main thrust being in 1141 to 1153 with no less than 17 new creations and 16 incorporations[259]. In Provence it was archbishop Guy of Vienne who introduced the white monks (at Bonnevaux) in 1119, the year he became Pope Calixtus II[260]. In Brittany, L'Aumône accounted for nine of fifteen Cistercian abbeys[261].

As Christian monarchs in Iberia slowly drove the Moors southwards throughout the twelfth century, the deserted lands which became available formed an ideal environment for Cistercian expansion. Monarchs like Alfonso VIII of Castile (1158–1214) and Alfonso II of Aragon (1164–96) were to the fore in endowing abbeys of white monks, partly as a deliberate strategy to secure the lands newly gained[262]. (The archbishops of Tarragona, the Premonstratensians of Bellepuig, and the Carthusians of Scala Dei also received great estates in New Catalonia.)[263] Fitero (1140) was the first Spanish Cistercian house, not Moreruela as previously supposed[264]. After victories in battle, Count Ramón Berenguer IV of Barcelona brought monks from Fontfroide to settle at Poblet (1150)[265]. Sited close to the 'no-man's land' of the political frontier, this great abbey consolidated its possessions in the Plain of Urgel and the lower Ebro valley, irrigated new lands, practised cattle-breeding, encouraged lay settlement, and initiated trade and industry. Closely associated with the royal house, Poblet repaid the generosity shown it by undertaking diplomatic services on behalf of the king and by practical assistance – redeeming Christian captives and helping to finance Alfonso II's quelling of Moslem rebellion[266]. Prince Ferdinand, his son, took the habit at Poblet in 1201[267].

Other Spanish monasteries of significance included Santes Creus, which developed the Gaia valley, and Carracedo, which played an important rôle in the kingdom of León[269]. Other monarchs who assisted the Order's growth included James I ('the Conqueror') of Aragon, who founded Benifazá (1233) and in old age took the habit at Poblet[270]. It was in the wake of James' conquest of the Balearic islands (1229) that his kinsman, Count Nunó Sanç, settled monks from Poblet at La Real in Majorca (1232), following on Augustinian, Dominican and Franciscan foundations on that island[271]. Whilst in much of Spain Clairvaux was the dominant force, in the northeast several abbeys were of the lineage of Morimond, having been formed from intermediary houses of that family in south-west France[272]. In Portugal, the first Cistercian abbey was either Tarouca or Alafões (there is some uncertainty as to which)[273], but it was Alcobaça (fd. *c.* 1153) that came to occupy a prominent political position *vis-à-vis* the Crown[274]. The country's sixteen abbeys and eight nunneries all were founded, or had the effective backing, of Alfonso I (1139–85)[275], a correspondent of St Bernard[276]. After his death, the Cistercians knew various tribulations at the hands of the Moors[277].

Cistercian expansion into Germany went hand in hand with that of the Premonstratensian canons; the latter by 1200 had sixty abbeys in the Empire compared with nearly one hundred houses of white monks[278]. Many of the Cistercian monasteries were of the lineage of Morimond, settled directly, or indirectly from its daughter-houses of Camp (fd 1123), Ebrach (1127), and Heiligenkreuz (1135). Lützel and Camp compete for the position of being the first house to be established in German territory[279]. The line of Clairvaux was also significant – especially in the Rhineland and Bavaria: La Chalade (1128) and Eberbach (1135) being its first filiations on what was then German soil[280]. The weakness of imperial rule before the advent of Barbarossa meant that noblemen were to the fore in endowing early abbeys, often in partnership. Duke Frederick I of Swabia and Count Reinhold of Lützelburg founded Neuburg (1131)[281], Counts Eberhard and Adolph of Altena settled Altenberg (1137), whilst two other nobles, Bern and Rivin, established Ebrach (1127)[282].

Eastern Europe, and the Balkans

A significant line of demarcation in the twelfth century was the river Elbe. It divided established Christendom from heathen peoples such as the Wends, and separated to a marked extent the areas of influence of the older orders of monks (Benedictines and Cluniacs) from those of newer foundation (Cistercians and Premonstratensians)[283]. The very abundance of land, often quite poor marsh and forest, encouraged Cistercian settlement, as did the generosity of princely benefactors, the willingness of many white monks to 'germanise' the lands obtained, and their desire to assist in 'christianising' peoples still largely pagan[284]. The large estates given by Polish princes to the Cistercians was one factor explaining their possession (contrary to their ideals) from the outset of villages and serfs. The other was the lack of vocations. *Conversi* were few as there was a high degree of serfdom which inhibited freedom of action and mobility; choir-monks were in short supply as every son was entitled to inherit a portion of his father's estate[285]. This lack of vocations caused the General Chapter (1231) to permit boys as young as fifteen to be received as novices in 'remote' regions (such as Poland, Livonia, Frisia, Hungary, and Bohemia), where, it was said, 'adult vocations are rare'[286]. This was a problem which led to the importing of monks from France and Germany throughout the Middle Ages, including wayward monks sentenced to banishment from their own houses. They could have an unsettling effect, and so the Chapter (1275) ordered that 'no delinquent monks are to be sent to Hungarian abbeys, saving those which have a strong community'[287].

Both Germans and Danes played a rôle in Cistercian expansion along the Baltic coast. After peace in the Empire between Church and State (1168) and with the expedition of Valdemar I, there came in rapid succession: Doberan (1171), Dargun (1172), and Kołbacz (1175)[288]. The last two, daughter-houses of the Danish abbey of Esrum, were endowed by Pomeranian nobles but were part of a political process of securing (short-lived) Danish supremacy in their region[289]. Kołbacz, in turn, founded Oliwa (1186), thus helping to pave the way for the mission to Prussia. In Silesia conflicts in the Piast family delayed the foundation of some abbeys, but the Cistercians eventually became the most powerful Order[289a]. The favour shown to the Cistercians by the Polish princes was exemplified in 1270 when King Boleslas V created the abbot of Morimond (whose houses held sway in his realm) a noble of the first class[290]. In Bohemia and Moravia, too, all the abbeys were of the family of Morimond[291] and royal or noble patronage assisted both Cistercian and Premonstratensian settlement. The earliest Cistercian house in Moravia, Sedlec (fd 1143), was settled by Duke Miroslav with monks from Waldsassen[292]. One-and-a-half centuries later it sent monks to the abbey of Zbraslav (Königsaal, 1292) founded for it by King Wenceslas II ('The Old') of Bohemia. Zbraslav became the mausoleum of his entire dynasty. During the search for a suitable site for the monastery Masses of the Holy Spirit were said in all the churches of Prague. Later Queen Elizabeth of Bohemia (*c.* 1338) added a southern aisle with nine chapels[293]. Other royal foundations included Velehrad (1202)[294] and Zlatá Koruna (Goldenkron, 1263)[295].

By the time Cistercian expansion flowered in Hungary under the auspices of Béla III, there were already some eighty Benedictine houses there. By 1320, compared to eighteen Cistercian abbeys, the Premonstratensians had no less than thirty-nine in that kingdom. In the thirteenth century the Dominicans and Franciscans also made rapid progress[296]. For the Cistercians, life in Hungary was not easy. Novices were in short supply – so often unsuitable monks were imported – and the journey to the General Chapter at Cîteaux was both lengthy and dangerous. In 1196 the abbots did not reach France, being 'wounded, robbed, and taken prisoner' en route[297]. The Order was badly affected by the Tartar invasions, and only survived by welcoming recruits from

Austria and France[298]. During the second wave of incursions (1259) some of the community of Koprzywnica (then in the kingdom) were murdered, Egres was besieged and burnt, and no more was heard of Keresztúr[299]; that same year, the abbots of not only Hungary but also Poland and Livonia dared not travel to the General Chapter 'out of fear of the Tartars'[300]. General visitations of the Order in Hungary were made in 1274 to 1275 (when widespread deviations from Cistercian custom and discipline were alleged)[301], and in 1356 (when a very depressing state of affairs was revealed)[302].

One monastery in the Balkans yet more remote was Cîrţa, perhaps the earliest Gothic edifice in the foothills of the Transylvanian Alps, founded by King Imre (1202). There can be little doubt that he saw it as a bastion on the borders of his realm. In its day it was said to be 'a long way from the other abbeys of Hungary' (1216)[303] and 'at the limits of the kingdom' (1343)[304]. Its abbot attended the General Chapter only very infrequently[305]. It had to endure devastation by the Tartars (1259)[306], as well as hostility from the local Orthodox population[307], and probably those Wallach herdsmen whose land had been given to the monks[308]. It may be that its foundation was partly influenced by the Fourth Crusade, Innocent III (1212) later expressing the hope that 'the Order propagate itself in Romania'[309]. Further east, the capture of Constantinople during that Crusade (1204) meant not only the establishment of the short-lived Latin Empire but also that of the Roman Church. Cistercian abbots (Luke of Sambucina and Peter of Locedio) had helped preach the Crusade[310], and in its wake (probably with Innocent III's backing) some twelve abbeys of white monks were founded in Constantinople itself, or elsewhere in Greece and Crete, mostly in abandoned Orthodox monasteries. Amongst them were Chortaïton – given to Locedio in return for abbot Peter's services – and St Stephen' s, founded from St Thomas of Torcello by Venice[311]. Further afield were Daphni (*Laurus*) on the outskirts of Athens, and Zaraka in the Peloponnese[312]. Greek monks had returned to some of the houses before the Empire fell in 1261; apart from two Cretan houses only Daphni survived – until Mahomet II entered Athens in 1458[313].

The Mediterranean Lands

The first foundations in Italy were settled from La Ferté: Tiglieto (1120) and Locedio (1124) – the latter playing a significant rôle in Cistercian settlement in Syria. There followed colonisation from Cîteaux and Morimond, but, following the journeys of St Bernard to Italy, it was the lineage of Clairvaux which dominated (save in the Piedmont)[314]. There were to be almost ninety monasteries of the Order in Italy – a number of them being reformed and incorporated institutions. Distance from Cîteaux and Clairvaux led – as with the Hungarian houses – to a weakening of administrative ties; this was particularly true of the houses of southern Italy. General visitations of the Order in Calabria and Sicily were ordered (1226, 1232, 1272)[315]; some abbeys had a problem with vocations (1228)[316a] – as Roccamadore, 1232)[316b]; some were not represented for 'many years' at the General Chapter[317] (though this was also true of the abbeys of Lombardy and Tuscany, 1252)[318], and some fell behind with their financial dues (1344)[319]. Discipline could be poor in abbeys further north: several shortcomings were alleged at Trefontane (1199)[320], and 'horrible excesses' noted at a group of monasteries centred on Chiaravalle Milano (1291)[321]. It would be a mistake, though, to think all was unrelieved gloom[322]. Calabria was also the home of the noted theologian, biblical commentator, mystic, and prophet, Abbot Joachim of Corazzo[323]. He did not find the Cistercian fold the most perfect form of religious life and set about founding a new monastery, Fiore (1188), at a height of about one thousand metres[324]. This became the centre of a new congregation, dedicated to absolute renunciation of the world[325]; it essentially represented a schism in the Order, but received papal approval (1196)[326]. After his death (1202), some of Joachim's views were condemned by the Lateran Council (1215) and others, but he was eventually numbered among the *beati* of the Cistercians[327].

Citing the pagan and climatic environment, St Bernard had once declined a site offered at the tomb of Samuel overlooking Jerusalem[328], but in the wake of the Crusades and with his restraining hand removed by death, Cistercians from Morimond settled at Deir Balamand (Belmont) in 1157[329]. After a former monk of La Ferté, Peter, became Patriarch of Antioch in 1209, he nostalgically arranged for the incorporation as a daughter-house of La Ferté of the Syrian (Orthodox) monastery of St George of Jubin on the Black Mountain[330]. Yet another incorporation, also under the oversight of La Ferté, was the Greek abbey of St Sergius near Byblos (1233)[331]. Balamand, Jubin, and St Sergius were all sited at some altitude – perhaps to avoid the heat of the coast or for reasons of security. The incursions by Sultan Baibars in northern Syria saw an end to Jubin (perhaps in 1268), its monks moving to Genoa, and later of St Sergius and Balamand (1289)[332]. Balamand had four daughter-houses: two in the kingdom of Jerusalem[333] of which virtually nothing is known, Salvatio (fd 1161)[334] and St John in the Wood (fd 1169)[335]; one in Sicily (Refech, settled about 1188, perhaps by monks of Balamand fleeing from Saladin)[336], and one in Cyprus (Beaulieu; founded in 1237, it later changed its site to the neighbourhood of Nicosia [1256])[337]. Once again, the foundation of abbeys in distant, troubled lands meant a relaxation of visitation procedures and hence of good discipline[338].

Northern Europe

In the time of King Stephen (1135–54) almost forty Cistercian abbeys were established in England, including the incorporation of eleven Savigniac houses (1147). This proliferation did not escape the notice of the chronicler, William of Newburgh (d. 1208)[339]. Stephen himself, as Count of Mortain, had a preference for the congregation of Savigny, founding Furness (c. 1124) and Coggeshall (1140), but semi-autonomous barons made the bulk of foundations – especially the ambitious Earl Ranulf of Chester[340]. It is commonly held that they did so for political gain and prestige, taking advantage of the anarchy which marked Stephen's reign[341]. This view may be too simplistic: other factors may have played a part since seven of the new foundations were made in the 'wonderful year' of 1147 alone. The restoration of strong rule in the reign of Henry II (1154–72) saw only six new abbeys founded between 1154 and 1200[342]. Abbeys of the 'generation' of Cîteaux were mostly in the Midlands and fringing the south coast of England; Savigniac expansion lay close to the Welsh border and in the plain of Cheshire; houses of the family of Clairvaux graced the Pennines region and East Anglia. Amongst the latter was the great abbey of Fountains (1132) whose first community was akin to that of Cîteaux: a group of Benedictines dissatisfied with life at St Mary's, York[343]. West of the Pennines lay the princely abbey of Furness; with considerable influence in the Isle of Man, it settled a daughter-house there at Rushen (1138)[344].

Cistercian settlement in Scotland owed much to King David I (1125–53) whose seneschal and friend, St Aelred, entered Rievaulx in 1134. There followed a series of royal foundations; the first, Melrose (1136), had David's step-son, Waltheof, as first abbot[345]. All the eleven Scottish abbeys of the Order derived from Rievaulx, *via* Melrose or Dundrennan (1142)[346]. King David settled other religious as well: Augustinian Canons at Jedburgh and Tironian monks at Kelso[347]. Semi-independent lords colonised Glenluce (1192) and Saddell (c. 1207)[348]. The prosperity of the Scottish abbeys lying close to England was shattered during the wars of Edward I, when they suffered severe damage – especially by the burning of granges[349]; in turn, the Border abbeys of northern England (such as Calder and Holm Cultram) were despoiled repeatedly by the Scots[350]. The campaigns of Edward I also badly affected the Cistercians in Wales. The first abbey to be founded was Anglo-Norman Tintern (1131), but eight of the thirteen abbeys in the Principality were not only all of the line of Clairvaux, deriving from the premier Welsh abbey of Whitland (1140), they were also all nationalistic in sympathy, strongly supporting the native princes throughout the thirteenth century[351]. At Strata Florida (1238) Prince Llywelyn the Great convoked a meeting of all the lesser 'princes' to secure the succession, and at Cwmhir (1282) the body of the slain Prince Llywelyn the Last was buried[352]. Despite their ardent nationalism, the Welsh Cistercians – unlike their brethren in Ireland – seem to have owed very little to the ancient Celtic *clas* system of monasticism[353].

Penetration of the white monks into Ireland owed much to the influence of St Malachy, papal legate, archbishop of Armagh (1140–48), and friend of St Bernard – who after Malachy's death at Clairvaux wrote his biography[354]. Impressed by what he saw of continental monasticism during a journey to Rome whilst Bishop of Down (1139), Malachy encouraged the foundation of both Augustinian and Cistercian houses. On his travels he had stayed with the Augustinian Canons at Arrouaise, and before his death there were twenty Arrouaisian houses in northern Ireland[355]. His visits to Clairvaux led to the foundation of the first Irish Cistercian house of Mellifont (1142); its first monks included some Irishmen who had been in Malachy' s party and remained at Clairvaux for training[356]. Over two-thirds of the thirty-three lasting Cistercian foundations in Ireland derived from Mellifont[357]. There was a slackening (as in England) in Cistercian colonisation of Ireland between 1154 and 1170[358], but over the turn of the century (between 1180 and 1220) Anglo-Norman settlement saw the establishment by the newcomers of ten Cistercian abbeys[359]. There came to be rivalry between Mellifont and St Mary's, Dublin (inc. 1147)[360].

The Anglo-Norman abbeys (of which the latter was one) tended to be in more favourable areas than the Irish[361], and to adopt Early English rather than Romanesque architecture[362]. A number of British mainland abbeys had contacts with Ireland; where some (like Tintern and Whitland) established daughter-houses[363], some sought food supplies (Furness and Glenluce)[364], and some owned property – even French Beaubec did so (in County Meath)[365]. As with other remote areas, affairs in the Irish Cistercian houses (as distinct from the Anglo-Norman foundations) caused frequent concern to the General Chapter. Irish monks claiming to be bishops were travelling abroad (1184), some were becoming bishops without leave of the Order (1199), and the conduct of these drew adverse comment (1234)[366]. There were rebellions in some houses especially directed at abbot-Visitors (as at Jerpoint and Mellifont; 1217)[367]; there was a paucity of personnel in others (1221)[368]; there was widespread absenteeism from the General Chapter[369] – one abbey went unrepresented for twenty years (1270)[370] – and there was a marked lack of regular observance (1227)[371]. Several general visitations had to be ordered[372], the most notable by Stephen Lexington, abbot of Stanley, at the time of the 'Mellifont Conspiracy' (1227–28).

Archbishop Eskil of Lund (1138–77) was also a friend of St Bernard, a visitor to Clairvaux, and interred there. His jurisdiction as metropolitan included Sweden and his influence was wide[373]. He founded Herrisvad (1144), supported the foundation of Esrum (*c.* 1150) and of Øm (1172), as well as influencing the colonisation of Løgum (1171) and of Holme (1172)[374]. Like Malachy, he also introduced other religious Orders – Carthusians and Premonstratensians[375]. During Eskil's exile (1161–67) and after his resignation (1177) his mantle fell on his successor, Absalom, who encouraged the incorporation of Benedictine Sorø[376]. Royal figures also played their part, especially King Sverker and his queen, Ulvilde, who founded Alvastra and Nydala (1143)[377]. It was indeed because royalty and ecclesiastics saw them as a settling political influence that the Cistercians perhaps first came to Scandinavia, in the period of civil war and social unrest prior to 1158[378]. Contact with Cistercians elsewhere (as by the bishop of Bergen) led to penetration into Norway from monasteries in England. Fountains settled Lyse (1146)[379], and Kirkstead sent monks to Hovedøya (1147)[380], both sited on fiord islands. The short-lived Munkeby (1161–1207) was the most northerly Cistercian house in Europe – at 64°N[381]. The chief problems for the Norwegian houses stemmed not solely from the severe climate (the first abbot of Hovedøya returned to Kirkstead)[382], but more from the distance from the motherhouses in England: sometimes no visitation was possible (1210) or had to be made by delegation – when the monk-Visitors might abuse their powers (1211)[383]. Lack of strong control near at hand could also cause rebellion – as at Hovedøya (1243)[384].

Two major cartographic endeavours have attempted to portray the locations of all medieval, and indeed modern, Cistercian monasteries and nunneries. The first, F. Van Der Meer's *Atlas de L'Ordre Cistercien* (1965)[385], is a valuable publication – not only on account of its maps but also by reason of the many photographs it contains and the summary notes afforded on each house. It is now virtually unobtainable. It has its errors and limitations, listed by Cocheril[386] and by Vongrey and Hervay[387] in detailed reviews, by Cattana dealing with Italy[388], Guerin as concerning Iberia[389], Krausen and Zakar listing German and Hungarian houses[390], and Schrader for the dioceses of Magdeburg and Halberstadt[391]. Lekai also emphasises its drawbacks[392]. The second work of note is Cocheril's *Cartes Géographiques* (1976)[393], being the first volume of the proposed *Dictionnaire des Monastères Cisterciens*.

Incorporated Monasteries

The appeal of the Cistercian Order was such that a number of existing religious houses either adopted the way of life it proposed, or else had their buildings transferred – not always voluntarily to the white monks. Of the 650 male abbeys established by 1350, almost one-third were incorporated in these ways. This was a major factor in the rapid expansion of the Order, but perhaps brought a certain weakening of the ideals of the early fathers[394]. The most notable country for incorporations was Italy – where, of a total of nearly ninety monasteries in 1340, almost one-half had previously housed other religious. Incorporations in Italy reached their zenith from 1217 to 1253, and owed much to the active encouragement of Popes Gregory IX and Innocent IV[395]. Incorporations were also significant in Denmark and Ireland, Greece and the Near East. The most notable year was the 'wonderful year' of 1147, when at the General Chapter (attended by the Cistercian Pope Eugenius III) the congregations of Savigny and Obazine were absorbed – though many Cistercians doubted the wisdom of the move[396] – but that of Sempringham was rejected, perhaps primarily because it was intended as a double monastery. (Obazine was also a double house, but the nuns there were subjects of the monks rather than partners)[397]. The influence of St Bernard was again significant: his peregrinations brought several incorporations in their wake, amongst them Grandselve in Aquitaine, the Dunes in Flanders, and Casamari and Fossanova in Italy[398].

The commonest reason adduced – sometimes much later in date – for the transference of existing monasteries to the white monks was the alleged decadence, economically or spiritually or both, of the house in question. This frequent assertion may sometimes have been Cistercian self-justification of the action[399], in other instances a large measure of truth may have been involved. The bishop of Byblos, requesting La Ferté to settle monks at St Sergius (1231), talked of it being 'a convent incontinent'[400]; Pope Gregory IX (*c.* 1230) said of the pilgrim hospital of Lovadina, that 'the only hope of saving it is to introduce the Cistercians'[401]. Similar reasoning applied to the assimilation of: Buonsolazzo (economic collapse)[402], Kalvø (paucity of numbers)[403], and Rivalta Piedmont (the effect of wars)[404]. More positively, in many cases there was perhaps a genuine desire on the part of existing religious 'to live a regular life, in silence, and following Cistercian observances' – the motives which the General Chapter (1237) cited when agreeing to the union of Palazzuolo to SS. Vincent and Anastasia[405]. There may have been mixed motives, the wish of some unaffiliated monasteries and hermitages to share in the Cistercian privileges of tithe-exemption and removal from episcopal jurisdiction. The Order may have welcomed the membership of some abbeys which brought considerable endowment and personnel with them[406] – like the 'second generation' great houses of Casamari, the Dunes, Grandselve, and St Mary's, Dublin. The allegations of previous decadence may sometimes have been true, but should be treated with caution[407].

When an incorporation of an existing community was mooted, two abbots would be appointed to hold an on-the-spot enquiry as to the proposed takeover. This would cover the suitability of the site and the monastery's material prosperity, the feelings of the existing religious, the views of the founder of the house in question, and the willingness of the diocesan bishop to give his consent. If all these proved satisfactory, then papal approval might be sought (it had to be from 1229)[408], a Cistercian abbey named as mother-house of the incorporated monastery, and Cistercian personnel sent there to instruct the new members of the Order, and to arrange for alterations to the existing buildings should that be necessary. When Klaarcamp (1216) wanted to cistercianise a Benedictine abbey, the abbots delegated to make enquiries were those of Aduard (a filiation of Klaarcamp) and Heisterbach (also of the lineage of Clairvaux)[409]. When Obazine was incorporated (1147), five monks and *conversi* went from Cîteaux to make sure its liturgy conformed with Cistercian usage, and to advise on pastoral farming. Another way of trying to achieve uniformity was for some monks of a house newly added to the Order to go for training to their new mother-house. On the incorporation of Silvanès (1136) some of its community underwent a year's formation at Mazan, whilst technically competent *conversi* from Mazan went to Silvanès to adapt the buildings[410]. The 'desire manifested by the brothers of Valmagne' was cited by Eugenius III (1149) on its entry into the Order[411], but not all religious affected were so happy. At Casamari (inc. 1140) a group of disaffected black monks occupied part of the buildings for eight years[412], whilst some of the monks of the former Benedictine house of Canales (inc. 1157) were trying to regain independence from Melun as late as 1203[413]. The process of incorporation could be abandoned – as at S. Maria de Maniace (1297)[414], delayed – as at Casalvolone (from 1169 to 1240)[415], or reversed – as when black monks returned to Slesvig from Guldholm (1190s)[416]. Some religious houses were merged completely into Cistercian abbeys rather than incorporated as individual units (Chapter 8).

An incorporated monastery might be recognised by its site – Cistercian abbeys were generally built on valley floors, but inherited houses (as several in Italy) might be upland, even hill-top, foundations. Cistercian abbeys were usually named after the Blessed Virgin Mary, but an adopted house might incorporate in its dedication the previous title or patron saint: Benedictine houses might retain a dedication to St Benedict (as, at first, did *Monte* Favale)[417]; Savigniac abbeys an ascription to the Holy Trinity (as at Aunay)[418]. As to the position of the former superior, practice varied. On the incorporation of his hermitage at Silvanès, Pons de Léras stayed on in the humble rôle of a *conversus*[419]. The Benedictine abbot Vivien of Hautecombe (inc. 1139) resigned, and went to live as a monk at Clairvaux[420], but when Santo Stefano del Bosco joined the Order (1150) its Carthusian prior, William, became the first Cistercian abbot[421]. Incorporation could bring disputes regarding both ownership of property and status within the Order. The possession of the grange of Vaudoncourt had to be settled by arbitration after Cistercians replaced Canons Regular at L'Isle-en-Barrois (1151)[422]. There was prolonged argument as to whether Waverley (fd 1128) or Furness (fd 1127, but not incorporated until 1147) should have seniority in England. The General Chapter (1232) eventually decided, inexplicably, that Furness should have priority in England in the families of L'Aumône (Waverley's mother house) and Savigny (its mother-house), but that Waverley should take precedence in general abbatial congregations[423]. The importance given to seniority is clear in a ruling by the General Chapter (1225) that, pending a final decision, the name of Furness was to 'be written in the "tabula" in that place from which it has been lately erased'[424].

An important component in Cistercian expansion was the eremitical movement – at its height from about 1075 to 1125[425]. A hermit was rarely alone: disciples gathered around him and living quarters were built. As such groups grew they frequently became institutionalised – as in the charterhouses – or by absorption into new Orders, such as those of Cîteaux and Prémontré[426]. Numerous Cistercian abbeys had their roots, directly or indirectly, in eremitism – including Espina, Fontenay, Morimond, and Waldsassen – to name but a few. Notable hermits who paved the way for a Cistercian foundation included Vitalis of Savigny (ob. 1122), Stephen of Obazine (ob. 1159), and Christian of L'Aumône (ob. *c.* 1165)[427]. The foundation of the Cistercian nunnery of Vallbona dates back to two communities, one of men and one of women, founded by the hermit Ramon, who (in 1173) gave himself 'body and soul' to Poblet[428]. At least two abbeys of the Order reflect their eremitical orgins in their names: *Bégard* – after the forest hermitage of Raoul Bégar[429] – and *Reclus* – from the recluse who previously lived there[430]. Not all the hermits who had occupied the final site of Kirkstall (1152) became Cistercians: some accepted financial compensation for dispossession[431]. Some incorporated hermitages were not transformed into monasteries but were retained as granges, and their lands became a welcome addition to the estates of the absorbing abbey. Such land extensions took place when the anchorites of Gaia were incorporated by Santes Creus (*c.* 1170)[432], when the Welsh hermitage of Llanfair Cilgoed was granted to Dore (1201)[433], and when the hermits of Swarnogata, taking the Cistercian habit at Oliwa (1303), transferred their lands to that abbey[434].

A principal figure in the eremitical movement was Géraud of Sales (d. 1120) who established several groups of hermits in SW France which came to form a 'Geraldine congregation', following the *Rule of St Benedict*. After his death it broke up: some hermitages became Benedictine, some remained autonomous, and some disappeared altogether, but others re-grouped around two leading hermitages in new, small, congregations – those of Cadouin and Dalon[435]. A bull of Innocent II (1143) required the Cadouin congregation to follow Cistercian observances[436]. Two of the abbeys (Ardorel and Grandselve) resented the control which Cadouin attempted to exercise, and they (as also Gondon, Fontguilhem and Faise) were absorbed into the Cistercian Order (in 1146/47). Cadouin itself had become an abbey in 1119, with a monk of Pontigny as its first Cistercian superior, but thereafter the link with Pontigny was at best tenuous and all but forgotten[437]. Innocent III (1201) ordered the reluctant monks of Cadouin to 'return' to the Cistercian Order, which suggests that the monastery had long been estranged. After this final incorporation the abbot of Cadouin was accounted the eleventh most senior in the Order, and his house placed firmly in the lineage of Pontigny[438]; its monks were obliged to conform to the habit and liturgy of the Cistercians, whilst their appropriated parish churches were to be served henceforth by secular chaplains, no longer by monks. They were, however, allowed to retain any tithes they owned, and the abbot of Cadouin continued to have the right to confirm the election of abbots of, and officially visit, all the eleven or so houses of his family[439], which thus remained 'a clan within a tribe'[440]. Such concessions were not helpful to maintaining uniformity within the Order, and resentment surfaced at the General Chapter of 1244[441].

The smaller congregation of Dalon also became an abbey following Cistercian custom after Géraud's death, with again a a monk of Pontigny as abbot[442]. The congregation was formally incorporated into the Order in 1162, though, contrary to Cistercian custom, Dalon retained its salt grange in Saintonge as a priory[443]. Also originating in a forest hermitage was the eremitical congregation founded (about 1127) by Stephen of Obazine. Like Silvanès, his group of hermitages was rejected by the Carthusians, but accepted at the notable Cistercian General Chapter of 1147 – though earlier declined because of the association with nearby Coyroux nunnery. The incorporation was conditional upon all non-Cistercian customs being gradually suppressed. Four of Obazine's cells, which ranked previously as priories, were grouped into the new abbey of Grosbot-Fontvive (its double name stemming from two of the absorbed cells)[444]. Obazine was placed in the line of Cîteaux, a *conversus* of which appears to have played a leading rôle at Obazine from 1168 to 1184, witnessing twenty-seven of its charters[445]. The ancient Celtic monasteries of Ireland were more akin to eremitical establishments than the five or so Cistercian abbeys (and fifty-seven houses of Augustinian Canons) which came to occupy their sites[446]. Other incorporated Celtic sites (not necessarily absorbing Celtic personnel) included Culross (St Serf's)[447], possibly Rushen (St Leoc's)[448], and perhaps a Welsh *clas* at Margam[449].

Very few Carthusian houses became Cistercian. Both Orders had similar austere ideals and there had been an empathy between them since the days of St Bernard; mutual respect was echoed in the pacts (of 1195 and 1210) whereby they normally declined to receive vocations from each other's houses[450]. The same mostly held good for the Premonstratensians. Not a few monasteries, however, had previously housed Augustinian Canons, amongst them *Canonica* (inc. 1223), its name betraying its origins[451]. Some quite large houses had once been Benedictine – such as the Dunes, Esrum, and Lubiąż. When an abbot of the former Benedictine monastery of Carracedo (1222) tried to disaffiliate his house from the Cistercian Order, Honorius III wrote to him urging him to refrain from such a step, and 'not to be like the wife of Lot who looked back'[452]. A wide variety of other incorporations included the Orders of St William (1279) and of the (Castilian) Penitents of Jesus Christ (1280)[453]. As the need for small leper hospitals and hostels for travellers lessened, these too were sometimes absorbed – like La Piana (*c.* 1235)[454]. The short-lived incorporation of several Orthodox houses during the ascendancy of the Latin Empire in the East has been noted; the Orthodox did not take this lying down, and contested the occupation by Cistercians of Chortaïton and Rufiniano[455]. Venetian Torcello received the Cretan Orthodox monastery of Gergeri (1217); matters did not work out successfully, for a few years later (1223) the Italian monks were seeking to build 'a place where they can lay their heads'[456].

The greatest single catch for the Cistercians was the Order of Savigny which had evolved out of a group of hermits in the far south-western border of Normandy and numbered some thirty houses at the time of its incorporation[457]. The Savigniacs already followed Cistercian custom in part – an annual general chapter, regular visitation, and exemption from payment of most tithes. There were major differences – the Savigniacs possessed manors, serfs and tithes, and, in theory, the abbot of Savigny ruled all the houses of the congregation absolutely[458]. There were disputes within the Order (as between Calder and Furness concerning the paternity of Byland, 1142)[459] and it may have been such crises that led abbot Serlo to apply for his congregation to become Cistercian. This was agreed at the General Chapter of 1147, and confirmed by

Eugenius III at the Council of Rheims, though abbot Peter of Furness resisted the move[460]. The Savigniac houses were placed in the line of Clairvaux, and its abbot was ranked as the fifth in seniority in the Cistercian Order – displacing from that position the 'venerable member'[461], a resentful abbot of Preuilly. The abbot of Savigny was given the privileges of being attended by monks rather than *conversi*, and of having a party of three horses when he rode to the General Chapter[462]. The Savigniacs retained a certain degree of independence. One of the best-known abbots of Savigny, Stephen of Lexington (1224–43), referred to the former congregation as 'our whole derivation', and held separate Savigniac abbatial conventions[463]. Some houses of Savigny continued to possess their manors and churches, and Alexander III (*c.* 1170) criticised them, saying that they had promised to observe Cistercian custom in every respect, but had not been doing so[464]. Such retention of sources of income rejected by the early fathers of Cîteaux, together with the customs retained by other absorbed congregations, cannot but have weakened the maintenance of the Order's cherished 'simplicity' and 'uniformity'[465]. Be this so or not, the accession of so many former monasteries and hermitages to the Order played a prominent rôle in its numerical growth and apparent success.

This quick and widespread growth of the Cistercian Order brought both praise and resentment: praise for its spiritual life, resentment of its privileges and considerable land ownership. Some critics voiced both. William of Malmesbury (*c.* 1120) said that the Cistercians were 'a model for all monks, a mirror for the studious, an inspiration for the indolent'. Peter the Venerable (ob. 1156), once at logger-heads with St Bernard, praised their fasts, vigils and labours. Archbishop Richard of Canterbury (ob. 1184) saw the Order as more appropriately called 'holy' than any other[466]. Gerald of Wales (*c.* 1200), also a stern critic at times, praised the Order as 'a strong pillar of the Church'[467]. As the Order spread like a tidal wave through Europe, it did arouse strong passions, but its critics perhaps too often forgot the confidence placed in it by several supreme pontiffs, its fidelity to severe and demanding discipline and liturgy, the emergence of many undoubtedly holy lives, and its constant work of charity. It was easy to forget that many other monasteries sought to join the white monks, and that, in the words of Orderic Vitalis (*c.* 1140), 'many noble warriors and profound philosophers flocked to them'[468].

Notes

1. Knowles (1969) 13–20, 33–37.
2. Lackner (1972) 6–40, 56, 85–86, 90.
3. Lekai (1977a) 24.
4. *Statuta* III, 196 (1280/9), 352 (1321/3).
5. Lackner (1972) 216.
6. Hilling (1992) 30, 33.
7. Leyser (1984) 101, Locatelli (1975) 178; *cf.* RBM I, *passim.*
8. *Cf.RD* I, 568 (No. 3344).
9. Lackner (1972) 131, 152–53.
10. *Ibid.* 122–24, 155–58.
11. *Ibid.* 93.
12. *Ibid.* 90; *cf.* Mikkers (1988) 742.
13. *LSB* 77 (No. 49).
14. *Inter alia: CDS* III, 75 (Walkenried, 1134); Archivum Panstowe w Poznañiu, *Lekno Cyst. 1* (Lekno, 1153); CE *87* (Esrum, 1173); *RBM* I, 187 (No. 415; Plasy, 1193); *cf. CDAC* 106 (No. 116; Cîteaux, 1140).
15. Lackner (1972) 45–50, 168–76.
16. *Ibid.* 187–96, 201, 208–09.
17. *Ibid.* 220–24, 238–39; *cf.* Mikkers (1988) 736.
18. Lackner (1972) 217, 255.
19. *Ibid.* 233, 244.
20. *DHGE* XXII (1988) 682, Dimier (1982f) 689–92.
21. Lackner (1972) 240–41, 266–67.
22. *Cf. CHA* I, 240.
23. Lekai (1977a) 14, Wulf (1944) 22–23.
24. Knowles (1963a) 199, Wulf (1944) 24.
25. Lackner (1972) 218–19, 257; Waddell (1982) 256–57; *cf.* Mikkers (1988) 736.
26. *Cf.* Załuska (1989) 69.
27. Lekai (1977a) 16–17.
28. *Statuta* II, 15–16 (1222/13: Feast of Twelve Lessons); II, 398 (1254/1: name added in the Litany).
29. Lekai (1977a) 16.
30. Waddell (1982) 247–48, 259–63, 268; *cf.* Lekai (1977a) 457–58 ('Roman Privilege').
31. Lackner (1972) 259.

32. *WMG (1)* 380 (2) 347; *SRD* IV, 558; *cf. CP* I, 243–44.
33. Lackner (1971) 6–8.
34. Casey (1988) 288.
35. Knowles (1963a) 209.
36. James (1957) 18, 23.
37. Dimier (1952) not paginated.
38. Lekai (1977a) 18–19.
39. Stéphan (1970) 41.
40. Lekai (1977a) 34.
41. Williams (1935) 162, 166.
42. *LSB* x.
43. James (1957) 91.
44. *Ibid.* 93–96.
45. *Ibid.* 104.
46. *LSB* 182–211 (Nos. 127–43; including letters to Henry I of England, Emperor Lothair, and Louis VI of France).
47. Lekai (1977a) 35, Williams (1935) 97.
48. James (1957) 107–08, 112, 123; *cf.* Carlson (1987).
49. Williams (1935) 51, 135.
50. James (1957) 70.
51. Bedini (1964) 21.
52. James (1957) 123–25.
53. Lesher (1984) 261–62.
54. Chauvin (1989) 43.
55. Barber (1994) 12–23; *cf.* Carlson (1987) 142.
56. James (1957) 74–75.
57. Moore (1974) 1–10.
58. Paulsell (1976) 72–74.
59. James (1957) 165–66.
60. *LSB* 463–64 (No. 392).
61. Paulsell (1976) 73–74; *cf.* Lekai (1977a) 35.
62. *KDS* I, 43–46 (No. 17), *RBM* I, 125 (No. 281); *cf.* Dunin-Wąsowicz (1988) 533.
63. *SB (2)* 567–619 (De Warren, 'Tables chronologiques').
64. Williams (1935) 136–58.
65. Carlson (1987) 133–34, Connor (1988) 173, Moore (1974) 10, 61, 86; Williams (1935) 273, 62; *cf.* Holdsworth (1990) 86–101.
66. *DHGE* VI (1934) 555, Canivez (1928) 29–40, Moore (1974) 1–10.
67. Bedini (1964) 21, King (1954) 211–18; *cf.* Paulsell (1976) 72–74 (chapel dedicated to St Bernard in Florence).
68. Leclercq (1976) 11.
69. Connor (1988) 173, Dimier (1952) not paginated, and (1982d) 650–52; King (1954) 218.
70. Dimier (1952) not paginated.
71. Williams (1935) 85, 167.
72. Luddy (1937) 674.
73. *LSB* 259–62, 265–84 (Nos 187–88, 193, 195–208).
74. Lekai (1977a) 231, Paulsell (1976) 74.
75. James (1957) ix–xviii, *cf. CHA* (2–3) 157–58 (No. 850).
76. Leclercq (1978) 137, Lekai (1977a) 231, Mikkers (1988) 743.
77. Leclercq (1978) 214.
78. Lekai (1977a) 231.
79. *LSB* xvii.
80. *Cf.* King (1954) 234, Paulsell (1976) 72–74.
81. James (1957) 134–41.
82. *LSB* 402 (No. 326).
83. Moore (1974) 9–10, Williams (1935) 162, 166; *cf. LSB* 212–15 (Nos 144, 146).
84. *LSB* 472 (No. 399).
85. *LSB* 270 (No. 201).
86. *Ibid.* 270 (No. 201).
87. Leclercq (1978) 213, *Cf. inter alia, LSB:* 215 (No. 146), 270 (No. 201), 442 (No. 372), 519 (No. 464), 521 (No. 469).
88. *Cf.* Holdsworth (1990) 90–91.
89. Lackner (1978b) 21.
90. King (1954) 234, Zarnecki (1972) 70; *cf.* CMM *I, 153–54.*
91. McCaffery (1978) 200–08.
92. *LSB* 289–93 (No. 215); *cf.* King (1954) 109, Knowles (1963a) 513.
93. Constable (1971) 51–52, Leclercq (1976) 35–36.
94. Holdsworth (1990) 86.
95. Bredero (1978) 85, 89–90, 98–99.
96. *Statuta* I, 528 (1220/55), *cf.* I, 70 (1159/7).
97. James (1957) 20.
98. *Statuta* II, 461 (1260/4).
99. *Statuta* III, 200 (1280/26).
100. *FRB* II, 262.
101. Hill (1971) 65.
102. *Cf. CDAC 81–82 (No. 69).*
103. Lekai (1977a) 68.
104. *DHGE* XII (1953) 894, Lekai (1977a) 63–64.
105. *DHGE* XII (1953) 895, XIV (1960) 1282; Marriott (1963) 99–93, Thompson (1920) 78–79.
106. *DHGE* XII (1953) 895, Lackner (1978b) 18; *cf. LMT* 235 (No. 249).
107. *DHGE* XII (1953) 933.
108. *DHGE* XVII (1971) 1209; Bolton (1990) 149.
109. *DHGE* XII (1953) 934–35.
110. *Ibid.* 862.
111. *FHL* I, 21.
112. *DHGE* XII (1953) 934.
113. *Ibid.* 935.
114. *Ibid.* 936.
115. *Ibid.* 936–37; *Statuta* II, 214 (1240), 230–31 (1241/3); *cf. CM* 183.
116. *DHGE* XII (1953) 937–38.
117. *Ibid.* 938–39.
118. Desmond (1971) 144.
119. *Statuta* I, 527 (1220/49).
120. *Statuta* II, 86 (1230/11), 121 (1233/49), 192 (1238/39), 217 (1240/6), 260 (1243/5).
121. De Ganck (1975) 265; *cf.* McCrank (1975) 265.
122. *Statuta* II, 187 (1238/12); *CDH* 208–06 (No. 18).
123. *Statuta* II, 411, 419 (1255/7, 40–41); *DHGE* XII (1953) 938–40.
124. *Cf. CMH* 70–82 (No. 51 of 1189) with *UKS* 44–47 (No. 43 of 1275); *see too:* Chapter 12.
125. *CAF* 5–98, *cf. CE* 1–40.
126. *DSMP* 166–68 (No. 196); *cf. RHC* 96–102.
127. *RBM* II, 753 (No. 1753).
128. McGuire (1985b) 260.
129. *KD* I, No. 1.
130. France (1992) 201; *cf.* 200.
131. *CDB* (2) 391–92.
132. *CD* I, 26–28; *cf.* Kornerup (1879) 112, 131.
133. *CDEM* I, 276; *cf. CD* I, 145–46.
134. CDEM I, 118 (No. 265); *cf. CE* 87.

135. VCH, *Kent* II (1926) 153.
136. *DHGE* XII (1953) 157.
137. *SBC* I, 17.
138. *DHGE* XIV (1960) 314–15.
139. VCH, *Hampshire* II (1903) 140.
140. VCH, *Stafford* III (1970) 230.
141. *FRB* V, 111.
142. *Cf.* VCH, *York* III (1974) 142 (Kirkstall); *FRB* IV, 36–37 (No. XXIX), 46 (No. XXXVI; Zbraslav).
143. Carville (1981) 43.
144. Hockey (1976) 95.
145. *CPR* 1294/62; VCH, *Chester* III (1980) 156.
146. Van Der Meer (1965) 300.
147. Williams (1984) I, 193.
148. Carville (1984) 31.
149. *DAM* I, 15, 319.
150. Bedini (1964) 188, Serra (1984) 224.
151. Dimier (1965) 214–22.
152. Williams (1978) 233.
153. Locatelli (1975) 185.
154. Grégoire (1985) 225.
155. *RCH* 63.
156. Dupont (1982) 655–55.
157. *DHGE* VI (1932) 629.
158. *DHGE* XV (1963) 850.
159. Campbell (1899) 122–21.
160. Gwynn (1970) 124.
161. Williams (1984) I, 9.
162. Velehrad guide, 17*n*.
163. *CCR* 1232/122, 1233/220–21.
164. Richardson (1951) 1.
165. Jarry (1864) 230–32.
166. *Statuta* II, 351 (1250/25); *cf.* II, 363 (1251/16, 18, 20); 367 (1251/38); 379 (1252/12–13, 15); 444 (1258/28); III, 201 (1280/38).
167. McGuire (1982) 38, 51, 61–62.
168. Da Silva Barros (1972) 5.
169. Stalley (1987) 14.
170. Bernard (1967) 133–34.
171. Szacherska (1977) 97, 128–29, 144–45.
172. Hill (1968) 29, 54; Lekai (1977a) 286–88.
173. *Statuta* I, 181–82 (1195/3).
174. *DHGE* II (1914) 25, 27; *cf.* Jansen (1984) 79.
175. *DHGE* XII (1953) 940–41, Dimier (1954) 10–11, Southern (1970) 261–62.
176. Richards (1968) 99, Sowell (1982) 71.
177. *DHGE* XII (1953) 941–43.
178. *Ibid.* 944–42; Dimier (1954) 1011.
179. Dimier (1954) 8, Lohrmnan (1980) 120; *cf.* *Statuta* II, 25 (1223/16), 32 (1224/14), 57 (1227/11), 66 (1228/5).
180. Dimier (1954) 120–21; *DHGE* XII (1953) 942.
181. Dimier (1954) 53, 56, 58; *cf.* Jansen (1984) 76.
182. Dimier (1954) 67, 71–74.
183. *DHGE* XII (1953) 862, 944–42.
184. Dimier (1954) 116–17.
185. *DHGE* XII (1953) 942–43.
186. Hümpfner (1927) 8; *cf.* *DHGE* XII (1953) 891.
187. *RCH* 29, *cf.* Gerevich (1977) 166.
188. *RCH* 28–29, Lekai (1976) 41, 256.
189. *RCH* 19, Lekai (1976) 258.
190. Hümpfner (1927) 9, Ostojić (1965) III, 638–40.
191. *RCH* 91–92, Fuxhoffer (1969) 92.
192. *DHGE* VII (1934) 494, Lekai (1976) 259–60, Sinor (1959) 60.
193. VCH, *Lancaster* II (1908) 114.
194. Cottineau (1935) I, 1650; *cf.* *Statuta* II, 348 (1250/13).
195. VCH, *Essex* II (1907) 125.
196. Jansen (1984) 76, 79.
197. *Ibid.* 76.
198. *CPR* 1350/484, 560.
199. Schittekat (1966) 28.
200. Talbot (1960) *passim.*
201. VCH, *Sussex* II (1973) 72.
202. *DHGE* IX (1937) 1099; *cf.* CBP III, 31 (No. XXXIV).
203. Hockey (1970) 21, (1976) 11–12, 23; Williams (1984) I, 171.
204. *CPR* 1226/40, *AF* 84, *AM* II, 348; *cf.* Madden (1963) 357.
205. Carville (1973a) 30, 33.
206. Talbot (1939) 42.
207. *DHGE* II (1914) 892; Jansen (1984) 79; respectively.
208. Attwater (1965) 218–19.
209. Williams (1978) *passim*; *cf.*Dubosz (1995) 244, 257.
210. *RBM* IV, 322 (No. 819).
211. Buczek (1971) 99.
212. Barnes (1982) 70–71.
213. O'Dwyer (1976) 78, 84–85.
214. Buczek (1971) 99–103.
215. McCrank (1975) 269, *cf.* 273.
216. *SMD* II, 206–52; McGuire (1976a) 76–107.
217. McGuire (1982) 149.
218. Lackner (1972) 109–10.
219. Barnes (1982) 68, Hill (1968) 44.
220. Birch (1897) 173.
221. Hays(1963) 20.
222. *AF* 203.
223. Williams (1984) I, 12.
224. Lekai (1977a) 288.
225. *DHGE* VII (1934) 164.
226. Williams (1984) I, 9.
227. *CPR* 1272/673, 1279/337, 1280/358.
228. Lekai (1976) 264.
229. *CC* (3) B. 53–56.
230. Williams (1984) I, 55–57.
231. *CAF* 153, Lekai (1976) 264.
232. Lackner (1972) 110.
233. Donkin (1967) 279–81.
234. *Ibid.* (1967) 284, (1978) 27.
235. *Statuta* I, 35–37.
236. *LSB* 403–08 (No. 328); *cf.* *Statuta* I, 39; 173 (1194/12), 230 (1198/42), 344 (1207/54), 498 (1218/63); II, 99–91 (1230/33), 108 (1232/42), 206 (1239/17), 344 (1249/49); Coomans (1995), Dimier (1952); Péchenard (1883) 97–98.
237. Birch (1870) 282.
238. *Statuta* I, 63 (1157/34); *cf.* *Statuta* I, 37 (of 1142); 63 (1157/34), 71 (of 1163). *cf.* Parisse (1994) 10.
239. *Statuta* I, 71 (1159/*n*).
240. Donkin (1978) 28.
241. Donkin (1967) 285–86, (1978) 28.
242. *Ibid.* (19867) 285–86, (1978) 28; Kinder (1980) 10–11.

28   *The Cistercians in the Early Middle Ages*

243. Dimier (1958) 112–16, with map.
244. Donkin (1967) 286.
245. Bligny (1960) 330, 357.
246. *DHGE* XI (1949) 621–22; Donkin (1978) 28.
247. Donkin (1978) 21–22, Wulf (1944) 73.
248. Waddell (1994) 28; *cf. AM* II, 235.
249. Barnes (1982) 3, Williams (1935) 395.
250. Barnes (1982) 3, Lekai (1977a) 287–88.
251. Hill (1971) 66–63, Lekai (1977a) 287–88.
252. *CTB* 11; *cf.* King (1985) 130.
253. *Statuta* I, 488–83 (1217/76); *cf. OC* XIII–XIV.
254. Conbhuř (1963) 293.
255. Dugdale (1846) V, 71.
256. *Statuta* II, 204 (1239/11), 83 (1270/13).
257. *E.g.:* Birch (1870) 281–99, 352–69; *CSMD II*, 217–18.
258. Locatelli (1975) 181–82, 184, 192–200, 208, 213–14; *cf.* Chauvin (1989) 5, 12, 55, 67.
259. Barrière (1983) 77, Berman (1981) 195.
260. Berman (1983) 43.
261. Warren (1946) 59, 61.
262. Cocheril (1964) 267.
263. McCrank (1973) 60–61, (1976) 138–39.
264. Lekai (1977a) 41, *cf. DHGE* XV (1963) 948, Donkin (1967) 279.
265. Grèzes-Ruelff (1977) 258, McCrank (1973) 60.
266. McCrank (1973) 50–59, 68–65.
267. *Statuta* I, 271 (1201/38).
268. McCrank (1973) 61*n*.
269. *DHGE* (1949) 1122.
270. *DHGE* XII (1953) 891, *cf.* Bouton (1959) I, 230.
271. *DSMLR* 173–185 (Nos 3–4).
272. *DHGE* XV (1963) 948–59; Cocheril (1959b) 55–56.
273. *DHGE* XII (1953) 891; Cocheril (1959b) 40, 54–55.
274. Cocheril (1959b) 41, 64; Durand (1983) 108.
275. Durand (1983) 102.
276. *LSB* 469 (No. 397).
277. *DHGE* XV (1963) 951, Cocheril (1964) 234.
278. Thompson (1920) 70; *cf.* Clapham (1941) 365.
279. Schulz (1982) 168.
280. Thompson (1920) 73; *cf.* Lekai (1977a) 37.
281. Schulz (1982) 168–69.
282. Thompson (1920) 72.
283. Thompson (1920) 74.
284. Williams (1978) 229–30.
285. Lekai (1976) 252, 254.
286. *LCC* (1) 116, (2) 314.
287. *Statuta* III, 141 (1275/9).
288. Bouton (1959) I, 163; *cf.* Schich (1979b) 138.
289. Szacherska (1977) 122, 154–55.
289a. Grüger (1996) 103.
290. King (1954) 354.
291. Čechura (1996) 37–38, Charvátová (1991) 178.
292. *CDEM* I, 221–22; *cf.* Charvátová (1987) 113.
293. *CDEM* II, 274–76; *cf.* Ječný (1987) 138–40.
294. *CDEM* II, 19–13, 45–48, 112–16, 121–22, 193–201.
295. Charvátová (1987) 123; Boháč (1996) 105–14 (for Lusatia).
296. Lekai (1976) 255, 267–68.
297. *RCH* 29–30, 83; *cf. RCC* II, 369.
298. *RCH* 24.
299. *RCH* 112, 121–22, 125; *cf.* Koslowska–Budkowa (1983) 75.
300. *Statuta* II, 449 (1259/4).
301. *Statuta* III, 131–32 (1274/21), 143–44 (1275/19).
302. *RCH passim.*
303. *Statuta* I, 458 (1216/42).
304. *RCH* 113.
305. *Statuta* I, 458 (1216/42); III, 40 (1266/25), 118 (1279/29); *RCH* 30.
306. *UGDS* 93–94 (No. 107).
307. Entz (1968) 144.
308. Matei (1974) 53; *cf. UGDS* 356–60 (No. 388); Reissenberger (1894) 9.
309. Clair (1961) 262.
310. Panagopoulos (1979) 6–8; *cf.* Clair (1961) 211.
311. Brown (1958) 63, 76–78, 82–84; Clair (1961) 262, 269–70; *cf. Statuta* I, 397 (1212/36).
312. Bon (1969) 79, 480; Clair (1962) 266–65.
313. Bon (1969) 554, Brown (1958) 90, 116–18, Clair (1961) 276–77; *cf. Statuta* III, 14 (1276/12).
314. *DHGE* XVII (1971) 1209, Bedini (1964) 9–25, Dimier (1957) 63–67.
315. *Statuta* II, 50 (1226/13), 59 (1227/19), 105 (1232/25), 118 (1233/34); III, 110–11 (1272/32).
316a. *Statuta* II, 65 (1228/4).
316b. *Statuta* 105–06 (1232/27).
317. *Statuta* II, 149 (1235/43), 408 (1254/39); III, 40–41 (1266/25).
318. *Statuta* II, 388 (1252/54).
319. *Statuta* III, 480 (1344/14).
320. *Statuta* I, 242–43 (1199/56).
321. *Statuta* III, 255–56 (1291/40).
322. Gosso (1940) 80.
323. *DHGE* XIII (1956) 805, McGinn (1985) 21, 26–28; *cf.* Burger (1986) *passim.*
324. McGinn (1985) 20, 25.
325. Wulf (1944) 234; *cf. OC* LXXI–LXXII.
326. *DHGE* XIII (1956) 805, McGinn (1985) 27.
327. Bett (1931) 16, Cross (1957) 727; *CHA* (2–3) 171 (No. 939).
328. Pringle (1992) 183, *cf. LSB* 294 (No. 216).
329. Williams (1974) 61–62.
330. Hamilton (1976) 409, (1980) 219; *cf.* Richard (1969) 25.
331. Williams (1974) 72.
332. Richard (1969) 72, Williams (1974) 74; *cf. Statuta* III, 248 (1290/16).
333. Pringle (1992) 184–85.
334. *OC* 144, *cf.* King (1985) 128.
335. *OC* 139.
336. White (1938) 172–77.
337. Williams (1974) 67.
338. Williams (1974) 68–69, *cf.* Millet (1899) 32.
339. *CRSHR* I, 53.
340. Barnes (1982) 3, Hill (1968) 97–98, 102.
341. Fergusson (1984) 17–19; *cf.* Hill (1968) 36, 39.
342. Hill (1968) 63.
343. Knowles (1963a) 229, (1969) 87; *cf.* LSB 235–43 (Nos 168–73).
344. VCH, *Lancaster* II (1966) 117, 128.

345. Easson (1957) viii-ix; *cf.* Barnes (1982) 3.
346. Easson (1957) viii, Talbot (1939) 23.
347. Easson (1957) ix, 65.
348. Carrick (1907) 28–29, Easson (1957) 7.
349. Easson (1957) 63–66; *cf.* Campbell (1899) 175.
350. Gilbanks (1899) 22, Midmer (1979) 231, 278.
351. Williams (1984) I, 5, 7, 1–10, 34–41.
352. *BC* 163.
353. Williams (1984) I, 4.
354. James (1957) 178–74.
355. Gwynn (1970) 3, Stalley (1987) 10–12.
356. James (1957) 172–73.
357. O'Dwyer (1975) 271, *cf. Statuta* I, 122 (1190/17).
358. *Cf.* Carville (1973a) 40; Stalley (1987) 12 (fig. 2), 13–14.
359. Stalley (1987) 16.
360. *DHGE* XIV (1960) 932–38.
361. *Ibid.* 10, 16, 31.
362. *Ibid.* 107–08.
363. Williams (1984) I, 193.
364. *Cf.* VCH, *Chester* III (1980) 159; *Lancaster* II (1960) 114*n*; *RHC 138*, Talbot (1939) 56.
365. *Cal. Documents relating to Ireland* (Rolls Ser., 1875) (1171–1251) 341 (Nos 2293, 2295), 342 (2302); (1293–1301) 110–111 (No. 260); (1302–07) 94 (277), 253 (713), 263 (714), 298 (722).
366. *Statuta* I, 97 (1184/14), 244 (1199/59); II, 133 (1234/31); *cf.* I, 192 (1195/68), 518–19 (1220/12); II, 278 (1244/22), 305–06 (1246/25).
367. *Statuta* I, 470, 483 (1217/25, 78–79).
368. *Statuta* II, 4–5 (1221/21).
369. *Statuta* II, 110 (1232/50), 120–21 (1233/47), 138–39 (1234/53); III, 267 (1294/37).
370. *Statuta* III, 86 (1270/29).
371. *SL* 44, O'Dwyer (1975) 273.
372. *Statuta* I, 509–10 (1219/33); II, 5 (1221/22), 50 (1226/15), 61 (1227/28), 97 (1231/32).
373. Schonsgaard (1953) *passim*.
374. France (1988) 244–45, (1992) 527; McGuire (1982) 38–40; Schonsgaard (1953) 231.
375. France (1992) 77, McGuire (1982) 66–68.
376. France (1992) 243, McGuire (1982) 92, 108.
377. France (1992) 28–29, McGuire (1982) 41–43.
378. McGuire (1982) 6, (1985b) 259–60, 271.
379. France (1992) 78–79, Knowles (1963a) 248.
380. Johnsen (1967) 7.
381. France (1993) 261–75.
382. France (1992) 88.
383. *Statuta* I, 376 (1210/35), 376 (1211/41); *cf.* 396 (1212/32), 406–07 (1213/11), 422 (1214/24); II, 144 (1235/25).
384. *Statuta* III, 267 (1243/43).
385. Paris: Brussels (1965).
386. Cocheril (1966b) 119–44.
387. Vongrey and Hervay (1967) 115–52.
388. Cattana (1969) 359–63.
389. Guerin (1966) 67–69.
390. Krausen and Zakar (1966) 279–90.
391. Schrader (1970) 265–78.
392. Lekai (1977a) 402.
393. Rochefort Abbey, Belgium (1976).
394. Lekai (1977a) 49.
395. Bedini (1964) *passim*; *Statuta* I, 85–234 *passim*.
396. Golding (1990) 129–28, 139–40; *cf. DHGE* XII (1953) 866.
397. Golding (1990) 139–41.
398. Dimier (1957) 65, *cf.* Locatelli (1975) 188, 190; Mousnier (1983b) 66–66.
399. McGuire (1985b) 251.
400. Breycha-Vautier (1967) 9.
401. *DHGE* XII (1953) 943.
402. *DHGE* X (1938) 1222.
403. McGuire (1982) 75.
404. *CR* 184, *cf.* Gosso (1940) 79–80.
405. *Statuta* II, 171 (1237/14).
406. Berman (1986) 33.
407. *Cf.* McGuire (1974) 7–11.
408. *Statuta* II, 74 (1229/42).
409. *Statuta* I, 463 (1216/65).
410. Barrière (1986) 89–90.
411. *RD* I, 642 (No. 3829).
412. Dimier (1957) 65.
413. Hermano Juan (1960) 18–19.
414. Bedini (1964) 60.
415. *DHGE* XI (1949) 1256.
416. McGuire (1982) 101.
417. *OC* 250 (DCLIII).
418. Auvry (1898) III, 321.
419. Barrière (1986) 76–78, 83; Kienzle (1989) 215. *cf.* Wildhaber (1986) 35.
420. Dimier (1952) not paginated.
421. Dimier (1957) 68.
422. *CSB* 58–59.
423. *Statuta* II, 103 (1232/20); *cf.* 98 (1231/37); *AF* 196, *RSL* II, 271–72; *DHGE* XIX (1981) 46.
424. *Statuta* II, 40 (1225/28).
425. Kinder (1980) 14, Leyser (1984) 34.
426. Berman (1981) 75, 194.
427. *Cf.* Cocheril (1966) 154–55, Collin (1978) 122–23, Leyser (1984) 35–37, Mikkers (1963) 45.
428. Mikkers (1975) 367; *cf. DP* 352 (No. 470).
429. *DHGE* VII (1934) 425.
430. Dimier (1966) 45.
431. VCH, *County of York* III (1974) 143; Barnes (1982) 7.
432. Fort i Cogul (1965) 76–77.
433. Williams (1984) II, 232.
434. *MPH* VI, 316–17.
435. Lenglet (1978) 7, 39; *cf.* Barrière (1983) 76–77, (1986) 74–75; Mousnier (1982) 60.
436. Barrière (1986) 82; *cf. DHGE* XI (1949) 119.
437. Lenglet (1978) 10; *cf.* Barrière (1986) 80–81, 94–95; Mousnier (1982) 60, (1983b) 66.
438. *DHGE* XI (1949) 119; Barrière (1983) 77–78, King (1954) 152.
439. Barrière (1983) 77–78, 90; (1986) 96.
440. *DHGE* III (1924) 1617.
441. *Statuta* II, 278 (1244/24).
442. *DHGE* XIV (1960) 38, Barrière (1986) 79.
443. *DHGE* XIV (1960) 38; Barrière (1983) 77, (1986) 80, 86, 91.
444. Barrière (1986) 75, 84, 86, 92; *cf.* K i n g (1954) 23.
445. Barrière (1986) *passim*.
446. Carville (1982b) 2, *cf.* 84–87, 118; Stalley (1987) 38–39.
447. Douglas (1927) 67, Talbot (1939) 57–58.

448. McIntire (1943) 2; Butler (1988) 63 exercises caution.
449. Williams (1984) I, 16–17.
450. *Statuta* I, 188–88 (1195/41), 368–69 (1210/1); *cf.RD* I, 368–69 (No. 4520, of *c*. 1175).
451. Van Der Meer (1965) 275.
452. Goutagny (1963) 150–52; *cf. DHGE* XI (1949) 1122.
453. *Statuta* III, 188 (1279/32), 201 (1280/3), *cf.* 228 (1282/66).
454. Owen (1971) 55–56.
455. Brown (1958) 80–81, 87–89.
456. *Ibid.* 84–85; *cf.* Bedini (1964) 104.
457. *DHGE* XII (1953) 890, Hill (1968) 82, 84, 89–93.
458. Hockey (1970) 12, Wulf (1944) 109–10.
459. *Statuta* I, 37, 131 (1190/72); Hill (1968) 98–99.
460. Auvry (1898) III, 7–17, Hill (1968) 101, 104, 106–07.
461. *Statuta* III, 186 (1279/19).
462. *LCC* (1) 647, (2) 262; *Statuta* I, 48 (1152/22), III , 321 (1309/3).
463. *SL* 217, *cf.* Hockey (1970) 27, Lekai (1977a) 308.
464. Hill (1968) 107–08.
465. *Cf.* Barrière (1986) 93, Hill (1968) 108–09.
466. Lackner (1978b) 17–18.
467. Williams (1984) I, 31.
468. Lekai (1977a) 33.

Chapter 2

ADMINISTRATIVE ORGANISATION

The Rule of St Benedict

Pope Calixtus II (1119) noted how the first Cistercians had as their aim 'the observance of the Rule of Blessed Benedict'[1]. They saw themselves, undoubtedly, as reformed Benedictines, having as their model the original *Rule* free of subsequent modifications[2]. Aiming at uniformity amongst the abbeys of the Order, the *Rule* was to be 'interpreted and kept in one and the same way' (*c.* 1119)[3]. Once the first generation of white monks had passed away, the Order still insisted that the *Rule* was to be observed 'in every particular, as our holy fathers understood and kept it' (*c.* 1170)[4]. Their keeping of the *Rule* aroused the criticism of such as William of Malmesbury (*c.* 112/35) who wrote of the white monks 'following the *Rule* to such an extent that they think no iota or dot should be overlooked'[5]. In fact, the Cistercian keeping of the *Rule* meant several significant variations. The *Rule* knew nothing of a lay-brotherhood, nor of the rejection of churches and tithes, nor yet of severe diminution of local autonomy by a General Chapter[6]. Contrary to Cistercian practice, the *Rule* did give a rôle to the diocesan bishop in the appointment of an abbot, and it did assume the presence of boys – and hence of education – in a monastery[7]. So it was that the Cistercian way of life was seen not only as reformed, but also as distinctive. The monks were referred to as following 'the Rule of St Benedict and the institution of the Cistercian fathers'[8]. In all this, the Cistercians worked for 'the simplicity of our Order': a theme which will recur throughout this book, and an ideal which was frequently lost or varied.

One outcome of 'simplicity' was that the Cistercians used undyed wool for their habits, and so (perhaps as early as 1115 and certainly by 1123) they earned the name of 'the white monks', a term that endured[9]. It is noteworthy – perhaps due to the several shades of 'white'- that the monks of several Central European Cistercian abbeys were called the 'grey monks'[10]. Mostly these monasteries were of the lineage of Morimond. A general listing of the religious orders in Brandenburg (1279) referred to 'the Cistercians, the Greys, the Blacks ...'[11]. The *Chronicle of Pforta* said of the Cistercians in general that 'their habits are grey, and so, from the beginning, they have been called Greys'[11a]. The Savigniacs were also reputedly 'grey monks' before their incorporation, whilst a fourteenth-century satirical verse referred to an Irish Cistercian house as 'a fair abbey of white monks and of grey'[12].

Exemption from Episcopal Jurisdiction

The ability of the Cistercian Order to develop its especial ethos lay partly in the almost total exemption its monks came to enjoy from episcopal control. This gave it the freedom to utilise to the full its two principal institutions: an annual General Chapter and a peculiar system of statutory visitation[13]. Local bishops had a quite substantial rôle in the evolution of the Order, as no new monastery could be founded (by ancient custom stretching back to the Council of Chalcedon, AD 451) without the consent of the diocesan[14]. Early Cistercian practice insisted that not only the bishop's consent be obtained, but also his approval of the administrative arrangements outlined in the *Charter of Charity*[15]. These included the General Chapter and the system of visitation within the Order – both of which limited the relationship between a Cistercian monastery and its local diocesan. The bishop's consent thus implied acceptance of a degree of independence on the part of the white monks, and contained within it the seeds of increasing exemption from his jurisdiction[16].

In the early years of the Order (1119) the *conversi* were admitted to the ranks of the white monks 'with the licence of the bishops', and appeal might be made to the diocesan by a father-abbot dealing with a recalcitrant subordinate superior[17]. By the mid-twelfth century the situation was changing quite rapidly. Innocent II (1132) not only dispensed all Cistercian abbots from attendance at diocesan synods, he also removed the *conversi* of the Order from episcopal jurisdiction[18]. Alexander III (1165) forbade any episcopal interference in the election or deposition of a Cistercian abbot: all this was to be left to the Order's own machinery. This ruling was reflected in the later version of the *Charter of Charity* (c. 1170) which omitted the recourse of an appeal by an abbot-Visitor to the diocesan[19]. A series of papal bulls (Chapter 1), perhaps reflecting de facto situations, eventually made the white monks to all intents and purposes exempt from episcopal control. They needed to seek from the diocesan only the consecration of altars, the blessing of their abbots, the ordination of their monks, and their supplies of holy oils[20]. A notable instance of exemption was Poblet (1221) with total immunity in its *vere nullius* status[21].

As some bishops perhaps tried to re-assert ancient rights long in desuetude[22], further privileges were granted by the papacy. If the local bishop refused, after three requests, to bless a newly elected abbot, then the latter could legitimately assume office (1165), or else a passing bishop could give the blessing (1185)[23]. Bishops who had retired to a monastery could perform episcopal functions within it (1179)[24], and the white monks were freed from canonical visitation by the diocesan (1184)[25]. Hence all a bishop could do was to make representations when he felt not all was well at a particular monastery[26]. The bulls granted to individual monasteries reveal further restrictions on the diocesan bishops. They might not use the precincts of Cistercian abbeys for their business[27], nor for ordinations, trials, or public meetings[28], nor for consecrating holy oils[29], nor were they to interfere in the selection of novices[30]. The bull *Parvus fons* (1265), with its explicit rules governing the election and deposition of abbots and the Cistercian system of visitation, makes no reference at all to the local diocesan, and shows that exemption from episcopal jurisdiction was by then complete[31]. Later (1260), some abbots were allowed to confer the minor orders (acolyte, etc.) on their monks[32].

Newly-elected Cistercian abbots normally had recourse to the diocesan for their sacramental blessing. They made a profession to the bishop of 'submission, reverence, and obedience, 'as commanded by our holy fathers'[33]. (Episcopal exemption was not sought in the early years[34] and was disfavoured by St Bernard[35]). On the authority of Honorius III (1224) this promise was qualified by the additional clause, 'saving our Order', thus reflecting the actual situation *vis-à-vis* episcopal control[36]. There was not infrequently considerable tension between Cistercian communities and their diocesans (Chapter 1). Despite a papal prohibition to the contrary (1184)[37], a bishop of Worcester laid an interdict on an abbot of Hailes (1275)[38], and a bishop of Exeter excommunicated an abbot of Ford (1276)[39]. Another source of potential friction concerned the hospitality and dues expected by a bishop when on visitation to Cistercian-held parish churches. Bishops of Worcester received hospitality or a fee *in lieu*[40]; archbishops of York stayed at Kirkstall on their first visitation of that diocese[41]. The bishop of Kamień (1347) claimed from Kołbacz an annual tribute of wine, beer, oats, and money[42]. No clear pattern can be deduced from the available published evidence.

The General Chapter

The most famed institution of the Cistercians was the annual General Chapter when all the abbots of the Order were expected to visit the New Monastery, 'to meet one another, and to tend to the affairs of the Order'[43]. The discussions held endeavoured to ensure a high spiritual tone and uniformity of life within the many monasteries. Though intended to be held always at Cîteaux, the meetings could be held elsewhere, should there be criticism of the abbot of Cîteaux himself[44]; that of 1162 was held, belatedly, at a grange of Foigny, political considerations making access to Cîteaux difficult[45]. The chairman was the abbot of Cîteaux, save in 1240 and 1241 when he was in captivity and the abbot of La Ferté, the senior proto-abbot, acted in his stead[46]. For many years the General Chapter was the truest international assembly known to Europe, and Archbishop Richard of Canterbury (1178–84) praised it as 'uniting sons from every nation'[47]. It was copied by the Carthusians, Premonstratensians, and others[48]. The Fourth Lateran Council (1215) ordered all religious orders not holding general chapters to initiate them at least triennially in every province, to use the Cistercian Chapter as a model, and to invite two Cistercian abbots to explain procedure[49].

The Chapter was held, at least by 1162, around Holy Cross Day (14 September)[50]. On the first day, the abbots heard read the statutes promulgated in the previous year and any letters received. On the second day, after the examination of faults and before Sext, representative abbots (the definitors) were appointed; on the third day there was a sermon and prayers for the dead. In the intervals, for three or four days, enquiry was made into shortcomings within the Order, and petitions of various kinds discussed, the definitors drafting the Chapter's response in between sessions[51]. On the last day, after prayers for earthly rulers and protectors, the statutes agreed were promulgated, and the abbots started to disperse[52]. The extant manuscripts detailing the statutes of successive Chapters (as published by Canivez, and currently being revised by Waddell)[52a] have hardly any specific references to individual abbeys before 1180, by which time the Chapter acted as both a legislative body for the whole Order, and as a judicial tribunal – investigating the affairs of individual houses and proposed new foundations[53]. Those decisions affecting the whole Order were to be reported to the monks of each house on their abbot's return from the copy he brought. They were to be read in every monastic chapter a further three times each year[54]. No appeal was allowed from decisions of the General Chapter, not even to the Holy See[55].

In a typical year, that of 1200, some 45 of the then 525 monasteries of the Order found mention: seven abbots were criticised for non-attendance, seven commissions were appointed to consider proposed new foundations or incorporations, five commissions were set up to investigate disputes between abbeys or with houses of other Orders; seventeen statutes were personal rebukes to abbots – as for breaches of custom or discipline in their houses – and six referred to trouble within individual monasteries[56]. When the abbot of a house under censure was absent from the Chapter, its decisions were transmitted to him by abbots who were most conveniently placed geographically to do so. Such cases form one of the few pointers as to which abbots were present at a particular Chapter[57]. Several questions remain to be asked with regard to the work of the Chapter. Were the assembled abbots informed of everything they ought to have known? How did the Chapter acquire its information? How much of its knowledge was 'hearsay' evidence (as implied by the frequency of the word *dicitur*)? Were the only commands recorded in relation to individuals those which had to be passed on by a third party? Were all decisions communicated in writing, or some by word of mouth? How far were letters employed? Such conveyance of messages took time – weeks if not months[58]. How well were the instructions of the Chapter obeyed? Sometimes the work of the Chapter was impeded when abbots failed to deliver a message[59], or neglected to carry out a commission[60], or omitted to report findings back to the Chapter[61].

As the Order expanded, the attendance of individual abbots became less frequent, and the composition of one Chapter was increasingly very different from that of the previous year. This perhaps explains why important statutes might be repeated in a subsequent year – not so much because of non-compliance, but to ensure all knew of them. It also helps to explain the passage of contradictory rules, revoking statutes promulgated in the previous Chapter[62]. In the earlier years some 'laws' were proposed on an experimental basis and little heeded, like the prohibition (1152) against further new foundations. Many later regulations left loop-holes, like the statute (1182) concerning houses over fifty marks in debt, with its saving clause – 'unless there should be real necessity'. The need for common consent was underlined by the bull *Parvus fons* (1265), which stipulated that no law passed by a Chapter was to be regarded as binding unless confirmed by the following year's Chapter[63]. Differing interpretations of individual statutes appear in the eight extant original collections; until Waddell's critical edition appears, caution is necessary in using Canivez's published collection[64].

From the late twelfth century the Chapter was assisted by a steering committee of 'definitors' named by the abbot of Cîteaux. The origins of this system – not mentioned in the *Charter of Charity*[65] – may date from 1176[66]. Firm evidence comes with the requirement for a small advisory body to assist the president of the Chapter (1185)[67], and then for a representative body of fifteen abbots (1190)[68] – to meet where convenient to discuss the affairs of the Order, and to bring significant matters before the next Chapter. As well as the five proto-abbots, the superior of Preuilly was included on account of seniority, and those of Savigny and Dalon as heads of incorporated congregations. The considerable number of abbots who were potential members of the Chapter, and the need to expedite business, all contributed to necessitate such a steering committee. The definitors played an increasingly important rôle, which was at once both judicial and legislative. They decided difficult cases [69] (especially if the Chapter could not reach an agreed opinion[70]), and they edited the work done by the abbots in plenary session, drawing up each year's statutes for promulgation[71]. They were responsible for revising the codification of all those statutes in force (1214–18)[72] and for approving similar work done later (1234–35)[73]. Three of their number were to hear applications for the proposed incorporation of nunneries into the Order (1228)[74]. They had the duty to exhort the abbots assembled at Chapter to charity when Cîteaux itself fell on hard times (1235)[75], and they were to inspect the list of absentee abbots (1270)[76].

The choice of the definitors, technically nominated by the abbot of Cîteaux, became a major cause of tension between that personage and the four proto-abbots – reaching the ears of Innocent III (1202) and Honorius III (1216–17), and culminating in the schism in the Order lasting from 1263 to 1265. This necessitated the bull of Clement IV (*Parvus fons*, the 'Clementina') of the latter year[77]. The abbot of Cîteaux had (in 1197) been encouraged for the sake of 'good peace and charity' to enquire of the proto-abbots as to 'wise followers of the Order' in their respective 'families' before he made his choice[78]. Later (1215–18) the council came to consist of the abbot of Cîteaux, the four proto-abbots, and 'others they shall summon'[79]. The bull of 1265 made precise arrangements which brooked no misunderstanding[80], but which were modified (with the approval of Clement IV) after arbitration at the Chapter that autumn by Cardinal Guy of Burgundy, himself a former abbot of Cîteaux. The twenty-five definitors were to consist of the abbot of Cîteaux and the four other proto-abbots; two abbots – whom the abbot of Cîteaux could not reject – to be appointed by each of the proto-abbots from their respective lineages; and a further two from each generation chosen by the abbot of Cîteaux from short-lists of three supplied by each proto-abbot[81]. By the late-thirteenth century it is probable that the Chapter did little more than ratify the decisions of the definitors. This situation reduced the active rôle of the abbots present, discouraged regular attendance[82], and gave rise to resentment. At the Chapter of 1275 nine abbots voiced vigorous opposition to the definitors, one (Abbot Ponce of Le Reclus) calling them tyrants. The grumblers were instantly deposed[83].

The position of the abbot of Cîteaux was more than that of being 'first among equals', but it was early kept in check both by the rules of the Order, and by the influence of other significant abbots – not least St Bernard[84]. At first the General Chapter was little more than a meeting of the daughter-abbots of Cîteaux, and at the New Monastery they were to 'reverently and humbly obey the lord abbot of Cîteaux'[85]. The Chapter was superior to him, occasionally rebuked an abbot of Cîteaux, and even deposed Abbot Guy (1134)[86]. Moreover, his own abbey of Cîteaux, early described as 'the mother of us all' (*c*. 1119)[87], was subject to annual visitation (fixed in 1265 for 22 July, St Mary Magdalene's Day) by the four proto-abbots[88]. As a last resort, they could depose an incorrigible abbot of Cîteaux[89]. At first the abbot of Cîteaux was chosen by the monks of Cîteaux alone – but in the presence of as many daughter-abbots of the house as could attend, who perhaps brought pressure to bear. By the late-twelfth century these daughter-abbots participated fully in the election with the monks of the house. The bull of Clement IV (1265) again confined the election solely to the monks of Cîteaux, though the abbots could act as advisers[90]. By this time the General Chapter increasingly delegated decisions and negotiations to the abbots of Cîteaux, some of whom consciously amplified their own powers. The General Chapter addressed him as 'our venerable father' (1270)[91], his monastery being that to which 'honour and singular reverence' were due (1286)[92].

As the Order expanded, the annual Chapter at Cîteaux became an increasing burden on the resources of the New Monastery[93]. The *potential* numbers attending grew rapidly; twelve abbots in 1120, forty in 1130, no less than three hundred in 1150[94]. Not all came yearly, and the chapter-hall (built 1193) held only three hundred people – an indication of the numbers then expected[95]. At the close of the twelfth century perhaps about two hundred and fifty abbots attended each year[96]; add to this at least one or two travelling companions, and the total company to be lodged and entertained rose to at least six hundred persons.. The consequent problems in hospitality were clearly not envisaged by the founding fathers when the concept of the annual Chapter first surfaced. They were, in part, solved by obtaining specific grants of income and of food towards the maintenance of the Chapter, by limiting the numbers of colleagues and servants a participating abbot might bring with him, by restricting the length of their stay at Cîteaux, by prohibiting other guests at the monastery during the Chapter, by out-housing some of the servants (the boys particularly) in nearby Dijon, and by (from the mid-thirteenth century) levying a tax on each monastery of the Order.

Monarchs might make financial grants for the upkeep of the Chapter, as did Alfonso II of Aragon (1181)[97], and Sancho I of Portugal (1206)[98]; or give the revenues of churches – Richard I of England (1195) gave Scarborough church (amplified by a share of the tithes of the fish of Dogger Bank)[99], and Alexander II of Scotland (1189) the church of Airlie[100]. Béla IV of Hungary (1246) gave the profits of four churches[101], and Alfonso IX of León (1211) rents from royal salt-mines[102]. Several of the Order's own abbeys gave income from rents, (including L'Arrivour, Disibodenberg, Rievaulx, and Val-St-Lambert)[103]. The general taxation of the Order finds fuller mention later. Food, in the form of fish, was another means of assistance. As early as about 1150 Cîteaux received a grant to enable it to buy fish for the Chapter[104]; and, later, Cistercian fishing rights in Lake Geneva were reserved for food for the Chapter (from 22 July to 14 September each year)[105], and in a stretch of the Saône (from 23 August to 13 September)[106].

The restriction on the number of travellers varied from time to time and with geographical location. From 1134, monks were not allowed to accompany their abbot to Chapter, the company of one *conversus* or familiar (but not a boy) being felt to be sufficient. An exception was made for an abbot from overseas or south of the Alps: his party could number two horses with a boy or familiar in attendance if no *conversus* was available[107]. In the thirteenth century a party of two horses with two servants (in practice often including boys) was generally permitted, but no monk was to be brought[108]. This last regulation was later often breached, the Chapter of 1266 providing for monks accompanying their abbots to stay in the monastic dormitory[109]. Abbots from a distance – as those of England (1204)[110] and Majorca (1278)[111] – might have an extra companion, and the abbot of Savigny (1152, 1215), because of his prestige, could be accompanied by a monk[112]. A statute of 1285 implies that by that date three horses and three servants were generally allowed, though the four proto-abbots could exceed this number[113]. In the early fourteenth century, the usual rule was one *conversus* and one familiar in attendance, or two familiars if a house had insufficient *conversi*[114].

The visiting abbots were not allowed to remain at Cîteaux for longer than absolutely necessary[115]. Their attendant grooms were lodged in the stables, but from the mid-thirteenth century had to be left in Dijon[116]. Companion *conversi* also slept in the stables, but separately from the boys[117]. *Conversi* could be troublesome, as implied in a ruling (1189) that they were only to drink water, not alcohol, until they were back in their own abbey[118]. Senior abbots, like those of Clairvaux, Ourscamp[119], Eberbach and Himmerod[120], came to have their own reserved chambers at Cîteaux (1258). Because of the strain on hospitality (and perhaps the need for secrecy during deliberations)[121] no guest-monks were to be received at Cîteaux during the Chapter; any found were to be publicly flogged[122].

The term 'boys' (*pueri*) covered not only teenagers but grooms, in the same sense as stable 'lads' in Britain to-day. The General Chapter was keen to limit the number travelling to Cîteaux, and not only because of accommodation problems[123]. The 'boys' – of differing nationalities and languages – had come to gain a reputation for unruliness. The abbots were instructed not to bring 'quarrelsome' boys (1186)[124], to see that they were decently attired and did not carry sharp knives (1237)[125]. Coming to Cîteaux or the four proto-abbeys[126] they were to surrender at the gate-house any weapons they might be carrying (1257)[127]. Later, all attendants were forbidden to come armed (1317)[128]. Such arms might be a necessary precaution on a dangerous journey, but could be perilous if used in a brawl – as at Vauluisant (1241) by boys riding to Cîteaux with four abbots from the south of England[129]. It was encounters such as these, as well as the boarding difficulties, that led to the insistence that all 'boys' were to be left in Dijon during the time of the Chapter with a maximum of five shillings to cover their expenses (1239, 1257)[130]. Being left to themselves, they became a public nuisance in Dijon (1251)[131]. The Chapter had to rule that no 'boys' were brought at all unless the abbots concerned had no *conversi* – increasingly the case at this date (1267)[132] – and that 'boys' who engaged in fighting were to have their employment terminated (1278)[133].

The journey to Cîteaux was a lengthy one. From Portugal a distance of some 1400 km (900 miles) was involved. For the abbots from the west of Ireland it meant a three month absence from their monasteries[134]. It took the Polish abbots, leaving Chapter in 1289, four weeks to get as far as Silesia[135]. Valuable as the institution of the General Chapter was, it was to an extent self-defeating in frequently taking an abbot away from his monastery for lengthy periods[136]. This was perhaps a factor which led to increasing mitigation of the attendance rules. English abbots mostly met in London and then set out in convoy not later than mid-August, a month before the Chapter. For them, from the mid-thirteenth century on, permission to travel from the English monarch was usually necessary, together with royal letters of protection and of authority to change money[137]. The journey was a lengthy and costly one also for Welsh abbots. The abbot of Cymer (in 1274) borrowed £12 from the prince of Wales to assist his travel as early as 9 July, two months before the Chapter[138]. The abbot of Whitland (in the far west of Wales), and his company, paused at Chepstow Castle (about 21 July, 1217) to obtain letters of protection[139].

The abbots minimised expense by staying *en route* at abbeys and granges of the Order. To lessen the burden of hospitality, the Chapter limited their stay in any one abbey to one or two nights at most[140], and bade them be moderate in their demands (1257)[141]. At Clairvaux, a noble gift of 2,000 marks allowed the abbots of its line to gather for the feast of the Nativity of Our Lady (8 September) before they went on to Cîteaux[142]. A number of daughter-abbots of Cîteaux and Clairvaux stayed preceding and following the Chapter in their halls in Dijon[143]. Clairvaux, for its hall, received 120 bushels of wheat and six hundred gallons (2,700 litres) of wine yearly from the duke of Burgundy (*c.* 1180), and fishing rights in the lordship of Reynel for eight days before and after the time of the General Chapter (1204)[144]. Abbeys near sea-ports (as Boxley near Dover), or near Cîteaux itself (as Auberive) received many travelling abbots. For their support at Auberive, the lord of Villars-Montroyer granted the right of fishing in all his ponds during the two days preceding the Chapter (1198, 1253)[145]. At Auberive, the abbots of Ourscamp, Longpont, and Vaucelles bought up exclusive rights to lodge in a chamber by the infirmary of the monks (1258)[146], and the abbot of Cambron the right to a chamber by the infirmary kitchen (1259)[147]. These locations – by the infirmary – suggest a certain relaxation in diet and freedom of speech for the visitors. Detailed lodging arrangements were also spelt out for the abbot of Ourscamp and his daughter-abbots at Longuay (1277), also proximate to Cîteaux, in return 'for money received from them'[148]. Longuay (1321) received many other abbatial guests, as from Brabant and Flanders[149].

The welcome accorded the travelling abbots occasionally left much to be desired. On arrival at Chapter, when there had been serious discourtesy shown at an abbey or grange *en route*, the abbots affected complained, though only two or three cases at most were noted each year[150]. Whilst the *conversi* generally took the blame, it has been suggested that their abbots or cellarers encouraged them[151]. The rebellious attitude of some *conversi* was shown by one who was guest-master at Barbeaux (1220), who said that he was not afraid of the abbots, and that he wasn't bothered about serving them well[152]. This makes one wonder how effective were the penalties for such offenders decreed by the Chapter[153]. Common complaints included: disrespect – a Spanish abbot kept waiting all night outside the gate-house of Bouras (1196)[154]; lack of provisions – no wine served at Fontmorigny (1197)[155], no fodder supplied for the horses at Boxley (1219)[156]; theft of horses – as at Fiães (1204)[157]; a refusal to receive a guest – an abbot of Lehnin turned away at Riddagshausen (1198)[158]; a refusal to guide abbots in strange territory – as by a monk of Aiguebelle (1196)[159]; worse still, assault and robbery – as when the *conversi* of Les Pierres (1207) armed themselves and lay in wait for the approaching abbots[160].

A hostile reception was not the only hazard. Assault and robbery were potential dangers, and abbots travelled in the company of others for mutual protection[161]. Even so, coming to Cîteaux in convoy, Hungarian abbots were 'seized and robbed' (1197)[162]. An abbot of Doberan (1274) was excused attendance until he could have the company of other abbots[163]. The Chapter (1204) expected those abbots who were robbed on the way to complete their journey, with assistance from the abbeys visited on their route[164]. Passing through the diocese of Bourges the Iberian abbots of Moreruela and Salzedas (1252) were both robbed and badly beaten[165]. An abbot of Kirkstall (1301–12), forewarned, evaded robbers lying in wait in the woods near Roche[166]. For some there was an additional peril – the sea journey, dreaded by an unnamed Scottish abbot[167] and feared by an abbot of Calder (1238)[168]. Stormy weather in the North Sea could delay the passage of the abbot of Lyse (1236)[169]. Another problem was the crowd of beggars – often fraudulent – who sought alms as the abbots reached Cîteaux. The Chapter (1260) ordered that all such charitable monies be used to help needy abbots[170]. Some abbots failed to complete the journey because of illness, like the abbots of Lilienfeld and Zwettl (1306) – both of the lineage of Morimond and travelling together[171]. Other abbots died *en route*, frequently in an abbey where they had halted: as Richard of Fountains at Clairvaux (1143)[172], Geoffrey of Dundrennan at Auberive (1222)[173], and Elias of Whalley at Boxley (1318)[174]. Three abbots of Croxden died in France, one being buried at Cîteaux[175]. Most deaths took place on the return journey: the strain of many days spent on horseback told. Burial was usually at the abbey where death took place.

The cost, effort, and time involved in undertaking such journeys meant that well before the close of the twelfth century numerous abbots absented themselves without leave. The General Chapter (1270) ordered their excuses were to be examined, and their names noted[179a]. Some were said not to have attended for 'many years' – as those of Georgenthal (1190))[176] and distant Nydala (1192)[177]. The Chapter commented upon widespread geographical absences (1194)[178], and (in 1206) twenty abbots who should have attended were missing[179]. Failure to attend was a recurring problem throughout the thirteenth century, the Chapter ordered an enquiry (1275)[180] and saw absenteeism as 'endangering the unity of the Order' (1329)[181]. After 1152 only infirmity was accepted as an excuse for non-attendance[182], and from 1183 an absent abbot had to send a letter of explanation and a substitute – at first this was the prior, later any 'suitable' monk[183]. Abbots absent without good reason were disciplined by the Chapter[184] and usually expected not to use their stall in choir, and to eat only bread and water every Friday, until they presented themselves at Cîteaux[185]. The papal constitution for the Order (of 1335) expected absentee abbots to pay into its funds whatever sum would have been expended upon their journey[186].

The reasons proffered for absence included illness (Rufford, 1217)[187], poverty (a frequent excuse)[188], and dangers: wars *en route* (Øm and Tvis, 1215)[189], fear of the Tartars (Hungary, 1259)[190], trouble from the Scots (Sallay, 1327)[191]. Some abbots were excused at the behest of the pope – as several of southern Italy (1197)[192] and Luke of Sambucina who was away on a preaching tour (1198)[193]. Some gave dubious excuses – as an abbot of Rueda (1222) with his 'broken rib and forearm'[194], and an abbot of Midleton (Chore, 1194) who said he was too old and ill, although the Chapter heard 'he was able to ride'[195]. A few abbots were hindered from making the journey by rebellious monks or *conversi* stealing their abbot's horses and money (as Monfero, 1218)[196]. More properly, a monarch might request or explain an abbot's non-appearance at Chapter because he needed him for political or other business in his realm – as did the king of Bohemia for the abbot of Plasy (1217)[197], and the king of England for the Welsh abbot of Aberconwy (1293, 1298)[198]. An absence of abbots from Spain was explained in a letter from Alfonso X of Castile and León (1255)[199].

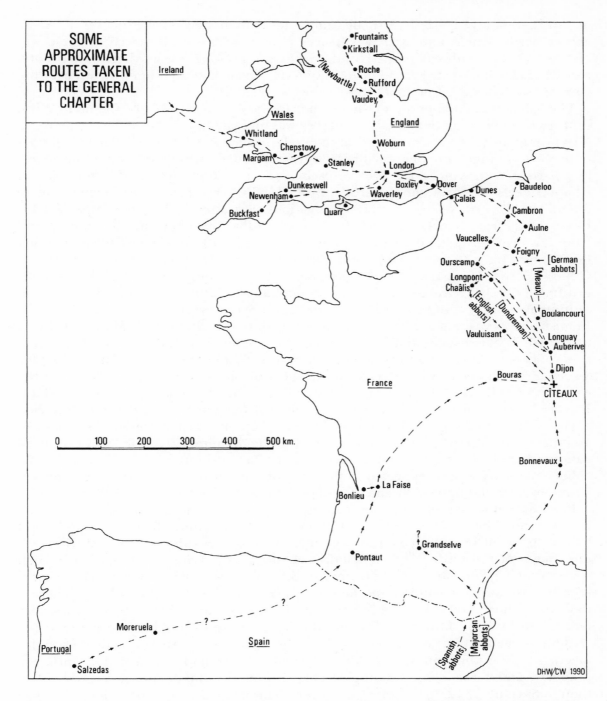

SOME APPROXIMATE ROUTES TAKEN TO THE GENERAL CHAPTER

More than one English monarch made attendance very difficult for abbots of his realm. King John (1210, 1212) forbade their presence because of the Interdict laid on his country, and because the Cistercians had refused him a financial subsidy[200]. For much of the reign of Henry III and thereafter travel was difficult because of the wars with France. Attendance might be completely forbidden or permissible only on a licence being granted[201]. In the reign of Edward I on average up to ten abbots were allowed to go[202], but in 1299 only Garendon, of several already 'congregated in London', did so[203]. Port officials could be tough: the abbots of Byland and Warden (in 1293) reached Dover but 'fearing assaults and hearing sinister rumours' returned home[204]. Those without licence caught on returning were imprisoned (seven abbots in 1308)[205]. Those who did go were not to carry any money or silver which might be of use to the enemy[206] – only a small sum to meet their necessary expenses[207]. Some abbots tried to hide money in wool sacks (1301), so a careful search of these was ordered[208]. The outbreak of the Hundred Years War (1337) meant that of the twenty-two Chapters held between 1344 to 1365 only seven had an English presence: the Chapter saw its control of the Order further weakened[209].

The 'labours and expenses' of the journey to Cîteaux meant that by the mid-twelfth century the obligation of annual attendance was mitigated for those abbots 'who live in distant regions': they were to come 'at intervals decided in Chapter'[210]. Such dispensations were arranged on a national basis with sometimes a stipulation that some abbots of a particular province were present each year – this to ensure the dissemination of Chapter decisions throughout Europe. From 1157 the Scottish abbots needed only to attend every fourth year[211]. By 1183 mitigations were a marked feature, especially for those abbots from 'across the seas', from south of the Alps ('beyond Mt. Bardo'), and from Eastern Europe and Iberia[212]. The remoter the region, the greater the mitigation. Abbots from Germany and Lombardy came every other year, by 'ancient custom' (1206)[213]; from Hungary (1211)[214] and Iberia (1229)[215] every third year; from southern Italy (1227)[216], Greece (1217)[217] and Pomerania (1229)[218] every fourth year; from Scandinavia every fifth year (1217)[219], and from Syria, every seventh year (1232)[220]. English abbots wishing to attend only every fourth year (1201) were told to abide by an unrecorded 'old dispensation'[221]. The abbot of Mellifont (1190) had to ensure that some abbots from Ireland were present each year[222]; a petition from Wales (1209) for a similar arrangement was referred to the abbot of Clairvaux[223]. Those rulings of the early thirteenth century were modified, often relaxed, in later decades, and (in Iberia[224]) very much simplified, whilst certain isolated abbeys[225] and a few individual abbots[226] received special dispensations. The Chapter (1270) ordered the names of absentees to be listed and the roll presented to the definitors[227]. As no apparent mitigation applied to the abbeys of France and the Low Countries, a total of some 420 abbots might have been expected at the close of the thirteenth century; the annals of Croxden seem to imply an attendance of over four hundred abbots in 1274[228].

Regional gatherings of abbots were rarely permitted, and never allowed to formulate new policies. The abbot of La Ferté (1191) was ordered to invalidate the chapters held by the abbots of Lombardy and to urge them to 'observe with courage and with zeal' the usages of the Order[229]. The English abbots (1248, 1250, 1260) and their Irish counterparts (1248) were told, at times of difficulties with King Henry III, 'to meet together for common counsel and help'[230]. Meetings of the English and Welsh abbots took place near Oxford (1274)[231] and at Northampton (1277)[232] to discuss levies demanded by King Edward I. Provincial chapters were ordered as a prelude to the Order's new taxation system (1326)[233] – the abbots of Germany and Silesia also meeting at Frankfurt-am-Main (1336)[234]. The General Chapter guarded its authority jealously, and forbade the holding of chapters by its component 'generations'[235] – though Savigny (c. 1230) did so[236], and even Clairvaux (1264) during a time of schism in the Order[237]. The objections of the Chapter were both to gatherings and to the promulgation of edicts[238]. When English travel to the Continent was greatly restricted, and the abbots of the province of Canterbury met in chapter (1342) 'forming their own statutes', the General Chapter realised that 'if this continues the unity of the Order will be lost'[239].

Schism was by no means unknown in the Order, but it stemmed chiefly from the growing influence of the abbots of Cîteaux, sometimes resulting in bad relations with the proto-abbots. A lengthy dispute between Cîteaux and Clairvaux (1202–13) culminated in the dismissal of the abbot of Clairvaux without the other proto-abbots being consulted[240]. Reconciliation came in a written pact (1223) following the intervention of Cardinal Conrad d'Urach, himself formerly abbot of Cîteaux[241]. It was short-lived. By

1237 Cîteaux was in dispute with the 'proto-abbots', (a 'great scandal', the abbot of Savigny termed it), their discontent allegedly fomented by the abbot of Preuilly. There was 'no small discord' in the Order[242], and peace-loving abbot John of Cîteaux resigned[243]. A major breach was that which lasted from 1263 to 1265, and which even St Louis could not heal. William of Newburgh suggested that no General Chapter was held in 1264[244]. The trouble arose partly because the abbots of Clairvaux[245] and Pontigny[246] refused to accept the disputed election (by the monks of Cîteaux alone) of James II as their abbot. It culminated in Clement's IV's bull, *Parvus fons* (the 'Clementina') which sought to address underlying problems[247].

Visitation

If the annual General Chapter was of the essence of the Order, so too was the provision for regular inspection of its monasteries, a system foreshadowed in the congregation of Vallombrosa (*c.* 1070) and in the Accord of Molesme concerning Aulps and Balerne (1110)[248]. Every Cistercian abbot was responsible for an annual visitation of each daughter-house founded directly from his own monastery, or placed under its wing[249]. During the visitation the abbot of the house under scrutiny was to cede precedence to the Visitor[250]. The procedure to be adopted was drawn up between 1152 and 1175, written into the *Book of Usages* of the Order, and amended in later years[251]. The Visitor was to make careful enquiry as to the state of the monastery, 'charitably correct' anything he found amiss, diligently encourage peace and good order, lead the monks to respect their abbot, and to practise mutual charity in Christ[252]. Opportunity was given for each monk to make known, publicly or privately, what needed correction – the faults of his abbot not being excepted[253]. The Visitor would enquire as to the satisfactory observance of the liturgy, of silence, and of stability, and would ensure that the house had a copy of the edited statutes of the General Chapters[254]. He could dismiss under-age novices[255], and would seek for evidence (certainly in later years) of simony, sorcery or sodomy[256]. He would check that the correct diet was followed[257], and that the sick and guests were cared for[258]. He might not punish or expel monks save after consulting some of the senior monks (1265)[259]. He was not to act hastily in deposing the abbot, and only to do so after taking 'great and wise counsel' (1197)[260]; later this meant the acquiescence of two coadjutor Visitors.

A Visitor also enquired into the temporal well-being of the monastery, especially where it was burdened by debt[261]. He could depose unworthy officials[262], he might fix the number of monks that the house could sustain, he would be informed of the value of its possessions, and he would give appropriate advice[263]. Visitors were reminded not to be overbearing, or to decree anything against the local abbot's will – unless absolutely necessary[264], or to divulge the names of adverse witnesses – if this could be avoided[265]. A Visitor's findings and prescriptions for reform were made known to the community in chapter, and committed to parchment[266]. This 'charter of visitation', endorsed by his seal, was kept by the precentor of the house, and was to be read to the monks by way of reminder at least thrice in the ensuing year[267]. A visitation was meant to be a positive, not a negative exercise[268], but by their very nature visitation charters generally stressed the failings found, ignoring the mass of genuine devotion and true spirituality[269].

The proceedings of a visitation are best illustrated by reference to the few extant reports which have been published. As at Holy Cross in Ireland (1228)[270] and at Stams (1328–45)[271], an inventory of an abbey's possessions (including stock) was drawn up in advance; (the same was done on the creation of a new abbot)[271a]. The injunctions of Visitors might refer to the liturgy: at Hailes (1261)[272] the monks were reminded to rise and bow during the *Gloria Patri* at the end of each psalm; at Heiligenkreuz (1287)[273] the *Salve Regina* was to be sung with greater reverence. At both abbeys, the cellarer was urged to a better performance of his duties: 'he ought to be like a father to all'. The problems of monastic stability and of contact with women surfaced at Hailes and at Dore (1318)[274]. Other prescriptions at Heiligenkreuz reiterated the prohibition on the eating of meat and of unduly long visits by parents, and referred to a lack of charity between the older and the younger monks. The number of religious who could be supported was fixed at 50 monks and 20 *conversi*. A later visitation (1315) forbade astrological speculation. The Visitor at Dore told the monks not to evade their weekly duty on rota in the church. The Register of Holm Cultram refers to its 'yearly visitation' by the abbot of Melrose[275], and the records of Sibton (1345) tell how it was 'visited by the abbot of Warden as superior'[276]. The counsel of the father-abbot was necessary for major property transactions – as when the abbot of Riddagshausen attended at Marienrode (1260)[277]. Coadjutor visitors accompanied a father-abbot if it might be necessary to depose a superior – five abbots met at Stanley (1235) to receive its abbot's resignation[278] and the presence of three abbots at Vyšší Brod (1320) might imply similar business[279]. An abbot might die whilst on visitation: Stephen of Sawley did so at Vaudey (1252) and was buried in its chapter-house[280].

Not unnaturally, some monks disliked the visitation procedures, whilst some father-abbots viewed their forthcoming duties with mixed feelings. Bl. Gerard I of Clairvaux ('proto-martyr' of the Order) was assassinated by a rebellious monk whilst on visitation at Igny (1175)[281]. Assaults on Visitors became so numerous[282] that the General Chapter (1268) was greatly disturbed by them[283]. As at Løgum (1191), the abbot of the daughter-house might be party to such opposition[284]; or, as at Tarouca (1217), the monks might pressurise the Visitor into deposing their abbot[285]. The Visitors themselves might be to blame – by being unduly harsh (as at Morimondo Milano, 1195)[286], by outstaying their welcome (Pilis, 1199)[287], by making a false unhelpful report (Chiaravalle di Milano, 1250)[288], or by deposing an abbot without proper enquiry (Fontmorigny, 1225)[289]. A common complaint was that some Visitors were susceptible to bribery: abbots of Boxley (1198)[290] and Berdoues (1221)[291] accepted gifts (notably of horses). The abbot of Acey visiting Hungary (1232) told of attempts to bribe him into making good reports on sub-standard monasteries[292]. The papal constitution of 1265[293] restricted the powers of Visitors, warned against the malicious deposition of abbots, insisted on adverse evidence against monks being publicly presented, limited any visitation to three days in length, and allowed only necessary expenses[294] to be received. The constitution of 1335 made similar provisions[295], whilst the Chapter (1287) laid down the quantity and quality of food served to Visitors[296].

Where a monastery had several daughter-houses, and perhaps some of them at a great distance, it was not always feasible for a father-abbot to inspect all of them each year. Even if he were able, the frequent absences on visitation did not make for good discipline or leadership back home. Gregory IX (1228) and Benedict XII (1335–42) noted that the visitation of the many daughter-houses of Clairvaux meant that its abbot was absent for much of the year[297]. There were individual derelictions of duty – as when an abbot of Tarouca had not visited his daughter-house for three years (1198)[298], and when an abbot of Heiligenkreuz left Bors Monostor for three years without a superior (1212)[299]. For the most part (as shown by the records of Lilienfeld) annual visitation was the norm[300]. The problem was most acute when daughter-houses lay far away – as Daphni in Greece (1259) unvisited from Bellevaux for ten years[301]. By the mid-twelfth century, later versions of the *Charter of Charity* allowed delegation: an abbot might visit 'either in person or through one of his co-abbots' – who might be closer at hand[302]. By the early-thirteenth century a father–abbot might delegate his duty to two of his own community. Abuses by such monks led the Chapter (1277) to rule that they might not become abbots of the houses they inspected, nor could a visitation be delegated to monks more often than every second year[303].

The acute problem faced by Clairvaux could only be solved by delegation. Its Welsh foundation at Margam was visited on at least three occasions by the abbot of Rievaulx (1208, 1228, 1307)[304], though by monks from Clairvaux in some years (1213, 1326)[305]. The abbot of Boxley (1233) was once commissioned to visit the monasteries of the Order in Wales[306]. When travel from France was difficult the Chapter (1324) ordered its over eighty daughter-houses to be visited from neighbouring abbeys[307]. The same pattern was true elsewhere: an abbot of Hungarian Pilis visiting Pásztó (1279)[308], an abbot of Hailes deputising for Morimond at Dore (1318)[309], and an abbot of Irish Tracton taking the place of Welsh Tintern at De Voto (Tintern Secunda; 1346)[310]. As early as 1210, the abbot of Fountains was accustomed to visit Norwegian Lyse 'by means of monks'. The two then sent took over the abbey for nearly a year, much to its detriment[311]. The abbot of Nydala (1226) could send monks on visitation to Gudvala on the Baltic island of Gotland, but was told that he must go in person every third year[312]. Remote abbeys might have an *annual* visitation entirely dispensed with. The father-abbots of monasteries in Greece, Livonia, and Norway (1217) were told to provide for their visitation every third year; nothing was said about monks being sent in the intervening years[313]. The same mitigation applied to La Real (1243) on the island of Majorca[314]. The abbots of two Syrian houses, Jubin and Balamand (1219), might inspect each other's houses, 'as otherwise they cannot be visited'[315].

Neglect of visitation by a father-abbot caused the oversight·of Lyse (1213), during the troubles there, to pass from (English) Fountains to (Swedish) Alvastra, but the difficult overland journey from Alvastra meant that by 1235 Lyse was again subject to Fountains[316]. For the same reason, default of inspection, the paternity of Chalivois passed from Bouras to Pontigny (1277)[317]. The distance from La Ferté meant that oversight of Syrian Jubin (1238) was transferred to Italian Locedio – also of La Ferté's lineage[318]. Financial difficulty saw the paternity of Val-Dieu (1295) pass from Eberbach to Clairvaux[319]. Malice on the part of the monks of Heiligenkreuz was adduced when Zlatá Koruna (1277–81) was taken from its jurisdiction and made subject to Plasy[320]. Malice on the part of a local lord led to moves to break the links between Whitland and Strata Marcella (1323–33)[321]. Oversight of Canonica (inc. 1223) soon passed from Fossanova to Clairvaux because the cardinal-founder was dissatisfied with its progress[322]. Following the incorporation of the congregation of Savigny, Basingwerk and St Mary's, Dublin, resented being placed under the care of Buildwas[323]. Other disputes related to the paternity of Monte de Ramo (1216–18)[324], Dünamünde (1239)[325] and Calder (1277)[326].·

Where the state of the Order required it, special general visitations might be held, generally at the behest of the General Chapter. Such took place in England and Wales (in 1188, resulting in the deposition of three abbots[327], and perhaps again in 1217[328]), in Iberia (1221)[329], and in Southern Italy and Sicily (1227, 1232, 1272, 1331)[330]. Also at a distance from Burgundy, with its monastic discipline suffering somewhat, was the kingdom of Hungary. The Order there was said to be in 'a disorderly state', and the Chapter enjoined general visitations there in 1277–75 and again in 1288. A later visitation by the abbot of Rein (1356), ordered by the Elector and King Louis I, was not completed[331]. Other special visitations, by lineage, included those of a new abbot of Clairvaux (Peter) in France, Germany and Italy (1180's)[332], and by Stephen Lexington, as abbot of Savigny, in much of his congregation (1230–33)[333].

Communications

Abbots travelling far afield could encounter language difficulties – so St Bernard, visiting Germany, used for interpreter a Clairvaux monk who hailed from Freiburg, and Gervase of Louth Park used an interpreter in Ireland[334]. The decisions of the General Chapter and the findings of Visitors were in part transmitted by sealed letters sent by messengers. Letters from the Chapter to Richard I of England (1194) were carried by the abbot of Pontigny[335], a letter to Innocent III (1206) was borne by the abbot of Pforta[336]. Letters might be intercepted on the way. An abbot of Morimondo Milano (1195) detained letters of the abbot of Cîteaux affecting his daughter-house[337]; an abbot of L'Estrée (1199) tore up letters *en route* from the king of Hungary to the abbot of Cîteaux[338]. After a visitation of the lineage of Clairvaux in Ireland (1229), its abbot kept the original visitation reports, sending the monasteries copies only: 'on account of the many dangers of the roads'[339]. Many decisions of the Chapter affecting individuals may have been conveyed by word of mouth: hence the phraseology in its statutes: 'The abbot of X. here (present) to tell him'[340]. Communications regarding tax assessments were to be made 'by word of mouth, or in sealed letters'[341]. One could say in words things which one had no time or wish to put in writing. Abbot Stephen Lexington in Ireland (1228), writing to the abbots of Buildwas, Furness and Mellifont, said that he had asked the bearers to convey 'that which we cannot include in the brevity of a letter'[342], and in his report to the abbot of Clairvaux he wrote: 'the bearer will intimate in more detail certain secret matters'[343].

Constitutions

The knowledge of the origins of Cîteaux and the customs of the Order came to be supported by the written word, in a loose compilation of several works. Of this two versions are extant, each forming essentially a 'Book of Usages' or of 'Customs'[344]. The one, dating from about 1133–35, is entitled the *Usus cisterciensium*; the other, written about 1152 and thereafter, is known as the *Consuetudines cisterciensium*. Each edition contained an historical prologue (the *Exordium Cistercii* or the *Exordium Parvum*), one version or another of the *Charter of Charity*, the *Institutes* (statutes of successive General Chapters), the *Ecclesiastica Officia* (liturgical and domestic arrangements), and the *Usus Conversorum* (the way of life of the *conversi*). All these component parts underwent frequent revision[345]. In theory at any rate, the entire *corpus* did not jettison the *Rule of St Benedict* – to which (as in 1222)[346] the General Chapter often made recourse and appeal; rather, the Usages were the Cistercian patrimony built upon it.

The *Charter of Charity* was, from the outset, the basic constitution of the Order. It sought its essential unity whilst allowing modest autonomy to each abbey. It underpinned Cistercian spirituality, basing the life of the monks upon austerity and seclusion from worldly affairs, as well as upon the labours of their own hands[347]. It therefore swept aside any dependence upon ecclesiastical and secular possessions, such as churches and tithes, manors and serfs[348] – an idealism soon to be lost. The Charter influenced the later *Charter of Charity* of the Order of Chalais (*c.* 1148)[349] and the *Rule* of the Valliscaulians (*c.* 1205)[350]. The original Charter, with its prologue and eleven chapters, the *Carta caritatis prior*, evolved whilst Stephen Harding was abbot of Cîteaux[351], and it was the version approved by Calixtus II (1119)[352]. In his own day, William of Malmesbury (*c.* 1125/35) praised abbot Stephen as the guiding light and originator of the Charter[353], though some modern critics play down his rôle[354]. The Charter underwent modification, as shown in two later editions. The first, now called the *Summae cartae caritatis*, reflects change, and received confirmation by three successive pontiffs between 1152 and 1157, enabling its further development to be traced[355]. The second, now known as the *Carta caritatis posterior*, followed upon important amendments made after the death of St Bernard[356], and received papal sanction in 1163. This final version of the Charter was modified by the papal bull, *Parvus fons* (1265), and later restructured into five chapters (1316)[357]. The Charter was to be read at every General Chapter and a copy was to be kept in every abbey (1201)[358]. Its authority, as late as 1318, was described as 'fundamental from the beginning and as valid as ever'[359].

Prefacing the *Charter of Charity* were the *Exordia*, apologetic works, which gave reasons for the foundation of Cîteaux and told of its early history. The earliest form, the *Exordium Cistercii*, which some would attribute to Stephen Harding, consists of only two chapters and comes to an end about the year 1115. Views differ as to the authorship of the later *Exordium Parvum*, perhaps not Harding's work as once thought: the oldest copies of it date from about 1152. A much longer work – a prologue and some eighteen chapters – it is an endeavour to defend the secession of the monks from Molesme, and backs its stance with relevant letters and, above all, the 'Roman Privilege' of 1100[360]. The much later *Exordium Magnum*, the work of Conrad of Eberbach (ob. 1221), is sub-titled the 'Book of illustrious men of the Cistercian Order'. Apart from describing the development of the Order, it relates a number of vision and miracle stories originating at Cîteaux and Clairvaux[361].

As the Order expanded, the General Chapter issued disciplinary decrees (the *capitula* referred to by Calixtus II in 1119[362]), to meet situations hitherto not envisaged[363]. There were twenty such statutes in 1119[364], and when an enlarged collection was codified about 1147 it comprised eighty-four decisions. About 1155 a revised total of ninety-two statutes were listed as the 'Institutes of the General Chapter'. Further revisions (in 1179 and 1189–90) omitted many original decisions by now incorporated into the 'Book of Usages'. Waddell shows that the dating of the statutes in Canivez's published edition needs to be treated with caution. Of the collection dated 1134 only twenty-eight belong to that period: the rest correctly derive from between 1134 and 1147[365]. Some of the twenty-eight partly derive from the *Summa cartae caritatis*[366], and may be an attempt to portray an idealised past which perhaps never existed. Further, the statutes placed under the year 1157 belong variously from 1157 to about 1179[367].

By the late twelfth century the General Chapter had issued many new injunctions and an abundance of case law had been established, leading to the codification of statutes made in 1202, the work mostly of Abbot Arnauld of Cîteaux, and published as the Order's first *Libellus Definitionum* ('Book of Definitions')[368]. Each monastery was ordered to acquire a copy 'as quickly as they can'[369]. The topics covered, in fifteen sections, included: the abbey churches, granges, liturgy, visitation system, monastic life, trade, and officials, the *conversi*, and so on[370]. It was revised over a five-year period (1214–18) by the definitors, and published anew in 1220[371]. As successive General Chapters issued new statutes, so further revisions were necessary[372]. The next, commencing in 1234, was entrusted to the abbots of Savigny, Chalivois, Maizières, and Valloires, meeting in Paris[373]. Each lineage within the Order was thus represented, apart (seemingly) from that of Morimond. In 1235 a further meeting (with an adjustment of personnel) took place at a grange of Preuilly[374]. The new version was published in 1237 and, for the first time, referred to the nunneries of the Order[375]. Another re-drafting was ordered twenty years later; led by the abbot of Preuilly (at whose monastery the work was undertaken) and published in 1257, it served to underline the senior position of the abbots of Preuilly in the Order[376]. Both new editions were ordered to be read once a year in their entirety to every community[377].

A third revision followed somewhere between 1287[378] and 1292[379], and a fourth edition in 1316[380]. This last, entitled the *Libellus antiquarum definitorium* ('the Book of Old Definitions'), was amended again in 1321[381], whilst the papal constitution of 1335 necessitated yet a further revision undertaken by the abbots of Champagne and Hautecombe (1338)[382] and ratified by the General Chapter (1339)[383]. The pope as well as the cardinal-protector were dissatisfied with the drafting, and the old version (of 1316) was reverted to[384]. Finally, after much trouble, the *Novellae Definitiones* ('the New Definitions') were issued (1350)[385], and used alongside the Old[386]. Other documents of the Order, kept by the precentor of Cîteaux, included the 'table of the Order' (list of abbeys with foundation dates and showing seniority), the 'roll of Cîteaux' (persons and bodies to whom spiritual fraternity had been granted), and the list of absentees from General Chapter – as well as the bursar's accounts for the whole Order.

Financial Support

The annual General Chapter, which came to cost nearly 1,000 *livres tournois* to stage (1338), was not the only claim on the income of the Order[387]. There were national levies on monasteries, such as King John's exactions on the English Cistercians (1200–16) and Philip IV of France's levies for an invasion of Flanders and a crusade in Aragon (1284)[388]. Some were common to the entire Order, as the subsidy agreed for 'the redemption of the Holy Land' in 1276[389] – a modest taxation compared to that demanded in 1290, when the Order in France alone was expected to find 100,000 *l.t.*[389]. Other outgoings included: monies given to the Holy See for confirmation of the Order's privileges (100,000 *l.t.* demanded in 1274)[391]; the annual grant made to the cardinal-protector (3,000 *l.t.* expected, but not always received); fees to the Order's procurators at the Curia[392], and the expenses of the definitors, as well as large amounts spent on the maintenance of St Bernard's College in Paris[393]. The Chapter (1264) had to send the abbots of La Ferté and L'Aumône to Rome to plead 'the poverty of the Order'; at that date greater burdens were yet to come[394].

In 1235, when the needs of the Order were modest (4,000 marks), all abbots attending the General Chapter were urged to bring voluntary alms[395], but it was not long before compulsory taxation proved inevitable (1250), one of the reasons cited being 'the debts of the Order which are accumulating interest'[396]. Each father-abbot became responsible (1262) for the contributions of his daughter-houses, and could enforce payment by suspending abbots and officials of defaulting monasteries[397]. Various bases were used for assessing individual payments: the revenues of a monastery (1262), its size and wealth (1293), the number of monks it could support (1300)[398]. There might be appeals: Whalley (1318) had its contribution cut from £100 to £80[399]. Complaints about assessments by father-abbots led to provincial assessors being appointed (1326)[400].

The bursar of Cîteaux had over-all charge of Cistercian taxation[401] and revenues were transmitted to him in a variety of ways, especially as attendances at the General Chapter declined and it became more difficult for monies to be paid in directly at Cîteaux. A frequent device was for monies to be passed over to a monk-collector – sometimes the bursar himself – at the fairs of Troyes (as in 1290) and of Provins (as in 1294). Travelling collectors worked from central offices in Paris, Avignon and Metz[402]. From 1335, after each meeting of the General Chapter, the definitors met in Dijon to consider the Order's finances and appoint collectors and sub-collectors of taxes. A special seal was engraved for receipts attesting payments[403]. In 1276, and again in 1335, precise rules were laid down for the safe-keeping of monies received – in a chest with several different locks[404].

To assist the raising of revenue the General Chapter (1318) laid down that the assessed value of each monastery should be recorded in a book[405], and later (1326) provincial assemblies of abbots were ordered as a prelude to a survey to determine

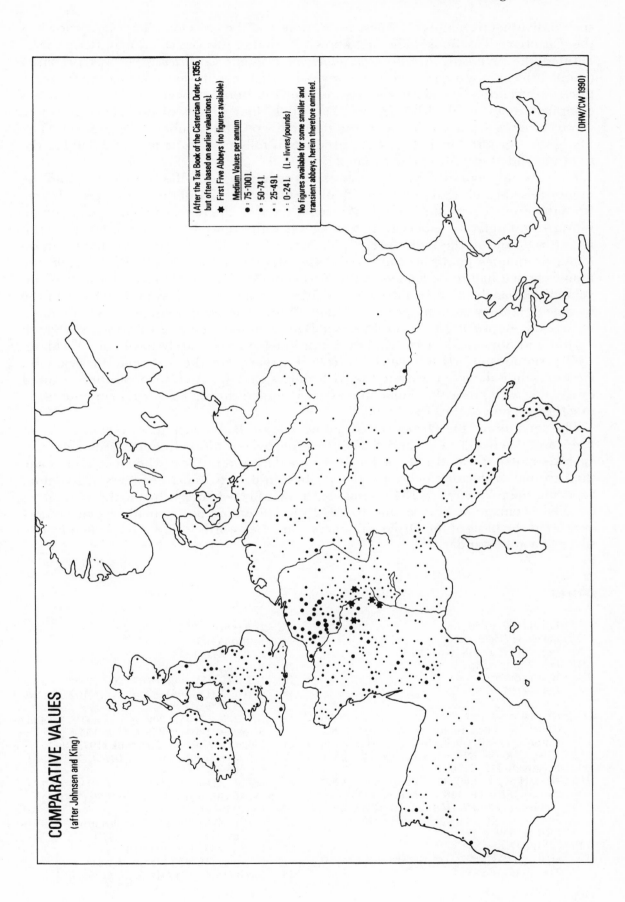

COMPARATIVE VALUES
(after Johnsen and King)

(After the Tax Book of the Cistercian Order, c.1355, but often based on earlier valuations).

★ First Five Abbeys (no figures available)

Medium Values per annum

● : 75-100 l.

● : 50-74 l.

● : 25-49 l.

· : 0-24 l.   (l. = livres/pounds)

No figures available for some smaller and transient abbeys, herein therefore omitted.

(DHW/CW 1990)

such individual payments[406]. These injunctions laid the basis for what is now known as the 'Cistercian Tax Book'. The first known version of this is a Dijon manuscript, later entitled the *Secundum Registrum monasteriorum ordinis Cisterciensis*. It was prepared (about 1354–55) by a scribe who used several earlier inventories, some dating from the thirteenth century[407]. Another version of the 'Tax Book' survives at Modena and was compiled about 1370–85[408]. In the 'Tax Book' four grades of potential values are given, ranging from 'moderate' through 'mediocre' and 'double' to 'excessive' . The first grade (ordered in 1348) would produce (if fully paid up) a levy of 9,000 l.t., the last (demanded in 1340) no less than 24,000 *l.t.*[409].

Perhaps only half of the abbeys paid taxes regularly – 356 did so in 1342 – and the money raised rarely covered the needs of the Order[410]. 42% of the taxes received came from the French monasteries, only 8% from Iberia[411]. There was difficulty in obtaining funds from England – especially in time of war with France – when it was feared that it might 'redound to the king's prejudice'. Edward I frequently laid a complete ban on monastic monies going abroad, as did the Statute of Carlisle (1306). In 1298 the monies raised had to be loaned to the Exchequer[412], but in 1343 five houses circumvented the ban[413]. The Hundred Years' War also meant the loss to the Order of the income of Stanley church, given it in 1240[414]. Monasteries in remote areas were often in arrears. Between 1337 and 1347 six Danish houses made no payments, though Esrum and Sorø paid thrice[415]. The Scottish abbeys may rarely have paid[416]. About 1340 strenuous efforts were made to collect arrears. For the first time dues came in from certain Balkan houses, and the Irish abbeys paid up after the interruption caused by the war with France[417]. Some monasteries slipped through the net, being not listed in either version of the 'Tax Book'[418].

The fortunes of the Order varied. Some years it had a surplus of revenue – as in 1345 and 1346 (3,644 *fl.* and 2,371 *fl.* respectively). More frequently its expenses exceeded income – as in 1340 (a deficit of 3,438 *l.t.*), and in 1341 (when it could not pay the cardinal-protector's pension). It was often in debt to Italian bankers at Avignon, repaying them 7,000 *fl.* in 1340–41 alone. It was affected latterly by the debasement of the silver coinage of France, and by 1342 the Florentine florin finally replaced *livres tournois* as the basis of the Order's finances – in other words, there was a switch from a silver to a gold standard[419].

Notes

1. Lekai (1977a) 20.
2. Zarnecki (1972) 69.
3. Lekai (1977a) 448 (No. IX).
4. *Ibid.* 462 (No. 3).
5. *WMG* (2) 349.
6. Lekai (1977a) 33–32.
7. Lackner (1978b) 22.
8. Cf. RBM *I*, 103 (No. 231; Sedlec, *1142*); *CSBW* 73 (St Benoît-en-Woëvre, *1182*), Anton (1986) 361 (No. 57; Moreruela, *1208*); *UKS* 44 (No. 43, Scharnebeck, *1275*).
9. Fergusson (1984a) 6.
10. Hlaváčková (1996) 305, Všetečková (1996) 290; *cf. FRB* II, 348 (Hradiště, *1279*), 463 (Sedlec, *1169*); *UKSH* 142, 216 (Nos CXLVI and CCXXXIV; Heilgenkreuz, *1259, 1278*).
11. *FRB* II, 349.
11a. *CP* I, 247.
12. Stalley (1987) 22; *cf. OC* 139 (CCCLIV, Tripoli nunnery).

13. Lawrence (1984) 156.
14. Bouton (1959) I, 181.
15. *DHGE* XII (1953) 902.
16. Knowles (1963a) 633.
17. Lekai (1977a) 450; *DHGE* XII (1953) 902.
18. *DHGE* XII (1953) 902–03; *cf. CMH* 79 (No. 51, of *1189*).
19. *DHGE* XII (1953) 902; *cf.* Lekai (1977a) 446.
20. Knowles (1963a) 633; *cf. CDH* 195.
21. Lekai (1977a) 386, McCrank (1975) 267.
22. Knowles (1963a) 591; *cf. DHGE* XII (1953) 903, 939.
23. *DHGE* XII (1953) 903–04; *cf.* Lekai (1977a) 68, McGuire (1974) 34, *CMH* 79 (No. 51).
24. King (1954) 256.
25. *DHGE* XII (1953) 904; *cf.* Bouton (1959) I, 176; Swietek (1983) 296; *CDH* 192–200.
26. *Cf. Statuta* I, 392 (1212/14).
27. McGuire (1974) 34 (Sorø, *1186*).
28. Birch (1897) 173 (Margam, *1179*).

29. *CMH* 79 (No. 51; Huerta, *1189*).
30. *CDH* 200–01 (Herrera).
31. *Statuta* III, 23–30; *cf. DHGE* XII (1953) 939.
32. *DHGE* XII (1953) 939, XXII (1988) 1257; *cf.*
      Statuta II, 462 (1260/8).
33. Stéphan (1970) 89.
34. Lekai (1977a) 453, 458.
35. James (1957) 94.
36. Stéphan (1970) 89, 105, 107, 110, 114–15.
37. *DHGE* XII (1953) 904, *cf. RBM* II, 135.
38. VCH, *County of Gloucester* II (1907) 96.
39. Snell (1967) 37–38.
40. VCH, *County of Gloucester* II (1907) 96; *cf.*
      RHC *100*.
41. Barnes (1982) 70–71.
42. Allendorff (1971) 272.
43. Lekai (1977a) 445.
44. Lekai (1977a) 466.
45. Bouton (1959) I, 100.
46. *Statuta* II, 214, 230 (1241/3), 233 (1241/8).
47. Lackner (1978b) 18.
48. Lekai (1977a) 30; Sayers (1964a) 22, 27; *cf.*
      EOC *461*.
49. *SC* 999–1000, Sayers (1964a) 27.
50. Bouton (1959) I, 100; D'Arbois (1858) 152.
51. Mahn (1945) 194–45, *cf. Statuta* I, 23.
52. *Statuta* I, 23 (1134/XLV), 182 (1195/3);
      D'Arbois (1858) 154.
52a. Waddell (1993) 389–412.
53. Lekai (1977a) 50, (1978) 15–16.
54. *LCC* (2) 270, *cf.* Buhot (1936) 186–87.
55. Sayers (1964a) 32, (1964b) 179.
56. *Statuta* I, 253–63.
57. Barnes (1982) 78, O'Dwyer (1975) 287.
58. Dimier (1982b) 531.
59. *Cf. Statuta* II, 258 (1242/66; Jerpoint).
60. *Cf. Statuta* II, 147 (1235/36; Bruern).
61. *Cf. Statuta* II, 257–58 (1242/65; Osera).
62. Lekai (1977a) 50.
63. Lekai (1978) 17–18.
64. Waddell (1993) *passim.*
65. Buhot (1936) 186.
66. *Statuta* I, 85 (1176/44).
67. *Statuta* I, 99 (1185/12).
68. *Statuta* I, 132–33 (1190/76), 174 (1194/21);
      LCC (2) 5 (*n*.3).
69. *Cf. Statuta* I, 481 (1217/68).
70. *Statuta* I, 221 (1197/57); *LCC* (2) 5 (*n*.3),
      Buhot (1936) 187.
71. *Statuta* I, 423 (1214/31); *LCC* (2) 7; Buhot
      (1936) 186.
72. *Statuta* I, 423 (1214/31), 437 (1215/15), 460
      (1216/52), 478 (1217/54), 495 (1218/52).
73. *Statuta* II, 131–32 (1234/27), 141–42
      (1235/19).
74. *Statuta* II, 68–69 (1228/17).
75. *Statuta* II, 142–43 (1235/20).
76. *Statuta* III, 80 (1270/2).
77. Mahn (1945) 233–35, *cf.* Dimier (1982c)
      535–39, King (1954) 42–44.
78. *Statuta* I, 221 (1197/57); *LCC* (2) 269.
79. *Statuta* I, 423 (1214/31), 437 (1215/15), 460
      (1216/52), 478 (1217/54).
80. *Statuta* III, 26–27; Mahn (1945) 234–35.
81. *Statuta* III, 31; *Cf. DHGE* XII (1953) 951;
      Buhot (1936) 186, Lekai (1977a) 71.
82. Lawrence (1984) 160, Lekai (1977a) 72.
83. Dimier (1966) 47; *cf. DHGE* XII (1953) 539.
84. Knowles (1963a) 214, Lekai (1977a) 29.
85. Lekai (1977a) 445.
86. *DHGE* XII (1953) 863.
87. Lekai (1977a) 445.
88. *Statuta* II, 27; *cf.* Lekai (1977a) 71, 463.
89. Lekai (1977a) 446–47, 466.
90. Lekai (1977a) 446; *cf. DHGE* XII (1953) 863.
91. *Statuta* III, 85–86 (1270/27); *cf.* De Ganck
      (1971) 9.
92. *Statuta* III, 236 (1296/13); *cf.* De Ganck
      (1971) 5–6.
93. *Statuta* I, 174 (1194/21).
94. Bouton (1959) I, 100.
95. King (1985) 30, Lekai (1977a) 50; *cf. Statuta*
      II, 27.
96. Lekai (1977a) 50.
97. *CDAC* 193–94 (No. 245), *cf.* 185 (No. 234).
98. *Statuta* I, 333–34 (1206/76).
99. Richard (1946) 262–67, Talbot (1960)
      95–158.
100. King (1954) 31, (1956) 50–55.
101. King (1985) 36; *cf.* Lekai (1976) 260.
102. King (1985) 36.
103. *Ibid.* 37–39.
104. Schich (1987) 39.
105. King (1954) 33.
106. Poloni (1981) 49.
107. *Statuta* I, 23 (1134/XLII, XLVIII), 32
      (1134/1), 71 (1159/12), 89 (1182/2); *cf.* 213
      (1197/16).
108. *Statuta* I, 321 (1206/6); *LCC* (1) 64.
109. *Statuta* III, 39 (1266/11).
110. *Statuta* I, 89 (1182/2), 300 (1204/21), 321
      (1206/6); *LCC* (2) 262.
111. *Statuta* III, 180 (1278/32).
112. *Statuta* I, 48 (1152/22), 435 (1215/5); *LCC* (2)
      262.
113. *Statuta* III, 323 (1285/11).
114. *Statuta* III, 321 (1309/3).
115. *Statuta* I, 49 (1153/22–29); *LCC* (2) 262.
116. *LCC* (2) 264; *cf. Statuta* I, 49 (1153/28–29).
117. *Statuta* I, 275 (1202/5), 466 (1217/5).
118. *Statuta* I, 111 (1189/4).
119. *CO* 3–4 (No. III).
120. Schneider (1975) 33.
121. King (1985) 30.
122. *Statuta* I, 30 (1134/LXXVI); *LCC* (2) 265–66.
123. *Statuta* I, 111 (1189/4), 165 (1193/43).
124. *Statuta* I, 105 (1186/16).
125. *LCC* (2) 263–64.
126. *Statuta* I, 503 (1219/2).
127. *LCC* (2) 266–64.
128. *Statuta* III, 333 (1317/3).
129. *Statuta* II, 234 (1241/25).
130. *LCC* (2) 264.
131. *Statuta* II, 360 (1251/1).
132. *Statuta* III, 49 (1267/8).
133. *Statuta* III, 177 (1278/13).
134. Stalley (1987) 15; *cf.* Lawrence (1984) 159.
135. *Cf.* Grüger (1987) 171.
136. Lawrence (1984) 159.
137. *CCR passim, CPR passim.*
138. Williams (1984) I, 188.
139. *CPR* 1217/80.
140. *Statuta* I, 71 (1159/12); *cf.* I, 503 (1219/6);
      McNulty (1943) 161.

141. *LCC* (2) 260–61.
142. Dimier (1954) 25.
143. *Cf. Statuta* I, 65 (1157/44); *LCC* (2) 272; *RCC* II, 259, 263.
144. *RCC* I, 314.
145. Grandmottet (1958) 11.
146. *CO* 3–4 (Nos III, VIII).
147. *CAC* 134 (No. XLVII).
148. *CO* 14–15 (No. XX).
149. *CAC* 208–09 (No. LXXXV); *cf. Statuta* I, 155, 219, 324; II, 327.
150. Mahn (1945) 183–85.
151. Donnelly (1949) 79.
152. *Ibid.* 80; *cf. Statuta* I, 526 (1220/46).
153. *Cf.* (for penalties) *Statuta* I, 414 (1213/50), II, 271 (1228/27), III, 144 (1275/22).
154. *Statuta* I, 202 (1196/27); *cf.* 198 (1196/3), 414 (1213/50), 494 (1218/48).
155. *Statuta* I, 213–14 (1197/20).
156. *Statuta* I, 512–13 (1219/48), *cf.* 261 (1200/64).
157. *Statuta* I, 293 (1204/41).
158. *Statuta* I, 230 (1198/44).
159. *Statuta* I, 203 (1196/31).
160. *Statuta* I, 345 (1207/61), *inter alia.*
161. *LMT* 189 (No. 70), *cf. Statuta* I, 155, 219, 324; II, 327.
162. *Statuta* I, 220 (1197/50).
163. *Statuta* III, 135 (1274/45).
164. *Statuta* I, 298 (1204/12).
165. *Statuta* II, 386 (1252/49).
166. Clark (1895) 207.
167. Hockey (1970) 23.
168. *Statuta* II, 194 (1238/45).
169. France (1992) 316.
170. *Statuta* II, 463 (1260/10).
171. *Statuta* III, 314 (1306/6).
172. Knowles (1963a) 255.
173. *CM* 58.
174. McNulty (1943) 161*n*; *cf.* Millard (1994) 243.
175. *ACA* 298–99
176. *Statuta* I, 128 (1190/50).
177. *Statuta* I, 155–54 (1192/39–40), 160 (1193/16).
178. *Statuta* I, 179–80 (1194/54).
179. *Statuta* I, 320–34 *passim.*
179a. *Statuta* III, 80 (1270/2).
180. *Statuta* III, 139–40 (1275/3).
181. Desmond (1971) 153; *cf. Statuta* III, 384 (1329/15).
182. Bouton (1959) I, 207; *cf.* Lekai (1977a) 446.
183. *Statuta* I, 92 (1193/8), 95 (1194/1).
184. *RPR* II, 1559 (No. 19259), *cf.* Lekai (1977a) 446, 464.
185. *Cf. Statuta* I, 323–24 (1206/22); D'Arbois (1858) 15.
186. McNulty (1943) 161–62.
187. *Statuta* I, 469 (1217/20).
188. *Cf. Statuta* I, 336 (1207/11); III, 140 (1275/4).
189. McGuire (1982) 285 (No. 26); *Statuta* I, 438 (1215/19).
190. *Statuta* II, 449 (1259/14).
191. *CS* II, 188.
192. *Statuta* I, 216 (1197/33).
193. *Statuta* I, 221 (1198/4).
194. *Statuta* II, 17 (1222/22).
195. O'Sullivan (1945) 11.
196. *Statuta* I, 493 (1218/42), *cf.* 304 (1204/31).
197. *Statuta* I, 470 (1217/23).
198. Williams (1984) I, 51.
199. *Statuta* II, 418 (1255/38).
200. *RC* 163; *CM* II, 531; *Statuta* I, 400 (1212/51); Hockey (1970) 23.
201. *AM* III, 163–64; *CM* IV, 235; *CCR* 1229/199; *CPR* 1264/340.
202. *Cf. inter alia: CPR* 1288/292, 297, 299; 1289/316–19; 1300/514–15, 518, 521, 524–25, 529.
203. *CPR* 1299/431.
204. *FH* III (1890) 86.
205. Desmond (1971) 150–51; Sparks (1978) 64.
206. Desmond (1971) 138; *cf. Statuta* III, 384 (1329/15).
207. Desmond (1971) 151–54; *cf.* CCR 1332/586; 1334/121.
208. Desmond (1971) 152.
209. *Ibid.* 153; Hockey (1976) 108.
210. Lekai (1977a) 464.
211. Lawrence (1984) 159; *cf. Statuta* I, 67 (1157/62); *LCC* (2) 261.
212. *Statuta* I, 92 (1183/8), 95 (1184/1).
213. *Statuta* I, 321 (1206/11).
214. *Statuta* I, 458 (1216/42); *cf. LCC* (2) 261, RCH 22.
215. Statuta *II, 88–82 (1229/37)*; cf. D'Arbois (1858) 151.
216. *LCC* (1) 63, (2) 261.
217. *Statuta* I, 459 (1216/49); *LCC* (2) 261; *cf.* Brown (1958) 110–11.
218. *Statuta* II, 82 (1229/41).
219. *Statuta* I, 468 (1217/14).
220. *Statuta* II, 103 (1232/18); *cf.* I, 459 (1216/49), *LCC* (2) 261.
221. *Statuta* I, 272 (1201/45), *cf.* 400 (1212/51).
222. *Statuta* I, 122 (1190/17), *cf.* 196 (1195/91), *LMT* 203–04 (No. 132).
223. *Statuta* I, 367 (1209/50).
224. *Statuta* III, 177 (1278/15), *cf.* 83 (1270/15).
225. *Cf. Statuta* I, 349 (1208/12), 458 (1216/42); II, 194 (1238/45), 266 (1243/38); III, 40 (1266/25).
226. *Cf. Statuta* II, 221 (1240/28), 298 (1245/45), 54 (1259/33); III, 12–13 (1263/18).
227. *Statuta* III, 80 (1270/2).
228. *ACA* 299.
229. *Statuta* I, 136 (1191/13); *cf. EOC* 46.
230. *Statuta* II, 328 (1248/5), 352 (1250/28), 469 (1260/33).
231. Hockey (1970) 121–22.
232. *CBK* xxvii, 43–44 (No. LIX); *cf. AF* xliii-xlv.
233. *Statuta* III, 373–74 (1326/4).
234. Grüger (1987) 171*n*; Jażdżewski (1992) 85.
235. Lekai (1977a) 464.
236. *Ibid.* 308.
237. *AM* II, 357–58.
238. *Cf. Statuta* I, 136 (1191/13), 258 (1200/48).
239. *Statuta* III, 469–70.
240. *DHGE* XII (1959) 945–50; Lekai (1977a) 69–70, (1978) 69.
241. *Statuta* II, 24–25 (1223/13).
242. *RSL* II, 314, King (1954) 39.
243. *AM* II, 319.
244. Mahn (1945) 232–35.
245. *AM* II, 357–58.
246. Lekai (1977a) 70; Mahn (1945) 232, 234.

247. *Statuta* III, 211–30; *cf. DHGE* XII (1953) 940.
248. Lekai (1977a) 29.
249. *Ibid.* 463 (No. 7), *cf.* 464 (No. 18).
250. *Ibid.* 445 (No. III).
251. *Statuta* I, 85 (1175/43).
252. Lekai (1977a) 445 (No. III); *cf. Statuta* I, 20–21 (1134/XXXIII); *LCC* (2) 284.
253. *Statuta* I, 20 (1134/XXXIII); *cf. CHDM* (1) 165–66.
254. *Statuta* I, 399–91 (1212/7).
255. *Statuta* I, 62 (1157/28).
256. Harper-Bill (1980) 104.
257. *Statuta* I, 158 (1193/2).
258. Harper-Bill (1980) 104–05.
259. *Statuta* III, 29 (1265/6).
260. *Statuta* I, 210 (1197/3).
261. *Statuta* I, 82 (1175/5); *LCC* (2) 288.
262. *Cf. Statuta* I, 111 (1189/12), *cf.* 264–65 (1201/6); III, 28–29 (1265/*bulla* No. 6).
263. *Statuta* I, 120 (1190/13).
264. Lekai (1977a) 71, 445 (No. III).
265. McNulty (1943) 161.
266. *Statuta* I, 321 (1206/10); *cf. RSL* II, 1200 (No. 4; *1231*), 206 (Nos 2, 6), 219 (No. 6), 223 (No. 11).
267. *LCC* (2) 284.
268. Knowles (1963a) 638.
269. Conbhuí (1958) 28.
270. *SL* 23 (no. 5), *cf. 36 (No. 15)*.
271. VKS 196–99.
271a. Clay (1895) *passim*.
272. Harper-Bill (1980) 107.
273. *HCVP* 45–52.
274. Harper-Bill (1980) 105–06.
275. *RHC* 13.
276. *SBC* II, 12 (No. 8).
277. *UKS* 32 (No. 23).
278. Hockey (1970) 44.
279. *RBM* III, 244 (No. 592).
280. Holman (1986) 109.
281. *DHGE* XVII (1971) 852; King (1954) 254.
282. *Cf. Statuta* II, 450 (1259/10); III, 212 (1281/33); *DHGE* XV (1963) 1001, XVI 1967) 1091, XVII (1971) 852.
283. *Statuta* III, 60 (1268/6).
284. *DHGE* XV (1963) 1001; *cf. Statuta* I, 190 (1195/58); II, 252 (1242/51); III, 78 (1269/70).
285. *Statuta* I, 477 (1217/48); *cf.* Tomkinson (1985) 62.
286. *Statuta* I, 188 (1195/46).
287. Lekai (1976) 261.
288. *Statuta* II, 350 (1250/22).
289. *DHGE* XVII (1967) 983–84.
290. *Statuta* I, 226 (1198/21), *cf.* 338 (1207/24; L'Escale-Dieu).
291. *Statuta* II, 5 (1221/26), 12 (1221/59).
292. Lekai (1976) 261.
293. *Statuta* III, 24–29 (Nos 2, 6, 7).
294. *Cf. VRL* 31 (for those of abbot of Dore, 1329).
295. McNulty (1943) 161.
296. *Statuta* III, 237 (1287/3).
297. King (1954) 267, 281.
298. *Statuta* I, 228 (1198/33).
299. *Statuta* I, 398 (1212/38).
300. *HCVP* 43–52.
301. *DHGE* XIV (1960) 79–80.
302. Lekai (1977a) 463 (No. 7), *cf.* 445 (No. III).
303. *Statuta* III, 163 (1277/1), *cf.* III, 151–52 (1276/2).
304. Birch (1897) 119, 181; *RSL* I, 22–23; *SL* 19–20 (No. 3).
305. Williams (1984) I, 190.
306. *CPR* 1233/14.
307. King (1954) 281.
308. *RCH* 23.
309. Harper-Bill (1980) 105–06.
310. Williams (1984) I, 194.
311. *Statuta* I, 375 (1210/33), *cf.* 376 (1210/35), 387 (1211/41), 396 (1212/32).
312. *Statuta* II, 53 (1226/24); *DHGE* XXII (1988) 643.
313. *Statuta* I, 468 (1217/14).
314. *Statuta* II, 266 (1243/38).
315. *Statuta* I, 150 (1219/37).
316. France (1992) 321–22; *cf. Statuta* I, 400–07 (1213/11), 422 (1214/24), 474 (1217/38).
317. Bedini (1964) 69.
318. Williams (1974) 69.
319. Ruwet (1966) 13.
320. *RBM* II, 466–65 (No. 1101), 541–42 (No. 1255).
321. Williams (1984) I, 56, 190.
322. *DHGE* XI (1949) 758.
323. Gwynn (1970) 131; Williams (1984) I, 10.
324. *Statuta* I, 462–63 (1216/63), 479 (1217/58), 497 (1218/61).
325. *Statuta* II, 209 (1239/33).
326. *Statuta* III, 172 (1277/51).
327. Cowley (1977) 116; Williams (1984) I, 189.
328. *CPR* 1217/68, 70–71.
329. *Statuta* II, 6–7 (1221/33).
330. *Statuta* II, 50 (1226/13), 59 (1227/19), 105 (1232/25); III, 110–11 (1272/32); IV, 397 (1331/15).
331. *RCH* 23, 27, 34; *Statuta* III, 242 (1288/10); Lekai (1976) 262, 265–66.
332. Péchenard (1883) 153.
333. *RSL* II, 192–233, *passim*.
334. Dimier (1952) 1152.
335. *Statuta* I, 178–79 (1194/50).
336. *Statuta* I, 332 (1206/67).
337. *Statuta* I, 188 (1195/46).
338. *Statuta* I, 248 (1199/81); *cf. RCC* II, 50 (No. 559).
339. *SL* 203–04.
340. *Cf. Statuta* III, 14 (1263/34), 227 (1282/43), 232 (1284/10).
341. *CTB* 27.
342. *SL* 33 (No. 14), 35 (No. 15), 38 (No. 17).
343. *SL* 86 (No. 38).
344. *LMP* 87–302.
345. Altermatt (1990) 295–304, Lackner (1976) 54; *cf. LCC* (2) 7.
346. *Statuta* II, 15 (1222/11), *cf.* 14 (1222/7).
347. Lekai (1977a) 27, 31–32, 298–300.
348. Knowles (1963a) 210.
349. Van Damme (1963) 103; *cf.* Knowles (1963a) 225.
350. Easson (1957) 8.
351. *CDU* 285.
352. Knowles (1963b) 222, *cf.* Lekai (1977a) 27.

353. *WMG* 380.
354. Lekai (1977a) 27.
355. Altermatt (1990) 298–99, Waddell (1978a) 49.
356. Bouton (1959) I, 126.
357. Altermatt (1990) 299.
358. *Statuta* I, 265 (1201/9).
359. *Statuta* III, 341–42 (1318/12).
360. Altermatt (1990) 299–96, Auberger (1986) 42, Waddell (1982) 257–58; *cf.* Lekai (1977a) 457–58 (for transcription of the 'Roman Privilege').
361. Altermatt (1990) 296–97.
362. Lekai (1977a) 19–20.
363. *Ibid.* 26; Knowles (1963a) 12–20.
364. Altermatt (1990) 301 (*n.* 49).
365. Waddell (1993) 384–412, (1994) 28; *cf.* Statuta *I, 13–32 (1134/I-LXXXV)*.
366. Auberger (1986) 343–54.
367. Waddell (1993) 405–07, (1994) 28.
368. Altermatt (1990) 303; *cf. LCC* (1) *passim*; (2) 3, 13.
369. *Statuta* I, 296 (1204/8).
370. Altermatt (1990) 303, *cf. LCC* (2) 3.
371. *Statuta* I, 423 (1214/31), 437 (1215/15), 460 (1216/52), 478 (1217/54), 495 (1218/52).
372. Holdsworth (1986) *passim*.
373. *Statuta* II, 131 (1234/27); *LCC* (2) 4 (*n.* 3).
374. *Statuta* II, 141–42 (1235/19); *LCC* (2) 4 (*n.* 3), 21.
375. Altermatt (1990) 304; *LCC* (2) 4–5 (*n.* 4), 22, 32.
376. *Statuta* II, 424 (1256/11).
377. *LCC* (2) 21, 39–40, 356.
378. *Statuta* III, 237 (1287/3; ref. to the 'definitions edited of old').
379. *Statuta* III, 259 (1292/3; ref. to 'the new compilation of definitions'); *cf.* Lekai (1977a) 75–76.
380. King (1954) 51.
381. *Statuta* III, 355 (1321/14), *cf.* 404 (1333/9).
382. *Statuta* III, 453 (1338/11).
383. *Statuta* III, 456 (1339/5).
384. *Statuta* III, 460–61 (1340/3); Lekai (1977a) 76.
385. King (1954) 55, (1985) 179.
386. Lekai (1977a) 76.
387. King (1973) 135; Lekai (1977a) 325.
388. Desmond (1971) 140–-42, King (1985) 94, *CTB* 25.
389. *CBK* xxvii-xxviii; *AF* 86.
390. *CTB* 25.
391. Desmond (1971) 147.
392. King (1973) 136, (1985) 173.
393. King (1973) 136, (1985) 184, 187–88; Lekai (1977a) 325.
394. *DHGE* XVI (1967) 1305.
395. *CTB* 22–23; King (1973) 127; *cf. CPR 1224/460*.
396. King (1985) 49–50; *CTB* 19, 24.
397. King (1973) 128.
398. *CTB* 25, 27.
399. VCH, *Lancaster* II (1908) 135.
400. King (1973) 128.
401. Hart (1977) 172, King (1985) 175, *cf.* (1956) 55–54.
402. *CTB* 24–26, King (1973) 134, (1985) 8, Lekai (1977a) 324.
403. *CTB* 26; King (1973) 130–31, (1985) 9.
404. *Statuta* III, 159 (1276/32); (for 1335): McNulty (1943) 162.
405. *CTB* 27.
406. *Statuta* III, 373–74 (1326/4); *cf.* King (1973) 132, 141; Lekai (1977a) 324.
407. *CTB* 7–9; *cf.* France (1992) 386.
408. King (1985) 15.
409. *CTB* 28; King (1973) 129–30, (1985) 75, 78.
410. King (1973) 112; Lekai (1977a) 325.
411. Wamba, J.P.E., at 1993 Fontfroide Conference.
412. Desmond (1971) 142–47; King (1954) 48.
413. *AF* 87, King (1973) 132.
414. *DHGE* XII (1953) 858.
415. King (1973) 133; *cf.* France (1992) 383–88.
416. King (1956) 54, (1973) 132–33.
417. King (1985) 74–75; *cf.* Conbhuǐ (1964) 144–60.
418. King (1985) 81, 129.
419. King (1973) 137–41, (1985) 161.

Chapter 3
RECRUITMENT

Numerical Strength

The minimum number of monks in a Cistercian house was fixed at thirteen (the abbot and twelve others), representative of Christ and the twelve disciples; 1134[1], 1205[2]). This was the basic number sent forth, together with a sufficient number of *conversi*, to make a new foundation. Later (1190) a community of thirty monks was felt to be necessary for a monastery to be a viable entity[3], whilst a (now lost) early statute of the General Chapter did not allow an abbey to found a daughter-house unless it itself had achieved a complement of sixty[4]. This was the number of monks required or recorded at Marienstatt (1215)[5] and Meaux (1249)[6], aimed for at Royaumont (1236)[7] and Zwettl (1285)[8], and claimed by three Welsh abbeys in their hey-day[9]. It was also the number deemed sufficient for a monastery to sustain a 'lecturer' of the Order (1300)[10]. In time, differing cultural backgrounds and economic fortunes meant that the size of Cistercian communities differed greatly.

In the later twelfth century many communities greatly exceeded the ideal number of sixty; indeed Alexander III (1179) advised the General Chapter to limit the number of religious[11]. Some figures ascribed, as, for example, 500 monks at Bellevaux and 600 at Cherlieu, are perhaps grossly exaggerated or include the large number of *conversi* each house had[12]. Yet there might be very considerable numbers – witness the 888 slips of profession found at Clairvaux after St Bernard's death[13]. At Rievaulx the number of monks was so great that its church 'swarmed with them like a hive of bees'[14]. Altenberg, Vaucelles[15], and Villers[16] each had over 100 monks at the close of the century. In the thirteenth century some abbeys continued to recruit well: Vaucelles's community rose from 110 monks (1200) to 130 (1252)[17]; that of the Dunes from 120 (c. 1233) to 181 (1300)[18]. Many monasteries had more moderately-sized communities, and indeed the General Chapter (1196) cautioned that it was better to settle for a small community, and then let it grow as funds became available[19]. To create a strong community several monasteries (as Aulne, 1229[20]; Zwettl, 1285[21]; and Roche, 1345[22]) sought further endowments enabling them to take in additional recruits.

The Chapter (1198) also ordered numbers to be proportionate to revenue, and to be fixed by the father-abbot, and insisted that abbeys should not exceed the quota of monks allocated to them[23]. This 'quota system' is reflected in the prescriptions of thirteenth-century visitations: maxima were fixed in 1228 for Byland (80 monks and 160 *conversi*)[24] and Mellifont (50 monks + 50 *conversi*)[25], and in 1231 for Longvilliers (1231; 40 monks + 60 *conversi*)[26]. Monthéron (1340) might have 40 monks[27], and St Bernard-opt-Scheldt (1301) 39[28]. Several monasteries seem to have had a target of fifty monks: as Amelunxborn[29], Froidmont[30] and Lilienfeld[31]. The Chapter ordered temporary or partial halts to recruitment in 1190, 1205 and 1268[32].

Some monasteries remained small or even reduced their numbers. In Ireland, Southern Europe and the Balkans, numbers sometimes fell below the requisite thirteen. The Chapter ordered the reduction of such abbeys to grange status (Chapters 8, 12), or the entire dispersal of the monks (1189), placing the initiative in these situations on the abbot-visitor (1189, 1275)[33]. Small communities might be amalgamated with larger ones, as Sauveréal with Valmagne (1321)[34]. Economic circumstances forced Margam (1329) to reduce its potential complement by ten monks[35], and Troisfontaines (1335) to twenty monks in total[36]. A few small abbeys made no effort to increase their community size, despite having the potential to do so: as Faleri (1199)[37] and Szepes (1356)[38]. The early fourteenth century saw a decline in vocations but there remained many respectably sized communities, such as Bordesley (1332, 34 monks)[39], Henryków (1336; 44 monks)[40], Camp (1316; 72 monks)[41] and Poblet (1316; 92 monks)[42]. Clairvaux (1331) still had 100 monks and 200 *conversi*[43], and Salem (1311) could boast 130 monks. Vaucelles (1316) and the Dunes (1317), however, saw dramatic falls in numbers to 32 and 25 monks respectively[44].

An indication of potential community numbers comes in the size of the monastic dormitory. It was ruled at Jerpoint (1228) that there could be 36 monks since its dorter was 110 feet long, thus allowing 6 feet per monk in a double row of beds[45]. Using this basis, there was accommodation for 48 monks at Mellifont, 79 at Vitskøl and 44 at Lyse[46]. Given the figure of at least thirteen monks in the early communities (and some had many more), there must have been some 5,000 monks at the very least in 1151; taking a conservatively estimated average of thirty monks per house a century later, then around 1250 the total was in the order of 20,000. In the early thirteenth century the numbers of *conversi* were usually at least double those of choir-monks[47]. There must, therefore, have been well over 50,000 Cistercian personnel at any given time for much of the thirteenth century: a spiritual and an economic force to be reckoned with!

Origins

In the early decades of the Order's history it was successful (particularly on the Continent) in attracting many entrants of noble birth or of intellectual attainment; these were the recruits who often found quick promotion. Royal blood was to the fore when Prince Otto of Austria led a complement of young German nobles into the novitiate at Morimond (1132), and when Prince Henry of France entered Clairvaux (1146) at the age of twenty-five[48]. Other houses with noble representation included Poblet[49], Stürzelbronn[50] and Grandselve[51]. Such membership of high birth could not help but bring prestige, and attract other vocations and benefactors. In the thirteenth century (with exceptions, as at Salem)[52] recruitment from the nobility declined. When nobles[53] and others of 'gentle birth'[54], did enter the Order they were (from 1188) only accepted as monks, and not as *conversi*. Serfs, if allowed by their lord to enter[55], could only be *conversi*; it was felt (certainly in 1308) that people of low birth might cast a shadow on the Order's reputation[56]. The Cistercian pope, Benedict XII (1334–42), had been a baker's son[57].

Into the Order from the ranks of the clergy came men like Archdeacon Baldwin of Totnes who became abbot of Ford and a noted spiritual writer[58]; from the military world came soldiers like Évrard de Berg – who entered Morimond incognito – and became abbot of Georgenthal[59], and from the world of the arts came the troubadour, Foulques, later abbot of Thoronet[60]. Some entrants owed their admission to a 'gift' of land made by their parents; this was a contractual obligation by which a father could help secure the future of a son[61] – but how genuine was the vocation? Berdoues (1171) promised one benefactor that his sons would be received 'one after the other *if they so wished*'[62]. One donor gave Himmerod (1325) Simon 'his only son'[63]. Whole families might embrace the religious life. One early 'donor' to Fountains insisted that he be

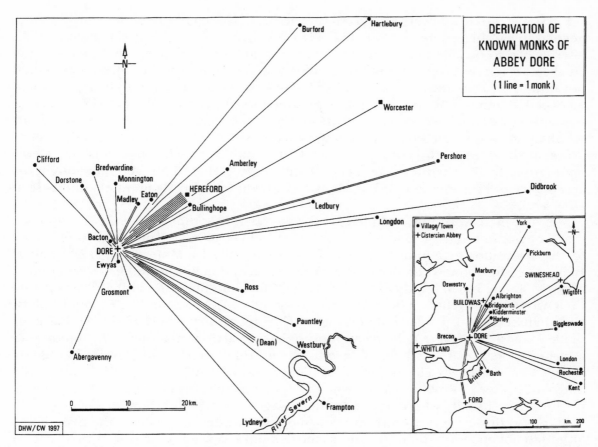

DERIVATION OF
KNOWN MONKS OF
ABBEY DORE
(1 line = 1 monk)

accepted as a *conversus*, his son (perhaps better educated) as a monk, and his wife be settled in a nunnery[64]. Three brothers who gave lands for the site of Bloemkamp (1191) became, after a year's probation at Klaarcamp, founding abbot, prior, and a *conversus*, of the new abbey[65].

Where recruits brought income and possessions to an abbey, there could be problems if such recruits had creditors (Poblet, 1166)[66], young children (Moreruela, 1210)[67], aggrieved heirs (Walkenried, 1278)[68] or lords (Cherlieu, 1222)[69], or were wanted by the civil authorities (Furness, 1231)[70]. It was important to obtain papal backing not only to receive free-men, but also that 'no-one interfere with them' after profession – as enjoined in numerous papal bulls[71]. Prince Llywelyn ab Iorwerth disallowed any claim made against Aberconwy (1199) relating to a man once he had been professed[72]. Such privileges did not extend to the probationary year, but during that year the novices made their will and on profession those wills took effect[73].

In the formative years of the Order many entrants were young adults and students, even older men[74], for the Cistercians refused to admit children to the cloister[75] until they were at least fifteen (1134)[76]. If novices were found to be, or seemed to be, under that age, the abbot-visitor could expel them (1154)[77]. The minimum age was soon raised to eighteen years (1157): novices were to be 'fully grown and of man's age' (1160)[78]. This rule, often breached (1201)[79], was frequently re-iterated by the General Chapter, but (from 1175 to 1231) younger boys wrongly received could stay[80], though their abbots might be deposed (1201)[81]. From 1237 there was one major exception: the age limit was lowered again to fifteen years for monasteries 'in remote regions', as eastern Europe, 'where adults rarely choose to become monks'[82]. Three Cistercians of note, Pope Benedict XII (1334–42), Patriarch Peter II of Antioch (1209)[83], and Thorkellus, sixth abbot of Øm (1199–1216)[84], all told of being with the white monks 'from their youth up'.

Physique and health were also taken into account. None were to become novices who needed to eat three times a day (1157, 1184). At Berdoues (1174) and Gimont (1161), novices had to be able to come 'sound in body, riding or walking'[85]. Sickness was not an absolute barrier: some might be received who on account of 'bodily sickness' could not fulfil their crusading vows (c. 1170)[86]. Novices who were found to be lepers could be expelled, but out of mercy might be provided for in secular habit (1191)[87]. Literacy was not an essential requirement in the early days – it was said of St Aelred's choir-monks at Rievaulx that amongst them were 'simple men who could not read or write'[88] – but in the thirteenth century the need for a sufficient education was repeatedly emphasised by the Chapter[89] and, later, by Benedict XII (1335)[90]. A donor sought the acceptance of his son as a monk at Huerta (1200) 'if found truly literate', otherwise as a *conversus*[91].

Married men were not excluded from Cistercian life, though the Order enjoined that a novice found to be 'bound in marriage' was to be expelled, unless his wife agreed to the separation[92]. Nunneries were founded at Jully by Molesme (1112)[93] and at Belfays by Morimond (1128[94]) for the wives of married men who wished to enter those abbeys. Married men admitted to Silvanès (1136)[95] and Staffarda (1234)[96] also placed their wives in convents. Others (if there was good cause) obtained a decree of nullity, as did an entrant to Poblet[97]. The General Chapter also ruled (1308, 1324) that none of illegitimate birth were to be received without special dispensation[98]. The importance attached to legitimate birth was shown by the need for a bishop of Hereford (1320) to certify that the newly-elected abbot of Tintern was born within wedlock and was a native of his see[99]. Problems arose when a 'donor' sought the admission of one ineligible for entry, usually where boys were under-age[100].

Many twelfth-century Cistercian choir-monks were not ordained to the priesthood, although abbots normally were, and as more monks aspired to be priests the Chapter (1189) ordered that their requests be delayed for two years. Some humble recruits to the Order, attempting to become not monks but *conversi*, tried to conceal the fact that they were ordained. If their true status was discovered they were to be expelled (1214), though this ruling of the Chapter was tempered the next year (1215) by allowing them to be retained as 'familiars'[101]. At differing times mutual agreements were reached with the Premonstratensians (1142)[102], the Carthusians (1195)[103], the Franciscans (1266)[104] and the Carmelites (1274)[105], whereby vocations were not normally accepted from each other's personnel. A relaxation allowing the admission of members of the mendicant orders (1287)[106] was soon severely restricted. It may be that the potential numbers of such aspirants were too great and seen as a disturbing influence (1306)[107]. Relations with the Franciscans were especially variable, particularly after the Franciscan-inspired beating and imprisonment of the abbot of Mataplana (1275)[109]. Among those who did become white monks were a Franciscan who had attacked his Guardian (Waldsassen; 1259)[109] and some apostate Dominicans (at Sawtry; 1306)[110].

Would-be Cistercians stayed in the guest-house for a few days before thrice seeking admission from the community in chapter. If accepted they were led to the 'cell of the novices' [111]; such novitiate buildings or *probatoria*, are on record in Ireland (1228)[112], at Staffarda (1251)[113] and at Croxden (1260)[114]. At Maulbronn, an early-thirteenth century hall complete with picture of Christ holding birch and scourge, may have been its novitiate[115]. The number of novices was sometimes in single figures: Meaux, 6 novices in 1160, Beaulieu, 7 in 1270[116], Stams, 3 in 1345[117]. Clairvaux had many more in St Bernard's day when there was an average of over 22 professions a year; at Croxden, much later (1242–74), professions averaged but four a year[118]. During an obligatory probationary year[119], the novices came under the supervision of a monk novice-master[120] and wore a cloak and mantle[121]. St Aelred based his *Speculum caritatis* on the instructions he gave when novice-master[122]. Though they normally ate in the novitiate or in the refectory[123], it is possible that – by way of penance – the novices sometimes ate in the cloister[124]. Should one run away, so long as he returned the same day, he did not lose rank[125].

At the end of their probation those who wished to remain and were accepted, were summoned to the chapter-house and made their wills; three such testaments made by novices of La Real (1270–1301) show these new recruits to have been quite well-off[126]. After the sacristan had cut their hair[127], the new monks were tonsured and blessed at a special Mass celebrated by the abbot at which they received Communion[128]. The novitiate was not meant to be easy: it was only for those whom God had called. St Bernard counselled one young novice to be ready to endure the sufferings of Christ[129]. A novice of La Real (1279), realising that the Cistercian life was not for him, more than reimbursed the abbey for his keep on leaving[130]. Even Waltheof of Melrose, previously Augustinian prior of Kirkham, found the probationary year very trying[131]. If there was doubt about a candidate, the year's probation might be extended[132].

Racial Compositions and Tensions

The foundation of the earliest monasteries entailed many French monks going to foreign parts, but thereafter recruitment was generally on a local basis. There were always a few monks in most houses from further afield, who may have come into contact with a particular abbey on their travels, or by being brought up on the lands near the granges of an abbey, or may have entered a foreign house because there was no Cistercian monastery in their own region (as the early English monks at Clairvaux), or because they had been sent there as a punishment. Evidence of local recruitment comes in those names of monks which bear their place of origin; as Peter de Morigny at Cherlieu (1208)[133], and Philip of Kenfig at Margam (1203)[134]. Matthew of Colle (La Real; 1337)[135] and Philip Kingstone (Grace Dieu, W; 1366)[136] came from the vicinity of granges so named. At Grandselve most recruitment was from the Midi, but some monks were of Italian or Spanish origin[137]. In Germany, numerous natives of Cologne were professed at Altenberg or Eberbach close by[138]. Clairvaux sent English monks of its community to be the first abbots of Vaucelles (1132)[139] and Vauclair (1134)[140]. An Englishman was the first abbot of Øm (1166)[141]. Other recruits from far afield included 'a noble Greek' at Corazzo (1170)[142], a saintly Englishman, Richard de Busto, at Aduard (1236–66)[143], and a Saxon abbot, Frederick, at Sedlec (d. 1330)[144]. By the thirteenth century foreign monks were (in Western Europe) very much the exception, though, following the Battle of Benevento (1266), thirty-seven French monks from Royaumont were settled at Real Valle in Italy (1273)[145].

It was the will of the General Chapter that race was not to be a factor in refusing recruits: there was to be 'impartial reception, especially of natives, since these have the greater claim' (1275)[146]. In Hungary there were many French, and more especially Germans, in the monasteries, and the abbot of Rein's visitation report (1357) implied a policy of exclusion in his time[147]. This might have stemmed earlier from the reported lack of local vocations, and the same may have been true in Poland. The monasteries of Little Poland were well stocked with French monks, and those of Greater Poland with Germans[148]. A fifteenth-century chronicler asserted that two monasteries, Wąchock and Jędrzejów, only accepted French vocations[149]. At Sulejów (1298) were 'the Gallic brothers, called from Gaul'[150]. Only natives of Cologne were admitted at Łekno, Ląd and Obra – all deriving from Altenberg[151]. Throughout the Middle Ages there was hardly an abbot of Polish birth[152], although the foundation charter of Lubiąż had envisaged 'Poles, Germans, or French'[153]. At Whitland (fd 1140) the monks, Welsh in sympathy, spoke the language and took it over to Ireland. Abbot Lexington on visitation there (1228) noted that some monks of Whitland were more concerned that those of Tracton (a daughter-house) spoke Welsh 'than that they do the will of God and the Order'[154]. The monks of Basingwerk, often recruited from Cheshire, on the other hand, said they had 'no knowledge of the customs of the Welsh' (1281)[155], admitting they were aliens living 'among them' (1346)[156].

Where monks settled in border territories or in foreign parts, racial tensions could result. Poblet's community split for a time (1204–13) into pro-Catalan and pro-French factions[157]. English monks settled by Edward I at Coupar were alarmed and fled when visited by the Scots leader Wallace (1297)[158]. At Doberan most monks were Slavs, but its mother-house (Amelunxborn) tried to ensure that the Saxon members held the chief positions. The Slavs (1345) alleged that when the Saxons could not get their own way, they tried to poison them or use witchcraft against them. One Slav *conversus*, expelled from Doberan (1337), returned there with armed men and amputated one of the prior's legs, alleging that he had treated him harshly[159].

There was a serious divide in Ireland between the Anglo-Norman and Irish Cistercian foundations – a reflection of the English invasion of the country in 1169 to 1170[160]. A long history of trouble started when the abbot of Mellifont (1192) tried to be independent of the mother-house of Clairvaux[161]. When the state of the monasteries in Ireland required a special visitation (1217), the gates of Mellifont were closed so that the Visitors could not leave, whilst four abbots (all of the family of Mellifont) encouraged a riot at Jerpoint[162]. Further 'enormities' in the Mellifont 'generation' led to two further special visitations (1219, 1220)[163] and, later (1227), the sending of the abbots of Froidmont and Trois Fontaines to Ireland. They deposed four abbots and removed four abbeys from the oversight of Mellifont[164], but they, and the new abbots they appointed, met with great resistance[165]. The General Chapter named five abbots as being the leading partners in what it called 'the Mellifont Conspiracy'[166]. A new visitation was ordered and the lot fell on abbot Stephen Lexington of Stanley, aided by the abbots of Buildwas and Margam, and occupied much of 1228[167].

Lexington, too, was obstructed: attacked by robbers near Kilcoooly[168], barricaded out at Maigue[169], and waylaid by the prior of Suir (whose monks had beaten up the messenger he sent ahead)[170], he felt that monastic observance in the Irish houses was negligible and 'only the habit remained'[171]. He held a council of abbots in Dublin which further broke up the Mellifont 'generation'[172] (though in 1278 it was partly restored)[173], transferring its filiations in small groups to the paternity of Clairvaux, Fountains, Furness, and Margam. He reconciled forty rebels but banished others (some for two years training) to French and English monasteries[174]. He installed thirteen new abbots and brought in replacement monks from France[175]. He ended the visitation to Ireland at the Anglo-Norman *De Voto* abbey by drawing up a memorandum, sealed by seventeen abbots[176]. He had issued thirteen common articles to be read in each Irish abbey every month for a year[177]. His visitation had been thorough, and the charter lists ninety-seven points needing reform[178]. To raise cultural standards, he insisted that only novices who could understand French or Latin were to be received[179].

The Irish problem was diminished but not solved[180]. Further rebellions (1230) saw the abbot of Fermoy and a monk of Suir killed, and the abbot of Monasterevin and a *conversus* of Jerpoint blinded[181]. Gregory IX denounced the trouble-makers as monks 'only in name'[182]. The settlers of Cashel said that Hore Abbey was 'filled with robbers who kill Englishmen' (1272)[183], but the native princes alleged that the English monks of Abbeylara and Inch hunted Irishmen with spears[184]. In the early-thirteenth century some Anglo-Norman houses (including Inch) had tried to exclude Irish recruits[185], but, much later (1321), Mellifont refused to accept any of the English race. Edward II (1321) ordered that the abbeys of Ireland were to receive 'not only Irish, but all who wish'[186], and he was backed by the General Chapter which reiterated that vocations were to be accepted 'indifferent of nation'[187].

Apostasy

Many monks and *conversi* perhaps embraced the religious life in the early Middle Ages without a God-given calling, but rather because they, or their parents for them, sought security and a better material life than they might otherwise have had. Those without a true vocation will have found the vows and life-style irksome and constraining. They might either endeavour to abandon the monastic life, or else become focal points of discontent within it. Even in the early Cistercian communities, Orderic Vitalis (*c.* 1135) wrote, there were 'tares with the wheat'[188]. Apostasy was a marked feature by the time of Innocent III (1203), who forbade the harbouring of run-away monks[189], and by 1266 the General Chapter noted 'the enormous harm' it was doing to the Order[190]. Sometimes whole groups of monks abandoned their monastery – as in Central Wales (*c.* 1210)[191], at Stanley (1259)[192], Dobrilugk (1268)[193], and Tintern Secunda (1282)[194].

Fugitive monks often spurned their habit, as those from Stanley (1259)[195] and Dunkeswell (1346)[196]. A few might join other religious orders, like three monks of Silvacane (1289) who became Benedictines[197]. A dissatisfied monk might try to find excuses when seeking to leave his house, such was the monk of Rievaulx (1279) who pretended to have contracted leprosy but who stabbed the monk appointed to examine him[198]. Some monks left for good cause, as thirteen from Bonnefont (1334) who only absconded because the abbot had put them in fear of their lives[199]. Fugitives who returned voluntarily could be readmitted, but did penance[200]. If they were brought back forcibly they were flogged[201] – one such at Rievaulx (1279) so severely that he died[202]. Disaffected monks might well return not in penitence but to wreak havoc. A Flemish apostate raised an armed band in Bruges, Ghent and Ypres, chased away the abbot and twenty monks from the Dunes (1338) and did damage to the value of 7,000 gold florins[203].

Internal Disorders

A monk lacking a true vocation, or bearing a grudge, might cause trouble within his abbey, or, worse still, conspire with others and foment discontent. It has been calculated – from the statutes of the annual General Chapter – that there were 123 serious disturbances in the houses of the Order between 1190 and 1308, involving the collusion of a group within a monastic community[204]. In fact there were more, as not all occasions of rebellion reached the attention of the Chapter. Those that did were sufficiently numerous to cause it concern (1268), and to comment that they often occurred during visitations or abbatial elections[205]. Many disturbances were caused by *conversi*: 49 out of the 123 cases cited, with monks colluding with them in a further 27 instances[206]. Attacks on abbots were quite frequent[207]: they were after all the superiors whose disciplinary decisions might well be resented. Often a dagger was used (as at Jouy in 1226)[208]. Abbot Gerard of Alvastra (1153–93) was struck as he descended the dormitory stairs by a monk he had been obliged to punish[209]. An abbot might be tied up by his monks (Oliva, 1213)[210], imprisoned by them (Bélakút, 1282)[211], or evicted by them (Ferrara, 1198)[212]. Worse still, at least thirteen Cistercian abbots were murdered by one or more of their community[213]. When Simon, a monk of Trefontane (1180), had killed his abbot, he calmly went to say Mass but finished it by confessing[214]. A monk-bystander might come to the rescue of his assailed abbot (as at Heilsbronn in 1246) or else turn a blind eye (as at Boschaud in 1247)[215].

Difficult monks might also assault fellow-members of their community[216]. A monk of Combermere (1307) killed a *conversus* with a knife[217]; a monk of Zwettl (1275) lost his nose[218]. Brutal as these instances may seem, they need to be set in the often turbulent background of their time. Nor was it unknown for monks to attack seculars: children were allegedly murdered at Auberive (1240)[220], whilst a nobleman staying at Lehnin (1339) was killed in his bed with, it was said, monastic complicity[221]. Rebellious monks could cause schism in a community (Bonnecombe, 1234; Obazine, 1277)[222]. They might violently dispute an abbatial election (Sobrado, 1213[223], Nepomuk, 1243[224]), or disturb a visitation[225]. At Hovedøya (1242) some monks stripped the Visitors of their clothing, and stranded their prior, sacristan and succentor, on an offshore island to die of starvation[226]. Some monasteries underwent protracted periods of trouble[227], like Schönau (1202)[228]. Other problems of indiscipline included sorcery (Fontenay, 1199)[229], necromancy (Doberan, 1345)[230], sodomy (Boulbonne, 1267)[231], and eccentric behaviour (Veruela, 1259: two monks exhuming bodies)[232]. There were frequent arson attacks by disaffected monks which did grave damage[232]. One monk of Jouy (1227) not only threatened a fire, he also placed a sharp razor in his abbot's choir-stall[234]. The General Chapter (1273) became much troubled by the reports of ill-living which reached it[235].

Such behaviour was not typical within the Order, and the recorded lapses of discipline are surprisingly few, considering the thousands of religious. Nonetheless, the Order took steps to preserve its well-being and good name. A Visitor might engage armed lay assistance to help put matters right or, as Abbot Lexington (1228) put it: 'to summon heaven and earth, the divine vengeance and the secular arm'[236]. Such external force might be essential in times of conspiracy, as at Cliente (1211)[237] and Monfero (1218)[238], or when an abbatial election was violently contested, as at Vaudey (1280)[239]. English kings ordered their sheriffs to arrest wandering monks and return them home[240]. Some considerable time may have elapsed before the monarch received and granted such a request; a monk might by then have travelled far away, whilst the expenses of taking such fugitives had to be borne by their own monastery (1284)[241].

The punishments imposed on delinquents included a combination of: excommunication (a solemn denunciation against conspirators, thieves and arsonists, was pronounced in every abbey each Palm Sunday)[242]; expulsion from the Order for fugitive monks who during their apostasy had married or sired children[243]; banishment to a distant house (sometimes for ever)[244] for sexual offenders, arsonists, assailants, and rebels[245]; imprisonment (sometimes perpetual, and usually in chains) for arsonists, conspirators, forgers, thieves[246]; flogging: a very common penance[247]; bread and water diet every Friday (for striking a lay-man[248] or for alcoholism[249]), or for life (for murderers)[250]; taking the lowest place in the community[251]; eating one's meal on the refectory floor and remaining unshaved for a year (returned runaways)[252]; removal of religious habit from thieves[253] and apostates returned involuntarily[254]; bar on ordination for complicity in murder[255]; abstention from saying Mass for sorcerers[256]. Such offenders were at least spared the death penalty: if a monk committed crime outside the precincts, Cistercian privileges usually meant that he was handed over to his abbot for justice[257].

Specific excommunications were issued by the General Chapter for the kidnappers of the prior of Hoveydøya (1243)[258] and the exhumers of bodies at Veruela (1259)[259]. A monk of Combermere (1207) who killed a *conversus* was imprisoned 'according to the custom of the Order'[260]. *Conversi* who killed an abbot of Baudeloo (1226) were expelled to other houses for life[261]. Two monks of Signy (1196) served three years' exile, for conspiring against their abbot[262]. Three rebellious monks of Clairvaux (1223) were sent away: one to the Dunes, another to Aubepierre, and the disposition of the third lay with the abbot of Cîteaux[263]. To help monasteries to which such monks were sent, their own abbots were to give them some money and necessary clothing and shoes (1317)[264]. Expulsion of a monk who had assaulted a lay-man served to spare the culprit's monastery from embarrassment if he had killed a local person. A jury suggested that Velehrad (1333) should make generous compensation to the widows of three men killed by some of its *conversi* and forestry workers[265].

Spirituality

The short-comings of some members of the Order must not conceal the very great number of dedicated monks. The statutes of the General Chapter reflect only offences brought to its attention, and give a distorted impression of the true state of affairs. The Cistercian historian can truly say: 'Behold, the half was not told me' (1 Kings 10:7). Contemporaries told of the Cistercian way of life as 'shining out in the world like lanterns in a dark place' (Orderic Vitalis, *c.* 1135)[266]; wrote of the 'rare piety' of the Order's monks (Gregory IX, 1227)[267]; spoke of the 'sanctity of the monks of Clairvaux' (Count Baldwin of Flanders, 1202)[268], and of the 'vigils, prayers and fasts' at Dargun (Duke Barnim of Pomerania, 1266)[269]. It was a life which, as St Aelred put it, 'had no moment of idleness or dissipation'[270].

Basic to such a life were solitude, silence, simplicity, and stability. Solitude meant not only siting monasteries in remote locations, for not all could be. It did mean detachment from worldly affairs, an interior solitude. St Bernard wrote: 'Withdraw in mind, in spirit, not in body'. William of St Thierry (d. 1148) (quoting Ecclesiastes 4:10: 'Woe to him that is alone') praised the 'common life' of the Cistercians, and saw them as 'solitaries living in a crowd'[271]. That common life, Stephen Lexington stressed (1232), meant that monks were to have no private property, nor were they to receive letters or gifts without permission[272]. That detachment from worldly contacts meant that Cistercians were not to engage in pastoral duties. They were not to hold the cure of souls (1234) nor to preach (1191)[273], nor to baptise any save Saracens[274], unless there was danger of death (1157)[275]. The General Chapter saw abbots baptising as 'an extremely grave matter' (1186). They were not 'to hold infants in baptism' (i.e. be god-fathers), nor were they to bless the baptismal water[276]. External preaching was forbidden – whether in parish churches (1191), or to gain alms for church construction (1198, 1212)[277]. All this detachment was vital for an Order which Eugenius III (1145–53), himself a Cistercian, saw as being a contemplative one[278].

The background to such a life of meditation was, as Orderic Vitalis wrote, 'the silence they maintain at all times'[279] – a silence which lifted the mind to a spiritual plane, and was vividly expressed by the gagged Christ sculptured in the cloister at Lạd. Silence was especially enjoined at night, from Compline on; at all times in the church, cloister, scriptoria, refectory and dormitory[280], and everywhere within the precincts whilst Lauds, Mass, and Vespers, were being chanted in the church[281]. Monks travelling or staying on the granges were to maintain silence, as if in the monastery[282]. Essential conversation was held in the parlours, and there were concessions for the *conversi* at work. Necessary questions concerning the liturgy could be asked even in the cloister[283]; in the infirmary the master could talk to the gravely ill, even after Compline[284]. The 'keeper of the order' might lead small spiritual discussion groups[285]. There were breaches of the rules[286], and in time the General Chapter (1298) observed that silence was often wanting[287]. A Visitor at Hailes (1261) saw silence as obviating 'vain chatter and quarrels among the brethren'[288].

Monastic silence led to sign-language. A monk of Cluny had been able to draw up in 1068 a list of almost 300 signs then in monastic usage[289]. Extant Cistercian codifications are quite late, being manuscripts surviving from the fourteenth and fifteenth centuries for Vyšší Brod (Hohenfurth), Fürstenzell, and Lubiąż[290]. Cistercian custom provided for sign-language at the work-place[291], in the refectory[292], and on the granges[293]. It could be mis-used: monks might circumvent the rule of silence by talking in signs[294]. The *Ecclesiastica Officia* bade monks at work 'not to make many signs between themselves'[295]. Sign-language could be used for jocularity; it could also be half-hearted. The monks of Barbery (1231) were warned against 'making syllables and sounds between signs'[296].

A keynote of the Cistercian reform was simplicity: that ' holy simplicity' which William of St Thierry and Guerric of Igny (d. 1157) praised as 'the humility which ensures the search for God alone, the will turned towards God'[297]. Abbot Charles of Heisterbach (1199) remarked to his novices: 'Let the simplicity of our Order suffice you'[298]. This idea of simplicity – in buildings, in worship, in food, in economy, and indeed in numbers – was not easy to sustain. Reforming abbots, like Stephen Lexington (1230s), were constantly emphasising this 'simplicity of our Order'[299]. His, and like endeavours, were aimed at maintaining not only simplicity but also uniformity[300].

Simplicity in clothing disallowed 'furs, vests and shirts' (1134)[301]. Each monk was rationed to three tunics, two cowls, two pairs of hose, and a scapular 'on account of work' (1246)[302]. The scapular (rather like an apron) was seen as having practical significance. The clothing store was the domain of the wardrobe-keeper[303]. Working boots were of cloth, not hide[304]; day-shoes of cow-skin, and not goat-skin or cordwain; belt-buckles were of wood, or (later) horn or iron. Gloves were worn only by masons, waggoners, fishermen and vintners[305]. Simplicity was also reflected in the habits of undyed cloth; the Order saw white as 'a sign of purity' (1312) and 'of the contemplative life' (1356)[306]. The Camaldolese and the Carthusians already wore white habits, but the early Cistercians were criticised for spiritual pride in so doing by Orderic Vitalis ('white draws attention') and by Peter the Venerable ('you are white while the rest are black')[307]. White may have been a preferred custom by 1115[308], but what was essential (1134[309], 1181[310]) was that habits were undyed in keeping with the 'character' of the Order. This meant variations in shade helping to account for the alternative phrase, 'the grey monks'. The Chapter of 1269 ordered white habits of correct regulation length to be worn – especially in the cloisters and in choir, but impracticability meant that in 1271 it allowed cowls of coarse or grey cloth to be used everywhere, except in choir (save perhaps at nocturns)[311]. At Beaulieu (1270) white scapulars were worn in summer but those with dirty jobs could wear grey ones[312]. The 1335 Constitution decreed a white cowl and a brown scapular[313].

Closely associated with the wearing of the habit was the tonsuring of a monk, using water heated by, and 'combs, scissors, and razors' sharpened by, the monastic kitchener[314]. At first tonsuring and shaving took place mostly before the principal feasts, but their periodicity was gradually increased (partly 'on account of reverence for the sacrament of the altar') until (in 1293) it became a fortnightly event – an indication of concern for the dignity and reputation of the Order[315].

Simplicity of life was also asserted in the extended period of fasting kept from Holy Cross Day (14 September) through to Easter, and in the rule of complete abstinence from meat and any food containing fat, both at a monastery and on its granges, save by the gravely ill[316]. Meat was also forbidden to Cistercian monks whilst travelling, even on ships[317]. Breaches of abstinence were noted at Altenberg (1205: meat served to workers)[318]; Bonmont (1205: meat offered to the diocesan bishop)[319]; and Frienisberg (1207: meat served to masons)[320]. The Chapter had frequently to reiterate the law of abstinence[321]. The papal Constitution of 1335 made concessions: meat could be eaten in the abbot's company and by visiting and retired abbots, but not in the refectory [322].

Profession as a Cistercian monk was for life, normally in the monastery where his vows were made. This stability, coupled with obedience, was emphasised in the *Rule*: no-one was 'to go anywhere or do anything, without the approval of the abbot'[323]. St Bernard wrote: 'There are two things for especial observance. One is submission to the abbot, the other is stability in our monastery'[324]. When there was a need for monks to be away, it was only to be for as long as was necessary[325].To encourage stability, the General Chapter ordered the bounds of each abbey 'to be conscribed in letters patent' so that its monks were aware of them (1200)[326]. Monks were not to go out of bounds to talk[327], nor to external bathing-places[328], nor home to their parents[329], nor to have a horse (unless on monastic business)[330]. Breaches of stability became frequent[331], and the General Chapter of 1281 referred to 'false religious who went out at night'[332]. Nor was going on pilgrimage encouraged. The abbots of Cherlieu and Gard (1236) were rebuked for spending six days in Canterbury visiting the shrine of St Thomas Becket[333]. Cistercian writers (including St Bernard and William of Chaâlis)[334] saw no need for a monk to travel abroad as a pilgrim: his earthly and lifelong pilgrimage was his progression in sanctity within his own house.

At the heart of Cistercian life was night-prayer (Matins, or Nocturns or Vigils), which commenced at about 1.30 a.m. in winter, about 2 a.m. in summer. Even so, the monks had the best part of nine hours in the dorter in winter, six hours in summer[335]. Vigil was watching: waiting for the Lord and guarding against temptation. Abbot John of Ford (d. 1220) wrote: 'We keep perpetual vigil for what is at stake is our own soul'[336]. It is possible that the infirm were excused, for St Bernard underlined the physical fitness of a monk of La Crête sent to Clairvaux who had 'always been present at vigils with the rest'[337]. At Cîteaux (1270) young and old monks might be excused Vigils twice a week[338]. Apart from the normal daily services, there were frequent calls to especial prayer. The General Chapter (1195) ordered that every Friday each community was to say, prostrate in their church, the seven penitential psalms, and to take the discipline privately. Amongst the objects of this prayer and penance were 'the tribulations of the Holy Land, and the invasion by Saracens in Spain'[339]. In 1245 no less than 23 grants of obits and special Masses were made by the Chapter, including a Mass of the Holy Trinity to be said by every priest-monk for Princess Isabella of France, and a Mass of the Holy Spirit for the royal family of Castile[340]. In 1261 special prayers were ordered daily against the Tartars[341].

Following the maxim in the *Rule* that 'they are truly monks when they live by the labour of their hands'[342], St Bernard comprehended work within Cistercian spiritual life as being 'to cultivate silence, to exert ourselves in fasts, vigils, prayers, *manual work*, and, above all, to keep the way of charity'[343]. After the daily chapter, the clapper (*tabula*) was sounded in the cloister[344], the prior allocated work and tools[345], and the monks went forth in silence[346]. If labouring in the fields, they chanted their office and ate their food where-ever they might be[347]. Manual labour could come close to six hours in summer, but less than two hours in winter[348]; only essential work was done on Sundays and many feast-days[349]. Most farming work was done by the *conversi*, especially as the monks were not allowed to live on the granges for any length of time, though they could go to assist with harvesting[350]. Monks of Cwmhir (1231)[351] and of Monthéron (1313)[352] are on record as labouring on their granges. The General Chapter rebuked the abbot of Casalvolone (1194) for sending out monks at night as watchmen in its cornfields[353], and the abbot of Iranzu (1195) for making monks take part in the grape harvest[354].

The sanctions for those who fell short of the high standards Cistercian custom demanded, were meant not only to punish the offender but to advance him in the spiritual life. St Bernard said: 'it is a mark of innate humility not to mind correction, if sometimes you are in error'[355]. Disciplinary matters were dealt with at the daily chapter, when monks were not to show 'indignation' at a penance awarded them by the abbot, nor was such a sentence to be made public outside the chapter-house[356]. No-one could be accused merely on suspicion, and a more senior monk could plead for mercy for an offender[357]. Faults were graded as 'lesser' – which might involve eating moderately outside the refectory and lying prostrate during much of Mass[358], or 'grave' – which usually incurred a flogging. Flogging, which St Bernard saw as a last resort[359], was much resorted to in the Order as late as 1303[360]. Those the General Chapter itself ordered to be flogged included a *conversus* of Theulay (1218) for serving meat on a grange[361], and a cellarer of Mores (1220) for spreading false views concerning the Virgin Birth[362]. A monk ordered to be flogged lay prostrate in the chapter-house, having bared his back, and the punishment continued until the abbot felt it to be sufficient. A junior could not be called upon to flog a more senior monk, nor could the accuser flog the accused[363]. After the penance the monk left to sit elsewhere with the company of an older monk to console him, so that (said the Rule) he be not 'overwhelmed with excessive sorrow' (2 Corinthians 2:7)[364]. When all else failed, a monk might be expelled[365], lest (as St Bernard put it) 'by one sick sheep the whole flock should be contaminated'[366].

Cistercian Saints

The disciplined life of prayer, work, fasting and penance produced many holy men within the Cistercian Order. Such were Waltheof, second abbot of Melrose (1145–59), whose tomb when opened in 1171 showed 'the body to be entire and the vestments unchanged'[367]; Abbot William of Øm (1180–93), said to be 'occupied day and night, reading and praying'[368]; Henry I, abbot of Baumgartenberg and then of Heiligenkreuz (1252), noted as a worker of miracles[369]. and Abbot Richard of Croxden (1294–97) with a special devotion to the Trinity[370]. Those endowed with the 'gift of tears', echoing the words of Our Lord – 'Blessed are those who mourn'[371] – included abbots Henry of Tintern (1148–57)[372], Turgis of Kirkstall (*c.* 1196)[373] and Walter of Villers (1214–21)[373a]. It was a Cistercian writer (*c.* 1309) who could refer to: 'weeping – the proper work of a monk'[374]. Of well over one hundred Cistercians to gain a reputation for sanctity[375], many had made their initial profession at Clairvaux[376]. Villers counted twenty-four of its religious as *beati*[377].

Next to St Bernard, and like him often in poor health, the best-known Cistercian saint was Aelred of Rievaulx. In lay life steward to King David I of Scotland, he entered Rievaulx, became abbot of Revesby, and later returned to the mother-house as abbot (1146–67)[378]. Called the 'Bernard of the North', he did for Rievaulx, vocation-wise, what Bernard had achieved at Clairvaux[379]. He shared Bernard's reluctance to expel an erring brother: 'Do not kill the soul for which Christ died. Do not drive our glory out of this house'[380]. He was a famed spiritual writer, his *Speculum Caritatis* and his *De spirituali amicitia* deriving from friendships enjoyed in his youth, but the suggestion that he had homosexual tendencies is baseless[381]. He was a noted preacher – giving the sermon at Westminster (1163) at the translation of the relics of the recently canonised Edward the Confessor[382]. Other saints worthy of note included Bl. David of Himmerod, who was always smiling with 'the face of one going towards Jerusalem'[383]; Bl. Vincent Kadłubek, bishop of Cracow, who dedicated the abbey church at Jędrzejów and later (1218) retired there as a monk[384]; St Maurice of Langonnet (d. 1191) at whose grave at Bégard miracles were cited[385]; and St Robert of Newminster (d. 1159) whose soul Blessed Godric saw in a vision being transported to heaven[386]. Amongst noted visionaries were Prior Wigan of Volkenrode (*c.* 1133)[387], and Simon, a *conversus* of Aulne (d. 1215)[388]. There were also martyrs on the Prussian mission and Baltic crusade: at Oliwa (1224), and Dünamünde (1228), and, at the hands of the Tartars, at Koprzywnica (1241)[389].

Hermitages

The solitude inherent in Cistercian life had an especial appeal to hermits, and a number of hermitages were incorporated into the Order (Chapter 1). Not a few Cistercians themselves became hermits: St Benedict had remarked that the solitary life should only be embarked upon by those who had learned discipline under an abbot[390]. St Aelred of Rievaulx, equally warning of inherent dangers, wrote at the request of his sister – herself an anchorite – his *De institutis inclusarum*[391]. There is also extant a Cistercian-attributed rule for recluses[392]. Some Cistercians-turned-hermits had a reputation for sanctity, as Albert, a *conversus* of Sestri (d. 1239) who spent the last thirty years of his life living in a monastic wood[393], and Benedict, a *conversus* of Ferrara (d. 1278) who lived on a hill near Venafro[394]; both were reputed as workers of wonders. Amongst those who had been solitaries before entering the Order was St Famian (d. 1150). Originally a recluse named Quardus he became a monk of Osera, but later resumed his eremitical life at Gallese[395]. Amongst abbeys which had hermitages on their lands – either granted them or taken under protection – were Aiguebelle, Newminster[396], and Georgenthal[397]. Bl. Hazeka (d. 1261) spent thirty-six years as a recluse at Sittenbach[398].

Spiritual Fraternity

Numerous bodies (including the Carthusians and Premonstratensians), as well as individuals, sought to gain spiritually from the prayers and labours of the white monks without becoming Cistercians themselves[399]. A donor to Veruela (1166) was received 'into all benefits of our Order, in masses, vigils, fasts, almsgiving, prayers, psalms, hymns and spiritual canticles'[400]; further all members of this extended fraternity were prayed for during the General Chapter[401]. A grant of fraternity was frequently a recompense for favours granted. A count of Flanders was taken into association for giving the white monks freedom from toll (*c.* 1182)[402]. Even a small gift might warrant a deed of fraternity: Fitero (1182) gave one in return for a mill[403]; Warden (1205) in return for one acre of land[404]. Monarchs favoured included Wenceslas II of Bohemia (1292, for gifts to the General Chapter)[405]; the young Henry III (admitted at Waverley in 1225)[406]; and Prince David of Wales (1280) – promised benefits 'in life and in death, as for one of us'[407].

   The abbey of St-Waast at Arras early entered into fraternity (1224) following a visit by St Stephen Harding[408]. Religious in Paris seeking fraternity included the Canons of St Victor (1212)[409], and the Benedictines of St Denis (1261)[410]. Every 20 November a *Commemoratio Fraterna* was observed at Clairvaux with prayers for the abbeys and chapters of canons and others in spiritual association with it. These were termed its *familiars*, in a different sense of that name from its tertiary workers[411]. Individual religious included the noted and aged twelfth century Premonstratensian abbot Godescalc of Želiv, who sought admission after having a vision of St Bernard[412]. Requests from other religious communities were reciprocated. The calendar of commemorations of associated monasteries at the abbey of St Remi included the Cistercian monks of La Chalade and of La Crête[413].

Local grants of fraternity were noted in the calendars of the relevant abbeys, but those given by the General Chapter would additionally be inscribed in 'the roll of Cîteaux'[414]. In time batches of deeds were prepared ready for use, leaving spaces for the insertion of the names of the beneficiary and the sponsoring abbot[415]. Some grants of fraternity carried the right of burial at the abbey, as when Riddagshausen (1310) promised to fetch the body of the knight concerned from wherever he might die in the Duchy of Brunswick[416]. Even if burial was not sought, an obit (anniversary masses and office) might be granted[417]. Obits, too, were carefully recorded, and in 1183 the General Chapter enjoined: 'After the name of Count Theobald of Champagne write the name of Henry (III), King of England'[418]. Others of royal blood listed in the Order's *Commemoration of the Dead* and *Calendar of the Order* included Béla III of Hungary (enrolled 1183)[419], and Mary, dowager duchess of Burgundy (1185)[420]. For them, and many individuals of lesser stature, the prayers of the white monks seemed an assured way of obtaining eternal happiness.

Notes

1. *Statuta* I, 15 (1134/XII), 111 (1189/3); *LCC* (1) 30, (2) 208.
2. *Statuta* I, 313 (1205/29).
3. *Statuta* I, 118 (1190/1).
4. *Cf.* Altrichter (1979) 15; Fergusson (1984a) 7; this may be an inference from that of 1190 requiring thirty monks and a suitable number of *conversi*.
5. Flink (1980) 31.
6. Toepfler (1983) 54.
7. Davies (1984) 149 (*n.* 6).
8. *LFZ* 217.
9. Williams (1984) I, 148.
10. *Statuta* III, 299–300 (1300/2); Clairmarais (1321) acquired *sixty* silver spoons for its refectory (De Laplane 377, No. LXI).
11. Conbhuí (1958) xxxiii.
12. Locatelli (1975) 211.
13. D'Arbois (1858) 256, 261.
14. Platt (1984) 41.
15. Davies (1984) 131, 149 (*n.* 6).
16. Toepfer (1983) 54.
17. Davies (1984) 149 (*n.* 6).
18. *CCD* 55–56; Cocheril (1964) 271.
19. *Statuta* I, 207–08 (1196/53–55).
20. *DNC* III, 391.
21. *LFZ* 217.
22. VCH, *York* III (1913) 153–54.
23. *Statuta* I, 225 (1198/9); III, 233 (1285/6); *cf.* Lekai (1977a) 303.
24. *RSL* II, 205 (No. 15).
25. *SL* 164 (No. 80/56).
26. *RSL* II, 194 (No. 28).
27. Sommer-Ramer (1982) 318.
28. *OLSB* vii.
29. Wiswe (1953) 90.
30. Toepfer (1983) 54.
31. *HCVP* 48.
32. *Statuta* I, 118 (1190/2), 307 (1205/5); III, 62 (1268/16).
33. *Statuta* I, 111 (1189/3), 295 (1204/1); III, 140 (1275/4).
34. Van Der Meer (1965) 296.
35. Williams (1984) I, 55, 148.
36. *RCCH* 13.
37. Bedini (1964) 29.
38. Lekai (1976) 275–76.
39. Toepfer (1983) 55.
40. *Ibid.* 56.
41. Janssen (1983) 207.
42. Toepfer (1983) 56.
43. *DHGE* XII (1953) 1056.
44. Toepfer (1983) 56.
45. Carville (1982a) 61.
46. France (1992) 140*n*.
47. *Cf.* Southern (1970) 7.
48. D'Arbois (1858) 246–47.
49. Richards (1968) 97.
50. D'Arbois (1858) 251.
51. Fort i Cogul (1972) 43; Mousnier (1983b) 64, 67–69.
52. Schreiner (1982) 99.
53. *Statuta* I, 108 (1188/8).
54. *LCC* (1) 117.
55. As at Arnsburg in 1287 (*UKAR* 147–48 [No. 217]).
56. *Statuta* III, 318 (1308/1).
57. King (1954) 52*n*.
58. Hill (1968) 133–34.
59. King (1954) 336.
60. Sumption (1976) 30.
61. Lynch (1973) 297.
62. *Ibid.* 296.
63. Storch (1958) 27–28.
64. Platt (1969) 213.
65. *DHGE* IX (1937) 212, XII (1953) 918.
66. McCrank (1975) 260.
67. Anton (1986) 365 (No. 58).
68. Wiswe (1953) 95.
69. Kempf (1976) 55.
70. *AF* 195–96.
71. *Cf. AF* 152–53 (of 1175), *CAF* 139 (of 1226), *CDEM* II, 130–31 (of 1230), *CDH* 194 (of 1245).
72. Williams (1984) I, 133.
73. McCrank (1973) 66–67.
74. D'Arbois (1858) 260.
75. Lynch (1973) 282–86.

76. *Statuta* I, 31 (1134/LXXVIII); *cf.* I, 24 (1134/I); *LCC* (2) 334.
77. *Statuta* I, 57 (1154/16).
78. *Statuta* I, 62 (1157/28), 72 (1160/12); *LCC* (1) 90.
79. *Cf. Statuta* I, 400 (1212/49), 422 (1214/23); II, 87 (1230/16).
80. *Statuta* I, 84 (1175/26); II, 93–94 (1231/12); *cf.* I, 487 (1218/11); III, 115 (1273/4), 318 (1308/1), 320 (1309/1); Lynch (1973) 287–88.
81. *Statuta* I, 264 (1201/4), 209 (1196/65).
82. *LCC* (1) 116, (2) 314; *RCH* 32; *cf. Statuta* III, 320 (1309/1).
83. Richard (1969) 64.
84. *SMD* II, 193, 196; *cf.* France (1992) 120.
85. Lynch (1973) 294*n*; *cf.* Hermans (1947) 33.
86. *CW* 23–24 (No. 20).
87. *Statuta* I, 145 (1191/80); *cf.* I, 308–09 (1205/9, 12).
88. Merton (1988) 51; *cf. EOC* 318 (CXIII/11); Saward (1980) 71.
89. *Statuta* II, 93–94 (1231/12); III, 115 (1273/4); *LCC* (2) 314.
90. McNulty (1943) 162.
91. *CMH* 115.
92. *EOC* 296–97.
93. Lynch (1973) 295.
94. King (1954) 338.
95. Lynch (1973) 295.
96. *CAS* I, 209–10 (No. CCXXVI).
97. Tort (1974) 400.
98. *Statuta* III, 318 (1308/1), 368 (1324/7).
99. Williams (1984) I, 153; *cf. RPR* II, 1545 (No. 19058).
100. *Cf. Statuta* I, 190 (1195/55), 264 (1201/4).
101. Lackner (1981) 57–58.
102. *Statuta* I, 35–37 (1142); *cf.* III, 210 (1281/25); King (1954) 217.
103. *Statuta* I, 187–88 (1195/41); *LCC* (1) 118, (2) 314.
104. *Statuta* III, 37 (1266/5), 59 (1268/4).
105. *Statuta* III, 127 (1274/3).
106. *Statuta* III, 238–39 (1287/7).
107. *Statuta* III, 315 (1306/2), 368 (1324/3), 390 (1330/6).
108. *Statuta* III, 142 (1275/14), 152 (1276/3).
109. *CDRB* VI, 286–87 (No. 180).
110. VCH, *Huntingdon* I (1926) 391.
111. *EOC* 294–95; Hermans (1947) 51.
112. *SL* 169.
113. *CAS* II, 42 (No. CDXX).
114. *ACA 298*; VCH, *Stafford* III (1970) 229.
115. Anstett (1987) 52.
116. Lekai (1977a) 304, 315.
117. *VKS* 198.
118. *CC* 9–17; VCH, *Stafford* III (1970) 227.
119. *EOC* 294–95; *Statuta* I, 487 1218/11); *cf.* I, 292 (1203/37), 337 (1207/19), 386 (1211/35); III, 188 (1279/32).
120. Barea (1977) 215; *cf.* Anton (1986) 406.
121. *EOC* 299–95, 318–19 (esp. Nos 12–13).
122. Hermans (1947) 97.
123. *EOC* 318 (No. 12); *Statuta* I, 57 (1154/7); *cf.* Hermans (1947) 86–87.
124. *EOC* 305–10 (No. CVIII).
125. *Statuta* I, 487 (1218/10); *cf.* Whone (1987) 53.
126. *DSMLR* I, 311–17 (No. 87; 1270), 365–66 (No. 118; 1284); 398–99 (No. 143; *1301*).
127. *EOC* 296–97.
128. *Statuta* I, 110 (1189/1), 186 (1195/24); III, 342 (1318/13).
129. *LSB* 449 (No. 378).
130. *DSMLR* I, 345–47 (No. 104).
131. Merton (1988) 53–55.
132. Hermans (1947) 91.
133. Sommer-Ramer (1982) 183.
134. Williams (1971) 184, 208.
135. *DSMLR* 500 (No. 197).
136. Williams (1971) 208.
137. Mousnier (1986) 110–11.
138. Giessler-Wirsig (1979) 98–99.
139. *Vaucelles*, 54.
140. Dimier (1966) 45.
141. *SMD* II, 192.
142. McGinn (1985) 19.
143. Brugmans (XXIV 1902) 43–44, Uitterdijk (1874) 226–27.
144. *PZKZ* XXIV, 302.
145. Bedini (1964) 168–70, Serra (1984) 225.
146. *Statuta* III, 141–42 (1275/13).
147. Lekai (1976) 266.
148. Williams (1978) 243.
149. Kłoczowski (1970) 128.
150. Mitkowski (1949) 336.
151. Bouton (1959) I, 166; David (1934) 212, Kłoczowski (1970) 128–20, Schneider (1974) 77, Williams (1978) 244 (*n.* 135).
152. Williams (1978) 244 (and *n.* 138).
153. *KD* I, 26–28.
154. *SL* 206; *cf.* O'Dwyer (1976) II, 26, 96–97.
155. *Cal. Chancery Rolls var.* 198.
156. *ACW* 185.
157. McCrank (1973) 71.
158. Rogers (1880) xviii-xix.
159. McGuire (1976b) 69–71; *cf. DHGE* XIV (1960) 533.
160. Stalley (1987) 6.
161. *Statuta* I, 151 (1192/29); *cf. LMT 203–04*.
162. *Statuta* I, 456 (1216/32), 470–71 (1217/25), 483 (1217/78–79).
163. *Statuta* I, 509 (1219/33), 518–19 (1220/12).
164. O' Dwyer (1975) I, 291–92, 294, 296; (1976) II, 28, 32; *cf. Statuta* II, 50 (1226/15), 61 (1227/28).
165. O'Dwyer (1975) I, 294–95, (1976) II, 289.
166. *Statuta* II, 61 (1227/29).
167. O'Dwyer (1975) I, 296–97; *cf. CDK* 51, *CPR* 1228/176.
168. O'Dwyer (1975) I, 298.
169. Stalley (1987) 18.
170. O'Dwyer (1975) I, 298; (1976) II, 13–14.
171. *RSL* II, 35–36; *cf.* O'Dwyer (1976) II, 45.
172. O'Dwyer (1976) II, 10.
173. *Statuta* III, 179 (1278/24).
174. *SL* 129; Conbhuí (1958) 66–67, 71–72.
175. Keenan (1969) 89–91.
176. NLW, Penrice and Margam Charter 133.
177. Carville (1979) 62–63; Watt (1979) 59.
178. *RSL* I, 99 *et seq.*
179. *SL* 62, 68.
180. Conbhuí (1958) 59.

181. *Statuta* II, 87–88 (1230/20), 96 (1231/27); *cf.* III, 86 (1270/29); O'Dwyer (12975) I, 295–96; (1976) II, 100.
182. *Statuta* II, 104 (1232/21).
183. Conbhuï (1961) 310.
184. Gwynn (1970) 124.
185. Carville (1984) 35, *cf. CDK* 16.
186. *CCR* 404.
187. *Statuta* III, 353 (1321/6).
188. King (1954) x.
189. *Cf.* Birch (1897) 173 (No. 35).
190. *Statuta* III, 37 (1266/4).
191. Williams (1984) I, 26.
192. *CHS* 60; *cf. CPR* 1280/399 (Vaudey).
193. *DHGE* XIV (1960) 538.
194. *Statuta* III, 220 (1282/12).
195. *CPR* 1265/481.
196. Sparks (1978) 76n.
197. *Statuta* III, 244–45 (1289/144), 247 (1290/12); *cf.* Yañez Neira (1977) 267–68.
198. VCH, *County of York* III (1913) 151.
199. Fachinger (1986) 62; *cf. DSMLR* 389–90 (No. 136); *MF* 187.
200. *Statuta* III, 262 (1293/4).
201. *CPR* 1259/45, 1280/399.
202. VCH, *County of York* III (1913) 151.
203. Berlière (1905) 48–49; *DHGE* XV (1963) 29–30.
204. O'Dwyer (1976) II, 25.
205. *Statuta* III, 60 (1268/6).
206. Donnelly (1949) 62.
207. Donnelly (1949) 37, 75–79; France (1992) 152; Goutagny (1965) 44.
208. Dimier (1972a) 40.
209. France (1992) 111.
210. *Statuta* I, 408 (1213/19).
211. *Statuta* III, 219 (1282/9).
212. Donnelly (1949) 73.
213. Dimier (1972a) 40–43; *DHGE* VI (1931) 668.
214. Dimier (1972a) 40.
215. Donnelly (1949) 76.
216. *Cf. CPR* 1296/216; Dimer (1972a) 47–48.
217. BL, Harl. MS 2079, f.127.
218. *Statuta* III, 145 (1275/24).
219. *Cf. CPR* 1287/287, 1292/516.
220. Dimier (1972a) 47.
221. *CDB* 241.
222. Donnelly (1949) 75, 78.
223. *Ibid.* 75.
224. *CDB* 241.
225. *Cf.* Donnelly (1949) 72–78.
226. France (1992) 153; *Statuta* III, 267 (1243/43).
227. *Cf. Statuta* II, 455 (1259/35); III, 180 (1279/19); PRO, SC 7/15 (34); Donnelly (1949) 72–79.
228. Donnelly (1949) 73.
229. *Statuta* I, 232 (1199/49); *cf.* Lekai (1976) 263.
230. McGuire (1976b) 70.
231. *Statuta* III, 54 (1267/46).
232. *Statuta* II, 455 (1259/35).
233. Leclercq (1970) 346–47.
234. *Statuta* II, 60 (1227/25).
235. *Statuta* III, 116–17 (1273/9); *cf.* III, 189 (1279/36).
236. *SL* 94.
237. Donnelly (1949) 73.
238. *Statuta* I, 493 (1218/42).
239. *CPR* 1280/399.
240. *E.g.: CPR* 1259/45, 1265/481, 1266/533; *cf.* McGuire (1982) 107, Wagner (1976) 128.
241. *Statuta* III, 231 (1284/8).
242. *Statuta* I, 93 (1183/11); *LCC* (1) 77.
243. *Cf. Statuta* I, 185 (1195/21); III, 167 (1277/21).
244. *Cf. Statuta* I, 62 (1157/30), 185 (1195/19); II, 438 (1258/8); *LCC* (1) 122–23, (2) 317–18; *CRSHR* II, 545.
245. *Cf. Statuta* I, 98 (1185/6); *LCC* (1) 121; Harper-Bill (1980) 107.
246. *Cf. Statuta* I, 106 (1187/2), 108 (1188/2); III, 145 (1275/24), 205–06 (1281/1); Conbhuï (1980) 228–29; Dimier (1972a) 40–42, 47–48.
247. *Cf. CPR* 1259/45, 1280/399; *RCH 121.*
248. *Statuta* I, 65 (1157); *LCC* (1) 79–80, (2) 276.
249. *SL* 158, 166.
250. *Statuta* I, 106 (1187/2).
251. *LSB* 102 (No. 73).
252. *Statuta* III, 93 (1271/3).
253. *Statuta* III, 205–06 (1281/1).
254. *Statuta* III, 232 (1285/3); *LCC* (2) 279.
255. *Statuta* I, 170 (1193/63).
256. *LCC* (2) 277; *cf.* Lekai (1976) 263.
257. *Cf.* Conbhuï (1980) 228.
258. *Statuta* III, 267 (1243/43).
259. *Statuta* II, 455 (1259/35).
260. BL, Harl. MS 2079, f. 127.
261. Dimier (1972a) 40.
262. *Statuta* I, 178 (1194/16), 203 (1196/29).
263. *Statuta* II, 26–27 (1223/20).
264. *Statuta* III, 336 (1317/13).
265. *CDEM* VI, 349–50.
266. Lackner (1981) 60.
267. *CAF* 144.
268. *RCC* II, 308.
269. *MU* 136.
270. Stalley (1987) 2.
271. Constable (1987) 29.
272. *RSL* II, 206 (No. 6), 211 (No. 8).
273. *Statuta* I, 137–38 (1191/20); II, 126 (1234/1).
274. *Statuta* I, 131 (1190/74).
275. *Statuta* I, 60 (1157/7); *LCC* (1) 39, (2) 215.
276. Lackner (1981) 59.
277. *Ibid.* 59–60.
278. *Statuta* I, 34–41 (1151/I).
279. McGuire (1982) 49.
280. *Statuta* I, 32 (1134/XXXV), 46 (1152/3), 465 (1217/1); III, 190 (1279/38); *SL* 160 (No. 23).
281. *LCC* (1) 44.
282. *SL* 169 (No. 93).
283. Knowles (1963a) 612.
284. *RCOC* 1649 (Cap. V).
285. *RSL* II, 202 (No. 1).
286. *E.g.: Statuta* I, 184 (1195/11), 362 (1209/25), 484 (1218/85); II, 206 (1239/20); *SL* 44, 160 (No. 23), 164 (No. 52), 169 (No. 93).
287. *Statuta* III, 295 (1298/6).
288. Harper-Bill (1980) 108.
289. Barakat (1975) 25.
290. Bibl. MS (Ferenc Hervay); *cf.* Jarecki (1988) 329–99.
291. *RCOC* 1651–52 (Cap. XIII).
292. *RCOC* 1648 (Cap. IV).

293. Sullivan (1989) 186.
294. Trout (1974) 52–53.
295. *EOC* 221.
296. *RSL* II, 210 (No. 4).
297. Leclercq (1978) 254.
298. Lawrence (1984) 151.
299. Fergusson (1979) 75–77, Walker (1983) 51.
300. Lekai (1977a) 448 (IX-X).
301. *Statuta* I, 13 (1134/IV); *LCC* (1) 152, (2) 336; *cf.* Stalley (1987) 2.
302. *Statuta* II, 303 (1246/7).
303. *Cf. ABB* 214–24.
304. *Statuta* I, 31–2 (1134/LXXXIII).
305. *LCC* (1) 153, (2) 336.
306. *Statuta* III, 326 (1312/6), 517 (1350/3).
307. Lawrence (1984) 148.
308. Fergusson (1984a) 6*n*.
309. *Statuta* I, 89 (1181/11).
310. *Statuta* I, 89 (1181/11).
311. *Statuta* III, 69 (1269/4), *cf.* 79–80 (1270/1), 92–93 (1271/1); *RSL* II, 302.
312. *ABB* 215, *cf.* 53.
313. Wulf (1944) 33–34.
314. *EOC* 244–46 (No. LXXXV).
315. *Statuta* I, 136 (1190/12), 449 (1215/68), 465 (1217/74); II, 426 (1257/4), 440 (1258/12); III, 234–40 (1287/14), 241 (1288/7), 265 (1293/24); *LCC* (1) 218; *EOC* 245–46.
316. *Statuta* I, 61 (1157/14); *LCC* (1) 146–47, (2) 332–33.
317. *Statuta* II, 82 (1270/10), 101–02 (1232/6).
318. *UKA* 43 (No. 56).
319. *Statuta* I, 316 (1205/42).
320. *Statuta* I, 338 (1207)23).
321. *Cf. Statuta* I, 94 (1183/20), 183 (1195/10), 186 (1195/28), 323 (1206/12); II, 104 (1232/22); III, 103 (1271/73), 190 (1279/38), 230 (1284/7), 323–24 (1311/2), 324–25 (1312/1).
322. McNulty (1943) 162–63.
323. *RSB* 185 (Cap. LXVII).
324. *LSB* 35 (No. 8/15).
325. *Statuta* I, 14 (1134/VI).
326. *Statuta* I, 251 (1200/14).
327. *SL* 157 (No. 3).
328. Lekai (1977a) 374.
329. *SL* 160 (No. 25).
330. *Statuta* I, 184 (1195/16); *cf. LCC* (2) 307; *RSL* II, 212 (No. 13).
331. *Statuta* II, 425 (1257/2), *cf.*440 (1258/3, 13).
332. *Statuta* III, 206 (1281/4).
333. *DHGE* XIX (1981) 1218.
334. Keenan (1976) 175; *cf.* Leclercq (1961) 47, 49.
335. Lekai (1977a) 364.
336. Corkell (1985) 312.
337. *LSB* 506 (No. 437).
338. *CDCS* 144.
339. *Statuta* I, 181–82 (1195/1).
340. *Statuta* II, 292 (1245/11–17).
341. *Statuta* II, 475–76 (1261/3).
342. *RSB* 130 (Cap. XLVIII).
343. *LSB* 220 (No. 151).
344. *Cf. SL* 164; *RSL* II, 196 (Nos 2, 3).
345. *EOC* 218–21 (LXXV *passim*).
346. Lackner (1978a) 70, Seward (1972) 26.
347. *RCOC* 1650 (Cap. 10); *EOC* 221, 42–44 (No. LXXXIV).
348. Lekai (1977a) 365.
349. *EOC* 124–25 (XXXIII, XXXIV, XXXV) – where feasts listed.
350. Lekai (1977a) 367, Sullivan (1989) 194.
351. Williams (1984) II, 285.
352. Sommer-Ramer (1982) 316, *cf.* Occhipinti (1985) 335.
353. *Statuta* I, 177 (1194/42).
354. *Statuta* I, 195 (1195/87).
355. *LSB* 70 (No. 36).
356. *Statuta* I, 467–68 (1217/10); *EOC* 208 (LXX/77).
357. *EOC* 206 (LXX/48, 68, 71).
358. *LCC* (1) 77, (2) 275–76.
359. *LSB* 150 (No. 103).
360. *Statuta* III, 321 (1309/3).
361. *Statuta* I, 489 (1218/23).
362. *Statuta* I, 525 (1220/43).
363. *EOC* 206 (LXX/50, 69, 71, 76).
364. *LCC* (1) 77, (2) 275–76.
365. *RSB* 89 (Cap. XXVIII); *cf. Statuta* I, 166 (1193/47), 185–87 (1195/19, 30, 96), 429 (1214/59), III, 263 (1293/12).
366. *LSB* 451 (No. 380).
367. Rogers (1880) 6, *CM* 133–34.
368. France (1992) 126.
369. *DHGE* VI (1932) 1487.
370. *CC* (2), B 41.
371. Williams (1984) I, 27–28.
372. St Matthew 5:4.
373. Clark (1895) 186; VCH, *York* III (1913) 144.
373a. *CHDM* I, 98–101.
374. LMT 200 (No. 117).
375. Wulf (1944) 341–43 (where listed).
376. *DHGE* XII (1953) 908.
377. Pineault and Coomans (1994) 121–51.
378. Squire (1969) 97–99, *cf.* Knowles (1963c) 34–38.
379. *Cf.* Knowles (1963c) 51.
380. Merton (1988) 61.
381. Yohe (1995) 338 *et seq.*
382. Knowles (1963c) 42–47.
383. Leclercq (1978) 69.
384. Bar (1985) 47–48.
385. De Warren (1946) 91–94.
386. *CNM* x.
387. *RBS* I, 56.
388. Millard (1994) 515.
389. *DHGE* XII (1953) 959.
390. Talbot (1951b) 173.
391. *Ibid.* 168–217 (where transcribed); *cf.* Squire (1969) 112–28.
392. Griesser (1949) 81–93 (where transcribed).
393. Bedini (1964) 13, Merton (1965) 135, Wulf (1944) 340.
394. Bedini (1964) 74.
395. Wulf (1944) 339.
396. Merton (1965) 138–40.
397. Winter (1868) II, 186.
398. Merton (1965) 137.
399. *Cf.* Clark-Maxwell (1925) 19–60.
400. Mariotte (1963) 340.
401. *Statuta* III, 196 (1284/9); *cf.* Clark-Maxwell (1925) 29.
402. *CDAC* 191 (No. 241).
403. Monterde Albiac (1978) 490.
404. *CW* 64 (No. 85).

405. *PZKZ* 55 (No. XLIV).
406. Fergusson (1984a) 22.
407. Williams (1984) I, 42.
408. *CDAC* 83–84 (No. 74).
409. *Statuta* I, 391 (1212/10).
410. *Statuta* II, 25 (1223/14).
411. *DHGE* XII (1953) 1056.
412. *FRB* II, 500–05; *CDEM* I, 311–12; *cf.* LSB 405 (No. 328).
413. *BHC* I, 562 (note by Falkenstein, L.).
414. *Cf. Statuta* III, 196 (1280/9).
415. Clark-Maxwell (1925) 28, (1929) 185.
416. *CRD* 40.
417. *Cf. RD* I, 802 (No. 4802/220).
418. *Statuta* I, 94 (1183/21).
419. *Statuta* I, 94 (1183/19).
420. *Statuta* I, 101 (1185/26).

Chapter 4

THE MONASTIC COMMUNITY

The Abbots

The superior of each Cistercian community was the abbot, who occupied the first place in choir (on the south side), chanted the solemn mass on major festivals, blessed the candles, ashes, palms, and paschal fire; received novices, heard confessions, presided at the daily chapter and collation, and gave holy water to the brethren after Compline[1]. His rôle was far from being solely ceremonial, nor was he merely the chairman of the community. *The Rule of St Benedict* saw the abbot as occupying 'the place of Christ' in the monastery, and he was, therefore, a personage to whom the utmost respect and obedience were due. In a Cistercian monastery the absolute power of a Benedictine abbot was tempered by the decisions of General Chapters and of Visitors. Nor did the abbot act alone. The *Rule* had insisted that, before making a decision, in all matters of importance a superior should consult his whole community; in lesser affairs his senior monks[3]. By the close of the twelfth century a Cistercian abbot might turn to them for advice on quite important matters. They constituted his 'abbot's council', which always included the prior, sub-prior, and cellarer[4]. In particular, abbots had to seek the advice of their 'council' before demising land (1220)[5].

No-one too young was to be made a Cistercian abbot[6] – yet Maurice of Langonnet was little more than twenty-three when assuming his lengthy rule there[7]. The religious duties of an abbot pre-supposed that he was an ordained priest, but Thomas Woodstock, the first abbot of Croxden (1178–1229), was elected whilst a deacon[8]. As late as 1275, a bull of Gregory X (to Scharnebeck) implied that not all abbots elected were priests[9]. If one was of illegitimate birth, a dispensation might be sought (Cîteaux, 1236[10]; Tintern, 1320[11]). In the thirteenth century an emphasis was placed on the need for Cistercian abbots to be educated[12], literate[13], and to have preaching ability[14]. Monks elected as abbots had usually held a responsible position within their monastery, most commonly that of cellarer or prior. If their election was to the oversight of a daughter-house their going might weaken the standards of the mother-house[15]. The General Chapter (1185) therefore ruled that no abbot could be *forced* to lose his prior or cellarer to the abbacy of another monastery[16].

Their experience of temporal oversight meant that at least four cellarers of Esrum became abbots, one going to its daughter-house at Vitskøl (1290) and another to Øm, settled in turn from Vitskøl (1320)[17]. Four thirteenth-century abbots of Newbattle had previously been cellarers there or at Melrose[18]. Having ruled wisely, the abbots of daughter-houses elected abbots of their mother-house included three early abbots of Clairefontaine translated to Morimond[19] and three early abbots of Furness promoted from Swineshead[20]. Other officials of experience from whose ranks new abbots were chosen included not only priors[21], but also sub-priors[22], sub-cellarers[23], masters of novices[24], masters of *conversi*[25], and porters[26]. Some abbots had been just ordinary members of the community[27]. In the early years the first abbots were naturally from the founding house. At Kirkstall five of its first six abbots were monks of Fountains[28]. Outstanding religious might experience a triple translation. Such were Arnauld Amaury of Poblet, moving first to Grandselve, then to be tenth abbot of Cîteaux (1201–1212) and later archbishop of Narbonne[29]; and Ralph of Tintern, promoted first to Dunkeswell and then to Waverley, (1252–66)[30]. An abbacy was for life unless resignation or deposition intervened, but an abbot who had resigned might find himself abbot yet again. Bl. Peter I was twice abbot of Morimond (1178–81, 1184–98)[31]; and so was Richard, at Croxden (1309–13, 1320–29)[32].

The father-abbot (until 1265, thereafter the prior) fixed the date of election of a new abbot, and summoned the abbots of any daughter-houses of the monastery concerned[33]. They, together with the community of the house, then proceeded to an election 'according to the will and counsel of the father-abbot'. He could very much influence the outcome of the proceedings. Where a vacant daughter-house lay over fifteen days' journey from the mother-house its senior monks could send their votes to the father-abbot and he could then make the appointment (1215)[34]. An alternative for a busy Visitor was to delegate other abbots (at least two) to conduct the election for him[35]. The papal bull of 1265 ruled that at least fifteen days' notice had to be given of an election, and the abbots of the daughter-houses were no longer summoned: the choice was to be the community's own, but the prior, sub-prior and cellarer were to play a prime rôle in deciding upon nominations[36]. At the time of an abbatial election, the Visitor was enjoined (1329) to make a diligent record in writing of the economic state of the monastery[37]. Before the election the monks might take an oath to vote for none other but the monk they thought most suitable[38]. The quasi-episcopal office of an abbot was shown by his presenting himself to the local diocesan (wherever he might be) for a formal blessing (Chapter 2), and on these occasions the General Chapter forbade abbots from making offerings to the bishop[39] or kissing his feet[40]. In England the blessing was frequently received in episcopal manor chapels[41]. At Melrose the bishops of Glasgow blessed several abbots in the abbey church[42], and on one day alone (13 December 1211) the bishop of Connor blessed there three abbots (for Fountains, Furness and Calder)[43].

In the fourteenth century it sometimes became customary for an abbot to be 'provided' rather than freely elected; this was the policy in certain instances of John XXII (1316–34)[43a]. New abbots – by papal appointment in his reign – included those of Aiguebelle, Casanova, Ebrach, Fontfroide, Fossanova and Val-Sainte[44]. An abbot of Nepomuk (1310) was instructed by the General Chapter to arrange for a new abbot of Žďár 'by canonical election *or otherwise*'[45]. A commission of four abbots chose a new abbot of Doberan (1337)[46]. From the thirteenth century, external pressure might be brought to bear by secular parties with vested interests (family, economic or political), the General Chapter (1258) noting that princes and other magnates were influencing abbatial elections[47]. On the accession of a new abbot of Poblet the kings of Aragon expected him to perform homage[48], and on the election of a new abbot of Zbraslav the rulers of Bohemia looked for a monetary offering[49]. There were irregular elections, as at Fitero (1198) when two abbots were elected[50]. A similar situation at Lehnin (1324–39) resulted in a lasting split in the community[51]. The General Chapter (1268) referred to trouble often arising at elections[52], and there were several instances of abbots being intruded by armed force (as at Nepomuk in 1243[53] and Moreruela in 1297[54]).

Early Cistercian abbots had little in the way of privileges. They took part in manual labour and slept in the common dormitory, but ate in the guest-house[55]. From the thirteenth century, they came to have their own substantial quarters (Chapter 11), where the papal bull of 1335 permitted them to eat meat and entertain visiting abbots and members of their own community[56]. From the outset Cistercian abbots received the pastoral staff[57], and, although St Bernard had said they should not aspire to pontificals[58], the right to wear mitre and ring and other episcopal insignia was eventually granted to some abbots – like those of Preuilly (1282), Santes Creus and Poblet (1336–37), but apparently only later (1380, 1392) to the abbots of Cîteaux and Clairvaux[59]. Some Cistercian abbots had been allowed by the pope, in 1260, to confer the minor orders (reader, exorcist, acolyte and sub-deacon) on their monks[60], but the General Chapter forbade any use of this privilege – lest it led to bad relations with the local bishops[61]. Certainly in England and Wales ordinations of monks as acolyte or sub-deacon were performed by the diocesan[62].

Cistercian abbots were frequently employed by popes and kings as messengers and diplomats. Their ecclesiastical status, their white habits, and their membership of an international Order helped them to enter 'no-go areas' reasonably safely, and even to penetrate behind enemy lines. Successive pontiffs named Cistercian abbots as members of commissions acting in a judicial or arbitral rôle; so much so, that Fountains (1185) complained to Lucius III that such tasks burdened the monastery with expenses, and earned it the enmity of powerful men[63]. They were also time-consuming, involving lengthy absences of abbots from their monasteries. Such were the missions of an abbot of Newbattle (1190) judging an advowson dispute between William the Lion, king of Scotland, and Bishop Joscelyn of Glasgow[64], and of three abbots (Lilienfeld, Cîrţa and Egres; 1225) charged with looking into the 'grave conflicts' between the king of Hungary and the Teutonic Knights[65]. Pope Gregory IX sent the abbot of Fálleri, 'a man in awe of God, prudent and discreet', on missions to the king of France (1238) and the queen of Navarre (1239)[66]. More spiritual duties accorded Cistercian abbots included the visitation and reform of Benedictine monasteries, especially during the reigns of Gregory IX (1227–41) and Innocent IV (1243–54)[67], and membership of commissions sifting the evidence in causes for canonisation: as for Caradog the Hermit (abbots of Strata Florida and Whitland, 1200)[68], St Wulfstan (Woburn, 1203)[69], and St William of York (Fountains and Rievaulx, 1223)[70].

Service to kings was to the fore in the case of Richard I of England (1189–99). An abbot of Le Pin was his almoner[71], an abbot of Perseigne (the son of a serf) an adviser[72], an abbot of the Dunes helped to negotiate his release from captivity[73], whilst the abbots of Boxley and Robertsbridge went to Bavaria to find him[74]. King John made much use of abbot Hugh of royal Beaulieu, sending him both to France and to Rome (concerning the Interdict, 1208, and attending the Fourth Lateran Council, 1215)[75]. Abbot Straddell of Dore went thrice to France on Crown affairs (1330, 1334, 1335), amounting to a cumulative absence of one year from home. He was paid expenses and was permitted to take 'the silver vessels of his household'[76]. Cistercian abbots employed on the French side included those of Belleperche and Grandselve (1294)[77]. Other spheres of diplomatic activity lay within the British Isles themselves. Abbots sent to Ireland included those of Buildwas (representing the king at the Synod of Cashel, 1172)[78] and of Rewley (one of a commission inspecting the new Irish coinage and exchange, 1284)[79]. Abbots of Waverley (1304) and Rievaulx (1327) were amongst those sent to treat for peace with the Scots[80]. In the troubled land of Wales – where Prince Llywelyn the Great (1195–1240) had seen abbots as 'men of great authority'[81] – Cistercian superiors were again employed by both sides. Notable in their support of Prince Llywelyn the Last (1246–82) were the abbots of Aberconwy and Strata Florida[82], whilst English monarchs made use of the abbots of Vaudey (1230), Grace Dieu (1236), Tintern and Stanlaw (1268), Dore (1273) and Vale Royal (Darnhall, 1275), in negotiations with the Welsh[83].

A small minority of English and Welsh abbots were summoned from time to time to sit in Parliament[84]; they might occasionally be expected to go on circuit with the justices of the Common Pleas (as an abbot of Furness, 1272)[85], or be appointed as custodians of royal interests (as an abbot of Tintern named 'keeper' of the Crown demesne south of the Trent, 1266)[86]. An unpopular task was the collection of a tenth or subsidy granted to the pope or the king. The levying of such taxes, usually on a diocesan basis, saw the bishop appoint sub-collectors from abbots and others who held substantial spiritual income (tithes, etc.) in his diocese. Such duty was seen as 'a manifest burden': it involved large sums of money, it was time-consuming, and a serious financial liability – failure to raise the money (as in Wales in times of unrest) meant distraint on the goods of the abbey[87]. The abbot of Holm Cultram handled nearly £1,000 from 1294 to 1296 (a tremendous sum then); he claimed £33 for the expenses of his officials in collecting the money and forwarding it to London[88].

The General Chapter, concerned about the potential detriment to good monastic order, warned its abbots to be cautious in the amount of secular business they undertook. They were not to become involved in conflicts between 'princes of the earth', and especially not in the tensions between the kings of England and France (1224)[89]. Cistercian abbots did continue to act as messengers and peace-makers. Pope Gregory IX (1229) requested the abbots of Cîteaux and La Ferté to negotiate a peace between the young kings of England and France then preparing for battle[90]. King Hâkon of Norway (1217) sent the abbot of Lyse to England to conclude a treaty of friendship and commerce with Henry III[91]. An abbot of Poblet was at a Council held in Barcelona (1228) by James I of Aragon, which decided upon the conquest of Majorca[92]. Emperor Henry of the Romans (1313) asked the abbot of Zbraslav to persuade King John of Bohemia to bring an army to Italy[93]. Abbots of Val-Dieu negotiated in disputes between the townsfolk of Aix-la-Chapelle and Liège[94].

Diplomacy was not always easy: it needed abbots of courage to stand up to kings, such as the abbot of Meaux who led the refusal of the Cistercians to pay a tax to King John (1200)[95], and the abbot of La Faise (1335) who asked Edward III to end depredations committed by his troops in Gascony[96]. Some abbots assisted in royal marriage settlements, as the abbots of La Charité (1206, the wedding of Count Stephen of Burgundy to the sister of the king of Aragon)[97]; Morimond (1209, the proposed marriage of Otto IV to the daughter of Philip of Suebia)[98]; Lyse (1283, the wedding of King Erik of Norway and Margaret of Scotland)[99]; Zbraslav (1310, the union of Princess Elizabeth of Bohemia and John of Luxembourg)[99a]. Many abbots undertook the executorship of wills[100]. An abbot of Fontmorigny was an executor of no less than six wills in eight years (1243–51)[101].The will of Agnes, a widow of Kutná Hora, was sealed by the abbot of Sedlec and the abbess of Frauental in 1336, and confirmed by the abbots of Osek, Waldsassen, and Zbraslav[102].

The sundry duties of Cistercian abbots meant that they were 'in journeyings often' (2 Corinthians 11:26). Peter the Venerable (d. 1156) could quote a popular saying: 'The white monks are always in motion'[103]. The frequency of travel led the General Chapter to issue regulatory injunctions. Non-essential journeying was frowned upon in Advent and Lent[104]. Abbots and monks on a journey could sing the hours of the Blessed Virgin Mary and the office for the dead[105], save on a few major feasts[106]. Travelling abbots were to be properly attired[107]. Travelling monks were later allowed to wear grey skull caps (1288)[108] and dispense with the cowl (1295)[109]. Abbots were generally accompanied by a monk or *conversus* or by grooms[110]. If the latter carried sharp weapons, they were to abstain from wine (1182)[111]. The grooms were often the cause of brawls, and unless travelling 'well into Saracen country' were forbidden to carry sharp knives or swords (1202)[112]. In time, some lay-servants might have the duty of riding with their abbot written into their contracts as, at Buildwas, Alan (1255) and his son-in-law, Edmund of Lenham (1302)[113].

Long journeys were wearisome, and infirm and elderly abbots sought to avoid them. More than that, there were dangers: of being robbed (as an abbot of Pipewell, 1230)[114], kidnapped (Hulton, 1271)[115], murdered (Eaunes, 1209)[116], falling from one's horse – and breaking one's legs (Riddagshausen, 1246)[117], being drowned (Fermoy, 1301)[118], weakened by sea-sickness (Stephen Lexington, 1228)[119], ship-wrecked and drowned (Balmerino, 1281)[120], beheaded by pirates (Lyse, 1337)[121]; the last two cases both in the North Sea. Abbots whose monks did not see them again because of death abroad, included Richard I of Fountains (at the Second Lateran Council in Rome, 1139)[122], an abbot of Poblet at far-away La Ferté (1229)[123], an abbot of Coupar (1243) at distant Rheims[124], and an abbot of Villers (1317) at Clairvaux *en route* from Rome[125].

The Cistercians recognised that an abbot might not wish to hold office for life[126], though resignations had been frowned upon by St Bernard[127] and St Hildegarde[128]. Father-abbots were not allowed to consent too readily to the resignation of abbots of their filiations: there was to be 'compelling reason', and the counsel of neighbouring abbots was to be sought[129]. In the first half of the twelfth century, there were some very lengthy abbacies: only three abbots of Cîteaux, but as many as thirteen in the second half of the century; only two abbots of Pontigny between 1114 and 1165, but seven then before 1201. Such later rapid changes of proto-abbots meant little consistent leadership for the Order at a time of protracted problems[130]. Of the six abbots of Clairvaux following St Bernard only one died in office naturally: one was deposed, one murdered, one resigned, and three were translated to bishoprics[131]. At Øm the tenth abbot, Magnus ('the tenth and the first'; 1233–35), was for similar reasons the first to die in office[132]. The average length of an abbacy varied : 16 years at Kirkstall (in 1147–1231)[133], 14 years at Margam (in 1147–1360)[134]. At Furness[135], and generally later[136], at least ten years was regarded as making an abbacy worthwhile. There were some much longer abbacies, such as those of Roger at Byland (1142–96, fifty-four years)[137], and Gerard of Utrecht at Alvastra (1153–93, forty years). Retiring home to Clairvaux, too old and ill to ride, he undertook the long journey suspended between two horses[138]. A number of noteworthy abbacies spanned over thirty years, as those of Adam at Perseigne (1188–1221)[139], Otto Grill at Zwettl (1330–62)[140], and Llywelyn Fychan at Strata Florida (1344–80)[141]. These lengthy abbacies, under wise leaders, were of great profit to their monasteries.

The reasons for resignation included, the later *Charter of Charity* pointed out, 'inefficiency or timidity'[142] in the face perhaps of mounting external pressures – raids by armed bands, threats to one's life, increasing debt. It was because of such troubles that Abbot Bo of Øm (1262–63) resigned 'with delight and pleasure', as did his successor, Ture (1263) following 'much adversity and anguish'[143]. For the good of the Order, the General Chapter (1202) ruled that 'abbots, who for reason of age or feebleness of body or blindness, cannot properly perform their office or attend Chapter' were to retire[144]. Such included the aged Abbot Hugh of Deer (1235)[145], and two blind abbots of Newenham[146]. One infirm abbot of St Bernard-opt-Scheldt (1343) was not pressed to resign but allowed a co-adjutor instead[147].

A twelfth century abbot who resigned became an ordinary monk again, with no especial precedence but ranking in the community according to his date of original profession[148]. He might transfer if he wished to another house of the Order (Serlo of Savigny retiring to Clairvaux, 1158)[149]: there he was to be received 'benignly and not turned away' (1228)[150]. If he was 'quiet, humble, and obedient' he could stay in the monastery he had once ruled (1195)[151]. Either way, he had to 'make his profession again', fully and unreservedly, to the (new) superior within thirty days (extended later to two months)[152]. Many retiring abbots returned to the house of their profession, as William of Santes Creus (1157) going to Grandselve[153], and Simon of Coggeshall (1168) to Melrose[154]. Adam of Newbattle (1213), resigning 'in the beauty of humility', continued there as an ordinary monk until his death (1229)[155]. Resignation from an abbacy was not always the end to major responsibility. Gilbert of Glenluce became novice-master at Melrose, and later bishop of Galloway[156], Philip of Hovedøya (*c.* 1150) prior of Kirkstead and later abbot of Meaux[157]. Retired abbots came later to have definite privileges. They were to be shown 'proper consideration and respect' (1202), 'honour and kindness' (1260)[158]. They were excused, in 1260, from normal labour and duties – and could have a suitable place in the infirmary if they wished, but the next year's General Chapter revoked this statute, seeing these concessions as detrimental to monastic humility[159]. In 1285 the Chapter ruled that retired abbots were to remain in the house they had ruled[160] (receiving a pension if they had ruled it profitably)[161] or return to the abbey from which they had been translated. The papal Constitution of 1335[162] provided that a 'good abbot' who resigned was to be 'sufficiently provided for', and allowed a place where he could eat meat.

An unsatisfactory abbot might be deposed (unless he resigned voluntarily) by a father-abbot (acting in concert with other abbots)[163], his monks being released from their profession of obedience to him[164]. An erring superior had to be given four chances to mend his ways[165], and, to preclude malicious depositions, the papal bull (of 1265) stipulated that the General Chapter should review the evidence supporting depositions and consider all doubtful cases[166]. Grounds for deposition included heresy, simony, immorality, sorcery, perjury, allowing buildings to fall into disrepair, and wholesale alienation of property[167]. Abbots deposed included Stanley (1204) for founding a daughter-house (Duiske) without permission[168], Holm Cultram (1223) for misusing monastery funds[169], and Signy (1238) for heretical views concerning Our Lady[170]. At least three deposed abbots (Tuterø, 1217[171], Sauveréal, 1280[172] and Ferrara[173]) tried to cling to office. Other abbots who attracted attention at the General Chapter included the superior of Aguias (1217) for misconduct in the guest-house at Marmoutiers[174], and of Gerka (1297) for bringing up a boy in the gate-house[175]. A former abbot of Escarpe (1280) who had incurred large debts was restricted in his movements[176]. There were irregular depositions, as at Esrum (1229) where the Visitor acted without the counsel of another abbot[177], and Melrose (1261) where the abbot's deposition was pronounced in the chapter-house of Rievaulx (its mother-house) without his knowledge[178]. An abbot of Holm Cultram (1266) unjustly deposed was reinstated by the General Chapter[179].

A deposed abbot was not to remain in his own monastery (1195)[180] but to transfer to another of his own choice (1228)[181], unless the father-abbot thought otherwise (1202)[182]. A deposed abbot was to make his profession in his new monastery within thirty days[183] (later two months)[184], or else be accounted a fugitive (1196). Abbot Gilbert of Margam (1213) being deposed was 'made a monk' at Kirkstead[185]. A short-lived abbot of Ferrara (1319), being deposed, left with his cronies and led an unedifying life[186]. The General Chapter ruled that former abbots, retired or deposed, were not to take away goods belonging to their monastery (1283)[187] as had a deposed abbot of Bouillas[188]. Deposed abbots who were guilty of grave faults might be further disciplined – as an abbot of Chalivois (1277) ordered to be incarcerated[189], and an abbot of Escarpe (1281) told to take the lowest place in the community[190]. A deposed abbot who had made enemies in his community might well be fearful of his future, as Stephen of Dore (1236–57)[191]. Not all deposed abbots were hard done by: one father-abbot (1190) told a newly-elected subordinate abbot to show his deposed predecessor 'every kindness and consideration to make up for his loss of office'[192]. The General Chapter (1308) was to rule, however, that abbots who had been deposed, or 'resigned out of fear of punishment', were not to be shown any special favours[193]. Abbots deposed because of 'turpidity' (1267) or other serious crimes (1268) were, if at all possible, not to be appointed prior, sub-prior, or cellarer[194]. The great majority of Cistercian abbots were honourable and wise religious. Many monasteries in later life would hark back nostalgically to the days of outstanding superiors – like Stephen Lexington of Savigny and

Clairvaux (1243–55)[195], or Richard Straddell of Dore (1312–46) – well remembered there two centuries on[196].

An abbot's second-in-command, and stand-in when he was absent, was the *prior*, sitting opposite him in choir[197]. Priors were chosen by the abbot after consulting with 'God-fearing brethren' (1217)[198], and were to be monks of such calibre that they were themselves potential abbots (1238)[199]. In the absence of the abbot, the *prior* presided at the daily chapter[200]. His regular duties included presiding in the refectory, arranging and leading the daily labour, and making the periodical arrangements for blood-letting[201]. Priors were not excused kitchen duties[202], and could be deposed for mis-using their office (1195)[203], or for unsatisfactory life (1183)[204]. Seniority meant that priors might be given special commissions[205], and they came to the fore especially when taking charge during inter-regnums between abbots[206]. A prior of Pontigny (1233) so acting was rebuked for admitting in one day seventeen unsuitable persons as *conversi*[207].

The prior was sometimes termed the 'grand prior' (*prior maior*) to distinguish him from his deputy, the *sub-prior*[208], who took over if the prior was ill, or engaged on other duties (e.g. serving the mid-day meal)[209]. The sub-prior had an especial concern for the discipline of the community[210], and for the worship in church. He was 'to animate' the brethren in choir, and make good any short-comings on the part of the precentor or sacristan[211]. Other specific duties might be assigned to a sub-prior, as the hearing of confessions[212], and (at Hautecombe, 1209) the distribution of shoes to servants[213]. Sub-priors might play an occasional rôle outside the precincts, such as a sub-prior of Morimond on visitation at Dore (1204)[214], and a sub-prior of Meaux (1260) negotiating between the men of Holderness and the forces of Prince Edward[215]. At Waldsassen, one Christian was sub-prior for thirty-two years[216]. Another official with disciplinary duties was 'the keeper of the order' (*custos ordinis*), to the fore in Savigniac houses (1231–36)[217]. In the absence of the abbot, he was to remove the habit from a returning apostate monk, and, in the absence of the prior and sub-prior, to lead spiritual discussion groups[218]. At Beaulieu (1270) the weekly accounts of the various departments were rendered in his presence[219]. The duties of a 'keeper' evolved before the thirteenth century[220], and impinged on those of the prior and the hebdomadary of the week. At Zbraslav (1344) his was an office to which rents pertained and was quite distinct from that of all the other monastic officials[221].

Monks in the World

Not only abbots and priors, but also ordinary monks were asked to undertake duties outside their monastery by both ecclesiastical and lay dignitaries, and this impelled the General Chapter (1157, 1175) to remind them that such demands were a negation of their stability[222]. Unless the Chapter gave leave, no Cistercian was to live with persons not of his Order – save with the pope, a cardinal, or their diocesan bishop[223]. In 1220 rules were relaxed: monks and *conversi* could be made available to bishops and kings as almoners and confessors, but they were to be recalled immediately if employed in secular affairs[224]. It had long been the custom for a Cistercian bishop to have religious of his own Order living with him: now there could be a wider deployment. The bishops of Tournai and Winchester were each permitted one monk and two *conversi* living in (1237)[225], and the bishop of Brno was to be given two monks 'of good character' (1242)[226]. A queen of Germany was allowed two monks or *conversi* in her household (1274)[227], a king of Sicily had a monk of Ourscamp (1280)[228]. A king of Hungary was allowed as companions two monks and a *conversus* when he set out for the Holy Land (1213)[229]. Abricius of Sulejów (1298) was not only chaplain, but also 'procurator' to King Wladislas[230].

When monks were engaged in 'unfitting tasks', secular business, the General Chapter took action. It rebuked monks of Bonport and Perseigne (1197) for being involved in 'wars of the kingdom'[231], and noted the mis-use of a monk of Beaupré (1269) by the duke of Lotharingia[232]. The privileges granted to monarchs were also taken up by nobles: Cistercian monks officiated in the chapels of the count of Brittany (1259)[233] and the count of Foix (1262)[234]. In Poland the monks of Sulejów were chaplains to the dukes of the line of Casimir the Just (ob. 1194)[235]. Such religious performed other spiritual and appropriate offices which accorded with their calling – in particular, that of almoner[236]. Monks might be engaged on diplomatic missions. Monks of Mellifont (1206) were sent with a substantial sum of money to King John of England for the restitution of the temporalities of the see of Armagh[237]. Reginald, a monk of Melrose (1265) sent to Norway by King Alexander III, achieved the sale to Scotland of the Isle of Man[238]. Cistercian lack of personal interest in financial affairs meant that by the later thirteenth century a monk of San Galgano often acted as chamberlain of Siena[239], a monk of Settimo helped to keep the accounts of the government of Florence[240], and monks of Sestri administered the port of Genoa[241]. James of Pareres, a notable monk of La Real, was procurator-general to James II of Majorca (1281–1306), and then retired to Poblet with a royal pension[242].

Cistercian Bishops

A number of Cistercians were translated to the episcopate, the first being Peter, abbot of Locedio, as archbishop of Tarentaise (1124–41)[243]. It was a sign of Clairvaux's eminence that in St Bernard's life-time it alone gave the Church no less than ten bishops, five cardinals, and a pope[244]. By 1227 the Order had provided nineteen cardinals and over 130 archbishops and bishops, but this number was small compared with the total strength of the episcopate[245]. The first Cistercian pope was Eugenius III (1145–53): abbot of Trefontane and formerly a novice of St Bernard at Clairvaux, he continued to wear his white Cistercian habit[246]. Two short-lived Cistercian pontiffs were Gregory VIII (1187) and Celestine IV (1241)[247]. Benedict XII (1334–42), who gave the Order its 1335 Constitution, had been abbot of Fontfroide (1311–17)[248]. Two Cistercians declined election as supreme pontiff: Henry de Marcy, bishop of Albano (1187) and formerly abbot of Clairvaux[249], and Conrad of Urach, bishop of Tusculum (1227) and previously abbot successively of Villers, Clairvaux and Cîteaux[250].

Only in Ireland did Cistercian bishops reach a sizeable proportion of the local hierarchy – some thirty between 1200 and 1300[251]. The see of Cashel was occupied by Cistercian archbishops from 1183 to 1289 with only one break[252]. The first abbot of Mellifont, Gilla Crist, who had been a novice at Clairvaux with Eugenius III, was consecrated by that pontiff as bishop of Lismore (1150), and, as legate in Ireland, presided over the Synods of Kells (1152) and of Cashel (1171)[253]. Five of Pontigny's first six abbots became bishops: of Auxerre (twice), Lyon, Bourges, and Arras[254]. Melrose provided six bishops, mostly to Scottish sees[255]. The English abbey of Furness was given by King Olaf of the Isles (1134) the right of nominating the bishops of Man; this privilege was confirmed by Celestine III (1194) but lost amidst growing resentment of it by the mid-thirteenth century[256]. The antipathy to Furness's right of nomination meant that twice at least the see of Man had two rival bishops[257]. English Cistercian bishops included the spiritual writer Baldwin of Ford who, as archbishop of Canterbury (1184–90), crowned Richard I in Westminster Abbey, and, accompanying him to the Holy Land, died in Tyre[258]. Perhaps the oldest bishop in the Order was Gunner, abbot of Øm, and then bishop of Viborg, dying (about 1265) at the age of ninety-nine[259]. Not all bishops were a credit to the Order, certainly in Ireland where some were condemned by the General Chapter (1234, 1235) for their 'detestable life'[260].

The General Chapter had mixed feelings on the appointment of its monks as bishops. None were to accept election without the approval of their own abbot and of the Chapter, unless acceptance was strongly urged upon them by the pope[261]. Those monks who were consecrated were to observe Cistercian customs: in diet, clothing, fasting, and recitation of the canonical hours[262]. They were not released from their monastic vows, and were expected to attend General Chapter – though not all did so[263]. They could have two monks and three *conversi* living with them, called from monasteries of the Order, thus forming a mini-community. The aim was to give the prelate spiritual strength ('solace')[264]. In order to avoid jealousy among monks, because of the privileges accorded them, Cistercian bishops were to visit the monasteries of the Order only infrequently. When they did so, monks might only eat with them in the refectory (1134)[265], and were not to talk with them after Compline (1237)[266] – a rule which had been breached. Some Cistercians accepted election without leave of the Chapter – especially in Ireland (1194, 1199)[267]. Gerard, the cellarer of Mellifont, had been excommunicated in the troubles of 1227, yet managed to become bishop of Dromore for eighteen years[268]. Some Cistercians, like St Bernard, declined episcopal consecration, preferring conventual life[269]. Some saw their elections quashed – either by the pope (as in 1307, when the abbot of Flaran was elected to Tarbes)[270], or by a monarch (as about 1220 when Hâkon of Norway rejected Sigurd of Tautra as archbishop of Nidaros)[271], or by the General Chapter (as in 1193, when it prevented the abbot of Berdoues from becoming bishop of Auch)[272]. As late as 1307, the Chapter referred to 'the ambitious of our Order fraudulently procuring bishoprics'[273].

Affection for their former life saw Cistercian bishops retiring to a house of the Order, perhaps that of their profession or where they had served as abbot. Some retiring bishops greatly benefited their eventide home – as Archbishop Felix of Tuam (1135) who leaded the roof and tower of St Mary's, Dublin[274]. Another group of bishops were those who, nominally at least, became Cistercians upon resigning their sees – as Bl. Vincent Kadłubek of Kraków (1218–23) retiring to die at Jędrzejów[275], and bishop Conrad of Halberstadt who became a monk of Sittenbach (1208–25) but continued to travel on papal missions[276]. The presence of retired bishops in a monastery, probably with especial privileges, could create resentment among some of its community, accusing them of ill-keeping of the usages; there were such instances at Clairvaux[277], and at Dore and Dublin (1239)[278]. Like any other bishop (from 1179) a Cistercian bishop could be invited to perform episcopal functions in a monastery[279]. A Cistercian bishop of Ferns dedicated the infirmary chapel (1201)[280] and five altars (1214) at Waverley[281]. Monk-bishops living at Clairvaux were allowed by Gregory IX (1227–41) to ordain monks and consecrate altars[282]. Cistercian bishops were not, however, to hold visitations of monasteries or bless their novices: only abbots did that[283] – a rule breached in Southern Italy (1211)[284].

The Conversi

Cistercian economy was basically agrarian, but since the Order renounced a labour supply in the form of serfs, and as its monks could not leave the cloister to work lands increasingly granted to it at a distance[285], the first Cistercians quickly realised that without assistance 'they would be unable to observe fully the precepts of the Rule by day and by night'[286]. So, early in the twelfth century, and with episcopal[287] and papal[288] permission, the Order came to rely heavily upon these hard-working men of 'inherent simplicity', as the founders thought them[289]. Known as *conversi*[290], they were already a feature of the congregations of Camaldoli, Hirschau and Vallombrosa[291]. St

Aelred saw their rôle as that of the industrious Martha in contrast to the contemplative monks whom he equated with Mary (St Luke 10:38–42)[292]. The cartulary of Gimont (1142–1233) listed its *conversi* as 'cobblers, cowherds, stablemen, masons, smiths, reapers and vine-growers'[293].

The *conversi* were not accorded the status of monks, but were seen as otherwise being with them 'equals in life and in death'[294]. They did not wear the cowl[295], only a cloak; nor were they tonsured. Yet they were true religious for they vowed obedience, lived a common life and, if they left the Order, might not marry. Once professed as *conversi*, they could not aspire to becoming choir-monks or priests[296] (and so were sometimes called *conversi laici*)[297] – though there were exceptions[298]. From 1181, they were prohibited from attending abbatial elections – probably to avoid rebellious interruptions[299] – and, from 1188, the admission of nobles as *conversi* was discouraged[300] – perhaps because differences of birth created problems. These rules highlighted and accentuated the sharp divide (in worship, education, work, living and sleeping arrangements) which became firmly established in the twelfth century between the monks and the *conversi* – a class-distinction which forsook the equality the first fathers perhaps envisaged[301].

The name of *conversus* in the Cistercian context implied one who had 'converted', changed inwardly in his spiritual life and transferred from a purely lay to a religious state[302]. Whilst the 1202 codification of statutes occasionally used the term *frater laicus* alongside *conversus*[303], the General Chapter (1234) later ruled that whilst an individual *conversus* might be referred to as 'brother X', the generic term for these religious was 'not brothers, but *conversi*', and ordered those calling them otherwise to be flogged[304]. Some resented being called *conversi* (St André-en-Gouffern, 1231)[305], whilst the General Chapter (1275) in time allowed those of 'Provence, Gascony, and beyond' to be termed 'brothers', as the name of *conversus* had become associated with heretics in the Cathar Midi[306] and elsewhere[307].

Unlike the monks, and emphasising their non-clerical status, the *conversi* (*fratres barbati*) grew beards[308] not more than two fingers long[309]. Burchard of Balerne (*c.* 1160), in his *Apologia De Barbis*, acclaimed the beard as a sign of fortitude, grace, and wisdom[309] but, none too happily, he described the beards of the *conversi* as 'showing the law' but the shaving of the monks as 'declaring grace' (*cf.* 2 Corinthians 3:16)[310]. *Conversi* gravestones show both a sharp, pointed beard (Obazine, *c.* 1280), and, later, a broad and long growth (Ebrach, *c.* 1348)[311]. The General Chapter (1303) ordered the removal of beards from all *conversi* who had shortened them, or had shaved their moustaches, 'contrary to custom'[312]. Save for one year (1255–58), the *conversi* were shaved at the same intervals as the monks[312]. It seems that they were not tonsured like the monks, yet, in 1229, they do appear to have had a distinctive hairstyle[312a]. Abbot Burchard tried to show that the beards of the *conversi* and the tonsures of the monks were complementary. 'You', he declared, 'bear the beard without the "crown", we the "crown" without the beard'[314].

The life of the *conversi* was regulated primarily by the *Usus conversorum* ('the Use of the *Conversi*') drawn up by St Stephen Harding, perhaps in the period of 1125 to 1132, as a response to what he perceived to be differing attitudes to their *conversi* by the abbots of the several monasteries then constituting the emergent Order[315]. The *Usus* constituted the third part of the *Consuetudines* ('the Customs of the Order'), and with its twenty-six divisions or chapters was a comprehensive guide[316]. It dealt with their time of rising (later than the monks), and their diet (somewhat more abundant): both were a response to the hard manual labour expected of them. It outlined the pattern of their worship – far less time in church; assuming them to be illiterate (i.e. not knowing Latin), it forbade them to possess books, but enjoined them to learn by heart the *Pater, Credo, Gloria, Miserere* and, later, the *Ave Maria*[317]. A number of medieval copies of the *Usus* are known, of varying editions due to the incorporation of later statutes of General Chapter touching upon the *conversi*[318]. The other important source governing the life of the *conversi* of the lineage of Clairvaux was a detailed commentary upon the *Usus*, the *Regula conversorum*, written after 1174 but alleged (by one edition emanating from Aulne) to have derived its origins from St Bernard himself[319]. The institution of the *conversi* (and some of the problems arising therefrom) seems to have been copied from the Cistercians by the Gilbertines[320], whilst the regulations of the *Usus* are reflected in the provisions for lay-brothers in the first Dominican Constitution (1216)[321].

The large numbers of *conversi* at the peak of the institution coincided with and greatly aided the expansion of the Order. Eastern Europe apart, the great majority of *conversi* were locally born. This is demonstrated by their surnames (when known), and was a reflection of their peasant origins. Several studies have shown this to be the case[322]. Shortage of native vocations, given the intense degree of serfdom, accounts for many *conversi* in Poland being of German stock – brought from German monasteries or coming from German settler families on Cistercian lands. A similar paucity of aspirants in Hungary meant an import from France also[323]. In Western Europe many laymen took advantage for genuine spiritual reasons of this particular form of vocation which the Cistercians had to offer, and gained holiness and sanctification thereby. Very many such entrants, however, may have been farmers or labourers exchanging the uncertainty of life on a small-holding for security in a monastery[324]. They frequently brought lands with them, enabling an abbey to enlarge its estates, and it is possible that some abbeys had a predilection for potential *conversi* who could benefit them in this way, rather than for aspirants who were destitute. As farmers they brought practical skills as well[325].

The motives of such entrants were, at best, mixed: by the close of the twelfth century, Conrad of Eberbach saw peasantry as driven to the Order 'more by necessity than by the fear of God'[326]. A later Dominican preacher (d. 1277) saw numerous *conversi* as 'seeking white bread and often'[327]. Mid-twelfth century donors of land to Berdoues and Gimont often made conditions that they, or their sons, or both, be admitted as *conversi*[328]. Two entrants as *conversi* at Silvanès gave lands which formed the nucleus of its later Promillac Grange (1162)[329]. Some gifts were not small. One donor gave Margam (*c.* 1200) no less than twenty-four acres on admission[330]. Olaf of Øm (*c.* 1240) gave 'his woods, lands, houses, and animals'[331]. Gifts of land, as a form of dowry on a son or brother becoming a *conversus*, marked the entry of Hugh the Palmer at La Ferté (*c.* 1130)[332], and Arbert of Maranville at Clairvaux (1228)[333]. Family consent was sought for gifts made by a *conversus* on entering St Bernard-opt-Scheldt (1352)[334].

Not all twelfth-century *conversi* came from the peasant class. There is plenty of evidence of noble or knightly admissions at Grandselve[335], Himmerod[336] and Salem[337]. Prince Alexander of Scotland spent his last years as a *conversus* at Foigny (d. 1229)[338]. Some fifty nobles or knights were admitted as *conversi* at Himmerod[339]. The General Chapter came to disapprove and, whilst not absolutely prohibiting the admission of nobles as *conversi*, did insist (1188) that all such who would be useful as monks should be so professed[340]. What was necessary (so far as the outside world was concerned) was that aspirants should be free-men. Aberconwy (1311) was fined for receiving two of the king's villeins as *conversi*[341]. What was necessary (so far as a monastery was concerned) was that entrants should be free of financial difficulties: at Margam the three sons of one postulant promised to meet their father's debts[342]. Most, but not all, *conversi* were illiterate, and so for much of the fourteenth century Cistercian *conversi* were employed in sealing papal bulls at Avignon, on the supposition that being unlettered they could not read the documents they were handling[343]. There were exceptions, and those *conversi* who must have had a high degree of literacy included Imbert of Cîteaux, one of two attorneys appointed by its abbot (1280)[344], and Robert of Vale Royal (1290–92), rendering account as royal escheator for the county of Chester[345]. Tue, a thirteenth century *conversus* of Løgum, was a skilled copyist[346].

The General Chapter disapproved of secular priests who came surreptitiously and, pretending to be lay-men, gained admittance as *conversi*. Once their true status was discovered they were to be expelled (1214)[347]. A *conversus* of Grandselve (1204) who hid the fact that he was a deacon was similarly dealt with[348]. Alternatively, an abbot could place such a cleric (retaining his tonsure) amongst the familiars[349]. There were many examples of married men becoming *conversi*, but they had to forgo the marital state. A donor of land to Bonnecombe was promised admission 'if his wife absolved him from their marriage vows'[350]. A married man was guaranteed entry at Gimont (1196)[351], but a would-be *conversus* at Margam was only acceptable 'if not debarred by marriage'[352]. It seems likely that many *conversi* became such in widowhood, or voluntarily withdrew from their wives and offspring. Where such a novice was a generous donor, there is some evidence that the monastery made provision for his family. Certainly there is mention in Wales (1344) of 'Matthew ap David, son of a Cistercian laybrother'[353].

Age was also a determining factor. Whilst Simon of Aulne (1160) became a *conversus* at the age of sixteen[354], and the grandson of a donor to Clairvaux was admitted there (1178)[355], the General Chapter (1201) fixed the minimum age of novice *conversi* and monks alike at eighteen years[356], probably reiterating earlier blanket provisions. Vital to the hard work of a *conversus* was physical capability. Berdoues (1161, 1183) insisted that prospective *conversi* should be fit and well, 'all their limbs intact'[357]. Gimont (1196) promised admission to a donor provided that he entered within five years 'sound and entire in all his members'[358]. Time limits (sometimes of only a few months) may have been meant not only to ensure physical capability, but also so that labour was available for grange creation to go forward[359]. The General Chapter (1224, 1261) insisted that none be received unless they could accomplish the same work as a hired hand[360]. Rather than lose substantial lands which were the nuclei of its later Stormy and Resolfen Granges, Margam (*c.* 1170) promised admission as a *conversus* to a married man 'when he became infirm', and (*c.* 1200) to a blinded tribesman[361].

Aspirants who fulfilled the necessary entry conditions were presented to the monks in their chapter by the cellarer, and on the following Sunday were introduced into the chapter of the *conversi*[362]. A novice then served a year's probation, aided by an experienced *conversus* able to teach him the usages and customs of the Order. If he survived the novitiate the cellarer again led him into the monks' chapter; there, lying prostrate, he begged 'the mercy of God and that of the Order', and, raised up, made before the abbot his profession of obedience, chastity, and renunciation of personal property. For a short period a new *conversus* also took an oath written into the *Usus* after 1160, but struck out in 1183 'because it begs many questions'[363]. The entry of men of mixed motives or unsuitable nature was countered by General Chapter (1220) making would-be *conversi* serve six months' preliminary probation in secular clothing[364].

At the peak of the Order's growth the ratio of *conversi* to monks in many abbeys may have been in the region of two to one, though some of the figures quoted for the twelfth-century are perhaps exaggerated. There were a reputed 500 *conversi* (as opposed to 140 monks) at Rievaulx in St Aelred's day (1147–67), but it is not clear whether this is the number for any particular year or for the duration of his abbacy[365]. Vaucelles shows an increase in *conversi* numbers from 130 (1152, as opposed to 103 monks) to 180 (1181, in contrast with 107 monks)[366]. The late-twelfth century extension of the *conversi* range at Fountains by nine bays was indicative of their large numbers[367]. If an average of 80 *conversi* per abbey in the year 1200 is assumed, then a total of at least 40,000 in Europe at that time is suggested, and this could be an underestimate. In the thirteenth century numbers of *conversi* could still be considerable: 200 reputed at Himmerod (1224, as opposed to 60 monks)[368], and 150 at Louth Park (1230, compared with 66 monks)[369]. The *Chronicle of the Dunes* lists the admission of 1441 *conversi* (as opposed to 884 monks) over the 350 years between its foundation (1128) and the editing of the chronicle (1487); this casts some doubt on the high numbers sometimes attributed to it[370].

An idea of maximum possible numbers comes from the 'quota' system operated by Visitors: 160 at Byland (1231, compared with 80 monks); and 60 at Longvilliers (1231, as opposed to 40 monks)[371]. Such numbers were (in these instances) fixed by Stephen Lexington who (1230) noted that at Savigny only one or two *conversi* at most manned some of the granges[372]. Beaulieu (1270) with a total of 68 *conversi*, had at most eight on its leading grange at St Leonard's[373]. Even in the hey-day of *conversi* a monastery with twelve to twenty granges soon found itself stretched and in need of hired workers[374]. In the fourteenth century the numbers of *conversi* showed wide variations. Salem is credited with 180 in 1311, declining to 160 in 1323. Poblet also showed a decline from 85 (1311) to 55 (1316)[375], but even Margam (1336) still boasted 40 (compared with 38 monks)[376]. Henryków had 30 (opposed to 44 monks) in that year – but the *conversi* population of many Polish abbeys was perhaps always modest[377]. Some houses went down to single figures: there were only 7 *conversi* at Bordesley (1332), Viktring (1335), and Meaux (1349 – this before the Black Death)[378].

The *conversi* were dressed in a tunic retained by a belt, with hose, scapula and smock[378a] and shod with sandals[378b]. Overall they wore a cloak (of old cloth or skin)[379] with a hood, but not the cowl of the professed monk[380]. Their habit was supposed to be of undyed coarse cloth, but divergences led the 1335 Constitution to insist that it be grey or russet[381]. They were allowed four tunics each year, whilst the clothing of herdsmen, ploughmen and waggoners could be of more ample measure. The smiths could have rounded black smocks[382]. Boots (and then old ones) were only allowed to *conversi* 'on account of vigils' – presumably referring to those attending vigils in a cold abbey church (the context suggests this), but possibly referring to those keeping watch in the fields[383]. The restriction on boots caused resentment and trouble in at least one monastery (Schönau)[384]. Woollen vests were forbidden, as in general were gloves. Only masons could wear leather gloves; waggoners, fishermen, and vine-growers could wear mittens[385].

When the *conversi* retired to their dorter it was to mattress beds like those of the monks, but for bedclothes they could use only the hides of sheep and goats, not woollen blankets nor bed-spreads (1175)[386], though this ruling was mitigated for monasteries in cold regions (1187)[387]. If so unwell as to have missed choir for three days, the *conversi* could enter their own infirmary[388]. They were bled at the abbey, not on the granges[389]. The *conversi* resident in an abbey ate in their own refectory, sitting in order of seniority. The meal was presided over by the senior *conversus* who led the responses and the Lord's Prayer before, and the *Miserere* after, eating (1189)[390]. They ate in silence, wearing their cloaks (1161)[391], but there were no readings. They ate the same quantity of food as the monks[392], and, if their abbot allowed, could have for breakfast (*mixt*) water and $\frac{1}{2}$lb. of white bread ('convent bread') or a greater quantity of coarser bread. On the granges this allowance was doubled, and fasting (from breakfast) was moderated[393]. When the *conversi* from the granges went to the abbey for Sundays they were placed either with the residents according to seniority, or, if there were too many, at a separate table[394]. Alcoholic drink could be a problem, and at Savigny Stephen Lexington enjoined (1230) that their drinking bowls were to be of the prescribed size, but on the granges (where hard work was done) they could be somewhat larger[395].

The *conversi* worshipped within their own choir, the western portion of the abbey church. On Sundays and some thirty holy-days they assisted at the two sung conventual masses, but on other working feast-days they heard only the first Mass[396]. On ordinary days they were not present at all. If essential work (or residence on the granges) kept them from an obligatory Mass, they were to recite the Lord's Prayer fifty times instead[397]. They took part in the Candlemas, Palm Sunday, Ascension Day and Assumption Feast processions in the cloister, walking in pairs behind the community and the abbot[398]. Unless engaged on essential work, they were expected to attend the anointing of the dying and the obsequies for the departed[399]. The *conversi* communicated only seven times a year: Christmas, Candlemas, Maundy Thursday, Easter, Pentecost, the Nativity of Our Lady, and All Saints Day[400]. Those communicating on Maundy Thursday were to continue to eat only 'Lenten bread' until they had received Holy Communion again on Easter Day (1189)[401]. Those living on distant granges could receive Holy Communion (and the imposition of ashes on Ash Wednesday) elsewhere (1202)[402]. Otherwise, the *conversi* not on essential duty were expected to return to their monastery for Sundays and festivals. This meant that (including leave for blood-letting and the four days of Christmas) the grange *conversi* spent theoretically one-quarter of the year back at their abbey[403]. In their choir the 'first of the senior *conversi*' occupied the stalls nearest the altar. The head *conversus* before Communion received the Peace from the sub-deacon and conveyed it to his fellows in their stalls[404].

As for the divine office this was shorter than that of the monks, but recited at the same time so that 'a union of prayer' was achieved[405]. The senior *conversus* intoned the opening and closing responses and said the Lord's Prayer (once silently, once aloud) at all offices, which basically consisted of the repetition of the Lord's Prayer and then the *Gloria Patri*: twenty times at Vigils (but forty times on greater feasts), ten times at Lauds and Vespers, and five times at the Lesser Hours and Compline[406]. In summer, the Lesser Hours and even Vespers might be chanted in the fields, but all went to Compline in the abbey church. On Sundays and other holy-days when no work was done, the *conversi* rose at the same time as the monks. On working days from mid-September to Maundy Thursday their rising bell was sounded as the monks started the last psalm of the first nocturn at vigils, and they went to work at the close of nocturns. In the summer months, since they did not get a siesta on account of work, they did not rise until Lauds. *Conversi* on the granges rose in summer at daybreak, in autumn and spring in time to complete vigils before dawn, and in winter they kept vigils 'about the fourth part of the night'[407].

Save for essential conversation concerning their work, the *conversi* were enjoined to keep silence in the monastery[408], on the granges[409], and going to and from the fields – especially if wayfarers were in the vicinity[410]. They could give directions to lost travellers and ask questions if searching for stray animals. Talking was permitted to ploughmen when turning their ploughs, shepherds watching their flocks (very quietly, 'so others may not understand'), fullers in their mill ('because of the noise of the water'), and smiths in their forge – perhaps to avoid accidents[411]. Sign-language was encouraged[412]. Stephen Lexington had to remind the *conversi* of Chaloché (1231) to keep silence – 'between the church and the door of the dorter' – it seems they wanted to talk on their way to bed[413]. One *conversus* noted for his non-communicative nature was Bl. Everard 'the taciturn' of Villers[414].

On Sundays the *conversi* had their own weekly chapter under the presidency of the abbot or his delegate – often the master of the *conversi*[415] – but on those feasts when a sermon was given in the monks' chapter the *conversi* went to listen (either entering, or from the cloister). This meant that at Christmas, Easter and Pentecost, their own chapter was held the next day[416]. At the chapter a talk on the Order was given[417]; a novice might be presented, and a brother appointed to guide him. Lastly, came the punishment of faults, when excuses were not permitted[418], and those guilty of grave offences were flogged[419]. Additional penances might include: for disobedience – eating on the floor of the refectory for three days, without their cloak (1186)[420]; for sexual offences – exile to granges of other abbeys and deprivation of religious habit (1242)[421]; for rebellion, and refusal to work as directed – reduction to the status and habit of a 'familiar' (1244, 1261)[422].

The cellarer was responsible for the work and discipline of the *conversi*, aided by the 'grangers' : it was he, therefore, who presented would-be *conversi* for admission and profession in chapter. Their spiritual director and confessor was the 'master of the *conversi*': a monk of 'experience and prudence who would set a good example', and who not infrequently became an abbot himself . Whilst it was laid down (1237) that such an official was to be appointed 'where the number warranted it', few monasteries would have been without him. The master attended the chapter of the *conversi*, and heard the confessions of his subjects in 'a suitable place' on the Saturdays and vigils of days when they received Holy Communion; the frequency of confession was increased (1232) to once a week, as for the monks. The infirmarian of the *conversi* was to notify him if any sick needed his ministrations[423]. The master was also, once a week, to visit the workplaces of the *conversi*, and give them (singly or in groups) a spiritual conference. Apart from that, the master was not to speak to the *conversi*, nor to assign them duties, nor give them licence to speak. Another duty was to visit the *conversi* on the granges where he would hold a chapter, hear confessions, give spiritual instruction and take counsel with the granger[424]. The 'master' at Dore went to its Welsh grange at Trawscoed to communicate the brethren there at Easter[425]. Stephen Lexington ordered the master at Duiske (1228) to visit its five granges monthly[426].

It was on the basis of *conversi* labour that the Cistercians farmed so many granges and shepherded their large flocks[427]. They were the backbone of the Order's agricultural economy, but fulfilled numerous other rôles – as merchants, miners, craftsmen, kitchen staff and house cleaners, wardens of town houses, abbatial attendants on journeys, couriers and arbitrators, and economic advisers to the Order's nunneries; some were even medical men[428]. *Conversi* had oversight normally of the monastic bakery, brew-house, weaving-room, forge, and most other offices, and such heads of department might gain suffixes such as 'Gerald the tailor' (La Ferté, 1170)[429], 'Martin the smith' (Pilis, 1199)[430], 'William the shepherd', (Tintern, 1261)[431] and 'Adam the carpenter' (Combermere, 1307)[432]. The versatility of an individual *conversus* was shown by Bertrand of Clairvaux (adm. 1140): skilled in water-way construction, he was also no mean blacksmith and farrier; as a merchant he went to markets and fairs, and was used by St Bernard as a courier – despatched with letters as far afield as Southern Italy[433].

The liturgical usages suggest that work started for the *conversi* at the conclusion of Vigils in winter and about the close of Lauds in summer[434]. The day of the *conversus* was a long one, and when animals were put out to graze it could mean watching over them at night[435]. Only essential work was expected on Sundays, the four days of Christmas, Easter Monday, Whit Monday, the Epiphany, Good Friday, Ascension Day, Michaelmas, All Saints Day, the five principal feasts of Our Lady, seven or eight feasts of the apostles, and some five other holy-days – making at least eighty days holiday in total[436]. Work was expected on lesser feasts and transferred festivals (1157)[437]. Through this life of silence and discipline, of worship and of work, many *conversi* gained a reputation for holiness of life, and some were especially endowed as visionaries and prophets. Conrad of Eberbach told of a *conversus* who dreamt that as he ploughed a field Christ was walking beside him[438]. Heinrich of Himmerod saw devils loose in the monks' choir, but also the Holy Spirit as a dove hovering above a novice during his ceremony of admission[439]. Gerekin of Alvastra saw the figure of the Christ-child in the priest's hands during the elevation at Mass[440]. Many visitors came to see Simon of Aulne (adm. 1160) who foretold the questions and answers of the 1215 Lateran Council[441]. Other holy *conversi* included Arnulf of Villers (1180–1228) who practised severe corporal mortification[442]; John of Sagramenia (d. *c.* 1150)[443] and Peter of the Dunes (d. 1280) who ate only bread and water[444]. The abbey of Villers counted seven of its *conversi* as of great sanctity[445], and some Scandinavian *conversi* had a similar reputation[446].

Much of the trade of Cistercian monasteries was in the hands of experienced *conversi*, and by 1195 the larger abbeys at least had a senior man who was called 'the merchant'[447]. Such *conversi* held posts of considerable responsibility, involving frequent travel[448]. The General Chapter issued more than one statute prohibiting sharp practice by merchants of the Order, noting (1214) English *conversi* who had bought wool in order to sell it at a profit[449]. Cistercian merchants might go far afield: two from Øm with a monk were sent to Horsnæs with cloth, copper and silver coins, in order to buy grain when food was short in Denmark[450]. Berthold, a merchant of Salem, was involved in at least sixty transactions – purchase of lands and goods, contracts, litigation for damages, etc.[451]. Journeying could be hazardous: a *conversus* of Furness (1246) was drowned when he fell from his horse whilst crossing Leven Sands[452]. As arbitrators, *conversi* were involved in settling a land dispute between Bouras and Fontmorigny (1178)[453] and in arranging a land exchange between Cambron and the Dunes (1234)[454]. As a business agent of his house, a *conversus* of Heiligenkreuz (1278) had an audience of King Ladislas IV of Hungary[455]. *Conversi* of Salem (1259, 1260, 1276) appeared as procurators of their monastery in litigation; they were also frequently on record as witnesses to charters[456]. Other houses whose *conversi* witnessed charters included Cymer (1209)[457], Chorin (1267)[458], and Kołbacz (1233)[459].

The households of Cistercian bishops often included resident *conversi*. Eventually, even non-Cistercian bishops could borrow *conversi* for appropriate employment, often as almoners (1220[460]). They were not to be used for secular business, and when assigned inappropriate tasks might be recalled (Silvanès, 1200[461]; Wettingen, 1252[462]). A *conversus* engaged by the Franciscan archbishop of Milan (1243) to head his guard (*dux exercitus*) was ordered home immediately[463]. The skill, expertise and probity of many *conversi* led to frequent demands for their services by kings and nobles, a pressure which the General Chapter resisted well into the thirteenth century[464] (ordering many home)[465], but which individual monasteries found it difficult, perhaps impolitic, to refuse. In order perhaps not to offend powerful patrons and benefactors the Order had to make concessions, allowing *conversi* to be at the service first of monarchs (as almoners, 1220)[466] and then of 'princes' (1233)[467]. Such *conversi* were to be, the Chapter ruled, 'of praiseworthy life, mature age and good report' (1242)[468]; they were not to engage in secular business (1238)[469], only in tasks appropriate to their religious profession (1250)[470].

Emperor Frederick II asked for *conversi* of Ferrara (1223) to guard his flocks[471]. Henry III of England sent a secret message by word of mouth – using an unnamed *conversus* – to the count of Ponthieu (1234)[472]. He had as his 'carpenter' Randolph of Combermere, said to be 'constantly engaged on the king's affairs' (1266)[473]. King Diñiz of Portugal (1279–1325) employed a *conversus* of Alcobaça to drain swampland[474]. A *conversus* of Warden (1245) advised on the construction of royal fish-ponds at Windsor[475]. Numerous *conversi* served as almoners, as to the countess of Brittany (1246)[476] and the duke of Bavaria (1262)[477]. Others served, in unspecified capacities, the king of Germany (1250)[478] and the king of Aragon (1266)[479]. The trend troubled the General Chapter (1235) almost from the time of relaxing its rules[480]. It ordered the recall of monks and *conversi* borrowed from Casanova (1236) by the king of Sicily, 'if possible without scandalising him'[481], and the withdrawal of *conversi* of Heiligenkreuz (1281) from keeping the flocks of layfolk[482]. The concession granted to nobles was terminated in 1270[483].

In the early years most *conversi* were perhaps highly motivated, seeing their work in the fields as a form of prayer[485], yet long before the twelfth century ended a number were disobedient and rebellious. The reasons included:

1. *Mixed motives for entry* (lamented by Caesarius of Heisterbach)[486] – insecurity in the world, insistence of parents: 'difficult' characters became *conversi*, not truly called by God. Archbishop Peckham (1289) told how known wrongdoers sought refuge by becoming *conversi*[487].

2. *Later regret of an impulsive decision to enter*, coupled with the loss of previous independence[488].

3. *Class distinction* – Stephen Lexington (1228) reminded the Irish *conversi* that they did not have parity with the monks, and that they were 'not to pull their sleeves or harass them'[489].

4. *Long working day and strict discipline*[490].

5. *Intoxication*, and

6. *The consequent refusal of alcohol.* For some fifty years (1184–1238) the General Chapter sought to avoid disturbances by forbidding wine or beer to the *conversi*, especially in England and in Wales where they were to have only 'simple water' (1184)[491], but this led to rioting (Cwmhir, 1195[492]; Ireland, 1228[493]). Because three of its *conversi* were drunk, a granary of Meaux (1225) burnt down[494].

7. *Resentment* felt by the *conversi* as a growing tenantry led to their replacement[495].

As St Hildegard (d. 1179) had observed, some *conversi* – of Eberbach – did not want to work[496]. Masters of granges, therefore, were encouraged to 'urge and compel' them (1224)[497]. Arrogance of *conversi* in supervisory rôles at Meaux (1225) led to their transfer to more menial tasks[498]. Lazy *conversi* were to be reduced to 'familiar' status and fed on coarse bread (1261)[499]. The next year it became permissible for granges to be entrusted to full control by *conversi*, whose only obligation was to return a regular rent (1262)[500]; this may have been because of difficulty in controlling them or a means of giving them greater incentive to work. *Conversi*-related problems also affected the Gilbertines and Grandmontines[501].

The recorded incidences of rebellious *conversi* were, in total, minimal compared with the thousands of *conversi* in the Order at any one time, but they caught the headlines. Even so, as late as 1272, the Chapter could refer to 'the frequent excesses of *conversi* in many abbeys'[502]. Incidents occasioned by *conversi* ranged from serious affrays to relatively minor assaults. Conspiracies against authority (especially in times of visitations) were widespread as at Walkenried (1196)[503], Pontigny (1230)[504] and Casanova (1260)[505]. Even Cîteaux was not immune from trouble (1220)[506]. There were intermittent disturbances at Eberbach in which two abbots were wounded (1241, 1269) and one murdered (1254)[507]. At Gard (1193) *conversi* occupied a grange[508]. At Margam (1206) they barricaded themselves in their dormitory[509]. When monks in Flanders decided to sell or lease lands rather than use *conversi*, there was much trade-union type opposition. One *conversus* of Ter Doest (1308), 'a man of great strength' who had been a hero in the Battle of Courtrai, killed the cellarer and then took refuge in the church tower at Lisseweghe[510].

Attacks on abbots were not surprising, given their disciplinary authority. St Hildegard noted the disrespect for authority. There were, she wrote, '*conversi*, of whom many do not convert to God, who say of their superiors: "Who and what are they?"'[511]. Assaults on abbots with sticks or stabbing with knives were not uncommon. *Conversi* rendered the abbot of Heilsbronn (1246) useless[512], and murdered an abbot of Baudeloo (1226)[513]. Assailants, if apprehended, were subject to severe punishment, including perpetual imprisonment on bread and water, expulsion or dispersal. It is no wonder that some abbots laid 'violent hands' on erring *conversi*: Buzay (1206)[514], Walderbach (1209)[515], and Amelunxborn (1213)[516], amongst them. Jealousy may account for attacks by *conversi* on the monks in their communities. For self-defence the monks of some abbeys in Germany and Poland, as well as in Hungary, armed themselves in such situations[517]. *Conversi* mutilated monks at St Gotthard (1195)[518], practised 'unheard of cruelty' at Aulps (1272)[519], and at Zwettl (1275) cut off a monk's nose[520]. An apostate *conversus* of Kołbacz (1329), not content with setting fire to its church and razing three granges, killed two of the monks and hung their bodies on a gibbet[521]. Cellarers, the immediate bosses of the *conversi*, were also particular objects of hostility – killed at Rivalta (1267)[522]. *Conversi* might even kill one of their own number[523]: at Pilis (1213) they were alleged to have buried a fellow-*conversus* alive[524]. They might attack lay-people[525]: *conversi* of Beaulieu (1274) raided a lay manor, killing a horse and damaging crops[526]. Lesser peccadilloes by *conversi* included adultery and fornication (Fountains, 1307)[527], magic and sorcery (Bonnecombe, 1354)[528].

In addition to individual punishments awarded, the General Chapter might order the dispersal of *conversi* from troubled houses (1185, 1196)[529], and a ban or restriction on the recruitment of more (1195)[530]. At Pontigny (1230), a very senior house, those who had been expelled were never to be allowed to return, nor were any more to be immediately recruited[531]. Affairs in the line of Pontigny became so bad that the formulary used by abbots in composing visitation charters included a paragraph 'against rebellious lay-brothers'[532], as if they were taken for granted. The Chapter regulated for some time the numbers of *conversi* that could be admitted at the trouble-prone abbeys of Baudeloo (1226–36)[533] and Eberbach (1261–74)[534].

Whilst some continental abbeys maintained large numbers of *conversi* well into the fourteenth century, a general decline was evident by the second quarter of the thirteenth. In 1237 this caused the General Chapter to allow abbeys with no more than eight *conversi* to employ lay-servants in the kitchens[535], a practice hitherto strictly forbidden[536]. (It may be that the ruling refers to the number resident in the monastery itself, not the grand total of *conversi* a house had). In 1274 the Chapter, referring to a considerable general fall in *conversi* numbers, allowed lay-servants of good character in all monastic kitchens[537]. The decline also meant that abbots travelling to the Chapter could now be accompanied by lay-grooms ('youths') rather than by *conversi* (1267)[538].

The reasons for the diminution of *conversi* numbers included perhaps the growing prosperity of peasants – who no longer needed to seek cloistered security; the attraction of the newer Mendicant Orders – with less manual work and greater freedom of movement[539]; a feeling of inequality *vis-à-vis* the choir-monks, and resentment of restrictions ; the rapid increase of grange size – rendering their numbers insufficient[540]; the bull of Boniface VIII (1302) allowing Cistercian lands to remain tithe-free, even if not worked directly but by tenants and labourers – making *conversi* not so essential[541], and possibly the reluctance of some superiors to take on potential trouble-makers. By 1341 even the head-carpenter of Sedlec was a lay-servant[542]. After the Black Death (1348–49) the institution of the *conversi*, which had been the bulwark of the Order's economic growth two centuries before, was in rapid decline.

The Familiars

The somewhat shadowy institution of the 'familiars' which had evolved by the late twelfth century (certainly by 1190)[543] represented a half-way stage between the professed *conversi* (with whom they lived and worked in close association) and the hired paid workers and servants (sometimes referred to as 'mercenaries'). In fact the Cistercian Order used the word 'familiar' to describe two different groups of people. Benefactors might have their names inscribed on a monastery's 'roll of familiars' (1192–1234) and receive the prayers of the brethren and perhaps the right of burial.

These were non-resident 'familiars', the recipients of spiritual fraternity[544]. The resident 'familiars' were essentially people who gave themselves to the monastery – hence, as at Ferrara (1272)[545] and Fontmorigny (1249, 1252)[546], they might be called 'oblates'. They also gave all they possessed in the way of houses and lands – and so might be termed 'donors' (*donati*) – though those so called at Poblet[547] could keep their wives. True 'familiars', in return for the grants they had made, received food, clothing and residence for life, and – at their death – burial and prayer. In their abbey they communicated at a side-altar[548].

An injunction (of not later than 1147) ordered that would-be monks who died before formally requesting admission in chapter be counted as familiars rather than as novices – but the reference is ambiguous and might simply refer to the status afforded an ordinary benefactor[549]. Hugh le Barbu was a familiar at Rievaulx in St Aelred's time before becoming a *conversus*[550]. Resident familiars were a recognised group, alongside the monks and *conversi*, when the General Chapter limited the size of communities (1190)[551]. 'Brothers, familiars, and mercenaries' worked on the lands of Clairefontaine in 1198[552]. An abbot of Locedio (1193) was rebuked for engaging a familiar in politics[553]. So little is on record regarding resident familiars in the twelfth, and even the thirteenth, centuries, that perhaps not all monasteries had such an arrangement, but familiars were certainly seen as a necessary complement to the community when Torcello (1205)[554] and La Real (Majorca; 1232)[555] were founded.

Into the ranks of the familiars came men unfitted (perhaps by age or health or disinclination) for the rôle of *conversi* (Cherlieu; 1202)[556]. *Conversi* who had broken silence (1221)[557], or who were guilty of theft (1228)[558], or who didn't want to work (1261)[559], or who had absconded (1272)[560], might be reduced to the status of familiars. The case of a *conversus* of St André-en-Gouffern (1242) so degraded was reviewed[561]. Monks who had run away two or three times and wished to return had to wear the habit of a familiar but were to attend vigils (though out of choir) and keep the monastic fasts (1267)[562]. This implies the more relaxed régime of the familiars. *Conversi* voluntarily returning after leaving their monastery were to hold familiar status for a period equal to their length of absence, but were meanwhile to keep to the observances of the lay-brethren (1272)[563]. This regulation was later revoked (1284)[564].

It is clear that by 1213 the familiars wore some kind of habit and had their hair cut short[565]. Those who received this habit in one monastery could not transfer to another unless their abbot agreed. There were some ten familiars at Beaulieu (1270) wearing a special habit[566]; tunics and hose were issued to familiars at Carracedo[567]. The General Chapter (perhaps for the sake of uniformity) attempted to turn the familiars into *quasi-conversi*, insisting (1233) that on admission they renounced private property, took vows of obedience and chastity before their abbot, and wore the habit and tonsure life-long[568]. There is no knowledge of the nature of their tonsure (presumably a shaven head), nor of the colour and style of their habit. As for their diet, Stephen Lexington ordered that the familiars at Clairmont's Corcelles Grange (1236) were not to be served wine, lest it make the *conversi* jealous[569].

Other familiars are on record in the thirteenth century: at Clairmarais (1208)[569a], at Cîteaux (1230)[570], Toplica (1252)[571], Ferrara (1272) – where some had apostasised[572], and Doberan (1282) – where one (John of Brunswick, a 'faithful familiar'), witnessed a charter[573]. The familiars of Beaulieu (1270) had special regulations drawn up for them[574]. There were female familiars – though it is not certain that they were resident: at Fontmorigny (1252) one Agnes, who had given a house to the monastery[575], and at the Dunes (1260) Adeliza Veys of nearby Ramscapple, who gave lands and a silver chalice for the daily Mass in the gate-house chapel, where eventually she was buried[576].

As the number of *conversi* declined, it may be that an increasing number of lay-folk opted for the life of a familiar – less rigorous than that of a *conversus*. The presence of too many familiars following a not so demanding régime was felt by the General Chapter not to be conducive to good discipline in the communities. Consequently, the Chapter first forbade their admission save with the consent of the father-abbot of the house concerned (1292)[577], and then tightened up further, making leave of the Chapter itself necessary (1293)[578]. This all but ended the familiars' rôle, but it did survive in at least some houses. Yet another female familiar, Sister Marguerite Goys, a widow and benefactor and described on her tombstone as a 'familiar', died at the Dunes (1348) only a month after her contract of admission was drawn up. The monastery's obligations to her included the grant of 'white cloth for making a habit' – perhaps an indication of the colour of a familiar's garb[579].

Mixed Communities

There was no place in Cistercian life for co-habitation with women[580]. There were no double-monasteries as allowed by the Gilbertines, though many convents of nuns were served by chaplains and *conversi* resident outside the enclosure. Some Cistercian monasteries had their origins in dual-houses. A grant to Balerne by two brothers on condition that their mother was made a nun, *may* refer to a dual-monastery there before its incorporation into the Order (1136)[581]. When the joint community of monks at Obazine and nuns at Coyroux (only 600 metres apart) were incorporated into the Order (1147), instead of being partners the nuns were made subject to the abbot[582]. The first hermits at Vallbona (fd. 1157) were called 'brothers and sisters' but after the founder's death and the adoption of Cistercian life (1176) it became purely a female house[583]. 'Brothers and sisters' were also living at Bon Repos (1204) but the monks ceded the property to a benefactor who established (by 1215) a nunnery with his daughter as first abbess[584]. When the double Benedictine community of Menterwolde was incorporated (1247), separation of the monks and nuns into two abbeys was enjoined. The male abbey later moved to Termunten, the nuns were established at Midwolde – only twelve kilometres distant. Their house had to be abandoned (1299) on account of flooding[585].

Other Cistercian nunneries which originated from dual-houses were Vivegnis (incorporated 1238, the nuns moving from Beaufays on the order of the local bishop)[586], Lübeck (inc. 1245, the monks transferring to Cismar)[587], and the English nunneries at Catesby and Swine[588]. Stephen Lexington (1228) was offended to find that in Ireland monks and nuns were sharing different sections of the same buildings at Jerpoint, Mellifont, and Suir[589]. This was in line with Celtic tradition but he ordered the removal of the abbot's house at Mellifont from within 'the courtyard of the nuns'[590]. When it was reported that women were received as *conversae* in a house owned by La Crête (1266), the General Chapter ordered an end to the practice save with its special leave[591].

Notes

1. *EOC* 310–13.
2. *RSB* 17 (Cap. II), 34 (Cap. V); *cf.* 19 (Cap. II); D'Arbois (1858) 156–57.
3. *RSB* 24–25 (Cap. 3).
4. Leclercq (1988) 17–23; *cf. Statuta* I, 106 (1187/4), 310 (1205/15); III, 94 (1271/7); the 'council' at Margam in 1228 consisted of 14 monks (*SL* 19 [No. 3]).
5. *Statuta* I, 517 (1220/5); *LCC* (2) 331.
6. *Statuta* I, 62 (1157/23); *LCC* (1) 94.
7. *DHGE* XI (1949) 1106.
8. VCH, *Stafford* III (1970) 230.
9. *UKS* 46.
10. *LCC* (2) 8*n*.
11. Williams (1984) I, 153.
12. France (1992) 237.
13. *Statuta* II, 246–47 (1242/6).
14. *SL* 217 (No. 102), *AF* 85.

15. Sullivan (1989) 195.
16. *Statuta* I, 102 (1185/30).
17. France (1992) 123–24, 134.
18. *CRC* 13, Clay (1952) 10.
19. *Cîteaux* XLVI: (1995: 1–2) 163.
20. *AF* 170.
21. *Cf. CM* 58 (Warden, *1223*), 91 (Newbattle, *1256*), *CRC* 12 (Coupar, *1243*); Fachinger (1986) 64 (Thoronet, *1345*); France (1992) 123–24 (Alvastra, *1153*).
22. *Cf. ACA* 300 (Croxden, *1293*), *CM* 32 (Melrose, *1206*), 58 (Dundrennan, *1223*).
23. *CM 28* (Holm Cultram, *1192*); Hockey (1976) 99–100: (Newenham).
24. *MA* V, 343 (Roger was, successively, monk of Furness, subprior of Calder, novice master of Hood, then abbot of Byland – *1142*), *CRC* 5 (Coupar, *1200*).
25. *RBS* 68 (Waldsassen, 16th abbot); *RHC* 134 (Holm Cultram, *1233*); Carrick (1907) 42 (Newbattle, *1201*).
26. *CM* 88 (Balmerino, *1252*); Davidson (1843) 75 (Newenham, *1338*).
27. *CM* 58 (Deer, *1223*), 88 (Dundrennan and Kinloss, *1250*).
28. Lawrence (1984) 158.
29. *DHGE* XII (1953) 866.
30. Williams (1984) I, 155.
31. King (1954) 348–49.
32. *ACA* 305.
33. *LCC* (1) 93; *Statuta* I, 29 (1134/LXVII), *cf.* I, 391 (1212/9).
34. *Statuta* I, 436 (1215/9).
35. *Cf. RSL* II, 298–99; De Laplane (1863) 380.
36. *Statuta* III, 25 (1265/3); *cf.* III, 97 (1271/7), Lekai (1977a) 72.
37. *Statuta* III, 385–86 (1329/4), 389–90 (1330/4), *cf. CMM* II, 176, and De Laplane 380–82 (No. LXIII).
38. *CWK* 55.
39. Waddell (1994) 33.
40. *Statuta* II, 327 (1248/2).
41. *Cf. AF* 267 (Furness), Stéphan (1970) 89, 107, 110 (Buckfast); Williams (1976) 26.
42. *CM* 11, 20, 86.
43. *CM 35*.
43a. Lekai (1977a) 101–02.
44. Fachinger (1986) 60–64; *CDAA* 299.
45. *Statuta* III, 323 (1310/5).
46. *CDB* 240.
47. Buczek (1971) 108.
48. McCrank (1975) 257.
49. *RBM* IV, 305 (No. 772).
50. *Statuta* I, 226–27 (1198/24).
51. *CDB* 241–43, *Cf. DHGE* XIX (1981) 318.
52. *Statuta* III, 60 (1268/6).
53. *Statuta* II, 273–74 (1243/70–71); *cf.* Jażdżewski (1992) 55–51.
54. *Statuta* III, 290 (1297/15).
55. *EOC* 313; *cf.* 308–09; Lackner (1978a) 71, McGuire (1976a) 117.
56. McNulty (1943) 163.
57. Lackner (1981) 53, *cf. ACA* 300.
58. James (1957) 94, Lackner (1976) 54.
59. *DHGE* XII (1953) 978, *cf.* Bouton II (1964) 308, De Maillé 262 (1930; Preuilly); Lekai (1977a) 256.
60. Lackner (1971) 34.
61. *Statuta* II, 462 (1260/8).
62. *Cf.* Williams (1984) I, 155.
63. Hill (1968) 141, 144–45.
64. Carrick (1907) 42.
65. Entz (1968) 11–18; *DHGE* XV (1963) 28; *cf. CDEM* III, 28.
66. *DHGE* XVI (1967) 448.
67. *DHGE* XII (1953) 944, (1971) 537.
68. Williams (1984) I, 32.
69. VCH, *County of Bedford* I (1904) 366.
70. Clay (1952) 20–22.
71. Clair (1961) 98.
72. *Cistercian Studies* XII (1977:2) 328 (note 541 by P. Hart).
73. Southern (1970) 267, Meyerus (1561) 59.
74. VCH, *County of Kent* II (1926) 153.
75. VCH, *County of Kent* II (1903) 140–41; *Statuta* I, 445 (1215/48); Hockey (1976) 23–24.
76. Williams (1976) 17–18.
77. Taupiac (1878) 102.
78. VCH, *Shropshire* II (1973) 51.
79. *CPR* 1284/127.
80. Baigent (1882) 256, Mullin (1932) 85.
81. *BT* (1955) 295.
82. Williams (1984) I, 38, 41–42.
83. Williams (1984) I, 38; *CPR* 1268/254, 1275/104.
84. *Cf. AF* 220, 247–48; De Varabeke (1972) 18–19, Mullin (1932) 86, Williams (1984) I, 52.
85. *CPR* 1272/614.
86. *CPR* 1266/568.
87. Williams (1984). I, 59–63.
88. *RHC* 102–03, 128.
89. *LCC* (2) 306–07; *Statuta* II, 32 (1224/15); *cf. LCC* (1) 103.
90. Dimier (1954) 26–27.
91. France (1992) 121.
92. Shelley (1926) 136.
93. *RBM* III, 51 (Nos 119, 121).
94. Ruwet (1966) 11.
95. Clay (1952) 29.
96. *DHGE* XVI (1967) 414.
97. *Statuta* I, 32 (1206/66), 337 (1207/16).
98. King (1954) 351.
99. France (1992) 122.
100. *Cf. CCR* 1231/474, *DAC* (1978) 486, *RBC* 37, *RCCH* 122–23.
101. *CAF* 183, 191, 198–99, 207, 215, 218.
102. *RBM* IV, 122 (No. 307), 168 (No. 417).
103. Lackner (1978b) 24.
104. *Statuta* I, 64–65 (1157/40).
105. *Statuta* I, 60 (1157/1).
106. *Statuta* I, 171 (1194/1).
107. *Cf. Statuta* I, 395 (1212/26).
108. *Statuta* III, 241 (1288/4).
109. *Statuta* III, 280 (1295/9).
110. *Cf. Statuta* I, 217 (1197/32).
111. *Statuta* I, 90 (1182/3).
112. *LCC* (1) 108.
113. VCH, *Shropshire* II (1973) 54.
114. VCH, *Northampton* II (1908) 117–18.
115. Tomkinson (1985) 61.
116. *DHGE* XIV (1960) 1263–64.
117. *CFC* 136.

118. Gwynn (1970) 132; O'Sullivan (1946) 175.
119. *SL* 81.
120. Campbell (1899) 176–77, *cf.* Talbot (1939) 64.
121. France (1992) 365.
122. Gilyard-Beer (1987) 45.
123. King (1954) 119.
124. *RCA* xlix.
125. *OLSB* 46.
126. France (1992) 127.
127. Bouchard (1980) 255.
128. France (1992) 129.
129. Bouchard (1980) 250–52.
130. *Ibid.* 251, 255.
131. King (1954) 247–58.
132. *SMD* II, 195.
133. Lawrence (1984) 158.
134. Williams (1971) 189.
135. Dickinson (1965) 15.
136. *Cal. Letters and Papers, Domestic (Henry VIII)* X, 170 (No. 424).
137. Clay (1952) 10–11, 41–43.
138. France (1992) 114.
139. *DAC* (1975) 7–8.
140. *UKZ* 384–85.
141. Williams (1984) I, 67–68.
142. Lekai (1977a) 465 (No. 23).
143. France (1992) 127, 130.
144. *Statuta* I, 280 (1202/39).
145. *CM* 61.
146. Davidson (1843) 75.
147. *OLSB* 170.
148. *Statuta* I, 30 (1134/LXXV), 65 (1157); *LCC* (1) 95, (2) 294–95.
149. D'Arbois (1858) 252.
150. *Statuta* II, 74 (1228/43); *cf. LCC* (2) 294.
151. *Statuta* I, 187 (1195/37); *cf. LCC* (2) 294–95.
152. *LCC* (2) 294–95.
153. Mousnier (1983b) 67.
154. *RC* 16.
155. *CM* 38.
156. *CM* 60–61.
157. Clay (1952) 28.
158. *Statuta* I, 280 (1202/39); II, 461 (1260/2).
159. *Statuta* II, 461 (1260/2), 475 (1261/1).
160. *Statuta* III, 233 (1285/9).
161. *Statuta* III, 241 (1288/6), 245 (1290/3); *cf.* 353 (1321/8).
162. *Statuta* III, 424–27 (1335/*bulla* 22, 27).
163. Lackner (1981) 53–54.
164. *Cf. CM* 97.
165. Lekai (1977a) 465 (No. 24).
166. *Statuta* III, 29–30 (1265/*bulla* 8); *DHGE* XII (1953) 950.
167. *Statuta* III, 30 (1265/*bulla* 8).
168. Conbhuï (1958) 49.
169. *RHC* 133.
170. *Statuta* II, 200 (1238/75).
171. France (1992) 90–92.
172. *Statuta* III, 203 (1280/63).
173. *DHGE* XVI (1967) 1222.
174. *DHGE* I (1912) 1061.
175. *Statuta* III, 290 (1297/18).
176. *Statuta* III, 196 (1280/8).
177. France (1992) 131.
178. *CM* 103.
179. *Statuta* III, 45 (1266/51).
180. *Statuta* I, 187 (1195/37).
181. *Statuta* II, 74 (1228/43).
182. *LCC* (1) 95, (2) 295.
183. *Statuta* I, 208 (1196/60).
184. *LCC* (1) 95, (2) 295.
185. Birch (1897) 375.
186. *DHGE* XVI (1967) 1222.
187. *Statuta* III, 229–30 (1283/5).
188. *DHGE* IX (1937) 1505.
189. *Statuta* III, 170 (1277/37).
190. *DHGE* XV (1963) 850.
191. Williams (1976) 11.
192. *LMT* 204 (No. 133).
193. *Statuta* III, 319 (1308/2).
194. *Statuta* III, 48 (1267/4), 59 (1268/3).
195. King (1954) 270–74.
196. Williams (1976) 15–18.
197. *EOC* 314–15 (Cap. CXI).
198. *Statuta* I, 468 (1217/12); *LCC* (2) 296.
199. *Statuta* II, 200 (1238/76).
200. *Statuta* I, 100 (1185/14), 467 (1217/10).
201. *Statuta* I, 47 (1152/9), 87 (1180/2).
202. *EOC* 314 (Cap. CXI).
203. *Cf. Statuta* I, 186 (1195/27; in matter of pittances).
204. *Cf. Statuta* I, 92 (1183/6; sorcery).
205. *Cf.* Reissenberger (1894) 11 (Cîrţa); Williams (1984) I, 41 (Strata Marcella).
206. *Cf. CAS* II, 38–41 (CD XVIII-IX; Staffarda), Williams (1984) I, 86–87 (Aberconwy).
207. *Statuta* II, 125 (1233/68).
208. *Cf.* Anton (1986) 332 (No. 25, Moreruela), *CAS* II, 38–41 (Staffarda).
209. *EOC* 316–19.
210. *SL* 161 (Nos 29–30), 163 (No. 47).
211. *EOC* 316–19.
212. *Ibid.* 316 (Cap. CXII).
213. *Statuta* I, 359 (1209/13).
214. *Statuta* I, 302 (1204/30), 319 (1205/64).
215. *AF* 28–29.
216. *RBS* I, 59.
217. *RSL* II, 202 (No. 1), 212 (No. 2), 219 (No. 3).
218. *LCC* (2) 279, 299.
219. *ABB* 47, *cf.* 174, 180, 254, 260, 272, 276.
220. *Cf. LECU* 34 (No. XXVII), 35 (XXVIII), and see: 477 (No. CCCLXXIV).
221. *RBM* IV 574 (No. 1418); *cf. MEB* 134–37 (Ebrach, 1340).
222. *Statuta* I, 66 (1157/47), 84 (1175/33); *LCC* (1) 102.
223. *LCC* (1) 132–33, (2) 327.
224. *Statuta* I, 516–17 (1220/3), *cf.* 509 (1219/30).
225. *Statuta* II, 170 (1237/10).
226. *Statuta* II, 253 (1242/43).
227. *Statuta* III, 186 (1274/48).
228. *Statuta* III, 202 (1280/43).
229. *Statuta* I, 404 (1213/66).
230. Mitkowski (1949) 338.
231. *Statuta* I, 219 (1197/46), 226 (1198/23), *cf.* 286 (1203/13).
232. *Statuta* III, 73–74 (1269/28).
233. *Statuta* II, 453 (1259/28).
234. *Statuta* III, 4 (1262/26).
235. *Cf.* Mitkowski (1949) 338.
236. *E.g.: Statuta* III, 4 (1262/26).
237. Conbhuï (1958) 53.
238. *CM* 102–03.

239. Canestrelli (1896) 126–27.
240. Lesher (1984) 264–65.
241. Penco (1961) 435.
242. *DSMLR* I, 364–62 (No. 114), 412–13 (No. 153); *cf.* 356–59 (Nos 110–11), 593 (No. 257).
243. Dimier (1982b) 529.
244. King (1954) 222.
245. Lipkin (1980) 63, 69.
246. *DHGE* X (1938) 67, XVII (1971) 902; Bedini (1964) 30.
247. D'Arbois (1858) 266.
248. *DHGE* XVII (1971) 974.
249. King (1954) 255.
250. *Ibid.* 37; Pineault and Coomans (1994) 129.
251. Conbhuí (1980) 219, 221.
252. Mellifont (1980) 17.
253. Conbhuí (1958) 13, 40, 217; (1980) 218–19.
254. Bouchard (1980) 254; *DHGE* XXII (1988) 777–78.
255. *CM* 98 Talbot (1939) 23.
256. *AF* 122–24, Kinvig (1950) 70; McIntire (1943) I, 2', 4 , 8.
257. *AF* 117; *cf. Statuta* I, 179 (1194/51).
258. Cross (1957) 121, Fergusson (1984a) 125.
259. France (1992) 348.
260. *Statuta* II, 133 (1234/31, 32); 143 (1235/22).
261. *Statuta* I, 22 (1134/XXXVIII), 486 (1218/9); *LCC* (2) 295–96.
262. *Statuta* I, 27 (1134/LXI); III, 82 (1270/10).
263. *Statuta* I, 149 (1192/17), *cf. LMT* 188 (No. 62); Bouton (1959) I, 183.
264. *Statuta* I, 27 (1134/LXI); *LCC* (2) 278.
265. *Statuta* I, 27 (1134/LXI).
266. *LCC* (2) 296.
267. *Statuta* I, 177 (1194/39), 244 (1199/59).
268. O'Dwyer (1976) 82–83.
269. Dimier (1982b) 530.
270. *DHGE* XVII (1971) 369.
271. France (1992) 91–92.
272. *Statuta* I, 166 (1193/47).
273. *Statuta* III, 317 (1307/4).
274. *DHGE* XIV (1960) 937.
275. *DAC* (1978) 726–27.
276. Andrea (1987) 60–91.
277. King (1954) 261.
278. Williams (1984) I, 28.
279. King (1954) 256.
280. *AM* II, 253.
281. *AM* II, 282.
282. *DHGE* XII (1953) 1056.
283. *LCC* (2) 215.
284. *Statuta* I, 380 (1211/12).
285. Knowles (1969) 74, Roehl (1972) 86, 89–91; Sullivan (1989) 179, 183.
286. Lekai (1977a) 335–36, 459.
287. *Statuta* I, 14 (1134/VIII).
288. *E.g.:* Birch (1897) 173 (Innocent III, 1203).
289. Sullivan (1989) 188.
290. For a full review of the *conversi*, see: Othon (1929), Toepfer (1983).
291. Clapham (1941) 74, Donnelly (1949) 61–62, Lekai (1977a) 334–35.
292. Hockey (1976) 57.
293. Barrière (1994) 66 (*n.* 10).
294. *Statuta* I, 14 (1134/VIII); Lekai (1977a) 450 (No. XX).
295. Leroux (1990) 19.
296. Sullivan (1989) 180.
297. Thompson (1920) 88.
298. *Statuta* II, 174 (1237/22); III, 453 (1338/13); France (1992) 120.
299. *Statuta* I, 88 (1181/2); *cf.* II, 265 (1243/41), Donnelly (1949) 24–25.
300. Othon (1929) 162.
301. *Cf.* Lescher (1988) 74–77.
302. Othon (1929) 147.
303. *LCC* (1) 160 (No. 8).
304. *Statuta* II, 127 (1234/4).
305. Walker (1983) 55.
306. *Statuta* III, 140 (1275/5).
307. Wiswe (1953) 94.
308. Waddell (1988) 34, *cf.* France (1992) 145.
309. *BDB* 21–22.
310. *Ibid.* 19.
311. Othon (1929) 177–78.
312. *Ibid.* 178.
312a. *Statuta* II, 76 (1229/7).
313. Othon (1929) 179.
314. *BDB* 19.
315. Othon (1929) 159–98 (for the *Usus*).
316. *DHGE* XII (1953) 922.
317. Othon (1929) 191; *LCC* (1) 157, (2) 339.
318. Othon (155–59.
319. *RCOC* col. 1647; *cf.* Donnelly (1949) 18, Othon (1929) 156–60.
320. Knowles (1979) I, 67.
321. Donnelly (1949) 14.
322. *E.g:* Toepfer (1983) 84; France (1992) 148 (Denmark), Mousnier (1986) 111–11 (Grandselve), Williams (1984) I, 156 (Wales).
323. Lekai (1976) 261, (1977b) 127.
324. Berman (1986) 55–54, Roehl (1972) 88, Waddell (1988) 37.
325. Toepfer (1983) 188.
326. Lekai (1977a) 338.
327. *Ibid.* 339; *cf.* Lawrence (1984) 150–51.
328. Lekai (1977a) 339
329. Berman (1986) 19, 19*n*, *cf.* 22 (*n.* 41), 49.
330. Williams (1984) II, 202.
331. France (1992) 147.
332. Duby (1965) 75.
333. *RCC* III, 67.
334. *OLSB* 52.
335. Mousnier (1986) 110–11.
336. Lekai (1977a) 339.
337. Toepfer (1983) 84.
338. *DAC* (1978) 486.
339. Lekai (1977a) 339.
340. Roehl (1972) 87, Waddell (1988) 37.
341. Hays (1963) 90.
342. Williams (1984) II, 157.
343. Donnelly (1949) 20.
344. *CPR* 1280/382.
345. *CPR* 1290/391, 1291/429, 1292/471.
346. France (1992) 148, McGuire (1982) 31.
347. *Statuta* I, 429 (1214/59).
348. *Statuta* I, 277 (1204/14).
349. *LCC* (2) 320.
350. Berman (1986) 19.
351. *CG* 245.
352. Williams (1984) I, 157.
353. *Cal. Papal Registers (Petitions)* I, 77.
354. Barry (und.) 29.

355. *RCC* I, 151.
356. *Statuta* I, 264 (1201/4).
357. Berman (1986) 55.
358. *CG* 245, *cf.* 329 (of 1178).
359. Berman (1986) 55.
360. *Statuta* II, 30 (1224/1), 476–77 (1261/7).
361. Williams (1984) I, 157; II, 202.
362. *LCC* (1) 157, (2) 339.
363. Othon (1929) 166–67, 169.
364. *Statuta* I, 516 (1220/1).
365. Roehl (1972) 89; *cf.* Othon (1929) 171–73.
366. Fergusson (1984a) 33*n*; *cf. AM* II, 244 (Waverley); Kempf (1976) 48 (Cherlieu).
367. Lawrence (1984) 150.
368. Storch (1958) 39, Toepfer (1983) 54.
369. Fergusson (1984a) 33*n*.
370. *CD passim.*
371. *RSL* II, 194 (No. 28), 205 (No. 15); *cf. HCVP* (Lilienfeld), *OLSB* VII (St Bernard-opt-Scheldt).
372. *RSL* II, 231.
373. *ABB* 17–19, Talbot (1958) 196.
374. Lekai (1977a) 342; *cf.* Higounet (1983b) 172.
375. Toepfer (1983) 56, *cf.* Richards (1968) 103.
376. Williams (1984) I, 159.
377. Toepfer (1983) 56; *cf.* Lekai (1977a) 343, (1977b) 124; *UKZ* 385 (for Zwettl).
378. Toepfer (1983) 55–56.
378a. *pectus.*
378b. *pedules.*
379. *Statuta* I, 70 (1159/3), 83 (1175/19).
380. *Statuta* I, 83 (1175/19); *LCC* (1) 167, (2) 346.
381. Othon (1929) 175–76.
382. *Statuta* I, 68 (1157/71); *LCC* (1) 167, (2) 346.
383. *LCC* (1) 167, (2) 346.
384. Donnelly (1949) 34–35.
385. Othon (1929) 176–77.
386. *Statuta* I, 29 (1175/29); *LCC* (1) 167, (2) 347.
387. *Statuta* I, 106 (1187/6).
388. *RCOC* 1647 (Cap. I).
389. *Statuta* I, 88 (1180/11); *LCC* (2) 345.
390. *Statuta* I, 111 (1189/7); *LCC* (1) 163, (2) 343–44.
391. *Statuta* I, 73 (1161/10).
392. *Cf. RCOC* 1649 (Cap. IV).
393. *LCC* (1) 163, (2) 343–44.
394. *LCC* (1) 166, (2) 346.
395. *RSL* II, 231.
396. *LCC* (2) 341; *RCOC* 1648 (Cap. II).
397. *RCOC* 1648 (Cap. II); Othon (1929) 187.
398. Othon (1929) 190, Waddell (1988) 34–35.
399. *RCOC* 1648 (Cap. II); Waddell (1988) 34–35.
400. *LCC* (1) 160, (2) 341.
401. *Statuta* I, 111 (1189/8), *cf.* Othon (1929) 180*n*.
402. *LCC* (1) 161, (2) 342.
403. Hockey (1976) 67, Othon (1929) 196.
404. *RCOC* 1647 (Cap. I).
405. Waddell (1988) 35–36.
406. Othon (1929) 185; *LCC* (1) 165, (2) 345.
407. *LCC* (2) 340.
408. *LCC* (1) 161–62, 168–69; (2) 343, 347.
409. *LCC* (1) 161–62, (2) 343.
410. *RCOC* 1651–52 (Cap. XIII).
411. *RCOC* 1651 (Cap. XV); *cf. LCC* (1) 161–62, (2) 343.
412. Sullivan (1989) 186.
413. *RSL* II, 194 (No. 1).
414. Pineault and Coomans (1994) 137.
415. *RCOC* Cap. III; *cf. Statuta* I, 149 (1192/16; Clairvaux).
416. *LCC* (1) 160–61, (2) 342; Waddell (1988) 35.
417. *Statuta* I, 83 (1175/9).
418. *LCC* (1) 161, (2) 342; *RCOC* Cap. III.
419. *Statuta* I, 104 (1186/8), 149 (1192/16).
420. *Statuta* I, 104 (1186/8); *LCC* (1) 161, (2) 342.
421. *Statuta* II, 247 (1242/12).
422. *Statuta* II, 30 (1224/1), 476–77 (1261/7).
423. *LCC* (2) 300–01, 333–39; Othon (1929) 187.
424. *LCC* (2) 301, 338–39.
425. Williams (1984) I, 158.
426. Carville (1979) 71.
427. *Statuta* I, 14 (1134/VIII).
428. Donnelly (1949) 19.
429. Duby (1953) 132.
430. *Statuta* I, 234–35 (1199/13).
431. Williams (1984) I, 158.
432. BL. Harl. MS 2079, f. 127.
433. Waddell (1988) 37.
434. *Cf. Statuta* I, 83 (1175/12); *RCOC* 1647, 1650 (Caps. I, X).
435. *RCOC* 1650 (Cap. X).
436. *LCC* (2) 340.
437. *LCC* (1) 160, (2) 341; *Statuta* I, 68 (1157/68).
438. Lawrence (1984) 151.
439. McGuire (1976b) 52–53; *cf. CHDM* I, 10.
440. France (1992) 148–49.
441. Barry (und.) 29.
442. De Moreau (1909) xxvii-xxix.
443. Millard (1994) 317.
444. *CCD* 68.
445. *DHGE* XII (1953) 923; *cf.* Canivez (1926) 87–88.
446. France (1992) 149.
447. *Statuta* I, 187 (1195/34).
448. Toepfer (1983) 92–93; *cf. Statuta* I, 194 (1195/79), 199 (1196/10).
449. Donnelly (1949) 19.
450. France (1992) 153–54.
451. Toepfer (1983) 93.
452. *AF* 207.
453. *CAF* 46.
454. *CAC* 421–22 (No. V).
455. *UKSH* 213–14 (No. CCXXXII).
456. *CDSL passim.*
457. Williams (1984) I, 157.
458. *CBR* II, 406.
459. *CDB* (2) 394.
460. *Statuta* I, 516 (1220/3), *cf.* II, 188 (1238/18, 20).
461. *Statuta* I, 256 (1200/37).
462. *Statuta* II, 387 (1252/50).
463. *Statuta* II, 267 (1243/41).
464. *Statuta* I, 66 (1157/47), 84 (1175/33), 169 (1193/57).
465. *E.g.: Statuta* I, 261 (1200/66), 399–400 (1212/45, 48), 414 (1213/53); II, 99 (1231/43).
466. *Statuta* I, 516 (1220/3).
467. *Statuta* II, 111 (1233/3).
468. *Statuta* II, 256 (1242/58).
469. *Statuta* II, 188 (1238/20).
470. *Statuta* II, 347 (1250/7).
471. *DHGE* XVI (1967) 1221.

472. *CPR* 1232/47.
473. *CPR* 1266/602, 678; 1271/538, 1272/658.
474. Yañez Neira (1970) 566.
475. *CCR.* 1245/293.
476. *Statuta* II, 305 (1246/21).
477. *Statuta* III, 4 (1262/28).
478. *Statuta* II, 347 (1250/7).
479. *Statuta* III, 40 (1266/19, 20).
480. *Statuta* II, 140 (1235/5).
481. *Statuta* II, 160 (1236/37).
482. *Statuta* III, 216 (1281/75).
483. *Statuta* III, 83 (1270/14).
484. Lekai (1977a) 393.
485. Berman (1986) 82.
486. Donnelly (1949) 64.
487. Fletcher (1919) 156–57.
488. Berman (1986) 59, Othon (1929) 163.
489. Carville (1979) 70–71; *cf. SL* 170 (No. 97), Othon (1929) 180–81.
490. Lescher (1988) 74–77.
491. Williams (1984) I, 24; *cf.*   Donnelly (1949) 32.
492. *Statuta* I, 191 (1195/66).
493. *SL* 65 (No. 64).
494. *AM* I, 432; *CC*, B. 25–26; *cf. Statuta* I, 360 (1209/19; grange of Le Val).
495. *AGN* 90–91; Donnelly (1949) 27, 64.
496. Gimpel (1977) 49.
497. *Statuta* II, 30 (1224/1).
498. *AM* I, 432.
499. *Statuta* II, 476–77 (1261/7).
500. *Statuta* III, 3 (1262/10).
501. Donnelly (1949) 25–26.
502. *Statuta* III, 104 (1272/5).
503. *Statuta* I, 206 (1196/49), 207 (1196/52), 218 (1197/40).
504. *Statuta* II, 86 (1230/13).
505. *Statuta* II, 466–67 (1260/25); *cf. DHGE* XIX (1981) 469 (Furness), Donnelly (1949) 72 (Quincy).
506. *Statuta* I, 519 (1220/14).
507. *Statuta* II, 195 (1238/52), 233 (1241/19), 482 (1261/32); *DHGE* XIV (1960) 1282–83; Donnelly (1949) 33, 73 (No. 25).
508. *Statuta* I, 164 (1193/40).
509. *Statuta* I, 324 (1206/23).
510. *AGN* 90–91, Donnelly (1949) 59–60, 69.
511. Gimpel (1977) 49.
512. *Statuta* II, 307 (1246/31).
513. *AM* II, 301; *Statuta* II, 52–53 (1226/23).
514. *Statuta* I, 329 (1206/50).
515. *Statuta* I, 359 (1209/14).
516. *Statuta* I, 408–09 (1213/20).
517. Lekai (1976) 261.
518. *Statuta* I, 194 (1195/79), 199 (1196/10).
519. *Statuta* III, 105 (1272/7).
520. *Statuta* III, 145 (1275/24).
521. *AC* 718.
522. *Statuta* III, 54 (1267/47), 58–59 (1268/1); *cf. SL* 170 (No. 97).
523. *Cf. CPR* 1232/473; *Statuta* I, 401 (1212/52), 406 (1213/9); Dimier (1972a) 46.
524. *Statuta* I, 413 (1213/46).
525. *Cf. Statuta* I, 409 (1213/22), Barnes (1982) 49.
526. Hockey (1976) 81.
527. *MF* xxxii.

528. *DHGE* IX (1937) 1029.
529. *Cf. Statuta* I, 98 (1185/6); *DHGE* XIX (1981) 1262; Donnelly (1949) 32–33.
530. *Statuta* I, 185 (1195/20); *cf.* I, 401 (1212/52).
531. *Statuta* II, 86 (1230/13); *cf.* 195 (1238/51).
532. Lekai (1977a) 342–43.
533. *Statuta* II, 52–53 (1226/23), 91 (1230/36), 159 (1236/32).
534. *Statuta* II, 482 (1261/32); III, 76 (1269/42), 85 (1270/25), 135 (1274/44).
535. *Statuta* II, 169 (1237/3).
536. *Statuta* I, 115 (1189/27), 183 (1195/6).
537. *Statuta* III, 128 (1274/12).
538. *Statuta* III, 49 (1267/8).
539. Berman (1986) 56–57, Knowles (1979) II, 77.
540. Higounet (1983b) 172.
541. Conbhuí (1958) xxxiv; *cf.* Knowles (1979) II, 126.
542. *RBM* IV, 340 (No. 859).
543. *Statuta* I, 118 (1190/2).
544. A series of statutes from *Statuta* I, 148 (1192/12); II, 129 (1234/17).
545. *DHGE* XVI (1967) 1222.
546. *CAF* 210, 225.
547. McCrank (1973) 66.
548. *EOC* 419.
549. *LCC* (1) 126, (2) 320.
550. *EOC* 419.
551. *Statuta* I, 118 (1190/2).
552. Affolter (1978) 55.
553. *Statuta* I, 163 (1193/30).
554. *Statuta* I, 319 (1205/65).
555. *DSMLR* 181 (No. 3).
556. Kempf (1976) 113; *cf. LCC* (2) 320.
557. *Statuta* II, 1 (1221/3).
558. *Statuta* II, 67–68 (1228/14).
559. *Statuta* II, 467 (1261/7); *cf.* Lekai (1977a) 342–43.
560. *Statuta* III, 47 (1267/1), 103 (1272/1).
561. *Statuta* II, 256 (1242/58).
562. *Statuta* III, 47 (1267/1).
563. *Statuta* III, 103 (1272/1).
564. *Statuta* III, 231 (1284/6).
565. *Statuta* I, 404 (1213/1); *cf.* Hugues (1863) 162, Theurot (1995) 17.
566. *ABB passim*; (they included *conversi* reduced in status for misbehaviour).
567. Wamba (1986) 180.
568. *Statuta* II, 114 (1233/14), *LCC* (2) 320.
569. *RSL* II, 212 (No. 16).
569a. De Laplane 361 (XXXIV).
570. Theurot (1995) 17.
571. *CDCDS* 521.
572. *DHGE* XVI (1967) 1222.
573. *DD* 1529.
574. *ABB* 131, 305, 307.
575. *CAF* 225.
576. *CCD* 58; Dublois (1957) 48.
577. *Statuta* III, 259–60 (1292/5).
578. *Statuta* III, 261 (1293/3).
579. Dublois (1957) 43, Schittekat (1966) 105.
580. *LCC* (1)126, (2) 321.
581. Locatelli (1975) 212.
582. Barrière (1977) 99–93.
583. *CV* 72.
584. Fort i Cogul (1965) 90–94.

585. *Statuta* II, 321 (1247/36), Van Der Meer (1965) 288.
586. Bouton (1986) 87, Canivez (1926) 265–66,
587. Bouton (1986) 111.
588. Thompson (1984) 142.
589. Carville (1979) 63, O'Dwyer (1976) 14, 20, 58–59.
590. Gwynn (1970) 140.
591. *Statuta* III, 41 (1266/28).

Chapter 5

CULTURAL ACTIVITY

The Cistercians and Education

The statutes of the General Chapter broke with Benedictine tradition in forbidding the education of secular youths within monastic precincts[1]. There was practical training for boys over twelve years old working in the 'workshops of the weavers, tanners, and tailors', but such youths were not to be brought up in the abbey[2], and when Obazine was incorporated (1147) its two priory-schools became granges[3]. The prohibition placed by the Chapter (1205) shows that the abbeys of Frisia were providing secular education[4], as did then the monasteries of Aduard[5] and Esrum[6]. Two future Silesian dukes were educated in the 'outer school' of Henryków (c. 1270)[7], and individual boys possibly at Meaux[8] and certainly at Osek (1334)[9]. The monks of Grandselve played a dominant rôle in the foundation of the university of Toulouse (1229)[10], and an abbot of Alcobaça (1291) in the establishment of that of Coimbra (Lisbon)[11]. Alcobaça also opened a public school teaching grammar, logic, and theology (1269)[12].

Many early Cistercians were learned men, and despite St Bernard's apparent strictures to the contrary, he did praise learning undertaken for the right reasons and of a spiritual nature[13]. There remained an emphasis on avoiding unnecessary studies, particularly canon law (1188)[14], and as late as 1230 the noted Cistercian preacher Hélinand of Froidmont, could say: 'Learning that does not aid salvation is worthless'[15]. By this time, however, the need to combat heresy, involvement in missionary activities, the rise of scholasticism and the emergence of forceful preaching and learned writing by the friars, led to a re-think of Cistercian attitudes[16]. As Matthew Paris put it, the Order wished no longer to be held in contempt by the Mendicant Orders[17].

The General Chapter (1245) decided that in every province at least one monastery should have a study-centre (*studium*) for theology, to which other abbeys could send students[18]. Greater abbeys (1281), with eighty or more monks, could provide lectures in other faculties besides theology[19]. All abbeys (1287) with twenty or more monks were to send one to such a monastic school; those with forty or more were to send two. Monks could be sent to the Paris college instead[20]. Rather than send several monks away (1300) a monk-lecturer was to be maintained in every abbey with sixty or more monks[21]. At Arnsburg (1321) the granger, Hartman, doubled up as *lector monachorum*[22]. Further lecturers were to be appointed (1331) in abbeys with over forty monks to teach grammar and logic to their juniors and those sent to them[23]. The new Cistercian emphasis on education was reflected in 1322 when eight out of twenty-two recorded statutes at that year's General Chapter related to the topic[24].

A leading proponent of education for the good of the Order was Stephen Lexington, though at least one modern commentator has depreciated his rôle[25]. On visitation in Ireland (1228) and as abbot of Savigny (1231), he insisted that junior monks were to be primarily occupied in reading and meditation, in memorising the services and studying the Book of Usages[26]. He also addressed a letter (*c.* 1236) to the abbot of

Pontigny urging the need of theological training because of charges of heresy brought against members of the Order[27]. By the time Lexington became abbot of Clairvaux (1243) that abbey already maintained a house for student-monks in Paris[28]. It was the nucleus of the more formal college which Lexington established early in 1245 with the blessing of the pope[29]. The General Chapter that year, somewhat reluctantly, allowed the college 'now started, to remain undisturbed'[30].

Innocent IV was a strong supporter of the Paris college[31], allowing a Dominican theologian to teach there[32], confirming its foundation, and insisting that its students be granted a licence in public preaching[33]. The General Chapter (1248–50) decided that the Paris house was to be a constituent member of Clairvaux, that the superior was to be termed the 'provisor' and not 'prior', and in any monastery he was visiting to take precedence in choir after any abbots present[34]. These regulations firmly established 'the house of St Bernard in Paris', but many Cistercians, including Arnulf of Villers (1240–48)[35], were unhappy with the project[36]. After Innocent's death (December 1254) the next General Chapter deposed Lexington from the abbacy of Clairvaux. Matthew Paris asserted that this was because of his foundation of the Paris college[37]. The new pope (Alexander IV) ordered his re-instatement and called him 'a burning lamp of religion'[38].

The Paris college started in a hospice owned by Clairvaux[39], but purpose-built buildings were necessary and lands (vineyards) in Paris were bought up (1246)[40]. Half-a-century later a new site was bought (1321) and new buildings erected[41]. The foundation stone of the college chapel was laid in 1338 by the queen of France[42]. Cardinal William Curti (*c.* 1345) bequeathed a fine library[43]. The refectory is now used as a garage (24 Rue de Poissy)[44]. The year 1321 also saw the sale of the college by Clairvaux to the Order as a whole[45]: henceforth the definitors chose each year the provisor and the cellarer[46]. A high-level visitation was ordered (1322)[47], and its findings were adopted by the General Chapter (1323)[48].

The students at Paris (and other Cistercian colleges) were allowed (in 1281) to study other works in addition to theology[49], but this permission was revoked in 1318[50], and as late as 1335 Benedict XII forbade the study of canon law[51]. The General Chapter insisted repeatedly that students were to be capable – in terms of age, character and intelligence – of undertaking higher education[52]: unsuitable ones were to be sent back home[53]. Students were to swear faithfulness to the Order (1327)[54], but not all were plaster saints. Some monk-scholars at Toulouse had to be expelled (1334)[55]. Whilst Matthew Paris described the Paris students as being of good character[55a], some – in later years – liked to go out at night in secular dress and cause trouble, so the college gates had to be locked after Compline (1339)[56]. Reform of the college had been ordered in 1334, and new rules were drawn up[57].

In 1314, the General Chapter ruled that abbots were not to study at the colleges, unless they resigned their abbacies first[58]. This was tempered the next year, in one of the about-turns a different Chapter could take, by allowing an abbot to attend if he had leave of the head of his 'family' within the Order and of his Visitor, and also the agreement of his community[59]. Not all Cistercian students remained theologically correct, or blindly loyal to established authority. Jean de Mirecourt of Cîteaux (1347), an exponent of William of Ockham, had some of his writings condemned. His fellow-student Peter Ceffons of Clairvaux, both defended and outdid him. His works included *Parvum Decretum*, a dissertation on the limits of papal authority, and *Somnium*, in which he attacked the decision by the 1348 General Chapter that once a year monks must disclose to their abbot their already confessed sins[60].

A Paris or other doctorate was often the stepping-stone to an abbacy[61]. The first student to be awarded one was Abbot Guy of L'Aumône (1256), but this was at the command of Innocent IV. The first to receive the distinction in the normal way was

John de Weerde, monk of the Dunes, in 1274[62]. The next year the college was incorporated into the University of Paris[63]. The statutes of 1321–22 refer to no less than six abbots as 'doctors of sacred theology': all perhaps former students at Paris[64]. When (in 1341) the General Chapter noted that the Paris college 'glorifies our whole Order'[65], it was a complete *volte-face* from the criticism Stephen Lexington endured a century before. True, the Chapter had then spoken in endearing but disingenuous tones.

St Bernard's, Paris, was the precursor of similar establishments there by the Premonstratensians (1252) and the Cluniacs (1261)[66], and of Cistercian colleges in other university cities. The first, at Montpellier, was founded in a hospice of Valmagne and came under the jurisdiction of its abbot[67]. A reality by 1262[68], it was enjoined to continue its customary hospitality to Cistercian personnel[69]. A college at Toulouse emerged from the fusion of two hospices of Grandselve in that city (1270)[70]. Approved by the General Chapter (1281), it had its own church and cemetery from the start[71]. The dorter was 78 metres long, and by 1328 each student had his own cell[72], but all that remains today is the street-name, Rue Saint-Bernard. The officials included the syndic (representing the abbot of Grandselve) and the cellarer (administering the finances and property of the house). Cistercian guests were to be received as of old[73]. Students were not to miss a lecture without valid reason, nor go into the city without permission[74]. As at Montpellier, the appointment of 'capable and erudite' lecturers was enjoined (1329)[75].

For British monks, Rewley Abbey (fd 1280) was designated as the college for Cistercian students at Oxford[76], though some abbots seemed reluctant to send monks to it (1291)[77]. The fifteen original students were augmented to sixteen in 1294[78]; the seal of the house depicted an abbot and fourteen students[79]. A more formal study-centre came with the foundation of St Bernard's College, Oxford, in 1437[80]. A college established at Estella in Navarre (by 1289)[81] was transferred to Salamanca in 1335[82]. Poblet set up a house for Cistercian students in Lérida and Alcobaça did so in Lisbon (1294)[83]. A minor college was founded by Ebrach in Würzburg (1281) and a house for Cistercian students appeared in Cologne (1285)[84]. A college for the study of grammar and natural philosophy was established by Morimond in Metz (then in Germany) (1332)[85]. A Cistercian theology school was founded in Prague (1350) two years after the university there[86]. Monarchs seeking the establishment of Cistercian colleges included the kings of Castile (1260)[87] and of Portugal (1294)[88].

The constitution of Benedict XII (1335), himself a former Paris student, maintained the international character of St Bernard's, Paris[89]. Only monasteries with less than thirty monks were to send a student elsewhere: those with over forty were to send two monks to Paris[90]. The pontiff named the catchment areas of the other *studia generalia*. Bologna was to serve Italy, Salamanca was to cater for Iberia (excluding Navarre); Montpellier and Toulouse served the whole of the Midi, and Toulouse Navarre also; Metz was to provide for the German monasteries of the line of Morimond, and Oxford served Britain[91]. The academic year was to start on 1 October at Paris, 18 October (St Luke's Day) or 1 November (All Saints Day) elsewhere; a biblical expert and a spiritual director were to be appointed in each college; a sliding-scale of payments for college staff was laid down and proper expenses for the students; the provision of food by relatives was restricted, and a humble lifestyle enjoined for the masters[92]. Theology courses lasted at least six years[93].

Cistercian Libraries

Early Cistercian monasteries started with the bare minimum of liturgical books, as well as the *Rule*, brought by the founding fathers coming from the mother-house[94]. Such necessary works were taken, for instance, from Pontigny to Egres (1179)[95], from Nepomuk to Žd’ár (1252)[96], and from Wilhering to Vyšší Brod (1259)[97]. The small number of volumes an early Cistercian house possessed meant that they could be accommodated in the book-cupboard (*armarium*), usually a carved recess in the eastern walk of the cloister[98]. Several fine examples include those at Boquen (with shelves of stone), Silvacane (grooves for supporting wooden shelves), and Escale-Dieu (a three-arched recess)[99]. At La Real (Majorca) there was an *armarium* in or off the dorter[100]. As libraries grew, sacristies were sometimes divided, that portion nearest the cloister becoming the book-room[101]. At Calder it projected into the chapter-house[102]. Early Cistercian usages provided for a lamp in the book-room, so that works could be read more easily 'on certain days and at certain times'[103].

Many early Cistercians were gifted scholars, and as Abbot Richard of Melrose (1148) put it: 'A cloister without literature is a grave for living men'[104]. The white monks began to accumulate books, by purchase or donation or by copying. By 1170 the book-cupboard of Pontigny was said to be 'well-stocked'[105]; by the close of the century Clairvaux had some 340 works in its library[106], and other significant collections included those of Marienfeld[107], Signy[108] and Vaux-de-Cernay[109]. Heiligenkreuz, which had 93 books in the late-twelfth century, numbered 353 by the fifteenth[110]. The combined libraries of Ter Doest and the Dunes came, in later years, to number over 1200 volumes. They included 259 works of the Fathers, 93 medical books, 77 writings of St Augustine (a favourite author with the Cistercians) and 33 by St Bernard[111].

Many additions to monastic libraries came by gifts. A dean of York, on entering Fountains (1135), brought his large library[112]. The royal founders of Hailes (1246)[113] and Darnhall (1271)[114] wrote to other abbeys asking them to donate books to the new foundations. King Wenceslas II gave money to the abbot of Zbraslav (1292), *en route* to the General Chapter, to buy books in Paris[115]. Mother houses might donate additional books to their daughter-abbeys, as Doberan to Pelplin[116] and Fontfroide to Valbonne – sixty volumes, including biblical and liturgical works[117]. Books were bequeathed – as to Wettingen (*c.* 1285)[118], and by that great Majorcan scholar, Ramon Llull, to La Real (1313)[119]. Former abbots translated to the episcopate made gifts of books to Fontfroide (1225, 1348)[120]. Biblical works were given to Zwettl (1347) 'for the edification and encouragement of the monks'[121]. Croxden (1268) bought (for fifty marks) a nine-volume bible[122]; Øm paid 'quite a sum of money' for books to Bishop Peder of Århus (d. 1246)[123]. Gerald of Wales (*c.* 1200) pawned his books to Strata Florida and was not allowed to re-possess them[124].

Care was taken in the safe-keeping of books. The official responsible, because the early books were mostly liturgical works, was the precentor[125] aided by the succentor[126]. Books lent out by Clairvaux to Vaux-de-Cernay (1180) were returned in a poor condition[127]. Stephen Lexington (1231) enjoined that books were only to be lent to trustworthy people, and that a record of loans was to be kept[128]. Lest their books fall into wrong hands, or a borrower be disinclined to return them, Cistercian library books usually had a prominent *ex-libris* inscription on the fly-leaf, with a caution added, such as: 'let him who deceitfully takes it be anathema'[129]. *Ex-libris* were in use at Cîteaux by 1135, and were often multi-coloured[130]. The earlier *ex-libris* at Lubiąż (*c.* 1215) were in black ink, but later (*c.* 1250) in red[131]. Altzelle did not confine such warnings to fly-leaves (which could easily be removed) but continued them across two facing pages of text[132].

A check could be kept on monastic books by cataloguing them. Twelfth-century catalogues exist for Cheminon and Vaux-de-Cernay, and in the thirteenth century for Chaâlis and Vyšší Brod[133]. Pontigny's catalogue marks those books given to its foundation at Egres (1179)[134]. No catalogue is known for Cîteaux's library until the fifteenth century[135]. The first known catalogue of La Real was drawn up in 1386 by a

Majorcan notary[136]. Dore appears to have been without a catalogue in 1318. When ordered to compile one, its Visitor said that any monk who did not hand in a book for cataloguing was to be treated as a thief[137]. Despite all precautions, books could be lost: in an armed raid (Aberconwy, 1215)[138], by fire (Newry, 1162)[139], by the need to sell to raise money (Ford, 1210)[140], or perhaps by theft (Pontigny)[141]. Books could be damaged and need repair (Champagne, 1230)[142].

Despite the mistrust of books of canon law (1188) and the restriction placed on the possession of such works (1237)[143], such volumes did find a place – as at Vaux-de-Cernay by 1200[144]. Books (many medieval) of canon law are known from the library of the Dunes[145]. Books on medicine were to be found – especially at Sorø, which had a variety of such treatises[146]. Kirkstall included a recipe for the 'falling sickness' in its Coucher Book[147], and Vale Royal had prescriptions for curing various diseases[148]. Amongst interesting works in Cistercian hands by the thirteenth century were a *Computus planetarum* (at Vyšší Brod)[149], and abridgements of the Domesday Book (at Margam and Strata Florida)[150]. Other works in British Cistercian libraries included biblical commentaries, Latin grammars, scientific treatises and architectural notes[151]. Dore had its *Panormia* (Latin Dictionary)[152]. Monks might make jottings on fly-leaves, quite unconnected with the subject matter: musical notations (in a work of Dore)[153], letters close of Edward I (Rewley), the dated record of the building of a mill (Llantarnam)[154], and notes of the abbot's manorial court (Margam)[155].

Cistercian Scriptoria

Many of the books in a Cistercian library were copied in the monastery, the work of the scribes in the scriptorium. At Beaulieu the binders worked in the parchment-making workshop[156]. It has been suggested that the scriptoria were sited in the north walk of the cloister[157], and a monk of Fountains was noted as laying out freshly inscribed parchment in its cloister to dry. Other evidence, such as the rule that silence be kept in the scriptoria 'as in the cloister' (1134)[158], and the prohibition of monks from entering the scriptoria (study-places as well as writing-rooms) when the community gathered in the cloister (1278)[159], may suggest that the writing-rooms were located elsewhere – as in the calefactory or 'day-room' or dorter undercroft[160]. Precentors and copyists might enter the monastic kitchens, 'for planing a tablet, for liquefying ink, and for drying parchment'[161]. Copying spiritual books was seen as a praiseworthy form of manual labour[162].

The best known early writing room was that of Cîteaux, where Stephen Harding encouraged book-making. A two-volume bible was completed there in his day, the work of three scribes. One of them also took part in its fine edition of the *Moralia in Job*, which depicted scenes of monastic labour (hewing a tree, harvesting grain, gathering grapes, weaving cloth)[163]. Several early works of Cîteaux had illuminated and decorative initials, whilst the Jesse tree found a place in at least two[164]. Some time after Harding's death a perhaps divided General Chapter (1134/1145–51) restricted the making of books without its leave[165] and forbade any form of illumination: letters were to be 'made of one colour and not decorative'[166] – a rule lost sight of in the next century[167]. At Pontigny late-twelfth century initials were coloured in red, green and blue, and were up to 20 cm long[168]. The Chapter prohibited monastic scribes from 'writing or binding books, or making covers' outside the monastic precincts (1154)[169], but their skills became known and sought after[170]. Cistercian scriptoria may have been modest in output, but that of Himmerod produced some 200 volumes before 1200[171].

The thirteenth century saw continued literary activity. The abbey of Rein (*c.* 1210) produced a textbook for illuminators, illustrating handicraft techniques and giving patterns from fishing and hunting scenes and the animal world[172]. Mariental also had its sample-book (*muster-buch*)[173]. Noteworthy scriptoria included those of Alcobaça (a training ground for many Cistercian scribes)[174], Altzelle (where over fifty decorators may have worked between 1175 and 1215)[175], Lubiąż (which produced an antiphonal with representations of the Man of Sorrows and Our Lady as Queen of Heaven, as well as St Benedict and St Bernard, and a gradual with a miniature of the Birth of Christ)[176], Øm (where Abbot Bó was a copyist and painter)[177] and Sambucina (noted for its calligraphy)[178].

Liturgical works are sometimes datable from the calendars they include. A calendar of Ląd, attributed to the twelfth century, must post-date the canonisation of St Malachy (in 1190) whose feast it includes[179]. A liturgical work of Dore must pre-date the later addition of the feast of St Thomas Aquinas, canonised in 1323[180]. Calendars are known from six English houses, including Boxley (with astronomical tables down to 1386) and Waverley (followed by the rules and tables for determining the date of Easter)[181]. Fontfroide had a martyrology detailing the 'Passions' of seventy-four saints (their feasts ranging from 6 August to 6 February)[182]. A similar work (a 'Lectionary', latterly in the hands of Osek) may have had Cistercian origins[183]. Copying the Scriptures (as at Camp[184] and Croxden[185]) was a common task, and a study of thirty-five early medieval Cistercian bibles shows a division into four or five volumes, corresponding to the categories of scripture as defined in patristic sources[186]. Despite the Order's apparent distaste for canon law studies, no less than thirty-three legal works were copied at Marienfeld by Abbot Nicholas (1321–44)[187]. In interesting developments, the monks of the Dunes evolved a system of pagination using letters and dots[188]; those of Aulne and Vaucelles popularised a system of ciphers denoting numerals up to 9,999[189]. Other aids to study included the *Angelus* or bible dictionary of Abbot Garnier of Clairvaux (1186–93), the *Flores Bernardi*, an early-thirteenth century compilation at Clairvaux of extracts from St Bernard's works with an alphabetical index, and the *Flores paradysi* of Villers (*c.* 1216–30), a collection of sentences from the Fathers[190].

In binding books, the Order rejected expensive clasps and binding materials[191]. At Morimond-by-Milan (1237) raiders stole 'the tools of iron and wood used for the binding of books, and all the clasps and the measures of hide'[192]. A 13th-century Byland copy of Bede was in oak board covered with ox-hide, 'having brass knobs to protect the hair'[193]. The books of Pontigny were bound in thick wooden covers over which was stretched vellum or parchment. Protection was given to the covers by placing five studs, cross-wise, on both front and back[194]. The accounts of Beaulieu (E) suggest that in its workshop much more parchment was made from sheep-skin than from calf-hide (vellum). In 1270 sixty-three mutton skins were received from the monastery's tannery alone, but some skin had to be purchased, as did 20 lbs of dry ink, an ink-well, binding thread and book clasps. Some parchment was sold, taken it would seem to markets and fairs[195].

Cistercian Writers

In so far as there was a Cistercian tradition of spiritual writing, it was a mystical tradition, Christ-centred, and based upon allegorical reading of the Scriptures. It was more concerned with faith, love and contemplation, than with doctrine. Its motivation was to make God known to men, and to bring them closer to Him[196]. Its principal exponents were St Bernard (Chapter 1) and St Aelred (Chapter 3), but there were other writers who had been monks of Clairvaux in St Bernard's day and continued in his tradition[197]. Noteworthy were William of St Thierry (d. 1148) and Guerric of Igny (d. 1157) who, with SS. Bernard and Aelred, have been called 'the four evangelists of

Cîteaux'[198]. William became a Cistercian and monk of Signy, after his term of office as Benedictine abbot of St Thierry. He wrote his *Speculum Fidei* attacking Abelard's understanding of the nature of the Trinity; a 'Golden Epistle' or *Letter to the* (Carthusian) *brothers of Mont-Dieu* – a treatise on the solitary life; and, unusual in Cistercian literature, an *Exposition on the Epistle to the Romans*[199]. Guerric, abbot of Igny, looked forward to the Coming of Christ, as in his *Second Sermon for Advent*. His teaching on redemption offered a two-fold reward: 'contemplation in this life, heaven in the next'[200]. On his death-bed he was troubled in conscience for having had a volume of his sermons bound without leave of the General Chapter[201].

Another notable author was Isaac of Stella (d. *c.* 1168, abbot of L'Étoile), who perhaps wrote mostly in retirement at the island monastery of Châtelliers. Said to have 'known his bible backwards'[202], he is best remembered for his *Sermons in Sexagesima*, treating of the Divine Nature, and his *Letter on the Soul*, classifying spiritual and intellectual faculties[203]. This group of early writers in the Bernardine tradition included, of course, the saint's secretaries, Geoffrey and Nicholas of Clairvaux[204]. It is clear that Cistercian writers of the thirteenth century, like Stephen of Sawley, knew well not only the works of Bernard and Aelred, but those too of William of St Thierry and Isaac of Stella[205]. The second half of the twelfth century saw the work of writers such as Caesarius of Heisterbach (d. *c.* 1200) whose principal work was written as a dialogue between a monk and a novice, based on his own experience as a novice-master[206]; and Conrad of Eberbach (d. 1226) who wrote the first four volumes of the *Exordium Magnum* treating of the early history of the Order[207]. The principal writer of the period was Baldwin, abbot of Ford and, later, archbishop of Canterbury (d. 1190). His notable work was *De sacramento altaris*, in which he used texts from the Old Testament to express the realities of the New, and defended the term *transubstantiatio*, though not precisely in the Church's present understanding of it[208]. A thirteenth-century copy of it was made at Clairvaux for transmission to Alcobaça[209].

Amongst the Cistercian literature of the early-thirteenth century were the treatises of monks as far afield as Thomas of Perseigne and Adam of Kinloss[210]. There was an equal diversity of subject matter. Oger of Locedio (d. 1214) meditated on the love of Christ in the Eucharist[211] and defended the Immaculate Conception[212]; Adam of Chaâlis (d.1217) prepared a sermon on the text, 'Cast thy bread upon the waters..' (Ecclesiastes 11:1)[213]; Robert of Olmütz (d. *c.* 1240) prepared a manual for confessors[214], and Alain of Lille (d. *c.* 1203) wrote a textbook for preachers, one of the first in this field[215]. He ended his days as a *conversus* at Cîteaux, and his *Oculus sacrae Scripturae* was in the library of the Dunes[216]. Abbot John of Ford (1191–1220) used perhaps more names of Christ than any other Cistercian author[217]. As confessor of the monarch, he also wrote a missing *Acts of King John* as well as the life of the anchorite saint, Wulfric of Haselbury[218]. Hélinand of Froidmont (d. 1237), a former court singer, prepared at least fifteen sermons for the feast of the Ascension. A preacher against the Cathars, he emphasised in a sermon for the Rogation Days that the conversion of heretics can only be achieved if example supports word[219]. Hugh of Barzelle, concerned for monastic peace, wrote on the text from the Psalms: 'Behold how good and lovely a thing it is: when brethren dwell together in unity' (Psalm 133:1)[220].

Stephen of Sawley (d.1252) prepared a *Mirror for Novices*. He wrote that: 'A monk should jump up quickly from his bed when the signal is given', and at the close of each day should enter his bed 'as if it were his grave'[221]. He gave practical advice for those who could not sleep: 'Say seven times the Athanasian Creed or the seven penitential psalms'. Following the establishment of St Bernard's College, Paris (1245), the late Edmund Mikkers discerned a new phase in Cistercian writing, a more scholastic approach. It started with the work of John of Limoges (monk of Clairvaux, *c.* 1250–70), and encompassed the writings of many scholars, such as Guy of L'Aumône (*c.* 1260), and Humbert of Preuilly (d. 1298). It culminated in the *Commentary on St Matthew* and thirty-one extant sermons by Jacques Fournier, monk of Boulbonne, later to be Pope Benedict XII (1334–42)[222]. Entering the Order in the mid-fourteenth century, a monk of Sawley, William of Rymington, became noted for his attacks on the teachings of Wycliffe[223].

Several Cistercian writers apart from St Bernard (eighty-six sermons on the book) had a predilection for studies on the Song of Songs. They included William of St Thierry, Gilbert of Hoyland, abbot of Swineshead (d. 1172) and John of Ford[224]. So valued was the Song of Songs that it was translated into French, but the General Chapter (1200) ordered such books in the vernacular to be burnt[225]. Writers who devoted part of their works to Our Lady included: Odo of Morimond (d. 1161; her sufferings at the Cross)[226]; Guerric of Igny (nearly eighty different epithets for her)[227]; Amadeus of Lausanne (d. 1159; homilies in her praise)[228], and Stephen of Sawley (fond of the title, 'Mother of Mercy')[229]. Hagiographical works included St Bernard's life of St Malachy[230], Walter Daniel's account of St Aelred[231], and lives of St Patrick, St Kentigern and Waltheof of Melrose by Joscelyn of Furness[232]. Roger of Pontigny (where the saint had stayed) wrote perhaps a life of Thomas Becket, and Philip of L'Aumône a sequence in his honour[233].

Some Cistercian literature contained accounts of alleged miracles and visions. This was especially true of Caesarius of Heisterbach's late-twelfth century compilation, *Dialogus miraculorum*, collated out of happenings reported from the Order[234]. Herbert of Mores (d. 1180) wrote three books, *De miraculis*[235], and Herbert of Clairvaux (*c.* 1180) penned his *Liber Miraculorum*: once again stories (by no means all historically accurate) meant for the edification of monks[236]. A 'Book of Miracles' based on Herbert's work was copied at Ląd and later passed to Kołbacz[237]. Ten visions at Stratford found place in the *Liber revelationum* of Prior Peter, O.S.A. of Holy Trinity, Aldgate, (fl. 1200–06)[238]. Fürstenfeld compiled a *Liber visionum* in the thirteenth century[239]. A number of vision stories emanated from Waldsassen, especially during the abbacy of John III (1306–13); one related to an appearance of Our Lady and her Child above the high altar[240].

Cistercian Chronicles

The keeping of annals and chronicles was a monastic literary activity often taken for granted, but for which there might be especial motivation. When Bishop Absalom founded Sorø (1162) he may have hoped for annalists to record the history of the kingdom for posterity[241]. The Øm Chronicle, started in 1207, may have been written to safeguard the rights and property of that abbey, for it includes transcriptions of bulls and charters[242]. After a fire destroyed the charters of Løgum (*c.* 1185), the early history of the monastery was recorded in a mini-chronicle[243]. The *Chronicle of Silvanès*, written about 1165, may have been to assist promotion of the founder's (Pons de Léras) canonisation[244]. The same was partly true of the *Chronicle of Zbraslav* which gave special emphasis to the life of King Wenceslas II (d. 1305)[245]. Edward I of England (d. 1307) asked the monks of Furness to incorporate in their chronicles facts relating to the Scottish wars, so that they would be known for all time[246].

The early sections of many monastic chronicles detailed events long before the abbeys existed, and depended for this information on other sources[247]. Thereafter scribes were able to record events more or less as they happened. Three successive writers followed the first scribe and kept the Croxden annals between 1320 and 1377[248]. In the chronicle of Melrose, from the date of 1140 onwards, are 'numerous and progressive variations in hand-writing'[249]. That chronicle itself bears witness to the change of hands, the scribe of 1262 referring to 'those annalists who have had charge of our chronicles before myself'[250]. One compiler of the chronicle of Zwettl notes the years of his ordination as deacon (1145) and priest (1147); his successor as scribe notes his own ordination as sub-deacon (1170)[251]. Some later chroniclers improved upon existing monastic manuscripts. This must have been the case when Thomas Burton (d. 1437) – during his lengthy retirement after resigning as abbot – compiled the extremely detailed *Chronicle of Meaux*[252].

Eye-witness accounts were useful to chroniclers, though not entirely reliable, as memory becomes dulled with time. Hugh of Kirkstall (about 1206) writing the history of the early years of Fountains, made use of a living witness, Serlo, a ninety-seven year old monk of the house[253]. Travellers staying at a monastery could furnish information. Ralph of Coggeshall thus gained from Hugh de Neville particulars of an engagement between King Richard I of England and the Saracens, whilst the king's chaplain, Anselm, supplied details of the capture of Richard on his way home from Palestine[254]. That chronicles are not infallible is evident from that of Silvanès which diverges from some of the facts as recorded in its early charters[255]. The compilation of chronicles may have been shared with non-Cistercian sources. Strata Florida wrote up the *Brut y Tywysogyon* ('the Chronicle of the Princes') in Welsh sometime after 1282, using annals previously kept at St David's and Llanbadarn Fawr[256]. The annals of Kołbacz were completed at the monastery after it took over the codex from Lund about 1200[257]. Tintern made additions (for the period 1302–23) to a copy of the *Flores Historiarum* emanating from Norfolk[258]. The *Annales Placentini Gibellini* obtained information concerning the betrayal of King Henry IV from 'secret writings' kept at Fontevivo[259]. The originals of some chronicles are lost and known only from copies – like the foundation narratives of Guldholm and Vitskøl[260]. Some chronicles end abruptly[261] – possibly on the death of a chronicler and a subsequent loss of interest After the Conquest of Wales (1277–82), once the native princes were no more, the *Brut y Tywysogyon* faded away[262]. The chronicle of Rushen ceased in 1316, the year of a devastating English raid on the Isle of Man[263]. The annals of Dore finished in 1362, the year of a change of abbot[264].

Cistercian chronicles devoted much space to national and political events well beyond the walls of the monastery. St Aelred compiled a *Genealogy of the Kings of England*[265]. In the *Brut y Tywysogyon* Strata Florida completed 'the succession and acts of the Princes of Wales'[266]. Bl. Vincent Kadłubek did much for Polish history in his *Chronicon Polonorum*[267], John of Viktring (d. 1345) for the history of the Hapsburgs in his *Liber cartarum historiarum*[267a], and Peter of Zbraslav (d. 1339) for the history of Bohemia in writing his monastery's annals, the *Chronicon Aula Regiae*[268]. The *Cronaca di Fossa-nova*, possibly emanating from its daughter house at Ceccano, is a useful source for Italian political and ecclesiastical history[269]. At Oliwa was written the *Exordium ordinis Cruciferorum*, the history of the Teutonic Knights in Prussia[270]. More than one Cistercian chronicle (those of Øm, Sorø, and Ryd) related the main political events in Denmark[271]. No less than three Cistercian chronicles dealt with the Crusades. Günther of Pairis (d. 1220), in his *Historia Constantinopolitana*, described the Fourth Crusade – his abbot, Martin, had taken part[272]; Ralph of Coggeshall (d. 1227) who wrote (some have thought) the *Libellus de expugnatione Terrae sanctae per Saladinum*, had himself received a head-wound in Palestine[273]; and Alberic of Ter Doest wrote (in 1272) a *Chronicle of the Holy Land*, basing it on an old book kept at the Dunes[274]. Peter of Vaux-de-Cernay (d. 1218) wrote his *Historia Albigensis*, an eye-witness account of the Cathar crusade. The chronicle of Rushen told how Godred became king of Man in 1079[276], whilst that of Dieulacres recounted Richard II's deposition[277]. The annals of Margam was the only British chronicle to give a detailed account of the murder of Arthur of Brittany in 1204 by his uncle, King John – who, with his army, had twice encamped at the abbey[278].

Chronicles also recorded events within the monastery: giving perhaps the succession of abbots (as in the annals of Dore)[279], or noting special occasions (as the raising of 'the great bell' at Strata Florida)[280], or dating the foundation of daughter-houses (as in the annals of Zwettl)[281]. There could be an exact account of the architectural history of an abbey, as in the chronicle of Meaux[282]. There might be references to the election and deposition of abbots, as in the chronicle of Melrose[283]. Many chronicles noted in passing external events beyond the monastery's control. Ralph of Coggeshall notes from time to time, 'floods, frosts, thunderstorms, pestilences, earthquakes, comets, and eclipses'[284]. Eclipses of the sun were also recorded in the chronicles of Melrose (in 1191)[284a], of Waverley (in 1263)[284b] and of Croxden (in 1330)[284c]. Strong earthquakes, and their effects, are noted in the annals of Zwettl (25 January 1348)[285] and the chronicle of Meaux (27 March 1349)[286]. The annals of Kołbacz tell of such an extremely cold winter in 1323 that many people died and the Baltic completely froze[287]. The annals of Waverley note 'thunder and lightning all day long' on 16 May 1270[288], and the chronicle of Hailes tells of a great flood at Corpus Christi in 1337[289]. Late medieval marginal notes added to the annals of Dore tell of 'a comet in the east', visible for much of February 1516[290]. Cistercian annals are thus a valuable source for the history of climate and tectonics.

Most books emanating from medieval Cistercian houses are now widely dispersed, as those of Italy and Spain[291]. Forty-nine volumes of Buildwas are known, many of them at Trinity College, Cambridge; a lesser number from Fountains are more widely scattered[292]. Some five hundred Cistercian manuscripts from Belgian abbeys such as the Dunes, Orval, and Villers are in the Royal Library of Albert I in Brussels. Illuminated manuscripts from Pairis are in the municipal library of Colmar, and from Vauclair in that of Laon[293]. Manuscripts from Tintern (only one known book is extant) may have perished at Raglan Castle during the Civil War[294]. The library of Ebrach was lost during World War II and earlier conflicts[295].

Cartularies

Cistercian scriptoria produced edited collections of the many deeds kept in an abbey's muniment room or chest. Meaux kept duplicates of its early charters, lest some were lost or became damaged or faded with the passage of time[296]. Other monasteries copied their charters on to rolls of parchment, like the eighteen charter-rolls of Margam containing some five hundred entries[297]. Other houses entered their charters and deeds into bound volumes variously referred to as cartularies, coucher-books, ledger-books, or registers. Such compilations meant easy reference to essential information in times of land disputes or encroachments on monastic rights. Stephen Lexington referred to the need to transcribe charters and other documents 'word by word' into registers in order to determine truth[298].

An early cartulary was that of Silvanès incorporating over 450 charters granted to the monastery between 1132 and 1169, and compiled shortly afterwards[299]. The fine illuminated *Oculus Memorie* of Eberbach treated of the period from 1131 to 1213[300]. Other early-thirteenth century compilations included the 'coucher-book' of Kirkstall[301] and the lost 'register' of Strata Florida[302]. The great two-volume cartulary of Clairvaux dates from about 1260[303]. Later comes note of the 'Formelbuch' of Baumgartenberg (1300)[304], the 'register' of Cîrţa (1306)[305], and the 'book of privileges' of Zwettl (1311)[306]. A lost 'great register' of St Mary's, Dublin, survived into modern times[307]. The cartulary of Gard (1350) was dated on its penultimate page[308]. Other fourteenth century editions included the first 'register' of Newenham (c. 1320)[309], the 'coucher-book' of Whalley (c. 1365)[310], and the 'ledger-book' of

Stoneleigh (*c.* 1392)[311]. The 'white register' of Buckfast noted in 1446, and its 'black register' referred to in the sixteenth century, could be of much earlier date[312]. The cartulary of Rivalta Scrivia (1244) was compiled by a public notary[313].

In the compilation of cartularies, changes of hand-writing frequently show a succession of different scribes to have been involved. Such evidence indicates four scribes to have been involved in the cartulary of Obazine[314], and the cartulary of Warden to have been compiled in at least five stages[315]. No less than nineteen hands drew up the *Oculus Memorie* of Eberbach prior to 1248[316]. The *Güterbuch* of Tennenbach, a detailed review of its possessions, was completed by Abbot John Zenlin in 1341 (after many years' work) but was added to by later scribes[317]. Some cartularies were composite works, as that of Melrose with its two sections dealing (1) with charters down to the time of King Alexander III, and (2) charters down to the reign of King James IV[318]. Three editions of the cartulary of Pipewell are known[319], and two of that of Sibton[320].

Cartularies might be edited for easy consultation[321]. The early deeds of Revesby were grouped into 'funds', e.g. 'stable', 'refectory', 'wine for masses'[322]. The cartulary of Gimont[323] was arranged grange by grange[323]; that of Fontfroide separated the gifts of magnates from those of lesser gentry[324]. The *Güterbuch* of Tennenbach reviewed the history of its benefactors and its entitlement to lands[325]. The 'old cartulary' of Cambron had fifteen sections, the first containing ninety papal bulls dating from 1172 to 1351. Other sections dealt with alms, tithes, the office of porter, and exemptions from tolls, as well as lands and concords[326]. The cartulary of Bonnevaux included details of recruitment of new members, and of obits for benefactors[327]. Where its monks had only a copy of a papal bull, the register of Holm Cultram noted where the original might be found, perhaps at Boxley or Louth Park[328].

A typical cartulary was that of Berdoues. It measured 35 x 25 cm, contained 526 pages of parchment giving 825 entries ranging from 1150 to after 1264; it was enclosed in wooden covers lined with sheepskin dyed green[329]. The normal arrangement of parchment pages, as at Sibton, was for 'flesh side opposite flesh side, and hair opposite hair, with hair outwards'[330]. The cartulary of Gimont, totalling 290 folios, was set in two large quarto volumes[331]. Cartulary entries might be arranged across an entire page (as at Sibton)[332], or in two columns (as at Cambron)[333]. Cistercian austerity might restrict illumination to the title (given in red at Ourscamp and Gard)[334], and to the initial letters to rubrics and paragraphs (red at Obazine[335], vermilion or blue at Ourscamp[336]). The *Oculus Memorie* of Eberbach has multi-coloured floral decoration for the initial letters of each section.[337]. The *Güterbuch* of Tennenbach has a fine contemporaneous illuminated fly-leaf depicting both its abbot and his cellarer[338].

Numerous cartularies have been lost, as the 'register' of Neath referred to as late as 1595 and 1707[339]. Either because their subjects never had a cartulary, or more often perhaps because it is no longer extant, a number of modern printed 'cartularies' are, in fact, a compilation of relevant monastic charters culled from various archives. This is true of the 'cartulary' of Léoncel which relies heavily on the archives of the prefecture of Drôme[340], whilst the modern 'cartularies' of Bonport[341], and Casanova[342], derive their deeds from several sources. Cartularies served to defend monastic rights: an abbot of Egres (1367) displayed before the deputy governor of Transylvania 'certain quires compressed into one volume'[343]. They assist the modern scholar (as in the case of Salem) to trace the process of monastic estate building[344]. They are of value to the political historian, as the cartulary of Fitero with its lengthy documents relating to the kingdom of Navarre[345]. Some collections of deeds (like those of La Real) tell much of the social and economic life of their region[346].

Closely associated with cartularies, in that they list the dates of death not only of abbots and monks but also of benefactors, are the monastic 'obit-books', 'martyrologies' and 'necrologies'. A number have been transcribed[347], and remind us that on 11

January the houses of the Order commemorated all their deceased abbots and on 21 May all their departed monks[348]. They tell of a donor who gave Alderspach 'a good palfrey'[349], and one who gave Raitenhaslach 'a great tankard of 5 quarts'[350]. A benefactor of Sibton (1394) had 'the day of his death put in the martyrology', so that the monks did not forget his obit[351].

Seals

No business transaction, or other deed or letter of significance, was of any worth in medieval days unless attested by an appended impression of the distinctive seal especial to the grantor or writer. The importance attached to the seal was of no less moment in the affairs of the Cistercian Order as a whole, and of its individual monasteries, though Cistercian restraint meant that seal design and size was modest compared with the seals of some Benedictine houses[352]. This simplicity did not lessen the weight the Order attached to the seals of its abbeys, and several statutes of successive General Chapters gave instructions for their design and custody, made provision for their eventual destruction or mutilation, quoted instances of their theft or unlawful retention, or referred to the problems stemming from their misuse[353]. Excavation evidence at Alvastra suggests that seal-matrices may have been made in the monastery workshops[354]. Many monasteries could, like Beaulieu (E, 1270), produce their own beeswax[355], but Kirkstall purchased 'wax for charters' (1262/3) including 'green wax' (1315)[356].

In the twelfth century most Cistercian abbeys employed, by tradition or general consent, an abbot's seal rather than a common seal. These were usually pointed-oval in shape, and commonly depicted a cowled fore-arm holding erect a pastoral staff (as at Clairvaux, 1150[357], and Orval, 1192[358]). This device, intentionally or otherwise, underlined the prime rôle of the abbot in monastic life[359]. Such seals were sometimes inscribed: SIGNVM, rather than the later SIGILLVM, as at Newminster (1140)[360]; and Rievaulx (1191)[361]. In the second half of the century another common form appeared: the three-quarters length image of an abbot holding his pastoral staff (as at Longpont[362], Margam[363], and Rein[364]). There was, however, some diversity in seal devices employed, and, noting 'a certain discord in the seals of the Order', the General Chapter (1200) ordered a considerable degree of uniformity (generally well observed thereafter). Each monastery was to use only the abbot's seal, and this was not to bear his personal name[365]. Later (1218), any house which retained a common seal was to destroy it[366]. These regulations occasioned misgivings as to the validity of deeds so sealed. Consequently, Cwmhir (1235) when sealing a document, felt constrained to say that 'it is not a custom of our Order to have a common seal except the seal of the abbot'[367]. Le Miroir (1243) did likewise[368].

The statute of 1200 further provided that by the following Easter only two designs would be acceptable on Cistercian seals: either the simple effigy of the abbot alone holding his staff, or the continuance of an emergent hand grasping the staff. Quite soon the former became the more popular type, and was already in use at Fountains and Kirkstall (1196)[369]. The hand-and-staff device was replaced at Warden and Neath by 1208[370]; Waverley 'changed' its seal in 1221[371]. By the mid-thirteenth century the 'hand-and-staff' was temporarily a seal of the past, though it survived in use at Tintern until 1253[372], and at Dore, where two seals may have been in use, until 1263[373].The abbatial seals normally showed the abbot standing full-length, holding a book in his left hand and his pastoral staff in the right. A seal of the abbot of Morimond (1215) exceptionally showed him seated[374], and a seal of Roma (1317) shows the abbot giving a blessing[375]. The abbatial seals were generally of pointed-oval type and early in the thirteenth century, whether by coincidence or unrecorded instruction, were of similar size – averaging 40 x 27 mm. By the close of the century new seals engraved were larger (55 mm length at Bénissons-Dieu[376] and Kirkstall[377]). Hand-and-staff seals had occasionally been circular (Llantarnam, 1203: 32 mm[378], L'Aumône, 1225: 35 mm)[379].

The statute of 1218 provided that no abbot was to have two seals[380]; this rule *may* have meant that abbots were to have one *official* seal, but did not disbar a second *private* seal[381]. It was later enjoined (1237) that no prior or obedientiary was to have a seal bearing the name of the abbey[382]. In contrast to a multiplicity of departmental seals in great Benedictine houses[383], few are extant for medieval Cistercian houses, and probably few existed. There are notes of a prior's seal (perhaps for use in a vacancy), as at Thame (1250)[384] and Sept-Fons (1303)[385]. A fourteenth-century *conversus* of Fossanova had his own seal, including on it the abbey's name, perhaps because he had frequently to do business on its behalf[386], as did Baldwin, master of the *conversi* at Signy (1303)[387].

The 1257 codification of statutes allowed an abbot two seals, one (the effigy-type) for major business transactions, and a second for lesser affairs and letters[388]. No longer was the 'hand-and-staff' to ornament the abbot's official seal, but it *was* to be the design for the lesser seal, which was to be inscribed CONTRASIGILLVM henceforth. Examples with this legend (but not with the appointed device) occur at Longpont by 1261[389] and Lorroy by 1263[390]. Correct examples known from many houses include the counterseals of several Swedish abbeys[391]. The return of the 'hand-and-staff' meant that Biddlesden had, over the years, at least four matrices of this type engraved, two being its major seal, two its counter-seal[392]. The inscription required was almost uniformly adhered to, but there were exceptions: S'MINVS ('the lesser seal') at Melrose[393], and S'SECRETVM ('the privy seal') at Newminster[394]. These counter-seals were sometimes circular (as at Culross[395], and Byszewa (1288[396]), their diameters averaging 25 mm. Others were pointed-oval (averaging 33 x 23 mm), as at Flaxley (1315)[397] and Holm Cultram (1301)[398].

Change was to come. It was heralded (in England and Wales) by the Statute of Carlisle (1307) which provided that 'there be a common seal for religious houses'[399]. The consequence was that an abbot could no longer obligate his monastery by the sole use of his own seal which he had been wont to carry with him: others were now involved in decision-making and sealing[400]. Contrariwise, a community could not escape obligation by shouldering blame on a deceased superior. It became the practice of Edward II when requiring a house to grant a corrody to a retiring royal servant, to demand that its monks did so 'by letters patent under their seal' (as Tintern, 1314)[401]. Not all monasteries obeyed the statute immediately. Flaxley in 1316, Furness in 1329, and Holm Cultram in 1331 still used unchanged their abbatial seal[402], perhaps more mindful of Cistercian statute than that of Carlisle, which may have lost some of its force with the death of Edward I.

Others did make the change. At Croxden (1313) the new seal was engraved in deliberate accordance with the royal command when a vacancy occurred in the abbacy[403]. Buckland had a common seal by 1310[404], Rievaulx by 1315[405]. The latter seems to have shared a common designer with Byland, Jervaulx and Fountains – all Yorkshire houses. These common seals were generally pointed-oval in shape, and often continued to have the abbot's effigy as the principal device. Common seals also now appeared on the Continent, as at Chaâlis (1307)[406] and Lekno (1309)[407]. The need for a common seal was reinforced by Benedict XII's Constitution (1335). This enjoined that each Cistercian abbey was to have its own 'special' (i.e. common) seal[408]. The General Chapter ordered that it be 'made rounded of copper, and engraved with the image of the Blessed Virgin, in whose honour are founded all the monasteries of the Order'[409]. New circular seals engraved in response to the papal command were in use at Sedlec by 1336[410] and at Monthéron by 1337[411]. Their diameters averaged 42 mm, ranging from 36 mm at Savigny[412] to 59 mm at Orval[413]. By design or accident, a number were close to the mean, as at Paradyż (40 mm) and Mogiła (41 mm)[414].

The effigy of Our Lady on the new common seals generally showed her holding her Child. She is sometimes seated, as at Aduard[415], Eberbach[416], and Zbraslav[417]. The seals of Bordesley[418] and Robertsbridge[419] depict her Coronation. Some seals had the motto AVE MARIA added (Newminster[420], Pipewell[421]). In the field might be an abbot kneeling in supplication (Aberconwy)[422], or monks in prayer (Boxley)[423]. An abbot might be depicted praying in a niche at the base of the seal, as at Dieulacres[424], and Hore[425]. As common seals became more elaborate additional devices might be found to either side of Our Lady: the heads of SS. Benedict and Bernard (Boxley)[426], a king and an abbot (Holm Cultram)[427], a kneeling angel swinging a censer (Orval)[428]. The seal of Royaumont also added angels and a bust of its royal founder, St Louis[429]. The seal of Dargun had an inverted M, interpreted as indicating its lineage from Morimond[430]; that of Robertsbridge had the letters P R (for *Pons Roberti*)[431]. Grace Dieu (W), perhaps because of poverty, changed its abbot's seal into its common seal simply by adding the words *ET CONVENTVS* in the field[432].

A number of common seals included heraldic devices. Cwmhir impaled the arms of Burgh and Mortimer, barons of the March[433], Strata Marcella displayed the lion rampant of Powys[434], Furness the arms both of England and of Lancaster[435]. Such shields generally reflected close associations with noble founding families and patrons. Some common seals bore allusive devices. Bridges occur on those of Long*pont*[436], *Pont*igny[437], and Roberts*bridge*[438]. A boar's head ornamented the seal of *Swineshead*[439]; candles that of Cîrţa (*B.M.V. de Candelis* being its Latin name)[440]. A few abbeys had double-sided common seals, as Boxley and Robertsbridge which displayed on their reverse image (at Boxley) the figures of SS. Benedict and Bernard[441], and (at Robertsbridge) the abbey church[442].

The 1335 papal Constitution provided that where major transactions were involved, necessitating agreement of both abbot and community, then both the common seal of the house and the abbot's seal were to be appended to the relevant deed[443]. Sometimes this was done (as earlier at Roche, 1329)[444] by impressing the abbatial seal on the reverse of the common seal. This rendered the 'hand-and-staff' type superfluous. Further, since the common seal might be in use for centuries and to avoid fraud, it was also enjoined that the abbot's personal name be henceforth inscribed on his seal. In this way it would be easier to tell 'by whom and in whose time' a deed had been executed[445]. This provision in turn led the General Chapter (1350) to order the destruction of such abbatial seals on the cession or death of their owner, to avoid any misuse[446]. This explains the rarity of extant matrices today. Such a seal, bearing the abbot's name, was used at Dargun in 1337 by Abbot Johann Billerbeck who had only been installed the previous year[447]. Where several abbots were a party to an adjudication (Wales, 1256)[448], or involved in decisions of a provincial chapter (Poland, 1289)[449], their several appended seals form an impressive array.

In the fourteenth century the Order came to have a few especial seals. Until 1318 decrees and licences of the General Chapter were sealed with the matrix of the abbot of Cîteaux[450], but thereafter the Chapter had its own corporate seal[451]. From 1318 to 1390 the definitors used the counter-seal of the abbot of Cîteaux, but thereafter had their own common seal[452], on which the abbot of Cîteaux appears mitred[453]. From 1335 the three abbot-collectors were to use a special seal with which to receipt taxes paid by the monasteries of the Order[454]. Throughout the thirteenth century the seal of the abbot of Cîteaux was rounded, showing the abbot vested in chasuble with book and staff, but more than one almost identical matrix was engraved in this period[455]. St Bernard had been content with the 'hand-and-staff' matrix of Clairvaux, but this was easy to forge. In 1151 he had a new seal engraved, showing himself seated, because of 'many false letters under our false seal'[456]. Unlike his earlier seal, his personal name now also appeared.

Fraudulent or unauthorised use of a conventual seal (as in the sale or demise of land) could mean severe economic loss to houses of the Order. One most likely opportunity for this to happen came upon the death, deposition or resignation of an abbot. Stephen Lexington told the monks of Longvilliers (1231) that their abbot's seal was only to be fixed to a deed with 'the knowledge and consent of the greater and senior (*alt*: wiser) part' of the community 'after mature and great counsel'[457]. The General Chapter (in 1238, at a time when the abbot's seal bore no personal name and was therefore more at risk of misuse) ordered that during a vacancy the seal was to be 'diligently guarded, so that no peril could come from thence'[458]. At Cîteaux (from 1265) the seal was to be guarded by the prior during a vacancy, at other monasteries by the father-abbot or another abbot[459]. At the election of a new abbot the seal was passed to him. When two abbots were deputed to install the new abbot of Vaucelles (1269), they were 'to give up to him the seal with the cure'[460]. Once abbatial seals bore a personal name, on the election of a new abbot the seal of his predecessor was broken up in the presence of the Visitor and the community, and a new one engraved (1350)[461].

So far as the common seal was concerned, the Statute of Carlisle (1307) provided that it be kept 'in the custody – not of the abbot, but of the prior and four worthy monks, and be placed in safe keeping under the private seal of the abbot'[462]. Consequently, when at Croxden (1313) its first common seal was cut, the Visitors enjoined that it be kept by 'four of the most reliable monks of the house'[463]. The papal Constitution (1335) and the General Chapter (1336) later varied these instructions. Of four keys, differently cut and fitting different locks of the seal chest, one was to be held by the abbot, one by the bursar, one by the prior, and the fourth by another monk[464]. The three abbot-collectors were also each to have a differently designed key to safeguard their seal (1336)[465]. Fraud was also obviated by the requirement (1237) that no abbot was to seal letters without reading them, nor to seal an empty parchment – the equivalent of signing a blank cheque today[466]. An abbot of Pontrond (1223) had been guilty of the former offence[467], an abbot of Loccum (1249) the latter[468].

Despite all precautions seals were frequently stolen, sometimes during rebellions by monks or *conversi*, as at Alvastra (1216)[469], and Acquafredda (1273)[470]. Stephen Lexington (1228) told how two Irish abbatial seals had been pawned, one in a tavern, and how the respective monasteries were thereby in straitened circumstances[471]. Deposed abbots like Malachy of Baltinglass (1228)[472] and Theodore of Olivet (1200)[473] walked off with their seals. A similar situation arose at Bordesley (1257) where the late abbot 'proposed with it to contract divers debts and consequently to confound and destroy that house'[474]. The new seal then engraved shows a close likeness to the 1256 seal of Tintern, suggesting a common engraver[475]. Raids by seculars (as at Bindon, 1331) could also mean theft of the seal[476].

The forging of seals (commented upon by St Bernard) was another hazard. The abbot of Cîteaux (1228) noted that as a seal of the abbot of Buzay had his personal name engraved, then not the custom, it must be regarded as false[477]. Brother James of Paradyż (1247) was the alleged forger of many seals[478], whilst vagabond monks of Beaulieu (1265)[479], and Eberbach (1294)[480] wandered abroad with 'false seals like the seal of the house' concerned, to their potential and feared detriment. The problem was such that the General Chapter (1287) inhibited any such forger from receiving any office or dignity within the Order or his own monastery[481]. As common seals continued in use for centuries (at Julita from at least 1349 down to 1506)[482], they might become so worn (as that of Cymer) as to give only an indistinct image[483].

Notes

1. Lawrence (1984) 152; *cf. Statuta* I, 31 (1134/LXXVIII), 275 (1202/2), 320–21 (1206/5).
2. *Statuta* I, 184 (1195/15).
3. Barrière (1977) 87–90, (1986) 92.
4. *Ibid.* I, 313 (1205/26).
5. *KKA* 37–8, *VDA* 4, 17, 29; Uitterdijk (1874) 217, 228.
6. McGuire (1982) 68.
7. Jażdżewski (1987) 358, Grüger (1978a) 253, but note *CHA* (2–3) 115 (No. 590).
8. Snape (1968) 147.
9. *RBM* IV, 14–5 (No. 40).
10. Mousnier (1986) 123.
11. *DHGE* II (1914) 27, Da Silva Barros (1972) 7.
12. Cocheril (1959a) 57, Yañez Neira (1970) 564.
13. Stéphan (1970) 46, Lackner (1976) 60.
14. France (1992) 234.
15. Kienzle (1985) 234.
16. Lekai (1977a) 79, 236.
17. *MPHA* 57, *cf. MPCM* 529.
18. *Statuta* II, 289–90 (1245/3).
19. *Ibid.* III, 207 (1281/9).
20. *Ibid.* III, 238 (1287/6).
21. *Ibid.* III, 299–300 (1300/2).
22. *UKAR* II, 356 (No. 539).
23. *Ibid.* III, 392–3 (1331/2).
24. *Ibid.* III, 357–60 (1322/1–8).
25. O'Dwyer (1965) 243.
26. *RSL* II, 195; *cf. SL* 68; Lacorte (1995) 291–92.
27. *RSL* I, 116–18.
28. *Statuta* II, 170 (1237/9).
29. *RCC* V, 246 (No. 1545); D'Arbois (1858) 65–6.
30. Statuta II, 290 (1245/4).
31. Lacorte (1995) 297–99; *cf. RCC* V, 247 (No. 1581); *Statuta* II, 399 (1254/2).
32. Lacorte (1995) 300.
33. *Ibid.* 301–03.
34. *Statuta* II, 348 ((1250/9); LCC (2) 256.
35. Lawrence (1984) 165–67; *cf.* Pineault and Coomans (1994) 130.
36. Talbot (1963) 214.
37. *DHGE* XII (1953) 946; *MPCM* 596..
38. Lawrence (1960) 173; *MPCM* 651–52.
39. *SL* 13.
40. *RCC* V, 249 (No. 1581), 250 (No. 1585), 252 (No. 1609)
41. *Statuta* III, 353–54 (1321/9), 358 (1322/4), III, 316 (1306/7).
42. De Montgolfier (1986) 18, Lekai (1977a) 83.
43. De Montgolfier (1986) 18.
44. King (1954) 271.
45. Obert-Piketty (1986) 148.
46. *Statuta* III, 354 (1321/9).
47. *Ibid.* III, 359–60 (1322/8) – the first five abbots together with the abbot of Preuilly.
48. *Ibid.* III, 363–64 (1323/6).
49. *Ibid.* III, 207 (1281/9).
50. *Ibid.* III, 342 (1318/14).
51. McNulty (1943) 166.
52. *Statuta* III, 175 (1278/2); III, 316 (1306/7), 326 (1312/7), 387 (1329/9), 466 (1341/2).
53. *Ibid.* III, 175 (1278/2).
54. *Ibid.* III, 376–77 (1327/4).
55. *Ibid.* III, 406 (1334/3).
55a. *MPHA* 529.
56. *Ibid.* III, 457–59 (1339/6–8).
57. *Ibid.* III, 400–08 (1334/5), 449–50 (1338/1), 466–67 (1341/3).
58. *Ibid.* III, 329–30 (1314/8).
59. *Ibid.* III, 331 (1315/8).
60. Lekai (1977a) 239.
61. Cf. *Statuta* II, 360 (1251/3).
62. De Montgolfier (1986) 18, Lekai (1977a) 238.
63. King (1954) 273, cf. 267–68.
64. *Statuta* III, 354 (1321/9), 359 (1322/7, 8).
65. Lekai (1977a) 237; N.B: see: Békefi (1896) 565–87, for an account of St Bernard's, Paris, written in Hungarian.
66. Dautrey (1976) 192–93.
67. *Statuta* II, 473 (1260/55); III, 188–89 (1279/33), 211 (1281/27).
68. *Ibid.* III, 2 (1262/6).
69. *Ibid.* III, 473 (1260/55).
70. Lekai (1977a) 145.
71. *Statuta* III, 212–13 (1281/40).
72. Lekai (1971a) 145–47.
73. Gérard (1957) 202–04.
74. Lekai (1971a) 146–67.
75. *Statuta* III, 387 (1329/8); cf. 367–68 (1324/4), 381–82 (1328/9).
76. *Statuta*. III, 200 (1280/26), 209 (1281/19), 213 (1281/42), 217 (1282/2); *cf.* Little (1893) 83–4.
77. *Statuta* III, 254 (1291/28), *cf.* VCH, *Oxford* II (1907) 80–82.
78. VCH, *County of Oxford* II (1907) 88–82.
79. *Ibid.* 82.
80. *Ibid.* 86.
81. Obert-Piketty (1986) 142, D'Arbois (1858) 69; *cf. Statuta* III, 307 (1302/5).
82. Schneider (1992) 145.
83. *Ibid.* 130.
84. Scherg (1976) 99; Kottje (1992) 130.
85. *Statuta* III, 399 (1332/7), 429 (1335/*bulla*, 31).
86. *DHGE* XIV (1960) 88–9.
87. Statuta II, 473 (1260/57).
88. *DHGE* XII (1953) 947.
89. Lekai (1977a) 238.
90. McNulty (1943) 164–65.
91. *Statuta* III, 429 (1335/*bulla*, 31).
92. *Ibid.* III, 423–35 (1335/*bulla*, 32–40).
93. Statuta III, 435 (1335/*bulla*, 41).
94. France (1992) 244–45; Hillgarth (1959) 23.
95. Peyrafort-Bonnet (1984) 92–3.
96. *FRB* 529.
97. Friedl (1965) 64.
98. *Cf.* France (1992) 252–53.
99. Aubert (1933) 74, 77–8; Dimier (1964) 52–3; Péchenard (1883) 40.
100. Hillgarth (1959) 48.
101. France (1992) 252–53.

102. Visual observation.
103. D'Arbois (1858) 60.
104. King (1954) 221.
105. Talbot (1954a) 107.
106. *DHGE* XII (1953) 910.
107. Werland (1968) 12, 349.
108. *DHGE* XII (1953) 910.
109. Aubert (1931) 9.
110. Jażdżewski (1992) 120–21.
111. Isaac (1984) *passim*; *Cf.* Załuska (1992).
112. Fergusson (1984a) 40.
113. BL, Add. MS 48,984.
114. CPR 1271/505.
115. Seibt (1974) 362.
116. Wetesko (1991) 159, Karłowska-Kamzowa (1987) 384.
117. Bell (1995) 82–87.
118. *CHA* 4–5, 51 (No. 216).
119. *DSMLR* 442 (No. 165).
120. Bell (1995) 81–2, 93–5.
121. *CZ* 684.
122. *CC* (2), B. 30; *ACA* 299.
123. France (1992) 251–52.
124. Williams (1984) I, 30.
125. *RSL* II, 210 (No. 1).
126. Harper-Bill (1980) 105.
127. King (1954) 250.
128. *RSL* II, 199 (No. 6).
129. Trinity Coll. Camb. MS 1272, *cf.* Williams (1984) I, 160 (*n.*101); France (1992) 250.
130. Załuska (1989) 26, Pl. XV.
131. Jażdżewski (1992) 127.
132. Dupont (1982) 651–54.
133. *DHGE* XII (1953) 911; *cf.* Friedl (1965) 20–1, 64.
134. Peyrafort-Bonnet (1984) 92–3; *cf.* Talbot (1954a) 108.
135. Jażdżewski (1992) 127.
136. Hillgarth (1959) 57.
137. Harper Bill (1980) 105–06.
138. Williams (1984) I, 35.
139. Gwynn (1970) 142.
140. Bell (1984b) 223*n.*
141. Talbot (1954a) 111.
142. *RSL* II, 219 (No.1).
143. *LCC* (2) 211.
144. *BDB* 162; *cf.* Canestrelli (1896) 125–26.
145. Isaac (1984) clxxxi.
146. McGuire (1982) 33–4.
147. *CBK* xxviii (No. LII).
148. Bell (1992) 207.
149. Friedl (1965) 20–1, 64.
150. Jack (1972) 86.
151. Bell (1992) 166–69, 207.
152. Hereford Cathedral MS P. v. 5. (The copyist was a monk of Dore, John of Bath).
153. Exeter Coll. Oxford, MS 1 (now kept at the Bodleian Library); *cf.* AF 145.
154. BL, Add. MS 48984 (Llantarnam), Thompson (1928b) 238 (Rewley).
155. BL Royal MS 13, D ii; *cf.* Lewis and Williams (1976) 20.
156. *ABB* 37–8, 195–98.
157. St Clair Baddeley (1964) 7.
158. *Statuta* I, 32 (1134/LXXXV); LCC (1) 171–72.
159. *Ibid.* III, 177 (1278/11), 184 (1279/3).
160. Stalley (1987) 217, *cf.* 46.
161. *EOC* 212–14 (LXXII/2).
162. Stéphan (1970) 47.
163. Talbot (1986) 57, Załuska (1989) 67, 69; Pl. II.
164. Załuska (1989) Pls. V, VII, X, XII.
165. *Statuta* I, 26 (1134/LVIII); LCC (1) 171–72.
166. Norton and Park (1986) 5; *cf.* Statuta I, 31 (1134/LXXX).
167. King (1954) 17–8.
168. Norton and Park (1985) 5.
169. *Statuta* I, 58 (1154/3).
170. *RCC* III, 59 (No. 670).
171. CHA (4–5) 49 (No. 208).
172. Elm (1980) 172, Rappold (1979); *cf.* CHA (4–5) 339 (No. 2770).
173. Leyrer (1988) 107–08.
174. Cocheril (1959b) 41, 44–5.
175. Kinder (1982) 397.
176. Wetesko (1991) 111–14, 156; *CHA* (2–3) 96 (No. 495); Jażdżewski (1992) Pls. 3, 21.
177. France (1992) 187.
178. Bedini (1964) 58–9.
179. Zakrzewski (1907) 12.
180. Exeter Coll. Oxford, MS 1.
181. Bell (1992) 163–64.
182. Bell (1995) 99.
183. Všetečková (1996) 286, 288, 299.
184. *CHA* (4–5) 49 (No. 210).
185. VCH, *Stafford* III (1970) 227.
186. *CHA* (2–3) 115 (No. 592); *DHGE XII* (1953) 912.
187. Werland (1968) 350.
188. King (1995) 184, 187, 196.
189. *Ibid.* 184–88.
190. Rouse (1976) 123–34.
191. Holdsworth (1986) 54.
192. Occhipinti (1985) 335.
193. Fletcher (1919) 163.
194. Talbot (1954a) 110.
195. *ABB* 37–8, 195–98, 304–05.
196. Matarasso (1993) xiv-xvi.
197. Mikkers (1988) 745–49.
198. Matarasso (1993) 127.
199. *Cf.* Anderson (1978) 137, Leyrer (1988) 107–08, Mikkers (1988) 745, Tomasic (1972) 75–6, Waddell (1978b) 126.
200. *Cf.* Costello (1966) 283, Mikkers (1988) 747, *CHA* (2–3) 175–6 (No. 979).
201. Matarasso (1993) 127.
202. McCaffery (1978) 205.
203. McGinn (1973) 4, Mikkers (1988) 750–51, Trout (1974) 207, 247.
204. *DHGE* XII (1953) 912, Mikkers (1988) 748–49.
205. Holman (1986) 109–10.
206. *CHDM* (1) 1–2.
207. *DHGE* XII (1953) 915, Mikkers (1988) 764.
208. Bell (1987) 217, Leclercq (1978) 103.
209. Bell (1984b) 227–34.
210. *DHGE* XII (1953) 958.
211. Mikkers (1988) 761–62.
212. Millard (1994) 222.
213. *DHGE* I (1912) 466.
214. Mikkers (1988) 815.
215. *DHGE* XII (1953) 913, Elm (1980) 171, Trout (1974) *passim*.

216. Isaac (1984) 13, 55–56.
217. Mikkers (1978b) 220, 237.
218. *DHGE* XII (1953) 959, Sherwin (1927) 252.
219. *CHA* (2–3) 173 (Nos 953–55).
220. *Analecta Monastica* 4 (Studia Anselmiana 41: 1957) 119–40.
221. Holman (1986) 110–12.
222. Mikkers (1988) 742, 748, 778.
223. O'Brien (1965) 278–304.
224. Mikkers (1988) 745, 755, 777; *cf.* McCorkell (1985) 307.
225. *Statuta* I, 255 (1200/34).
226. Lekai (1977a) 234.
227. *CHA* (3–3) 159 (No. 865).
228. Mikkers (1988) 748.
229. Holman (1986) 115.
230. *DHGE* XII (1953) 915.
231. *Ibid.* 915.
232. *AF* 177–77; VCH, *Lancaster* II (1908) 129–30.
233. *DHGE* XII (1953) 911–16.
234. Finucane (1977) 51, Mikkers (1988) 758–59.
235. *DHGE* XII (1953) 915.
236. McGuire (1983a) 26.
237. Szacherska (1977) 153n.
238. Holdsworth (1962) 152–205.
239. France (1992) 245.
240. *RBS* I, 56–61.
241. *DHGE* XII (1953) 915, Lekai (1977a) 235–36.
242. McGuire (1976a) 20–26.
243. *Ibid.* (1982) 105.
244. Berman (1978) 282, Kienzle (1989) 215.
245. *PZKZ* 1–337.
246. VCH, *Lancaster* II (1908) 130.
247. *Cf.* CM (2) xiv.
248. *ACA* 297, *CC.* (1) B. 4.
249. *CM* (2) xiv.
250. *CM* 94.
251. *ACA* 297n, *cf.* 537–38.
252. Clay (1952) 27–28.
253. Baker (1975) 2, Gilyard-Beer (1986) 147–48.
254. *RC* xii-xiii.
255. Berman (1978) 281.
256. Cowley (1977) 148.
257. McGuire (1982) 19.
258. Williams (1984) I, 162.
259. Marriotti (1927) 172.
260. McGuire (1982) 12–20.
261. *Cf. CRC* 13.
262. Williams (1984) I, 161.
263. Butler (1988) 63.
264. BL, Egerton MS 3088; *Monumenta Germaniae Historica, Scriptorum* XXVII, (Hanover, 1885) 514–31 (where transcribed).
265. *DHGE* XII (1953) 915, Glidden (1987) 183.
266. Williams (1984) I, 161–62.
267. *DAC* (1978) 726–27.
267a. *New Catholic Encyclopaedia* (New York, 1967) VII, 1076.
268. *PZKZ* 1–337.
269. *CFN* 489–549.
270. Williams (1978) 247.
271. France (1992) 242–43, McGuire (1982) 18–19.
272. *DHGE* XII (1953) 914, Spence (1978) 262–73.
273. *DHGE* XII (1953) 914, *RC* 162–63, Gardner (1955) 20.

274. *DHGE* I (1912) 1413.
275. Lekai (1977a) 236.
276. Kinvig (1950) 51.
277. VCH, *Stafford* III (1970) 233.
278. *DHGE* XII (1953) 914.
279. Williams (1976) 7.
280. Williams (1889) Appx. ii.
281. *AZ* 679, 681.
282. *CMM passim.*
283. *E.g.* CM 103.
284. *RC* xv.
284a. *CM* 28.
284b. *AM* II, 355.
284c. *ACA* 305.
285. *AZ* 684.
286. *CMM* III, 69.
287. *AC* 717.
288. *AM* II, 376; *cf.* ABB 24–25.
289. Winkless (1990) 39.
290. Exeter Coll. (Oxford) MS 1, f. 3d.
291. Leclercq (1949a) 91–120, (1951) 71–77, (1954) 302–07.
292. Sheppard (1997) xlix; *Collectanea Ord. Cist. Ref.* XIV (1952) 267–77.
293. *CHA* (4–5) 46 (No. 192), 47 (No. 198), 139 (No. 943); Gand (1990) *passim.*
294. Williams (1984) I, 160.
295. *CHA* (4–5) 48–49 (No. 205).
296. *CMM* I, xx-xxi.
297. NLW, Penrice and Margam Charters 288–296, 543–546, 2089–2093.
298. *RSL* II, 225–26 (Savigny, 1230).
299. Berman (1978) 282.
300. *OM passim.*
301. *CBK passim, cf.* Barnes (1982) 55.
302. Williams (1984) II, 262.
303. Hümpfner (1946) 138.
304. Van Der Meer (1965) 271.
305. Reissenberger (1894) 10.
306. *LFZ* 586.
307. Benoît and Sportes (1991) 181.
308. Destombe (1969) 130.
309. Davidson (1843) 131–32, *cf.* 106.
310. *CBW* I, xi-xii.
311. *SLB* ix.
312. Stéphan (1970) 20–21.
313. *CRS* II, 22.
314. *CG* xv-xvi.
315. *CW* 2–3.
316. *OM passim.*
317. *TG* xvi.
318. *LM* iv.
319. VCH, *Northampton* II (1906) 116 (*n.* 9).
320. *SBC* I, 150–60.
321. This allowed quick reference if lands or privileges disputed.
322. Donkin (1965) 165.
323. *CG* xv-xvi.
324. Grèzes-Ruelff (1977) 253.
325. *TG passim.*
326. *CAC passim.*
327. Berman (1983) 44.
328. *RHC* 96–102.
329. *CB* 10*-11*.
330. *SBC* I, 151.
331. *CG* xv-xvi.
332. *SBC* I, 151.

333. *CAC* xvi.
334. *CO* 5, Destombe (1969) 130.
335. *CCO* 30.
336. *CO* 5.
337. *OM passim.*
338. *TG* (fly leaf).
339. Williams (1984) II, 266.
340. *CL passim.*
341. *CBP passim.*
342. *CADC passim.*
343. *RCH* 92.
344. *CDSL passim.*
345. *CSMF* 5.
346. *DSMLR passim.*
347. *NG* II, 1; IV, 3–26, 106–27, 239–59, 447–72; *OLSB passim.*
348. *NG* II: 1, 261, 269; IV, 240.
349. *NG* IV, 8.
350. *NG* II:1, 275.
351. *SBC* IV, 104 (No. 1179).
352. Heslop (1986) 267.
353. Williams (1984b) 249.
354. Hallberg (1965) 113.
355. *E.g. ABB* 83, 194.
356. *DCK* 216, 246.
357. Walford (1857) opp. 48, *cf.* Heslop (1986) 267.
358. Halkin (1970) 79 (No. 24).
359. Heslop (1986) 267.
360. *CNM* xix.
361. Clay (1928) 6; Birch (1887) I, No. 3907.
362. Douët D'Arcq (1868) 95 (Nos 8808–8803 of 1151–1223).
363. Williams (1987) 142 (No. 220, of 1170–1249).
364. Rappold (1979) 431, Pl. 42 (of 1195).
365. *Statuta* I, 251–52 (1200/15, 17).
366. *Statuta* I, 487 (1218/13).
367. Beverley Smith (1970) 91.
368. Clay (1928) 2–3.
369. *Ibid.* 5, Heslop (1986) 269.
370. NLW, Penrice and Margam Charters 101.
371. *AM* II, 295.
372. BL, Harleian Ch. 75 D. 11; Heslop (1986) 269*n.*
373. Williams (1997) 212.
374. Birch (1887) V, 305 (No. 18,696).
375. Hallberg (1965) 96 (No. 81), 110 (though with his left hand).
376. Douët D'Arcq (1868) 59 (No. 8538).
377. Ellis (1986) 47 (No. 444), *cf.* Heslop (9186) 271.
378. BL, Harleian Ch. 75 A. 32; *cf.* Williams (1987) 144 (No. 228).
379. Douët D'Arcq (1868) 54 (No. 8503).
380. *Statuta* I, 487 (1218/13).
381. Heslop (1986) 272.
382. *LCC* (2) 297–98.
383. Snape (1968) 133.
384. PRO, E 212/28; *cf.* Ellis (1986) 87 (No. 833).
385. Douët D'Arcq (1868) 170 (No. 9341).
386. Muzzi (1990) 226 (No. 580).
387. Archives Nationales (Paris); Seals Dept: ST 959.
388. *LCC* (2) 297–98.
389. Douët D'Arcq (1868) 95 (No. 8804).
390. *Ibid.* 96 (No. 8809).

391. Hallberg (1965) 99, 106, 108; *Figs.* 32, 62, 72.
392. Birch (1887) I, 447 (Nos 2649, 2650, 2653, 2655).
393. *Ibid.* IV, 176 (No. 15,383).
394. *CNM* xix.
395. Birch (1887) IV, 141 (No. 15, 249).
396. Gumowski (1966), Pl. XL, No. 407.
397. Ellis (1986) 35 (No. 325).
398. *Ibid.* 41 (No. 381).
399. Clay (1928) 4, Heslop (1986) 282–83.
400. Heslop (1986) 274.
401. *CCR* 1314/192.
402. Heslop (1986) 274.
403. *ACA* 303, *CC*, B 43.
404. Heslop (1986) 274.
405. *Ibid.* 274–75.
406. Douët D'Arcq (1868) 8 (No. 9177).
407. Wyrwa (1989) 2.
408. *Statuta* III, 411 (1335, *bulla* 2), 414–15 (*bulla* 8).
409. *Statuta* III, 437 (1335/2), *cf.* Bony (1987) 201–40.
410. Stehlíková (1996) 332.
411. Heslop (1986) 278.
412. Douët D'Arcq (1868) 41 (No. 8408).
413. Halkin (1970) 107 (No. 106).
414. Gumowski (1966) 79, Pl. XL (No. 406).
415. Rijksarchief Groningen (Holland) Seal No. 471.
416. Staab (1987) 61.
417. Stehlíková (1996) 331.
418. Heslop (1986) 278.
419. Birch (1887) I (No. 3912 R).
420. *Jnl. Brit. Archaeol. Assoc.* VII, Pl. 8 (No. 2).
421. Birch (1887) I, 678 (No. 3726).
422. PRO, E 42/321.
423. *Jnl. Brit. Archaeol. Assoc.* XLVIII, 168.
424. Ellis (1986) 30 (No. 286).
425. Stalley (1987) 224 (No. 270).
426. *Jnl. Brit. Archaeol. Assoc.* XLVIII, 168.
427. Ellis (1986) 41 (No. 380).
428. Halkin (1970) 86 (Fig. 29).
429. Douët D'Arcq (1868) 33 (No. 8362).
430. Schlegel (1980) 61.
431. Birch (1897) I (No. 3912).
432. Williams (1993) 24 (D. 13).
433. PRO, E 329/244.
434. NLW, Wynnstay Deeds (1945 Deposit) Box 3; Antony House, Cornwall: BD/13/102 (kind information of Mr Graham Thomas).
435. Birch (1887) I, 561 (No. 3177).
436. Douët D'Arcq (1868) 29–30 (No.8336), 95 (No. 8804).
437. Birch (1887) V, 324 (No. 18,763); Coulon (1912) 226 (No. 1283).
438. Birch (1887) I (No. 3912 R).
439. *Ibid.* I, 765 (No. 4136).
440. Reissenberger (1894) 28*n*, *RCH* 117.
441. Heslop (1986) 276.
442. Birch (1887) I (No. 3912).
443. *Statuta* III, 415 (*bulla* 9).
444. Meekings (1979) 15.
445. *Statuta* III, 415 (*bulla* 9; 1335/9).
446. Heslop (1986) 283 (No. 13).
447. Schlegel (1980) 82–83.
448. BL, Harleian Ch. 75 A. 37.

449. Grüger (1987) 171.
450. *Cf.* Clark-Maxwell (1925) Pl. V (Nos 3–4).
451. *Statuta* III, 343 (1318/20), 409 (1334/9); *cf.* Douët D'Arcq (1868) III, 222 (No. 9713).
452. *Statuta* III, 343 (1318/20), 573 (1390/2).
453. Rossignol (1851) 26.
454. *Statuta* III, 422 (1335, *bulla* 18); *cf. CTB* 26.
455. *Archaeologia* LXXV (1925) Pl. V-4; Marilier (1982) 364–66.
456. Walford (1857) 48–52.
457. *RSL* II, 202 (No. 5).
458. *Statuta* II, 185 (1238/3).
459. *Statuta* III 24.
460. *Statuta* III, 70–71 (1269/13).
461. Clay (1928) 5, Heslop (1986) 283 (*n.* 13).
462. Heslop (1986) 282–83.
463. *CC* (2) B. 43.
464. *Statuta* III, 413 (1335/*bulla* 5); 441 (1336/1).
465. *Statuta* III, 422 (1335/ *bulla* 18).
466. *LCC* (2) 299–98.
467. *Statuta* II, 28 (1223/24), *cf.* 374 (1251/69).
468. *Statuta* II, 346 (1249/55).
469. *Statuta* I, 461 (1216/56), *cf.* II, 346 (1249/55).
470. *Statuta* III, 118 (1273/16).
471. *SL* 44.
472. *Ibid.* 58.
473. *Statuta* I, 254 (1200/27).
474. *CPR* 1257/565.
475. Heslop (1986) 270.
476. Desmond (1971) 160–61.
477. Clay (1928) 3.
478. *Statuta* II, 317 (1247/15), 334 (1248/36).
479. *CPR* 1265/481.
480. *Statuta* III, 271–72 (1294/26).
481. *Statuta* III, 240 (1287/18).
482. Hallberg (1965) 109–10.
483. NLW, Dolrhyd Deed 1; Peniarth (Hengwrt) Deed 208.

Chapter 6

THE SECULAR COMMUNITY

Medieval monasteries were surrounded by precinct walls, and access was by means of a gate-house. This structure was the first impression travellers gained of a monastery, and when they reached it they might well have echoed in spirit the words of the Psalmist: 'Open to me the gates of righteousness' (Psalm 118:19), for beyond lay what was meant to be a haven of peace and holiness. The gate-house was the immediate point of contact between the enclosed monastic community and the outside world, and to it came all classes of people: not only those whom God was calling to make here their profession, but also the traveller seeking shelter, the pilgrim fulfilling a vow, the refugee fleeing from war, the wrong-doer seeking sanctuary, the pensioner looking for an eventide home, the sick and aged and poor hoping for relief and care, the dying wishing a holy end, the would-be servant needing a position, and the local miscreant to be incarcerated in the gate-house cells. All these might well find admission within the gates, but for practical reasons the great mass of the deserving poor received their charity, alms or dole, at the gate, whilst outside it (as later at Tintern) the local ne'er-do-wells might hang around and cause trouble, or fight or amuse themselves with sports[1]. Business transactions might be done at a Cistercian gate-house (Salem, 1265)[2], or a court held there (Løgum, 1343)[3]. A medieval monastic gateway was, as in Old Testament times, a favourite meeting-place.

The gate-house was the domain of the monk nominated as porter, who according to the *Rule of St Benedict* was to be 'a wise old man'[4], for his was a responsible position with his own semi-independent department. Some porters were elected directly from that office to an abbacy. A porter of Melrose (1249)[5] became abbot of its daughter-house at Balmerino, and a porter of Beaulieu (1325) became abbot of Newenham[6]. The *Rule* provided that the gate-house was to be continually manned: the porter 'was to have a cell near the gate, so that persons who arrive may always find some-one at hand to give them a reply'[7]. The *Charter of Charity* included the 'gate-keeper's cell' amongst the first regular places to be constructed[8]. The ancient usages of Cîteaux required the porter to be at his post from the end of Lauds until after Compline, except when he was at meals, being bled, at Mass, or taking the rest allowed him in the dorter during summer after Prime and None, when another monk, the sub-porter, was to take his place[9]. The 'chief porter' is noted at Moreruela (1254)[10]; at Beaulieu (1270) he was assisted by a *conversus* and servant[11].

The porter's primary function was to distribute alms, food and clothing to the poor. He was the monastery's almoner; his zeal could flag, and so Stephen Lexington reminded porters 'to show themselves more merciful and humane towards the poor'[12]. To the gate-house came left-overs from the refectories, the daily portion (for a month) of dead monks, and other food provided by custom. In addition, the *Usages* bade the porter keep bread for travellers. Unless it was a time of famine, women of the neighbourhood were not to be fed, and any women with young children were to eat outside the gate-house[13]. The porter received gifts of lands, rents and tithes, as those presented to the porters of Perseigne (1212)[14] and Ter Doest (1231)[15] 'for the use of the poor'. At Perseigne the procurator of the gate drew up a list of the rights and privileges in money and lands pertaining to it. At Villers charters of relevant donations were often addressed directly to the porter, and though purchases by him might mention his abbot's consent they were made on his own initiative. He was also the abbey's agent for the payment of life annuities[16]. A porter's other significant task was to receive guests and callers – with a cry of *Deo gratias*: genuine visitors he admitted with a genuflexion and notified the abbot of their arrival, the needy sick he would direct to the lay infirmary. When a guest left he was treated as humbly as when he arrived[17]. The Cistercian porter was almoner, businessman, watch-man and gaoler[18].

Charity at the Gate

There are many passing references to the good deeds of the Cistercians. King Béla noted the 'sustenance of the poor' at Toplica (1225)[19], the foundation charter of Paradyż (1236) envisaged that its monks would be 'diligent in serving the poor'[20], and there was reference to 'the true compassion' shown at Eldena (1276)[21]. Visitors demanded that 'charity at the gate' remain unabated (Champagne, 1231[22]; Dore, 1318[23]), though recognising that it would be proportional to 'the means of the house'. The work of almsgiving at Cîteaux necessitated a special chamber, an almonry, for 'the generator of charity' (1258)[24]. This official was perhaps an adjutant to the porter, and paralleled in the 'dole-giver' of Ebrach (1340)[25]. A new almonry was being built at Beaulieu in 1270[26]: the site of the almonry at Byland, attached to the gate-house, is still visible[27]. Charity was also given on the granges (Dunes, 1245[28]; Zwettl, c. 1270[29]). A house in reduced circumstances might be 'no longer able to perform its distribution of alms' (Flaxley, 1281)[30]. Two pontiffs praised Cistercian charity: John XXII lauded the good works of Salem (1322)[31]; Benedict XII (1335) saw the Order as 'outstanding and prompt' in good deeds[32].

Assistance to the poor was at its greatest in years of famine, when hundreds of starving peasants might crowd around abbey gates. In the great European famine of 1315 to 1317, the abbot of Chaâlis told how because of 'hunger and death many more persons flocked to the abbeys of the Order for alms and shelter'[33]. These certainly included Aduard (1315)[34] and Riddagshausen (1316)[35]. The figures quoted of people afforded such urgent charity may be exaggerated. Morimond (1147) was said to have fed its whole neighbourhood for three months[36], and later (1303) to have killed 3,000 cattle to feed the starving[37]. Margam (1188) sent a ship to Bristol to obtain corn for 'a very large crowd of beggars'[38]. Other abbeys to display wholesale charity in famine years included Clairvaux (1125)[39], Melrose (1154)[40] and Heisterbach (1217)[41].

Even in normal years there was substantial and systematic giving. Relief mostly took the form of food, drink, and clothing, and each house had its own specific arrangements. In the line of Pontigny the porter was always to keep alms ready, including discarded clothing, and dole out daily at least 100 loaves from the abbey's bakery[42]. Villers (1240) dispersed 300 loaves a day[43]. The porter of Meaux (1240) received yearly from its tannery twenty hides for new shoes for the poor and the repair of old ones, as well as cloth for their clothes from its lanary, and one-tenth of the cheese produced at its dairy at Felse[44]. The porter of Beaulieu (1270) gave out bread on Mondays, Wednesdays, and Fridays; sometimes he cooked pottage in the gate-house for the needy, and every six months he distributed thirty pairs of new, and forty of old, shoes as well as new clothing and yearly 70 old tunics and 60 pairs of hose. At harvest-time the poor who were fit were expected by Beaulieu to 'work in the fields for their bread'[45]. Riddagshausen (1317) encouraged the poor to help themselves by giving them sickles to cut the ripened corn[46].

Such a scale of charity was one reason why the Cistercians were forced to expand their estates, but it was also supported by grants from philanthropic benefactors. Cambron received seventeen charters (1222–1331) aiding its alms-giving[47], Clairvaux no less than thirty grants in as many years (1216–1247) specifically to help the work of the porter[48]. Grants could take the form of money (Amelunxborn, for the purchase of food and clothing, 1254)[49]; lands (Zwettl, for the sustenance of thirty poor, 1208)[50]; fishing rights (Fontmorigny, 1180)[51]; rents (Bonnevaux, 1220)[52]; a share in tolls (L'Aumône, 1235)[53]; mills (Warden, for the provision of shoes, 1205)[54]; churches and tithes (Dunkeswell, 1242)[55]. Grants for specific purposes allowed Heiligenkreuz (1196) to distribute 300 loaves twice a week[56], and Doberan (1324) some 60 loaves each Friday[57]. Sometimes such extra dole was on a yearly basis: as 1 shilling each to 100 poor boys at Furness[58]. The obit of a benefactor who had so provided would be marked by especial charity (Waverley, 1310)[59].

Certain feast-days might be designated for supplementary dole: Corpus Christi (a gallon of base beer at Esrum)[60]; St Crispin's Day (5 oxen distributed at Furness)[61]; St Catherine's Day (two oat-cakes and two herrings to each of one hundred poor at Newminster)[62]. In time for winter (at Martinmas, 11 November) clothing was distributed at Melrose (1320)[63]. Lent was a particular season for charity at Bonnevaux[64], and, throughout the Order, that great day of Christian charity, Maundy Thursday, was marked by the washing in the cloister of the feet of as many poor people as there were monks in the monastery; each also received a piece of silver[65]. Supplementary alms were given on this day at many houses, as at Combe, Merevale and Stoneleigh (money, bread, beer and herrings)[66] as well as Tintern[67] and Zwettl[68]. So great was the crush of the poor outside the gate of Fontfroide on Maundy Thursday in 1322, that people were stifled to death[69].

Lay Hospitals (Secular Infirmaries)

Only a small fraction of the sick, aged and poor, could be allowed within the gates of a monastery, and these were housed in a purpose-built complex referred to as the 'hospice', 'hospital of the poor', or 'secular infirmary'. By the early thirteenth century these buildings were present in the larger monasteries throughout Europe, and in some cases replaced earlier edifices. A secular infirmary is on record at Warden by about 1180[70], and at Furness by about 1190[71]. One was founded at Fountains in 1199 and extended or re-built a few decades later[72]. A lay hospital was built at Alcobaça[73] and at Heiligenkreuz[74] about 1200, and new ones were built at Zwettl in 1218[75] and at Santes Creus by 1230[76]. Throughout the thirteenth century come frequent references to secular infirmaries, as at Staffarda (1234)[77] and Bonport (1248)[78]. Hiddensee had a hospital for the poor and the ship-wrecked[79]. At the nunnery of Bijloke in Ghent was the second largest medieval hospital ward in Europe[80]. The secular infirmary stood usually inside the monastic precincts – within the outer court[81]. Often it stood close to the abbey gate (as apparent at Fountains[82] and noted at Sibton[83] and Zwettl[84]), so that the inmates would not distract monastic life.

The inmates of such lay-hospitals were perhaps extremely poor (*penuriosa*: Heiligenkreuz, 1205)[85]; bed-ridden in part (*decumbentia*: Sibton, 1235)[86], and long-term residents (*stagiarii*: Sibton)[87]. There may have been some separate provision for those of better quality (like Gruffydd ap Gwenwynwyn at Strata Marcella[88] and Duke Henry the Lion at Loccum)[89], who may have expected a place consonant with their rank. The numbers of inmates were never very great. Zwettl (1218) could house thirty of the needy infirm[90], whilst Beaulieu (1270) gave food and shelter nightly to sixteen poor men[91]. The pressure on available places could be great (Sedlec, 1343)[92]. Dying patients might benefit the monastery in a will (Rivalta Scrivia, 1258–61)[93]. The infirmary refectory at Beaulieu had on great festivals to give meals to the monastery's grooms[94].

The monk or *conversus* in charge of the lay hospital was termed the *provisor* at Walkenried (1200)[95], the *master* at Châtelliers (1248)[96]. At Gimont (1206) he was a monk[97], at Villers (1220) a *conversus*[98]. When the hospital at Zwettl (1218) was founded ten attendants were envisaged[99], but the accounts of Beaulieu suggest a slim-line staff. Its *keeper* of the lay-hospital had every Monday morning to render his accounts at the weekly heads of department meeting. He also had to arrange the digging of the graves of dead inmates[100]. The *Usages* of the Order bade 'the monk of the hospital' treat all guests, whether poor or infirm, with equal solicitude. On Maundy Thursday it was his task to get ready those who were to have their feet washed in the cloister[101].

The account rolls of Beaulieu (1270) tell of the diet in its lay infirmary, whose inmates consumed broth prepared from gruel, herbs and vegetables, and received daily a measure of beer and a small white loaf. Meat was also served, clearly anticipating the General Chapter's licence of that year for it to be eaten in hospitals of the poor. It was primarily mutton or lamb and was served with beans and peas. Fish eaten included herring, cod, hake and mackerel – a reflection of Beaulieu's marine position and shipping interests. Hens (for eggs) and pigs were kept, and fed in part on dregs from the monastic brewery. Bowls, pitchers and dishes were bought, canvas and straw provided – presumably for bedding – and turf and firewood for cooking and to keep the inmates warm[102]. Father-abbots on visitation took an interest in the lay hospitals: Stephen Lexington inspecting Jerpoint (1228)[103] laid down that linen and better food be provided, and at St André-en-Gouffern (1232)[104] better bread.

The maintenance of a lay hospital was a considerable undertaking, and cost Beaulieu more than twice as much to run as did the monastic infirmary[105]. This care was met in part by income stemming from donations or bequests. These included grants of lands (as to Warden, *c.* 1180[106] and Bebenhausen, 1277)[107]; vineyards (Himmerod, 1307)[108]; churches and tithes (Valasse, 1203[109]; Sibton, 1263[110]); pasture for sheep (Meaux, *c.* 1240)[111]; rents (Michaelstein, 1218)[112], and bridge tolls, (Santes Creus, 1229)[113]. Salt was provided for Scharnebeck[114]. Lands were given to Villers (1231) to help shoe the poor[115]. There were also gifts of money – as to Santes Creus (1229) to help with clothing[116], and to Poblet (1263–68) for the upkeep of bedding[117]. Bonport had no less than twenty-four charters aiding the work of its lay hospital[118]. Newminster[119] and Stanley[120] had practically-minded benefactors who endowed a lamp in their hospitals. Some grants were aimed at increasing the potential number of inmates (Vyšší Brod, 1347)[121].

Nor was spiritual provision neglected: larger secular infirmaries came to have their own chapel, as at Furness[122], Zwettl[123], and Margam[124]. The infirmary chapel at Poblet was dedicated to St Catherine[125], and at Sibton to St John the Baptist[126]. At Santes Creus (1229) a donor, wishing to be buried in the portal of the lay hospital, made a bequest for the erection of an altar of St Peter in its chapel[127]. Earlier the General Chapter had discouraged the saying of Mass in such chapels, even ordering the blocking of the entrance to the hospital chapel of Stürzelbronn (1205), and enjoining its poor to hear Mass in the guest-house chapel[128]. Daily Mass was instituted in the hospital chapel of Waverley in 1228[129], and, that year, a chalice and other necessities were provided for the hospital chapel at the Dunes, possibly just built[130]. Arnsburg (1278) received a grant to maintain the sanctuary light in its chapel[131].

Some secular infirmaries were sited at a little distance from the monastery. This may have been because of local need, or to keep infectious diseases at arm's length. It is possible that some external hospitals catered for lepers, the General Chapter (1204) having ordered that they were not to live near abbeys of the Order[132]. (The fear of leprosy forbade the reception of the diseased into the community [1191–1205][133], and the leper house at Bruges once issued a certificate that a monk of the Dunes did not have the disease[134].) Monasteries with lay hospitals on one or more of their granges included Moreruela (1208)[135], Casanova (1254)[136], and Zwettl[137]. Aiguebelle's hospital at Roussas was 1½ leagues from the abbey[138]. In Wales, Tintern's lay-hospital (its 'Secular Farmer') and Neath's (Cwrt-y-clafdy) both lay over a mile away[139]. Beaubec built an external infirmary by St Lô near Rouen[140]. Clairvaux was given a leper-house at Lanty (1216)[141]; Villers (1224) took over that at Ter-Banck which served Louvain[142]; Hore (1272), previously Benedictine, inherited a leper-house on incorporation[143]. Alcobaça cared for lepers on its grange at Gafa[144], Grace Dieu (1256) at Benon in Saintonge[145]. Igny bought distinctive clothing for the lepers of the neighbourhood[146]. The lepers of Douvaine looked to Aulps (1314) for help[147]. Whitland may have cared for lepers at St Leonard's chapel, in a healthy situation by the Tywi estuary[148].

The reputation of the Cistercians for their care of the sick and poor meant that a number of hospitals were put under their supervision, or even built with that purpose in mind. Such grants of hospitals, usually accompanied with their assets, might prove attractive to a monastery. Sallay (1174) received an allegedly ill-managed hospital at Tadcaster, the brethren who ran it agreeing to adopt Cistercian rule[149]. Pforta (1193), given a hospital in Erford, inherited brethren who entered into spiritual fraternity with the Order[150]. Later the citizens of Erford (1212) were far from happy when the abbot demolished the hall of the hospital and discontinued Mass in its chapel[151]. Given another hospital, the Magdalen at Naumburg, Pforta withdrew, feeling the work contrary to the ethos of the contemplative life[152]. Gregory IX gave to Požega a hospital in Bačka, and requested that two of its *conversi* 'suitable for the work'[153] take over one founded by the bishop of Kalocsa (1234)[154]. A bishop of Patras (1273) gave a band of two monks and two *conversi* custody of a hospital he had newly built[155].

A hospital of the Order of the Holy Ghost was given 'with its assets' to Michaelstein (1218)[156]. A hospital was erected near the cloister at Žďár (1273) with an 'old woman' as *rectrix*[157]. Queen Blanche of Aragon, building a hospital at Fortis del Perelló, sought 'a good and circumspect' *conversus* of Santes Creus as its keeper[158]. Some hospitals doubled up as pilgrim hospices: 'poor pilgrims' could stay at Chorin's two external hospitals (Bardsin and Oderberg, 1258)[159], and at Volkenrode's hospital of St George in Salza (1272)[160]. A new hospice for the sick and poor at Port-Saint-Ouen was put under the supervision of Bonport (1293)[161]. Kamieniec had such hospices at Wrocław, Świdnice, Nysie, and Kłodz[162]. Other Cistercian-managed hospitals included those in Cree (run by Dundrennan), in Seaford (by Robertsbridge)[163], and in Goslar (by Walkenried, Riddagshausen, and the dean of Goslar)[164].

It is not certain whether the sick and poor in Cistercian lay hospitals received any real medical attention, or simply care and shelter. The accounts of Beaulieu would seem to suggest the latter. There were medical men amongst the ranks of both monks and *conversi*, including the Cistercian Cardinal John of Toledo (*c.* 1255) – both a medical writer and papal physician[165]. Religious who had gained medical skills before entering the Order sought to put them to good effect, and the General Chapter (1157, 1175) had to forbid qualified monks and *conversi* from going out at night to treat the sick or give them medicine[166]. Cistercian writers came to distinguish between those medical monks who kept the rules of the Order, and those vain ones who did not[167]. Caesarius of Heisterbach told of one monk who was constantly at the call of the sick, to the neglect of his monastic vocation[168]. Gerald of Wales attacked both black and white monks who set themselves up as physicians – allegedly without medical skills, and sometimes with disastrous results[169]. One monk of San Galgano (1255) was described as being a surgeon[170]. Alcobaça[171] and Casamari[172] came to have noted pharmacies. The monks of Alcobaça[173], Écharlis[174], and Fontaines-les-Blanches[175] sought out local mineral waters.

Corrodians

Permanent guests were the corrodians, who for past services rendered or for financial help afforded, had been granted a 'corrody' or 'exhibition' or 'livery' by a particular abbey[176]. The Council of Oxford (1222) frowned on the practice[177], and not all corrodies granted by British Cistercian houses that century were full corrodies. A true corrody consisted of residence within the walls, regular meals and drink, heat and light, and sometimes other benefits – as clothing, shaving, laundering, tailoring, and stabling. The provision afforded varied with the down-payment made (if any) and with the rank and class of the recipient. A true corrody was for life, and was conveyed by letters patent attested by the common seal. It was a way in which long-time servants might be pensioned off, or other lay-people find a retirement home, their grant or down-payment being an insurance policy for their old age. For the abbey concerned, it could be a means of obtaining substantial lands, or ready cash when needed, or both[178].

Early corrodies, of the late twelfth century, were granted by Furness to William Gever, who gave a half carucate of land in return for the monks 'caring for my soul and providing for old age', and to Warin the Little and his wife who 'becoming very decrepit' gave land which formed the nucleus of Beaumont Grange[179]. In the thirteenth century grants do not always specify residence – though Dore (1263) allowed Walter de Homeness a corrody 'in its walls'[180], and Furness (1264) gave Adam de Merton 'food and clothing in the convent'[181]. A knight (Geoffrey de Brachefort), who provided the second site of Vaudey, was rewarded with food and clothing for his wife, himself, and two servants, for their lives – with a certain class distinction: 'Geoffrey and his wife to receive the same food as the monks, the servants the same as the *conversi*'[182]. Residence near the monastery is implied, though perhaps not within the precincts. Three lady benefactors of Margam (1241–1320) received daily or weekly rations of food and drink, but without apparent residence[183]. At Arnsburg (1253) a benefactor received substantial quantities each year of cereals, fish, and cloth, as well as money; the amounts were to be reduced on the death of his wife[184]. At Pforta (1292) a knightly benefactor received daily, for life, supplies of bread, ale, cheese, herrings, and pottage for himself and his servant; residence is implied but uncertain[185]. The provisions made by Quarr (1300) to Walter de Blackland allowed residence in the monastery, but his entitlement (bread, beer and pottage, daily) applied 'wherever he might be, within or without the Island' (Isle of Wight). Shoes, gown, pittance, turf and firewood were also afforded him, as well as a silver mark yearly[186].

In the early fourteenth century came further evidence of residential corrodies – as the 'prebendaries' of Hautcrêt (1299–1319)[187] and Monthéron (1323 on)[188]. The former included a woman who was bedded out in a convent at Maudon. Setting the scene for general practice later in England, Sibton gave three grants of corrody in 1323 alone[189]. One was residential ('a chamber within the close of the lay infirmary'), the other two were to chaplains whose abode is uncertain. All three corrodians paid the abbey in advance for their 'corrody or livery', the monastery benefiting in total by £70. The food provisions included bread, ale and herrings[190]. At Meaux (c. 1350) a burgess of Hull brought with him his chaplain and his servant, but (together with the sale of two other corrodies) the monastery benefited by £110[191].

In England most is known at this period of the 'royal' corrodians, imposed on a house by the king claiming rights because of its royal foundation or benefaction. The practice of Henry III (1271) in endeavouring to place aged or sick retainers in a monastery[192], gained momentum in the reign of Edward I. It was resented because there was no concurrent grant of land or financial aid: the corrody was an absolute charge on the abbey and a drain on its resources. The monarch rarely claimed more than one place in any house, but careful records were kept, and when one such corrodian died the Crown was not slow to find a replacement. So Edward II sent a royal servant to Buckfast (1325) 'in place of William de Brigstwyt, deceased'[193], and Edward III to Robertsbridge (1348) 'instead of Thomas Breton, deceased'[194]. A succession of corrodians can thus be traced at Pipewell (1310–30)[195]. Such retiring royal servants were often said to have 'long served the king, faithfully and well' (Rufford, 1307[196]; Croxden, 1318[197]). They included royal officials of lesser rank, such as 'the king's scullion' (Pipewell, 1310)[198], 'the king's cook' (Stratford, 1317)[199], 'the king's messenger' (Stoneleigh, 1330)[200], and 'the king's yeoman' (Robertsbridge, 1348)[201]. Buckfast (1325) received a royal huntsman who had been 'maimed in the king's last hunt in the New Forest'[202]. Henry III (1255) had sought, unsuccessfully, to settle Jewish 'converts' at religious houses including Dore and Tintern[203].

A monastery might be expected to make substantial provision for 'royal' corrodians. It had to be worthy of the retiring official: 'according to the requirements of his estate' (Vaudey, 1310[204]; Croxden, 1318[205]). He might be accompanied by one or more grooms[206], and these also had to be catered for. The royal missive might simply demand for the pensioner 'the necessities of life in food and clothing', or spell out precise requirements. When John de Sutton, Edward II's cook, was sent to Stratford (1317) he was to receive not only 'food and clothing, two robes yearly, and a chamber in the monastery', but also maintenance for two attendant grooms and two horses, as well as 'candles, litter, firewood, and other necessaries'[207]. Such demands led houses to avoid too great a burden. Henry III promised Stanley (1271) that it need take one 'exhibitioner' only[208], and a similar promise was made to Warden (1272)[209]. Some monasteries resisted such royal impositions, and, to ensure that they complied, the Crown letters of commendation insisted that a monastery write back to the king stating what had been arranged[210]. A 'royal' corrodian sent to Coggeshall (1299) received only food from the monks, and the king had to press for clothes and shoe-leather to be given him[211]. When Edward II sent David Gough to Aberconwy (1315) armed with his royal grant, the monks replied that they could not comply because they had fallen on bad times[212]. An abbot of Boxley (1331), summoned before the King's Bench for refusing to admit a royal servant, successfully produced charters upholding his case[213]. Edward III (1335) excused Dore from providing corrodies because of its abbot's 'great labours' in royal service[214].

Hired Servants

The white monks realised, early on, that as well as the labour of *conversi*, the assistance of paid 'mercenaries' was also necessary. This is made clear in the *Exordium Parvum* written soon after 1134[215]. These employees worked in the fields and craft buildings, later still in the domestic quarters. It is clear from the provision made for their diet (meat was allowed them)[216], and from their reception of the last rites and burial[217], that some at least were resident within the walls or on the granges. They worked the same number of days as did the *conversi*[218], finished work early on the eve of great festivals, and had rest periods in summer when the working-day stretched from dawn to dusk[219]. Restrictions came to be placed on their admission: they were not to be 'suspicious persons' (1230)[220], nor were they to be blood-relatives of a member of the monastic community (1195)[221], and they had to be at least twelve years old (1195)[222]. The Order tried to keep its servants at a distance from the daily routine of the monastery, but the regulations were neither absolute nor enduring. Lay servants were forbidden to work in the guest-hall (1152) – unless there was a large number of guests; they were not to wait on the abbot's table – unless the needs of guests demanded it (1181)[223]. They were forbidden duties in the kitchens and infirmaries of the monks and *conversi* (1189)[224] (a rule sometimes breached)[225] until the numbers of *conversi* declined. The restriction on kitchen work was mitigated in 1237[226] and 1257[227], and in 1274 abandoned completely[228]. The number of servants varied: Poblet, at one stage, had 60 – seemingly Moorish prisoners – compared with 92 monks and 55 *conversi*[229]; Bordesley (1332) 17 compared with 34 monks and 7 *conversi*[230].

The thirteenth century saw hired servants occupying important posts, including (at Kingswood, 1256) those of baker, brewer, and miller – each a position once held by a *conversus*, and each now attracting its own rate of pay. Casual labour was needed at seed-time and harvest, and all told the monastery expended some £80 on its servants' wages[231]. At Beaulieu (1270) there was also casual labour, but many workers were semi-permanent, the winter harrowers doubling up as summer marlers, and the reapers both sowing the corn and harvesting it. Higher summer than winter pay reflected the longer hours then worked[232]. The accounts of Beaulieu make clear a gradation amongst its resident workers: servants, grooms, and pages, in that order of importance. The grooms (over forty of them perhaps)[233] were based in the stables, but ate on greater feasts in the lay hospital. The pages were their assistants. All Beaulieu's workers had a special meal on Shrove Tuesday, before the Lenten fast commenced[234]. Payment of servants could be in kind. Warden (1185) gave one labourer two loaves a day for looking after its crops and pastures[235]. Contracts survive for two servants of Newenham (1249, 1280). The first worker (probably a widower) gave land to the abbey and entered its service, the monastery undertaking to keep his three sons also in its employ until they became of age, and to find his daughter a place outside the walls[236]. The second labourer separated from his wife, who went to live with their married daughter in Axminster[237]. Both were perhaps 'familiars' rather than hired servants. A 'free sergeant', a leading servant, appointed by Margam (1325) gave the abbey lands in Kenfig and received a stipend as well as food[238].

Guests and Guest-houses

Prince Llywelyn of Wales (1199) noted in a charter to Aberconwy that 'it behoves the monks to give food and lodging to travellers and guests'[239], whilst Gerald of Wales told how the white monks 'incessantly exercise, more than any others, the acts of charity and beneficence towards the poor and strangers'[240]. The *Rule of St Benedict* had dictated that 'all who arrive as guests are to be welcomed like Christ'[241]. Resident visitors were accommodated in a purpose-built complex, the guest-house or hospice, set apart from the conventual buildings – so as not to interfere with monastic calm. It was often close to the gate-house, the point of entry[242]. That at Bonlieu stood on the bank of a pond[243], that of Staffarda by a bridge[244], those of Fountains by the river Skell[245]. Guests were also lodged on the granges. As early as the mid-twelfth century the Empress Matilda constructed two large guest-houses at Mortemer[246], and by 1187 Kołbacz had a hospice for 'rich and poor'[247]. Note was made at Boyle (1202) of 'the great stone house of the guests'[248]. At Kingswood a new one was being built in 1242[249]. The guest-halls at Buckfast[250] and Kirkstall[251] were extended in the late thirteenth century.

The Buckfast hospice was of considerable size (115 feet x 35 feet) and had a lead-pipe water-supply[252]; that at Kirkstall was built around a small courtyard, and excavation has uncovered something of the drainage plan[253]. The hospice at Vaux-de-Cernay comprised refectory, dorter, and infirmary[254]. The complex at Vauclair included kitchen, cool-house, and fish-pond[255]. Armorial floor tiles have been found in the hospice of Pilis[256]. Stables for guests' horses were noted at Kingswood (1263)[256]. At the annual visitation the guest-house was inspected – as at Lilienfeld (1316) when better provision of bedding was suggested[257]. Guests probably heard Mass in the gate-house chapel, but Orval had its own guest-house chapel (dedicated to St Marguerite)[258], and a 'chapel for the guests' was built at Hauterive by Abbot Guy (1268–95)[259].

The guest-house was the responsibility of the monk designated as guest-master, and he was assisted by at least one *conversus*[260]. The names of some are known: 'hostilars' included Miguel Sanchez at Rueda (1308)[261]; Lambert (1306) and later Berthold (1336) were 'guest-masters' at Doberan[262]; Jacob was 'provisor' of the hospice at Velehrad (1232–34)[263]. Sometimes, *conversi* took charge – as at Coggeshall (*c.* 1190, a visionary)[264], and Barbeaux (1220, an insolent character)[265]. Contrariwise, a knight-turned-monk guest-master at Himmerod (Walter, d. 1222) won others to the religious life by his affability and tact[266]. In the early years lay-servants were discouraged in guest-houses unless there were more guests than usual (1152)[267], but by 1264 boy-servants were an accepted fact in the hospice of Furness[268].

When a guest arrived, the porter sent a message to the abbot, and on his approval, the visitor was escorted to the church for prayer and then to the guest-house, to be received by the guest-master with a deep bow or complete prostration[269] – the marks of humility demanded by the *Rule*[270]. At night a sconce might be used to give light for the reading of the formal sentences of welcome[271]. The guest-master decided who ate when and where, and who slept where, and aided by two brothers he washed the hands and feet of the guests at the time of the weekly maundy in the monastery[272]. At Beaulieu the type of persons who could be received, the food they would eat, and the length of their stay, were all carefully laid down in writing[273]. Relatives could make a two-day visit three or four times a year: if they remained longer they had to care for themselves[274]. Sometimes parents or families of monks exceeded their stay by far and had to be asked to leave[275].

Monks and *conversi* serving at the guest tables were to speak only if absolutely necessary (1258)[276], and the diet was a disciplined one. No meat was served[277]: even visiting legates had to be content with Cistercian fare[278]. Guests were, however, supplied with white (better-quality) bread[279]. In Advent and on fast-days they were to have the same 'Lenten fare' as the monks[280]. No butter, cheese or eggs were allowed on Fridays and other customary fast-days[281], but in 1276 milk products were permitted on Ember Days and vigils[282], whilst at Sibton (1323) the guests came to have a different diet from the community on fast-days[283]. In the earlier years, before abbots came to have their own establishment, they generally ate in the hospice with the guests, but they were not to dawdle over their meals[284]. Gervase, the first abbot of Louth Park, as he approached death confessed in his *Lamentations* how he had eaten 'sumptuously with the guests while his brethren were famishing with hunger in the refectory'[285].

The accounts for Beaulieu (1270) give a picture of its guest-house[286]. Nobles, ecclesiastics, and others of distinction were entertained there. 'Decent' travellers of lesser rank who arrived 'by the third hour of the day' remained perhaps only to eat; those coming after lunch stayed the night. In addition, the guest-house gave shelter each night to thirteen poor people selected by the porter. Hospitality was also afforded from Christmas Eve until after dinner on St Stephen's Day to as many poor people as there were monks in the monastery. There was provision for feeding women relatives, and other ladies who could not be refused without causing offence, though it is not clear where they ate. In Beaulieu's guest-house there was class distinction in the grades of bread and beer provided to the different ranking guests, as also in the type of broth, and the frequency of pittances of fish, butter and cheese. Only guests of rank, dining with the abbot, could have wine served to them. Herring was the common fish eaten, but cod, eels, mackerel, ling, hake, and salmon – for the more important guests – were also served. The accounts mention gruel, salt, and honey, and refer to bedding, towels, turf, firewood, and straw. The poor guests on leaving could take with them any bread left over, but grooms were not to take drink to the stables.

The duty of hospitality could be a heavy burden, costing Vale Royal (1336) nearly one-quarter of its gross annual income[287]. The guests at Savigny (1232) ate as much bread as was consumed by twenty monks[288]. At Beaulieu the food and drink consumed in its guest-house in 1270 included 12,500 loaves of 'hospice bread' and 7,500 of better-grade 'convent bread', 8,640 gallons of good beer and 6,000 of 'mixed beer', and the greater part of 900,000 herrings, as well as 1,600 mackerel and 850 hake[289]. Several monasteries referred to the demands such hospitality made upon their resources. The monks of Doberan (1269) carried 'a most heavy burden of costs and expenses on account of guests and travellers'[290]. This was always true of monasteries adjacent to well-travelled routeways[291]. Margam (1336), on a coastal route to Ireland, grumbled that 'being on the high road, and far from other places of refuge, the abbey is constantly over-run by rich and poor strangers'[292]. No small number of mariners expected hospitality at Bindon (1348) – close to Poole Harbour[293] – and Netley (1338) – adjacent to Southampton Water[294]. Huntsmen frequented the Cheshire abbeys of Combermere and Vale Royal (1331)[295], Altzelle in Germany, and Lubiąż in Silesia (1280)[296], where, the monks said, they were 'as hungry as wolves'[297].

The provision of hospitality was met in part by grants and benefactions. The General Chapter (1190), trying to restrict undue acquisition of lands, excepted instances where such were necessary to meet the expenses of hospitality[298]. When times were difficult monasteries might successfully petition the Chapter for permission not to receive guests for a fixed term, usually one, two, or three years[299]. The count of Geneva freed Tamié (1191), which stood on a major routeway, from all tolls and taxes because of 'its custom of giving hospitality to voyagers'[300]. A bishop of Schwerin granted a forty-days indulgence to those supporting the guest-house of Doberan (1269)[301]. Sibton (1240) received grants of tithes to help its work of hospitality[302], as well as a grant for 'utensils and cloth' to help with the reception of guests 'converging there'[303]. Flaxley received rents for income to mend the bed-clothes of poor guests, and to repair its hospice[304].

A mixed bag, a motley crowd, could be found in Cistercian guest-houses. No wonder that Gerald of Wales (c. 1204) complained about 'the noise of the people' in the hospice at Strata Florida. There could be unpleasant incidents. A young man was killed in a brawl in the 'guesten-hall' of Margam (c. 1180)[305], whilst visiting grooms stabbed guests to death during stable-brawls at Furness (1246)[306] and Croxden (1273)[307]. A mob destroyed the guest-house at Zbraslav (1308)[308]. Little wonder that Cistercian houses were ordered not to give hospitality or provisions to warriors (1157)[309], and Savigniac houses enjoined 'not to keep any suspicious person or dangerous substance'[310]. Also prohibited as guests were hostages held as prisoners on behalf of nobles (1275)[311].

The customary of Cîteaux ordered the guest-master to treat kindly 'all guests whether sick or poor'[312]. The guest-house at Kołbacz (1278) was said to be a place where 'many benefits are disbursed to the nobles and the common people, to rich and poor'[313], but there was class distinction. At Beaulieu the guests were graded at the gate-house, and those arriving on horse-back were kept separate from those coming on foot, and given preferential hospitality[314]. Gerald of Wales objected to being treated as an ordinary traveller at Strata Florida, and at being placed 'in the public hall among the common guests'[315]. At Salem (1300) there were two guest-masters, one to look after the 'decent folk', the other to care for the 'lower guests'[316]. At Sorø (1347) there were 'guests, greater and lesser'[317]. At Sibton (1323) a corrodian ate in the guest refectory 'with the better sort of people'[318]. Discrimination was perhaps reflected in the accommodation provided, as seemingly at Fountains[319], Savigny[320], and Tintern[321].

The more important guests included royalty. In Wales, after the death of Prince Llywelyn the Last (1282), some of his chattels were found at Cymer. He being dead, and Wales conquered, it was Edward I of England who stayed for some time at Aberconwy[322]. A frequent visitor to Cistercian houses throughout his kingdom he was, during his Scottish campaign, at Holm Cultram the day before he died[323]. Other English monarchs visiting houses of the Order included John and Richard II, who both encamped with their troops at Margam *en route* to, and returning from, Ireland[324]. John and Edward III visited Flaxley whilst hunting in the Forest of Dean[325]. Henry III, at the head of his army, called at Robertsbridge and extorted a large sum of money[326], whilst at Stratford he received the papal legate[327]. A most assiduous monastic visitor was Louis IX of France (St Louis) who, when calling at his own foundation of Royaumont, would visit the sick monks and even help serve the community in the refectory[328]. Emperor Frederick II stayed at Ferrara whilst journeying to, and from, the Holy Land[329]. Margrave Přemysl of Moravia stayed at Velehrad, issuing charters there[330]. Monarchs and prelates were received with dignity. A Cistercian community went out to meet them in procession with lights, thurible and holy water preceding them[331].

Hospitality to monarchs and their retinue was a mixed blessing, but some good could result. King John excused Margam from a heavy tax imposed upon other abbeys of the Order[332]. Henry III visiting Fountains presented it with wine, and gave twenty oak trees to Croxden on calling there[333]. Visiting Combermere he granted the abbey the right to hold a market and fair on its manor at Drayton ('Market Drayton' today)[334]. Not all royal visits were happy ones. King Sverker of Sweden was murdered on Christmas Day 1156 by his stable-boy, whilst on a visit to Alvastra[335]. In later years, a rumour spread that King John had died (1216) not from dysentery, but from being poisoned by the monks of Swineshead where he had just stayed[336]. A royal stay might be facilitated by special accommodation, like that built by Edward I at Stanley (1290)[337], and Kings Peter III (1276–85) and James II (1291–1327) of Aragon at Santes Creus[338].

Monasteries formed useful meeting-places for kings and others. The closing sessions of the Synod of Kells (1152), which divided Ireland into ecclesiastical provinces, took place at Mellifont[339]. After Dublin became the Anglo-Norman capital of Ireland (1171), the parliament and privy council might meet in the chapter-house of St Mary's Abbey[340]. At Poblet (1228) James I of Castile planned the conquest of Majorca[341]. At Strata Florida (1238) Prince Llywelyn the Great called together the Welsh princes to ensure the succession of his eldest son, David[342]. At Stratford (1267) Henry III made peace with the Barons, following their revolt[343]. At Boulbonne (1272) Philip III of France and James I of Aragon discussed peace terms[344]. At Ås (1286) a meeting took place between Norwegian and Danish protagonists after the murder of King Erik of Denmark[345].

Papal visitors included Innocent II (1131) and Eugenius III (1148)[346] at Clairvaux, and Clement V at Bonnefont (1308–09)[347]. Again, a large retinue had to be entertained. When Innocent III dedicated the high altar at Fossanova (1208) he arrived with a party of two hundred – their horses also needed fodder[348]. Alexander IV (1259) insisted that Cistercian abbeys should receive papal legates and nuncios and their diocesan bishop, notwithstanding any previous privileges to the contrary[349]. Papal representatives were led on arrival into the church and chapter-house and greeted

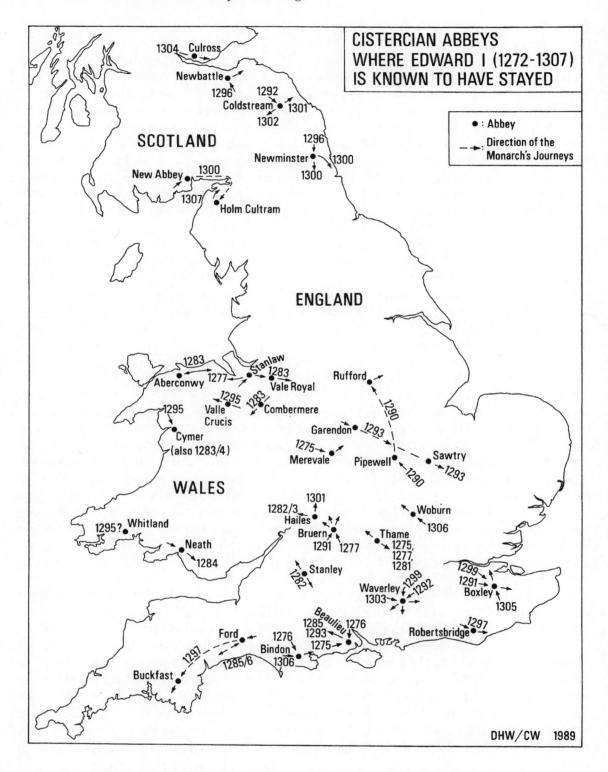

CISTERCIAN ABBEYS
WHERE EDWARD I (1272-1307)
IS KNOWN TO HAVE STAYED

● : Abbey
- - -→ : Direction of the Monarch's Journeys

1304 Culross
Newbattle
1296   1292
   Coldstream ● 1301
        1302
SCOTLAND   1296
           Newminster ● 1300
New Abbey ● 1300
        1307
         ● Holm Cultram

ENGLAND

1283   Stanlaw
   1277   ● 1283   Rufford
Aberconwy   Vale Royal
     1295 1283 Combermere
1295   Valle
        Crucis   Garendon 1293
Cymer   1275 →   Sawtry
(also 1283/4)   Merevale Pipewell 1293
                              1290
WALES
                   1301
                1282/3   Woburn
          Hailes   1306
1295? Whitland Bruern →   Thame
              1291 1277   1275,
Neath   1277,
   1284   Stanley   1281
            1282   Waverley 1299   1299
                     1303   1292   1291
                          Boxley   1305
                    Beaulieu
              Ford 1285 1276   1297
         1276 1293   Robertsbridge
         Bindon 1275
1297   1285/6 1306
Buckfast

DHW/CW   1989

with a blessing; non-Cistercian bishops were conducted to the guest-house after a formal welcome and not to the cloister. Only a pope could be received solemnly more than once[350]. There was accommodation for visiting diocesan bishops at, or close by, Løgum, Øm and Sorø[351]. Bishop Guy of Noyon (1278) had a house within the precincts of Ourscamp where he could escape from the pressures of the world[352].

Guests admitted to the cloister were mainly visiting abbots and monks of the Order, especially numerous in houses closest to Cîteaux and the General Chapter. It was the duty of the monastic wardrobe-keeper to place a cowl, habit and socks at the beds provided for such fellow religious[353]. Houses adjacent to routeways were also prone to a number of Cistercian visitors. The abbot of Whitland (like Margam, on a coastal route to Ireland), obtained a decree (1220) limiting the free stay of Irish and English abbots to fifteen days[354]. Margam's guests in these years had included Abbots Gregory of Mellifont and Isaiah of Jerpoint[355]. Not all Cistercian abbots visiting their brethren were well received[356]; English, Welsh and Scottish houses, being singled out in this respect (1219)[357]. An abbot of St Mary's, Dublin, was rebuked at Chapter (1199) because he did not wish bishops and abbots in his house[358]. Eventually (1287) the General Chapter limited the stay of travelling abbots to two nights[359]. Another group of religious who had to be made welcome were monks from dispersed communities (1282)[360]. A monastery with twenty monks was bound to receive one displaced religious; a house with forty monks, two; and so on up to a maximum of five refugees (1315)[361]. Many houses will have had one or two religious dismissed from their own monastery for some serious offence. Nor were religious of other Orders turned away, and, in especial, Premonstratensian canons were ordered to be honourably received (1281)[362].

Pilgrims and Shrines

An important component among the visitors in a Cistercian guest-house might well be pilgrims[363]. Pilgrims might call for an over-night stay *en route* to their destination, or be attracted by a well-known shrine or famed relic held at a monastery, or by indulgences promised to those who visited an abbey and gave alms towards its maintenance. No less than fifty-one British bishops made a grant of indulgence in favour of Furness[364]. No fewer than ten bishops (the bishop of Prague leading the way in 1270) granted forty days or more indulgence to those visiting Vyšší Brod on the anniversary of the dedication of its church and on specific feasts of Our Lady[365]. Similar indulgences (often adding the feast of St Bernard) were granted to a number of houses[366]. Innocent IV gave an especial indulgence in favour of Bonport (1244) for the feast of the Assumption[367]. Specific needs might be cited in a grant of indulgence, e.g. the upkeep of the monastery buildings (St Benoit-en-Woëvre, 1257)[368]; the building of a new church and cloister (Fontguilhem, 1309)[369]; or renovation following a disastrous fire (Llantarnam, 1398)[370]. External monastic chapels might also attract pilgrims, e.g. St Margaret's by Neath[371], St Volcmar's of Michaelstein[372], and St Mary-by-the-Sea next to Cleeve[373].

As for relics and 'miraculous' images, there is some evidence that these were not always genuine, but fulfilled a need for hard-pressed communities to attract pilgrims and thereby obtain additional finance[374]. Pride of place went to relics of the Holy Cross, which accounted for the names of certain abbeys: Holy Cross[375], and perhaps Heiligenkreuz and Keresztúr[376]. (Santes Creus owed its name, however, to the several crosses placed to delimit its first site)[377]. Royaumont was dedicated to the Holy Cross, St Louis having given it a considerable portion[378]. Nobles returning from the Crusades gave relics of the Cross to Dore[379], Perseigne[380] and Wilhering[381]. A relic of 'the wood of God' was inserted at its dedication into the high altar of Fiume (1196)[382]. Ownership of a relic of 'the Wood of the Cross' caused a dispute between Poblet and the cathedral chapter of Lérida (1247)[383]. Other abbeys claiming such a relic included La Boissière[384] and Strata Marcella[385]. There were altars dedicated to the Holy Cross at Engelszell[386], Neath[387] and Sorø[388]. A late twelfth century writing emanating from Nepomuk contains a legendary tale about the Holy Cross[389]. 'Miraculous' crosses attracted pilgrims to Aduard[390], Meaux[391] and Mogiła[392]; Boxley had a weeping statue of Christ on its rood-loft[393]. Other relics connected with Our Lord included the Precious Blood at Hailes[394] and the Holy Shroud at Cadouin[395]. Zlatá Koruna took its name from a spine of the Crown of Thorns given it by St Louis[396]. The Corpus Christi altar at Doberan witnessed eucharistic manifestations, and was also a place of pilgrimage to the 'Holy Blood'[397].

A number of abbeys had 'miraculous' images of the Blessed Virgin Mary, as Cambron (profaned by a Jew in 1322)[398], Écharlis[399] and Meaux (in their gate-houses)[400], and Tintern (in its Galilee porch)[401]. The multitude trying to observe the image of Our Lady at Meaux in 1361 was such that 'many were brought to death by reason of the crush'[402]. Cîteaux received from Daphni in Greece an arm of St John the Baptist[403]; Osek had one of his fingers[404]. Fossanova gave a fore-arm from the body of St Thomas Aquinas to the Dominicans[405]. More localised Cistercian shrines, with liturgical observance in their house, included those of St Robert, first abbot of Newminster[406], Bl. Maurice at L'Arrivour[407], and the holy martyrs Faustus and Eustachius at La Prée[408]. The mid-thirteenth century was significant in this outpouring of devotion; the treasured possession of relics came much earlier. Newbattle (*c.* 1170) enclosed its relics in a silver chest[409]. An abbot of Zinna (1195) sent out monks and *conversi* begging with relics[410]. Jurors determining the boundaries of a forest swore on the relics of Melrose (1184)[411]. Deeds were attested on 'the relics of Margam' (1235)[412]. External shrines owned included one honouring St Leonard at Fürstenfeld[413], whilst St Benoît-en-Woëvre had a shrine at Ansoncourt Grange[414], and Bégard one on Maudez Island[415].

Pilgrims from afar came to the shrine of St Edmund Rich at Pontigny, which had also a chapel dedicated to St Thomas Becket[416]. Both archbishops had been refugees there for a time. St Edmund Rich was buried at the monastery in 1240[417], and after his canonisation St Louis attended the solemn translation of his remains (1247)[418]. Despite his earlier differences with the saint, Henry III of England gave gifts[419] and visited the shrine himself (1254)[420], as did a stream of Englishmen[421]. So great was the crowd, especially of women, that about 1249 an arm was separated from the body and placed in a reliquary to be venerated at the monastery gate; some said that after this mutilation miracles became fewer[422]. St Edmund's Day (16 November) was observed throughout the Order[423]. Alms were collected in England for the shrine, but some collectors were fraudulent[424].

Pilgrims might be attracted to monasteries by the reputation of miracles wrought there. There were sufficient of these reported by the 1180 to form the basis of the *Book of Visions and Miracles* compiled by Herbert of Clairvaux[425]. There were traditions of blind monks regaining their sight at Dieulacres[426] and Melrose[427], and of healing miracles at tombs – including those of Roger of Élan (*c.* 1170)[428] and of Matilda de Bohun at Dore (1318)[429]. Miracles worked at Cambron (1331) by Our Lady on the third Sunday after Easter were later commemorated by a procession on that day[430]. In Wales, the fame of healing wells drew pilgrims. Most frequented were St Winefride's Well (belonging to Basingwerk) and St Mary's Well (the property of Llantarnam). Three other Welsh Cistercian abbeys had their *Ffynnon Fair* ('Mary's Well')[431].

Refugees, and Sanctuary

Several prelates in political difficulties took refuge in Cistercian houses, as notably three archbishops of Canterbury at Pontigny, all at variance with their monarch: Thomas Becket (1166–66), living there a life of austerity[432]; Stephen Langton (1207–13), refused entry to England after his consecration[433]; and Edmund Rich (1234–40), who found there his last resting-place[434]. Becket's name was added (in

1214) to the Cistercian Litany of the Saints[435], and a relic of his clothing was inserted in the high altar of Fiume (1196)[436]. Archdeacon Gerald of Wales (*c.* 1205) told how he often retreated to Strata Florida 'in the hour of violent persecution'[437]. Bishop Everard of Norwich, in disfavour with Henry I, fled to Fontenay (1134) and financially aided the building of its church[438]. A bishop of Cremona, forced to leave his see city during civil strife, found sanctuary at far-away Aduard (*c.* 1295–98) and consecrated its infirmary chapel[439].

Secular foes, too, might retreat to a monastery. King John noted that the Welsh abbey at Strata Florida 'harbours our enemies' (1212), and Henry III said of a grange of Cwmhir that it was 'a refuge for Welshmen to fly to'[440]. So far as both political foes and run-of-the-mill criminals were concerned, the proverbial forty days was the limit to the protection ecclesiastical sanctuary gave[441]. This became clear when Richard Marshall took refuge at Flaxley (1234) and an armed watch surrounded the monastery walls[442]. Monasteries might give asylum to thieves (Bruern, 1266), even murderers (Louth Park, 1279)[443]. The right to harbour criminals might be challenged by secular or royal authority[444], or even be actively violated (Waverley, 1240)[445]. Some abbeys had more specific and wider rights of sanctuary within a defined area, 'chartered sanctuary'[446]. This was true in England of the Great Close of Beaulieu[447] and, in Wales, of Neath, bounded by its 'sanctuary wall' (1700)[448].

Prisons, and Prisoners

There were 'guests' held involuntarily: prisoners detained in the gate-house cells. Substantial remains exist of the medieval prison at Villers whose dungeons, each with its own latrine, overlooked the channel bounding the abbey. A gate-house prison has been postulated at Bordesley[449], and there are traces of the secular prison at Clairmarais[450]. The note of 'prisons' at Pforta (1344) indicates a separate prison for erring religious[451]. A prisoner at Mellifont (1217) was kept in the stocks until he died[452]. At Kingswood (1240) the cellarer paid the porter sixpence for the maintenance of a prisoner[453]. Robbers were held in irons at Beaulieu's Faringdon prison, and one was hung (1270)[454]. A woman escaped from the prison at Robertsbridge (1278)[455]. A clerk complained that he had been held for five weeks at Zlatá Koruna (1347) 'in foul prisons, kept in chains'[456]. On the other hand, a generous allowance of grey or white cloth was made to the poor at Pforta (1350) – even to those 'confined and hidden in prison'[456a]. Experience perhaps led to the appointment of the sub-prior and 'a good monk' of Fontfroide (1306) as 'keepers' of the prison of Albi[457]. In modern times several former Cistercian monasteries are, or have been, used as prisons (amongst them Clairvaux), police barracks (Fürstenfeld), army barracks (Hemiksem), borstals (Droiteval nunnery), detention centres (Valloires), asylums (Eberbach), orphanages (Kappel), and old people's homes (Lehnin)[458].

The Cistercians and Women

The earliest injunctions of the Order forbade any women to pass through a monastery gate[459], whilst monks and *conversi* were completely forbidden ever to live under the same roof as them[460]. As new abbey churches were built, women were allowed to enter such a Cistercian church, but only on the day of its dedication or within the octave[461], nor were they to stay overnight within the precincts[462]. Frequently they overstayed their welcome[463]. The general prohibition remained, and women were forbidden employment as monastic milk-maids[464]. When women did breach the enclosure the community were enjoined (1197) to fast that day on bread and water. The conventual Mass was not to be said, and those by whose consent the women entered were to be severely punished[465].

The injunctions against women were repeated frequently in the thirteenth century[466], and strongly reinforced by Stephen Lexington of Savigny (1230–32)[467]. He also ruled that monks must only speak to female relatives at the gate and 'in the open'[468]. Gregory IX (1227–41) forbade nobles to take women into a Cistercian abbey[469], but Innocent IV (1250) allowed noble women and their retinue to enter[470], once a year[471], but they were not to eat meat or stay the night. Such would have included foundresses, and the wives and daughters of founders[472]. Papal dispensation (as when Princess Eleanor attended the chapter sermon at Waverley, *c.* 1245)[473] weakened the stance of the General Chapter (1262)[474]. A Visitor at Dore (1318) enjoined that women pilgrims were to be provided for at the abbey gate, and that the practice of allowing women in to wash and prepare flax was to cease[475]. As late as 1311 and 1320 widows wishing to visit their husbands' tombs at Aiguebelle[476] and Melrose[477] needed papal permission.

There were frequent breaches of the rules[478], as when women entered Barbeaux (1190) on the anniversary of Louis VII's burial there[479]. When they entered Bellevaux (1192) on the anniversary of St Peter of Tarentaise, each monk had to take the discipline privately[480]. Women entered Heiligenkreuz (1193) during the Sacred Triduum and received Holy Communion[481]. Three infringements were alleged at Egres (1200–12)[482] – possibly because the shortage of vocations in Hungary led to female servants[483]. Worse still, an abbot of Knockmoy (1240) had his hair washed by a woman[484]. There were prominent transgressions: the queen of France spent two nights in the infirmary at Pontigny (1205) and heard the sermon in chapter[485]. Queen Eleanor spent three weeks at Beaulieu (1246) nursing a sickly Prince Edward, but the prior and cellarer lost their jobs in consequence[486].

It was difficult to keep women out, especially when, as at Vaux-en-Ornois (1193)[487] and at Beaulieu-en-Bassigny (1216)[488], they wanted to place alms on the altar. It was more difficult still when they made a violent intrusion, as when (perhaps at Queen Christina's instigation) scantily dressed women disturbed the Palm Sunday cloister procession at Varnhem (*c.* 1156)[489]. There was a wave of forcible entries by females between 1193 and 1210[490]. At Carnoët in Brittany (1195) the monks had to take refuge on a grange[491]. At Pontigny the monks need not have bothered to sever St Edmund's arm; a few years after they did so, English women (and later still, females of all nationalities), were officially permitted to enter the precincts to visit his shrine[492].

The General Chapter (1154) prohibited women from staying in houses outside an abbey gate[493], but in the thirteenth century there was an increasing tendency for this to happen. At three monasteries in Aquitaine (Berdoues, Gimont and Perseigne; 1246) Arab women, concubines of their Arab workers, lodged in houses near their gates[494]. In 1278 the abbot of Wettingen was told to get rid of the women living near its gatehouse[495]. Special buildings for females without the gates did come to be built as at Staffarda[496], La Ferté (1231)[497] and Aduard (by 1350)[498]. St Bernard-opt-Scheldt (1341) had such a house by its mill[499]. The widow of its patron, Theobald de Verdun, remained at Croxden (1316) for a month after his funeral[500]. From 1344 to 1349 St Bridget lived in a house at Alvastra[501]. General Chapter also forbade huts being built for women during the harvest season in front of the gates of granges (1154), but did not prohibit such huts at a distance, implying acceptance of women harvesters[502]. Women were not allowed within the precincts of a grange complex (1134)[503]; they were forbidden entry 'wherever *conversi* stay' (1180)[504]; they were to be kept well away from the gates of granges (1237)[505]. Later the rules were relaxed. Women could enter grange precincts providing no *conversi* or monks were living there (1284)[506]. By now some granges had no resident *conversi*. In 1297 women were not allowed to enter 'abbeys, granges, or vineyards in which they are not accustomed to live or enter'[507], suggesting that at some it was accepted practice.

The Dying and the Dead

Towards the close of the twelfth century, Abbot Leonard of St Mary's, Dublin, angered the local clergy – who could see a loss of income – when he proclaimed the spiritual advantages that would accrue if one chose to die in Cistercian habit and be buried in a Cistercian cemetery[508]. His statement was a reflection of current practice which extended well into the thirteenth century, whereby quite a number of lay-folk who were at death's door were indeed clothed in the habit, formally admitted to the noviatiate, and placed directly in the monastic infirmary. The practice brought benefits in terms of bequests and property, it by-passed the Order's disapproval of death-bed donations, and it circumvented the prohibition (until 1217) on the burial of seculars[509]. What happened if death did not come, and a monk so professed regained his strength and vigour? Would he wish to continue as a religious? Clothed (apparently) only as a novice, he could presumably leave.

Among those so clothed and buried were the great and mighty, as Prince Llywelyn ab Iorwerth at Aberconwy (1240) and his son, David, beside him (1246)[510]. James I of Aragon on dying at Poblet (1276) left the abbey a substantial legacy[511]; his double effigy shows him both as king and as monk[512]. The tomb of the saintly monk, John of Montmirail, at Longpont (d. 1217) depicted him both as knight (which he had been) and monk (clothed shortly before death)[513]. Other notabilities dying in the habit included: Prince Owain Cyfeiliog at Strata Marcella (1197, 'at a great age')[514], and Earl Patrick of Dunbar at Melrose (1232, a kinsman of its abbot)[515]. Irish kings were clothed and buried at Assaroe (1224)[516] and Knockmoy (1224; 'in the habit of a grey monk')[517], as were counts of Foix at Boulbonne[518], and Welsh nobles at Strata Florida (1176–1249)[519]. Gerald of Wales asserted that dying folk were carried off from local villages to Dore (*c.* 1205) 'by corrupt persuasion'[520]. A dying parson, 'made a novice' at Meaux (*c.* 1190), gave the abbey more than £200[521]. Lesser folk might take the habit of a *conversus*. A grantor to Furness of a 6 shilling rent was promised admission as a *conversus*, 'in his life or at his death'[522].

Gerald of Wales said that amongst the dying so clothed at Dore were two women of substance, one the mother of the founder of its daughter-house at Grace Dieu. He alleged that each was 'made a monk, with tonsure and cowl complete'[523]. The practice of clothing dying women – also reported from Valroy (1196)[524] and Fontguilhem (1205)[525] – earned censure from the General Chapter (1201)[526]. Blanche of Castile (d. 1252), received as a Cistercian nun in Paris a few days before her death, vowed obedience to the abbess of Maubuisson – where she was buried in the nuns' choir[527]. Not all sick benefactors were so clothed. One donor of Furness, having given his manor to the monastery and intending to take the habit, withdrew and returned to his estate (which his son now rented from the abbey), and lived there 'as a guest and not as lord'[528]. When a local knight was dying, the abbot of Louth Park (1342) sent a covered cart to bring him to the monastery, and there, in his death-chamber, was signed and sealed his grant of a manor to the abbey[529].

When a guest was dying a priest-monk gave him viaticum. After giving the host he was to 'sprinkle his fingers with wine in the chalice, and minister it to him holding his left hand under his chin' – this late-twelfth century usage shows Holy Communion in both kinds as still common practice[530]. As for the dead, the earliest injunctions allowed guests and hired workers to be buried within the precincts[531]. These came to include 'travellers detained by infirmity'[532]. The burial of most guests was a relatively simple affair: chanting was afforded (at the abbot's discretion) only to people of rank[533]. There was class distinction even in death. Dying guests included St Thomas Aquinas at Fossanova (1274) – taken ill en route for the General Council at Lyons[534]. The bishop of Sodor returning from the same Council fell ill in Copeland and was buried at Furness[535]. Other travelling bishops buried included Peter of Roskilde (1218) and Torfinn of Hamar (1284), both at Ter Doest[536] – its coastal location attracting travellers. A monk of Fossanova (1226) beat and robbed a dying Tuscan bishop who was eventually buried less his mitre and ring[537]. Moreruela (1236–54) had a monk, Pelagius, as 'inquisitor of the dead' – perhaps coroner and receiver of the property of the deceased[538].

Only kings and queens, bishops and founders (and in practice their families) might be buried in a Cistercian abbey church[539], though the right of founders varied in the twelfth century[540]. Where such richer people were concerned, individual monasteries became associated with specific dynasties. From 1196 Poblet was the pantheon of the Crown of Aragon[541]. It had a special cemetery for nobles, whilst several had their own chapels and family crypts there, amongst them the chapel of the Holy Evangelists, the burying-place of the counts of Urgel from 1209[542]. Hautecombe was for centuries the last repose of the House of Savoy[543], and a chapel was built there (1330–42) to receive them[544]. Members of the Hohenzollern dynasty found a last resting-place at Heilsbronn (1297–1625)[545]; Lubiąż was the burial place of the dukes of Silesia[546]. Count Roger IV of Foix had a mausoleum chapel built at Boulbonne (1262) for his family, and dedicated to SS. Philip and James, but a later count (1302) had all the remains translated to tombs before the high altar[547]. The list of such dynastic associations is endless.

Other royal burials included: at Rushen, Norse kings of Man and the Isles, such as Olaf the Black (1225) and Magnus (1265)[548]; at Egres, Andrew II of Hungary (d. 1235), his second wife, Yolande (d. 1232), and Queen Hoilenz (1233)[549]; at Santes Creus, Peter III (1285), James II (1327), and Blanche of Castile (1308)[550]. Queen Gertrude of Hungary was interred 'in the monastery of the grey monks' at Pilis (1213)[551]; Alexander II of Scotland at Melrose, but his wife, Queen Marie, at Newbattle (1241)[552]. Kingswood (1327), refusing the body of King Edward II after his murder, lost a potential source of income[553]. Many founders (and their family members) were buried in the monasteries they had endowed, as: Bishop Svend at Øm (1191)[554], Earl Malcolm of Fife at Culross (1217)[555], and Baron Záviš at Vyšší Brod (1284)[556]. The burial of Matilda Marshall at Tintern (1248) saw her carried into the church by her four knight-sons[557]. The burial of the last of the de Verduns at Croxden (1334) was attended by four other abbots and two priors[558]. The Käfenbergs, descendants of the founder, constructed their mausoleum chapel at Georgenthal in 1285[559]. When the new choir was built at Žďár the body of its founder, Count Boček, was transferred there on the day of consecration[560].

Burial in a chapter-house was normally restricted to abbots, but kings, queens, and bishops, might be interred there 'if they chose' (1180)[561]. There were irregular burials of others in chapter-houses[562], whilst at Melrose (1219) a noble was buried in its chapter-house 'contrary to the wishes of the monks'[563]. From 1222 to 1275 at least ten burials of Welsh nobles took place in the chapter-house at Strata Florida[564]. The rules were relaxed, and the Chapter (in 1252), disallowing the burial of a count in the church of Pforta, permitted interment in the cloister or chapter-house instead[565]. Infringements of the rules regarding burial in abbey churches were noted at, amongst others[566], Le Miroir and Perseigne (1219), where, obviously wary of upsetting benefactors, the Chapter ordered that the bodies be transferred to a more appropriate resting-place 'at an opportune time'[567]. Eventually (1322), any who contributed towards the construction of a Cistercian church could be buried in it[568].

Within the monastic external cemetery, the Order tried to limit burials to benefactors, guests, paid employees, and those in spiritual fraternity[569]. There were numerous infringements which raised the ire of local bishops and clergy because of the surplice fees lost[570]. Innocent III (1198) reminded the Cistercians to bury only their own subjects, not strangers[571]. Even women were received for interment, as at Vieu Ville (1201)[572]. Pressure to take account of what was by then a prevalent and lucrative practice caused the Chapter to review its policy in 1217. Henceforth the burial of seculars was permitted if their parish priest agreed[573]. Gregory IX (1228) allowed the burial of the faithful so desirous, 'saving however justice to those churches from whom the bodies of the dead are taken'[574]. It was a contentious issue. Dunbrody (1217) buried seculars without reference to the local bishop[575], Mazan an excommunicated nobleman (1225)[576], and Kirkstall (1314) allegedly interred parishioners from nearby Leeds[577]. In 1283 La Real promised the bishop of Palma not to bury boys under the age of fourteen nor girls under the age of twelve – a sign perhaps of the low expectancy of life[578].

Many monasteries (as Dore and Margam) received grants of land in return for promise of burial[579]. Furness gained land in Craven from a miller and his wife, though they lived over fifty miles from the abbey where they sought interment[580]. A benefactor in Yorkshire quitclaimed land to Sallay (*c.* 1176) in return for a monk bringing his body on death to the abbey 'if such a course be possible'[581]. One donor wishing to be interred at Perseigne (1246) gave various goods to the abbey including his bed and two feather mattresses[582]. A female donor to Sorø (1292) ordered that the velvet pall on her coffin be afterwards used to make a chasuble for the monks[583]. Reception of the bodies of debtors could cause problems, and Gregory IX (1240) had to protect Hautecombe from the claims of creditors[584]. Grants were made to Doberan (1268, salt rights)[585], Dunkeswell (1257, a manor)[586], and Tintern (1224, a grange)[587], in return for a candle burning 'day and night' at the tomb of the donor's parents. Count Čák gave Borsmonostor (1237) a serf and his son to care for his tomb[588].

Excavators have plotted the interments at Øm, and have shown a number of wounded and palsied people interred in the cemetery north of its church[589]. At Lekno a large multi-layered burial ground has been uncovered with 121 inhumations of males and females[590]. Calder had a cemetery dedicated to St Andrew within the precincts[591], and Strata Florida a large walled cemetery burying folk from a wide area[592]. During the Interdict servants of Meaux were buried outside the precincts, its monks in the garden[593], and at Waverley a special cemetery for the 'excommunicated dead' was blessed[594]. At St Angelus in Petra the graves of French crusaders constituted a problem when the site had to be abandoned (1222)[595]. At Fontmorigny (1209) an heir objected because his mother had not been placed next to his father, but the monks countered that she was interred at the place chosen by those accompanying her corpse[596].

As for burials within an abbey church, excavations at Rushen have shown adults and children to be buried throughout the choir and transepts[597]. A medieval listing of the interments at Sorø mentions the mausoleum of King Valdemar, notes two rows of burials in its choir, refers to women, and to burials in the choir of the *conversi*, even to a grave by the night stairs[598]. An earl of Angus was buried before the high altar at Newminster[599], and a prince of Powys (the founder) in like manner at Strata Marcella[600]. Petronilla, a benefactress of L'Escale Dieu, was interred in the last chapel of its south crossing[601]. From the thirteenth century, prominent personages might be interred in special tomb recesses, as seen in the north wall of the presbytery at Cymer and Dundrennan[602], and in a transept chapel at Strata Florida. Countess Agnes of Ahsperch sought burial under the presbytery step at Zwettl[603]; an Hungarian royal official was interred in the sacristy at Ercsi[604].

Circumstances might dictate, especially in the case of death far afield, that some who wished to be buried in a Cistercian church had to be buried elsewhere, as Peter II of Aragon (unable to be interred at Poblet)[605], and John of England (who had desired Beaulieu, his foundation)[606]. Monasteries might jealously guard their traditional links. A lengthy dispute (1214–20) followed the burial of a duke of Lorraine at Clairlieu although he had opted for Stürzellbronn; Clairlieu was slow to hand over his remains[607]. After litigation, the body of Hugh de Lacy was transferred from Bective (1205) to St Thomas' Priory, Dublin, and with it went the lands claimed by Bective at the original burial ten years before[608]. A cellarer of Boyle intercepted the body of the archpriest of Tech Baethín (d. 1229) on its way to burial at the Premonstratensian abbey of Holy Trinity, Loch Cé, but arbitration upheld the canons' claim[609]. There was 'agitation' over the body of King Andrew of Hungary (d. 1235): buried first in the city of Várdai, it was reclaimed by the monks of Pilis and eventually interred at Egres[610].

The Scripture says: 'Where your treasure is, there will your heart be also' (St Matthew 6:21). Heart-burials were not uncommon, for when one's body might need to be buried in one place, the heart detached could be interred in another which the deceased held dear. The heart of Robert Bruce I was interred at Melrose (1329) which he had greatly endowed. When the foundress of New Abbey (1289) died, the heart of her husband, John Balliol, was buried with her, and the monastery gained the colloquial name of Sweetheart[611]. The body of Bishop Peter des Roches of Winchester was buried in his cathedral, but his heart at Waverley Abbey (1238)[612]; the heart of Bishop John de Breton of Hereford was interred at Dore (1275), where his parents lay[613]. The heart of Pope Calixtus II (d. 1124) was buried at Cîteaux[614], as was that of Queen Jeanne of France (1348)[615]. Ranulf de Blundeville, Earl of Chester and Lincoln, left his heart and the manor of Leek to Dieulacres (1232)[616].

Benefactors often sought an annual obit after their earthly demise. Count Mrocha gave Paradyż (1301) a village in return for a chantry in the monastery[617]. Hubert de Burgh gave Dore a grange-cum-chantry at Llanfair Cilgoed (*c.* 1235) where Mass would be said for his soul[618]. Such provision was expected to meet the approval of the General Chapter. The abbots of Preuilly and Les Sellières (1205) were disciplined for conceding to the countess of Champagne a daily Mass 'contrary to the form of the Order'[619]. A later Chapter (1251) approved an annual obit for the counts of Foix buried at Boulbonne[620]. Benefactors could also have their name perpetuated, and seek continuing prayers, by bequeathing provision for a pittance on their obit day[621].

Settlement adjacent to monasteries

The coming and going of so many different groups of people to a monastery could invade upon the privacy and solitude of the community unless there were safeguards. The General Chapter (1217) found it necessary to insist that in large abbeys two religious be stationed at the doors leading into the cloister, to prevent unauthorised entry. When one went to church for service, the other was to remain on duty[622]. Necessary talking was allowed with those wishing to enter the cloister, but 'in a proper place not far from the cloister door'[623]. In time it was noted (1257) that at some monasteries layfolk were living 'next to the cemeteries and infirmaries', and, worse still, eating meat within the precincts: they were to be removed 'if possible'[624]. It seems as if in some houses these were by now ingrained customs, to end which would have provoked much local resentment and hostility.

A monastery seems to have attracted more than one group of people wishing to live 'without the walls'[625]. This may have been for purposes of employment, trade, security, or spirituality. As the numbers of *conversi* declined their replacement lay-workers, especially married men, may have lived in part in dwellings deliberately set up not far from the gate-house. Settlements next to Zwettl[626] and Alcobaça[627] were growing by 1200. At three (aforesaid) monasteries in Aquitaine there were, by 1246, Arab settlements outside the gates[628]. By 1284 the village of Froideville stood close to Monthéron; it had thirty households in 1308[629]. Cîrţa had its 'abbey town' in 1311[630], as later did Holm Cultram. Building of a village was taking place outside the walls of Ábrahám in 1343[631]. Dwelling houses were erected outside the gates of Waverley (1316) by a retiring clerk of the bishop of Winchester[632]. 'Great Gate vill' developed north-west of Croxden. The early ideal of complete solitude of the white monks was based upon isolation from the world and self-sufficiency, but as more people flocked to the monasteries, and especially as the need for lay workers grew, the people of the world impinged increasingly upon Cistercian communities.

Notes

1. Williams (1984) I, 144; *cf.* Williams (1991) 87–117.
2. *CDSL* I, 463.
3. McGuire (1982) 217.
4. *RSB* 180.
5. Campbell (1899) 164.
6. Davidson (1843) 70.
7. *RSB* 180.
8. Lekai (1977a) 448.
9. *EOC* 334–37 (CXX).
10. Anton (1986) 243.
11. *ABB* 175.
12. *SL* 165 (No. 65); *RSL* II, 229 (Savigny, 1230).
13. *EOC* 334–37 (CXX).
14. *CDP* 186 (No. CCCXXXVI).
15. *OHZ* II, 133; *CDNS* 384–85.
16. De Moreau (1909) 233.
17. *EOC* 334–37 (CXX).
18. PRO, LR 1/228, f. 6d.
19. *CDCDS* III, 250.
20. *KD* I, 145–46.
21. *PU* II, 322–23.
22. *RSL* II, 198 (No. 1).
23. Harper-Bill (1980) 108.
24. *CO* 4 (No. III).
25. *MEB* 141.
26. *ABB* 176.
27. Between the inner and outer gates.
28. Kluit (1780) 497.
29. *LFZ* 477.
30. VCH, *Gloucester* II (1907) 95; *cf. CPR* 1348/199.
31. Rösener (1974) 157.
32. McNulty (1943) 159.
33. King (1985) 94.
34. *VGA* 15, Post (1922) II, 165.
35. Wiswe (1953) 110.
36. Lekai (1977a) 385.
37. King (1954) 357.
38. Williams (1984) I, 180.
39. Wulf (1944) 105.
40. Wright (1905) 383–84.
41. D'Arbois (1858) 204–05.
42. Lekai (1977a) 383.
43. *Ibid.* 384.
44. *CMM* II, xiv–xv.
45. *ABB* 32–3, 172–77; *cf.* Talbot (1958) 195.
46. Wiswe (1953) 110.
47. *CAC* 877–894.
48. *RCC* III, 59 (No. 672)-V, 251 (No. 1597).
49. Winter (1868) II, 41; *cf. OMA* 232, 236–7.
50. *LFZ* 64; *cf.* Talbot (1939) 31; Grebenc (1973) 31 (No.50).
51. *CAF* 50; *cf. DHGE* XVII (1971) 983; *RHC* 5.
52. *RD* II, 127 (No. 6557); *cf. DHGE* X (1938) 59–60; *CAF* 215.
53. Cuissard (1885) 424.
54. *CW* 211.
55. *MEX* 393; cf. SBC IV, 53 (No. 1005, iii).
56. *UKSH* 28–9 (No. XXI).
57. *DD* 1614–15.
58. Carville (1981) 39.
59. Baigent (1882) 26–7.
60. *CE* 102.
61. Carville (1981) 39.
62. *CNM* xvi, 108.
63. Lekai (1977a) 384–85.
64. RD II, 127 (No. 6557).
65. *EOC* 301–02, *cf.* Lackner (1978a) 72–3.
66. VCH, *Warwick* II (1908) 74, 77.
67. *Valor Ecclesiasticus* IV (Record Commission, London; 1821) 371.
68. *LFZ* 477.
69. *DHGE* XVII (1971) 973.
70. *CW* 228–30; *cf.* Bell (1989) 170 (No. 18), and see pp. 168–71 for other examples.
71. *CDL* 179.
72. Gilyard-Beer (1986) 151.
73. *DHGE* II (1914) 27.
74. *UKSH* 28–8 (No. XX), 74 (No. LXIII); *cf.* Grill (1961) 22n.
75. Lekai (1977a) 381.
76. *RBC* 59.
77. *CAS* I, 205 (No. CCXXI).
78. *CBP* 172 (No. CLXVIII).
79. *DHGE* XXIV (1993) 390.
80. Dustin (1973) 16–17, *CHA* (2–3) 237 (No. 1360).
81. *Cf. AMA* 40–42; *CDB* (2) II, 494; *RBM* IV, 505–06 (No. 1269).
82. Mullin (1932) 93.
83. *SBC* I, 2; IV, 11 (No. 952).
84. Lekai (1977a) 381; *cf.* D'Arbois (1858) 217.
85. *UKSH* 27–8.
86. *SBC* II, 285 (No. 391), 305 (No. 418); *cf. CDB* (2) II, 494 (for Chorin).

87. *SBC* I, 2.
88. Williams (1984) I, 182.
89. Heutger (1971) 149.
90. Lekai (1977a) 381, 448.
91. Hockey (1976) 71.
92. *RBM* IV, 505–06 (No. 1269).
93. *CRS* II, 75–6 (No. CCXXVIII), 244–45 (No. DCCXVI) *cf. ABB* 181.
94. *ABB* 177–80.
95. *UKW* 233; *cf.* Winter (1868) II, 143.
96. Lenglet (1978) 35, *cf.* D'Arbois (1858) 217.
97. Lekai (1977a) 382.
98. De Moreau (1909) 262.
99. Lekai (1977a) 111–12.
100. Talbot (1958) 195.
101. *EOC* 333–34 (CXIX).
102. *ABB* 34, 177–82, 233; *cf. Statuta* II, 80 (1270/3).
103. *SL* 169 (No. 87), *cf.* 165 (No. 63); O'Dwyer (1976) 48.
104. *RSL* II, 208 (No. 5).
105. Bell (1989) 168; *cf. RSL* II, 214 (No. 4); Wiswe (1953) 39.
106. *CW* 38, 80–1, 227–30; *cf.* 167–68.
107. Sydow (1984) 93; *cf. CDP* 189 (No. CCCXXXVI), *UKSH* 27–8 (No. XX).
108. Schneider (1954) 187.
109. *CVL* 70.
110. *SBC* II, 270 (No. 371, *c.* 1230), 285 (No. 391, *c.* 1240); IV, 11 (No. 952 of 1263).
111. *CMM* II, ix.
112. *Statuta* I, 500 (1218/75).
113. Fort i Cogul (1975) 76.
114. *UKS* 58.
115. De Moreau (1909) 263.
116. Fort i Cogul (1969) 48.
117. Altisent (1970) 111–12; *cf. CF* v.
118. Bouton (1959) II, 256.
119. *CNM* xv, 171.
120. *CHS* 251.
121. *UKH* 88 (No. LXXXVIII).
122. Jones (1981) 8–9, *cf.* CBFA (1) xii.
123. Lekai (1977a) 381.
124. Jones (1981) 8–9.
125. Richards (1968) 108.
126. *SBC* I, 2; *cf. CVL* 70.
127. Fort i Cogul (1969) 48, (1975) 76.
128. *Statuta* I, 310 (1205/16).
129. *AM* I, 305.
130. *CDN* 533–33, 836.
131. *UKA* 107 (No. 162).
132. *Statuta* I, 296 (1204/5); LCC (2) 320.
133. *Statuta* I, 145 (1191/80), 172 (1194/6), 308 (1205/9), 309 (1205/12), 312 (1205/25); *cf.* I, 58 (1154/25).
134. *CDNS* 218.
135. Anton (1986) 361 (No. 57).
136. *Statuta* II, 398 (1254/37), 432 (1257/41).
137. *LFZ* 553.
138. Bouton (1959) II, 256.
139. Williams (1984) I, 182.
140. Deck (1974) 134.
141. *RCC* III, 59 (No. 670).
142. Canivez (1926) 222–23, Willems (1957) 165.
143. Conbhuí (1961) 309.
144. *DHGE* II (1914) 27.
145. Bouton (1959) II, 256.
146. Péchenard (1883) 209.
147. Ménabrea (1843) 235.
148. Williams (1984) I, 223.
149. *CS* II, 102–05; *cf.* Bell (1989) 170; Anton (1986) 324 (No. 27).
150. *CP* I, 100; *cf. PU* I, 76 (of 1183; for hospital in Gorna granted to Kolbacz).
151. *CP* I, 103.
152. Winter (1868) II, 197.
153. *RCH* 101.
154. *DHGE* XII (1953) 944.
155. *Statuta* III, 123 (1273/50), *cf.* Bouton (1959) II, 256.
156. *DHGE* I (1912) 762–67.
157. *FRB* 538, 541.
158. Fort i Cogul (1975) 412.
159. *CDB* (2) II, 397–98; *cf. DHGE* XII (1953) 656, Winter (1868) II, 144–45.
160. *DHG* I, 762–67.
161. De Durainville (1856) 189–91.
162. Kaczmarek (1987) 427–28.
163. Bell (1989) 170.
164. *UKW* 119 (of 1227).
165. France (1992) 226.
166. *Statuta* I, 65 (1157/46), 84 (1175/32).
167. D'Arbois (1858) 224–26.
168. *CHDM* 531.
169. Owen (1904) 184.
170. Canestrelli (1896) 16.
171. Yañez Neira (1970) 563–64.
172. Caputo and Torre (1972) *passim,* it still functions today.
173. Cocheril (1959a) 57.
174. *DHGE* XIV (1960) 83.
175. *DHGE* XVII (1971) 851.
176. Williams (1983) 77–78.
177. Snape (1926) 145.
178. Williams (1983) 78, 288–94.
179. *AF* 135; *cf.* VCH, *Lancaster* II (1908) 127.
180. *Catal. Ancient Deeds* I, 277 (B. 673).
181. *CDL* 176.
182. Fergusson (1984) 191.
183. *Cartae Glam.* II, 526–27, 536–37; NLW, Penrice and Margam Ch. 64.
184. *UKAR* 46 (No. 65).
185. *UKP* 297.
186. Hockey (1970) 74.
187. Sommer-Ramer (1982) 147.
188. *Ibid.* 317.
189. *SBC* IV, 100–06 (Nos 1180–82).
190. One corrodian received, as part of his benefits, 1,000 red herrings on St Nicholas' Day (*6 Dec.*).
191. Snape (1926) 144.
192. *CPR* 1271/507, 1279/305.
193. Stéphan (1970) 26–27.
194. *CPR* 1348/201 (No. 5).
195. VCH, *Northampton* II (1906) 117.
196. *Ibid.* 102.
197. *CC* (3), B. 55–53.
198. VCH, *Northampton* II (1906) 117.
199. VCH, *Essex* II (1907) 131.
200. *SLB* 81–83.
201. *CPR* 1348/201 (No. 5).
202. Stéphan (1970) 106–07.
203. Greatrex (1994) 19–20.
204. Hill (1961) 45, 85.

205. *CC* (3), B. 52–53.
206. Hill (1961) 45, 85.
207. VCH, *Essex* II (1907) 131.
208. *CPR* 1271/507.
209. *CPR* 1272/695.
210. *Cf. CCR* 1314/192; *CC* (3) B. 52–53; *SLB* 81–83.
211. VCH, *Essex* II (1907) 126.
212. Hays (1963) 91–92.
213. VCH, *Kent* II (1926) 153.
214. *CPR* 1330/513; *cf. CCR* 1335/370.
215. Lekai (1977a) 459.
216. *Ibid.* 448–49 (No. XIII), *cf.* Sullivan (1989) 190.
217. Lekai (1977a) 450 (No. XXIV).
218. *ABB* 21; *cf.* Wiswe (1953) 93.
219. *ABB* 315–16.
220. *RSL* II, 228 (Savigny, 1230).
221. *Statuta* I, 184 (1195/15).
222. *Cf. Statuta* I, 183 (1195/6); *RSL* II, 203 (No. 8).
223. Sullivan (1989) 194–95.
224. *LCC* (1) 81; *Statuta* I, 115 (1189/27), 183 (1195/6).
225. *Statuta* I, 128 (1190/51), 148 (1192/13), 364 (1209/37).
226. *Statuta* II, 169 (1237/3).
227. *LCC* (2) 279, 279*n*.
228. *Statuta* III, 128–29 (1274/12).
229. Richards (1968) 103.
230. VCH, *Worcester* II (1906) 153.
231. *DCK* 211–13.
232. *ABB* 20, *cf.* Talbot (1958) 196.
233. *ABB* 20.
234. *ABB* passim. (See Index for 'Shrove Tuesday').
235. *CW* 35–36.
236. Davidson (1843) 11–19.
237. *Ibid.* 51–52.
238. Birch (1897) 348.
239. Williams (1984) I, 170.
240. Cowley (1977) 73.
241. *RSB* 40.
242. Aubert (1947) II, 146–47.
243. Martin (1893) 115.
244. *CAS* II, 46 (No. CDXXIII of 1251).
245. *Fountains Abbey* (National Trust, 1989) Plan.
246. Musset and Aubreton (1979) 6.
247. Allendorff (1971) 27.
248. Stalley (1987) 44.
249. *DCK* xii, 202.
250. Brown (1983) 9; MS Notes (Arch. Dig Open Day, 24–9–1983).
251. Bond (1989) 96.
252. MS Notes (Buckfast Arch. Dig Open Day, 29–9–1983).
253. Bond (1989) 96, Gilyard-Beer (1976) 40.
254. Aubert (1947) II, 146–47.
255. Courtois (1982) 327.
256. Gerevich (1982) 392.
257. *DCK* 220.
258. Halkin (1970) 58.
259. *DHGE* XXIII (1990) 576.
260. D'Arbois (1858) 223–24, *cf. Statuta* I, 526 (1220/46).
261. Barea (1977) 215.
262. *DD* 1587, 1619.
263. *CDEM* II, 263.
264. VCH, *Essex* II (1907) 125.
265. *Statuta* I, 526 (1220/46).
266. Millard (1994) 575.
267. *Statuta* I, 48 (1152/17).
268. *AF* 219.
269. *EOC* 246–48 (LXXXVII).
270. *RSB* 140.
271. Ker (1984) 105.
272. *EOC* 304–05, 332–33; *cf.* D'Arbois (1858) 232–34.
273. *ABB* 269–76, *cf.* Talbot (1958) 194–95.
274. Talbot (1958) 195.
275. *Cf. Statuta* I, 371 (1210/12); *RSL* II, 192 (No. 12), 216 (No. 10).
276. *Statuta* II, 441 (1258/17).
277. *LCC* (2) 333.
278. *CAF* 122 (of 1218).
279. *LCC* (1) 145.
280. *Statuta* I, 83 (1175/8).
281. *LCC* (1) 148, (2) 334, *cf. Statuta* I, 83 (1175/8), 141 (1191/38), 148–49 (1192/5).
282. *Statuta* III, 157 (1276/27).
283. *SBC* IV, 106 (No. 1182 of 1323).
284. *Statuta* I, 282 (1203/19).
285. Talbot (1951a) 38.
286. *ABB* 33, 269–82; *cf.* Talbot (1958) 194–95.
287. VCH, *Chester* III (1980) 160.
288. *RSL* II, 227–28.
289. *ABB* 278–81.
290. Lekai (1977a) 381, *cf. UKZ* 423 (Zwettl).
291. *Cf.* Midmer (1979) 278, VCH, *Yorkshire* III (1974) 156.
292. Williams (1984) I, 171.
293. *CPR* 1348/52.
294. VCH, *Hampshire* II (1903) 147 (and 138–39 for Quarr).
295. Crossley (1939) 68; *cf.* VCH, *Stafford* III (1970) 232 (for Dieulacres).
296. *CDS* III, 89.
297. Thompson (1920) 93.
298. *Statuta* I, 118 (1190/1), *cf. UKZ* 423.
299. *Cf. Statuta* II, 308 (1246/35, 36), 238 1241/41), 475 (1261/2).
300. Bernard (1967) 21, Martin (1982) 20.
301. Lekai (1977a) 381.
302. *SBC* II, 32 (No. 29); IV, 97 (No. 1162).
303. *SBC* II, 303 (No. 417), 306 (No. 419).
304. *CF* v, *cf. CDB* (2) 392 (Chorin).
305. Williams (1984) I, 172, 175.
306. *AF* 207.
307. *CC* (2), B. 38.
308. *PZKZ* 166 (No. CVII).
309. *Statuta* I, 60 (1157/5), *LCC* (1) 133.
310. *RSL* II, 228.
311. *Statuta* III, 141 (1275/10), *cf.* 197 (1280/13).
312. *EOC* 332–33.
313. Thompson (1920) 93.
314. *ABB* 33.
315. Butler (1937) 236.
316. Schreiner (1982) 111.
317. *SRD* IV, 535, *cf.* Duval-Arnold (1968) 224.
318. *SBC* IV, 106 (No. 1182).
319. Coppack (1990) 105–07, Gilyard-Beer (1976) 151.
320. RSL *II, 229.*
321. Courtney (1989) 99, 125–26.

322. Williams (1984) I, 50–51, 172.
323. *RHC* 83, 139.
324. Williams (1984) I, 172.
325. *CF* 53; VCH, *Gloucester* II (1907) 95.
326. VCH, *Sussex* II (1973) 73.
327. VCH, *Essex* II (1907) 131.
328. Dimier (1954) 67, 71–74.
329. *DHGE* XVI (1967) 1221; *cf.* Bedini (1964) 76 (in 1223, 1227, 1229).
330. *RBM* I, 392 (No. 833).
331. *Statuta* II, 230 (1241/1).
332. Williams (1984) I, 172.
333. *C.C.R.* 1244/222–23, 225.
334. VCH, *Chester* III (1980) 152.
335. Swartling (1969) 20.
336. Hallam (1954) 33.
337. Fergusson (1984) 147; VCH, *Wiltshire* III (1956) 273.
338. Arenas (1985) 54, Rahlves (1966) 211, Rosenmann (1983) 229.
339. Gwynn (1992) 222.
340. *DHGE* XIV (1960) 936.
341. Richards (1968) 97.
342. Williams (1984) I, 172.
343. VCH, *Essex* II (1907) 131.
344. *DHGE* X (1938) 63.
345. France (1992) 361.
346. D'Arbois (1858) 222.
347. *DHGE* IX (1937) 1034.
348. *CFN* 531.
349. *CDH* 200–06 (No. 18).
350. *EOC* 246–47 (LXXXVI); *cf. Statuta* II, 308 (1246/34); Kempf (1976) 33; Lackner (1981) 63.
351. France (1992) 293.
352. *CO* 246 (No. CCCCVIII).
353. *SL* 165 (No. 62).
354. *Statuta* I, 521 (1220/22).
355. Birch (1897) 152.
356. *Cf. Statuta* I, 198 (1196/17), 202 (1196/27), 326 (1206/35), 365 (1209/40), 410 (1213/32), 444 (1215/46).
357. *Statuta* I, 504 (1219/7).
358. *Statuta* I, 248 (1199/80).
359. *Statuta* III, 239 (1287/12), 242 (1288/9), 277 (1294/8).
360. *Statuta* III, 218 (1282/4), 229 (1283/4).
361. *Statuta* III, 330 (1315/3).
362. *Statuta* III, 210 (1281/25), *cf.* I, 229 (1198/38).
363. *Cf. DHGE* II (1914) 755 (of 1206).
364. VCH, *Lancaster* II (1908) 120.
365. *UKH* 24 (No. XVIII), 48 (No. XLIV), 53–4 (No. L), 54 (No. LI), 61–2 (No. LVIII), 62 (No. LIX), 64 (No. LXII), 72 (No. LXXI), 87–8 (No. LXXXVI, of 1346).
366. *Cf. AW* 85 (Walkenried); *CDEM* V, 277 (Velehrad); *CDRB* V:2, 404 (No. 741; Fürstenzell), 443–44 (No. 772; Raitenhaslach).
367. *CBP* 133–31 (No. CXXXI).
368. *CSBW* 117–18.
369. *DHGE* XVII (1971) 981.
370. *CPL* V, 507–08.
371. Williams (1984) I, 179; *cf.* (1990) 138 (fig. 59).
372. *AMA* 104–06.
373. Hugo (1855) 43–4, Weaver (1906) 9–10.
374. Williams (1994) 14.
375. Stalley (1987) 115–17.
376. *RCH* 104, 120.
377. *OC* 133 (No. CCCXL).
378. Dimier (1954) 58.
379. Williams (1976) 15.
380. *CDP* 22–26 (No.   X), 75.
381. *NG* IV, 457.
382. *CFN* 524.
383. McCrank (1975) 277–72.
384. *DHGE* IX (1937) 584, Chevallier (1855) 336–68.
385. PRO SC 6 (Henry VIII) 5259.
386. *NG* IV, 243.
387. PRO C 1/213, m.106 (the '*cross auter*').
388. France (1992) 136.
389. Reindel (1969) 153–54.
390. *VGA* 15.
391. VCH, *Yorkshire* III (1974) 147.
392. *CHA* (3–3) 64 (No. 328).
393. VCH, *Kent* II (1926) 154, Sumption (1975) 270.
394. *Statuta* III, 149 (1275/69); VCH, *Gloucester* II (1907) 97.
395. *CHA* (2–3) 193 (No. 1083), 271 (No. 1530).
396. *OC* 256 (No. DCLXVII).
397. *CHA* 93–3) 98 (No. 507); Richter (1993) 162.
398. *DHGE* XI (1949) 586.
399. Régnier (1913) 341–42.
400. Midmer (1979) 218.
401. Williams (1984) I, 177.
402. Midmer (1979) 218.
403. *Statuta* III, 12–13 (1263/18).
404. *CHA* (2–3) 24 (No. 74).
405. *Statuta* III, 385 (1329/2).
406. *CNM* 225, 229–32, 235–38 (all told 14 grants for providing lights around the tomb).
407. *Statuta* II, 347 (1250/4).
408. *Statuta* II, 347 (1250/5).
409. Carrick (1907) 41.
410. *Statuta* I, 193 (1195/78).
411. Coulton (1933) 69.
412. NLW, Penrice and Margam Ch. 293 (14).
413. Lekai (1977a) 389.
414. *CSBW* 117.
415. Goff (1980) 212–13, 385.
416. *PCP* 233–34 (No. 184).
417. *CMM* I, 441.
418. King (1954) 165–66.
419. *C.C.R.* 1247/497; *C.P.R.* 1264/318; *PCP* 252–53 (No. 211).
420. *AM* II, 346.
421. *Cf. C.P.R.* 1259/19, 1260/181, 1261/174, 1277/199.
422. *AM* II, 346; *cf.* Finucane (1977) 29, 139.
423. *Statuta* II, 315 (1247/2).
424. *C.P.R.* 1272/674, 1276/151.
425. McGuire (1982) 68–71.
426. VCH, *Stafford* III (1970) 231n.
427. *CM* 95.
428. *DHGE* XV (1963) 111.
429. Williams (1966) 72.
430. *Statuta* III, 392 (1331/12).
431. Williams (1984) I, 177–80; *cf.* Humphrey (1982) 54 (Garendon).
432. Hill (1971) 78–80); *cf.* Mikkers (1956) 245–63.

433. King (1954) 162.
434. *Cf. PCP* 274–81 (Nos 242–44, 276–81: gifts made by the archiepiscopal refugees).
435. *DHGE* XII (1953) 895–96.
436. *CFN* 524.
437. Williams (1984) I, 176.
438. *DHGE* XVII (1971) 902; Grégoire (1992) 418–25.
439. *KKA* 52, *cf.* Uitterdijk (1874) 227.
440. Williams (1984) I, 176.
441. Whitley (1920) 80.
442. *C.C.R.* 1234/554, *CF* 55–57.
443. *C.P.R.* 1266/645, 1279/346; *cf.* Harbison (1970) 135 (for Dunbrody).
444. *Cf. C.C.R.* 1234/393; Cauvet (1875) 511–12, O'Sullivan (1939) 4.
445. *AM* II, 325–27; *cf.* Harper (1930) 215–16.
446. Whitley (1920) 80.
447. VCH, *Hampshire* II (1903) 143, *cf.* St John Hope (1906) 175, Cook (1965) 167–68.
448. Williams (1984) I, 176.
449. Rahtz and Hirst (1976) 7.
450. De Laplane (1863) 74.
451. *UKP* 567.
452. *Statuta* I, 471 (1217/16).
453. *DCK* 196.
454. *ABB* 84–85.
455. Whitley (1920) 88.
456. *UKG* 102–03, 107–09 (Nos LIIIa, LVIa).
456a. *CP* I, 129–30.
457. Felten (1986) 212.
458. Van Der Meer (1965) *passim.*
459. Lackner (1981) 62.
460. *Statuta* I, 14 (1138/VII); LCC (1) 126, (2) 321.
461. *Statuta* I, 61 (1157/10), 156 (1192/50); LCC (1) 127, (2) 321–22; *cf. Statuta* I, 138 (1191/22); *DHGE* II (1914) 799.
462. *LCC* (2) 213.
463. *Cf. Statuta* I, 180 (1194/55; Cîteaux), 361 (1209/23; Longvilliers); 427 (1214/53; Bonmont and La Trappe); *DHGE* IX (1937) 1008.
464. *Statuta* I, 67 (1157/58); *LCC* (1) 126, (2) 321.
465. *Statuta* I, 211 (1197/6).
466. *Cf. Statuta* I, 144 (1191/73), 160 (1193/12), 171 (1194/70); III, 41 (1266/28), 131 (1274/18), 288 (1297/3); *LCC* (2) 321–22.
467. *SL* 158 (No. 9), 166 (No. 72); *cf.* Walker (1983) 53, (1984) 43.
468. *RSL* II, 212 (No. 13); 219.
469. *LCC* (2) 247.
470. *RPR* II, 1531 (No. 18,905); *cf.* 1545 (No. 19,066, of 1265); *CC*(3), B.55.
471. *Statuta* II, 350 (1250/23).
472. *CMM* III, 35–36.
473. Baigent (1882) 15.
474. *Statuta* II, 3 (1262/11), 107 (Hailes).
475. Harper-Bill (1980) 105.
476. *CDAA* 286–87.
477. Coulton (1933) 96.
478. *Cf. Statuta* I, 135 (1191/5), 138 (1191/22), 174 (1194/22), 175–76 (1194/31–32), 319 (1205/29), 522 (1220/27); *DHGE* XV (1963) 850.
479. *Statuta* I, 129 (1190/55).
480. *Statuta* I, 156 (1192/50); *cf.* Dimier (1978a) 59.
481. *Statuta* I, 165–66 (1193/41).
482. *Statuta* I, 257 (1200/46), 266 (1201/16), 338 (1207/22), 389 (1212/1); *cf.* I, 240 (1199/44), 248 (1199/81); *DHGE* XV (1963) 28–29.
483. Lekai (1976) 262.
484. *Statuta* II, 223 (1240/40).
485. *Statuta* I, 308–09 (1205/10).
486. Hockey (1976) 29–30, *cf. CC* (3) B. 55.
487. *Statuta* I, 161 (1193/18).
488. *Statuta* I, 453 (1216/18).
489. France (1992) 38–39, 163.
490. *Statuta* I, 162 (1193/28), 195 (1195/85), 224 (1198/4), 373 (1210/20).
491. *Statuta* I, 194–95 (1195/83), 199–200 (1196/11).
492. *CMA* 113–14, *cf.* Finucane (1977) 29, 87.
493. *Statuta* I, 58 (1154/24).
494. *Statuta* II, 308 (1246/33); *DHGE* XX (1984) 1415.
495. *Statuta* III, 183 (1278/67).
496. Boyd (1943) 73.
497. King (1954) 121; *cf. Statuta* II, 235 (1241/27), Aubert (1947) II, 146–47.
498. Post (1922) II, 162.
499. *OLSB* 37.
500. *CC* (3), B.55.
501. France (1992) 36.
502. *Statuta* I, 58 (1154/24); lecture notes by Fr C. Waddell at Fontfroide Conference (1993).
503. *Statuta* I, 14 (1134/VII).
504. *Statuta* I, 88 (1180/13).
505. *LCC* (2) 322.
506. *Statuta* III, 230 (1284/9).
507. *Statuta* III, 288 (1297/3).
508. Stalley (1987) 105.
509. *Cf.* Lekai (1977a) 292, Knowles (1963a) 636, Stalley (1987) 205.
510. Williams (1984) I, 183.
511. McCrank (1975) 262.
512. Arenas (1985) 63.
513. Zarnecki (1972) 87.
514. Williams (1984) I, 183.
515. Coulton (1933).
516. Gwynn (1970) 127; *cf. CTA* 52 (No. 381).
517. O'Dwyer (1976) 35*n*.
518. *DHGE* X (1938) 59, 61, 63–64.
519. Williams (1984) I, 183.
520. Williams (1976) 8.
521. *CMM* II, 234.
522. Cottam (1928) 65–66.
523. Williams (1976) 8.
524. *Statuta* I, 202 (1196/27).
525. *Statuta* I, 313 (1205/28).
526. *Statuta* I, 266 (1201/15).
527. Kinder (1976) 167.
528. Cottam (1928) 63–64.
529. *CPL* 59–61.
530. *EOC* 292 (CI).
531. *Statuta* I, 19 (1134/XXVII); *LCC* (1) 127; Lekai (1977a) 450 (No. XXIV).
532. *LCC* (2) 322.
533. *EOC* 292–95; *cf. Statuta* I, 72 (1160/13; 1161/4).).
534. *AM* II, 382; *cf.* Millard (1994) 541.
535. *AF* 222.
536. Dendooven (1972) 20.
537. *Statuta* II, 51 (1226/17).

538. Anton (1986) 406 (No.96).
539. *Statuta* I, 47 (1152/10), 68 (1157/63), 87 (1180/5), 356 (1208/49); *LCC* (1) 128, (2) 245.
540. *Cf. Statuta* I, 87 (1180/5), 356 (1208/49).
541. *DHGE* XVII (1971) 972, Arenas (1985) 63.
542. McCrank (1973) 67.
543. Williams (1935) 55.
544. *DHGE* XXIII (1990) 565.
545. Van Der Meer (1965) 282.
546. Bouton (1959) I, 165.
547. *DHGE* X (1938) 63.
548. Cumming (1868) 38, Kinvig (1950) 70.
549. *DHGE* XV (1963) 29; *RCH* 142.
550. Rosenmann (1983) 230–31; *cf.* Fort i Cogul (1972) 69.
551. RCH 91, 142.
552. Carrick (1907) 47, Richardson (1981a) 35.
553. Midmer (1979) 183.
554. Garner (1973) 17.
555. Talbot (1939) 58.
556. *FRB* V, 171.
557. Williams (1976) 102.
558. *Jnl. Brit. Arch. Assoc.* XXI (1865) 302.
559. *DHGE* XX (1984) 577.
560. *FRB* V 539.
561. *Statuta* I, 87 (1180/5), *LCC* (1) 128.
562. *E.g: Statuta* I, 212 (1197/14), 215 (1197/26), 225 (1198/18), 247 (1199/78), 409 (1213/24), 507 (1219/19).
563. *CM* 54.
564. Williams (1984) I, 184.
565. *Statuta* I, 161 (1193/19).
566. *Cf. Statuta* I, 161 (1193/19), II, 373 (1251/68).
567. *Statuta* I, 508 (1219/26).
568. Fergusson (1984a) 10.
569. *Statuta* I, 19 (1134/XXVII); *LCC* (1) 127– 28.
570. *Cf. Statuta* I, 129 (1190/59), 139 (1191/26), 161 (1193/19), 410 (1213/28, 30), 421 (1214/20); *DHGE* XIV (1960) 1030.
571. *DHGE* XVI (1967) 448.
572. *Statuta* I, 266 (1201/15).
573. *Statuta* I, 465 (1217/3); *LCC* (2) 322; *cf.* *DHGE* XIV (1960) 1030.
574. *LCC* (2) 245, *cf. CDEM* III, 302 (Velehrad, *1261*); Anton (1986) 394 (No. 82; Moreruela, *1228*).
575. *Statuta* I, 472 (1217/29).
576. *Statuta* II, 39 (1225/19); *RD* II, 168 (No. 6802).
577. Barnes (1982) 53.
578. *DSMLR* 364 (No. 117).
579. Williams (1984) I, 200–03.
580. *AF* 134, *cf. CDL* 181.
581. *CS* I, 36.
582. *CDP* 129 (No. CLXXII).
583. McGuire (1976a) 170–71.
584. *RD* II, 339 (No. 7809).
585. *DD* III, 1511. 855.
586. PRO, DL 25/214.
587. Williams (1984) I, 185.
588. Lekai (1976) 257.
589. Garner (1973) 25, 34.
590. Wyrwa (1984) 35.
591. PRO, DL 25/40.
592. Williams (1984) I, 183.
593. *CMM* I, xl.
594. *AM* II, 282.
595. Clair (1961) 272.
596. St Clair Baddeley (1964) 12.
597. Butler (1988) *passim*; *cf.* Hirst and Wright (1989) 307 (Bordesley).
598. *SRD* IV, 539–44 *(Catalogus illustrium Sorae sepultorum).*
599. *CNM* xvi, 304.
600. Williams (1984) I, 184.
601. *DHGE* XV (1963) 845.
602. Richardson (1951) 11; *cf.* Stalley (1987) 207 (Ireland).
603. *LFZ* 237.
604. *RCH* 98.
605. McCrank (1973) 67, *n.38.*
606. Hockey (1976) 13, 26.
607. *DHGE* XII (1953) 1044; *Statuta* I, 422 (1214/21), 439–50 (1215/26), 450–51 (1216/7), 482 (1217/75), 488 (1218/21), 516 (1220/63).
608. Gwynn (1970) 128.
609. *CTA* 52 (No. 390).
610. *RCH* 91.
611. Carrick (1907) 29, Talbot (1939) 25, 67; (Bruce's casket was found in 1996).
612. Baigent (1882) 14.
613. Williams (1976) 5.
614. King (1954) 20.
615. King (1985) 49.
616. *C.C.R.* 1232/122, 1233/220–21.
617. *KD* II, 200.
618. Williams (1976) 35.
619. *Statuta* I, 314–15 (1205/34–35).
620. *DHGE* X (1938) 61.
621. McGuire (1982) 177–71.
622. *Statuta* I, 466 (1217/7).
623. *LCC* (2) 302.
624. *Statuta* II, 428 (1257/12).
625. *Cf.* Williams (1984) I, 186.
626. *LFZ* 503.
627. Cocheril (1964) 275–76.
628. *Statuta* II, 308 (1246/33).
629. Sommer-Ramer (1982) 316–17.
630. *UGDS* 301 (No.   328).
631. *RCH* 49.
632. Baigent (1882) 30.

Chapter 7

THE TROUBLED BACKGROUND

Physical Disasters

Cistercian life in the early Middle Ages had to contend with a variety of external pressures, in the wake of which it was surprising that abbeys badly affected had the tenacity to survive. Physical attacks on monasteries, their property and personnel; natural or accidental or deliberate disasters, especially fire, heavy financial levies and subsidies exacted, and a burden of consequent debt and litigation, affected many abbeys from time to time. A major part of a community's energy might well be expended on dealing with such issues, to its spiritual detriment. Some abbots found the strain too much and resigned. The vision to-day of peaceful monastic ruins, often carefully landscaped, belies the considerable turmoil they perhaps once knew. Prince Llywelyn's charter giving protection to newly-founded Cymer (1209) gave an idea of what monks might expect: 'burning of houses, shedding of blood within the monastic precincts or also of the granges ... fire, theft, irreverence'[1].

In the Scottish campaigns of English kings monasteries on both sides of the Border suffered grievously. At Melrose (1322) Edward II's troops killed a monk and two blind *conversi*, wounded many more, set fire to buildings, drove off cattle, plundered granaries, and stole church plate[2]. It was a typical catalogue of what a monastery might endure in war. Badly affected 'by frequent forays of the Scots' was Holm Cultram (as in 1216, 1315, 1331)[3]: its lands laid waste, it had to import food from Wales, Ireland, and even Gascony[4]. Rushen's position on the Isle of Man saw it plundered by both Scottish (1275) and Irish (1316) invaders[5]. The Welsh wars of Henry III and Edward I meant abbeys burnt in whole (Grace Dieu, 1233) or part (Strata Florida, 1294); granges burnt (Cwmhir, 1228, 1231); monasteries plundered (Aberconwy, 1245); lands sacked (Basingwerk, 1282)[6]. Only the novitiate and dorter remained intact at Boyle (1202), damaged in the Anglo-Norman wars against the Irish[7].

Particularly devastating were the Tartar invasions of Eastern Europe. In Poland the first wave of attacks (1241) ruined the monasteries of Henryków and Mogiła[8]. In the Balkans the monks of Pilis fled[9], whilst the monks of Egres besieged in their partly fortified monastery were massacred[10]. In the second invasion (1259–60) fifty monks of the six Cistercian houses in Little Poland were killed[11], and Velehrad's community found it safer to live on its granges[12]. The intensity of the second invasion of the Tartars led the General Chapter to order prayers and a special collection for the affected houses, and to request its monasteries to provide clothing for members of the Order 'fleeing from the face of the Tartars'[13]. Egres suffered further (1297) at the hands of the heathen Curmans whom Ladislas IV had settled on lands laid waste by the Tartars[14]. After Danish supremacy had ended in Pomerania, Prussians burnt Oliwa in 1224 (killing twenty of the community), and again in 1235 (six *conversi* and thirty-four servants massacred)[15]. The Prussians also killed the monks of the short-lived abbey at Szpetal (1242)[16].

The wars of Frederick II in Italy saw the burning of Fontevivo, and the sacking of Morimondo Milano (*al.* Coronato) and of Chiaravalle della Colomba (1248)[17]. Rivalry between city states found abbeys in Lombardy frequently in battle-zones. Morimondo (1237) was attacked by Pavian troops who burnt the home grange, destroyed vineyards and mills, ruined crops and broke up the high altar of the church – throwing the sacred Host to the ground[18]. Chiaravalle della Colomba (1307–14) also suffered from inter-city feuding[19]. The grave damage done must have taken years to recover from. In a war zone, too, was Santo-Spirito di Palermo in Sicily. At the moment a revolt broke out there against the Angioni (31 March 1282) the abbey bell happened to ring for Vespers, giving that bloody rebellion the name of the 'Sicilian Vespers'[20]. Further east Moslem ravages under Saladin put an end to conventual life at St John's and 'Salvatio' in the kingdom of Jerusalem (1187)[21], the incursions of Sultan Baibars and his son Qalun did the same for Jubin (by 1271), St Sergius (by 1279), and Balamand (by 1289)[22].

A number of abbeys suffered from attacks by neighbouring hostile lords or communities. The economic success of the white monks irritated those who felt threatened, particularly those who had little land of their own. Innocent III (1214) reminded the Order why it was becoming unpopular: non-payment of tithes, buying up of land and then re-selling at a higher price, rich people able to buy right of burial in Cistercian churches. All these factors, he told the Cistercians, were 'against your Order's initial statutes'. Stephen Lexington (1230) noted that the Order had 'many sly detractors'. The General Chapter commented (1248) that 'in these days of growing malice, our Order is exposed to frequent vexations on account of our privileges and immunities'[23]. There was envy and ill-will: monasteries and their lands became frequent targets; none was totally immune or safe.

The Dunes (1245)[24] and Orval (1276)[25] were badly plundered by local pillagers. Attacks on granges of Monthéron (*c.* 1207) left the monks having to beg their bread 'from door to door'[26]. Locals destroyed the corn of Bindon (1283, 1297) and killed some of the abbey's workers[27]. Men of Nantwich attacked Combermere (1309), burnt its houses in their town, and laid ambushes so the abbot dared not return home[28]. Firm and unpopular administration by Vale Royal of its manor at Darnhall saw an abbey servant slain and his head used as a football (1320)[29], and ultimately the killing of its abbot and cellarer(1339)[30]. At Croxden (1319) the gate-ways were blocked with thorn hedges and the monks besieged for four months[31]. Buckland (1301) saw Devon miners strip five hundred acres of its woodland[32]. Abbot Jens of Øm (1246–49), giving pursuit to German soldiers, was thrown from his horse[33]. The theft by neighbours of firewood, mules and sheep was a recurring problem for Poblet[34]. During disturbances in Bohemia (1278) new buildings at Zlatá Koruna (fd 1263) were razed to the ground[35]. A state of anarchy in Germany allowed Lehnin to be captured and held by a marauding band for twenty years (1319–39). When Salem (1314) took the wrong side in the double-election of Louis of Bavaria and Frederick of Hapsburg as Emperor, the abbot was twice kidnapped and had to pay large sums for ransom and 'protection money'[36]. Kołbacz (1329), threatened by an armed band, paid over 70 marks and 50 pounds of pepper 'as the lesser of two evils'[37]. These instances illustrate the hazards monasteries might face – the Hundred Years War was yet to come.

The white monks were not always the innocent party. Stanley (1276) blocked the Pewe stream, leading to the flooding of the highway between Chippenham and Calne[38]. Men of Dunkeswell (early 14th century) having injured property of the Hospitallers at Bodmescombe, had to present themselves there stripped and barefoot for absolution[39]. Buckfast (1333) denied the allegations of Philip de Columbariis that its monks had hunted on his land and stolen his deer[40]. The master of the hospital 'without the East Gate of Oxford' complained that monks of Stoneleigh (1350) led a band which attacked its property at Westcote, Tysoe, and badly beat its servants there[41]. Peter IV of Aragon suspected the loyalty of some of the monks of La Real (1345)[42]. In the many disputes, though, in which Poblet (1166–1275) was engaged, and settled by arbitration, only five were decided against the monastery[43].

Monasteries might be recompensed, in part at least, for damages suffered in war, either in cash or by the grant of additional lands. Count Raymond VII of Toulouse (1229) paid Grandselve 1,000 silver marks, Belleperche 300, and Candeil 200[44], and aided the expenses of Cîteaux and Clairvaux at the time of the General Chapter[45]. Duke Barnim I of Pomerania gave Oliwa (1254) 120 marks (at the rate of 8 stettin marks per year)[46]. Edward I of England (1284), after making due enquiry, awarded war damages to five Welsh Cistercian houses, Valle Crucis receiving most (£160)[47]. Additional lands were given to Velehrad (1236)[48] and to Osek (1250)[49] by Wenceslas I of Bohemia, and by Ottakar II to Zwettl (1252)[50]. Sovereigns (and also popes)[51] repeatedly took monasteries 'under their protection'. The kings of Aragon (1160–1269) gave at least eighteen warnings to transgressors afflicting Poblet[52]. King Philip Augustus of France (1221) took fourteen Cistercian houses under his wing[53]. Emperor Frederick II (1227) did the same for Heiligenkreuz and its 'line' of Lilienfeld, Zwettl, and Baumgartenburg[54]. Such guarantees might have only limited effect[55]. In Britain, monasteries looked to the king for 'letters of protection'[56], issued also to abbots travelling to General Chapter and elsewhere. Such letters might be 'without term'[57], or valid for one[58] to three years[59] only, or even less[60].

Fire was a serious hazard as monastic buildings had a high degree of timberwork – especially in the domestic ranges. Abbeys ruined by fire were exempt from Cistercian controls on new building when a monastery was heavily in debt[61]. By the close of the thirteenth century the General Chapter (1302) noted an increasing incidence of abbeys 'which are burnt or otherwise destroyed'[62]. Restoration was a major expense and a serious drain on resources. Fires might result from military strategy (as by Edward II's troops at Barzelle; 1314)[63]; arson by disgruntled monks or *conversi* (as a precentor of Perseigne; 1194)[64]; or by seculars with a grudge or out of envy (as frequently at Ląd[65] and on granges of Kołbacz; 1326[66]). A grange was an easy target for arsonists and pillagers, and at best a high fire risk. Sir John Herries set alight a grange of Newbattle (*c.* 1350) and so burnt to death two monks 'in intrigue' with his daughter and widownurse[67]. Some fires were clearly accidental: a barn of Coupar (1215), full of corn, was set ablaze by a candle 'badly and carelessly placed'; the granger perished[68]. Fire also resulted from natural causes, particularly lightning striking the church bell-tower, as at Kołbacz (1253)[69], Strata Florida (1284)[70], and Doberan (1291)[71]. Such fires spread quickly to the church roofs[72]. Seven Scandinavian Cistercian abbeys knew devastating fires[73], and the General Chapter (1293) asked neighbouring abbeys to help ease 'the intolerable poverty' so caused to Vitskøl (1287) and Herrevad (1291)[74]. In drier climes there was a greater risk of fire, and when La Real (1360) demised a grange, a condition was that no fires be started on its lands without its consent[75].

Monastic chronicles may give details of the origin and progress of a fire. At Sorø (13 May, 1247) the conflagration started at 'the third hour after mid-day' and swept through the domestic ranges including the guest-houses, weaving-room and subcellarer's office[76]. At Kołbacz (1248) a fire started 'after Compline', and lightning struck (1253) 'during the time of chapter'[77]. At Strata Florida lightning struck at night and the belfry and roofs were alight without the monks immediately realising it. Melted roof lead flowed down, and 'only the presbytery was spared'[78]. At Toplica 'in the vigil of St Agatha [4 February 1342] in the middle of the night, thunder was heard and lightning set on fire the tower'[79]. At Oliwa (1350) an accidental fire, on Good Friday, destroyed the gate-house and most of the ancillary buildings. Financial help came from Kołbacz (its mother-house) and the Master of the Teutonic Knights, whilst the abbey of Pelplin sent gifts in kind including rye and barley[80]. When fire destroyed Pásztó (1230) grain stored above the cellarium fell in, and still forms an archaeological floor-level[81].

Flooding was a natural hazard for monasteries sited by rivers, as were most Cistercian abbeys. Despite banks and ditches, in times of great storms much damage could result. Waverley (1201, 1203) twice saw major floods invade the conventual buildings[82]. Abbeys sited by tidal waters could be gravely affected, as at Stanlaw by the Mersey estuary (1287; the tower blown down, and fire and flood causing the monks to leave for Whalley)[83]; Meaux by the Humber estuary (1253; a 'great flood' drowning many of its men and animals)[84]; and Margam by the Bristol Channel (1336; repeated flooding destroying its crops)[85]. The bad weather years of 1315–17 were a particular trial for Louth Park[86] and Cleeve[87] – crippled by bad harvests. The dampness was accompanied by widespread outbreaks of animal disease, 'murrain', decimating the stock of Hailes[88], Thame[89] and Newenham[90]. Strong winds destroyed the orchards of Croxden (1300)[91] and the roofs of its claustral buildings (1330)[92]. Earthquakes severely damaged the church fabric[93] at Alcobaça (1222)[94], and Sambucina (1296)[95], struck with fear the monks of Croxden (1331)[96], and severely shook those of Meaux in their choir-stalls (1349)[97].

Disputes with Neighbouring Religious Houses

Pressure of territorial space in western Europe meant that the estates of some monasteries of different Orders were too close for comfort. Contentions arose regarding land ownership and encroachments, and could spill over into violent behaviour. Despite the Peace of 1142 negotiated with the Premonstratensians, there were intermittent quarrels between its monasteries and neighbouring Cistercian houses. These might concern land[98], mills[99] or the close proximity of granges[100]. A *conversus* of Igny burnt a farm belonging to Braine[101]. The Benedictines of Montmajour, jealous of Cistercian privileges, occupied Silvacane (1289) but were forced to withdraw[102]. The Friars Minor caused trouble for the Cistercians in Spain (1275), not least when they captured the abbot of Mattalana in the city of Toledo, beat him and held him prisoner in chains[103]. Arbitration was necessary in difficult situations – as between Léoncel (1192) and the charterhouse of Val-Ste-Marie[104], Poblet (1275) and the Knights Templar of Barbará[105], Rueda (1309) and the Hospitallers of Calanda[106].

Bitter disagreements could arise between neighbouring abbeys of the Cistercian Order itself. The General Chapter noted no less than thirteen major internecine disputes in 1209, fourteen in 1218 and 1239, and as many as fifteen in 1276. The Chapter (1223) strongly condemned those monasteries which 'harmed the unity of the Order by dissensions and quarrels'[107]. Such intra-Order disputes were commonplace in Britain in the first half of the thirteenth century. Combermere (1191–1252) had contentions with Buildwas, Croxden, Dieulacres and Merevale[108]; Cwmhir (1199–1252) with Aberconwy, Strata Florida, Strata Marcella, and Valle Crucis[109]. Matters seemed to have stabilised after 1250, perhaps because land rights were more clearly defined and accepted. Problems arose when abbeys (such as Croxden and Dieulacres) were too closely sited[110], but more commonly because of difficulties stemming from adjacent granges. This was true of some of the granges of Silvacane and Sénanque (1190)[111], Beaubec and Bonport (1206)[112], and Sestri and Rivalta (1207)[113]. Fontenay (1209) 'newly built' a grange close to one of Maizières[114]. Furness (1219) built Winterburn Grange only five miles from Sawley's Stainton Grange[115]. The consequence was pasture disputes, as between Clairefontaine and Cherlieu (1215)[116]. Other disputes might centre on woodlands: L'Île-Dieu and Montier-en-Argonne (1192)[117], water-courses:

Pforta and Reifenstein (1289)[118]; mills: Altzelle (1292)[119]; tithes: Clairvaux and La Ferté (1198)[120], and mines: Byland and Fountains (1226)[121].

Jealous concern for its rights might lead one abbey to perpetrate physical attacks on the property of another. Bitter disputes between Margam and Neath (*c.* 1210) saw their prize horses set to fight each other as their abbey champions[122]. Monks and *conversi* of Mazan (1215) stole sheep belonging to Aiguebelle[123]; and a monk of Maizières (1215) took bundles of hay from a field of Cîteaux[124]. The communities of Eaunes and Feuillant (1246) came to blows[125]. Furness (1338) accused the abbot of Jervaulx of leading a night assault at Horton, where both houses shared pasture, 'with swords, staves, bows and arrows'[126]. The General Chapter (1134) had early insisted that such disputes should be settled peacefully by a meeting of neighbouring abbots. If an impasse was reached the matter was to be referred to the Chapter which then appointed appropriate abbots as arbitrators and judges[127].

An analysis has been made of the principles upon which investigating abbots were appointed[128]. In a dispute between Margam and Neath (1208) seven abbots drawn widely from England and Wales met at the former's Orchard Grange, three as arbitrators, four as assessors; no apparent reason appears for their selection, save that the abbot of Combermere (a Savigniac house) was brought in to safeguard the interests of Neath[129]. A dispute between Cwmhir and Strata Marcella (1227) saw three abbots (of Dore, Whitland and Llantarnam) nominated. Whitland was the mother-house of both monasteries, the other two were impartial. No less than fifty senior monks of the Order, including two further abbots, sat as 'associates' at Radnor[130]. The Horton issue between Furness and Jervaulx (1338) saw the abbots of Sawley and Dieulacres appointed as judges. (Dieulacres, like Furness, was of Savigniac lineage). The arbitrators were from Byland (on the part of Jervaulx), Stanlaw (on the part of Furness), and the prior of Roche (on the part of the judges)[131]. Contrary to the rules of the Order one abbey might take another to secular justice, as Trefontane against Fossanova (1206)[132]. An abbot of Armentera (1274) was deposed because he took the abbot of Valverde to judgement before the king of Castile[133].

Levies and Subsidies

Cistercian houses had no option – whatever exemptions their charters may have given but to comply increasingly with burdensome exactions demanded of them, by their monarch, the Holy See, and the General Chapter (Chapter 2). Throughout the thirteenth century there were repeated demands for money to assist the crusades. Financial aid was also sought towards the expenses of the Fourth Lateran Council (1215)[134], and for the papal war against Frederick II (1240) – this the British Cistercians declined to pay[135]. From the reign of John XXII (1313–34) a wide range of payments was expected by the papacy, as on the confirmation of abbatial elections – when Grandselve had to find 4,000 florins, Clairvaux 3,000, and others lesser amounts[136]. In Britain, royal exactions were much to the disadvantage of monastic economy. The process started when Richard I (1193) demanded that all Cistercian houses give him a year's clip of wool (their most valuable asset), to help pay the exorbitant ransom for his release from captivity[137]. When King John (1210) placed a heavy tax on the British houses to assist his Irish expedition, the monks refused to pay[138]; furious, he fined the Order 30,000 marks. Meaux had to sell buildings and stock in order to comply[139], and when the royal henchmen approached Waverley the abbot fled in fear[140]. The arrears of £800 demanded of Strata Florida were still being paid as late as 1248, so careful was Crown accounting[141].

Henry III frequently expected financial help, but an abbot of Buildwas (1256) told him: 'We cannot give you both money and prayers'[142] – summing up the effect on conventual life that such demands brought. When the General Chapter (1243) forbade such payments, he stopped the sale of Cistercian wool abroad[143]: wool from Margam was impounded at Bristol[144]. Edward I (1275) did exempt the Order's houses from paying a fifteenth, but demanded a 'courtesy payment' of £1,000 for the privilege – this to aid his Welsh wars[145]. Further demands followed: a fifteenth (1292), money for the recovery of Gascony (1294) and defence against the Scots (1297)[146]. Whitland complained that it had paid its fifteenth but this had not been 'written in the great roll'[147]. Edward III (1332), levying money for the marriage of his sister, Eleanor, sent clerks to the monasteries demanding to know what amount each would give[148]. Philip the Fair imposed taxes on all religious houses in France; this became part of a running battle with Boniface VII (1294–1303)[149]. He particularly sought money for his war with Aragon (1285) and for the defence of France (1286–1303)[150]. In all he taxed the French Cistercian houses 20,000 *livres* each year. Some reluctant to pay were ransacked by royal tax-collectors[151]. Other forms of aid might be expected. With the advent of the Hundred Years War, Edward III (1337) expected Beaulieu to provide a ship and mariners to patrol the south coast of England, but the abbot pointed out that he was already finding ten men-at-arms as well as archers[152].

Very detrimental to a British monastery's well-being could be the appointment of its abbot as a royal tax-collector. Not only was it time-consuming, but if the abbot found other monasteries or clerics unable or unwilling to pay, his own house might well be distrained in consequence. The varied objectives included a tenth imposed to find revenue for the Scottish war (1309), 'crusading tenths' – as that enjoined by Clement V (1318–20) – and a triennial tenth on account of the war with France (1344–45). In most cases an abbot acted as a sub-collector for the diocesan bishop. His 'qualification' for appointment was his monastery's possession of appropriated churches in the relevant diocese[153]. An abbot of Aberconwy (1294) found the local clergy so affected by war that they could not pay their tenth, even if they had been willing[154]. As the abbot of Valle Crucis was often in arrears, distraint on that monastery's property was ordered five times (1316–34)[155]. As a prior of Cluniac Bromholm noted, collecting tenths was 'a shrewde labor, a grete cost, a shrewde juparde'[156].

The Burden of Debt

The abbot of Margam reported to the General Chapter in 1336 the reasons for its 'pressing debts': marine incursions, animal disease, enemy attacks, and a multitude of guests[157]. To which he might have added: the burden of tenths, unwise dealings with money-lenders, acting as sureties and credit banks, and, sometimes, poor administration and the burden of litigation[158]. The list of Cistercian monasteries suffering severe debt problems at one time or another is endless. It included houses experiencing 'intolerable poverty' (Nogales, 1207[159]); 'manifold collapse' (Fontainejean, 1277)[160]; 'saddled with debt' (Barona, 1219)[161]; 'bound in debt' (Fontmorigny, 1241)[162]; 'poverty and penury' (Beaugerais, 1201)[163]; 'an abyss of debts' (Longvilliers, 1231)[164]. Monastic debts were often very considerable, as at Meaux (1269), owing nearly £4,000 (equivalent to some £200,000 today)[165]. Far worse was the proto-abbey of Pontigny (1260): owing 10,000 *tours pounds*, it's abbot was deposed for maladministration[166]. The problems increased rather than got better. The General Chapter of 1278 referred to many abbeys as being in a state of 'irreparable destruction', and ordered that where debts amounted to more than the annual value of the house the abbot was to be deposed, and the cellarer and bursars removed from office[167]. In 1303 the Chapter still had to note the 'considerable debts and credit obligations' of many of its monasteries[168].

A recurring problem was involvement with Italian wool merchants-cum-moneylenders. With the development of the wool trade the houses of Italian bankers flourished in England. They bought up monastic wool 'and launched out into all forms of banking enterprises'[169]. Many a monastery found that to sell the next year's crop of wool in advance (permitted by the Order in 1181) was a simple way of getting ready cash. Unfortunately if (perhaps because of murrain) sufficient wool was not then produced the houses became indebted to the moneylenders. This was especially true at Fountains which in 1276 sold the next four years' crop to merchants of Florence for a down-payment of almost 700 marks. Fountains was already in debt to Flemish dealers, and the Italian merchants insisted on mortgaging the abbey. The Crown had to come to the rescue, taking the monastery into secular custody[170]. The problems in England caused the Chapter (1277) to reiterate that no more than one year's wool crop might be sold in advance, but then (1279) permitted a longer period 'if the money was to be used to pay outstanding debts'[171]. It was a vicious circle. Other houses which borrowed money included Tilty (1296) – £64 from the Ricardi of Lucca. Tilty maintained it repaid this debt, but – when Edward I confiscated the goods of the Ricardi – Tilty had to pay it over again, this time to the Exchequer[172]. Meaux (1280) owed £2,500 to foreign moneylenders and merchants[173].

The General Chapter forbade the taking of usurious loans from Jews (1189–90)[174]. This may have stemmed from the realisation that when Aaron of Lincoln died (1189) nine English Cistercian abbeys owed him in total over 6,400 marks[175]. The building programmes of those monasteries had probably been a major factor in this dependence on Jewish financiers[176]. The earlier injunctions conveniently forgotten, monastic borrowing from Jews was to the fore much later – as at Stratford (1275) and Fountains (1273). The king pardoned Stratford the interest due on its debt, but insisted it repaid the principal[177]. Fountains, owing the Jews of York £2,700, raised the money partly by borrowing from Flemish and Italian merchants[178]. In the year before they were expelled from England (1290), the General Chapter ruled that no deposit was to be held in safe-keeping for Jews[179].

A series of regulations was aimed at containing the problem of debt. Father-abbots were to punish abbots and officials of daughter-houses in excessive debt (1157)[180] for no good reason (1181)[181]. 'Enormous debts' were to be repaid by the sale of property (1184)[182]. Abbeys owing more than fifty marks were not to buy new lands or commence new building works, but work already started was not affected (1188)[183]. Later (1240) the debt limit was raised to £100 and exemptions were given if the cost was covered by a specific ear-marked donation, or if the abbey was a new foundation[184]. No loans were to be taken at an usurious rate of interest, because it became too difficult to repay (1189)[185]. This ruling was later mitigated if a loan was to pay off previous debts or intended for some other 'great and urgent necessity'[186]. As often happened, speedy turnabout or revision of Chapter legislation left many loop-holes and the ability to circumvent the rules.

In bad cases of debt a community might be dispersed or the monastery taken into secular custody. Abbots who broke the rules might be deposed[187]. Visitors were reminded to deal with problems of debt (1237)[188]. Stephen Lexington on visitation at Longvilliers (1231) instituted proper procedures for book-keeping and ordered austerity measures – including limiting the numbers in the community. At the same house (1236) he approved a ten-point plan to reduce the still heavy debt. It involved a cut-back in expenses – wine was forbidden, and more careful supervision by the cellarer[189]. When Heisterbach (1277) was in financial difficulties the abbots of Camp and Val-Dieu held a meeting there with its creditors[190]. Debts could be reduced: at Vaux-de-Cernay from 2,000 *paris pounds* in 1232 to 200 only four years later[191], and at Kirkstall from over £5,000 in 1284 to only £160 by 1301[192]. To pay their debts,

Fountains sold wool at Boston Fair (1276)[193] and Meaux (1280–86) demised granges[194]. The papal constitution of 1335 tightened matters up considerably[195].

Litigation in Secular Courts

As the estates and privileges of the Cistercians grew, so too did the complaints of those lay-folk who felt aggrieved in one way or another, and who sought remedy in civil courts of justice. As early as 1180 Abbot Peter of Clairvaux drew attention to 'the great number of false claims successfully made against our houses'[196]. Abbots and senior monks needed to have the ability to defend the rights of their houses[197]. It was said of Abbot Thomas of Meaux (1182–97) that he was 'too soft and mild, too much at home in the cloister rather than in the law court'[198]. The burden of litigation became so great that Gregory IX (1227) ruled that Cistercian monks could not be summoned to a tribunal more than two days' journey from their monastery[199]; a privilege of which the monks of Dore (1266) reminded the Knights Hospitaller who wanted to sue their abbey in London[200].

Litigation was both time-consuming and expensive. The expenses of an abbot of Croxden (1263) attending Stafford Assizes for seven weeks came to £30[201]. When an abbot of Sibton (1340–42) pleaded exemption from taxation on 200 acres of land, it involved court hearings in both King's Lynn and Norwich, a personal appearance by the abbot at the former, the appointment of an attorney and a sergeant, searching of rolls and memoranda at the Exchequer, and the empanelling of a jury. All this took over two years[202]. When, after the Edwardian Conquest, the Cistercian houses of Wales saw their ancient exemptions challenged, the monks of Valle Crucis (1290) complained of 'the hardship to them in being obliged always to go to seek remedy where the king may be'[203]. Deferral of cases made matters even more expensive. Strata Marcella (1279–81), involved in protracted litigation before several sessions of the Welsh Assize, was partly to blame for postponements as frequently it was not represented[204]. The white monks were not only sued, they often initiated cases. Jervaulx had to sue tenants for neglect of services due (1284), men who had rescued goods impounded by the abbot (1298), and those who had pulled down a wall on monastic land (1300)[205]. To withdraw from a suit after issuing a writ also cost money, as an abbot of Midleton (1293) found[206].

Whilst an abbot might appear in person in important cases, it became more usual for him to be represented at secular courts by attorneys, frequently obtaining royal approval for their nomination. The 'Coucher Book' of Kirkstall contains a set form for the appointment of such monastic proctors 'for all business'[207]. An attorney appointed by Bonrepos (1267) was to 'gain or lose for it in all pleas and plaints'[208] A proctor nominated by the monks of Sibton (1305) had 'authority to bind them, their house and goods, to the sum of £10, and to do all things which may be done by proxy'[209]. Royal approval for the appointment of attorneys was given to Clairvaux (1259) to maintain its interests in English courts[210]. Attorneys were approved for many English houses when their abbots travelled overseas[211]. A monastery might appoint two of its monks as its attorneys, as Beaulieu (1271)[212]. More often, one monk and a layman were nominated as at Bonrepos (1267)[213] and Robertsbridge (1280)[214]. At Salem (1259–76) *conversi* were procurators at court[215]. One of the attorneys might be the cellarer (Roche, 1230)[216]. At Beaulieu (1270) a 'Keeper of Pleas' handled all litigation, as well as recording its results and costs. His expenses included the purchase of two chests to keep charters safe, and the cost of pleas in London, Winchester (the Forest Eyre) and Cornwall (where it had land and revenues in the Lizard peninsula)[217].

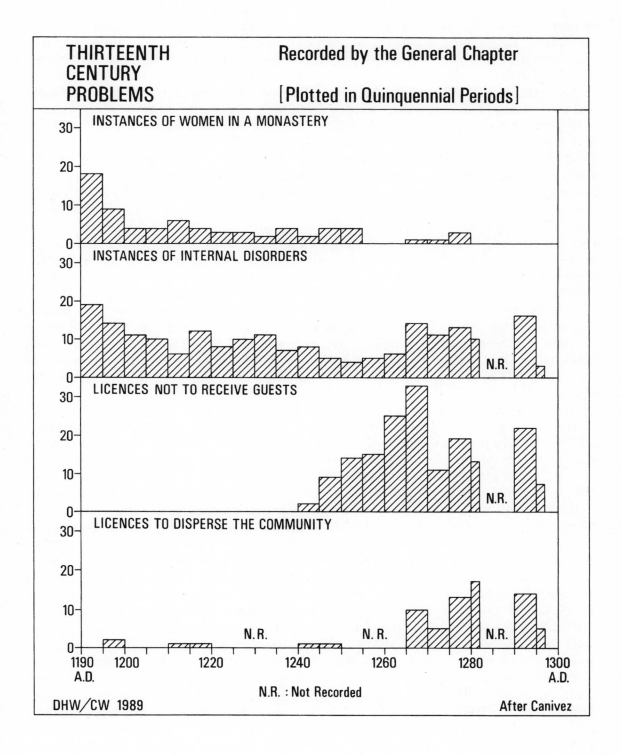

THIRTEENTH CENTURY PROBLEMS

Recorded by the General Chapter

[Plotted in Quinquennial Periods]

INSTANCES OF WOMEN IN A MONASTERY

INSTANCES OF INTERNAL DISORDERS

LICENCES NOT TO RECEIVE GUESTS

LICENCES TO DISPERSE THE COMMUNITY

N.R. : Not Recorded

DHW/CW 1989

After Canivez

Preventive Measures

An abbey beset by debt or other serious problems, might well petition the General Chapter to allow it not to receive guests (a heavy economic burden) for a stated period of years, or even for permission to disperse its monks temporarily to other houses of the Order. In England a concerned monarch might take a troubled monastery into 'secular custody'. These were only partial solutions, but they did give monasteries a breathing-space in which to recoup their losses.

Available records suggest that between 1239 and 1297 some 120 abbeys of the Order had to resort to obtaining a dispensation from receiving guests[218]. Some houses had to seek permission three times, as Bujedo[219] and Bellevaux[220], whilst Tamié (1267–94) had a protracted series of dispensations[221]. Ten houses received dispensation in 1262[222], no less than fourteen in 1281[223]. The period granted varied from one to five years, but three years was most common. Sometimes the permission was conditional, being granted on the understanding that the community was not dispersed, as for Bronnbach (1274)[224], or, if already dispersed, on the monks being recalled, as at Pforta (1277)[225]. Chiaravalle di Milano (1262) was granted a four-year dispensation from receiving guests, so long as it was maintaining twelve monks from its afflicted daughter-house at Cerreto[226]. Sometimes (and perhaps implied in other instances) the dispensation was only from receiving persons of the Order, as for La Clarté-Dieu (1239)[227]. Debt was cited as the reason for non-reception of guests at Mores (1251)[228], wars at Pairis (1251)[229]; and bad weather at four French houses in 1249[230]. A king of Bohemia (1338) freed Sedlec from giving hospitality 'to all men of whatever status' because of the economic collapse of that monastery[231]. The General Chapter (1261, 1306) ruled that during the period of dispensation no novices were to be received at the abbey concerned and no new and 'sumptuous' buildings erected, only old ones repaired[232].

In extreme circumstances, a father-abbot was permitted (1190) to disperse the monks of a distressed abbey to other houses, provided that they were not similarly afflicted. If the dispersal was likely to last long then the General Chapter was to be consulted. The abbot of a receiving house was to welcome refugee monks 'with joyful love'[233]. Later (1237) the permission of the Chapter became necessary for all dispersals, unless the matter was very urgent. This saving clause was omitted in the codification of 1257, which insisted on the Chapter's permission being obtained[234]. When communities were dispersed without leave of the Chapter (1276) then no abbey was obliged to receive any of their monks[235]. To spread the burden, it had ruled (1258) that no abbey should maintain more than two refugee monks[236]. Later (1315) a sliding-scale was introduced: a monastery with at least twenty monks was to receive one refugee, an abbey with forty, two; and so on, up to a maximum of five at a house with one hundred monks[237]. At least sixty monasteries suffered dispersions between 1260 and 1300. The year with the greatest known number of dispersals (as well as of exemptions from receiving guests) was 1281 (twelve cases)[238]. Some dispersals were noted in non-Chapter records, e.g. those affecting Žďár (1280)[239] and Sedlec (1282)[240].

Time limits were placed on the length of dispersal or slowness of recall, three years being the most common. So long as a house was maintaining refugee monks it might be excused from receiving guests[241]. The Chapter (1281) became aware of the harm numerous dispersals did to the reputation of the Order[242]. Some monks were dispersed for longer than was good[243], and father-abbots were urged (1284) to 'recall them by their industry'[244]. Dispersals usually took place within the 'generation' to which a house belonged, as when the monks of Rievaulx (1291)[245] and Camp (1295)[246] were disseminated. This to an extent might make refugee monks feel at home, and their plight was further mitigated by the Chapter's ruling (1281) that monks were not to be dispersed out of the region in which they lived[247]. That statute was revoked the next year[248], but successive Chapters did insist that monks of Cerreto (1273) were to be dispersed only 'through Lombardy'[249], and monks of Bruern (1292) 'through the kingdom of England'[250], whilst monks of Buch (1294) were to remain within Germany[251]. Refugee monks could thus stay in their own cultural environment.

The monks of Meaux were dispersed three times (*c.* 1160, 1196, 1210) - a humiliation for the abbots who in each case resigned[252]. The monks of Waverley were dispersed twice (1203, 1210); first because of crop failure, and then because of King John's impositions[253]. Other reasons ascribed for dispersal included: poverty (the most common)[254], economic collapse (Himmerod, 1297)[255], debt (Kirkstall, 1284)[256], storm effects (Fontenay, 1249)[257], and physical attacks (Rievaulx, 1291)[258]. A skeleton staff remained[259]: at Rivalta (1269) two monks as overseers rendering quarterly accounts[260]; at Sedlec (1282) three or four monks[261]. When the monks of Vaux-de-Cernay returned from sheltering in Paris (1195) during English-French conflict, they found their abbey badly damaged[262]. Sometimes dispersion was a finality: monks never returned to Stirpeto (1348) after leaving when the Hungarian army invaded its region[263]. No Cistercian guests (1189)[264] and no novices (1196)[265] were to be received in an abbey whose community had been dispersed, unless their standing was such that rejection would cause scandal (1237)[266].

To avoid the dispersal of monks, and to right the economic situation of a troubled monastery, English monarchs (at least from the time of Edward I) might take such a house into royal custody. This assistance and protection meant the appointment of persons of standing to temporarily manage the finances[267] and fabric[268] of the house, whilst allowing the monks sufficient income for their upkeep[269]. The 'keepers' (who deputed officials) included: the earl of Lincoln for Kirkstall (1276)[270], the earl of Devon for Bindon (1348)[271], the bishop of Durham for Rievaulx (1288)[272], and the neighbouring abbots of Bordesley and Dore for Flaxley (1335)[273]. The most common reason for secular custody was indebtedness – true of thirteen abbeys between 1274 and 1305[274], Flaxley (1277) because of debt to the king 'in a very large sum' – partly due to a loan contracted in the Jewry[275]. Combermere underwent several periods of custody between 1275 and 1328[276]. Bindon (1348) was placed under protection because of French marauders[277]. Secular custody removed economic freedom for a time from the monks of the house, but it did allow them to remain there and continue the daily round of worship unimpaired.

Fortifications

Several Cistercian abbeys found it expedient to adapt their buildings for defensive purposes. King Andrew II of Hungary (1205–35) fortified Egres, and there the local populace took refuge from the Tartars (1241). Unfortunately, the abbey was besieged and 'many armaments' set up against it[278]. In the wake of the Tartar invasions, defensive towers were built by Pilis at Vepruch near Poszony (Bratislava)[279], and by Toplica on the island of St Ladislas[280]. King Přemysl of Bohemia garrisoned a fortress on Velehrad's island of St George[281]. In the Baltic region the monastery of Dünamünde, either after its sacking by the Semgallians (1228) or possibly later by the Teutonic Knights, was re-modelled with a moat fed from the Dvina river surrounding two walled and turreted enclosures. A similar style was developed at Falkenau[282]. After the wooden buildings of Padis had been burnt in the Wars of Liberation (1343) stone structures were erected with rectangular outer walls[283].

Other more or less fortified abbeys in Eastern Europe included Hiddensee and Pelplin[284]. The Hundred Years' War (1337–1453) saw similar measures taken in

France. The monks of Flaran built a precinct wall on the south side with a battlemented gate-house pierced by loop-holes; to the east, north and west, the river Baise and the mill-canal gave sufficient protection[285]. Boulbonne was defended by high towers and strong walls[286], and other abbeys to take protective measures included Vaucelles[287] and Bonport[288]. The granges of Bonneval were fortified against looters[289], as were two granges of Fontfroide: Fontcalvi and Gaussan[290]. In Spain the Puerta Real at Poblet with its towers was erected in the reign of Peter IV of Aragon (1338–87)[291]. In the Lebanon the fortress-like nature of Balamand, and a hidden chamber there, may relate to the Moslem enemy[292].

Edward III (1327) bade Roche and other monasteries in Northern England protect themselves against the Scots[293], and gave leave for Whalley (1348) 'to crenellate its church and close'[294]. Holm Cultram (1348) was permitted to crenellate its manor-house at Wolsty nearby[295], and Furness (1327) its 'dwelling-house of Fotheray'[296]. Both the latter, Wolsty Castle and Piel Castle to-day, were defensive towers suitable for the storage of valuables, and as guards and look-outs against both Scots and pirates. Piel had the additional advantage of being sited on an island. Newminster had its Rothley Tower[297]. In Southern England the danger of French landings saw Buckland (1337) given permission to crenellate[298], whilst Beaulieu and Quarr (1339) provided men-at-arms and archers to help defend the New Forest and the Isle of Wight[299]. (Unfortunately, soldiers appointed by the Crown to guard the coastlands of Netley [1341] stole its sheep and wool)[300]. The seal of Robertsbridge showed an embattled tower at each end of the abbey bridge[301]. Stephen Lexington (1228) advised the use of laymen to guard woods and cornfields[302]. Armed with bows and arrows[303], servants protected granges of Fontenay (1233)[304], Holm Cultram (1235)[305] and Margam (1246)[306].

Monasteries as Repositories

In an age before banks, large sums of money were held in monasteries, partly because of the relative security they afforded, and partly because their abbots were frequently collectors of subsidies. All abbeys had a safe-room or treasury for the storage of monies and valuable deeds and documents in a Cistercian house often at dorter level. At Meaux precious ornaments and relics were kept by the sacristan 'in a chamber within the dormitory'; at Whalley 'in a little chamber in the dorter'[307]; the treasury at Croxden (1344) was contiguous to the new dorter[308]. The treasury at Whalley (1265) must have been at ground-level, for it was flooded out[309]; that at Boyle was subterranean, in the crypt[310]. The abbot of Tintern as collector of a tenth (1320) was enjoined to keep the money 'in a safe place'[311]. Caesarius of Heisterbach (*c.* 1225) mentions an usurer depositing money in the safe of a monastery 'by the side of the monastic money', and refers to the locks of the safe and the seals of the bags[312]. The treasury of Poblet (1316) guarded 87,667 *sueldos*, a hoard which contained nine kinds of currency[313]. The 1335 papal constitution bade monies be 'kept in a safe place under four different locks and keys', the keys being held by the abbot, bursar, prior, and one other monk elected by the community[314]. A few monasteries had external strong-rooms as did Holm Cultram at Wolsty Castle where was an 'evidence house' or muniment chamber[315], and Valle Crucis at Y Tŵr near Castell Dinas Brân – where valuable records were kept[316].

Popes and kings might use Cistercian strong-rooms to bank money from subsidies securely, as well as crown jewels and other valuables. Ter Doest (1231) received in safe-keeping (being close to the coast) a coffer containing 1,000 silver marks collected in Denmark by a papal scrivener, and there also (1227) the queen of France deposited a chest containing 549 marks whilst it awaited carriage to the king of Denmark[317]. King

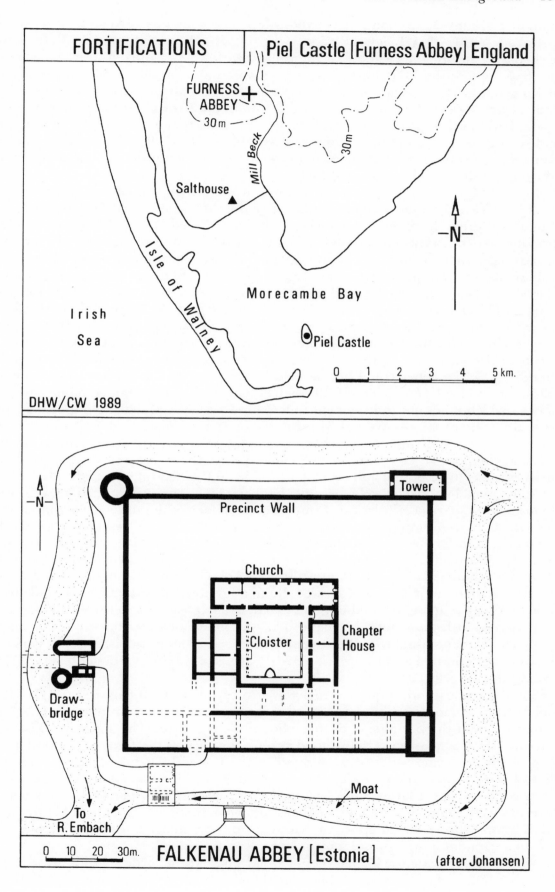

FORTIFICATIONS — Piel Castle [Furness Abbey] England

DHW/CW 1989

FALKENAU ABBEY [Estonia]   (after Johansen)

John of England (1215) had jewels, gold, silver, and wine in safe-keeping at fourteen Cistercian houses[318]. When Crown wine was stored at Holm Cultram (1299), the royal exchequer paid for the cleaning of the cellar and for a lock affixed to it[319]. At Egres (1280) King Ladislas IV deposited the crown jewels and regalia[320]; the same was true of King James II of Aragon at Santes Creus (1307)[321]. Much money levied as tenths and subsidies was lodged in monastic houses until the Crown had need of it. Furness (1345) had to safeguard the monies levied by the collectors in Lancashire 'in a proper and strong room'[322]. Crusade monies were held at Pilis (1200–04) for King Imre of Hungary[323]. Dore (1245) received money 'for the redemption of crusading vows' which the bishop of Hereford sent for[324].

In time of war even a monastic strong-room was at risk. On Christmas Day, 1215, King John's army ransacked Tilty, 'broke open the chests, and carried off the booty'[325]. When the 'great army' of the justiciar of Ireland raided Boyle (1235), the soldiers 'broke open the crypt and carried off its treasure'[326]. Men of the earl of Hereford broke open coffers of Sir Hugh Despenser placed in safe-keeping at Stanley (1321) and stole money, jewels, gold and silver plate[327]. After the Battle of Byland (1322) silver plate left at Rievaulx by Edward II was plundered by the Scots[328]. The abbot of Margam (1320) on the south coast of Wales protested that 'the place of the abbey is too perilous to receive or keep treasure'[329]. Despite such risks numerous layfolk deposited their savings, and the General Chapter (1183) legislated to save abbeys any embarrassment. Deposits greater than £5 were to be received only on condition that should there be loss, the abbey could not be held liable[330], but the abbot was to provide for 'faithful custody'[331]. An abbot of L'Île-Dieu (1206) 'who had commuted money held on deposit which he ought to have kept unimpaired' was disciplined[332]. Deposited sums were often spent, or re-invested in loans; this was forbidden by the Chapter (1209) unless the depositor agreed[333]. Abbot Lexington (Savigny, 1230) expanded on the rules: any deposit received was to be handed over to the treasurers, the year and day of receipt was to be noted, and also 'by whose hand the deposit was made'[334].

Cistercian abbeys frequently became bankers for their area[335]. 80 marks were deposited at Quarr (1227) by the Templar commander of the navy at Portsmouth[336]; 200 marks by a bishop of Avranches at Savigny (1235)[337]; £80 at Thame (1265) by Simon de Montfort before his death[338]. A layman deposited a large sum 'in the treasury of Staffarda' (1274)[339]. Other goods which might be deposited[340] included grain (as at Staffarda, 1247[341] and Holm Cultram, 1325)[342]. Abbot Lexington ruled that if the storage of corn or wine was allowed, then, as granges in Britain had recently been destroyed, it was to be received not 'in the name of deposit' but 'in the name of grant', so that no satisfaction need be made if it was stolen or deteriorated[343]. Casanova d'Abruzzo was entrusted with the keys of the local city, and its public seals[344]. Personal deeds were deposited at Basingwerk (1328)[345], Duiske (1289)[346], Fürstenfeld (1338)[347] and Strata Marcella (1230)[348].

Some religious were requested to act as a surety or to stand bail. Urban III (1186) ruled that 'no monk or *conversus* was to become a surety', and Innocent III (1203) added 'without the permission of the abbot and chapter'[349]. The abbots of L'Isle-en-Barrois (1205) and Buzay (1206) stood surety 'contrary to the form of the Order'[350]. The practice became widespread and led to the General Chapter (1260) reiterating that Cistercians were not to undertake such obligations[351]. An abbot of Beaupré (1277) became surety 'for a large sum of money'[352]. An abbot of Cymer (1276) was one of several sureties for the release of a noble's son from prison[353]. An abbot of Holy Cross (1297) stood surety for an episcopal bad debt to the Lombardi; called to account, he had to surrender a grange and a manor to the merchants[354].

Monasteries frequently loaned money to layfolk, but the Order (1180) insisted that when lending to those *in need* an abbey should not take their possessions in pledge, nor in that way gain interest on the principal lent[355]. The Chapter (1204) also ordered that 'chests or treasuries which for the purposes of indecent gain have been placed in abbeys' were to be removed immediately[356]. When three German abbots (1202) were rebuked for lending money for the building of a settlement, their action may have been viewed as an improper or risky venture[357]. The Chapter (1226) did allow the advance of money to seculars for farm improvements (as stock numbers) in return for a share of the profits[358]. Margam (1252–58) loaned monies in return for gifts of land, one donor giving it an acre of land for one mark 'with power of redemption on paying the mark and the cost of improvement'[359].

Indirect banking transactions were evidenced at Furness (1219), the kings of Man paying there an annual 'recognition' to the Holy See[360]. The hospital of Sandon received an annual rent *via* the abbot of Sallay (1246)[361]. The good offices of the abbot of Aberconwy (1280) enabled Prince Llywelyn to transfer 100 marks to his brother's use[362]. Sedlec (1312) handled large sums of money on behalf of the duke of Austria[363]. Those who borrowed money from a Cistercian house ranged from people in 'great necessity'[364] to nobles and monarchs. Poblet assisted financially Alfonso II's subjugation of the Moors (in the 1170's), and helped James I in his conquest of Majorca (1229)[365]. Netley (1242) lent £100 towards the expenses of Henry III's rearguard in leaving Portsmouth[366]. After 1300 Danish abbeys lent money in return for lands mortgaged to them as collateral[367].

Some visitors to, or even officials of, a monastery, might have mislaid or secreted cash which they were unable later to reclaim. Hoards have been found at Cwmhir: thirteen *deniers* dating from the reigns of Henry II (1154–89) and Richard I of England (1189–99), issued in their capacity as dukes of Aquitaine[368]; at Neath: 166 English silver pennies hidden beneath the first floor of the west range, whose concealment may be connected with the flight of Edward II who stayed at the abbey shortly before his capture nearby in November 1326[369]; and, five miles from Rushen (at Ballayelse in the mountain land of Arbory), Edward I silver pennies – which might relate to the English raid on that abbey in 1316[370]. At Longueroye Grange of Longvilliers (in a wall being demolished in 1913) a parchment enclosing about sixty gold and silver coins, dating from no later than the first half of the fourteenth century, was discovered – perhaps hidden during a time of English invasion[371]. At Melrose[372] and San Galgano[373] monastic tokens issued for local transactions have been found.

The Knights of Calatrava

The white monks did not shrink from settling in difficult 'frontier' areas. They met in this way the Moor in Spain, the Saracen in Syria, and the pagan Slav in the Baltic littoral. These contacts led to Cistercian influence in the growth of military orders, whilst some abbots and monks played no small part in the crusades – although monks and *conversi* were forbidden to take up arms or become involved in war areas (1197)[374]. In time (1237) *conversi* were officially allowed to accompany military expeditions – but only to care for the animals[375]. As late as 1282 the General Chapter reiterated that 'no monk or *conversus* was to bear arms of any kind, because it is not agreeable to the purity of our religion – which is to be angels of peace and an example in the Church'[376]. Clearly some religious had been doing so.

Early Cistercian influence in warfare and the crusades stemmed from St Bernard's presence at the Council of Troyes (1128) and his work on the rule of the Knights Templar[377]. Bernard thought of the Templars as being military monks: 'They can fight the battle of the Lord, and indeed be soldiers of Christ'. There were parallels to Cistercian custom: white cloister habit for the knights, brown for the lesser brethren;

emphasis on silence – including sign language in the refectory; simplicity in weapons and saddlery. There were Cistercian dissentients from the idea of holy war, not least Isaac of Stella who wrote of 'this dreadful new military order, that someone has called the order of the fifth gospel'[378]. Bernard's rôle in the evolution of the Templars formed a precedent for other new orders closely associated with the Cistercians, of which the most notable was the Order of Calatrava. After the Templars had abandoned their Spanish fortress at Calatrava in 1158, Sancho III of Castile gave it to Abbot Raymond of Fitero, a daughter-house of Morimond in Navarre. The abbot, supported by the archbishop of Toledo, brought as many monks as possible from Fitero and assembled with them at Calatrava a very large band of armed men. The abbot acted as Master of the new Order until he retired and died near Toledo (1163)[379].

Having Cistercian roots, the knights (1187) with royal backing, requested the General Chapter for a firm union with the Order. They were accepted as 'true brethren of Cîteaux' and affiliated to Morimond[380]. Two monks of Morimond were to reside at Calatrava, and the fortress was to be visited annually by the abbot of Morimond or his delegate; from 1195 to 1234 this was usually the abbot of Gumiel[381]. From 1209, the knights when visiting abbeys of the Order could stand at worship in the retro-choir or even in the presbytery; in monastic infirmaries they were to be cared for in a separate place[382]. From 1222 they could be with the monks in choir, chapter, refectory and infirmary[383]. Their status had become intermediate between that of the choir monks and the *conversi*: they were neither lay-brethren nor yet clerics; they were military knights, but truly Cistercian. They wore a tunic of undyed wool to facilitate riding, over which they wore a black or white scapular with hood attached. Outdoors, over tunic and scapular they wore a mantle, indoors a cloak, but in choir (from about 1222) a cowl. Theirs was a modified Cistercian habit. Clothing restrictions chafed the knights, but Gregory X (1275) insisted that no changes be made. Only in 1397 were they allowed to add a red cross of woollen cloth on their left breast if they so wished[384].

The General Chapter of 1249 referred to the Order of Calatrava, after its successful exploits, as 'a noble and special part of the Order'[385]. From 1247 the Prior was to attend the Chapter every third year, the Master every sixth[386]. Like all Cistercian houses, the commanderies of the knights were exempt from the jurisdiction of diocesan bishops, and generally speaking from the payment of tithes. Until 1245 this latter privilege led to a long-running battle with the archbishops of Toledo[387]. Special constitutions for the knights were drawn up by a monk of Cîteaux, Guy de Paray (ob. 1206). At first the knights, unmarried, were drawn from any class except serfs. From 1325 on, only the offspring of knights and squires were accepted, not humbler freemen[388]. The knights made their profession to the lay Master 'as if abbot'[389]. Absolute obedience to the Master was promised, and implicit in this were poverty and chastity. The chaplains were secular clergy who became monks of Calatrava, and their superior was the Prior[390]. Only one female house (San Felices de los Barrios, fd 1219) was attached to Calatrava: the General Chapter (1220) allowed dispersed nunneries to be united in this foundation as 'Calatrava sisters'[391].

The Master of the Order resided in one of the larger commanderies. His duties were manifold: to lead the knights in battle, and garrison them in strongholds, appointing their commanders; as a major vassal to give 'aid and counsel', when called on, to the kings of Castile; to arrange the internal organisation of the Order and to maintain discipline, governing it in matters both temporal and spiritual; to attend the General Chapter of the Cistercians, and to visit the affiliated Orders of Alcántara, Avis, and Montesa[392]. At first the Master was elected by all the knights and chaplains, but by the close of the thirteenth century only the commanders and perhaps a representative group of other electors met, so that the frontier was not left unguarded[393].

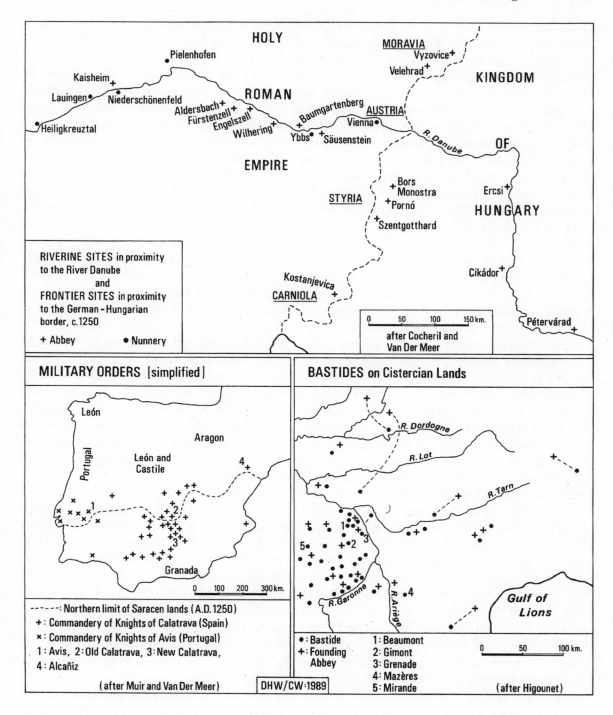

RIVERINE SITES in proximity
to the River Danube
and
FRONTIER SITES in proximity
to the German-Hungarian
border, c.1250

+ Abbey   • Nunnery

after Cocheril and
Van Der Meer

MILITARY ORDERS [simplified]

-----: Northern limit of Saracen lands (A.D.1250)
+ : Commandery of Knights of Calatrava (Spain)
× : Commandery of Knights of Avis (Portugal)
1 : Avis, 2:Old Calatrava, 3:New Calatrava,
4 : Alcañiz

(after Muir and Van Der Meer)

DHW/CW:1989

BASTIDES on Cistercian Lands

• : Bastide
+ : Founding
    Abbey

1: Beaumont
2: Gimont
3: Grenade
4: Mazères
5: Mirande

(after Higounet)

The Master originally lived in community with the knights but, increasingly a public figure, his standard of living and financial commitments were such that by the end of the thirteenth century half the revenues of the Order went to him. There were five great officers of the Order below the Master: the *comendador mayor*, the lieutenant-general of the Master in Castile; the *clavero*, the castellan of Calatrava itself; the *prior*, who cared for the spiritual welfare of the knights and acted as superior of the chaplains; the *sacristan*, responsible for liturgical arrangements; and the *obrero*, a sort of clerk of works[394]. Always a French Cistercian from Morimond, the Prior resided at Calatrava itself[395]. From time to time there was dissension concerning the positions of both Master and Prior. About 1200 the knights of Alcañiz elected their own Master.

Innocent III put an end to the consequent temporary schism. There were serious intermittent challenges to the mastership of Don García López (1297–1336) and the subsequent succession of Don Alfonso Pérez[396]. The abbots of Morimond found it necessary to visit Calatrava more frequently than in the past[397], and especially as the abbot of Gumiel, acting as Visitor, had in 1234 tried to usurp the powers of Morimond by appointing a Spanish monk as Prior at Calatrava[398]. There were also external quarrels, chiefly a natural rivalry between the Orders of Calatrava and Santiago, though pacts of brotherhood were concluded from time to time, dealing with ownership of properties, rights of pasture, mutual hospitality, and concerted military action[399]. There were problems too for Calatrava from 'many abbeys in Spain' (1249–50) concerning the passage and pasture of its flocks. Calatrava itself seems to have charged tolls on Cistercian flocks (of Tarouca and other abbeys) in passage across its lands[400].

The knights were garrisoned in a series of commanderies guarding the frontier of Christian Spain. Calatrava itself, governed by the *clavero* of the Order and the seat of the Prior, had a community of monks of the Order who prayed for the spiritual welfare of the knights and their success in battle[401]. Each lesser commandery had twelve knights and a chaplain. In time of war, able-bodied men of the district would supplement the fighting force. Each commandery was essentially a benefice comprising a unit of territory, the rents from which formed the income of the knight-commander[402]. Commanderies tended to be priory towns rather than isolated strongholds. The commandery itself was usually centred on a rectangular Spanish keep, with corner towers to facilitate arrow, fire and oil pouring, and a watch-tower outside the walls. Usually the castle and the conventual buildings were separate[403]. The original Calatrava was lost in battle in 1195, and the knights transferred to Salvatierra; this too was lost (1209) but retrieved by a crusading army. Finally the knights moved to a new site at Calatrava la Nueva (1217), a safer headquarters on a rocky eminence eight miles from Calatrava la Vieja[404]. Its church with a great rose window was one of several fine chapels of the Order[405]. Notable commanderies still to be seen include Alcañiz, elevated on a hill-top[406], and (in ruins) Zorita dominating the Tagus valley[407].

The daily life of the knights was akin to that of Cîteaux, with a novitiate of one year before profession[408]. Disobedience meant eating one's meals on the ground for three days, even the loss of horse and armour for up to six months. Infringements of chastity were punishable by flogging and bread-and-water diet[409]. [How did military men take to such a régime, and how far, given the exigencies of warfare, was it honoured in the breach rather than in the observance?] Silence was kept in church, refectory, dorter and kitchen[410], but a meat-dish was served on Sundays, feast-days, and two week-days[411]. For the canonical hours the Psalter was recited ten times a year, but on active service a specified number of *paters* and *aves* instead. Confession and Communion were enjoined three times a year, ideally during the General Chapter held at Calatrava at Christmas, Easter, and Pentecost[412].

In battle, the knights usually shared the offensive with others, rather than act alone, but they were useful also for their strategic knowledge of the local terrain and of enemy fortifications[413]. They could be fearless and merciless, like the third Master of Calatrava who on one foray pursued a marauding party of Moors who had killed seventy knights: he took two hundred prisoners and promptly cut their throats![414] Together with the knights of Santiago, the Calatravans, serving in the vanguard of royal armies, contributed substantially to the Castilian reconquest and the taking of Andalusia (1158–1252)[415], and were prominent in campaigns leading to the surrender of Córdoba (1236), and the capture of Seville (1248)[416]. Together with the knights of Santiago and of Alcántara, they helped to drive the infidels out of Ubeda (1234) and to liberate Tarifa (1340)[417]. The prowess of the Calatravans saw them assist briefly in north Poland during the 'Baltic Crusade' (1215)[418].

The Order of Calatrava became an economic force in its own right. By 1188, some thirty years after its foundation, the knights had accumulated a territory of 340 square miles. This region, later known as the 'Campos de Calatrava', covered much of the modern province of Ciudad Real. Around the northerly commandery of Zorita the knights possessed ten towns and villages, and in a third zone centred on the commandery of Martos they transformed a small estate of three villages, granted in 1228, into a territory of eleven settlements. Here were harvested cereals, olives and grapes[419]. Much of Calatrava's land expansion came from royal gifts to secure the loyalty and assistance of the knights in the defence, colonisation, repopulation, and administration of newly-taken territories. From the late-twelfth century there was a system of commissions by which the knights received a pre-determined share of campaign spoils. Such commissions included in 1175 a fifth of all the spoils of war, and in 1254 a tenth of the king's share in the conquest of Murcia. Two major royal grants came in 1246 (two-thirds of the tithes of Osuna, to be spent in repairing the fortifications of that town), and 1300 (the town of San Esteban del Puerto and its territory)[420].

The extensive lands the knights came to own could not be worked by them alone, and they largely cultivated with Moslem slaves the estates they did not lease out[421]. Alfonso VIII urged them to restrict to forty *yugadas* their arable holdings in any area, and to distribute the rest on a partnership basis – thus encouraging settlement[422]. As the reconquest took place, the knights thus helped in peopling the empty lands abandoned by the Moors, encouraging colonists by leasing out land on extremely favourable terms[423]. Alcañiz (1209) received the right of colonising the territory of Monroyo: by 1223 it established nine villages yielding rents, partly in kind – of grain and wine[424]. The knights did not work alone: other Orders peopling lands included the Templars and Santiago. To encourage settlement, residents on Calatravan lands were repeatedly exempted from head-tax (in 1215–64 at least), but the lands were not entirely tax-free. The residents of prosperous commanderies were expected to pay to the Crown yearly 900 *maravedis* or specified amounts of grain, stock, and wine (a tribute called *yantar*)[425].

The Calatravans possessed considerable herds, ranching half-wild on the barren *mesetas* cattle, horses, goats, pigs, and especially sheep, driving them into the cooler high sierras during the summer[426]. The knights were free of royal dues on their stock and had substantial rights of pasture. With the latter went (certainly in 1317) permission for their shepherds to cut timber for fuel to bake bread (a sign of transhumance), and to make bridges over rivers 'so that they and their cattle might cross'[427]. Problems came, especially from the late-thirteenth century, of towns enclosing fields or charging the knights for their use; this limited free passage and the use of common pastures. The great extent of Calatravan flocks raised concern amongst secular farmers of danger to their agricultural lands[428].

Animosity also existed between Calatrava and the *Mesta*, the organisation which regulated transhumance of sheep to southern (warmer) pastures each autumn. The knights complained (as in 1285) of the Mesta flocks causing damage; the Mesta countered that the knights were setting up enclosures (a barrier to free movement) and charging tolls. Eventually, by an agreement of 1328, the *Mesta* acknowledged the right of the Calatravans to five from every thousand sheep that came into their lands. This meant a gain for the knights at that time of just over 1,000 sheep a year. No wonder the Order had a share in the Castilian wool trade with Flanders![429]. Other substantial assets included tithes – in 1311 in the diocese of Jaén alone these were worth 20,000 *maravedis* to the knights; salt-mines – as at Peralejos near the commandery of Otos (1277–77); mercury mines – a monopoly from 1282 of those of Almadén (close to Chillón). The knights became (1286) the sole agents for exporting the mercury – mostly to Genoese merchants[430].

By the fourteenth century the Order of Calatrava had lost much of its earlier spiritual emphasis. In receiving vocations there was distinct class-consciousness: Masters had been transformed almost into princes with rich commanderies in their gift; commanders had become wealthy landowners. There was internal wrangling and vying for position, excessive wealth and personal ambition. Later still, loose living was alleged, and under-age commanders, even Masters, were appointed. But in the late-twelfth and early-thirteenth century, hand in hand with the Orders of Santiago and Alcántara, the Knights of Calatrava had been a spear-head of the Christian Reconquest of Spain[431].

Other Military Orders

The prestige of the Knights of Calatrava led other evolving military orders to seek close association with the Cistercians[432]. One small group, the brothers of Monfrag (*alias* Montegaudio or Alfambra) were fully incorporated into the Order (1215) under Calatrava, and lost their separate identity[433]. The knights of Trujillo (perhaps synonymous with those of San Julián de Pereiro founded about 1176)[434], were granted (in 1190) association with the Order 'just as Calatrava', and they were placed under the oversight of Moreruela[435]. In 1218 Calatrava ceded its newly-acquired fortress town of Alcántara (and other possessions in León) to the Order of San Julian which then became known as the Order of Alcántara[436]. The knights wore a white tunic, black hood and shortened scapular[437]. They came to own half of Extremadura[438], but also suffered from internal dissensions. The Master of Calatrava accompanied by two Cistercian abbots, deposed the Master of Alcántara in 1318, after unrest there and complaints from both knights and clerics of ill-treatment[439].

After the Council of Vienne (1312) confiscated the goods of the Templars, James II of Aragon (1317) founded a new order at the former Templar commandery of St George at Montesa. It followed the customs of Calatrava, and ten brethren of Calatrava instructed the new knights. The possessions of the hospitallers of St John as well as of the Templars passed to the new Order, which also in 1399 absorbed the knights of San Jorge de Alfama founded in 1201 by Peter II of Aragon[440]. The brethren wore white mantles, and their Prior and first Master were named by the Catalonian abbot of Santes Creus[441]. Like Calatrava, the territory of Montesa was divided into commanderies; a notable one, Peñinscola, was sited on a rock almost surrounded by the sea[442]. Loyal to the royal house, Montesa took the side of Peter IV of Aragon in the civil war with his brother, the count of Urgel, which ended in 1348[443]. [All the foregoing Orders had the Master of Calatrava for Visitor and formed part of the 'family' of Morimond.] At the request of the king of Castile (1273) the equestrian Order of Cartagena, employed in the closing stages of the Albigensian crusades, was affiliated to the Cistercians and made subject to Grandselve[444].

In Portugal, the principal Order of Avis (*alias* Aviz) stemmed from the Knights of Evora; their inspiration was Cistercian and by 1166 their Visitor was the abbot of Tarouca, though by 1187 they came under the jurisdiction of Calatrava. After Alfonso II (1211) gave them the town of Avis they became the Knights of Avis, and in 1218 Calatrava ceded all its Portuguese properties to them[445]. A short-lived Order under the jurisdiction of Alcobaça, that of San Michael de Ala (St Michael's Wing), took the name of the archangel credited with visibly assisting Alfonso I's victory over the Moors[446]; the Order (of uncertain foundation date) did not long outlive that monarch[447]. King Diñiz (1318) founded in former Templar preceptories the Knights of Christ. Their first Master was a knight of Avis, and the first knights were trained by ten Spanish brethren from Calatrava[448]. Also made subject to Alcobaça, Morimond listed the new knights as of its lineage[449].

Other military Orders with Cistercian input included the Order of SS. Lazarus and Maurice in Savoy[450], the Knights of Spata in Gascony[451], and the Knights of Our Lady of Montjoye in Outremer[452]. Cardinal Conrad of Urach, himself Cistercian, organised the Order of the Holy Faith (1221) to help combat mercenary soldiers and the Albigensians in south-west France[453]. When peace came they faded from view, St Louis (1261) authorising their union to the abbey of Feuillant near Toulouse[454]. In Prussia, Bishop Christian (1215), formerly a monk of Oliwa, together with Duke Conrad, established the Order of Dobrzyn ('the Dobriners'); not a great success, it was absorbed into the Teutonic Knights in 1235[455]. Theodoric, a monk of Loccum on the Baltic mission, was one of those instrumental in the foundation of the Militia of Christ ('the Sword-brothers') and their coming to Livonia in 1202[456]. Bishop Albert of Riga acquiesced in their rôle but had serious difficulties with them. Not all the Sword-brothers were saints: one murdered his Master in 1208[457].

The Cistercians and the Crusades

Their intrinsic life of contemplation and stability meant that the basic contribution of the Cistercians for the relief of the Holy Land lay in prayer and financial support. Yet there were some religious, notably St Bernard, who played a more active rôle[458]. He saw just war only as a last resort, but emphasised the spiritual side of crusading endeavours, the triumph of good over evil[459]. He was opposed to any active participation by monks, for whom 'the sign of the cross was always carried in their hearts'[460]. He disapproved strongly when Abbot Arnold of Morimond (1125) left his monastery to journey to Palestine, a progress rudely interrupted by his death at Camp[461]. Yet St Bernard, reluctantly but at the express wish of Eugenius III[462], did more than any other to stir up public support for the Second Crusade (1147) and to encourage many to take the Cross. He did so partly by his preaching tours commencing at Vézelay in 1146 when King Louis VII was marked with the Cross. The next year in Germany, assisted by the abbots of Ebrach and Rein, he secured the co-operation of Emperor Conrad IV and the German princes[463]. Bernard also sent letters all over Europe awakening support: they reached the English[464], Bretons, Bavaria, and Cologne[465]. He pressed for an assembly at Magdeburg to organise resistance against any pagan attacks in central Europe whilst the crusading armies were away[466]. He invited Duke Wladislas and the people of Bohemia to join the expedition to Jerusalem[467]. Bernard's was a household name, and his passionate support did much to get the crusade off the ground[468]. When it proved a failure he glossed over the disaster by representing it as one of the mysterious ways in which God works. The failure meant only lukewarm support for another such enterprise which Bernard and Abbot Suger of St Denis advocated in 1150. It also perhaps lessened popular esteem for the Cistercian Order, retarding its growth, and may have contributed to the delay in Bernard's canonisation[469].

Other Cistercian abbots to preach the Second Crusade included Rainald of Morimond in Bassigny[470] and Geoffrey of Igny in Germany[471]. The Cistercian prince-bishop, Otto of Freising, once briefly abbot of Morimond, commanded German knights in the Crusade[472]. (These early military connexions of Morimond may explain how later it took under its wing several of the military Orders.) Cistercian bishops played a major rôle in organising the Third Crusade (1184–92). It was preached by Archbishop Gerard of Ravenna in Italy; he died later in battle at Acre[473]. Cardinal Henry de Marcy persuaded the sovereigns of England (Richard Lionheart), France (Philip Augustus) and Germany (Frederick Barbarossa) to take the Cross[474]. Abbot Garnier of Clairvaux preached in France and Germany[475]. The archbishop of Canterbury, Baldwin of Ford (also to die at Acre) did so in England and Wales. His tour of Wales (1188) saw the abbots of Whitland and Strata Florida 'in faithful atten-dance'[476]. The abbots of Morimond and La Crête were rebuked by the General Chapter for allowing *conversi* to go to Jerusalem[477].

The General Chapter (1199) initially refused to undertake the preaching of the Fourth Crusade as not being consonant with the ideals of the Order[478], but under pressure from Innocent III it relented (1201), and four abbots with many supporters set out 'signed with the Cross'[479]. It also promised 2,000 marks towards crusade expenses, but pledges were still being collected from monasteries in 1214[480].This Crusade saw the sack of Constantinople (1204) and the replacement of Orthodox monks in several monasteries there by Cistercians and military knights[481]. Abbot Luke of Sambucina preached the Crusade in the kingdom of Sicily[482], and Martin of Pairis in Germany – he then led German volunteers to Constantinople[483]. Abbot Peter of Locedio travelled in the entourage of Boniface of Montserrat. Mixed loyalties (for he favoured the Venetians) meant that he omitted to proclaim the papal prohibition against an attack on the Christian city of Zara[484]. After the capture of Constantinople he stayed on, played a part in pacifying Greece, and later became Patriarch of Antioch[485].

Abbot Guy of Vaux-de-Cernay and the abbot of Cercanceaux accompanied Simon de Montfort. Disgusted by the capture of Zara, they made for Syria rather than Constantinople[486]. Adam of Perseigne took part, but his experiences turned him against such warfare[487]; so did lesser folk such as the *conversi* of La Cour-Dieu, some of whose enthusiasm soon waned[488]. Cistercian participation in later Crusades was smaller. The Fifth Crusade (1217–21) was preached by Bishop Conrad of Halberstadt, now a monk of Sittenbach[489], and by Abbot Foulques of Thoronet, whilst the abbot of Villers accompanied the duke of Brabant to Palestine. Abbot Frederick II of Aiguebelle organised the preaching of the Sixth Crusade (1228–29)[490]. In later crusades (1277–76) the Cistercians offered mostly prayer and alms[491], though an abbot of Netley went with Prince Edward to Tyre (1270)[492].

To escape repression in Flanders and the Rhineland heretical Cathars had fled to Languedoc from the 1160s onwards, and many settled in the diocese of Albi – this lending its name to the Cistercian-influenced 'Albigensian Crusade'[493]. Until it commenced, in 1208, ineffectual preaching missions had largely formed the Catholic means of attack, but the Crusade was to suffer from differences between Innocent III and his legates, difficulties in recruiting crusaders, and the short period (forty days) for which many of them served. It also degenerated into a personal war between Simon de Montfort the elder (d. 1218) and Raymond VI (d. 1222) for the viscounty of Toulouse; the last stage, the crusade led by Louis VIII (1226–28), probably did more to absorb Languedoc effectively into the French kingdom than it did to extirpate heresy[494]. The Crusade did, however, contribute to the annihilation of the Cathars and their doctrines, thousands of them perished; and it prepared the ground for the work of the Inquisition which followed it for a further fifty years[495].

Cistercians were closely involved in the Crusade: indeed its notable chronicler, Peter of Vaux-de-Cernay, who had seen something of the Fourth Crusade, was an eye-witness to much of the activity[496]. Long before, St Bernard had confronted a heretic from Provence at the Council of Pisa (1135), and had preached (1145) in Albi and Toulouse against the dualists, but with limited success[497]. It was to the General Chapter thirty years later that Raymond V of Toulouse wrote describing the position: 'Few believe in the Creation or Resurrection; the sacraments are despised, and the reli-gion of two principles has everywhere established its hold'[498]. Consequently, in 1178 the abbot of Clairvaux, Henry de Marcy, held theological debates with Cathar heretics in Toulouse; in 1181, now a cardinal, he took with a small army a Cathar stronghold, the hill town of Lavaur[499]. Cistercians continued to preach in Languedoc, and after the deposition in 1198 by Innocent III of seven bishops of the region, Cistercians were amongst those nominated to succeed them[500]. Innocent also appointed Cistercians as papal legates in Languedoc, and when one (Peter of Castelnau) wanted to retire to his monastery of Fontfroide, Innocent told him: 'Stay where you are: at this hour, action is better than contemplation'[501]. Peter was assassinated in 1208.

Another legate was Abbot Arnauld Amaury of Cîteaux who proclaimed the Crusade at the General Chapter of 1208, and when Carcassone was taken preached in its streets. He made much use of spiritual weapons – such as excommunication and interdict – as well as leading several of the battles in person[502]. A perhaps apocryphal tale (of a saying attributed to others as well) has it that when, at the siege of Béziers (1209), the problem arose as to how to distinguish between heretic and Catholic inhabitants, he responded: 'Kill them all, God will recognise His own'; a Solomonesque judgement[503]. Arnauld Amaury was made archbishop of Narbonne in 1211, but the following year (a Castilian himself, and former abbot of Poblet) he led French troops into Spain to help repulse a north African army which had captured the Calatravan fort of Salvatierra. In the victory over the Moors which followed, Arnauld was one of the principal advisers to the three kings of Castile, Navarre and León; he recounted the victory to that autumn's General Chapter[504]. Other appointments of Cistercian bishops in Languedoc included that of the veteran crusader, Guy of Vaux-de-Cernay, to the see of Carcassone (1210)[505].

Other lesser Cistercians accompanied Arnauld Amaury in numbers as missionaries in 1207, and preached every winter for some ten years in Northern France, the Low Countries and Germany, in partly successful efforts to recruit crusaders. They also accompanied Prince Louis in his abortive crusade in 1219[506]. It was the influence of the white monks during the Albigensian Crusade that perhaps led St Dominic to conceive his Order of Preachers[507]. After the unsuccessful expedition of Prince Louis, an interlude followed when a few Cistercians engaged in helping the political opposition (though not the heretics); the General Chapter (1218) sent three abbots to Languedoc to root them out[508]. Arnauld Amaury seemingly faded from the scene, but was still to the fore in 1226 when Louis VIII marched through Languedoc, and he went ahead of the army receiving surrenders. It was the abbot of Grandselve who in November 1228 took Raymund VII's offer of surrender to the French Court[509], and Grandselve co-operated in the foundation of the University of Toulouse, intended to ensure orthodoxy rather than heresy (1229)[510]. That year a moderate line was taken when Hélinand of Froidmont preached in Toulouse and emphasised that heretics would only be converted if example supported word[511]. The death of Catharism was slow and prolonged. Even the white monks may not have been immune, some houses of Tarragona being suspected of heresy (1236)[512]. At the turn of the century the inquisitor at Montaillou was the Cistercian bishop and later pope, Jacques Fournier[513].

In Eastern Europe a pagan environment also gave scope for Cistercian zeal. As early as 1147, and at St Bernard's instigation, a crusade against the Wends was decided upon following the Reichstag at Frankfurt[514]. Later, Danish monasteries helped to supplant Wendish paganism in Pomerania and Rügen[515]. Dargun tried to convert its local Slavs, its monks visiting the villages to baptise them[516]. The monks of Amelunxborn and Doberan attempted to christianise Mecklenburg, but the latter house was to have a number of martyrs. The first abbot of Zinna was also killed by pagans[517]. The missionary endeavour of Doberan continued undaunted, backed by Henry II of Saxony (1178–1227)[518]. In Poland, early abbeys, such as Łekno and Lubiąż, engaged in missionary work from the start. Such endeavour had the full support of at least two popes (Innocent III and Honorius III), but not always of all elements within the Cistercian Order itself[519]. In Little Poland, one of the motives of settling white monks at Mogiła (1222) may have been to ease the removal of pagan cults in the vicinity of the tomb of Wanda, a legendary princess[520]. In Pomerania, Wartislas II encouraged Danish monks to settle at Kołbacz (*c.* 1173) so that they might 'recall the barbaric Slavs from the error of their cult and superstition'[521]. The landmarks of the lands first granted to Kołbacz included 'the tumuli of the pagans'[522].

Work in Prussia was begun in earnest in 1206 by Abbot Godfrey of Łekno, backed by Innocent III who allowed the abbot to take others with him to assist in 'in this work of the ministry of salvation'[523]. Two of those who accompanied him were Philip (a monk of Łekno) and Christian (a monk of Oliwa). Philip was martyred but Christian was appointed first bishop of Prussia (1215)[524]. Innocent III in 1212 had criticised the antipathy within the Order to this missionary activity, a strong feeling which had apparently caused some Cistercians to withdraw from the mission field[525]. Honorius III in 1220, in like vein, requested the bishops of Eastern Europe to organise in their dioceses missionary groups of able preachers, preferably Cistercians[526]. Bishop Christian laboured for nearly twenty years amongst the Old Prussians near the Vistula. His work was of necessity accompanied by armed force. This involved the stationing for a time of Knights of Calatrava at Tymawa on the Lower Vistula[527]. With Duke Conrad, Bishop Christian also established the short-lived 'Dobriners'[528]. Christian's work had but limited results[529], whilst his own lengthy captivity (1233–38) paved the way for the Teutonic Knights to take over the Prussian mission[530].

Cistercian missions in the 'Baltic Crusade' had originated in the 1190's, and it too was a mission field which saw several martyrdoms. It was also supported by Innocent III (1204) who praised the work of the Cistercians in Livonia[531]. It was a remote sphere of activity, so Abbot Theodoric travelled there by sea[532]. It was a region which necessitated fortified monasteries such as Falkenau and Dünamünde. Difficult though the area was, a Cistercian presence was established which endured until the last Lithuanian monks were deported to Siberia in 1864[533]. Two former religious of Loccum played here a significant rôle. One was Bishop Berthold of Uexküll who, finding peaceful means ineffective, recruited a German army but was killed whilst leading it in battle (1198)[534]. The other was Bishop Theodoric of Estonia, who had assisted in the formation of the Sword-brothers and in the foundation of Dünamünde (1205), of which he became first abbot. He was killed mistakenly in time of battle (1219) when his tent was mistaken for that of King Valdemar of Denmark[535]. The Livonian mission passed to the Dominicans in the mid-thirteenth century, but meantime other Cistercians made their mark. These included Bernard de Lippe, seventy years old when he became second abbot of Dünamünde[536], the martyred Frederick of Altzelle (1215)[537], and Peter of Coblenz (monk of Himmerod, later abbot of Dünamünde) who has been called 'the Apostle of Livonia'[538].

The difficulty of their work is reflected in the history of Dünamünde. Sited on 'Saint Nicholas Mountain', on an estuarine site close to Riga, the abbey prospered at first. Indeed, 'pilgrims' (i.e. crusaders) came to the monastery for a year's stay and work[539]. It was attacked on St Bernard's Day, 1228, by the Kurs and Semigallians[540], and the monks massacred, but was able to shelter the legate Baldwin of Alna when besieged by the Swordbrothers three years later[541]. It may have gravely suffered from fire when Riga was burnt by the Letts in 1263[542]. Eventually, in 1303, the abbot sought leave from the General Chapter to sell out to the Teutonic Knights, 'because it is not possible to resist the pagans and the property is daily diminished'[543]. The sale, for nearly 3,000 marks, took place ten years later and was criticised by Pope John XXII[544]. The monks moved to Padis in Estonia, but twenty-eight of them were martyred there one night in 1348[545].

There remains to note the letters addressed by Gregory IX in 1241 jointly to the Cistercian abbot of Heiligenkreuz, the Dominicans and Franciscans of Vienna[546], and the Dominicans of Germany ('the German Preachers')[547], to preach a crusade against the Tartars, promising volunteers the same spiritual privileges accorded to those fighting in the Holy Land.

Notes

1. Williams-Jones (1959) 59.
2. *Ibid.* 24–5, Richardson (1951) 36.
3. *RHC* 128–29, 143.
4. Baxter (1914) 278–79.
5. Butler (1988) 63, Midmer (1979) 271.
6. Williams (1984) I, 34–6, 44–7; Harrison (1998).
7. O'Dwyer (1976) 35.
8. Williams (1978) 240.
9. *RCH* 259, *cf.* Lekai (1976) 259.
10. *DHGE* XV (1963) 29.
11. *MHP* I, 78; *cf. Statuta* II, 449 (1259/4).
12. *CDEM* III, 293–94; *cf.* 91–2, 127–31.
13. *Statuta* II, 475 (1261/3); III, 12 (1263/11).
14. *DHGE* XV (1963) 29.
15. Williams (1978) 241.
16. Kłoczowski (1970) 118–20.
17. Rocca (1936) 78–9.
18. Occhipinti (1985) 322–23, 327–28.
19. Bedini (1964) 15, Bertuzzi (1972) 34–5.
20. Bedini (1964) 69.
21. Gervers (1992) 184.
22. Williams (1974) 71, 74.
23. Lekai (1977a) 394–97.
24. Kluit (1780) 497.
25. Halkin (1970) 59.
26. *Statuta* I, 40 (1207/33–34), 385 (1211/32).
27. *C.P.R.* 1283/99, 1297/60.
28. VCH, *Chester* III (1980) 152–53.
29. *VRL* 51.
30. VCH, *Chester* III (1980) 159.
31. *ACA* 304.
32. *C.P.R.* 1301/624.
33. *SMD* 197, *cf.* France (1992) 130.
34. McCrank (1975) 279–80.
35. *FRB* II, 332.
36. Lekai (1977a) 94–96.
37. *AC* 718.
38. VCH, *Wiltshire* III (1956) 270.
39. Sparks (1978) 46.
40. Stéphan (1970) 111.
41. *C.P.R.* 1350/520.
42. *DSMLR* 524 (No. 215).
43. McCrank (1975) 282.
44. Mousnier (1986) 123, Cazes (1982).
45. Dimier (1954) 25.
46. *PU* II, 13.
47. Williams (1984) I, 45–6.
48. *CDEM* II, 511–21; *RBM* I, 418 (No. 889), 432 (No. 930).
49. *CDRB* IV:1, 331 (No. 180); V:1, 70–1 (No. 31); *RBM* I, 578 (No. 1244); II, 16 (No. 36).
50. *RBM* I, 598 (No. 1298).
51. *E.g: CAF* 131, *SBC* II, 328–29 (No. 460).
52. McCrank (1975) 259.
53. *CAF* 131.
54. *UKSH* 67 (No. LVI).
55. *Cf.* Occhipinti (1983) 550–51.
56. *Cf. C.P.R.* 1281/474.57.
57. *C.P.R.* 1217/66.
58. *C.P.R.* 1226/96.
59. *C.P.R.* 1223/369.
60. *C.P.R.* 1224/441.
61. *Statuta* II, 215 (1240/1); *LCC* (1) 87–88.
62. *Statuta* III, 308 (1302/9).
63. *DHGE* VI (1932) 1061.
64. *Statuta* I, 174 (1194/23).
65. *KD* I, 164–65.
66. *PU* I, 487.
67. Carrick (1907) 43–44.
68. *CM* 43.
69. *PU* I, 485.
70. Williams (1984) I, 49.
71. *RCH* 185.
72. As at Strata Florida.
73. France (1992) 342.
74. *Statuta* III, 263–64 (1293/14).
75. *DSMLR* 591 (No. 257).
76. *SMD* IV, 535.
77. *PU* I, 357, 485.
78. Williams (1889) 153.
79. *RCH* 185.
80. *MPH* VI, 348–49.
81. Valter (1993) 391, 394–95.
82. Baigent (1882) 9–10, Midmer (1979) 321.
83. *CBW* I, vii.
84. *CMM* II, xxi.
85. Williams (1984) I, 55.
86. *CPL* 24.
87. Gilyard-Beer (1960) 9–10.
88. Mullin (1932) 97.
89. Midmer (1979) 303.
90. Davidson (1843) 67–8.
91. *ACA* 301.
92. *CC* (2) B. 43.
93. Notable enough to be recorded in monastic chronicles.
94. *DHGE* II (1914) 792.
95. Van Der Meer (1965) 296.
96. *ACA* 302.
97. *CMM* III, 69.
98. Lohrmann (1983b) 246–48.
99. Desmarchelier (1974) 38.
100. *Statuta* II, 90–1 (1230/33).
101. Lohrmann (1983b) 246–48.
102. Pontus (1966) 22.
103. *Statuta* III, 142 (1275/14); *MGH* XIX, 716.
104. Wulschleger (1991) 30, 33.
105. McCrank (1975) 281.
106. Barea (1977) 124–28 (No. 157).
107. *LCC* (2) 254–55.
108. VCH, *Chester* III (1980) 152.
109. Williams (1984) I, 25.
110. VCH, *Stafford* III (1970) 226.
111. *DHGE* XVIII (1977) 1020; *Statuta* I, 126 (1190/41), 135 (1191/8).
112. *Statuta* I, 329 (1206/49); *cf. RCCH* 56–7.
113. *Statuta* I, 341 (1207/40), 355 (1208/45).
114. *Statuta* I, 365 (1209/42).
115. Cottam (1928) 68.

116. *Statuta* I, 446 (1215/55); *cf.* I, 353 (1208/36), 367 (1209/49); Giessler-Wirsig (1979) 145.
117. *Statuta* I, 154 (1192/42).
118. *Statuta* III, 242 (1289/11).
119. *Statuta* III, 261 (1292/11).
120. *RCC* I, 266.
121. Clay (1952) 36.
122. Cowley (1977) 124, *cf.* (for Meaux) *CMM* II, 100–02.
123. *Statuta* I, 440 (1215/ 27, 28), 472–73 (1217/32); *RD* II, 86 (No. 6331, of 1215).
124. *Statuta* I, 445 (1215/50).
125. *Statuta* II, 306–07 (1246/30).
126. VCH, *Lancaster* II (1908) 120; *cf. CDL* 182.
127. *Statuta* I, 29–30 (1134/LXX).
128. Sayers (1964) *passim.*
129. Birch (1902) 62; Williams (1984) II, 227.
130. Williams (1984) I, 25.
131. *CDL* 182.
132. *Statuta* I, 331 (1206/61); *cf. DHGE* XIV (1960) 1030.
133. *Statuta* III, 130–31 (1274/17).
134. *Statuta Ibid.* I, 471 (1217/28).
135. Sparks (1978) 54.
136. *DHGE* XII (1953) 962–64.
137. Madden (1963) 351, Mullin (1932) 59–61.
138. Knowles (1963a) 366–67.
139. Bell (1984a) 27, Lekai (1977a) 302.
140. *AM* II, 265.
141. Williams (1984) I, 33.
142. VCH, *Shropshire* II (1973) 57; *cf. CCR* 1229/178–71, 1233/217, 287, 293–95, 311; 1243/69.
143. Graves (1957) 40–1.
144. *CCR* 1250/304, 314.
145. *CCR* 1277/209, 216; 1278/264.
146. *CS* II, 187.
147. Jones (1950) 230.
148. *CC* (3), B. 53.
149. *DHGE* XII (1953) 960.
150. King (1954) 46, 49, 173.
151. Lekai (1977a) 326.
152. Hockey (1970) 135.
153. Williams (1984) I, 59–63.
154. Hays (1963) 84.
155. Williams (1984) I, 62–63.
156. *AF* 238.
157. Birch (1897) 305.
158. Madden (1963) 342.
159. *Statuta* I, 336 (1207/11).
160. *Statuta* III, 169 (1277/34).
160. *Statuta* III, 169 (1277/34).
161. *Statuta* I, 510 (1219/38).
162. *Statuta* II, 238 (1241/41).
163. *Statuta* I, 278–79 (1202/22), *cf.* 266 (1201/14).
164. Lekai (1977a) 305.
165. Midmer (1979) 216.
166. King (1954) 171.
167. *Statuta* III, 176–77 (1278/10).
168. *Statuta* III, 309 (1303/2).
169. Madden (1963) 355.
170. *Ibid.* (1963) 360, *cf.* Wardrop (1987) 24–5.
171. Wardrop (1987) 24–25.
172. VCH, *Essex* II (1907) 135.
173. Earle (1906) 14.
174. *Statuta* I, 113 (1189/15), 120 (1190/14).
175. Knowles (1963a) 353.

176. Barnes (1982) 11, Graves (1957) 42–44, Fergusson (1984) 20.
177. VCH, *Essex* II (1907) 131.
178. *CPR* 1274/63, 1275/97, 1276/151, 1278/259–60.
179. *Statuta* III, 244 (1289/12).
180. Lekai (1977a) 304–5.
181. *Statuta* I, 88 (1181/6).
182. *Statuta* I, 97 (1184/13).
183. *Statuta* I, 109 (1188/10), *LCC* (1) 86–7.
184. *Statuta* II, 215 (1240/1).
185. *Statuta* I, 113 (1189/15), 120 (1190/14).
186. *LCC* (2) 290.
187. *Statuta* I, 150 (1192/24); *cf.* III, 74 (1269/30); Davidson (1843) 58.
188. Graves (1957) 33–4.
189. *RSL* II, 222.
190. *Statuta* III, 169 (1277/34).
191. Lekai (1977a) 305.
192. VCH, *Yorkshire* III (1913) 144; Snape (1968) 135.
193. *CPR* 1276/141.
194. Lekai (1977a) 306.
195. McNulty (1943) 160.
196. *LMT* 174 (No. 1).
197. Berman (1986) 41.
198. Burton (1989) 41.
199. *CAF* 143.
200. PRO, E 135/21/5, m. 11; E 315/51/135.
201. *ACA* 300.
202. *SBC* II, 4–6 (No. 4).
203. *CAP* 455 (No. 13385).
204. *WAR* 183.
205. Fletcher (1919) 115–16.
206. O'Sullivan (1945) 110.
207. *CBK* 41 (No. LIV).
208. *CPR* 1267/118.
209. *SBC* IV, 103 (No. 1175).
210. *CPR* 1259/20; *cf.* 1267/118; *CCR* 1230/404, 1231/577.
211. *E.g: CPR* 1270/485, 1271/546, 589; 1272/648; 1280/386, 389.
212. *CPR* 1270/485, 1271/546.
213. *CPR* 1267/118; *CCR* 1231/577.
214. *CPR* 1280/386, 389.
215. Toepfer (1983) 91.
216. *CCR* 1230/404.
217. *ABB* 34, 256–57 (No. 67).
218. *Statuta* II, 203-III, 292, *passim.*
219. *Statuta* II, 452 (1259/19); III, 212 (1281/37), 287 (1296/19).
220. *Statuta* III, 51 (1267/20), 123 (1273/45), 212 (1281/37).
221. *Statuta* III, 51 (1267/20), 76 (1269/38), 148 (1275/53), 274–76 (1294/62).
222. *Statuta* III, 5 (1262/31–42, *passim*).
223. *Statuta* III, 212–14 (1281, *passim*).
224. *Statuta* III, 135 (1274/46); *cf.* II, 444 (1258/27); III, 5, (1262/31), 12 (1263/17), 235 (1286/5).
225. *Statuta* III, 173 (1277/71), *cf.* III, 148 (1275/48).
226. *Statuta* III, 5 (1262/42).
227. *Statuta* II, 203 (1239/6).
228. *Statuta* II, 363–64 (1251/21); *cf.* II, 238 (1241/41), 363–64 (1251/21).
229. *Statuta* II, 364 (1251/22).

230. *Statuta* II, 337 (1249/15–17), *cf.* II, 364 (1251/24), 378 (1252/10).
231. *RBM* IV, 213 (No. 530).
232. *Statuta* II, 475 (1261/2); III, 316 (1306/4).
233. *Statuta* I, 121 (1190/15).
234. *LCC* (2) 290.
235. *Statuta* III, 155 (1276/20).
236. *Statuta* II, 442 (1258/19); *cf.* III, 104 (1272/2).
237. *Statuta* III, 330 (1315/3).
238. *Statuta* III, 212 *et seq.*
239. *FRB* 543.
240. *PZKZ* 18–19 (No. XIII); *Statuta* III, 213 (1281/41)
241. *Cf. Statuta* III, 5 (1262/41).
242. *Statuta* III, 210 (1281/24).
243. *Cf. Statuta* I, 519 (1220/13); III, 198 (1280/17).
244. *Statuta* III, 231 (1284/3).
245. *Statuta* III, 258 (1291/61).
246. *Statuta* III, 281 (1295/18).
247. *Statuta* III, 210 (1281/4).
248. *Statuta* III, 223 (1282/26).
249. *Statuta* III, 118 (1273/18).
250. *Statuta* III, 266 (1292/31).
251. *Statuta* III, 274 (1294/46); *cf.* III, 275 (1294/56), 292 (1297/40).
252. *CMM* I, xxviii-xxix, 107, 352–53; Earle (1906) 24.
253. *AM* II, 255, 265; *cf.* Gasquet (1908) 239.
254. *Cf. DHGE* IX (1937) 1300, X (1938) 1449; *FRB* 543.
255. Lekai (1977a) 304.
256. *Ibid.* 304.
257. *Statuta* II, 337 (1249/16).
258. *Statuta* III, 258 (1291/61, 62); *cf.* McGuire (1982) 142.
259. *Statuta* III, 188–89 (1279/38).
260. *Statuta* III, 75 (1269/33).
261. PZKZ 18–19 (No. XIII).
262. Aubert (1931) 14.
263. Bedini (1964) 162–63, *cf.* Davidson (1843) 40–42.
264. *Statuta* I, 114 (1189/18).
265. *Statuta* I, 208 (1196/56).
266. *LCC* (2) 290; *cf. Statuta* III, 258 (1291/61).
267. Graves (1957) 36–37.
268. VCH, *Chester* III (1980) 153.
269. *CPR* 1282/39, 1283/78.
270. *CPR* 1277/208.
271. *CPR* 1348/52.
272. *CPR* 1288/294.
273. VCH, *Gloucester* II (1907) 95.
274. *CPR* 1274/59; 1275/76, 78–9, 103; 1276/120, 1291/431, 1291/491, 1295/154, 1348/199; VCH, *Hampshire* II (1903) 147; Graves (1957) 60.
275. *CPR* 1277/200.
276. VCH, *Chester* III (1980) 153.
277. *CPR* 1348/52.
278. *RCH* 91, *cf.* Fuxhoffer (1869) II, 91.
279. *RCH* 143, *cf.* Fuxhoffer (1869) II, 114..
280. *RCH* 184.
281. *CDEM* III, 256–57; *cf.* Pojsl (1996) 166 (map).
282. Dimier (1982j) 832–33, (figs. 170–71); *cf. CD* 285.
283. Tuulse (1942) 287.
284. Dimier (1964) 174, *cf.* 173.
285. *DHGE* XVII (1971) 369, Benouville (1889) 233.
286. *DHGE* XII (1953) 965.
287. Dimier (1964) 173; *cf. CHA* I, 43–44 (No. 158).
288. De Durainville (1856) 215; *cf.* King (1954) 145.
289. Josephine (1976) 296.
290. Still impressive today.
291. Arenas (1985) 40.
292. Ward (1971) 46–7; Williams (1974) 66.
293. Mullin (1932) 55.
294. *CPR* 1348/124.
295. *CPR* 1348/194.
296. *CPR* 1327/169.
297. *CNM* xiii.
298. *CPR* 1337/529.
299. VCH, *Hampshire* II (1903) 89.
300. Midmer (1979) 226.
301. VCH, *Sussex* II (1973) Pl. opp. p. 74.
302. *SL* 158 (No. 12).
303. The weapons of the time.
304. Donnelly (1949) 75 (No. 49).
305. Platt (1969) 30.
306. *Cartae Glam.* II, 624–25; *cf.* Williams (1984) I, 37.
307. King (1954) 294.
308. VCH, *Stafford* III (9170) 229.
309. *AM* II, 368–69.
310. *CTA* 58–9.
311. *CFR* 1320/45.
312. *CHDM* I, 121.
313. McCrank (1973) 78.
314. McNulty (1943) 160.
315. *RHC* 135–36, *cf.* Platt (1969) 30.
316. Lhuyd (1910) II, 41.
317. Weale (1867) 103–09.
318. *Cf. CPR* 1216/3; *AF* 181; *CHS* 53, 291; 455. *MF* I, 166; VCH, *Dorset* II (1908) 83; Snell (1967) 42.
319. *RHC* 132.
320. *RCH* 92, *DHGE* XV (1963) 29.
321. Fort i Cogul (1975) 24–5.
322. *AF* 266, *cf.* 238.
323. Gerevich (1977) 168.
324. Williams (1976) 11.
325. Galpin (1928) 90.
326. *CTA* 58–9, 87.
327. VCH, *Wiltshire* III (1956) 271; (Stoneleigh is sometimes confused with Stanley).
328. VCH, *Yorkshire* III (1913) 151.
329. *Cal. Chancery Warrants* I, 517.
330. *Statuta* I, 93 (1183/13).
331. *LCC* (1) 135, (2) 329.
332. *Statuta* I, 326 (1206/34).
333. Lekai (1977a) 392.
334. *RSL* II, 227.
335. *Cf.* Gosso (1940) 78–9.
336. Hockey (1970) 131.
337. *RSL* II, 357.
338. *CPR* 1265/457.
339. *CAS* II, 124 (No. DXXIII).
340. *Cf.* Wollenberg (1984) 339.
341. *CAS* II, 14 (No. CCCLXXX).
342. *RHC* 142.

343. *RSL* II, 192 (No. 10).
344. Bedini (1964) 88.
345. Taylor (1899) 187–88.
346. *CDK* 77, 118.
347. Wollenberg (1984) 339.
348. *CH* 174–75 (No. 876).
349. Birch (1897) 58, 173.
350. *Statuta* I, 313 (1205/27), 330 (1206/58).
351. *Statuta* II, 463 (1260/11).
352. *Statuta* III, 166–67 (1277/18).
353. Williams (1984) I, 41.
354. Carville (1973) 50–51, (1984) 54.
355. Coulton (1960) 285.
356. *Statuta* I, 298 (1204/14).
357. *Statuta* I, 276 (1202/11).
358. Duby (1968) 150–51.
359. BL, Harleian Chs. 75 A, 38, 39.
360. VCH, *Lancaster* II (1908) 117 (fn.26).
361. *CS* II, 186.
362. Williams (1984) I, 145.
363. *RBM* III, 39 (No. 88).
364. *Cf.* Mullin (1932) 62.
365. McCrank (1975) 257–58.
366. Meekings (1979) 26.
367. Brown (1958) 93.
368. *BSFN* 1978, 372–74.
369. Lewis (1976) 26–27.
370. Butler (1988) 63, Davey (1978) 424–428.
371. Leroy (1972) 158.
372. Richardson (1981a) 40.
373. Canestrelli (1896) 11–12 ('quarteruoli').
374. Taylor-Vaisey (1976) 221; *cf. Statuta* I, 219 (1197/46).
375. *LCC* (2) 306.
376. *Statuta* III, 221 (1282/18).
377. O'Callaghan (1959) I, 172; *cf.* Seward (1972) 20–24.
378. Seward (1972) 22–27, 27–8.
379. *Cf.* Seward (1972) 134–40; O'Callaghan (1959) 181–86, (1961) 231; Estow (1982) 267.
380. O'Callaghan (1959) 188, 190.
381. O'Callaghan (1960) 48–50, 52; *cf.* (1959) 190, (1960) 48; *LCC* (2) 28.
382. *Statuta* I, 366 (1209/47).
383. *Statuta* II, 13–14 (1222/4).
384. O'Callaghan (1960) 28, 33–35; Seward (1972) 140.
385. *Statuta* II, 340 (1249/33).
386. O'Callaghan (1960) 51.
387. *Ibid.* 57–59, (1971b) 63–82.
388. *Ibid.* (1960) 11–12; *DHGE* XII (1953) 870.
389. O'Callaghan (1960) 13.
390. *Ibid.* (1960) 13, 15–16.
391. Forey (1987) 72.
392. O'Callaghan (1960) 6–8.
393. *Ibid.* 3–4, Seward (1972) 140–41.
394. O'Callaghan (1960) 9–9.
395. *Ibid.* 278, Seward (1972) 140–41.
396. Seward (1972) 148, 159–60, 162.
397. O'Callaghan (1961) 256.
398. *DHGE* XII (1953) 1151.
399. O'Callaghan (1969) 609.
400. *Statuta* II, 340–41 (1249/34); 349 (1250/18).
401. Dimier (1964) 170, Seward (1972) 140–41.
402. O'Callaghan (1960) 3, 9–10.
403. Seward (1972) 151.
404. Dimier (1964) 172, O'Callaghan (1959) 190–91, Wulf (1944) 117–18.
405. Dimier (1964) 172, Seward (1972) 151.
406. Dimier (1964) 172, Seward (1972) 142.
407. Dimier (1964) 171–72.
408. Seward (1972) 141.
409. O'Callaghan (1960) 20, 25.
410. Seward (1972) 141.
411. O'Callaghan (1960) 31.
412. Seward (1972) 141–43; O'Callaghan (1960) 10–11, 27–29.
413. Seward (1972) 150.
414. *Ibid.* 146.
415. O'Callaghan (1969) 609; *cf.* Estow (1982) 272.
416. O'Callaghan (1969) 614, 616; Seward (1972) 154–55.
417. Seward (1972) 153, 159, 163.
418. David (1934) 216–17; *cf. Statuta* II, 296–97 (1245/38) for a Polish duke's request for Knights of Calatrava.
419. Estow (1982) 271, 275–76, 283–84; *cf.* O'Callaghan (1971b) 63.
420. Estow (1982) 277–73.
421. Seward (1972) 152.
422. Estow (1982) 273; 'yugada'= 1 plough-land/carucate perhaps.
423. Estow (1982) 277–80.
424. Corbera (1986) 227–28, 231.
425. Estow (1982) 274.
426. Seward (1972) 152.
427. Estow (1982) 274, 286.
428. Gerbet (1986) 95, 101; Estow (1982) 287.
429. Estow (1982) 286, 288–89.
430. *Ibid.* 274–75, 282–85.
431. Seward (1972) 4, 158–59; O'Callaghan (1960) 285.
432. O'Callaghan (1959) 176.
433. *Statuta* I, 448 (1215/61); *DHGE* XV (1963) 952; (Wulf [1944], places Monfrac in the Orient).
434. *DHGE* XV (1963) 952–53; O'Callaghan (1962) 481.
435. *Statuta* I, 126 (1190/40); *cf.* Seward (1972) 145, 307; [Wulf (1944) 119, places 'Turgel' in the Orient].
436. Lekai (1977a) 57–8, O'Callaghan (1962) 485, Seward (1972) 151.
437. Wulf (1944) 118.
438. Seward (1972) 156.
439. *Ibid.* 159–60.
440. Gutton (1974) 98–100, 103; *cf.* O'Callaghan (1960) 7*n*, Wulf (1944) 118.
441. *DHGE* XV (1963) 952–53; Gutton (1980) 258.
442. Gutton (1974) 103–04.
443. *Ibid.* 110.
444. *Statuta* III, 122 (1273/37), *cf.* Grolleau (1932) 243.
445. Seward (1972) 145, 149, 152; *cf.* Cocheril (1959b) 54, O'Callaghan (1962) 474.
446. *DHGE* II (1914) 27.
447. Grolleau (1932), Wulf (1944) 118.
448. Wulf (1944) 11, *CMM* II, 390.
449. *DHGE* XV (1963) 953, Grolleau (1932) 243, King (1954) 225.
450. King (1954) 352.

451. Wulf (1944) 119
452. Seward (1972) 33.
453. Sumption (1976) 206.
454. *DHGE* XVII (1967) 1335.
455. Urban (1975) 134, Williams (1978) 236–37.
456. *FHL* I, 25; *Cf.* Williams (1978) 238.
457. *FHL* I, 58–9 (Nos 73–4); *Cf.* Seward (1972) 93, Urban (1975) 44.
458. Lekai (1977a) 62.
459. Leclercq (1976) 16, Renna (1980) 125, 127.
460. *LSB* 468–69 (No. 396); *cf.* Lackner (1976) 59*n*.
461. King (1954) 334–35; *cf. LSB* 19–22 (No. 4).
462. Gervers (1992) 29.
463. Constable (1953) 244–45, Gervers (1992) 8.
464. *LSB* 460–63 (No. 391).
465. Constable (1953) 245–47.
466. *CDEM* I, 253–55; *LSB* 466–68 (No. 394).
467. *CDEM* I, 255–57; *LSB* 463–64 (No. 392).
468. Constable (1953) 247.
469. Constable (1953) 276, Gervers (1992) 135.
470. King (1954) 341.
471. Péchenard (1883) 93.
472. King (1954) 340.
473. Lekai (1977a) 53.
474. King (1954) 255.
475. Bouton (1959) I, 187.
476. *GCIK* 119,
477. *Statuta* I, 128 (1190/52).
478. Constable (1953) 277.
479. *Statuta* I, 270 (1201/37).
480. Brown (1958) 72.
481. Seward (1972) 56.
482. *Statuta* I, 221–24.
483. Millet (1899) 25.
484. Andrea and Motsiff (1972) 17–18.
485. Lekai (1977a) 53.
486. Andrea (1985) 21–22, Brown (1958) 74–75, *cf. DAC* (1978) 568–69.
487. Andrea (1985) 37.
488. *Statuta* I, 268 (1201/24).
489. Andrea (1987) 23–53, 85.
490. Bouton II (1964) 262–63.
491. E.g: *Statuta* III, 126–27 (1274/1), 143 (1275/17), 152 (1276/4), 164 (1277/9).
492. *C.P.R.* 1270/485.
493. Sumption (1978) 42, 49.
494. *Ibid.* 68, 73, 77, 82, 100–01, 105, 108, 113–18, 126–30, 140–43, 212–25; *cf.* Lekai (1977a) 56.
495. *Ibid.* 229–35.
496. *Ibid.* 58, 64.
497. *Ibid.* 44–45.
498. *Ibid.* 54.
499. *Ibid.* 54–7; *cf. LMT* 174*n*, 176 (No. 11); 234 (Nos 58, 61).
500. Sumption (1978) 67–69, 76; *cf.* Lekai (1977a) 56.
501. Lekai (1977a) 55.
502. Sumption (1978) 79, 83, 85–86, 99–100, 226.
503. Sumption (1978) 68, 93–4; Richards (1968) 97.
504. *DHGE* XII (1953) 929. Dimier (1954) 11, Sumption (1978) 144.
505. Sumption (1978) 143, 175.
506. *Ibid.* 72, 105, 109; *cf.* Constable (1953) 277, Mousnier (1986) 120, Pineault and Coomans (1994) 132.
507. Dimier (1954) 11, Sumption (1978) 71.
508. *Statuta* I, 491 (1218/35); *cf.* Sumption (1978) 201.
509. Sumption (1978) 221, 223.
510. Lekai (1971a) 143–44.
511. *CHA* 3–3 (1988–89) 173 (No. 954).
512. *RD* II, 279 (No. 7463).
513. Mohs (1978) 53–5.
514. Gervers (1992) 36; *cf. LSB* 466–68 (No. 394).
515. Kornerup (1881) unpaginated.
516. Szacherska (1977) 131, 144.
517. *DHGE* II (1914) 1195, XII (1953) 898.
518. *DHGE* II (1914) 507.
519. Williams (1978) 235.
520. Mogiła Abbey MS.
521. *PU* I, 33.
522. *Ibid.* I, 177–78.
523. David (1934) 236, Lekai (1977a) 61.
524. Chase (1946) 9–10, Zakrzewski (1907) 4.
525. *KD* I, 66, 73; *cf.* Bouton (1964) 268.
526. Kłoczowski (1970) 132, Lekai (1977a) 62.
527. David (1934) 216–17.
528. Chase (1946) 9–10, Urban (1975) 134.
529. Bouton (1964) 268.
530. *Cambridge History of Poland* I (1950) 83–4.
531. Thompson (1920) 74.
532. Urban (1975) 26.
533. Lekai (1953) 117.
534. Brundage (1961) 6, Urban (1975) 36–7.
535. Brundage (1961) 40, Urban (1975) 43–4, 104.
536. Bouton (1964) 267–68, Lekai (1977a) 59, Urban (1975) 83, 99, 105.
537. Brundage (1961) 140–41, *cf.* 175–76.
538. Lekai (1953) 50, Van Der Meer (1965) 277.
539. Brundage (1961) 44, 76–7.
540. *AD* 109; *cf. LECU* 93 (LXXIX), 94–95 (LXXX), 178 (CXXXVIII), 476–77 (CCCLXXIV).
541. Urban (1975) 141, 144.
542. *AD* 109.
543. *Statuta* III, 310 (1303/7), *Cf. LECU* 20–23 (No. DCXIV, of 1305).
544. *Statuta* III, 327 (1313/3), 344 (1318/22); *LECU* 74 (DCXLII, of 1313), 108 (DCLXIII, of 1318); *PU* V, 105, 139.
545. Bouton (1964) 230, Dimier (1964) 174; *cf.* MPH VI, 338; for Padis, see: *LECU* 588–87 (CDLXXVIII, of 1281).
546. *RBM* I, 489–90 (No. 1043).
547. *CDEM* III, 5–7.

Chapter 8

ABBEY SITES

The sites chosen for Cistercian foundations were generally low-lying, almost always by running water, and frequently in remote situations. Riverine sites afforded means of water-supply, transport, drainage and sanitation, and food-supply. Many houses experienced one or more changes of site for a variety of reasons, which included growing awareness of the physical limitations of the original position and physical attacks by human agencies. In other cases there is evidence that the first site was deliberately a temporary one, occupied while the permanent conventual buildings were being erected.

The early principles of the Order demanded that its monasteries should be sited at least eight kilometres (5 miles) from a town[1] (unlike some Benedictine priories), and so be 'in places removed from the conversation of men'[2], for solitude was of the essence of the Order. The sites of numerous Cistercian houses were relatively remote, even if only because much of the best land was already settled and the white monks were pushed to the edges of a manor or parish or county. In their own day, Cwmhir (1232) was noted as being set in a 'remote mountainous district'[3] and Dieulacres (1334) 'in a lonely waste on the confines of the county of Stafford'[4]. Many monasteries were, however, sited in areas which had long been developed, where scope for monks to be far apart from other people was extremely limited. This was inevitable given the number of Cistercian abbeys – well over six hundred – and when the white monks settled, as often they did, in little-peopled marsh and forest areas, it was part of a general shift into new territories as European population figures rose[5]. There was also competition for space from other Orders: 64 Cistercian abbeys were founded in the plains of NW Europe where there were already 650 other ecclesiastical bodies[6].

Yet, based on a text sung on Saturdays at Lauds: 'He found him in a desert land, and in the howling waste of the wilderness' (Deuteronomy 32:10), some early Cistercian narratives, perhaps to enhance the prestige of the Order, referred to early Cistercian sites as being 'in a desert land, in a horrible place, and in a vast empty space'[7]. William of Newburgh saw Rievaulx as being 'in a horrid and vast solitude'[8]; the bishop of Ossory described the place of Duiske (1202) as one of 'horror and a vast solitude'[9]. Such stock-in-trade terms were often wishful thinking – especially when used of Cîteaux itself[10]. If areas were uninviting it was perhaps because the better lands had been used up; if areas immediately adjacent were empty of people, it was often because the Cistercians had moved them away. Many monasteries in western Europe were sited in favourable and by no means unpeopled areas. Charters granted to Aiguebelle described it as lying in a 'savage canyon', whereas in fact it is in an open, gently sloping valley[11]. The chronicle of Villers suggested that its monks too came to a 'savage' area, but in reality they inherited the hamlet of Villare and lands already assarted[12]. Previous occupation of land is obvious in the conveyance of vineyards to Bonnecombe and of olive-groves to Grandselve[13]. Virtually all the land acquired by Silvanès was settled before the Cistercians came, and needed little reclamation[14].

Archaeological evidence suggests a small village at the Dunes before its monks came[15], and there were also pre-monastic settlements at Amelunxborn and Loccum[16]. Alvastra was built on a site continuously inhabited since the Ice Age[17], Velehrad on the site of the ancient capital of Moravia, long since destroyed[18]. Excavation has demonstrated substantial building up to a century before the Cistercians came to Wąchock[19]. In England, the considerable number of monasteries meant that few could be really remote: from the first the monks had to work in close proximity with peasants extending village lands[20]. This is not to say that the Cistercians had no scope for marshland drainage and woodland clearance: they did – as at Fossanova in Italy, Kołbacz in Poland, and Valcroissant in the Alps[21].

An artificial isolation was created at some Cistercian houses by the clearance of the indigenous population, generally with recompense, to a new settlement. The Cistercians, suggested their critic, Walter Map, 'make a solitude that they may be solitaries'[22]. An archbishop of Canterbury (about 1155) mentioned 'those parishioners whom the monks of Coggeshall have driven from their lands and homes'[23]. Fountains 'reduced' Cayton to a grange (by 1146) and later cleared six hamlets[24]. The foundation of Rufford (1146) meant the disappearance of three villages, two of which became monastic granges. The displaced people were partly settled in a new planned village at Wellow, and some received individual financial compensation ranging from 10 shillings to 20 pence[25]. Such clearances facilitated not only provision for the monastic precinct, but also space for a consolidated home estate. It meant that lay-folk were removed from the doorstep of a monastery.

When Revesby (1142) was founded, the earl of Lincoln offered the villagers either fresh land or their freedom: 31 of 38 chose emancipation[26]. When Rievaulx (1132) was settled the home grange was sited on the destroyed village of Griff[27]. The eviction of inhabitants of Llanegwestl to give way for Valle Crucis (1200) saw them resettled in Northcroft and Stansty, near Wrexham[28]. Villagers removed for the second site of Byland were resettled at Old Byland and a church and green provided for them[29]. When the first site of Kirkstall was founded at Barnoldswick (1147), displaced inhabitants came back regularly to worship at their church; they were seen as a nuisance, and the monks, backed by pope and archbishop, pulled the church down[30]. Other evidence of depopulation included that at the sites of Combe[31], Croxden, Pipewell[32] and Woburn[33]. Published evidence from the Continent is less fulsome, but evictions accompanied the foundation of Bonnevaux[34] and Ourscamp[35], Pforta[36] and Henryków[37]. The monks of Aulne faced objections to the process, and had to compensate the peasants' loss of land by purchase or exchange[38]. Peasant removal is also documented at Žd'ár (1252)[39], Chorin (1274), and Dobrilugk (1297). The frequent granting of sites together with 'the men of that place', facilitated the removal of peasants, but on many occasions they remained as *conversi*, familiars, labourers, or even tenants[40].

Several Cistercian houses were placed by long established routeways, which proved to be a mixed blessing, – allowing ease of trade but attracting numerous travellers. The Order's rule that abbeys were to be at least half a mile (0.8 km) from the nearest public road was of little help in avoiding this burden of guests[41]. Fossanova was on the Appian Way between Rome and Naples (and so St Thomas Aquinas called and died there)[42]. Poblet was on one of the ancient Roman roads of Spain, the Via Aurelia between Tarragona and Lérida: travellers used the abbey as a staging-post[43]. Tamié, by a mountain col (at 952 m), was much used by travellers between Geneva and Turin: it was a pilgrim route to Rome[44]. Gimont and L'Escale-Dieu were near pilgrim routes to Compostella[45]. Position by such routeways could not but detract from an atmosphere of solitude and isolation. One monastic device, therefore, was to close local roads (as did S. Sulpice-en-Bugey)[46], or to re-route them (as did Pontigny, 1156[47], and Fontmorigny, 1193[48]). There could be worse problems. Maulbronn was sited near the old Roman and Imperial road towards Speyer; this attracted brigands and made the area unsafe[49]. Far-flung Cîrţa, sited on the left bank of the Olt river, the only waterway breaching the southern Carpathians, suffered later from every invading army, including the Turks in 1421 and the Wallachians in 1430[50]. More positively, the Via Emilia, not far distant from Chiaravalle della Colomba, may have helped its trade[51]. Ten Irish Cistercian abbeys were by routes of long-standing, 'vital for a successful economy'[52].

Isolation was diminished where abbeys, deliberately or otherwise, were built close to a major fortification. Such situations were not ideal, but might afford a measure of protection in troubled times. In Wales, Neath was close to Castell Nedd, and Valle Crucis stood under the shadow of Castell Dinas Brân. In Ireland, Bective (1228) was said to be in a 'strongly fortified place': the great castle of Trim was only four miles away[53]. In Germany, Buch stood near Liznik Castle[54], and Altzelle near Nossen Castle[55]. In Poland, Ląd was close to a castle which became more of a nuisance than a protection, in 1236 becoming its property[56]. In England, Rievaulx and Newminster stood near the castles of their patrons; Sawley was near Clitheroe Castle and Vaudey not far from Bytham Castle[57]. Some monasteries were sited in the foundations of fortifications – as Lekno[58], or inherited a fortified building – as Disibodenberg[59], or started life in a castle given to its monks – as Lubiąż[60].

The isolation of early Cistercian houses was facilitated by three twelfth-century pontiffs (Adrian IV, Urban III, and Celestine III) who forbade the foundation of any other religious or secular establishment within one league. Their economic well-being was safeguarded by the Order's early and continuing insistence that a new Cistercian abbey site was to be at least ten Burgundian leagues (40 km/25 miles) from an existing one[61]. It was a rule frequently breached, partly because the choice of site was restricted to lands a benefactor was willing to give, and sometimes because an incorporated monastery was already well within the prescribed limits. In Wales, Neath (fd 1130, previously Savigniac) and Margam (fd 1147) were but eight miles (11 km) apart, leading to protracted friction between the two communities[62]. When Neath thought of moving to its Exford manor in Somerset (1199), it found its way blocked by the new foundation then taking place at Cleeve, only twelve miles (19 km) distant[63]. When Stanlaw (1296) was transferred to Whalley, Sallay objected because the new foundation was only five leagues away, and its nearness had caused a general rise in prices[64]. In France, the settlement of Olivet (fd 1145), only fifteen kilometres from Barzelle (1138) and of Varennes (1148), only eight kilometres distant, did not work well for the economic prosperity of any of the three[65]. Beaupré-de-Beauvais (fd 1135) and Lannoy (1137) were only three kilometres apart, as the latter was originally Savigniac and not then bound by the regulations[66]. Pressure on available land made for such proximity in western Europe; in countries like Poland and Hungary the problem did not arise.

Frontier Sites

It has become fashionable to play down the idea of the Cistercians as being essentially monks who deliberately went to remote areas to build their monasteries, to be in effect 'frontiersmen'[67]. Yet it is a fact that numerous monasteries were sited close to boundaries – be they national, county, diocesan, or parochial. It was certainly true of Morimond, where the border between France and Lorraine passed through its refectory, so that one writer could say: 'The monks prayed and sang in France, but ate in Germany'[68]. The reasons for a frontier position are not always obvious, but they undoubtedly included the suitability of a remote position, the availability of little-used and thinly peopled land, and, sometimes, a deliberate placement for political reasons by a founder.

Close to the Hungarian border stood Ábrahám and Szent Gotthárd[69]. Lucelle (Lützel) was by the Swiss-German border[70]. Águiar was for long in territory contested by Spain and Portugal[71]. A bishop referred to the position of Kamieniec (1260) as 'on the borders between Poland and Bohemia'[72]. Cîrţa (1343) was also in its day described as being 'on the extreme confines of the kingdom of Hungary'[73]. The frontier character of Waldsassen (1181) was emphasised when Duke Frederick of Bohemia granted it a property called 'Ugiez in Bohemian, but Meringe in German'[74]. It also gained ducal permission for free access to its lands in Bohemia (1196)[75]. As the reconquest of Iberia proceeded, the founding of several monasteries in what were then 'frontier' situations, attracted colonists and re-peopled empty lands. The foundation of Alcobaça[76], Poblet[77], Ovila[78], and Vereruela[79] all had strategic aspects, intentional or otherwise. Zlatá Koruna (1263) was founded partly because the king of Bohemia wished to stop the expansion of the Rožmberk family in southern Bohemia, and so gave it a vast stretch of unoccupied territory which it assarted and settled[80].

In an unsettled Europe a location on political frontiers could mean severe difficulties, as noted before at Holm Cultram. Zwettl (1176) was burnt during conflict between the dukes of Austria and Styria[81]. Frederick II (1214) took Waldsassen under his protection because of 'frequent insults of the Bohemians'[82]. Ottakar II of Bohemia (1257) agreed to Velehrad's request for protection against possible Hungarian attack[83]. Stephen Lexington (1228) noted that Mellifont 'is in very bad and dangerous marchland between the English and the Irish', and suggested its transfer[84]. Dore (1345) 'had suffered by the wars between the English and the Welsh', and at the time of the Glyn Dŵr Revolt (1405) gained royal leave 'to treat with the (Welsh) rebels for the safety of the abbey which is in great peril of destruction and burning'[85]. Like other Border monasteries Dore walked a tight-rope, not wishing to give aid and comfort to the king's enemies, but not wanting either to suffer in the process.

Monasteries might stand on the boundaries of a county or later defined département, as Aubignac at the extremity of Indre, next to Creuse, and Fontaines-les-Blanches almost astride the border of Indre-et-Loire[86]. Stratford was described in its own day as lying on the confines of the counties of Middlesex and Essex[87]. Val-Dieu was transferred (in 1216) from Hocht to the mutual frontier of the county of Dalhem and the duchy of Limburg; both lords gave land for the new monastery precinct and its home estate[88]. Monasteries sited at diocesan boundaries could experience conflicting loyalties. The boundary between the sees of Bourges and Limoges passed through the claustral buildings of La Colombe[89]. Because of a dispute between the bishops of Valence and of Die as to which diocese Léoncel (1183) belonged, the pope allowed its monks to be ordained by the archbishop of Vienne[90]. The bishops of Amiens and Thérouanne jointly consecrated the new abbey church of Cercamp (1262) sited on their mutual borders[91]. A similar situation nearly arose at Dore (1284), the bishops of St David's and Hereford both laying claim to it. The General Chapter sat on the fence, and decided that Dore should acknowledge the *de facto* diocesan[92].

Topography

The saying is often quoted: *Bernardus valles, colles Benedictus amabat*[93], and the valley position typical of Cistercian houses was reflected in numerous monastic place-names, both official – as *Longa vallis* (Cwmhir), and colloquial – as Clair*vaux*, and *Vau*dey. Such a low-lying situation could lead to problems such as flooding, as attested at Sénanque[94], and Boyle[95]. The advantages of proximity to a river were many – for food-supply (fish) and transport – while a leat led off the river could form a drainage channel and provide power for the monastic mills[96]. Better still was a site where a small tributary flowed down a fairly steep slope into the main river giving a powerful motive force; this was true at several Irish houses[97]. Cymer gained its name from its position near the confluence ('cymer' in Welsh) of a river and its tributary[98], as did Alcobaça from the proximate meeting of the Alcoa and Baça rivers[99]. In Ireland 25 out of 34 Cistercian sites were close to rivers, whereas only 56 out of 96 houses of Augustinian canons were so[100]. A medieval monk travelling on the river Danube through Austria and Hungary could have broken his journey at several Cistercian abbeys close to its banks, such as Engelszell, Wilhering, Ercsi and Czikádor.

Rivers could form a natural defence – as on the northern side of Newminster, facing the Scots[101]. Rivers might lend their name to a monastery, as St Bernard-opt-*Scheldt*; Santo Stefano del *Corno* referred to a bend (*cornu*) of the river Po, close to its first site[102]. The usual Cistercian abbey plan meant that abbeys were ideally sited on the left bank of a river, but considerations of relief, land availability, or politics might make that impracticable, and a right bank site was a feature of most Irish houses and of several Danube monasteries. A riverine site meant scope for a monastery's own sailing vessels. Cymer, sited by the river Mawddach, had thereby a sea connection to its granges in Llŷn. Tintern on the river Wye could send its boats to trade in Bristol; it was also an entrepôt for goods being shipped upstream to Monmouth[103]. A riverine site had its hazards: a monk of Cymer[104] and a benefactor of Wilhering[105] both met their death by drowning. To avoid flooding of riverside cloisters, drainage channels were essential[106].

Valley floors were frequently marshy – and riverine sites were therefore often on bluffs raised above the flood-plain, as at Ląd in Poland and Maenan in Wales[107]. Marshland sites were not uncommon[108] – hence such abbey names as Clair*marais*[109] – but they were not deliberately sought out[110]. Swineshead in the Fenland, Holm Cultram by the Solway Firth[111], and Brondolo near low-lying Venice[112] were all surrounded by marshy tracts. Marshland sites could mean mosquito infestation, 'marsh fever', and death – documented at Franquevaux in the Camargue[113], Trefontane close to the Pontine marshes[114], Sawtry in the Fens[115], and Zaraka by Lake Stimfalias[116]. Numerous monasteries undertook drainage works – not least Fossanova (its name meaning 'the new ditch') and Byland[117]. To avoid flooding, the precincts of Louth Park were moated. A charter granted to the abbey (1314) referred to 'the island where the monks dwell and the marsh as the outer dyke surrounds it'[118]. To ensure firm foundations it was essential to find dry sites, 'islands', within the marsh – as did Holm Cultram[119]. Grey was sited on a drumlin overlooking the salt marshes of Strangford Lough[120], and Obra on a dry hill site overlooking Lake Bezyńskie[121]. Part of the monastery at Bordesley was built on cobble and pebble rafts[122]; oak piles were driven into swamp at Velehrad to support an oak lattice which carried its foundations[123].

A lacustrine site also facilitated water-borne transport and fishing. In northern Italy, Capo*lago* took its name from a lakeside position[124], as did *Acqua*fredda on a cliff edge by Lake Como[125], and *Ripa*lta Scrivia – by a marshy pond[126]. In Greece, part of Lake Stimfalias, adjacent to Zaraka, has silted up since monastic days[127]. A lacustrine situation was common in the fluvio-glacial deposits of the North European Plain, as at Chorin (Stagnum S. Mariae[128]) and Marienwalde. Lekno I (fd *c.* 1142) stood on what was then an island close to the western bank of Lake Lekno[129]. In Savoy, Hautecombe, by Lake Bourget, had its Water Grange (the thirteenth century 'La Voûte') capable of receiving its boats[130]. In Scandinavia, the name of Esrum meant 'the open place on Ese Lake'[131]. It was a monk of that house, Stephen, who helped the Augustinians of Æbelholt lay a water conduit[132]. Skill in waterworks enabled Martin, a monk-artificer of Øm, sited between Lakes Mosse and Gudensø, to realise that the water-level of the former was slightly higher than at the latter[133]. Øm excavated three canals to connect

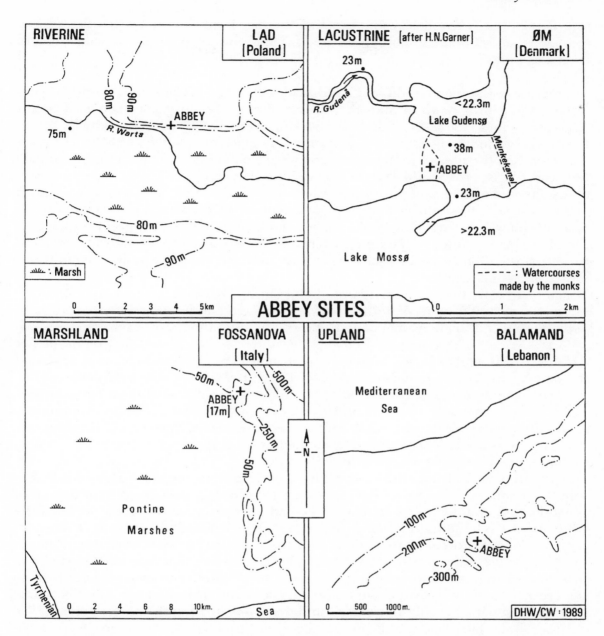

RIVERINE   LAD [Poland]

LACUSTRINE [after H.N.Garner]   ØM [Denmark]

- - - - : Watercourses made by the monks

ABBEY SITES

MARSHLAND   FOSSANOVA [Italy]   UPLAND   BALAMAND [Lebanon]

DHW/CW : 1989

the two lakes, but one abbot (Jens, in the 1240s) had to block the mouth of the western canal (which was navigable) 'with stakes and great tree trunks' to deny access to attackers[134]. At Sorø (*c*. 1200–03) a dam was built to create an artificial difference in height between Lakes Sorø and Tuel: this allowed the cutting of the Møllediget Canal, yielding both running water and mill-power[135]. Some of the monks of Nydala suffered martyrdom (1521) by being drowned in Lake Rusken adjacent[136].

Coastal sites also enabled monastic trade – as by the boats of Beaulieu on the Solent, whose daughter-house at Netley could easily be reached across Southampton Water[137]. Marine situations might also afford the privilege of wreck of sea. The position of some abbeys close to the sea or by tidal estuaries, suggests that their situation played a part in their emplacement, for ease of access[138]. Three British Cistercian houses sited on, or near, its western coasts, gave rise to daughter-houses across the sea in Ireland: Grey (founded from Holm Cultram), Inch (from Furness), Comber and Tracton (both from Whitland). The first three were all sited on the shores of Strangford Lough[139]. To the south of Ireland, Tintern Minor and Dunbrody stood at the head of ria inlets[140]. In

Galicia, Oia had a striking position by the Atlantic Ocean[141]. Ter Doest's site, on the coast of Flanders, made it not only a base for papal and royal envoys travelling to and from Scandinavia, but also for messengers and visitors to King John of England (1213)[142].

A marine position had its difficulties: climatic – flooding of the Dunes (1280)[143]; gales – the tower blown down at Stanlaw (1289)[144]; thefts – of sheep and lambs of Netley (1314) by sailors[145]; access – pedestrians walking across the sands of Morecambe Bay to Furness drowned[146]; hospitality – demanded by mariners (Netley, 1314)[147]. In post-monastic days the site of the Dunes was completely obliterated by blown sand, and only rediscovered in post-World War II excavations. The danger of pirate attacks meant that some monasteries were purposely sited somewhat inland – as La Real in Majorca and Fontfroide in southern France[148]. Innocent IV (1250) noted the dangers to La Real 'of the waters surrounding the island, and of frequent incursions of pagans [i.e: the Moors] and pirates'[149]. Pirate raids saw monks on Isola Trémiti murdered[150], and caused those of Ponza and of Santo-Spirito di Zannone (on offshore islands) to trans-fer to the mainland[151].

The Cistercian monks on the island of Hiddensee (fd 1292) were not long in build-ing a chapel (1302) on its eastern coast for fishermen and traders. Each year (from 8 September to 1 May) they maintained a beacon light on the chapel tower as a guide to sailors[152]. A cell of Val-Richer sited (by 1309) on a rocky island, Maître Île of Les Ecrehou, north-east of Jersey, kept a lamp burning all night 'that mariners might avoid the dangerous reef contiguous to the chapel'[153]. A hill-top convent of Cistercian nuns did the same at Koszalin by the Baltic[154]. Other island sites included Torcello (inc. 1206) in the Venetian lagoon[155], and Châtelliers (on the island of Ré)[156]. Scandinavian island sites can be recognised by the suffix Ø, as Kalvø, Sorø, Tuterø, and Hovedøya[157]. The latter was not that remote: being situated in the shipping lane leading to Oslo its monastic peace was frequently disturbed[158].

It was inevitable that in the early Middle Ages many monasteries were founded in woodland situations, as forest land was then extensive, gave a substantial degree of isolation, and might be the only land to be had. Orderic Vitalis (*c.* 1135) wrote of the white monks as building their monasteries 'in lonely, wooded places'[159]. A forest situa-tion was ideal for timber production, pannage for pigs, honey extraction and, later, hunting and hawking. There were disadvantages – not least friction over forest rights, or robbers hanging out in the woods (Roche, 1304)[160]. Entire forests were granted for the creation of the German abbeys of *Wald*sassen and Fürstenfeld[161]. The first name reflects its situation, as do those of Grand*selve* (*Grandis silva*)[162] and Sauveréal (*Silva regalis*)[163] in France. Amongst the numerous other Cistercian houses set in a forest envi-ronment were Herrenalb in the Black Forest, Zirc in Bakony Forest, and Santa Maria Incoronata (in 'a great oak forest')[164]. Rufford stood in Sherwood Forest, Beaulieu in New Forest, and Flaxley in Dean Forest. Express mention of a forest site came when a bishop of Metz, addressing a charter to St Benoît-en-Woëvre (1138) mentioned: 'your monastery situated in Richismanil Wood'[165], and when the bishop of Orleans gave to La Cour-Dieu (1166) 'the wood which is around the monastery'[165a].

Some abbeys were to be found, exceptionally, in upland positions – reflected in place-names such as *Alto*fonte (near Palermo) and *Mon*fero (in Galicia)[166]. In the Lebanon, Balamand (Bel*mont*) stood at 312 m above the Mediterranean, possibly for reasons of security, or to avoid the heat and mosquitoes of the salt-marshes below[167]. Hradiště in Bohemia was built on a ridge which gave it the appearance of a fortress (*gradišt*)[168]. Some upland sites derived from a pre-Cistercian foundation as Santo-Spirito d'Ocre (850m.)[169], Santa Maria di Preallo (835m.)[170], and St Sergius (600m above Byblos)[171]. In the Massif Central, Chambons, Mazan and Mercoire all stood over 1,000 m, as did Du-Jau in the mediterranean Pyrenees[172]. Some abbeys had a valley situation but at a considerable altitude, as Cwmhir in Wales, Hautcrêt in Switzerland, and Léoncel in the foothills of the French Alps.

Some monasteries were obliged to adjust to the limitations of their site. At Hoveydøya the east range could not be built in line with the church transept because of a large outcrop of rock[173]. The steep site of Le Thoronet meant that three ranges of the cloister were built on a lower level than the south range, which itself was on a lower level than the church[174]. A steeply-dipping bedrock at Mellifont was circumvented by having a crypt (later filled in) at the west end of the church, to keep the floor level[175]. Considerations of slope at Rievaulx[176], and restricted space at Sénanque[177], caused their churches to have a north-south axis; that of Furness was orientated from south-west to north-east[178]. At Clairvaux (1135) the course of the Aube was changed to allow for a new site for the abbey church[179].

Site Names

The variety of environments in which Cistercian houses were sited found expression in their place-names – both the official Latin forms recorded on the *tabula* at Cîteaux and the more local colloquial usage[180]. Pipewell was early called St Mary *de Divisis* due to its situation on the old bounds of Rockingham Forest[181]. Woodland sites were denoted at Boschaud (*Boscum* cavum), Castagnola (indicative of chestnuts), and Haute-*Seille* (Alta *silva*) to name but a few[182]. Forest clearings were indicated in Scandinavia by the suffix -*ryd* (-*rud*, *rød*), as in Ryd[183]. Coastal sites included Hidden*see*; Comber*mere* tells of a proximate lake. Inland sites included *Quart*azzola (*four* miles from Piacenza)[184]. The names of Roche and Les Roches reflect a rocky situation[185]. Numerous names reflected a water-point, spring or well as *Fontevivo*, Maul*bronn*, and Žďár (*Fons* S. Mariae)[186]. Tre*fontane* referred to the three springs said to have issued forth when St Paul was beheaded. *Aigue*belle meant 'beautiful water', Sén*anque* – 'clean water', and *Font*froide – 'cold spring'[187]. Bridge sites were denoted at *Ford* and Long*pont*. The coastal sand-hills gave their name to Ter *Duinem* (The Dunes). The alleged beauty of a site accounted for names such as *Beaulieu* and *Bon*port[188]. Twenty-seven abbeys had such a prefix in their name[189]. Beauty was also suggested in names such as *Clair*vaux ('valley of light') and Cleeve ('Vallis *florida*': 'valley of flowers')[190].

Many official names referred to Almighty God, especially in Ireland: *Castrum Dei* (Fermoy, 'the camp of God'); *Flumen Dei* (Abbeyshrule, 'the river of God'), and *Lex Dei* (Abbey*leix*, 'the law of God')[191], but also *Dieu*lacres ('may God grant increase')[192] and La Real (Fontis *Dei*). The prospect of heaven was reflected at Mironice (*locus coeli*) and at Tišnov nunnery (*porta coeli*)[193]. Official names frequently honoured the Blessed Virgin as at Croxden (Vallis S. *Mariae*), Marienfeld (Campus S. *Mariae*), and Przemęt (Lacus S. *Mariae*)[194]. The white colour of the Cistercian habit was alluded to at Herren*alb* ('the white lords'). *Espina*[195] and Zlatá *Koruna* (Golden*kron*)[196] possessed relics from the Crown of Thorns; Lieu*croiss*ant, relics of the Three Kings (*Les Trois Rois*)[197]. A royal foundation was alluded to by *Royau*mont and Vale *Royal*. Other names indicating a monastery's origins included *Canon*ica (inc. 1223), previously a college of *Canons* of the Lateran[198].

The precentor of Cîteaux kept a list (*tabula*) of the official Latin names of each Cistercian monastery, and the chronicler Orderic Vitalis (*c.* 1135) told how these were chosen with great care[199]. Confusion could arise when several monasteries shared the same name: no less than three abbeys were called 'Grace Dieu', and another four 'Beaulieu'. No less than four nunneries enjoyed the name of Gnadental (*vallis gratiae*)[200]. There was uncertainty in medieval records as between Stanley and Stoneleigh[201], and in modern indices as between Buch and Buków[202]. There might be contemporaneous attention drawn to the difference between official and colloquial names. There was reference (about 1210) to 'Vallis Florida commonly called Cleeve'[203]. King Wenceslas I (in 1238) of Bohemia noted that a Czech nunnery had the colloquial name of Oslavany, but that, transmuted, its equivalent was *Vallis sancte Mariae*[204]. Where a monastery had a site change it might carry with it its original name, leading to alternative colloquial names. This was true in Wales of Llantarnam (also called Caerleon or Duma), and of Aberconwy (also known as Maenan)[205].

Water Supply (see Chapter 11)

The importance of water in monastic economy was well attested in a twelfth-century manuscript describing its use at Clairvaux, in its mills (both corn and fulling), brewery, tannery, kitchen, and the like[206]. The Clairvaux manuscript also pointed out that water 'carries away the waste and leaves everywhere spotless'. Monasteries which did not have easy access to a river from which water could be immediately diverted had to remedy this defect in a number of ways – by building reservoirs, canals, aqueducts, even tunnels. Some were fortunate to be sited by springs. La Real (Majorca) had its first site by a massive spring at Esporles; the abbey's official name was consequently *Fontis Dei*[207]. Fontguilhem was sited at William's Spring above the Lysos valley[208]. The head of such a spring would (as at Clairvaux) be protected by a well-house, to keep the water clean[209]. Wells could be used to supplement water-supply. In dry limestone areas they became imperative – as for Abbeydorney[210] and perhaps Corcomroe[211]. Louth Park received water in a canal from St Helen's Spring in Louth town[212], Cherlieu in a stone-lined canal from St Bernard's Spring[213]. Kingswood (1301) was allowed to augment its water-supply from a spring in Haw Park. The landowner made a condition that when monks came to repair the pipes they were not to bring dogs nor carry bows and arrows, so that no harm came to the deer[214].

To store water, Walkenried built a walled and vaulted reservoir on a slope of the Harz Mts. It had a massive layer of gravel and sand, perhaps to act as a filter. Water reached the abbey by means of a walled subterranean canal[215]. At Maulbronn the monks dammed upstream to make a reservoir. The fact that the water-level was as high as the roof of its buildings did not seem to have worried them[216]. Numerous monasteries (as Bordesley[217] and Strata Marcella[218]) diverted streams into artificial channels. Melrose took water from the Tweed river at a point over 500 metres to the east of the monastery; it fed the mill and abbey drain before rejoining the river[219]. In Portugal, Alcobaça (1187) bought up land specifically to modify a river course[220]. Canals channelling monastic water from a river could be considerable engineering feats. Its water supply from the river Renkelbach becoming insufficient, Henryków (c. 1270) diverted water from the river Ohle into a canal over 2½ km long and cut some 6 m deep[221]. Drinking water was brought to Alcobaça through a long stone tunnel deriving from a 3½ km leat[222]. The twelfth-century monks of Obazine channelled water 1½ km to the monastery from the river Coyroux in a drain bored in places in the mountain rock; it served also the monastic fish-pond and three mills[223]. Some large canals served primarily to transport goods, including stone for building the monastery. This was especially true at Meaux – the Eschdike joining the abbey to the river Hull – whilst at Sawtry the 'Monk's Lode' linked it to the river Nene[224].

A notable aqueduct was that built (1212–21) by the monks of Cîteaux: running for over 10 km (over 6 miles), with a fine bridge at Arvaux, it took water from the stream of La Cent-Fons[225]. Aqueducts carried water on or above the surface, but it was sometimes necessary to make tunnels through solid rock, as did Rein boring through the Ulrichsberg[226]. Such feats of engineering meant that some monks and *conversi* became noted for their skill, as Martin of Øm and Stephen of Esrum. There were others, like Syrian, a monk of Waverley (1215), who channelled water through underground conduits to his abbey[227], and Gnolo, a monk of San Galgano (1267), called upon for hydraulic advice by the city of Siena[228]. Mechanical aids might help assure a sufficient water-supply[229]. Pelplin had a bucket-wheel to raise the water of the river Ferse to the desired level[230]. Sorø had a pump-house with an ingenious framework for supporting wheels[231]. Fountains had two conduit-houses to allow a head of water to build up. Conduit-houses appear attached to infirmaries – as at Beaulieu and Waverley[232].

Excavation and geophysical survey can reveal, as at Walkenried[233], a complex system of subterranean channels fed from the main monastery canal. The system at the Dunes was described (in 1203) as 'an aqueduct, very well and ingeniously constructed'; the 'aqueduct' (*sic*) was described as conveying its water 'by an underground course and leaden canals'[234]. Carefully planned conduits at Orval led to the kitchen and fountain-house[235]. Stone-lined channels were common (as at Kirkstall[236] and Tintern[237]). Clean water was distributed at Kirkstall by lead pipes deriving from a series of cisterns which may also have acted as filters[238]. Lead pipes have been commonly found, as at Cwmhir[239] and Varnhem[240]. A monk of Mortemer (about 1190) came to England to buy lead for its water-courses[241]. Lead pipes meant that late-twelfth century taps, as well as brass stop-cocks, have been found at Kirkstall. Water conduits at Alvastra, Beaulieu and Waverley included hollowed elm trunks[242]. At Glenluce earthenware pipes were used, and changes of direction were made by means of earthenware junction boxes with removable lids[243]. A stepped depression in the choir at Strata Florida was a conduit inspection chamber[244]. Villers had a remarkable 'water-clock'[244a].

Changes of Site

Despite the care taken in selecting the site for a new Cistercian house, about one-third of the Order's communities found it expedient to move to a new location. Very often this was close at hand, but sometimes quite far afield. The need was recognised by the General Chapter (1152+) which allowed any abbot, having the consent of his father-abbot, to transfer his monastery to a better site if any 'intolerable incommodity' was experienced at the first. The new site was to be at least ten Burgundian leagues (about 40 km/25 miles) from an existing Cistercian house[245]. Later (1214) the agreement of the Chapter became necessary before a move could be made[246], and later still royal or papal consent might be deemed advisable. Many site changes occurred in the early years – as in the monasteries of the Rhineland[247]. Such early changes perhaps reflected a quick realisation of the physical limitations of an ill-judged site[248]; if so, the process casts doubt on the supposed ideal of the white monks seeking for 'desert' and 'difficult' sites[249]. Other early changes of site were made simply because the first location had been intentionally provisional, occupied whilst the permanent abbey was being built. Some moves though took place decades, occasionally centuries, after the first foundation: a response to more specific external factors or to some grave calamity. Very often site changes ('cloister translation') led to later confusion, as to (i) a monastery's date of foundation: some records might give that of the first site, others that of a later site; (ii) an abbey's name (official or colloquial): sometimes a new name was adopted, sometimes the old name was transferred; sometimes both might be used.

Some abbeys had two or more changes of site before a lasting foundation was made, notably in the cases of Byland and Øm. Monks who had settled at Calder (1134–38) and were troubled by the Scots, moved to Hood (1138–43), but finding the site there too cramped moved on to Ryedale (1143–47). Too close there to Rievaulx (allegedly the two communities were able to hear each other's bells) they moved again to Stocking

(1147–77). Water shortage there prompted the final settlement at New Byland (1177)[250]. Monks who first settled at Sminge (1165) soon migrated, first to Veng (1165) and then to Kalvø (1168), before making a final settlement at Øm (1172)[251]. Its own chronicle told how in the days of its first abbot, Brian (1167–73), 'the cloister moved from place to place to the place where it now is'[252]. When Cistercians settled at Vitskøl in 1158, they were moving for the fifth time[253]. A commonly ascribed reason for a site change was 'limited space', the inability to expand. This was especially true of island sites, and was a factor in monastic migrations from the island of Lurö (fd 1150) in Lake Vänem to Varnhem (1154)[254], and from St James' island in the river Sava (fd *c.* 1272) to a site close to Zagreb (*c.* 1310)[255]. Other factors played a part: storm and ice made crossing Lake Skanderborg difficult for the community of Kalvø, whilst political considerations perhaps helped prompt the move to Zagreb.

An alleged lack of water was a frequent cause of site transfer. 'Arid' sites caused the monks of Eckenweiher (fd 1138) to go to Maulbronn (1146/47)[256], and those of Cantávos to Huerta (1162)[257]. A lack of water was shown at La Bussière when there was insufficient to quell a fire[258]. Monasteries sited on ridges of permeable limestone found it advantageous to move down to a spring-line: as Hazleton to Kingswood. The abbeys established in years of high precipitation at Loxwell (1151) and West Lulworth (1171) found that when normal conditions prevailed there was a water-shortage, and moved site to Stanley and Bindon respectively[259]. Too much water, especially stagnant water with associated 'insalubrity of air' and 'marsh fever', led several marshland communities to seek a change of site – as the monks of Saint-Aire transferring to Barbeaux (1156)[260], those of St Matthew in Rieti migrating to San Pastore de Greza (1234)[261], and those of Bellofonte moving to Valparaiso in Zamora (1232)[262]. The community of Vremde moved to Hemixsem (1246) after some of its monks had died from 'the deadly vapours of marsh water'[263]. St Bernard had little sympathy when the monks of Trefontane, by the Pontine marshes, wrote to him complaining of the putrid air[264].

A liability to flooding, consequent upon riverine or marine locations, obliged several site changes – as at Épinay (fd 1144) whose monks left for Bohéries after only two years because of inundations from the Oise[265]. Flooding by the Isère caused the monks of Commiers to move (1221) and be replaced by nuns[266]. Flooding and pestilence encouraged the monks of San Pastore (1236–55) to move from the valley floor to a hillside site overlooking the Plain of Rieti[267]. In Britain, the danger of flooding played a part in site changes from Bytham to Vaudey[268], and from Otley to Thame[269]. The monks of Haverholme (sited at only 8 m.O.D.) migrated to a slightly more elevated position at Louth Park[270]. The monks of Pyle in Frisia left (first for Timèla and later for Klaarcamp) because of 'devastation from flooding by the sea'[271]. The weather, too, played its part. The 'snow and rigorous climate' led the monks of Cabadour, established in 1137 at about 1050 m in the Pyrenean valley of Campan, to move down three years later to a new forest site at L'Escale-Dieu. A great fire, which had burnt its shepherds' huts and killed many of its sheep, was another factor[272]. The notably wet years of 1151 and 1152 helped to spur on the move from Barnoldswick (at some height in the Pennines) to Kirkstall (in the Aire valley). Summer rains delaying its harvest caused Fors in Wensleydale (1156) to move down the Ure valley to Jervaulx[273]. Some such moves may have been an unduly hasty response, a knee-jerk reaction, to unusually wet years.

A combination of factors, rather than one specific reason, frequently caused site changes, and these might include: fire: occasioning transfers from Azeraule (1131) to La Bussière[274], and Munkeby to Tautra (1207)[275]; 'sterility of soil': Ferrière to Clairlieu (*c.* 1158)[276], and La Harperie to Fontaine-Daniel (1204)[277]; wild beasts: the nuns of Suc-Ardu (in the Auvergne) to Bellecombe (*c.* 1200)[278]; and too close a proximity to well-travelled routeways: Pussac to Bonneval (1143)[279]. The need for a site 'fitting for contemplatives' was emphasised when Alexander IV sanctioned the transfer of the monks of Pyrgos to Beaulieu (Cyprus, 1256)[280]. Broadly political considerations governed other site changes. Edward I helped build a new abbey at Maenan (1284) for those monks whose strategic site at Aberconwy he required for a castle[281]. Hostile attacks by pagan Slavs caused Schmölln to move to Pforta (1132)[282], and Doberan (fd 1171) to migrate some distance (1179/86)[283]. Welsh raids caused the monks of Poulton to migrate (after sixty-one years) to Dieulacres[284]. The Welsh also burnt and razed to the ground the Border monastery of Grace Dieu (1233), causing the monks to move site across the Troddi stream[285]. 'Bad men' caused the monks of Salz to move to Junqueira (*c.* 1173)[286]. After the monks of Osek had moved (1207), a disgruntled founder attacked their new monastery and expelled the community[287].

A site change could be a lengthy process, with the views of several interested parties to be taken into consideration. On petition to the General Chapter an inspection of the new site would be ordered, and this took time. When (in 1277) the king of Bohemia wished to translate the destroyed monastery of Zlatá Koruna the Chapter appointed the abbot of Morimond to investigate: the abbey was of his lineage[288]. Any site change certainly needed the approval of the father-abbot: the transfer to Chorin (1273) from Mariensee came only after consultation with the abbots of Kołbacz and Lehnin (its mother-house)[289]. The diocesan bishop might be closely involved, as in the protracted move from Vremde to Hemixsem of St Bernard-opt-Scheldt: the grant of Hemixsem was made in 1243, but matters were still not finalised in 1251[290]. A very protracted site change was that of Stanlaw to Whalley. Sited by the Mersey estuary, Stanlaw suffered a series of privations: severe flooding (1279), its church tower blown down (1287), a fire and yet more flooding (1289)[291]. In 1283 the earl of Lincoln granted the abbey the church of Whalley, and the king's consent (necessary because of the Statute of Mortmain, 1279) was forthcoming. The bishop of Lichfield's consent was not obtained until 1285, nor that of Pope Nicholas IV until 1289. It was conditional on the death of the aged rector of Whalley, which did not take place until early in 1295. Negotiations with interested parties, and compensatory payments, followed, so that the monks only moved to Whalley in 1296[292].

Stanlaw had promised the pope (1289) that some monks would remain at the first site so long as it was habitable, and indeed three did so right down to the Dissolution[293]. The same was true at early sites deserted by Belleperche[294] and San Pastore[295]. At some abandoned sites other religious communities moved in: nuns replaced the monks at Hocht on their move to Val-Dieu (1216)[296], and at Isenhagen on the change to Marienrode (1261)[297]. A hermitage occupied the first site of Georgenthal (1144)[298], and Furness re-took the site of Calder when its monks moved to Byland (*c.* 1140)[299]. In the Stanlaw agreement (1283) the earl of Lincoln stipulated that the ashes of those buried there were to be removed to the new abbey at Whalley[300]. When the monks of Weng left for Kalvø, they carried 'their relics and the bones of their founders'[301]. To the new monastery of the Dunes (1237) were translated the bodies of Bl. Idesbald (d. 1156) and other religious[302]. All this was not unusual: when an avalanche of snow and rocks (in the winter of 1133–32) all but destroyed the Grand Chartreuse and killed six of its monks, the bodies of the dead Carthusians were transferred to their new place[303].

A grange normally remained on site when a community moved. On its replacement (*c.* 1135) the old abbey at Clairvaux became the home grange[304]. The first site of Jervaulx (at Fors) is still known as Dale Grange today[305]. Other instances are many, as at Esporles (first site of La Real)[306], Munkeby (of Tautra)[307], Otley (of Thame)[308], and Rhedynog (of Aberconwy)[309]. Both the first two temporary sites of Duiske became granges[310], as did four former abbey sites in Lorraine[311]. A number of early abandoned sites might, then or now, bear the name of 'old abbey'. The place names of Abadia Velha (in the case of Salzedas)[312] and of 'Hen fynachlog' (in the instance of Strata

Florida)[313] mark the location where their monks dwelt during the construction of their permanent abbey. The modern place-names of *Vieux*-Briostel and *Vieux*-Montier mark the first sites of those abbeys. The term 'old abbey' or 'old court' or 'old cloister' occurs in deeds referring to the first sites of Cambron (1228)[314], Champagne (1239)[315], Froidmont (1256)[316], Whalley (1333)[317], and Llantarnam (1291)[318]. A field-name of 'old abbey' occurred close to Grace Dieu (W, 1536)[319]. A transferred abbey might continue to use its earlier name (as did Strata Florida), or else adopt a new one ('Vale Royal' replaced 'Darnhall' at the king's insistence)[320].

A number of site changes were simply moves from buildings being temporarily occupied whilst a permanent cloister was being built. The monks of Morimond sent to Morimondo Coronato (1134) first occupied a grange for two years[321], and Mitjana Grange was the temporary home of Poblet's community[322]. It may be that the monks of Huerta saw Cántavos as a temporary stage. A papal bull of 1152 refers to 'the monks of Cántavos and the grange of Huerta', but a bull of 1164 to 'the monastery now called Huerta and the grange called Cántavos'[323]. The religious installed at Esporles (1239)[324] and at Barnoldswick (1147)[325] were so perhaps in anticipation of their definitive monasteries at La Real and Kirkstall, respectively. The monks of Rushen (1192) moved into Douglas town for four years whilst building work took place[326]. The monks of marshland Stratford temporarily evacuated to Burstead Grange after the abbey was 'with sore floods defaced'[327].

Not all mooted site changes were in fact accomplished. The community of Fountains (1135) prepared to move to a grange in Haute-Marne, France, but their fortunes changed and they stayed in England[328]. The abandonment of Acqualonga was debated by the Chapter in 1219 and 1225 but its monks stayed put[329]. A change in site was envisaged for Roccadia (1224) by Frederick II; he even began building the new church, but for some reason construction came to a halt at a height of 3 metres, and went no further[330]. Franquevaux's (1262) planned move (because of putrid marsh air) to its Campagnoles Grange was never fully accomplished; moreover, the delegates on the enquiry commission were very tardy[331]. A further move hoped for by La Real (1303), which cited some 'great inconvenience' to the General Chapter, seems to have petered out[332].

United and Ephemeral Sites

The rapid growth of the Order in the twelfth century inevitably meant that a number of monasteries, established with goodwill and high hopes, fell short either in material possessions or numbers of personnel and found it difficult to survive. This seems to have been particularly true towards the close of the twelfth century, when the General Chapter referred to the small numbers of monks in some abbeys as a grave scandal. The Chapter provided (1189, 1190, 1204) that if a house had less than the requisite thirteen monks and could not sustain that number, it was to be either reduced to the status of a grange or closed down altogether, and the monks sent to another abbey. If it was sufficiently prosperous the father-abbot was to endeavour to make up its numbers (1204). The consequence was that several smaller monasteries were united to larger ones[333]. The situation was especially serious in Ireland, where by 1221 it appears some monasteries had next to no monks[334].

An abbot of Froidmont (1227) on visitation in Ireland, and 'finding the abbey of Killenny in debt and its monks obliged to beg', ordered its union with Duiske, but enjoined that its abbot and monks be well treated[335]. Objections to the union were persistent, and came from Mellifont (head of line) and Jerpoint (mother-house of Killenny), but the amalgamation was confirmed by the General Chapter (1231, 1261),

Countess Matilda Marshall (1246), Henry III of England (1252), and the cardinal-protector of the Order (John of Toledo, 1261)[336]. In the Isle of Man, by 1196 Miresco had been united to Rushen, perhaps because it lay in the ill-drained boglands of the Curragh[337]. In Poland, the General Chapter (1191) ordered the amalgamation of Ląd with its mother-house of Lekno, but ducal intervention put paid to this plan. The Chapter had decreed: 'From two let there be one, and let there be one sheep and one shepherd'[338]. After pillaging by the count of Toulouse, the French abbey of Frayssinet was united to Aiguebelle (1228), its benefactors receiving compensation[339]. On the union of Santes Salvatore with Oliva (1270) the Chapter enjoined that a skeleton staff of monks was to remain to offer divine service for those monks buried there[340].

Dispersed or united sites commonly became granges of the absorbing monastery. The abbot of Casanova was allowed to have divine service celebrated at its St Bartholomew's Grange, which had once been a conventual abbey and where three monks lived[341]. After the invasion of the kingdom of Naples in 1348 by the king of Hungary, Sterpeto became a grange of the mother-house of Arabona[342]. In Spain, the General Chapter reduced San Vicente (1216) to a grange: it was so poor it could only sustain two monks[343]. In France, Boulbonne received as granges the monasteries of Tramesaigues (1209) and Vajal (1225)[344]. Contrariwise, granges might be elevated into abbeys. Ląd (*c.* 1175), formerly a grange of Lekno, became its daughter-house[345]; the abbey of Vaux-la-Douce (1168) was founded at a grange of Clairefontaine[346]. Some abbeys threatened with closure were spared, as St Sebastian in the Catacombs (1191)[347]. Some sites reduced to granges might be revived as conventual abbeys: Du-Jau (1230)[348] and Kilbeggan (1281)[349] amongst them.

There were a number of other transient foundations[349a]. The Welsh abbey of Trawscoed (fd *c.* 1173) had been endowed with rents and fisheries, 'provided that it shall remain in Cantrefselyf for ever', but by about 1200 it had been degraded by the mother-house of Dore to grange status[350]. Italian houses which failed to thrive because of unfavourable topography included S. Maria di Sala (1217)[351] and S. Giusto di Tuscania (1255)[352]. The monks of Holy Trinity of Palermo saw their abbey given in 1197 to the Teutonic Knights by Emperor Henry VI[353]. Some Cistercian foundations were extremely short-lived. Kilshane (1198) failed almost immediately and became a grange of Monasternenagh[354]. Barona (fd 1192), an Italian daughter of La Ferté, never really got under way and by 1224 was perhaps no more than a far-flung grange[355]. A foundation made by Pforta at Jarosław (by 1201) was said to have been 'erected and thrown down'; its property passed to Lubiąż[356]. Some Cistercian sites have been lost to human knowledge, or their whereabouts are at best uncertain; this is true of Ábrahám, Egres, and Jubin.

Some Cistercian foundations were unauthorised, some were delayed, and some never got off the ground. When the abbot of Buzay (1202) transformed one of his granges into an abbey without proper authorisation, the Chapter ordered its closure[357]. The same ruling applied when Santa-Maria de Caritate was founded (1211) without permission[358]. A monk of Fontfroide, Peter de Serre, established without leave a monastery of St Victor at Montueyre. When the dissident monks were reintegrated at Fontfroide (in 1206), St Victor and its possessions were organised into two granges[359]. Years of delay might elapse between the intention of a founder being expressed and the actual fulfilment of his promise. In about 1178 monks of Kołbacz prepared to settle at Oliwa, but the recrudescence of hostilities between Denmark and Pomerania delayed this foundation until 1186[360]. Monks of Woburn founded Medmenham in 1204 but returned home that year and a lasting settlement was only made by about 1212[361]. The Barons' War delayed the royal charter for Vale Royal[362]. Knardrup was founded in 1326 by King Kristoffer II, but he went into exile later that year, the monks were ejected and did not regain the property until 1343[363]. King Sancho VII of Navarre intended to build an abbey for one hundred monks, but he died (1234) before his plan could be realised[364]. An abbey was to have been founded at Dénesvölgy in Hungary, but the Tartar invasion of 1241 saw the project fall through[365].

Seasonal Sites

A few monastic communities, desiring cooler air or wishing to be away from malarial marshes, took pains to relieve the discomfort each summer brought by transferring temporarily to a grange away from stagnant water and at a higher altitude. A skeleton staff would have been left behind, and to these the provision of the General Chapter (1191) applied that when a community was staying on a grange the observances of the Order were nevertheless to be maintained by those remaining in the abbey[366]. The monks of Matina (by 1235) spent three months each summer in a grange of Sambucina, possibly at that abbey itself[367]. The monks of Franquevaux, sited by Lake Scamandre in the Camargue, suffered there from 'corrupt and unbearable air' and (from 1270) migrated from 1 May to 1 October each year to their Campagnoles Grange, keeping there the normal conventual life, but making sure the safe-keeping of their abbey. There was even thought of moving there permanently[368]. The monks of Trefontane in its earlier days transferred in the summer months to the castle of Nemi, because of the malarial hazards of the Pontine marshes, and later (1237 onwards) to Palazzula, on the slopes of Monte Cavo by Lake Albano. This became an abbey in its own right (1244) but remained as a summer-house until 1391[369].

Other monasteries with granges used for seasonal or recreational purposes included Salley (1289) at Hartlepool[370], Fossanova (1297) at Petra Grange[371], and (later) Poblet at Milmande Grange[372] and Whitland at Maenor Forion[373]. Conversely, the abbey of Léoncel, sited at 900 metres in the foothills of the Alps, had a winter dwelling at Pardieu, about 200 metres below in the Plain of Valence; originally a monastery of hermits, it was fused with Léoncel in 1194. The Cistercians lived there from St Andrew's Day (30 November) to Easter each year, keeping a skeleton staff of four to six monks at Pardieu through the summer[374]. A vaulted cellar and spiral staircase still remain.

Mechanics of Foundation

The foundation of a new Cistercian house required an *invitation* to settle, *approval* of the diocesan, *agreement* of the General Chapter, *appraisal* of the ground and *selection* of the site[375]. An invitation to settle implied an appropriate benefaction. At Coggeshall, this meant three carucates of land, a woodland, fishponds and a fishery on the sea[376]. At Valbonne, the dowry included 300 silver florins, 18 sets of sacerdotal vestments, one hundred sheep and one hundred goats, as well as gifts of oil, butter and cheese[377]. King Andrew of Hungary, giving land for the building of Toplica, commanded the men there, 'free and serfs,' to obey the monks as they had obeyed the king[378]. There could be confusion: the founder of Pipewell raised its first buildings before inviting a community. His ambiguity led to two communities setting out for the new house, from Garendon and Newminster; argument ensued and the monks of Garendon withdrew[379]. Some grants might be disputed: Biddlesden (1147) was settled on land confiscated during the civil war; this ended, the owner laid claim to the land and the monks satisfied him with ten marks[380]. The brothers of Coëffort contested the land granted for the foundation of L'Épau (1229) by Berenger, the widowed queen of Richard I of England, and were also indemnified[381].

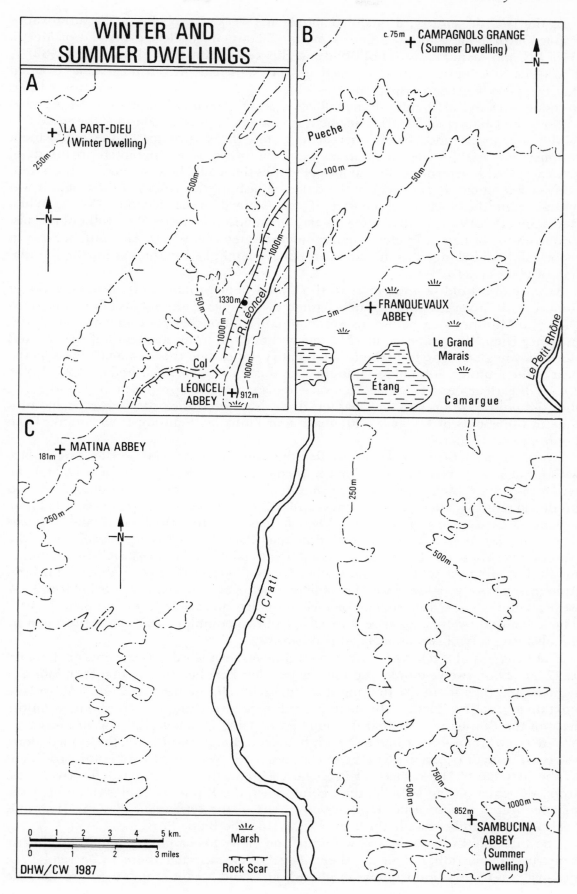

WINTER AND SUMMER DWELLINGS

A

LA PART-DIEU
(Winter Dwelling)

250m

500m

1000m

750m

R. Léoncel

1000m

1330m

1000m

Col

LÉONCEL
ABBEY 912m

B

c. 75m CAMPAGNOLS GRANGE
(Summer Dwelling)

—N—

Pueche

100 m

50 m

5 m

FRANQUEVAUX
ABBEY

Le Grand
Marais

Étang

Le Petit Rhône

Camargue

C

MATINA ABBEY
181m

—N—

250 m

R. Crati

250 m

500m

750m

500m

500m

852m

1000m

SAMBUCINA
ABBEY
(Summer
Dwelling)

0 1 2 3 4 5 km.

0 1 2 3 miles

Marsh

Rock Scar

DHW/CW 1987

In the twelfth century, a qualified monk or *conversus* probably made an advance inspection of a site offered. Adam, a monk of Fountains, selected the site of Meaux (1151)[382], and Alan, a *conversus* of Buildwas, checked out the site of Dunbrody (1182)[383]. The General Chapter (1194), aware that some sites had proved unsuitable, decided that two abbots were to inspect all sites which were being offered[384], and were (1203) to report back to the Chapter of the following year[385]. No new house was to be founded without the Chapter's leave[386]. The abbot-investigators were to consider the suitability of the site, its distance from other abbeys, and the sufficiency of the endowment promised[387]. In 1267 these regulations were reinforced, as the potential prosperity of an abbey would 'determine the number of monks that could be sustained'[388]. It was also necessary to obtain the consent of the diocesan bishop; this ruling of the Chapter was in line with the ancient injunction of the Council of Chalcedon (451)[389]. When Buckland (1278) was founded from Quarr, the monks celebrated Mass without permission from the bishop of Exeter, who excommunicated them[390]. In England, because in theory all land belonged to the king, royal leave might be sought – as for the foundation of Hailes (1245)[391].

Benefactors could be evasive as to the endowment promised, as seemingly Count Robert IV of Auvergne who had to be visited three times by the abbots of La Bénissons-Dieu and Montpeyroux before his foundation of Le Bouchet got under way (1199)[392]. At Grace Dieu (W), proposed in 1217, delay came first from the abbots of Bruern and Bordesley neglecting to fulfil their investigatory duties, and then from tardiness on the part of the founder, John of Monmouth , but the house was established in 1226[393]. The abbots of Kołbacz and Łekno (1232) were to inspect the site proposed for Paradyż, but they did not report back to the Chapter; three years later, the order was repeated, this time to the abbots of Kołbacz, Sittenbach and Zinna, with authority for monks from Lehnin to settle there[394].

It was an early provision of the Order that 'no abbot shall be sent to a new place without at least twelve monks': this complement clearly representing Christ and the twelve apostles[395]. At Calder[396] and Termunten[397] the names of the founding abbot and his dozen monks (coming from Furness and Aduard respectively) are on record. Those leaving Aduard were seen as having 'their names written in the book of life'[398]. It was whilst he was at Beaulieu's consecration that Earl Richard of Cornwall chose the community of thirteen for his new monastery at Hailes[399]. Some *conversi* also accompanied a founding party: ten in the case of Kirkstall (1134)[400], five at Villers (1147)[401]. Amongst the twelve *conversi* who left Villers to settle at St Bernard-opt-Scheldt in 1237 were a tailor, a cook, a smith, and one who doubled up as launderer and fisherman[402]. The abbot and twelve monks sent to Žďár from Nepomuk in 1252 were preceded by an advance party of two monks and two *conversi*[403].

The progress of a few founding communities is on record. When, on 2nd January 1247, an abbot, twelve monks and four *conversi* left Beaulieu for the first foundation at Newenham, they spent the first night at Christchurch, the next at Bindon Abbey, the next on a grange of Netley, the next at Ford Abbey, reaching their destination on the feast of the Epiphany (6 January), a journey of some 70 miles (120 km) in four days. When a new community came to Newenham from Beaulieu in 1265, they sailed along the coast from St Leonard's Grange to Charmouth[404]. When monks of Himmerod went to the first site of Heisterbach at Petersberg (1188), they did so partly by river: first from Mönchen on the Moselle, then going down the Rhine to Königswinter[405]. A sea journey (often perilous) perhaps played a part in the settlement of some Irish and Welsh abbeys, and certainly those of Norway and the Baltic Provinces.

The first monks to settle a new foundation came to temporary buildings already constructed for, rather than by, them. The Order expected there to be ready: 'an oratory, a refectory, a dormitory, a guest-house, and a gate-keeper's cell, so that the monks may immediately serve God and live in religious discipline'. The statutes are silent as to who was to pay for and to construct them, and as to the form or plan: presumably the founder was held responsible[406]. Sometimes the temporary buildings were at a distance. The monks of Øm 'erected houses or rather huts' there, whilst still resident at Kalvø[407]. At some houses the early buildings were dual-purpose, as at Foigny where one building served as dorter and refectory[408]. The first buildings would have been largely, if not entirely, of timber (Chapter 9). At Bordesley, excavations have shown that the timbers from the first (temporary) church were used to bury the founder monks[409]. The chronicle of Signy records that materials from the first buildings which were not reused in the new were buried within the precincts of the monastery by Abbot Alard (1156–74). Relics of the earliest buildings were seemingly treated with reverential awe[410].

The actual date of a foundation as recorded in the *tabula* kept by the precentor of Cîteaux, might differ from that given in other sources. It depended on the point from which the foundation was seen as being effective: the original promise, the inspection of the site, the approval of the bishop, or the granting of a confirmatory charter[411]. The exact date of foundation of some abbeys is therefore a matter of debate[412]. A monastery such as St Bernard-opt-Scheldt might take its foundation as the year of the original charter (1235) or be thought of as founded in the actual year of settlement (1237)[413]. The dates given in one known copy of the *tabula* are at variance with dates given in contemporary chronicles and annals. This list was written in two portions: from 1098 to 1190, then with a new scribe entering the portion from 1191 to 1234, when the list abruptly concludes. Among the 348 abbeys given precise dating, whilst foundations were made throughout the year, the winter months were the least popular – especially December [only 13]. May led the way [43], followed by March (with the onset of spring) and July [both 39], whilst the number of foundations in November [32] suggest a desire to get foundations established before winter set in[414]. Some monasteries may have been settled on dates which bore a significance of which we know nothing. The official ingress at Dargun on 15 June 1172, the anniversary of the solemn translation of Duke Knud Lavard, canonised two years before, suggests that the Danish monks were well aware not only of their religious but also of their political aims[415]. The settlement of monks at Grace Dieu on 24 April, 1226, came almost on the exact anniversary of the foundation date of its mother-house at Dore (25 April, 1147)[416].

Notes

1. Waddell (1994) 29.
2. *Statuta* I, 13 (1134).
3. *Cal. Papal Registers (Letters)* I, 131.
4. VCH, *Stafford* III (1970) 232.
5. Berman (1986) 292.
6. Fossier (1983) 59.
7. Berman (1986) 88–9, King (1954) 3.
8. Compton (1892) 20.
9. Carville (1982b) 57–8.
10. Lekai (1977a) 14.
11. Berman (1983) 45.
12. Despy (1983) 194.
13. Berman (1986) 24.
14. Berman (1978) 296–97; *cf.*283–84, 286–87.
15. Thoen (1975) 228–29.
16. Rösener (1983a) 138.
17. France (1992) 29.
18. *FRB* V, 16–17.
19. Bialoskórska (1962) 199–203.
20. Donkin (1964) 48–9.
21. *Cf.* Williams (1978) 255; Berman (1983) 44.
22. Holdsworth (1980) 37.
23. Hill (1968) 112.
24. Muir (1982) 86.
25. Barley (1957) 75, 80–81, 84, 87; *cf.* Muir (1982) 88.
26. Donkin (1978) 42, *cf.* Barley (1957) 79.
27. Wright (1972) 1768.
28. Williams (1984) I, 15.
29. Muir (1982) 87–9.
30. Barnes (1982) 5.
31. Donkin (1964) 42.
32. Knowles (1963a) 350–51.
33. Fergusson (1984a) 9.
34. Berman (1983) 45.
35. *Cîteaux* (1978: 1–2) 121.
36. Coulton (1960) 224*n*.
37. Grüger (1987) 167.

38. Despy (1974) 65.
39. *FRB* 529.
40. Roehl (1972) 103–04.
41. Waddell (1994) 29.
42. Dimier (1957) 67.
43. Richards (1968) 99.
44. Bernard (1967) 15, 134.
45. Leblanc (1949) 604, Lecaze (1993) 168.
46. Goutagny (1965) 47, *cf. PCP* 157–58 (No. 86).
47. *PCP*. 156 (No. 85).
48. *CAF* 67.
49. Anstett (1987) 2–3.
50. Lekai (1977a) 272.
51. Rocca (1936) 291.
52. Carville (1982b) 22.
53. Stalley (1987) 242.
54. *DHGE* II (1914) 179.
55. Speiss (1959) 275.
56. *KD* I, 166–65; *cf. CB* No. 41.
57. Fergusson (1984a) 18.
58. Wetesko (1991) 156.
59. *DHGE* XIV (1960) 519.
60. *KD* I, 26; *cf. CDM* I, 263–64 (Arnsburg).
61. *LCC* (1) 31, (2) 211, 241; *cf.* Waddell (1994) 29.
62. Cowley (1977) 1224–25.
63. Butler (1976) 6.
64. *CS* I, 155–56.
65. *DHGE* VI (1932) 1061.
66. *Ibid.* VII (1934) 232.
67. Berman (1986) 8.
68. King (1954) 330.
69. Van Der Meer (1965) 269, 295.
70. *Ibid.* 291.
71. Cocheril (1966) 232.
72. *CDRB* V:3, 139 (No. 1167).
73. Reissenberger (1894) 17.
74. *RBM* I,166 (no. 373).
75. *CDRB* I, 321–22 (No. 357).
76. *Cf.* Wamba (1994) 122, 150 (*n*.16).
77. McCrank (1973) 57, 60; (1976) 138*n*.
78. Burke (1982) 78.
79. Martinez (1984) 281–82, and map opp. 284.
80. Charvátová (1987) 123.
81. *AZ* 541.
82. *CDRB* II, 109 (No. 116).
83. *Ibid.* V:1, 288–89 (No. 136).
84. *SL* 57.
85. Williams (1976) 20, 44.
86. Devailly (1973) 288.
87. *CPR* 1290/397.
88. Ruwet (1966) 7–9.
89. Devailly (1973) 289.
90. *RD* I, 812 (No. 4875).
91. *DHGE* XII (1953) 157.
92. Williams (1976) 2–3.
93. Dimier (1964) 36.
94. See later flood-levels marked in its cloister.
95. *Cal. Patent Rolls* 1300/52.
96. *Cf.* Williams (1990) 132 (fig. 50), 89 (fig. 10).
97. Carville (1982b) 42, *cf.* Williams (1984) I, 13.
98. Williams (1990) 86 (fig. 6).
99. Van Der Meer (1965) 270.
100. Carville (1982b) 2.
101. *CNM* xv.
102. Bedini (1964) 129.
103. Williams (1984), I, 13; II, 317.
104. Williams-Jones (1957) 49.
105. *NG* IV, 456.
106. Often silted up today.
107. Williams (1984) I, 14; *cf.* Carville (1982b) 85–7 (Holy Cross).
108. *Cf.* Donkin (1964) 51–53.
109. Dimier (1974a) 56–57.
110. Dimier (1964), *cf.* Carville (1982b) 17.
111. *RHC* 21 (No. 50a of 1185).
112. Donnelly (1949) 79 (No. 118).
113. *DHGE* XVIII (1977) 1020.
114. Bedini (1964) 30, Bell (1989) 142.
115. VCH, *Huntingdon* I (1926) 392*n*.
116. Clair (1961) 266.
117. McDonnell (1965) 32–5, *cf.* Darby (1940) 101 (Sawtry).
118. Donkin (1978) 116, 118.
119. *Ibid.* 116 (and Meaux).
120. Carville (1982b) 86, *cf.* 67 (Abbeydorney).
121. Wyrwa (1992) 379.
122. Rahtz (1976) 14, 89, 104.
123. Petrù (1972) 20.
124. Van Der Meer (1965) 275.
125. Clair (1961) 266.
126. Bedini (1964) 78.
127. Clair (1961) 266.
128. Van Der Meer (1965) 276.
129. Wyrwa (1984) 39, (1992) 373.
130. Dimier (1973) 53, 56; David-Roy (1973) 62.
131. McGuire (1973) 123.
132. McGuire (1974) 28–9.
133. *SMD* II, 176; *cf.* McGuire (1976a) 40, (1982) 100–03.
134. *SMD* II, 197; *cf.* France (1994) 173.
135. France (1998) in press; McGuire (1974) 298–9, (1976a) 39.
136. Van Der Meer (1965) 290.
137. Hockey (1976) 20.
138. Williams (1984) I, 7–8.
139. Carville (1981) 37–9.
140. Stalley (1987) 38.
141. Tomé (1991) 95.
142. Van Nerom (1984a) 34.
143. *CCD* 68.
144. Fergusson (1984a) 147.
145. Butler and Given-Wilson (1979) 306.
146. VCH, *County of Lancaster* II (1908) 119*n*.
147. Butler and Given-Wilson (1979) 306.
148. Comment by Mme. B. Barrière at the Fontfroide (1993) Conference.
149. *DSMLR* 264 (No. 46).
150. Bedini (1964) 87 (No. 38).
151. *Ibid.* 145–48.
152. *DHGE* XXIV (1993) 390.
153. Balleine (1962) 6; kind information of Fr G. Flood, Biggin Hill.
154. Guide leaflet at site.
155. Bedini (1964) 104.
156. McGuire (1982) 4.
157. France (1992) 25.
158. Johnsen (1977) 55.
159. McGuire (1982) 49.
160. Clark (1895) 207.
161. *DHGE* XII (1953) 918.
162. Mousnier (1983b) 58.
163. *RD* I, 755 (No. 4526).

164. Bedini (1964) 131.
165. *CSBW* 37.
165a. Jarry (1864) 182–83.
166. Laurent (1928) 117, *cf.* Van Der Meer (1965) 270, 288.
167. Williams (1974) 63.
168. *DHGE* XXIV (1993) 1347.
169. Bedini (1964) 151.
170. *Ibid.* 141.
171. Williams (1974) 65, 72.
172. Leblanc (1949) 585, 589.
173. Johnsen (1977) 59.
174. Esquieu (1986) 15.
175. Carville (1982b) 52, Mellifont (1980) 31–3.
176. Butler and Given-Wilson (1979) 141; Lillich (1982a) 141.
177. Pontus (1966) 28.
178. Fergusson (1984a) 61.
179. Leclercq (1977) 139–40.
180. For a full review of Cistercian place-names, see: Laurent (1928) *passim*; *cf.* France (1992) 19–26.
181. VCH, *Northampton* II (1906) 116.
182. Van Der Meer (1965) *passim*.
183. France (1994) 169.
184. Van Der Meer (1965) 292, 295.
185. *Cf.* Van Der Meer (1965) 293.
186. *Ibid.* 303.
187. Whone (1987) 7.
188. Laurent (1928) 190, 192.
189. Van Der Meer (1965) 271–73.
190. Laurent (1928) 191–92.
191. Stalley (1987) 40.
192. VCH, *Stafford* III (1970) 230.
193. Rymar (1987) 207.
194. Laurent (1928) 194–96.
195. *DHGE* XV (1963) 969–70.
196. Kuthan (1982) 224.
197. Van Der Meer (1965) 285.
198. *DHGE* XI (1949) 758.
199. Stalley (1987) 40.
200. Van Der Meer (1965) 281.
201. VCH, *Wiltshire* III (1956) 269.
202. *DHGE* X (1938) 1020.
203. VCH, *Somerset* II (1911) 116.
204. *CDEM* II, 351.
205. Williams (1984) I, 21–2.
206. Gimpel (1977) 3–6.
207. *OC* 239 (No. DCXXIII).
208. Traissac (1960) 142–43.
209. Lillich (1984) 142–43.
210. Carville (1982b) 82.
211. Stalley (1987) 31.
212. *CPL* lxi.
213. Kempf (1976) 10.
214. Lindley (1955) 39.
215. Grüger (1984) 202.
216. Richards (1968) 85.
217. Rahtz (1976) 14, 33; *cf.* Astill (1994) 541, 546.
218. Williams (1976) 68.
219. Butler and Given-Wilson (1979) 293; Richardson (1981a) 29.
220. Mascarenhas (1994) 156.
221. Grüger (1984) 203.
222. Mascarenhas (1994) 159.
223. Barrière (1992) 28.
224. Aston (1993) 123–25 (and map), 130–31 (and Fig. 87).
225. Sonnet (1984) 285–90.
226. Amon (1979) 140.
227. Bond (1989) 86.
228. Canestrelli (1896) 17.
229. Evans (1977) 143–44.
230. Grüger (1984) 202.
231. France (1998) in press; *Cf. SRD* IV, 535.
232. Bond (1989) 86; Coppack (1990) 85.
233. Heutger (1985) 148; *cf.* Dimier (1964) 108.
234. *CCD* 50.
235. Grüger (1984) 202.
236. Lillich (1984) 146.
237. Robinson (1995) 58.
238. Coppack (1990) 88.
239. Williams (1890) 150–52.
240. France (1992) 17.
241. Lillich (1984) 146.
242. Coppack (1990) 92, Lillich (1984) 146.
243. Cruden (1950) 71–72.
244. Information of Mr Stuart Harrison.
244a Gand (1990) No. 22.
245. *Statuta* I, 45 (1152/1); *LCC* (1) 31, (2) 208.
246. Bouton (1959) I, 136.
247. Rösener (1983a) 138–39.
248. Donkin (1978) 31.
249. Rösener (1983a) 138.
250. VCH, *Yorkshire* III (1974) 131–32; Donkin (1978) 34.
251. France (1992) 65.
252. *SMD* II, 192–93.
253. McGuire (1976a) 13, 15.
254. France (1992) 35.
255. Lekai (1976) 258.
256. *DR* 786.
257. *OC* 78–80 (CXCVII); *cf.* Cocheril (1964) 252.
258. Colombet (1976) 281.
259. Donkin (1978) 34.
260. Bouton (1959) I, 136.
261. *DHGE* XXII (1988) 192; *cf. Statuta* II, 130 (1234/22), 155 (1236/5), 174 (1237/3).
262. Cocheril (1961a) 69–70.
263. *OLSB* VI.
264. Dimier (1957) 65–6.
265. *OC* 64 (CLVI), *DHGE* IX (1937) 510.
266. *RD* II, 137 (No. 6613), 145 (No. 6664), *cf.* 465–66 (No. 8506).
267. Bedini (1964) 115.
268. Hill (1968) 48–49.
269. Fergusson (1983) 78.
270. Donkin (1978) 35.
271. *CFC* 135.
272. Bouton (1959) I, 136.
273. Donkin (1978) 33; *cf.* VCH, *Yorkshire* III (1974) 143 (for Barnoldswick).
274. *DHGE* X (1938) 1426; Colombet (1976) 281.
275. France (1993) 270.
276. Grégoire (1985) 225.
277. *DHGE* XVII (1971) 831.
278. Cocheril (1964) 252, Bouton (1959) I, 136.
279. Josephine (1976) 296.
280. Williams (1974) 68-8.
281. Williams (1984) I, 11–18.
282. Speiss (1959) 274.
283. *DHGE* XIV (1960) 532; Roehl (1972) 97–8.

284. VCH, *Stafford* III (1970) 230; Donkin (1978) 36–37.
285. Williams (1984) I, 18., Harrison (1998).
286. Tomé (1991) 162–63.
287. *DHG* II, 59; *CDRB* II, 634–4 (No. 69).
288. Kuthan (1982) 224*n*.
289. *CBR* II, 391, 393, 396, 412–13.
290. *OSBS* (1) 46–7 (No. 39), 77 (No. 69), 103–09 (Nos 87–93), 143–44 (Nos 136–37).
291. Hand (1919) 22.
292. VCH, *Lancaster* II (1908) 132–34; Ashmore (1962) 6, 56.
293. VCH, *Lancaster* II (1908) 132; *Trans. Hist. Soc. Lancs. and Cheshire* CXIV (1963) 68*n*.
294. Berman (1986) 34.
295. *DHGE* XXII (1988) 192.
296. Brouwers (1983) 218–19.
297. *CTB* 16–7.
298. *DHGE* XX (1984) 577.
299. *AF* 124–26, 137.
300. VCH, *Lancaster* II (1908) 132.
301. *SMD* 167.
302. *CCD* 31–2.
303. *RD* I, 589 (No. 3473), 591 (No. 3496).
304. Leroux (1990) 21, *cf.* Williams (1935) 20.
305. VCH, *Yorkshire* III (1974) 140.
306. *DSMLR passim*.
307. France (1993) 269.
308. VCH, *County of Oxford* II (1907) 83.
309. Williams (1984) I, 17, 125.
310. *CDK* 13.
311. Parisse (1981) 80.
312. Campos de Sousa Real (1986) 77.
313. Williams (1984) I, 20.
314. *CAC* IV, 419.
315. Philippe (1991) 122.
316. Bonnet-Laborderie (1985).
317. *CBW* II, 408.
318. *Taxatio Ecclesiastica* 281b.
319. Owen (1935) 191.
320. *C.P.R.* 1294/62.
321. Bedini (1964) 15.
322. McCrank (1976) 143.
323. *CMH* 3–12 (Nos 3–5).
324. Blanco Trias (1953) 61–2.
325. Barnes (1982) 7.
326. Cumming (1868) 37.
327. VCH, *Essex* II (1907) 131.
328. Fergusson (1984b) 40.
329. Bedini (1964) 100.
330. *Ibid.* 73.
331. *DHGE* XVIII (1977) 1020, *Statuta* III, 8 (1262/67).
332. *DSMLR* 410 (No. 151).
333. *Statuta* I, 111 (1189/3), 121 (1190/15), 295 1204/1, 2); III, 140 (1275/4); *LCC* (1) 310–1.
334. *Statuta* I, II, 4–5 (1221/21, 22); *cf. SL* 23, 26; Conbhuí (1958) 56.
335. *CDK* 43–6, 48, *cf.* 56–57; *RSL* I, 82.
336. *CDK* 63–6, 83–4, 93–5, 100–01; *cf.* 114–18, 120–22; Thompson (1931) 16.
337. Butler (1994) 185–86.
338. *Statuta* I, 137 (1191/17); Kłoczkowski (1970) 116.
339. Hugues (1863) 161, 164–68.
340. *Statuta* III, 72 (1269/20), 84 (1270/22).
341. *Statuta* II, 99 (1231/45).
342. Bedini (1964) 162–63.
343. *Statuta* I, 459 (1216/50); Lekai (1977a) 44.
344. *DHGE* X (1938) 66.
345. Wetesko (1991) 156.
346. Affolter (1978) 20, 47.
347. *Statuta* I, 137 (1191/15); II, 413 (1255/16).
348. *Ibid.* II, 86–7 (1230/14).
349. *Ibid.* III, 209 (1281/15).
349a. *Cf. OC* LXVII-LXXXII.
350. Williams (1984) I, 5–6.
351. Bedini (1964) 81–2.
352. *Ibid.* 45.
353. *Ibid.* 83.
354. Carville (1982a) 39.
355. Bedini (1964) 108.
356. *Statuta* I, 274 (1201/54).
357. *DHGE* X (1938) 1448–49.
358. Bedini (1964) 109.
359. Grézes-Ruelff (1977) 258–59, 267, 275.
360. Szacherska (1977) 152.
361. VCH, *Buckingham* I (1905) 376.
362. Colvin (1963) I, 248.
363. McGuire (1982) 194–95.
364. De Oyaga (1967) 49.
365. *RCH* 40–1.
366. *Statuta* I, 145 (1191/83), 181 (1194/61).
367. *Statuta* II, 145–46 (1235/29).
368. *Statuta* III, 84–5 (1270/23), 98 (1271/29); *DHGE* XVIII (1977) 1020.
369. Tower (und.) 5.
370. *CS* II, 100–01.
371. *Statuta* III, 291 (1297/29).
372. McCrank (1976) 143.
373. Williams (1984) II, 223.
374. *CL* 58 (No. LIII); *Cf.* Berman (1986) 73; Wullschleger (1991) 29–30.
375. Donkin (1965) 276.
376. *CDF* I, 292 (No.   808).
377. Grèzes-Ruelff (1977) 258.
378. *CDCDS* III, 54–5, 123, 250.
379. Fergusson (1983) 78.
380. VCH, *Buckingham* I (1905) 365.
381. *DHGE* XV (1963) 546.
382. Fergusson (1984) 8.
383. Stalley (1987) 36–7.
384. *Ibid.* 36–7.
385. *Statuta* I, 285 (1203/5), 291 (1203/33).
386. *LCC* (1) 31, (2) 208.
387. *Statuta* I, 258 (1200/50).
388. *Statuta* III, 47–48 (1267/2).
389. *Statuta* I, 464 (1216/68), *cf.* France (1992) 13.
390. *MEX* 380.
391. Hill (1968), Meekings (1979) 35.
392. *DHGE* IX (1937) 1465.
393. *Statuta* I, 48 (1217/67); II, 19 (1222/32), 27 (1223/21), 43 (1225/39).
394. *Statuta* II, 107 (1232/35), 122 (1233/53), 149 (1235/44).
395. Lekai (1977a) 448 (No. IX).
396. *AF* 121.
397. *VGA* 8.
398. *KKA* 46–7.
399. Meekings (1979) 35, *cf. Statuta* II, 262 (1243/20).
400. Barnes (1982) 34.
401. *DHGE* XII (1953) 919.
402. *OLSB* (2), 52, 172.

403. *FRB* II, 533–34.
404. *MEX* 357–58, *cf.* Davidson (1843) 8–9.
405. Kraus (1980) 51.
406. Fergusson (1983) 75.
407. France (1998) in press; *cf.* Fergusson (1983) 75*n*.
408. Gilyard-Beer (1986) 175.
409. Coppack (1993) 19.
410. Fergusson (1983) 102*n*.
411. France (1992) 37; *cf.* Hill (1968) 43.
412. *DHGE* XV (1963) 1089–91.
413. *OLSB* VI; (the first grant of land had been made in 1233: *OSBS* (1) 9 (No. 8).
414. Birch (1870) 281; for Scottish dates, see: Easson (1957) *passim*; for some English dates, see: *AM* II, 221–33.
415. Szacherska (1977) 141.
416. Williams (1976) 59.

Chapter 9

THE MONASTIC BUILDINGS

Building Materials

The first buildings erected, prior to the arrival of the monks, were often no more than intentionally temporary wooden huts. Timber was therefore used[1]: it was quicker to work than stone, and it reflected Cistercian simplicity[2]. The biographer of St Aelred of Rievaulx told how its first monks 'set up their *huts* by the Rie'[3]. The chronicle of Øm (1172) records how its monks moved to their new home 'having erected houses, or rather *huts*'[4]. The monks of Dargun (1172) lived in wooden accommodation for years, their brick monastery only being commenced in 1225[5]. In the course of time, and generally starting with the church, wooden monastic buildings became wholly or partly replaced by stone or, sometimes, brick. The early timber buildings were not always completely destroyed because of their sentimental value[6]. At Cîteaux (1106) a stone church and cloister were ready within a few years of its foundation (1098)[7]. Elsewhere, the substitution of stone for timber took longer. Vaux-de-Cernay (fd 1118) was partly raised in wood, to be replaced from 1145 by stone[8]. In the early-thirteenth century, Varnhem (tr. 1154) still boasted a wooden church[9]. The cloister of Meaux (fd 1151) was not rebuilt in stone until about 1200[10], those of some Irish houses not until the fourteenth century[11], and that of Obra (fd 1237) not until 1618[12]. The cloister of Tautra endured as a wooden structure[13], as did perhaps the *conversi* ranges at Basingwerk and Cymer[14].

Even where stone was employed, timber still played a salient rôle. When the west end of Louth Park church was completed (*c.* 1240) it was chronicled that its 'great cost and labour may be estimated from the timber work'[15]. Valmagne (1181) had freedom from toll on the Rhône for timber being used to build Sauveréal Abbey[16]. St Bernard-opt-Scheldt (1250, 1277) was allowed freedom from toll in Holland and Zeeland for 'all timber and stone' needed, implying the mix of building materials[17]. At Valle Crucis all the main construction timbers were of oak, and halved trunks were used in the refectory and kitchen as a strengthening raft[18]. Timber was essential for carving choir-stalls, as well as for scaffolding (many a ruined monastery still displays the necessary post-holes). Scaffolding timbers have been found in excavations at the sites of Bordesley and Fountains, and were possibly used in the fashioning of coffins[19].

Each community numbered in its ranks a 'master-carpenter'[20]. When Dondslébi Oh Inmainéin of Boyle died in 1230 he was described in its annals as 'chief master of the carpenters'[21], but this may not mean that he was a carpenter himself[22]. In some cases, lay craftsmen helped to fashion the early timber buildings before a community's arrival[23]. The chronicle of Meaux tells that before the monks came its founder, the count of Aumale, provided a great house of mud and wattle with an adjacent building – the upper floor of which served as the church, the lower storey as the dorter[24]. When Žďár (1233) was founded, Count John of Polna provided, to aid the construction, six carpenters as well as help from the local serfs[25]. The Øm chronicle, and the biographer of St Aelred (for Rievaulx), suggest a monastic involvement by an advance party in setting up their first buildings[26]. *Conversi* certainly helped to do so at Barnoldswick and at Louth Park[27].

Monasteries sited in woodlands (as Cîteaux itself)[28] had a ready supply of timber, but when Kirkstall was built, the long-ruling Abbot Alexander (1152–85), to conserve the monastery's own forests, brought wood from elsewhere[29]. Monasteries might, for better timber at least, seek out grants from benefactors, as Coupar (beams from Atholl forest)[30], and Roche (for its cloister)[31]. Some English monasteries benefited from the generosity of Henry III (and occasionally of King John). Stanley received by royal gift sixty-five oaks in one decade (1214–24), mostly from Chippenham Forest[32]. Beaulieu received timber from the New Forest and Savernake Forest[33]. Monasteries were often restricted to taking 'dead' trees, or those not 'bearing fruit or foliage'. Other grants allowed 'good' timber, as at Waverley (1234)[34]. Grants with other qualifications attached included that to Biddlesden (1232) – fifty oaks in Handley Forest, Towcester, but to be extracted widely in the forest, not all from one stand[35]. Grants might specify a particular purpose, as at Bindon (for the roof, thirty loads of lead and fifty oak logs, 1213)[36] and (for choir-stalls) to Cleeve (1230)[37], Biddlesden (1237)[38] and Stanley (1246)[39]. Stoneleigh (1241) received forty oaks from Kenilworth Wood for repairs after a severe fire[40], and Thame (1235) thirty oaks from Brill forest 'for making a framework to renew the collapsed chancel'[41].

As timber buildings came to be replaced, the building stone employed was mostly of local origin – bulk alone determined that. Many a monastery was therefore a reflection of its geological surroundings and blended well into the local physical environment; Tintern (with much Wentwood Old Red Sandstone), Bélapátfalva (of calareous rock hewn from Mount Bélko behind), and Léoncel (of local karst limestone), were fine examples of this[42]. Many monasteries employed a mix of stone, and some needed to import from a distance – if only to accomplish finer work[43]. There were those abbeys too which used a different stone in thirteenth century rebuilding from the more local stone employed in the first stone edifices of the twelfth century. The choice of stone in different building periods (as at Rievaulx) may have reflected (i) availability, (ii) the quality required, (iii) knowledge imparted by other monasteries, and (iv) the personal preference of master-masons[44].

Sandstone was dominant in seven Irish abbeys[45], as at Boyle (from a quarry only 130 metres [1/8 mile] north)[46]. It was also much used at Fountains (from nearby Upper Carboniferous strata)[47], Herrenalb (from the Schwarzwald)[48], and Maenan (red and white stone from nearby Creuddyn)[49]. Abbeys employing much limestone included Alvastra (from quarries ten miles [16 km] away)[50], Stanley (from its own Cotswolds quarry)[51], and La Ferté (from its quarry on nearby St Martin's Hill)[52]. Sixteen Irish houses employed limestone, like the local grey stone used at Corcomroe[53]. Roma was built entirely of limestone quarried on the island of Gotland, where it was situated[54]. Igneous rocks were to the fore at Newry (granite and basalt rubble)[55], Cabu Abbas (trachyte)[56], and Zinna (granite)[57]. Arabona owed its white complexion to travertine[58]. A mix of stone was mostly employed, as at Bordesley (sandstone as well as oolitic limestone)[59], Cymer (glacially derived rocks as well as local Cambrian strata)[60], and Sweetheart (red sandstone for the church, but granite for the claustral foundations)[61]. Early building at Mellifont employed much local slate, but Caen and Dundry stone later[62]. Bélapátfalva used volcanic rock for earlier Romanesque stages, but limestone in later gothic architecture[63]. Rievaulx at first made much use of oolitic limestone, later of crinoidal limestone[64]. The nature of the stone affected the finer detail: the coarse-grained, hard Bramley Fall stone used at Kirkstall accounts for the bluntness in the rendering of its capitals[65].

It is clear that most monasteries had their own quarries, but the available lifting gear and tackle limited the potential depth of stone extraction. Old quarries in close proximity to Irish monastic sites were seldom more than 30 feet (9 m) deep[66]. Meaux (c. 1185) was granted a quarry at Hessle, and bought another at Brantingham; its area was 1600 square feet[67]. For building its monastery, Ramón de Cevere gave Poblet (1166) leave 'to break up, extract, and carry away rocks and stones' from his honour of Espluga[68]. Henry III allowed Stanley (1222) to excavate for stone in Chippenham Forest[69], and Count Burchard of Lauterberg gave Walkenried (1256) a quarrying trench at Widagrode[70]. Stratford bought stone in London[71]. Stone was granted to Beaulieu (1243)[72], and bought by Quarr (1293)[73], from royal quarries in the Isle of Wight. For Beaulieu this involved transport by water across the Solent – probably in its own vessels.

Water transport frequently played a decisive rôle in the choice of building stone. Five abbeys in south-eastern Ireland, lying close to the sea coast or a river estuary, imported Dundry sandstone from quarries sited a few miles from the Bristol river Avon in England[74]. The access to building stone may have been a major factor in their choice of site[75]. Mellifont (three km upstream on the river Boyle) did the same, and is also credited with importing Caen stone from Normandy[76]. Stone for Medmenham in Buckinghamshire was carried from Windsor by boat on the river Thames[77]. At Kirkstall, sandstone was brought from quarries across the river, and landed at a wooden jetty[78]. Tradition has it that freestone for Strata Florida came from Somerset to the port of Bristol, and then by boat to the monks' own harbour at Llanddewi Aberarth[79]. Sawtry brought in building stone on 'the great channel which runs from Whittlesea Mere' (1192)[79a].When Meaux received its quarry at Brantingham, grant was given of way-leave to the river Humber[80]. The so-called 'canals' of Rievaulx probably did not transport stone, as once postulated[81].

Where building stone was scarce, recourse had to be made to brick. This was especially true of the north European Plain where deep fluvio-glacial deposits masked the bedrock, but provided plenty of sand and clay. A series of fine brick abbey churches (as at Aduard, Chorin, Kołbacz, and Sorø) punctuate the northern parts of Holland, Germany and Poland, as well as appearing in Denmark and southern Sweden[82]. The raw material for brick-making was also to be found in the flood-plain alluvium of parts of Lombardy. In northern Italy, therefore, brick predominated at several monasteries including Casanova, Chiaravalle and Morimondo Milano, and Valserena. Other largely brick edifices included Gimont in France[83], and the Dunes – set by the coastal sands of Flanders[84]. At some monasteries the claustral buildings were in brick, though the church (being given priority) was built in stone – as at Alvastra (limestone)[85] and Zinna (granite)[86]. A late medieval chronicler, Długosz, noted of Wąchock that it was built 'partly of stone, partly of baked brick'[87]. A brick church might be quicker to build: the construction of that at Himmelpfort (1300–07) lasted less than eight years[88]. Most monasteries fired their bricks on, or near site, as certainly did Camp[89], Dargun[90], Eldena[91] and Ourscamp[92], and perhaps others – like Chorin and Zinna[93]. Chiaravalle Milano had a brick and tile works close to its *Creta*rolo Grange (so called from the clayey nature of the soil)[94]. Craftsmen from northern France or the Low Countries may have produced (from about 1150 to 1225) a range of brick and other building materials for Coggeshall[95]. A brick and tile works (at *Til*key) remained there until 1845[96].

The Builders

There is plenty of evidence that monks and *conversi* played a substantial rôle in the construction of Cistercian monasteries. The Benedictine historian, Ordéric Vitalis (c. 1135) said of them:'They have built monasteries with their own hands', whilst William of Saint-Thierry (*c.* 1147), reported of the monks of Clairvaux that 'some felled trees, others cut the stones, others built the walls'[97]. Amongst the first community at Viktring (1147) were five *conversi* of Clairvaux, who had just worked at Villers and who were 'experts in several skills'[98]. The chronicle of Meaux recorded that Abbot Adam (*c.* 1155) and his monks 'built that great house', and said of the abbot that he was 'a man of the greatest knowledge'[99]. When monks left Ford (1201) to build Dunkeswell, it was with the workman, Gregory, at their head[100]. Abbot Henry III of Walkenried (1223–31) employed twenty-one *conversi* as 'stone-cutters, masons, architects, and iron smiths' in raising its abbey church[101]. It was said of St Louis that as Royaumont church was being built (1223–35) he liked to help the monks carry the stones 'in great silence'[102]. A monk of the Dunes (1310), James of Biervliet, made the bricks for its cloister's wash-house[103].

The monastic clerk-of-works, the *custos operis* (Furness, 1231)[104], or *magister operis* (Salem, 1264)[105], or simply the *operarius [ecclesie]* (Rueda, 1309)[106], was generally a religious. The chronicle of Maulbronn tells of the *conversi* who succeeded each other as 'masters of the work' during the whole time of the construction of its church[107]. At San Galgano from 1218 to 1276 the 'masters of the work' were mostly, if not always, monks[108]. A statute of the General Chapter (1159) presupposed that the 'master of the mortarers' would be a religious[109]. One *conversus* at Moreruela (1215–1238) was 'master of the work' there for at least twenty-three years[110]. At Rueda (1266) the designation of a monk, Giles, as *operarius maior* supposes he had a deputy[111]. In Wales, as late as 1307 there was 'a master of the works at the New Church' of Margam, and in 1340 there was still a 'keeper of the work of the church of Tintern'[112]. Ebrach (1340) had its 'master of the fabric', whose dues included money, wine and pasture[113]. By 1270, the works department at Beaulieu was mostly concerned with maintenance such as the repair of the church tower and the *conversi* cloister; it also afforded training to an apprentice carpenter and an apprentice plumber, both stipendiary[114]. Occasionally, secular masters of work are on record[115], most notably in the early-fourteenth century building of Vale Royal[116].

Whilst an early statute (1157–75) forbade Cistercians from working on projects for lay-folk, their acquired experience meant that they were much sought after[117]. Henry III had a *conversus* of Combermere as a 'keeper of the works' at Westminster from 1266 to 1271[118], and a monk of that house, suitably named Thomas *le Plumer*, was engaged in plumbing work at Chester and other royal castles from about 1299 to 1304[119]. Emperor Frederick II (1221) sought Cistercian building experts for the construction of his palace[120]. From 1257 to 1295 the 'masters of the work' in the construction of Siena Cathedral were almost entirely monks of San Galgano, and *conversi* helped in its building[121]. Conversely, given the numbers of *conversi* employed on the granges, most Cistercian monasteries needed to employ from the outset a number of secular masons. There is early note of this at Fountains (1134) and Clairvaux (1135)[122]. Secular masons are also known from witness names to deeds[123], statutes of the General Chapter[124] and the accounts of Beaulieu[125]. A noble lady loaned La Real (1272) a young white Saracen to help in the building of the monastery and to be taught 'the art of stone-cutting'[125a].

Evidence for 'imported' masons comes at Quarr (from Holland)[126], Stična (from France)[127], Loc-Dieu (from Pontigny)[128], Clairmarais (from other Cistercian houses)[129], and Maulbronn (from Alsace)[130]. An indication of secular masons comes in the incision of masons' marks: unmarked stones were probably the work of monastic personnel or resident labourers[131]. No less than 3,000 signs have been identified at Rueda, the marks of 373 different masons[132]. Some 680 marks have been found at Noirlac, the signs of 35 different masons: one of the marks occurs 169 times[133]. The similarity of some masons' marks at the abbeys of Strata Florida (*c.* 1160–1200) and Strata Marcella (*c.* 1174–1200) suggests that some masons were employed at both houses[134]. The same is true of four signs found both at Fontmorigny and Noirlac[135].

In a semi-fictitious account of the building of Le Thoronet (fd 1136) the architect is pictured as saying:'All my life I was more mason than monk, more architect than Christian'[136]. This was certainly not true of the trio of monks sent out by St Bernard from Clairvaux to counsel on the foundation of other abbeys. Their duties usually included not only planning advice, but instruction on perhaps all aspects of Cistercian custom and liturgy[137]. Achard, a monk of Clairvaux from 1124 and its novice-master, is credited with the initiation of several monasteries – including Himmerod (1134)[138]; Geoffrey d'Ainai was sent in 1135 to lead constructional work at Fountains, but he also helped at other monasteries in France and Flanders[139]; and Robert was sent in 1142 to Mellifont, specifically to give architectural advice[140]. Achard and Geoffrey had been leading figures in the construction of Clairvaux's first stone church[141]. Three monks who had all been in the community of Fountains when Geoffrey visited it, themselves became notable abbot-builders: Adam at Meaux, Alexander at Kirkstall, and St Robert at Newminster[142].

Much has been made of a Cistercian rôle for the French architect, Villard de Honnecourt (fl. 1225–50), who perhaps gained early experience working as a boy at the site of Vaucelles[143], and patterns from his album may well have been copied in Cistercian architecture in Greece[144] and Hungary[145]. Recent scholarship suggests, however, that he was neither a member of, nor an architect especially concerned with, the Order[146]. An architect who was a monk and whose influence linked both Italy and Poland was one Simon, active in Little Poland from about 1217, and by 1239 third master of the works at San Galgano. His name is inscribed on the fabric of both Koprzywnica and Wąchock, and similarities of style from that period are alleged as between Koprzywnica and San Galgano. The fifteenth century chronicler, Długosz, noted Italian influence in the building of the abbeys of Little Poland[147]. The architect for Lucelle's new church (1340–46) was a *conversus*, Bubuc, whose effigy was engraved on an interior wall[148].

Little is known of the actual planning of a Cistercian house. At Corcomroe, preparatory architectural drawings occur incised on plaster surfaces on two walls within the church; a similar drawing occurs on the west end of Byland[149]. At Newminster (1136) and Woburn (1145)[150] the monastery was laid out 'after our manner'. When work commenced at Walkenried (1207) two monks, Berthold and Jordan, 'laid out the plan and supervised the work'[151]. The use of pattern-books (as that of Villard) perhaps suggests why 'the intricate never-ending interlaces, the solomon knots, the vigorous vegetal growth recur with such consistency ... in a Spanish fountain-house, on a Polish vault, a Danish keystone, a Yorkshire floor'[152].

The overall planning by early monk-architects, the use of a common supply of masons, and the knowledge of the lay-out of houses already built, taken together with the Cistercian spirit of restraint and simplicity, account for the many likenesses that are to be found between abbeys of the Order, especially where their churches are concerned. Indeed, the chronicle of Kinloss suggests that its infirmary, kitchen, fish-house, and other working offices, were constructed on models taken from English houses[153]. Cistercian architecture has been frequently seen as in its turn influencing the building styles of other ecclesiastical edifices, but it must be a moot point as to whether the effect was not sometimes in the reverse direction[154]. Longpont, for example, has been said to be 'a monastic spin-off of Soissons Cathedral', and Saint-Denis a model for Altenberg[155], but the Cistercians have been praised for introducing gothic architecture into countries such as Greece, Poland and Hungary[156]. Fossanova (and perhaps Casamari) influenced the architecture of, amongst others, the cathedrals of Piperno and Sezze[157].

Despite the notion of simplicity and restraint in building, of which the General Chapter reminded the Order[158], the abbeys raised by the Cistercians were to become notable architectural achievements, and brought comment in their day. Unaccustomed to such large buildings in stone, the native Irish called Mellifont *An Mhainistir Mhór*, 'the Great Monastery'[159]. Hélinand (*c.* 1230), himself to become a monk of Froidmont, criticised the white monks for constructing superfluous buildings when they ought to be giving to the poor[160]. Eye-witnesses commented upon the 'splendid workmanship' at Strata Florida[161], and 'the magnificent stonework' at Roche[162]. All this cost money. Luckiest were abbeys with royal founders[163], but donations from other benefactors[164] and offerings from pilgrims all helped. Abbot Frederick of Walkenried (1216–23) sent out two monks to other monasteries of the Order, and to the 'maritime cities', to collect successfully a large sum for its new cloister[165].

The construction of a monastery was a long-drawn-out affair, with most white monks living for generations cheek-by-jowl with a building site – a place of noise and dust. The chronicle of Meaux relates its building history[166]. Dating successive stages by the reigns of its abbots, it records (1182–97) the construction (in stone) of the refectory, kitchen, and calefactory, and the church started but begun anew by the next abbot; (about 1195) the refectory and dorter of the *conversi* commenced; (1197–1210) work on the monastic cloister and a new reredorter; on Palm Sunday, 1207, the foundation stone of the new church laid; (1210–20) the cloister of monks and dorter of the *conversi* finished; (1220–35) the monks' infirmary commenced; (1235–49) the church completed and covered with lead; (1249–69) the bell-tower completed; and (1285–1310) the abbot's chamber built. Later, the monks' dorter was covered in lead. A less detailed account is known for Croxden[167]. Changes of architectural style also reflect a building programme: at Valcroissant, a Romanesque church but a Gothic refectory[168]; at Dore, a Romanesque nave but Gothic presbytery[169]. Only a few abbeys (as Cymer) were swiftly completed and of one style[170].

Precinct Walls

The first view of an abbey a traveller gained would often be obstructed by a high wall surrounding the abbey 'court' or 'close'. Within the precinct so formed lay not only the monastery but also a variety of ancillary buildings – such as the bake-house, brewery and guest-house – well exemplified on a sixteenth-century drawing of the Dunes[171]. The enclosure could therefore be of some size, and precincts ranged in area from nearly 30 ha (75 acres) at Clairvaux[172] down to but a modest 3.85 ha (9.6 acres) at Pilis[173]. Other large precincts included, in England, Fountains[174], Furness[175], and Garendon[176] – all in the region of 24 ha/60 acres. In time, it might be necessary to increase the size of a precinct, as (in 1299) did Rewley (by 6.4 ha/16 acres)[177], and Vaudey (by no less than 12 ha/30 acres)[178]. Buckfast enlarged its enclosure by demolishing part of the precinct wall and delimiting its new extension by a large ditch[179].

Precinct walls were not solely a monastic phenomenon: many great abbey walls come from a time when many towns were so surrounding themselves[180]. The precinct wall kept at bay unwanted strangers and wild animals, but, more importantly, it reminded the monks of their vow of stability and enhanced their sense of vocation. Greater or lesser remnants of precinct walls are still to be seen, though some walls known from documentary evidence have vanished. At Sweetheart are stretches of a wall composed of large unhewn granite boulders[181]. Remnants of a massive stone wall at Newbattle are rightly or wrongly ascribed to the time and provision of William the Lion (1165–1214)[182]. There are fine remains also at Beaulieu[183], Fountains[184], Vauclair[185], and Esrum – the latter of red brick[186]. A description of 1537 tells of the precinct at Furness being 'enclosed with a great stone wall in circuit by estimation near about a mile'[187]; of great length, too, were those at Eberbach (1100 m)[188], and Poblet (1500 m)[189].

It is possible to trace the building periods of some walls. Visiting Furness in 1231, abbot Stephen Lexington ordered its wall to be completed by Holy Cross Day (14 September) that year[190]. The chronicle of Croxden tells that abbot Walter (1242–68) began the building of its wall 'in his latter days', and that it was completed by abbot Henry (1274–84)[191]. It was obviously some time a-building. At Hauterive, abbot Guy (1268–94) 'encircled the monastery with a wall'[192]. The wall of Mortemer (still trace-able) was early raised between 1164 and 1174[193]; that of Koprzywnica was being built in 1346[194]. Stanley was allowed stone from the forest of Pewsham for building its wall in 1292 to 1297[195]. Some walls were seemingly insubstantial, as those at Pipewell (1275) – thrown down by disaffected persons[196], and Kołbacz (1349) – damaged by tempest and flood[197]. Some walls were moated, and so the gate-house had to be approached by a causeway – as at Kirkstead[198] and Louth Park[199]. Water-filled ditches also helped to delineate the precincts at Bordesley[200], Stratford[201], Maulbronn[202] and Sorø[203].

Gate-houses

Lawful entrance to a monastic precinct was by means of a gateway penetrating the precinct wall. Edward I commanded that no one was to enter the abbey of Vale Royal but by its gates[204]. The *Rule of St Benedict* and the Cistercian *Charter of Charity* envisaged a gate-house structure from the outset of a community's existence. Little is known of early gateways, but one was constructed at Mortemer about 1160[205], that of Bellevaux finds mention around 1158[206], whilst vestiges of a twelfth-century gate are to be seen at Gimont[207]. As substantial precinct walls came to be built, so too did an often massive gate-house, 'the great gate', protecting the outer court and monastery, and often sited west or north-west of the abbey church[208]. In England, from the mid-thirteenth century on, several early gate-houses were modified, enlarged, or replaced. By 1246 an extra chamber for the porter had been added to the gate-house at Louth Park[209]. Croxden had its lasting gate-house erected by abbot Walter in about 1260[210]. The gate-house of Beaulieu was rib-vaulted about 1300[211]. The substantial gate-house at Stoneleigh was finished in 1346[212]. The same pattern was perhaps true on the Continent. Hauterive had an 'old gate' with stables adjacent about 1270, and a 'new gate' with chapel adjoining about 1290[213]. The Great Gate at Croxden lent its name to the village of Greatgate to the north-west of that abbey[214], whilst lands adjacent to the gate of Newenham are still called 'the Yeatlands'[215].

Great gates had two entrances: a large opening intended for horse-drawn vehicles, and to the side a smaller access for pedestrians, as is to be seen at Whalley and Roche. The *Chronicle of Melrose* refers to the 'larger gate' and the 'postern gate' there in 1262[216]. Most gate-houses had a chamber over the entry arches. At Mellifont there were three storeys reached by means of a spiral staircase[217]. At Roche there survives an alcove at the foot of the stairs intended for a lamp to burn at night. The gate-house of Fontenay has a guard-dog cubicle. Great gates were usually double-gated, with exterior and interior openings. The space between at Roche is finely vaulted, its floor cobbled[218]. At Casamari (as at Byland) a chamber served as the almonry. At Beaulieu the accounts for 1270 imply the existence of several chambers in the gate-house complex – one for storage, one for cooking, and one for eating[219]. At Maulbronn a 'chimney-house' built about 1220 provided warmth for the gate-house[220]. An abbey's secular prison was often incorporated into the gate-house, and near it stood lay-infir-mary and guest-house.

The size of a gate-house obviously varied: the main structure at Zaraka measured 7.4 x 7.8 m[221], but at Whalley 22.9 x 11.3 m[222]. The external walls at Vauclair were 1.75 m thick, making its gate-house 'a veritable defensive facade'[223]. The substantial nature

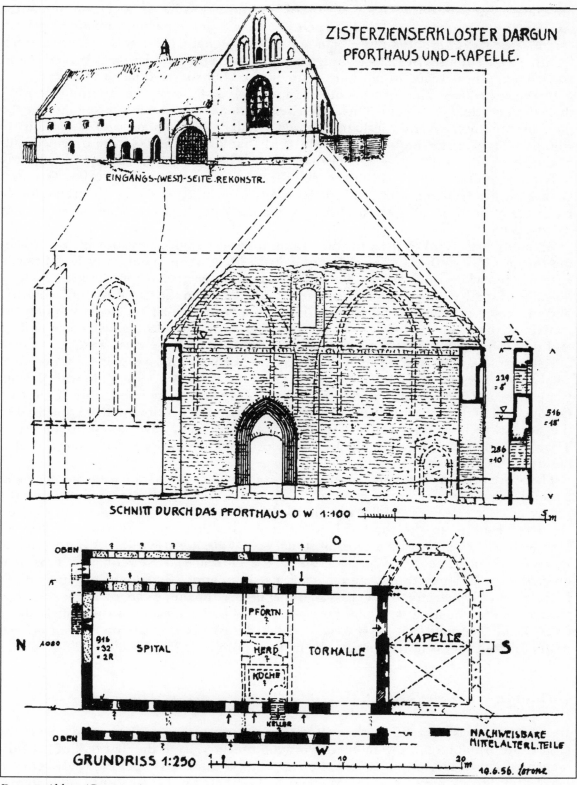

Dargun Abbey (Germany):
Plan and Elevation of the Gate-House:
(Reproduced by kind permission of Dr Gerhard Schlegel, from his book:
Das Zisterzienserkloster Dargun, 1172–1552 [St Benno-Verlag GmbH, Leipzig, 1980.]

means that at monasteries like Kingswood[224] and Zaraka the gate-house is practically all that is left of the abbey. Conversely, the site of the gate-house is sometimes revealed only by excavations – as recently at Coyroux[225] and Silvacane[226]. At certain monasteries – as Strata Marcella and Valle Crucis in Wales – there are no remains or certain evidence or lasting tradition of a gate-house. Occasionally there was a moat or ditch fronting a gate-house. In 1223 a young boy fell outside the gate-house at Waverley and was carried downstream 'under four stone bridges' but survived his ordeal[227].

By the late thirteenth century some precinct walls had means of entry and exit other than the guarded great gate. This gave rise potentially to breaches of stability on the part of the monks, and perhaps allowed unqualified persons into the claustral complex. Stephen Lexington ordered in 1231 that all such exits in the precinct walls of the abbeys of Champagne and Furness were to be quickly blocked up[228]. An affray took place at Ourscamp in 1309 between 'the great gate and the gate called Gambart Gate'[229], whilst troubles occurred in 1350 at Aduard's 'northern gate'[230]. Strata Florida had its 'southern gate'[231], Heisterbach its 'middle gate'[232], whilst Clairmarais had its 'Forest Gate'[233].

Greater privacy and security for the community were sometimes afforded by providing the entrance to the cloister or 'inner court' with an inner gatehouse, as at Chorin, Cleeve, Henryków, and Poblet. Beaulieu had an outer gate before its great gate, a distance of some 60 m separating the two[234]. Tintern, from the late-thirteenth century, had an inner gate whose porch was lined by a stone bench on the south side. It contained the outer parlour, a vaulted chamber where monks could receive visitors and do business[235]. Where a monastery was adjacent to a large river and had its own boats for trade, then another major entry to the precinct was essential: the water-gate. That still to be seen at Tintern[236] gave access to the river Wye (for trade with Bristol, Chepstow, and Monmouth), and to its ferry leading across the river to its Modesgate Grange and Manor of Woolaston. A gateway in the north precinct wall at Quarr led to the Solent[237]. The water-gate of Rewley, noted in 1300, gave access to the river Thames[238]. The water-gate at St Bernard-opt-Scheldt had, in 1330, a large chapel beside it[239]. Clairmarais, too, had its water-gate[239a].

There are occasional references to crosses erected outside the monastic precinct, and generally in proximity to the great gate. There was, early, 'a stony crosse beside the Abbey of Door' (*Dore*)[240], whilst at Tintern the 'Abbey Cross' stood as late as 1651 on the road leading to the local village[241]. Amongst other 'good works' an abbot of Hauterive (1268–96) set up a cross of stone[242]. At Vale Royal, Edward I put a cross to mark the limit of the early precinct[243]. At the entrance to Newenham a cross was erected in 1347, exactly a century after its foundation, in commemoration of its founders and benefactors[244]. A cross standing before the outer gate of Stanley marked the boundary adjoining Pewsham Forest[245]. A field by Dunkeswell is still called 'Abbey Cross Field'[246]. About 1350, a *conversus* of Aduard was affixed to a temporary or permanent cross outside its northern gate, by men of Groningen[247].

Gate-house Chapels

It is not surprising that as the gate-house was a meeting place, and given the Cistercian prohibition on women entering the precinct, from the first half of the thirteenth century onwards many gate-houses came to have a chapel built adjacent. As early as 1196 a church was dedicated to St Matthew by the enclosure of Fiume[248]. There was initial disapproval. In 1225 the General Chapter heard a complaint against the abbot of Neubourg, that 'he had permitted Mass to be celebrated in the gate by a monk'[249]. Three years later (1228) Stephen Lexington halted building work on a gate-house chapel at Jerpoint[250]. It may be partly a result of his visitation of the Irish houses that no gate-house chapels are to be seen in that country[251]. Architectural evidence, however, suggests that the *capella extra portas* at Coggeshall was built about 1220[252], and there was such a chapel at Sibton by about 1235[253]. The chapel at Louth Park was built in abbot Richard's time (1227–46)[254], and that at Croxden probably by abbot London (1242–68)[255]. The chapel at Waldsassen was dedicated in 1259[256], and that of Beaubec in 1266[257]. John of Antwerp paid in 1264 for the building of a gate-house chapel at St Bernard-opt-Scheldt, with the intention of Mass being said there daily[258].

Some gate-house chapels not constructed until the fourteenth century may have been more grandiose replacements of earlier edifices. The chapel of Aduard dates from the time of abbot Frederick (1329–50)[259]. In addition to the normal chapel, Meaux had another built over its Great Gate. The work was started by abbot Adam (1310–39) but demolished by his successor in about 1340[260]. Other upper chapels included those at Kirkstall[261] and at Whalley[262]. Beaulieu had two parallel chapels above its Great Gate[263]. Tilty's chapel, built in about 1220, was extended a century later by the addition of a chancel[264]. Known gate-house chapel dedications include ascriptions to Our Lady (as Kingswood[265], Merevale[266], and Robertsbridge[267]), to St Nicholas (Coggeshall[268] and Louth Park[269]), and to St Ursula (Beaubec[270] and Morimond[271]); other dedications included those to St Anne (Tintern)[272] and St George (Loccum)[273].

The chapels were occasionally sited away from the great gate: that at Clairvaux was at the inner gate – perhaps because the outer gate was so far from the abbey. On the other hand, the north wall of the chapel at Furness formed part of the precinct wall[274]. Nydala had its 'chapel without the walls', implying it lay technically without the enclosure[275]. At both La Boissière[276] and Loccum[277] a small doorway allowed a priest to enter directly from the abbey precincts. In the chapel at Coggeshall are to be seen a brick-lined sedilia, a double piscina, and a mural consecration cross[278]. Similar features exist in the chancel extension of the chapel at Tilty, its slightly stepped sedilia bearing carvings in stone of the heads of a Cistercian monk and of a layman[279]. Coloured decoration of gate-house chapels is evidenced by remnants of red masonry patterns at Coggeshall and of grey at Kirkstead[280]. The gate-house chapel at Hailes has been described as having 'the finest display of decorative painting in an English Cistercian context'. Upon its walls are remains of paintings attributed to the reign of Edward I, who attended the funeral of his cousin Edmund, earl of Cornwall, at Hailes in 1301. They include, *inter alia*, the arms of Castile (the monarch having married Eleanor of Castile) and the German-Roman Eagle (the founder of the abbey, Earl Richard of Cornwall, having been crowned King of the Romans)[281]. The early fourteenth century extension at Tilty boasts a fine rose east window[282]. At Merevale the east window contains part of a fine Tree of Jesse, dated to about 1335[283]. A grant was made to Sibton (*c.* 1235) to maintain 'the lamp of the chapel at the gate'[284].

The primary function of gate-house chapels was undoubtedly to serve those who could not enter the precincts, as well as passing travellers and poor guests. It was noted at Fontmorigny (in 1281) that women could go to such a chapel[285]; at Aduard the chapel was built by abbot Frederick (1329–50) 'on account of women and the poor'[286]. Daily Mass was celebrated in the gate-house chapel at the Dunes by 1240, and a silver-gilt chalice was given for this purpose[287]. The rector of Leeds alleged (in 1314) that Kirkstall admitted some of his parishioners to the Sacraments in the chapel above its gate-house[288]. In the fourteenth century at least two gate-house chapels became places of pilgrimage to miraculous images of Our Lady – at Écharlis[289] and at Merevale[290]. Kingswood's gate-house chapel also became noted for miracles[291]. Haila of Rutelingen was interred in the gate-house chapel at Bebenhausen, she having had it built for the monks[292]. Grave-yards adjoined the gate-houses at Dunbrody and Inch[293]. Divine worship is still held in former monastic 'chapels-without-the-gates' at: Coggeshall, Hailes, Kirkstead, Merevale, and Tilty, in England; at Riddagshausen and Schöntal in Germany, and Velehrad in Moravia. The chapel at Tintern in Wales is a private residence. The chapels existing at Bordesley until 1805 and at Croxden until 1886 have long been demolished.

The Outer Court

Within the precincts of a monastery, outside of the claustral complex, and between the outer and inner gate-house, lay an often large area loosely known as 'the outer court'. It was here that the bustle of normal life was to be found – though much of the work was done in silence. It was here that the guest-house and secular infirmary stood, as well as a wide range of ancillary buildings providing for the everyday needs of the abbey. It had been the ideal of the *Rule of St Benedict* that 'the monastery should be so arranged that all necessary things, such as water, mill, garden, and various crafts may be within the enclosure, so that the monks may not be compelled to wander outside it, for that is not expedient for their souls'[294]. The *Institutes* of the Cistercians re-iterated this need for seclusion[295]. Stephen Lexington on visitation in Ireland (1228) went a step further, and ordained that no buildings should be erected in the centre of the precincts but 'along the sides in a circle, on account of thieves and other dangers that might arise'[296]. This was an exceptional provision. The visitor to a ruined abbey today witnesses usually only the church and cloister, and goes away unaware of the numerous other workshops and offices that were formerly to be seen in the west range and the outer court.

Contemporaneous records tell of the variety of these ancillary buildings. At Sorø (1247) were 'the greater and lesser guest-houses, bakehouse, brewhouse, tailor's house, subcellarer's house, cellarer's chamber, stores for building and gardening tools, the weaver's house, stabling for horses, the gatehouse, a barn and the mills'[297]. Within the precincts of Morimondo Milano (1237) stood 'the store for the bakery holding at least 100 wagon-loads of firewood, the store of the farrier where the animals were shod (containing about 40 wagon-loads of hay), and the stable'[298]. The accounts of Beaulieu (1270) list no less than thirty-one monastic departments[299]. Documents of the sixteenth century refer at Rievaulx to a double water-mill, the barkhouse or tannery, the tailory, the slaughter-house, the cart sheds and the waggon houses[300]. Aerial photography at Kirkstead, Sawtry[301], and Tintern[302], bears witness to the considerable acreage of a monastic precinct taken up by economic activity. The best preserved Cistercian precinct dating from the Middle Ages is that of Maulbronn – with stables, cooperage, storehouse, wheelwrights, forge, mill, bakehouse, dairy shed, and fountain[303]. Many of the departments of the outer court (the guest-house, the lay infirmary, the granary, the mills and the forges) find detailed report in previous or succeeding chapters; here we review the remainder.

The monastic *bakehouse* produced the considerable amounts of bread required for the monks, *conversi*, servants, guests, the sick, and the poor at the gate. At Clairmont (1231) repairs were ordered to the chimney of the bakehouse, seemingly in imminent danger of collapse[304]. About 1260, a new bakehouse was made at Meaux, and roofed with lead[305]. Former bakehouses are still to be seen at Fontenay[306] and Inch[307]. At Savigny (1230), in addition to the 'keeper of the bakehouse', there was at least one *conversus* who acted as delivery boy. Its bakehouse received, in addition to poorer grains, an allocation of 25 qts (317 kg) of wheat each week from mid-September to Easter, but 30 qts (381 kg) in the summer[308]. The granger of Beaulieu's (1270) home grange supplied its bake-house with four grades of flour, of which the *familia* flour was

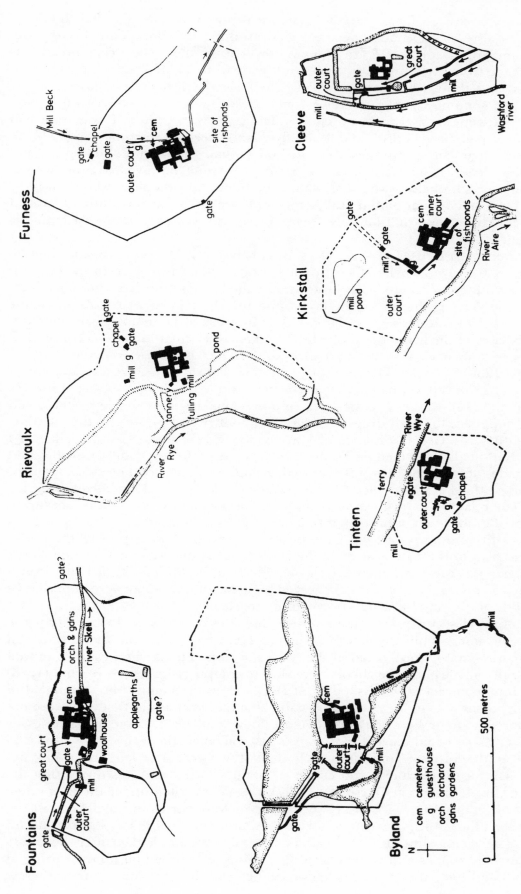

Plans of precincts of Cistercian abbeys: Fountains; Rievaulx; Furness; Byland; Tintern; Kirkstall; Cleeve. (Reproduced by kind permission of Batsford Books and Prof. M. Aston from his *Monasteries* [1993]).

made from a mixture of rye, barley, beans, peas and vetches[309].The bakehouse of Pipewell, as also its brewhouse, received daily supplies of thorns and briars from Rockingham Forest for fuel[310]. In the twelfth century most Cistercian bread was perhaps made from rye flour, with wheat producing white bread reserved for the sick, the guests, and those who had been bled. In the early thirteenth century matters changed: the community might receive white bread by way of pittance and it soon became more general as 'convent bread'[311]. The coarsest bread of all was served to *conversi* doing penance (1220)[312] and to fugitive monks seeking re-admission (1272)[313]. By 1270 Beaulieu had four grades of bread: conventual, guest-house, 'clermatin', and familiar. Two loaves of 'convent' bread were worth 1 penny, but five loaves of 'hospice bread' could be supplied for the same sum. The bran and sweepings were sent to its piggery[314]. A corrodian at Sibton (1323) received weekly 'seven conventual loaves of the best dough and weight', and also seven loaves called *Prikkedeloves* – a monastic brand-name![315].

A well-known *brewhouse* is that of Villers. Built between 1270 and 1276, and sited on the banks of the river Thyle which provided water, it measures 42 m by 12 m, is divided by a range of round pillars into two vaulted aisles, and has a granary floor above. At the entry is the site of the boiler and the chimney arcade[316]. Another fine brewery (in brick) is to be seen at Chorin. The brewery of Fountains has been excavated, the bases of the copper and of a brick-cemented circular tank demonstrated[317]. The brewery at Meaux was served by a 'malt-kiln in which our barley is made ready'[318]. At Savigny (1230) 24 qts (305 kg) per fortnight of barley and oats were allocated for its brewhouse. Its sub-cellarer had charge of the beer and had to liaise with the brewer[319]. At Beaulieu (1270), where a cooper was employed making barrels, clean wheat and oats were supplied, the malt dregs going to feed poultry and pigs[320]. By the late thirteenth century the German houses of Marienfeld, Riddagshausen, and Walkenried had their hop-fields[321]. In medieval times beer was one of the few drinks available, and several grades of monastic beer were brewed; Beaulieu had its good beer, second beer or 'lag', and a third grade – called 'Wilkin le Naket'. There was also a 'mixed beer' for the sick. The quantity to be given to every grade of recipient was carefully laid down, but the third grade was not measured because of its 'weakness and uselessness'. It was useful notwithstanding, since 400 gallons (1800 litres) of it were sent to the guest-house, and also to the gate-house for the poor[322]. (It is uncertain as to whether the medieval *galo* was the same as to-day's gallon[323].) In 1306 the monks of Hude grumbled about the poor quality of the beer served to them, and the abbot agreed to change the methods of brewing by using more oats and barley[324].

For reasons of security and monastic stability, the *stables* were to be within the precincts and not without the gates[325]. The General Chapter, noting that disgraceful behaviour was taking place, ordered the stables of some English houses to be moved within the precincts, but some abbots were slow to comply (1222)[326]. In Ireland (1228) a similar injunction had to be issued[327]. At Dore (1318) the monks were reminded to keep their horses only in the communal stable: the implication was that they were not to have horses of their own, enabling them to ride out at will[328]. Large monasteries, as Beaulieu (1270), would have three stables: the abbot's, the conventual, and the guests'[329]. At Maulbronn[330] and Rievaulx[331], the last two were sited fairly near the gate-house, which meant less noise and clatter near the cloister, and less dirt within the outer court itself, though at Ourscamp (1277) a stable was sited under the west range dorter[332]. At Stams (1333–45), there were three or four horses in the abbot's stable, some ten for other officials, a couple for general use, and (in 1333) a stallion and (in 1345) four steeds for hunting[333]. At Beaulieu the stable grooms looked after the horses of travellers and monks and carters, as well as being responsible for all the carting of grain, wool and fuel, and the repairing of saddles and the greasing of the leather[334].

The Order permitted the *conversus* in charge of stables to talk as necessary[335]. At Savigny (1230) the grooms or 'boys' ate in the guest-house[336], at Beaulieu (1270) in the stables, save on feast days (when at the guest-house). There were a dozen or so of these young men employed at Beaulieu; they may have been somewhat difficult to handle, as they were not allowed into the kitchen unaccompanied. They received each year two or three pairs of shoes from the abbey, and their other duties included accompanying members of the community on journeys[337].

Within the outer court or in the western range were the workshops of the *skinner*, the *tanner*, and the *shoemaker*. At Beaulieu[338] and Henryków[339], if not in most houses, the last two offices were combined. It was the skinner's job to dehair the raw hides and skins received from the granges and cure them ready for distribution as leather for belts, sheep-skin blankets, and lamb-skin hoods. Hides were also used for making parchment – vellum from the skins of sheep and calves[340], and perhaps for the burial of the dead (as a lay-person at Tintern)[339]. An early Chapter statute appears (1157+) to inhibit the sale of hides, but it could be taken as forbidding only the re-sale of hides bought for profit[342], which was soon to be the case (1202)[343]. Hides were later widely sold, but also bought if necessary. A worldly-wise *conversus* of Neath (1205) had cancelled a sale of hides promised to Quincy Abbey in favour of a better price from another quarter[344]. At Kingswood, 'white skins' were bought in 1241, but in 1288 the monastery sold horseskins, calfskins, cowskins, oxskins, and mare skins[345]. Quite a variety – but Cistercians were forbidden by Chapter statute from working on the skins of wild beasts, wild cats, rabbits, squirrels, and miniver – a note of conservation and animal welfare?[346].

Clairvaux had a *tanning-mill* by 1136[347], and Candeil in 1192[348], but for many abbeys there is no record of them before the thirteenth century[349]. Tanning pits are to be seen within the precincts at both Rievaulx (close to the monastic reredorter and the Milne Beck)[350], and at Melrose (three brick-lined pits in the vaulted undercroft of the *conversi* reredorter)[351]. In both cases there was proximity to water. Beaulieu[352], Holm Cultram[353], and Tintern[354] had local supplies of bark in their own or other woodlands. Kirkstall its 'bark mill' in 1288[354a]. Henryków (*c.* 1260) bought extra lands to give income for its tannery[355]. A count of Toul gave Cherlieu (1209) an experienced 'skinner-tanner'[356]. An adolescent, seemingly skilled in the craft, aided the shoe-maker of Waverley (1239)[357]. Conversely, Salem (1272), which had a *conversus* skilled as skinner and tanner, offered a burgess of Freiburg practical experience and instruction as a cordwainer or furrier[358].

The 'master of the *shoemakers*' at Arnsburg (1247) was one Wigand, a *conversus*[359]; John, the *conversus* shoe-maker at Krzeszów, died in 1302[360]. A shoe-maker's tombstone is to be seen in the cloister at Hautecombe. The shoe-making workshop at Morimondo Milano (1237) contained shoes, unworked leather, lasts and knives, 'which the cobblers use in their work'[361]. Beaulieu (1270) produced yearly around 500 pairs of shoes. Each monk and *conversus* received a pair for summer and a pair for winter, whilst the abbot gave away 120 pairs as presents. Leather of lesser quality was used for the shoes of the servants. All the old shoes were sent to the gate-house for distribution to the poor, plus 30 new pairs[362]. In the twelfth century the monks of La Ferté paid for some of their purchases with home-made shoes: early-medieval barter[363]. The Order regulated the types of shoes its monks wore: day-shoes were to be made from cow-hide, not from goatskins or cordwain (1237). Later (1257) the quite early insistence on cow-hide was dropped: day shoes were simply to be not 'out of the ordinary'[364]. Stephen Lexington (1228) insisted that a monk be attached to the workshop 'who is informed of all the things the cobbler does in selling, buying, giving and lending. He will put these down in writing'[365] – a *conversus*, skilled in manual work, might be unable to keep the books! At Beaulieu the cobbler was not only using leather, he was also the tanner, preparing leather for his workshop. Since he himself needed tallow and grease in quantity, his department supplied the tallow for the candles in the dorters and the grease for softening the leather boots in the calefactory. Herring dripping was supplied to him as well as lard, reflecting Beaulieu's maritime interests[366]. At Morimond Milano (1237) too, animal fat was used in treating leather[367].

In the *weaver*'s shop, wool was combed, spun and woven on a loom before it passed to the fuller[368]. At Fountains, the 'wool-house' stood in a range which included the malt-house and the brew-house, with (by the end of the thirteenth century) a fulling-mill in its western aisle. In the fourteenth century dye-vats were added with provision for a hot water supply. It was now a multi-purpose structure for the finishing of cloth[369]. At the Dunes (*c.* 1255)[370] and Staffarda (1349)[371] the weaver's shop was in the west range. Abbot Idesbald of the Dunes (1155–67) sent boats to England for wool[371a]. Meaux's lanary was sited on its Wawne Grange[372]. Alcobaça had its aptly-named 'Vestiaria Grange[372a]. A weaving-house was meant to provide the clothing the community required. Some abbeys had a surplus for sale; others might need to buy in cloth for special purposes – as Kingswood (1240–62) for sacks and harnesses[373]. A grant of tithes to Scharnebeck (1286) ensured that each monk got an additional cowl and each *conversus* an extra cloak[374]. An annual rent was assigned to Salem (1355) so that a summer tunic of white cloth could be given to each monk and *conversus*, and rougher garments for the winter[375].

At Beaulieu (where eleven hundred ells of cloth were produced yearly) each monk and *conversus* received a new tunic and hose yearly, new cowls every second year, and new scapulars every third. In 1270 , 25 cowls, 22 scapulars, 160 tunics, and 139 pairs of hose were produced. For winter wear white or grey woollen cloth was used (the latter being slightly more expensive to produce); summer garments were made from warp – cheaper to produce and lighter to wear. Blankets were also made for the dorters[376]. The weaving-house was perhaps under the immediate supervision of a *conversus*. Arnsburg (1247) had its 'master of the tailors'[377], and Tennenbach (1326) its 'tailor, or overseer of clothes'[378]. They could give necessary instruction to one new in the craft; otherwise the weavers kept silence as they wove[379].

Cistercian cloth-making might take advantage of technological advance. Towards the close of the thirteenth century the Silesian monastery at Henryków built a weaving-house operating several mechanical looms, and producing substantial quantities of undyed white and grey cloth,. This led to complaints of unfair competition from the clothiers of Ziębice (Münsterberg). After arbitration (in 1293) it was agreed that the monks would in future only use one such loom, save between Christmas and Easter when they might operate two[380]. Similar disputes between Riddagshausen in north Germany and the town of Brunswick ended in 1325 when its monks promised to produce cloth only according to their age-old custom: either quality or quantity put on the local market had upset its traders[381].

The general oversight of the skinning and tanning, shoe-making, and cloth-weaving departments was the province of the monk-*vesturer*. Brother William held this position at Staffarda (1245)[382] and Gilde Luche at Rueda (1315)[383]. The vesturer could speak to the 'masters' of the several workshops, both in their work-place and where they 'stored and cut clothes'. When necessary he was excused from the common labour of the community. He had the duty of providing bedding for the guests, distributing clothes and shoes to the community, and seeing all was necessary, habit-wise, at the blessing of a novice[384]. The departments of the vesturer's concern were but three of the many in the outer court: a hive of activity – not simply because of the rules of the Order regarding enclosure and stability, but also because, like any large village in those days, self-sufficiency was of the essence. Other offices at Beaulieu included the 'minor store', a general stores which provided a range of goods (including towels and carpets) primarily to the lay-infirmary and the guest-house[385]. The variety of business concerns within the outer court were carefully overseen by the cellarer and the bursars of the community, and weekly accounts had to be presented. All this made for good management.

The Monastery Garden

Monastic gardens within the precincts are on record at Escarpe (1243)[386] and Sénanque (1297)[387]. At Cîteaux (1258), the gardener's office was near the stables[388]. The abbey garden at Dore (1286) was next to the cemetery[389]. Melrose had a garden which ran down to the Tweed[390]. The gardens of Palazuelos (1274) were irrigated[391]. Many abbeys had external gardens, and orchards within or without the enclosure (Chapter 16). Around 1200, Caesarius of Heisterback tells of the monks planting cabbages in its garden, and of the *conversi* harvesting peas[392]. By 1273, Doberan had a semi-greenhouse for plant experimentation[393]. The vegetable-garden at Beaulieu was perhaps divided into lots between the several workshops. Controlled by the 'keeper of the curtilage', assisted by five paid workers and a boy, and aided by manure from the stables, their prime function was to provide beans, vegetables (including leeks and onions), and herbs, for pottage, but the gardeners also produced honey and cider, and dug the graves of the deceased[394]. Growing on the walls of Beaulieu is still to be seen the hyssop plant used in medieval times to strew on floors – on account of its scent-releasing qualities[395].

Notes

1. *FRB* II, 534; *FRM* 529, 532.
2. Fergusson (1983) 74.
3. Daniel (1950) 12.
4. *SMD* II, 177.
5. *DHGE* XIV (1960) 88.
6. Fergusson (1983) 77; Weatherill (1954) 348–49.
7. Fergusson (1984) 3.
8. Aubert (1931) 7–9.
9. Dimier (1954) 112.
10. Fergusson (1984a) 134.
11. Stalley (1987) 160.
12. Wyrwa (1992) 379.
13. France (1992) 89.
14. Visual observations and discussions on sites.
15. Fergusson (1984a) 51–2 (quoting *CPL*).
16. Berman (1986) 82.
17. *OSBS* (1) 140 (No. 132), 342 (No. 360).
18. Butler (1976) 93–4, 115–16.
19. Information of Dr. David Robinson.
20. *Cf. CB* 429 (No. 630).
21. *CTA* 84 (No. 391).
22. Stalley (1987) 41.
23. Gilyard-Beer (1986) 150.
24. Fergusson (1983) 80–1.
25. *CDRB* III:1, 116 (No. 100).
26. France (1998) in press.
27. Fergusson (1984a) 24.
28. *Ibid.* (1983) 74.
29. Barnes (1982) 58.
30. *CRC* xv–xvi.
31. *CRA* 20.
32. *CHS* 53–55.
33. *CCR* 1232/58, 1233/222.
34. *CCR* 1234/72, *cf.* 1245/329, 1246/486.
35. *CCR* 1232/387, *cf.* 1244/209.
36. VCH, *Dorset* II (1908) 33; *cf. CCR* 1232/195.
37. Gilyard-Beer (1960) 9.
38. *CCR* 1237/470.
39. *CCR* 1246/461.
40. VCH, *Warwick* VI (1951) 79.
41. *C.C.R.* 1235/245.
42. *Cf. RCH* 53; Wullschleger (1991) 13; Pl. III.
43. *Cf.* Carville (1982b) 54–5.
44. Senior (1989) 230.
45. Carville (1982a) 62–3.
46. *Ibid.* (1982b) 55.
47. Senior (1989) 230.
48. Kohler (1994) 20.
49. Butler (1963) 37.
50. Swartling (1969) 34.
51. Brakspear (1908) 544, 576 (at Haslebury, pa. Box); *cf.* Rahtz (1976) 19 (Bordesley, at Combe Grange).
52. Duby (1953) 10.
53. Carville (1982a) 63, Stalley (1987) 34.
54. Swartling (1967b) 9.
55. Carville (1982a) 62–3, (1984) 7.
56. Zanetti (1959) 68.
57. Van Der Meer (1965) 303.
58. Bedini (1964) 106.
59. Rahtz (1976) 19.
60. Neaverson (1949) 281.
61. Richardson (1977) 7.

62. Stalley (1987) 34.
63. Gergelyffy (1960) 275–76.
64. Senior (1989) 232, 235.
65. Barnes (1982) 58.
66. Carville (1979) 31.
67. *CMM* I, 228.
68. Tort (1974) 500.
69. *CHS* 292.
70. *UKW* 218.
71. *C.C.R.* 1241/291.
72. *C.C.R.* 1243/107.
73. *C.P.R.* 1293/25.
74. Stalley (1987) 65.
75. *Ibid.* 34.
76. Carville (1982a) 50–1.
77. *C.C.R.* 1245/325.
78. *CBK* xiii, 57, 82; *cf.* Barnes (1982) 58.
79. Williams (1887) 105, 107.
79a. Darby (1940) 101.
80. *CMM* I, 28.
81. Senior (1989) 233–34.
82. Van Der Meer (1965) *passim.*
83. Wildhaber (1986) 33.
84. Schittekat (1966) 110.
85. Swartling (1969)
86. Van Der Meer (1965) 303.
87. Bialoskórska (1965) 14.
88. *DHGE* XXIV (1993) 582.
89. Lohrmann (1983a) 216*n.*
90. Szacherska (1977) 62.
91. *DHGE* XV (1963) 125; *cf.* Mohr (1977) 19.
92. Lohrmann (1983a) 216*n.*
93. *Cf.* Schneider (1974) 332.
94. Mauri (1985) 292.
95. Drury (1985) 460–61, but *cf.* Gardner (1955) 30–31.
96. Cutts (1858) 182.
97. Dimier (1964) 108, McGuire (1982) 49.
98. Fergusson (1984a) 171.
99. *Ibid.* 18–9, (1983) 82–84.
100. Sparks (1978) 1.
101. *CWK* 87, *cf. CMM* I, 432–33.
102. Dimier (1964) 110.
103. *CCD* 72.
104. *RSL* II, 203 (No.12).
105. Rösener (1974) 153.
106. Barea (1977) (2) 125 (No.157).
107. Dimier (1964) 110.
108. Canestrelli (1896) 17.
109. *Statuta* I, 70 (1159/6).
110. Anton (1986) 243.
111. Barea (1977) (2) 30.
112. Williams (1984) I, 133.
113. *MEB* 140.
114. *ABB* 35, 205.
115. Fergusson (1984a) 72, 139.
116. VCH, *Chester* III (1980) 157.
117. Stalley (1987) 42.
118. VCH, *Chester* III (1980) 152; *cf.* Colvin (1963) I, 108, Fergusson (1984) 154.
119. Hall (1896) 5; *cf.* Colvin (1963) II, 560.
120. *DHGE* XVI (1967) 1221.
121. Canestrelli (1896) 20, 128; *cf.* Lekai (1977a) 273.
122. Fergusson (1984b) 15.
123. Harrison (1986) 39.
124. *Statuta* I, 338 (1207/23: Frienisberg, Hautcrêt, Sankt Urban).
125. Talbot (1958) 196.
125a. *DSMLR.* 320–21 (No. 90).
126. Fergusson (1984a) 139
127. Zadnikar (1980) 269.
128. Steger (1985) 88.
129. Fergusson (1984b) 22.
130. Richards (1968) 87.
131. Coulton (1933) 192, Stalley (1987) 42.
132. Lopez (1987) 137–39.
133. *CHA* I, 305; Hugoniot (1985) 500, 510, 516.
134. Williams (1984) I, 136.
135. *CHA* I, 305.
136. Pouillon (1970) 47.
137. Fergusson (1983) 80–1, Gilyard-Beer (1986) 174–75.
138. Dimier (1964) 108.
139. *Ibid.* 108–09, Fergusson (1984b) 19–20.
140. Dimier (1964) 101–10, Stalley (1987) 317.
141. Fergusson (1984b) 12–20.
142. *Ibid.* 19, 83.
143. Gimpel (1977) 120.
144. Panagopoulos (1979) 36–7.
145. Entz (1963) 6.
146. Kinder (1982) 398.
147. Bialoskórska (1965) 15–7.
148. Chèvre (1973) 88.
149. Stalley (1987) 49.
150. Fergusson (1984) 36.
151. *Ibid.* (1984b) 21.
152. Lillich (1982b) xv.
153. Talbot (1939) 44.
154. Eydoux (1958) 97–9.
155. Davies (1984) 141, 146, respectively.
156. Entz (1963) 6.
157. Fotheringham (1890) 46.
158. *Statuta* I, 147 (1192/4).
159. Conbhuí (1958) 14.
160. *CHA* (2–3) 144 (No.768).
161. *CRA* 11–12.
162. *BT* (2)183.
163. *Cf.* VCH, *Hampshire* II (1903) 140–41 (Beaulieu); Colvin (1963) 158 (Vale Royal).
164. *Cf. CDS* III, 103, *KZ* 690.
165. *CWK* 83.
166. *CMM* I, 106–07, 326, 380, 433; II, 64, 119, 238; III, 36.
167. *CC* (2) B. 30; *cf. ACA* 306–07.
168. Jobin (1980) 137.
169. Visual observation.
170. Radford (1965) 2.
171. Van Der Meer (1965), Figs. 230–232.
172. Bibolet (1986) 12–13.
173. Gerevich (1982) 388.
174. Coppack (1986) 46.
175. Dickinson (1965) 16.
176. Humphrey (1982) 7.
177. *CPR* 1299/445.
178. *CPR* 1299/411.
179. MS Notes (Arch. Dig, Open Day; 24-1-1983).
180. Anstett (1987) 9.
181. Dalrymple (1899) 3, Richardson (1951) 7–8, Stewart (1989) 68.
182. Carrick (1907) 34, 76, 83–4.
183. St John Hope (1906) 141.
184. Kind information of Dr David Robinson.

185. Courtois (1982) 305.
186. Kornerup (1879) 16.
187. Coppack.
188. Einsingbach (1988) 5–6.
189. Arenas (1985) 36.
190. *RSL* II, 203 (No.12).
191. *CC* (2), B.31–32; *ACA* 298..
192. Waeler-Antiglio (1976) 235.
193. *Abbaye N-D. de Mortemer* (Site Guidebook, 1976) 6.
194. Kozłowska-Budkowa (1983) 49, 55.
195. Donkin (1978) 134.
196. *C.P.R.* 1275/122.
197. *MGH* XIX, 719.
198. Owen (1971) 58.
199. *CPL* xlvi, lxi.
200. Rahtz (1976) 33–4, 123–32. *cf.* Bond (1989) 99.
201. *Cf. CPR* 1280/380.
202. Seward (1972) 75.
203. France (1992) 16.
204. *VRL* 12.
205. Musset (1979) 23.
206. Chauvin (1989) 56.
207. Wildhaber (1986) 33.
208. Morant (1995) 42, 44.
209. *CPL* 14.
210. *CC* II, 31.
211. Butler and Given-Wilson (1971) 150.
212. VCH, *Warwick* VI (1951) 231.
213. Waeber-Antiglio (1976) 235.
214. *CC* II, B.31.
215. Davidson (1843) 83.
216. *CM* 94.
217. Stalley (1980) 314.
218. Visual observation.
219. *ABB* 173.
220. Anstett (1987) 12, 20.
221. Panagopoulos (1979) 41.
222. Ashmore (1962) 13.
223. Courtois (1982) 329.
224. *Trans. Bristol and Glos. Arch. Soc.* 63 (1944) 131–32.
225. Barrière (1986b) 178–80.
226. Fixot (1980) 194.
227. *AM* II, 298.
228. *RSL* II, 199 (No.7), 203 (No.12).
229. De Montesquiou (und.) 197.
230. *KKA* 58.
231. Hartwell Jones (1912) 379.
232. *CHDM* (2) 184.
233. De Laplane (1863) *cf.* Plates III and IX.
234. St John Hope (1906) 143.
235. Robinson (1995) 63.18–19.
236. Robinson (1995) 18–19.
237. Hockey (1970) 65.
238. *C.P.R.* 1300/552; *cf.* Squires (1928) 118–19, Pl. LXX.
239. *OLSB* VII.
239a. De Laplane (1863) 82.
240. Kentchurch Court, Herefs., *Herald's MS* p. 21–2.
241. NLW, Badminton Manorial 2445, f. 9.
242. Waeber-Antiglio (1976) 235.
243. *VRL* 12.
244. Davidson (1843) 85.
245. VCH, *Wiltshire* III (1956) 274; *cf.* PRO, E 32/225.
246. Sparks (1978) 20.
247. *KKA* 58.
248. *CFN* 524.
249. *Statuta* II, 45 (1225/53).
250. *SL* 169 (the reference could be to Duiske: Carville [1979] 71).
251. Stalley (1987) 313.
252. Gardner (1955) 29; *cf.* Edwards (1964) Pl. 10.
253. *SBC* II, 307 (No. 421).
254. Fergusson (1984a) 132.
255. VCH, *Stafford* III (1970) 229; *cf. Archaeologia* XLIX, 434–38.
256. *CDRB* V: 3, 131 (No. 1153).
257. Deck (1974) 142*n*.
258. *OSBS* (1) 262–63 (No. 257), 274–75 (No.268); it cost 80 *Louvain pounds*.
259. *KKA* 55, *cf.* Post (1922) 162.
260. *CMM* III, xi.
261. Barnes (1982) 71.
262. Ashmore (1962) 13.
263. St John Hope (1906) 146–47.
264. Dickinson (1981) 2.
265. Lindley (1954) 133.
266. VCH, *Warwick* II (1908) 77.
267. VCH, *Sussex* II (1973) 72.
268. Gardner (1955) 21.
269. *CPL* 14.
270. Deck (1974) 142*n*.
271. Van Der Meer (1965) 289; *cf.* Aubert (1947) II, 146.
272. NLW, Badminton Manorial 1524, m.44.
273. Karpa (1963) 18.
274. Dickinson (1965) 9.
275. Swartling (1969) 34.
276. Aubert (1947) II, 146.
277. Heutger (1985) 149.
278. Gardner (1955) 21, Park (1986) 196.
279. Dickinson (1981) 2.
280. Gardner (1955) 29, Park (1986) 196.
281. Park (1986) 196 *et seq.*
282. Dickinson (1981) 2.
283. Marks (1986) 219.
284. *SBC* II, 307 (No.421).
285. *CAF* 327.
286. *KKA* 55.
287. Dublois (1957) 48.
288. Barnes (1982) 53, 71.
289. Régnier (1913) 344–42.
290. Midmer (1979) 218.
291. Lindley (1954) 133.
292. Eydoux (1950) 16.
293. Stalley (1987) 176, 273.
294. France (1998) in press.
295. Lekai (1977a) 448 (No. IX).
296. *SL* 160 (No. 21).
297. France (1998) in press.
298. Occhipinti (1985) 327.
299. *ABB* passim.
300. Coppack (1990) 100.
301. Aston (1993), Pl. 58.
302. *Ibid.* Pls. 60, 87; Williams (1990) 84 (Pl.4).
303. Luipold (1993; (Fontfroide Conference handout).
304. *RSL* II, 198 (No.1).

305. *CMM* II, 119.
306. Fontenay (guide, undated).
307. Pochin Mould (1976) 54.
308. *RSL* II, 225.
309. *ABB* 36, *cf*. 283–89.
310. VCH, *Northampton* II (1906) 118.
311. Einsingbach (1988) 82, *cf. LCC* (1) 145.
312. *Statuta* I, 525 (1220/44).
313. *Statuta* III, 103 (1272/1).
314. *ABB* 36, 54–55.
315. *SBC* (4) 105 (No.   1181).
316. Dimier (1973) 61, summarised in (1964) 178.
317. Coppack (1993) 99–97.
318. *CMM* III, 36.
319. *RSL* II, 225.
320. *ABB* 36, 39, 233–37.
321. Wiswe (1953) 77.
322. *ABB* 38–39, 230.
323. *ABB* 39.
324. Jaritz (1985) 59.
325. *LCC* (2) 212.
326. *Statuta* I, 523 (1220/30); II, 16 (1222/14).
327. Stalley (1987) 46.
328. Harper-Bill (1980) 106.
329. *ABB* 37.
330. Luipold (1993; Fontfroide Conference handout).
331. Coppack (1990) 101.
332. *CO* 15 (No.XX).
333. *VKS* 196–99.
334. *ABB* 37, 258–60.
335. *LCC* (1) 169, (2) 347.
336. *RSL* II, 228.
337. *ABB* 20
338. *Ibid*. 37.
339. Grüger (1978a) 133.
340. *ABB* 37–38.
341. Williams (1984) II, 302.
342. *Statuta* I, 61 (1157/19).
343. *LCC* (1) 141.
344. *Statuta* I, 310 (1205/4).
345. *DCK* 194–98, 233–34, *cf*. 211.
346. *LCC* (1) 166, (2) 344; *Statuta* I, 69 (1158/5).
347. Donkin (1978) 172*n*.
348. Berman (1986) 91*n*.
349. *Ibid*. 69, Donkin (1978) 172.
350. Cruden (1960) 71; Fry (1986) 6.
351. Richardson (1981a) 31.
352. Linnard (1982) 48.
353. Donkin (1978) 127.
354. Williams (1984) II, 270.
354a. Bond (1994) 373.
355. Grüger (1978a) 133.
356. Kempf (1976) 55.
357. *AM* II, 325.
358. Pillet (1934) 220.
359. *UKAR* 36 (No.52).
360. *AGM* 542.
361. Occhipinti (1985) 325.
362. *ABB* 17, 20, 38; *cf*. Wamba (1986) 180 (for use of shoes as presents).
363. Duby (1968) 154.
364. *LCC* (2) 336; *cf*. Lekai (1977a) 448 (No.XI).
365. *SL* 165 (No. 66).
366. *ABB* 38.
367. Occhipinti (1985) 325.
368. Talbot (1958) 199.
369. Coppack (1990) 115, (1993) 95.
370. *CCD* 61.
371. *CAS* I, 162 (No.CLXV).
371a. Schittekat (1966) 28.
372. *CMM* II, 63.
372a. Cocheril (1959) 57.
373. *DCK* 190, 214; *cf*. Donkin (1978) 136.
374. *UKS* 58.
375. *CDSL* 142–43.
376. Talbot (1958) 201, *cf. ABB* 214–19.
377. *UKAR* 36 (No.52).
378. *TG* 407.
379. *RCOC* Col. 1649, Cap. VI.
380. Grüger (1978a) 94, 132.
381. Wiswe (1953) 78.
382. *CAS* I, 289 (No. CCCXXIV).
383. Barea (1977) 215.
384. *LCC* (1) 101–02, (2) 302.
385. *ABB* 38, 245–53.
386. *Statuta* II, 265 (1243/34).
387. Moyne (1981) 275.
388. *CO* 4 (No. III).
389. Williams (1976) 5.
390. McLean (1981) 41.
391. Espinos (1982) 129.
392. *CHDM* 185, 385.
393. Lekai (1977a) 319.
394. *ABB* 37, 199–94; *cf*. McLean (1981) 27.
395. McLean (1981) 177.

Chapter 10

THE ABBEY CHURCHES

Church Building and Re-Building

The abbey church was the building which epitomised the whole purpose of conventual life, the worship of Almighty God, and those of the Order have attracted frequent national or regional studies[1]. There was no Cistercian 'style' of architecture, but there was a Cistercian 'attitude' towards buildings[2] – one of 'humility and simplicity' – observed by the first churches of the Order, and reiterated by the General Chapter as late as 1263[3]. As early edifices were rebuilt, size grew. The final churches at Longpont (105m), Royaumont (105m), Alcobaça (105m) and Clairvaux (105m) showed great similarity in their length[4]. The longest built by the Cistercians was Vaucelles (132m)[5]. Other churches were much more modest: those of Little Poland[6] and of Provence ranging only from 37 to 41 m[7]. There was no common Cistercian size: length reflected the prosperity of a house, both in terms of finance (enabling ambitious building) and community size (to be accommodated at worship). The Pontigny/Clairvaux group also showed close likeness in the width of their transepts (*c.* 48 m) and of their naves (*c.* 24 m).

The early simplicity of Cistercian church-building – dating from St Stephen Harding's time at Cîteaux – was later underpinned by the writings of St Bernard (as in his *Apologia*), by St Aelred (in his *Speculum Caritatis*) and in other works (including the *Vita prima* concerning St Bernard). The arguments used were that large churches were costly and the money might be better spent in helping the poor, and that paintings and sculptures were unnecessary and might even detract from prayer[8]. The General Chapter prohibited any colouring – even of church doors (1157), decorative tile pavements (1218), or altar-pictures (1240)[9]. Each of these dated injunctions shows that such features were creeping in. The 1257 codification of statute-law viewed matters less rigidly, and – by the 1289 and 1316 compilations – such prohibitions had become almost ritualistic[10].

The first stone churches in England, as at Waverley and Fountains have been shown to have had long aisleless naves with a square-ended choir[11] – which might be deepened as the years progressed – notably at Byland[12], and with flanking transepts – each with one or two chapels. Aisles were introduced (to provide side-altar space) in a large church from the mid-1130s, in smaller churches from the 1150s[13]. By the 1150s, too, the concept of an apsidal east end had begun to appear – as at Georgenthal (1150), or a greater complex of chapels – as at Fountains (1147)[14]. In the late twelfth century some notable churches terminating in hemicycles or polygons included Clairvaux III and Pontigny III[15]. The earlier square-ended presbytery was typical of other churches which, like Noirlac, adopted or never grew out of, the so-called 'Bernardine plan'[16].

It has been said that Cistercian churches were 'fundamentally modular in plan, the result of accumulating and combining a few square geometrical forms', with (Hahn wrote) two squares determining the key points of such plans: the larger determined the width of the nave and aisles and if multiplied by three gave the total length of the entire church, the smaller defined the width of the transepts and when multiplied by two gave the total length of the transepts[17]. Such proportions, whilst true of many twelfth-century foundations from Clairvaux, are not always proven elsewhere – notably at Cîteaux[18] and Furness[19]. Wiemer, using computer analysis, demonstrated the proportional relationships at Ebrach, suggesting that the total length of its church was seven times the breadth of the nave, whilst the ratio between the length of the choir (including the presbytery) and the total length of the church was in the proportion of $\sqrt{3}:2$[20]. Such careful planning was not obvious at Mellifont, where the width of the church varies by over two feet, nor at Corcomroe, where the east crossing piers are not aligned to each other[21].

Certain early churches had considerable influence on those built later. In particular the plan of Fontenay (1147) was reproduced widely elsewhere – though with local variations – as at Águiar[22], Bebenhausen, and Strata Florida[23]. Seven Irish abbeys adopted the Fontenay plan, but the similarity is disguised by differences in scale, proportions and elevation[24]. The measurements of Sorø are almost identical with those of Fontenay[25]. The Norman west front of Margam bears a striking resemblance to that at Fontenay, Margam was founded in the year Fontenay's church was consecrated[26]. A number of Italian monasteries – including Casamari and Fossanova – were based upon the plan of Pontigny II, and, with variations, this was copied in Little Poland[27]. The church of Cercamp was meant to be a replica of Pontigny III and, when the latter's design changed during the course of building, its daughter-house kept to the original model[28]. The churches of Ebrach, and (in large measure) Schönau, were a 'veritable copy' of that at their mother-house at Morimond[29]. The corona of radiating chapels at Croxden repeated the plan at its mother-house of Aunay[30]. There is evidence to show that these similarities were in part at least deliberate, and fostered by monk-architects and masons with experience on an earlier building programme. The rebuilding, after fire, at Fountains was carried forward by abbot Richard (1150–70) who had previously been for six years at Vauclair, and this may help to account for the 'transmission of architectural detailing from the Laonnais to Yorkshire'[31]. The chronicle of Aduard tells explicitly how, in 1224, abbot Wigold sent a *conversus* master-of-the-work (accompanied by his son) to sketch and measure Clairvaux, so that there should be a likeness. It wasn't exact, but when he died the brother was rewarded with burial at the entrance to the choir[32].

Some sites knew three successive churches: an early one (usually of timber) giving way to a modest stone edifice replaced in time by a much larger building. This sequence of events has been demonstrated at Clairvaux[33], Fountains[34] and Meaux[35]. It is usual to refer to the churches in their chronological order as, for example, Clairvaux I, II, or III. Such extensive rebuilding is to be ascribed to increasing numbers in a community, wealthy patrons, and an abbey's economic prosperity. The General Chapter tried to curtail the tendency, criticising the 'costly and superfluous' rebuilding at Vaucelles (1191)[36], but by the thirteenth century it had become accepted practice. The most common cause attributed for rebuilding was the destruction of the early edifice by fire as at Stanley (1212)[37] and Orval (1251)[38], to name but a few. An armorial frieze depicting the coats of the White family was painted around the church at Sorø – marking their contribution to its restoration after the great fire there in 1247[39]. Other physical factors making for reconstruction included decaying stone-work (Altenberg: 'consumed with age')[40], collapse of structure (the presbytery at Thame)[41], the weight of the crossing tower (Bordesley)[42], shaking by earth movements (Lützel)[43], gale force winds lifting off the roof (Croxden)[44], marine inundations (the Dunes)[45], and physical attacks as by the Saracens (Alcobaça)[46] or the Scots (Calder)[47].

The replacement of early Cistercian churches was usually planned so that the monks could continue to worship in the old choir until their new one was ready. At Ourscamp the second church was built to the south of the first one, which was left standing. At Waverley it was built to the north, and the site of the old nave was incorporated into the new cloister[48]. A similar methodology was used at Tintern[49]. At Doberan[50] and Lubiąż[51] the great church was built around and beyond the earlier edifice, which was then demolished. At La Chalade[52] and Vauclair[53] masonry from the earlier building was reused in the construction of the later. At Cîteaux successive enlargements of the church dictated the absence of a western aisle on the south arm of the cloister[54]. At the Dunes – where the monastery was rebuilt by the side of its former emplacement – the remains of Bl. Idesbald were transferred to the new church[55].

Especially in the thirteenth century, the laying of the foundation stone of a new church might be done with some dignity – by abbot or patron. King Henry III placed the foundation stone of Netley in 1242 at the base of the north-east pier of the crossing[56]. Edward I laid that of Vale Royal (1277) at the spot 'where the great altar was to be built' and, after him, other dignitaries laid stones[57]. The foundation stone of the new church at Altenberg (1259) was placed by the duke of Limburg and his brother[58], that of St Bernard-opt-Scheldt (1330) by the duke of Brabant[59] and that of the new choir at Zwettl (1343) by the count of Oeting[60]. Abbot Alexander laid the foundation stone of Meaux's new church on Palm Sunday, 1207[61]; the abbot of Pforta – in the exterior wall of his church's choir – on 21 March 1251[62]. Both were so placed on the anniversary day of the foundation of Cîteaux.

A phrase in a chronicle such as: 'The church was completed', might in fact refer only to the monastic choir. The date of consecration came sometimes years after the monks had full use of their church – perhaps because it was only partly finished or had an outstanding debt. Cercamp[63] and Dore[64] were not consecrated for about a century after building work had commenced. Precise evidence may come from chronicles as for the church of Waverley – started in 1203 and ready for use in 1231 – but not consecrated for another forty-seven years[65]. Other churches with a thirty-odd year building programme included Pontigny (1185–1210)[66] and Longpont (c. 1200–1227)[67]. Others took longer, or had their dedications delayed, as Tarouca (1152–1207)[68] and Ourscamp (1154–1201)[69]. The completion of a church was often delayed as, once the monks' choir was completed attention was paid next to the cloister, and only then was the western part of the church finished[70]. This is evidenced by stylistic breaks between the transepts and the naves, as at Sweetheart[71] and Roma[72]. Breaks in construction might also result from invasion (by the Tartars at Bélapatfálva)[73], lack of resources (Knockmoy)[74], lack of skilled man-power (Loc-Dieu)[75], partial collapse of the structure (Walkenried)[76] or by interdict (Beaulieu)[77]. At Noirlac the nave walls were started, but completed upwards only after a lengthy break[78]. Løgum, Søro, and Øm had naves uncompleted, probably because of a lack of *conversi* to occupy them once that stage of building was reached[79]. The longest known building gap was at Vitskøl, where the west end was completed only twenty years before the Reformation closed the monastery[80].

The long years of construction – for what-ever reason – were reflected by differing building styles within an abbey church. At Maulbronn no less than six building periods can be distinguished stretching from 1147 to 1424, even so the church was consecrated in 1178[81]. Fossanova exhibits features from early Romanesque through transitional stages into pure Gothic[82]. Silvanès, basically Romanesque, bears signs of that transition[83]. In the east facade of Knockmoy (commenced c. 1210) the lower lancets are round-headed, the later upper ones pointed[84]. At Boyle the first four bays of the south arcade have cylindrical piers, their counterparts on the north side clustered piers[85]. As building progressed at Pontigny groin vaulting gave way to rib vaulting[86]. At La Chalade gothic rib vaulting rests on Romanesque round piers[87]. On rebuilding or extension the choir was normally given priority, the nave often left untouched: a

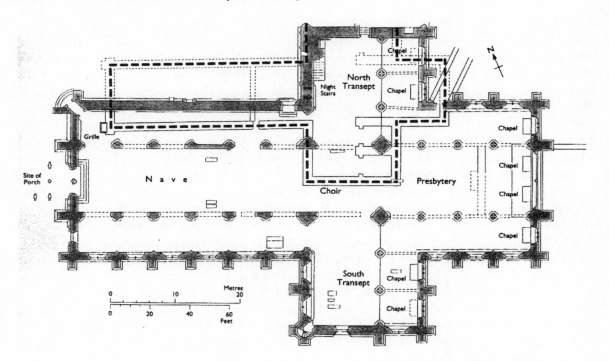

Tintern Abbey, Wales: the Norman Church (outlined) set against that of the 13th Century. *By courtesy of Cadw: Welsh Historic Monuments. Crown Copyright Reserved.*

Romanesque nave can therefore lead into a Gothic choir – as at Dore[88] and Heilsbronn[89]. Some churches which were built, or rebuilt – relatively rapidly or early or late – are very largely of one style: Romanesque – as at Cadouin[90] and Eberbach[91], late Romanesque – as at Buildwas[92], Gothic – as at Altenberg[93]. The Cistercians have been called 'missionaries of Gothic' – a term first coined by De Roisin in 1859[94] – but 'the old view that they were *pioneers* of Gothic is now generally rejected'[95]. They did though help to *diffuse* Gothic ideas – especially in the more distant parts of Europe – as in Ireland (as at Grey)[96], Italy (Fossanova)[97], Spain (Rueda), Germany (Walkenried)[98], Rumania (Cîrţa)[99] and Little Poland (Wąchock)[100]. In many abbeys the original Gothic is today masked by later Baroque adornment.

The rebuilding of choirs allowed the introduction of ambulatories, with chapels providing altars for private Masses. Morimond – and some churches in Germany, Austria, and Czechoslovakia – did this, but retained the square east-end to the church[101]. So, too, did Dore[102] and Henryków[103] - both of the lineage of Morimond. A number of abbeys in Western Europe (as Poblet) followed the plans of Clairvaux II and Pontigny III, with radiating chapels in a rounded or polygonal chevet[104] – sometimes enclosed by a continuous wall (as at Beaulieu and Sénanque), sometimes projecting outwards (as at Croxden and Hailes)[105]. The naves received the least attention, and were often unprepossessing[106]. Naves were often eight bays long, occasionally more (nine at Beaulieu) or less (seven at Pontigny); some were shorter still (five bays at Beaulieu [Tarn-et-Garonne])[107].

Church building cost money: it could lead monasteries into debt, as happened (by 1189) to ten abbeys in northern England[108]. This despite the prohibition of the General Chapter (1182, modified in 1192) against abbeys in debt erecting new buildings[109]. Especially in the wave of rebuilding finance had to be raised – for perhaps few patrons could afford to cover the cost of larger churches, as they might have done for the smaller edifices of earlier days. There were royal benefactions as for Maenan (by

Edward I)[110] and for Melrose (by Robert I)[111], whilst Andrew II of Hungary helped to renovate no less than five abbeys[112]. The earl of Norfolk completed the rebuilding of the church of Tintern (1301)[113]. The Chapter (1198) allowed the collection of alms towards church construction, so long as no preaching by monks was involved (1212)[114]. Grants of indulgences to those who visited an abbey and gave alms on the day or within the octave of its dedication – or on the anniversary thereafter – helped to raise funds. Such indulgences were granted by the pontiff to Belleperche (1263)[115] and Vyšší Brod (1267)[116], and by diocesan bishops to Dore (1260)[117], and Pforta (1268)[118]. Honorius III (1221) both granted an indulgence and sent Osek several relics, to encourage pilgrims to attend the dedication of its church[119].

The completion of a new abbey church heralded the solemn ceremony of its consecration. Pope Eugenius III dedicated Fontenay in 1147[120], and then in 1151 consecrated Casamari; the latter's new church was dedicated in 1217 by Honorius III[121]. More often the diocesan bishop assisted by other ecclesiastics would pontificate, as when the bishops of Thérouanne and Tournai dedicated the church of the Dunes (1262)[122]. When the new church at Fiume was dedicated (in 1197) by a former abbot (Cardinal Jordan) he was assisted by six bishops. The procession included twenty smoking silver thuribles, seven pairs of torches, and a multitude of men and women[123]. The day of dedication was an occasion when women were permitted into the enclosure (as at Volkenrode in 1347[124]), but they were not to outstay their welcome. The incised crosses in the walls of Waverley were 'anointed with oil and blessed' as early as 1214[125]. When its church was ready for use (in 1231) the monks entered it in solemn procession, but the consecration and a great banquet given by the bishop of Winchester were delayed until 1278[126]. The church at Beaupré was re-consecrated (in 1192) because some of the *conversi* had moved the high altar from its place[127], and that at Champagne (about 1270) after being ruined in Anglo-Norman wars[128].

The General Chapter early decreed that, because the founding fathers had dedicated Cîteaux to the Blessed Virgin Mary, all Cistercian abbey churches were to be dedicated to her: 'Queen of heaven and earth'[129]. There were some dual dedications – especially to the Holy Trinity within the incorporated Order of Savigny. Several Polish monasteries are credited with a dual dedication[130], but their secondary ascriptions may have been added at a later date. Aduard[131] and Hemixsem[132] were always called 'St Bernard's monastery'. Fossanova (1218), ten years after its consecration, was allowed by the Chapter to make commemoration of St Stephen 'in whose honour the church is dedicated'[133]. So set apart for the worship of Almighty God, the new Cistercian churches had to be kept clean: this was a duty laid upon the *conversi* every Good Friday[134]. The Visitor at Hailes (1261) had to remind its community to see the church was washed at least once a year[135].

Internal Simplicity

The interior of Cistercian churches was meant to be in keeping with the 'simplicity' of the Order[136]. A statute of 1158 allowed the doors of the 'house' to be painted white or black; by 1179 this statute had been revised to the doors of the 'church'; black was no longer an option[137]. This emphasis on the *doors* being painted may imply that much of the interior was, in the twelfth century, extremely bare. By the thirteenth century most abbey churches appear to have had a white masonry pattern on their walls, simulating the system of joints with paint or simply by limewash on a ground of plaster or stone[138]. Remnants of such masonry patterns survive at Obazine and Longpont[139]. In remoter parts of Europe – as Wales, Sweden, Brittany and Ireland – where walls were often of undressed masonry, once plastered, white-washed and marked out with false masonry 'there would be little to show that the walls were not built of ashlar'[140]. About 1275, the second church at Žďár was noted as being 'plastered white'[141]. But, by the start of the thirteenth century, other colours had begun to appear – as red masonry patterns at Léoncel and Sénanque[142]. The transepts of Clairmont display early decorative patterns[143], whilst a painting of red roses in white circles in the sanctuary of Maulbronn may be late-Romanesque[144]. Wall, and other, paintings (technically forbidden as late as 1316, save for representations of the Saviour) became common. By the late thirteenth century Trefontane had paintings of the Nativity of Our Lord and of the Coronation of Our Lady in the sacristy, and of a secular nature in the dorter. By the mid four-teenth century a Majesty and the Resurrection of the Dead were portrayed at Ląd[145].

Relief from a monotonous interior might be provided by device-bearing tympani above doorways or leaf-moulding on the capitals of pillars. Carved on many twelfth- or early thirteenth century tympani was but a simple cross, as is to be seen (in differing locations) at Bonmont, Riddagshausen[146], and Sulejów[147]. Tympani might bear the *Agnus Dei* as at Haina[148] or the Coronation of the Virgin as at Cwmhir[149]. Tympani might decorate the west front of a church – as the Christ in Majesty at the Czech nunnery of Porta Coeli[150], and the crucifixion (upside down) of St Peter at Aulnay[151]. Tympani bearing vegetative designs ornament the west doorways of Casamari and Heiligenkreuz[152]. At Herrenalb an inscribed tympanum above the west door (of *c.* 1180) recorded the name of the founder, another in the Galilee porch (of *c.* 1200) bore three quasi-geometrical designs – possibly symbolic of the Trinity[153]. A Romanesque tablet at Amelunxborn shows a cross nimbus between two axe heads, as if to say: 'Pray and work'[154]. At Stürzelbronn, engraved in stone, is the table for determining the date of Easter[155].

The piers of the church of Fontenay (1147)[156] – and other early buildings as at Eberbach and Bonmont[157] – had partly plain imposts. Later in the twelfth century capi-tals at houses such as Boyle and (in the nave of) Dore were scalloped or had a chevron design[158]. By the close of the century capitals and consoles in most Cistercian churches (and other parts of a monastery) were often sculptured with plain leaf patterns[159]. The earlier the design (as in the church of Fontenay[160]) the plainer the leaves, those sculp-tured later (as at Marienfeld[161]) could be more elaborate[231]. No less than fourteen such different leaf mouldings occur at Henryków[162]. The tall slender gothic piers of the crossing at Dore each terminate with a capital bearing a different leaf-pattern[163]. Such leaf designs are to be found widely, as far afield as Pilis[164] and Zaraka[165]. Certain simi-larities suggest that pattern-books (as that of Villard de Honnecourt) may have been used[166]. Variants in the thirteenth century included capitals depicting an *Agnus Dei* (as at Arabona)[167], or monastic figures (Eberbach)[168], or animal figures (Boyle)[169].

Roofs

Some churches had entirely timber roofs (Chapter 9), others were, in part at least, stone-vaulted. The naves might remain in timber and stone vaulting be restricted to the presbytery, either on account of cost or to enhance its dignity and to be a precau-tion against fire[170]. Early churches had pointed barrel vaults (as the 'Three Sisters' of Provence)[171], but these gave way in Cistercian architecture first to groins (as at Eberbach and Fossanova) in the mid-twelfth century[172], and then to Gothic rib vault-ing by the close of the twelfth century[173] – a feature of so many churches of the Order[174]. The interior might also be enhanced by sculpted bosses placed at the inter-section of the ribs. Flower, foliage and fruit designs occur on the bosses of Henryków[175]. Dore's bosses portrayed a Majesty, the Coronation of the Virgin, and St Catherine with her wheel[176]. A boss at Hailes shows Christ as a spiritual Samson rending the lion's jaw[177]. Elevations of the interior varied, but church roofs were indeed lofty: the crown of the vaults stood over 24 metres above floor level at Altenberg and Longpont[178].

Where it could be afforded the church roof (and other roofs of the claustral buildings) were covered by lead. This was early the case at Clairvaux (1178)[179] and Pontigny (1199)[180].The church of Meaux was leaded by Abbot Michael (1235–49), as also the monks' dorter and the granary[181]. Near the time of its great fire – when much of the lead melted – it was said of Strata Florida (*c.* 1284) that 'the whole church was completely covered with lead'[182]. Lead was costly, so Henry II of England paid for the roofing of Clairvaux[183] and the archbishop of Tuam for St Mary's, Dublin[184]. Bindon (1213)[185] and Netley (1251)[186] both received royal grants of thirty cart-loads of lead for roofing work. The need of the new foundation at Vale Royal (1283) for lead saw its abbot appointed 'keeper of mines and miners in Englefield'[187]. In earlier decades – and permanently where a house had no access to lead – a monastery roof was generally tiled, as at nearly all the Irish abbeys[188]. At Bordesley the roof tiles were at first made in the precinct using local clay[189]. The church and conventual buildings at Kirkstall (by 1182) were 'all covered excellently with tiles'[190]. Blue roofing slates and clay roof tiles have been found in excavations at Maenan, some of the slates still having nails in position[191]. The re-roofing of Croxden church (1332–34) was done with shingles[192].

Crypts

Few Cistercian churches are known to have had crypts: exceptions included Boyle (used as the treasury)[193], Padis (used for worship until the church was vaulted)[194], Pásztó (under the east end)[195] and Villers (a burial crypt)[196]. A sloping land surface at both Heisterbach and Mellifont[197] meant a crypt at the west end, with the main entrance to the church being a doorway in the north wall. The crypt at Mellifont clearly also had a practical purpose: possibly as a treasury or prison. A three-bay vaulted crypt at Buildwas may have served to carry the north transept over a dip in ground level[198]. The crypt at San Giusto predated its incorporation into the Order[199]. Other crypts occur at Falkenau[200], Velehrad[201], and (possibly) at Tintern[202].

Floors

In the twelfth century – and in some instances for much later – the floors of Cistercian churches were largely untiled. Many abbeys had stone flag or beaten earth floors which would be strewn with reeds or rushes[203]. An abbot of Froidmont (1197) was rebuked because he laid down carpets to beautify its presbytery floor[204]. The church at Meaux was not completely tiled until the late thirteenth century[205], that of Bordesley not until the early fourteenth[206]. Even when tiling became common, many naves had but plain tiles laid down – as excavated at Glenluce[207] and uncovered at Savigny[208]. Some churches remained completely untiled – like Rushen (earth floor in choir, slate paving in transepts)[209], Varnhem (limestone flags)[210], and also Cwmhir, Cymer and Maenan[211]. Tile studies have been hampered by plunderers – as at Jervaulx following its 1807 clearance[212] and at Strata Marcella – in the course of its 1890 excavation – by Sunday afternoon sightseers[213]. Tiles from Tilty were used in paving Dunmow Church (1538)[213a].

By the early thirteenth century – certainly in the abbeys of northern France – tiling had become common. The General Chapter did not look askance at this, what did concern the Order was the use of tiles of different colours and designs[214]. Such 'varieties of pavement' (1213)[215], 'superfluous and curious' (1205, 1237)[216], did not accord well with 'the ancient simplicity of the Order' (1205, 1235)[217] – and were to be amended[218] or removed altogether[219]. A monk of Beaubec (1210) constructed a tile pavement (but not at his abbey) which was said to be 'lacking in gravity and out of the ordinary'[220]. From 1236 onwards the opposition to variegated pavements diminished rapidly. As time progressed, a new floor might be laid over another: no less than seven medieval floor levels are identifiable at Bordesley[221]. Notable tile pavements have been found at Byland[222] and Newminster[223], as well as in the gate-house chapels of Bordesley[224] and Coggeshall[225]. The earliest known English tile mosaic was laid at Fountains in the abbacy of John of Kent (1220–47)[226]. In several French abbeys (like Bonmont and Fontmorigny) late-twelfth century decorated tiles had simple geometrical designs. In the thirteenth century appeared birds and animals[227], and common (as at Acey and, Bonport) was the fleur-de-lis[228]. Simple heraldic designs included the cross of Languedoc at Grandselve[229]. In Wales a variety of motifs included Saladin (at Neath), the griffin (at Strata Marcella) and an Agnus Dei (at Whitland)[230]. Tiles bearing heraldic devices became common in Britain in the thirteenth century. Those at Newminster ranged in date from the reign of Henry III (1216–72) down to Edward II (1307–27) and included the arms of families with connections with the monastery: those of De Clare, Percy, Vescy, and Warrenne[231]. Heraldic tiles at Neath also included the arms of early patrons[232].

A common source may explain the similarities in tile design found at certain houses of mid-Wales, as also at Tintern and Cleeve, Basingwerk and Buildwas[233]. Similarities also occur in pavement design between the central European houses of Dobrilugk, Heiligenkreuz, Walkenried, and Zwettl[234]. Two floor patterns at Pilis were identical with patterns found in the album of Villard de Honnecourt[235]. Scientific analysis of tiles recovered at Bordesley show that its supply of tiles changed with time: at various times the tiles were produced on site, at other times they came from a source which supplied other Cistercian houses, and at other times from a west Midlands source which supplied a variety of sites in the region[236]. One of the best known Cistercian tileries was that belonging to Chaâlis at Commelles in the forest of Chantilly, its timber affording a supply of fuel. Remains exist, including a perhaps thirteenth century chimney. By 1228 this tilery was in full production and surplus tiles were marketed[237]. Other French houses with kilns included Aiguebelle – one, at Montlucet, was producing (in 1341) 600 tiles annually for la Cour de Réauville[238]; Cheminon, at Renauval – work there led to a dispute with Trois Fontaines in 1192[239]; Igny – tiles and pottery produced at Coincy by 1307[240]; and Vauclair – three kilns in the precinct demonstrated by excavation[241]. There were tile-works close to Herrevad[242] and Fürstenfeld – the latter bought out by the abbey in 1342[243].

At Byland, Old Byland became the tilery of the monastery and was later known as Tile House Grange[244]. Textual differences suggest that the tiles of Byland, Fountains, Meaux and Rievaulx were made at different kilns but by the same men – itinerant tilers or *conversi* – thus accounting for their similarity of design and technique but difference of fabric[245]. The presence of tileries on granges away from the monastic precinct is in part to be explained by the availability of local clay, as for the Dunes at Bogaerde Grange[246]. Meaux's North Grange had both boulder clay and marine sand readily at hand[247]. (The tilers working on the church of Meaux used at least 265 differently shaped templates for cutting out curvilinear tiles[248].) Chaâlis (1148–1228)[249] and Dore (from 1148)[250] received grants allowing the extraction of clay. The production of tiles at St Sulpice-en-Bugey was aided by a mid-thirteenth century grant of 'workers of glass and tiles'[251].

Windows

The 'simplicity' of the Order demanded that church windows were 'white' (uncoloured) without any imagery (*c.* 1149)[252]: windows which broke this rule were to be changed[253]. An exception was made (1202) in the case of windows *already* in a monastic church at the date of incorporation of a non-Cistercian community[254]. Such a dispensation was not helpful to uniformity.The Cistercians largely resorted to using grisaille glass, (Fr: *gris* = grey), perhaps under the influence of Romanesque art[255]. This form of blank glazing was relieved by leadwork forming patterns, though in a number of non-French abbeys – as Doberan[256] and Heiligenkreuz[257] – paint, rather than lead, was used to define them. Such 'white glass' had a large percentage of soda salts which produced greenish tones[258]. Grisaille glass – common in the twelfth century – persisted in large measure in Cistercian churches in the thirteenth, with a cross-hatched background becoming common in France and Germany[259]. In France examples of grissaille glass survive widely, as at Bonlieu[260], Pontigny[261] and La Chalade[262]. Geometrical arrangements (as interlacing circles superimposed upon a diagonal lattice) and vegetal displays (as a palmette pattern encircled by a heart-shaped frame) were common. Thirteenth century grisaille (elaborated with convoluting plant stems bearing fruiting foliage) still adorns German and Austrian churches, such as Altenberg and Heiligenkreuz[263]. Similar window patterns suggests the use of pattern-books: one such, the thirteenth-century *Reiner Musterbuch* – named after the Austrian abbey of Rein – has patterns also used at Heiligenkreuz and Walderbach[264]. Grisaille with plant motifs – dating from about 1275 and donated by Queen Margaret of Denmark – is still to be seen at Doberan[265].

Coloured glass may have appeared early in some Cistercian churches (as at Fountains), impelling the Chapter to rule against it[266]. The regulations were never absolutely obeyed: some German houses used limited colour in forming grisaille patterns, whilst red was used for the same purpose at La Bénissons-Dieu[267]. By the late thirteenth century the regulations were widely ignored, and the 1316 codification of statutes contented itself with forbidding unnecessary and too elaborate imagery[268]. By this time large figures on coloured grounds were appearing. At Hauterive were portrayed figures of the apostles, and at Doberan of Our Lady and the two Saint Johns[269]. Scenes from the life of Christ appeared at Kappel and Wettingen[270], and at Royaumont episodes from the Old and New Testament[271]. In the early fourteenth century heraldry also appeared: the arms of Navarre at La Chalade[272] and those of Earl Roger Bigod at Tintern[273].

In the twelfth century, and later, a frequent Cistercian custom was to insert an oculus (containing a rose or wheel window) over three lancets (or round-headed windows, according to the period) on the west front or east end of an abbey church. Some see in this an expression of God's unity (in the oculus) and of the Trinitarian nature of that unity (in the three lancets)[274]. Examples include the west front of Longpont[275]. The oculus surmounting three round-headed windows at Trois Fontaines may owe something to the abbot of Fountains (where there was a similar arrangement) who became abbot there in 1151[276]. The arrangement is also to be seen at the east end of Sulejów and Koprzywnica[277]. It is not as common as has been supposed: there are variants – as when an oculus is placed above *two* windows – as on the west fronts of Fontfroide and Søro, and at the east ends of Bélapátfalva and Marienfeld[278]. A complex arrangment involves an oculus above two other levels of windows, as at Casamari – where it partly replaces an earlier larger wheel[279].

Rose- and wheel-windows were not restricted to the Cistercians, but they appear to have had an especial predilection for them. Some scholarship sees the wheel window as developing out of the rose[280], other studies the converse[281]. The oculus often contains features of both types, or has been subject to a high degree of elaboration, which makes it difficult to classify. A great wheel-window is that of Fossanova formed by a hub of twelve arches sustaining twelve slender colonettes radiating towards the circumference. Valvisciolo's window has twelve such radiating spokes, and was copied almost exactly at Fiume and Chiaravalle di Castagnola[282]. The rose window, primarily a French feature, was perhaps symbolic of the Blessed Virgin: 'the mystic rose'[283]. Notable examples occurred at Byland (8 m in diameter)[284], Vaux-de-Cernay (6.8 m diameter)[285], and Kołbacz (a 'blind window')[286]. Rose windows also frequently appear in positions other than the west front, as in the transepts of Obazine and Silvacane[287].

Window construction could be helped by glass-making on site: as at Doberan (helped by plentiful supplies of local sand)[288], Vale Royal (which gathered ferns from Delamere Forest)[289] and Pásztó (where glass workshops have been excavated)[290]. Vyšší Brod had its 'Glashof' by 1373[290a]. Poblet (1189) had at least one glazier-tenant paying an appropriate kind rent[291]. Nor were the Cistercians without their own painters: at Haina one window pane is signed: *lupuldus frater*; at Hude a glass-painter *conversus* is known. Painters and glass-painters may have lived in a house adjacent to Salem[292]. The elaborate windows of Altenberg made a lasting impression on the glass painters of Cologne[293]. The great rose of Byland may have influenced window construction at Beverley Minster and Durham Cathedral[294]. A stone mould for casting leaden window ventilators has been found at Neath[295].

Bells and belfries

Cistercian statute forbade 'stone towers for bells' (1157)[296] and wooden ones of immoderate height[297]. Timber for tower construction was supplied by royal grant to Croxden (1244, twenty oaks from Sherwood Forest)[298] and to Stanley (1237, four oaks from Chippenham and Melksham Forests)[299] – thus dating this stage in their building programmes. The resultant wooden edifices usually rested on a stone base at the crossing (of choir and transepts) or elsewhere[300]. The insistence on wooden towers (despite their susceptibility to gales and lightning) was demonstrated – as late as 1274 – when Valloires was allowed to build a stone tower because of the strong local winds[301]. Low stone towers had been built at the crossings of Buildwas and Kirkstall from the mid-twelfth century on[302] – possibly because the work started before the relevant injunctions were promulgated – or perhaps because they were empty and purely decorative, thus not infringing the wording of the statute: 'towers *for bells*'[303].

Very commonly the unsegregated crossing, with the nave roof carrying across the choir, did not allow for a crossing tower[304]. The crossing towers at Fountains and Furness imposed strain on the fabric necessitating the erection of buttresses against the crossing piers[305]. Some towers stood in other positions: the west end (as at Cymer)[306], or the side of the south transept (as at Casanova in Piedmont)[307]. Simple bell-turrets adorn Balamand[308] and Le Thoronet[309]. Octagonal turrets occur at Duiske[310] and Sénanque[311]. Ascent within a tower was usually by a spiral staircase – as at Calder and Tintern. A bell-tower, apart from its primary use, might be seen as a symbol of authority and prestige[312]. Its solid nature and small windows might make it a place of refuge, not only for monks but also for seculars – like Richard O'Nolan beseiged in the tower of Duiske in 1330[313]. The character of Cymer's west end tower suggests a similar rôle.

Historical record enables the building of some towers to be traced. Stephen Lexington told Coggeshall (1232) not to exceed the customary low height in building its tower and not to let it be a drain on its resources: it was 'to fix the cost solemnly in chapter'[314]. A youth working on the new tower of Waverley (1248) fell from it, but escaped fatal injury[315]. It is clear that the period of 1230 to 1250 saw substantial

Cistercian tower raising in England[316]. Later came the lead-covered belfry of Meaux, built about 1260[317]. As part of an ongoing restoration a campanile was built at Žďár about 1295[318]. The tower of Bonlieu was built between 1302 and 1305, the abbey calling in experienced workers and hauling the materials by oxen[319]. The tower of Clairmarais was completed in 1325[320].

A Cistercian church possessed two principal bells, the 'great' and the 'lesser'[321]. They were to be rung separately – never together, and neither bell was to exceed 5 cwt (226 kg) – so that one monk could ring it[322]. It is possible that in the twelfth century the 'lesser' bell surmounted the refectory: if not, the latter had its own bell[323]. In Britain the building of towers was accompanied by the acquisition of bells. Henry III had two bells made for Netley (1240): of 40 lb (18 kg) and 20 lb (9 kg) weight[324]. Kingswood (1241) borrowed money to pay for its great bell[325], Strata Florida (1255) paid 97 marks and two cows[326]. At Louth Park, a 'great bell' was made in 1283 (it weighed 1819 lb/ 820 kg), a 'lesser bell' in 1289, and a 'collation bell' in 1306[327]. When the Pavians attacked Morimondo Milano in 1237 they removed a total of five bells[328]. Fragments have been found at Kirkstall of two sets of moulds for casting small bells[329]. Beaulieu (1270) used leather for making bell-ropes[330]. When the great bell of Croxden broke in 1313, a new one was cast on site by a Lichfield founder[331]. The blessing of a great bell was an occasion of some dignity, performed by the bishop of Bangor at Strata Florida[332]. An abbot of Val-St-Lambert was rebuked for blessing a bell 'too simply'[333]. Great bells might have names: as the 'Benedict' at Meaux[334] and the 'Grandisson' at Newenham[335]. The second great bell of Waverley, hung in 1239, had an inscription naming it in honour of 'The Virgin, the handmaid of the Lord'[336].

The great bell was rung for the conventual Masses, for Vigils, Prime, Lauds and Vespers, before and after meals and for drinkings, and also after the mid-day rest: in other words, when personnel might be widely dispersed or need their attention aroused. The lesser bell was rung for the Lesser Hours, for collation and for Compline[337]. It was also rung (once only) at the elevation of the Host at all masses in the abbey church, and then all who heard it were to genuflect[338]. It was also rung twice to mark the burial of a guest[339]. Minor bells might include a small bell – the *nola* – used both in choir and at the prior's table in the refectory[340]. In the cloister hung a wooden clapper (the *tabula*) or (perhaps) a metal cymbal to summon the monks to gather for mixt, and when one of their number was dying[341]. Stephen Lexington ruled that 'no-one shall be excused from sounding the gong'[342]. The monastic day came to an end with the great bell being rung urgently ('with double effort') after the singing of the *Salve Regina*[343].

The High Altar

The focal point of the abbey church was the 'great altar', free-standing in the presbytery, though set up at Santa Maria a Fiume (1197) 'in the middle of the church'[344]. It was on the high altar that 'the Eucharist, the body of the Lord' was kept under lock (Mellifont, 1228)[345]; here Christ was 'daily immolated' at the conventual Mass (Esrum, 1237)[346]; here, despite contrary provision of the General Chapter (1157)[347], benefactors might lay their charters (Margam)[348]; and here a Christian knight about to do battle might rest his sword (as Simon de Montfort at Boulbonne, 1213)[349]. Built of stone, the solemn dedication of the high altar (to Almighty God the Blessed Trinity, and Saint Mary, at Fiume[350] and Newenham[351]) saw relics inserted within the *mensa*: no less than twenty at Fiume. An abbot of Walkenried (1255–67) collected relics in preparation for the dedication of its new church[352]. Known remains of medieval Cistercian altars include those at five Irish abbeys[353], as also at Dore[354], Preuilly[355], and San Galgano[356]. Upon the high altar stood a wooden cross which might be painted: crosses of gold or silver were discountenanced

(1134–1237)[357], as for a time were processional crosses (1157)[358]. Such restrictions did not outlive the mid-thirteenth century, perhaps to avoid giving offence to would-be donors[359]. By the close of the twelfth century (1185) it was customary to place a reliquary as well as the cross on the high altar for Mass on festivals[360]. Later (1237) two wax lights burnt by the relics in addition to other altar lights, thus enhancing their dignity[361]. An abbot of Zwettl (*c.* 1256) made a point of collecting relics whenever he travelled, including them in its 'great silver cross'[362]. Relics which might be displayed included those of St Denis the Areopagite (brought back from the Fourth Crusade) at Longpont (1205)[363], and of St Maurice and his Companions at Hautcrêt (1253)[364].

Pride of place on the high altar went to the Blessed Sacrament, described variously as 'the Body of the Lord' (Mellifont, 1228)[365], 'the Eucharist' (statute of 1238)[366], and 'the Most Holy Sacrament' (Osek, 1340)[367]. Its presence in a Cistercian church is clear by the mid-twelfth century, though reservation on the altar is not explicit until about 1180[368]. A lamp *might* (1152)[369], indeed *must* (1237, 1257), burn day and night before it[370]; it was to be kept under lock and key (1238)[371], and the pyx was to be placed in an appropriate vessel[372] of one colour[373]. At Trois Fontaines 1212) it rested on a pillar[374]. The reference at Osek (1340) to 'the Most Holy Sacrament of the Body and Blood of God' reflected perhaps acceptance of the teaching of St Thomas Aquinas that both sacred species were fully present in either the consecrated Bread or Wine, rather than be meant to imply reservation in two Kinds. At Doberan 'the eucharist or body of the Lord' was described as 'hidden in our altar'[375] – this suggests a tabernacle of some kind – as does the reference to the 'ark of God' at Hardehausen[376]. A thirteenth century octagonal wooden tabernacle survives at Sénanque[377], and a fine fourteenth century example at Arabona[378]. Despite such security precautions acts of sacrilege did occur, as when the Pavians attacked Morimondo Milano (1237)[379] and English forces raided Melrose (1322)[380]. Conversely, in the great fire at Strata Florida about 1284, the 'great altar' was adjudged spared because there lay 'the body of the Lord under lock'[381]. Abbeys to which grants of land, rents, or money, were made to maintain the light continually burning before the Blessed Sacrament, included Esrum (1237)[382] and Doberan (1306)[383]. The candle granted to Esrum was to be seven marks in weight and to hang before the altar; Doberan's (of six mark-talents) was to have, as 'custodians of the light', the abbot, cellarer, chamberlain, infirmarian and keeper.

In the twelfth century, Cistercian altars were largely undecorated[384], but pictures were not forbidden so long as they were of the Saviour[385] and of 'one colour'[386]. By 1240 a perhaps widespread practice led the General Chapter to 'command that all panel paintings in diverse colours on the altars of our Order be removed or painted in white'[387]: did this mean a grisaille technique or painting over in white? Despite this general injunction worse was to come: the Chapter of 1263 ordering the privileged abbey of Royaumont to return to 'the ancient humility and simplicity' of the Order by removing all those 'newly made pictures, images and sculptures, hangings, and pillars with angels about the high altar'[388]. Such regulations were soon disregarded, although moderation was called for as late as 1316[389]. At its dedication in 1277 Newenham had an altar-frontal panel bearing six images given it by the mother-house of Beaulieu[390]. About 1300 a (stone) reredos depicting the Crucifixion was set up at Fontenay[391], and Løgum acquired a carved and coloured wooden altar-frontal showing Christ bearing the stigmata[392]. In 1309 'a new work about the high altar' was painted at Louth Park by a layman[393]. A carved wood and polychromed altar-piece was made for Doberan about 1310[394]. Abbot Adam of Meaux (1310–39) replaced earlier altar paintings with ones depicting the Gospels and the Prophets – painted by one of the community[395]. There was now in these respects, in at least some monasteries, an abandonment of early Cistercian 'simplicity'. Further, in 1256, silk altar coverings had been allowed on greater festivals, rather than the 'ordinary' ones hitherto[396].

Subsidiary Altars

Well before the close of the twelfth century, it perhaps became increasingly the practice for each priest-monk to offer a daily private Mass[397]. This necessitated the construction of several subsidiary altars within an abbey church, and their eastward extension (sometimes with an ambulatory arrangement of radiating chapels) in part reflected this need[398]. Side-chapels would also be found in the transepts (generally against the eastern walls)[399], in the nave (against the pulpitum)[400], in chapels formed by cross-walls in the aisles[401], and in the Galilee porch[402]. In a disused monastery the site of such altars can be determined (as at Noirlac) by the piscinas still evident in the adjacent walls. At least ten altars at Valmagne had double-piscinas, at Buildwas two chapels shared a common floor-piscina[403]. Sometimes the footings of such altars are apparent (as at Vitskøl)[404] or the tile pavements around them (as at Strata Florida)[405]. Clairvaux came to have no less than thirty-two such altars, ten of them in the nave[406]. For a time at least, whilst its high altar was in stone, the side altars were of timber[407]. Between 1217 and 1294 no less than twenty-two subsidiary altars were consecrated at Villers, five of them in 1280 alone[408]. An inscription at Sénanque tells that some of its chapels were consecrated by Bishop Benedict of Cavaillon (d. 1178)[409]. When Hailes was consecrated in 1251 by the bishop of Worcester, thirteen other bishops assisted – each dedicating a side altar[410]. Between 1251 and 1288 eighteen side-altars were consecrated at Grandselve[411]. Even a modest church would have had twelve or so.

Each subsidiary altar had its own dedication, and the names given to all Villers' twenty-two altars are known[412]. Dedications favoured in Cistercian houses included the Holy Trinity – as at Villers (where it stood by the tower door)[413], the Holy Cross – as at Coggeshall[414] (in all known cases it stood – as was usual – in the choir of the *conversi*); the Blessed Virgin Mary – as at Hautcrêt (where it stood in the sacristy)[415], St Mary Magdalene – as at Margam[416], St Catherine – as at Pforta[417], St James – his name incised in whitewash – at Fountains[418], St Margaret – as at Hulton[419], and St Nicholas – as at Esrum[420]. Local saints commemorated included St Dennis (at Savigny)[421], St Elizabeth (at Georgenthal)[422], and St Cuthbert (at Furness)[423].

Private Masses were meant to be relatively low-key affairs: for many years no candles were lit during them and Stephen Lexington (1228) reiterated this rule[424]. Change was already taking place. Benefactors provided wax for candles for private Masses at Clairvaux (1222, one wax light per monk)[425] and at Meaux (1215–35)[426]. Burning a tallow candle or other lamp (but not of wax) was permitted (from 1189) before side altars on the night of the feast of the saint in whose honour they were dedicated[427]. When Mellifont was dedicated in 1157 cloth for each of its nine side-altars was given[428]. In 1164 relics were placed in all the altars of Morimond, (which suggests they may have been of stone)[429]. Side-altars enabled a monastery to fulfil chantry obligations – as at Esrum – where from the fourteenth century three altars were fully occupied in this way. One had a requiem Mass on four days with a Mass of the Holy Spirit on Tuesdays, of Our Lady on Saturdays and of the solemnity on Sundays[430].

Statuary

Not only pictures, but also images (save later of the Saviour) were forbidden in Cistercian churches by a series of statutes stretching from 1119 to the codification of 1257, because the attention paid to such things might detract from 'godly meditation and religious gravity'[431]. Images set up at Lorroy (1204)[432] and San Prudencio (1216)[433] were to be removed. The exception made accounted for an 'image of Christ' at Duiske (1228/1232)[434]. In the later thirteenth century the rules were ignored: images of the

Blessed Virgin were set up at Aduard (at the entry to the church by 1266)[435], and at Newenham (near the high altar at its dedication in 1277)[436]. Before the century ended abbeys with like statues included Aulps[437], Maulbronn[438], and Osera[439]. Extant also are images of Our Lady (from Cîteaux)[440], and Christ as Judge (from Heilsbronn)[441] – both of the early- to mid-fourteenth century.

Sculptured Detail

Frequently to be seen in Cistercian sanctuaries are the remains of the triple-sedilia where the sacred ministers sat during Mass: notable examples occur at Baltinglass[442], Furness[443], and Kappel[444]. The sedilia at Žďár was sculpted about 1300[445]. A presbytery might also be enhanced by finely carved double-piscinas (as at Cymer and Dundrennan)[446]. At Alvastra piscina drains remain[447]. The stone base of a lectern survives at Basingwerk[448] and at Mellifont[449]: the usages of the Order mention 'the pulpitum for the reading of the lessons at Vigils'[450].

Funerary Monuments

From the early-thirteenth century substantial monuments might mark the burial-places of the great, thus detracting from the simplicity of a church interior. Buried at Lubiąż before the high altar was Duke Bolesław (d. 1201): his tomb inscribed with a verse praising him as 'prince of Poland, the glory of the country'[451]. The tomb at Pilis of Queen Gertrude (d. 1213), wife of Andrew II, may have been designed by Villard de Honnecourt[452]. Over the grave of its founder (Queen Bérengère, who died in 1230), arose in the middle of the choir at L'Épau a tomb of white marble[453]. Magnificent tombs were erected at Royaumont (for the family of St Louis)[454], whilst one of the largest collections of monuments (of the Hohenzollern dynasty) occurs in the nave at Heilsbronn[455]. In the choir of Santes Creus are the impressive tombs of Peter III of Aragon (d. 1285), James II (d. 1327), and his queen, Blanche of Anjou (ob. 1310)[456]. More imposing still are the royal monuments at Poblet[457]. In the presbytery at Cymer and a side-chapel at Strata Florida, are arched recesses which once contained a funerary monument long since vanished.

The Nave

The choir of the monks was placed in the eastern portion of the nave: at Bordesley the stalls occupied the two bays nearest the crossing, but extended into the crossing for much of the thirteenth century[458]. Excavation has shown several changes in extent of its stalls, and recovered fragments of them[459]. The stalls at Roche were described (in the sixteenth century) as being 'like the seats in minsters'[460]. Royal grants of timber aided the making of choir-stalls, including those at Thame (1232)[461]. The monks' stalls at Meaux were erected about 1245[462], new stalls were completed at Louth Park in 1315[463], and at much the same time those at Stoneleigh were renewed[464]. Thirteenth century stalls survive at Kappel[465] and Loccum[466]: at the latter the screen bears a typical Cistercian pattern of interlacing vegetative growth. Below the late medieval stalls at Fountains have been excavated resonance pits containing vases of earthenware[467].

The western part of the nave was occupied by the choir of the *conversi*, and separating the two choirs was a substantial screen (sometimes of stone) known as the pulpitum. It is not clear how early this rigid separation of the monks and *conversi* took place, nor is it recorded where the *conversi* worshipped before their portion of the nave was completed – sometimes long after the monastic choir. A pointer perhaps comes in the reminder the General Chapter gave Sobrado, in 1191, to 'make a partition in the church between the monks and the *conversi*'[468]. The restored stone pulpitum of Maulbronn, dating from about 1175, is 3.2 m high and has two round-arched door-ways leading into the monastic choir[469]. The stone pulpitum of Tintern (completed about 1330) reached a height of 5.5 m[470]. The pulpitums of Fountains[471] and Furness[472] had altars flanking their western face. The pulpitum at Rievaulx bore a statue of Christ in Majesty[473].

Eastwards of the screen, or between two parallel screens (where the pulpitum was a substantial edifice with a loft above) was the retro-choir: here those who had been bled, as well as sick and elderly monks, and perhaps visiting chaplains from nunneries of the Order, might worship[474]. From a reference (at Cîteaux, 1270) to 'the lamp of the novices in the retro-choir', it may be that they were also sometimes accommodated here[475]. In the retro-choir, too, might assemble the *conversi* for the final prayers after a funeral[476]. Westwards of the screen might stand the altar of the Holy Cross, and it was in the choir of the *conversi* at Meaux that abbot Hugh (1339) set up a 'miraculous' cruci-fix[477]. The stalls of the *conversi* ranged on either side, the senior of them having the stalls nearest the altar[478]. The *conversi* had their own doorway through which to enter their choir: normally in the nave wall towards its western end but sometimes differently positioned – as a doorway in the west facade at Silvanès, noted (in 1181) as 'the door of the church of the *conversi*'[479]. Another exit from the church was the so-called 'door of the dead' off the ambulatory, leading to the infirmary or the grave-yard, or both[480]. Such door-ways are to be seen at Dore, Orval[481], Loccum[482], and Tintern.

Galilee Chapels

Early Cistercian churches may have been intended to have had no western door as, given the purpose of the building, an entrance for the laity was hardly thought neces-sary – and the monks and *conversi* had their own separate doorways piercing the nave wall. There was though a place reserved for guests in some abbey churches[483], and in time secular folk did have greater access. The west door at Varnhem[484] may be a later insertion and the absence of west doors at Buildwas and Mellifont was the consequence of the immediate relief, but the church of Sénanque never had a west entrance[484a]. West doorways became general, however, and reflected the style of their times: Romanesque at Fontenay and Flaran, a fine multi-ribbed late-Norman archway at Strata Florida[485], Gothic at Ebrach and Vaux-de-Cernay, and with dog-tooth orna-mentation at Dunbrody and Grey[486]. Without the west door stood, in some but not all abbey churches, a porch, usually of stone, and referred to alternatively as the 'galilee' (as at Hauterive, 1329)[487] or the 'paradise' (as at Maulbronn, 1288)[488]. Sometimes this porch has almost completely disappeared, its former presence only indicated by brack-ets marking its roof-line on the west facade of the church (as at Fontenay)[489]; or by foundations in the ground (as at Tintern, where it may have been free-standing)[490]. Such an arrangement was not Cistercian in origin: porches or vestibules were known in the eleventh century at Monte Cassino (where called the 'paradise'), and at Cluny and at St Gall (where called the 'galilee')[491].

The pillared porch at Fountains was erected about 1170[492], the three-bayed paradise at Maulbronn about 1210 to 1220, (showing a transition from Romanesque to Gothic architecture)[493]. The porch of Herrenalb, built first about 1200 was later raised in height, and thus shews a similar transition in style[494]. At Waldsassen (1357) a wall connected the 'galilee' and the guest-house[495]. As for measurements: in 1667 the porch of Ourcamp was said to be 'thirteen paces long by ten in width'[496], that of Herrenalb rose 12.5 m high[497]. Other 'galilees' included those at La Ferté (built about 1210–20)[498], Pontigny (with Romanesque pillars), and Staffarda (with an open brick arcade). The known building dates suggest that galilee-building was particularly favoured in the early thirteenth century. The 'galilee' often contained one or more altars – where perhaps strangers and guests might hear Mass[499]. At Fiume was consecrated in 1196 'the altar of St Paul in the portico of the church, and the altar of St Quiricus in the other portico'[500]: this may be a clumsy way of referring to two altars in the same 'galilee'. The chronicle of the Dunes (1355) refers to the 'the porch of the church, with two chapels made superbly and expertly'[501]. Two altars are yet to be seen in the porches of Maulbronn, Poblet, and Valmagne. Burials took place in the paradise of Herrenalb[502] and the porch of Melrose[503].

Church Lighting

As well as liturgical lighting, the usages of the Order made provision for the general lighting of the abbey church. Early references, such as 'a light may burn day and night in the oratory if you wish and if it is possible'[504], probably refer to a quasi-liturgical purpose – perhaps to indicate the presence of the Blessed Sacrament. The general lighting of the church was subdued – the monks knowing the psalms by heart[505]. The *Institutes* (1134) and the *Book of Usages* (c. 1185) provided for five lamps for general lighting purposes: one to illuminate the step of the presbytery, another in the middle of the choir, another in the retro-choir, another in the choir of the *conversi*, and yet another in the place reserved for the guests[506]. There is note at Cîteaux (1270) of 'the lamp placed between the stalls of the abbot and the prior – i.e. in the middle of their end of the choir[507]. Lamps were used until 1222 at Clairvaux, but not altar candles, to allow the monks to say their private Masses[508]. A lamp would have been placed by the night-stairs in the transept. Grants towards the cost of lighting the church were made to, amongst others, Arnsburg (1245)[509] and Clairvaux (1210)[510]. Cresset stones have been found at Calder and Furness[511].

The Liturgy

In early-twelfth century Cistercian usage there was ritual simplicity. Mass began (as every Cistercian office) with the saying of the Lord's Prayer, elevation of the Blessed Sacrament and genuflections were (at first) unknown[512] and the Last Gospel was never said[512a]. It was the custom 'not to prostrate, but to pray standing or kneeling'[513]. The chalice was prepared after the Confession, at the commencement of the Collect or Gloria[514]. This led to an unfortunate incident at Trois Fontaines where – in the dim light – the absence of wine from the chalice was not noticed until the time for Communion[515]. No pall or veil covered the chalice – only the corner of the corporal[516]. A Cistercian priest acting as a deacon wore his stole around the neck (as a priest) and not across the shoulder (deacon-wise)[517]. At the pax, the peace was exchanged with seculars present as well as with clerics[518]. By 1152 the host was elevated after its consecration, but the chalice was not so until 1444[519]. By 1210 it was provided that at the elevation candles might be raised, the lesser bell rang out, and all who heard it were to genuflect: 'making the prayer which God inspires'[520]. The monks were enjoined (1134/47) to receive the Blessed Sacrament every month, less or more frequently if the abbot thought fit[521]. The Precious Blood was given from the chalice using a reed: chalice and reed might be of silver-gilt but never of gold (1202)[522]. From 1261 Holy

Communion was given in one Kind only – save to the sacred ministers – on account, the General Chapter ruled, 'of grave danger from receiving the Blood of the Lord in the chalice'[523]. Did the danger come from alcoholism, or infection, or sacrilegious reception? It was in tune with the eucharistic teaching current at the time.

At first only one conventual Mass was celebrated[524], but by about 1185 two Masses were sung on Sundays and about 47 feast-days. The first Mass, 'the morning mass', was sung (or said) after Prime and attended by officials (as the porter) who might find it difficult to be present at the High Mass after Terce[525]. By the late twelfth century every monk-priest who wished might say his own private Mass (save on Ash Wednesday) – either during the period of reading (after Vigils) or after the Offertory during the conventual Mass – presumably leaving the choir to do so[526]. In 1239 the count and countess of Flanders gave Clairvaux an annual rent worth 30 Flanders pounds on condition that no monk left the abbey for the fields at harvest-time until he had said his private Mass[527]. The hosts for the Eucharist were to be made only from 'pure wheat'(1191)[528]. Grants of money for buying the necessary grain were made to Clairvaux[529] and Flaxley[530], whilst Quarr received a practical gift – an acre of wheat[531]. Bonport (1223) received annually 8 bushels of 'better wheat' to enable the sacristan to have prepared 'the most holy bread to sacrifice on the altar'[532]. At Heisterbach (*c.* 1200) the hosts were impressed with the 'sacred letters'[533]. In England a few abbeys received yearly a tun of wine for Mass by royal grant: as Coggeshall[534] and Netley[535]. Wine for Beaulieu came from the king's wine imported at Southampton[536].

Chalices were not to be of gold (1119)[537], but might be of silver (Staffarda, 1223)[538] or silver-gilt (Rufford, *c.* 1185)[539]. Despite the regulations, gold chalices were possessed by Mellifont (1157)[540], Kirkstall (*c.* 1185)[541] and Beaulieu (1204 – given by King John)[542]. Censers were to be of iron or copper only (1119)[543]: gifts of censers were made to Netley (1239)[544] and Staffarda (1223)[545]. Queen Elizabeth of Bohemia (*c.* 1330) bequeathed a crystal incense-boat to Waldsassen[546]. There is note of the censing of the altar during Lauds at Strata Florida (1202)[547]. Altar cloths and vestments were to be either of linen or wool[548]. Chasubles in particular were to be of one colour, and without orphreys (1207)[549]. These rules were breached in Poland and Hungary, where vestments were ordered to be 'humble and ordinary' (1204)[550]. Later (1226) silk chasubles were allowed, providing that they were *donated* to a house[551]. It was papal pressure (1257–60) that ended Cistercian simplicity in vesture and caused the General Chapter to allow abbots to wear copes in processions and carry their pastoral staff, and for the deacon and sub-deacon of the conventual Mass to wear dalmatic and tunicle[552]. A 'low-church' tradition of one and a half centuries had come to an end!

At Mass but one wax candle stood (in early Cistercian decades) in an iron candle-stand in the sanctuary, later two candles were allowed – one to each side of the altar. On solemnities, from 1237, two candles were allowed *on* the altar by the relics – in addition to the two lights 'fixed on the walls to either side'. The candlesticks were to be of wood or iron and uncoloured[553]. From 1195, instead of the usual one oil lamp[554], three oil lights might burn before the high altar on solemnities[555]. At Zwettl (*c.* 1300) poppy-oil[556] was used for altar lamps[557]. Grants of oil included those made to Tilty[558] and Žďár[559]. For candle-making Sedlec received annually a gift of 3 stones (22 kg) of pure wax[560]. The candles lit at the elevation of the Host were to be small and not of wax (1270)[561]. Later, large candles were allowed (1288)[562], and grants made included those to Esrum (for 'two great candles', 1299)[563], and to Zwettl (for 'great lights', 1317)[564].

The early Cistercians rejected the accretions of centuries to the liturgy: they chanted all the psalms each week, omitted various commemorations of saints, held no processions (save for Candlemas and Palm Sunday) and they retained alleluias in Lent[565]. Processions were reintroduced on Ascension Day (in St Bernard's time) and on the Assumption (in 1223)[566]. Further departures from simplicity came with the addition of the daily offices of the Dead and of Our Lady. By the late twelfth century, the daily Mass for the Dead was omitted only on Good Friday, Holy Saturday, and Easter, Whitsun, and Christmas Days[567]. The daily office for the Dead was omitted somewhat more often[568]. It was said in winter in the interval which followed Vigils, but in summer after Vespers[569]. The office of the Blessed Virgin Mary was used on the granges from 1157 and in the monastic infirmary from 1185. Rules were drawn up in the later-twelfth century for the commemoration of Our Lady at Lauds and Vespers at certain seasons[570]. The Mass of Our Lady, 'whether private or sung in community', became a feature in the same period[571].

The Church's Year

The Cistercian calendar was that of the universal Church, but with appropriate additions. It is noteworthy that whilst the Assumption of Our Lady was observed, there is no mention of her Conception in the narratives of the *Ecclesiastica Officia*, nor in the earliest known Cistercian calendars[572]: possibly this reflected St Bernard's unease concerning it. To the calendar were added the feasts of the principal founding fathers and early notables of the Order (as St Aelred on 12 January, St Gerard on 30 January, and St Stephen of Obazine on 11 March)[573]. The calendar also included the Commemoration of dead bishops and abbots of the Order on 11 January; dead monks, *conversi* and novices, of the previous year, on 17 September (the day after General Chapter ended), and dead parents were remembered on 20 November[574].

The passage of the Christian year was kept fresh by customary changes. In Advent, the Book of Isaiah was read in its entirety, not only at vigils but also in the refectory[575]. On Christmas Eve night a fire was lit in the calefactory so that the monks could warm themselves in the interval between vigils and the Mass, *Dominus dixit ad me...* (perhaps erroneously called today the 'Midnight Mass')[576]. Christmas Day was of course a feast of Sermon. It was a matter of great concern to Abbot John Bridesall of Kirkstall, travelling to Cîteaux in the summer of 1304, that he might not return in time to preach on Christmas Day – nearly five months later![577]. On Candlemas Day there was the usual procession in the cloister: Margam's church was especially illuminated[578], and income from a mill provided candles for Cherlieu[579]. Layfolk might attend Mass in an abbey on this day and (like Mary and Joseph in the Temple) make offerings[580].

On the First Sunday of Lent the precentor distributed the Scriptures to each monk for their spiritual reading. After Compline all the crosses were veiled and the curtain before the presbytery was drawn across (save on Sundays) until the Wednesday in Holy Week[581]. On Palm Sunday branches from trees were blessed on the step of the presbytery, and distributed for the procession in the cloister[582]. On Maundy Thursday the abbot washed in the cloister the feet of four monks, four *conversi*, and four novices (to represent the twelve disciples); others washed the feet of the remainder of the community. There were also washed the feet of as many poor people as there were monks in the monastery, and they were given refreshment[583]. On Good Friday the wooden tabula, not the bell, called the brethren to worship[584], and Holy Communion was received by the sacred ministers only. The Kiss of Peace was neither said nor given (as Judas betrayed the Lord in that way)[585], and (from 1289) a genuflection was made at the mention of the death of Jesus in the proclamation of the Passion[586]. After Vespers the *conversi* gave the church its annual spring-clean. During the Easter Vigil the precentor fixed the five grains of incense into the paschal candle[587]: the weight of which was first regulated by Innocent III (1199)[588] and fixed by the *Usages* of the Order – at 10 *trecenses pounds*[589].

At Pforta there was a liturgical blessing of bread on Easter Day and of wine on 24th June (St John Baptist's Day)[590], and at Lubiąż of plants on 15 August (the Assumption)[591]. The Litany of the Saints was sung on the Rogation Days[592] and a procession held on Ascension Day. From 1241 in France, and then throughout the Order from 1292, Corpus Christi was kept as a solemnity with two Masses[593]. By 1355 there was a Corpus Christi procession at Lilienfeld[594]. From 1223 a procession outside each church marked the Assumption[595]. From 1273 the seven penitential psalms, sung each Friday 'for the state of the Church', were chanted in procession in the cloister[596]. The Order showed concern for the feast of St Barnabas. His day (11 June) was to be kept as for an apostle but the *conversi* were to work (1203), readings were prescribed (1204), and if it fell on the vigil of Pentecost it was to be transferred to the Thursday thereafter (1261)[597].

In the thirteenth century abbeys in a number of countries were increasingly permitted to observe the days of saints dear to them as feasts of 12 Lessons (i.e. of three nocturns at Vigils). Such special days included in Poland the feasts of SS. Albert and Wenceslas (28 September) and of St Stanislaus (11 April)[598]; in England the feasts of St Edmund (20 November), St Edward the Confessor (13 October), and St Augustine of Canterbury (27 May)[599]; in Scandinavia the feast of St Olaf (30 July)[600]; and in the kingdom of Castile the feast of St Marina (18 July)[601]. More local commemorations permitted included those of SS. Crispin and Crispinian (25 October) at Longpont[602], St Maurice (22 September) at Hautcrêt[603], and St Winefride (3 November) at Basingwerk and Buildwas[604]. Particularly favoured was St Margaret (July 20): her feast was observed first in Austria (1228), then at L'Épau and Neath (1259), and then throughout England, Wales and Scotland (1268)[605].

It was said of the monks of Doberan (1255) that they spent their time 'night and day in prayers, fasts, vigils and other divine obsequies'[606]. That day was punctuated from rising (perhaps around 2.00 a.m.) to bed-time (perhaps about 7.30 p.m.) by alternating periods of worship and work. There were variations between summer and winter, and probably from abbey to abbey, so it is difficult to give a precise time-table. Monks rose earlier in summer, and retired later, than in winter[607]. After Vigils there was an interval – during which a monk might wash or work. After Prime came the conventual Mass and time for reading (in winter), but Chapter and work (in summer). After Terce came chapter and work (in winter) but Mass and reading time (in summer). Mixt (for some) would follow Sext in winter but Mass in summer. Mid-day meal followed None in winter but Sext in summer. In winter, after the meal, came reading-time, Vespers, drinking-time, collation reading, Compline and bed. In summer came a siesta followed by None, drinking-time, work, Vespers, supper, collation reading, Compline and bed[608]. Glimpses of this daily round come in a quote from Kirkstall: 'We *stood* at vigils'[609]. On Saturday evenings, before Compline, the monks appointed washed the feet of the community in the cloister: a ceremony witnessed at Zwettl on 1 July 1341, by Duke Albert of Austria[610].

Cistercian Chant

St Stephen Harding (1109–33) is credited with being instrumental in the preparation of the first Cistercian hymnal[611]. This in turn was revised – under the influence of St Bernard – between 1140 and 1147, and came to include over fifty hymns[612]. The reform of liturgical chant may have been early undertaken by William of Clairvaux, later founding abbot of Rievaulx (1132)[613]. The General Chapter, not being convinced that the Cistercian gradual and antiphonary were as accurate as might be, set up what was in reality a 'music committee': headed by St Bernard, but with Abbot Guy of

Cherlieu and Guy d'Eu, a monk of Longpont, and other experts, to revise it further. This also was done by 1147. The revised chant, St Bernard said, was intended to obviate attention being paid more to 'feats of voice than to the meaning of the words'. Simplicity was aimed at, and exuberant phrases – as in alleluias – were simplified[614]. What was sought was 'a virile pitch of recitation and not the theatrical effects of falsetto'[615]. In the thirteenth century a series of statutes of the Chapter prohibited singing in parts (1217)[616] or too loud a voice (1258)[617], or novelties in choir·(1302) – such as the 'hocket' (1320)[618]. Chanting was to be moderate, dignified, and devotional (1258)[619]: it was to be 'as of old' (1302)[620], 'from St Bernard' (1320)[621]. The monks of Dore and Tintern (1217) were rebuked for singing in three-or four-part tones[622]. A Visitor at Hailes told its monks to sing the psalms more slowly, and, at Prime, to make the hymn *Luce matutina oriente,*'the song of jubilation it was, rather than a dirge of lament'[623].

Liturgical Supervision

The general arrangements for the monastic liturgy, and much else, devolved primarily upon the sacristan and the precentor. The sacristan rose early and saw to the lights of the dorter, church and cloister, as well as to the opening and closing of the church doors. He was also responsible for the sounding of the bell for all offices and meals. He had the general care of the church, making sure that it and the sacred vessels were kept clean, and that the necessary candles and oil were available. He had to prepare the abbot's stole and staff as required; and candles, ashes, and palms, for blessing at the due seasons. In all this he had a deputy, his 'helper', and perhaps other assistants[624]. Notable sacristans included Bl. Adam, a twelfth-century visionary at Loccum[625], and Maurin of Boulbonne (1213): the latter advised the visiting Simon de Montfort prior to his victory at the Battle of Muret[626]. The sacristy was generally positioned off a transept end with a connecting door into the presbytery, as at Løgum – where it was lit by two lancet windows)[627]. At the new church of Melrose the sacristy, at a lower level than usual, became known as 'the wax cellar'[628].

The office of the sacristan was a financially semi-autonomous department of the monastery[629]. Grants might be made to, or through, the sacristan for the provision of sanctuary-light oil[630], altar candles[631], and hosts for the Eucharist[632]. At Moreruela the income from the grange of Palazuelos pertained to the work of the sacristan[633]. At Beaulieu (1270) the sacristy account shows that 68 gallons of oil were handled: 23 went to the church, 21 to the dormitories, and 24 to the infirmaries. Almost all the wax from the numerous bee-hives in the enclosure went to the work of its sacristan. Half-a-tun of wine was received for Mass, as well as 140 lbs (64 kg) of wax used for making candles, and 3 lbs (1.4 kg) of incense. A panel was being made for the high altar. A painter was engaged for fifteen weeks, and gold and silver leaf were bought. A clock-maker was employed for five weeks, and there was a stipendiary lay-servant (paid 4 shillings and sixpence p.a.). The church was swept out before all Feasts of Sermon[634]. The most revealing words in the sacristy account are perhaps: 'charcoal for the church in winter in sufficient quantity'[635]. 3 qtrs (38 kg) were obtained, the season suggesting its use to take the chill off the church, as well as to burn incense[636].

The precentor also had an aide: the 'sub-chanter' or succentor. Their duties were primarily concerned with 'encouraging watchfulness and singing' in choir, and they were responsible for the necessary books being in place. The precentor stood on the right-hand side of the choir, the succentor opposite him on the left. The precentor commenced all antiphons and alleluias at the Office, all the sung parts at Mass (as Offertory Verse and Sanctus), and led in with *In terra pax* after the celebrant had intoned *Gloria in excelsis*. Because of his concern with the liturgical books, the precentor was in charge of the book-cupboard. It was he who distributed reading books for Lent, and who closed the armarium each evening. He had other duties: he drew up the rota of readers at Mass, he fixed the grains of incense into the Paschal Candle, he took care of the deeds of profession of new monks, and he sent out the death notices of deceased members. If his abbot so decided, he also safeguarded the charters of the house[637]. Finally, the precentor of Cîteaux had the additional task of keeping the list of all the abbeys of the Order with their dates of foundation and official Latin names. The post of precentor was a responsible one: William Arley who held the position at Dore (1258) had previously (1245) been one of its bursars[638].

The work of precentor and succentor was supplemented by that of two other monks, both appointed on a weekly basis. The hebdomadary celebrated the conventual Mass and led the offices at the Hours. He blessed those going on and returning from journeys. If the abbot was absent, he blessed the candles, ashes, palms, and new fire on the appointed days. He took general charge if abbot, prior and sub-prior, were all away[639]. These latter duties were akin to those of the 'keeper'. The Server of the Church was responsible for the lighting in church, cloister and chapter, for having water ready for the lavabo before Mass, for preparing salt and water for blessing on Sundays before Terce, and for kindling the charcoal in the thurible before the Gospel[640]. He had the specific duty at Cîteaux (1270) of lighting the choir and retro-choir lamps[641].

The early Cistercian statutes contained a number of provisions concerning the church, its furnishings and its vessels – insisting that all abbeys used the same liturgical books[642]. These prescriptions concerning the liturgy were collated into the *Ecclesiastica Officia*. In its earliest form it may date from the time of St Stephen Harding, but it underwent radical reform about 1147 and was modestly revised about 1185 when it came to include the Order's *Book of Usages*. The *Ecclesiastica Officia* thereafter continued to be amended as new relevant statutes were promulgated by the General Chapter[643]. In 1175 the recent canonisation of St Bernard necessitated a revision of the *Book of Usages*: in that year, too, the form for official Visitors to follow was written into the Book[644]. Further corrections were made in 1191 and 1217. Stephen Lexington (1228) therefore called it the *Book of Usages and of New Provisions*[645].

The other safeguards, aimed at promoting decorum and uniformity, came in the injunctions laid down in visitation charters. Most is known of visitations at Hailes in the late-thirteenth century. These dealt with attendance: no monk should be out of choir on a Sunday or feast-day without permission. They related to behaviour: all monks who were not solemn and devout in choir were to be beaten. They regulated for the 'further education' of the juniors: young inexperienced monks were to recite part of the office every day to those appointed to supervise them. They safeguarded the conduct of the services: the Office was not to be rushed with the words slurred together. They ruled as regarding posture: the monks were to genuflect more deeply when crossing before the high altar, and with their cowls drawn back. 'More deeply' may suggest a low bow rather than a bending of the knee. During the last verse of any Psalm all were to rise from their stalls and bow (for the *Gloria Patri*)[646]. The early simplicity of Cistercian worship may have partly disappeared, but there was still a great concern that the humble worship of Almighty God should be worthy of Him. To that end, and for that purpose alone, did the General Chapter legislate and Visitors and abbots regulate, and perhaps for that reason too were such great churches raised.

Notes

1. As by Fergusson and Park (for England), Stalley (for Ireland), Aubert (for France), Holtmeyer (for Thuringia), Kuthan (for Bohemia and Moravia), Kutzner (for Silesia), Fornari (for Italy), and Lorenzen (for Denmark and Sweden), whilst others (as Hahn) write on a broader basis.
2. Stalley (1987) 2.
3. Fergusson (1984b) 15.
4. Cocheril (1982) 242.
5. Lekai (1977a) 269.
6. Grüger (1987) 210.
7. Muheim (1987) 10.
8. Park (1986) 9–10.
9. Lekai (1977a) 264.
10. *Cf.* Park (1986) 6.
11. Fergusson (1984a) 27.
12. Beuer (1957) 280–85 (for Hude and Marienfeld).
13. Fergusson (1984a) 27.
14. Beuer (1957) 268–74.
15. *Ibid.* 285–88.
16. Meslé (1980) 22–29.
17. Hahn (1957) *passim*; *cf.* Stalley (1987) 68.
18. Cocheril (1982) 242.
19. *DHGE* XIX (1981) 470.
20. Wiemer (1982) *passim*, especially pp. 442–43.
21. Stalley (1987) 49.
22. Cocheril (1959b) 74.
23. Beuer (1957) 274–80.
24. Stalley (1987) 58.
25. France (1992) 191.
26. Dr. F.G. Cowley, in a Cardiff lecture in May 1979.
27. Białoskórska (1962) 348, Pajzderski (1916) 60–62.
28. Kinder (1984) 18.
29. Eydoux (1958) 68–74.
30. Platt (1984) 53.
31. Fergusson (1983) 15.
32. *VGA* 5–6, *cf.* Davies (1984) 144–43.
33. Fergusson (1984b) 26*n*; timber church foundations have recently (1996) also been excavated at Buków Abbey (Poland).
34. Coppack (1990) 46.
35. Burton (1989) 41.
36. *Statuta* I, 146 (1191/90), *cf.* 147 (1192/4), 151 (1192/31).
37. Fergusson (1984b) 147.
38. Dustin (1973) 26.
39. France (1992) 343.
40. Davies (1984) 131.
41. Fergusson (1984b) 150.
42. Coppack (1990) 57.
43. Chèvre (1973) 88.
44. Fergusson (1983) 123.
45. Dustin (1973) 31.
46. *DHGE* II (1914) 26.
47. Fergusson (1984b) 61, 128.
48. Gilyard-Beer (1986) 177.
49. Robinson (1995) 32–33.
50. Gloede (1965) 53.
51. Łużniecka (1995) 46, 191.
52. Steger (1984) 149.
53. Courtois (1982) 324.
54. Jansen (1987) 80.
55. *CDN* 28, *cf.* Schittekat (1966) 29.
56. Meekings (1979) 27–28.
57. *VRL* 5.
58. Davies (1984) 131.
59. *OLSB* VII–VIII.
60. *AZ* 683, *KZ* 691.
61. Fergusson (1984a) 134.
62. *CP* I, 109.
63. *DHGE* XII (1953) 157.
64. Williams (1976) 3.
65. Baigent (1882) 13.
66. Dimier (1964) 102.
67. Dimier (1954) 54.
68. Cocheril (1982) 632.
69. De Rouey (und.) 7.
70. Stalley (1987) 45.
71. Gilyard-Beer (1986) 177.
72. Swartling (1976b) 9–10.
73. *RCH* 57, Gergelyffy (1960) 269.
74. Stalley (1987) 44.
75. Steger (1985) 88.
76. *CWK* 92.
77. VCH, *Hampshire* II (1903) 147–41.
78. Zakin (1979) 57–58.
79. France (1992) 155–57; Schiorring (1986 Noirlac Conference).
80. Schiorring (1986) Noirlac Conference.
81. Anstett (1987) 22–26.
82. Fotheringham (1890) 13.
83. Durand (1984) 81.
84. Stalley (1987) 106–07.
85. *Ibid.* 90.
86. Kinder (1982) 397, (1983) 326.
87. Zakin (1979) 71.
88. Butler and Given-Wilson (1979) 322.
89. Schmidt (und.) 3–4.
90. *DHGE* XI (1949) 120.
91. Einsingbach (1988) 6.
92. English Heritage Guide, *Buildwas Abbey* (1985) 3.
93. *DHGE* II (1914) 792.
94. Wilson (1986) 86.
95. Stalley (1984) 71, (1987) 12, 68.
96. Stalley (1984) 69, (1987) 12, 92.
97. Fotheringham 1–46 *passim*.
98. Lekai (1977a) 273–74.
99. Visual observation.
100. Białoskórska (1962) 347–48.
101. Dimier (1964) 103–04.
102. Williams (1976) 5–6.
103. Łużniecka (1995) 106–07.
104. Dimier (1964) 102, Kinder (1992) 77.
105. Gilyard-Beer (1976) 19.
106. Stalley (1987) 112.
107. *Cf.* Davies (1984) 131, Fergusson (1984a) 142, Gallagher (1982) 53, Jansen (1987) 80, Zakin (1979) 17.
108. *Downside Review* 104 (Jan. 1986) 61.
109. Fergusson (1984b) 15.
110. Williams (1984) I, 17–18.
111. Coulton (1933) 265.
112. *RCH* 32.
113. Williams (1984) I, 133.

114. Lackner (1981) 59–60.
115. *RPR* II, 1503 (No. 18,530).
116. *CDRB* V:2, 47 (No. 502).
117. PRO, C 115/D 19/1895.
118. *CP* I, 70.
119. *FRB* II, 196–97 (No. 211).
120. Fontenay guide-book (non-paginated).
121. *DHGE* X (1949) 1256.
122. *DHGE* XIV (1960) 1040.
123. *CFN* 523–24.
124. *Statuta* III, 507 (1347/8).
125. *AM* II, 282.
126. Baigent (1882) 13, 21.
127. *Statuta* I, 151 (1192/53).
128. Philippe (1991) 115.
129. *Statuta* I, 17 (1134/XVIII); *LCC* (1) 29, (2) 207.
130. Wyrwa (1992) 365–404.
131. Rijksarchief Groninger (Ho.) *OA* 3.
132. *OSBS* (1) 14 (No. 12).
133. *Statuta* I, 499 (1218/70).
134. *EOC* 108–9 (XXII/38).
135. Hockey (1976) 97.
136. *Statuta* I, 404 (1213/1).
137. Waddell (1993 Fontfroide Conference).
138. Park (1986) 124–25.
139. *Ibid.* 124–25, 186–89; *cf.* Wetesko (1991) 158.
140. Stalley (1987) 47–48.
141. *FRB* 540.
142. Park (1986) 189–91.
143. Information of Dr. David Robinson.
144. Anstett (1987) 34–36.
145. Park (1986) 182, 197–99.
146. Van Der Meer (1965) *passim.*
147. Białoskórska (1995) 636, Pl. VI.
148. Arens (1982) 17–21.
149. Visual observation.
150. Král (1987) 23.
151. *Daily Telegraph* (London), 6-01-1985.
152. Zakin (1979) 346–48.
153. Kohler (1994) 31–32, 126–27, 137–41; Pls. 16, 47–48.
154. Gloede (1965) 13.
155. Peugniez (1994) 149.
156. Zarnecki (1972) 76–77.
157. Information of Dr. David Robinson.
158. Stalley (1987) 89–90.
159. Carville (1982a) 52.
160. Van Der Meer (1965) Pl. 98.
161. *Ibid.* Pl. 380, *cf.* Pl. 140.
162. Łużniecka (1995) 87–95.
163. Visual observation.
164. Gerevich (1982) 382.
165. Panagopoulos (1979) 34.
166. Gerevich (1982) 382.
167. Negri (1981) 38.
168. Visual observation.
169. Stalley (1987) 184–87.
170. *Ibid.* 129.
171. Zakin (1979) 18.
172. Information of Dr. David Robinson.
173. Stalley (1987) 130, Zakin (1979) 28, 36.
174. Muheim (1987) 12–22.
175. Łużniecka (1995) 96–97.
176. Morgan (1971) 6.
177. Winkless (1990) 10.
178. Davies (1984) 136.
179. King (1954) 254.
180. Clair (1961) 97.
181. *CMM* II, 64; *cf.* Earle (1906) 21.
182. Williams (1984) I, 138.
183. Colvin (1963) I, 90; *LMT* 177 (No. 18).
184. Stalley (1987) 48, (he was buried there in 1238).
185. Fergusson (1984b) 112, (the king staying there at the time).
186. Meekings (1979) 30.
187. *CPR* 1283/69.
188. Stalley (1987) 48, but *cf. SL* 168 (No. 82).
189. Astill (1994) 542.
190. Fergusson (1984b) 48–49.
191. Butler (1963) 37.
192. Crossley (1939) 88.
193. *CTA* 58–59.
194. Tuulse (1942) 278.
195. Valter (1994) 394.
196. Jacob (1970) 15.
197. Stalley (1980) 293.
198. English Heritage guide, *Buildwas Abbey* (1985) 3.
199. Tobin (1995) 62–63.
200. *DHGE* XVI (1967) 443.
201. Böcek (1938) 29.
202. Heath (1828) non-paginated.
203. Coppack (1990) 55–57, Fergusson (1984a) 139.
204. *Statuta* I, 200–01 (1197/17).
205. Beaulah (1993) 8.
206. Coppack (1990) 57.
207. Cruden (1951) 179.
208. Aubert (1947) I, 313.
209. Butler (1978) 1, (1979) 2.
210. Edenheim (1982) 64.
211. The abbeys were Cwmhir, Cymer, and Maenan.
212. Park (1986) 229.
213. Williams (1992) 78.
213a. Park (1986) 228*n.*
214. Cothren (1982) 119.
215. *Statuta* I, 404 (1213/1), 486 (1218/5).
216. *Statuta* I, 309 (1205/10); *LCC* (2) 208.
217. *Statuta* I, 309 (1205/10); II, 146 (1235/30).
218. *Statuta* I, 309 (1205/10).
219. *Statuta* II, 146 (1235/30).
220. *Statuta* I, 375 (1210/34).
221. Coppack (1990) 55–56.
222. Midmer (1979) 92.
223. Honeyman (1929) 100.
224. Rahtz (1976) 178.
225. Garnder (1955) 31.
226. Eames (1956) 264–65, 276.
227. Bouton (1959) I, 153.
228. Aubert (1947) I, 313; Chappée (1922) 36–55.
229. Cazes (1982) 239.
230. Lewis (1976a) 14–15, 30, 34.
231. Honeyman (1929) 100.
232. Knight (1850) *passim.*
233. Lewis (1976a) 3.
234. Cothren (1982) 116.
235. Gerevich (1977) 183.
236. Astill (1994) 541–42.
237. Blary (1989) 339, 352; (1990) 47; Lohrmann (1983a) 214–16 (where illustrated).

238. *CDAA* 125.
239. *RCCH* I 66.
240. Péchenard (1883) 347.
241. Courtois (1982) 349.
242. Arvidsson (1986) 26–29.
243. Wollenberg (1984) 251.
244. Platt (1969) 224.
245. Eames (1956) 271–72.
246. Van Nerom (1993) 50.
247. Eames (1961) 141–43.
248. Beaulah (1993) 9, *cf.* Eames (1956) 273–76.
249. Blary (1989) 338–39, (1990) 47.
250. PRO, E 315/54, f. 209; 315/48, f. 293.
251. Bru (1982) 215.
252. *Statuta* I, 31 (1134/LXXX); *LCC* (1) 29.
253. Park (1986) 5, Fergusson (1984b) 10.
254. *LCC* (2) 208, *cf.* Park (1986) 10.
255. Lymant (1980) 345; Zakin (1979) 198, 204.
256. Richter (1993) 169.
257. Zakin (1979) 204.
258. Brisac (1982) 133.
259. Lillich (1993) 238.
260. Zakin (1979) 47–52.
261. *Ibid.* 38–42.
262. *Ibid.* 72–75.
263. Elm (1980) 346–49.
264. Zakin (1979) 200, 356–68 (illus.).
265. Richter (1993) 165–68.
266. Coppack (1986 Noirlac Conference).
267. Richter (1993) 170–71, *cf.* Zakin (1979) 7, 30.
268. Zakin (1979) 5.
269. Richter (1993) 170–72.
270. Aubert (1947) I, 313*n*.
271. *Ibid.* I, 313.
272. Zakin (1982b) 147.
273. Williams (1984) I, 138–39.
274. Lillich (1982) xii, Muheim (1985) 26.
275. Van Der Meer (1965) Pl. 118.
276. Fergusson (1984b) 44.
277. Van Der Meer (1965) Pls. 504, 522.
278. *Ibid.* Pls 156, 685, 576, 379, respectively
279. *Ibid.* Pl. 855, *cf.* Pl. 861 (San Galgano).
280. Fotheringham (1890) 25.
281. Muheim (1985) 26.
282. Fotheringham (1890) 24.
283. Muheim (1985) 26, Stalley (1987) 75.
284. Harrison and Barker (1987) 134–49.
285. Aubert (1931) 78.
286. Information of Dr A. Wyrwa.
287. Aubert (1947) I, 299.
288. Schich (1979b) 157–58, *cf.* Elm (1980) 231.
289. Donkin (1978) 134, *cf. VRL* 24, 44, 131, 138–40; Crossley (1939) 72.
290. Valter (1994) 391.
290a. Charvátová (1987) 122.
291. Vila-Grau (1993) 158–59.
292. Schneider (1974) 311, 314.
293. *Ibid.* 315.
294. Harrison and Barker (1987) 148.
295. Rigold (1977) 334–36.
296. *Statuta* I, 61 (1157/16); *LCC* (2) 207.
297. Fergusson (1984b) 47, *cf. Statuta* I, 471 (1217/27), 495 (1218/53).
298. *C.C.R.* 1244/209.
299. *C.C.R.* 1237/470.
300. Aubert (1947) I, 369.
301. *Statuta* III, 135 (1274/39).
302. Malone (1984) 60.
303. Fergusson (1984b) 47.
304. Information of Dr David Robinson.
305. Gilyard-Beer (1976) 27.
306. Visual observation.
307. Bedini (1964) 152–53.
308. Williams (1974) 64–66.
309. Esquieu (1986) 12.
310. Carville (1982a) 47–48.
311. Muheim (1987) 10.
312. Stalley (1987) 148.
313. *CDK* 134.
314. Dautrey (1982) 87.
315. *AM* II, 340.
316. Tardieu (1980) 112.
317. Earle (1906) 21.
318. *FRB* 544.
319. Peyron (1982) 218*n*.
320. De Laplane (1863) 24.
321. The *Ecclesiastica Officia* (*EOC* 405) distinguishes between the great bell (*signvm*) and the lesser (*campana minor*).
322. *Statuta* I, 62 (1157/21); *cf.* Leclercq (1954) 77.
323. *Cf. EOC* 405 where: '*nec signvm in ecclesia nec campana in refectorio*'.
324. Meekings (1979) 24, *cf.* Hockey (1976) 22.
325. *DCK* 199.
326. Williams (1889) 144.
327. *CPL* xxxviii–ix, 13, 20.
328. Occhipinti (1985) 335.
329. Moorhouse and Wrathmell (1988) 150.
330. *ABB* 207.
331. *ACA* 303; *CC* (2) B. 43.
332. Williams (1889) Appx. ii.
333. *Statuta* I, 296 (1204/9).
334. Earle (1906) 21.
335. Davidson (1843) 85.
336. *AM* II, 321.
337. *LCC* (1) 35, (2) 211.
338. *Statuta* I, 49 (lit. '*seek forgiveness*'), 429 (1214/61), 434 (1215/1).
339. *Statuta* I, 72 (1160/13).
340. *EOC* 405–06.
341. *Ibid.* 405–06.
342. *SL* 164 (No. 59).
343. *Statuta* III, 369 (1325/1: '*trino*').
344. *CFN* 524 ('in medio').
345. *SL* 165 (No. 66).
346. *CE* 101–02 (No. 93).
347. *Statuta* I, 68 (1157/70).
348. Williams (1984) II, 206.
349. *DHGE* X (1938) 60.
350. *CFN* 524.
351. Davidson (1843) 47.
352. *CWK* 96.
353. Stalley (1987) 276.
354. Williams (1976) 3.
355. Van Der Meer (1965) Pl. 11.
356. Albergo (1980) 31, 81 (reconstruction).
357. *Statuta* I, 17 (1134/XX); *LCC* (1) 29–30, 32–33; (2) 209.
358. *Statuta* I, 61 (1157/15).
359. Holdsworth (1986) 54.
360. *Statuta* I, 98 (1185/4); *LCC* (1) 32–33.
361. *LCC* (2) 209.

362. *LFZ* 137.
363. De Montesquiou (und.) 15.
364. Sommer-Ramer (1982) 149.
365. *SL* 165 (No. 66).
366. *Statuta* II, 185 (1238/1).
367. *RBM* IV, 325 (No. 829).
368. Richardson (1981a) 36; *cf.* Aubert (1947) I, 148*n*.
369. Pontus (1966) 55.
370. Aubert (1947) I, 148.
371. *Statuta* II, 85 (1238/1).
372. *Statuta* III, 2 (1262/8).
373. Leclercq (1954) 77.
374. *Statuta* I, 399 (1212/43).
375. *DD* 587.
376. *CHDM* (1) 75.
377. King (1965) 76.
378. Negri (1981) 37.
379. Occhipinti (1985) 327.
380. Richardson (1981a) 36.
381. Williams (1889) 153.
382. *CE* 101–02 (No. 93).
383. *DD* 587.
384. Fergusson (1984b) 9, Park (1986) 183.
385. *Statuta* I, 404 (1213/1).
386. *LCC* (1) 208; *cf. RSL* II, 213 (No. 1), 214 (No. 1).
387. Park (1986) 184, *Statuta* II, 218 (1240/12).
388. *Statuta* III, 11 (1263/9).
389. Park (1986) 387.
390. Davidson (1843) 47.
391. Sadler (1993) 101–02.
392. Smidt (1931) 61, 96–97.
393. Owen (1971) 82.
394. Ehresmann (1984) 178–200.
395. *CMM* II, 237, *cf.* Earle (1906) 21.
396. *Statuta* II, 422 (1256/6); *cf.* Swartling (1969) 37.
397. *Statuta* I, 33 (1134/1).
398. Fergusson (1984b) 74–77.
399. *AM* II, 301–02, 309–10.
400. Gilyard-Beer (1987) 49.
401. Fergusson (1984b) 44–45.
402. Waeber-Antiglio (1976) 236–37.
403. English Heritage guide, *Buildwas Abbey* (1978) 3.
404. Van Der Meer (1965) Pl. 681.
405. Williams (1889) 224–27 (with plates).
406. *DHGE* XII (1953) 1058.
407. King (1954) 253.
408. Laeman (1898) 88–89, *cf. AM* II, 282, 301–02, 309–10 (Waverley); *KKA* 45, *VGA* 7, 10 (Aduard).
409. Muheim (1985) 15.
410. VCH, *Gloucester* II (1907) 95.
411. Cazes (1982) 233–34; *cf. AZ* 684, *CZ* 865 (Zwettl).
412. Laeman (1898) *passim*.
413. *Ibid*. 88–89.
414. Beaumont (1921) 71.
415. Sommer-Ramer (1982) 148.
416. NLW, Penrice and Margam Charter 2067.
417. *CP* I, 112–13.
418. Park (1986) 187.
419. Lancaster (1984) 7.
420. *CE* 158.
421. Auvry (1897) 305–06.
422. *DHGE* XX (1984) 577.
423. *AF* 142–43.
424. Walker (1983) 55.
425. *RCC* III, 424 (No. 1176), *cf.* Aubert (1947) I, 148*n*.
426. *CMM* I, 361; *cf. CP* I, 112–13 (Pforta).
427. *Statuta* I, 112 (1189/12); *LCC* (1) 34, (2) 210.
428. Stalley (1980) 268–69.
429. King (1954) 346–47.
430. *CE* 99–100 (No. 92), *cf.* 102 (No. 93).
431. *Statuta* I, 17 (1134/XX) – even the image of Christ disallowed at first; I, 85 (1177/45), 404 (1213/1); *LCC* (2) 208; *cf.* Stalley (1987) 47, 179.
432. *Statuta* I, 304 (1240/40).
433. *Statuta* I, 458–59 (1216/45).
434. Dautrey (1982) 87.
435. *VGA* 10.
436. Davidson (1843) 148.
437. Ménabrea (1843) 233; (another at Fontenay: Van Der Meer [1965] Pl. 99).
438. Anstett (1987) 34.
439. Yañez Neira (1977) Pl. 34.
440. Lillich (1993) 260.
441. Schmidt (und.) 32.
442. Beuer-Szlechter (1970) Pl. opp. 208; Carville (1984) 17.
443. Dickinson (1965) 12.
444. Van Der Meer (1965) Pl. 469.
445. *FRB* 544.
446. Richardson (1994) 18.
447. Lillich (1982a) 147*n*.
448. Information of Dr. David Robinson.
449. Stalley (1980) 283.
450. *EOC* 401–02.
451. Jażdżewski (1992) 108.
452. Gerevich (1977) 179–85, (1982) 390.
453. *DHGE* XV (1963) 547.
454. Lekai (1977a) 269.
455. Van Der Meer (1965) 282.
456. Arenas (1985) 32, Rosenman (1983) 325–26.
457. *Cf.* Van Der Meer (1965) Pl. 742.
458. Coppack (1990) 56–57.
459. Walsh (1982) 102–08.
460. Crossley (1939) 39.
461. *C.C.R.* 1232/38 (and see Chapter 9).
462. *CMM* II, 64.
463. Fergusson (1984a) 132.
464. VCH, *Warwick* VI (1951) 80.
465. Van Der Meer (1965) Pl. 466.
466. *Ibid*. Pl. 362.
467. Coppack (1990) 20–21.
468. *Statuta* I, 139 (1191/30).
469. Anstett (1987) 4, 28.
470. Robinson (1995) 48.
471. Gilyard-Beer (1987) 48.
472. English Heritage guide (1985) 3.
473. Coppack (1994) 6.
474. *EOC* 401–02.
475. *CDCS* 146.
476. *EOC* 286 (XCVIII/34).
477. *Statuta* III, 35 (1339/49); *CMM* III, 35, *cf.* II, 119 (for the stalls).
478. *RCOC* col. 1647, cap. I.
479. Durand (1984) 5.
480. *Cf.* Stalley (1987) 65, Swartling (1969) 47–48.
481. Halkin (1970) 40.

482. Heutger (1985) 150.
483. *EOC* 190–91; *cf*. Aubert (1947) I, 148.
484. Edenheim (1982) 40–41; *cf*. (1987) 64 (for Ireland).
484a. Muheim (1985) 24, (1987) 48.
485. Robinson and Platt (1995)
486. Stalley (1987) 64.
487. Waeber-Antiglio (1976) 236–37.
488. Anstett (1987) 10, 20.
489. Richards (1968) 69.
490. Robinson (1995) 42.
491. Kohler (1994) 147–50 (and footnotes).
492. Whone (1987) 142.
493. Anstett (1987) 10, 20; Richards (1968) 87.
494. Kohler (1994) 124, 134.
495. *RBS* I, 69.
496. Bruzelius (1981) 35.
497. Kohler (1994) 124.
498. King (1954) 119.
499. Anstett (1987) 4.
500. *CFN* 524.
501. *CCD* 73.
502. Kohler (1994) 156 (recorded in 1300).
503. Richardson (1981a) 7.
504. *Statuta* I, 36 (1152/5); *LCC* (1) 34, (2) 210.
505. Aubert (1947) I, 48; Pontus (1966) 55.
506. *EOC* 190–91 (LXVII, *passim*); *cf*. *Statuta* I, 200–01 (1196/17).
507. *CDCS* 146.
508. Aubert (1947) I, 148*n*.
509. *UKAR* 31 (No. 46).
510. *RCC* II, 53 (No. 599).
511. *Trans. Cumberland and Westmorland Antiq. Arch. Soc*. VII (1884) 310–11; Kelly (1926b) 266–67.
512. Lackner (1971) 29.
512a. Lekai (1977a) 255.
513. *Statuta* I, 32 (1134/LXXXIV).
514. *EOC* 158 (LIII/24–30).
515. *LSB* 100 (No. 72).
516. Lekai (1977a) 254–55.
517. *Statuta* I, 58 (1154/27).
518. *Statuta* I, 83 (1175/10).
519. Lackner (1971) 33.
520. *Statuta* I, 369 (1210/5), 434 (1215/1); *LCC* (2) 229 ('*petant veniam*' : colloq.'bend the knee').
521. *Statuta* I, 33 (1134/12), *cf*. I, 116 (1189/36).
522. *LCC* (1) 32.
523. *Statuta* II, 477 (1261/9); *DHGE* XXII (1988) 1257.
524. Lekai (1977a) 254.
525. *EOC* 32–33, 184–85 (LX).
526. *Cf*. *EOC* 180–81 (LXIIII/3), 200 (LIX/1).
527. *RCC* IV, 173 (No. 1452).
528. *Statuta* I, 146 (1191/92), 148 (1192/9); *LCC* (1) 35, (2) 209.
529. *RCC* II, 308.
530. *CF* 138.
531. Hockey (1970) 62.
532. *CBP* 59 (No. LVIII).
533. *CHDM* (2) 117.
534. VCH, *Essex* II (1907) 127.
535. *CCR* 1242/79; VCH, *Hampshire* II (1903) 148.
536. VCH, *Hampshire* II (1903) 140, 144; *cf*. VRL 55.
537. Fergusson (1984a) 10.
538. *CAS* I, 171 (No. CLXXVIII).
539. Fergusson (1984a) 142.
540. *Ibid*. 44*n*.
541. Barnes (1982) 52.
542. Hockey (1976) 22.
543. Fergusson (1984a) 10.
544. Meekings
545. *CAS* I, 171 (No. CLXXVIII).
546. *RBS* I, 69.
547. Williams (1984) I, 140.
548. Lekai (1977a) 254.
549. *Statuta* I, 335 (1207/7); *LCC* (1) 31–32.
550. *Statuta* I, 298–99 (1204/16)
551. *Statuta* II, 48 (1226/2), *LCC* (2) 209, *cf*. Lekai (1977a) 254, *Statuta* I, 93 (1183/12).
552. *Statuta* II, 425 (1257/1); *DHGE* XII (1953) 939.
553. Aubert (1947) I, 148; *cf*. *Statuta* I, 98 (1185/4); *SL* 160 (No. 24).
554. *Cf*. *PCP* 188 (No. 124 of 1189).
555. *Statuta* I, 186 (1195/25); II, 84 (1230/1).
556. '*oleo papaverino*'.
557. *LFZ* 538.
558. Waller (1903) 357.
559. *CDEM* VI, 240–41.
560. *RBM* II, 463 (No. 1097).
561. *Statuta* III, 82 (1270/11).
562. *Statuta* III, 254 (1288/1).
563. *CE* 122, 130.
564. *LFZ* 15.
565. Lekai (1977a) 248–49; all of which Peter Abelard described as 'novel' (Waddell [1976] 80–83).
566. Lekai (9177a) 256.
567. *EOC* 182–83 (LVIX:17).
568. *EOC* 148 (L:1).
569. *EOC* 148 (L:2); p. 407 gives a differing arrangement: in winter, Vespers of Dead after regular Vespers, and Nocturns-Lauds of Dead after regular vigils; in summer, Vespers- Nocturns after regular Vespers, Lauds after regular Lauds.
570. *Statuta* I, 46–47 (1152/6), 101–02 (1185/28); *cf*. Lekai (1977a) 256.
571. *Statuta* I, 48 (1152/19); *cf*. *CNM* 239, Harper-Bill (1980) 109.
572. *LMP* 302.
573. Kaul (1949) 52–61.
574. *EOC* 397, *cf*. 154, and *NG* IV, 240.
575. *EOC* 66 (I:1).
576. *EOC* 70 (IV:1), 71 (No. 4).
577. Clark (1895) 207.
578. Birch (1897) 139; *cf*. *EOC* 142 (XLVII:6).
579. Kempf (1976) 52.
580. *Statuta* I, 19 (1134/XXVII).
581. *EOC* 92 (XV: 1, 3–4, 6–7).
582. *EOC* 96–97 (XVII: 2, 4).
583. *EOC* 102 (XXI: 7–23, 33).
584. *EOC* 100 (XX: 2), 102 (XXI: 24–25).
585. *EOC* 108 (XXII: 239–30, 32).
586. *Statuta* III, 242 (1289/1).
587. *EOC* 112 (XXIII: 8).
588. *Statuta* I, 232 (1199/53).
589. *Statuta* III, 82 (1270/11).
590. *CP* 255–59.
591. Jażdżewski (1992) 150.
592. *EOC* 118 (XXVIII: 2).
593. *DHGE* XII (1953) 957–58; *cf*. *Statuta* III, 357 (1321/19).

594. *TL* 89.
595. *LCC* (2) 223; *cf. DMLH* II, 190 (No. 402), 311 (No. 486).
596. *Statuta* III, 114 (1273/1).
597. *Statuta* I, 284 (1203/1), 298 (1204/15); II, 476 (1261/4).
598. *Statuta* I, 482 (1217/74); II, 420 (1255/48).
599. *Statuta* II, 10 (1221/50), 141 (1235/15); III, 56 (1267/64).
600. *Statuta* II, 172 (1237/21).
601. *Statuta* II, 465 (1260/20).
602. *Statuta* I, 482 (1217/72).
603. Sommer-Ramer (1982) 149.
604. *Statuta* II, 394 (1253/24).
605. *Statuta* II, 72 (1228/32), 453 (1259/29); III, 63 (1268/24).
606. *DD* 1498.
607. *EOC* 36.
608. *EOC* 33–34; 236 (LXXXII: 6).
609. Clark (1895) 185.
610. *KZ* 691.
611. Lackner (1971) 6–7.
612. *CHA* (2–3) 191–92 (Nos 1070, 1074).
613. *DHGE* XXII (1988) 997–98.
614. Lekai (1977a) 250–52.
615. *Statuta* I, 30 (1134/LXXIII).
616. *Statuta* I, 472 (1217/31).
617. *Statuta* II, 435 (1258/2).
618. Lekai (1977a) 252.
619. *Statuta* II, 435 (1258/2).
620. *Statuta* III, 306–07 (1302/14).
621. *Statuta* III, 349 (1320/9); *cf. SL* 167 (No. 76).
622. *Statuta* I, 472 (1217/31).
623. Harper-Bill (1980) 108.
624. *EOC* 318–21.
625. *DHGE* I (1912) 466.
626. *DHGE* X (1938) 60.
627. Van Der Meer (1965) Pl. 705.
628. Richardson (1981a) 26.
629. *Cf. ABB* 240–43, De Moreau (1909) 231.
630. *Cf. CW* 240–41.
631. *Cf. CNM* 239.
632. *Cf. CBP* 59 (No. LVIII); *CF* 138.
633. Antón (1986) 390–91 (No. 78).
634. *ABB* 240–43, *cf.* 235, 299.
635. *ABB* 240.
636. *ABB* 242.
637. *EOC* 322–24, *cf.* Harper-Bill (1980) 105–06.
638. Williams (1976) 10–12.
639. 298–300 (CIII).
640. *EOC* 303 (CV).
641. *CDCS* 146.
642. *Statuta* I, 13 (1134/III); *cf.* Lackner (1971) 12.
643. Waddell (1978a) 35, 39–46; (Exeter Coll. Oxon., MS 1, is an example).
644. *Statuta* I, 85 (1175/43–44).
645. *SL* 162 (No. 4), *cf. Statuta* I, 109 (1188/9), 145 (1191/85), 495 (1218/52).
646. Harper-Bill (1980) 107–08.

Chapter 11

THE CLAUSTRAL COMPLEX

The Cloister

The cloister was in a real sense 'the home of the monk', from which he had direct access to the chambers of the monastery as well as to the church. Ideally it was sited to the south of the church – so gaining for the north range (mostly used for sacred reading) extra sunlight and protection from cold northerly winds[1]. Relief dictated that some cloisters were placed to the north of the church – to solve problems of drainage and water supply – as at Alcobaça[2] and Pontigny[3]. Cloisters were generally square, but exceptions included those at Le Thoronet – trapezoidal[4] and Basingwerk – rectangular[5]. Size varied proportionally to the length of the church. Early cloisters of the Romanesque period were barrel vaulted, as at Aiguebelle[6]. Gothic period cloisters were often rib vaulted – as at Fontenay (where subdued leaf moulding on the consoles)[7] and Royaumont (where in brick with fluted columns)[8]. The cloister of Canonica has an unusual thirteenth century network of stone tracery[9]. Relief considerations caused the cloister at Le Thoronet to be stepped, and that at Buildwas to be well below church floor level. The simplicity of a cloister might be relieved by roof bosses and by carved consoles – as those of Ląd, which include the head of a silent Christ and of a thirsty Christ. A cloister console at Maulbronn tells of Prior Walter (d. 1303): 'Let us remember Prior Walter with due devotion, since he completed this building. *Valete in Domino*'[10].

Early cloisters were often timber erections replaced later in stone, though those at nine houses in Ireland remained wooden edifices for three centuries[11]. At some abbeys (as Byland and Jervaulx) stone cloisters were built before the final and great church was complete[12]. Chronicle evidence dates the first stone cloister of Meaux to about 1197–1220[13], and tells of the new cloister being roofed at Croxden in 1332[14]. When (shortly after 1272) work on a new cloister was started at Žďár everything from the old one was transferred there[15]. When Santes Creus had its cloister rebuilt – in the first half of the fourteenth century – the work lasted for thirty years[16]. The custom of burying benefactors in a cloister meant that there was a danger of monks tripping on the gravestones, the General Chapter (1191) therefore ordered that all such slabs be made level with the surface[17]. The floors might in time be tiled (as at the Dunes)[18] or paved (as at Pairis)[19]. The 'door of the cloister' (as noted at San Galgano, 1244)[20] was usually an archway penetrating through the west range[21]. In large abbeys two monks were stationed here to prevent the unauthorised entry of layfolk[22]. The entrance might have a porch – like that built at La Real in 1258[22a].

The north walk of the cloister (or the south walk – if the cloister position was reversed) saw the nightly gathering of the community for the collation reading. This necessitated a stone bench on which the monks could be seated: remains of such benches are visible at Dundrennan[23] and at Løgum – where of brick[24]. The burial of a deposed abbot of Croxden (1308) took place 'in the monks' cloister, outside the church door, *near the bench*'[25]. That 'church door' – the processional entrance for the monks into their choir – was generally carved enhancing its dignity. (The entrance doorway for the *conversi* stood near the west end of the north range – or even beyond it – allowing direct access to their choir). When the founder of Chassagne (1242) was buried it was 'in the cloister of the collation'[26]. When the founder of Le Gard (1176) was interred it was 'in the great cloister, where takes place the Compline reading'[27]. Traces are often visible – as at Cleeve – of the abbot's 'collation seat' recessed into the cloister wall[28]. Opposite was the lectern for the reader – projecting into a bay extending into the cloister garth – as at Strata Florida[29]. A new lectern was built at Boxley in 1373[30]. The monks might sit in the cloister when free or to study, and here too took place the weekly Maundy and the Palm Sunday and other processions.

The Chapter-House

In the east range of the cloister was one of the finest and most important chambers of the monastery, the chapter-house: so called because during the daily meeting here of the community a chapter of the *Rule of St Benedict* was read[31]. This meeting (also called 'chapter') commenced with the reading of the martyrology and concluded with the commemoration of the departed. On Sundays and solemnities, instead of the reading of the *Rule*, a Sermon was preached[32]. There also took place – during chapter – the correction of faults; it was this aspect of the building that caused a twelfth century monk to name it: 'That house where all things are hard'[33]. It was as well that it was forbidden to reveal 'the secrets of chapter' to outsiders[34]. Increasingly, as the centuries passed by, business transactions were agreed – and demises of property made – in the chapter-house. As early as 1170 a grant to Fontmorigny of freedom from toll was made by Count Guy II of Nevers, 'Before the community assembled in chapter'[35]. This suggests that, when necessary, lay-folk were admitted to part of the chapter meeting. The monks could sit and read if they wished in the chapter-house in the interval between Vigils and Prime. The Server of the Church for the week was to kindle a light before the armarium (for books to be borrowed) and in the chapter-house (for them to be read). The monks were not to go to sleep, and they were to have their hoods on in such a way as for others to tell whether they were sleeping or not[36].

The sturdy interior piers of chapter-houses gave way to rib or fan vaulting and bore the weight of the dormitory above. The chambers might be square or polygonal (with one central pier – as at Zwettl) or rectangular (necessitating two or more piers). Two columned chambers included that of Noirlac, four piers – Bebenhausen, six piers – Furness, and eight piers – Tintern[37]. The chapter-houses were lit by windows in the outer wall, usually round-headed Romanesque openings or Gothic lancets. Around the room the monks sat on stone benches, sometimes arranged in tiers – as may still be seen at Fountains[38] and Le Thoronet[39]. Arnsburg and Eberbach, as many abbeys, had one bench with foot-rest[40]. The abbot had a special place, called: 'The place or seat of the president'. It was at this spot that three abbots of Fountains[41] and an abbot of Sawley (interred at Vaudey)[42] were buried. The stone lectern used for reading and preaching can still be seen at Osek and the nunnery of Tišnov, the sockets of their former lecterns survive at Byland and Waverley[43]. An abbot of Fountains was buried close to such an 'analogium'[44]. The chapter-house at Vaucelles, built about 1175 and measuring 18.5 × 18.2 m, was one of the largest in Europe[45].

Any floor space in a chapter-house not taken up by the grave-slabs of abbots might be tiled – as at Tintern[46]. The walls of the chamber at Newminster were colour washed and marked out as ashlar – with joints formed by chocolate and white lines[47]. As beautiful as the interior was, it could be surpassed by the three great carved arches in the wall fronting the east walk of the cloister: these formed the doorway and the windows through which the *conversi* listened to the Sunday Sermon. Growing numbers of monks, or perhaps a desire for a greater ceiling elevation with more air space – not possible below the dorter, meant that some chapter-houses were extended eastwards beyond the outer wall of the east range – as at Garendon – where it projectecd as a semi-poylgon[48]. At Margam, Dore and Whalley the old chapter-house became a vestibule to an entirely new polygonal building[49]. At Aduard (about 1340) an altar of the Holy Souls was erected in the chapter-house[50].

Monastic Burials

It was the privilege of abbots to be buried in the chapter-house, as were nineteen of the superiors of Fountains: their bodies arranged in sequence in rows of four or five graves[51]. It was perhaps because the chapter-house had no space left that at Croxden (1332) an abbot was interred in the church before the altar of St Benedict[52], and at Newenham (1339) under the first arch of the cloister which he had constructed[53]. All the evidence is that by the early fourteenth century grave space in chapter-houses was scarce. When (the later St) Hugh of Bonnevaux died (1183), or soon thereafter, his monks buried him in its church: 'On account of the fame of his holiness'. The General Chapter disapproved, but allowed his body to rest undisturbed[54]. It ordered, however, that the bones of a reputedly holy abbot of Locedio (1218) – who had been interred in its church – were to be transferred to the chapter-house[55]. At Cîteaux (1270) a dead abbot lay for his obsequies in the presbytery of the church with one candle alight at his head and another at his feet[56]. The names of dead abbots, as of other deceased monks, would be inscribed on a mortuary roll sent to other houses asking for prayers: one such survives from Silvacane[57].

The graves of abbots were covered by a stone slab on which was engraved (as on an abbot's seal) either a cowled fore-arm with a hand grasping the pastoral staff or a full length effigy. When Abbot Otto died at Zwettl (1362) its chronicle recorded his interment under 'A stone on which is the image of a pastoral staff'[58]. At Dargun the brass on the grave-slab of Abbot John von Rostock (d. 1336) bore his full length effigy, but that of John Billerbeck (d. 1349) reverted to the hand-and-staff image: the staff appears broken for he was no longer abbot[59]. As on seals of the time the slab of 1336 used Lombardic Capital lettering, that of 1349 showed the current change to Black Letter script. Early slabs might record little more than the name and status of the abbot concerned[60], but later gravestones gave his name, length of rule and date of death: they might also laud his life or seek prayers for his soul[61]. The gravestone of Abbot Jacob of Aulne (d. 1331) outlined his monastic career[62].

The cemetery for ordinary monks lay in the angle between the presbytery of the church and the east range of the cloister: tombstones are to be found in this position at Newbattle and Strata Florida. One former cellarer of Fountains was interred at Furness (1314): 'In the cemetery against the great church of the abbey, namely in the east as it goes to the sacristy'[63]. Sometimes cemetery chapels were built: as at Santes Creus[64] and San Galgano[65]. A *conversus* of Bonnevaux (1194) was buried outside its cemetery because three pence were found on his body when he died, suggesting that he had breached his vow of poverty. He was said to be simple in mind: so the General Chapter allowed his reburial in the cemetery[66]. During the Interdict special arrangements were made for the burial of the dead at Meaux (in the orchard)[67] and Waverley (in a special cemetery)[68]. Interment of the body of a deceased Cistercian did not always mean a final resting-place. When the chapter-house of Melrose was finished (in 1240) the bones of its abbots – which had previously lain near its entrance – were reburied

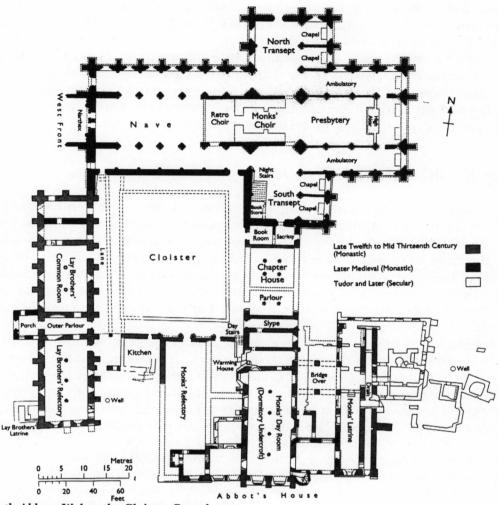

Neath Abbey, Wales: the Cloister Complex.
Reproduced by kind permission of Cadw: Welsh Historic Monuments. Crown Copyright Reserved.

'with great solemnity' in the eastern part of the chamber (i.e. near the president's seat)[69]. At Clairvaux the bones of the first community were transferred in 1148 to a new cemetery, and then – in 1269 – to a charnel crypt[70] under the chapel of the count of Flanders[71]. When cemeteries became full the bones of those a long time dead were often lifted and placed in such charnel houses. These sometimes had a window: the 'death-light', for illumination – as in the 'bone-house' of Doberan which dates from about 1250[72]. A charnel house was built (in 1274) next to the infirmary of the monks at Zwettl: a salutary reminder to its inmates of their ultimate end. It had an altar dedicated to St Andrew the Apostle[73]. An ossuary is to be seen at Sedlec and on record at Velehrad.

Parlours

Next to the chapter-house in the east range – but further away from the church – was the inner parlour: here monks could engage in necessary conversation without infringing the rule of silence. The parlour may also have served as an office for the prior and as a place for the monks to hang their cowls[74]. Business transactions might take place in the parlour. At Rivalta Scrivia (1232) a deed was drawn up: 'In the cloister of our monastery, in the parlour'[75]. The parlour was usually a narrow stone chamber, sometimes piered and vaulted – as at Buildwas[76] and Neath[77]. *Conversi* might have their own parlour between the kitchen and their refectory[78]. At Léoncel (1192) a grant was finalised by a dying female, and confirmed by her son, 'In front of the parlour of the *conversi*'[79]: here it might have been differently positioned. At Tintern the 'outer parlour' (serving perhaps *conversi* and layfolk) formed part of the complex containing the inner gate-house[80]; at Neath the passage at the entry of the cloister served this purpose. Beyond the parlour – at the end of the east range – was a narrow vaulted passage way – the slype – leading to the infirmary complex[81].

The 'Day Room' and the Calefactory

Beyond the slype a sometimes quite long undercroft stretched to the end of the east range. Stone vaulted – to support the dorter above and to lessen the risk of fire – it was not only the largest building of the cloister, but was also one of the most beautiful. Magnificent examples of such sub-dorters include those at Fontenay[82], Neath and San Galgano[83]. At Tintern the chamber – extended by about 1200 – had its own latrine adjacent to the drain complex[84]. This architecturally often splendid building may have been partitioned and employed for more than one purpose – as perhaps novitiate and scriptorium.

The warming-house or calefactory stood at the commencement of the south range (north, where the cloister was so arranged) between the 'day-room' and the refectory. An account of the building of Žďár (c. 1273) described the erection 'after the new cloister, of the chapter-house and also the house where the monks rest'[85]. The calefactory is well-preserved at Fountains (a superb example)[86], Longpont (where it has a central chimney supported by four piers)[87], Silvacane (where the pier capitals are ornamented by flat leaves and acanthi)[88] and Maulbronn (where it was erected about 1250, and its fire fuelled from an adjacent 'heating house' now demolished)[89]. The rooms above the calefactory at Wąchock gained direct central heating *via* air ducts in the stone vaulting[90]. A fire appears to have been lit in the calefactory through the winter months[91], and there is early mention of the *conversi* of Waldsassen collecting wood for it[92]. Apart from enabling the monks to keep warm in rest periods (as after Vigils on Christmas night) it was in the calefactory that scribes prepared their ink[93], monks were bled and shoes were greased – the heat allowing the grease to penetrate the leather[94].

The Monastic Refectory

Beyond the calefactory stood the dining-room or refectory, often a building of some size: 37 m long at Melrose[95], 45 m at Eberbach[96]. Early refectories were aligned parallel to the cloister with an east–west axis – and some so remained (as at Cymer and Sawley), but from about 1170 – in new cloisters being built or in old ones remodelled – there was a tendency to build the refectory with a north-south axis[97]. This allowed the calefactory and the kitchen – situated to either side – to comfortably fit into this range of the cloister[98]. This change (possibly, but not certainly, to accommodate increased numbers of monks) was made, *inter alia*, at Kirkstall[99] and Melrose[100]. Fine examples of Cistercian refectories include open halls – as the barrel vaulted Romanesque dining rooms of Aiguebelle and Poblet and the Gothic refectory of Huerta, and double-aisled early Gothic edifices – like those at Maulbronn and Royaumont[101].

At Croxden the refectory had its own belfry[102]. At Fountains the raised foot-paces and the stubs of stone table-legs can still be traced around the walls[103]. At Poblet a

1. Lacustrine Site: Buków Abbey, Poland

2. Precinct wall: Sweetheart (New) Abbey, Scotland

3. Gatehouse, with adjacent Chapel: Riddagshausen Abbey, Germany.

4. Gatehouse remnant: Zaraka Abbey, Greece.

5a. Abbot's Chapel, Pforta Abbey, Germany.

5b. Monastery Church, Cîrţa Abbey, Rumania.

6. Monastic Church and Cloister: Casamari Abbey, Italy. (*Reproduced by kind permission of the Abbot and Community*).

7. Rose Window ('blind'): Kołbacz Abbey, Poland.

8. The Third Church on Site: Pontigny Abbey, France.

9. Estuarine Site: Dunbrody Abbey – by an inlet of the river Barrow, Ireland.

10. Cistercian Nave: Bélapátfalva Abbey, Hungary.

11. Subsidiary Chapels: Pontigny Abbey, France.

12a. Pier Capitals: Santes Creus Abbey, Spain.

12b. Pier Capitals: Santes Creus Abbey, Spain.

13. Cloister and Fountain House: Santes Creus Abbey, Spain.

14. Cloister Console: Maulbronn Abbey, Germany (telling of Prior Walter).

15. Galilee Chapel: Maulbronn Abbey, Germany.

16. Monastic Prison for Lay Offenders: Villers Abbey, Belgium.

17. Chapter House, Margam Abbey, Wales (as it was until 1799). (*S.H. Grimm, 1777*).

18. Monastic Refectory: Poblet Abbey, Spain.

19. Monastic Infirmary: Ourscamp Abbey, France.

20. *Conversi* Lane: Byland Abbey, England.

21. *Conversi* Dorter: Clairvaux Abbey, France.

22. Estate Enclosure Bank and Ditch: Buków Abbey, Poland.

23. Tanning Pits: Melrose Abbey, Scotland.

24. Dovecot and fortified Barn: Vaulerent Grange (belonging to Chaâlis Abbey, France).

25. Fortified Outpost: Piel Island (belonging to Furness Abbey, England).

26. Vineyard Complex: Colombé-le-Sec (the property of Clairvaux Abbey, France).

27. Vaulted Cellar: Colombé-le-Sec Vineyard.

28. Cistercian Nunnery: *Porta coeli*, Tišnov, Czech Republic – the West Front.

29. Chapter House: *Porta coeli*, Tišnov.

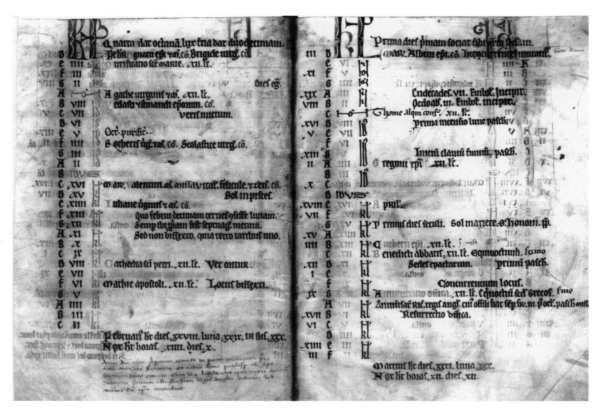

30. Cistercian Calendar (showing February and March) in Exeter College, Oxford, MS1 (formerly belonging to Abbey Dore, England). At the bottom-left has been added a record of the appearance of a comet in 1517. (*Reproduced by the kind permission of the Master and Fellows of Exeter College*).

1.   2.   3.   4.

5.   6.   7.

31.   Cistercian Seals.
1. Abbot's Seal, Buildwas Abbey, Early 13th C.   2. Abbot's Seal, Froidmont, 1225.
3. Abbot's/Common Seal, Grace Dieu (W), mind-14th C.
4. Common Seal, Paradyż, by 1386.   5. Seal of Abbot of Cîteaux, 1227.
6. Second Seal of St Bernard, 1151.   7. Seal of a *conversus* of Fossanova, mid-14th C.

washing fountain stands in the middle of the dining room[104]. A noteworthy feature of every refectory was the raised pulpit from which the monk appointed read during meals to the community seated beneath him: in this way his voice carried above the bustle of the servers and the clatter of plates. Such are still to be seen – often with carved arcading over the steps leading up to them – at Casamari[105], La Bussière[106] and Rueda[107]. At Jerpoint the pulpit necessitated a gable projection in the exterior wall[108]. The floors of refectories were often tiled: as at Cleeve[109] and Rievaulx[110]. The walls might be painted: white, yellow, red and other colours survive at Beaulieu[111]. Above the entrance to the refectory at Aduard was inscribed (in 1268) a rhyming verse: *Sordes mentales magis ablue quam manuales / Inficiunt tales, quia plus qua materiales / Hoc non carnales / sapiunt sed spirituales*[112]. Another feature of many refectories – as at Basingwerk, Huerta[113] and Valcroissant[114] is the hatch-way which allowed food to be served quickly and hot from the adjacent kitchen. The refectory of Beaulieu (1270) had gadgets for catching flies[115].

Monastic Diet

In the summer months Cistercian monks took two meals: dinner (the main meal) after Sext with supper at the setting of the sun, but in the winter months dinner came after None and no supper was taken[116]. In Lent, too, only one meal was eaten and that at the setting of the sun. Breakfast (mixt) consisted of a quarter of a loaf of bread and about one-third of a litre of wine (beer presumably in northern lands): it could be taken by the novices and young monks and (save on fast days)[117] by those *conversi* who had to labour[118]. Those working in the fields ate there, and took a siesta afterwards[119]. At dinner in the refectory the prior presided[120]. The book most commonly read was the bible (in Latin): the Scripture readings in Trinity-tide alone included the 4 Books of the Kings, the parable of Job and the Books of the Maccabees[121]. The monk on duty was to read in such a way as not to provoke levity amongst his hearers[122]. The meal being ended: 'None were to wash their bowl by hand, but those who wish with a cloth', nor 'to wipe their hand or cutlery by cloth unless first wiped with bread'[123]. That done, the community chanted the *Miserere* (Psalm 51 [50]) en route to the church to give thanks[124]. Meanwhile the readers and servers took their meal[125]: this was the 'second table'[126]. In between dinner and supper the monks could go to the refectory for 'drinkings' – after None[127] and after Vespers[128] – the latter perhaps when there was no supper. A monk of St Bernard-opt-Scheldt (1348) was given money: 'for the drinkings of the community'[129]. Silver and gold utensils were forbidden to 'the poor and humble servants of God'[130] – but an abbot of Pipewell once replaced his monks' wooden spoons with silver ones[131]. Pottery used might be local earthenware fired on the premises (as at Kirkstall)[132] or imported (as at Glenluce)[133].

The diet of the early Cistercians was plain and meatless. Meat was only allowed to those who were sick, and even then it was discouraged on Saturdays and in the extended fast from mid-September to Easter[134]. Vegetables (such as beans and peas), bread and water or beer, salt and locally produced herbs (but no pepper or cumin)[135] all formed part of a Cistercian's food supply. Dairy products – milk, cheese and eggs – could be taken, but not in Advent and Lent, nor on the September Ember Days, nor on the vigils of solemnities[136]. Fish – though little eaten at first – became general in the late twelfth century[137], and herrings were common fare in Advent and Lent[138]. The 'black fast' was kept on Fridays in Lent until the late thirteenth century, thereafter only on Good Friday[139]. Abbot Matthew of Melrose (1246–61) won praise from its chronicler: 'It is through him that we have pittance-loaves upon the Fridays in Lent – when we fast on bread and water'[140]. In the twelfth century only coarse bread was usually eaten[141], but 'white bread' was allowed to the sick and those who had been bled – and became general fare in the thirteenth century. Beer was commonly drunk in northern lands, and wine – perhaps little used at first – was widely drunk elsewhere by the late twelfth century[142]. A grant was made to Bonport (as early as 1225) of freedom from toll for 100 tuns of wine – solely intended for the monks' own consumption[143], but at the Dunes Abbot Lambert (who died in 1344) was the first to allow his monks to drink wine. He gave them a pint each day: his successor (Walter Stryc) doubled this allowance, and – as a later chronicler put it – 'He was for ever remembered because of this'[144].

The monotony of the Cistercian diet was varied from the mid-twelfth century (if not earlier) by the addition of supplementary dishes – or better quality food – on certain days. By about 1150 such 'pittances' came to be accepted, if only not to offend the donors[145]. The Order insisted that they were not to be expected as of right, that they were only to be served at the abbot's discretion, and then never on more than two consecutive days. Such days were usually feasts specified by the donor or his or her obit day[146]. Sixty pittances were granted to Villers between 1209 and 1274[147], whilst – by the late fourteenth century – the monks of Zwettl enjoyed 98 days of such extra nourishment[148]. All pittances due were recorded in a monastery's calendar[149] or obit book[150] or cartulary[151]: Henryków had its 'pittance register'[152]. In earlier decades the sub-cellarer might be responsible for arranging the serving of pittances on the appointed days, but by the early fourteenth century a number of large abbeys had their monk-'pittancier'[153].

The numerous pittances granted to the monks of Villers – mostly in the thirteenth century – included fish and wine on St Agnes' Day (21 January), Maundy Thursday – but later transferred to Holy Saturday, and on the feast of the Annunciation (25 March)[154]. Duke Leopold of Austria (1196) made provision for the monks of Heiligenkreuz to receive fish on the four solemnities of Our Lady, oil throughout Advent, and to have – twice a week – more and better quality bread, cheese and wine than was usual. He made one condition: the monks were to give to the poor what was left of the three hundred loaves he provided on pittance days[155]. (This is a pointer to the size of the abbey's community at the time). The Assumption (15 August) brought a pittance at Newminster of 'good bread and ale, salmon and other fish'[156]. Esrum's community enjoyed German ale at Corpus Christi[157]. In addition to its other pittances, money was set aside at Vyšší Brod (1320) so that once a week the community could fish in its fish-pond, because: 'After work it is necessary to have recreation'[158] – an attitude perhaps not shared in the early days of the Order. Such a stance was offset by a benefactor of Sénanque (1297) who refused a pittance to a non-celebrating monk: 'Because he who does not work does not eat'[159]. The effect of pittances was to bring to the monks a wide and nourishing variety of food and drink, making for better health.

Washing before Meals

Cleanliness was extremely important in the Middle Ages – especially before meals – as forks were a rarity and eating was accomplished using only knives, spoons and fingers. Most monasteries had a lead-lined washing trough set in or against the inside wall of the cloister by the refectory door. Emplacements of such troughs – still to be seen – include those of Kinloss (contained in an arched recess)[160], Ourscamp (which has thirty taps above a lead trough)[161], Tintern (two troughs – one to each side of the door)[162] and Whalley (with a stone canopy above and a drain below)[163]. Poblet had an octagonal fountain set in the middle of its refectory: dating from about 1200, it may have outlived its usefulness when the abbey's fountain house was built[164]. A fountain house – set opposite the entrance to the refectory and projecting into the cloister garth – was the later alternative to a washing-trough. It is possible that in some cases they were more decorative than utilitarian[165].

In central Europe some thirty Cistercian abbeys have been identified as having a fountain house. Their shape differed: some were square, some hexagonal, some octagonal, some nine-sided – yet others had a rectangular vestibule terminating in a polygon[166]. Fairly complete remains exist at a number of monasteries including Bronnbach (built in 1411 but replacing an older edifice)[167], Lilienfeld (built about 1287 and restored after a fire in 1810)[168] and Maulbronn (built about 1345 – the second on the site – its upper storey half-timbered)[169]. In western Europe square fountain houses included that at Fossanova, hexagonal – at Santes Creus, and octagonal – at Valmagne. Save for Mellifont there were few fountain houses in northern Europe – perhaps because winter frost would have cracked the basin[170]. In Poland some cloisters were too small to accommodate such a building: the existence of others (as at Kamieniec) has been demonstrated by excavation[171]. The chronicle of the Dunes tells of the building of its fountain house – now long vanished – about 1310[172]. Fountain houses might have a single bowl cut from a block of stone – like at Pontigny[173], or a double-tiered structure – as at Poblet[174], or even a three-tiered edifice – the case at Maulbronn[175]. Some fountain houses are exquisite and still have flowing water.

The Monastic Kitchen

At the west end of the refectory walk of the cloister stood the principal kitchen of a monastery: there were other kitchens attached to the abbot's lodging, guest-house and infirmaries and – in later centuries – a meat kitchen. The main kitchen was conveniently sited – lying as it did between the dining-hall of the monks on the one side and that of the *conversi* on the other – and therefore able to serve both. The building of stone kitchens is chronicled at Meaux (*c.* 1190)[176] and Croxden (*c.* 1225)[177]. Several fine examples survive including those at Chorin (in brick)[178] and at Villers (where a great ventilating shaft)[179]. Kitchen drains are to be seen at Tintern (a stone-lined channel from which late medieval pottery has been recovered)[180] and at Fountains (with a stone-grid covered chute for the disposal of waste)[181]. Immediately south of the principal kitchen at Kirkstall dripping pans have been excavated – indicating (at a late date) the cooking of meat[182]. Access to the kitchen in a Cistercian abbey was restricted[183] – for obvious reasons if a monk was feeling hungry. The usages of the Order directed that two brethren were to be employed each week, on a rota, to serve (and do all that was necessary) in the kitchen[184]. They were probably intended to be monks – though the 'kitchener' at Fontaines-les-Blanches (in 1231) was a *conversus*[185]. Their week ended with a busy Saturday: they had to clean out the reredorter and the washing trough in the cloister, wash in warm water and rinse in cold the towels used for hands and feet, tidy the kitchen itself, get water ready for the Saturday evening washing of feet and bring in wood for Sunday's kitchen fire[186].

The Monastic Dormitory

The dorter of the monks was often of great length – 73 metres at Eberbach[187], 46 metres at Santes Creus[188] – stretching as it did over chapter-house, parlour and 'day-room'. Early dorters might be single chambers (as at Poblet)[189], but the dorters of the thirteenth century were generally two-aisled with a central row of piers (ten at

Eberbach)[190]. Some dorters were vaulted in stone (as Le Val)[191], others had timber roofs at least in part (like Mortemer)[192]. The dorter of Meaux – which may date from 1164 – was not leaded until 1340[193]. Light entered dorters from a range of windows on either side – Romanesque or Gothic – according to the date of construction. The dorter was approached by the 'day stairs', sometimes situated in the angle of the east and south ranges of the cloister[194]. At Walkenried (1323) comes mention of: 'The steps which lead from the porch up to the dorter'[195]. At Santes Creus and Le Thoronet the steps emerge in the middle of the dorter, a low wall around them for safety reasons.

In their dormitory the monks slept (on straw mattresses) fully dressed, as if prepared for the coming of the Lord[196]. They might detach their wood-knife, so as not to injure themselves. It was ruled (in 1272) that all bedclothes were to be of one colour – either white or black[197]. Blankets may have been of serge. Pillows were to have a maximum width of half-a-metre (1237) though later (1257) a 'moderate size' was stipulated[198]. Two or three times a year the prior and sub-prior inspected the beds of the monks and *conversi* to ensure that they were not holding any private property hidden away[199]. There was no privacy in a dorter – as individual cells were forbidden[200]. To prevent any 'irregular behaviour' at night one or two lamps were always kept burning[201]. The hook on which a lantern hung survives at Cleeve: a squint in the end wall allowed it to illuminate the reredorter as well[202].

On rising for Vigils in the early hours, the monks proceeded down another flight of steps ('the night stairs') directly into their choir. At Bordesley these were originally in timber, but were replaced in stone after an early thirteenth century fire[203]. Impressive flights of steps are still to be seen at Holy Cross[204] and Alvastra[205]. At Dore and Valle Crucis the stairs are no more, but the doorway opening on to them remains. The vacant space (seen at Noirlac[206] and Silvacane[207]) under the night stairs might have found use as the monastic prison. Chambers might also exist under the day stairs: like the twelfth century cylindrical vault at Flaran and the thirteenth century rib-vaulted room at Vauclair. It was in the chamber under the day stairs at Clairvaux that St Bernard's secretary, Nicholas, worked. That at Noirlac has traces of fastenings for iron bars – suggesting its use as a prison – but the windows were usually so small that bars were not really necessary[208].

At the far end of the dorter was the latrine or '*necessarium*', literally the reredorter. This was placed over a body of running water: sometimes natural – like the river Sénacole at Sénanque[209], sometimes artificial – as the stone-lined channel at Furness[210]. The privy shafts of the early twelfth century reredorter still exist at Fountains[211]. The usages of the Order allowed Cistercian monks to go to the reredorter 'whenever they have need' and to use 'modesty and discretion when undressing and dressing'[212].

Prisons

Erring monks needed to be secured. By 1188 abbots held in chains those guilty of arson or theft[213]. The murderer of an abbot of Trois Fontaines (1181) was kept under close guard until he could be brought to justice: he was not to be allowed 'to escape or die of hunger'[214]. The troubles that stemmed from religious with false vocations led the General Chapter to permit (1206) and then insist (1229) that where it was possible 'solid and strong' prisons be made to hold criminal and apostate monks[215]. Incarcerated monks were held in chains, unshaved and deprived of their habit, and often on a diet of bread and water: 'the bread of adversity and the water of affliction' (Isaiah 30:20)[216]. Those sentenced to perpetual imprisonment could only have their term ended by order of the General Chapter: 'Life' imprisonment meant just that![217] Amongst those refractory monks detained were arsonists, murderers (Cherlieu,

1226)[218], conspirators (Garendon, 1196)[219] and forgers (Paradyź, 1247)[220]. Frequently the sentence had to append the words: 'If he can be taken', for – not unnaturally – many fled before punishment could be exacted. Former prisons can be seen at Fountains (in the basement of the abbot's house)[221], Noirlac (under the day stairs)[222] and Santes Creus (off the infirmary cloister). At Fontenay the prison was a semi-dungeon: inscribed on its walls are the telling words of Psalm 121: 'The sun shall not strike thee by day, neither shall the moon by night'.

The West Range

Fronting the west walk of the cloister was another lengthy two-storeyed building – the west range – the domain of the cellarer and the *conversi*. Where it was in line with the west front of the church, it formed an imposing aspect. The range was 108 metres long at Melrose[223], 95 metres at Fountains[224] and 93 metres at Eberbach[225]. The upper storey consisted of the dorter and reredorter of the *conversi*; the lower floor or undercroft contained their refectory, chapter room, calefactory and infirmary, as well as the cellarer's office, store rooms and workshops. The range might be pierced by the main cloister entrance – thus separating the refectory from the rest of the building. The extension of the range at Fountains in the late twelfth century may reflect the large number of *conversi* at that time[226], but in Denmark the west ranges were not built until there were few *conversi* left – and were presumably primarily intended for storage and craft purposes[227].

The undercroft might be an open chamber (as at Fontfroide)[228], but frequently a central row of stone piers divided it into two aisles[229]. At Clairvaux two rows of piers made three aisles with both undercroft and dorter vaulted in stone. The length of time taken to build the range is reflected by changes in architectural style: round-headed Romanesque windows in the undercrofts of Clairvaux and Kołbacz, but pointed Gothic lancets in the later dorters above[230]. The outstanding beauty of some undercrofts today was lost in the Middle Ages – since they were divided by wooden (even stone) partitions to form the necessary rooms for eating, meeting and work[231]. The alley-way or *conversi* 'lane' – which in some monasteries insulated the west walk of the cloister from the bustle of the west range – may also have served as an area where the *conversi* could rest and congregate. It led directly to the *conversi* entrance into the church – at Hovedøya *via* a western porch[232]. The 'lane' at Byland had thirty-five stone recesses for seats[233], that at Fontfroide was covered[234].

In their refectory the *conversi* ate the same food at the same time as the monks, and shared in any available pittances. They sat wearing their cloaks, the senior of them leading the responses and the Lord's Prayer before and after meals[235]. Before their dining-halls were built they presumably ate in wooden structures or even with the monks – for some reason a practice at Chaloché in 1231[236]. The question also arises as to where the *conversi* slept before their own especial dorters were constructed[237]. As late as 1202 the General Chapter ordered them 'not to sleep near the grooms in the stables, but separately in another place assigned to them'[238] – suggesting that at that date a number of monasteries did not have a purpose-built dormitory for them. Their dorter at Fountains dates from the 1170s[239]; at Meaux it was built about 1210[240] and at Poblet around 1235[241]. At the Dunes two 'towers' (presumably having spiral staircases) led up to the dorter[242]. The night stairs remain at Tintern[243]. At Staffarda – by 1349 – there were cells in the dorter, and (perhaps because of the decline in *conversi* numbers) various offices (including the tailor's workroom) were linked to it[244]. The *conversi* reredorter at Fountains spanned the river Skell and had two rows of seats back to back, a wooden partition between them[245].

A statute of the General Chapter in 1189 assumed that there were separate infirmaries for the monks and the *conversi*[246], but in some instances (as perhaps at Longuay[247] and Sorø[248]) the building may have been a shared one. The *conversi* infirmary at Roche stood close to their reredorter[249], that at Meaux was built about 1260[250], and those of Fountains and Furness had a series of arched recesses into which the beds fitted[251]. At Aduard Abbot Gijlard (1305–29) built an altar in the infirmary[252]. The infirmarian of the *conversi* might speak to a sick bed-bound patient – but only to one at a time – and in such a way that 'others may not hear what is being said'. To patients able to get up he could speak in an area set somewhat apart[253]. One infirmarian of Zwettl (Hainricus) was praised by his abbot for his 'industry and care'[254]. No *conversus* could enter the infirmary – unless obviously gravely ill – until sickness had kept him out of choir for at least three days[255].

The Monastic Infirmary

The *Rule of St Benedict* insisted that: 'Before all things and above all things care must be taken of the sick'[256]. The monastic infirmary was sited to the south-east or north-east of the cloister (depending on the position of the latter) and usually at a little distance away: this allowed for a relaxation of monastic discipline without this disturbing or infecting the main body of the community. The infirmary was (in large abbeys at least) a self-contained complex consisting of the hospital hall – with rooms attached for eating and for the infirmarer, a latrine block, a kitchen and – sometimes – a chapel. Additionally the infirmary might have its own small cloister. Some of the infirmaries built in stone in the thirteenth century may have replaced earlier timber structures[257]. The two principal infirmary halls still to be seen practically in their entirety are at Aduard – now the local parish church, and at Ourscamp – now the monastery church of the Servants of Jesus and Mary.

The hospital hall could be of great size and elevation: that of Ourscamp measures 46 × 16 metres and – above the stone vault borne by two rows of lofty piers – is an immense roof cavity approached by a spiral staircase[258]. The large dimensions caused the buildings to be sometimes called the 'great infirmary' (Aduard, 1297)[259] or the 'great hall' (Croxden)[260]. The number of beds might be determined from the number of recesses ranged (as at Furness)[261] along the wall, or from the niches (seen at Fossanova and Villers) in the walls – one per bed. The niches were perhaps the 'bedside lockers' of those days. At Louth Park Abbot Richard's (1220–47) first step was to build the monastic infirmary together with a chamber for those who were seriously ill[262]. At Waverley the infirmary comprised a hall of six bays with a central hearth. It had a small cloister garth – to the north of which lay the chapel and to the south-east the kitchen[263]. A covered passageway led from the infirmary at Tintern to its abbey church[264]. It was through the infirmary door at Amelunxborn (in 1279) that the community fled from rebellious and threatening *conversi*[265].

Sick monks fit enough to do so worshipped in the retro-choir of the abbey church, but by the early thirteenth century many Cistercian infirmaries had their own chapel where presumably the daily office of the Blessed Virgin Mary – ordered in infirmaries by statute of 1185 – was said[266]. The first chapel at the Dunes was built about 1215[267], that at Santes Creus in 1220[268] and that at Beaubec was dedicated in honour of St Lawrence in 1248[269]. In 1232 Stephen Lexington ordered the removal of coloured glass and variegated floor tiles from the chapel of Aulnay[270]. In 1263 Matilda of London – a benefactor of Waverley – was buried in its infirmary chapel (consecrated in 1201), but later – due to flooding – the chapel became no longer usable and (in 1339) her remains had to be removed[271]. Remains of other chapels include those at Byland, Heiligenkreuz[272] and Loccum[273].

The duties of the infirmarian (and his *conversi* helpers) were laid down in the *Usages* of the Order. He was to light a candle for Matins and bring with him the necessary books for the daily recitation of the Office of Our Lady[274]. Later he attended the 'morning mass', thus freeing him for his work. He was to ensure that each new patient had an eating bowl and a drinking flagon. He might talk as necessary with one patient at a time, especially the very sick. On Saturday he washed the feet of those who wished and beat their clothes[275]. No one might enter the infirmary without his permission[276]. At Hailes (1270) the care of the sick was found wanting by the Visitor: he ordered that 'the president of the chapter' (the abbot normally) should visit all the sick at least once a day, appoint an infirmarer to tend them and ensure that delicacies were given them to build up their health[277]. The inhabitants of an infirmary included the chronically sick (those unable for at least three days to go into choir), the very aged and feeble and those who had been bled[278]. They could do some work if fit enough: any grumblers were to be punished[279].

Stephen Lexington's injunctions for the Savigniac houses give a picture of potential shortcomings in infirmary life. He insisted on silence being kept[280], he forbade games and levity[281], he stopped the erection of separate cells[282], he would not allow goose to be eaten[283] and he enjoined that – save for the bed-ridden and the blind – the sick monks were to eat at a common table[284]. Known monastic patients included a delirious monk of Strata Florida (1202) who had seen a vision during Whit-Sunday Lauds[285], and a dying monk of Glenluce (1235) who was stripped of his clothing by Scottish knaves[286]. Contact with lepers was discouraged[287], but those contracting the disease were not abandoned or thrown out – though they might be isolated. The obit of one leper monk was kept yearly at Wilhering[288]. Those who became mentally ill might be separated from the community – either in the monastery or on a grange[289]. A subdeacon of Vauclair (1204) suffering from 'weakness of the head' was reduced to the status of a *conversus*[290].

Meat might be eaten by patients in the infirmary but this was restricted: no meat was allowed on Saturdays – save for the gravely ill (1185)[291], nor from Septuagesima until Easter – with no apparent exception (1237)[292]. From 1288 the sick might eat after Terce and have an evening meal – even in winter-time when only one meal was taken in the monastery[293]. At Beaulieu (1270) abstinence was carefully maintained in Advent and Lent, fish then being served. When meat was eaten there it included chicken, pigeon and dove – from birds kept by the infirmarian. Delicacies offered included almonds, liquorice and sugar[294]. Gifts for infirmaries – on a regular basis – included wine (Beaulieu)[295], fish (Arnsburg)[296], pepper (Sawley)[297] and venison (Tintern)[298]. Financial aid was given by benefactors to enable the purchase of helpful commodities like butter, eggs and cheese for the infirmary of Bebenhausen (1325)[299]. St Bernard-opt-Scheldt (1278) received a bed with bedding[300], Berdoues (1210) was given tithes for revenue to maintain a lamp burning in its infirmary by night[301].

When a Cistercian monk was at the point of death the infirmarer placed a cloth on the floor on which he was laid to die[302]. The 'tabula' was sounded in the cloister so that the community might gather around for the viaticum and extreme unction administered by the abbot, and to chant the Litany of the Saints and the Penitential Psalms[303]. The corpse was washed in warm water[304] – as once viewed by St Louis at Chaâlis[305] – on a stone slab like that still to be seen at Cadouin[306]. Unless his body was fetid, the monastic choir divided into two to keep vigil over it by night in the church. The next morning a Requiem Mass was said after Prime followed by the burial. If a monk died early in the day interment was after Terce, if somewhat later then during the second sitting in the refectory. During the burial a few monks remained to watch over the church and cloister – a necessary precaution against thieves. A brother stood in the grave ready to receive the corpse and to cense it after the abbot had sprinkled it with holy water, the abbot finally throwing earth on to the deceased[307]. The formalities were concluded by giving – for thirty days – the deceased's portion of food to the poor at the gate, as well as his old clothes and footwear[308].

Monastic Medicine

The early Cistercian attitude to medicine – especially of St Bernard – is a matter for debate[309], but – well before the close of the twelfth century – some of the Order's monks were acting as physicians. The General Chapter (1157–1202) forbade such religious to stay away from their monastery overnight for such work, or to give medicines to layfolk[310]. Gerald of Wales (c. 1200) criticised those black and white monks who practised medicine without any skill – and sometimes with disastrous results[311]. In the thirteenth century there is sporadic evidence of Cistercian doctors: several were known at San Galgano including Abbot Rainer (1288)[312]. The Cistercian Cardinal John of Toledo was not only Protector of the Order but also physician to Alexander IV (1254–61)[313]. A somewhat notorious chemist and physician was Adolph Gishorn of Walkenried (c. 1318). Detested by his community since becoming addicted to necromancy, he left – and went to stay in turn at the abbeys of Amelunxborn, Marienrode and lastly Loccum – after living there for several months he was found dead 'in a secret place'[314].

Evidence of Cistercian interest in medicine has been demonstrated at Øm where skeletal remains have shown its surgeons' ability to heal limb fractures and to trepan skulls[315]: the same excavations have produced there 'a whole arsenal of surgical instrmuents'[316]. A number of herbs – not indigenous to Scandinavia – are still found growing wild around former abbeys like Løgum and Vitskøl, suggesting herb gardens used for medicinal preparations[317]. At Sorø (c. 1310) a monk, Knud Jul, copied a treatise dealing in part with the healing properties of herbs[318]. Such knowledge led to a medieval pharmacy at Orval[319] and the dispensary of Casamari[320]. Other medical works in Cistercian libraries included a late twelfth century *Book of Healing* at Rievaulx, a *Book of Physic and Surgery* given to Meaux in 1305[321] and a fourteenth century manuscript – *Traktaty medyczne* – at Pelplin[322]. Scribbled on a fly-leaf of a twelfth century Waverley manuscript are prescriptions for curing kidney stones[323]. Kirkstall had a recipe for the 'falling sickness' in its *Coucher Book*[324].

Blood-letting

A regular feature of monastic life was the letting of blood as a means of encouraging good physical and mental health[325]. Bleeding took place in the calefactory – especially heated in winter – in the early morning[326]. Monks were bled quarterly, the prior naming in chapter a small group to be bled that day[327]. He was discouraged from naming too many at once – as the daily life and economy of the abbey would suffer[328]. Bleeding (a weakening experience) was not supposed to take place on fast days (including the whole of Advent and Lent)[329] – though some accounts suggest that it did[330], nor during the Christmas, Easter and Whitsun festivals. A twelfth century account refers to the 'blood-letter' (presumably a monk – as at Dore in 1500)[331] coming at the behest of the prior and forewarned by the infirmarian[332]. Blood-letting instruments have been found at Varnhem[333].

Some monks may have been fearful as their turn approached – it could mean the loss of four pints of blood[334] – and monks were known to faint during the process or even to die (as one abbot of Boyle)[335]. Bleeding was a risky business with the possibility of infection setting in. Some monks[336] and *conversi*[337] tried to avoid or postpone their turn.

Once bled the patients could take mixt in the refectory: this breakfast was timed for 'after the Gospel' in 1154[338], but 'after Mass' in 1160[339]. To help regain their strength one pound of white bread was allowed them[340] and – for three days – a pittance at both meals[341]. For those three days they were also excused from reading, work and choir[342]: they might lie on their beds in the dorter or sit in the cloister or chapter-house[343]. If they did come to choir – perhaps for a funeral – they might stay seated, presumably in the retro-choir[344]. Those three days of rest, four times a year, were the nearest to a holiday that a Cistercian monk ever got.

The Abbot's Lodging

Early Cistercian abbots slept in the dormitory with their community and ate with the guests in the hospice, but later came to have their own quarters. These were sited (at Fountains and Tintern[345]) adjacent to, or at the east end of, the monks' reredorter – so that the abbot and his guests might also use it. Such was the position by the early thirteenth century when – at a number of monasteries – free-standing abbots' houses were built. These were in existence at Bithaine – perhaps by 1211[346], Kirkstall by about 1230[347], Flaxley by around 1232[348] and at Foucarmont – well before 1233[349]. Coggeshall's complex – by the dorter – may date from as early as 1190[350]. Abbot Matthew of Melrose (1246–61) built there 'the great chamber of the abbot which stands by the river'[351]. The foundations (by the river Lade) survive: a building measuring 26 × 15 metres with two rows of piers[352]. The abbot's house at Croxden (rebuilt about 1335) stood between the monks' infirmary and the dorter[353]; that at Meaux lay east of the infirmary[354]. At Tintern the abbatial complex was greatly enlarged in the fourteenth century – with a great hall, kitchens, chapel and dovecot[355]. Other abbatial chapels built included those at Coggeshall, Netley[356], Pforta and Zwettl[357].

It was perhaps the need to entertain – as Cistercian abbots became increasingly men of commercial, political and social stature – that necessitated separate accommodation: sited – like the infirmary – away from the cloister so that the monks living there on simple fare might not become unduly jealous. A separate residence necessitated servants and better quality utensils. By 1273 the abbot of Croxden had his 'whole household'[358]. At Dore (by 1335) silver vessels and cutlery were used at the abbot's table – and carried with him even when he travelled abroad[359]. At Osek (in 1340) some of the poultry received in kind rents were reserved for the abbot's kitchen[360]. At Sibton (in 1323) one corrodian had a share 'of all the left-overs in the abbot's chamber'[361].

Drainage

Cistercian abbeys – being lowlying – were susceptible to flooding, requiring a system of drains both to take away excess water and to remove waste. The drainage system was carefully planned, was in part subterranean, and presumably executed before the various buildings it served were erected over it. The chronicle of Meaux tells how its water channels were laid out from about 1220 to 1235 in the relatively early stages of a lengthy building programme[362]. Drainage channels were often stone lined, but some (as at Kołbacz) might be in brick[363]. The waterway passing outside the woolhouse at Fountains had banks of gritstone blocks originally lined by timber and sheets of lead[364]. The water was usually derived from nearby rivers – as the Oise at Ourscamp[365] and the Merse at San Galgano[366]. The lesser water channels are today sometimes hardly visible: their course determined only from aerial photography (as at Grace Dieu in Wales), from scorch marks in grass in a dry summer (like at Byland in 1983)[367], by means of geophysical survey (lately pursued at Kirkstall) or by excavation (undertaken at Tintern Secunda – also in 1983)[368].

In a typical arrangement, water at Kirkstall came from a hillside stream, ran in a large stone drain beneath the guest-house and entered a sluice – whence a channel served the *conversi* reredorter and then passed south of the kitchen, under the refectory, the monks' reredorter and the abbot's house before joining the river Aire[369]. The great drain of Melrose was over 450 metres long and arched underneath buildings[370]. The subterranean drain at Garendon had an internal depth of 1.5 metres with sides of sandstone blocks and with chutes coming down from the latrines and kitchens[371]. One of the finest subterranean vaulted channels can still be seen at Maubuisson nunnery. The impressive drainage system of Fountains culminated in four parallel stone tunnels passing under the infirmary complex – but how healthy and hygienic was this – some of the water having previously drained the *conversi* latrines?[372] It is worth recalling the use of these drains in later years: at Tintern (1528) tenants had to be restrained from: 'Washing any dirty things, clothes or other corrupt matter, in the stream which flows through the middle of the abbey'[373]. The channel survives but the stream, alas, no longer flows today.

Notes

1. Stalley (1987) 56.
2. King (1954) 203.
3. *Ibid*. 203.
4. Esquieu (1986) 15.
5. Butler and Given-Wilson (1979) 199.
6. Van Der Meer (1965) Pl. 188.
7. *Ibid*. Pl. 95.
8. *Ibid*. Pl. 63.
9. *Ibid*. Pl. 864.
10. Anstett (1987) 11.
11. Stalley (1987) 154–55, 160.
12. Gilyard-Beer (1986) 176.
13. *CMM* I, 326.
14. *ACA* 306.
15. *FRB* 538.
16. Rahlves (1966) 211.
17. *Statuta* I, 145 (1191/78), 172 (1194/7); *LCC* (2) *322*.
18. *CCD* 73.
19. *Statuta* I, 333 (1206/72).
20. Canestrelli (1896) 71.
21. *Statuta* I, 466 (1217/7), *LCC* (2) 302.
22. Visible at many houses – as in the foundations at Cymer.
22a. *DSMLR* I, 291 (No. 68).
23. Richardson (1981) 12.
24. Sterum (1983) 312.
25. *CC* (2) B. 42.
26. Goutagny (1964) 208.
27. Thoen (1975) 153.
28. Hamlin (1983) 156–58.
29. Robinson and Platt (1995) 53.
30. Gilyard-Beer (1981) 129.
31. *Cf. SL* 44.
32. Lekai (1977a) 366.
33. Coulton (1967) 123, 182.
34. *RSL* II, 197 (No.   1).
35. *CAF* 24.
36. *EOC* 217.
37. Van Der Meer (1965) *passim*; Robinson (1995) end-plan.
38. Whone (1987) 49.
39. Van Der Meer (1965) Pl. 29.
40. *Ibid*. Pls. 291, 280.
41. Gilyard-Beer (1987) 47.
42. *CS* II, 186.
43. Gilyard-Beer (1976) 34.
44. Gilyard-Beer (1987) 48.
45. Peugniez (1994) 36–37.
46. Robinson (1995) 55–56.
47. Park (1986) 190.
48. Butler (1983) 80.
49. *Ibid*. 80.
50. *VGA* 16, *KKA* 55.
51. Gilyard-Beer (1987) 46.
52. *ACA* 307.
53. Davidson (1843) 75.
54. *Statuta* I, 176 (1194/33).
55. *Statuta* I, 491 (1218/36).
56. *CDCS* 142.
57. Pontus (1966) 20–21.
58. *KZ* 691.
59. Schlegel (1980) Pl. 18–19, pp. 58–59.
60. *Cf. CWD* 65, Van Der Meer (1965) 165.
61. Schlegel (1980) 58–59.
62. *CA* I, 31–32.
63. *AF* 250.
64. Arenas (1985) 26.
65. Albergo (1980) 55, 78; Canestrelli (1896) 73.
66. *Statuta* I, 177 (1194/41).
67. *CMM* I, xl.
68. *AM* II, 282.
69. *CM* 65–66.
70. *RCC* III, 247 (No. 859).
71. *DHGE* XII (1953) 1056.
72. Gloede (1965) 121.
73. *LFZ* 255–56.
74. *EOC* 402–03, Dimier (1964) 55.
75. *CRS* II, 24 (No. 11).

76. *Buildwas Abbey* (English Heritage, 1978) 6.
77. Butler (1976) 18.
78. *EOC* 402–03.
79. *CL* 48 (No. XLVIII).
80. Robinson (1995) 63.
81. Aubert (1947) II, 73.
82. Information from Dr D Robinson.
83. Information from Dr D Robinson.
84. Robinson (1995) 51–58.
85. *FRB* 539.
86. Information of Dr D Robinson.
87. Dimier (1964) 57.
88. Pontus (1966) 44.
89. Anstett (1987) 50.
90. Information from Dr K Bialoskórska.
91. The evidence of *EOC* in this respect is conflicting.
92. *RBS* 59.
93. Stalley (1987) 169.
94. *EOC* 214 (LXXII/6).
95. Richardson (1981a) 27.
96. Einsingbach (1988) 12.
97. Fergusson (1986) 168.
98. Watson (1946) 180.
99. Barnes (1982) 11, 60.
100. Richardson (1981a) 27.
101. Van Der Meer (1965) Pls. 185 (A), 744 (P), 307 (M), 64 (R), 771 (H).
102. *CC* II, 44.
103. Coppack (1990) 74.
104. Van Der Meer (1965) Pl. 744.
105. Dimier (1962) 84.
106. Information from Dr D Robinson.
107. Soriano (1979) 37.
108. Stalley (1987) 170.
109. Butler and Given-Wilson (1979) 193.
110. *Ibid.* 323.
111. Park (1986) 189.
112. Uitterdijk (1874) 222.
113. Martinez (1982) 82–83.
114. Jobin (1980) 137.
115. *ABB* 34.
116. *EOC* 238 (LXXXIII/25).
117. *Statuta* I, 24 (1134/L); *cf.* D'Arbois (1857) 276.
118. D'Arbois (1857) 275–76.
119. *EOC* 243.
120. *EOC* 224–27.
121. *EOC* 132 (XL, *passim*); *cf. Statuta* III, 189 (1279/34), 326 (1312/8), 393 (1331/4).
122. *RSL* II, 214 (No. 4).
123. *EOC* 225.
124. *EOC* 226–27.
125. *Cf. SBC* IV, 106 (No. 1182).
126. *EOC* 225, 228–31, 276–77.
127. *EOC* 233–39 (LXXXIII/35–43).
128. *EOC* 232 (LXXX), *cf. CDCS* 1453.
129. *OLSB* 56.
130. *Statuta* III, 346 (1290/4).
131. VCH, *Northampton* II (1906) 118.
132. Mitchell (1959) xv, 94–95.
133. Cruden (1960) 76.
134. D'Arbois (1857) 271.
135. *Statuta* I, 27 (1134/LXIII), *LCC* (1) 147–48.
136. D'Arbois (1857) 273, Lackner (1978a) 69.
137. D'Arbois (1857) 272–73.
138. *Statuta* I, 186 (1195/26); *cf. LCC* (1) 148, (2) 334; *SBC* IV, 107 (No. 1183).
139. D'Arbois (1857) 277.
140. *CM* 97.
141. *LCC* (1) 145.
142. Lackner (1976) 57, Walker (1984) 42.
143. *CBP* 62 (No. LXI).
144. Meyerus (1561) 156b, *cf.* Southern (1970) 268.
145. D'Arbois (1857) 279.
146. *Statuta* I, 66 (1157/50); *LCC* (1) 149, (2) 335; D'Arbois (1857) 278–79, 282.
147. De Moreau (1909) 233.
148. Jaritz (1985) 57.
149. D'Arbois (1857) 281.
150. Grüger (1978a) 224.
151. D'Arbois (1857) 282.
152. Grüger (1978a) 224.
153. D'Arbois (1857) 282, *cf.* Grüger (1978a) 224, Rösener (1974) 155.
154. De Moreau (1909) 233.
155. *UKSH* 28–29 (No. XXI).
156. *CNM* 118.
157. France (1992) 409–10.
158. *RBM* III, 244 (No. 592).
159. Moyne (1981) 275.
160. Cruden (1960) 79.
161. Lillich (1982a) 140–41.
162. Robinson (1995) 60.
163. Ashmore (1962) 17.
164. Arenas (1985) 47–48, *cf.* Dimier (1964) 57.
165. Arenas (1985) 47–48.
166. Grüger (1984) 205.
167. *Ibid.* 2005–09.
168. *HVCP* 49.
169. Anstett (1987) 12.
170. Lillich (1982a) 140–41.
171. Grüger (1984) 210, *cf.* Łużyniecka (1995) 136.
172. *CCD* 72.
173. Lillich (1982a) 141.
174. Van Der Meer (1965) 745.
175. *Ibid.* Pl. 312.
176. *ACA* 98.
177. Dimier (1964) 59.
178. Van Der Meer (1965) Pl. 348.
179. Jacob (1970) 8.
180. Lewis (1976) 32.
181. Lillich (1982a) 139.
182. Moorhouse and Wrathmell (1987) 107–08.
183. *EOC* 213–15.
184. *EOC* 305–10 (CVIII).
185. *RSL* II, 201 (No. 8).
186. *EOC* 305–10 (CVIII).
187. Dimier (1964) 59–60.
188. Arenas (1985) 22.
189. Van Der Meer (1965) Pl. 743.
190. *Ibid.* Pl. 281.
191. *Ibid.* Pl. 15.
192. Musset (1979) 6.
193. *CMM* III, 36.
194. Stalley (1987) 168.
195. *CWK* 130.
196. *EOC* 236–37 (LXXXII/8), *cf.* Lackner (1978b) 19.
197. *Statuta* II, 108 (1272/14); *LCC* (2) 336.
198. *LCC* (2) 336.
199. *RSL* II, 218 (No. 5).

200. Coppack (1990) 73, McNulty (1943) 163.
201. *RSL* II, 201, 218.
202. Butler and Given-Wilson (1979) 193, Midmer (1979) 113.
203. Coppack (1990) 56.
204. Stalley (1987) 65.
205. Swartling (1969) 50.
206. Aubert (1947) I, 303.
207. Pontus (1966) 44.
208. Aubert (1947) II, 77–73.
209. Lillich (1982a) 135*n*.
210. A double channel ultimately.
211. Whone (1987) 125.
212. *EOC* 214–15 (LXXII/13).
213. *Statuta* I, 108 (1188/2).
214. *LMT* 179–80 (mm. 27–28).
215. *Statuta* I, 320 (1206/4); II, 76 (1229/6).
216. *Statuta* I, 202 (1196/24).
217. Stalley (1987) 175.
218. *Statuta* II, 53 (1226/26).
219. *Statuta* I, 202 (1196/24).
220. *Statuta* II, 317 (1247/15).
221. Gilyard-Beer (1976) 44–45.
222. Aubert (1947) II, 742–43.
223. Richardson (1981a) 29.
224. Gilyard-Beer (1976) 50.
225. Dimier (1964) 180.
226. Lawrence (1984) 150.
227. France (1998) in press.
228. Dimier (1964) 60.
229. *Cf.* Dimier (1966) 46, Gilyard-Beer (1976) 50.
230. Borkowska (1995) 133–34.
231. Gilyard-Beer (1976) 50.
232. Johnsen (1977) plan.
233. Midmer (1979) 92.
234. Van Der Meer (1965) Pl. 154.
235. *LCC* (2) 344–44 (Nos 13–14).
236. *RSL* II, 195 (No. 4).
237. We know so little about *conversi* life in practice in the twelfth century.
238. *Statuta* I, 275 (1202/5).
239. Coppack (1990) 73.
240. *CMM* I, 326; II, 327 (it lost its lead about 1300).
241. Arenas (1985) 42.
242. *CCD* 73, *CDN* 13–14.
243. Robinson (1995) 63.
244. Comba (1978) 404.
245. Bond (1989) 95, Coppack (1990) 98.
246. *Statuta* I, 115 (1189/27).
247. *CO* 15 (No. XX).
248. Hall (1989) 30*n*.
249. Gilyard-Beer (19876) 43.
250. *CMM* II, 119.
251. Bell (1989) 166–67.
252. *KKA* 54, *VGA* 15.
253. *Statuta* I, 31 (1134/LXXVII; *RCOC* 1649 (Cap. V).
254. *LFZ* 330–31.
255. *RCOC* 1647 (Cap. I).
256. France (1992) 226.
257. Bell (1989) 162.
258. De Rouey (und.) 10, *cf.* Lekai (1977a) 375.
259. *KKA* 51, *VGA* 13.
260. *CC* (2) B. 31.
261. Bell (1989) 162–63.
262. *CPL* 13.
263. Coppack (1990) 77.
264. Robinson (1995) 64–66.
265. Donnelly (1949) 77–78 (No. 97.
266. *AF* 74.
267. *CDNS* 343–44.
268. *Statuta* I, 529 (1220/64).
269. Deck (1974) 142*n*.
270. *RSL* II, 211 (No. 7).
271. Baigent (1882) 18, 33–31.
272. Only a few examples can be named here.
273. Heutger (1985) 149.
274. *Statuta* I, 171 (1194/1); *LCC* (1) 49, (2) 221.
275. *EOC* 262–65 (XCII), 326–29 (CXVI); *cf. Statuta* I, 30 (1134/LXXVII); *LCC (1) 101, (2) 300–02; SL* 65; *RSL* II, 203 (No. 11).
276. *EOC* 262–63 (XCII).
277. Harper-Bil (1980) 108.
278. *Cf.* Bell (1989) 163*n*.
279. *EOC* 266–65 (XCII).
280. *RSL* II, 195 (Nos 4–4).
281. *RSL* II, 240 (No. 5).
282. *RSL* II, 217 (No. 3).
283. Walker (1983) 53.
284. *SL* 164 (No. 55).
285. Williams (1984) I, 142.
286. *CM* 62.
287. *Cal. Papal Registers (Letters)* I, 81.
288. *NG* IV, 464.
289. Whone (1987) 94.
290. *Statuta* I, 298 (1204/13).
291. *Statuta* I, 98 (1185/3); *LCC* (1) 147.
292. *LCC* (2) 333.
293. *Statuta* III, 240–41 (1288/2), 244 (1289/9).
294. *ABB* 34, 255.
295. *CCR* 1243/12.
296. *UKAR* 58 (No. 90).
297. *CS* II, 60.
298. Williams (1984) I, 182.
299. Sydow (1984) 154.
300. *OSBS* (2) 382 (No. 392).
301. *CB* 157 (No. 216).
302. Othon (1929) 199.
303. *EOC* 266–69.
304. *EOC* 328–29 (CXVI).
305. Dimier (1982k) 836.
306. King (1954) 296.
307. *EOC* 275–81, 284–91; *Statuta* I, 105 (1186/14), 335 (1207/6).
308. *EOC* 286–87.
309. Bell (1989) 141–51, Williams (1935) 69–70.
310. *Statuta* I, 65 (1157/46), 84 (1175/32); *LCC* (1) 173.
311. Williams (1984) I, 30.
312. Canestrelli (1896) 16–17, Caputo and Torre (1972) 23.
313. Caputo and Torre (1972) 22–23.
314. *CWK* 126.
315. France (1992) 230.
316. Elm (1980) 176.
317. France (1992) 231.
318. McGuire (1982) 34.
319. Defrance (1988) 47.
320. Caputo and Torre (1972) *passim.*
321. Bell (1989) 145–59.
322. Wetesko (1991) 128, 135.
323. Bell (1989) 156.

324. *CBK* xxviii, LII.
325. Bell (1989) 164*n*.
326. *EOC* 328–29.
327. *EOC* 254–60 (XC).
328. *Statuta* I, 47 (1152/9).
329. *EOC* 254–60 (XC).
330. *Statuta* I, 72 (1160/14); *cf.* Ker (1984) 105.
331. PRO, E 315/405 (2), m. 22.
332. Ker (1984) 105.
333. France (1992) 230.
334. Bell (1989) 164.
335. Stalley (1987) 169.
336. *SL* 160 (No. 26).
337. *Statuta* I, 95 (1184/6); *LCC* (1) 66, (2) 345.
338. *Statuta* I, 57 (1154/17).
339. *Statuta* I, 72 (1160/14).
340. Lekai (1977a) 448 (No. XII).
341. Knowles (1963a) 641–42, *cf. CDCS* 145, *KDS* 27 (No. 266), *MEB* 59 (No. 7).
342. Ker (1984) 105.
343. *EOC* 258–60 (XC).
344. *Statuta* I, 105 (1186/14).
345. Robinson (1995) 67.
346. *Statuta* I, 389 (1211/50).
347. Barnes (1982) 60.
348. Donkin (1978) 127.
349. *RSL* II, 214 (No. 3).
350. Fergusson (1984a) 120, Gardner (1955) 28.
351. *CM* 97.
352. Richardson (1981a) 28.
353. *ACA* 307.
354. *CMM* II, 238.
355. Robinson (1995) 68.
356. Butler and Given-Wilson (1979) 309.
357. *KZ* 691, *UKZ* 384.
358. *CC* (2) B. 38.
359. Williams (1976) 17.
360. *RBM* IV, 331 (No. 848).
361. *SBC* IV, 107 (No. 1184).
362. *CMM* I, 433.
363. Cnotliwy (1987) 300.
364. Coppack (1986a) 56.
365. De Rouey (und.) 14.
366. Canestrelli (1896) 71.
367. Harrison (1986) 27–29.
368. Stalley (1987) 169.
369. Mitchell (1959) 28–29.
370. Richardson (1981a) 29.
371. Humphrey (1982) 12–20.
372. Lillich (1982a) 146–47.
373. NLW, Badminton MS 1663, m. 4d.

Chapter 12

LANDED PROPERTY

The size of the initial estates granted to the Cistercians varied in proportion to the wealth and interest of the founder and the amount of available land. Abbeys in well settled areas – perhaps with other religious orders competing for territory – had relatively small endowments, whilst in eastern Europe – where undeveloped land was more abundant, and where political motives may have played a greater rôle – there were some very large estates from the outset. In England Swineshead received only 100 ha/240 acres at its foundation[1], but King Ottakar II of Bohemia gave Zlatá Koruna territory measuring 48 km (30 miles) northwards and eastwards[2]. Abbeys founded relatively late might find it difficult to obtain much land: as Königsbronn (1303) unable to create even a grange[3]. St Louis, founding Royaumont (1228), gave it no lands but regular supplies of wheat, wine and other food – so that its monks might 'wholly abstract themselves from the world'[4].

Land acquisition during the formative years of a monastery – coupled with the initial benefaction – made eventually for some large monastic estates. It was again in central and eastern Europe that these might be of immense size. So large was the estate of Lubiąż in Silesia – estimated at 245,000 ha (600,000 acres) – that it is noticeable even on a small scale atlas map[5]. Stams in Austria owned a territory larger than the state of Lichtenstein[6]. In western Europe few monasteries could compete with such areas though some estates were of significant size: as that of Furness (80,000 ha/200,000 acres)[7]. Poblet – in lands newly occupied after the Reconquest – owned 29 villages, 30 or more mills, 60 orchards and olive groves and 27 granges[8]. Estates in well developed areas remained moderate: as those of Villers – 10,000 ha (25,000 acres) in Belgium and Dutch Limburg[9], and of Valloires in Picardy – only 800 ha (2,000 acres)[10].

Where no later mapping exists the precise size of medieval estates can be open to question – especially as the value of measurement units differed from one region to another. Chorin received at least 160 'hides' of land and Lehnin well over 100[11], but the 'hide' varied from 32 to 48 hectares (80 to 120 acres). Land units might also be expressed in central Europe in terms of 'morgen', fluctuating in value from about 0.25 to 0.31 of a hectare[12]. Grants of property might refer not to an areal measurement but rather to the number of 'hufen' or peasant holdings owned: each of which may have been equivalent to about 10 ha (25 acres). Lubiąż was credited with 5,000 'hufen' in the duchy of Great Poland and 900 in the duchy of Silesia[13]. In France a grant might refer to the number of 'manses' being given – and thereby to the total of day-works the several holdings provided[14]. Little is known as to how area was assessed, but, in 1188, the General Chapter ruled that: 'From now on the measurement of leagues is never to be done with measuring lines or rods, but by eye survey of arbitrators'[15]. In Britain former Cistercian estates can be accurately mapped by reference to the mid-nineteenth century tithe-maps.

Grantors and their Motives

Benefactors ranged in scale from royalty and nobility – who could afford to make generous grants, down to those who urgently needed ready cash and might sell to a monastery practically all they owned. In Poland of 75 charters analysed for Sulejów, 43 were given by Polish dukes, 14 by clergy and 2 by royal officials[16]. In France Auberive included bishops, cathedral chapters, other religious orders and the Templars amongst its benefactors[17]. In England over 300 people are known to have made grants to, sold to, or exchanged property with Sibton. Many of its benefactors were quite small landowners, and some gave to other religious houses as well[18]. In the thirteenth century many donors were no longer people of great financial resources and grants were often modest[19]. In Denmark royal and noble women now played the rôle of benefactor which had been the preserve of men in the twelfth century[20].

In many instances the motives which impelled grants of land are not stated, but where a cause is assigned it often parallels one of those given at the foundation of a house, and a spiritual background may again be discerned: in Wales Prince Llywelyn ab Iorwerth granted a confirmatory charter to Cymer (1209) 'In the hope of eternal recompense'[21]. Closely allied were those grants made in recompense of wrongs done: when Frederick Barbarossa (1179) did penance – for his long and bloody opposition to the papacy – he made Fossanova the especial object of his bounty[22]. The most common returns expected of the Cistercians were the right of burial and an annual obit thereafter. Some 6% of grants to Poblet were made to secure interment[23]. The wording of such grants employed phraseology such as: 'With my body' (Warden, 1185)[24]. The mode of burial desired was sometimes expressed: 'Burial as for a monk' (La Ferté, *c.* 1155)[25]. Such a request was made to avoid the simple funeral given to a passing guest. The place of burial sought might be specified: in the case of William III of Lancaster at Furness (1240), 'In the presbytery by the tomb of my grandfather'[26]. Lands or rents were given by nobles to Tintern (*c.* 1219)[27] and Doberan (1268) in return for a light burning day and night at the tombs of their parents[28].

The promise of an annual obit could bring substantial grants to a monastery: Bishop Robert of Langres gave to Clairvaux (1245) all the revenues of the churches of Maranville and Rouvre: in return the monks were to pray yearly for his predecessor, Hugh[29]. Hauterive found itself obliged to offer fifty solemn Masses for deceased donors each year[30]. The *Todtenbuch* of Lilienfeld lists the obits of monks and benefactors[31]. Some donors (as at La Ferté[32] and Margam[33]) sought the inclusion of their names in this 'martyrology' of a monastery so that their obit was not forgotten. Regular chantry provisions were sought by Bertram de Verdun who gave Aunay (*c.* 1178) Great Limber church in Lincolnshire, on condition that two monks should always be received into the abbey to say Mass for 'The weal of his soul and that of his father'[34]. Hubert de Burgh, as lord of the Three Castles, gave Dore (*c.* 1235) the granges of Llyncoed and Llanfair for chantry Masses: in the first instance by 'four priest-monks' in the abbey church, in the second at the grange chapel[35]. Other external chantry chapels served included Seething Chapel – where monks of Sibton said daily a Mass of Our Lady and a Mass for the Dead[36].

A number of grants were made by knights about to go on crusade or by others on pilgrimage. Especially important were the years running up to the Second Crusade (1145), the Third Crusade (1189–90) and the Albigensian Crusade (1205–15)[37]. Four motives played a part: the need of knights for money for equipment and for the journey; the hope for good health on the way, of victory in battle and then a safe return home. Crusaders who granted property included Roger de Mowbray – who received 120 marks from Fountains to aid his journey[38], and a knight to whom Bonnevaux gave 30 *sous* with which to buy his weapons[39]. Some crusaders trusted to return: one grant to Cheminon (1228) was for five years only[40], another (1245) was to be given back if the knight returned[41]. In a like instance at Cheminon (1233) a knight did return and tried to reclaim his land, but: 'Counselled by wise men', he gave other property to the abbey instead[42]. Some realised that they might never come back: one knight going to Jerusalem gave lands to Igny (1173) 'If he died there'[43]. Crusading grants might include: meadowland (for La Ferté)[44], salt rights (Cherlieu)[45] or a vineyard (Clairvaux)[46]. Berdoues[47], Bonnevaux[48] and Grandselve[49] benefited from knights leaving to fight the Albigeois, and Léoncel from knights leaving for Spain to fight the Saracens[50]. French pilgrims going to Compostella settled lands and mills on Fontmorigny (1220)[51] and Igny (1222)[52]. The curé of Autreville, journeying to Rome (1224), gave property to Clairvaux: 'In case he does not return'[53]. A pilgrim to the Holy Land, Sir James Douglas, bestowed lands on Newbattle (1329) to aid its work of charity[54].

A number of donors stipulated entry into the community as the condition of their making a gift (cf. Chapter 3). No less than 16% of grants made to Poblet were so by monks and *conversi*, sometimes when making their wills before profession[55]. Around the close of the twelfth century several (seemingly needy) benefactors of Margam became numbered amongst its *conversi*[56]. If not truly called by God – but by economic circumstances – what effect might their presence have had on the spiritual life of the house? Richard de Southill gave Warden (1180) 7 acres (2.8 ha) of land on the reception of his son, John, as a *conversus*. The grant was made with the assent of 'his son and heir', Hugh: so John was the younger son – for whom perhaps there was little land to inherit[56a]. The need for ready cash also stimulated many grants. Such 'urgent' or 'great necessity' made one donor give 500 measures of land in Flanders to the Dunes (1310)[57]. Paying off a person's debts – in return for land – was favoured by Poblet: it was indemnified by royal decrees (in 1166 and 1256) against any claims for money owed by debtors entering its community[58]. Meaux adopted a similar policy[59]. A ploy which might be used was to allow a person in financial difficulties to mortgage his lands to a monastery: this may have been more common than the scanty evidence suggests – as if redeemed the contract would have been perhaps destroyed[60]. One house which accepted lands in mortgage was Berdoues which, in little over a century, entered into well over two hundred mortgage contracts. For the most part these pledges seem to have remained unredeemed – and the abbey thus acquired much extra land. Berdoues used the system primarily to consolidate and extend its property rather than to lend money. Between the mid-twelfth and the mid-thirteenth century Berdoues spent only 13,845 *solidi* on outright purchases, but lent 26,622 against lasting mortgages[61].

In the late twelfth century many grants were made by those approaching death and formally clothed in Cistercian habit (Chapter 6). Others, in their last illness, would also ease their entry into heaven by favouring the monks. In this way St Benoît-en-Woëvre (1222, 1226) received tithes and vineyards[62]. Some grants were made by a husband whose wife was ill, as one gift to Léoncel (1220) when a mother was in child-birth[63]. Three years after a dying Lambert of Wislar had given land to St Bernard-opt-Scheldt (1238) the grant was challenged by a nephew. The questions put to the witnesses, at the eventual inquiry (1245) held on papal orders, asked – where the grant was made, at what time of day and year, whether Lambert was in his right mind, whether he was in bed, whether he was sitting up or lying down, and whether he was naked or clothed. The answers given generally agreed: save as to the time of day – one witness saying 'At mid-day', another 'After vespers', yet another 'At dusk'[64]. Grants of lands might also come from corrodians and pensioners given rights by a monastery. By 1272 no less than 297 people received pensions from Villers in return for previous donations: their entitlement was worth over 10,000 gallons of grain. The abbey functioned 'almost like a modern insurance agency'[65].

Nature of Land Grants

Even when the land was 'given' to a monastery, some form of return was frequently expected – even if only an obit after death. A so-called 'gift' might expect a cash or kind payment, a yearly rent or an annual 'acknowledgement'[66]. This might be clearly expressed in the preamble of a grant, like one to Silvanès: 'I give, award, and sell'[67], or when additional lands were bought up by Tintern: 'For which gift the monks have paid twenty-five marks'[68]. Even when lands were described as being given 'In free alms' (*frankalmoign*) the term was perhaps used to imply that no conditions attached to the grant, rather than that no return of any kind was to be made. Only when the phrase 'Free and pure alms' was employed did the grant perhaps incur neither rent nor military service obligation[69]. The earlier the grant (as in the first half of the twelfth century) the more likely it was to be given in 'pure frankalmoign': thereafter 'gifts' with burdens attached became commonplace[70]. Gifts in frankalmoign might later be challenged: Strata Florida and Whitland (1336) claimed certain privileges by virtue of their estates being granted in frankalmoign. They were told to prove it by producing their charters[71].

Royal charters to some English houses – as Holm Cultram (1190)[72] and Warden (1199)[73] – might contain a list of exemptions from services and taxes an abbey might otherwise have been required to fulfil – as carriage duty, castle guard, bridge building, and scutage. Abbeys so honoured might signify their privileges by setting up a wooden cross before their exempted granges – as did Cîteaux (1119)[74] and Perseigne (1240)[75]. Charters releasing monasteries from feudal obligations often gave only partial immunity. Grants to Doberan (1237) cited the usual freedom from services – 'except in defence of the land'[76]. Prince Swantopolk freed the men of Oliwa (1224) from every exaction – 'except rebuilding of the castle of Gdańsk'[77]. It was such an exception to their privileges that saw the abbots of Balmerino and Coupar (1336) contributing towards the cost of rebuilding the walls and towers of Perth[78], and the abbot of Warden (1266) paying towards castle-guard at Rockingham[79]. Combermere and Dieulacres (1266) gained exemption from carriage service during the siege of Kenilworth Castle[80], and so did Buildwas, Croxden, Hailes and Pipewell (1277) from carrying food to the royal army in Wales[81]. An inquisition of 1166 showed that a number of Cistercian abbeys in England did pay scutage – a tax in lieu of military (*forinsec*) service – arising from holdings granted to the monks[82]. Scutage formed a significant enough item to warrant *A Table of Reliefs at 100 shillings for the knight's fee* to be included in the Coucher Book of Kirkstall[83], and a detailed *Memorandum* to be placed in the cartulary of Sibton[84]. Great abbeys with substantial holdings might actually provide men in defence of the realm: such were Furness[85] and Quarr[86].

Many 'gifts' of lands to monasteries – even if in free alms – might be subject to claims from potentially disgruntled heirs. To ensure their goodwill when Geoffrey Sturmi sold land to Margam (*c.* 1200) his three sons each received a cloak and four gold pieces[87]. The favour of heirs was also encouraged by the payment of a perpetual annual 'acknowledgement' by a monastery, even though this might be quite small – like a pair of gloves by Margam[88], a pair of gilt spurs by Roche[89], a pound of white incense by Sibton[90] and a 'muid' of wheat by Fontmorigny[91]. Stephen Lexington warned the Irish houses not to buy land: 'Unless careful inquisition has first been made, so that any entry or possession shall be fully legal and secure in title'[92]. This might mean the acquiescence of a superior lord and certainly the approval of the donor's immediate family.

There were many cases when, in later years, the heirs of a grantor wished that their ancestor had not been so generous. King Alfonso I of Portugal gave generously to Bouro (inc. 1148) but a century later his descendants entered into negotiations to get some of the property back[93]. Two sons – irritated that their father on 'being made a monk' at Boulancourt (1157) had given some of his best possessions to the abbey – plundered all they could carry away[94]. Such problems might end in arbitration – resulting in confirmation of the grant and a partial climb-down by the disaffected heirs on receiving some compensation[95]. It was to try to avoid such situations that when the tithes of Longchamp were granted to Clairvaux (*c.* 1170) it was with the agreement of the donor's wife, son and daughter[96]; and when a benefactor of La Trappe (1191) gave it land it was 'with the assent of all his sons, of his wife Mary, and his eldest son's wife, Annette'[97]. It was important not to forget interested parties who might be abroad or in their minority. Deeds in favour of Cherlieu (1235, 1254) note the absence of one of the sons with promise of his consent on his return[98]. A widow and four of her children, making an important grant to Fontmorigny (1276), promised to have the sale ratified by the two younger sons and brothers when they became of age[99].

Much land was of course *bought* by monasteries as they sought to increase their estates and to make them viable economic propositions. This was especially true in the thirteenth century when the age of large 'gifts' had all but passed. Between 1163 and 1250 Bonnecombe expended over 135,000 *solidos* on property acquisitions: the later the date the more money spent (56,000 *solidos* in 1230–49 alone)[100]. To encourage Clairvaux to buy his land, one benefactor gave the abbey (1223) one-third of it as a gift – successfully tempting the monks to expend 1,000 *livres provinois* on buying the remainder[101]. In the wake of the Albigensian Crusade and the confiscation of lands held by heretics, Fontfroide (1255–65) – in ten years – expended 140,000 *sous melgoriens* in buying six lordships[102]. Casanova (1266) bought the major part of its Raccongi Grange – for 557 *Astesi lire* – from the Commune of Raccongi which needed the money to build its city walls[103].

The Cistercians not infrequently acquired lands belonging to other religious houses. Clairvaux (1196) spent the not inconsiderable sum of 500 *livres* in purchasing its grange of Blinfay from the Premonstratensians[104]. Haina (1225) bought (perhaps cheaply) the properties of a cell (of nuns and brothers) in Huckele (Werberg) which had been devastated by an 'invasion of wild beasts'[105]. Bonnecombe bought lands from Mazan and Bonneval – including La Serre Grange for 12,000 *solidi*[106]. Some purchases of land were made wholly or partly in kind rather than in cash. It accorded well with Celtic custom when Gunnilda Sturmi gave Margam (late 12C.) her dower-land for £4 of silver, twenty sheep and some lambskins for making a pellice[107]. Between 1139 and 1169 Silvanès gave, on six occasions, a horse as part payment in purchasing land: one was 'A nag with bit and bridle'[108]. A cellarer of Léoncel (1238) bought land for a 'quarteron' of wool[109].

Land Acquisition in Time

For those abbeys where a complete cartulary exists, it is possible to draw graphs showing the build-up over the years of the monastic estates. The peak towards 1180 (coinciding with the run up to the Third Crusade) at houses such as Bonnefont[110] and Fontfroide[111] has been noted. Land acquisition at Poblet peaked about 1195, then fell steadily to 1225 with a later mini-peak about 1235 to 1240 corresponding to the military victories of James I over Majorca and Valencia[112]. It was in these years that the substantial growth of their estates gained the white monks several critics[113], and Abbot Stephen Lexington of Savigny realised what was happening. He wrote: 'These days our Order has its share of enemies who lie in wait to catch it at a disadvantage'[114]. It was the alleged wealth of the Cistercians that caused King Richard I to seek money for his ransom from the Order, and that led his successor, King John, to tax it savagely. On the Continent the Order was satirised in verse. An early critic was Nigel de Longchamp in his *Speculum Stultorum* (*c.* 1180)[115], whilst Guiot de Provins (*c.* 1205) devoted no less than one hundred and forty verses in derogation of the economic prosperity of the white monks[116].

From 1182 to 1240 a series of statutes of the General Chapter sought to limit the rate of land acquisition by monasteries of the Order: basically these injunctions allowed property given in 'free gift' to be accepted but forbade any further purchasing of land[117]. The rules – partly intended to avoid monasteries getting into debt and perhaps partly in response to the Order's critics – did prove a temporary check, but they could often be circumvented because of the exceptions made. In 1182 'poorer houses' were absolved from obeying the regulations[118], in 1190 abbeys where thirty monks and sufficient *conversi* could not be sustained were excepted[119], in 1206 monasteries in 'urgent necessity' were excused[120] and in 1240 new communities not fifteen years old were exempted[121]. From the reign of Henry III efforts were made in England to limit the amount of land alienated by ecclesiastical persons and institutions, but the Cistercians at first generally managed to circumvent them[122]. Secular dissatisfaction became widespread, and the eventual consequence was the Statute of Mortmain – *De viris religiosis* – passed by Parliament in 1279. It sought to greatly diminish lay fees passing into (literally) the 'dead hand' of the Church[123]. The statute came too late – most abbeys had already acquired the bulk of their estates, and abbeys continued to receive lands – because of the exceptions the Act made. Land could still be acquired if an inquisition *ad damnum* showed that there was no harm (literally, 'no damage') likely to ensue to the Crown[124]. Between 1282 and 1292 seventeen Cistercian monasteries gained 30 such licences between them, not a great number[125]. The process was costly: fees were payable both for the inquiry and for the licence itself[126].

Land Exchanges

The Cistercians endeavoured to increase the efficiency of their holdings by grouping them where possible into compact estates. This allowed of careful land management and economic efficiency, gave freedom of movement and avoided certain duplication of expenses. Lands which lay adjacent to, or within those acquired initially by the monks might be bought up or gained by exchanging another property. Lynge Grange was described in the 'Donation Book' of Sorø as being founded 'partly by purchase, partly by just exchange'[127]. Rivalta (Piedmont, 1291) exchanged a piece of land at Torino 'having in mind the advantage to the monastery'[128]. Such exchanges did not necessarily mean an increase in acreage, at most it might only be 'acre for acre' (Rievaulx)[129]. Distant properties might be exchanged for alternative lands much nearer the monastery. In Denmark Esrum early exchanged the far away property of Asserbø for land in Orvid Forest[130], whilst Sorø (1205) gave up the grange of Undløse in return for nearby Pedersborg[131]. In Wales Neath (*c.* 1200) obtained the local fee of Walterston (Gower) in place of a distant property at Hornblotton (Somerset)[132]. Not all distant properties were surrendered: in some cases the opportunity for rationalisation did not arise, in other instances they were specialised granges of the utmost importance.

Charters and Confirmations

Monastic possession of land might well be disputed in the years and centuries which followed its acquisition: proof then of rightful ownership would depend upon a monastery being able to produce its original charters, properly sealed and witnessed. Prince Gwenwynwyn of Powys (1191) – in giving a grant of land to Strata Marcella – pointed out that 'Nothing resisteth forgetfulness and false claim more effectively than a

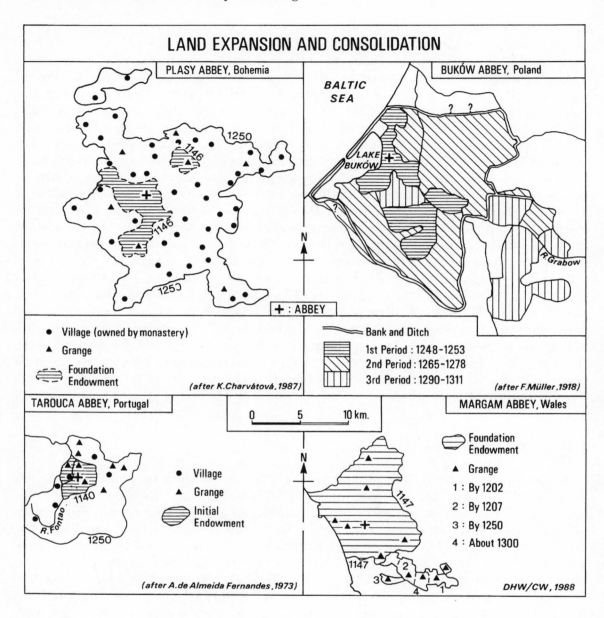

LAND EXPANSION AND CONSOLIDATION

PLASY ABBEY, Bohemia

BUKÓW ABBEY, Poland

BALTIC SEA

LAKE BUKÓW

R. Grabow

+ : ABBEY

- Village (owned by monastery)
▲ Grange
Foundation Endowment

(after K. Charvátová, 1987)

Bank and Ditch

1st Period : 1248-1253
2nd Period : 1265-1278
3rd Period : 1290-1311

(after F. Müller, 1918)

TAROUCA ABBEY, Portugal

0 5 10 km.

MARGAM ABBEY, Wales

R. Fontao

- Village
▲ Grange
Initial Endowment

Foundation Endowment
▲ Grange
1 : By 1202
2 : By 1207
3 : By 1250
4 : About 1300

(after A. de Almeida Fernandes, 1973)

DHW/CW, 1988

written record'[133]. He confirmed his gifts: 'By means of the signatures of witnesses, and the protection of my seal'[134]. An abbot of Zlatá Koruna (1293) granted a charter so that the nature of the gift did not 'disappear from future knowledge through forgetfulness'[135]. Charters were vital records, and – partly to have easy access to their contents and partly to guard against the loss of the originals – many monasteries enrolled their charters in a cartulary (Chapter 5). One donor to Bonnevaux (*c.* 1150) prepared three copies of his charter, giving one to the abbey and depositing two in other places – a necessary precaution against the loss which could ensue from armed raids in troubled times[136].

If a charter was a concord between two parties, or gave rights to the donor, two copies of the agreement would be made on the same piece of parchment which would then be cut in twain along an indented line – thus creating 'indentures'. The veracity of a deed could later be determined by ascertaining whether the two parts fitted together. It was a simple device against fraud. When an agreement was reached regarding boundaries between Bonnevaux and the Chartreuse, the local bishops sealed 'two charters separated by an alphabet'[137]: for sometimes the letters spelling 'CHIROGRAPHVM' were written in the space between the two copies. Stephen Lexington

(Savigny; 1230) ordered that any cirograph or charter granted by an abbey was to be written out 'word by word in the register' before it was handed over[138]. He also laid down regulations for the care and custody of monastic charters: they were to be kept under lock and key and not lent out unless a copy had been made and the abbot's permission obtained[139]. Who wrote the charters giving lands to the Cistercians? Sometimes the last witness to a charter was the monk who wrote it, as in a grant to Whalley attested by 'Henry, prior, who made this charter'[140]. Another deed was witnessed at Berdoues (1244) by 'brother Deusadiuvat who wrote this charter'[141].

Instances of affidation or 'faith-pledging' whereby a grantor promised in the hand of a third party to observe the terms of his charter occur in some late twelfth century grants. The third party was a person of equal or higher rank, or in the case of a lady another woman. At Warden (*c.* 1180) 'Eudo made affidation in the hand of William de Almo and offered the gift on the altar'[142]. Two grants to Léoncel (1191) were made 'On the Book (of the Gospels) and between the hands (*inter manus*) of abbot Peter'[143]. At this time, too, it became common to include within charters a clause of warranty guarding against future claims on the land granted[144]. A number of early charters given to Léoncel between 1169 and 1220 were publicly granted in the chapter-house, indicating that as early as the late twelfth century laity entered the cloister for this purpose[145]. One such grant was witnessed: 'In the common chapter, in the presence of all the brothers, monks and *conversi*'[146]. Charters – as given to Kirkstall – and addressed 'To all seeing or hearing this writing', suggest that the deed was recited aloud before the assembled gathering[147]. It was common to make a grant touching the Book of the Gospels [148], or the relics of the house[149] and not least: 'The most precious wood of the True Cross'[150]. It was commonplace to lay the charter on the high altar as a further sign of good faith, as happened at Léoncel (1169)[151] and Igny (1198)[152]. This meant layfolk entering even the presbytery of the abbey church.

Almost as important as the initial grants of land were the subsequent confirmations of original charters, and some original deeds – now lost – are known only through such confirmations. Confirmatory charters can be of interest in that they sometimes expand upon details given in the originals: this may reflect monastic expansion in their economy, or simply the monks' concern to spell out precisely what had previously been taken for granted. Amongst the foundation grants of Tintern (1133) was the land of 'Merthyr-gerain'. Earl Gilbert of Pembroke's confirmation a few years later notes: 'Merthyr-gerain with the church', whilst Gilbert Marshal's confirmation a century on lists: 'Merthyr-gerain with the church and the wood'[153].

In the case of royal confirmations these would be issued wherever the Court might be. St Louis visiting Perseigne (1248) confirmed there its possessions[154], whilst the monks of Whitland (1399) took advantage of Richard II being nearby at Haverfordwest for the same purpose[155]. In England confirmations meant costly fees to the Crown: Furness paid 800 marks to Richard I, £100 to King John, and 400 marks to Henry III[156]. Especially where lands were 'given' to the monks, the repeated need to renew charters meant that the original value might be paid several times over. There was a tendency to safeguard monastic possessions by seeking a confirmatory charter early in the reign of a new monarch. Such charters were granted to Holm Cultram by Henry II (1158), Richard I (1189), John (1201), Henry III (just after he achieved his majority, 1227) and Edward I (1307) – the latter at the close of the reign[157]. A charter of Henry VII (1508) – in favour of Strata Florida – listed eleven previous confirmations[158]. A similar pattern prevailed on the Continent: after the incorporation of Bebenhausen (previously Premonstratensian) Emperor Henry VI of the Romans (1193) confirmed its possessions and privileges, as did Frederick II (1232) and four later kings of the Romans: Henry (1233), William (1255), Rudolf (1274) and Albert (1299 and 1305)[159]. Monasteries whose properties lay in territory subject to a boundary change, or to capture, would seek charters from both monarchs concerned. Lands of Heiligenkreuz granted by Béla IV of Hungary (1230, 1246) received later confirmation by Duke Albert of Austria and Styria (1290)[160].

It was often felt important to obtain confirmation of a grant by the donor's superior lord. Arnoul de Parigny promised Fontmorigny (1189) that he would obtain ratifying charters 'from his over-lord and the lord of whom he was especially the vassal'[161]. King Philip II of the Romans confirmed the property of Altzelle (1207) with particular regard to the time when Margrave Theodore of Meissen was no more[162]. It might also be necessary to obtain confirmation of a father's grant from his heir when he became of age, as did Léoncel (*c.* 1175)[163] and Warden (1306)[164].

The final court of appeal in Christian Europe was the Holy See, and the cartularies of many abbeys have an entire section reciting papal bulls confirming their charters (Chapter 5). Innocent III issued numerous such bulls – as for Osek (1207)[165] and Otterberg[166]. They spelt out a monastery's lands and rights – including privileges general to the Order. During Innocent III's reign the abbots of both Chassagne (1212) and La Bénissons-Dieu (1213) travelled to Rome to seek such charters[167]. Despite the comprehensive bulls he issued, the growing importance of canon law meant that monasteries were 'well advised to seek out new legal forms for old privileges'[168]. Abbeys seeking charters from later pontiffs included Villers (1239) from Gregory IX[169] and Lehnin (1336) from Benedict XII[170]. Papal charters might be vital evidence: a rector of Wigton desisted from seeking tithes from Holm Cultram (*c.* 1250) – 'Having seen the papal privileges releasing the abbey'[171].

Confirmatory charters might arise from specific needs – the most common being the loss of original charters or their wear and tear with the passage of time. Edward I confirmed a charter of Quarr (1278) after it had been deliberately torn by a malcontent[172]. The nuns of Ivanics – having lost their copy of a charter given them (in 1246) by the bishop of Zagreb – asked his successor not only to confirm it but also to 'Renew and transcribe it'[173]. The abbot of Neath (1336) petitioned Edward III: 'To view and confirm the charter of King John, which charter has been much ruined and worn by the wars in those parts'[174]. Llantarnam (1398) sought confirmation of the papal bull – granted it in 1257 – because the abbey had 'great need of the said letters, which are beginning to be consumed with age'[175]. After the seal of Henry III was changed, Furness (1267) had an *inspeximus* of its charters – given under the former seal – 'Fortified with the impression of the seal now used'[176].

Before the drafting of a charter the bounds of the territory granted needed to be defined. A common early medieval practice was for this to be done by 'Law-worthy and trustworthy men' (as at Kirkstall) walking around the boundaries of the land concerned[177]. Prince Henry of Scotland, granting land to Holm Cultram (1150), personally undertook such a perambulation 'with several true men'[178]. On giving land to Sallay (*c.* 1160) a donor walked around it, with the monastery's cellarer, placing boundary markers[179]. In a dispute regarding lands of Holm Cultram a perambulation was ordered to be undertaken by: 'Elderly men of the district who know the right ancient bounds'[180]. Other perambulations on record include those delimiting properties of Toplica (1242)[181], Doberan (1268)[182] and Tennenbach (1318)[183]. Boundaries were often in dispute, leading to lengthy arbitration procedures – as for Altzelle (1224)[184] and Herrera (1290)[185].

In defining boundaries natural features, especially rivers, played a major rôle – as the river Dünupe separating the territory of Dünamünde from that of the adjacent city of Riga[186]. 'A certain river' in Germany delimited the pasture rights of Pforta from those of Riffenstein[187]. The limits of the lands of the Dunes were defined by reference to streams, banks and trees: the latter including a burnt oak (*quercus combustus*) and a honeyed oak (*quercus melliflua*)[188]. A willow and an oak – both contorted somewhat like a cross – helped to define Toplica's lands at Lakuč[189]. Trees marked with crosses were employed by Newminster[190]. Where no obvious natural features were present, artificial markers might be placed – as wooden crosses by Casanova (1142)[191]. A line of posts marked the limits of Meaux's rights in the West Marsh: by 1339 they had deteriorated and large stones replaced them[192]. Eighteen stones were set up in 1303 to indicate the home demesne of Léoncel – two still survive[193]. Stone crosses were employed by Toplica[194]. The chronicle of Øm – giving the boundaries of its property of Djursø in Jutland – refers to 'the sea, the fosse, big stones, streams, and the great stone – where is the beech-tree – to which is infixed a cross'[195]. Whether in stone, or in timber, the sign of the cross played a prominent rôle in indicating monastic ownership. The first true extant English survey map – in a Kirkstead Psalter and dating from about 1240 – delimits the rights of pasture of Kirkstead and Revesby in Wildmoor Fen. It is the first map known to have north at the top[196].

Land Disputes and Accords

Despite carefully worded charters monastic lands were often the subject of disputes with other interested, perhaps resentful parties (Chapter 7). Powerful lords might wrest lands from the Cistercians with apparent impunity: Count Otho I of Burgundy appropriated Cherlieu's village of Montigny – after his death in 1200 it took the abbey a dozen years to reclaim it[197]. Land disputes were often protracted, as in Denmark, when the consequent litigation was transferred from father to son[198]. There were disputes too with neighbouring religious houses, even Cistercian – as (from 1239 down to 1291) between Bonrepos in France and Sawtry in England regarding lands in Lincolnshire[199]. When an abbot of Léoncel – accompanied by three monks and four *conversi* – reached an accord with the Carthusian house of Boucantes, the monks of Léoncel not present refused their consent and the treaty had to be renegotiated[200]. To protect themselves against appearance in the law-courts, one course open to monastic houses was to have written into charters given them a clause inhibiting any future litigation concerning a grant. A donor to Tilty agreed to be publicly excommunicated if she reneged on her charter[201]. The need to defend an abbey's rights saw an abbot of Holm Cultram (1278) forced to take his case before the king's justices at Carlisle[202], an abbot of Vale Royal (1328) appear personally at a parliament held at Northampton[203] and an abbot of Furness (1337) before the justices of the Pleas of the Forest (of Lancaster)[204]. The frequent need to sustain monastic interests at law meant that large abbeys might have, as did Beaulieu, a monk holding the office of 'Keeper of the Pleas'. He took charge of all litigation as well as recording its results and expenditure[205].

A more sensible way was to submit to arbitration. When it was agreed to divide disputed territory equally between Furness (*c.* 1200) and Alan de Penington, it was after referral 'to the oath of twelve knights chosen on either side'[206]. Not all cases – whether settled in court or by mediation – were decided in an abbey's favour, but generally the Cistercians won the day. Of 53 land disputes between 1166 and 1275 concerning Poblet, thirty-five were resolved in its favour, 15 were compromise agreements, only 3 were adverse decisions[207]. The need to compromise appears frequently in monastic concords. When a young man entered Meaux as a novice he surrendered to the abbey the 7 ox-gangs of land his father had given him, but the would-be monk died and his father disputed the gift: the abbey surrendered to him one-half of the property[208]. To go to law might mean that a case was lost entirely, as by Croxden[209] and Merevale[210] at the Staffordshire Assizes of 1227 and 1247 respectively, and by Furness at the Lancaster Assizes of 1291[211]. It was better to accept arbitration and a binding concord.

Tithe Exemption

A 'hidden benefit' of great advantage to the Cistercians was their exemption from paying tithes on the produce of their own lands – a potential saving of one-tenth of their harvest which otherwise might have fallen into other hands[212]. Such exemption was not solely a Cistercian right: Pope Calixtus II gave the privilege to the Benedictines of Honcourt (1122) and referred to the teaching of Gregory VII (1073–85) that priests and 'the poor of Christ' should not pay tithes to other priests[213]. Cistercian exemption may have arisen from like considerations, as well as the fact that the white monks did not seek to own tithes themselves – though this ideal faded away[214]. Tithe-exemption was given early by diocesan bishops to Bonnevaux (1120)[215] and Clairvaux (1128)[216]. Shortly thereafter Innocent II (1132) exempted Cîteaux and its 'entire congregation' from paying tithes on: 'Produce from your own hands and for your own use, in order that you may be able to serve God more securely and freely'. The papal decision was supported by the Council of Pisa (1135)[217] but alarmed those to whom such tithes had previously been due[218]. Adrian IV (1154–59) restricted the policy severely, only allowing exemption on the produce of land which the Cistercians had *newly* brought into cultivation: the monks were to pay all other tithes previously due[219]. This restriction encouraged the white monks to accelerate the clearance of woodland and bring virgin land under the plough.

Alexander III (1174) completely reversed his predecessor's policy, giving once again widespread tithe-exemption to the Cistercians[220]; he was backed in this by later popes like Lucius III (1181–85)[221] and Urban III (1185–87)[222]. Continuing criticism had found focus in a letter from the archbishop of Canterbury (about 1180) to the General Chapter threatening to excommunicate those 'who gave or sold to the Cistercians lands from which tithes were owed'[223]. In a parish where the Cistercians might have one or two large granges the loss of income to the rector could be considerable. The Chapter took note and enjoined its abbeys to pay tithes on lands acquired where tithes had previously been due, until and unless such tithes were peacefully acquired[224]. The bitter animosity shown to the Cistercians by Archdeacon Walter Map of Oxford (d. 1210) perhaps stemmed in part from diminishing tithes in his parish of Westbury-on-Severn – because of land owned there by Flaxley[225]. As 'more and more voices' were raised in protest, the Fourth Lateran Council (in 1215) took up the issue[226]. It decreed that tithe-exemption was to be maintained in respect of land acquired and/or brought into cultivation before the Council – and still cultivated by the monks, but thereafter only to land they brought newly into cultivation[227]. Honorius III (1224) extended Cistercian tithe-exemption to possessions leased out to tenants and to the produce of gardens, orchards and fisheries[228]; and Innocent IV (1244) to sheep and cattle and the output of forests, salt-mines and mills[229].

The widespread feeling – which archbishop Peckham of Canterbury alleged in 1284 – that: 'Plenty of people have a very great horror of the approach of the Cistercians, for they take away tithes'[230], did not stop Boniface VIII (1302) – grateful for their support during his struggle with Philip IV of France – from extending to the whole Order a right previously granted to eight French abbeys. This meant that all Cistercian lands – whether under domestic cultivation or leased to others – were not to be subject to tithe if no one had been collecting tithes from those possessions up to that time[231]. As a result the Order could demise land without fearing claims from local rectors and other tithe-owners: with the decline in their own labour force of *conversi* this was an opportune development[232].

Despite their theoretical and blanket privileges of tithe-exemption most monasteries found it advisable to clear their lands of any claim for tithe-payment, so that their granges were free and unencumbered[233]. There is much evidence that whilst in theory

Cistercian lands may have been excused the payment of practically all tithe, yet in practice numerous agreements were reached with tithe-owners by which the latter quitclaimed their rights in favour of the white monks[234]. The cartularies of many abbeys list concords relating to the settlement of tithe-payment disputes[235]. Despite, or because of, such agreements, some tithes were payable: Hulton (1237) paid tithes even on newly-cleared land at Mixon[236], and Fountains (1245) gave tithes out of a portion of Bradley Grange[237].

In England and Wales tithe-exemption was long enduring and was enjoyed – by the monks' successors in the ownership of such lands – until the final abolition of tithe payments in 1936. Perusal of the nationwide mid-nineteenth century survey of tithes – each parish having its map and apportionment schedule, is of considerable assistance in delineating medieval Cistercian lands – especially where the original monastic estate has been subject to later sub-division[238]. Deriving from – and coterminous with – certain tithe-free lands in Britain were areas of later *extra-parochial* status. These too are of the greatest assistance in Cistercian mapping. The centuries of monastic possession – with no external parochial involvement nor payment of tithes – meant that after the Dissolution these lands were not viewed as belonging to any particular parish. On the Continent the same Cistercian preservation of their privileges resulted in an archbishop of Mainz forbidding any priest to expect parochial rights within the granges of Walkenried (1224)[239], and led a parish priest of St Magnus, Brunswick to renounce his claims against three granges of Riddagshausen (1226)[240]. It was in these ways that some grange lands lost from human memory their original parochial association.

Until 1845 the extra-parochial demesne of Kingswood formed an island of Wiltshire within the county of Gloucester[240a]. Grace Dieu owned a chapel in the extra-parochial woodland of Trivel[241], whilst – in a like situation in wild, lonely country at Kidland on the Scottish Border – the *conversi* of Newminster resided and worshipped at the Memmerkirk[242]. Some such extra-parochial areas gave way to new ecclesiastical parishes after the Suppression, like Gwenddwr and Monknash in Wales. At least two parishes in England and one in Scotland – all now called 'Grange' – derive from former Cistercian holdings. In Ireland Mellifont's 'Salt Grange' became the later parish of Salterstown[243].

The Cellarer

Pivotal to the economy of any Cistercian house in its earlier decades was the monk appointed as 'cellarer', for to him fell the oversight of all its granges and other property as well as the supervision and deployment of the *conversi*[244]. He was effectively the business manager of the monastery, and its well-being and prosperity depended in large measure on him. Indeed, the early *Institutes* of the Order forbade an abbot from handing over administration of monastic property to anyone other than the cellarer[245]. This meant, as the Rule emphasised, that a cellarer was to be 'prudent and of mature character'[246]. The Order insisted (1238) that no monk was to be appointed prior or cellarer unless he was of such quality that he might be considered fit to be promoted abbot[247]. A cellarer shared with his abbot and prior in many major decisions, and when rules were broken or things went wrong he might be disciplined along with them[248].

The early statutes provided that a cellarer was to render a monthly account of all the receipts and expediture of his house – whilst the grangers and heads of the several workshops were to do likewise in his presence[249], but his financial rôle declined with the advent of 'bursars' and 'treasurers'. The cellarer kept careful accounts, fragments of which are extant – as for Kingswood (1240)[250] and Tintern (1412)[251]. The cellarer of Savigny (1230) rendered account twice yearly of all receipts of corn and monies, and of the stock on the granges – noting the reasons for any improvement or deterioration. He checked the yearly accounts for each grange, noted any gifts the abbey received, and wrote out 'all his business and each article in his records'[252]. A cellarer might negotiate an agreement concerning tithes (St Bernard-opt-Scheldt, 1264)[253], receive fines imposed on erring villeins and tenants (Tintern, 1263, 1341)[254] and preside at the abbey's manorial court (Quarr, 1336)[255]. Not for nothing was the cellarer also known as the 'procurator' (Riddagshausen, 1288)[256] or the 'procurator-general' (Fontmorigny, 1275)[257].

The cellarer had oversight of the *conversi*, apportioning their work and labour, and so had a general responsibility for all the various workshops within the precincts[258]. He presented would-be *conversi* for admission and profession, and he led the *conversi* on Days of Sermon to the chapter-house and on Maundy Thursday to the cloister for the *mandatum*. He appointed those *conversi* who were to prepare the Christmas Eve night fire in the calefactory, who were to heat the water for the Maundy Thursday foot-washing, and who – on Good Friday – were to clean the church (after Vespers) and the cloister and chapter-house (after Compline). The cellarer had an especial oversight of the kitchen and refectory, ensuring that both were properly stocked with food and drink, and that all necessary utensils were at hand[259]. In the twelfth century his rôle may have incorporated all that a later 'refectorer' undertook[260]. The cellarer of Beaulieu (1270) also had control of the monastic brewery[261].

Cellarers (who could talk relatively freely when necessary) ate their meals at the second sitting and could take a rest in the dorter when they wished[262]. They had occasion to travel frequently – on business and inspecting the granges. In one year the cellarer of Kingswood (1240–41) went thrice to the nearby port of Bristol and twice to Gloucester; he also visited Bath, Cirencester, and Priddy Fair (in the Mendips)[263]. The cellarer of Lyse in Norway (1233) journeyed to King's Lynn (in England) to negotiate on behalf of King Håkon the release of two Norwegian ships impounded there[264]. One of the best known cellarers was Gerard of Clairvaux, praised by St Bernard for his 'masterly competence': 'nothing ever escaped his skilled eye'[265]. Cellarers may have been forceful personalities, perhaps chosen on that account. A cellarer of Sobrado (1241) was at the heart of a rebellion there[266]. A cellarer of Tintern (1318), jealous for his monastery's rights, went with his greyhounds to a neighbouring Augustinian manor and killed ten of its pigs[267].

In the fourteenth century the influence of some cellarers waned. Their early fiscal responsibilities were now largely in the hands of 'treasurers', there were few *conversi* left to supervise, some granges were demised and no longer under their control, and – with the advent of lay-Stewards – they took second place at the manorial court. In their hey-day cellarers – with their varied and considerable responsibilities and their need to be frequently absent – were allowed a deputy[268]. Generally known as the 'sub-cellarer', this monk might also be referred to as his 'associate' (Pforta, 1271)[269] or 'lesser cellarer' (Arnsburg, 1252)[270]. The sub-cellarer was to obey the directives of the cellarer and 'do absolutely nothing contrary to his will'[271]. The evolution of sub-cellarers in the twelfth century meant that the cellarer himself often came to be styled the 'greater' or 'major' cellarer, as at Eusserthal (1206)[272].

Apart from acting as the cellarer's deputy, the particular duties which came to be the lot of a sub-cellarer largely stemmed from the early responsibility of his master for maintaining the food-supply of the monastery. In especial he was charged by statute (1195) with the custody of the keys of the wine cellar and the ministration of wine[273]. In practice he was also frequently the pittancier – responsible (as at Beaulieu) for the supply of eggs, cheese and fish. As the provision of pittances multiplied, his duties in this respect might in a large monastery be delegated to a separate 'pittancier'. The sub-cellarer was certainly the pittancier at Beaulieu (1270) whilst much of his accounts there related to his rôle as fishmonger. He handled in that year some 8½ 'lasts' of red herrings (about 1 million fish) and 4 'lasts 'of white herrings (about 530,000 fish). He saw to the salting and preservation of fish, and he supplied herring dripping for grease to the shoe-maker[274]. The sub-cellarer of Croxden – also concerned with its fish supply – had the duty of periodically emptying and renewing the fish-pond[275].

During a visitation at Lilienfeld (1316) its sub-cellarer was advised to perform his duties with 'benevolence and gentleness', so that the monks didn't show animosity towards him[276]. The duties of a sub-cellarer, which began as a helping hand to the cellarer, became by the fourteenth century very specific ones. At Sibton (1328)[277] and Ebrach (1340)[278] rents in money or kind were reserved for him to fulfil his rôle adequately. At Sorø (1347) he had his own office[279]. Sub-cellarers might undertake business transactions, and this could involve travel – as for the sub-cellarer of Kingswood (1240) going to Gloucester and even as far afield as London[280].

In large monasteries the 'major' cellarer might share his work-load with officials more senior than a mere 'sub-cellarer'. By 1211 Salem had a 'major', a 'medium' and a 'sub-cellarer'[281]. The 1237 codification of statutes refers to 'two cellarers – major and middle'[282]. By 1311 Moreruela had its major cellarer – responsible for overall administration, a second cellarer who controlled the economy and the granges, and a third who was responsible for the kitchen (and presumably the refectory)[283]. Alcobaça had four cellarers: the major cellarer, another responsible for the lands in the Tagus valley, another who was 'cellarer of work', and yet another who was 'cellarer of flocks'[284]. Senior assistant cellarers might be termed 'con-cellarer' – as at Dore (1312)[285] or 'coadjutor-cellarer' – as at Vaux-de-Cernay (1233)[286]. Unfortunately the latter absconded with some of the monastery's money: later arrested and held in chains, he was banished 'to a remote house'.

Other Officers

From the early thirteenth century each Cistercian house had (usually) two 'bursars' or 'treasurers' who handled all the income and expenditure of their monastery. The *Institutes* of the Order had previously referred to 'the keeper of all deposits'[287]. The General Chapter (1217) insisted that all incomings were to be committed to the custody of 'the keepers of the common depository'[288]. Stephen Lexington, in his injunctions for houses of the family of Savigny (1230–31) made clear that all monies received – from whatsoever source and from whomsoever – were to be wholly paid to these treasurers and any expenses drawn from them. They were to keep a careful record of all monies received and expended: the nature of the currency, the amount, the source or destination, the date, and 'by whose hand'. The purpose was 'to avoid any suspicion of fraud'[288a]. The need for 'one or two faithful bursars' in each house was reiterated by the General Chapter of 1308[289]. The father-abbot was to ensure that they had been appointed, and they were to receive and expend all monies 'at the will of the abbot and the cellarer'. The papal Constitution for the Order in 1335 further codified their duties. The treasurers were to be appointed by the abbot after consulting with the senior monks (his 'council'), and one of them was to be the principal (hence the term 'sub-bursar' for the other)[290].

In some monasteries (as at Beaulieu) the senior bursar was known as the 'keeper of the treasury'[291] or as the 'chamberlain' (Velehrad)[292]. At Zbraslav (1344) the bursars seem to have been subordinate to its 'chamberlain'[293], but at Ebrach (1340) the offices of the 'chamberlain' and the 'bursars' were separately funded – with lands, money and kind rents reserved to assist their departments[294]. In the early fourteenth century there are isolated instances of lay treasurers being appointed: Dunkeswell (1326) found difficulty in obtaining accounts from its lay treasurer[295]. Lay 'stewards' appeared at Margam by 1333[296] and at Furness by 1339[297]. Such stipendiary officials – usually local people of substance and influence – presided (often through a deputy) at the monastery's manorial court[298].

Accounting

Cistercian accounting is best understood by reference to particular examples – as the rules drawn up by Stephen Lexington for Savigny (1230). The annual review (made after All Souls' Day, 2 November) was wide-ranging and sought information on twelve points: (i) debts, (ii) expenses, (iii) receipts of wool and stock, (iv) numbers in the community, (v) extent of lands, (vi) full details of the well-being of each grange, (vii) the number of all animals, (viii) rents in money, (ix) rents in kind, (x) all expenses to do with cereal production, (xi) all domestic, industrial and other agricultural expenses, (xii) expenses in pleas and litigation[299]. Lexington also enjoined that quarterly accounts were to be submitted by the grangers and herders to the abbot and his council[300]. At Furness (1231) he insisted that the treasurers, cellarers, bakers and brewers were to render account weekly ('within the circle of six weekdays'), lesser officials quarterly. On these occasions at least twelve other monks were to be present[301]. A weekly meeting was also held at Beaulieu (1270) every Monday morning (after Mass in winter, after Chapter in summer) presided over by the 'keeper of the rolls' and in the presence of the 'keeper of the Order'. At this all departments of the monastery made statements which made for harmonious working. Every Michaelmas each department submitted its annual accounts, and four times a year the chamberlain presented an outline of the general situation of the monastery to the abbot[302].

Amongst those accounts extant are the bursars' accounts for Kingswood for the year of 1 August 1240 to 1 August 1241[303]. These suggest a considerable profit noting £320 received and £263 spent. Most of this profit (if such it be) came from the sale of wool. In the accounts of the 1260s there were several instances of expenses exceeding receipts. The cellarer's rolls for the 1240–41 period tells of his travel expenses, and of payments for many miscellaneous items – as for the carriage of hay, for threshing and beating corn, for fish and salt and the repair of roads[304]. For Boxley a series of annual acounts exist, as yet untranscribed, stretching from the 1270s down to the late fifteenth century[305]. They include the rolls of the cellarer, sub-cellarer, keeper of the mills, keeper of the granary, and the infirmarian.

Summary surveys are extant for Stams and stretch from 1328 to 1345[306], made ready for visitations and elections of new abbots. They show that sometimes (as in 1331) receipts exceeded expenses (854 marks to 797 marks that year), but at other times (as in 1340) expenses were greater than receipts (by 52 marks in part of the year alone). The accounts tell how in 1333 Herman ceased to be abbot and Ulrich took his place, that the abbey had 41 monks and 10 *conversi*, that it was in debt to the tune of 136 marks, and that the stock of the home grange included 52 oxen, 82 cows and 201 she-goats. There was enough grain to suffice until Martinmas for the community and the guests. The annual accounts for Vale Royal (1336) describe an annual income of £249 but outgoings of £200. Of the income – £101 came from spiritualities (tithes and the like), of the expenditure – £60 went on hospitality, £50 in 'gifts, damages and contributions' (levies, subsidies, etc.) and £30 'in defence of the monastery' (legal fees and expenses). Only £48 remained for the support of the community[307].

The fullest annual Cistercian account yet published is that stretching from Michaelmas 1269 to Michaelmas 1270 for Beaulieu[308]. It includes thirty-one accounts not only for the granges but for every aspect of monastic life and economy – the portery, the infirmaries, the parchment maker, the brewer, the forge, the granary, and so on[309]. The published version is based upon British Library Additional MS 48978, but includes material from Barlow MS 49 at the Bodleian Library, Oxford[310]. It may be a copy of that year's accounts made as a guide to checking future accounts: it is doubtful that such a work was compiled each year, but that rather departmental records were normally presented orally with the aid of tallies, counters or rough notes[311]. It has also been pointed out that comprehensive and valuable as the accounts are, yet 'the whole picture is static: there is nothing to show whether developments are being planned, or whether the weather had provided a poor or an outstanding harvest'[312].

The Beaulieu Account Book still retains its medieval binding of oak boards and measures 52 × 54 cm. Each page was elegantly written in red, green and black ink, accompanied by a series of sepia-wash drawings illustrating the activities of the various monastic departments – mostly now sadly missing[313]. The Account Book opens with detailed 'Rules for the Account' outlining the procedures to be followed[313a]. No cash passed between the various officials, but all money transactions were carried out by a system of tallies. Following the 'Rules' comes the 'Table for Reckoning External Expenses and Receipts' – a valuable guide to prices in those years[314]. The carcass of an ox was valued at 6 shillings, a quarter of coarse salt was worth 12 pence and a cask of best beer was reckoned at 15 shillings. The accounts also reveal the measures used: for grain, 8 bushels = 1 quarter; for beer, 240 gallons = 1 cask; and for wool, 30 stone = 1 sack[315].

Notes

1. Hill (1968) 49.
2. Southern (1970) 262.
3. Rösener (1983a) 140.
4. *CM* 120.
5. *Cf.* Lekai (1977a) 296.
6. Köfler (1978) xxviii.
7. Much of it barren mountainous land.
8. McCrank (1973) 77.
9. Jacob (1970) 41.
10. Fossier (1975) 279.
11. Roehl (1972) 99–100.
12. Janssen (1983) 211–12, Zakrewski (1907) 74.
13. Cocheril 1964) 271.
14. Duby (1968) 29.
15. Waddell (1994) 29–30.
16. Mitkowski (1949) 386.
17. Grandmottet (1958) 3–9.
18. *SBC* I, 25.
19. Lekai (1977a) 289.
20. McGuire (1982) 78, 168–71.
21. Williams (1984) II, 201–02.
22. Fotheringham (1890) 17.
23. McCrank (1973) 67.
24. *CW* 180, cf. 199–93 (of *ca.* 1237).
25. Duby (1953) 53–4.
26. *AF* 203–04.
27. *CChR* III, 104.
28. *DD* 1511.
29. *RCC* V, 68.
30. Lekai (1977a) 291.
31. *TL* passim.
32. Duby (1953) 53–4.
33. *Cartae Glam.* VI, 2380–81.
34. *CDF* 187 (No. 531).
35. Williams (1984) II, 203.
36. *SBC* IV, 51 (No.   1,003 of 1268).
37. Grèzes-Ruelff (1977) 264; *cf. PCP* 127–28 (No. 55), 140–41 (No. 69), 197–98 (No. 138), 218–19 (No. 165) , 245–46 (No. 200), 256–57 (No. 217), 283 (No. 251), 368 (No. 382).
38. Fletcher (1919) 109.
39. *RD* I, 847 (No. 5096).
40. *RCCH* 105.
41. *RCCH* 118.
42. *RCCH* 98.
43. Péchenard (1883) 562.
44. Duby (1953) 114.
45. Kempf (1976) 30.
46. *RCC* III, 168.
47. Berman (1982) 257.
48. *RD* I, 798 (No. 4792).
49. Berman (1986) 124, *cf.* (1979) 218; Samaran (1970) 25.
50. *CL* 76.
51. *CAF* 130.
52. Péchenard (1883) 214–15.
53. *RCC* III, 371.
54. Carrick (1907) 49.
55. McCrank (1973) 66–7.
56. Cf. NLW, Penrice and Margam Ch. 2008; Williams (1984) II, 202.
56a. *CW* 30–1.
57. *CTD* 74–5.
58. McCrank (1973) 70.
59. Southern (1970) 147.
60. Berman (1982) 264.
61. *Ibid.* 251–64.
62. *CSBW* 95–7.
63. *CL* 87 (No. LXXXV).
64. *OSBS* (1) 221–22 (No. 20), 22–23 (No. 21), 45 (No. 38), 94–97 (No. 80).
65. Lekai (1977a) 291.

66. Williams (1984) II, 204.
67. Berman (1986) 95 (*n.* 6).
68. *CChR* III, 99–100.
69. *Cf.* Barnes (1982) 24.
70. *Cf.* D'Arbois (1858) 286, 288.
71. Williams (1984) I, 54.
72. *RHC* 20.
73. *CW* 290.
74. *CDAC* 80 (No. 67).
75. *CDP* 57 (No. XX).
76. *DD* 1482, *cf.* 1473.
77. Lingenberg (1982) 124–25.
78. Talbot (1939) 65.
79. *CW* 206–07.
80. *CPR* 1266/678.
81. *CPR* 1277/224 (B+P), 226 (C), 232 (H).
82. Hill (1968) 61, Lekai (1977a) 286.
83. *CBK* 203–05 (No. CCLXXXIX).
84. *SBC* II, 1–2 (No. 2).
85. Carville (1981) 39, Gasquet (1908) 78.
86. Hockey (1970) 134.
87. NLW, Penrice and Margam Charter 1978.
88. *Cartae Glam.* II (1910) 527–28.
89. *CRA* 24, *CPR* 1295/150.
90. *SBC* II, 283 (No. 389).
91. *CW* 122.
92. Carville (1979) 63.
93. *DHGE* X (1938) 245.
94. *Ibid.* 53.
95. *Cf. CAF* 109; *RD* I, 834 (No. 5013), II, 386–87 (No. 8075); Berman (1982) 255–56.
96. *RCC* II, 153.
97. *CDF* I, 245 (No. 694).
98. Kempf (1976) 80–84.
99. *CAF* 10.
100. Berman (1979) 205.
101. *RCC* III, 245.
102. Grèzes-Ruelff (1977) 269.
103. Gosso (1940) 88.
104. *RCC* II, 263.
105. *CDM* I, 492.
106. Berman (1979) 205n, (1986) 38n.
107. Williams (1984) II, 205.
108. Berman (1986) 95n; Bourgeois (1973) 141.
109. *RD* II, 310 (No. 7647).
110. Samaran (1970) 25.
111. Grèzes-Rueff (1977) 265.
112. McCrank (1973) 70–71.
113. *Cf.* Williams (1984) I, 29–31; II, 210–12.
114. Walker (1984) 40.
115. Batany (1964) 5–6.
116. *Ibid.* 8.
117. Lekai (1977a) 301, *cf. Statuta* I, 142 (1192/42).
118. Lekai (1977a) 301.
119. *Statuta* I, 117–18 (1190/1), *cf.* 118 (1190/2).
120. *Statuta* I, 321 (1206/9).
121. *LCC* (2) 285.
122. Desmond (1974) 138.
123. *Ibid.* 137–38.
124. *Ibid.* 139–40, 146.
125. *Ibid.* 150.
126. *Cf. SBC* I, 130–32.
127. France (1994) 73.
128. *CR* 232–35.
129. Donkin (1978) 61.
130. McGuire (1973) 122–23.
131. France (1994) 174, McGuire (1974) 29–30.
132. Cowley (1977) 76.
133. Jones (1947) 50–1.
134. *Cf.* BL, Add. Ch. 26727.
135. *UKG* 38 (No. XII).
136. *RD* I, 645 (No. 3856).
137. *RD* I, 827 (No. 4972), *cf.* NLW, Penrice and Margam Charters 279, 532.
138. *RSL* (2) 226.
139. *SL* 161 (No. 31), 210 (No. 2).
140. *CBW* 420.
141. *CB* 291.
142. *CW* 135–36.
143. *CL* 4747 (No.XLII), 48 (No. XLIII).
144. *CW* 8–9; *SBC* I, 147.
145. *CL* 19–20, 47 (No. XLII), 86 (No. LXXXIV).
146. *CL* 69 (No. LXIV).
147. Barnes (1982) 21, *cf.* Anton (1986) 322 (No. 25).
148. Douglas (1927) 73.
149. Birch (1897) 198.
150. *Ibid.* 227.
151. *CL* 19–20.
152. Péchenard (1883) 176–77.
153. Williams (1984) II, 210.
154. *CPR* 1399/575.
155. Williams (1984) II, 210.
156. *AF* 160, 165; *VCH*, *Lancaster* II (1908) 191n.
157. *RHC* 73–6.
158. Williams (1984) II, 209.
159. *DR* 362–64.
160. *UKSH* 172 (No. CLXXXVI), 182–83 (No. CXCVIII), 265 (No. CCXCV).
161. *CAF* 61–2.
162. *CDS* III, 88–89.
163. *CL* 13 (No. XI).
164. *CW* 211.
165. *CDRB* II, 59–61 (Nos 64–5).
166. *UKO* 10–14.
167. Goutagny (1964) 206.
168. McGuire (1982) 117.
169. De Moreau (1909) 130–35.
170. *CDB* 240 (No. CXXIV).
171. *RHC* 72.
172. *CPR* 1279/314.
173. *RCH* 110.
174. Williams (1984) II, 208.
175. *Cal. Papal Registers (Letters)* V, 164.
176. *CPR* 1267/116.
177. Barnes (1982) 21–2.
178. *RHC* 21.
179. *CS* I, 137–38.
180. *RHC* 49.
181. *CDCDS* 167–68.
182. *DD* 1511.
183. *TG* 358.
184. *CDS* III, 235–36.
185. *CDH* 232–37 (No. 34).
186. *FHL* 100.
187. *Statuta* III, 242 (1289/1).
188. *FHL* 101.
189. *CDCDS* 519–20.
190. *CNM* xviii.
191. *CADC* 6–7; (its markers also included a *cerum crucis*).
192. Blashill (1892) 106.
193. Wullschleger (1986) 29.

194. *CDCDS* 519–20.
195. *SMD* II, 263–64.
196. Bell (1994) 256, Hallam (1986) 71–81.
197. Kempf (1976) 35–5.
198. McGuire (1982) 172.
199. *DHGE* IX (1937) 1099.
200. *RD* I, 860 (No. 5181).
201. Waller (1903) 358.
202. *RHC* 25.
203. VCH, *Chester* III (1980) 159.
204. Cottam (1928) 79.
205. *ABB* 34.
206. Lindley (1954) 177.
207. McCrank (1973) 65.
208. Blashill (1892) 105.
209. *CHS* IV, 50.
210. *Ibid.* 104.
211. *AF* 230–31.
212. Berman (1986) 83.
213. Dubled (1959) 778.
214. Conbhuí (1958) xxxiii.
215. *RD* I, 559 (No. 3282).
216. Constable (1964) 251.
217. *Ibid.* 240–42.
218. *Ibid.* 289.
219. *Ibid.* 279–80.
220. O'Callaghan (1960) 58–9, Constable (1964) 296–303.
221. *AF* 153–54.
222. Rocca (1936) 77.
223. Constable (1964) 293.
224. *Ibid.* 303, Berman (1981) 200–01.
225. VCH, *Gloucester* II (1907) 94.
226. O'Callaghan (1960) 58–9.
227. Donnelly (1949) 68–9.
228. Lekai (1977a) 67.
229. *Ibid.* 67; *LCC* (2) 248, cf. 251.
230. Donnelly (1954) 409.
231. *Ibid.* 421.
232. *Ibid.* 422.
233. Berman (1986) 51–2.
234. Berman (1978) 288.
235. Berman (1978) 288, *cf.* Constable (1964) 270–72.
236. Tomkinson (1985) 60.
237. Clay (1929) 101.
238. Williams (1984) II, 240–41.
239. Wiswe (1953) 64.
240. *Ibid.* 65.
240a. Lindley (1954) 115.
241. Williams (1976) 71–2.
242. *CNM* xviii, 77, 164.
243. Conbhuí (1958) 52.
244. *Statuta* I, 29 (1134/LXVIII), *LCC* (1) 99; Sullivan (1989) 182.
245. Roehl (1972) 89–91.
246. France (1998) in press.
247. *Statuta* II, 200 (1238/76).
248. O'Sullivan (1989) 185.
249. *Statuta* I, 45 (1152/27).
250. *DCK* 193–99.
251. NLW, Badminton Manorial 1575.
252. *RSL* II, 226, 230–31.
253. *OSBS* (1) 261.
254. Williams (1984) II, 255.
255. Hockey (1970) 171.
256. *CRD* 39.
257. *CAF* 302.
258. *Statuta* II, 245 (1241/75).
259. *EOC* 328–33.
260. *EOC* 333 (CXVIII/18), 469 (*n.* 256).
261. *ABB* 230–37.
262. *EOC* 232–238, *cf.* 328–32.
263. *DCK* 193–99.
264. Johnsen (1977) 50–51.
265. France (1998) in press.
266. *Statuta* II, 243 (1241/68).
267. PRO, C 115/K 2/6683, f. 94.
268. *EOC* 331 (CXVII/26).
269. *UKP* 239.
270. *CDM* V, 19.
271. *EOC* 331 (CXVII/27).
272. *Statuta* I, 331 (1206/59).
273. *Statuta* I, 184 (1195/17).
274. *ABB* 304–05, 308–12.
275. *CC* (2) B. 46.
276. *HVCP* 52.
277. *SBE* 43, 53, 68–9.
278. *MEB* 137–38.
279. *SRD* IV, 535.
280. *DCK* 215.
281. Rösener (1974) 155.
282. *LCC* (2) 335.
283. Antón (1986) 242.
284. Durand (1983) 112.
285. Williams (1976) 51 (*n.* 19).
286. *RSL* II, 216 (No. 28).
287. *D'Arbois* (*1858*) *236.*
288. *Statuta* I, 465 (1217/4).
288a. *RSL* II, 192 (Nos 6–7), 203 (No. 16), 204 (No. 21), 226 [where one reading would give 'treasurers of the year' – as if referring to an annual appointment].
289. *Statuta* III, 319 (1308/3), *cf.* 383 (1328/11).
290. McNulty (1943) 160–61.
291. *ABB* 313.
292. *CDEM* II, 263.
293. *RBM* IV, 574 (No. 1418).
294. *MEB* 131–33, 138–39.
295. Sparks (1978) 54.
296. Birch (1897) 303.
297. *AF* 266; an earlier Steward in 1234 may have been more of a personal officer of the abbot (*AF* 199).
298. Hockey (1970) 171.
299. *RSL* II, 232–33.
300. *RSL* II, 29.
301. *RSL* II, 204 (Nos 19–20).
302. *ABB* 41.
303. *DCK* 199–201, *cf.* 219.
304. *DCK* 193–99.
305. PRO, SC 6/1251–56.
306. *VKS* 196–99.
307. VCH, *County of Chester* III (1980) 160.
308. *ABB* passim.
309. *ABB* 44–5.
310. *ABB* 1–9.
311. *ABB* 9.
312. *ABB* 24.
313. Talbot (1958) 190; *cf. ABB* 3.
313a. *ABB* 46–51; Talbot (1958) 194.
314. *ABB* 52–55.
315. *ABB* 40–1.

Chapter 13

THE GRANGES

The ideal system by which the Cistercians exploited their lands was through a series of 'model farms' – quickly known as 'granges': a generic term in the early Middle Ages for buildings – especially store-houses – devoted to agricultural production[1]. The white monks gave the term new emphasis, for their granges were centres where *conversi* lived and laboured in company with hired workers. A grange might be called a 'court' (*curia*) of the abbey concerned. The terms were interchangeable: monarchs confirming the properties of Neubourg called its farms 'courts', but papal bulls referring to the same entities termed them 'granges'[2]. In later medieval times, and in modern mapping, granges have become colloquially known as 'cwrt' or 'mynachty' (in Wales – with variants such as 'hengwrt' and 'quirt'), 'uithof' (in Holland), 'hof' (in Germany), 'dvór' (in Bohemia)[3] and 'ladegård' (in Denmark)[4]. In France 'court' appears as a suffix as in Biche*court* and Tremon*court* – granges of Cherlieu[5]. The term 'court' was also more narrowly used with respect to the building complex at the heart of a grange.

Some granges were little more than sheep runs, with a bare minimum of essential buildings[6]. Larger granges might be almost miniature monasteries – with precinct wall, gatehouse, hostelry, chapel, calefactory, refectory and dorter, as well as having a barn, animal shelters and possibly a mill. Some abbeys (as Grandpré)[6a] evolved from being a grange of their mother-house. Contrariwise, an abbey which could not attract or sustain a sufficient community might be reduced to grange status (as Trawscoed)[7]. The original site from which a community moved to a new location generally remained in the monks' hands as a grange, as in the case of Asseraule[8]. A number of granges incorporated earlier hermitages: when Fontfroide received the hermitage of St Arnoult – which became its Parvoneval Grange – it also inherited his tomb and chapel[9]. As the Middle Ages progressed – and monastic lands expanded – granges in close proximity frequently came to form part of a larger unit and were henceforth jointly managed[10].

Grange Sites

Granges were sited in a wide variety of topography – allowing specialised forms of farming, a diversity of produce, labour saving by seasonal transfer of workers and the minimising of risk as disease or bad weather might hit one grange rather than another[11]. Granges were established on widely differing soil-types, as those of Cîteaux – ranging from soils developed on lowland Recent Alluvium to upland Jurassic Limestone[12]. Granges might be sited on coastal marshland – which no-one else might have wanted (as the Moor Grange of Meaux) – helping to drain it. Some granges were elevated in the uplands, as La Baltière of Beaubec at 1200 metres[13]. Granges by the sea (as several of the Welsh abbeys) allowed coastwise movement of agricultural produce to the monastery, and gave potential for fishing

In settled areas of western Europe the pressure on available land meant that

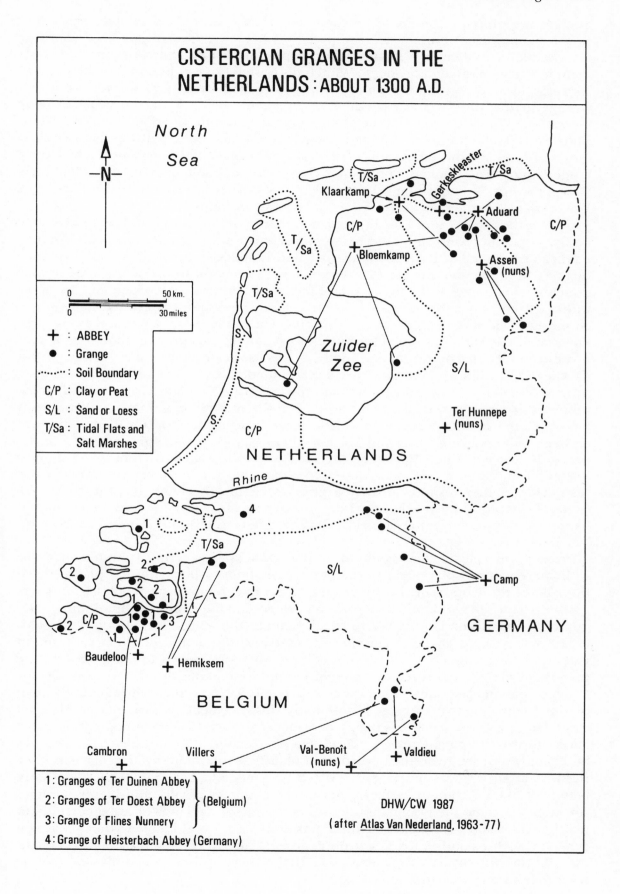

CISTERCIAN GRANGES IN THE
NETHERLANDS : ABOUT 1300 A.D.

North
Sea

N

0 ___ 50 km.
0 ___ 30 miles

+ : ABBEY
● : Grange
..... : Soil Boundary
C/P : Clay or Peat
S/L : Sand or Loess
T/Sa : Tidal Flats and
Salt Marshes

T/Sa

Klaarkamp
Gerkeskleaster
T/Sa
Aduard
C/P
C/P
Bloemkamp
Assen
(nuns)

Zuider
Zee

S/L

Ter Hunnepe
(nuns)
+

NETHERLANDS

Rhine

4
1
T/Sa
2
S/L
2
2
1
Camp
2 C/P 1 1 3
1   1
GERMANY
Baudeloo
+ Hemiksem

BELGIUM

Val-Benoît
(nuns)
+ Valdieu

Cambron
+ Villers
+

1: Granges of Ter Duinen Abbey
2: Granges of Ter Doest Abbey } (Belgium)
3: Grange of Flines Nunnery
4: Grange of Heisterbach Abbey (Germany)

DHW/CW 1987
(after Atlas Van Nederland, 1963-77)

granges were often to be found on the edge of parishes: indeed granges frequently over-rode parochial boundaries – especially where the grange consisted more of detached lands rather than of one large compact block. Oia's Silva Grange had lands in no less than eighteen parishes[14], Whitland's Castell Cossam in nine[15]. A shortage of land saw numerous granges established in well-wooded areas – as Balerne's Montorge Grange in the Jura[16]. Not a few abbeys (as Altenberg[17] and Casanova[18]) had their 'Forest' or 'Wood' Grange. Other grange names reflecting their site included Holm Cultram's 'Sandenhouse' – on a sandy ridge[19], and Clairvaux's 'Outre-Aube' – close to the abbey but on the other side of that river[20]. Kingswood and Tintern had their 'upper' and 'lower' granges – reflecting relative altitude[21]. Sibton and Meaux had their 'North Granges' – indicating orientation[22]. 'New Granges' – like those of Villers[23] and Walkenried[24] – might suggest a relatively late date of foundation.

So that the *conversi* could readily return to their monastery for Sundays and Greater Festivals, granges were supposed be no more than a day's march away. This distance has been computed at 15 to 20 kilometres (9 to 12 miles)[25]. By the late twelfth century this was an injunction difficult to observe as most monasteries had a few quite distant granges – sometimes fulfilling especial functioms. Øm had fifteen granges, ten were within 16 km but one (Radmos) was 90 km removed and a source of limestone[26]. Grandselve had seventeen granges within 15 km but another was a pastoral grange 140 km away[27]. The early statutes of the Order also enjoined that granges should be at least two Burgundian leagues from one another. This has been computed as between 8 and 11 km (5 to 7 miles)[28], and was specifically intended to reduce friction between the *conversi* of neighbouring granges. It was only in 1278 – a bit late in the day as *conversi* numbers had greatly waned – that the General Chapter rescinded this regulation[29]. It was the close proximity of granges which – more than any other factor – led to disputes between neighbouring Cistercian houses. There had to be some give-and-take in the concords reached: when Valmagne (by 1161) set up its Cambert Grange too close to one of Silvanès, the grange was allowed to remain but the movement of its flocks was restricted[30]. Other disputes involving granges 'within the limits constituted by the General Chapter'[31] meant that (in 1233) the abbots of Clairmarais and Villers had to fix the bounds of Cambron's Stopeldic Grange *vis-à-vis* the Dunes' Zande Grange[32] and Ter Doest's Groda Grange[33].

Pressure on available land could mean that granges came to incorporate entire vills with consequent displacement of the population. Some scholarship has played down the rôle of the Cistercians in this respect[34], but that removal of peoples from lands given to the white monks did take place is evidenced in the efforts of King John to safe-guard inhabitants on lands given to Neath[35] and to Kingswood[36]. A bishop of Glasgow (1222) was worried at the expulsion of tenantry by the monks of Holm Cultram 'in making their granges'[37]. At least nine villages were suppressed to make way for the granges of Plasy[38], and three for some of Esrum[39]. Fountains developed its Baldersby Grange out of no less than three former settlements[40]. Numerous quitclaims at the turn of the twelfth century suggest a substantial displacement of peasants as Margam extended its estates[41]. There is plenty of evidence of such Cistercian population clearance, but it was a patchy process. Displaced peoples might be resettled elsewhere (as by Byland)[42], or be given their freedom (Lubiąż)[43], or become *conversi* (Margam)[44] or resident hired workers (Furness)[45]. Evicted peasants may have found that they were better off: their lot might be pleasanter[46]. The churches of vills absorbed by granges sometimes became the grange oratory – as on some of the lands of Aubepierre[47], but in other cases an existing parish church was destroyed – as at Llangewydd by Margam (1202)[48]. Such examples led Guiot de Provins (1206) to comment of the Cistercians that: 'In the churchyards, over men's bodies, they have built pigsties and their asses lie where men were wont to chant Mass'[49].

Grange Numbers and Size

Many of the abbeys founded in the early twelfth century rapidly set up at least five or six granges, and continued to add to this number – and to enlarge their existing granges – down to about the middle of the thirteenth century. Ourscamp set up seven granges between 1130 and 1153, but only one after 1240[50]. Fontfroide had but five or six granges in 1162, but possessed at least twenty-four by the end of the thirteenth century[51]. The county of Yorkshire had forty-six granges before 1200 but 72 by 1220[52]. The turning-point of the mid-thirteenth century came perhaps because most abbeys then had as many granges as they needed or could handle: with the common decline in *conversi* numbers it was now difficult to staff in the traditional manner even those they had. Charter evidence helps some granges to be dated precisely and to trace the build-up of Cistercian estates. A grant to Bonport (in 1190) shows that it was currently 'making the grange' of Ardouval[53]. A papal bull in favour of Sulejów (1234) mentions the grange of Łęczno 'which the monks had constructed'[54].

The number of granges held varied greatly, and abbeys founded relatively late generally had the least[55]. The largest numbers – twenty-five or more – belonged to the abbeys of southern France[56], Flanders[57] and Yorkshire[58]. In Burgundy great abbeys (like Cîteaux and Cherlieu) approached to twenty, the average number (as at Fontenay) was ten to twelve, some modest abbeys (like Lieucroissant) had only seven or eight[59]. In Bohemia Plasy and Sedlec each had over twenty granges, but Osek had only ten and the rest lay in between[60]. Granges might be a marked feature of the regional cultural landscape: Burgundy boasted over 200 Cistercian farms and vineyards[61]. In eastern Europe – where there were relatively few granges – the paucity was more than balanced by other forms of land holdings.

The size of granges also varied greatly – with the nature of the land surface and soil, as well as the amount of land available. Granges which were primarily arable concerns were smaller than those mostly devoted to pastoralism. It has been estimated that the Dunes had 25 granges absorbing 10,000 ha (25,000 acres) of land, giving an average grange size of 400 ha (1,000 acres)[62]: on this basis Villers had an average grange size of 500 ha (1200 acres)[63]. Poblet's Cérvoles Grange totalled 1000 ha (2500 acres) but part of this was irrigated or pastoral land[64]; Aberconwy's Nanhywnain Grange comprised some 4850 ha (12,000 acres) but was mostly barren mountainous land[65]. Some monasteries had a much smaller average grange size like the farms of Altenberg (150 ha/370 acres)[66], Bebenhausen (190 ha/470 acres) and Eberbach (350 ha/860 acres)[67]. Bebenhausen had some large granges – as Geisnang (530 ha/1500 acres), but also quite small ones – as Vesperweiler (50 ha/125 acres)[68]. Whilst Meaux had two large granges (Skerne and Wharram) others were much smaller – one only 69 ha (170 acres, another but 39 ha (95 acres) – giving it an average grange size of 188 ha (464 acres). Its smaller granges were not compact but consisted of widely scattered strips: its Moor Grange lay partly in Doddington fields, partly in Beeforth fields and partly in an enclosure of its own[69].

Large compact granges frequently grew out of relatively small holdings: they were consolidated by the abbey concerned buying out parties who had interests there or exchanging other lands for theirs, and extended by adding adjacent plots. This process was especially helped by the General Chapter's permission (from 1200) for distant and useless lands to be discarded[70]. Staffarda's Luagnasco Grange grew by the year 1300 to some 1300 'giornate' of land from the original benefaction of 120 'giornate' in 1138[71]. Margam (from 1150 to 1320) used the two-fold process of exchange and of acquiring contiguous lands to develop a valuable strip of land, east of Pyle, which came to encompass several granges. Around 1200, for example, it gained an additional thirty acres 'nearest to its land of Llanfeuthin'[72]. Meaux's Moor Grange (founded about 1170) was extended when its neighbour, Acer, gave it: 'The land he has nearest the grange, on every side of the grange'[73]. Some fifteen grants and deeds (from before 1154 to 1210) enabled Warden to consolidate its grange at Myddlehoo[74]. At least ten grants helped St Sulpice-en-Bugey (1145 to 1162) to build up its grange at Chassagne[75]. Oia, in completing its estates, received 62 grants (1270–1305), but also made 273 purchases or exchanges[76].

Michaelstein (1284) made an exchange for 'enlarging its grange' in Helsinge[77]. Sallay (1298) exchanged 1½ acres it held in Barrowby for the same acreage adjacent to its grange there[78]. Cîteaux acquired fifteen strips of land in one Burgundian village (Ouges) in a single year (1322): 'Between seed-time and harvest'[79]. Where individuals still held rights as grange lands began to surround their holdings and hem them in, they were bought out. This was done in seventeen different acts in the case of Bonnevaux's Landrins Grange[80], and by more than twenty agreements as Igny (*c.* 1200) developed its Villardelle Grange[81]. Two men gave strips of land to Meaux which they held within 'The court of its grange' of Moor[82]. Dore (*c.* 1240) consolidated Llanfair Grange by buying up lands lying 'within the lands of the monks'[83]. It was the chronicle of Meaux which noted that its monks – by merging its 'cultures' in Arnold Grange – were able to 'hold them more conveniently'[84]. The white monks clearly realised that consolidation and extension made economic good sense.

Grange Enclosures

The bounds of early granges were often delineated by a ditch around the perimeter – lined by an embankment formed with the earth excavated. Such a 'fosse' (if hedged) also served to exclude wandering animals. In the late twelfth century Fountains made at Greenbury (near Scorton): 'A fosse to enclose all the land'[85]. Doberan (1313) received a grant to aid maintain: 'The fosse around its court of Gawetzowe'[86]. At least five of Meaux's granges had moated nuclei[87], whilst the main enclosure of Cwmhir's Mynachty Grange was a moat almost four metres wide[88]. Roche had 'a ditch before the gate of the grange of Thurnscoe'[89]: in such cases a perimeter ditch meant that the approach to the gate of a grange took the form of a causeway or bridge. In large granges there might be an inner and an outer court, both having earthwork surrounds. Such great double enclosures can be seen at Fountain's Sutton Grange and Garendon's Burton Grange[90]. Within the inner enclosure stood the homestead of the grange, itself sometimes moated – as at Sibton's Jurdyz Grange (1325)[91]. The great earthen embankment surrounding Neath's Monknash Grange encompasses several other enclosures within the square mile formed by the main precinct[92].

The precinct banks of granges might in time be replaced with stone walls. Chiaravalle di Milano's Valera Grange had a moat around it by 1236 and encircling walls by 1255[93]. By the fifteenth century Plasy's Třebekov Grange[94] and Chaâlis' Vaulerent Grange[95] were enclosed by stone walls: that at the former measured 110 × 90 metres, that at the latter was fortified with small turrets. A massive boulder wall still encircles the territory of Garendon's Roystone Grange[96]. Precinct walls presupposed the need for a gateway entrance: Sibton's North Grange had its 'north gate' and its 'south gate'[97]. The remains of stone gateways can be seen at Tintern's Merthyr Gerain Grange[98] and Ourscamp's Warnavillers Grange[99]. Some grange gateways consisted of little more than an entrance with a cell attached for the porter, but others were so substantial that business transactions were done there – as by Staffarda (1228) at 'the gate' of its Pomerolo Grange[100]. The work of charity at the gate (like in a monastery) was emphasised by donors who gave thirty loads of turf annually to Furness: 'To warm the poor who are entertained at the gate of Winterburn Grange'[101].

Grange Buildings

The buildings sited within the inner court varied from little more than rudimentary accommodation for the *conversi* (though usually with a substantial barn)[102] to a complex of domestic and functional structures making the grange almost a monastery in miniature[103]. The Order assumed the presence on its granges of at least an oratory, dormitory, refectory, calefactory and hospice[104]. Some scholars today insist that the grange was *not* the reduced version of an abbey[105] – but several medieval descriptions tell otherwise. In 1237 Morimondo Milano's Fornace Grange had its refectory, two dorters (one being for the cow-herds), a kitchen, two store-houses (of hay and straw), stock buildings and a cheese-making unit[106]. In 1307 Pipewell's Causton Grange had a cloister (as did Staffarda's Pomerolo Grange in 1245)[107] dorters for monks and *conversi*, kitchen, refectory and chapel, with separate chambers for the abbot and the brewer[108].

Not all early granges had purpose-built dorters. A General Chapter statute of 1202 enjoined that *conversi* resident on the granges were not to sleep with the grooms in the stables, but 'in another place'[109]. This injunction may have stimulated the construction of dorters on the granges. Medieval dorters can still be seen at Clairvaux's Fraville Grange and Orval's Prouilly Grange[110]. The Chapter (1220) also legislated regarding the refectories on granges: the *conversi* were to eat in silence and wearing their cloaks[111]. Plasy's refectory at its Kázňov Grange was noted (in 1346) as being 'a chamber of stone'[112]. Essential was the kitchen: that of Pipewell's Causton Grange (in 1266) baked – in its two large ovens – enough bread (both common and of better quality) to serve nine granges of the monastery[113]. Deeds were executed in the 'lower porch' (sub-portico) of the kitchen of Staffarda's Morre Grange (in 1291)[114]. A few granges might have their own infirmary since they lay at a considerable distance from their abbey: like Casanova on St Satrone Grange (in 1254) – the hospital soon transferred to its St Agatha's Grange (in 1257)[115] – and the Dunes (1258) on its island Zande Grange[116].

Hospitality on the Granges

The giving of accommodation to travellers – especially members of the Order – was implied by the General Chapter (1134+) which early assumed the presence of guest hospices on the granges[117]. The brother 'hospitaller' – who could talk quite freely, especially with guests and servants[118] – is on record at Fontainejean's Mosily Grange (1196)[119]. Abbot Richard of Louth Park (1224–46) built in all its granges: 'Dormitories and dining rooms for guests'[120]. Morimondo di Milano's Basiliano Grange (1237) had: 'A house in which guests were lodged'[121]. A grant of timber enabled Obazine's Graule Grange (1366) to have firewood to warm its hospice in the village of Ventaillac[122]. At Départ was a hospice-grange of Sauvelade receiving pilgrims *en route* for Compostella[123]. Doberan (1313) received guests – 'Even lords and knights' – at its grange of Gawetzowe[124]. Accompanied sometimes by their army (as at Morfa Mawr in 1256)[125] or retinue (as on the granges of Pforta)[126], hospitality afforded to a prince or a bishop could prove a considerable burden. Granges might get caught up in local warfare. An earl of Gloucester (1202) used Strata Florida's Aberduhonw Grange as a base whilst trying, unsuccessfully, to storm Builth Castle[127]. During a rebellion of the men of Holderness, its sheriff posted men in Meaux's Sutton Grange[128].

Granges were places where business of the Order might be done, like the meetings to codify statutes or to solve pasture disputes. Fifteen abbots were to meet (in 1190) at 'Caleium', a grange of Pontigny: if their business was protracted – to spare undue burden on that grange's resources – they were to move on to 'Cerelegio', a grange of

Vauluisant[129]. A visiting abbot was allowed (from 1187) to 'eat in a fitting place, in the refectory or otherwise as he wishes'[130]. Incidents of a 'less than respectful' welcome to, or 'inhumane' treatment of, such abbots included those at granges of Fontainejean (1196)[131] and Pilis (1222)[132]. Visiting monks and *conversi* were not to tarry overlong[133] and were to eat as the brothers of the grange: they might talk with the granger and the hospitaller but not to the other resident *conversi*[134]. Secular business might also be transacted: in the mid-thirteenth century 'love-days' (occasions to settle disputes without recourse to law) were held at Dore's Kingstone Grange and Tintern's Trelech Grange[135]. It was forbidden for women to enter the 'court' of a grange, unless by leave of the abbot, and even then no one was to talk alone with a woman[136]. Women might come into granges to milk the cows – but only in regions where milk-men could not be hired[137]. Women worked combing wool on a grange of Le Reclus (1215) – but were to do so outside the precinct[138]. Women baked bread on a grange of La Merci-Dieu (1217)[139]. As late as 1283 and 1297, however, the General Chapter reiterated that women were not 'to enter, live or pass the night' on granges[140].

Agricultural Buildings

The most solidly built edifice on a grange was usually the barn. Sited some way from the domestic quarters (to minimise the risk of fire)[141] it frequently remains a notable feature even where all the other grange buildings have disappeared. The side walls were each broken by an opposing large opening – to allow the entry and egress of carts, and the floor might in part be hardened by a mixture of limestone and clay – to allow the passage of horses and the threshing of sheaves[142]. The timber roof was upheld by one or two rows of stone, brick or wooden piers. A twelfth century barn survives at Preuilly's Beauvais Grange[143], whilst the longest Cistercian barn known is that of Beaulieu's St Leonard's Grange (seven bays comprehending 74 × 20 m)[144]. In the Beauvais region of France grange barns averaged 47.6 × 16.2 m with a mean height of 13.6 m: the number of bays formed by the supporting piers averaged ten, but Ereuse Grange had thirteen[145]. Other notable surviving barns include those of Beaulieu's Coxwell Grange[146] and Kingswood's Calcot Grange (the erection of the latter being dated on a stone as in the year 1300)[147], Pontigny' s Villers-la-Grange (with eleven central piers)[148] and Whalley's Stanlaw Grange (built of great sandstone blocks, its roof consisting of oak rafters locked together by oak pegs)[149]. The size of such barns was implied from the 150 wagon-loads of hay stored (in 1237) in the barn of Morimondo Milano's Basiliano Grange[150]. The need for such barns was emphasised by the production at Coxwell (in 1270) of nearly 500 qtrs of cereals[151].

Stone vaulted cellars commonly occur under the principal buildings of former granges: in them wine might be stored and other foodstuffs kept cool. At Plasy's Kázňov Grange (1346) the granary was built over: 'A cellar of stone'[152]. Morimondo Milano's Coronate Grange (1237) had two cellars – one for the storage of wine, another for cheese[153]. Carracedo's Villaverde Grange (1243) had: 'A wine cellar with its press'[154]. Above ground-level timber played the major rôle in the construction of grange buildings: consequently only the original stone vaults have sometimes survived. Meaux (*c.* 1240) used 'incorruptible oak' for its farm buildings[155]. Several monasteries received grants of timber to help in grange construction, repair and maintenance: these included Gimont (for its Grange du Hour, 1158)[156] and Biddlesden (for its Gorhal Grange, 1232)[157]. At Beaulieu's granges of Hartford and Beufre timber buildings were raised on large stone foundations[158]. Timber buildings – especially those which might contain dried out hay and corn – were susceptible to damage by fire, whether accidental or deliberate. A candle 'carelessly placed' caused a barn of Coupar

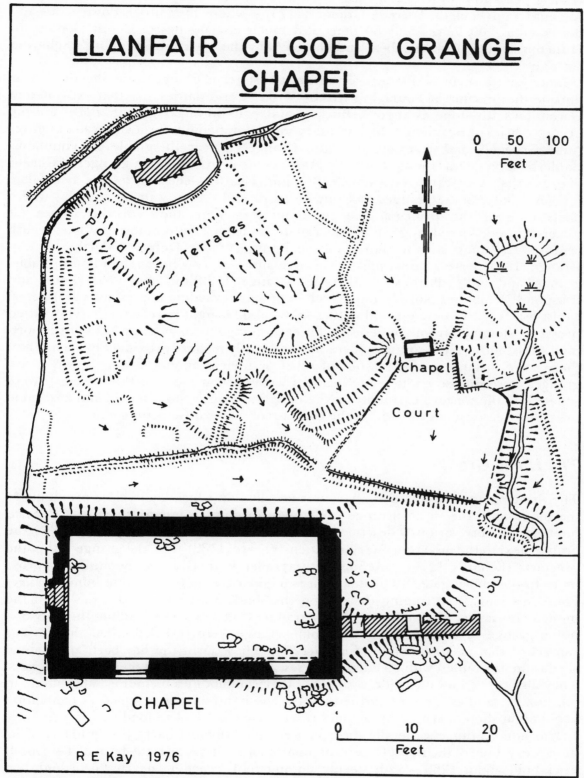

LLANFAIR CILGOED GRANGE CHAPEL

Ponds

Terraces

Chapel

Court

0   50   100
Feet

CHAPEL

R E Kay 1976

0   10   20
Feet

This plan was especially surveyed for the author's *Atlas of Cistercian Lands in Wales* (University of Wales Press, Cardiff, 1990)

(1215) to be destroyed[159]. Three granges of Vale Royal (1340) were burnt down by a restless peasantry 'with all the corn that was in them'[160]. Physical attacks saw men of Almenar raid Poblet's Torredà Grange (1175) – where they broke down gates and doors, stole 300 loaves and 60 hens and much else besides[161]. Count Godfrey of Huneburch (1175) robbed, beat and chased away the *conversi* of Neuburg's Selhoven Grange[162].

Amongst the many buildings found on a Cistercian grange were sheepcots – as outside the precinct at Fountain's Kirkby Wiske[163], and dairies – as that excavated at Garendon's Roystone Grange[164]. Buckets and pails were bought (in 1270) for the grange dairies of Beaulieu[165]. Stables find contemporaneous note at Clairvaux's Outre-Aube Grange[166] and Pipewell's Causton Grange[167]. Near the stable on Fountain's Balderby Grange was the cattle-shed[168]. Dove-cots still to be seen on granges of Chaâlis (Troussures), Ourscamp (Warnavillers)[169] and Neath (Gelligarn)[170] may be of late medieval date. Many granges had one or more mills. Two 'water-granges' – where boats entered the principal grange building – were those of the Dunes (at Allaersthuisen, served by an adjacent canal)[171] and of Hautecombe (the late twelfth century 'La Voûte' on the shore of Lake Bourget)[172]. At Tintern's Merthyr Gerain Grange (1387) were garden, pigsty, old byre and new, cow-house, hen-house, stable, granary and mill[173]. Bordesley's Shetwood Grange (1529) included a bake-house and fish-pond[174]. Sibton's North Grange had an orchard (yielding apples, nuts and pears) whilst osiers – with herbage and nettles sold – also brought in revenue[175]. This varied provision stemmed from the necessity for each grange to be more or less self-supporting. Whilst most of the grange offices were normally in close proximity to each other, there were instances – for reasons of relief or their economic history – why a few granges were diffuse entities. At Neath's Cwrt-y-carnau the 'court' and chapel were situated on the western extremity by the Loughor estuary, but the mill and coal-mine towards its eastern edges – within the confines of modern Gorseinon[176].

The Home Grange

The principal grange of a monastery was usually that which lay in close proximity to the monastery, the western range sometimes forming an integral part of it[177]. Such home farms were variously described as 'the court of the cloister' (Stams, 1333)[178], 'the grange next to the monastery' (St Benoît-en-Woëvre, 1182)[179] or 'the grange within the precincts' (Écharlis, 1219)[180]. At Sibton it was called Porta Grange – because of its proximity to the abbey gate[181]. Greater houses might have more than one home grange: Fountains had three ringing the site on the south, west and north sides[182]. In the immediate vicinity of Maulbronn lay six granges – all in a sense fulfilling the duty of a home grange[183]. The contents of a home grange were revealed when the Pavians ransacked that at Morimondo Milano (1237). They burnt the hay barn and animal sheds and absconded with 35 oxen, 5 horses, 120 pigs, an ass and 60 hens and capons. They also carried away a wide variety of other commodities including salt, salted fat, oil, honey, candles, pepper and chestnuts. The hen-house is revealed as containing about 50 bushels of crushed grain and cereals used for chicken food[184].

The home grange generally incorporated the principal barn, the granary, of its monastery. One of the finest Cistercian monuments in Europe is the barn of Ter Doest: brick-built about 1250 – with steeply sloping roofs reaching nearly 20 m high – it measures 60 × 24 m. The interior is divided into three naves by two rows of oak pillars set on bases of brick and Tournai stone[185]. In England – previously reckoned as one the earliest surviving timber framed buildings of the country[186] – is the Grange Barn of Coggeshall, the dating of which is now open to question[187]. An aisled structure of some six bays, it measures 37 × 14 m and reaches an internal height of nearly 11 m. The existing king-post roof structure dates from about 1290. The granary of Doberan, illuminated by gothic windows, was built by Abbot Conrad III (1283–90)[188]. The 'Elephant' granary of Loccum exceeded fifty metres in length: dating from about 1300 it had three floors[189]. The 'new granary' at Walkenried (1323) had a chapel dedicated to St Anthony built within it[190].

The granary was the domain of the *conversus* or monk appointed as 'keeper of the granary': a term sometimes confused with 'granger' (*infra*). The 'keeper of the granary' – otherwise called the 'grain-receiver' – is noted in deeds at Raitenhaslach (1290)[191] and at Hautcrêt (1344)[192]. The monks who were 'grain-receivers' at Savigny were to measure the grain – using tallies – in the presence of those who brought it: 'So that the occasion for theft is excluded, and there is no disagreement between senders and recipients'. They also kept a record of rents paid in kind on the granges[193]. The keeper of the granary at Beaulieu was (in 1270) responsible that year for receiving nearly 2,000 qtrs of wheat (mostly destined for the bake-house) and over 1,300 qtrs of oats (much going to the stables as fodder). He supplied all the monastery departments with grain as required. If corn was brought from its Cornish lands he had to pay the pilot of the boat 2$^{1}/_{2}$ pence for each quarter shipped[194].

Fortified Granges

The frequent insecurity of the countryside of medieval Europe due to war and unrest and the valuable nature of the contents of many Cistercian granges, meant that defensive measures had sometimes to be adopted. Many of these came later than the period of this study – a consequence of the Hundred Years' War between England and France. In Spain at least five of Poblet's granges when received were already obsolete defence towers or small castles[195]. They included Milmande – elevated in a commanding position – it was further strengthened and fortified in the abbacy of Ponç de Copons (1316–48): a fine vaulted gate-house resulted[196]. Other granges of Poblet were 'masies', where the farm buildings were placed around a central court-yard forming a fort-like enclosure with windowless exterior walls[197]. Other houses with granges which were previously forts included Nonenque nunnery (Peyre-sur-Sorgue)[198] and Zbraslav (Chocni)[199].

The weakness of most grange enclosures was demonstrated in 1329 – when the people of Pagny attacked Cîteaux's grange of Tontenans, breaking down the palisade[200]. In areas of especial difficulty normal defences had to be supplemented. Fontfroide may have initiated the imposing fortress-like nature of its Gaussan Grange in the early thirteenth century[201]. A century later it turned its Fontcalvi Grange (closer then to the Mediterranean) into a small fortress with eight high square towers: perhaps as a defence against looters from both land and sea[202]. Between 1270 and 1276 ramparts were supplied to four of the Brabant granges of Villers[203]. Heiligenkreuz (1282) was allowed to build in the churchyard of Gundramsdorf (where it had a vine-yard) a store-house to protect its property 'in time of war'[204]. A fortified gate-house is implied by the use of the term 'propugnaculum' to describe (in 1346) the principal building on Plasy's Kâzňov (Kaznejov) Grange[205]. Defensive measures might also include employing armed servants – with bow and arrows – on the granges: as did Fontenay (1233)[206], Holm Cultram (1235)[207] and Margam (1246)[208]. The commissioner of the Cour de Valréas in 1336 set up above the dorter of Aiguebelle's Fraysinnet Grange a banded red and white pontifical flag as a sign of protection[209].

Grange Chapels

On the granges an oratory was a necessity where the *conversi* could chant their office, but – as they were supposed to return to their monastery for Sundays and greater feast-days – it was not meant to be a 'chapel' in the sense that Mass was said there[210]. A statute of the General Chapter in the 1150s, referring to an earlier lost 'sentence', makes it clear that some granges did have chapels at an early date[211]. This may have been because they were part of lands given or acquired by an abbey[212] – perhaps when a hermitage was incorporated[213]. The Chapter – in the late-twelfth century and beyond – tried repeatedly to stop Mass being said on the granges but it was a losing battle. In 1180 it enjoined that no new altars might be built on the granges: those in place could remain but Mass was no longer to be chanted[214]. Despite this injunction – written into the 1202 codification of statutes[215] – Quarr (1190) had a chapel on its Forwood Grange and Furness (1199) at Hawkshead Grange[216].

These were not isolated examples for the Chapter took firmer action. In 1204 it ordered *all* altars on granges to be destroyed: Mass was only to be said on a grange by special leave of the General Chapter[217]. This statute was modified the next year (1205), perhaps after protests from benefactors and bishops: altars which had been consecrated might remain, but Mass was not to be said at them and no more were to be built[218]. Ten years on the rules were relaxed for those granges which had previously contained churches *with cemeteries*. Such chapels could be restored and Mass said in them twice a week[219]. Further relaxation was to come in 1236: abbeys which had non-parochial chapels before their incorporation into the Order might maintain worship in them[220]. Chapels which *were* held were not to be served by monks, but by secular chaplains specially appointed[221] or clergy enjoying the spiritual fraternity of a community[222].

Times were changing. By 1221 St Benoît-en-Woëvre had a chapel on its Bouzonville Grange where Mass was sung on Sundays and feast-days[223]. By 1228 Mass was said on Cistercian granges in Ireland[224]. The General Chapter itself gave leave for Mass in grange chapels where there were extenuating circumstances: on a grange of Casanova des Abbruzes (Civitella Casanova) – because it 'had been an abbey' (1231)[225], and on island granges of the Dunes and Ter Doest (1236) – because of their inaccessibility and the danger the sea posed to travellers[226]. Innocent IV (in 1245) allowed Mass in the grange chapels of St Bernard-opt-Scheldt (not long founded) because, he said, this had been newly proposed at the General Chapter[227]. In especial the monks had a grange called 'Castrum' (1244), where: 'The altar ought to remain, where the abbots and brothers on coming, as is the custom of the Order, are able to celebrate'[228]. Alexander IV (1255[229], 1257[230]) gave blanket permission for Mass to be said on granges 'far from a parish church', but only for their residents: strangers wishing to receive the sacraments there required the permission of the diocesan bishop. (This safe-guard protected the local parochial clergy from the loss of financial oblations.) The bishop of Lincoln (1236) allowed Thame to have a chapel at Oddington[231], and the bishop of Winchester (1249) permitted Waverley to have Mass at Neatham Grange[232].

Even after the papal concession of 1255 not all granges had chapels[233]. In Wales Margam had thirteen chapels (including those of at least two pre-existing ecclesiastical sites), Tintern and Llantarnam had seven chapels each, but two is the maximum known for any other Welsh house[234]. Jerpoint had nine grange chapels (one on each grange it possessed)[235], Jouy had eight[236], Froidmont had six[237]. In Majorca La Real's chapel at Esporles Grange (in 1360) had a silver chalice, altar cloth and hangings, missal, breviary and psalter[238]. No thorough survey has ever been attempted of grange chapels, but it is fair to say from visual observation that they were generally modest in size. Tamié's chapel at La Bridoire measured 10 m × 6 m[239].

The Order disallowed the ringing of bells on its granges, save for a small refectory bell to call the *conversi* to meals[240]: chapel bells were forbidden[241]. There was a bell-turret (in 1256) at Boulbonne's Tramesaigues Grange[242] – but its purpose is unknown. Burials on granges were also discountenanced by the Order: an abbot of Dalon (1190) was rebuked for consenting to a cemetery on a grange[243]. The first and second codifications of statutes (1202/37) ruled that no cemeteries were to be made on granges – and that none were to be buried there – unless a right of burial existed[244]. Some of Altenberg's grange chapels, however, were undoubtedly used (in 1236) for burying the dead[245]. It may have become a common practice: in Wales there is plenty of evidence for grange burials afforded by tradition, by finds of human bones and from field-names. Chapel Farm Terrace in Abercarn, on a former grange of Llantarnam, was once locally called 'Skeleton Row'[246].

As for the living, the attitude of both the Order and the bishops was that grange chapels were meant for the *conversi* and not for outsiders. Even the lay workers might only receive the sacraments at a grange chapel if they lived far from a parochial church. The pontiff or the diocesan bishop did allow relaxations where such was the case. As Cwmhir (1232) was: 'In a mountainous district, remote from parish churches', it received leave to administer the sacraments to its servants[247]. At Altenberg's Eppinghoven Grange (1236) men living within the bounds of the grange could communicate in its chapel – except at Christmas, Easter and Pentecost – when they were to repair to the parish church[248].

Grange chapels frequently received a formal dedication. The saints so patronised included St Bernard (at Altenkamp's Bergharen Grange)[249], St Catherine (Aiguebelle's Fraysinnet Grange)[250], St John (Stams' Home Grange)[251] and St Lawrence (Morimond's Vaudinvillers Grange)[252]. Other chapel dedications included those to (the Celtic) St Bridget on a grange of Llantarnam[253], St Gertude on a grange of Aulne[254] and St Sylvester on a grange of Hauterive[255]. There is little or no physical evidence now of some former grange chapels. In Wales the evidence of a former chapel comes partly through field-names – as 'Cae Capel' (Chapel Field) – or in the finds of burials[256]. The chapel at Tintern's Woolaston Grange has been demolished in modern times, and that at Dore's Llanfair Cilgoed Grange has severely deteriorated until little is left. Architectural features may indicate a chapel which has fallen into ruin or been converted for other purposes – as a fourteenth-century piscina in the modern kitchen at Kingswood's Estcourt Grange[257].

The Granger

The day to day running of a grange was in the hands of the *conversus* appointed as 'granger' or 'master' or 'keeper' of the grange: in so doing he was subject to the monastery's cellarer. Other alternative terms employed included 'rector' – on granges of Osek (1343)[258] and 'procurator' – on a grange of Heiligenkreuz (1318)[259]. Granges were meant to be the domain of the *conversi*, and it was rare to find a monk heading a grange in the twelfth century: there was an instance (about 1150) on a grange of La Ferté (La Valotte)[260]. Ardorel had a grange (in 1201) – La Rode – with a resident prior: a consequence of its membership of the incorporated 'family' of Dalon[261]. When *conversi* numbers dwindled in the second half of the thirteenth century there was little option – if the granges were to remain directly managed by an abbey – but for monks to sometimes take over the rôle of granger. Melrose employed a monk (by 1243) to look after its distant lands at Kylesmuir[262], whilst Beaulieu[263] and Hailes[264] had monk-wardens (in 1270 and 1300 respectively) supervising their remote Cornish lands. Lay, stipendiary grangers were rare, though there was one on Kingswood's Baggeston

Grange (1240)[265]. It may be that such lay grangers received both a wage and perquisites – in the form of income from part of the land. There pertained to the 'office of granger': 'The Granger's half-acre' at Sibton's North Grange (1325)[266], 'Certain acres' at Fountain's Bradley Grange (1331)[267] and eleven acres of meadow 'by custom' at Tintern's Merthyr Gerain Grange (1387)[268]. *Conversi* (or monks) were still supervising most granges at the close of the thirteenth century and beyond[269].

Grangers had the right to talk (when necessary) to their *conversi*, familiars and any guests[270]. They were normally to do so standing and to no more than two *conversi* at a time[271]. Their privileges were limited: they were not allowed the use of a horse when going to the abbey but had to walk on foot like the other *conversi*[272]. In the Savigniac houses a horse was permitted (1232) and a companion-servant – if the grange was remote[273]. Apart from their general oversight of their grange[274] and their obligation of submitting proper accounts, grangers might be involved in relevant business activities[275]. A granger of Clairvaux (at Outre-Aube, 1222) negotiated the sale of a piece of land[276], a granger of Staffarda (Luagnasco, 1273) took possession of land in the name of his monastery[277] and a granger of Bonneval (Fraysinnet, 1291) helped negotiate an end to various problems with other parties[278]. Rents due, in cash or kind, to their respective monasteries were paid in to the masters of many granges, as at Beaulieu's Otterwood (1270)[279].

Grangers – like cellarers – might be selected not only because of their business ability but also because of a forceful character – in order 'to get things done'. Theirs could be a difficult task: a granger of Fountains (at Kayton, 1270) was wounded during a pasture dispute[280], and a granger of Baltinglass (at Rosnalvan, 1299) was assaulted with a hatchet when trying to rescue cattle from marauders[281]. In their turn, grangers might not always be innocent parties: a granger of Kirkstall (at Micklethwaite) was accused of taking part in the beating to death of the forester of Clifford[282], and its granger at Barnoldswick (1276) allegedly cut off an ear of a serving-boy who had stolen two loaves of bread[283].

The Labour Force

The total numbers of *conversi* in a monastery might have seemed great but when spread around several granges – especially in an age of little mechanisation – their labour supply became somewhat stretched. Hired labourers were always very necessary. As early as 1230 Savigny had no more than one or two resident *conversi* on some of its farms[284]. By 1276 Villers operated 20 granges with the help (reputedly) of 300 *conversi*: this meant an average at most of 15 *conversi* per grange, less if taking into account those resident at the abbey and running its work-shops[285]. By 1352 at Buch's Amelgostewitz Grange one monk and two *conversi* supervised numerous servants and labourers[286]. Monks might go to help on the granges – especially in time of harvest[287], but they were not to spent the night on a grange – unless it was far removed from their abbey[288]. There is note at Beaulieu (1270) of monks staying 'in autumn' (harvest-time) at its distant Coxwell and Wyke Granges[289]. Monks so staying on remote granges were to 'eat as the brothers of the grange'[290].

On the granges the *conversi* kept silence in the dorter, refectory, and calefactory 'and within the appointed bounds'. They might talk to the granger and to those assisting them at work[291]. They returned to the abbey for Sundays and festivals – returning (on foot and in silence) the next day[292] – and also in order to be bled[293]. The régime was less severe than in the monastery: rising in summer at dawn and in winter after sleeping for three-quarters of the night. Except in fasting times the *conversi* had breakfast (mixt) each morning: consisting of half-a-loaf of bread and water[294]. Each *conversus* was entitled to a pound of best bread per day and as much coarser bread as might be necessary. The *conversi* permanently resident on the granges of Beaulieu (in 1270) received eight loaves of bread weekly, save in Advent and Lent (when seven) making a total of 400 loaves per person each year. They also received half-a-gallon of 'mixed beer', made up in equal proportions from the best beer and from the 'second' beer of the abbey. Each, therefore, received 183 gallons per year[295]. The grange *conversi* of Beaulieu also received an allowance of butter (increased in summer) for their pottage, and pittances (including fish at harvest-time)[296] were enjoyed. Shrove Tuesday saw a pre-Lenten feast for the servants[297]. The General Chapter of 1202 lamented that 'in some lands they have wine or beer in the granges, and it is not possible to revoke this', but elsewhere alcohol was to be prohibited 'irretractibly for ever'[298]. It was not.

As for hired labour, Beaulieu's leading St Leonard's Grange (1270) had 55 paid workers including ploughmen and shepherds. Some of its granges employed milk-maids and washerwomen[299]. At Tintern's Merthyr Gerain Grange food and drink were provided for its labourers where they worked: 'Lest they go from the field to their own'[300]. The Cistercians of northern Italy used extra labour in the grape-harvest and for reaping corn and making hay[301]. An act of the Commune of Piacenza (in 1243) sanctioned particular granges of Chiaravalle di Colomba and of Quartazzola to which men might freely come from other districts to work[302]. Semi-corrodians assisted on the granges like the 'sergeants' of Margam and the 'donatos' of Poblet. Serfs, inherited or given, might form part of a labour force. Extant grange accounts tell something of the wages paid to stipendiary workers. At Kingswood, for the winter of 1254–55, they received amounts varying from just under 2 shillings for ploughmen down to a shilling and sixpence for cooks and herdsmen. In the ensuing summer half of the year, probably because of the longer hours worked, wages showed an average increase of 1 shilling per head[303]. At Beaulieu – where no work was expected on Sundays and perhaps some twenty-five feast-days – there was greater disparity as between winter and summer wages. Herdsmen received, for example, a shilling and fourpence for winter work but over twice as much – 3 shillings to three shillings and sixpence – for summer labour. Its best paid servants were the grange wheelwrights or carpenters who received no less than 10 shillings per year[304].

Agricultural Economy

In the circumstances of the Middle Ages a mixed economy was essential – both for each grange to be self-supporting and for the good of the monastery. Even where a grange tended to be a pastoral property there was still a need for corn to be produced – for bread production, and hay – for winter fodder for the animals. A typical example of a mixed economy is noted (in the mid-fourteenth century) at Zwettl's Ratschenhof. It had 2,000 sheep, 60 cows, 24 horses (12 of them unbroken) and 40 oxen. Lambs, calves, goats and pigs were kept for food for the servants and for 'others of the cloister'. Also there were 'sown for the community at the will of the abbot' 40 measures of oats, 20 of rye and 3 of barley, as well as poppy seed and rapeseed. The grange was expected to send yearly to the monastery 4,000 cheeses, 12 urns of butter, 2,000 fleeces, 70 measures of rye, 80 of oats, 10 of barley, 15 of poppies and 3 of rape[305]. Varying conditions of relief, soil and climate meant that some granges, especially those more remote from their monastery, did tend to specialise. Chaâlis had three groups of granges: those on the plateau of Picardy producing grain for sale, those in the forest of Senlis with pastoral and forestry activities as well as cultivation, and its vineyards close to the rivers Marne, Seine and Oise[306].

True pastoral granges were often in uplands, as Obazine's Graule Grange – 1250 m high on the Limon Plateau[307]. Because the granges of Furness were mostly pastoral (dampness and altitude being the causes) the abbey had to rely heavily on grain imports from Ireland[308]. Other monasteries with much upland property sought to have granges in areas of low-lying and better soils. These were literally their 'bread-baskets'. This was true of Sedlec and Hradiště's granges in the Labe valley[309] and of Strata Florida's coastal granges (adjacent to Cardigan Bay) of Morfa Mawr and Morfa Bychan – they had the mildest weather and longest growing season of all its granges, coupled with relatively fertile boulder clay soils and the gentle relief of their raised beaches. They produced much wheat, its upland granges oats[310]. Diversity in arable farming was also displayed on the granges of Fontmorigny: Andres produced primarily wheat and barley, Jouet – barley and rye; Givry – rye and Raymond – oats[311].

The best picture of a grange's economy comes in the grange accounts where they survive. At Zwettl the grangers (and other officials) took an oath on entering office, which included the promise to make faithful accounts of receipts and expenses[312]. At Savigny (1230) the grangers were to account at least four times in the year before the abbot and the cellarer[313]. As the grangers were *conversi*, frequently unable to read or write, they were presumably given help in making up their accounts. The Account-Book of Beaulieu (1270) includes a 'Table for the Granges' as a point of reference for those drawing up its grange accounts. The account for its Coxwell Grange shows that nearly two-thirds of its income came from the sale of grain. Food – like fish and salt bought – formed a major item of expenditure. Miscellaneous payments included those to a (perhaps visiting) blacksmith for shoeing horses and making horseshoes[314]. The grange accounts for Tintern's Merthyr Gerain (1387/89) tell of its old byre being repaired, of a chamber being made for the keeper of oxen to lie there and of candles bought for his use in winter-time.The keeper of its granary paid sixpence on food for men who had caught a thief and held him overnight. The upkeep of agricultural machinery necessitated 'the mending and greasing of wagons and ploughs'[315]. Other guides to grange economy come in periodical surveys, like the 'extents' and 'rentals' made in the early fourteenth century for the granges of Sibton[316] and Zbraslav[317]. These give details of all kind rents due to those monasteries from the tenants in their vills and granges, and thus some indication of their agricultural production.

The Granges Today

Since the Middle Ages Cistercian granges have undergone a varied history. Some have been badly damaged in warfare: as Longpont's Viviers during the Great War (1914–18)[318]. Some have fallen slowly into decay: as Dore's Llanfair Cilgoed. Some have seen buildings demolished on safety grounds: like the mill at Tintern's Rogerstone Grange. Some have medieval buildings surviving: as Chaâlis' Vaulerent Grange. At others a series of earthworks remain and the plan is recoverable by aerial photography (as at Neath's Monknash)[319] or by excavation (like Santes Creus' Ancosa)[320]. The site may now be uncertain – as in the case of three granges of Sibton[321]. At Fossanova's Home Grange the barn is now a restaurant, that at Strata Florida's Morfa Bychan Grange is the club house of a holiday camp, and that at Roche's One Ash Grange offers simple camping accommodation[322]. Granges frequently leave their mark in place-names. In Wales 'Grangetown' in Cardiff perpetuates the former Moor Grange of Margam, whilst 'Grangemouth' in Scotland owes its name to the 'Abbot's Grange' of Newbattle formerly sited in that shipping town[323].

Land Communications

The movement of carts and animals to and from their granges meant that the Cistercians frequently had a need to create roads. Warden received several grants of lands between 1180 and 1250 in order to make approaches to its properties[324] – notably for a road 30 ft (9 m) broad leading from Myddelhoo Grange to neighbouring land at Stirt[325]. It also made 'a path for those coming on foot from Bedford to Salpho at sowing-time, leading to the great road'[326]. When Furness (1318) demised its manor of Penyton, it was to retain: 'A way of the width of fifty feet (15 m) with liberty to take stones, earth and other necessaries for repairing it'[327]. The quarrier of Ozleworth was paid by Kingswood (1240–41) for several weeks work in the upkeep its roads[328]. Igny (*c.* 1205) made a wagon road from Pelongerot Grange to Rochetaillêe[329].The 'Salter's road' was constructed by Newbattle – from the monastery to the coast – to assist in the export of coal[330].

Monastic roads might be cobbled or paved. A paved road approached Kirkstall's gate-house from the south[331]. A cobbled lane led from Duiske to its fisheries at Castle Ford[332]. There was a 'Stony Way' between the lands of Croxden and Rocester Priory[333]. Tintern had a cobbled 'Stony Way' leading from the gate-house to its vill at Porthcaseg[334]. Other roads remained largely unpaved – the 'greenways' – as that of Sibton coming from its land in Huntingfield[335], and Mastiles Lane in the Pennines which allowed Fountains' sheep to pass from Kilnsey Grange to Malham Moor. The bases of stone crosses – used as guide-stones – survive along the route[336]. Such crosses were also erected on the 'Abbot's Way' crossing Dartmoor to Buckfast[337]. Former crosses are also implied (in the Pennines) by minor place-names along the way connecting Whalley to properties further east[338]. Several former monastic green-ways are yet traceable in Wales[339]: becoming a popular walk to-day is the alleged monastic route through the mountains from Cwmhir to Strata Florida[340].

Bridges

Where a road passed through marshy land it was necessary to construct causeways. Sibton made two in the Suffolk marsh of Wenhaston – each 1½ roods broad – 'to carry hay and turf'[341]. In south Wales Margam's New Grange in the marsh of Afan was approached by a paved causeway[342]. In the English Fens Revesby was once alleged to have failed to maintain the North Dyke causeway; as a consequence it was claimed: 'Divers persons drown every year'. It was said that when two men were carrying a corpse from Stickney to Sibsey for burial, the deceased toppled over into the water[343]. Where a monastery or grange precincts were enclosed by ditches and moats, as at Kirkstead[344] and Louth Park[345], a causeway approach might result.

To cross streams bridges were needed: several enduring into modern times had their origins in monastic days. One was the bridge 'de la Guillotière' over the Rhône at Lyon, reconstructed in timber by Hautecombe (1308–14) after being given the care of it by the archbishop of that city. Hautecombe passed the responsibility over to Chassagne abbey, which stationed two religious and three servants there to maintain the hospice for travellers attached to the bridge. The bridge lasted until 1957[346]. The 'Long Bridge' at Coggeshall, dating from about 1220, is said to be the 'oldest brick bridge in England'[347]. Evidence for now vanished or replaced bridges comes in medieval deeds – as the 'great bridge before the gate' at Ourscamp (1180, 1266)[348]; and in place-names – as 'pont-y-fynach' and 'pont-mynach' ('the monk's bridge') occurring in Wales[349].

Auberive (1200) built a bridge over the Aujon river to bring flocks to and from

Pelongerot Grange[350]. A bridge built by Fontmorigny (*c.* 1208) was destroyed by an irate layman because he had not known of his late mother giving her consent[351]. Meaux (*c.* 1230) came to agreement with local lords for making two new bridges beyond the recently excavated Forth-dyke[352]. One was to be built by the lords, the other by the monastery: it would serve its fishery and help pasture its flocks. Both bridges were to be so raised that small boats without high prows ('beaks') could pass under them. In 1270 Beaulieu was making or repairing several bridges on its lands – it bought lime-stone to burn for lime for making a bridge at Sowley in Hampshire[353], but it repaired with timber a bridge at Colbury in the same county[354]. The construction of water-mills also necessitated bridge-building over the adjacent river or the leat. A series of these (in stone) exist in Ireland at Assaroe, Abbeyleix and Holy Cross[355]. There is some evidence that Grandselve (1175) and Beaulieu (1270) charged tolls on those using their bridges[356].

There was a constant need to maintain bridges: even those in stone could be washed away in floods – as at Waverley in 1233[357]. Henry III (1227) gave Fountains eight oaks from Knaresborough Forest to mend the bridge of Hewick: 'Lately broken in water inundation'[358]. The upkeep of bridges was frequently a vexed question – sometimes surfacing in litigation – especially where local folk accustomed to use the bridges felt aggrieved. In such court cases Coggeshall (1308; in respect of Stratford bridge between Braintree and Coggeshall)[359], and Fountains (1310; concerning Bradley bridge – then in a bad state)[360] both proved they had no such responsibility. Stratford (1315), however, found itself obliged (after years of controversy in the matter)[361] to maintain the bridge and causeway between Stratford-atte-Bow and Ham Stratford[362].

Where large rivers and estuaries interfered with their commerce and travel, the monks might resort to ferries. Aberconwy had ferry privileges on the Conwy river and Menai straits leading to their granges[363]. Tintern had a stipendiary ferryman to man its boat crossing the Wye from the abbey to its lands in Gloucestershire. (In 1282 he was one appropriately named Henry *le Passur*: it was alleged that he had conveyed poachers coming out of the Forest of Dean)[364]. Meaux had free passage across the river Humber at Paul, and maintained a house at Hedon for those waiting whilst going to and from Salthaugh Grange[365].

Notes

1. D'Arbois (1858) 303–04, Donnelly (1954) 405, Higounet (1983b) 157.
2. Dubled (1959) 770.
3. Charvátová (1987) 112.
4. France (1992) 257.
5. Kempf (1976) 44, 47, 49.
6. Donkin (1978) 63.
7. Williams (1984) I, 56–6.
8. Colombet (1976) 288.
9. Deladreue (1871) 52–58.
10. *E.g. DCK* 232–33, Mauri (1985) 300, Williams (1990a) 46–47 (No. 70).
11. Berman (1986) 74.
12. Poloni (1981) 8–9.
13. Deck (1974) 135.
14. *CHA* (2–3) 263 (No. 1490).
15. Williams (1984) II, 228, 240.
16. Chauvin (1977) 268.
17. *UKA* 37 (No. 48, of 1201).
18. Gosso (1940) 88.
19. Baxter (1914) 275.
20. Bibolet (1986) 10.
21. Lindley (1954) 182 (K), Williams (1990a) 63 (Nos 178–179: T).
22. Donnelly (1954) 434 (*c. 1152*); *SBE* 55–53 (of *1325*).
23. De Moreau (1909) 194.
24. Winter (1868) 189 (from 1259); *c. RBM* IV, 325 (No. 829, of 1340: 'new court' of Osek).
25. Dimier (1973) 53, Donnelly (1954) 405, Higounet (1983b) 158.
26. France (1994) 174–75.
27. Mousnier (1983a) 10, 21; Pressouyre and Kinder (1990) 103.
28. *Statuta* I, 20 (1134/XXXII); *LCC* (1) 35; Waddell (1994) 29–30.
29. *Statuta* III, 175 (1278/1).
30. *CSV* 244–46; *cf. CDVG* 118 (of 1244) for Rhion Gr. of Val-Saint-Lambert).
31. *Cf. Statuta* I, 268 (1201/26); VCH, *County of Stafford* III (1970) 232.
32. *CAC* 425–26 (No. VIII), *CDN* 513–14, 848.
33. *CAC* 423–24 (VI), 426–27 (IX).
34. Higounet, quoted in *Cîteaux* (1978: 1–2) 131.

35. Cowley (1977) 79.
36. Donkin (1978) 49.
37. Donnelly (1954) 410.
38. Charvátová (1994) 182.
39. France (1992) 270.
40. Clay (1952) 339.
41. Cowley (1977) 80.
42. Donkin (1978) 40.
43. Coulton (1960) 156.
44. Donkin (1978) 40.
45. Donnelly (1954) 411; *cf.* Rösener (1983a) 141–42 (for this phenomenon in west Germany).
46. Coulton (1960) 224*n*.
47. Martin (1893) 60–62.
48. Cowley (1977) 80–81.
49. Coulton (1960) 224.
50. Nazart (1978) 121.
51. Grèzes-Ruelff (1977) 274.
52. Higounet (1983b) 165.
53. *CBP* 2 (No. II).
54. Mitkowski (1949) 326.
55. Higounet (1983b) 165.
56. Pressouyre and Kinder (1990) 102.
57. Southern (1970) 268.
58. Barnes (1982) 18–20, 32–33.
59. Chauvin (1983a) 23.
60. Charvátová (1987) 132.
61. Chauvin (1983a) 23.
62. Southern (1970) 268.
63. Lekai (1977a) 296.
64. McCrank (1976) 144.
65. Williams (1984) II, 219.
66. Roehl (1972) 31.
67. Rösener (1983a) 143.
68. Elm (1982) 147.
69. Bishop (1936) 209.
70. Fossier (1983) 61.
71. Gosso (1940) 72.
72. Williams (1984) II, 215.
73. Platt (1969) 51.
74. *CW* 143–48.
75. Nelson (1986) 92–95.
76. *Cîteaux* (1978: 1–2) 149.
77. *AMM* 47.
78. *CS* II, 45.
79. Duby (1968) 235.
80. Berman (1983) 46.
81. Péchenard (1883) 177, 217.
82. Platt (1969) 52.
83. University of Kansas, Spencer Research Library, MS Flat 1/11 (3).
84. Donkin (1978) 62.
85. *Ibid*. 48.
86. *DD* 1599.
87. Platt (1969) 73.
88. RCAHM, *Radnor* (1913) 376.
89. Aveling (1876) 148.
90. Platt (1969) 72.
91. *SBE* 41.
92. Williams(1990a) 124–25 (Plates 43b–c).
93. Mauri (1985) 292.
94. Charvátová (1987) 131.
95. Blary (1989) 107.
96. Hodges (1990) 6.
97. *SBE* 52, 56.
98. Parkes and Webster (1974) *passim*.
99. Bonnet-Laborderie (1985) 11, 20.
100. Comba (1978) 401*n*, *Cf. CAS* I, 288 (No. CCCXXII).
101. Cottam (1928) 69–70.
102. Higounet (1983b) 170–71.
103. *Cf.* Berman (1986) 62.
104. *Statuta* I, 30 (1134/LXXII), *LCC* (1) 161, (2) 343.
105. Berman (1986) 52, Higounet (1983b) 170–71.
106. Comba (1983) 127.
107. Combet (1978) 401*n*.
108. VCH, *Northampton* II (1906) 117–18.
109. *Statuta* I, 275 (1202/5).
110. Grégoire (1969) 62, ill. opp. p. 57; *cf. CDAA* 309.
111. *Statuta* I, 524 (1220/38).
112. *RBM* IV, 693 (No. 1733).
113. VCH, *Northampton* II (1906) 116–17.
114. Comba (1978) 401*n*.
115. *Statuta* II, 398 (1254/37), 432 (1257/41), 418 (1255/36).
116. *CDN* 590–91, 873–74.
117. *Statuta* I, 30 (1134/LXXII).
118. *RCOC* col. 1650 (Cap. IX).
119. *Statuta* I, 198 (1196/2), *cf. Statuta* I, 261 (1200/64).
120. Owen (1971) 64.
121. Occhipinti (1985) 328.
122. Chalvet (1888) 50.
123. Treuille (1978) 31–32.
124. *DD* 1599.
125. Williams (1984) II, 39.
126. *Statuta* I, 332 (1206/67).
127. Williams (1984) II, 33.
128. Blashill (1892) 105.
129. *Statuta* I, 132 (1190/76); *LCC* (2) 5 (No. 3).
130. *Statuta* I, 107 (1187/8).
131. *Statuta* I, 198 (1196/2).
132. *Statuta* II, 18 (1222/25).
133. *LCC* (1) 109.
134. *Statuta* I, 30 (1134/LXXII), *LCC* (1) 111.
135. Williams (1976) 36, 134.
136. *LCC* (1) 168, (2) 321.
137. *LCC* (1) 126, (2) 321; *cf. Statuta* I, 68 (1157/68).
138. *Statuta* I, 444 (1215/43).
139. *Statuta* I, 471 (1217/26).
140. *Statuta* III, 230 (1283/9), 288 (1297/3).
141. Bonnet-Laborderie (1985) 12; Blary (1989) 116.
142. David-Roy (1973) *passim*.
143. Dimier (1964) 178.
144. Holdsworth (1994) 355.
145. Bonnet-Laborderie (1985) 12.
146. Horn (1965) 1.
147. Holdsworth (1994) 356, 358.
148. *CHA* (2–3) 141 (No. 756).
149. Hand (1919) 26–27.
150. Occhipinti (1985) 328.
151. Holdsworth (1994) 359.
152. *RBM* IV, 693 (No. 1733).
153. Occhipinti (1985) 328.
154. Wamba (1986) 180.
155. Donkin (1978) 124.
156. Lacaze (1993) 171.
157. *CCR* 1232/75.

158. *ABB* 16.
159. *CM* 43.
160. Donnelly (1954) 443.
161. Altisent (1972) 16–17.
162. *ADP* 261.
163. Platt (1969) 214.
164. Hodges (1990) 6.
165. *E.g.: ABB* 110, 115, 121, 140; (bolting-cloth, canvas and well as rennet also acquired).
166. Dimier (1973) 62–63.
167. VCH, *Northampton* II (1906) 117.
168. Donnelly (1954) 413.
169. Bonnet-Laborderie (1985), *cf.* Blary (1989) 109.
170. Williams (1990 a) 136–37 (Pls. 57–58).
171. Dimier (1973) 63, (1978b) 139–40.
172. Dimier (1973) 56, (1964) 180.
173. Williams (1984) II, 239.
174. Astill (1994) 546.
175. *SBE* 57.
176. Williams (1984) II, 239.
177. Dimier (1964) 180.
178. *VKS* 196.
179. *CSBW* 73.
180. Régnier (1913) 253.
181. *SBC* 116.
182. Coppack (1990) 125.
183. Elm (1982) 149.
184. Occhipinti (1985) 324–27.
185. Dimier (1964) 186.
186. *Coggeshall* (Offical Guide) 14.
187. Andrews and Boutwood (1984) 150–53.
188. Gloede (1965) 52.
189. Heutger (1971) 30.
190. *CWK* 128–29.
191. Krausen (1977) 353.
192. Sommer-Ramer (1982) 148.
193. *RSL* II, 27, 232.
194. *ABB* 283–89.
195. McCrank (1976) 150.
196. Altisent (1972) opp. p. 112; McCrank (1976) 143–44.
197. McCrank (1976) 151–52.
198. Berman (1990) 56.
199. *LKZ* 6.
200. Poloni (1981) 14.
201. MS notes (at Gaussan); *cf.* Grèzes-Ruelff (1977) 254–55.
202. David-Roy (1973) 54, Dimier (1964) 186.
203. Platt (1969) 31.
204. *UKSH* 228–29 (No. CCL), 246–47 (No. CCLXXIII).
205. *RBM* IV, 693 (No. 1733); Charvátová (1987) 130.
206. Donnelly (1949) 75 (No. 49).
207. *RHC* 129, Baxter (1914) 278.
208. Clark (1910) II, 544–45.
209. *CDAA* 309.
210. Othon (1929) 196, Williams (1984) II, 234.
211. *Statuta I*, 49 (1152/27).
212. Martin (1893) 60–62.
213. Deladreue (1871) 52–58.
214. *Statuta* I, 87 (1180/6).
215. *LCC* (1) 35–36.
216. Hockey (1970) 48–49 (Q); VCH, *Lancaster* II (1908) 121 (F).
217. *Statuta* I, 299–97 (1204/11) .
218. *Statuta* I, 301–08 (1205/7).
219. *Statuta* I, 428 (1214/55); *LCC* (1) 35–36; *cf. Statuta* I, 49 (1152/27), 436 (1215/8); II, 65 (1228/1).
220. *Statuta* II, 153 (1236/3).
221. *SL* 159 (No. 14).
222. *LCC* (2) 309.
223. *CSBW* 93.
224. *SL* 159 (No. 14).
225. Higounet (1983b) 161.
226. *Statuta* II, 153 (1236/3).
227. *OSBS* (1) 92 (No. 78).
228. *OSBS* (1) 75 (No. 67).
229. *DMLH* II, 297 (No. 479).
230. Deladreue (1871) 91.
231. Platt (1969) 27–28.
232. *AM* II, 342.
233. Higounet (1983b) 171.
234. Williams (1984) II, 234.
235. Pochin Mould (1976) 55.
236. Lefevre (1983) 33–37.
237. Deladreue (1871) 36, 39–40, 42–44, 53.
238. *DSMLR* 593 (No. 257).
239. Bernard (1967) 56.
240. *LCC* (1) 166.
241. *Cf. AM* II, 342, *RSL* II, 295, Canestrelli (1896) 31.
242. *DHGE* X (1938) 62.
243. *Statuta* I, 124 (1190/25).
244. *LCC* (1) 35–36, (2) 211.
245. *UKA* 99 (No. 126).
246. Pugh (1934) 19–20; Williams (1984) II, 235–36.
247. *Cal. Papal Registers* (*Letters*) I, 131.
248. *UKA* 99.
249. 'Kapel in Bergharen', *Hier en Ginder* 17 (1976) No. 7, 75–77.
250. *CDAA* 117 (dedicated in 1310).
251. *VKS* 198 (recorded in 1345).
252. Dubois (1879) 116.
253. Williams (1984) II, 237.
254. *Wavriesia* (1974) 51–74.
255. Sommer-Ramer (1982) 181.
256. Williams (1984) II, 234–36.
257. Platt (1969) 238.
258. *RBM* IV, 493 (No. 1241).
259. *RCH* 106.
260. Duby (1953) 9.
261. *DHGE* III, (1924) 1618.
262. Easson (1957) 68.
263. *ABB* 14.
264. Snell (1967) 28.
265. *DCK* 210–13.
266. *SBE* 52–53.
267. Clay (1929) 100.
268. NLW, Badminton Manorial 1571; Williams (1976) 130.
269. *E.g.* Barea (1977) (2) 125 (No. 157), Chalvet (1888) 28, 43.
270. *LCC* (1) 162, (2) 343.
271. *RCOC* col. 1649 (Cap. VIII).
272. *RCOC* col. 1650 (Cap. IX); D'Arbois (1858) 232–33.
273. *RSL* II, 208 (No. 7).
274. No small responsibility.
275. Toepfer (1983) 89.
276. *RCC* III, 246.

277. *CAS* II, 120 (No. DXVII).
278. *CABR* 241, 244 (No. 225).
279. *ABB* 158.
280. Donnelly (1954) 416.
281. Fitzgerald (1906) 386.
282. Donnelly (1954) 416.
283. Barnes (1982) 35; Platt (1969) 189.
284. *RSL* II, 231.
285. Lekai (1977a) 296.
286. Platt (1969) 80, Thompson (1920) 90.
287. *DHGE* XII (1953) 922, *cf.* Dimier (1964) 182.
288. *Statuta* I, 60 (1157/3); *LCC* (2) 310.
289. *ABB* 79, 91.
290. *Statuta* I, 30 (1134/LXXII).
291. *LCC* (1) 161, (2) 343.
292. Dimier (1964) 181.
293. *LCC* 310.
294. D'Arbois (1858) 307.
295. *LCC* (1) 163, (2) 344.
296. *ABB* 126–27, *cf. RCOC* 1651 (Cap. XII).
297. *ABB* 125.
298. *Statuta* I, 276 (1202/10).
299. *ABB* 22.
300. NLW, Badminton Manorial 1571; Williams (1976) 130.
301. Comba (1983) 128.
302. Rocca (1936) 217.
303. *DCK* 209–12.
304. ABB 311–19.
305. *LFZ* 540–43.
306. Higounet (1965) 17.
307. Barrière (1990) 16.
308. Donkin (1978) 64.
309. Charvátová (1987) 114, 118.
310. Williams (1990) 107 (fig. 25).
311. *CAF* 113, 115, 120, 204, 206, 223, 339.
312. *UKZ* 395.
313. *RSL* II, 229.
314. *ABB* 88–97.
315. Williams (1984) II, 294–96 (after: NLW, Badminton Manorial 1571).
316. *SBE* 12–13.
317. Charvátová (1987) 57–59.
318. Dimier (1974a) 56.
319. Williams (1990) 123–25 (Pls. 43a–c).
320. *CHA* (2–3) 93 (No. 480).
321. *SBC* I, 117–18.
322. *The Universe* (21–8-1988), 26.
323. Carrick (1907) 73.
324. *CW* 75–76.
325. *CW* 145–47.
326. *CW* 184–88.
327. *CDL* 167.
328. *DCK* 194.
329. Grandmottet (1958) 5.
330. Carrick (1907) 105.
331. Owen (1955b) 2.
332. Carville (1979) 77–79.
333. Hill (1865) 304.
334. Williams (1976) 133 (plan)-134.
335. *SBC* II, 142 (No. 186; '*viridem viam*').
336. Wright (1972) 1767, *cf.* McDonnell (1963) 76, 423.
337. *Daily Telegraph* (31-12-1988).
338. Moorhouse (1989) 37.
339. Williams (1984) II, 231–32.
340. RCAHM (Wales) III, *Radnor* (1913) No. 412a.
341. *SBC* II, 248 (No. 344).
342. RCAHM (Wales), *Glamorgan* III: 2 (1982) 274.
343. Dugdale (1777) 219–20.
344. Richards (1968) 94.
345. *CPL* xlvi, lxi, *cf.* 56.
346. *DHGE* XII (1953) 576, Goutagny (1964) 210.
347. RCAHM, *Essex* III (1922) 168; Cutts (1858) 170.
348. *CO* 99 (No. CXLVII), 260 (No. CCCCXXV).
349. Williams (1984) II, 232.
350. Grandmottet (1958) 5.
351. *CAF* 102.
352. *CMM* I, 408.
353. *ABB* 15, 137; *cf.* 141, 154.
354. *ABB* 121.
355. Carville (1982b) 40.
356. Mousnier (1986) 111, 125 (fn. 13) [G], *ABB* 79 ([B]: at Wyke Grange).
357. *AM* II, 312.
358. *CCR* 1227/11.
359. VCH, *Essex* II (1907) 126.
360. Wardrop (1987) 112*n*.
361. *CPR* 1297/375.
362. VCH, *Essex* II (1907) 130.
353. Williams (1984) II, 231.
364. VCH, *Gloucester* X (1972) 105.
365. *CMM* I, xix.

Chapter 14
SETTLEMENT ON CISTERCIAN LANDS

Changes in Grange Management

The early injunctions of the Cistercian Order forbade its monks to release any of their lands to seculars – whether by way of lease or of mortgage – but a wide variety of factors meant that there were numerous breaches of this rule long before the close of the twelfth century. Abbeys might find themselves with lands too far distant to work directly, or with estates too large to be managed entirely by their *conversi*. Monasteries which had a need for money (because of a building programme, or after a fire or some other disaster or due to heavy debts incurred) might be tempted to raise ready cash by disposing of some of their lands. It wasn't an ideal solution: it was really 'selling the family silver' for short-term gain[1]. Poblet leased out an entire grange in 1180 (Cérvoles) to the bishops of Huesca and Pamplona, receiving annually 500 measures of wheat and barley[2]. Life-leases of minor properties were a feature of the 1190s at Fountains[3] and Margam. In a charter to Margam Innocent III (1203) insisted that the consent of a majority of its community – and especially of the 'wiser' monks – be given before any alienation of land[4].

The process became so widespread that the General Chapter attempted to regulate it by forbidding *any* demises of monastic land (1200[5], 1205[6]). Pressure to be able to do so remained, and in 1208 the Chapter allowed poor land – land not able to be cultivated – and remote land to be demised for half the produce, or 'in any other way'[7]. This concession was reversed in 1214 and forbidden again in 1215 and 1216[8]. From 1220 lands 'of little profit' could be rented out – but only for a fixed period – if the senior monks and the father-abbot consented[9]. In 1224 a more general permission was given – providing 'the lease be expedient'[10]. By 1237 it became necessary to seek the additional consent of the diocesan bishop if tithe rights were in any way affected[11]. For the congregation of Savigny Stephen Lexington (1230) ruled that a maximum of seven years was to be the term of any such lease: 'So that there may be recent memory of the transaction'. He also insisted that all leases were to be entered into the abbey Register and a sealed receipt given, and that no leasing was to take place without: 'Mature counsel and careful deliberation, and with appropriate precautions having been taken in public with due solemnity'[12]. In other words there were to be no behind-the-scenes deals, or any likelihood of the permanent loss of that land to the monastery.

From the early thirteenth century Beaubec demised lands which brought it rents in kind of wheat, barley and oats, hens, salt, wine and fish[13]. Leases can be traced at Hauterive (by 1217)[14], at Herrenalb (by 1220)[15] and at Aubepierre (by 1229)[16]. In the second half of the century, impelled by the rapid decline in *conversi* numbers, entire granges came to be leased. Alcobaça demised Bombarral Grange (in 1248) on a renewable four year contract[17]. Vaucelles leased out Ceule Grange (in 1263) for nine years[18] – provision being made for regular inspection by the abbey's cellarer[19]. The General Chapter (1261) – seeing potential pitfalls – ordered that when entire granges were demised to seculars traditional hospitality to visiting monks was still to be practised on those farms[20]. When whole granges were demised they were sometimes broken up, perhaps because there were few tenants capable of taking on single-handedly a large complex property. In cancelling its earlier ruling, and now forbidding those granges to be 'sold or broken up' which were 'accustomed to provide hospitality to persons of the Order', the Chapter (in 1269) referred to the practice in passing[21]. When Herrenalb gave up direct working (in 1220) of its Ottersweiler Grange it divided the lands between four tenants. They came to possess hereditary rights, but could be removed for bad management or if the abbey wished to resume direct working of the grange[22]. When (in 1336) because of Scottish incursions Fountains leased out its granges at Balderby and Marton, it fragmented them – leasing the lands to several tenants-at-will[23].

By the late thirteenth century some monasteries leased a grange – not to a layman – but to one of its own *conversi*, who managed it and made a fixed annual payment in kind. The General Chapter (1262) ordered that nothing of the residue of income left after rent had been paid in this way be disposed of, except at the will of the abbot[24]. There was an opportunity here for the misappropriation of funds. One such lease was made when Fountains appointed brother Robert of Morton (in 1310) to have charge of its remote but important Cowton Grange[25]. Granges were occasionally demised (for a fixed term) to a company headed by a monk or *conversus*. In 1351 (perhaps as a consequence of the Black Death) Dore demised all its properties in Cantref-selyf for ten years (in return for 40 marks p.a.) to a five-man body headed by two of the monks, with three layman completing the board of directors[26]. In 1360 La Real leased out for five years its principal grange (Esporles) to one of the community and a layman, in return for an annual rental of 120 Majorcan 'lesser pounds' and supplies of timber, lime and olive oil[27]. All this was not in accord with the early emphasis of the *Charter of Charity* that: 'In raising our animals and cultivating our lands we do not have joint dealings with laymen, such as giving or receiving shares or profits'[28]. This ruling was reiterated by the General Chapter in the years of 1214 to 1217[29], but it did make exceptions: for San Galgano (1226) – 'on account of its needs'[30], and more generally (1237) – if consent of the Chapter were obtained[31].

In the early fourteenth century the secularisation of Cistercian lands was quickened by the bull (of 1302) of Boniface VIII which extended the privilege of tithe exemption to cover those lands from which tithes had not been collected previously. This meant that lands brought under cultivation by the monks could now be demised without fear of tithes being claimed[32]. The General Chapter continued to endeavour to exercise control. A grange was not to be leased to a layman for life or in perpetuity since: 'By this comes the danger of total loss' (1312). If possible management was to be by members of the Order[33]. Three years later (1315) life-leases and in perpetuity arrangements were allowed, but only if it was for the 'manifest utility' of an abbey – as in cases of granges remotely located.[34]

In the first half of the fourteenth century numerous granges were demised. Tennenbach (by 1342) had leased out its 'court' at Mundiger: 'Which used to be cultivated by our *conversi*'[35]. Rebellious *conversi* accelerated the process at Ter Doest and the Dunes, whilst war, plague and famine resulted in leases by Villers[36]. King John of Bohemia made great financial demands on Sedlec, Plasy and Zlatá Koruna causing them to demise properties[37]. Chassagne (1344) assigned a grange to a former abbot for life, by way of pension[38].The period of leasing now was often five years, as demanded by the papal constitution of 1335, but a number of houses (especially in 1344) sought permission for an extended term. These included Cercamp (because of debts), Barrois (because the land was distant) and Neuenkamp (because it was 'less useful')[39]. The extent of leasing varied according to the circumstances of individual houses. Whilst

Stams had but two granges directly worked in 1333[40] and St Sulpice virtually none[41], Hardehausen demised no grange before 1322[42] and Osek still managed ten in 1350[43].

Some monasteries actually *sold* granges outright, generally when there was an urgent need for ready cash. As early as 1269 the Chapter reluctantly countenanced sale as an alternative to leasing[44], but it took exception if the community had not consented and the father-abbot had not agreed – as in instances affecting Theulay (1269)[45] and Buzay (1297)[46]. Monthéron sold Cugy Grange to Hauterive Abbey for 5,000 *sols laus*[47] and Lieucrossant (1258) sold Courcelles Grange to Thibaut IV of Neuchâtel for 200 *livres*[48]. Few people could afford to buy a grange at these sort of prices, which is one reason why the more common course taken was to demise for an annual return. Some authors see the sale or leasing of granges as stemming not only from the effects of debt, of war and the shortage of *conversi*, but also as a consequence of the persistent decline in the price of corn, of the need to augment the wages of hired labourers and of agriculture being no longer viewed by the white monks as a central pivot of their life[49].

For whatever reasons it occurred, the off-loading of granges from direct monastic management – whether by sale or by leasing – resulted in the transformation of the typical Cistercian grange economy of the twelfth century to the manorial system of orders like the Benedictine[50], which the early white monks had so flatly rejected. Now they had a tenantry paying money and kind rents, and owing services of one kind or another. With the passing of granges into lay hands the *conversus*-granger gave way to the lay-bailiff. This is clearly enunciated in a charter of Vitskøl (1263) which says that, because of a shortage of monastic personnel, it had: 'To place lay bailiffs on those farms which the *conversi* used to manage'[51]. Once each year, from 1230, 'two discerning and God-fearing monks' were despatched from Savigny to go through all the lands of the monastery, call together all the reeves and the tenants they supervised, and make a diligent survey as to the lands held and by what service[52]. This is a clear indication of how far piecemeal demising had gone even quite early in the thirteenth century. Lay officers might be lacking in their duty: Sallay (1300) had difficulty in obtaining from Richard Boredbayn 'a reasonable account of the time when he was bailiff of its manor of Sunderland'[53].

As the grangers had done, reeves and bailiffs kept annual accounts. The reeves of Savigny (1230) were each 'to write down at the end of every year what rents and services they have exacted and what is owing'. Their records of rents received were to be handed to the abbey treasurers, and of corn received to the keeper of the granary. Any increase or diminution in rents was to be recorded in the accounts ('the rolls') kept by those officials[54]. At Beaulieu (1270) three reeves had charge of granges and making account, two more held subordinate positions on other properties. Their usual stipend was 5 shillings p.a. Its manor of Great Faringdon had a lay steward, bailiff and reeve all assisting the monk in charge. Despite the presence of lay reeves, on at least two of the granges they managed *conversi* came to help with the harvest in autumn[55].

Tenants' Services

The General Chapter (1208) in permitting certain lands to be demised laid down that half the produce of those lands was to be rendered up by the tenants to the monastery, or else rent was to be paid 'in some other way'[56]. All the evidence is that whilst such substantial payments in kind brought valuable and varied food supplies to the monastic communities, yet from the start there were monetary offerings as well[57]. The men of Santes Creus' vill of Ponton (1319) paid money rents as well as yielding wheat and barley in mid-summer and poultry at Christmas[58]. The dues payable to Osek (1340) by the inhabitants of Černochov were partly in money and partly in measures of oats, as

well as specified numbers of sheep and poultry[59]. The wide variety of kind rents an
abbey might expect each year was well exemplified on the lands of Ebrach (1340) which
rendered substantial quantities of rye and oats, butter and cheese, eggs, lambs and
poultry, as well as of flax and wax[60]. When Morimondo Milano's Fallavecchia Grange
was split up (1297) the kind rents due included cereals, turnips, wine and poultry[61].
The tenants of Cymer's coastal grange at Neigwl (1350) provided that abbey with
wheat, oats, pigs, butter, cheese and herrings[62].

Cereals were everywhere an essential return. The tenants of Rueda's newly acquired
property at Romana (1211) were to deliver each year directly to the abbey a proportion of their best cereals[63]. Kind rents of wheat came to the monasteries of Meaux[64] and
Margam[65] from coastal granges, and to Cwmhir from those by the river Wye[66].
Amongst the kind rents of Bellevaux were wheat, oats and millet[67]. Tennenbach (1342)
received – from the lease of part of one grange alone – 36 measures of wheat and 27
of rye[68]. An outstanding wheat producing grange was Vaulerent, rendering yearly to
Chaâlis about 70 'muids' (nearly 200 hectolitres) of corn. Its reception was staggered
over the winter months, perhaps due to a shortage of storage space[69]. Every household
on the home estate of Toplica (1208) rendered three times a year (at Christmas, Easter
and the Assumption) a loaf of bread to the monastery[70].

Animals and dairy products also featured in kind payments, notably at Stams (1336)
which could expect yearly 5,400 head of cattle and over 1,000 cheeses. The bulk of the
cheese came from its Schwaig estates, and each cheese may have averaged 1 kg in
weight. As leasing moved apace the number of eggs it expected annually rose from 100
(in 1284) to 680 or more (in 1294) to no less than 7,590 (in 1336)[71]. Rents in kind came
also from new settlers on Cistercian lands. Those of Tarouca at Figueiro (1243) gave
up an eighth part of their wine, vegetables and flax, as well as some of their best
wheat[72]. Those of Rueda at Val de Mallatz (1244) had to part with one-eleventh of their
harvest of cereals and grapes[73]. In Wales, in the later Middle Ages, a number of kind
rents – but by no means all – were commuted to cash payments[74].

Kind rents were complemented by fixed rents payable in ready cash, by taxes
imposed ('tallage') and occasional dues of various kinds. Rents due to Sibton (1328)
were payable quarterly (at St Andrew's Day, Easter, St John Baptist's Day and
Michaelmas): in some places there was a fifth date – Candlemas[75]. In 1270 Beaulieu
received from its tenants over £100 in fixed rents, £21 by way of 'recognition' on the
'first coming' of the new abbot, nearly £15 in tallage, over £12 from those entering
upon new tenancies and nearly £8 from fines and perquisites of its manorial courts.
Small amounts were derived from tenants giving away their offspring in wedlock
('merchet'), or whose sons wished to become tonsured clerics – and would therefore be
of no profit to the estate. Several people who sold young horses without leave were
fined a total of six shillings and eightpence. A man (at Coxwell) who wished to build a
wall by the adjacent lane (presumably to protect his land from wandering animals) paid
4 shillings for the privilege. There are traces of 'relief' – sons paying a fine on taking
over the holding of their deceased father, and of 'heriot' (death duty) – an ox[76].

Entry fines at Tintern were about three times the annual rent: Nicholas Hathol
(1303) paid 2 shillings on entry into a holding but only gave 8 pence yearly thereafter.
They might be payable in kind: Nicholas le Wyte (1312) gave the abbey two gallons of
wine on entry into a plot of waste land, paying a 1 shilling annual rent from then on.
Fines for unlicensed marriages and on the fathers of children born out of wedlock
('lairwite') feature in the manorial court rolls of Tintern in the 1340s[77]. Two inheritors
to lands of the Dunes (1222) paid a total of 50 Flanders shillings for 'relief'[78]. The
nephew and nearest heir of a tenant of Warden gave security for the 'relief' of 4
shillings due: because of his poverty the abbot reduced the amount payable to 1
shilling[79]. As other houses, Warden (1232/40) expected the 'best beast' by way of

heriot[80]: in another tenancy (1288) specifying the worth of the animal payable – 'an ox valued at 10 shillings'[81].

By the early fourteenth century detailed conditions might be written into monastic leases. Tenants were expected to care for the property demised to them: a lessee of Tintern promised to rebuild: 'The house which he has allowed to fall into ruin'[82]. A lessee of Kingswood undertook to 'maintain his tenement in (good) condition'[83]. The improvement of a holding (buildings and land) might be expected: when St Benoît-en-Woëvre (1221) demised to an attorney and his wife for life the grange of Bougonville they were to pay an annual rent of 102 *sous de provins*, and to build there within three years a mill and a house in stone[84]. Land demised by Morimondo Milano (1218) had to be brought under cultivation by the lessees within ten years[85]. Nor was property to be alienated lest an abbey find it difficult to claim back: non-alienation was written into leases of Kingswood[86]. From the mid-thirteenth century Sibton excluded transfer of a lease to Jews (because of the king's over-riding interest in Jewish property), or to other religious houses (to avoid land falling into mortmain)[87]. La Ferté (*c.* 1160) forbade tenants to give away any of its property as dowry for their daughters[88]. Tenants of Tennenbach's Rogenbach Grange (1319) were expected to continue the accustomed hospitality to visiting monks and to permit existing rights of way[89]. There were general requirements for tenants to perform 'suit of court' (as by Kingswood, 1319)[90] and 'suit of mill' (Santes Creus, 1319)[91] – both obligations more fully evidenced in later centuries.

Labour services at time of harvest can be traced (by 1269) on lands of Tintern[92]. By this time Alcobaça required a few days work from its tenants, but never more than four[93]. Furness (1318) expected its tenants at Lindale Grange to reap one day in harvest time and (if they possessed a plough) to till half-an-acre there each year. Food was provided for them by the abbey[94]. Some tenants had carriage duties written into their leases. The commodities transported included stone (for Santes Creus)[95], grain (Hradiště)[96], wine (Tennenbach)[97], turf (Mellifont)[98] and salt (Strata Florida)[99]. The decline in available *conversi* free to accompany travelling monks saw a tenant of Osek (1343) obliged to ride with its abbot when necessary[100]. Tenants of Santes Creus' estate at Pontons (1319) had to keep its castle in good repair and defend it in time of war[101].

Several monasteries experienced difficulties in the thirteenth century in obtaining full satisfaction from their tenants. The 'work, services and labours' due to Staffarda had to be safeguarded by secular authority[102]. Tilty (1237)[103] and Kirkstall (1241)[104] had to go to law to obtain 'customs and services' from recalcitrant tenants. Balmerino (1291) had a number of tenants (including nobles) in arrears of rent to its considerable detriment[105]. The first half of the fourteenth century, with growing restlessness on the part of the peasantry, saw resentment by both tenants and serfs at what monasteries expected of them. In one ugly incident (in 1320) at Vale Royal's manor (and former grange) of Darnhall an abbey servant was slain, and his head then used as a football[106].

Manorialism

The *Charter of Charity* had said: 'Our very name, and the constitution of our Order, prohibit manors and serfs, land rents and all other incomes of this kind as contrary to the purity of the monastic vocation'[106a]. Alexander III (1159–81) ordered Furness and Swineshead not to accept manors or any kind of patronage as such were 'contrary to the institutes of the Order'[107]. Despite such ideals and injunctions not only were granges gradually transformed into manors, but lands with an existing manorial structure were acquired by the Cistercians (either by gift or purchase) and thereafter frequently maintained the *status quo*. By 1322 Neath's former grange at Exford had become a manor 'with services both of free tenants and of villeins'. When (in 1350) Aberconwy ceded Friwlwyd it was no longer described as a grange but as a manor and a vill. Transition might be gradual, and the terms of 'grange' and 'manor' for a time interchangeable: Strata Marcella's lands at Bronrotpol were called both a 'manor' (1342) and a 'grange' (1344) within the space of a few years[108].

In north Wales manorialism was already developed when Aberconwy received lands at Cornwy Llys and Penmynydd (1284) with villeins, rents and other customs and services there[109]. At Sibton (late 13th century) a grant of land carried with it homages, services and rents owing from some two dozen men: each man's dues are itemised but the mechanics of collection and oversight must have been considerable[110]. Early thirteenth century charters suggest widespread transfer of tenants and lordship to Berdoues and Bonnecombe with gifts of land[111]. Tenants of Verdu were acknowledged by the Crown as 'vassals' of Poblet (1273)[112]. The men of Aranga were declared by the courts as bound in obedience to Sobrado (1349) 'as vassals are to their lord'[113].

In England the most notable Cistercian manor was perhaps that of Beaulieu at Faringdon which – because of its distance from the abbey – worked as a separate entity with its own monk-warden and treasury, steward, reeve, bailiff and catchpole. At the grange of Great Faringdon was held the manorial court and here stood the prison and the gallows. Whenever the king levied tallage so did the abbot on his tenants. The lands of those who could not pay fines or render services due were confiscated. The profits of the manor were paid over to the abbey in a single livery (£120 in 1270) as was the entire crop of wool. During that year of account Edward I with his queen and son made overnight stays on the manor, which King John had intended as the site of Beaulieu itself[114].

Tintern came to organise two of its Welsh Border properties along manorial lines, and built up both estates (Porthcaseg and Woolaston) as compact entities: the monks could traverse from one end of each manor to the other without leaving their territory. An intermittent series of extant court-rolls for Porthcaseg from the mid-thirteenth century on suggest that its manorial court was ideally held at three-weekly intervals. Only seven courts were recorded in 1269 – possibly because they were held just when required and less frequently in winter and during harvest-time[115]. The rolls (for 1262–63) tell of Brebelof who had taken a wife without permission, and of John Mason who (along with his sons) had given a severe beating to Richard of St Briavel's[116]. A court, in the autumn of 1262, excused absentees 'because of the state of the weather'[117]. In 1340 Philip Ryband was convicted of using a short measure (it was to be confiscated), John William of allowing his boat (used for monastic business on the river Wye) to fall into disrepair, and a resentful villein of saying 'abusive words' about the community[118].

By this time Tintern was experiencing difficulties on its most valuable manor of Acle (far removed in Norfolk). In 1306, only four years after the abbey had received the manor, the men of Acle sued the abbot alleging that each of them held eight acres (3.2 ha) of land 'by the service of doing suit at the abbot's court of Acle every three weeks', heriot on the death of an ancestor, a penny rent per acre, and labour (mowing) services, which – they said – had been customary since the Norman Conquest. They complained that their new masters (the abbot and community) now required of them the carriage of hay, taxed them heavily, and took from them 'merchet' for the marriage of their children and heriot at will. The men lost their case: their complaints probably reflected the business-like nature of the new abbot Hugh de Wyke (1305–20) once sub-cellarer of the monastery. The same difficulties with the Acle tenantry surfaced again forty years later (1346)[119].

Changing social conditions and a growing independence of the rustic population played their part in the resistance Tintern encountered[120]. Similar difficulties were experienced by Vale Royal on its Cheshire manor of Darnhall. The firmness of its abbot with his bondsmen led to rebellion and uprisings (1307, 1336), but their personal complaint to the king (1328) led to the rebuff: 'As villeins you have come, and as villeins you shall go'. The abbey drew up a custumal (in 1326) to recall its historic rights. Extensive duties were required of its villeins in caring for the abbey's pigs, horses, bees and dogs, as well as the more usual services. When a serf died at Darnhall the heriot payable was not only the best ox, but also all his pigs, goats and mares, and a portion of his standing corn[121].

In eastern Europe the traditional grange system was, from the outset, submerged in a manorial-type economy[122]. This was in part because of the large estates German and Polish princes gave to the Cistercians – including many villages with their rent-paying peasants and serfs, and in part because of the lack of vocations here to the Order[123]. In addition, there were numerous villages settled by the Cistercians with immigrants from further west. In Bohemia the fees collected from the villages formed the backbone of Cistercian economy[124]. In Hungary a confirmatory charter for Pilis (1254) shows that, seventy years after its foundation, its monks lived not from their own labour but that of serfs, rents, tolls and a share of royal taxation[125]. The duke of Mecklenburg (1232) gave Doberan three Wendish villages: it purchased the village of Bork (1260) for 90 marks and the villages of Gross and Klein Jestin (1290) for 1,925 marks[126]. In other words the monks not only accepted and settled villages, they went out of their way to acquire them. Zlatá Koruna (fd 1263) came to be master of 150 villages in all, one hundred of them perhaps founded by the abbey itself on waste land given by the king of Bohemia[127]. Zinna (1285) bought the town and castle of Luckenwalde – with eleven villages and the local forest – for 2,500 Brandenburg silver marks[128]. Chorin, with only four granges, built up its village strength (to nearly twenty) until after 1350. As it did so, and developed its rights and privileges, it was necessary for the abbey to come to agreements with the citizens of neighbouring New Angermünde and Oderberg[129].

All this does not mean to say that some abbeys of the east did not have as many granges as houses in the west of Europe: they did, but they were minority holdings. Of some 30 possessions of Oliwa only four were granges – and one of those was its home farm[130]. In Bohemia Zlatá Koruna, Plasy and Sedlec each had 20 granges or more, but also around over 100, 70 and 50 villages respectively. Vyšší Brod had 70 villages but only 13 granges, Osek had 50 villages but only 10 granges[131]. Such granges as there were operated in the normal fashion, supervised by 'grangers' (Ląd, 1328)[132] or 'masters of the grange' (Osek, 1340)[133]. The monastic-owned villages had their lay bailiffs in most cases.

Serfdom

The early institutes of the Order forbade the ownership of serfs (bondmen, *nativi*, *neifs*, villeins) owing services to the abbot (as lord of the manor) and not free, without agreement or payment, to leave his service. In so refusing to have serfs it has been said that the Cistercians 'were not only turning their back on what was a universal institution, they were also asserting the dignity of man'[134]. Another potent reason was perhaps that serfs would detract from the emphasis given in the Order to manual labour on the part of the monks and *conversi*. The ideal was soon shattered. Before the mid-twelfth century villages (with their existing serfs) were given to abbeys of central and eastern Europe like Jędrzejów and Walkenried[135]. So far as Cistercian lands were concerned, serfdom perhaps reached its apogée in eastern Europe. Zlatá Koruna, for example, had its 'court of the serfs' at Weichselx Grange[136]. The enduring nature of serfdom until late dates was clearly enunciated by Abbot Ghyselbert of Ląd (1353):

'The serfs are bound to do to us all and singular services which the serfs of the king and other barons of Poland do', and by his successor Abbot John (1367): 'To all things to which the serfs of knights are bound, our serfs are obliged to us similarly'[137]. No suggestion of emancipation or freedom there!

In the second half of the twelfth century serfs were known at numerous houses in western Europe including: Rievaulx (1154)[138], Fontfroide (1166)[139] and Grandselve (1174)[140]. In the thirteenth century they were common-place. Kirkstall (*c.* 1230) received a family group: four brothers and a sister (perhaps orphaned) 'with all their goods'[141]. King Alexander II of Scotland (1248) empowered Coupar to recover those of its serfs who had absconded[142]. Sibton (1328) had numerous villeins compared to freemen: at Sibton itself – 18 villeins to 2 free though at Yoxford – only five bondmen compared to 15 free[143]. One of Sibton's serfs (at Cookley Grange, 1325) was relatively fortunate – holding 24 'acringges' of land. He paid a rent of 7 shillings p.a., he performed one boon-work in the time of sowing wheat and another in the time of sowing oats; he had to perform 16 days work during the harvest, and had to render to the abbey one cock and four hens at Christmas and ten sheep at Easter[144]. He was relatively well off – but still a bond-man. In Poland the men of five of Ląd's villages paid annually at Michaelmas fixed quantities of wheat, oats, rye, malt and flax; they had to reap two cart-loads of hay, and cut down the same quantity of timber as well as two trunks of pine; and, in addition, they had to weed the cornfields for three consecutive days with their families, and to stack corn for another day[145].

The vast majority of serfs on Cistercian lands undoubtedly came with the acquisition (by gift or purchase) of those lands. It has been said: 'To get the land, the monks took the serfs'[146]. The king of Offaly gave Monasterevin (1189) certain property 'with the men belonging to the same lands'[147]. Some dozen donations to Fontfroide (between 1166 and 1231) mention the gift of serfs and the land they cultivated[148]. Fountains received the gifts of villages with their bondmen at Rygton (1244) and at Litton (*c.* 1250)[149]. Herrenalb (1296) bought the vill of Mercklingen 'with the men residing there'[150]. Some serfs were purchased for ready money. When Simon de Beauchamp set free three villeins (about 1190) he sold them to Warden (for £1 each) together with their chattels. Their freedom was short-lived: in effect they were freed only from his service, their villeinage was transferred immediately to the abbey[151]. Furness bought at least eight serfs in the thirteenth century (at again a perhaps normal payment of £1 per head)[152].

Some serfs were acquired perhaps because of the skills they possessed – as a tanner by Cîteaux (1170)[153], a skinner by Clairvaux (1237)[154] and a carpenter by Sibton (1162)[155]. Some serfs came from vanquished people – as Mohammedan villeins of St Sergius[156] and Saracen serfs of Poblet[157]. Some serfs obtained were females: at Cheminon (1238) these may have been widows acquired with their bereaved children[158]. Walkenried (1184) leased out an acre of land in return for a woman and her children[159]. Furness early bought for 4 shillings a female serf 'with all her family'[160]. These were probably not acts of kindess – to set them at liberty – for women were useful as washer-women and milk-maids. Serfdom passed down from generation to generation. Kirkstall received Ivo: 'with all his sequel'[161]. St Sergius acquired: 'The villeins, Brain, Moufarege and Seit with all their heirs'[162]. When Clairvaux (1237) bought its skinner, the rights to his heirs were kept by the seller. It was the enduring nature of servitude that led a Polish duke to confirm the bondage of the serfs of Sulejów: 'Lest the facts are lost with the passage of time'[163].

There is patchy evidence of Cistercian serfs acquiring their freedom. As early as 1175 a serf of Fontfroide bought his liberty with a few *sous* and some land he had acquired[164]. An intriguing statute of the General Chapter (1215) enjoined that: 'The will of the late abbot of Salzedas was not to be held valid, except in that which pertains to the manumission of serfs'[165]. There are several traces of serfs buying their freedom from Sibton: one paying £5 for the privilege[166], whilst, in 1281, Sibton gave to Robert of Peasenhall: 'Full freedom of his person'[167]. The bursars's acounts of Kingswood (1241–42) include receipt of 21 shillings and 8 pence: 'From entry of land *and from freedom*'[168]. Purchases of freedom are also recorded in the Ledger Book of Vale Royal[169]. Happier still, but at a time when some British and Polish abbeys were firmly asserting their rights, Pontigny granted charters of enfranchisement to its serfs of Montigny (1345) and of Venouse (1346): they were now 'free men all'[170].

Legal Jurisdiction

Most Cistercian monasteries were (by their charters) entrusted with wide powers of oversight of those living on their lands. The monks of Tintern held some of their lands: 'With soc and sac (*jurisdiction of a manorial lord*), and tol and them (*the right to buy and sell, hold a market, and determine the ownership of goods*), and infangenethef (*right to judge a thief taken on one's land*)'. They were free of all secular exaction and summons, and; 'From toll, pontage, pannage, passage, tallage, blodwyte (*fine for shedding of blood*), flith-wyte (*fine for violence in public*), hengwite (*fine for wrongfully hanging a thief*) and flemenswite (*a fine for harbouring fugitives*)'[171]. Their residents were also free from these sanctions, but instead owed them to the abbey as their lord. Granted to Aberconwy[172], Dunkeswell[173] and Mellifont[174] was 'utfangenethef' – the right for a lord to judge one of his own men taken for felony elsewhere. Other common manorial rights were: 'view of frankpledge' – supervision of freemen who were mutual pledges for each other's good behaviour[175]: as an abbot of Dunkeswell pointed out this was 'for observing the king's peace'[176], and 'assize of bread and ale' – the regulation of the price and quality of corn, ale and bread: as exercised by Tintern which fined those who 'sold bread without licence'[177].

A distinction was drawn – especially in France – between 'high', 'medium' and 'low' justice. 'High' justice was the cognisance of cases which might involve capital punish-ment – as for murderers and thieves, 'low' justice – offences which merited a fine no greater than 60[178] or 65 *sous*[179]. Some monasteries had the right to exercise all three, as Fontenay[180]. Elsewhere the privilege might vary from grange to grange, according to the terms of benefaction. Cîteaux could exercise 'high' justice on all lands pertaining to four granges and within the walls of a further two granges, but at another grange might only exercise 'low' justice[181]. Penalties concerning 'life or limb' might not be heard in the abbot's court of Santo Spirito, Palermo[182]. In such cases more serious offences had to go to the courts of the nobleman concerned, though frequently the offender would be sent back to the monastery for punishment.

The Order (1205) itself discouraged any monastic exercise of capital punishment[183], secular aid was to be sought where necessary (1206[184], 1240[185]): its monks were not to exercise 'judgement of blood' (1237)[186]. The General Chapter also forbade other punishments meted out to thieves, such as branding or lopping off of a hand[187]. It also rebuked monks (1201) – especially those of eastern Europe – who beat their serfs to the point of drawing blood[188]. Wide judicial powers, including capital punishment, were exercised by the early fourteenth century at Sorø (1328)[189], Velehrad (1334)[190] and Doberan (1350)[190a]. In eastern Europe it was common for Cistercian abbeys to follow accepted local custom and employ trial by ordeal. On the lands of Doberan (1190) alleged thieves had to prove their innocence by walking over nine red-hot plough-shares, or by carrying a red-hot iron, and come through unscathed[191]. Even Honorius III (1222) encouraged trial by ordeal of white-hot iron at Dünamünde and elsewhere: if it burnt the suspects they were adjudged guilty and suffered accordingly[192]. On the lands of the nunneries of Polish Ołobok and Czech Oslavany trial might be by: 'Duel with staffs, ordeal by iron, passing over plough-shares, ordeal by water'[193]. Seemingly brutal, but the accepted practice of the times!

There are many references to judicial courts on Cistercian lands, but little evidence as to their organisation and procedures. The earls of Gloucester gave Neath (*c.* 1150) leave 'to freely hold its courts anywhere over its men'[194]. The men of Ląd (1251) were to be tried in the abbey's courts – 'unless a difficult case arose' – and even then the judgement given in the superior lay-court was to be remitted to the abbey for implementation[195]. At Wąchock (1260) only major cases involving bloodshed were remitted to the ducal court of Kraków and Sandomierz[196]. Obra and Koprzywnica had complete judicial rights, including the death penalty for murderers[197]. Because of the Order's prohibition on its monks administering justice, the appointment of lay judges became necessary – certainly during the thirteenth century. As early as 1201 the General Chapter ordered that when monastic serfs had to be flogged, they were to be so by a lay-man[198]. Lay judges on monastic lands might be referred to as the 'advocate' (Doberan, 1237)[199], or 'attorney' (Fürstenzell, 1276)[200] or 'sołtys' (Sulejów, 1296)[201] of the abbey concerned. The 'judge at the gate' of Lilienfeld (1328) was the father, or step-father, of one of its monks[202]. The manorial courts of Beaulieu[203] and Tintern[204] were held every three weeks. At Ląd's village of Covalew (1353) three 'great judgements' were held each year, its bailiff there receiving as a perquisite the third penny of all fines imposed. The bailiff had to provide a dinner, and the serfs – two, for the abbot or his delegate presiding at the judgements[205].

Capital punishment was noted when irregularly exercised by an abbot of Longuay (1263)[206], and when a robber was hung at Beaulieu's Faringdon manor (1272)[207]. It has been said that Glenluce might punish felons: 'Men by hanging, women by drowning'[208]. Tintern (1302) was given the right to: 'Gallows and judgement of life and limb'[209]. Dieulacres had a gallows at Leek, but might only execute offenders when there were 'certain signs of guilt' and after trial by jury[210]. Similar safeguards for offenders – as being taken in the act, or having stolen property on them – were enjoined at Velehrad, 1238[211]. Gallows existed on lands of Igny (at Monthazen Grange)[212], of Furness (at Dalton[213] and Hawkshead[214]) and of St Mary's, Dublin (in perhaps ten different localities)[215]. An abbot of Loos built a gibbet around 1290[216]. The gallows of Dunkeswell at Hackpen (1299) was thrown down and burnt by local men[217]. Evidence of long-vanished gallows comes in field-names: as on lands of Dore ('scaffold meadow')[218], Sibton ('gallowyhclose')[219] and of Tintern ('hanging acre', 'hangman's field')[220].

Prisoners awaiting trial or execution had to be securely confined. Monastic prisons appeared on Cistercian lands as well as at an abbey itself, like that of Vale Royal (at Weaverham)[221], of Furness (at Dalton)[222] and of Beaulieu (at Faringdon). The latter was (in 1270) being repaired and iron shackles were being made for the prisoners[223]. Stocks (pillories) were known on the lands of Ford (at Charmouth, 1320)[224] and of Velehrad (at Němčice Velké, 1334)[225]. A serf put in the stocks ready for whipping (at Kirkstall's Berdseye, 1289) was forcibly rescued[226]. A gang of seven men threw down by night a pillory of Merevale (at Orton, 1299)[227]. Tumbrils (stools for the punishment of women by ridicule or ducking in water) were additionally noted at Dalton[228], Rotherham[229] and on lands of St Mary's, Dublin[230].

Colonisation

When and where the Cistercians failed to have a sufficient supply of *conversi*, the monasteries concerned became active colonisers of those lands which would otherwise have been only partly worked: not only by leasing out lands to peasant tenants but by bringing in new settlers and by affording scope for the building of villages. This was especially true of monastic foundations in Iberia and eastern Europe, where large tracts of territory given to the Cistercians could not possibly be developed by the monks alone. The General Chapter statute (of 1208) encouraged the settlement of lay-people by allowing the demise of distant and useless properties for a kind rent[231]. Later in the thirteenth century the rapid decline in *conversi* numbers saw many abbeys enter into contracts of *paréage* (sharing) with the Crown or local nobles, by which new villages were created: this process was most marked in the *bastides* of south-west France, but was not restricted to that region, nor indeed to France. The monasteries yielded land surplus to their requirements, the lords provided defence, and both parties shared the profts. The people received a charter listing their rights and obligations. A king of Majorca (1309) summed matters up when he noted that La Real: 'On account of the lack of labouring serfs' did not have sufficient personnel to cultivate the lands of Colle Grange. He persuaded the abbey to give him the grange in return for substantial kind rents. His first argument was that he could settle people there to farm the land, his second reason betrayed his real motive: settling people, the monarch said, would 'promote security'[232].

In England Stanlaw early settled cultivators on its vill of Acton[233], and Dieulacres placed serfs given it on its lands at Rossall (in distant Lancashire)[234]. Rufford (in 1207) built houses to settle men near Wellow in an effort to protect its wood there from trespassers, and travellers on the high road from robbers. This was not to the liking of the villagers of Wellow who knocked the houses down[235]. Buckfast established a village with market at Kingsbridge: granted a charter by the king (in 1219) it came to be reckoned as a 'borough'[236]. Meaux founded Wyke-upon-Hull at Myton Grange, but its success led to Edward I taking it over (in 1293): henceforth it was '*King*ston-upon-Hull'[237]. Vale Royal's manors of Kirkham (in 1296) and Over (about 1300) were elevated to borough status[238]. Holm Cultram obtained a borough charter for Wavermouth – a port which victualled the Scottish fleet of Edward I. Marine incursions meant that, in its place, a borough (with royal charter, church and fair) was established at *New*ton Arlosh (on the abbey's Arlosh Grange) in 1305[239]. Ford's manor of Charmouth became a 'free borough' about 1325[240]. Other important boroughs of the period included those of Furness (at Dalton)[241] and Dieulacres (at Leek)[242]. In Ireland the village of *New*town – to the north-west of Duiske – had its provost and burgesses by 1280[243].

In Iberia the availability of land in the wake of the retreat of the Moors – but without a compensating number of *conversi* – meant that abbeys such as Alcobaça in Portugal and Poblet in Spain became important agents of colonisation[244]. Alcobaça created several settlements in a process lasting well over a century: some on newly cleared lands around the monastery and some on existing granges[245]. It gave a series of charters to the new inhabitants – as for Aljuarrota (1230), Évora (1285), and Santa Catarina (1342)[246]. Each settler normally received an average of 10 ha (25 acres) of land, and was expected to clear it and have it under cultivation within ten years – paying one-fifth of the produce to the abbey[247]. The number of households was specified: Maiorga – 100, Cela – 87, Santa Catarina – 31, and so on. Restrictions might be imposed: Maiorga had to be a cereal-producing village, its tenants were not allowed to grow fruit, vegetables or grapes on any scale[248]. Tarouca populated its granges of Figueiro (1243) and Tauça (1269)[249]. Fifty households were settled at Figueiro, a criminal code of fines was drawn up, and the manner of electing judges defined[250]. In granting a new charter to Figueiro (in 1281) the abbey demanded various dues from the tenants, as well as one-eighth part of all bread, wine, vegetables and flax produced[251].

Settlers on the lands of Poblet were encouraged by ample land-grants, tax exemptions and loans for home construction. There are no instances of Poblet destroying vills, rather villages thus formed around its farms or 'masies'[252]. Rueda, founding the town of Jaulin (1217), expected the settlers to build their own houses (this was normal practice), and reserved to itself the right of justice and the baking monopoly. Each settler was to pay the abbey tithes and half of the first-fruits, delivering this in Saragossa. The other half was reserved for building Jaulin church and for irrigation and other necessary works[253]. Settling colonists from Lagata at Val de Mallatz (in 1244), Rueda required of them tithe, and one-eleventh of their cereals, fruits and grapes, as well as monetary payments and fairly large quantities of wheat from those areas sown communally. The offer of places was open to both Christians and Moors[254]. The first grange to be settled by Rueda was Romana (1211)[255]: it also granted charters to Seña (1235) and Valimaña (1340)[256].

In northern Italy Chiaravalle di Milano abandoned direct cultivation on some of its lands – installing 26 familes at Vione, 18 on Vallera Grange (in 1255) and 53 on Villamaggiore Grange (in 1275)[257]. In 1327 the 'new town' of Villanova Solaro was created jointly by Rivalta and Philip of Savoy[258]. Early villages founded by Cistercian abbeys on grange lands also included that of Münchendorf in Austria (by Heiligenkreuz, 1187)[259]. In Switzerland at least three villages were settled on lands of Hautcrêt, with tenants paying rent to the abbey[260]. The Belgian abbey of Orval founded (jointly with Count Arnulph of Looz and Chiny) the village of Gérouville (1258), which had all the hall-marks of the 'bastides' of SW France. The seigneurial rights were divided between the two founders: tithes passed to the abbey, and profits of justice to the count[261]. The process of repeopling granges was clearly widespread throughout western Europe.

There is much evidence, too, in France from the late-twelfth century on. The village of Landouzy-la-Ville was founded by Foigny as early as 1168[262]. New villages were also established by Grâce-Dieu (Poitevin, 1234) at Surgères (thirty holdings)[263], by St Sulpice-en-Bugey (1242–45) at Hostiaz and Prêmilieu (a reversion to pre-grange status)[264] and by Aiguebelle (1280) at Barret and Saint-Nizier (with the lord of Valaurie)[265]. When Fontmorigny (1272) received leave to instal 'all the men it wishes' in the lordship of the Guerche, there was a division of juridical rights. If a person was convicted of serious crime (worthy of death or corporal punishment) then the delinquent's lands were to pass to the abbey, his other goods went to the secular lord[266]. When Beaubec (1305–26) formed the village of Criquiers on the plateau of Bray – on lands pertaining to three of its granges – each tenant was given a plot of land 6 perches broad, on which to erect their houses along the road-side: a 'street village'. Each had to pay a rent of 10 *sols* per acre, and grind their corn at the abbey mills. They were subject to the 'low justice' of the abbot but the 'high justice' of the local lord. Rules drawn up for inheritance included the equal division of goods between brothers and sisters. The abbey was to build a church, and dig a well and a pond there[267].

Several abbeys in Lorraine were active colonisers in the thirteenth century including La Crête and its daughter-house of St Benoît-en-Woëvre. The former, between 1223 and 1314, established a series of new villages including – in conjunction with the count of Champagne – those of Chantrains (1223) and Bourdons (1240) in Bassigny[268]. (One of its new villages, St Julien-en-Rayon, has now disappeared[269].) St Benoît, in partnership with the counts of Bar, founded new villages at Lahaymeix (1255), Wassecourt (Hazavant; 1276) and Hadonville (1284)[270]. The agreement for Wassecourt survives, and shows that the monks retained their grange complex with sufficient arable land for sixty days ploughing, and meadow-land for twenty days mowing[271]. Also in Lorraine Cherlieu built a church for the new village on the borders of its Cornot Grange (1257)[272] and Isle-en-Barrois helped to found the village of Deuxmonds (1279)[273], whilst new villages also occupied Morimond's former granges of Angoulancourt

(Lavilleneuve; 1310) and Grandrupt (1285)[274]. Cistercian colonisation in Lorraine must not be exaggerated: the new villages of the white monks were but few compared to the total settled in the period[275]. The need for security and to fill empty lands in such a 'frontier' country may have prompted some of the foundations.

The Bastides

The growth of new villages on Cistercian lands in France reached its apogée in Aquitaine, not least because of the density of Cistercian abbeys in that area, and because little other land was available there for such development[276]. Between 1252 and 1325 44 Cistercian-sponsored bastides were founded, mostly in the country between the rivers Garonne and Ariège[277]. 'Bastide' had meant originally a 'fortified place' but as peace came it lost its military connotations, becoming simply a term for new centres of settlement, 'bastides or populations'[278]. Bastides were also founded on other church lands, especially of the Premonstratensians[279]. The monks gave over part of their granges to establish these (sometimes fortified) villages, in partnership both with the seneschals of the Capetian kings (thirty were so founded) and with local Gascon barons. Some bastides were founded jointly with the English, but none so by a Cistercian abbey[280]. The earliest bastides, at Mazères (on lands of Boulbonne, 1252) and Labessière (on territory of Candeil, 1255), may have been genuine efforts by the monks to populate lands which might otherwise have gone unworked due to the declining numbers of *conversi*[281]. When Carbonne (1256) was founded, it was said to have been so 'at the request of the Cistercians' of Bonnefont[282].

In many instances the initiative came largely perhaps because the Crown wanted to continue more effectively the deepening of royal authority in Gascony – which had started with the Treaty of Paris (in 1229), and with the hope that bastides might contribute to peace. Once bastides were founded by the Capetian kings, local barons wishing to maintain their independence did the same[283]. A leading rôle in the process was played by Alphonse de Poitiers, count of Toulouse, brother of St Louis and royal Steward, who needed to assert his authority (and that of the king) in border areas such as Agenais, Guyenne and Rouergue[284]. In the time of a later Steward of Toulouse, Eustace de Beaumarchais (1272–92), ten (of the thirty Capetian-inspired) Cistercian bastides were founded[285]: this at a time of renewed Albigensian attacks on church property[286]. Several bastides (not just Cistercian) took their names from cities of Flanders, Italy and Spain, and 'it would be interesting to establish with what criteria the name was chosen'[287].

Bonnefont concluded five contracts of joint-ownership, two with the king (for Plaisance on its Minhac Grange, 1285, and Beauchalot at Apas Grange, 1325); two with the count of Comminges (for Lestelle, also on Apas Grange, 1256, and Boussens, on Pentens Grange, 1269), and one with the count of Toulouse (Carbonne on Carnet Grange, 1256)[288]. The count of Comminges also joined with Nizors in the establishment of Mondilhan (1260) and Nénigan (1282). The counts of Foix participated with Boulbonne to found the first bastide (Mazères, 1252), and also co-operated with Nizors (Blajan, 1283) and L'Éscale-Dieu (Avezac, 1305)[289]. A count of Astarac founded Mirande, in company with Berdoues[290]. The bastides assisted by Eustace de Beaumarchais, on behalf of Philip IV, included Beaumont (1279) and Grenade (1290) with Grandselve, Saint-Lys (1280) with Gimont and Beaufort (1291) with Feuillant[291]. Gimont also ceded to Philip VI (1323/25) 300 ha (750 acres) of its grange of Franqueville for the bastide of Solomiac[292]. Obazine founded, with Philip VI (1331), the bastide of Mont-Sainte-Marie on its Calès Grange – seemingly the last Cistercian bastide[293].

Lengthy and extremely detailed agreements were drawn up on the foundation of each bastide: these spelt out the relevant rights of the founding parties, and also acted as charters listing the privileges and obligations of the settlers. The contract of *paréage* between Grandselve and Philip IV of France (through his Steward of Toulouse, Eustace de Beaumarchais) for the bastide of Beaumont was settled in July, 1279[294]. Its many provisions included: (1) Grandselve gave the king one-half of the thousand house-building plots, one-half of the thousand holdings for gardens and one-half of the thousand 'arpents' for viticulture. Ownership of the other half was retained by the abbey. Profits from feudal dues, including bakeries and stalls, were likewise shared. (2) The profits from 'low justice' (incurring penalties of up to 60 *sous*) were also divided, but 'high justice' was reserved to the Crown. (6) Both sides were to share one bailiff, who on taking office was to swear on oath to serve both parties well, but there could be two bailiffs if the parties could not agree on a common choice. (7) Edicts and proclamations were to be jointly instituted. (10) The abbey could build a church and manse. (12) No 'Clerics or knights or other religious' could settle in the bastide without leave of the abbey. (14) Any judges and beadles appointed were to swear loyal service to both abbey and king. In another lengthy document (of eighty-nine articles) Philip VI (1327) recorded the customs of the bastide of Solomiac[295].

The contract for Grenade (1290) saw similar arrangements. Feudal dues and most rights of justice were divided between the Crown and Grandselve, the bailiff of the bastide was to be common for king and monastery, and all other officers (as judges, court notaries, consuls, sergeants and town-criers) had to swear faithful service to both[296]. The customary of the bastide (1291) made the consuls responsible for judging criminals such as robbers and murderers, and the bailiff for executing the sentences[297]. A revised contract for the bastide of Villefranche (founded in 1311) – perhaps made necessary by the accession of the new abbot of Silvanès – was confirmed by Philip IV after negotiations between the monastery (represented by the abbot and two monks) and the royal steward of the Rouergue, Peter de Ferrières. The new agreement left the abbey with substantial rights of justice and dues, but cost it 250 *livres l.t.* – payable to the Crown in five equal annual instalments[298]. The allocation of judicial rights formed a major part of the acts of *paréage*. The contract for the bastide of Pierrefiche (1306), sited on La Roquette Grange by Bonneval and the king, mentions some of the more serious punishments envisaged: 'Impressment, flogging, mutilation of members (*possibly branding*), exile or death'[299].

As the bastides were new villages, it was possible for them to be carefully planned. Ideally they had a rectangular lay-out of streets, an arrangement seen at its best in Grenade and Mirande[300] – 'bastides of the plains'[301], but modified where laid down on an earlier infrastructure (as at Beaumont)[302], or where relief dictated (as the large meander of the Garonne at Carbonne), or where there was a need to rebuild (as also at Carbonne)[303]. In the centre of the bastides was a town square with a medieval hall – indicative of craftsmanship, and arcaded surrounds – suggestive of commerce, with frequently the church on one side[304]. [The contract for Grenade (1290) specified the building of its church, which soon came to have a Confraternity of the Blessed Virgin Mary: its rules and statutes, drawn up in 1304, are extant[305].] The main through roads of the bastides might be quite large (an advantage to traders), whilst all the principal streets were prolonged into the surrounding agricultural lands, giving them too a geometric plan[306]. The whole might be surrounded by protective walls[307] – as those built at Grenade in 1341, but which failed to keep out English soldiery eight years later[308] – built upon defensive ramparts, banks and ditches, as still evident at Beaumont[309] and Plaisance[310].

A number of bastides, especially those in the plains, became important centres of trade and still have lively markets and fairs today[311]. Beaumont had a Saturday market and two fairs a year, Grenade a Wednesday market and also two fairs each year, and Comberouger, a Thursday market[312]. As for individual holdings, each tenant at Gilhac had land for house, garden, meadow, vine-plot and arable land[312a]. At Grenade 3,000 tenants each received a building plot (measuring 27 × 9 m [90 × 30 ft]), an allotment and garden and shared 2,000 vine-plots. For each holding a rent of 5 *d.t.* was payable yearly at All Saints, and for each vine-plot a rent of 10 *d.t.* was due on St Thomas' Day[313]. Whether the bastides were great or small, they were clearly an important source of income to the monasteries and secular parties concerned, but they represented a complete *volte-face* from the ideals of the early Cistercians who deliberately cleared peoples off their lands: now the wheel had turned full circle.

Eastern Europe

The Cistercians played a part, with other Orders and lay lords, in colonising lands beyond the Elbe, during the active Germanisation of parts of eastern Europe in the twelfth and thirteenth centuries: a mass movement of peoples partly motivated by the increasing population of the continent, which rose from 61 million people in 1200 to about 75 million in 1300[314]. Settlers (not only Germans) were actively encouraged, indeed recruited in the west, conducted upon their journey and housed in monasteries on the way[315]. Both conquering German princes in Brandenburg and native Slav princes (Christian since the crusade against the Wends in 1147) actively facilitated such settlement[316]: any native criticism was in part overcome by the resulting visible improvements to the relatively poor lands of the east[317]. For the Cistercians it was another means of utilising the large estates given them in this region. One grant to Kołbacz stated that as the abbey did not have 'sufficient brothers to utilise the land it might place there settlers, as many as it wishes'[318]. So it was, for most abbeys in eastern Europe, that the inherited serf and the imported colonist formed the vast bulk of their labour supply and tenantry.

In Pomerania monasteries such as Doberan (fd. 1171)[319], Dargun (1174), Eldena (1209) and Neuenkamp (1231) could not bring in Danish and German settlers quickly enough, and so were allowed to place Slav colonists as well[320]. In almost identical language, the charters given to Dargun (1176)[321] by Casimir I and to Eldena (1209)[322] by Jaromir I allowed those abbeys to settle: 'Danes, Germans, Slavs; men of different trades, create parishes and appoint priests, and have trading booths'. Another important coloniser was the abbey of Buków: founded in 1259, it had settled 11 villages by 1277 with Germans and Wends[323]. All the abbeys of the region were busy settling immigrants almost from their foundation. Eldena's settlers from Lower Germany fused with Dane and Slav labour in the salt-region to create the nucleus of the future town of Greifswald[324]. Some granges were transformed into villages to accommodate settlers: Dargun (1213–33) did this at *Neu*kalen[325] and Zinna (not a great coloniser)[326] at its *Neu*hof, close to the abbey[327].

In Poland the older abbeys were the most important colonising agents[328]. Łekno (fd 1143), with its strong links with Altenberg and Cologne, peopled 30 villages with Rhenish Germans by 1300[329]. Ląd (1143), whilst given 14 villages at its inception, built a new village (by 1155) peopled with Germans and free Poles[330]. The thirteenth century abbeys were not so significant. Przemęt (1210) took over existing 'German villages in the wood'[331]; Obra (1243) 'did not succeed in germanising the local population, though this was a principal objective'[332]. Paradyż (1236), however, settled Germans after draining the marsh of Meseritz[333], and Mogiła placed settlers on lands laid waste by the Tartars[334]. Pride of place in Silesia must go to the colonising activity of Lubiąż, which brought in settlers 'from Flanders and Eastphalia, from Hesse and

Thuringia'[335]. Boleslas the Lanky implied this activity in the abbey's foundation charter (1175)[336]. Under Abbot Günther (1203–39) it placed immigrants on nearly 400,000 ha (950,000 acres) of (generally) poor land, and the process continued with the backing of Duke Mesko (1239–46)[337]. Doberan established four 'towns' (including Müncheberg) as well as innumerable villages[338]. There was racial segregation on the lands of Lubiąż, the new German villages were kept separate from the settlements of Polish peasants[339]. Opposition from the Polish clergy helped to being this mass colonisation to a standstill in the later thirteenth centry[340].

In Bohemia large-scale colonisation of entire regions undertaken by the sovereign or the aristocracy overshadowed the efforts by houses such as Osek, Plasy and Sedlec[341]. Only Zlatá Koruna played a major rôle – with over one hundred villages founded on waste land – at the behest of the king[342]. Granted a substantial area of woodland by the counts of Freiberg, Velehrad (1302) founded a new 'town': 'Theodoric's town', in the neighbourhood of Freiberg[343]. In Germany, Dutch and Flemish settlers were colonists on lands of Pforta (1250)[344] and of Walkenried – the latter settling them in Thuringia in the Riet marshland between Ocher and Rode[345]. Waldsassen (fd 1133) germanised the Eger region and came to have 20,000 subjects in the 'Stiftland'[346], whilst Grünhain (fd 1235), despite its late foundation, colonised three 'towns' and 56 villages[347].The Austrian abbey of Heiligenkreuz undertook colonising tasks on the Hungarian border – backed by King Andrew of Hungary[348] – like Königshof (near Bruch on the Leitha) and Mönchhof (north-east of Lake Neusiedel)[349].

Colonisation in eastern Europe was encouraged, and the efficiency of the monastic estates facilitated, by the privilege often granted whereby the men of villages given to, or settled by, the Cistercians, were placed under Teutonic law and thus exempted from Slav and Polish laws and a whole range of customary dues and services owing to Crown and noble. It was not always a complete immunity. Whilst all the villages of Wąchock and Sulejów came to be 'under Teutonic law'[350], only three of the nine belonging to Żarnowiec nunnery were so[351]. The convent of Ołobok also had lands enduring under Polish law and custom[352]. Over thirty of Koronowo's fifty or so villages came to be under Teutonic law (alias 'the law of Magdeburg')[353]. The same was true of Obra where thirteen villages had to pay corn rents, whereas others did not[354]. But, in general terms, Cistercian villages were normally exempt from Polish law and custom.

The men of Ląd (1181): 'Whether freemen or bondmen or tenants' were immune from duties to the State of carriage, of guiding and of keeping guard, from tribute and kind payments in cattle, from toll and pontage, and from the building and maintenance of castles and bridges[355]. A general exemption was from conscription for military service away from the local magnate's territory, but there was rarely any immunity from joining in the defence of the home front. At Lubiąż (1175): 'If a hostile army enters the land, then the colonists of the abbey (the villeins on foot, the officials on horseback), shall proceed to the common defence'[356]. Duke Barnim gave the men of Dargun (1266) freedom from all exactions due to him and his barons, including: 'The building of towns, placing of bridges, all expedition, and from toll when on monastery business'[357]. Settlers were also encouraged by monasteries waiving rents for the first few years, and by giving practical help[358]. Obra gave its peasants 4 horses and 30 sheep each to set them up on their holdings[359]. Pforta (1250) made a pact with its Flemish settlers of non-eviction if they faithfully tilled the land and paid their rents on time[360].

Notes

1. Rösener (1983a) 154–55; Williams (1984) II, 348; *cf. Statuta* I, 14 (1134/IX).
2. McCrank (1976) 146–47; *cf.* 160, 163, 165.
3. Wardrop (1987) 87.
4. Birch (1897) 173, Williams (1984) II, 348.
5. *Statuta* I, 251 (1200/11).
6. *Statuta* I, 309–10 (1205/13).
7. *Statuta* I, 346 (1208/5).
8. Donnelly (1954) 421; Roehl (1972) 107.
9. *Statuta* I, 517 (1220/5).
10. Donnelly (1954) 68; *Statuta* II, 31 (1224/10).
11. *LCC* (2) 231.
12. *RSL* II, 210 (No. 5), 226.
13. Deck (1974) 143.
14. Lekai (1977a) 309.
15. Elm (1982) 153.
16. Aubrun (1978) 117.
17. Durand (1984) 116*n*.
18. Higounet (1983b) 179.
19. Lebecq (1983) 205.
20. *Statuta* II, 477 (1261/10).
21. *Statuta* III, 69 (1269/5).
22. Elm (1982) 153.
23. Bishop (1936) 197.
24. *Statuta* II, 3 (1262/10); Donnelly (1954) 426; Higounet (1983b) 162, Platt (1969) 97.
25. Platt (1969) 96.
26. PRO, DL 25/1285, 1346.
27. *DSMLR* 589–94 (No. 257).
28. Lekai (1977a) 449.
29. *Statuta* I, 428 (1214/57), 448 (1215/64), 463 (1216/66), 481 (1217/68).
30. *Statuta* II, 54 (1226/30).
31. *LCC* (2) 326–27.
32. Donnelly (1949) 69.
33. *Statuta* III, 326 (1312/9).
34. *Statuta* III, 330 (1315/4).
35. *TG* 358.
36. Platt (1969) 95.
37. Charvátová (1987) 128.
38. *Statuta* III, 479 (1344/12).
39. Donnelly (1954) 423, [*Statuta* III, 485–93 (1344/30–32, 34–35, 38, 40–48, 53, 57–58)].
40. *VKS* 196–99.
41. *Cîteaux* (1978:1–2) 124.
42. Lekai (1977a) 309.
43. Charvátová (1987) 119.
44. *Statuta* III, 69 (1269/5).
45. *Statuta* III, 74 (1269/29).
46. *Statuta* III, 289–90 (1297/13).
47. *Statuta* III, 203 (1280/62).
48. Sommer-Ramer (1982) 318.
49. Rösener (1983a) 154–55.
50. *Ibid.* 153, Donkin (1978) 17–18.
51. France (1992) 157.
52. *RSL* II, 232.
53. Donnelly (1954) 437.
54. *RSL* II, 232.
55. *ABB* 58, 60–61, 63, 65, 68, 70–71, 85, 114.
56. *Statuta* I, 346 (1208/5).
57. Williams (1984) II, 355.
58. Fort i Cogul (1972) 114–15.
59. *RBM* 331 (No. 848).
60. *MEB* passim.
61. Occhipinti (1985) 335.
62. Williams (1984) II, 294.
63. Barea (1977) 265–66.
64. Bishop (1936) 197.
65. Williams (1984) II, 357.
66. Williams (1984) II, 294.
67. Redoutey (1982) 731.
68. *TG* 358.
69. Higounet (1965) 52–53.
70. *RCH* 182.
71. Köfler (1978) 169.
72. Almeida Fernandes (1976) 93–96.
73. Barea (1977) (1) 267.
74. Williams (1984) II, 357.
75. *SBE* 16–17.
76. *ABB* 58–158 *passim*.
77. Williams (1976) 135.
78. *OHZ* II, 3–4 (No. 426).
79. *CW* 254.
80. *CW* 199–96.
81. *CW* 254.
82. NLW, Badminton Manorial 1639.
83. Lindley (1954) 169.
84. *CSBW* 92–93.
85. Occhipinti (1985) 334.
86. Lindley (1954) 169 (No.   43).
87. *SBC* I, 133.
88. Duby (1968) 439.
89. Elm (1982) 154.
90. Lindley (1954) 169 (No.   43).
91. Fort i Cogul (1972) 115.
92. Cowley (1977) 239*n*; Williams (1984) II, 358.
93. Durand (1983) 112.
94. Donnelly (1954) 414.
95. Fort i Cogul (1972) 114.
96. Charvátová (1987) 118.
97. *TG* 358.
98. Conbhuí (1958) xxxv.
99. Williams (1984) II, 358.
100. *RBM* IV, 493 (No. 1241).
101. Fort i Cogul (1972) 114.
102. *CAS* I, 274 (No. CCC).
103. *CCR* 1237/525.
104. *CBK* 18 (No. XXII).
105. Campbell (1899) 184.
106. *VRL* 51.
106a. Lekai (1977a) 450.
107. Lackner (1978b) 25.
108. Williams (1984) II, 243–44.
109. *Ibid.* 244.
110. *SBC* (4) 47–48 (No. 1000).
111. Berman (1978) 20.
112. McCrank (1975) 262.
113. Silva (1981) 126.
114. *ABB* 12, 14, 84–86; Hockey (1976) 58–61.
115. Cowley (1977) 253–57; Williams (1984) II, 251.
116. NLW, Badminton Manorial 1639; Williams (1976) 134 (where transcribed).
117. NLW, Badminton Manorial 1639.
118. NLW, Badminton Manorial 1645.
119. Williams (1976) 137.
120. Cowley (1977) 255.
121. VCH, *Chester* III (1980) 159; Coulton (1960) 489–91.
122. Wetesko (1991) 156.

123. Lekai (1976) 60, 62.
124. Charvátová (1994) 180.
125. Lekai (1976) 259.
126. Thompson (1920) 90.
127. Charvátová (1987) 123.
128. Speiss (1959) 278.
129. *CDB* II, 419–20, 432, 434, 459, 496–99.
130. *PU* III, 142.
131. Charvátová (1987) 114, 123; (1994) 181– 83.
132. Archivum Państowe w Poznaniu, Kl. Ląd A 4.
133. *RBM* IV, 325 (No. 829).
134. Conbhuí (1958) xxv.
135. Lekai (9177a) 293.
136. Platt (1969) 87–88.
137. Staats Archiv, Cologne: Kl. Lond. I (Ląd Copialbuch) ff. 45d–46r.
138. Graves (1957) 6.
139. Grèzes-Ruelff (1977) 270.
140. Mousnier (1986) 114.
141. Kitson (1895) 49 (No. 10).
142. *CRC* xiv; Morgan (1929) III, 442.
143. *SBE* 16.
144. *SBE* 149.
145. Staats Archiv, Cologne: Kl. Lond. I, 45d–46r.
146. Graves (1957) 6.
147. Conbhuí (1958) xxxiii.
148. Grèzes-Ruelff (1977) 270.
149. Donnelly (1954) 412.
150. *DR* 147–48.
151. *CW* 136–37.
152. Graves (1957) 7.
153. *CDAC* 156 (No. 193).
154. *RCC* VI, 164.
155. *SBC* IV, 97 (No. 1162).
156. Williams (1974) 73.
157. Tort (1974) 359.
158. *RCCH* 107.
159. Wiswe (1953) 56.
160. *AF* 112–13.
161. *CBK* lxxxiv.
162. Williams (1974) 73.
163. Mitkowski (1949) 319.
164. Grèzes-Ruelff (1977) 270.
165. *Statuta* I, 445 (1215/51).
166. *SBC* I, 122–23.
167. *SBC* III, 69 (No. 575).
168. *DCK* 201.
169. *VRL*. passim.
170. King (1954) 175.
171. Williams (1976) 114, 143 (n. 95).
172. Williams (1984) II, 247.
173. Sparks (1978) 56.
174. Conbhuí (1980) 238.
175. *Ibid*. 226–27.
176. Sparks (1978) 56.
177. Williams (1976) 135–36.
178. Sommer-Ramer (1982) 144.
179. Poloni (1980) 42.
180. *DHGE* XVII (1971) 903.
181. Poloni (1980) 41–42.
182. White (1938) 170.
183. *Statuta* I, 306 (1205/1).
184. *Statuta* I, 321 (1206/8).
185. Lekai (1977a) 393.
186. *LCC* (2) 303 (IX).

187. Waddell: Comment at 1993 Fontfroide Conference.
188. *Statuta* I, 272 (1201/46).
189. McGuire (1982) 205.
190. *RBM* IV, 17 (No. 46).
190a. *DD* 1625–26; *cf. DD* 1468 (of 1190) 1482 (of 1237).
191. Dolan (1909) 3; *cf. DD* 1469.
192. *FHL* 76 (No. 100).
193. *KD* I, 276–77.
194. Williams (1984) II, 247.
195. *KD* I, 264–65.
196. *MHP* I, 79–80.
197. *KDM* II, 156, *MPH* I, 79.
198. *Statuta* I, 272 (1201/46).
199. *DD* 1482.
200. *DHGE* XIX (1981) 318.
201. Mitkowski (1949) 336–37.
202. *TL* 58.
203. *ABB* 12.
204. Williams (1984) II, 247.
205. Staats Archiv, Cologne: Kl. Lond. I, 45d–46r.
206. *Statuta* III, 14–15 (1263/37).
207. *ABB* 85.
208. Morton (1936) 230.
209. Williams (1984) II, 248.
210. *CD* 297.
211. *CDRB* III:Pt. 2, 262–63 (No. 204).
212. Péchenard (1883) 359.
213. *AF* 233–36.
214. VCH, *Lancaster* II (1908) 121.
215. Conbhuí (1980) 239.
216. Coulton (1960) 191.
217. Sparks (1978) 44.
218. Williams (1976) Plan 2.
219. *SBC* IV, 63 (No. 1116).
220. Williams (1984) II, 248.
221. *VRL* 57.
222. *AF* 17.
223. *ABB* 85.
224. *MEX* 352.
225. *RBM* IV, 17 (No. 46).
226. Fletcher (1919) 127.
227. *CPR* 1299/475, 1300/552, 1301/632.
228. *AF* 235–36.
229. VCH, *Nottingham* II (1910) 102.
230. Conbhuí (1980) 239.
231. *Statuta* I, 346 (1208/5).
232. *DSMLR* 419–28 (No. 157).
233. Desmond (1975) 249.
234. *Ibid*. 249.
235. *RFC* xxix–xxx.
236. Beresford (1967) 133.
237. *Ibid*. 132.
238. Donkin (1978) 161.
239. Beresford (1967) 415–16; *cf. RHC* 95–96.
240. *MEX* 340, 352.
241. Donkin (1978) 161; VCH, *Lancaster* II (1908) 121.
242. *CD* 300.
243. Carville (1970) 75–77.
244. Lekai (9177a) 300.
245. Cocheril (1964) 274, Yañez Neira (1970) 562, 566.
246. *DHGE* II (1914) 26.
247. Durand (1983) 114.

248. Cocheril (1964) 274–75.
249. Almeida Fernandes (1976) 52–55, 95–96.
250. *Ibid*. 95–96.
251. *Ibid*. 95–96.
252. Lekai (1977a) 300.
253. Barea (1977) I, 266.
254. *Ibid*. I, 267.
255. Wamba (1994) 139.
256. Barea (1977) I, 269–70.
257. Comba (1983) 122, 129.
258. Higounet (1986) 128.
259. *Ibid*. 128.
260. Sommer-Ramer (1982) 146–47.
261. Berckmans (1973) 79–92.
262. Higounet (1986) 128.
263. Barrière (1994) 67 (fn.19).
264. *Cîteaux* (1978: 1–2) 124.
265. *CDAA* 234–36.
266. *CAF* 293 (No. DCIV).
267. Deck (1974) 144–47.
268. Higounet (1986) 128.
269. *DHGE* XIII (1956) 1032.
270. *CSBW* 20, 115–16, 142–44, 156–60.
271. *Ibid*. 142–44.
272. Chauvin (1983b) 41.
273. Maas (1944) 47–48.
274. Higounet (1986) 129.
275. *Cf*. the lists in Maas, *passim*.
276. Higounet (1950) 76.
277. Higounet (1950) 70, (1986) 27.
278. Roblin (1937) 44.
279. Higounet (1950) 70, 81.
280. Berman (1994) 213 (fn. 8).
281. Higounet (1986) 134–35.
282. *Ibid*. 130.
283. Barrière (1990), Higounet (1950) 75.
284. Higounet (1950) 74, (1986) 131.
285. Higounet (1986) 132.
286. Rumeau (1896) xv.
287. Guidoni (1978) 270.
288. *Cîteaux* (1978/1–2) 81–82.
289. Higounet (1950) 75.
290. *DHGE* VIII (1935) 351.
291. Higounet (1950) 73.
292. *Ibid*. 79.
293. Barrière (1977).
294. *LJ* 35–39.
295. Dubord (1879) 101–19, 175–85.
296. Rumeau (1896) xv, 10 (Nos 62/1, 62/6).
297. *Ibid*. 12–14 (No. 63).
298. *CSV* 450–56.
299 *CABR* 274.
300. Higounet (1950) 81.
301. *Ibid*. 81.
302. Berman (1994) 208.
303. Roblin (1937) 43, 46.
304. Cazes (1982) 231.
305. Rumeau (1896) 11 (No. 62/11), 36 (No. 2).
306. Higounet (1950) 82.

307. Roblin (1937) 45.
308. Rumeau (1896) vii, xvi.
309. Higounet (1948) 122.
310. Roblin (1937) 48.
311. Higounet (1950) 83.
312. Mousnier (1983c) 239.
312a. *Ibid*. 223.
313. Rumeau (1896) xv.
314. Speiss (1959) 112.
315. Lekai (1977b) 125, Thompson (1920) 77.
316. Carsten (1941) 61.
317. Thoma (1904) 137.
318. Chlopocka (1953) 62.
319. Bouton (1959) I, 163.
320. Carsten (1941) 62.
321. Kunkel (1911) 42–43.
322. Winter (1868) II, 252.
323. *DHGE* X (1938) 1109; *cf*. Winter (1868) II, 253–54.
324. Mohr (1977) 15.
325. Higounet (1986) 128.
326. Hoppe (1914) 132.
327. Higounet (1986) 128.
328. Williams (1978) 234.
329. Van Der Meer (1965) 285.
330. Schneider (1976) 76.
331. *KD* I, 64–65; Lekai (1977b) 124–25.
332. Krason (1950) 174.
333. *KD* I, 65–66.
334. Winter (1868) II, 395.
335. Thompson (1920) 571.
336. *Ibid*. 77.
337. Thoma (1904) 87, 137.
338. Grüger (1982) 98, Sculze (1979) 107.
339. Grüger (1982) 98, Schneider (1974) 108.
340. Thoma (1904) 149.
341. Charvátová (1994) 183 (fn. 7).
342. *Ibid*. 179.
343. *CDEM* V, 143.
344. *CP* I, 108.
345. Sebicht (1888) 39–40, Winter (1868) II, 194.
346. Van Der Meer (1965) 302, *cf*. Higounet (1986) 128.
347. Van Der Meer (1965) 281.
348. *UKSH* 63 (No. L, of 1222).
349. Roth (1986) 532.
350. *MPH* I, 79; Mitkowski (1949) 336–37.
351. Dąbrowski (1970) 142.
352. *KD* I, 276–77.
353. Kozlowski (1972) 127–28, 249.
354. Krason (1950) 172.
355. *KD* I, 32; *cf*. I, 264–65.
356. *KD* I, 27–28.
357. *MU* 136.
358. Schneider (1974) 108, Thoma (1904) 87, Thompson (1928a) 657.
359. Krason (1950) 173.
360. *CP* I, 108.

Chapter 15

LAND UTILISATION AND TITHES

The Cistercians, possessed of consolidated estates and (in the *conversi*) of a relatively large labour supply, were able to farm economically on an extensive scale, and to practise such agricultural improvements (as manuring) which might be feasible[1]. They did not perhaps employ any technological methods which were not known to their contemporaries, but they did set an example of successful farming to their neighbours, who sometimes sought their advice and expertise[2]. Success brought jealous critics (as Gerald of Wales) who, almost in one breath, both praised and condemned the white monks[3]. The Cistercians had, too, a discerning eye, as the monks of Tintern who cultivated fertile soil but left acidic soil forested[4]. None of the statutes of the General Chapter suggest that farming methods were ever raised at at its meetings, and any exchanges must have been informal[5]. Transmission of knowledge did take place: John of Ford (d. 1220) lamented that when Cistercians gathered, their talk was of 'the progeny of bulls and the yield of crops'[6].

The medieval need for self-sufficiency meant that the Cistercians, of necessity, practised a mixed agricultural economy, though some granges specialised. This was reflected by the fact that Stephen Lexington (1230) ordered a review twice a year of the quantities of corn, butter, cheese, and other commodities available at Savigny[7], and that Beaulieu (1344) sold to the English royal fleet wheat and peas, beef and mutton, fish and eggs, cider and beer[8]. The produce of monastic lands might be insufficient (especially in years of bad weather or when laid waste by war), and then there was a recourse to purchase. Holm Cultram (1220) sought corn in Ireland[9]; Beaulieu (1221) sent by ship corn to needy monks in northern England[10]; Kingswood (1262–63) bought in oats, mutton, eggs and cheese[11]. A major source of food supply came in the right to take tithes as well as in rents rendered in kind. Food also came by means of pittances bequeathed, and in regular or occasional gifts. Henry III (1243) gave Netley 100 qtrs (1270 kg) of wheat[12], a lord of Montpellier (1266) promised Santes Creus 500 qtrs (6350 kg) of barley ('fine and fresh')[13], whilst Scharnebeck (1286) received rents to enable it to buy bread and butter, beer and pepper[14]. An archbishop of Rouen (1201) granted Pontigny 10,000 herrings yearly (from Dieppe)[15].

Woodlands and Forestry

The medieval need for timber, and the other useful functions of forest land, meant that Cistercian monasteries saw the acquisition of woodland as an attractive proposition. In eastern Europe forest land was especially plentiful, but even in the west abbeys such as Clairvaux (15,000 ha/37,000 acres)[16] and Cîteaux (3,240 ha/8,000 acres)[17] possessed large woodland tracts. The quality-timber forests of Eberbach lay in eighteen different localities, but amounted in total to in excess of 3,600 carucates (*iugera*)[18]. In England, where perhaps one-third of all land was under 'forest law' (though not of necessity still wooded), there were moderate but numerous royal grants of woodland[19], as to Beaulieu (100 ha/ 240 acres)[20], Dore (400 ha/1,000 acres)[21], and Netley (120 ha/300 acres)[22]. In Scotland, Alexander II gave the Forest of Alyth to Coupar[23] and the Forest of Ettrick to Melrose[24]. Common species of trees (apart from oak) included alder (sought by Ourscamp[25] and Sibton[26]), and beech (enjoyed by Bonnevaux[27] and Henryków[28]). Villeins of Ląd had their 'trunks of pine' to fell yearly and haul to the abbey[28a]. Former monastic woodland in Wales is evidenced by such place-names as 'coed-yr-abad' and 'coed-y-mynach'[29]. Apart from their own woodlands, abbeys might be granted pannage and timber rights in other woods, as Bordesley in Feckenham Forest[30] and Holm Cultram in Inglewood[31].

The possession of woodland was not without its inherent difficulties. Neubourg (1178) had to come to an agreement with Frederick Barbarossa regarding Hagenau Wood[32]. Arbitration gave to Rein (1285) only two-thirds of woodland given it long before by Conrad II[33]. Monks of Riddagshausen (1229) were beaten up by peasants objecting to their felling timber (by ancient custom) in Stuthe Forest[34]. The chronicler of Pipewell (1323) told of wanton theft, 'day and night', of its timber, especially by 'great men' it did not dare oppose[35]. Cultivated clearings lawfully made in royal forest land in England frequently suffered severe damage (as at Grace Dieu [1338][36] and Flaxley [1353][37]) from the 'free roving of the king's deer'. For their part, the English Cistercians made some forty unlicensed encroachments in royal forests[38]. Tintern (1212) was fined £133 for trespass in Dean Forest (involving the death of a boar), and (1282) £213 for clearing 200 acres (80 ha) there without leave[39], and Holm Cultram (1252) £133 for making unlicensed 'dykes and hedges' in Inglewood[40]. Ottakar II (1277) pardoned Plasy for wrongful use of his woods[41].

The monastic usages of timber were varied. A grant to Perseigne envisaged wood being employed in fencing, house-building and mill repairs, and in making barrels and casks for apples and pears[42]. Beaulieu's woods provided timber for charcoal and fire-wood, and for faggots and stakes[43]. Timber (usually oak) was given to many English monasteries for use in building their churches, and especially for constructing bell-towers, choir-stalls, and rafters[44]. Wood also played a major rôle in constructing grange buildings and bridges. Fontguilhem used timber for stakes and supports in its kitchen-gardens, orchards and vineyards[45], Holm Cultram for making sheep-folds and sheep-cots[46], Meaux for repairing its carts[47], and Furness for making 'implements of husbandry, as well as bows and arrows'[48]. Oak from the forests of Himmerod was sought for making a bridge over the Moselle near Coblenz, and for ship-building at Leiser[49]. Dore (1198)[49a], Rufford (1291–1359)[49b] and Croxden (1329)[49c] all profited by the sale of their timber. King John appropriated timber of Warden to make armaments[49d].

'Dead wood' for fuel was given by royal grant to houses such as Bruern and Flaxley[50]. Casanova (1202, 1268) received a wagon-load a day of timber for use in its kitchen ovens[51]; the store of firewood at Morimondo Milano (1237) amounted to at least 100 wagon loads[52]. Beaulieu (1270) expected to obtain, yearly, from an acre (0·4 ha) of wood twenty years old, 2,000 pieces (3 ft/1 m long) of firewood, and 4,000 faggots[53]. Its timber might be converted to charcoal on the spot[54]; this was valued at 33 pence per quarter (12·7 kg)[55]. Grandselve (1165) early received a wood 'for making charcoal'[56]. Flaxley required two oaks per week for use in its iron forges[58]. Another important timber product was bark for the monastic tannery. The plentiful supply of bark at Beaulieu was worth 2 shillings or more per cartload[59]. Holm Cultram had the right to bark in Inglewood[60], and Tintern in Wentwood[61].

Other forest products included nuts. Morimond gathered acorns and beech-nuts in neighbouring feudal forests[62]. Grandselve produced walnut oil for sale in Rousillon[63]. St Bernard-opt-Scheldt (1330) received money to buy almonds (their oil useful for sweetening and digestive purposes) for Lent[64]. Especially valued were chestnuts (useful for livestock feed) stored by Staffarda at Gambasca[65], and by Morimondo Milano (with walnuts) on its Home Grange[66]. Between 1198 and 1230 Rivalta Scrivia was given about eleven chestnut woods and bought three others[67]. Casanova, from 1253 to 1277, obtained four chestnut woods by bequest, gift, or purchase for its Alva Grange[68]. Flaxley (1152) was granted the tithes of chestnuts in the Forest of Dean[69], and grants of chestnut trees (their timber a valuable building material) were also made to Bonnevaux (1182)[70] and Tarouca (1186)[71].

In the Middle Ages, when sugar was unknown, honey was used for sweetening food, whilst bees-wax was valued for making candles and sealing-wax. Apiculture was, therefore, important. Several Welsh abbeys found honey in the local forests – as Cwmhir in Maelienydd and Margam in Resolfen. When the English army encamped at Rhuddlan (1282), Aberconwy sent Edward I a 'pipe' of honey[72]. Kind rents of honey were due to Kołbacz[73] and Przemęt[74]. Vyšší Brod (1323) had its 'bee farm' (*curia apum*)[75]. Pontigny (1143) could take 'the bees' of Othe Forest[76]. Bee-hives by the Long Mountain were granted to Salem (1222)[77]. Darnhall (1276) kept bee-hives in Delamere Forest[78], and Sallay took honey in the woods of Sunderland[79]. The bee-hives of Beaulieu (mostly in its kitchen-garden) produced 152 gallons (700 litres) of honey in 1270 – much of it was sold, along with 210 lbs (95 kg) of wax – most of it used by the sacristan[80]. The wax produced at Berdoues likewise went to the church, the honey to its infirmary[81].

Forest land was also an asset in the grazing of animals, especially pigs, and for hunting. The woods of Kappel (1152)[82], Chaâlis (1166)[83], and Escurey (1188)[84] were early used for pannage. Pipewell (1252) could graze 250 animals in Rockingham Forest[85]. Dore (1268) had common for fifty pigs (and more) in Grosmont Forest[86]. Holm Cultram (1298) protested when royal officers interfered with its pannage rights in Inglewood[87]. Prince Llywelyn gave Cymer (1209) the right to take 'birds and wild beasts and animals of every kind'. In later defending its privileges (1348), the abbey laid claim to retain 'falcons, sparrow hawks, and all other birds and beasts of the forest' – thus indicating actual monastic usage[88]. Robertsbridge (1278) had an 'eyrie of sparrow-hawks' in Lamberhurst Wood[89]. A rent due to Vale Royal (at Darnhall) might be paid in sparrow-hawks and bows and arrows[90]. An early donor of forest rights to Melrose, however, forbade its monks to hunt or take falcons into the forest, 'for that is not becoming to their Order'[91]. A long-standing medieval injunction of the General Chapter seemingly discouraged hunting by inhibiting Cistercian monks from 'working in skins of wild beasts, neither wild cats, rabbits, squirrels, nor miniver'[92].

From the twelfth century, however, abbeys such as Fountains (in Nidderdale)[93] and Furness (in the Forest of Furness)[94] had their huntsmen, dogs, bows and arrows. Where royal land had been given to an abbey, hunting rights might be excluded: a specific grant was needed, as that made by Alexander II (1234) in favour of Balmerino[95]. Beaulieu (1278) was fined for trapping royal deer which strayed into its 'Close' in the New Forest[96]. Dogs, for hunting, were noted on lands of Dore (1241)[97], Kingswood (1301)[98], and Tintern (1318)[99]. Henry III (1253) excused Stanley from having its dogs on granges within the royal forests 'hambled'[100]. The capture of dogs belonging to Ourscamp (1309) formed part of a protracted dispute between that abbey and the bishop of Noyon[101]. Monastic hunting was now common-place. Some abbeys enclosed 'chases' or 'parks' to enable the trapping of deer, as did Stanley[102] and Kirkstead[103]. Malefactors broke into the 'park' of Garendon at Dishley (1282) and hunted its deer[104]; an armed band stole deer of Stoneleigh (1288)[105]. Whilst Melrose was early (though temporarily) forbidden to hunt with packs in Eskdale, it was allowed to trap wolves[106]. When benefactors of Newminster promised not to hunt on lands they had given the abbey, they excepted the taking of 'wolves, foxes, and such like noxious animals'[107].

From the thirteenth century, conservation of timber was a common monastic practice. To avoid undue depreciation of woodland, cutting might be restricted – as at Beaulieu (1270), where it was forbidden to fell trees of less than twenty years growth[108]. It also employed an iron frame to check the quantity of timber cut: eight such measures formed a cart-load[109]. Sibton (1325) only allowed the 'amputation' of individual woods every fifth year[110]. Margam (1349) permitted just dead wood, not green wood, to be cut for making sea-defences[111]. Grazing might be controlled – goats were disallowed in the woodlands of Buckfast (1325)[112]. New woodland might be planted – as by La Trappe (1290)[113], and the need to conserve or replant written into tenants' agreements – as by Altenberg (1335)[114]. Abbey woodlands might be carefully perambulated and surveyed to guard against false claim, as by Velehrad (1321)[115], Sibton (1325)[116] and Rufford (1329)[117]. Boundary marks might be placed, and even watch-towers erected – as perhaps by Aubepierre (1261)[118].

Monasteries with much woodland appointed a 'forester', who had the oversight of their forestry workers and guards: they themselves were sometimes referred to as 'foresters'. Monk-foresters were noted in the twelfth-century at Cîteaux and La Ferté[119]; *conversi* were the foresters of Preuilly (1220)[120], Rievaulx (1285)[121], and Sallay (1306)[122]. Henry III (1251) allowed Rufford to station a forester to guard the abbey's woodland in Sherwood Forest[123]. In the better days of Pipewell its 'keeper of woods' was a mounted *conversus*, having three foresters under him. Long before 1323 this was no longer the case – hence the depredations made in its woods[124]. Foresters had sometimes an unenviable task. A knight abducted the forester of Preuilly (1220)[125], and Rievaulx's forester (1285) was beaten up[126]. By this time lay foresters were sometimes appointed – as at Fontmorigny (1247)[127] and Kingswood (1255)[128]. In 1336 William Redhod was appointed 'keeper of the woods and warren' of Sibton and granted a chamber and corrody at its South Grange – perquisites 'long assigned' to the keeper: clearly he was not the abbey's first lay-forester[129].

Woodland Clearance (Assarting)

A pre-requisite for English monasteries if they were to utilise to the full lands given them within royal forests, was to obtain a grant 'disafforesting' or putting 'outside the regard of the forest' those possessions[130]. Unless that was done, newly-assarted lands could not generally be enclosed and cultivated (so as not to interfere with the royal chase), and might have to remain as pasture or waste[131]. Earl Ranulf of Chester disafforested the site of Stanlaw and its grange of Stanney[132], whilst Alexander II decreed that Melrose and four adjacent granges should be 'free of his forest'[133]. The lands of Basingwerk in Derbyshire were exempted from 'regard' in Peak Forest, 'so that it might bring into tillage the woods and waste'[134]. Tintern was made 'without regard of the Forest of Wentwood, so that the monks may do in their woods what they will'[135]. Disafforestation was a technical, but vital, legal act giving monasteries complete freedom on such lands of theirs as might lie within royal forest bounds. It did not by itself imply assarting that had already taken place.

As regarding actual monastic clearance of woodland, there is little doubt but that the Cistercians (their abbeys often sited in wooded areas) did much in this respect, though modern commentators caution against exaggerating their rôle[136]. Place-name evidence alone confirms monastic activity. Woodland clearance, 'assarting', is reflected in the names of 'Essertes' Grange (of Hautcrêt)[137] and 'Assart' Grange (of Neath)[138]. The early name of Warden, 'Sartis', suggests perhaps a pre-monastic clearing inherited by its monks[139]. On some Cistercian lands in France, '-sart' forms a suffix indicating woodland clearance, as does '-rode' in the Netherlands[140] and '-ryd' in Scandinavia[141]. The

same root lends itself to the name of Ryd Abbey in Denmark[142]. In Middle English 'ridding' was likewise virtually synonymous with 'clearing'. Neath had its Rhydding Grange and Tintern its Ruding Grange (now 'Reddings Farm')[143]. Similar terminology occurred on lands of Croxden (Gibber*ydinges*)[144], Sibton (le *Redynge*)[145] and Whalley (grene*ruydyng* : 'green clearing')[146]. The French villages of Grandes *Ventes* and *Ventes* Saint-Rémy gained their names due to their exposure to the elements, after Cistercian clearance of part of the Forest of Eawy[147].

Other pointers to monastic assarting come in documentation of the times. Gerald of Wales (*c.* 1200) criticised Dore for 'changing an oak wood into a wheat field'[148]. The chronicler of Pipewell told how, in the twelfth century, four woods near the abbey were brought under the plough[149]. An abbot of Kingswood (1214) had to explain to the Crown why he had 'uprooted trees on land over which he had but custody'[150]. Local clergy (1232) referred to the woodland which Staffarda 'had felled from the day of building of the monastery (1135) until the present time'[151]. Many charters gave leave to assart, as to Chaâlis (1182) allowing it 'to uproot trees, and break open the land'[152]. Baumgarten (1187)[153] and Lehnin (1284)[154] might 'extirpate thickets and thorns'. Pollen analysis suggests woodland clearance by Fountains in Nidderdale[155], and by Strata Florida in Ceredigion[156]. Newly-cultivated Cistercian lands were exempt from the payment of tithe: a major inducement to assart[157].

Woodland clearance varied in scale, and could be a protracted process. Assarting by Kingswood lasted well over a century[158]. Herrenalb gained three granges by clearance in the upper Hartwald[159], and La Cour-Dieu a series of granges in the Forest of Orléans[160]. Clearance could be on a piecemeal basis – a few acres at a time – until compact estates were achieved[161]. Valloires took forty-five years to create one farm of 150 ha (400 acres)[162]. At Roche, Rievaulx and Fountains, there are contemporaneous references to 'the great clearing of the monks'[163]. Assarting persisted throughout the early Middle Ages. Between 1250 and 1287 Rufford cleared some twenty acres (7·4 ha) or more (7,000 oaks and 1,000 saplings, in all) within and without Sherwood Forest[164]. Buildwas (around 1277) cleared sixty acres (25 ha) in Wrekin Forest[165]. Jervaulx assarted in Wensleydale as late as 1330[166].

Some assarts had been initiated by other communities, (as the hermits of Boulbonne[167] and the Benedictines of Rivet[168]), before their incorporation. Some substantial clearings had been made and developed before being granted (perhaps by exchange) to a Cistercian house – like Tintern's Woolaston Manor[169] and Amelunxborn's Bruchof[170]. Hired labour played a considerable rôle, especially as *conversi* numbers dwindled: Kingswood (1263) paid wages 'to the assarters'[171]. Tenants of Tintern (1263–1393) contributed to the process, paying the abbey a fee for so doing[172]. In areas already well-settled (as those where a pre-existing populace had to be removed) little clearance might be necessary. Very few charters granted to the abbeys of south-west France gave leave to assart: there was no need[173]. Recent research reveals that some monasteries in Lower Saxony were endowed with land already well cultivated, and that the monks had no part in reclaiming it[174]. Nor was assarting a peculiarly Cistercian phenomenon: it was a widespread process as population expanded, and was also undertaken by other Orders such as (in Picardy) the Canons Regular, Cluniacs, and Military Knights[175].

Much Cistercian reclamation of land was of secondary waste, land formerly settled and developed but later abandoned. 40% of Yorkshire twelfth-century granges lay in the territories laid waste by the armies of William the Conqueror in 1069 to 1070[176]. In north Gwent Dore (1250) leased land 'previously cultivated, but gone to waste'. Grace Dieu (1338) received wasteland in the Forest of Dean, with leave to 'bring it back into cultivation'[177]. Deserted villages and their abandoned lands were exploited by Haina[178] and Zbraslav[179]. Clairlieu's grange in Bédon[180] and Salem's Maurac Grange[181] resulted from waste reclamation. When Lubiąż (1230) colonised Naklo with Germans, it was said that 'in the memory of no one living has there been cultivation of this waste-land'[181a]. 'Waste' in the English royal forests may sometimes have been simply pasture-land, or land lying fallow[182]. Stanley bought waste in Pewsham Forest[183] and Beaulieu leased waste in the New Forest[184]. It was easier to reclaim waste than to assart woodland. Some waste-lands may not have been fully reclaimed, being useful for grazing, turbary, and thatching materials[185]. Stanley, for example, had leave to culti-vate less than half the waste it gained in Pewsham[186].

Enclosures and Boundary Marks (See also Chapters 12 and 13)

Assarting woodland, or reclaiming wasteland, was of little point unless an abbey could obtain leave to enclose such improvements – either to keep stock in (on pasture land), or to keep stock and wild animals from straying (on to arable land). Where royal forest land was concerned or where common rights existed, there could be problems. Pipewell (1238) was only allowed to enclose Oldfield Wood in Rockingham Forest so long as 'the king's deer shall have free entrance and exit'[187]. Netley (1253) was given permission to enclose 300 acres in the New Forest, but almost immediately sought a special licence to exclude the royal deer[188]. Such grants commonly allowed enclosures to consist of 'a *small* dyke and a *low* hedge' – as for Holm Cultram in Inglewood (1225)[189], Stanley in Chippenham Forest (1290)[190] and Grace Dieu in the Forest of Dean (1334)[191]. The reason was made explicit in a grant to Rufford (1233) affecting Sherwood: it was so that 'the wild beasts of the Forest could pass': the royal chase was not to be lost[192]. When Roche enclosed land at Maltby, it was not to block two roads, 'namely Bolegate, and the way which comes from Blythe'[193].

There is much evidence of monastic enclosures. By 1190 comes mention of Holm Cultram's land in West Seaton, 'within the dyke which the monks made around that land'[194]. By 1200 Warden enclosed some land 'by ditch and dyke of seven feet width'[195]. Duiske (1265) might make a ditch of either twelve or six feet breadth; if of only six feet, the abbey gained an extra six feet of land, as the ditch was to be made on the land of the grantor[196]. Rufford (1280) was allowed to make around its woods a trench forty feet (17 m) wide[197]. In such grants might come wide-ranging leave 'to ditch, enclose, assart and fence' (Kingswood, 1241)[198], or 'to till, assart, enclose, and deal with at pleasure' (Dore, early 13th century)[199]. Such enclosing, particularly where common rights were lost, might lead to hostility from the peasantry, especially as (in the early-fourteenth century) they tried to gain greater freedom. Enclosures at Biddlesden (1308) in Syresham were broken down, and cattle depastured there[200]. No sooner had Beaulieu (1324) enclosed waste in the New Forest than local people pulled out the hedge, burnt the stakes, and filled in the ditch with stones and gravel[201].

About 1180, boundary markers were set up to delimit Foigny's woodland in Watigny Forest[202], and Poblet erected stone crosses to demarcate disputed pasture land it claimed[203]. Crosses (probably in stone) were known on lands of Perseigne (*c.* 1145)[204], Aunay (before 1273)[205] and Sibton (in 1325)[206]. Not only the Cistercians employed such markers: the Chartreuse (1212) delimited territory by crosses sculpted on the rocks[207]. Huerta (1169) placed crosses on mounds raised adjacent to disputed properties[208]. 'Big stones' were set up by Eberbach (1209)[209], Orval (1271)[210] and Quarr (1328)[211]. The metes of Velehrad's home estate (1228) included 'the western stone, which is called the *kralow stol*'[212]. In settling doubts about the bounds of Holm Cultram's Kirkgunzeon Grange (1289) the abbot and others perambulated them so that 'crosses, cairns, and other visible marks should be made'[213]. Early markers may have been in timber, and, for greater permanency, replaced later in stone[214]. Timber markers were perhaps essential in soft terrain, where heavy stones might sink in. Balmerino (1260) fixed stakes to delimit a portion of peat-moss in Swan Mere[215]; St Bernard-opt-Scheldt (1276) enclosed waste-land in Gastel with stakes, as 'a sign of greater certainty'[216]. When arbitrators defined the boundary between the lands of Vitskøl (1219) and those of the canons of Viborg on the island of Laesø, they removed bark from the trees on the frontier[217].

Marshland and Drainage

Several Cistercian monasteries not only had marshland sites but – like Stratford[218] and Swineshead[219] – sought to increase their marshland holdings. Aduard (1262) spent 2,800 Groningen pounds on buying up marsh and pasture rights[220]. Unimproved marsh was useful for turbary (as at Strata Florida), reeds (Basingwerk), fish (Fountains), water fowl (Kirkstead) and salt (Quarr)[221]. In the marshlands of Clair*marais* willows grew, rushes were plentiful, and a variety of fish (including perch) were caught[222]. Valloires obtained eels from marshes in the Authie valley[223]. Wild-fowl was an asset in the marsh-holdings of Przemęt[224]. Fresh-water marsh was especially useful for pasture-land and as a source of hay. In the marshes of Wawne and Sutton, Meaux grazed 2,000 sheep and built eight sheep-cots[225]. When lands were so drained, the dykes could be used for fishing and for watering cattle[226]. Beaulieu protected its marsh interests by having a monk as its 'keeper of the marsh'[227]. A monk or *conversus* of Vaucelles was 'master of the Cuvele', its polder in Flanders[228].

Coastal flooding could be disastrous, as when the lands of the Dunes in Flanders were inundated in 1245, 1265 and 1287[229]. Estuarine and coastal monasteries might build sea walls as a defence, as did Margam in Afan[230], Robertsbridge in the Winchelsea area[231], and Stratford in West Ham[232]. These might be joint efforts with other interested parties. The abbeys with lands in Flanders (notably the Dunes and Ter Doest) continued the work of drainage initiated before their time[233], participating in the 'wateringues' – co-operative associations engaged in draining and embanking[234]. The abbot of the Dunes was head of the wateringue of Furnes[235], and (by 1183) one of his monks was its port-reeve – rendering annual accounts to its management committee[236]. The monk of Ter Doest (1361) in charge of its wateringue was styled the 'Moormeister'[237].

In this way, and by a system of canals and sluices, the Dunes is credited with reclaiming 10,000 ha (25,000 acres) from the sea, and establishing twenty-five granges on the new land[238]. In recognition of 'its work of dyking', the lord of Voren (1220) gave extra lands to Ter Doest[239]. St Bernard-opt-Scheldt had (by 1332) reclaimed near Hulst 1700 ha (4,200 acres) of land[240]. Clairvaux (1234) was permitted to retain all the land 'which emerges from the sea' between Diepenmude and Biervilietmud[241]. On the Scottish coast Holm Cultram (*c.* 1275) was granted at Kirkconnel a field, and 'as much as the monks can reclaim towards the sea'[242]. Balmerino (*c.* 1300) was given, east of Anstruther, a strip of land 150 feet (45 m) long, 'so that the monks might extend their marshes seawards'[243].

In Holderness, the curve of the field boundaries on Meaux's Salthaugh Grange reveal their original purpose as water-filled ditches[244]. In the English Fens, Sawtry was newly reclaiming land for meadow as late as 1281[245]. Its major drainage channel was (by 1342) not well kept, and local navigation that year was particularly affected due to 'the dryness of the season'[246]. Louth Park (1314) made 'gutters, sewers, and openings, to drain the moors and the marshes'[247]. In Yorkshire, Rievaulx drained marsh in Pickering Waste (the site of a former glacial lake), and established two granges there[248]. Abbey sites when granted might need draining, as at Salem[249], Fontaine-Jean[250], and

Rivalta Scrivia[251]. *Fossa*nova was so called from the canal built to drain the Pontine Marshes[252].

Notable drainage works were executed by a group of four abbeys in Poitevin Marsh: by Grâce Dieu, Charron and St Léonard-des-Chaumes to the south of the river Sèvre, and by Moreilles to the north[253]. The work reached its climax between 1190 and 1220, but continued thereafter, and the skill and assistance of the local populace was engaged[254]. In draining the marsh of Alouettes, a difference arose between the monasteries which was referred to the General Chapter (1217)[255]. The early works (1192) involved the expulsion of peasant-fishermen[256]. Trizay and Bois-Groland also played a part[257]. In the south of France, abbeys like Franquevaux (in the Camargue) continued drainage works initiated by others[258]. Fontfroide's several drainage schemes included that at Coursan, and it helped to drain Lake Ouveillan, thus improving the health of the locality[259]. Other abbeys with successful drainage works included Buzay (in the Loire valley)[260] and Silvacane[261].

In Thuringia, the monks and *conversi* of Walkenried drained marshland granted to the abbey (in 1144) in the lower Helm valley: they had been promised tithe-exemption on land they so reclaimed[262]. On the resultant 'Golden Meadows' eleven granges were set up[263]. Emperor Frederick I then obtained the help of Jordan, a monk of Walkenried, in draining the lower Rieth valley, enabling six villages to be established there[264]. Emperor Otto expressed royal gratitude for what Jordan had done[265]. Alcobaça drained swamps in the high Extremadura, and King Diñiz of Portugal sought its brother Martinho to cultivate royal swamp-land at Ulmar[266]. Other notable monastic drainage works included those by Schönau on the Rhine plain beside the Neckar confluence[267]; by Chiaravalle della Colomba[268] and Chiaravalle della Milano[269] in the Po valley; by Zlatá Koruna in Bohemia[270], and by Paradyż in the marsh of Meseritz[271]. Haina[272], Oliwa and Pelplin[273], all played a part in river-control by building protective earth-banks and wooden dams. Not all went well. The tilers and brick-layers of Beverley, constantly taking mud from the banks Meaux maintained in West Carr, were at the centre of a brawl[274]. Local men deliberately broke the river banks of the Derwent Byland had built up at Rillington, with consequential and substantial flooding[275].

Irrigation

In the drier areas of the Mediterranean lands, irrigation was frequently practised, particularly to ensure satisfactory grazing meadows and pastures. In the Piedmont of northern Italy, Staffarda (1176[276], 1280[277]) derived water from the river Po to moisten its Morra Grange pastures: it was granted (1282) a water-course 'three men's feet broad' to irrigate its pastures at Envie[278]. Frederick II (1226) made helpful grants of irrigation water, or confirmed existing rights, to Chiaravalle della Milano[279], Morimondo Milano[280], and Fontevivo[281]. The irrigation works of Chiaravalle della Milano started when it acquired the waters of the river Vecchiabia in 1138[282]. From 1226, again by grant of Frederick II, it might take water issuing from the city moat of Milan to serve its lands in Vicomaggiore and near Pavia[283]. In southern France, Fontfroide received several rights of making irrigation ditches between 1176 and 1245[284]. Further north, La Ferté (*c.* 1150) led water in an aqueduct from the spring of Laives[285]. In Spain, Rueda built barrages to bring water to the fields of its settlers at Romana (1215) and Lagata (1268) in the Ebro Basin. Veruela's tenants in the Ebro valley based their horticulture on irrigation[286].

The usual result of such endeavours was improved hay-meadows and pastures for grazing stock – as achieved by Bonnevaux[287], Fontmorigny[288], and Tennenbach[289], amongst many such houses. Arable farming was also assisted (as on lands of Poblet)[290], or gardens enabled to flourish (as at Alcobąca)[291] or 'cotton' grown (as by Rivalta Scrivia)[292], or viticulture sustained (as by Huerta)[293]. A by-product of the necessary water-works lay in fishing, facilitated (for example) by the irrigation schemes of Igny (dams made on the Orillon stream)[294], Fontaine-Jean (water storage ponds)[295], Quartazzola (water led from the river Trebbio)[296], and Staffarda (in the commune of Revello)[297]. Monasteries might have to reach agreement with other concerned parties regarding the use of joint water supplies. Sharing a common water source for irrigation, Fitero (1156) and the municipality of Tudegen alternated its use in eight-day turns[298]. Rivalta Scrivia (1256) had the use of a canal (to bring water to its Goyde Grange meadows) for five days a week[299], and the right (1233) to a one-third part of water (for its home meadows) in a channel close to the monastery[300]. When Rueda (1328) wanted to open a new irrigation channel at Azaila, experts were brought in to see how much fruit its neighbours would lose[301]. The monks of La Real, in irrigating the fields of St Lawrence Grange, took so much water from the channel leading from the great spring of Esporles to Palma that the city experienced a water-shortage. In 1310, therefore, they were restricted to taking water through an opening the size of one double Majorcan penny. They were compensated for the partial loss of ancient rights, but it was pointed out that they still had the water-course leading from Basta to the abbey[302].

Soil Improvement

The medieval Cistercians were well aware of the need to fertilise their fields. This might be done by using organic manure or by marling. Beaulieu used dung to improve its orchard soil[303], and considered the value of the dung left by the sheep in its fields as covering the cost of food provided for its shepherds[304]. From the fourteenth century, Grandselve supplied manure for the market-gardeners of Toulouse[305]. Animal dung might be excepted, in whole or in part, in a grant of pasture. A benefactor of Rievaulx (1160) granting it pasture rights allowed the monks to keep the manure, another only ceded them half the droppings, whilst a third kept the lot. When Warden was given pasture from mid-April to Martinmas (11 November) in Sandy for 480 sheep, the abbey could only take manure should the animals be under cover; not a very likely possibility in that period of the year[306]. A duty expected (in later centuries) of tenants on Strata Florida's lands was 'the casting of dung' – perhaps inherited from monastic times[307]. Newminster collected sea-weed as manure[308]. Several houses of south Wales sought lime or marl (calcareous clay) to 'improve' land deficient in lime[309]. Pforta had a shell limestone quarry near Flemminge[310a]; Løgum obtained lime by collecting mussel shells from beaches[310b]. Lime helped the Belgian Cistercians assist in fertilising the Campine heath-land[311].

Crop rotation, on a triennial basis (of rye, spring grain, and fallow) was practised in the thirteenth century on the three great fields (all of roughly equal size) at Chaâlis' Vaulerent Grange[312], but this was already common in the region[313]. A triennial rotation has also been ascribed to lands of Ourscamp[314] and of Palazuelos[315]. On the other hand, the three fields of Fountains' Baldersby Grange (mentioned in 1296) do not appear to have formed the basis of a rotation system[316]. Berdoues[317] and Moreruela[318] inherited lands where a biennial rotation was already usual. A lease of land to Kingswood (1243), allowing for five crops in ten years, suggests the land rested fallow in alternate years[319].

Tithes and Appropriated Parishes

The *Charter of Charity* early forbade the Cistercians to be the receivers of tithes: 'Our very name prohibits tithes from the labour or harvest of others, as contrary to the purity of the monastic vocation'[320]. In this they were not exceptional: the Carthusians[321] and Grandmontines[322] at first adopted a similar policy, but the Cistercians persisted longer than most in rejecting tithes. When Louis VI (1133) gave Ourscamp a grant of tithes, the abbey exchanged them for a field[323]; when Benedictine Balerne (1136) was incorporated, it gave up its church of Cognos[324]; when Byland (1140s) refused the advowson of three Yorkshire churches, the donor gave them instead to Newburgh Priory[325]. By the mid-twelfth century this idealistic stance began to change[326], not least because of the incorporation of congregations which were allowed to retain the churches and tithes to which they were accustomed, like Savigny, Cadouin and Obazine (in 1147) – earlier, Trefontane (1140)[327]. At first tithes were acquired on portions of land, but as these increased whole parishes came into Cistercian hands[328]. An archbishop of Canterbury (1158) reproved Boxley for holding the tithes of the church of Rochester[329]. In 1180 the General Chapter – whilst urging the abbeys to pay tithes due – allowed their acquisition if by genuine gift or peaceful agreement[330].

From this decade can be traced numerous Cistercian possessions of tithes[331], and by the close of the century the statutes forbidding their acquisition were tempered by the saving clause 'unless by leave of the general Chapter'[332]. Once entire parishes were appropriated, the white monks came to obtain a valuable source of 'hidden income' – the 'greater' rectorial tithes, chiefly of corn, but also of vegetables and perhaps flax, lambs and fish. In addition they might receive burial dues and a variety of other offerings – whilst any problems relating to the payment of tithes issuing from their own lands in the parish were obviated[333]. The total value of the parish of Whalley to its monastery was no less than £173 p.a.[333a]. Tithe-collectors might be appointed (as by Beaulieu)[334], and tithe-barns necessitated (as that of Dore at Avenbury[335], and that of Aunay at Ashby Mares in Northamptonshire[336]).

In the thirteenth century and beyond, the acquisition of parochial churches and their tithes continued apace. By 1259, Orval had the tithes of ten churches[337]; by 1273, Doberan of forty-one villages[338]; by 1350, Bebenhausen of twenty-seven churches[339]. In Wales, nearly eighty parishes were eventually Cistercian-owned: only Cwmhir seems not to have been granted any such churches[340]. The reasons abbeys gave in seeking parishes for their income and tithes were several: poverty (the most common), as Furness (1194)[341] and Nydala (1248)[342]; to avoid dispersal of monks, as Sallay (1189)[343], or debts, as Sibton (1331)[344]; the cost of building the monastery, as Valle Crucis (1220)[345]; to increase the number of monks, as Whalley (1298)[345a]; to provide the monks with clothing, as Cleeve (1281)[346]; inroads made by the sea, as Robertsbridge (1309)[347]; devastation suffered in war, as Holm Cultram (1332)[348]; sterility of lands and murrain of animals, as Dore (1328)[349]; loss of income with ending of initial endowments, as Combermere (early 1180s)[350], or in the wake of the Black Death, as Hulton (1348)[351]; to allow greater charity to the poor, as Sibton (1214, 1263)[352]; to show hospitality to guests, as Beaulieu (1236)[353]; as a thank-offering by the donor, as the Dunes (c. 1195)[354], or in return for chantry services as Dore (1327)[355]. Frequently, a combination of several factors led to the grant of a church, as to Pipewell (1342)[356].

As late as 1214, the General Chapter still endeavoured to end Cistercian acceptance of parish churches[357], but perhaps more in regard to their spiritual oversight than for the tithes received. Cistercian monks were, in 1234, strictly forbidden to minister in those churches which belonged to the Order: secular priests were to be appointed as chaplains instead[358]. When the church of Levin was given to Dargun (1261), it was understood that, by Cistercian custom, it would be served 'not by persons of the Order,

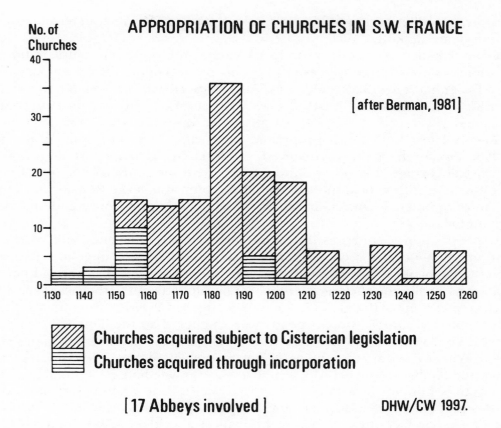

APPROPRIATION OF CHURCHES IN S.W. FRANCE

No. of Churches

[after Berman, 1981]

▨ Churches acquired subject to Cistercian legislation
▤ Churches acquired through incorporation

[17 Abbeys involved]   DHW/CW 1997.

but by secular clerks'[359]. There were occasional later breaches of this rule, as by monks of Riddagshausen at Wobek (1289)[360], and of Hailes at its distant Cornish churches of St Breage and St Paul[361]. Three monks successively served Whalley parish church in the early-fourteenth century, allegedly so that the claustral routine was not disturbed by the presence of secular clergy[362]. The secular clergy appointed to Cistercian parish churches were nominated by the abbot of the monastery concerned; Stephen Lexington recorded the formula employed when so presenting a priest to the diocesan bishop[363]. This right of patronage became a cause of dispute between Valle Crucis and a bishop of St Asaph (*c.* 1275), as the abbey preferred to appoint chaplains rather than 'perpetual vicars' – who had greater perquisites and security[364].

The acquisition of tithes and the appropriation of churches, involving as it might several interested parties, could be a complex, costly, and lengthy affair. A relatively small grant of tithes (in Eekeren) to St Bernard-opt-Scheldt (1257) necessitated no less than seven deeds: the grantor's charter, two deeds from the pastor of Eekeren, two from the bishop of Liège, and one from his chapter, as well as papal confirmation[365]. In the process of appropriation, the first preliminary was to obtain the advowson of the living, and await, and perhaps hasten, the voidance of the cure. Approval was necessary from both the diocesan bishop and his chapter, with papal confirmation often felt desirable[366]. Sibton wished to receive Westleton church in 1331, but the bishop's consent was not forthcoming[367]. It was only in 1356, in the time of a later diocesan, that within six months all stages were completed: approval came from the bishop and his chapter, the resignation of the rector was obtained, and the community were formally admitted to the living by the bishop. On 21 December, the deeds of resignation and admission were publicly proclaimed in Norwich Cathedral[368]. In England, the Statute of Mortmain (1279) necessitated the king's approval. Bindon (1292) paid forty marks for such licence[369]; Sibton (1320), having ignored the statute's requirements, was allowed to keep two churches nevertheless[370]; before Wigton church was granted to

Holm Cultram (1332) an inquisition was held before a jury which determined that it would 'not be to the king's hurt'[371].

Acquiring parishes was a costly process, and some outlays in fees, compensation, and other expenses were so large as to nullify for long periods of time any pecuniary advantages[372]. Bebenhausen (1326) paid out 650 *pfunds pfennig* in seeking the right to appropriate three churches[373]; Meaux (1337) spent £769 all told on two churches valued at £57 p.a. together[374]. Neither transaction was entirely a commercial success! When Meaux later (1345–53) appropriated two further churches, some of its monks objected because of the great cost involved, and foretold the losses it would bring upon them[375]. Robertsbridge (1309) was allowed to receive three churches, but it took twenty years of litigation with appearances in the king's court and at the Roman Curia before matters were completed. One abbot ran out of money whilst in Rome, and had to send to England for more[376].

The appropriation of churches also entailed several perpetual obligations: the provision and maintenance of a secular vicar or chaplain, the upkeep in good repair of the chancel, the payment of customary dues to the bishop and archdeacon, and potential nomination as a collector of clerical tenths[377]. The stipend paid to the vicar varied from £2 at a church of Tintern (fixed in 1274 and unchanged in 1535)[378] to as much as £12 in a parish of Sibton (1356)[379]. Most stipends were higher than the Tintern level[380], and perhaps differed according to the value of other perquisites – as the four oxgangs of land allowed to Whalley's vicar at Rochdale[381]. The incumbent also received the lesser tithes (as of hay and lambs) of his parish[382], as well as a parsonage house – a 'suitable mansion house' was to be built for Kirkstall's vicar at Bracewell[383], and a house 'sufficient according to the judgement of local men' for Margam's vicar at Newcastle[384]. Whilst the monastery (as rector) saw to the repair of the chancel, as evidenced at Beaulieu (1270)[385], the vicar might be expected to provide the altar lights (as by Kirkstall)[386] and to keep the books and ornaments in good repair (as by Sibton)[387]. Each appropriation was the subject of a formal agreement; two copies of this might be made (as by Dore in 1331), one for the abbey and one for the vicar, whilst it was also transcribed into the bishop's register[388]. Appropriated churches, unlike their parent monasteries, were subject to visitation by the diocesan, and on these occasions the bishop might stay at the abbey (as at Croxden in 1331[389] and Sibton about 1360)[390], and personally inspect 'the letters, instruments, and other muniments' concerning its churches.

The Cistercian acquisition of churches and tithes attracted frequent criticism – as by Gerald of Wales (*c.* 1200)[391], by Cardinal Ottobuoni presiding over the Legatine Council (1268)[392] and by Archbishop Peckham of Canterbury (*c.* 1284)[393]. Archdeacon Gerald also suggested that the white monks even 'razed churches' granted them. This was certainly true of Margam at Llangewydd (1202)[394], whilst it was alleged of Holm Cultram (1222) that it transformed Kirkgunzeon church into a grange chapel[395]. Dunkeswell (1242) on receiving Dotton (Doddeton) church closed it, and the bishop had to order its re-opening[396]. The ownership of tithes led to frequent disputes and contrary claims, as between Warden and the canons of Thetford[397], Dieulacres and Trentham Priory[398], Flaran and the chapter of Auch[399] and Margam and St Peter's Abbey, Gloucester[400]. It was not for nothing that Stephen Lexington (1228) had advised the Irish abbeys 'not to accept the patronage of churches, unless it has been established through a thorough inquiry that clear right of entry and secure title' might be had[401]. (Noteworthy, at that date, is the fact that he didn't object to such acquisitions so long as they were unlikely to lead to later problems.) Officials of Hailes (1337) going to oversee and receive profits at its Cornish appropriations were assaulted *en route*[402]. The General Chapter (1285) complained to Edward I that – since the coming of the Friars Minor and Preachers to Scarborough – its agents had much trouble in collecting the proceeds of the Order's church there[403].

Notes

1. Williams (1984) II, 197.
2. Roehl (1972) 94.
3. Williams (1984) I, 29–31; II, 197.
4. *Ibid.* II, 197.
5. Roehl (1972) 94.
6. Cocheril (1959b) 295.
7. *RSL* II, 227.
8. Hockey (1976) 90.
9. *CPR* 1220/234, 1222/339.
10. *CPR* 1221/285.
11. *DCK* 216–17, 220–21 (unless this is internal accounting).
12. *CCR* 1243/131.
13. Fort i Cogul (1972) 44.
14. *UKS* 58.
15. *PCP* 289–90 (No. 260).
16. Fossier (1991) 79.
17. Picard (1882) 208.
18. Haas (1966) 209–10.
19. Donkin (1978) 121–23.
20. VCH, *Hampshire* II (1903) 147.
21. Williams (1976) 33.
22. VCH, *Hampshire* II (1903) 147.
23. Morgan (1929) I, 146.
24. Talbot (1939) 22.
25. *CO* 57 (No. LXXXVI).
26. *SBC* II, 273 (No. 376).
27. *RDI*, 559 (No. 3285).
28. Grüger (1978a) 122.
28a. *KDI*, 15–16.
29. Williams (1984) II, 277.
30. Rahtz (1976) 18.
31. Gilbanks (1899) 82.
32. Dubled (1959) 775–76.
33. Amon (1979) 385.
34. Wiswe (1953) 40.
35. VCH, *Northampton* II: 1 (1906) 118–19.
36. Williams (1984) II, 279.
37. VCH, *Gloucester* II (1907) 95.
38. Donkin (1978) 130.
39. Williams (1984) II, 217, 272.
40. *RHC* 79, 129.
41. *CDRM* V: 2, 549 (No. 839).
42. *CDP* 23 (No. IX).
43. Linnard (1982) 48, Talbot (1958) 195–56.
44. Donkin (1978) 127.
45. *Cîteaux* XXV (1974:1) 84.
46. *RHC* 33.
47. Burton (1989) 36.
48. Cottam (1928) 78–80.
49. Schneider (1954) 123.
49a. Williams (1976) 33.
49b. *CPR* 1291/427, 1300/513; VCH, *Northampton* II: 1 (1906) 102–03.
49c. VCH, *Stafford* III (1970) 227.
49d. *RC* 207.
50. Donkin (1978) 124–27.
51. *CADC* 111–18, 356–57.
52. Occhipinti (1983) 327.
53. Linnard (1982) 48; of 775 vine-stakes produced, 200 were sold : *ABB* 199–200.
54. *ABB* 35, *cf.* Talbot (1958) 195–96.
55. Linnard (1982) 48.
56. Berman (1986) 98.
57. *CC* (2), B. 44.
58. VCH, *Gloucester* II (1907) 94, *cf.* Williams (1984) 273–74.
59. Linnard (1982) 48.
60. *RHC* 73.
61. Williams (1984) II, 273–74.
62. King (1954) 355.
63. Barrière (1983) 95*n*.
64. *OLSB* 97.
65. Boyd (1943) 141, cf. Gosso (1940) 73–75.
66. Occhipinti (1983) 324.
67. *CRS* I, 115 (CXXVII), 274–75, 385 (D III), 390; II, 78 (CCXXXII), 174 (DXXI), (DXXXV), 190 (DLXX), 204 (DCXVI).
68. *CADC* 288, 354, 366, 392; *cf.* Gosso (1940) 89.
69. VCH, *Gloucester* II (1907) 94.
70. *RD* I, 801 (Nos 4805, 4808).
71. Almeida Fernandes III (1975) 44 (No. 13).
72. Williams (1984) II, 270.
73. *PU* I, 173–78.
74. *KD* I, 64–65.
75. Charvátová (1987) 122, 134.
76. Benoît and Sportes (1991) 181.
77. *CDSL* I, 163.
78. *CPR* 1276/194.
79. *CS* I, 150–51.
80. *ABB* passim, *cf.* McClean (1981) 22.
81. *CB* 18.
82. Maas (1944) 34–35.
83. Quignon (1914) 397.
84. Maas (1944) 34–35.
85. Donkin (1978) 123.
86. Williams (1977) 34.
87. *CPR* 1298/378.
88. Williams (1984) II, 270.
89. *CPR* 1278/291.
90. Coulton (1960) 216.
91. Richardson (1981a) 35.
92. *Statuta* I, 69 (1158/5); *LCC* (1) 164, (2) 344.
93. Fletcher (1919) 109–10.
94. Fell (1908) 12, *cf. AF* 203, Cottam (1928) 72.
95. Carrick (1907) 122.
96. *CPR* 1278/270.
97. Williams (1976) 38.
98. Lindley (1955) 39.
99. Williams (1984) II, 271.
100. *CHS* 298 (had they been maimed, their hunting ability would have diminished).
101. *CO* 197.
102. *CHS* 256.
103. *CPR* 1299/413.
104. *CPR* 1282/48.
105. VCH, *Warwick* II (1908) 80.
106. *LM* xvi–xvii.
107. *CNM* 79.
108. Talbot (1958) 195–96.
109. Linnard (1982) 49, *cf. ABB* 35.
110. *SBE* 45–46.
111. Williams (1984) II, 276.
112. Stéphan (1970) 76.
113. Arnoux (1991) 20–21.
114. Roth (1986) 434.
115. *CDEM* VI, 134–35.
116. *SBE* 45–46.
117. *RFC* xxix.

118. Martin (1893) 82.
119. Chauvin (1983a) 20–21.
120. Clair (1961) 199–200.
121. *CPR* 1285/203.
122. *CS* I, 47.
123. VCH, *Nottingham* II (1910) 102–03.
124. VCH, *Northampton* II: 1 (1906) 118.
125. Clair (1961) 199–200.
126. *CPR* 1285/203.
127. *CAF* 196, *cf. BB* 201.
128. Donnelly (1954) 418.
129. *SBC* IV, 108–09 (No. 1186).
130. Donkin (1978) 131.
131. *RFC* xxix.
132. VCH, *Lancaster* II (1908) 131.
133. *CM* 63.
134. Donkin (1978) 131.
135. Williams (1984) II, 274.
136. As: Berman (1986) 9–10, Duby (1965) 97, Elm (1982) 143, Wiswe (1953) 43.
137. *DHGE* XXIII (1990) 561 (of 1154); Sommer-Ramer (1982) 147–47.
138. Williams (1984) II, 271.
139. Donkin (1964) 61.
140. Clapham (1941) 279.
141. France (1992) 169.
142. France (1993) 21.
143. Williams (1984) II, 271–72.
144. *ACA* 300, 307.
145. *SBE* 43.
146. Donkin (1978) 103.
147. Deck (1974) 10.
148. Williams (1976) 8–9, *cf.* King (1954) 3.
149. Clapham (1941) 78.
150. Donkin (1978) 49.
151. Gosso (1940) 77.
152. Lohrmann (1975) 179–80.
153. Dubled (1959) 777.
154. *CDB* 215–16.
155. Tinsley (1975) 158.
156. Moore (1968) 1009, Moore and Chater (1969) 374–75, Turner (1964) 83.
157. Donkin (1978) 109.
158. Barnes (1982) 36.
159. Elm (1982) 143.
160. Grand (1950) 250.
161. Donkin (1964) 67, (1978) 132.
162. Fossier (1983) 69.
163. Donkin (1978) 112.
164. *RFC* xxix.
165. *CPR* 1277/227.
166. Donkin (1964) 63.
167. Berman (1986) 28–29 (No. 6).
168. *Cîteaux* XXV (1974: 1) 85.
169. Williams (1976) 122.
170. Wiswe (1953) 43.
171. Donkin (1964) 60.
172. Williams (1984) II, 272.
173. Berman (1986) 25.
174. *Ibid.* 9–10.
175. Fossier (1983) 69.
176. Donkin (1978) 45, 56–57.
177. Williams (1984) II, 269.
178. Rösener (1983a) 145.
179. Tadra (1904) 143.
180. Lepage (1855) 169.
181. Elm (1982) 142–43.
181a. *KD* I, 107, *cf.* 133–34.
182. *Cf.* Donkin (1978) 121–22, 132–33; Berman (1986) 14.
183. *CHS* 63.
184. Hockey (1976) 76.
185. Donkin (1978) 114.
186. VCH, *Wiltshire* III (1956) 271.
187. Donkin (1978) 126.
188. VCH, *Hampshire* II (1903) 147.
189. *RHC* 83.
190. *CPR* 1290/374.
191. *CFR* 1338/65.
192. *RFC* xxviii.
193. *CRA* 20 (undated).
194. *RHC* 24, *cf.* 19, 28, 32–33, 64.
195. *CW* 74.
196. *CDK* 96.
197. *RFC* xxix.
198. Lindley (1954) 174.
199. Williams (1976) 47.
200. VCH, *Buckingham* I (1905) 366.
201. Hockey (1976) 76.
202. Buczek (1971) 91.
203. McCrank (1975) 276.
204. *CDP* 2 (No. 1).
205. Le Hardy (1897) 310.
206. *SBE* 47.
207. *RD* II, 61 (No. 6188).
208. *CMH* 27 (No. 15).
209. *UE* I, 139, 144.
210. Noel (1975) 285.
211. Hockey (1970) 80.
212. *CDRB* II, 322 (No. 321).
213. *RHC* 89.
214. As at two non-Cistercian houses: *RD* I, 743 (No. 4447, of 1171 A.D.).
215. Campbell (1899) 166.
216. *OSBS* (1) 356 (No. 352).
217. McGuire (1982) 131.
218. *RC* 187.
219. Dugdale (1777) 234–36.
220. Rijksarchief Groningen, Klooster MS 50.
221. Donkin (1978) 120.
222. *CDTA* 99.
223. Henocq (1970) 518.
224. *KD* I, 64–65.
225. Knowles (1979) I, 72.
226. Hockey (1970) 54, Thompson (1920) 79, *cf. ABB 21.*
227. ABB 318.
228. Lebecq (1972) 375.
229. Schittekat (1966) 30, *cf. OHZ* II, 404 (No. 754).
230. Donkin (1978) 119.
231. Williams (1984) II, 278.
232. *CPR* 1280/380, 1292/513.
233. Coulton (1960) 221, *cf.* 515.
234. Pirenne (1929) 310.
235. Dimier (1964) 185.
236. *CDN* XI, *cf. CCD* 66.
237. *CTD* 3.
238. Pressouyre and Kinder (1990) 106; *cf.* CDN *61, 166.*
239. *CTD* 435 (No. XV).
240. Lebecq (1972) 371–85.
241. *RCC* V, 72 (No. 1280).
242. *RHC* 48.

243. Campbell (1899) 191.
244. Dugdale (1772) 132; Platt (1969) 65.
245. Donkin (1978) 11–20.
246. Darby (1940) 104n.
247. Donkin (1978) 118.
248. Waites (1967) 22.
249. Rösener (1983a) 145.
250. *DHGE* XVII (1971) 837.
251. Bedini (1964) 78.
252. Dimier (1957) 67.
253. Sarrazin (1985) 337.
254. *Ibid.* 338, 346, 349n.
255. *Ibid.* 338, 351 (n. 46).
256. *Ibid.* 342.
257. *Ibid.* 337, 342, 352 (n. 58).
258. Berman (1986) 24–25, 29.
259. Cauvet (1875) 122–25.
260. *CHA* (2–3) 102–03 (No. 525).
261. Pontus (1966) 20.
262. Thompson (1920) 81.
263. Lekai (1977a) 298.
264. Winter (1868) II, 192–93.
265. *CWK* 79.
266. Yañez Neira (1970) 566.
267. Elm (1982) 143.
268. Rocca (1936) 283.
269. Menapace (1971) 304.
270. *DHGE* XVII (1971) 891.
271. Van Der Meer (1965) 291.
272. Ferling (1979) 137.
273. *Ibid.* 135.
274. Blashill (1892) 108–09.
275. Waites (1967) 29.
276. *CAS* I, 70–71 (LXI), *cf.* Gosso (1940) 73.
277. *CAS* II, 168–69 (DLXXXVIII).
278. *CAS* II, 177–78 (DXCVIII).
279. Fornari (1978) 18.
280. Occhipinti (1983) 550.
281. Mariotti (1927) 170–71.
282. Fornari (1978) 18.
283. Fumagalli (1792) II, 142.
284. Grèzes-Ruelff (1977) 279.
285. Duby (1953) 105–06, *cf.* 17–18.
286. Wamba (1994) 135, 140.
287. Berman (1986) 26–27, *cf.* 90.
288. *CAF* 69–70.
289. *TG* 415.
290. McCrank (1976) 144.
291. Durand (1983) 107.
292. *CRS* I, 68 (LXIII): '*gambas*' = (?) cotton, silk, flax. I am grateful to Mrs. Jean Jones for this elucidation.
293. *CMH* 92 (No. 56).
294. Péchenard (1883) 269.
295. *DHGE* XVII (1971) 838.
296. Mariotti (1927) 194–95.
297. *CAS* II, 177–78 (DXCVIII).
298. *CSMF* 66–67 (No. 106).
299. *CRS* II, 112–13 (CCCXL).
300. *CRS* II, 42–43 (CXXXIV).
301. Barea (1977) I, 271.
302. *DSMLR* 429–30 (No. 158, of 1300).
303. *ABB* 238.
304. *ABB* 16, *cf.* 126, 163, 192.
305. Barrière (1983) 98.
306. Donkin (1978) 95.
307. *EP* (2) 96.

308. *CNM* 55.
309. Williams (1984) II, 285.
310a. Speiss (1959) 274, *cf.* Ferling (1979) 136.
310b. France (1994) 175.
311. Pirenne (1929) 302.
312. Duby (1968) 94, quoting a Higounet study.
313. Berman (1986) 91n.
314. Chauvin (1978a) V.
315. Espinos (1982) 134.
316. Donkin (1978) 64.
317. Berman (1986) 92.
318. Wamba (1986) 173–74.
319. Lindley (1954) 168.
320. Lekai (1977a) 450.
321. Constable (1964) 137–38.
322. *Ibid.* 140–41.
323. *Ibid.* 190.
324. Chauvin (1983a) 38.
325. *HRA* xvi.
326. Constable (1964) 191–92.
327. Lekai (1977a) 294.
328. Berman (1981) 201–02.
329. Hill (1968) 112.
330. *Statuta* I, 86–87 (1180/1).
331. *Cf.* Fig. 2.
332. *LCC* (1) 130.
333. *E.g.:* *ABB* 27–28; *cf. LCC* (2) 242.
334. Platt (1969) 84–85.
335. Williams (1976) 42–43.
336. *CDF* 187–88 (No. 534, of 1186).
337. Halkin (1970) 150.
338. *DD* 1511.
339. Sydow (1984) 196–222.
340. Williams (1984) II, 332.
341. *AF* 159.
342. France (1992) 213.
343. Graves (1957) 11.
344. *SBC* IV, 85–86 (Nos 1145–47).
345. Price (1952) 69.
345a. *VCH, Lancaster* II (1908) 132.
346. *CPR* 1281/442.
347. *CPR* 1309/159, 1332/371–34/371, 1341/361; *cf. CMM* III, vi–x.
348. *RHC* 143; *cf.* Mullin (1932) 31.
349. Williams (1976) 42–43.
350. *VCH, Chester* III (1980) 151.
351. Desmond (1975) 257; *cf. CPR* 1348/413, 1362/536.
352. *SBC* IV, 11 (No. 952), 53 (No. 1005[1]).
353. *VCH, Hampshire* II (1903) 141, *cf.* Desmond (1975) 258.
354. Van Nerom (1983) 20–21, 26, 28–29, 40 (Eastchurch in Sheppey).
355. Williams (1976) 42–43.
356. Desmond (1975) 259.
357. *Statuta* I, 428 (1214/57).
358. Lackner (1981) 60; *cf. Statuta* III, 317–18; Lekai (1977a) 386.
359. *MU* 120–21.
360. Grüger (1978b) 66.
361. *VCH, Gloucester* II, (1907) 97.
362. Desmond (1975) 251.
363. *RSL* II, 269.
364. *Arch. Camb.* (1868) 156, *cf.* Price (1952) 78–79.
365. *OSBS* I, 200–06 (Nos 203–08), 212–13 (No. 214).
366. Desmond (1975) 254–55.

367. *SBC* IV, 88–86 (Nos 1145–47).
368. *SBC* IV, 89–90 (Nos 1150–52).
369. *CPR* 1292/475.
370. *SBC* IV, 100–01 (No. 1167).
371. *RHC* 45.
372. Desmond (1975) 253–54.
373. Sydow (1984) 219.
374. Desmond 253–54.
375. *CMM* III, vi-x.
376. VCH, *Sussex* II (1907) 72.
377. Williams (1984) II, 340–41.
378. *Ibid*. 343 (this was well below levels recommended by the Fourth Lateran Council [1215] and the Council of Oxford [1222]).
379. *SBC* IV, 88–90 (No 1150).
380. *Cf*. VCH, *Lancaster* II (1908) 132 (5 marks; Barnes (1982; 7 marks).
381. VCH, *Lancaster* II (1908) 132.
382. *Cf. RHC* 4–6, Hockey (1970) 35–36, Williams (1976) 42–43.
383. Barnes (1982) 73.
384. Randall (1955) 20.
385. *ABB* 70.
386. Barnes (1982) 73.
387. *SBC* IV, 88–90 (Nos 1150–52).
388. Williams (1976) 43.
389. *ACA* 306.
390. *SBC* IV, 101–02 (Nos 1168–72).
391. Cowley (1977) 181.
392. Desmond (1975) 252.
393. Williams (1984) II, 216.
394. *Ibid*. II, 338.
395. *RHC* 53–54.
396. *MEX* 394.
397. *CW* 173–75.
398. *CD* 358–60.
399. Durliat (1980) non-paginated.
400. Williams (1984) II, 345.
401. *SL* 211 (No. 7).
402. VCH, *Gloucester* II (1907) 97.
403. Talbot (1960) 105.

Chapter 16

ARABLE FARMING

It was of the essence of early Cistercian life that the monks subsisted through the labour of their hands, by 'tilling the earth and raising animals'[1]. Whilst all granges practised a mixed economy, some were predominantly arable and formed the 'bread baskets' of their monasteries. Such were Llantarnam's Pwl-pan Grange (with its twelve carucates) and Strata Marcella's Home Grange (with seven ploughlands)[2]. Monasteries with mostly cool and damp, upland territory, would seek arable granges in more favoured areas of clime and soil – as did Cwmhir and Strata Florida. Monasteries, as Kirkstall[3] and Walkenried[4], might have a *conversus* appointed as 'keeper' or 'master of the ploughs'. Help might occasionally be extended, when requested, for the ploughing of the lands of kings or nobles, as by Ląd (1299)[5] and Tintern (c. 1245)[6], in return for some favour granted. An abbey might plough too assiduously, like the monks of Ourscamp who furrowed a road belonging to the monks of Saint-Médard (1304)[7]. As for the implements needed for cultivation, an insight comes with the Pavian raid on Morimondo Milano (1237). The marauders took away not only fifty ploughs and fifty yokes for the oxen, but also hoes, shovels, scythes, vineyard knives, pruning shears, and whetstones (for sharpening blades)[8].

The types of cereal produced depended on local conditions of soil and weather, and varied widely, each house growing several grains. Wheat was favoured wherever possible: Beaulieu (1270) produced nearly 3,000 qtrs (8700 hl), but even more oats[9]. Poblet's monastery store (1316) contained 40 'measures' of wheat, 500 'measures' of 'corn', and a further 12,000 'septenas' of wheat – the latter figure alone represented a reserve worth more than 10,000 *sueldos*[10]. In the damp and cool climate of upland Wales oats formed the principal cereal crop[11]. Rye was widely grown, for example in France[12] and Italy[13], as a subsidiary crop, and was the principal culture of Aubepierre on cleared forest lands[14]. By the fourteenth century Schöntal might produce yearly 750 'malters' of rye as opposed to 565 of oats, but gained a further 340 of rye from rents-in-kind and yet a further 120 as tithe[15]. The burnt grain preserved at Pászto (following an early thirteenth century fire) comprised mostly barley with some rye but very little wheat[16]. Barley (a staple for brewing) was increasingly grown by Heiligenkreuz[16a]. Some millet was sown by Bohemian abbeys. Surplus grain might be sold, as by Osek which exported corn to Saxony[17] and by Grandselve which sent wheat and oats on the river Garonne for sale in Bordeaux[18]. Most of Beaulieu's oats went to its brewery and stables. When (as in 1270) output was insufficient to meet demand, the abbey had to buy in half as much wheat and oats as it produced[19]. Kingswood (1242) sold surplus corn, but bought in oats for seed[20].

Glimpses of cultivation are afforded in some charters and other deeds. Sedlec grew wheat as an autumn crop at its Poboř í Grange, while barley and oats were spring-sown[21]. An abbot of Casavolone was rebuked by the General Chapter (1194) because he sent monks out at night to guard its cornfields[22]. In summer monks went out to the granges to help the *conversi* bring the harvest in, as noted on the Wye valley farms of

Cwmhir (1231)[23]. Once harvested, the grain was gathered on the threshing floors, and, as at Rueda, 'threshed, winnowed, and purged'[24]. The costs of threshing and winnowing on its several granges are all carefully itemised in the accounts of Beaulieu[25]. The farming timetable could fluctuate from year to year because of weather changes. Heavy rain on and off for six months much retarded the harvest at Croxden in 1330 – wheat was still being brought in at All Saints (1 November), but two years later good weather allowed a rapid early harvest, completed in ten days. Good weather also prevailed in 1333: the harvest was gathered in before St Bernard's Day (20 August) and sowing started before St Denis (9 October)[26].

The carriage of corn to barn or mill required sturdy carts. The Pavians robbed Morimondo Milano (1237) of at least twenty carts[27]. In 1300 a cart of Holm Cultram was observed on the high road in the middle of Carlisle, drawn by oxen and laden with oats and other food[28]. In 1342 the abbot of Louth Park sent a covered 'iron cart' to bring a dying knight to the abbey[29]. Clairvaux (1247) had its 'master of carts'[30]. A refractory *conversus* of Whalley (c. 1300) was 'a very strong wheelwright'[31]. Monastic carts might be much sought after. The king and nobles of France had, in 1194, expected the Cistercians to loan them carts, but the General Chapter, the next year, forbade their provision to those engaged in warfare[32]. Edward I (1304) requisitioned local Cistercian carts 'to take the Exchequer from York to Westminster', and Edward III (1332–33) to assist his Scottish expedition[33]. About 1335 Newbattle promised a benefactor each year 'one new wagon of the same sort and quality as it manufactures for its own use'[34].

Milling

The early prohibition on the reception of tithes applied equally to Cistercian possession of mills[35]. Mills held were to fulfil monastic needs only, not to be a source of income[36]. Once again, the incorporation of monasteries already possessing mills weakened the first ideals. The General Chapter (1157) permitted such abbeys to retain mills which they held at the date of their absorption into the Order, but not any acquired thereafter[37]. The inhibition was repeated as late as 1205[38], but by this time there had been numerous infringements of the rule, and from 1215 monasteries might receive mills granted 'in free gift' but even these were to be rented out from the inception and not exploited directly by the monks themselves. This restriction had limited effect[39]. A papal bull addressed to Theulay (1228) concerned exclusively its mills and ovens[40].

Cistercian building of mills, if not on monastic land, meant acquiring not only the immediate site but also a sufficient area to be flooded to form the mill-pond, as well as way-leave[41]. Early mill-sites granted to Cîteaux (c. 1155)[42] and Cheminon (1183)[43] are on record. Llantarnam (1202) is noted as building a mill at its Maestir Grange[44], and Walkenried (c. 1209) at its Kaldenhausen Grange[45]. Stratford (1225) was given timber to help in mill-construction[46]. Furness[47], Holm Cultram[48] and Tamié[49] all had rights of quarrying for mill-stones. The Beaulieu accounts (1270) detail the money spent on stone, timber and ironwork in repairing the mill by its gatehouse[50]. A knight whose lands touched on those of Fontmorigny (1220) allowed it to construct a mill and pond on the boundary stream, in return for a share in the profits[51]. A donor gave Duiske (c. 1235) similar rights, but expected free grinding for his demesne corn[52]. Way-leave to their mills, by 'ancient ways' or 'common' or private roads, was granted to Sibton[53], Aberconwy[54] and Quarr[55] respectively.

Several monasteries (as Sorø[56], Zbraslav[57], and Žďár[58]) were described as having large mills with four wheels (or internal revolving mechanisms)[59]. The new mill at Morimondo Milano's Coronato Grange (1237) had its 'toothed gear-wheels' noted[60].

The bed of the mill-leat at Dunkeswell's Broadhembury Grange (1260) was 'cleansed', to enhance the motive power of the water[61]. Cistercian mills in south France included 'floating mills', operated by Grandselve, on the wide and slow-moving Garonne[62]. Dunbrody[63], Quarr[64], and Tintern Secunda[65] had their 'tide-mills' on coastal creeks. Marienrode (1296) bought a 'pumpemole', probably a water-mill[66]. Mills might acquire especial names, as Sibton's 'Chalkmelnes' in Norwich[67], and Pipewell's 'Thurnmill' in Little Lawford[68]. Innocent IV (1245), addressing a bull to Herrera, noted that its mills were locally called 'Rota'[69]. Mills were susceptible to destruction by fire, as unhappily experienced by mills belonging to Meaux (*c.* 1190)[70], St Bernard-opt-Scheldt (1268)[71], and Pipewell (1328)[72], or might be ravaged in war, as two of Grandselve ruined during the Albigensian Crusade[73].

Many Cistercian mills were acquired by grant, lease, or purchase. Emperor Conrad III (1139) early gave a mill to Volkenrode[74]. Rufford received a mill, the donor intending the income to be applied for stone-work for the abbey church[75]. William Baker gave Bordesley (1180) a mill in exchange for an annuity of 12 qtrs (35 hl). of wheat and 12 of rye[76]. Bindon (1200) also leased a mill[77]. Between 1302 and 1313 Marienrode bought four mills[78]. Doberan (1319) bought for 1300 marks a mill at Little Sprenz; with it went water and fishing rights[79]. By the close of monastic life the Cistercians in Wales had come to own nearly ninety water-mills[80], and those in south France in excess of one hundred[81]. Individual houses might possess (as Cherlieu[82] and Pforta[83]) twenty mills or more; Quarr had twelve mills on the Isle of Wight, four in mainland Hampshire, and one 140 km (88 miles) distant in Devon[84]. Valmagne had a complex with at least six mills (not all perhaps for grain) on the Hérault river[85]. Some abbeys strove to establish milling monopolies, a 'closed shop', meaning that all corn producers in wide areas had no alternative but to grind their corn at a Cistercian mill, and pay the relevant dues. Kołbacz had a monopoly of the mills on the Płonia river from about 1187[86]; Reinfeld bought the milling monopoly of Schwerin[87], and Zinna exercised a like monopoly elsewhere: its master-miller in Juteborg state was always a monk or *conversus*[88]. Occasionally an abbey might seek free grinding rights in lay-owned mills. Bonport was (in 1209) allowed to use the royal mill at Pont-de-l'Arche every Wednesday and Wednesday night; in 1215, this right was commuted to receiving one-seventh of the mill's revenue[89].

Tenants obliged to make 'suit of mill' usually paid their dues for grinding in kind. Such 'multure' meant to Beaulieu (1270) 24 qtrs (70 hl) of wheat, 74 (215) of barley, 32 (93) of 'mancorn', and 70 (203) of malt: small amounts compared to those produced from cultivation[90]. Certain tenants obliged to grind at Roche's mill paid over every twentieth bowl to the abbey[91]. Between 1295 and 1327, Bronnbach acquired the income generated from at least eight mills[92]. Sibton (1354), leasing mills at Weybread, required the lessee to maintain them, but would find for him the 'good timber needed for planks, beams and mill-wheel'[93]. The abbey millers of Obra received for their work very generous land and fishing rights, as well as one-third part of the ground corn[94]. The miller of Doberan (1336) in Little Sprenze had the discretion, in winter, to build up over a week a sufficient head of water at the sluice-gate, and to lessen outflow from the 'upper pond'[95]. Not all lessees were satisfactory: the tenant of Tintern's mill at Merthyr Gerain (1303) was in trouble for 'bad keeping' of the mill[96].

In numerous instances, monasteries undertook substantial hydraulic works to provide the necessary water supply for their mills (see also Chapter 8). At Mellifont a mill-race no less than 800 metres (2640 ft) long was cut to avoid the meander loops of the river Mattock[97]. At its Angolencourt Grange, Morimond took water of the river Meuse to work two mills separated by a leat about 600 metres (1830 ft) long[98]. Diversion of waters was common-place. Fitero (1183) paid 30 s. for the right to divert water to its mill in Tudege[99]; Stanlaw led water from the 'mere of Merton' to its mill at

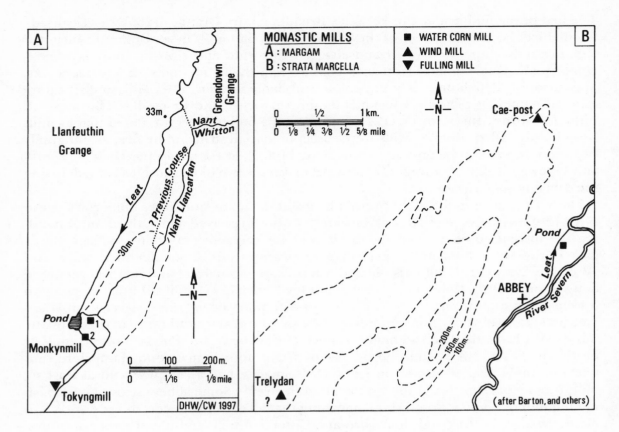

Steyning[100]; Aberconwy (1305) diverted the waters of Nant Gwyleth when building its mill at Rhedynog-felen[101]. There is note of Clairvaux (1224) constructing a breakwater at its mill in Bayel[102], and of Quarr (1206) making a sluice for its mill on the river Coly in Devon[103]. The storage of water in mill-ponds might require substantial dams. Even that at Bordesley's Grange Farm was 200 metres (610 ft) broad[104]. Both Kołbacz[105] and Neuenkamp[106] were blamed for so damming major rivers that subsequently there was widespread flooding. The waterworks associated with mill construction had subsidiary but valuable functions, as for fishing[107] and the watering of animals[108], and, in drier regions, for irrigation[109].

Cistercian development of milling rights could lead to disputes with aggrieved neighbours, especially where the diversion of water had reduced the flow downstream or where damming had caused flooding. A weir of Stanley (1213) near Faringdon caused flooding over lands of Beaulieu[110]; the diversion of water was a subject of contention between Alcobaça and the municipality of Leiria (1257)[111]; a lord of Miroglio complained of damage done to his fields when Locedio (1298) dug a water-course to one of its mills[112]. Poblet's efforts to monopolise the milling industry along the upper Francoli river led to rioting (1247) by the townspeople of Espluga, and their burning of abbey woodland[113]. More happily, Fitero (*c.* 1200) reached agreement with a local landowner who promised to stop taking water from a stream when the abbey needed it for its mill[114].

As for surviving mills, that in the outer court of Fountains and dating from the early-thirteenth century is still substantially intact[115]. The mill of Beaulieu had two chambers each with an undershot wheel[116]. A mill at La Crête dates perhaps from the thirteenth century, if not earlier[117], whilst a renovated mill-building is to be seen at Royaumont[118]. Numerous former Cistercian mills have been modified to form houses (as that of Llanllugan nunnery), or entirely destroyed on safety grounds (as that of Tintern's

Rogerstone Grange)[119]. Sometimes all that remains are earth-works from which one can deduce the mill foundations, the position of the dam and the course of the leat[120]. Mill-stones may remain on or near site, as in a lane by Tintern's Merthyr Gerain Grange, and forming a cottage doorstep at Byland. The phenomenon of 'industrial inertia' means that at several former Cistercian mill-sites in Wales some form of industry remains, though not the original milling practised there. The Gorseinon Packaging Works is now adjacent to the site of Neath's Cwrt-y-carnau grange mill, whilst the Ofrex Engineering Works occupies the place of Margam's Garw Mill[121].

Monasteries with lands in exposed maritime or estuarine positions might have one or more windmills, as Kołbacz[122], Oliwa[123], and Reinfeld[124], all in proximity to the Baltic; Ter Doest in Flanders[125], Altenberg in the Netherlands[126], Fountains at Boston by the Wash[127], Sibton not far from the North Sea[128], Quarr near the Solent[129], Meaux in Holderness[130], Stanlaw by the Mersey[131], Basingwerk above the Dee estuary and Aberconwy in Anglesey[132]. Inland houses might place windmills where elevated topography allowed, as Silvacane at La-Roque-d'Anthéron[133], Kingswood in the Cotswolds[134], and Strata Marcella above the upper Severn floodplain[135]. The first recorded Cistercian windmill in England was at Tostock, Suffolk – and a property of Sibton by about 1220[136]. Stanlaw's windmill had adjacent the necessary piece of land 'for cleansing the threshed grain in the wind'[137]. In 1270 the Beaulieu accounts reveal two newly-built windmills, and detail the items used in their construction – as the cloth for the sails and a pick for dressing the millstones[138]. Windmills were sometimes not very substantial: one of Meaux was later moved some 2 km from one site to another[139]. Disaffected local men easily broke down the windmill of Roche at Totewik (1329), and 'cut its timber into small pieces'[140].

Horse-mills are on record at Beaulieu (1270) – the horse was kept at its smithy[141] – Sorø (1347)[142], and Vale Royal (1337)[143]. Such mills were also insubstantial: the lessee of Vale Royal's horse-mill (at Kirkham) had to rebuild it within that lordship wherever the abbot wished. Abbot Burton of Meaux (1396–99) built a horse-mill there but with unseasoned timber, so that it soon deteriorated[144]. The mention of 'mill' in monastic records need not always imply a corn mill, though these formed the great majority. In addition to numerous fulling mills, there is not infrequent record of bark and malt mills, as well as iron hammers[145]. Two or more of these might utilise the same water source (as was frequent with corn and fulling mills in Wales)[146], or might (as at Rievaulx) stand on well separated sites[147].

Horticulture, and Fruit Production

Every monastery had its kitchen garden, but might also receive vegetables from plots scattered on its several properties – as did Palazuelos[148] and Poblet[149]. There is frequent note of those of Poblet throughout the latter twelfth century. Holm Cultram (*c.* 1225) was given a moss in Distington so that it could 'make a cabbage-garden'[150], and it had a field at Kirkconnel in Galloway (*c.* 1275) called '*Mustard*-garth'[151]. A tradition, right or wrong, has it that the monks of Newbattle popularised the Musselburgh leek[152]. As for orchards, these too might be widely spread. Pforta had nine orchards in different localities, but all supervised by its 'master of orchards'[153]. Salem had a religious designated as its 'fruiterer'[154]. Orchards were set up on granges of Bors Monostor[155] and of Zwettl[156]. A disputed orchard next to Bonport (1312) was adjudged to belong to the monastery and not to the French Crown[157]. At Deer a layer of stones was laid down well below the soil surface to stop its fruit trees developing tap roots[158]. Even Lyse in Norway not only sold fruit in Bergen, but also exported it to England[159].

In cooler lands, where viticulture was difficult to practise, apples were a staple fruit.

Walter Map (*c.* 1200) alleged that Tintern hanged a man caught stealing its apples[160]. Georgenthal (1227) accepted two manors, both abounding with apple trees, in settlement of a debt[161]. When a disastrous storm struck Croxden (1299), it uprooted no less than forty apple trees, as well as one very large pear tree[162]. Beaulieu produced cider[163], and sold some to the Normandy invasion fleet in 1344[164]. Cider was also a speciality of Gard in Normandy, and even of its mother-house at Bellevaux in Burgundy[165]. Rightly or wrongly, the Cistercians have been credited with introducing the grey rennet apple into eastern Europe[166]. The abbey of Warden gave its name to 'Warden pears', still sometimes so called[167]. Apples, pears, and cherries, were noted in the *Oculus Memorie* of Eberbach[168]; apples and cherries grew on Cistercian estates in León and Castile[169], whilst Alcobaça was famous for its oranges[170].

The olive-tree, typical of a 'Mediterranean' climate, was useful to the Cistercians in regions like southern France, Italy and Spain, since, when crushed by grinding stones, the oil yielded served not only as a commodity for trade, but also as lamp-fuel in the abbey churches[171]. As early as 1157, Grandselve had acquired or developed eighty olive groves in addition to holding rents on olive trees in fifty other localities A dozen of these groves were in the plain of Roussillon, near Perpignan, and nearly 200 km (125 miles) from the abbey[172], which sent down the Garonne river both olive oil and walnut oil for sale in Bordeaux[173]. Poblet built up its olive interests from 1151 to 1181, with rapid expansion in the short space of 1163 to 1166[174]. It also fostered trade in olive oil[175]. The nuns of Las Huelgas (fd 1187) received several olive groves in the first half of the thirteenth century[176]. Other Iberian monasteries with notable olive production included Fitero (granted the valley of 'Los Olivares' in 1183)[177], Rueda (at eight granges along the river Ebro)[178], and Santes Creus (with the tithe of olives on some of its lands)[179]. Alcobaça had olive oil presses in Lisbon[180]; a millstone and press are still to be seen at Le Thoronet[181]. St Sergius, in the Lebanon, had a partly walled olive grove outside Byblos[182].

Other monastic crops widely grown included flax and hemp for cloth making. There is frequent reference to them on Cistercian lands in northern Germany[183] as well as in Castile and León[184], and they were noted on Staffarda's Stupingi Grange[185]. The porter of Beaulieu bought linseed[186]. Crops on Cistercian lands in Bohemia included poppies and hops[187]; St Sergius (1238) had three sugar-cane patches by the Byblos river, close to the Mediterranean[188]; garlic was produced by thirteenth-century tenants of Alcobaça[189].

Viticulture and Wine Production

Claims have traditionally been made for the Cistercians that cannot be verified, suggesting that the white monks were responsible for introducing vines from Bassigny into eastern Europe[190], that Pontigny created Chablis[191], and that Lambrusco derived from vines originally planted by Chiaravalle di Milano[192]. What is certain is that the Cistercians (in appropriate areas) received gifts of vineyards from the outset and became notable wine producers. Cîteaux was given its Meursault vineyard on Christmas Day, 1098, by the duke of Burgundy[193]; Tamié (1132) received at its foundation a vineyard at Montmeillorat from the count of Savoy[194], and Longpont (founded the same year) was also endowed with two vineyards from the start[195]. Such early grants formed the basis for later prolonged expansion of Cistercian wine interests, with the emergence of notable monastic vineyards (like Cîteaux's Clos-de-Vougeot and Eberbach's Steinberg)[196], and the sale, sometimes quite far afield by river transport, of large quantities of wine, especially by monasteries sited in or close to the Rhine and Moselle valleys. All such abbeys (as Grandselve[197] and Salem[198]) appointed a monk or *conversus* as their 'vintner', to oversee this lucrative department of their economy.

In Burgundy there were (by 1250) some forty urban and rural 'celliers' – town houses and granges devoted to the storage and preparation of wine[199]. Cîteaux, which came to own fifteen vineyards[200], expanded its property at Clos-de-Vougeot between 1112 and 1336[201]; later the 125 acres (50 ha) there were enclosed with a high stone wall. The twelfth century cellar remains, though the present above-ground buildings are of sixteenth century date[202]. Clairvaux's oldest 'cellier' (wine-grange) was Morvaux vineyard (1143)[203], but that which became best known was at Colombé-le-Sec (1194)[204]. The cellar there is 33.8 metres (112 ft) long and 16.9 metres (55 ft) broad: stone-vaulted like most French monastic wine-cellars – the original height of the vaults was nearly 5 metres (some 16 ft)[205]. Such wine-granges had the buildings characteristic of any other grange: chapel, refectory, dorter, etc., and a *conversus* in charge. The known 'masters' of Colombé-le-Sec included Everard (1202), Martin (1222), and Girard (1250)[206]. Surviving charters trace Clairvaux's build-up of its vineyard acreage, especially between 1210 and 1240[207]. Granted some vine-plots, it bought others outright, but in several cases a gift was made of one-third of a vineyard, the abbey paying for the other two-thirds[208].

Other French abbeys with substantial wine interests included Longpont, acquiring vineyards from 1132 to 1301, and in 1270 greatly extending its vineyard at Presles by buying up episcopal land at Soissons for 3,000 *tours livres*[209]. A vigorous expansion of Preuilly's viticulture took place between 1200 and 1260, especially around Auxerre; purchases made might be of only one or two *arpents* (1½–3 acres) of vine-plots, and these were regrouped chiefly by exchange[210]. Léoncel expanded its vineyard at St Julien between 1218 and 1266: by 1308 its monks held fifty 'fosserées' under the vine there[211]. A note of 1266 refers to its gate-house, another of 1306 to its cellar, and several to its 'master'[212]. Froidmont built up, between 1173 and 1296, a total of over twenty vineyards[213]. Maizières owned the Beaune vineyard of Les Epenottes[214], Lützel had a vineyard at Hallstatt in the Colmar wine-growing area[215], and Tamié rendered yearly to the counts of Savoy sixty well-grown sheep in return for its large vineyard at Belmont[216].

In Germany, Eberbach, by 1232, cultivated vines on almost 30 ha (72 acres) of the steeply sloping Steinberg granted it a century before[217]: it too became a walled vineyard[218]. Early modern plans depict enclosure wall, gate-house and chapel at Himmerod's Siebenborn vineyard[219], granted to that abbey in 1157[220]. Another notable vineyard was that of Maulbronn at Eilfingerberg[221]. There is plenty of evidence of Cistercian viticulture in Spain[222], as at Fitero[223], with at least seven 'cellaria' noted amongst the granges of Moreruela[224], and also in medieval Hungary (as at Czikádor and Pilis)[224a]. Monasteries sited in regions not well suited for viticulture might obtain vineyards further afield. The Czech houses of Vyšší Brod and Zlatá Koruna, sited in the foothills of the Bohemian Forest, thus held vineyards in the Danube lands (not far distant) of Austria[225], particularly around Krems[226], where Zwettl too had vineyards[227]. Léoncel, high in the foothills of the French Alps, had its leading vineyard, St Julien, at a much lower altitude. Until the later thirteenth century, Villers in Belgium had vineyards in the Moselle and Rhine valleys, but because of transport difficulties gave these up and concentrated instead on producing wine in Brabant, notably at Louvain[228].

The relatively dry climate of north-east Europe, coupled with slightly warmer weather in the earlier Middle Ages than now[229], meant that the vine was cultivated even in the north of Poland. Cistercian vineyards were to be found on lands of Chorin[230], Oliwa, Pelplin[231], and the nunnery of Szczecin, all close to the Baltic[232]. In northern France, whilst Beaubec had vineyards in Normandy, including one by the sea-coast[233], Savigny, somewhat further west and perhaps damper, had no central vineyard but vines were grown on some of its granges[234]. In England, vineyards are evidenced (not

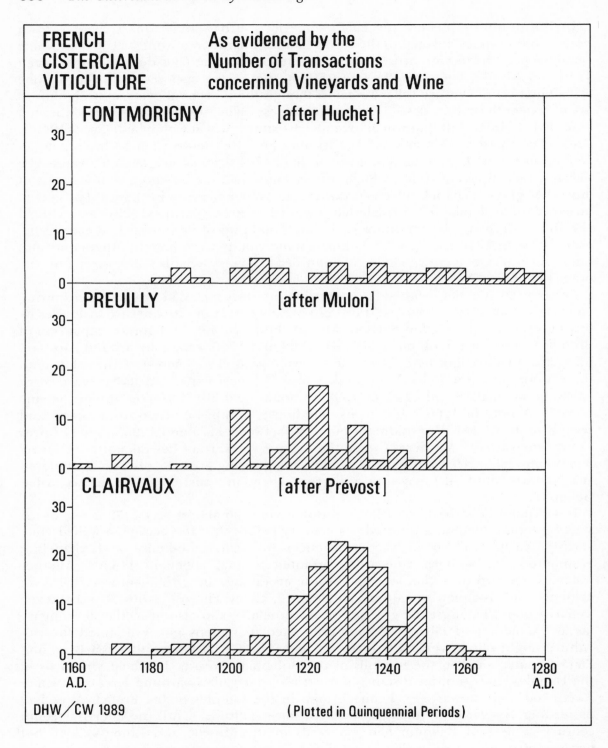

FRENCH CISTERCIAN VITICULTURE   As evidenced by the Number of Transactions concerning Vineyards and Wine

FONTMORIGNY   [after Huchet]

PREUILLY   [after Mulon]

CLAIRVAUX   [after Prévost]

1160 A.D.   1180   1200   1220   1240   1260   1280 A.D.

DHW/CW 1989   (Plotted in Quinquennial Periods)

always early) on lands of several abbeys in the drier and (in summer) warmer south-east, all within the bounds of the present-day 16°C July mean isotherm. The northernmost (noted in about 1240) was at Louth Park (beyond the 53° N line)[235]. There was an especial concentration in drier East Anglia (on lands of Coggeshall[236], Sibton[237] and Tilty[238]); in the south Beaulieu is credited with a vineyard planted in 1204[239]; further west there *may* have been viticulture on lands of Bordesley[240] and of Dore[241]. In Ireland, Lexington (1228) noted a wine-press at Jerpoint or Duiske[242]. A bull of Innocent IV in favour of Balmerino in Scotland (*c.* 1244) makes what must have been a purely routine mention of 'vineyards' in a standard form of confirmation of possessions, which does not prove that the abbey actually possessed any[243].

The vine was best grown on south-facing slopes, for the ripening grapes to gather maximum insolation. A margrave of Thuringia (1182) sold to Altzelle thirty acres of land 'on the side of a hill, to plant a vineyard there'[244], and there was contemporary note of vines of Altenberg (1197) growing on hill-slopes between Rhens and Kapellen[245]. A hillside vineyard was listed amongst the possession of Velehrad (1228)[246]. There are numerous references to monastic vineyards being sited in hilly areas: one of Heiligenkreuz was in 'Pfaffstätten mountain' (*c.* 1280)[247]; some of Froidmont's were on Mont César and Mont de Hermes[248]; a gift was made to La Ferté (1163) of a vineyard 'under St Martin's Mountain'[249]. Bonlieu had vineyards on the slopes of Cher[250], and Fontainejean on south-facing slopes in the Aveyron valley[251]. Morimond cultivated grapes on slopes of the Gouttes protected from northerly and westerly winds by the mountains and forests[252]. Casanova had several vineyards in the Chierese Hills[253]. Himmerod's Siebenborn lay in an abandoned incised meander of the river Moselle[254]. The monks of Eberbach (rightly or wrongly) have been credited with being the first wine producers to practise viticulture on terraced slopes[255]. Terracing, which *may* have borne vines, is to be seen on lands in England of Kingswood[256], and in Wales of Dore[257].

Both red and white wine were produced by Pforta (1243)[258] and Tennenbach[259]. When blight devastated the vineyards of Longpont (1379), it destroyed its white wine harvest but spared the red[260]. Pforta had, too, its 'good wine' (1226), its 'better wine' (1289), and its 'wine of the earth' (1340)[261] – possibly a 'vin ordinaire'. There was note of the 'better wine' of Altenberg (1191) at its Horchheim vineyard[262], whilst Walkenried (1202), finding that it could only produce poor quality wine at Bodenrode Thalheim, bought a large vineyard near Würzburg (Mittelheide) for 150 marks[263]. An abbot of Bronnbach (1340), implicitly criticising his predecessors, said that the abbey wine was of such poor quality because its vineyards had been neglected for years[264]. Himmerod safeguarded its wine output by making its long-lease tenants plant so many new vines each year: 25 or 50 or 100[265].

Monasteries might receive regular supplies of wine other than that produced on their own lands. Grants were made of wine for the celebration of Mass (as to Netley[266] and Wettingen[267]), and for the monastic refectory and infirmary (as to Fountains)[268]. King Albert of the Romans (1298) gave Zwettl a yearly gift of forty 'carrata' of wine from his Austrian vineyards[269]. Wine might be received as kind rents (as by St Benoît-en-Woëvre)[270], or in tithes (as by Altenzelle[271] and Dobrilugk[272]). Local inhabitants might have no alternative (as at Preuilly)[273] but to press their grapes in the abbey press, rendering a portion of wine to the abbey. Conversely, monasteries might pay their own outgoings in wine. Salem (1278) rendered yearly twenty 'urns' of white wine to a benefactor[274]; Lehnin (1196) had to make an annual delivery of wine to the duke of Brandenburg[275]. Pforta (1204) paid 200 'fuder' of wine as the purchase price for the village of Flemmingen[276]. Salem came to pay 'voluntary' compensation of a few tuns of wine to the counts of Werdenberg, in the time of King Ludwig of Bavaria; it was essentially 'protection money'![277]

An insight into vine cultivation is afforded by the grant to Beaubec to take timber in the forest of Andelys for vine props[278], the large quantities of vine stakes prepared by the forester of Beaulieu[279], and the willows probably used by Eberbach to bind vines[280]. The General Chapter (1195) rebuked the abbot of Iranzu for sending out monks 'to gather vines'[281]. The grape harvest over, monastic wine was pressed both at the abbeys and in the cellars of the vineyards and the monastic town houses. Bronnbach pressed its grapes both there and in its cellars at Würzburg and Marktheidenfeld[282]; Perseigne had several presses in different localities, including one (from an early date) in Neufchâtel[283]. Longpont (1143) received at Presles vineyard not only a press, but also some vats for treading grapes, and, for storage, 100 casks (each of nearly 240 gallons [about 10 hl]), giving an indication of that grange's potential wine-producing capacity[284]. The vaulted cellars of Clos-de-Vougeot, Colombé-le-Sec, Roches at Saint-Loup[285] and other vineyards allowed wine to be kept at a cool, constant temperature. At Fiastra, tunnels under the east end of the church, and rooms off tunnels under its home grange, served a similar purpose[286]. When local men drank more than their fill of wine stored by Poblet at Montroig (c. 1270), the cellar was set on fire[287].

Cistercian wine production had its difficulties. As vineyards expanded, tithes that were the perquisite of other bodies might be lost. Bonnevaux (1122)[288], Longpont (1194)[289] and Velehrad (1220)[290] were amongst those houses which had to come to terms in this respect. There were physical attacks on vineyards by aggrieved or jealous men, as on those of Longpont[291] and of Balerne[292]. Wine production at Longpont was curtailed by war (1358), blight (1379), and a hurricane (1391)[293]. Trading privileges led to conflict between Eberbach (1282) and the city of Cologne[294]. The mutual interests of Longpont and Ourscamp in viticulture at Montigny (1270) led to a weekly meeting of the grange-masters to smooth over difficulties[295]. The inhabitants of Montigny objected when Longpont blocked two local roads crossing its vineyards[296]. There might be difficulties with the local episcopate, as with bishops of Soissons[297] and Pécs[298] who objected to the scale of the wine sales of Longpont and Czikádor respectively, and with the archbishop of Bourges (1279) who questioned the measures used by Fontmorigny in its wine sales at Bernay[299]. When wine was sent on long journeys the ultimate sale price was increasingly raised by frequent tolls paid (unless clearances had been achieved); wine might be spilt by the rattling of casks on the road – on ships they had to be constantly packed and unpacked[300].

The consumption of wine within monastic precincts varied according to its local availability, but became increasingly common wth the passage of time (Chapter 11). The community of Longpont was always accustomed to have wine for their refreshment. A canon of Soissons (1143) gave the abbey its large vineyard at Presles to provide wine solely for the use of the monastery in 'the refreshment of the brothers, in the ministry of the poor, and in the reception of travellers'[301]. He gave a further four small vine-plots, the profits of which were to pay the workers in all its vineyards[302]. The wine of its home grange (in 1214) was reserved for the monks and for 'guests of honour', but by 1282 the wine of its two vineyards at Gorge Grange went to assist the work of charity at its gatehouse[303]. Wine was served (in the mid-thirteenth century) to the community of Vitskøl[304], and to the sick monks and *conversi* at Villers[305]. From the early-fourteenth century, if not before, wine in the refectory was commonplace at the Dunes[306] and at Preuilly[307]. The monks of the latter house were granted (from 1312) nearly a pint a day (about a half-litre) of good white wine in Lent. The problems of giving wine to rough and ready *conversi* have been noted (Chapter 4), but at Longpont's Moremboeuf Grange (1231) they were allowed some at the time of the grape harvest[308].

The great bulk of Cistercian-produced wine appears to have been intended for sale, and while the wholesale vending of wine never seems to have been forbidden to the white monks, the institutes and statutes of the Order did try to minimise its sale *retail*, or at least protect itself from having its monks take part in what might appear to be an unseemly occupation, and one open to moral pitfalls. As with some other early prohibitions, even the attitude to such retail sale of wine was modified in the course of time. In early days it was permitted, so long as the wine was not directly sold by monks or *conversi* themselves, but in the mid-twelfth century this leave was withdrawn[309]. In 1182, for the sake of abbeys labouring under 'intolerable indigence', retail sales were allowed on abbey property such as town houses, but not at a monastery or on its granges. Further, the sale had to be through a lay middleman, and no monk or *conver-*

sus was to eat, drink, or sleep in any part of such a wine-selling establishment[310]. Further statutes of the General Chapter reinforced (and somewhat adapted) these rules through to the early thirteenth century[311], noted infringements of them[312], and regularised wine storage[313]. By 1257 wine was openly sold in monastic precincts, but it was stipulated that such sale should not be accompanied by unseemly words or conduct[314]. As late as 1270 the Chapter again forbade any religious to be directly involved in such sales[315].

It was *wholesale* traffic in wine that became a marked feature of Cistercian trade in the later- twelfth century and thereafter. As both grapes and wine were bulky commodities, transport was wherever possible by river. Exemptions from tolls *en route* would be negotiated, and suitable houses with cellars would be acquired at journey's end. On the Rhine plied boats of such monasteries as Altenberg[316], Bronnbach[317], Eberbach[318], Heisterbach[319], Himmerod[320], Lützel[321] and Otterberg[322], all bearing wine from their vineyards destined for sale. Similar use was made by Chaâlis of the Seine, Marne, and Oise[323]; Vaucelle's boats also sailed on the latter river[324]; boats of Himmerod also plied on the Moselle[325]; those of Bronnbach on the Tauber[326], of Salem on the Neckar[327], of Preuilly on the Yonne[328], and of Grandselve on the Garonne[329]. The destinations (interim or final) were town houses with their storage cellars: as Cologne for Eberbach[330], Himmerod[331], and several other houses[332], and Provins for Preuilly[333]. Other urban property with a wine-trading function included the town houses of Auberive[334] and Clairvaux[335] in Dijon, Gard in Abbeville[336] and Amiens[337] (both on the Somme), Longpont in Noyon (three contiguous cellars) and Soissons[338], Châtelliers by La Rochelle[339], Fontainejean in Montargis[340], Vaux-de-Cernay in Montlhéry[341], Chaâlis in Beauvais (1240s)[342] and Thorigny[343], Lützel in Basle[344], Rein in Graz (by 1164)[345], and Walkenried in Würzburg (1206)[346].

Some wine went much further afield. Caesarius of Heisterbach (ob. 1240) told of the shipment down the Rhine of wine by Himmerod to Flanders and to Zeeland, with an attendant *conversus*[347]. Another monastery whose wine reached Belgium (Antwerp) and Holland (Utrecht) was Vaucelles[348]. It has been surmised that some of the wine of both abbeys may have reached England[349]. Cistercian wine was sent regularly to Benedict XII whilst the papal court was at Avignon; this was done (on behalf of the Order) by Maizières in 1339 (when valued at over 200 *livres tournois*), and by La Ferté in 1347 (some 300 *florins* worth)[350]. Normal Cistercian riverine traffic was on monastic-owned boats and barges, aided (to minimise the final cost and potential sale price) by the acquiring of toll-free rights. Between 1139 and 1270 Vaucelles obtained exemption from wine tolls in no less than thirty localities[351]. Charters granting such a privilege enable the sphere of monastic trade to be ascertained, and the route wine shipments took to be traced. Most of the lordships, for example, where Longpont had freedom from tolls lay to the north and north-west of the abbey, that is on routes supplying wine to the north of France[352]. Frederick II (1223) exempted Bronnbach from customs duties at Frankfurt on the Main, and at Boppard and Kaiserwerth (north of Dusseldorf) on the Rhine, suggesting that its wine trade stretched onwards for export well past Cologne. Its freedom of toll also at Oppenheim may suggest local monastic vineyards or some sales upstream[353]. Lützel was free of tax on wine at Eguishem and Woffenheim (by 1316) and at Basle (by 1352)[354].

Charters giving toll exemptions are also valuable in that they may indicate the quantities of wine that monasteries hoped to sell at a distance. The burgesses of Vienna (1270)[355], in a grant confirmed by the duke of Austria[356], allowed Heiligenkreuz to sell in that city, without any exaction, 72 'carratas' of wine; it might also sell 40 in Neustadt[357]. Lilienfeld (1272) received the right to sell up to 50 'carratas' in Vienna, and 30 at both Neustadt and Krems[358]. (The value of the 'carrata' is open to question, and all such medieval weights and measures varied from one locality to another, so that precise modern equivalents are not always possible.) The count of Troyes (1190) exempted Pontigny from all custom for up to 200 'muids' (nearly 12,000 gallons/about 540 hl) of wine taken each year to Troyes for sale[359]. The countess of Troyes (1210) allowed Preuilly free passage for the same amount to Provins, and the count of Provins (1223) allowed it to sell in Provins 50 'tuns' of wine[360]. By about this time, Vaucelles had the right of free passage in the Oise valley for some 33,000 gallons (1500 hl) of wine; this was later (1266) increased to over 60,000 gallons (nearly 3000 hl)[361]. In an agreement reached between Grandselve (1306) and the Steward of Gascony, the abbey could ship on the Garonne to Bordeaux, free of custom tolls, up to 300 'tuns' (perhaps 2500 hl/55,000 gallons), but dues had to be paid on what today would be called 'excess baggage'.[362]. Seen against these precise and documented figures, the claims that Eberbach in the thirteenth century was shipping some 2,300 hl (50,000 gallons) of wine down the Rhine seem eminently reasonable[363]. Such output, and the revenue gained, may not have been significant against the total wine trade of western Europe, but must have been of immense economic value to the monasteries involved. An accurate assessment is impossible, given the lack of precise figures of output for practically all the wine-producing Cistercian houses.

Notes

1. *Statuta* I, 14 (1134/5).
2. Williams (1984) II, 284.
3. Barnes (1982) 49.
4. Wiswe (1953) 99*n*.
5. Staats Archiv, Cologne, Kl. Lond. I, 39.
6. *C.Ch.R.* 1307/103–04.
7. *CO* 58 (LXXXVI).
8. Occhipinti (1985) 334–35.
9. *ABB* 25.
10. McCrank (1973) 78.
11. Williams (1984) II, 285.
12. E.g.: *Cîteaux* XXV (1974: 1) 81.
13. E.g.: Barea (1977) I, 275.
14. Aubrun (1978) 117.
15. Elm (1982) 149.
16. Valter (1994) 394–95.
16a. Roth (1986) 532.
17. Charvátová (1987) 132.
18. Mousnier (1982) 238.
19. *ABB* 26.
20. *DCK* 200–01.
21. Charvátová (1987) 132.
22. *Statuta* I, 177 (1194/42).
23. *C.C.R.* 1231/547.
24. Barea (1977) I, 202.
25. *ABB* passim.
26. *ACA* 305–06, *CC* II, 45–46.
27. Occhipinti (1985) 326.
28. Gilbanks (1899) 82.
29. *CPL* 59.
30. D'Arbois (1858) 241.
31. Crossley (1939) 33.
32. *Statuta* I, 180 (1194/57), 187 (1195/40).
33. Donkin (1978) 139.
34. Morgan (1929) III, 449, *cf.* Carrick (1907) 52, 73.
35. *Statuta* I, 14 (1134/IX).
36. Waddell (1994) 31.
37. Bond (1994) 369–70.
38. *Statuta* I, 312 (1205/21).
39. Bond (1994) 370, Hockey (1970) 40.
40. Chauvin (1983a) 31.
41. Berman (1986) 87.
42. *CDAC* 116 (No. 136).
43. *RCCH* 58.
44. Williams (1984) II, 286.
45. *CWK* 79.
46. Donkin (1978) 127–28.
47. Cottam (1928) 88–82.
48. *RHC* 69.
49. Bernard (1967) 58.
50. Bond (1994) 371; *cf. ABB* 282.
51. *CAF* 129–30.
52. *CDK* 74–75.
53. *SBC* II, 116 (No.   147, of *c*. 1230).
54. Hays (1963) 18.
55. PRO, E 40/B. 2542.
56. *SRD* IV, 535 (of 1347).
57. *CDRB* III: 1, 116 (No. 100, of 1232–34); it was the home mill.
58. *RBM* III, 163 (No. 406, of 1317); it was on the Labe by Kostelec.
59. *'quatuor rotas'*.
60. Occhipinti (1985) 328.
61. Sparks (1978) 28.
62. Berman (1986) 88.
63. Carville (1973c) 316.
64. Hockey (1970) 41.
65. Carville (1973c) 316.
66. *MUK* 107.
67. *SBC* IV, 32 (No. 980, of 1258).
68. Bond (1994) 371 (in 1328).
69. *CDH* 193–96.
70. Bond (1994) 371.
71. *OSBS* I, 291 (No. 284).
72. Bond (1994) 371.
73. Mousnier (1983c) 227.
74. *DHG* I, 751–52.
75. Bond (1994) 369.
76. *Ibid*. 367.

77. Graves (1957) 7–8.
78. Winter (1868) III, 30–31.
79. *DD* 1605–08; *cf.* 1617–19.
80. Williams (1984) II, 286.
81. Berman (1986) 88.
82. Kempf (1976) 50–52.
83. *UKP* passim.
84. Bond (1994) 369.
85. Berman (1986) 89.
86. Szacherska (1977) 153.
87. Thompson (1920) 83.
88. Hoppe (1914) 154.
89. *CBP* 46–48 (No. XLIV).
90. *ABB* 28.
91. Aveling (1876) 121.
92. Scherg (1976) 159.
93. *SBC* IV, 92 (No. 1156).
94. *KD* II, 237, 290–92, 307–08, 325.
95. *DD* III, 1618.
96. NLW, Badminton Manorial 1641r.
97. Carville (1982b).
98. Dubois (1879) 140.
99. *CSMF* 29 (No. 38).
100. *CBW* II, 424.
101. Hays (1963) 89.
102. *RCC* III, 369 .
103. Hockey (1970) 88.
104. Rahtz (1976) 24–25, and fig. 3.
105. Roth (1986) 531.
106. Thompson (1920) 84; Winter (1868) II, 252.
107. E.g. *SBC* II, 116 (No. 147).
108. E.g. *SBC* II, 185 (No. 257).
109. E.g. Berman (1986) 89.
110. Bond (1994) 370–71.
111. Durand (1983) 109.
112. Bellero (1985) 346.
113. McCrank (1975) 280–81.
114. *CSMF* 51.
115. Bond (1994) 365.
116. St John Hope (1906) 143.
117. Cailleux (1991a) 328.
118. Tosti-Croce (1994) 118 (fig. 8).
119. Williams (1984) II, 290.
120. Field-, and place-, names may also indicate deserted mill-sites.
121. Williams (1984) II, 290.
122. *PU* V, 329–30.
123. Surmised from a wooden disused structure still to be seen nearby in 1975.
124. Thompson (1920) 83.
125. Dendooven (1964) 6 (where shewn on a plan of 1561).
126. Ferling (1979) 137.
127. Mullin (1932) 47.
128. *SBC* I, 126; II, 69–70 (No. 72); IV, 42–44 (Nos 994, 997).
129. Hockey (1970) 33.
130. Earle (1906) 74, 77.
131. *CBW* II, 501–11 (Nos XXIV-XXVI).
132. Williams (1984) II, 291.
133. Pontus (1966) 20.
134. Lindley (1954) 182.
135. Williams (1984) II, 291 (where other Welsh examples).
136. *SBC* II, 69–70 (No. 72).
137. *CBW* II, 510 (No. XXIV).
138. Bond (1994) 373; *cf. ABB* 75, 91.
139. Bond (1994) 374.
140. *C.P.R.* 1329/478.
141. *ABB* 36, 263.
142. *SRD* IV, 535.
143. Bond (1994) 374.
144. *Ibid*. 374.
145. Lingenberg (1982) 223.
146. Williams (1984) II, 288.
147. Bond (1994) 371 (where further discussion).
148. Espinos (1982) 129.
149. Tort (1974) 388.
150. *RHC* 33.
151. *RHC* 48.
152. Carrick (1907) 103.
153. Lekai (1977a) 319.
154. Rösener (1974) 155.
155. *RCH* 65.
156. *LFZ* 540.
157. *CBP* 372 (No. CCCLII).
158. McClean (1981) 239.
159. Lekai (1977a) 319, Roth (1986) 536.
160. Williams (1984) II, 292 (where more details of fruit in Wales).
161. Thompson (1920) 87.
162. *CC* (2) B. 45.
163. McClean (1981) 27 *cf. ABB* 237–39.
164. Lekai (1977a) 319.
165. Chauvin (1983a) 26.
166. Winter (1868) II, 173–74.
167. McClean (1981) 230.
168. Staab (1987) 82.
169. Wamba (1986) 176.
170. Cocheril (1964) 267.
171. *Cf.* Gimpel (1977) 6, Tort (1974) 382.
172. Berman (1986) 24*n*, Mousnier (1982) 180.
173. Mousnier (1983c) 235.
174. Tort (1974) 382–86.
175. McCrank (1973) 58.
176. *DMLH* I, 102 (No. 57, of 1201); 175 (No. 109, of 1211); II, 9–11 (No. 260, of 1231); II, 239–31 (No. 437, of 1253).
177. *CSMF* 29–30 (No. 39).
178. Wamba: comment at 1993 Fontfroide Conference.
179. Fort i Cogul (1975) 68.
180. Durand (1983) 109.
181. Esquieu (1986) 21.
182. Williams (1974) 73–74.
183. Thompson (1920) 86.
184. Wamba (1986) 176.
185. Gosso (1940) 207.
186. *ABB* 176.
187. Charvátová (1987) 132.
188. Williams (1974) 73
189. Durand (1983) 114.
190. Thompson (1920) 80.
191. Seward (1974) 66.
192. Menapace (1971) 305.
193. *CDAC* 38 (No. 12), *cf.* 52–53 (No. 36).
194. Bernard (1967) 21.
195. Duval-Arnold (1968) 209.
196. Seward (1974) 77.
197. Higounet (1982) 698.
198. Staab (1987) 83, *cf. CDSL* I, 340; II, 427.
199. Chauvin (1983a) 26.
200. Seward (1974) 65.
201. *Ibid*. 66.

202. Dimier (1964) 188; (1974a) 48.
203. *RCC* II, 153–54.
204. Dimier (1974a) 49.
205. Corbet (1991) 269–270.
206. D'Arbois (1858) 315.
207. *RCC* passim.
208. E.g. *RCC* IV, 62 (Nos 1020–21, of 1227).
209. Duval-Arnold (1968) 209, 211, 215, 220. (Some 106 deeds relate to its wine interests).
210. *Cîteaux* (1978/1–2) 122–23.
211. Wullschleger (1991) 92–93.
212. Couriol (1980) 102–03.
213. Bonnet-Laborderie (1985) 10.
214. Seward (1974) 69.
215. Chèvre (1973) 57.
216. Bernard (1967) 58.
217. Lekai (1977a) 316–17.
218. Seward (1974) 73.
219. Stadt Archiv. Koblenz: 96/100 Akten; Abt. 1. C. Nr. 7739, Bl. 22.
220. Storch (1958) 12.
221. Seward (1974) 75.
222. Tomé (1991) *passim*.
223. *CSMF* passim; e.g: p. 55 (No. 91, of 1152).
224. Anton (1986) 362.
224a. *RCH* 143 (P), 174 (C); *cf.* 47–48, 63–64, 159.
225. Charvátová (1987) 133.
226. *UKG* 91–92 (Nos XLV–XLVI, of 1337).
227. *LFZ* 555–56.
228. De Moreau (1909) 213–15.
229. Carville (1972a) 352.
230. *CBR* II, 496 (of 1375).
231. Dąbrowski ((1970) 64.
232. *PU* II, 396.
233. Deck (1974) 138.
234. *RSL* II, 231 (of 1230).
235. *CPL* 13 (when a pond was made within it).
236. Cutts (1858) 183.
237. *SBC* IV, 102 (No. 1173, of 1330).
238. Galpin (1928) 92–94.
239. *Illustrated London News* 22-07-1967, p. 25.
240. Rahtz (1976) 31.
241. Williams (1984) II, 292.
242. Stalley (1987) 45.
243. Campbell (1899) 60.
244. *CDS* III, 323–24.
245. *UKA* 32 (No. 36).
246. *CDRB* II, 322 (No. 322).
247. *UKSH* 227 (No. CCXLVIII), *cf.* 12 (No. IX), 105 (No. XCVI).
248. Bonnet-Laborderie (1985) 10.
249. Duby (1953) 121.
250. Barrière (1983) 84.
251. Jarossay (1891) 322.
252. Dubois (1879) 59.
253. Gosso (1940) 87.
254. Storch (1958) 2–3.
255. Gimpel (1977) 47–48.
256. Lindley (1954) (1) 155.
257. Williams (1984) II, 292.
258. *UKP* 143.
259. *TG* 121.
260. Duval-Arnold (1968) 234–35.
261. *UKP* 119, 282, 528.
262. *UKA* 28 (No. 28).
263. Winter (1868) II, 172.
264. Scherg (1976) 154.
265. Schneider (1954) 117–18.
266. *C.P.R.* 1280/358.
267. *CDSL* II, 526 (of 1297).
268. *C.C.R.* 1244/222.
269. *LFZ* 215.
270. *CSBW* 101–02 (of 1239).
271. *CDS* III, 7 (of 1196).
272. *CDS* III, 120 (of 1210).
273. Mulon (1972) 85.
274. *CDSL* II, 203.
275. Schultze (1930) 30.
276. Winter (1868) II, 173.
277. Rösener (1974) 144–45.
278. Deck (1974) 142.
279. *ABB* 39–40.
280. Seward (1974) 73.
281. *Statuta* I, 195 (1195/87).
282. Scherg (1976) 154.
283. *CDP* 19 (No. VIII).
284. Duval-Arnold (1968) 210.
285. Dimier (1974a) 56.
286. Tosti-Croce (1994) 332–33.
287. McCrank (1975) 265.
288. *RD* I, 566 (No. 3331, of 1122).
289. Duval-Arnold (1968) 213–14 (of 1194 on).
290. *CDRB* II, 182–83 (No. 197, of 1220).
291. Duval-Arnold (1968) 218 (in 1196).
292. Chauvin (1983b) 183 (at Glenon).
293. Duval-Arnold (1968) 234–35.
294. *DHGE* XIV (1960) 1282.
295. Duval-Arnold (1968) 219.
296. *Ibid.* 218.
297. *Ibid.* 232.
298. Roth (1986) 529.
299. *CAF* 323–24.
300. King (1985) 181.
301. Duval-Arnold (1968) 233.
302. *Ibid.* 210.
303. *Ibid.* 223–26 (wine of its other vineyards was sold).
304. McGuire (1983b) 207.
305. De Moreau (1909) 213–15.
306. Notes on board in parlour of Grootseminaire, Bruges.
307. Mulon (1972) 84.
308. Duval-Arnold (1968) 224.
309. Waddell (1994) 35; *cf. Statuta* I, 25 (1134/LII).
310. *Statuta* I, 90 (1182/6).
311. *Statuta* I, 97 (1184/15), 99 (1185/9), 103–04 (1186/6), *LCC* (1) 142.
312. *Statuta* I, 125 (1190/36), 163 (1193/33), 312 (1205/21).
313. *Statuta* I, 173 (1194/11).
314. Thompson (1920) 92.
315. *Statuta* III, 82 (1270/8).
316. *UKA* 111 (No. 143).
317. Winter (1868) II, 173.
318. Steinwascher (1981) 99.
319. Amon (1979) 126.
320. *DHGE* XXIV (1993) 592.
321. Chèvre (1973) 84–85.
322. Elm (1980) 223.
323. Blary (1989) 292, 305.
324. Lebecq (1983) 204–05.
325. *DHGE* XXIV (1993) 592.
326. Winter (1868) II, 173.

327. Rösener (1974) 134.
328. *Cîteaux* (1978/2–2) 123.
329. Berman (1986) 93.
330. Lekai (1977a) 316–17.
331. *Ibid*. 317.
332. Chapter 19.
333. Mulon (1972) 86.
334. Grandmottet (1958) 10 (it was in rue Saint-Pierre).
335. Dimier (1973) 55.
336. Macqueron (1904) 55.
337. Fossier (1983) 69.
338. Duval-Arnold (1968) 230.
339. Barrière (1983) 93.
340. Jarossay (1891) 323.
341. Duby (1968) 133.
342. Quignon (1914) 392–93.
343. Blary (1989) 313–14.
344. Chèvre (1973) 54.
345. Amon (1979) 126.

346. Winter (1868) II, 172.
347. *CHDM* (1) 308, 515.
348. Lebecq (1983) 205–06.
349. *DHGE* XXIV (1993) 592 (H), Lebecq (1983) 205 (V).
350. King (1985) 181–82.
351. Map supplied by M. Lebecq at the Flaran Conference (16-01-1981).
352. Duval-Arnold (1968) 230.
353. Winter (1868) II, 173.
354. Chèvre (1973) 84–85.
355. *UKSH* 174 (No. CLXXXVII).
356. *UKSH* 253 (No. CCLXXIX, of 1286).
357. *Ibid*. (confirmed by the same ducal charter).
358. *RBM* II, 320 (No. 795).
359. *PCP* 368–69 (No. 382).
360. Mulon (1972) 86.
361. Lebecq (1983) 204–05.
362. Higounet (1982) 698.
363. Gimpel (1977) 47.

Chapter 17

PASTORALISM

The Cistercians (certainly in western Europe) became accomplished pastoral farmers, encouraged by considerable rights of pasture frequently afforded them, exemption from tithes which would otherwise have taken away every tenth newborn animal, and the acquisition of toll-free rights of way to markets. All this meant that they could rear their animals and sell them for a lower price than many of their competitors[1]. Animals, and their produce, became of prime significance in Cistercian economy, one abbot of Margam (1336) telling how he 'relied for support mostly upon his stock'[2]. In the early decades and later, cattle were important as they yielded dairy produce, gave raw materials for clothing and shoe manufacture, were essential in ploughing and transport, and when sold brought in ready cash[3]. They could also be used for barter, as when Cîteaux (c. 1140) paid 12 *Dijon pounds* and 'a brown cow' for some land[4], and when Strata Florida (1255) included two cows in the purchase price of its 'great bell'[5]. From the later twelfth century sheep-rearing often became more advantageous than breeding cattle. In the very early decades of the Order, it did have to forbid the raising of animals: 'Such as usually arouse curiosity or serve for vanity' – bears, cranes, and deer amongst them[6].

Even a relatively small monastery, Santa-Maria della Paludi in Sardinia, received at its foundation (1205) 10,000 sheep, 2,000 pigs, 1,000 goats, and 500 cattle[7], and later that century, Fountains, Rievaulx, and Jervaulx, were credited with 18,000, 14,000 and 12,000 sheep respectively[8]. Such numbers outshone some continental abbeys where grazing lands may have been limited, like Cambron, said at this period to have had only 4,000 sheep, 600 pigs, 400 calves, and 169 cows and oxen[9]. Animal statistics must be treated with caution. Do the figures relate to *all* an abbey's stock, or only that on the home estate? Poblet, for example, given its extensive lands, is quoted with quite low numbers (in 1316) of sheep (2,215) and goats (1,500)[10]. That year was a time when animal diseases were sweeping through Europe, and greatly affecting monastic flocks. It may be the effects of fatal disease, or the time of year when the figures were drawn up (whether before or after sales and slaughter), that explain the fluctuations of Meaux's stock figures: 11,000 sheep in 1280 but only 5,406 in 1310; nearly 1,000 cattle in 1280 but only 472 in 1286[11]. Knowledge of stock figures comes from surveys such as, for England and Wales, the *Taxatio* of Pope Nicholas IV (1291) – itself clearly defective in places[12] – or from accounts drawn up (as at Kirkstall) on the accession of a new abbot, or during the annual visitation by the father-abbot[13].

In empty countryside the Cistercians often owned large tracts of grazing territory. Such were Newbattle's Monkland property in Clydesdale[14], Furness' pastures of Brotherkeld and Southerscales in Cumbria and the Pennines[15], and the three areas of Dartmoor (South Holme Moor, Brent Moor and Buckfast Moor) owned by Buckfast[16]. Brotherkeld was some 14,000 acres in extent; Southerscales had cost £600. The alternative was for a monastery to obtain pasture rights, often in common with the flocks of the donor. This helped the latter for it encouraged cross-breeding and gave him perhaps a percentage of the newborn animals, as well as a ready source of dung[17]. Nearly half the pasture grants made to Meaux were of 'common of pasture'[18]. Kings of Aragon, Castile and Navarre all gave pasture rights to Veruela[19]. Jervaulx acquired exclusive rights of pasture north of the river Ure from the earl of Richmond[20]. Sibton, even in a well-developed area, acquired much pasture, as for 300 sheep near Mildenhall[21], and on its own lands frequently enclosed its pastures[22]. By no means were all pasture rights gifts: Berdoues received one grant as surety for a loan of 400 *sol*[23]; Clairvaux paid 15 *livres* for exclusive rights in two localities[24].

When rights in common pasture were granted, restrictions were often placed so that those lands did not become overstocked and overgrazed[25]. These limitations might specify the total number of animals allowed, refer to a closed season, and make provision for the animals to be counted. The earl of Richmond, giving Jervaulx common rights south of the Ure (in addition to exclusive rights north thereof), allowed 1,800 of the abbey's sheep and 1,100 of its other animals to graze there. His officers would count the stock thrice a year, and the monks were to pay a penalty per head for any numbers in excess[26]. Numerical restrictions applied to Meaux (in Sutton) – 100 sheep[27], and Silvanès (at Sarrus) – 1,000 sheep[28]. Cherlieu might pasture animals at Betancourt, but only from Martinmas (11 November) to Lent[29]; Holm Cultram at Wigton, between Martinmas and Easter[30]; Sibton at Shelfhanger, from Our Lady's Nativity (8 September) until Candlemas (2 February)[31]. This winter grazing meant that the land was naturally manured before perhaps being used for hay or arable, and did not interfere with the harvest season. Furness was granted common in Amounderness 'after the corn and hay harvest'[32]. At Shelfhanger, if Sibton's sheep strayed into a reserved area, the abbey was to make good any damage done. It may have been because Bonnecombe overexploited the pastures used from its Moncan Grange that by the mid-thirteenth century the heirs of the original donors attempted to restrict its rights. Eventually, its animals there were forbidden beyond the Muse river[33].

Upland pastures, where to be had, allowed (in summer at least) the grazing of large flocks, especially of sheep. Aberconwy had around 12,000 acres (4,850 ha) on the slopes of Snowdon, Strata Marcella 2,000 acres (800 ha) in Talerddig alone[34]. Forest grazing was primarily used for cattle, horses and pigs. Jervaulx had pasture rights in the forests of Wensleydale, Rievaulx in the woods of Teesdale and Helmsley[35]. Reclaimed marshland around the British coastline was sought after, because of the milder winter weather close to the sea and the constant freshness of the grazing. Several monasteries found good pastures in the English Fenland (as Kirkstead, Swineshead and Vaudey)[36]. Basingwerk[37] and Dieulacres[38] both grazed animals in Saltney Marsh by the Dee Estuary, Meaux in Holderness by the Humber, Holm Cultram on marshes next the Solway, and Boxley by the Medway[39]. Coastal marshland supported many of the animals of the Dunes and Ter Doest, as also Vaucelles (in the polder of Cuvele)[40]. Granges which had pastoralism as their prime concern included Fountains' Bouthwaite Grange (in Nidderdale)[41], Fontfroide's Parahou Grange (a gathering point for its transhumant flocks)[42], and Obazine's Graule Grange (at 1200 metres [4,000 ft] in the Monts du Cantal)[43].

Monastic flocks had frequently to be on the move, whether for dipping, shearing or watering, or to find fresh pastures, or to go to market for sale. Most abbeys had to enter into negotiations to obtain way-leaves, free of any charge if possible. Two brothers allowed Froidmont (1181) passage across their land for 'its flocks and wagons' going to and from Grandmesnil Grange[44]. Sallay (*c.* 1210) was given the use of a road 20 feet (6 metres) broad leading to its Stainton Grange[45]. William Pennington allowed Furness (1318) a fifty-foot (15 metres) broad way over Pennington Moor: materials from the moor could be used to maintain the road[46]. Ourscamp (1306) had passage from Carmey to Mares for five hundred sheep, but had to pay a small fee[47]. Free passage was given to Meaux across the river Hull (for its Salthaugh Grange)[48], and to Fontmorigny (1211) over bridges at Jussy[49]. Gimont[50] and Pontigny[51] (both in 1188) promised to make good any damage done during the transit of their flocks: such might, after all, stray and eat valuable crops. Animals and herders on long journeys needed permission to halt overnight, as given by local lords for the flocks of Furness going to Borrowdale[52], and to Fountains for those traversing Allerdale and Craven[53]. The flocks of Newbattle so resting were to 'avoid corn and meadow'[54]; those of Clairvaux might overnight in the woods of one grantor[55].

Monasteries with large flocks, especially when in transit, might seek additional sources of food and water. Bonport (1258) was granted 19 cartloads of hay yearly at Vaudreuil[56], whilst Jervaulx (1280) had leave to mow in Widdale[57]. Morimondo Milano (1237) stored 150 wagon-loads of hay on its Basiliano Grange alone[58]. Pontigny acquired the right for its flocks pastured locally to drink at the springs of Oisel (1181), Sormery (1197) and Champ Juignet (1218)[59]. Byland (1239) went to law when its cattle at Morton Grange were hindered from reaching the spring of Wudekelde[60]. Sallay (*c.* 1300) made a drinking-pond in Barrowby, 40-foot (12 metres) square[61]. In distant pastures housing for both flocks and their keepers needed to be built. Fountains had 8 acres (3·25 ha) of land in Allerdale 'to construct a shed for cattle going to and fro'[62]. By 1241 it had a chain of seven lodges in Langstrothdale[63]. Restrictions might be placed in areas where common rights were enjoyed. Shepherds' huts, but not a permanent dwelling, might be erected by Pontigny and Vauluisant (1155) on pastures they claimed between Sévy and Cérilly[64]. Clairvaux (1247) promised to set up only temporary, removable huts, in the lordship of Anglus[65]. The Order had early discouraged migration too far afield, by insisting that flocks were back on monastic territory by nightfall. Exceptions were allowed where pastures had to be sought far afield – as in the Alps, or by abbeys which were poor or had barren lands[66].

Pastoral farming was not without its hazards and problems, whether from animal disease or disgruntled peasantry or wild animals, or simply because most animals had a tendency to stray. The diseases commonly noted were 'scab' ('itch' today) and 'murrain' (perhaps 'anthrax' today)[67]. Both combined to reduce the number of lambs at Beaulieu by almost half in 1270[68]. In 1336 Margam told how 'a terrible mortality' had affected its animals[69]. It was in the years of great famine from 1314 to 1321 (throughout Europe) that murrain seems to have struck hardest[70]. In one year alone – 1316 – Croxden suffered nearly 200 marks (£133) loss because of its animals dying[71], whilst great inroads were made into the 1,000 plus sheep of Zbraslav in Bohemia[72]. Pipewell plummeted into debt[73]. The savagery of wild animals was recognised in those agreements which precluded monks from hunting any but 'noxious animals'[74]. At its remote Esklets Grange in Westerdale, Rievaulx (1185) 'set traps for wolves' and its shepherds carried horns 'because of wild beasts and bandits'[75].

In the lordship of Cardona (1195) rustlers absconded with many of Poblet's livestock[76], whilst the Welshry killed hundreds of the sheep of Margam (1223–24)[77]. Royal officials tried to collect special dues from Poblet's *conversi* herding its sheep on the grasslands of northern Valencia, but were rebuked by James I (1225)[78]; Henry III (1226–34) had repeatedly to order the Constable of St Briavel's to allow Flaxley to have its common rights in Dean Forest unimpeded[79]. Problems came too when other religious houses (of Valence) claimed tithes on the new-born animals of the transhumant stock of Léoncel[80], and when Bonneval, selling winter dairy produce in the markets of the Camargue, came into conflict with the merchants of St Gilles – who felt their trade was threatened[81]. In charters granted to Jervaulx (for its flocks in Uredale)[82] and to Margam (for those pastured on Newcastle Moor)[83], it was conceded that any abbey sheep which strayed were not to be impounded but to be chased back, or at least the monastery notified. The 'Coucher Book' of Furness told how many powerful barons gave the sheep of that abbey protection when sick or astray[84], but when two of Croxden's oxen (1271) strayed on to the high road, a royal writ was needed before their captor would release them[85]. The pasturing of animals in common, and the problem of sheep which strayed, meant that the ownership of all beasts needed to be easily identifiable. Hence references to the branding 'with a mark' of the animals of Aberconwy[86] and Pipewell[87].

Pasture Disputes

Not least of the difficulties which bedevilled the Cistercians, until at least the mid-thirteenth century, were the disputes when their pastures were contiguous with those of other religious houses. The matters of boundaries and stray animals had to be faced, as in the concords reached between Pontigny and the canons of Dilo (1146)[88], between Bonnevaux and the Chartreuse (1175)[89] and between Clairvaux and the Templars (1218)[90]. A lord of Bressingham accused Sibton (1227) of overstocking the pastures there[91], a lord of Chirinton enclosed part of a common so that Kingswood's animals lost grazing[91a], but Pipewell (1266) won its case at Warwick Assizes against 'the chief men' of Thurlaston who claimed common rights on Causton Common[92]. A dispute between Furness (1279) and Roger Hestholm was settled amicably after a duel by their champions had commenced before the justices in eyre[93]. Duelling had been reverted to in an earlier dispute between Margam and Neath[94].

Disputes between Cistercian houses with neighbouring pastures were far from unusual, and sometimes bitter. Early pasture agreements were reached between Pontigny (1150) and Reigny[95], and between Cîteaux (1150) and La Bussière[96]. Hulton entered into a number of inter-conventual agreements, principally with Dieulacres and (non-Cistercian) Trentham Priory[97]. The abbot of Fontfroide mediated between the proximate abbeys of Poblet and Santes Creus concerning conflicting pasture claims in the 'puertos' of Cerdaña (1177) and Peguera (1182)[98]. In counter-claims (1217) between Bonneval and Mazan on the one part and Bonnecombe on the other, to the pastures of Serre, Mazan (1225) ceded its rights there to Bonneval, which, almost immediately, sold Serre Grange to Bonnecombe. Bonnecombe paid out in cash (5,000 *sous* in local currency) or the equivalent in kind (84 cows or oxen) to both Bonneval and Mazan. Bonneval (1232) later attempted to retrieve the grange, but after an inquiry ordered by the General Chapter was told to desist[99]. Such disputes, with very little detail afforded, punctuate the statutes of the General Chapter down to about 1240, and include differences between Grandselve and Gimont (1208, 1225–29)[100], Clairefontaine and Cherlieu (1215)[101], Furness and Jervaulx (1226)[102], Furness and Fountains (1227–29)[103] and Merevale and Stanlaw (1238)[104]. Mediation might see definite boundaries placed between the respective 'spheres of influence' of abbeys with adjacent pastures, as the Rhondda Fawr separating pastures of Llantarnam and Margam, and a headwater of the Rheidol delineating those of Cwmhir and Strata Marcella[105].

Transhumance

The movement of flocks to summer pastures in the mountains or winter grazing lands by the coast was not a Cistercian invention, but it was a seasonal phenomenon which they utilised in no small measure, from (at latest) the mid-twelfth century[106]. Animals from abbeys in both Spain and France moved into the Pyrenees, and flocks from both France and Italian monasteries into the Alps. It may not have been shortage of pasture so much

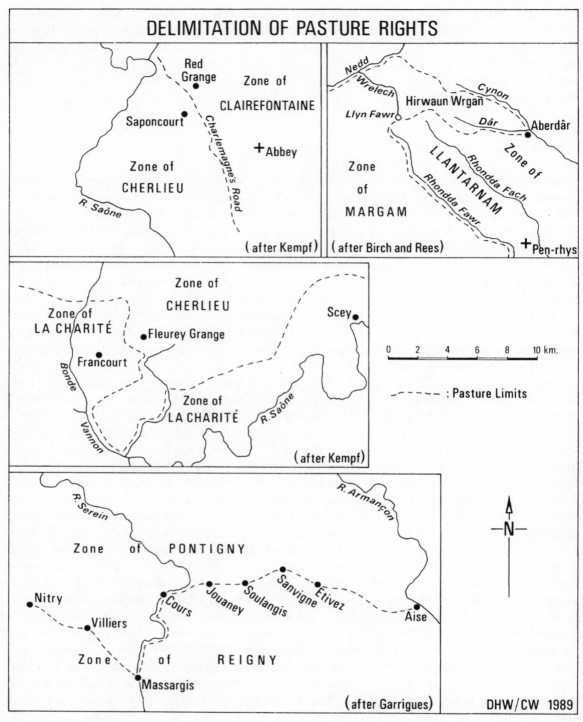

as climatic reasons (heat in summer especially) that prompted the practice[107]. Once again, it became necessary to secure rights to pasture, and wayleaves and halting-places *en route*. Such grants frequently specify the numbers of animals permitted, and allow the routes taken to be plotted[108]. The distances travelled could be considerable, but a word of caution is necessary, for the permission granted to an abbey for summer pastures might not mean that flocks walked all the way from the monastery, but perhaps only from a grange more proximate to those pastures. Transhumance involved the erection of suitable 'cabins' for the keepers, and resulted in a considerable production of cheese, as the milk produced in remote areas needed to be utilised on the spot.

Transhumance up to the Pyrenees was practised by Poblet and Santes Creus before 1177, when arbitration saw the *puertos* of Peguera and Lanos assigned to Poblet and the *puertos* of Portes and Barrades to Santes Creus[109]. The flocks of Poblet's Cérvoles Grange (1180) utilised summer pastures at Cerdaña and Bergaden[110]. Amongst other Spanish abbeys utilising the Pyrenees was Nogales, which was given exemption from transit tolls by Alfonso X in 1254 and Sancho IV in 1283 – who specified the numbers of animals so privileged: 1,500 head of cattle, 1,600 sheep, 500 goats and 100 horses. Some years before, Castañeda had been allowed 800 cattle, 1,000 sheep, and 100 mares[111]. From the French side of the Pyrenees came the flocks of Bonnefont, its highest pastures being over 2,000 metres in the valley of the Rioumajou. A deed of 1189 had allowed the passage at one point of 1,500 of its calves[112]. L'Escale-Dieu retained cabins for its shepherds at its first site, Cabadour (1,050 metres) in the Gripp valley[113]. Grandselve's animals, with transhumant pastures at Ravat, were allowed by the canons of Combelongue to rest and be fed and watered on their pastures, for three days on going up, and three days on coming down[114]. Fontfroide, from its grange of Parahou led flocks to pastures in the county of Foix, from its granges of Canemals and Poujolz to Py (then in Aragon), and also received rights in the valley of the Aude (then in Catalonia, now in France).

Grandselve also moved flocks up into the Central Massif[115], as did Chambons (with pasture on the plateau of Lugdanes and a halting-place near Joyeuse)[116], Aiguebelle (leading to conflicts with the shepherds of Mazan)[117], Fontfroide (to the Montagne Noire, in the Cevennes) and Valmagne and Silvanès (also in the Cevennes, well north of Béziers)[118]. Aiguebelle, moving its flocks to pasture by Lake d'Issarlis in the Alpine foothills, was accorded free passage by the priory of Croix-Géorand on condition that the number of beasts did not exceed 3,600 ewes, and that it paid the priory annually half a quintal of cheese and 9 *sols tournois*. The animals were to go up in late March or early April and come down in the autumn[119]. Bonnevaux (1122) might pasture flocks in 'the Charmenson alps' – the limits were fixed in the presence of Queen Matilda[120] – and at La Chaudière for its animals from Chomeane Grange[121]. Léoncel and Valcroissant also moved flocks high into the lower Alps[122]. Animals of Franquevaux (in the Camargue) came north to pastures in the Durance valley on the Montagne du Lubéron and near Sisteron[123]. Casanova[124] and Rivalta Scrivia[125] found pastures in the east of the Alps, as did San-Godenzo in the Appenines[126].

What has been termed 'inverse transhumance' – the movement of flocks to lower altitudes rather than to higher – was a feature of houses with adverse conditions in winter[127]. Chiefest of these was Léoncel, 900 metres high in the Alpine foothills, with extensive winter pasture rights in the Plain of Valence and further south as far as the Drôme valley[128]. One of its routes south lay across the plateau of La Vacherie[129]. Valmagne wintered its flocks in the Camargue (at Ulmet), with an intermediate stop *en route* in the 'garrigues' west of Montpellier[130]. Bonneval, too, sent its flocks in winter to the Camargue, where the local monasteries of Franquevaux and Sauvereal had their grazing[131]. Flocks of Santes Creus pastured in winter on its coastal pastures, acquired in 1177, at Albinyana, Roda and Salastre[132]. Little has been written about monastic transhumance elsewhere in Europe, though it has been postulated on a small scale in the mountains of Wales[133] and the Pennines[134].

Stock-rearing

As early as 1153, *conversi* of Clairvaux brought back home ten fine cattle from Italy for breeding purposes[135], and in the later Middle Ages pedigree cattle were raised for sale by abbeys such as Furness[136], Poblet[137] and Staffarda[138]. Despite the ascendancy of

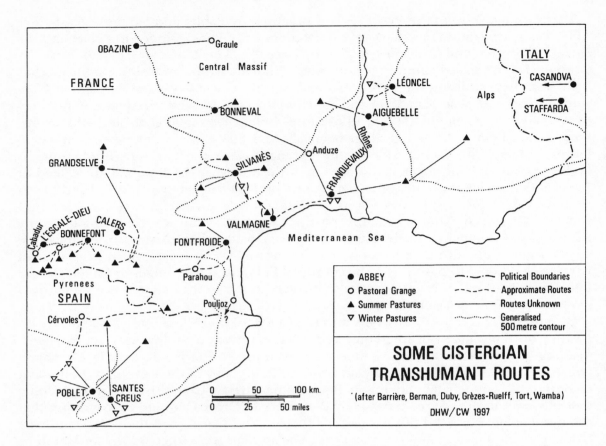

SOME CISTERCIAN TRANSHUMANT ROUTES

(after Barrière, Berman, Duby, Grèzes-Ruelff, Tort, Wamba)

DHW/CW 1997

sheep in the thirteenth century cattle remained vital for ploughing, skins, and transport. Beaulieu (1270) had some 1,300 cattle, of which 650 were oxen, 300 cows, and 16 bulls[139]. Margam had the right to pasture on Cefn Cribwr alone 50 oxen, 30 cows, and 40 steers and heifers[140]. Holy Cross (1297) had 42 oxen devoted to ploughing[141], whilst a charter granted to Rievaulx made it clear there were 8 oxen in one ploughteam[142]. The usages of the *conversi* demanded that when the oxen were grazing out in the fields, their herders were to watch over them by night[143]. Didier was 'keeper of the oxen' at Tamié (1216)[144]; at Tintern's Merthyr Gerain Grange (1388) candles were bought for the use of the drover by night, and a chamber made for him in the byre[145]. At Morimondo Milano's Home Grange the herdsmen slept in rooms around the sides of the large ox-house[146]. At Hailes a new byre was built in 1299[146a]. For Melrose Abbot Matthew (1246–61) built many 'cow-houses and houses for oxen'[147].

Such vaccaries were important for dairy produce. Immediately south-west of Léoncel was 'La Vacherie' – its dairy grange[148]. The vaccary of Cymer stood next to its cemetery[149]. Vaccaries might lie on lands well removed from the abbey; like Fountains' Stonethwaite dairy farm in Nidderdale[150], and Jervaulx's vaccaries at Blean and Mousethwaite in Wensleydale[151]. Vaccaries were prized possessions, and when a Welsh prince confiscated Strata Marcella's vaccary at Pennant-tigi in Mallwyd, the abbey persisted in reclaiming it[152]. Holm Cultram went so far as to gain permission from King John (1215) and Honorius III (1217) to convert St Hilda's hermitage at Islekirk into a vaccary for forty cows[153]..Berthold was 'master of the cows' at Salem (1274)[154]; Savigny (1230) had its 'dairy *conversi*'[155]. Dairying allowed the production of butter and cheese, supplied by five granges of Beaulieu to the abbey[156]. Obazine's distant Graule Grange specialised in cheese-making[157]; it was the norm on summer pastures, and there is record of cheese production on Morimondo Milano's Fornace Grange (1237)[158]. A 'good cheese' called 'Swaichaese' was regularly eaten in the refectory of Heiligenkreuz

(1196)[159], and Bildhausen made its 'Monks' Cheeses' – sought after by Fulda Abbey[160]. Eberbach (1219) produced several kinds of cheese[161]. Cheese could also be obtained in kind-rents: Raitenhaslach (1334) received 9,500 cheeses each year from its tenants[162]. A grant of 25 *Mans shillings* allowed Perseigne (1208) each St Andrew's-tide to buy in butter for its community[163].

Trading in horses was a Cistercian speciality from early days, judging by the careful provisions regarding it laid down by the General Chapter. It ruled in 1158 that, except for horses retained for an abbey's own use, all horses reared on monastic land were to be sold 'before bridle or saddle are put upon them', i.e. before they were 'broken'. Other versions of the same statute give 2½ years as the upper age limit, or stipulated that they must be sold by the time 'they have changed four teeth'. This somewhat later version of the 1158 statute allowed the horses to be broken before they were sold; they could be bridled but not yet saddled, still less trained to run. Further, horse sales were only to take place at the abbey or on the granges, not at markets and fairs[164]. Breaches of this rule led the General Chapter (1184) to demand that abbots who had sent colts to market bring the illicit money so received to Chapter for distribution amongst the poorer abbots of the Order[165]. A further statute (1233) reminded abbots, especially those of Gascony and Spain, that their horses' trappings were not to be ostentatious or out of the ordinary[166].

Horses needed pasture: granted to Holm Cultram in Allerdale[167], and bought by Furness in the Pennines[168]. Horses bore monastic officials on their duties: Michaelstein (1311) received pasture rights, saying that it could not hold a court without horses[169]. Horses took abbots and monks on the business of their house: a tenant of Holm Cultram in Carlisle (1300) had it, as a condition of his lease, that he build there: 'A stable for seven horses'[170]. Horses might be obliged to pull the monastery ploughs, as at Camp (1288)[171]. They could be used in barter: Bonnevaux (1165) received pasture rights in exchange for a horse[172]; Margam (1202) gave two horses in part-payment for the fee of Llangewydd[173]. A donor to Furness requested that its monks give him: 'A horse, such as might be honourable for them to bestow and for him to receive'[174]. Horses formed suitable gifts: as the dapple-grey palfrey Byland (1237) gave Henry III[175]. In their turn, monasteries might welcome bequests of horses. A descendant of the founder, wishing to be buried at St Bernard-opt-Scheldt (1266), left it a horse with its trappings[176]. Bishop Svend of Århus (1183) bequeathed to Øm all his wild horses grazing on the Djursland Peninsula[177]. Øm valued its horses; when Germans rustlers stole some (*c.* 1248), the abbot followed in pursuit of them and was badly wounded[178].

Quite early in the Middle Ages abbeys with wide open spaces, as Furness, Jervaulx[179] and Walkenried[180], were rearing fine steeds. Prince Gwenwynwyn (1190) expected an annual 'acknowledgement' from Basingwerk of two colts of its 'superior breed'[181]. Ter Doest had its 'excellent horses' noted as early as 1302[182]. Those of Jervaulx were later (1537) to be described as 'the tried breed in the north'[183]. When Henry III (1236) sought two palfreys, one from Jervaulx and one from Rievaulx, he specified that they were to be 'of the northern parts, good and fit'[184]. It was common practice for itinerant English monarchs to seek strong horses to move the treasury or the rolls of chancery from place to place. The abbot of Holm Cultram (1292), ordered to provide a horse to carry the rolls of chancery, promised to do so but referred to 'the wonderful scarcity of horses' that year[185]. As war with Scotland ended (1304), both Kirkstall[186] and Sallay[187] were commanded to provide a cart with four horses and two men to convey the exchequer from York to Westminster. Beaulieu (1309, 1332) was ordered to provide a 'strong horse' for like duty[188]. In Scotland, the Clydesdale breed may have descended from the horses of Newbattle[189]. In France, a notable horse-rearing house was Morimond: from its stables knights bought their steeds to ride to the Second Crusade (1146), and both Philip Augustus (1202) and Philip the Fair (1308) purchased mounts[190].

Bran from the monastic bakehouse, dregs from its brewery, and waste from its kitchen, could all form fodder for pigs, and thus be transformed into a source not only of meat and protein but also of lard, and of a valuable commodity for sale[191]. Piggeries were noted both at Rivalta Scrivia (1234) and on its lands[192]. On Morimondo Milano's Home Grange (1237) there were 120 pigs, and also 22 blocks of salted pork[193]. At Beaulieu (1270) the piggery had no less than four hired workers; 6 boars and 14 sows were kept, and of the 178 piglets born that year, 146 were sold and 26 went to the larder of the monastic infirmary[194]. The swineherd on one of Kingswood's granges (1288) was a *conversus*[195]. The General Chapter (1134, 1157) regulated regarding the pasturing of pigs, in the twelfth century at any rate, and so underlined their importance in monastic economy early on. As the grazing for pigs might be in distant woods, it was permitted for their sties to be up to two or three 'leagues' from a grange; the pigs could wander freely by day, but must be back in the sties by nightfall[196] – this to avoid loss, as was the injunction to ensure that newborn piglets were fattened only on monastic pastures[197].

Monasteries often received grants allowing their pigs glandage in forests, so as to feed on nuts and acorns. Oak and beech woods were especially suitable, and the relevant charters may, again, lay down numerical and seasonal restrictions – a touch of medieval conservation! From these a glimpse into the numbers involved is obtained. Morimond had 20 piggeries in the forest of Bassigny, each raising from 200 to 300 beasts, giving a total of some 6,000 head[198]. Cherlieu was granted pannage (in 1212) in Liége and Mouhy Woods for 100 pigs apiece, and (1270) in Preigney Wood for 120[199]. Fontmorigny (1212) had pannage rights, again for 100 pigs, in the woods of Lurcy[200]. In a grant of pannage to St Benoît-en-Woëvre (1165) at Tilly-sur-Meuse, in return for a 'recognizance' of 6 *deniers châlonnais*, its pigs could graze from Easter to St Remigius' Day (1 October), with timber to make a hut there for winter[201]. Holm Cultram had pannage in Allerdale and Engleswood from Michaelmas (29 September) to Martinmas (11 November), perhaps for fattening purposes[202]. Newminster received a like grant for 'about Martinmas'[203]. Pigsties were owned by Bordesley in Feckenham Forest and by Stanley in Chippenham Forest, both rich in oak and beech[204]. Beech was also abundant in Pomerania, allowing Loccum to have 133 swine at its hog-farm on the Böchenberg near Detmold[205].

In those regions with a relatively dry and warm 'Mediterranean' climate, and with sometimes thorny vegetation and scrub, goats came to the fore. In northern lands, they were seen as a nuisance, damaging as they did the woodlands of Strata Florida[206], and being excepted from some grants of common pasture such as those to Newminster (1297)[207] and Kirkstall (1329)[208]. In Spain and southern France they were numerous. Gimont had many, and Grandselve its 'goat-pen'[209]. Goats could be used in barter: Gimont (1176) gave thirty-five in return for some land[210]. At Poblet, in 1316, the number of goats (1500) even exceeded the number of sheep (1215)[211]. They are listed in transhumance way-leaves, as for Nogales (1293)[212]: their milk then must have been useful. In cooler and damper and better grassed northern lands, rabbits abounded. Many abbeys acquired rights of free warren – not least Clairvaux, which built up its interests in this respect by 1179 until at least 1250[213]. Free warren was often restricted to the lands actually belonging to a monastery, as at Boxley[214], Quarr[215] and Stratford – the latter enjoying the right in some fifteen localities[216]. Margam had a natural territory for rabbits, the nearby coastal Burrows (sand-dunes)[217]. Holm Cultram was given free warren in Flimby, with the stipulation that poachers there were to be fined 10 shillings[218]. Kingswood had a 'conygre' near Haselden[219].

The remains of dovecots are frequently to be seen within monastic precincts, as at Bonport, Fontenay, and Garendon[220], and on former granges, like the 'colver-houses' on lands of Neath[221], at Chaâlis Vaulerent Grange, and on the 'Granges' of Longpont.

Doves formed a source of egg-supply, of meat useful in winter, and of natural manure. There is note of their being built on lands of Newenham (1330)[222] and of Sibton (1325)[223]. The stream name of 'Nant Colomendy' at Whitland[224] points to a former dovecot there, and excavation has proved one at Tintern[225]. In Ireland, Mellifont had four dovecots, whilst the stone, circular, domed dovecot with central oculus still remains at Kilcooly[226]. In France, many dovecots were circular with a diameter around 8 metres[227], but those of Beaubec and Breuil-Benoît were octagons[228]. Some remaining (as at L'Aumône and Vaux-de-Cernay) date from the thirteenth century, but with conical tops fashioned in the sixteenth century or later[229]. The dovecot (octagonal and in red brick) at Vauclair dates from the seventeenth century, but is on the foundations of an earlier circular edifice. In Scotland, a dovecot was contained in the granary gable at Balmerino[230]. As for poultry, few figures exist, perhaps because they were common-place adjuncts. Beaulieu (1270) distributed over 17,000 eggs in pittances, but most were bought[231]. At Kingswood (1240)[232] and Beaulieu[233] geese were bought for the monastic infirmary.

The early statutes of the Order (1134) forbade its monks to 'go shares in the raising of cattle with seculars'[234], a restriction repeated as late as 1214[235]. Some authors see this as prohibiting the white monks from enjoying common in pasture owned by others without acquiring exclusive rights[236]. Could it, however, refer to more formal arrangements, whereby (as in the Alps by 1230) animals of other pastoralists contracted to share in grazing lands exclusive to the Cistercians?[237] The inclusion of such 'alien animals' in their flocks benefited the monks of Léoncel (1284), who received half of their new-born in return for guarding them and feeding them with pasture, water and salt[238]. The practice was clearly widespread by 1260, when Alexander IV exempted Grandselve from paying tithes on the new-born of such flocks entrusted to its care by others[239].

Sheep Rearing and Wool Production

By the close of the twelfth century, it was possible for the chronicler William of Newburgh to write that wool formed 'the chiefest part of the substance' of the white monks[240] – a view-point also taken by Matthew Paris in the next century[241]. The significance of wool in monastic economy was shown (again before the twelfth century was out) when each English Cistercian abbey gave one year's wool crop towards the ransom of Richard I[242], and by Meaux converting cattle byres into sheepfolds[243]. Its chronicler later wrote of those times that wool was more profitable a commodity than meat, for: 'Five sheep could find pasture where only a single ox could feed'[244]. In the thirteenth century the emphasis on rearing sheep was helped not only by Honorius III (1221) exempting the Order from paying tithes on its wool and lambs[245], but also by the ready and increasing market for good wool to be found in the textile industries of Flanders, and later in Italy. Sheep remained a mainstay in the welfare of many houses, and some (as Bruern[246], Combermere[247] and Meaux[248]) obtained rulings from several English sovereigns that when distraint had to be made on their goods, their sheep were not to be touched but rather their other livestock and goods. Sheep may not have 'always and everywhere' been dominant, and the Cistercian 'sheep age' may have lasted only from about 1175 to 1325[249], but Flaxley recorded (in 1281) that its monks 'mainly depended upon its sheep'[250].

Sheep could bring income, if sold: sheep and lambs from distant Bordesley and Vaudey were sought (about 1230) for the bishop of Chichester's estates[251]. They could be used in barter; as in transactions of Huerta[252] and of Netley[253]. Their milk was useful for cheese-making; Camp in 1312 produced some 500 sheep-cheeses each year (valued at 45 *guilders*) from one large flock alone at Hönnepel on the Rhine[254]. Wensleydale cheese may have evolved from the cheese of Jervaulx[255], whilst Bronnbach received sheep-cheeses (as well as half the lambs and wool) on leasing out a flock of sheep[256]. The sheep-skins of Himmerod[257] and Beaulieu provided parchment for documents; at Beaulieu (where half were sold) they were also used for making 'woolly blankets' and lining hoods[258]. Froidmont (1230) gained no small income by selling some 7,000 sheep-skins[259].

The value of monastic sheep was also shown in the efforts of rustlers. When some 400 sheep of the Dunes (1253) were stolen, the thieves had to pay 30 *flanders pounds* in compensation[260]. An aggrieved prior of (non-Cistercian) Stone (1264) raided Hulton's Normacot grange, driving away 300 of its sheep[261]. Sheep-rearing was sometimes precarious. In 1270, of the 1,313 lambs born on the lands of Beaulieu no less than 690 died from 'murrain', leaving only 623 new sheep[262] – a terrific loss. The flock would have been greater if a number of ewes had not been sterile and others had not aborted their offspring[263]. Murrain was to be at least partly responsible for the severe debts some sheep-rearing abbeys mounted up in the 1280s. As for 'scab', the *Annals of Waverley* told of the invention of a compound of quicksilver and pig grease to try to treat it[264].

Cistercian monasteries were not the only large herders of sheep. Fountains may have numbered some 18,000 sheep (in 1291), but (in 1259) there were 29,000 on the estates of the bishop of Winchester. Henry Lacy, earl of Lincoln (in 1303) could count 13,000 on his lands[265]. Yet the white monks often did have very large flocks, even on individual granges. Valmagne (1187) kept 1,000 sheep at Omellaz[266], and Zwettl (1311) 2,000 sheep on one of its properties[267]. A single benefaction to La Ferté (1217) by the countess of Chalon-sur-Saône numbered no less than 900 ewes[268]. Mellifont had its 'Sheep Grange'[269] and Jervaulx its 'Woolengrange'[270]. Amongst the grants of pasture to Melrose were rights for 1,500 wethers in Haddington, 700 ewes in Galloway and 500 sheep in Wedale[271]. Sallay might keep 480 sheep at Marton in the Aire valley in summer, but in winter 720 were brought down there from surrounding hill pastures[272]. A donor to Kirkstall required that 400 of the abbey's sheep be folded on his land, so as to manure it[273]. Kingswood practised careful breeding, buying in rams from as far afield as distant Lindsey[274]. The grant to Melrose in Wedale allowed a site there for 'a cow-house or sheepfold', and another house in which a fire could be lit for the *conversi* and their lay shepherds[275].

Sheepfolds (bercaries – though this is a variable term) were important to collect sheep together, and sheepcots to shelter them in bad weather. Meaux had eight sheep-folds in Sutton in Holderness, with over 2,000 sheep pastured[276]. Hulton (1237) enclosed a sheepfold at Mixon Hay with a ditch, and established a sheepwalk there of 240 acres (100 ha)[277]. The size of cots varied: ¹/₂ acre in one case of Rievaulx (1152), but 3 acres in an instance of Fountains (1180)[278]. A grant of pasture in Distington to Holm Cultram (1220) was accompanied by building materials for folds and cots[279]. Some cots had stone walls, as still evident on former lands of Casanova[280]. Other cots might be formed by no more than brushwood hedges. In Wedale Melrose made wattle cots[281]. Tilty (1251) made cots out of 'alder, thorns and dead wood'. Fountains roofed cotes with ferns: its Greenbury Grange had a roofed bercary 260 ft (80 metres) long. The bercary of Meaux's Wharram Grange extended for 160 ft (50 metres)[282]. At Sibton's North Grange (1325) was a bercary with 'gate and sheep-house'[283]. A sheep-house, 'Wether Cote', survives 200 ft (60 metres) above Rievaulx's Skiplam Grange[284]. Sheep-house names survive in Wales, as in 'Sheepfold Farm' on Margam's former manor at Bonvilston[285].

The *Bergerie* account for Beaulieu (1270) shows that it had oversight of the monastery's sheep, wheresoever grazing – save for those on its lands in Cornwall and

the Isle of Wight. The 'master of the bercary', either a monk or a *conversus*, had manifold duties. He paid the wages of the shepherds, and had to arrange and pay for the
building and repairing of sheepcots, the washing and shearing of the sheep, the sale of
wool and the carriage of some to the abbey, and the making of hay in autumn, as well
as the making of carts and wool sacks[286]. (A Beaulieu 'sack', when full, weighed 30 lbs
[13·5 kg][287]. Kingswood (1263) employed over thirty shepherds[288], and (like
Beaulieu[289]) gave them a special pre-Lenten meal each Shrove Tuesday. The duties of
the bercary-master at Beaulieu were probably paralleled by Martin, a monk and
'master of the flocks' of Léoncel (1212)[290], though lower down the Gervanne valley (at
St Julien) it had its 'master of the sheep' – one John of Bain (1244) – to care for those
pastured on the plateau of Font d'Urle[291].

When the time came for sheep to be sheared (twice a year for the lambs of
Waldsassen [1276])[293], the Order (1154/60) had early ruled that, whilst monks could go
to the granges to help in the corn harvest, they might not leave the cloister to assist in
shearing sheep[294]. These often had to be moved to a monastic shearing-centre, and
thus required especial way-leaves and grazing rights *en route*. From these it can be
ascertained that Fountains moved sheep in Wharfedale to Kettlewell[295], and Sibton
from its Tuddenham Grange (near Mildenhall) *via* Herringswell to the river Kennet
(Cambridgeshire). The latter grant (of 1200) was for up to 1,500 sheep[296]. Warden had
pasture in West Warden (1205) for 200 sheep, but double that number in shearing-
time[297]. Beaulieu washed sheep in the Thames near Radcot[298], and, for its lands in
Lancashire, Dieulacres had a right of way from Rossall to wash its sheep in Little
Bispham Mere[299]. Kirkstead had its 'Sheepwash Grange' on the south bank of the river
Witham: the wool then perhaps went downstream to the abbey and on to Boston[300].
Similarly, Buildwas had free passage for sheep from its Harnage Grange going to be
washed in the river Severn at Cressage. The permission given also allowed the loading
of barges there, suggesting shipment of the wool down the river to Bristol[301].

The Wool Trade

Much has been published regarding British Cistercian wool exports to the Continent,
but there was also a substantial home trade of which relatively little is known[302]. Holm
Cultram (*c*. 1200) sold wool to the towns of southern Scotland[303]. Dundrennan (1266)
had a two-way trade, taking wool for sale in England and bringing back corn to
Scotland[304]. Beaulieu[305], Combe and Pipewell sold wool to the English Crown (1297)[306],
Dieulacres[307] and Basingwerk (its 'excellent wool')[308] to the Black Prince (1347), and
Combe (1332) to a citizen of Coventry[309]. By this time, Roche, Furness and Kirkstall
were sending wool to northern cloth-making towns, such as Beverley, Doncaster,
Leeds and Pontefract[310]. A major outlet were markets and fairs. In one year, Holm
Cultram (1275) had available at Skinburness Fair £472-worth of wool: 31½ sacks of its
'best' wool, 7 of medium grade and 8 of the short 'locks'[311]. The greatest English wool
market was Boston Fair in Lincolnshire (with foreign merchants in attendance), and to
this came wool from at least eighteen Cistercian houses: some far afield – as Holm
Cultram and Melrose. Several of these abbeys, if not all, acquired accommodation and
warehousing in the town. There is specific note of the passage to Boston of wool from
Vaudey (50 sacks in 1275)[312], Fountains (to help, in 1276, to pay off its debts to the
Crown)[313], Combermere (in 1283, on its own carts)[314], and Stanlaw (in 1284, with safe-
conduct from the king)[315]. Such Cistercian trade was resented by other dealers, their
prices often undercut by monastic wool sold relatively cheaply as a result of freedom
from passage tolls and market dues[316].

There were objections in Lincolnshire to abbeys – like Louth Park and Meaux –

collecting wool from neighbouring estates and selling it with their own, thus depriving the Crown and the market towns concerned of revenue[317]. Such a practice had been outlawed by the Order (1157+), which ruled not only that monastic wool was not to be sold at exorbitant prices, but that wool was not to be bought from others for resale[318]. Some English *conversi* (in 1214) did exactly that, making a profit on their transactions[319]. It was with this in mind that King John (1212), giving customs clearance for Strata Florida to send wool overseas, allowed it 'only to declare its own wool'[320]. The Crown (1237) forbade the practice of sale and resale by the Cistercians in Rutlandshire because of 'public outcry'[321], and also prohibited it for a time in Lincolnshire (1262–68)[322]. The fifty sacks taken by Vaudey to Boston, and the seventy-two sacks later taken there by Meaux (1270/80), contained much wool collected from other producers[323]. It was a practice Kirkstead (1285–8), with royal leave, had to undertake in order to find the wool already paid for by foreign merchants – its own supply laid low because of the scourge of murrain[324]. In 1287 Meaux was under contract to sell to the Cerchi, merchants of Florence, no less than 108 sacks of such 'collected' wool[325]. The practice of taking in wool from other estates could of course be advantageous to smaller religious houses which may not have had the means perhaps to trade efficiently on their own behalf; for them, as for the prioress of Arden[326], the Cistercians were very necessary middle-men.

Overseas trade by the British Cistercians until the reign of Henry III may have been mostly with a variety of merchants – Danish, Hanseatic, Italian and Spanish – but at the latest by 1225 and until 1275 the emphasis was on the export of wool to Flanders[327]. Known licences from British monarchs for Cistercian trade in wool abroad date from the time of King John, and the large amount carried is implied in those permissions which allowed a whole shipload. Some refer in general terms to export 'overseas', as those in favour of Strata Florida (1212)[328], Melrose[329] and Kirkstall (1224)[330]. Others, like those to Garendon[331], Byland and Jervaulx (1225)[332], permit trade with Flanders, though Henry III disallowed any wool exports to those areas of Flanders controlled by the king of France. Trade with Flanders was certainly in progress two decades earlier, as evidenced by a dispute between several British wool-producing monasteries and the burgesses of St Omer (1207)[333]. Margam sold wool to Ghent (1250) and Douai (1271)[334], but the revolt of the Barons (1265) briefly interrupted the Flanders trade[335]. Kingswood, Pipewell and other houses were, by 1272, in debt to Flemish merchants[336].

Henry III (in 1272)[337] and Edward I (in 1275)[338] prohibited the sale of wool (save by Fountains) to Flanders, largely because of a disagreement with the countess of Flanders. Pipewell and Tintern, for example, were 'to take their wool elsewhere'. The Flemish market may also have become less attractive to British abbeys as the merchants of Flanders may not have been able to offer such large loans on wool sold in advance as the Italian traders-cum-money-collectors who largely replaced them[339]. Several abbeys (Kingswood, Neath and Stanley) continued to have dealings in Flanders, as with the burgesses of Ghent, in 1282[340], whilst Combermere was owing wool to a merchant of Ypres as late as 1313[341]. The political map of France by now allowed exports also to other centres, such as Bordeaux, Cahors and Montpellier[342], though the Gascon trade was rudely interrupted by war in 1294[343]. In a detailed contract with Pipewell (1290) meant to last for thirteen years, merchants of Cahors paid the abbey over £3,000 and effectively took control of 900 of the monastery's sheep (half ewes, half rams), which the monks were to care for as if their own. The wool of those sheep was each year to be 'prepared, packed and weighed' and delivered at Boston Fair, where a special wool-shed was to be built[344].

In France itself there was a substantial indigenous monastic supply of wool to the drapers of Douai, Liège and elsewhere, from very large-scale producers such as the abbey of the Dunes[345]. As early as 1160 four great abbeys, including Ourscamp, sent wool to the ancient textile centre of Arras[346]. In the course of time Clairmarais sold wool to drapers of St Omer[347], and Val-St-Lambert to those in Liège[348]. Cambron had some 4,000 sheep, perhaps grazing on its granges in eastern Zeeland, notably in the vicinty of Hulst[349]. Longvilliers sold (in 1279) 200 lbs (90 kg) of wool to two patricians of Douai alone. Ter Doest, in 1315, raised 877 *livres* in local currency from its wool sales, (almost as much as it normally received from selling grain); in addition, it gained that year 257 *livres* from the sale of sheep[350]. Little has been published regarding the wool trade of many houses, but Grandselve found an outlet amongst the clothiers of Languedoc at Toulouse[351], and Pforta in the markets of neighbouring towns[352]. Clairvaux (1340) was lent 150 *livres tournois* by the Order on the security of its wool[353].

British Cistercian wool trade with Italy was facilitated when, in the late thirteenth century, representatives of merchant companies (mostly based in Florence) such as the Bardi, the Frescobaldi and the Peruzzi, settled in England to collect papal taxes[354]. Florentine agents were buying wool from Bordesley by 1275[355] and Fountains not later than 1276[356]. Later that century merchants of Lucca were also heavily involved, and the Italian trade extended to Irish abbeys (as Duiske)[357] and Scottish monasteries (as Coupar and Melrose)[358]. The practice of selling several years' wool in advance in return for substantial monetary loans brought several monasteries into a state of grave debt, especially in the 1280s when murrain was widespread. Amongst those in debt to merchants of Lucca were Vale Royal (1288)[359], Kirkstall (by 1296)[360] and Duiske (in 1299). Debts varied from the £466-13-4 owed by Duiske[361] to the £6,473 in which Fountains (1291) was bound[362]. The system had too an inbuilt disadvantage, for after a price had been agreed and paid by the merchants, wool prices might rise and the monasteries thus lose out[363]. The *Register of Holm Cultram* (about 1294) listed in full 'the names of our merchants' – four agents or partners of the Society of Pullici and Rambertini[364] – suggesting perhaps that monasteries stuck with those companies with which they had become accustomed to deal.

An indication of the amount of monastic wool for sale is suggested by Pegolotti's late-thirteenth century list of wool-producing monasteries in Britain[365]. Its figures for the leading abbeys, Fountains, Rievaulx, and Jervaulx, of 76, 60 and 50 sacks respectively, tally well in proportional order with the numbers of sheep listed for those houses in the near contemporary *Taxatio Ecclesiastica* (1291) – 18,000, 14,000, and 12,000 animals respectively. Some houses had relatively little wool, as remote Calder – only four sacks[366]. The best quality wool (and, therefore, the higest priced) came from Dore and Tintern[367]. (Estimates of a 'sack' vary. If each contained 200 fleeces, then 6,000 sheep would be necessary to produce thirty sacks. Weights were not uniform until 1357: prior to that each sack was probably about 28 stone in weight[368].) Pegolotti's list is also of value in that it notes local conditions, as at Margam which (in the unknown year of survey) was making 'neither medium nor inferior wool'[369]. The list is best seen as a general qualitative guide rather than a precise indicator of monastic economy. Several questions are posed. Did the list include all the wool each monastery produced, or only that designated for sale to a particular merchant? Did it include not solely monastery wool but also wool which came to it by collection from smaller producers, and, in some cases, from tithes? Did it represent the figures of one year only – which might or might not have been affected by murrain?[370] It has also been pointed out that the prices Pegolotti quoted included the cost of carriage to Flanders and the profit due to the merchants[371].

Each producing abbey had a monk or *conversus* as its 'brother woolman' (as Vaudey in 1276)[372] or 'wool merchant' (as Tintern in 1272)[373]. They were responsible for negotiating with the merchants from Flanders and Italy, sometimes at their monastery, sometimes elsewhere: necessary arrangements in the 1270s for Darnhall (Vale Royal) and Newminster were drawn up in London[374]. The monastic 'wool-men' would oversee the preparation of the wool for sale, and its dry and clean storage. Merchants expected the wool to be 'well washed, dry and cleaned, and packed' (as by Pipewell, 1290)[375], and 'prepared and weighed' (as by Fountains, 1276)[376]. They looked to the quality of the wool and to its accurate measurement. When Dore's brand-new daughter-house of Vale Royal was selling wool to a merchant of Cambrai (1275), he laid down that it was to be: 'As good wool as the better crop of Dore, to be weighed by the weight of Dore'[377]. Meaux's 'woolhouse' on Wawne Grange was built (about 1240) of stone (to lessen the risk of such a valuable commodity being destroyed by fire), and roofed with lead (to keep the wool dry)[378]. The wool-house of Fountains, also rebuilt in the early thirteenth century, had two coppers giving a copious supply of hot water, possibly to help in dyeing[379] – though the colouring of wool had been proscribed by the Order (1195)[380]. Byland used its Thorpe Grange, strategically sited in the Coxwold/Gilling Gap, as a storage centre for 'collected' wool[381]. Beaulieu, perhaps by 1326, built a 'wool-house' in Southampton, a major outlet for trade with France[382].

Once ready for export, wool was transported by 'wagons, packhorses and carts' (Holm Cultram, c. 1280)[383]. Way-leaves were sought, and the wool taken either to riverside collecting points – where merchants would be waiting (as Hereford in the case of Dore[384], and Clifton-on-Ouse in the instance of Fountains)[385] – or direct to ports (as Bristol for Margam[386], Chester for Aberconwy[387], Hull for Meaux[388], Newcastle-upon-Tyne for Holm Cultram[389], Southampton for Beaulieu[390] and Margam[391], and above all, Boston with its fair). A number of abbeys sent wool to London for temporary storage before export overseas – as Bordesley (1224)[392], Vaudey (1276)[393] and Woburn (1265)[394]. Lesser inland river ports also used in the initial shipment of Cistercian wool included Lincoln[395] and Norwich[396]. The licences permitting wool export show that early summer and autmn were the commonest times for transhipment abroad. Alas! this great trade was to be severely cut back by the mid-fourteenth century, though by no means extinguished, and monasteries sold increasingly to English middlemen[397]. The age of great profits was over. The Hundred Years' War cutting off communication routes, the Black Death reducing direct monastic wool output, the bankruptcy of some great Italian merchants, and the growth of the monopoly of the wool-exporting Company of Staplers[398] brought to an end a potentially lucrative direct trade which had earned the Cistercians considerable income, but also made them the target of severe criticism, even of satire[399].

Fulling Mills

Cloth production taking place within or near abbey precincts has been described, but was sometimes to be found on granges as well – as at Alcobaça's aptly-named 'Vestiaria' Grange[400]. Little is known of Cistercian trade in cloth, though some monasteries as Amelunxborn[401] and Grandselve[402] were very active in this field. One indication of cloth-making comes in the possession of fulling mills: no less than twenty-seven eventually belonged to the Cistercians in Wales – four of them in the traditional cloth-making area of the Teifi valley[403]. Some fulling mills (especially in the later Middle Ages in England) were leased out for a cash return, so not all are proof of monastic cloth-making[404]. Fulling mills were known early in France at Perseigne (c. 1145)[405] and Silvacane (1164)[406]. In England they came to be owned by Cistercian houses from the late twelfth century on[407]. Quarr built an undershot mill on the Isle of Wight in 1198[408]. St Benoît-en-Woëvre received a site for a fulling mill in 1182[409], and Locedio had one at Ramezzana Grange from about 1220[410]. The account book of Beaulieu (1270) tells of repairs, and new wheels, for its fulling-mill, and contains a sketch of what appears to be such a mill[411]. Imported fulling clay has been excavated close to a mill at Løgum[412].

Corn– and fulling– mill might be in close proximity. This was true of those of Silvacane at Promillac (1164), where were noted: 'Two mills; one for fulling and the other for grinding, under one roof'[413]. In Wales where corn- and fulling- mill were often on the same water-course, the fulling-mill or 'pandy' was the less valuable 'poor relation'. Margam's 'Sheep's Mill' was on the same leat as its Cryke corn mill, and its mills in Llanfeuthin – the 'monkynmill' (corn) and the 'tokyngmill' (fulling) – both lay on Nant Llancarfan[414]. As with corn mills, there could be disputes regarding water-supply; Santes Creus (1226) came to agreement with the Hospital of Coctano regarding the water-course going from its fulling mill at Coctano Grange to the mill of the hospital[415]. Vanished fulling mills may sometimes be traced from place-name evidence (as 'pandy' in Wales), or from field-names (as that called 'tuckmill' near Baltinglass in Ireland)[416].

Notes

1. Berman (1986) 100.
2. Birch (1897) 305.
3. Donkin (1978) 83.
4. *CDAC* 9 (No. 102).
5. Cowley (1977) 84.
6. Waddell (1994) 31.
7. D'Arbois (1858) 56–57.
8. Gimpel (1977) 46.
9. Le Waitte (1673).
10. McCrank (1973) 78.
11. Earle (1906) 36.
12. Williams (1984) II, 305–06.
13. Clark (1895) 189, 203.
14. *RN* xxxv.
15. *AF* 206, 213–14; *cf*. 161.
16. Stéphan (1970) 62.
17. Hill (1968) 76.
18. Donkin (1978) 94–95.
19. Cabanes Pecourt (1982) 478–80.
20. *C. Ch. R*. III, 94.
21. *SBC* IV, 77 (No. 1134, of *c*. 1210).
22. *SBE passim*.
23. Berman (1986) 99*n* (in 1245).
24. *RCC* V, 242 (of 1242).
25. Berman (1986) 101.
26. *C.Ch.R*. III, 94 (of 1280).
27. Donkin (1978) 95, where other such examples.
28. Berman (1978) 303.
29. Kempf (1976) 48 (of 1197).
30. *RHC* 43 (of 1270); *cf*. 1–2, 71.
31. *SBC* II, 199–99 (No. 279; *c*. 1235).
32. Cottam (1928) 82.
33. Berman (1979) 212.
34. Williams (1984) II, 297.
35. Donkin (1978) 75–76.
36. *Ibid*. 76–74.
37. Williams (1984) II, 297–98.
38. *CD* 329.
39. Donkin (1978) 73–74.
40. Fossier (1983) 71.
41. Donkin (1978) 78.
42. Grèzes-Ruellf (1977) 278.
43. Barrière (1983) 83, 87.
44. Bonnet-Laborderie (1985) 16.
45. *CS* I, 41.
46. *AF* 254.
47. *CO* 33 (No. XLIX).
48. Burton (1989) 24.
49. *CAF* 105–06.
50. *CG* 401.
51. *PCP* 193 (No. 131; this grant was primarily for carts).
52. Cottam (1928) 84.
53. Donkin (1978) 75.
54. Morgan (1929) III, 449.
55. *RCC* V, 66.
56. *CBP* 235 (No. CCXXXI).
57. *C.Ch.R*. III, 94.
58. Occhipinti (1985) 327.
59. *PCP* 120 (No. 46), 115 (No. 41), and 340 (No. 335), respectively.
60. Fletcher (1919) 112.
61. *CS* II, 44–45.
62. Donkin (1978) 75 (undated).
63. Platt (1969) 213.
64. *PCP* 109 (No. 34).
65. *RCC* V, 252.
66. Waddell (1994) 31–32.
67. Eckenrode (1973) 257.
68. Donkin (1978) 92.
69. Birch (1897) 305.
70. Noted in more than one chronicle.
71. *CC* (2) B. 45.
72. Charvátová (1987) 125.
73. Eckenrode (1973) 258.
74. See Chapter 15.
75. McDonnell (1963) 436–37.
76. McCrank (1975) 259.
77. Cowley (1977) 83.
78. McCrank (1975) 261.
79. VCH, *Gloucester* II (1907) 94.
80. Berman (1986) 116.
81. *Ibid*. 122.
82. *C.Ch.R*. III, 94–95.
83. Williams (1984) II, 300.
84. VCH, *Lancaster* II (1908) 121.
85. *CC* 2, B. 37.
86. Williams (1984) II, 300.
87. Donkin (1978) 88.
88. *PCP* 135–36 (No. 62).
89. *RD* I, 756 (No. 4534).
90. *RCC* III, 166 (No. 713).
91. *SBC* I, 125.

91a. Lindley (1954) 168 (No. 37).
92. VCH, *Northampton* II (1906) 116.
93. *AF* 224–25.
94. Cowley (1977) 124.
95. *PCP* 118 (No. 45).
96. *CDAC* 180 (No. 226).
97. Wise (1985) vii.
98. McCrank (1975) 273.
99. *CABR* 117–19 (No. 136), 123–29 (No. 140–143), 135–37 (No. 151).
100. *Statuta* I, 353 (1208/36); II, 37 (1225/12), 71 (1228/25), 88–83 (1229/42).
101. *Statuta* I, 446 (1215/55).
102. *Statuta* II, 55 (1226/35).
103. *Statuta* II, 60 (1227/23), 78 (1229/18).
104. *CBW* (2) 512 (No. XXVIII); *Statuta* I, 183–84 (1237/72).
105. Williams (1984) II, 300.
106. Berman (1986) 103.
107. Mousnier (1983c) 225.
108. Berman (1986) 107.
109. Tort (1974) 147, *cf.* 401.
110. Higounet (1989b) 175.
111. Wamba (1986) 176.
112. Samaran (1970) 31.
113. Bouton (1959) I, 136.
114. Berman (1986) 109.
115. Berman (1983) 47.
116. Regné (1922) 245, 251.
117. Berman (1983) 47.
118. Berman (1986) 111.
119. *CDAA* 122–23; *cf.* Duby (1968) 147.
120. *RD* I, 566 (No. 3324).
121. *RD* I, 721–22 (No. 4312).
122. Berman (1983) 47.
123. Berman (1986) 111.
124. *RD* II, 400–01 (No. 8,146, of 1213/1245).
125. *CRS* II, 243 (No. DCCXV, of 1262).
126. Bedini (1964) 159.
127. Couriol (1980) 28.
128. Berman (1986) 105.
129. Couriol (1980) 28.
130. Berman (1986) 111.
131. *Ibid.* 122.
132. Fort i Cogul (1972) 441, (1975) 441.
133. Williams (1984) II, 302–03.
134. *E.g.* Donkin (1978) 75–77.
135. Grand (1950) 478, Roth (1986) 538.
136. *LP* XII: 2, p. 88.
137. McCrank (1973) 58.
138. Boyd (1943) 143.
139. *ABB* 30.
140. NLW, Penrice and Margam Ch. 2067.
141. Carville (1982b) 52.
142. Donkin (1978) 73.
143. *RCOC* 1650 (Cap. X).
144. Bernard (1967) 60.
145. NLW, Badminton Manorial 1571.
146. Occhipinti (1985) 327.
146a. Winkless (1990) 19.
147. *CM* 97.
148. Wullschleger (1991) 83.
149. PRO, LR 1/213, f. 119d.
150. Wright (1972) 1766.
151. *C.Ch.R.* III, 94.
152. Williams (1984) II, 302.
153. *RHC* 76, 78.
154. *CDSL* II, 106.
155. *RSL* II, 229.
156. *ABB* 30.
157. Barrière (1983) 867.
158. Occhipinti (1985) 328.
159. *UKSH* 282–29 (No. XXI).
160. Wagner (1976) 90.
161. Staab (1987) 82.
162. Krausen (1977) 196.
163. *CDP* 158–59 (No. CCLIV).
164. Waddell (1994) 30.
165. *Statuta* I, 95–96 (1184/7).
166. *Statuta* II, 111–12 (1233/4).
167. *RHC* 130 (of 1285).
168. Cottam (1928) 67, 85 (of 1250).
169. Wiswe (1953) 109.
170. *RHC* 16.
171. Jansen (1983) 213.
172. *RD* I, 88 (No. 4,110).
173. NLW, Penrice and Margam Ch. 62.
174. *CBFA* (2) xiv.
175. *C.C.R.* 1236/398, 1237/411.
176. *OSBS* (1) 272 (No. 267).
177. France (1992) 278.
178. McGuire (1976a) 63.
179. Cook (1965) 131–32, Graves (1957) 15.
180. Thompson (1920) 85.
181. Williams (1984) II, 305.
182. *AGN* 92.
183. Fletcher (1919) 114.
184. *C.C.R.* 1236/403.
185. *RHC* 131.
186. Barnes (1982) 63.
187. *CS* II, 187.
188. Hockey (1976) 88–86.
189. Talbot (1939) 29.
190. King (1954) 341–42, 354–55.
191. Astill (1989) 289.
192. *CRS* I, 70–71 (Nos LXVI–LXVII); II, 15 (No. XLVI).
193. Occhipinti (1985) 324.
194. *ABB* 22–29; *cf.* 37.
195. *DCK* 234.
196. Southern (1970) 256; *cf. Statuta* I, 26 (1134/LIX).
197. *Statuta* I, 60 (1157/8); *LCC* (1) 140; *cf. Waddell (1994)* 32.
198. Bouton (1959) II, 248.
199. Kempf (1976) 48.
200. *CAF* 110.
201. *CSBW* 65.
202. *RHC* 29 (No. 74).
203. *CNM* 17.
204. Donkin (1978) 134.
205. Thompson (1920) 84.
206. Williams (1984) II, 304.
207. *CNM* 10, 284.
208. Barnes (1982) 330.
209. Barrière (1983) 83.
210. Berman (1986) 37*n*.
211. Rahlves (1966) 209; *cf.* Tort (1974) 400.
212. Wamba (1981) 176.
213. *RCC* II, 155 (No. 192); III, 241 (No. 800); IV, 67 (No. 1603); V, 175 (No. 1475), 256 (No.1646).
214. VCH, *Kent* II (1926) 153.
215. VCH, *Hampshire* II (1903) 138.

216. VCH, *Essex* II (1907) 130.
217. Williams (1984) II, 304.
218. *RHC* 26.
219. Lindley (1954) 148.
220. Nuttgens (1967) 272.
221. Williams (1984) II, 304.
222. Davidson (1843) 74.
223. *SBE* 41.
224. James (1978) 71.
225. Robinson (1995) 68.
226. Stalley (1987) 175.
227. Aubert (1931) 102, (1947) II, 170–71.
228. Manneville (1979) 214.
229. Aubert (1947) II, 171.
230. Campbell (1899) 300.
231. *ABB* 29.
232. *DCK* 195.
233. *ABB* 29.
234. Waddell (1994) 32.
235. *Statuta* I, 425 (1214/58), 448 (1215/64).
236. Carville (1971) 280, Donkin (1978) 84.
237. Berman (1986) 115.
238. Berman (1983) 48.
239. Mousnier (1983c) 226.
240. Donkin (1978) 135.
241. Graves (1957) 20.
242. Burton (1989) 35.
243. Knowles (1979) I, 72.
244. *Ibid.* 72.
245. Waites (1967) 29.
246. VCH, *Oxford* II (1907) 80 (of 1233).
247. VCH, *Chester* III (1980) 152 (of 1253).
248. Waites (1967) 29 (from King John); *cf. DCK* 192–93; *SBC* II, 35 (No. 29).
249. Donkin (1978) 68.
250. VCH, *Gloucester* II (1907) 95.
251. Donkin (1978) 87.
252. *CMH* 92–93 (No. 57).
253. Meekings (1979) 12.
254. Janssen (1983) 220.
255. Wright (1972) 1769.
256. Scherg (1976) 155–56.
257. Schneider (1954) 124.
258. Hockey (1976) 86.
259. Bonnet-Laborderie (1985) 10.
260. *OHZ* II, 662–65 (Nos 984–85).
261. Tomkinson (1985) 60.
262. *ABB* 31.
263. Talbot (1958) 197–98.
264. Graves (1957) 22–23.
265. Stéphan (1970) 60.
266. Berman (1986) 96.
267. Roth (1986) 532.
268. *DHGE* XVI (1967) 1304.
269. Carville (1971) 283.
270. *Ibid.* 290.
271. *LM* xiv–xv (*n*).
272. Donkin (1978) 97 (*c.* 1200).
273. Barnes (1982) 38.
274. *DCK* 200. (in 1241).
275. *LM* xv (*n*).
276. Blashill (1892) 107.
277. Tomkinson (1985) 60.
278. Donkin (1978) 98.
279. *RHC* 33.
280. Clementi (1971) 167.
281. *LM* xv (*n*).
282. Donkin (1978) 99.
283. *SBE* 57.
284. Platt (1969) 234.
285. Williams (1984) II, 306.
286. Talbot (1958) 197; *cf. ABB* 163–70.
287. Talbot (1958) 199.
288. *DCK* 214.
289. *ABB* 165.
290. *RD* II, 58 (No. 6177).
291. Couriol (1980) 103–04.
292. Williams (1889), Appx. xvii.
293. *CDRB* V: 3, p. 421 (No. 1688).
294. *Statuta* I, 57 (1154/4), 71 (1160/3).
295. Donkin (1978) 97.
296. *SBC* IV, 80 (No. 1137a).
297. *CW* 87–88; *cf.* VCH, *Bedford* I (1904) 361.
298. Hockey (1976) 80.
299. *CD* 308.
300. Owen (1971) 58, 63.
301. VCH, *Shropshire* II (1973) 52.
302. Donkin (1978) 135–36.
303. *RHC* 54.
304. *CPR* 1266/8 (No. 16).
305. Hockey (1976) 86.
306. *CPR* 1297/311.
307. Midmer (1979) 128.
308. Williams (1984) II, 310.
309. Donkin (1978) 148.
310. *Ibid.* 142; Eckenrode (1973) 265.
311. *RHC* 96.
312. Donkin (9178) 93.
313. *CPR* 1276/141. (Early summer seems to have been a usual time.)
314. *CChR var.* 272.
315. *CPR* 1283/68, 1284/122.
316. *CPL* xxxi–ii.
317. Madden (1963) 355.
318. Barnes (1982) 59; *cf. Statuta* I, 60 (1157/4), 334 (1207/3), 421–28 (1214/54), 448 (1215/65).
319. *Statuta* I, 426 (1214/45).
320. Williams (1889) Appx. xix.
321. *CCR* 1237/532.
322. Donkin (1978) 92–93.
323. *Ibid.* 99–94.
324. *CPR* 1285/160.
325. Donkin (1978) 93–94.
326. *Ibid.* 99.
327. Eckenrode (1973) 260.
328. Williams (1889) Appx. xix.
329. *CPR* 1224/492.
330. *CPR* 1224/449.
331. *CPR* 1225/522.
332. *CPR* 1225/509.
333. *Statuta* I, 342–43 (1207/47).
334. Williams (1984) II, 309.
335. *CPR* 1265/400.
336. *CPR* 1272/648.
337. *CPR* 1272/689.
338. *CPR* 1275/86–87, 95.
339. Gimpel (1977) 102.
340. *Statuta* III, 227 (1282/55).
341. VCH, *Chester* III (1980) 152.
342. Donkin (1978) 151–52.
343. *ACA* 300.
344. Donkin (1978) 88; *cf.* Graves (1957) 30–32.
345. Dimier (1964) 185.

346. Lohrmann (1980) 122.
347. Espinas(1923) II, 316.
348. Verhulst (1972) 308.
349. *Ibid.* 307.
350. *Ibid.* 308, 319.
351. Mousnier (1983c) 235.
352. Schneider (1954) 127.
353. King (1973) 135.
354. Gimpel (1977) 46.
355. VCH, *Worcester* II (1971) 152.
356. Mullin (1932) 50.
357. *CDK* 124–27.
358. Donkin (1978) 152.
359. VCH, *Chester* III (1980) 159.
360. Fletcher (1919) 125.
361. *CDK* 124–25.
362. Knowles (1979) I, 68*n*.
363. Graves (1957) 28–29.
364. *RHC* 86.
365. Pegolotti (1936) .
366. Wright (1972) 1768.
367. Williams (1984) II, 310.
368. Graves (1957) 24–25.
369. Pegolotti (1936) 261.
370. Williams (1984) II, 310.
371. Donkin (1958) 2.
372. Owen (1971) 40.
373. *CPR* 1272/703.
374. Donkin (1978) 151.
375. *Ibid.* 88–89.
376. *Ibid.* 88–89.
377. *CCR* 1275/274.
378. Donkin (1978) 99.
379. Coppack (1993) 60–61.
380. *Cf. Statuta* I, 187 (1195/33).
381. Moorhouse (1989) 49.

382. Hockey (1976) 86.
383. *RHC* 39.
384. PRO, E 326/B, 9234.
385. Mullin (1932) 50.
386. *CCR* 1250/304, 314.
387. *CPR* 1277/235.
388. Mullin (1932) 44.
389. *RHC* 39.
390. Hockey (1976) 86.
391. *CPR* 1271/526.
392. VCH, *Worcester* II (1971) 152.
393. Graves (1957) 24.
394. *CPR* 1265/461.
395. Mullin (1932) 44.
396. Donkin (1978) 167.
397. Knowles (1979) II, 77.
398. Lekai (1977a) 314.
399. Donnelly (1949) 39*n*.
400. Cocheril (1959a) 57.
401. Rösener (1983a) 148.
402. Barrière (1983) 96.
403. Williams (1984) II, 307.
404. Bond (1994) 372.
405. *CDP* 4 (No. 1).
406. Berman (1986) 89.
407. Bond (1994) 372.
408. *Ibid.* 372.
409. *CSBW* 73.
410. Bellero (1985) 346.
411. Talbot (1958) 200; *cf. ABB* 219, 221.
412. France (1998) in press.
413. Berman (1986) 89.
414. Williams (1984) II, 308.
415. *RBC* 34.
416. Carville (1982b) 23.

Chapter 18

FISHING, MINING AND INDUSTRY

Fishing and Fisheries

In recent years debate has surrounded the part fishing played in the economy of the Cistercians. The general view now prevailing is that fish were widely eaten in their refectories before the close of the twelfth century, that this component of the diet became more marked in the thirteenth century – as fish frequently formed the numerous pittances then granted, that most of the white monks' fishing endeavours were for food for their own use and not for commercial gain, and, reflecting that, their many fish-ponds were more for storage than for breeding[1]. From the 1140s Pontigny was fishing the Serein and the Yonne rivers, and Valmagne was acquiring coastal fisheries[2]. By 1170 Byland was buying fish both for 'the monks and the sick'[3], whilst Fountains was given the fishing of Malham Tarn[4]. Not later than the 1190s Holm Cultram[5] and Melrose[6] received fisheries on the shores of the Solway estuary, and Lehnin obtained several nearby lakes for net-fishing[7]. As the twelfth century closed fish as a major item of Cistercian diet came to the fore when the General Chapter (1199) forbade any abbey to fish in Lake Geneva from St Mary Magdalene's Day (22 July) until Holy Cross Day (14 September), so that stocks were not depleted for the abbots attending the Chapter[8]. It became especially customary to eat fish in Advent and Lent and on major feast-days, and to place it before important guests[9]. Tombstones, as at Tintern, might depict fish, whilst at Himmerod is the tomb of a fisherman of Trier.

There is plenty of evidence to show that the *conversi* were much involved in fishing Cistercian waters. The Dunes (1233) had a house at Nieuwpoort on the nearby Flanders coast where 'the *conversi* can dry their nets'[10]. Salt was provided to the '*conversi* of the fishery' of Scharnebeck (1286) for preserving fish caught[11]. The skill of the *conversi* led Henry III (1263) to ask Waverley to send men and nets to fish for him in his vivary of Woolmer[12]. Tintern (1320) had a monk or *conversus* as 'guardian of its fisheries'[13]; Cherlieu (1209) had its 'fisherman' in charge at Befrenoa[14]. Fishing necessitated boats, nets and huts. Dargun received freedom from toll for twelve fishing smacks[15]; Santa-Maria della Paludi was given two fishing boats at its foundation[16]; Stephen Lexington (1231) insisted that the fishpond boat of Champagne be better maintained[17]. Two new boats were made (in 1270) for Beaulieu's Cornish fishery, and the nets there were repaired[17a]. Grants of fishing rights might, for conservation reasons, limit the number and size of boats and prohibit night fishing. Similar restrictions applied to net type and size. Lehnin (1317) in one lake could only use 'small' nets[18], Sallay (1247) was not to use 'the net called "wase"' at Ilkley[19], Raitenhaslach (1261) might fish on the Salzach but only with the 'Arich' net[20], Dargun (1292) fishing on Lake Verchenpenz was to use the 'worpenet' or 'stokenet'[21]. Buków might not use 'large seines' in the adjacent Baltic waters[22].

Some Cistercian holdings were primarily fishing establishments, with accommodation for the *conversi* and for fish to be dried and salted – like the Dunes' property at

Nieuwpoort and Vyšší Brod's 'Fisherman's Grange'[23]. William de Brus (1200) allowed Holm Cultram to 'build a house on the sand' to serve its fishery at Tordiff on the Solway[24]. Coupar had a house at Stichende Haven on the Tay[25]. Furness had a 'fishing booth' on Beaumont Grange, to store fish from its Lune fishery[26]. The lacustrine fishermen of Oliwa at Tuchom had a house for their residence[27]. In the medieval hut excavated at Byland's Oldstead Grange have been found a 7 lb lead measure (for weighing fish) and a number of lead weights (for stabilising nets)[28]. Meaux had a 'fishhouse' at Sutton in Holderness[29], whilst Quarr (1365) – during the threat of invasion from France – fortified its 'Fish House' on the Isle of Wight[30]. Out of Alcobaça's fishing interests grew the town of Pederneira[31].

Cistercian monasteries acquired fisheries and fishing rights in a variety of localities, whilst inland houses might seek to obtain salt water fish in addition to their local fresh water catch. Strata Florida had fishing for trout and eels in the nearby Teifi Pools, as well as herring fisheries on the coast of Cardigan Bay[32]. Øm obtained fresh-water fish from the lakes and rivers around it, but had salt-water fishing at its distant Vejleby Grange[33]. Rievaulx had rights on the Yorkshire coast at Teesmouth and Scarborough[34]. Numerous estuaries around the British coast had a Cistercian fishing presence, especially for obtaining salmon: like Sweetheart at the mouth of the Nith[35] and Tintern on the shores of the Severn[36]. Furness went far afield, acquiring a fishery in Marinerstown by the Boyne estuary in Ireland[37]. A royal grant to Balmerino (1318), of fishing on the north side of the Tay near Perth, allowed it to fix stakes for hanging and drying its nets[38]. Robert Bruce gave Coupar (1327) leave to fish for salmon in the Tay – even in the closed season[39] – and granted Kinloss (1310) a fishery near the abbey at Findhorn[40]. William de Brus, confirming to Holm Cultram (1210) a fishery by the Solway, reserved to himself any sturgeons or whales taken[41], but on the Baltic coast Dargun[42] and Oliwa[43] long enjoyed the right to retain sturgeons caught.

In the Baltic region the principal catch of monastic boats was the herring. Oliwa built two fishing stations, one north of the abbey and one at Kochon, for its boats bringing in herrings. Other ships could use the facilities but had to pay toll to the monks[44]. Dargun set up a yard on Usedom island for its deep-sea fishery[45]. Hiddensee's island site much enhanced its fishing capabilities[46]. Buków caught herrings in the adjacent haff and the open sea using small nets, baskets and hooks[47]. Various rulers exempted the Cistercians of houses close to the Baltic, such as Chorin[48] and Doberan[49], from paying toll on herrings they had caught and were transporting to their monasteries. The same privilege was granted Henry II of England (in 1180) to Foucarmont for herrings, ling and mackerel[50]. Herrings (both red and white) formed a major component of the diet at Sibton in the fourteenth century[51]: it had a fishery at Orford on the Suffolk coast[52]. Sibton's obligation to render yearly to Walden Abbey 2,000 well-cured herrings at its grange by the river Kennett, suggests it imported herrings there – perhaps by its own boat[52a]. In Yarmouth, also on the North Sea coast, Beaulieu, Boxley, Robertsbridge and Waverley owned property and had fishing interests, sending boats there to bring the herrings (kippered or dried) back to the monastery[53]. Fish were also sent to Beaulieu from its fishery in Cornwall[53a].

Riverine fisheries were important to most houses, especially where the streams were navigable or where weirs might be constructed, although the fisheries of Zinna in the Elbe[54] (as some of those of Raitenhaslach elsewhere[55]) were more often utilised by its tenants than by the abbey directly. Relevant charters can fix the limits of monastic fishing stretches precisely. Gard (1178) was given exclusive fishing rights in the Somme 'from the first wall of the monastery down to the millgate'[56]. Bonport (1199) might fish freely in the Seine from Pont-de-l'Arche to Martot[57], Raitenhaslach (1261) on the Salzach for a mile above and below the monastery[58]. Charter evidence also demonstrates the careful building up of fishing rights by Buch (1264 to 1288) on the Molda and other rivers[59], by Chorin (1281–1316) in the Oder at Oderberg[60], and by Val-St-Lambert (1211 to 1268) on the Meuse[61]. Pontigny made six dams on the Yonne at Auxerre[62]. Furness took timber on ox-drawn wagons from Lancaster Forest to maintain the weirs of its fishery on the river Lune[63]. Beaulieu, repairing its 'Kyndelwere', used thorn hedging[64]. Val-St-Lambert's first fishing rights (in the Ourthe) had been for one boat with two men[65]. Frederick II allowed Morimondo Milano to fish the Po and Ticino rivers with both small and large boats[66]. Especially helpful for fishing purposes was the possession of midstream islands, as by Eberbach in the Rhine[67], Fontmorigny in the Loire[68] and Pilis in 'the great Danube'[69].

In tidal river stretches salmon were again a favourite catch, as by Mellifont in the Boyne (where no less than four salmon fisheries)[70], Margam in the Afan (where gillings and sewin were also taken)[71], Tintern in the Wye (where it had several weirs)[72], Fontmorigny (at weirs in the Loire and Allier)[73], Altzelle (at its mills on the Mulde)[74], Lyse (at rapids in the river Drammen)[75] and by Oliwa (until 1343) in the Vistula estuary[76]. A much eaten migratory fish was the eel: many monasteries had access to substantial numbers. By the 1170s Carracedo had the right to a fourth of the eels leaving the local lake[77], whilst (in 1299) Furness was given half the eels issuing from Eshton Tarn[78]. Dalon trapped eels on the Charente at a grange in Saintonge[79]. Boyle claimed some twenty-four eel weirs on the river Boyle[80], and Vale Royal had eel weirs in the river Weaver[81]. When Croxden's main fish-pond was emptied in 1300, few fish were found but about five hundred eels[82]. Beaulieu (1270) gathered (and sold) over two hunded eels at its Kyndelwere[83]. The beaver was a valuable and protected animal and, in the thirteenth century, much sought after in the middle and upper reaches of the Oder, Warta, Vistula and their tributaries. At least seven Cistercian abbeys and three nunneries in south and east Poland enjoyed the right to hunt and take beavers[84], including Mogila[85], Sulejów[86] and Koronowo[87]. The abbeys of Lubiąż and Rudy and the nunnery of Trzebnica are known to have sold the profitable beaver furs in the local Silesian towns and cities[88].

Fish were also sought in natural lakes, and not least across the plains of northern Europe where rain and river water lay trapped in great depressions in the clay and sand left after the final Baltic ice-sheet retreat. Monasteries like Chorin (with eight lakes in the local scrubland, as Coldewater and Heiligensee)[89], Lehnin (a chain of fisheries by 1317[90], as in Havelland and Zauche)[91], and Zinna (with grants from several margaves, including Lake Steinitz near Hennickendorf and Lake Liebätz in Magdeburg territory)[92], all acquired substantial lacustrine fishing interests. So, too, did Walkenried (1234) which received from Landgrave Henry of Thuringia and his brother Count Conrad of Saxony, the right to fish in the Weissensee to provide the monastery with food at twelve festivals each year[93]. Salem fished in Lake Constance[94], and its daughter-house of Raitenhaslach in the Ibmsee and Höratigersee[95]. Furness was permitted to fish with one small boat, but also to have twenty nets, on both Coniston Water and Windermere in the English Lake District[96]. Furness (1299) was also granted Eshton Tarn to provide fish for its Winterburn Grange, with the right to build a hut there[97]: this upland lake was said then to be: '90 perches 20 feet in length, and 50 perches in breadth'[98]. In lowlying areas the ponds and reens of marshland tracts were important sources of fish. Stanlaw fished in the marshes by the Mersey estuary, Sawtry in the English Fenland[99], Meaux in Hornsea Mere[100] and Neath in the local Crymlyn Bog[101]. Auberive fished in the dykes surrounding its Perlonguet Grange[102], and Margam in Kenfig Pool – a sand-dune impounded lagoon[103].

Few abbeys were without one or more artificially constructed fishponds, which served to supplement fish derived from other sources. These might be pools dammed on a sloping valley bottom – with perhaps a series of ponds being consequently created at descending levels (as at Dunkeswell[104], Byland and Henryków), or they might be hollows excavated and embanked on the valley floor (as by Bordesley and Chaâlis)[105]. Such ponds attracted sedimentation and vegetative growth, thus allowing herbivorous and omnivorous species of fish to breed: bream and pike being particularly common[106]. Every few years – five years has been suggested but at Croxden there may have been a longer interval[107] – the earthen dam was breached to lower the water-level and harvest the bulk of the fish. Two of the recorded 'fractures' at Croxden (in 1318 and 1337) took place 'in Lent', making extra fish available for that penitential season. When the Croxden pond was emptied in 1300 the piece of wood called 'the bolt' was removed: it was found to be 40 ft (12 metres) long. When the dam was restored in 1346 it was with 'pipes and rings'[108]. In addition monasteries might have smaller masonry lined tanks for storing fish to meet seasonal fluctuating demands: like that excavated near the guest-house kitchen at Vauclair[109]. Both fishponds ('stanks' or 'stews') and tanks might be described as 'vivaries'.

Some abbeys had a number of fishponds: Morimond about twenty-one[110], Fontmorigny no less than twenty-seven[111], Heilsbronn 'controlled dozens'[112]. Some might be of considerable size: Waverley's 'Abbot's Pond' on heathland at Farnham covered about 14 acres (6 ha)[113], Fontmorigny's largest pond was 5 acres (2 ha) in extent[114], Byland's pond on Oldstead Grange was ½ mile (0·8 km) long, up to ¼ mile (0·4 km) broad and 30 ft (9 metres) deep[115]. Charters and other deeds may fix dates of construction: the great pond at Clairvaux is known to date from about 1146[116], Bonnefont made ponds in 1178 and 1212[117], Boxley enlarged its pond in 1234[118], Byland sought to make its pond at Cams Head Grange in 1235[119], and Rufford to dig a 'stew' in Sherwood in 1268[120]. Once made, the oversight of such ponds seems (as at Croxden)[121] to have formed part of the duties of the subcellarer. Beaulieu's subcellarer was its fishmonger[122].

Considerable engineering works might be involved: at Bordesley the river Arrow was diverted and the ground gained used for a series of fishponds and a millpond[123], at Kirkstall two ponds may have been formed out of a northern arm of the river Aire[124], and at Fontainejean an enormous embankment was built across the river Aveyron creating 'a magnificent lake'[125]. The expertise of the Cistercians in fishpond and tank construction was acknowledged when (in 1245) a *conversus* of Warden, skilled at the task, was required to assist in the making of a fishpond for Henry III at Windsor[126]. Some ponds might serve a dual purpose, being both fish- and mill-pond. The construction of dams and weirs to make millponds might halt there migrating eels and salmon[127]. Fishing in mill waters (leats sometimes as well as the ponds) is on record at Clairefontaine[128], Dünamünde[129], Ląd[130] and Tintern[131]. Moreruela, demising mills (in 1204) on a tributary of the Duero, reserved to itself the associated fishing potential[132]. Former monastic fishponds are still to be seen at Sawtry[133] and Szcyzrzycz[134], or may be evidenced by marshy depressions as at Coggeshall[135] and Tilty[136]. Sometimes their previous existence is only known from field-names – as 'Fishpool Meadow' at Grace Dieu (W), or from late medieval documents – like the 'fishpole water' of Tintern's Trelech Grange[137]. Others have given way to development: the site of the fishpond of Newbattle is now the Lothian private burial-ground[138], the fishponds of Mogiła (on the outskirts of Kraków) have given place to the Nowa Huta Sports Stadium[139].

It has been suggested that some monasteries used their fishponds and tanks for commercial gain, but there is scant evidence of this. Fish-breeding on a large scale has been suggested of abbeys lying very much inland: as at Waldsassen in Bavaria[140] and Svaté-Pole in Bohemia[141] – but in both instances that activity came after the period of this study. Other monasteries to which breeding has been attributed (but at late or uncertain dates) include Coupar[142], Morimond[143] and Krzeszów[144]. On the whole there is little evidence of any substantial trade in fish by the Cistercians. Their catch was mainly for home consumption. Adam de Brus II freed Byland from toll on fish it brought to his market[145], and Beaulieu (1270) both bought and sold a variety of fish[146], but nothing has been published to suggest any large-scale commerce. The one exception might be Grandselve in Bordeaux, but its freedom of toll for salted fish could relate to fish being taken to the monastery[147]. Yet the Cistercians perhaps took the greatest care to produce good quality fish. That they did is suggested – not only in the grants of bream from the royal pond of Fosse to stock abbey 'vivaries': sixty to Fountains in 1229[148] and ten 'mother breams' to Byland in 1245[149] – but also in the return compliment paid when (in 1299) Stanley gave both bream and pike to the royal fishponds at Marlborough Castle[150].

The Cistercians also obtained fish by grant, by purchase, and from tithes, tolls and rents in kind. It is not known as to how long Clairvaux received each St Andrew's Day the 'two tuns of herrings taken at Mardyck' promised (in 1188) by Count Philip of Flanders[151], or for how long Gard received a grant (for the first week of every Lent) of 2,000 herrings at Picquigny and 1,800 eels at Hangest[152], or whether Beaubec indefinitely enjoyed the 5,000 herrings from Tréport assigned it (in 1208) by the count of Normandy[153]. An earl of Warrenne (1240) gave to Roche the tithe of eels from most of his fisheries[154]. St Mary's, Dublin, claimed the 'best fish' from every fishing boat putting into the harbours on its lands at Blowich and Bullock, and also from every herring boat a 'mease' of herrings annually[155]. There were rents in kind due yearly to Byland (100 haddocks, but unpaid for eight years in 1239)[156]; La Garde-Dieu (two large lamphreys at specified late-spring dates)[157]; and Fürstenfeld (500 smoked 'whitefish')[158], whilst sardines were due to some of the monasteries of León and Castile[159]. Serfs of Przemęt (at Domnik and Dłużyn) had daily fishing duties for the monastery[160].

If all the available supplies still did not suffice a monastery's needs, then recourse was had to buying fish. Every year Lubiąż in Silesia sent boats to Pomerania to import fish, and boats also brought it salt for salting them[161]. Fountains (1267) bought herrings in the North Sea coastal port of Redcar[162]. Boxley (1225)[163] and Waverley (1284)[164] sent ships (either their own or hired) to Berwick and Yarmouth respectively for herrings. Nearly one-tenth of Kingswood's expenditure (in 1241) was on fish: a wide variety (including salmon, herrings, eels, oysters and mackerel) were bought at Priddy Fair. The purchases were made for the Feast of All Saints and in time for Easter[165]. Beaulieu (1270), which sometimes had much hake and mackerel in storage, also bought in fresh fish at times for both the monks and its guests[166].

The Cistercians did not always fish unimpeded. There could be disputes, especially when more than one party claimed rights in the same waters. An affray at a fishery on the river Lune (in 1314) between the boatmen of Furness and those of St Mary's Priory, Lancaster, centred on how many catches each monastery could make[167]. Joint ownership by Ås Abbey and Gudhem nunnery (both Cistercian) of the salmon fishery on the river Viskå also led (as in 1313) to tension between the two houses[168]. After a quarrel with the Teutonic Knights about fishing rights in the coastal haff of Zalew Wiślany, Oliwa (1317) could no longer fish in the mouth of the Vistula[169]. There were official objections when local navigation was impeded by Sibton (1280) putting its stakes in the port of Orford into deeper water[170], and when Tintern (1330) raised considerably the height of its weirs in the river Wye[171]. Poachers intruded into the fishing waters of Beaulieu (1278; and were only ejected after a physical struggle)[172], Coggeshall (1296; the local vicar who fished under cover of darkness)[173], and Velehrad (1320; some of its fisheries 'violently occupied')[174]. Strong waves (about 1240) destroyed Flaxley's 'Hynewere' in the river Severn[175], whilst coastal erosion or a rising sea-level (about 1290) saw Holm Cultram's fishery at the mouth of the river Derwent 'submerged and carried away'[176]. A monk of Bellebranche (1223) drowned whilst fishing on its pond[177], a melancholic *conversus* of another abbey (*c.* 1220) committed suicide by throwing himself into its fish-pond 177a, and a minor disaster occurred at Hailes (1337) when the sluice-gates of its fish-pond failed, and mud flowed through the cloister[178].

Wreck of Sea

The right to claim: 'The goods which, by shipwreck or tempest of the sea, happen to be upon any lands of the monks', was a privilege derived from royal and princely benefactors[179]. Around the shores of Wales it was a right enjoyed by several Cistercian houses[180], and the charters of Strata Florida early spelt out the variety of goods which might thus come a monastery's way: 'Wine, honey, beer, corn, fish, flesh, gold, silver, precious stones, rings. jewels ...'[181]. It was a right which was, in the case of Cymer (1209), unusually restricted to its 'own cargoes if wrecked by storm at sea', and to inquest by two jurors[182]. It was a right which might be challenged – as when a boat with three bales of wool was washed up on the shore near Margam (1333); its seven occcupants all drowned[183]. Holm Cultram claimed wreck of sea on its shores adjacent to the Solway by ancient usage, but as the right did not appear in its foundation charter it was to be the subject (from 1280 to 1294 and later) of lengthy enquiry[184]. Cleeve claimed wreck of sea by grant of Henry III[185], and Quarr claimed half the wreck stranded above low-water mark on its lands[186]. On the Continent abbeys with the privilege of wreck included Doberan (given by Prince Nicholas of the Slavs in 1190)[187], and Vitskøl (by grant of King Kristoffer I about 1255)[188].

Stone Quarrying

The importance of stone in the building of the many monasteries of the Order has been described. Many of the quarries – or rights of quarrying – granted to the Cistercians were in upland areas to facilitate the extraction: like Pforta's quarries in Mount Aldenburg[189] and 'at the foot of Mount Saelbergh'[190]. The term 'mountain' might encompass relatively small declivities, such as Zinna's valuable 'lime mountain' at Rüdersdorf near the river Spree[191]. Quarrying necessitated accommodation for the quarrymen, like Balmerino's house in Nidyn[192] and Ourscamp's 'habitation' in Mount Malconseil[193]. Stone might be used for a variety of purposes like mill and tannery construction by Sallay (1312)[194], and to repair mill-dams as by Rueda (1268) at Lagata[195]. Stone was a heavy and bulky commodity and, whilst water-transport might be used where possible, haulage might have to be in part by cart. This explains the grant to Balmerino (1285) not only of a quarry at Nidyn, but also of common pasture rights for 24 oxen there[196].

There could be external factors affecting monastic quarrying. Extraction of stone by Stanley (1232) in Chippenham Forest was halted 'by a certain oak', but once the monarch allowed it to be cut down quarrying went ahead[197]. The use of quarries at Tout-Vent (Oise) was the subject of disagreement between Ourscamp and the Benedictines of St-Médard Abbey, near Soissons[198]. When Emperor Charles IV drew up his 'Land Register' (in 1375) refused to declare the value of its Rüdersdorf limestone quarry, on the pretext that the depth of the limestone was unknown[199]. When a quarry had served its purpose it might be disposed of: Pontigny's church being all but finished, its abbot (in 1212) sold off a quarry situated near Chablis[200]. Others might value monastic stone. Zinna found a ready sale for its limestone to those building churches and fortifcations in its region[201]. Sixty-nine 'great freestones' from Merthyr Gerain quarry (perhaps the property of Tintern) went for building purposes to Llangybi Castle[202], and one of the sources of stone for Windsor Castle, in the building phase of 1350 to 1377, was Roche in far-away Yorkshire[203].

Peat Extraction

Those monasteries with marshland holdings or sited near fenland areas – as several were around the estuaries of the British coastline – had the advantage of an easy and ample supply of fuel to serve not only the abbey itself but also its granges. Beaulieu's porter used five cartloads of turf each year in cooking pottage for the poor[204], Furness had a grant of fifty cartloads annually for its Winterburn Grange[205]. Sibton had the right to turbary in no less than six localities in the Cambridgeshire Fens (serving its inland granges there) and the Suffolk coast (fuelling the abbey). It added to early grants of turf (as in 1163) as late as 1235[206]. Other grants of turbary in Britain included one hundred wagon loads yearly in Angerton Moss for Furness[207], peat and turf in Harras (Whitehaven) for Holm Cultram[208], and, for Balmerino, rights in the moss of Swan Mire near Leuchars[209]. In Ireland Holy Cross had a ready supply at its bog in Lisnagonogue[210], and in Wales Strata Florida owned the extensive Cors Goch Glan Tefi (Tregaron Marsh)[211]. In Flanders, abbeys like Ter Doest had a ready supply but it was still increasing its peatland holdings as late as 1259[212]. In Drenthe peat was not only extracted on a large scale by Aduard, but sent by the abbey (from about 1250) to Hamburg for sale[213].

With a grant of turbary might go a concomitant right of way, as for Sibton (1235): 'A free way, twenty feet in breadth' which led from 'the king's highway' to the marsh of Uggleshall (Suffolk)[214]. Once dried as solid peat marshland turf was obviously both less bulky and less heavy. It made sense, therefore, to dry it *in situ* before carting it away. Newminster – permitted to take as much peat as it wanted in Haverigg and Kirkstanton – was allowed by the grantor 'to pile it up in the fields and dry it there'[215]; Sibton, given turbary in Wenhaston (Suffolk), was permitted 'to dry it thoroughly on the land of the donor'[216]. Peat was a valued possession, and monastic peat might be stolen – as from turbaries of Byland[217] and Croxden (1232)[218]. Competing claimants to turbary might have recourse to arbitration – as by Meaux (1210) in dispute with the Cistercian nunnery of Swine[219], or even litigation – as by Baltinglass (1302) when others claimed turbary in Gilltown[220]. Kirkstall (1187), sharing the turbary of Bessacar with Peter of Bessacar, came to agreement with him that neither would give away or sell any turf. In this way supplies were conserved for both parties[221].

Coal Mining

A number of monasteries, fortunate enough to lie close to outcrops of carboniferous strata, made good use of the coal measures they contained. These seams of 'stone coal' might be alternatively called 'pit coal' (suggestive of the digging necessary to obtain it), or 'sea- coal' (the term originating in coal veins exposed in cliff-faces and wave-cut platforms along the British coast)[222]. By 1215 Newbattle was excavating coal at its Preston Grange[223], and later exported it from Morison's Haven[224]. The Scottish coal and iron district later known as Monkland derived its name from Newbattle's original ownership of the area[225]. Culross worked coal both at its Philpstoun Grange and 'in the common mure of Culross'[226]: it too was to develop a thriving export trade[227]. Both monasteries stood close to the Firth of Forth, and close to where the coal measures reached the sea. So, too, did Newminster, with its right along the coast 'from Snoc to Blythe, to take sea coal, where found'[227]. Margam and Neath in south Wales worked the locally outcropping coal measures. In one grant to Margam (1247) Owain ab Alaythur gave it 'all the carbon stone' in his land with 'ingress and egress for two-wheeled and four-wheeled carts'. The monks were to pay him five bushels of wheat yearly, and compensate him for any damage done to his farmland[228].

Other British monasteries with coal mining interests, included Basingwerk (in the Flintshire Coalfield)[229], Garendon (in the Leicestershire Coalfield)[230], Hulton (in the Staffordshire Coalfield)[231] and Kirkstall (in the Yorkshire Coalfield)[232]. The abbey of Cymer, close to the coast of Cardigan Bay but remote from any outcropping coal seams, still laid claim to 'sea carbon'[233]: perhaps drift material. On the Continent, amongst other abbeys fortunate also to be sited in coalfield areas, the mineral was mined by Carracedo in northern Spain[234] and by Grünhain in Saxony[235], whilst Aiguebelle exploited deposits of lignite near Fraisse[236]. Val-St-Lambert mined coal at Ans, Berleur and Marihaye, in the Meuse valley, but ran into opposition from local millers when it started mining on other lands, because the digging interfered with their water-supply. Nicholas, a *conversus*, was 'master of the colliers' of the abbey in 1317: dying in 1330, he was replaced by another *conversus*, Lambert de Freloux. By about 1350 the monastery was demising much of its coal mining interests[237].

Metallurgy

A typical grant of mining rights was one early made to Fountains of: 'All copper, iron, lead, and every kind of metal and stone, below ground or above'[238]. It was indicative of the varied mineral resources some abbeys might possess. The recently published charters of Strata Marcella rarely use the phrase 'above the land or below', but do so concerning properties where there was mining potential probably sought by its monks[239]. Based upon their own deposits, or using imported materials, all large monastic precincts were a hive of economic activity (Chapter 9). Even some granges (as Meaux's North Grange)[240] became veritable craft centres. When, in 1293, the local populace complained that the industrial production of Henryków in Silesia was leading to a shortage of raw materials, the community replied that monasteries everywhere practised 'mechanical arts', and that, without this means, they could not exercise hospitality and other works of mercy[241].

Copper was obtained by houses with easy access to Palaeozoic and metamorphic strata: like Sittenbach[242] and Walkenried who mined in the Harz Mountains. From 1188 Walkenried had a share in the copper mines of the Rammelsberg there, and by 1216 a *conversus* was in charge of its copper smelting operation in Goslar. It later mined copper in the Andreasberg, and obtained copper gravel between Lauenthal and Wildemann using tunnelling. It set up further smelting works between Seesen and Gandersheim (1226), near Brunebach (1237), in Sorge (1249) and near Grasdorf (1283)[243]. The monastery paid 12 marks yearly to the count of Hohnstein for its Harz operation[244]. Other Continental abbeys with copper mining interests included Mogiła[245], Rudy[246] and Wąchock[247]. In Britain a copper foundry has been excavated at Rushen on the Isle of Man[248], whilst copper and tin ores were smelted within the precincts at Kirkstall[249]. Tin was also produced by Grünhain[250]. Lead, so useful for covering church roofs and for water-piping, was mined by Fountains (in the Forest of Knaresborough)[251], Rushen (on the east coast of the Isle of Man near Laxley)[252] and by Strata Florida (in Cwmystwyth)[253]. Fountains had a lead-smelting works at a place still called 'Smelthouse' between Dacre and Pateley Bridge[254]. Perhaps in recompense for his murder of St Thomas Becket, Henry II (1180) had forty cart-loads of Derbyshire lead shipped from Boston to the monks of Cîteaux[255].

Silver bearing ores were quarried by monasteries in the Central European Highlands: Sedlec obtained silver in Kutten*berg*[256] and Rein in Silber*berg*[257]. After the discovery of silver ore – partly on the lands of Sedlec – in the late thirteenth century, the abbey prospered greatly – but not without litigation and demands for it to lend silver money for the public good[258]. Rein was permitted to have its own silver measure[259]. Silver found on territory belonging to Velehrad led to the development of Kutná Hora[260]. With a grant made to Žďár (1303), to assist it maintain its secular infirmary, of Heinrichsdorf (by Osoblaha) went: 'That mountain in which silver was formerly worked'[261]. Silver mining was also practised by Altzelle (but Margrave Otto the Rich took back from it the silver mines at Freiberg)[262], Grünhain (in the Erzgebirge, especially at a mine called Die Kutte – 'the Cowl')[263], and by Osek (from 1282 at the latest)[264]. In Wales Basingwerk (by 1153) was granted silver-bearing lands, but there is no record of it working the mineral[265]. In France Morimond mined surface silver ore of high quality at Chaligny[266], whilst Noirlac jointly owned with the lords of Charenton a silver mine at Puy-Dahert[267]. The monks of Fontfroide (1252) objected when a viscount of Narbonne started silver mining operations but a few metres from its precinct wall[268]. Žďár (1265) had leave from King Ottakar II of Bohemia to prospect for gold and silver[269], and later (1303) acquired a one-tenth part of the toll due in Chotěboř from the profits of silver and gold mined there[270]. Zbraslav (1339) was given profits from a royal gold mine near its Slapy Grange[271]. Plasy (1346) worked silver and gold ores at Kralovice[272] and Lubiąż at Złotoryja[273].

Iron Mining and Smelting

The essential mineral most widely worked was iron ore – whether in the carboniferous clay ironstone and red haematite deposits of Britain, or in the Jurassic oolitic limestones of France, or in the porous form of bog iron ore on the North German Plain. Iron was used in church construction[274], was needed for shoeing horses, for hoops on wheels and shares on ploughs, and for making knives and tools – all this was undertaken at the forge of Beaulieu (1270)[275]. The workshops of Bordesley produced objects such as nails and tenterhooks, as well as weapons: perhaps for sale as well as for domestic use[276]. At the smithy of Morimondo Milano (1237) were anvils and sledge-hammers, gratings, locks and handles, as well as grindstones to whet the metal[277]. Clairvaux used the phosphate slag resulting from smelting as fertiliser and road metal[278]. Žďár in Bohemia, with no less than twenty-one iron foundries, sold iron products as far afield as Augsburg and Nuremberg[279]. The income Furness (1291) gained from its forges was nearly double that from its flocks and herds[280]. Some granges specialised in iron-smelting, like Alcobaça's Quinta de Ferraria[281] and Clairvaux's La Forgeotte[282]: both aptly named. Because of the dirty and dangerous nature of their work, the *conversi* blacksmiths were allowed to wear a full black smock – allowing freedom of movement and giving protection from sparks and soot. They might talk reasonably freely – 'because they could scarcely carry out their work without harm in silence'[283].

Mining was either opencast or by means of tunnels cut into hill slopes. The requisite topography was noted when – in the late twelfth century – Duke Henry of Bavaria gave to Zwettl 'three ironbearing hills' at Chrumpenowe[284]; a benefactor of Tarouca granted it in Moledo 'my part of that hill from which iron comes'[285]. Smelting, if possible, took place near the mine – as the finished product was less bulky to transport than the untreated ore, and preferably in woodland – to have a ready supply of timber for charcoal. Such were the forges of Louth Park in the woods of Barley[286] and of Tintern in the Forest of Dean[287]. Stanley (1294) had leave in Chippenham Forest 'to dig, make into iron (*i.e. on the spot*), and carry away'[288]. Two oaks weekly were needed to fuel one of Flaxley's forges[289], but it has been estimated that one square acre of forest reduced to charcoal would scarcely suffice to yield two tons of malleable metal[290]. La Bussière (1211) was given a mine for iron ore, a place to build a forge, timber to make charcoal and way-leave to carry the iron to the abbey[291]. Rights of timber might be restricted to 'dead wood': as in grants to Holm Cultram[292], though (occasionally) greenwood might also be taken[293]. At the French Parliament (1299) royal foresters complained of the depredations made by Mortemer's ironworking in the Forest of Lyons, west of Beauvais[294].

An abbey might seek water for washing the ore – as granted to Furness (1235) at Orgrave[295]. Champagne abbey forge had its own lake[296]. Accommodation was necessary for workmen and equipment. Furness (1270) was permitted to erect huts for men and draught animals at Alinscale – 'as well by night as by day'[297], and on the Isle of Man (1146) it had a warehouse to store its ore mined there[298]. The earl of Richmond (1280) insisted that Jervaulx's forges north of the Ure should be protected only by rudimentary and easily dismantled sheds[299]. Way-leave was necessary: granted to Furness in respect of Alinscale together with halting-places for the beasts carrying the iron[300]. Fontmorigny had passage on a stretch of the Loire[301], Haute-Seille had freedom from toll across the Moselle at Port Saint Vincent[302]. Damage done had to be made good, or compensation paid: Kirkstall, engaging in opencast iron mining at Seacroft, promised to 'fill up the pits from which stone has been taken'[303]. Furness – at Alinscale – agreed to pay 'a reasonable price for arable land and corn disturbed'[304]. Iron ore was an exhaustible commodity: one grant to Margam was effective for 'so long as the mineral holds out'[305]. Cîteaux (1217), Longuay (1227)[306] and Villers-Betnach (1240)[307] all acquired prospecting rights for further ore supplies.

In France the leading region for Cistercian iron working was the Wassy area on the lower slopes of the Plateau of Langres. Here, within fifteen years, Count Henry of Champagne gave mining and smelting rights to La Crête (1156), Clairvaux (1157), Boulancourt, Igny (1158) and Trois Fontaines (1171)[308]. Clairvaux's forge in Wassy was attached to Blinfay, its leading iron making grange[309]. The monastery expanded its interests in the valley of the Blaise, along the Marne and around Chaumont: eventually owning at least eight forges in the Plateau[310]. It also acquired forges previously belonging to Beaulieu-en-Bassigny (1196)[311] and L'Arrivour (1292)[312]. Its output of iron by the late fourteenth century has been estimated as nearly 1,000 tons (1,000,000 kg) a year[313]. Other Burgundian houses with mining interests included Bithaine (with grant of ore and timber in 1186)[314], La Charité (selling iron in 1328)[315] and Cherlieu (near its Crayes Grange)[316].

From the mid-twelfth century there was also a Cistercian presence in the iron industry of the Moselle valley (Beaupré, Clairlieu and Morimond mining near Chaligny), and in its tributary of the Orne (Châtillon)[317]. Orval mined iron in the Chiers valley (a tributary of the Meuse) in the Buré d'Orval[318]. In the Forest of Othe, to the south-west of Troyes, Pontigny[319] and Vauluisant[320] had mining rights by 1143. Pontigny's workmen were based in a house at Sévy, a dependency of its Chailley Grange[321]. Unfortunately, in a riot by men of Vénisy (in 1316) the house was destroyed, iron ore stolen and the ropes used in mining broken[322]. In Normandy La Trappe smelted iron on La Gastine Grange and (from 1225) leased out lands for prospecting[323]. Monastic iron mining rights might be challenged: as by descendants of benefactors of Longuay (1312) and Cherlieu (1349)[324].

Amongst other continental iron working abbeys were Dobrilugk and Zinna which, like many North German monasteries, exploited bog iron ore[325]: indeed, it has been suggested that Zinna pioneered this development[326]. Dobrilugk ran two hammer-mills called Hammermühle and Buschmühle[327]. Further inland Grünhain mined iron in the Erzgebirge[328] and Walkenried in the south and west of the Harz[329]. At Waldsassen, Abbot Heidenreich (abbot from 1304 on, and seemingly a man with mining knowledge) strove to make its iron industry more viable[330]. Well before the close of the twelfth century Sorø was exploiting iron ore deposits in Halland[331] and Zeeland[332], whilst an iron furnace has been excavated at Alvastra[333]. Wąchock, in Little Poland – given leave to explore for iron ore in 1249 – created smelting works at Rejów,

Skarżysjka-Kamienna and Starachowice: still industrial areas today[334]. The remains of a forge of Wąchock have been excavated by the river Kamienna[335]. The forge of Pásztó in Hungary was destroyed by the fire there about 1230[336].

As – in the thirteenth century – some Cistercian houses turned to water-power to assist their iron manufacture, corn-mills might be adapted as iron-mills: as by La Charité (1242)[337] and perhaps also by Bellevaux (1218)[338] and Dobrilugk (1300)[339]. The best-known Cistercian iron forge in Europe, that of Fontenay, was built of the local oolitic limestone[340] and measured 53 metres (175 ft) long by 13.5 metres (45 ft) broad[341]. Originally two separate buildings – one a mill, the other having two chimneys[342] – it had a fall of water from the adjacent canal of 2.6 metres (8.6 ft)[343]. Fontenay had an 'iron mill' on record in the thirteenth century[344], but this may not have been it[345]. One of the earliest grants of iron forges to a Cistercian house was in England to Rievaulx in the 1140s[346]: one charter gave it 15 acres (6 ha) of land for erecting iron foundries[347]. Furness has been credited with no less than forty forges[348]: when the Scots raided Furness in 1316 they took some of the iron away[349]. The later forge of Maulbronn was a three-storeyed half-timbered building on a large stone base dating from about 1300[350].

Sources of Salt

In the Middle Ages salt was a much used and essential commodity. It formed a part (to what extent is not definitely known) in Cistercian diet: the monks being bidden to take salt with their knife, having first cleaned that utensil on bread and with their napkin[351]. It was the principal means of preserving food: for that reason 'the breeding of fish and the salt-trade of the Cistercians were inseparably linked'[352]. In an age when most beasts were slaughtered at Michaelmas, there was only salted meat available for the winter months[353]. When the monks of Maigue once had to prepare supplies to withstand a siege, they placed thirty dead bullocks, seasoned with salt, under their dormitory[354]. Salt was also used in the tanning of leather, the curing of skins[355], the manufacture of cheese[356] and even in the soldering of pipes and gutters[357]. It is not proven that it was given on a large scale to animals as part of their diet[358]. Salt could also be sold to gain cash, given as a gift to a benefactor or bartered. That was summed up well when Alfonso VIII of Castile (1175) granted salt rights to Huerta: it was, he said, so that it might have salt: 'To give, to sell, to exchange, to guarantee'[359]. Impetus to the white monks to acquire their own sources of salt was helped by local grants of freedom from tithe on salt, as to Huerta (1178–82)[360] and the entire Order (by Innocent IV; 1244)[361].

In the Middle Ages rock salt, as such, was rarely quarried or mined: salt was obtained by the evaporation of sea-water trapped at high tide in salt-pans (partly by the natural air, partly by artificial heat), or of naturally occurring brine in springs and underground water – usually in Triassic strata (using boilers of one kind or another)[362]. In northern Germany at least twelve Cistercian houses had rights to salt, if not their own pits, in the Lüneburg salt-field. There was a growing Cistercian presence here from at least 1230 onwards. There were two principal ducal salt-works in Lüneburg: 'Wechpanne' and 'Gungpanne' – the latter, divided into two, formed 'Gungpanne' and 'Guncpanne'[363]. Each was separated into sections called 'houses': probably the individual underground pits and workings. Monastic rights were spelt out very precisely in the relevant charters. Doberan received (in 1305) confirmation of two earlier grants of salt rights at Lüneburg. One entitled it to a specified amount of salt: 'In the house of Edinghe, on the left hand at the entrance of the said house, in the *sartagina* which is commonly called Wechpanne'; the other gave it salt: 'In the house of Grevinghe in the *sartagina* which is called Gungpanne, situated at the right hand when entering'[364].

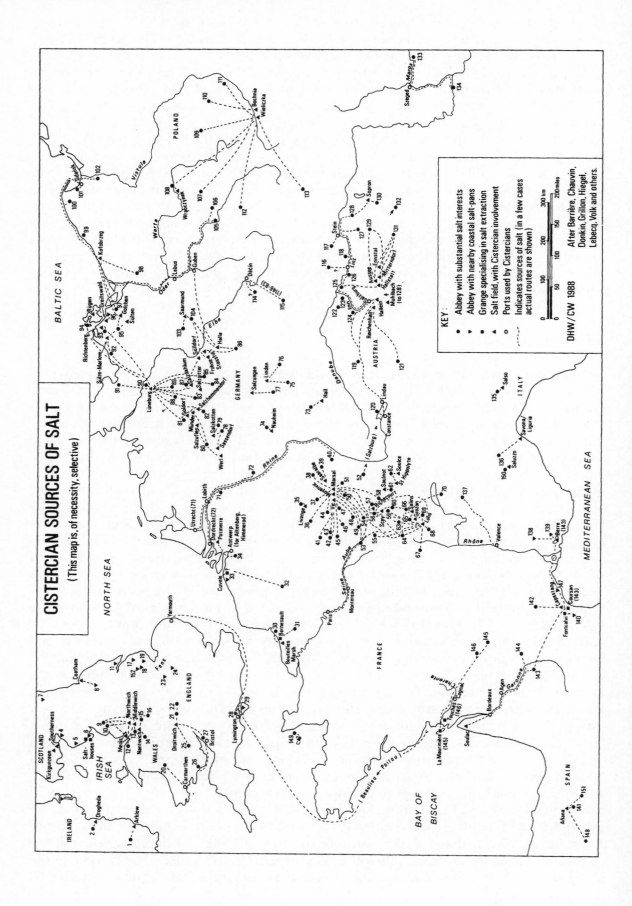

KEY TO ABBEYS AND NUNNERIES ON MAP

1. Baltinglass
2. Mellifont
3. Grey
4. Holm Cultram
5. Calder
6. Furness
7. Newminster
8. Byland
9. Sallay (Sawley)
10. Whalley (Stanlaw)
11. Meaux
12. Basingwerk
13. Vale Royal
14. Combermere
15. Dieulacres
16. Croxden
17. Louth Park
18. Kirkstead
19. Revesby
20. Strata Florida
21. Bordesley
22. Stoneleigh
23. Pipewell
24. Sawtry
25. Dore
26. Margam
27. Kingswood
28. Beaulieu
29. Quarr
30. Lieu Dieu
31. Beaubec
32. Vaucelles
33. Ter Doest
34. St Bernard-opt-Scheldt
35. Bonneweg
36. Châtillon
37. Villers-Betnach
38. Wörschweiler
39. Stürzelbronn
40. Neuburg
41. La Chalade
42. Montier-en-Argonne
43. L'Isle-en-Barrois
44. St-Benoît-en-Woëvre
45. Trois Fontaines
46. Vaux-en-Ornois
47. Clairlieu
48. L'Estanche
49. La Crête
50. Beaupré
51. Haute-Seille
52. Pairis
53. Clairvaux
54. Morimond
55. Auberive
56. Cherlieu
57. Clairefontaine
58. Bithaine
59. La Charité
60. Bellevaux
61. Lieucroissant
62. Lucelle (Lützel)
63. Acey
64. Cîteaux
65. Rosières
66. Bullion (Buillon)
67. La Ferté
68. Le Miroir
69. Balerne
70. Aulps
71. Camp (Altenkamp)
72. Heisterbach
73. Schönthal
74. Arnsburg
75. Ebrach
76. Langheim
77. Bildhausen
78. Bredelar
79. Hardehausen
80. Marienfeld
81. Loccum
82. Amelunxborn
83. Marienrode
84. Walkenried
85. Michaelstein
86. Pforta
87. Riddagshausen
88. Wienhausen
89. Isenhagen
90. Scharnebeck
91. Reinfeld
92. Doberan
93. Neuenkamp
94. Hiddensee
95. Dargun
96. Eldena
97. Stolpe
98. Kołbacz
99. Buków
100. Żarnowiec
101. Oliwa
102. Pelplin
103. Lehnin
104. Zinna
105. Lubiąż
106. Trzebnica
107. Ołobok
108. Ląd
109. Sulejów
110. Wąchock
111. Koprzywnica
112. Henryków
113. Velehrad
114. Osek
115. Plasy
116. Zlatá Koruna
117. Zwettl
118. Baumgartenberg
119. Fürstenfeld
120. Salem
121. Stams
122. Alderspach
123. Fürstenzell
124. Raitenhaslach
125. Engelszell
126. Wilhering
127. Lilienfeld
128. Heiligenkreuz
129. Neuberg
130. Bors Monostra
131. Rein
132. Szent Gotthárd
133. Egres
134. Pétervárad
135. Chiaravalle della Colomba
136. Casanova
137. Tamié
138. Sénanque
139. Silvacane
140. Fontfroide
141. Herrera
142. Silvanès
143. Grandselve
144. La Garde-Dieu
145. Obazine
146. Dalon
147. Valmagne
148. Las Huelgas
149. Écrehou (cell of Val Richer)
150. Staffarda
151. Cañas
152. Stixwould

'Houses' used by Scharnebeck at Lüneburg included in Guncpanne, Berndinghe (1315)[365] and Geminge (1281, 1299)[366], and in Wechpanne, 'Loteringe' (1320)[367] and 'Suderstinghe' (1276, 1294)[368].

The initial outlay could be very expensive. Doberan paid 400 marks (in 1262) to Dukes Albert and John of Brunswick for salt-rights in Gungpanne and Wechpanne, and (in 1281) acquired more rights for a further 180 marks[369]. When Duke Otto (in 1282) granted rights in the house of Seveninge to Scharnebeck the transaction was agreed in the monastery of the Friars Minor in Lüneburg: of the 210 marks expected the abbey made a down payment there and then of 60 marks, the remainder being paid later – in different places – by monks or *conversi* or lay intermediaries[370]. The amounts of salt granted are also spelt out precisely; and varied at different 'houses' from half-a-wagon load or 'plaustrum' (giving about 8½ tonnes) to three 'quires' or 'choris' (yielding about 156 tonnes)[371]. Some grants were made to generate income to fulfil specific needs of a monastery, like at Scharnebeck to provide bread and wine for Mass[372], or to service the needs of its 'office of keeper'[373]. Some rights were leased out[374]: in 1276 William Crane (perhaps the father of Gerhard Crane, a monk of Scharnebeck in 1282)[375] paid 350 marks to that abbey for exclusive rights in one of its pits[376]. Amelunxborn, which (in 1301) sold its village of Satow in exhange for two salt-pits in Lüneburg[377], disposed (in 1326) of at least one of them to Riddagshausen[378].

Monasteries gaining salt on or close to the Baltic coast included Eldena, whose salt-working colonists (Danish, German and Slav) founded the town of Greifswald – ceded (about 1250) by the abbey to Duke Wartislaw[379]. Dargun's salt rights included both Lake Tolense and Kołobrzeg[380] – where Buków, Kołbacz, and Oliwa, also had salt-works[381]. (Bukow's salthouse had four evaporating pans, and in 1265 it dug a new pit twelve feet square)[381a]. At Kołobrzeg even distant Trzebnica nunnery in Silesia had its saltworks, sending boats annually to collect the salt[382]. Inland Lubiąż (on the Oder) received salt midway – either from north Germany or the Baltic – at the river ports of Guben and Lebus, and was allowed two shiploads each year free from toll[383]. It has been calculated that each shipload may have amounted to about twenty cartloads, perhaps well over 300 tonnes[384]. Plasy (1146) was given a ducal grant of toll taken on salt entering Bohemia on the Elbe at Děčín, but dangers to its draught-animals and thefts by robbers on the long journey (130 km/80 miles) saw the abbey exchange this right (about 1183) for the village and lands of Kopidlo instead[385]. In the south of Poland at least seven Cistercian houses obtained salt from the 'Magnum Sal' close to Kraków: a saltmine which is a major tourist attraction today. Amongst those abbeys was Wąchock, the skill of whose *conversi* was shown in the promise made to the monastery (in 1249) by the duke of Kraków, that if they prospected and found new sources of salt as well as of metal ores in his duchy, the abbey would share in the profits[386].

Salem made its mark in salt production at Hallein in Austria. Granted a saltpit or well there (in 1201) by the archbishop of Salzburg – together with bucket elevators and boiler-house[387] (which it may have shared with its daughter-abbey of Raitenhaslach)[388] – the experienced *conversus* in charge was entrusted by the chapter of Salzburg (in 1237) with managing its saltworks as well[389]. By the end of the twelfth century Rein may have been producing about 500 tonnes of salt yearly at Ahornberg (Aussee), but a business-minded Duke Leopold VI took over the abbey's rights there, and thenceforth the monastery received yearly instead 100 bushels of salt (in total perhaps about 2,000 tonnes), as well as 10% of the duke's increase of yield in the saltworks[390]. Perhaps not a bad bargain for an abbey well over 100 km distant! Annual grants of salt were made to Heiligenkreuz by the archbishop of Salzburg (3 *talents* or *librae* of *nudi salis* to be taken at Muhlbach), and by King Béla III of Hungary (3,000 *zwani* of salt to be received at Sopron). The archbishop's grant, made in 1219[391], was confirmed as late as 1274[392]: the king's grant, confirmed about 1230[393], was a few years later commuted (in part) to a money payment by King Andrew[394]. The distance of the abbey from Sopron again probably made this advantageous. A grant of 30 *fuder* of 'dry salt' from Hallstatt, made to Engelszell in 1313, was received well into modern times[395].

Thirty or more French abbeys gained their salt where Mesozoic clays and marls outcropped at the foot of the Jura and the Vosges[396]. So great was this Cistercian involvement that (in 1237) the General Chapter ordered all abbeys with salt rights in Lons-le-Saunier to let the abbots of Balerne and Le-Miroir act as procurators there of their common interest[397]. Early grants in Lons to Cîteaux included 2 'monteys' of brine in 1170 and a further 2 in 1172[398]: a 'montey' equalled anywhere from 1,200 to 2,400 litres (265–530 gallons)[399]. The twelfth century grants in Lons to Balerne were often from nobles and made in return for spiritual services, but the later ones (and it considerably expanded its salt interests from 1234 to 1244)[400] were from lesser folk who usually expected monetary payment[401]. (Balerne expended in Lons 767 *estevenans* between 1234 and 1257)[402]. Some early grants had been in return for the services to the donors of one of its *conversi* Rudolph – an expert in salt production – and also of a monastic carpenter loaned to repair their shafts[403]. Fifteen Cistercian houses had rights in the episcopal saltfields of Marsal and Vic, paying the bishops (after arbitration in 1208) rent partly in cash and partly in salt. They also promised that two *conversi* would guard the entrances and maintain the passages and wells[404].

Around the coasts of western Europe monasteries obtained salt from lagoons and artificial salt-pans in coastal marshes, and several granges specialised in salt production. This was true of Brondolo's grange in Chioggia on the Adriatic[405], of Osera's saltpit by the haven of Marin[406], of Tarouca's grange in Alveiro by the marshes of Gafanha da Nazare[407], of Silvacane's Sauveplane Grange in the Camargue[408], of Fontfroide's fortified Fontcalvi Grange[409] and Grandselve's Coursan Grange[410] – both in the Capestang marshes, of Dalon's Touches Grange at the broad mouth of the Sendre in Saintonge[411], of Obazine's La Maurinière Grange set amidst the saltpans of the island of Oléron[412], and of Beaubec's Bernesault Grange adjacent to the marsh of Bouteilles[413]. Some 200 km (125 miles) and about 260 km (160 miles) separated Dalon and Obazine respectively from their coastal saltworks. These great distances reflected the importance of their salt to the monastic economy, and necessitated in part river transport upon the Charente upstream *via* Cognac (where Obazine had a salt store)[414] and Château-neuf (where Dalon was free of toll)[415]. Dalon's salt extraction at Touches had been enhanced by the salt tax exemption given it (in 1159) by Henry II[416]. Grandselve also received yearly three 'measures' of salt (forming at least one boatload)[417], and La Garde-Dieu two 'measures', from the royal saltworks in Bordeaux[418]: transport was upon the river Garonne. The archbishop of Narbonne gave ten muleloads of salt yearly to Silvanès[419] and the count of Barcelona five loads weekly to Silvacane from his marshes at Berre[420].

In inland Spain Herrera[421] and Las Huelgas had royal grants of salt from the pits of Añana and Atienza. Las Huelgas, at Atienza (1187), could extract one 'cargo' daily[422]; at Añana (1228) it was granted 100 'measures' of salt, fifty being for the monastery's own use and fifty for its lay hospital[423]. Huerta also acquired saltpits and rents at Atienza (1195)[424], as well as at Terceguela (1172)[425] and Medinaceli (1175) – with the latter grant went 'waters, and all that pertains to saltpits'[426]. Rueda had riverine saltpans at Escatrón, across the Ebro from the abbey[427]. Santes Creus (1289), finding that distance made it difficult to work directly its saltpits at Estanya de la Mora, leased them out in return for part of the salt produced[428]. The regal abbey of Poblet had access yearly from varied sources to about 12,500 kg (12½ tons) of salt[429]. Spanish monarchs made annual grants of salt to Monsalud (3,400 kg from 1180), Sacramenia (134,000 kg) and Valbuena (107,000 kg from 1173)[430]. In Majorca La Real was granted 50 quarters (630 kg) of salt yearly from the saltpits of Campos: a right confirmed as late as 1346[431].

In Italy Chiaravalle della Colomba had rights in the salt wells of Salso, and had timber in the neighbouring woods for fuel to evaporate the brine[432]. Cistercian coastal saltpans in Britain lay by the Firth of Forth (for Culross[433], Melrose[434] and Newbattle[435]), by the Solway Estuary (for Calder[436] and Holm Cultram[437]), in Amounderness[438] and Angerton Moss[439] (for Furness), by the Blythe Estuary (for Newminster)[440] and in Lymington Marsh (for Beaulieu[441] and Quarr[442]). Many monastic pans had purpose-built 'salt-houses', like Furness in Coupland and Furness[443] and Byland at Coatham on the Tees Estuary[444]. Extraction might be aided by grants of peat (for fuel to evaporate the salt water)[445], of sand (Kirkstead in the Fens and other houses extracted the mineral from salt-saturated sand)[446], and of timber (to construct the 'salt-houses')[447]. Beaulieu also bought salt from Poitou, perhaps directly, and certainly at Yarmouth to salt its fish there[448]. In 1270 Beaulieu bought sacks for its salt and repaired its salt-house[449]. The Cheshire 'wyches' (salt-springs) gave supplies of brine to abbeys such as Dieulacres with saltpans in Middle*wich* and Nant*wich*. Dieulacres had a house in Middle*wich* and was free from toll there and from suit at its 'wickmote'[450]. Basingwerk and more northerly houses had rights in North*wich*. Bordesley had a salt pit in Droit*wich* (Worcester)[451], from which town Dore – *via* Worcester(1233)[452], and Kingswood (1263) both bought salt[453]. Kingswood also purchased salt at Corsham[454], and Margam (1229) imported salt by ship from Bristol[455].

A bulky commodity, like wine and wool, salt was where possible transported on rivers: to keep costs down exemptions from tolls were again sought. The relevant deeds trace the routes Cistercian salt took from saltfield to monastery. Count Anthony of Valence (1190) allowed freedom from toll in his lands for six beasts carrying salt to Tamié[456], King Andrew II of Hungary (1203–35) exempted Egres from tolls on salt brought to it three times a year in six boats on the river Maros[457], and Duke Albrecht of Saxony (1237) allowed free passage for one ship yearly transporting salt from Lüneburg to Reinfeld[458]. (It has been suggested that such a ship bore over 17 tons [17,418 kg] of salt)[459]. Duke Otto III of Bavaria (1235–53) gave Salem both freedom from toll, and an escort for its salt coming from Hallein. The customs posts named show that the route taken was the so-called 'Lower Road' of Bavaria[460]. For the journey first on the river Inn and then on the Danube for salt going from Hallein to Heiligenkreuz, the complexity of medieval political and ecclesiastical boundaries meant that freedom from tax had to be sought (successfully) from not only the archbishop of Salzburg[461], but also the bishop of Passau[462], the dukes of Bavaria[463], and of Austria and Styria[464], the kings of Bohemia[465] and, later, the king of the Romans[466]. Moreover, as new monarchs or bishops acceded an abbey might feel it wise to have such toll exemptions confirmed: this happened repeatedly throughout the second half of the thirteenth century. A similar pattern can be traced for Zwettl's salt along the same route[467]. The large quantities of salt sometimes involved suggests that some of it was destined for resale. This is little documented, but salt surplus to requirements appears to have been sold by Salem (by 1207)[468], Reinfeld (by 1231)[469] and Raitenhaslach (by 1275) – by the latter down the Danube valley beyond Ybbs and Stein[470].

Notes

1. Currie (1988) 151–55, Hoffmann (1994) 402, Jones (1989) 151.
2. Hoffmann (1994) 402.
3. Currie (1988) 152.
4. *EAY* 33–35 (No. 23).
5. *RHC* 33–35.
6. *RHC* 35.
7. *CDB* (1) 188–83.
8. *Statuta* I, 234 (1199/9).
9. *Cf.* Currie (1988) 155–55; *Statuta* III, 477–75 (1344/8; for Advent); *SBC* IV, 106 (No. 1182, of 1323) for the 'fish-days' of Sibton.

10. *CTD* 47 (No. XIX).
11. *UKS* 58.
12. Baigent (1882) 18.
13. Williams (1984) II, 320.
14. Kempf (1976) 50.
15. Thompson (1920) 82.
16. Boyd (1943) 35.
17. *RSL* II, 199 (No. 11).
17a. *ABB* 104.
18. *CDB* (1) 231–32.
19. *CS* II, 82.
20. Krausen (1977) 185.
21. *MU* 193–94.
22. *PU* II, 99, 201.
23. Charvátová (1987) 120–21.
24. *RHC* 33–35.
25. Morgan (1929) 44.
26. VCH, *Lancaster* II (1908) 121.
27. *MPH* VI, 371–72.
28. Kemp (1984) 45–51.
29. Blashill (1892) 102.
30. *CPR* 1365/168, 1366/253.
31. Yañez Neira (1970) 566.
32. Williams (1984) II, 324.
33. France (1992) 281–82.
34. McDonnell (1963) 73, 112.
35. Stewart (1989) 59.
36. Williams (1984) II, 321.
37. Carville (1981) 60–61.
38. Campbell (1899) 191.
39. *CRC* xx.
40. Stuart (1872) xxxvi.
41. *RHC* 33–35.
42. *MU* 126–27.
43. *KD* II, 108–09; *MPH* VI, 337; PU III, 142, 437–38.
44. Lingenberg (1982) 215, 219.
45. Schich (1979b) 162.
46. *DHGE* XXIV (1983) 390; McGuire (1982) 153–54.
47. *PU* II, 99, 201.
48. *CBR* II, 433–31 (of 1288); *CDB* (2) 467 (of 1324).
49. *DD* 1469.
50. *CDF* 64 (No. 190).
51. *SBC* IV, 105 (No. 1181, of 1323); 107 (No. 1183, of 1376).
52. *SBC* II, 165–66 (No. 228 of *c.* 1233), *cf.* 168–69 (No. 233); IV, 35 (No. 984).
52a. *SBC* IV, 24–25 (No. 970), of *c.* 1225).
53. Donkin (1978) 163.
53a. *ABB* 309.
54. Hoppe (1914) 150–51.
55. Krausen (1977) 196.
56. *DHGE* XIX (1981) 121.
57. *CBP* 21–22 (No. XX).
58. Krausen (1977) 185.
59. *DHG* II, 189, 192, 195, 206, 222.
60. *CBR* II, 429–30, 450, 454, 496.
61. Van Derveeghde (1955) 64.
62. *PCP passim.*
63. Cottam (1928) 249, Donkin (1978) 128.
64. *ABB* 72.
65. Van Derveeghde (1954) 64.
66. Occhinpinti (1983) 550.
67. *UE* I, 198, 202, 211–12 (of 1218–19).
68. *CAF* 50 (of 1180).
69. Little remains today.
70. Conbhuí (1959) 119.
71. Williams (1984) II, 323.
72. *Ibid.* II, 320.
73. Vaslin (1990) 70.
74. Hoffmann (1994) 403.
75. France (192) 282.
76. Williams (1978) 259.
77. Hoffmann (1994) 403.
78. Cottam (1928) 71.
79. Hoffmann (1994) 403.
80. Conbhuí (1959) 120.
81. Crossley (1939) 72.
82. *CC* (2) B. 46.
83. *ABB* 75.
84. Williams (1978) 261–62.
85. *MPH* VI, 438.
86. *KD* I, 120–21; *KDM* II, 42.
87. Koslowski (1972) 123.
88. Grüger (1982) 95.
89. *CBR* II, 496.
90. *CDB* (1) 182–83.
91. Hoppe (1914) 149.
92. *Ibid.* 133, 149.
93. *UKW* 143.
94. *CDSL* I, 402–03.
95. Krausen (1977) 185.
96. Cottam (1928) 72, 203–04.
97. *Ibid.* 71, 239.
98. *C.P.R.* 1299/436.
99. Donkin (1978) 120.
100. Fletcher (1919) 66.
101. Williams (1984) II, 323.
102. Grandmottet (1958) 5.
103. Williams (1984) II, 323.
104. Bond (1989) 100.
105. Hoffmann (1994) 403–04.
106. *Ibid.* 403.
107. *ACA* 301, 304, 307.
108. *CC* (2) B. 46, (3) B. 59.
109. Hoffmann (1994) 403.
110. Dubois (1879) 146–51.
111. Vaslin (1990) 70.
112. Hoffmann (1994) 405.
113. Baigent (1882) 16.
114. Vaslin (1990) 70.
115. McDonnell (1965) 37–38.
116. Hoffmann (1994) 404.
117. Berman (1986) 90*n.*
118. *CCR* 1234/501.
119. Platt (1969) 196.
120. *CPR* 1268/211.
121. *CC* (2) B. 46.
122. *ABB* 36, 305, 308–09.
123. Bond (1989) 100.
124. Mitchell (1959) 56.
125. Jarossay (1891) 316.
126. *CCR* 1245/293.
127. Hoffmann (1994) 403.
128. Affolter (1978) 73 (in 1258).
129. *FHL* 101 (of 1226).
130. Staats Archiv, Cologne. Kl. Lond. I, f. 32v.
131. Williams (1984) II, 322.
132. Hoffmann (1994) 403.
133. Midmer (1979) 278.
134. Williams (1978) 261.
135. Cutts (1858) 183.

136. Galpin (1928) 94.
137. Williams (1984) II, 326.
138. Carrick (1907) 86.
139. Williams (1984) II, 261.
140. Hoffmann (1994) 406.
141. Charvátová (1987) 133.
142. Talbot (1939) 49.
143. Dubois (1879) 146–51.
144. Grüger (1982) 94–95.
145. Hill (1968) 67.
146. *ABB* 308–09.
147. Mousnier (1982)
148. *C.C.R.* 1229/278.
149. *C.C.R.* 1245/328.
150. VCH, *Wiltshire* III (1956) 273.
151. *RCC* II, 161.
152. Tribout (1966) 154.
153. Deck (1974) 140.
154. Aveling (1876) 28.
155. Conbhuí (1959) 119, (1962) 57.
156. Fletcher (1919) 122–23.
157. Hoffmann (1994) 402.
158. *Ibid*. 402.
159. Wamba (1986) 179.
160. *KD* I, 64–65.
161. Winter (1868) I, 114.
162. Donkin (1978) 163.
163. *C.P.R.* 1225/505.
164. Donkin (1978) 163; *CPR* 1284/136 ('with horses and carts' – so overland in part).
165. *DCK* 193–97, 200–01.
166. *ABB* 307, 309.
167. Cottam (1928) 80, 249.
168. France (1992) 283.
169. Lingenberg (1982) 221.
170. *SBC* IV, 36 (No. 985).
171. Williams (1984) II, 321.
172. Hockey (1976) 77.
173. *C.C.R.* 1296/474; *cf. C.P.R.* 1260/102.
174. *RBM* III, 244–45 (Nos 609–10, 612); *cf.* CDEM *VI, 155–56, 811–14*.
175. *C.P.R.* 1270/445 (for thirty years it lay unused).
176. *RHC* 22 (No. 52a).
177. *Statuta* II, 28 (1223/26).
177a. *CHDM* I, 239–40.
178. Midmer (1979) 156.
179. Williams (1889) Appx. xvii.
180. Williams (1984) 330–31.
181. *Ibid*. 147, Appx. lxx.
182. Williams-Jones (1957) 52–58, *Arch. Camb. 1846/453*.
183. Williams (1984) II, 331.
184. *RHC* 86 (No. 253), 92–94 (Nos 263, 263a).
185. Gilyard-Beer (1960) 6, Midmer (1979) 111.
186. Hockey (1970) 106.
187. *DD* 1469.
188. McGuire (1982) 130.
189. *UKP* 53, 60.
190. *CP* I, 93.
191. Speiss (1959) 280–81.
192. Campbell (1899) 182–83 (of *c.* 1285).
193. *CO* 221 (No. CCCLXIII, of 1193).
194. *CS* II, 51.
195. Barea (1977) II, 83.
196. Campbell (1899) 182–83.
197. *C.C.R.* 1232/100.
198. *CO* 58 (LXXXVI).
199. Speiss (1959) 265–66.
200. King (1954) 158.
201. Hoppe (1914) 156, Speiss (1959) 280–81.
202. Williams (1984) II, 329; info. of Mr J.K. Knight.
203. Colvin (1963) II, 881.
204. *ABB* 173.
205. Cottam (1928) 65, 69.
206. *SBC* 28 (No. 29), 85 (No. 96), 201 (No. 282), 208 (No. 294), 225–26 (No. 317–18), 242 (No. 282).
207. *CDL* 168–69.
208. *RHC* 32.
209. Campbell (1899) 166.
210. Carville (1973b) 106–07.
211. Williams (1984) II, 330.
212. Gottschalk (1955) I, 72–73.
213. Tromp (1989) 30–31.
214. *SBC* 85 (No. 96, of *c.* 1235).
215. *CNM* 200–01.
216. *SBC* 226 (No. 318; of *c.* 1200).
217. Fletcher (1919) 113.
218. *CHS* IV, 89.
219. Burton (1989) 36.
220. Fitzgerald (1906) 386.
221. *CBK* 160 (No. CCXXV).
222. *Cf.* Williams (1984) II, 327.
223. *RN* xxxiv.
224. Carrick (1907) 72–73.
225. *Ibid*. 76.
226. Douglas (1927) 84.
227. Talbot (1939) 58.
228. *CNM* 55.
229. Warwickshire C.R.O. CR 2017 (TP 704).
230. Aston (1993) 131.
231. Midmer (1979) 172.
232. Fletcher (1919) 126.
233. Williams (1984) II, 330.
234. Wamba (1986) 178–80.
235. Speiss (1959) 274.
236. *CDAA* 124.
237. Van Derveeghde (1955) 136–37; *cf.* (1946) *passim*.
238. Fletcher (1919) 109.
239. *E.g: CYM* 160–62 (Nos 18–19).
240. Platt (1969) 224.
241. Kaczmarek (1987) 422.
242. Roth (1986) 541, Speiss (1982) 272.
243. Speiss (1982) 265, 268–72; *cf.* Roth (1986) 542; *UKW* 153.
244. *Ibid*. 265.
245. MS info. at Mogiła.
246. Roth (1986) 542.
247. Elm (1980) 230.
248. McIntire (1943) 9.
249. Owen (1955b) 77.
250. Roth (1986) 543.
251. *Appendix to 30th Report of the Deputy Keeper of the Public Records*, p. 21.
252. Butler (1994) 187.
253. Williams (1984) II, 329.
254. Fletcher (1919) 110–11.
255. *Publns. Pipe Roll Soc.* XXIX (1908) xxix, 137.
256. Roth (1986) 543.
257. Amon (1979) 140.
258. Charvátová (1987) 113.

259. Amon (1979) 140.
260. Machilek (1973) 212–13.
261. *RBM* II, 855 (No. 1984).
262. Speiss (1982) 276–77.
263. Lekai (1977a) 322.
264. Machilek (1973) 213.
265. Williams (1984) II, 328.
266. Speiss (1982) 267.
267. Devailly (1973) 578.
268. *DHGE* XVII (1971) 972–73.
269. *RBM* II, 173 (No. 443).
270. *RBM* II, 855 (No. 1984).
271. *RBM* IV, 264 (No. 674).
272. *RBM* IV, 692–93 (No. 1733, of 1346).
273. Wetesko (1991) 157.
274. *E.g.:* Chauvin (1991) 147 (Clairvaux, *1168*); *CDEM* II, 343–44 (Velehrad, *1238*).
275. *ABB* 35, 72 (a pittance given to workers when colts shod and wheels fixed to carts).
276. Astill (1994) 540.
277. Occhipinti (1985) 328.
278. Chauvin (1976) 284, *cf.* Schubert (1957) 85–87, 100–07.
279. Machilek (1973) 212–13.
280. Cottam (1928) 73.
281. Yañez Neira (1970) 566.
282. Chauvin (1991) 147–48 (*grangia fabrica*).
283. Sullivan (1989) 190–91.
284. *UKZ* 412.
285. Almeida Fernandes (1973) I, 33 (No. 2; of 1182).
286. Schubert (1957) 107.
287. Williams (1984) II, 328.
288. *CPR* 1294/101.
289. *VCH*, *Gloucester* II (1907) 94 (of 1158).
290. Graves (1957) 17.
291. Chauvin (1991) 148–49.
292. *RHC* 21 (Nos 50c, 50d).
293. *RHC* 21 (No. 50b).
294. Arnoux (1991) 18, 29.
295. Cottam (1928) 74; Fell (1908) 14, 416.
296. Philippe (1991) 115–23.
297. Fell (1908) 17.
298. McIntire (1943) 9.
299. *CChR* III, 96.
300. Fell (1908) 17.
301. Vaslin (1990) 69–70.
302. Girardot (1970) 6–7.
303. Mott (1973) 157.
304. Fell (1908) 15, 417–18.
305. Birch (1897) 192.
306. Chauvin (1983a) 32.
307. Girardot (1970) 9.
308. Chauvin (1976) 283, Couvret (1969) 96–100.
309. Verna and Benoît (1991) 92–93.
310. Chauvin (1976) 283–84.
311. Verna and Benoît (1991) 93.
312. Couvret (1969) 100.
313. Chauvin (1976) 284.
314. Chauvin (1991) 148–49.
315. Chauvin (1982b) 70.
316. Kempf (1976) 9, 52–53.
317. Chauvin (1976) 281, Girardot (1970) 5, Verna (1983) 208.
318. Grégoire (1991) 125, *cf.* Girardot (1970) 14.
319. Benoît and Sportes (1991) 181.
320. Cailleux (1991) 194–95.
321. *Ibid.* 200.
322. Benoît and Sportes (1991) 186.
323. Arnoux (1991) 15, 18, 20.
324. Chauvin (1991) 164.
325. Schich (1979b) 157–58.
326. Speiss (1959) 278.
327. *Ibid.* 281–82.
328. Van Der Meer (1965) 281; *DHGE* XXII (1988) 426.
329. Rösener (1983a) 149.
330. Roth (1986) 542.
331. *SRD* IV, 471; McGuire (1982) 85–86.
332. Roth (1986) 541.
333. Swartling (1969) 154.
334. Wetesko (1991) 157.
335. Elm (1980) 230.
336. Valter (1994) 395.
337. Chauvin (1982b) 64.
338. *Ibid.* 67–68.
339. Roth (1986) 542.
340. Aquilina (1991) 299–314.
341. Cailleux (1991a) 316.
342. *Ibid.* 327–30.
343. Benoît (1991) 271.
344. *Ibid.* 275.
345. *Ibid.* 270; Cailleux (1991a) 330.
346. Schubert (1957) 101; *cf.* Barnes (1982) 70.
347. Hill (1968) 67.
348. Graves (1957) 17.
349. Fell (1908) 163–64.
350. Anstett (1987) 70.
351. Volk (1984) 28.
352. *Cf.* Donkin (1978) 120.
353. *CC* (1) B. 24.
354. Stalley (1987) 18.
355. Hockey (1970) 91.
356. Volk (1984) 29.
357. Hockey (1970) 91.
358. Volk (1984) 29.
359. *CMH* 38–39 (No. 24).
360. *CMH* 52 (No. 33), 71–72 (No. 44).
361. Lekai (1977a) 67.
362. Graves (1957) 19*n*.
363. *Cf. DD* 1537–88 (of 1288).
364. *DD* 1579.
365. *UKS* 113 (No. 154).
366. *UKS* 51 (No. 50), 85 (No. 102).
367. *UKS* 132 (No. 191).
368. *UKS* 47–48 (No. 44), 50 (No. 49), 74 (No. 83).
369. *DD* 1506, 1509, 1511.
370. *UKS* 52 (No. 52), 53 (No. 53).
371. Lindenthaal (1979) 22.
372. *UKS* 47–48 (No. 44, of 1276; Herman was 'custos').
373. *UKS* 50 (No. 49, of 1281).
374. *Cf. UKS* 48 (No. 45, of 1276).
375. *UKS* 53 (No. 53).
376. *UKS* 48–49 (No. 46).
377. Winter (1868) III, 32.
378. *Statuta* III, 375 (1326/8), 388 (1329/10).
379. *DHGE* XV (1963) 124–25.
380. *PU* I, 33–34 (of 1173).
381. *PU*, II, 127–28, 471; III, 142.
381a. *PU* II, 127–28.
382. Grüger (1982) 94.
383. *KDS* 30–31 (No. 267, of 1222).

384. Schich (1979b) 161.
385. *RBM* I, 118 (No.   265), 170 (No. 379).
386. Schich (1979b) 156.
387. Rösener (1974) 128.
388. Elm (1980) 232.
389. Toepfer (1983) 91.
390. Amon (127–28.
391. *UKSH* 55 (No. XXXIX).
392. *UKSH* 185–86 (No. CCI).
393. *UKSH* 75–76 (No. LXIV).
394. *UKSH* 82 (No. LXXI, of 1233).
395. Volk (1984) 41.
396. Chauvin (1983a) 33.
397. Chauvin (1987b) 90.
398. *CDAC* 156 (No. 193), 166–67 (No. 208).
399. Chauvin (1978b) 41*n*.
400. *Ibid.* 52–59.
401. *Ibid.* 71–107.
402. *Ibid.* 87–104.
403. Chauvin (1983a) 34–35.
404. Kempf (1976) 53.
405. Higounet (1983b) 176.
406. Yañez Neira (1977) 270.
407. Durand (1983) 113.
408. *CSV* 317–18 (of 1168).
409. Dimier (1964) 186; *CHA* (2–3) 259 (No. 1472).
410. Mousnier (1983a) 23.
411. Grillon (1963) 314–19.
412. Chauvin (1983a) 87 (*al.* Morinière).
413. Deck (1974) 139.
414. Pressouyre and Kinder (1990) 105.
415. Grillon (1963) 312.
416. *Ibid.* 311–13.
417. *C.P.R.* 1227/141; *cf.* Berman (1986) 102.
418. *C.P.R.* 1231/433.
419. Berman (1986) 102.
420. Pontus (1966) 20.
421. Yañez Neira (1975a) 42.
422. *DMLH* I, 22 (No. 11).
423. *DMLH* I, 325–26 (No. 223).
424. *CMH* 93–94 (No. 58).
425. *CMH* 28–29 (No. 16), 36 (No.23).
426. *CMH* 38–39 (No. 24), 42 (No. 26), 61 (No. 38).
427. Barea (1977) I, 274.
428. Fort i Cogul (1975) 79.
429. Tort (1974) 409.
430. Palenzuela (1978) 252.
431. *DSMLR* 531 (No. 220).
432. Rocca (1936) 285.
433. Douglas (1927) 79–87.
434. Richardson (1981a) 34.
435. Talbot (1939) 28.
436. Donkin (1978) 120.
437. De Brisay (1975) 72.
438. Cottam (1928) 82.
439. Donkin (1978) 120.
440. *CNM* xix, 45, 53–55, 201, 264; Donnelly (1954) 416 [in 1250 a *conversus* was stationed at Blythemouth].
441. *ABB* 36.
442. Donkin (1978) 120.
443. *CBF* (3) xix (No. CCCXCIV).
444. Donkin (1978) 120.
445. De Brisay (1975) 72.
446. Hallam (1954) 16.
447. *CBFA* (1) 90–91.
448. *ABB* 36.
449. *ABB* 188–89.
450. VCH, *Stafford* III (1970) 231.
451. Rahtz (1976) 18.
452. Williams (1976) 50.
453. *DCK* 246.
454. *DCK* 221.
455. Williams (1984) II, 268.
456. Bernard (1967) 21.
457. *DHGE* XV (1963) 29.
458. Volk (1984) 125.
459. *Ibid.* 125.
460. *Ibid.* 62.
461. *UKSH* 55 (No. XXXIX, of 1219), 73 (No. LXI, of 1230), 185–86 (No. CCI, of 1274).
462. *UKSH* 92 (No. LXXXI, of *c.* 1236), 106–07 (No. XCVIII, of 1243), 123 (No. CXIX, of 1252), 130 (No. CXXIX, of 1255), 170 (No. CLXXXIII, of 1269), 203–04 (No. CCXXI, of 1276), 226 (No. CCXLVII, of 1280), 231 (No. CCLII, of 1283), 249–50 (No. CCLXXVI, of 1286).
463. *UKSH* 107–08 (No. CI, of 1244), 134 (No. CXXXIV, of 1256), 186 (No. CCII, of 1274), 203–04 (No. CCXXI, of 1276), 263 (No. CCXCIII, of 1290).
464. *UKSH* 56 (No. XLI, of 1219); 110 (No. CIV, of 1245), 118 (No. CXI, of 1249), 123 (No. CXVIII, of 1251). 253 (No. CCLXXIX, of 1286).
465. *UKSH* 187–88 (No. CCIV, of 1274).
466. *UKSH* 205–06 (No. CCXXIV, of 1277), 207 (No. CCXXVI, of 1277).
467. *LFZ* 116, 119–22, 212–13, 284–85; *CDRB* V, 151–52 (Nos 1187–88, of 1260), 389 (Nos 1616–17, of 1274.).
468. Rösener (1974) 128, *cf.* (1983a) 149.
469. Volk (1984) 77, 124.
470. *Cf. RBM* II, 396 (No. 949).

Chapter 19

HOME AND OVERSEAS TRADE

An early institute of the Cistercian Order pointed out that 'it is dangerous and far from appropriate for religious to frequent the better known markets and fairs, but our poverty requires that we sell goods and buy necessities'[1]. Cistercian trade came to involve not only corn, fish, salt and wool, but a wide variety of other commodities. Kingswood (1240), for example, bought in cloth, pepper and spices[2], Clairvaux (1230) skins and wax from Denmark[3], Heisterbach (1217) butter and cork from lower down the Rhine[4], whilst Aduard (1280) sold dairy produce and even peat in Hamburg[5]. The importance of trade was reflected in the multitude of toll exemptions that the white monks acquired, in the obtaining of royal leave to set up markets and fairs, in the acquisition of ships, and the erection of dwelling-*cum*-warehousing in ports and other towns. An abbot of Buckfast (1236) was enrolled in the Merchants Guild of Totnes[6]. The commercial interests of Croxden (1318) led its chronicler to comment upon prevailing trade prices[7].

Throughout the twelfth century the General Chapter endeavoured to regulate Cistercian trade, partly to preserve monastic decorum and stability, partly to avoid houses falling into debt, and partly to stop any sharp practices by its own merchants. Its statutes implied that if any individual monk or *conversus* went away trading too often, it could lessen his spiritual fervour[8]. Before the twelfth century closed many abbeys had a *conversus* nominated as its 'merchant' and overseeing its trade. Such were 'Einulf the merchant' at Margam[9], Ancher at Clairvaux (1218)[10] and Berthold at Salem (1246)[11]. The Chapter provided that no more than two monks or *conversi* of any abbey were to be employed on trade: when away such 'merchants' were expected to live and eat as fitting for members of the Order[12], and any who were disobedient to their abbot or cellarer were to be removed from office[13]. Merchants were not to go on journeys of longer than four days[14] – except when seeking for hides or if crossing the English Channel – when a further two days from the coast was permitted, but attendance at fairs overseas was not[15]. Merchants were not to act dishonestly, nor buy at a low price to resell at a higher, nor negotiate long-term contracts[16], nor accept anything in exchange of goods but cash or 'trade tallies'[17]. Many of these stipulations entered into the early thirteenth century statute law of the Order[18], but thereafter there were few detailed regulations. The prohibition on distant journeying and long absences became of little relevance once abbeys had *conversi* resident at their urban trading-centres.

The many charters granting free passage through customs points give an indication of the nature of Cistercian goods, exported or imported, and the routes they took. Especially on long journeys – where there might be several sets of duty payable (as on rivers like the Danube and Rhine) – exemption from taxes became an extremely important asset. Had the Cistercians not gained the freedoms from tolls they did, their goods would have been much higher priced and not so able to compete in the open market: on the other hand, such exemptions lessened the revenue potential of the personages granting them. For this reason toll exemption was generally limited to 'their own goods only', and not to items collected and traded for other parties[19]. Alexander IV (1256) gave a blanket exemption from tolls to the entire Order for cereals and other goods, but this did not stop the Cistercians from feeling it advisable to secure such rights from individual authorities[20]. It was most helpful when monarchs and other feudal landowners gave a general exemption to an abbey covering the whole of their territories. This was true in northern France where, whilst under English rule, Henry II (between 1157 and 1175) gave freedom from toll to, amongst others, Aunay[21], Gard[22], Savigny[23] and Ter Doest[24]. Louis VI (1135) freed all Cistercian houses from toll throughout his lands[25], and Count Theodoric of Flanders (1142) to all abbeys of the 'generation' of Clairvaux[26].

Many abbeys needed to seek rights from several personages to whom tolls were due. Clairvaux received such grants not only from counts of Flanders[26], but also from dukes of Austria[27] and Valdemar II of Denmark[28] – indicating the far-flung nature of its trade. Ter Doest's eight relevant charters included toll exemption from not only Henry II, but also from counts of Cleves, Flanders, and Holland[29]. Some grants were more local and specific, like that of Thomas III of Savoy (1277) for traffic between Staffarda and its granges[30]. Some houses may have only gained widespread privileges late in life (as Loccum in 1331), or not at all (as possibly Marienrode and Michaelstein)[31]. In addition to freedom from passage and market tolls, exemption from bridge tolls (pontage) was also sought: it was a general right granted in numerous charters, as that of Henry I in favour of Beaubec[32]. Fontmorigny (1165) was free of toll on the bridge of Châtellerault – but only twice a year and on its own goods[33]. Mariental (1300) was exempt from paying 'bridge corn' (a toll in kind) at Offleben[34]. Land routes also necessitated way-leaves and halting-places. Alexander II of Scotland (1264) declared it to be of ancient custom and common law in his country that beasts of burden might have one-night stops *en route*[35]. In the lordship of Wigton Holm Cultram (1265) had leave at rest stops to unyoke 'the oxen from the wagons and the horses from the carts'[36].

The deeds giving free passage serve to emphasise the importance of water transport in the Middle Ages – when many 'roads' were rudimentary. Ships owned, or hired, by monasteries would economise by being loaded with goods on both the outward and the return journeys. The abbeys of the Rhineland (as Heisterbach[37] and Neuburg[38]) sent wine downstream, but brought back up river butter, fish and salt. The toll privileges of a ship of Altenberg (1228–1296) allowed it to bring to the abbey from Utrecht, duty-free, about 4,000 gallons (100 'ohms') of butter, 2 'loads' of herrings and ½ cwt (25 kg) of salt[39]. The two-way trade on the Rhine was underlined in Frederick II's grant for Pairis (1226) of toll exemption for one boat 'ascending and descending'[40]. (In many instances the leave was for one or two boats a year.) To sail the Rhine meant free passage being granted at several points within Germany alone: as for Bronnbach at Boppard, Frankfurt, Kaiserwerth and Oppenheim[41]. The rights of Eberbach on the Rhine (at Boppard, Coblenz, Cologne, and Mainz) were underpinned by several charters given it between 1185 and 1218[42].

A similar pattern can be traced on other great rivers of Europe, like the Danube and the Rhône: Léoncel was freed from paying toll at Valence[43] and Bonnevaux at Lyon[44] – almost from the date of their foundation. Crown documents noted how food was imported to coastal Holm Cultram both by sea, by 'fresh water' (1277) and 'by river'(1291)[45]. In Poland houses such as Przemęt[46] and Sulejów[47] had the right of passage *along* their local rivers, but the broad often unbridged waterways also necessitated rights of passage *across* rivers – as given to Paradyż over the Warta[48] and Lubiąż across the Oder[49]. The last abbey was privileged in being able to collect tolls on the Oder itself, as (in Wales) was Aberconwy for a time in the Conwy estuary[50]. Tintern, on the river Wye in Wales, seems to have served as a storage *entre-pôt* for goods destined for Monmouth upstream: the abbey making a charge[51]. The right to take toll – to help finance its hospice -was also given to Meaux (*c.* 1230) on the river Bek lying immediately east of the abbey[51a]. The right to take road passage tolls at La Vitarelle was bought up by Bonneval (1347): for every load of wax or wool or coloured cloth it could exact 10 pence, of fish – 6 pence, of butter – 4 pence, and so on[51b].

Overseas trade, again in ships belonging to or commissioned by an abbey, is well documented throughout the thirteenth century for abbeys on the western shores of mainland Britain seeking corn and other foodstuffs in Ireland. Political troubles meant restrictions on trade with Ireland at certain periods, and the Crown licences allowing monasteries to break the embargo[52], or (at other times) royal letters of safe-conduct, show how food was sought in Ireland perhaps when bad weather or war conditions made harvests on the mainland precarious. The import of corn by Furness from Ireland can be traced from 1200 down to 1348, and by Holm Cultram from 1220 to 1323[53]. Both abbeys also did much trade with the Isle of Man[54]. Dundrennan (from 1266) had the right to import into Scotland from Ireland 120 'crannocks' (perhaps about 350 bushels/140 hl) of wheat – and similar quantities of other foodstuffs – 'despite the prohibition'[55]. Holm Cultram could bring in up to 300 'crannocks' (about 900 bushels/330 hl) of corn[56]. Other monasteries *importing* corn from Ireland included (in Scotland) Glenluce[57], (in England) Stanlaw[58] and Vale Royal[59], and (in Wales) Aberconwy and Margam[60]. Irish *exporting* abbeys included: Grey (corn to England in 1222)[61], and St Mary's, Dublin (unspecified merchandise at Dieppe in 1265)[62].

Some English monasteries went still further afield, like Beaulieu which frequently sent a ship to Gascony laden with corn and returning with wine[63]. A burgess of Chester travelled 'beyond the seas' (in 1279) on behalf of Vale Royal, perhaps to Gascony, to bring it 100 tuns of wine[64]. In the south-west of Britain several Cistercian monasteries traded in the port of Bristol. These included Margam and Tintern[65], who had direct access there by water across the Bristol Channel, and two nearby houses – Kingswood (which bought wine there in 1263)[66], and Stanley (which was early freed from toll payments in the port)[67]. To the east coast ports of England came monastery ships from the Cistercian abbeys of Norway. From the early-thirteenth century ships of Lyse were free of tolls at harbours such as King's Lynn and Yarmouth, and went back home laden with goods like corn and cloth and wine. Political differences inhibited for a time the import of English corn into Norway, but Lyse (in 1223) was allowed to break that boycott[68]. (It was these commercial contacts and journeys which saw some Norwegian Cistercians appointed as emissaries from its king to the English Crown.) Dünamünde, in common with the citizens of Riga, traded with Novogorod in Russia[69]. Several inland monasteries in Spain found sea outlets like Meira at Ribaedo, Melón at Redondela and Sobrado at La Coruña[70].

Markets and Fairs

On the Continent a number of Cistercian merchants frequented the great fairs of places like Provins and Troyes[71], and hence these became collecting-points for dues owing to the General Chapter. Clairvaux was granted several stalls (1222–1231) – possibly permanent butchers' stalls – in Troyes Market[72]. Market privileges (such as freedom from tolls) were successfully sought by many houses, as by Silvanès at Lacaune and Millau[73], Bonnecombe at Albi, Gaillac and Rodez[74], Czikádor at Eszek[75] and (in England) Sallay at Ilkley[76]. When political conditions allowed the religious of Melrose traded at Carlisle Fair[77], and stayed with the monks of Holm Cultram as far away as Boston by the Wash to take part there in 'the great fair'[78]. A perquisite from that fair for Sibton (1180) was a grant of discarded empty wine casks[79]. Other local fairs patronised included those of Priddy (by Kingswood)[80], Ripon (by Fountains) and Helmsley (by Rievaulx)[81]. In northern Italy Rifreddo sold cattle in the market of Revello: so, too, did Staffarda in the markets not only of Piedmont but also across the French border in Dauphiné[82].

Over thirty Cistercian houses of England and Wales held markets and fairs on their own lands[83]: permission for this being necessary (usually from the Crown) because such trading activities meant a lessening of revenue elsewhere. There was a twofold advantage for the monasteries concerned. First, they had an additional outlet for their own produce, and for this reason the markets of northern abbeys (where harvest was latest) were mostly delayed until the autumn[84]. Second, they gained financially by renting out stalls and taking toll on goods sold. Usually a market was held on a specified day each week: the fairs – once (occasionally twice or more often) a year – were usually linked to a religious festival when people would be freer to attend. Many fairs lasted no more than three days – the vigil, day and morrow of the feast, but some remained in business for much longer. Most fairs were on manors belonging to an abbey (as Dieulacres at Leek[85], Furness at Dalton[86] and Newenham at Axminster[87]); less often at a monastery itself (and then without the precincts presumably) as at Graiguenamanagh[88], or (even within the walls) as at Holy Cross[89]; less frequently still on granges (exceptions including Stratford at Burstead and Waverley at Wanborough)[90].

Typical arrangements included those for Coggeshall: a Saturday market (from 1256) and a seven day fair (from 1250) held on its town manor of Coggeshall. The fair commenced on 31 July – the vigil of the feast of St Peter ad Vincula – the patron saint of Coggeshall town church[91]. Netley had (from 1251) a Monday market at Hound, and a two day fair (over the feast of St Margaret, 20 July) at Wellow[92]. Dunkeswell (from 1290) had Wednesday markets on both its manors of Broadhembury and of Buckland Brewer, as well as a three day fair over the feast of the Assumption (15 August)[93]. Several abbeys had Trinity fairs, including Basingwerk, Meaux and Swineshead[94]. So, too, did Beaulieu, which had a second fair over St Luke's Day (18 October)[95]. Its fairs were held on its manor of Faringdon, as was its Monday market. At the weekly market its stall holders paid a rent of $^1/_4$ penny a stall, but rates were doubled for the fair. All goods which sold for over 3 pence were subject to toll[96]. Both fair and market were relatively modest affairs, drawing an income in tolls of just under 30 shillings at each of the fairs, but over 52 shillings (in total throughout the year) from tolls charged at the weekly market. In addition tolls on salt, horseshoes and nails, were paid in kind[97]. A late fair to be granted (in 1301) was that for seventeen days annually (commencing on 23 June, the eve of the Nativity of St John the Baptist) in favour of Holm Cultram at Skinburness on the Solway coast. To this fair might come 'all merchants, English and foreign, by land or sea, except enemies'. Unfortunately only a few years later the fair (and burgh) had to be transfered inland to Newton Arlosh because of marine incursions[98].

In Wales, Strata Florida was (in the later Middle Ages) to be credited with three fairs a year at Rhos in the hills above the abbey: these may have been mostly concerned with the sale of cattle and horses. Whitland (at Eglwys Fair ar lan Tâf) came to hold five fairs each year at the principal feasts of Our Lady[99]. On the Continent King Andrew of Hungary gave Toplica (1213) a market in Bachusa[100]. Dobrilugk (1221) converted its village of Falkenburg into a market-place for trade with the Wends[101], whilst by 1241 Eldena had a weekly market in Rügen[102]. Marienthal opened a market on a strip of land it owned outside a gate of Magdeburg[103]. In the late thirteenth century Lubiąż and the nunnery of Trzebnica established a joint market[104]. A local market also facilitated the trade and revenue of Łekno[105]. Many of the Polish monasteries will have derived income from the village markets on their lands, as from the 'shambles' owned by Ląd[106]. Some Cistercian markets must have known times of difficulty, as when (in 1300, and at a time when unrest was beginning to make itself felt among the English peasantry) rioters stole both goods and toll-money from Meaux's market at Pocklington[107].

Urban Property

The early institutes of the Order allowed abbeys to maintain houses in neighbouring towns where this was necessary for the transaction of business, but no monk or *conversus* was to live in them on a permanent basis[108]. (Early conciliar decrees had recommended monasteries to have town houses, but as places of refuge in times of disturbances in the countryside[109].) The growth of trade by the white monks, and the desirability of having one of their own personnel to safeguard both property and business, meant that the regulations could not long be maintained. Long before the close of the twelfth century the General Chapter acknowledged the presence of religious in monastic town houses, but insisted (1189) that only *conversi* should be so resident – not monks, and that in a town where an abbey had acquired more than one house, only in one of them was there to be a resident *conversus*[110]. This remained the position, and the general practice, until in the late thirteenth century the numbers of *conversi* greatly dwindled. A further rule (1237) forbade women to live in any town house occupied by a *conversus*[111].

The first town houses acquired by the Cistercians were usually in cathedral cities, generally the most important centres of commerce in their regions[112]. At a time when exemption from episcopal control was far from complete, they gave the monks a residence if coming on business to the local bishop. By 1134 Himmerod had a house in Trier, by 1142 Ebrach and Heilsbronn a house in Würzburg[113], and by 1148 Altenberg a residence in Cologne[114]. The 1160s saw numerous town houses acquired or built by the white monks: Igny in Rheims (1161), Chaâlis in Senlis (1163) and Ourscamp in Soissons (1169), amongst them[115]. Later in the century, Bellevaux[116], Sawtry[117] and St Benoît-en-Woëvre[118] owned houses in the see cities respectively of Besançon, Ely, and Metz and Verdun. In Exeter three Cistercian abbeys owned residential property: Dunkeswell (in St Paul's parish)[119], and Buckfast and Newenham (in the cathedral close)[120].

The need for monks to have a place to stay was spelt out when Adam Seys gave the community of Dore: 'A piece of land that they may have a hostel when they come to Hereford'[121]. It was emphasised (in 1174) when Archbishop Guichard of Lyon, formerly abbot of Pontigny, confirmed a deed at Lyon: 'In the chamber which is called the Cistercian chamber'[122]. Other hospices included those given to Igny in Dieppe (1163)[123], Margam in Cardiff (by 1166)[124], Kirkstall in Pontefract (1178)[125] and Sénanque in Arles (1225)[126]. A house built by Berdoues (1188) in Auch catered for pilgrims *en route* to Compostella[127]: a hospice of Boulbonne in Toulouse for monks studying at the university prior to the more formal arrangements made there[128]. Mellifont (1348) acquired a residence in Drogheda for the abbot coming to meetings of the Irish Parliament[129].

Substantial town residences were erected by some 'proto-abbeys' for the large numbers of abbots of their 'generations' annually nearing Cîteaux for the General Chapter. Cîteaux itself had a large house in Dijon from 1162[130], and acquired a further property – outside the town walls on the banks of the Ouche – about ten years later. On that occasion the duke of Burgundy and the bishop of Langres met at the house and formally handed the keys to the prior[131]. Clairvaux extended its house in Dijon (1193–96) for abbots coming to Chapter and for meetings of the definitors thereafter[132]. Contributions towards its erection were sought[133], and the scale of the rebuilding raised some monastic eyebrows[134]. In addition to the provision made by Duke Hugh of wheat and wine for the abbots staying there, grants were made (1209) of a sack of salt and 400 eggs[135]. The first house of Morimond in Metz was given to it for abbots from northern Germany coming to Chapter: it also bought up three houses in Metz sold by debt-burdened Clairlieu. In 1261 Morimond further bought (for 84 *Dijon pounds*) a substantial property in Dijon[136].

Many charters granting town houses to the Cistercians do not specify the purposes for which the property was intended to be used[137]. Some however do, and it becomes clear that the principal urban granges or 'courts' were above all centres for the storage and sale of monastic produce, and places where formal business might be done. During the great famine years of the early fourteenth century, Zbraslav (1316), being 'indigent', had leave from the king of Bohemia: 'To sell and buy corn and wine at its court in Prague free of toll'[138]. Zlatá Koruna (1309) was granted a house in Krumau in east Austria for the specific purpose of 'selling its goods'[139]. Towns were safer in time of war than the rural areas, and so when (in 1319) Salem demised a house in Überlingen (but kept *part* in which to store goods) it retained the *whole* property for storage purposes until the war between Frederick of Hapsburg and the Landgrave of Bavaria had ended[140]. The urban houses were convenient places for meetings, and many of the business transactions of Rivalta Scrivia were carried out at its house in St Stephen's Gate in Tortona[141]. The abbot of Chambons (1289) was instructed to pay in his monastery's dues to the Order at the house of Bonneval in Lyons[142].

It was the need to trade that led abbeys to seek for their town houses exemption from import and other taxes, such as that given by the king of the Romans (1231) to Salem in respect of its hospices in Esslingen and Ulm[143]. It was for commercial purposes that monasteries sought houses in towns with major fairs: as did Clairvaux at Bar, Lagny, Provins and Troyes[144], and so many British abbeys in Boston. Within towns, for the same reason, Cistercian houses were often sited in market places: as by Garendon in Derby and Nottingham[145], Zlatá Koruna in Rožmberk[146] and St Bernard-opt-Scheldt in Antwerp[147]. Auberive had a house in Troyes in Croincels – the quarter of the drapers, tanners and butchers[148]. In town market-places abbeys would seek to set up their own shops or stalls, as did Coggeshall 'in the high street and market of Coggeshall'[149], Margam in Bristol[150], Sibton in Cambridge[151] and Strata Marcella in Shrewsbury[152]. In Leeds, Kirkstall had two shops 'at the head of the Fleshambles'[153]. Vale Royal owned thirteen shops in Chester[154], Alcobaça six in Santarém[155].

Monasteries with significant trading interests had urban property in a number of towns, some of them widely flung. Heisterbach had 'courts' not only all over the Rhineland, but also at Dordrecht on the mouth of the Rhine – a long way north, and at Linz by the Danube – far to the east[156]. Apart from Dijon, Paris and the fair towns, Clairvaux had distant property at Nieuwpoort on the Flanders coast, and by Boulogne close to the Straits of Dover[157]. Villers had houses in almost thirty towns, ranging from rent-paying domiciles to full-scale monastic 'courts'[158]. Sobrado's eleven urban houses included a house in Noya on the west coast of Spain and in La Coruña on the north[159]. Certain towns, as ports and capital cities, had a concentration of Cistercian property, like Paris (where nine abbeys had houses)[160], and London (where at least six, if not a number more, did)[161]. The London houses included those of Dieulacres (in Wood Street)[162], Thame (in 'Disteuelane')[163], Vale Royal (in Shoe Lane)[164], and Biddlesden (its abbot was assaulted there in 1280)[165]. Würzburg had a strong Cistercian presence, with thirteen abbeys represented: six by the mid-thirteenth century, the rest later – and all keen to sell their wine[166]. It made economic sense, especially in fair towns where houses might only be used for a short time each year, for two or more abbeys to share a property: as did (for a time at least) Buków and Dargun in Kotobrzeg[167], Silvanès and Valmagne in Montpellier[168], Ebrach, Heilsbronn and Langheim in Bamberg[169] and Würzburg[170], and Sallay and Jervaulx[171] (as well as Holm Cultram and Melrose)[172] in Boston. Other abbots shared Aubepierre's 'common house' in Limoges[173].

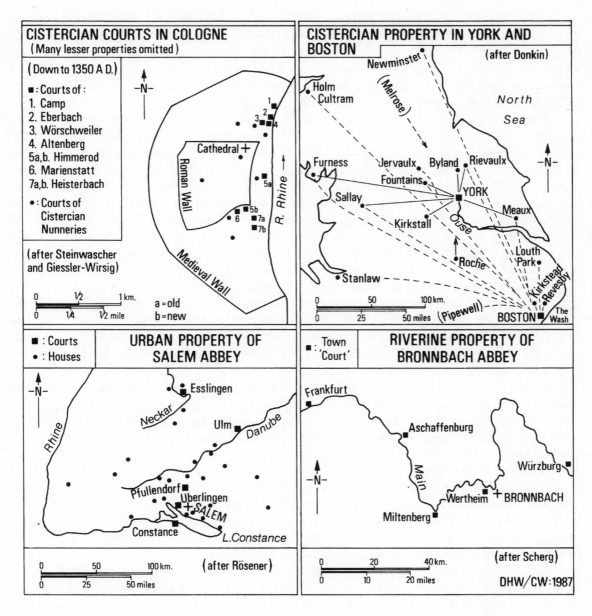

CISTERCIAN COURTS IN COLOGNE
(Many lesser properties omitted)

(Down to 1350 A.D.)

■ : Courts of:
1. Camp
2. Eberbach
3. Wörschweiler
4. Altenberg
5a,b. Himmerod
6. Marienstatt
7a,b. Heisterbach

● : Courts of Cistercian Nunneries

(after Steinwascher and Giessler-Wirsig)

0   ½   1 km.
0   ¼   ½ mile

a = old
b = new

-N-

Roman Wall

Cathedral +

Medieval Wall

R. Rhine

CISTERCIAN PROPERTY IN YORK AND BOSTON

(after Donkin)

Holm Cultram

(Melrose)

North Sea

Newminster

Furness   Jervaulx   Byland   Rievaulx

Fountains

Sallay   Kirkstall   YORK   Meaux

Ouse

Roche   Louth Park

Stanlaw   Kirkstead   Revesby

(Pipewell)   BOSTON ■   The Wash

-N-

0   50   100 km.
0   25   50 miles

■ : Courts
● : Houses

URBAN PROPERTY OF SALEM ABBEY

-N-

Rhine

Esslingen

Neckar

Ulm   Danube

Pfullendorf
Überlingen
+ SALEM

Constance

L. Constance

(after Rösener)

0   50   100 km.
0   25   50 miles

■ : Town 'Court'

RIVERINE PROPERTY OF BRONNBACH ABBEY

Frankfurt

Aschaffenburg

Main

Würzburg

Wertheim   + BRONNBACH

Miltenberg

-N-

(after Scherg)

DHW/CW:1987

0   20   40 km.
0   10   20 miles

Many of the sea-ports of Europe had one or more Cistercian urban 'courts', sometimes at a considerable distance from the parent abbey. The abbey of the Dunes on the Flanders coast owned a house in Dover[174]. The monastery of Gudvala, on the isle of Gotland in the Baltic, had a storage cellar at Tallinn (now in Estonia)[175]. Furness had a substantial complex across the Irish Sea in Marinerstown next to Drogheda[176]. Other properties were more local, as the houses of Amelunxborn[177] and Doberan[178] in Rostock, and that of Loccum in Bremen – the latter once violently occupied (in 1218) by fugitive monks[179]. By 1163 not only Igny but also Foucarmont[180] and Beaubec had property 'in the new port of Dieppe'; that of Beaubec was 'on the beach'[181]. Esrum had a house in Copenhagen[182], Lyse in Bergen[183] and Whitland in Carmarthen and Haverfordwest[184]. Gard[185] and Valloires had 'courts' at Abbeville, then at the mouth of the Somme: the latter's property was by the later St Paul's Quay[186]. By Lake Constance, Salem (1217) reclaimed land and built its large 'Salmansweiler Hof' on an artificially raised site[187].

River ports with a number of Cistercian owned houses included Cologne on the Rhine ('courts' of nine abbeys and seven nunneries of the Order)[188], Bristol on the

Avon (its access to the Bristol Channel making it an *entrepôt* for four Welsh monasteries)[189], York on the Ouse (some eight abbeys having interests)[190], Krems on the Danube (where Raitenhaslach[191] and other Austrian abbeys had interests[192]), and Verdun-sur-Garonne (for Grandselve)[193]. The houses of Kirkstead, Revesby and Vaudey in Lincoln had an outlet *via* the river Witham to the sea-port of Boston[194]. Of the ten urban 'courts' of Himmerod, four were in ports by the Rhine (as Cologne and Speyer) and three by the Moselle (as Trier and Zell)[195]. Monastic houses in river ports sought easy access to the water. In York, the holdings of Fountains, Furness[196] and Roche[197] extended to the bank of the river Ouse: indeed Fountains had a house on the principal bridge. In Cologne (where the Cistercian houses formed two clusters, one to the north and one to the south of the Roman walls) the 'court' of Camp was noted (in 1318) as being 'by the bank of the Rhine'[198]. In Würzburg on the Main, there was a similar grouping. The oldest Cistercian 'courts' were mostly to the south of the city as its walls stood in 1200: the houses acquired after 1250 were largely in the north, and there were only two 'courts' in the thirteenth century 'New City' extension[199].

In many towns the 'courts' were sited, if possible, near the walls; this made for easy access. Fontfroide's house in Carcassone (1194) stood 'under the walls' by the 'Money Tower'[200]. Most urban property was, like Doberan's 'court' in Rostock (1307), 'within the walls'[201]. This made the properties more secure, but some were outside town walls – as a house acquired by Fontmorigny (1261) near Montfaucon[202]. Holm Cultram, in the cathedral city of Carlisle, had property both 'within the walls' and 'in the suburb'[203]. Aduard's house in Groningen, 'Munnekeholm', had its own bridge leading over the town moat[204]. Especially sought were sites at the points of entry to towns, by their gates. Otterberg (1252) received the full use of a house in Worms 'before the Jewish Gate'[205]; a burgage in Bristol belonging to Stanley was 'beneath the gate'[206]; Balmerino acquired land in Perth in the Watergate and the street leading to the Inch[207]; Bonnecombe had a warehouse at the gates of Lodève[208]. There are numerous such examples. Settimo established a hospice called Cistello outside the Porta Pinti of Florence: not long afterwards it became the Cistercian nunnery of St Mary Magdalen the Penitent[209]. The Vallombrosan hospice of St Ermete outside the Oriental Gate of Pisa was taken over by the Cistercians, and became the little-known abbey of St Michael and St Ermete[210]. Eberbach's 'court' in Cologne stood opposite to 'St Servas-gate'[211], but both there and in Boppard, its 'courts' had their own 'gates' leading directly to the Rhine[212].

Some Cistercian town houses were existing properties bought for cash, as by Croxden (1308) in London for £20[213], and by Fontfroide (1218) in Narbonne for 2,000 *sous melgoriens*[214]. Six shops were acquired in Drogheda by Furness[215] and two houses in London by Tilty[216], in return for an obit made for the donor in the respective abbey church. Some urban property was built at the monks' behest. Adjoining sites were given to Santes Creus in Tàrrega, so that it could build first its 'cellar' (1188) and then its 'hospice' (1206)[217]. Clairvaux (1197) is noted as building a house at Neufchâteau, but without the local lord's consent[218]. Abbot Matthew of Melrose (1246–61) was praised by its chronicler: 'It was he who built our large houses in Berwick'[219]. There is plenty of evidence, especially from the mid-thirteenth century onwards, of early town 'courts' being reconstructed and extended[220]: like those of Riddagshausen in Brunswick (*c.* 1285)[221], Doberan in Rostock (1307)[222] and Fontfroide in Narbonne (1348)[223]. About 1249 Gard demolished its earlier property in Abbeville to build 'Little Gard', stretching for 24 metres (80 ft) along the bank of the Somme[224]. In 1279 Eberbach's 'court' in Cologne was reconstructed in such a way as helped to both protect the monastic property and to strengthen the city wall[225].

The urban 'courts' were normally walled for security reasons. There is contemporary note of the precinct walls of Pontigny's house in Chablis (1198)[226], Altenberg's court in

Cologne (1257)[227] and Tennenbach's property in Fribourg (1320)[228]. A dispute between Ourscamp and the Canons of St Bartholomew's, Noyon (1245) centred on a shared wall between their adjacent properties in Noyon[229]. Within a court's walls stood the principal hall over a vaulted storage cellar: this was the 'stone house' frequently referred to in relevant deeds. Warden had a 'stone house' in Norwich before 1200[230], Bebenhausen's property in Esslingen was called 'Steinhaus' (1257)[231] and there was note of Marienrode's 'stone house' in Hanover (1308)[232]. Such properties compared favourably to much surrounding timber-framed accommodation in the town. The medieval 'stone house' may have been much altered, even demolished, but the vaulted stone cellars often remain. Notable examples of cellars are to be seen at Ourscamp's 'great house in Paris'[233] (so-called in 1281)[234], at Chaâlis' cellar in the same street (rue François Miron)[235]; at that abbey's former properties in Senlis and Thorigny-sur-Marne[236], and at Pontigny's 'court' ('Little Pontigny') in Chablis. A vaulted cellar was described (in 1904) at Gard's house in Abbeville[237]. Finest of all is Clairvaux's 'court' in Dijon: a gothic stone-vaulted hall resting on a vaulted cellar of the late twelfth century[238].

The town 'courts' were often 'urban granges' in that they had a variety of other property to administer, and their customary position – near town walls or gate – was clearly helpful in this respect. Bronnbach (1206) was given a 'court' in Würzburg with which went: 'Merchants' chambers, winepress, wash-house, and the vineyard in Mount Steinbach'[239]. Vineyards were also held by the 'courts' of La Bussière in Beaune[240], of Fontmorigny in Aix[241] and of Tennenbach in Freiburg[242]. The latter house also had a mill, as did the 'courts' of Bonnecombe and Grandselve in Toulouse'[243]. Camp acquired a property with a brewhouse in Cologne in 1238[244], and beer was also brewed by Volkenrode at its 'court' in Mülhausen[245]. The 'court' of St Benoît-en-Woëvre in Verdun had a barn[246], that of Santes Creus in Cervera its bakehouse and garden[247]. The 'abbot's inn' of Vale Royal in Shoe Lane, London, included shops and cellars[248]. Large adjacent 'courts' may have been named separately – as, in Würzburg: 'Great' and 'Little' Ebrach (by 1325) and 'Great' and 'Little' Bronnbach (by 1340)[249]. Usually the prefix 'Little' was borne by the principal urban 'court', by way of contrasting it to the abbey proper: such was 'Little Doberan' in Rostock, so known by 1307[250]. The medieval Cistercian urban presence is still evident today in street-names[251], like 'Fountains Lane' in Boston[252], 'Monk's Lane' in Nantwich[253] and 'rue de Fontmorigny' in both Bourges and Nevers[254]. The south gate of Mussy-sur-Seine was nicknamed 'Auberive Gate', because that abbey's town house stood nearby[255].

An integral part of major urban 'courts', from the mid-thirteenth century, was a chapel for the resident monks and *conversi* to worship. Such chapels had been known earlier, as is suggested by the General Chapter's rebuke to the abbot of Aiguebelle (in 1191) for burying a dead person in one of its town 'courts'[256]. There were early chapels at Clairvaux's house in Dijon (1223)[257], at Lützel's property in Basle (1224)[258], and at Sénanque's hospice in Arles (1225)[258a]. As a common feature they do not appear until the opposition of the Order to grange chapels was breaking down. Alexander IV permitted Mass to be said, *inter alia*, in Fontfroide's house in Narbonne (1258)[259] and in the town houses of Velehrad (1261)[260]. Cheminon built a chapel in Vitry-le-Château in 1253[261], and Gard at Abbeville in 1263[262]. There are numerous later records of chapels being built, but some of these – if not most – may well concern rebuilding on a grander scale of earlier simpler oratories, and perhaps reflected the presence by that time in many town houses of monks rather than *conversi*. Such included Volkenrode's chapel in Mülhausen (1279)[263], Aduard's chapel in Groningen (1340)[264] and Heiligenkreuz's chapel in Pozsony (Bratislava; 1311)[265]. In that city Pilis also had a chapel, next to which (about 1335) a new synagogue was built: the monks complained that, because of the clamour the Jews made, they could not properly recite their office![266]

Town chapels, like grange chapels, if opened to the public, could be to the detriment of the well-being of the local parish clergy. It was stipulated, therefore, that any offerings made in Clairvaux's Dijon chapel (1223) were to be remitted to the parish of Saint-Etienne[267]. In a lengthy agreement between Santes Creus and the parish priest of Cervera (1289), detailed arrangements were made as to the liturgy and the offerings. There was always to be a resident priest-monk who was permitted to ring the chapel bells for the services, and perform the asperges before Sunday Mass, but the public were not to be admitted to the blessing of candles or of palms at Candlemas and on Palm Sunday[268]. As grange chapels, so too town chapels had a specific dedication: such as to Our Lady (Gard's chapel in Abbeville)[269], and to St Catherine (Grandselve's chapel in Bordeaux[270] and Zwettl's chapel in Vienna[271]). Himmerod's chapel in Cologne, grand and important enough to be dedicated by the archbishop of that see in 1355, was not short of patrons. It was consecrated not only in honour of Our Lady, but also of Saints Peter and Paul, Bernard, Catherine, Barbara, Mary Magdalene, Mary of Egypt and All Martyrs[272].

The immediate supervision of Cistercian town houses was, from the late twelfth century on, generally in the hands of resident *conversi*, though perhaps never more than one or two aided by lay servants. Such custodians included Eudo – a long-serving 'master' of Clairvaux's house in Dijon (1208–25)[273], and Sybotone – 'master' of Heiligenkreuz's 'court' in Baden (1263)[274]. Byland was given leave by the General Chapter (1238) to send two *conversi* to live in its house in London, but they were to be 'of proven life and behaviour'[275]. Such an isolated posting could present potential temptations. As the numbers of *conversi* dwindled, so monks increasingly took over the command of the town houses. In Cologne *conversi* were 'masters' for Altenberg's property until 1286 at least, but monks from 1301 on. *Conversi* cared for Camp's house there in 1238, but monks by 1290. *Conversi* had charge of Eberbach's court until 1307, but monks by 1330[276]. Other fourteenth century instances suggest that monks were now much to the fore[277]. Whether monks or *conversi* the 'court' managers had occasionally to be reminded of their duties. The General Chapter (1282) told them to receive charitably travelling personnel of the Order[278]. As part of an agreement between Aduard and the State of Groningen (1346), the abbot had to command the 'master' of its house in that town: 'To deal honestly as befits religious'[279].

To facilitate their trade, the white monks obtained wide-ranging privileges in respect of their urban 'courts': a practice which could lead to resentment from the other town dwellers – though the municipality of Berne affectionately referred (in 1386) to the monks of Frienisberg as 'our very old citizens'[280]. The exemptions granted Cistercian town houses, usually from all exactions (as customs and market dues) and services (as keeping watch), included those given by the landgrave of Thuringia in respect of Arnsburg (1230)[281], by the consuls of Stralsund (1257) in favour of Neuenkamp[282], by the town of Brunswick in favour of Riddagshausen (1266)[283] and by the duke of Austria in respect of Heiligenkreuz (1286)[284]. Salem's urban houses, whilst exempt in all other respects, had to pay the 4 *pfennig* property tax common to all householders[285]. Jealous of its rights, Altenkamp obtained a declaration of its privileges in 1285 from the archbishop of Cologne, and then inscribed a notice to this effect on the gates of its 'court' there[286]. Ourscamp (in 1267) placed a stone cross on the top of its Paris house as a sign of its immunity from exactions[287].

It may have been potential antipathy that led Louis IX to request Maubuisson nunnery to limit its urban holdings to one or two houses in any one place[288]. In Bordeaux there was a certain tension between the wine merchants and the trading interests of Grandselve[289]. In Abbeville (1259) criminals tried to escape justice by taking refuge in Valloires' 'court' there: in a concord agreed with the town, the monastery surrendered some of its rights[290]. In southern Germany there were disputes between abbeys such as Eberbach (with the citizens of Cologne)[291], Waldsassen (with those of Eger)[292] and Bebenhausen (with the townsfolk of Esslingen, Reutlingen[293] and Ulm[294]). A bull of Boniface VIII (in 1296), declaring the white monks free of customs dues, especially angered the people of Würzburg[295]. They were demanding from the numerous Cistercian houses in their town, 6 *pfennigs* for every imported bushel of corn, and one pound of '*hellers*' (pence) for every imported tun of wine. In a riot the town bells were rung and the people stormed the monastic 'courts', broke down the gates, took (it is said) the keys, and brought out the stored corn and wine for public sale[296].

Apart from the principal house or trading 'court', most abbeys had other town houses of a lesser scale which were – from the time of their acquisition – simply a source of income gained from rent-paying tenants. Neath held many houses in Cardiff (from 1289) as part of an exchange agreement with the earl of Gloucester: it had thirty-six burgages in St Mary Street alone[297]. Altenberg owned one hundred or so houses in Cologne[298]. Where property was mostly used as a hospice for abbots and monks staying only for short periods, it was advantageous to lease out the property but to retain the use of certain rooms and services for their needs when required. Kirkstall (in the 1180s) demised a house it had not long acquired in Pontefract, but on condition that the monks could stay whenever they wished[299]. Leasing out a house in Ulm (in 1241) Salem retained the use of a cellar and an upper room, perhaps for the storage of wine and corn: the tenant gave 30 marks for a life-lease, and had to maintain the roof[300]. Holm Cultram (1300) gave land for a secular to build a house at his own cost, but he had to accommodate and provide stabling for up to seven horses for any monks coming to Carlisle 'wearing their habits'[301]. Fontfroide (1305) demised property in Béziers on condition that the lessee gave any visiting monks a bed, food, fire and fodder[302]. When (in 1262) Fontfroide leased out a house in Aix-d'Angillon to a clerk, an inventory was made of its contents. They included two casks, four vats, three wash-tubs, and ten beds[303].

Ships and Harbours

The importance of shipping for the transport of bulky commodities as corn, salt and wool, is plain, and few monasteries would have been without a boat of some kind, even if only a small vessel plying on its fishpond. Inland monasteries (as, in England, Vale Royal and Waverley) may have commissioned or hired boats in undertaking overseas trade, or to transport commodities to a collecting port (such as Boston). Coastal monasteries, and houses by major rivers, generally owned their own boats – sometimes ships capable of being sea-going vessels. What it is difficult to ascertain is the nature and size of these ships, as there are very few contemporary descriptions. Meaux had one costly ship – probably a keel – to construct which the monks had felled an entire wood. Built about 1250 it was valued at 200 marks; but, debt-ridden, the abbey soon sold it for only 60 marks[304]. The larger boats of both Beaulieu[305] and Quarr[306] were felt suitable enough to convey Queen Eleanor to Gascony in 1254[307]. A survey, in 1325, of ships of over 100 tons reveal only four such on the English coast between the Severn and the Solway, but one of them – probably a cog – belonged to Furness[308].

British Cistercian seagoing vessels were frequently alluded to in Crown documentation. Royal letters giving safe-conduct or exemption from customs duties note, *inter alia*, a ship of Melrose (1225) taking wool to Flanders[309], a vessel of Boxley (1225) sent to Berwick for herrings[310] and a boat of Quarr (1327) in dock at Lescluse in Flanders[311]. Some such licences name a lay helmsman and an accompanying *conversus* as being in charge[312]. A ship might be mentioned as required by the Crown: like a boat of Beaulieu sent to Ireland in 1321[313], and vessels of Furness used by Edward III in 1334[314]. A boat might be noted as stolen (as one of Holm Cultram from Skinburness in 1300)[315], or forfeit (as one of St Mary's, Dublin, in 1194 – following acts of piracy by the hanged *conversus* who was its 'keeper')[316]. Boats of Holm Cultram (1175) went to fish in Ulster[317] and to trade in the Isle of Man[318]. King Godric of Man (1155–87) ordered that if any were wrecked, its goods were to be retained by the abbey[319]. In Wales, Aberconwy, Cymer, Margam, Neath and Tintern all had sea-going vessels[320]. Neath's boat (in 1235) was aptly named the *Hulc*[321], and other ship-names included (for Beaulieu) *La Mariote* (1254)[322], *La Stelle* or *La Stoyle* (1268)[323], and the *Salvata* (1270)[324]; (for Furness) the *Sealwe* (1258)[325], (for Netley) *La Russynole* (1271)[326], (for Quarr) *La Nicholas* (1327)[327] and *La Mariote* (1336)[328] and (for St Mary's, Dublin) *Le Rodship* (1294)[329]. The *Salvata* made two long-distance trips in 1270: one being to Gascony, the other to 'the northern parts' – probably meaning Yarmouth[330].

Ships were essential in Norway to the fiord island monasteries of Hovedøya and Lyse. King John (1212) exempted ships of Lyse from tolls in English ports[331], but royal officers detained temporarily a boat of Hoveydøya (1237) because of an alleged debt of King Håkon to the Crown[332]. A ship of Lyse coming across the North Sea (in 1337) was taken by pirates, and the abbot and his company beheaded[333]. Boats of Aduard plied up the Elbe estuary to Hamburg, with a stopping point *en route* at Stade[334]. The scale of its trade there, free from tolls, led a merchant of Hamburg (1273) to complain to the archbishop of Bremen – whose port Stade was – asking that the abbey's vessels called there less often[335]. In Hamburg itself protracted wars interfered with Aduard's shipping and trade. The upshot was a treaty of friendship (1347) between the monastery and the citizens[336], as well as satisfaction made to Aduard (1348) for damage done to its vessels and property[337]. In France, Beaubec kept a seagoing vessel at Le Tréport (by 1170)[338], and its ships sailed as far afield as Drogheda in Ireland (by 1218)[339] and Bristol in England (1237)[340]. In Flanders the Dunes was given leave by Henry II (1187) to 'make new ships and sell old ones'[341]. There are frequent mentions of its vessels[342], one of which conveyed up the Rhine the English envoys seeking the release from captivity of Richard I[343].

Caesarius of Heisterbach (*ob.* 1240) told of its ships suffering from pirates and tempests as they plied down the Rhine to Zealand[344]. On the Rhine were also boats of Altenberg (noted in 1183)[345], of Neuburg (with the customary downstream cargoes of wine and corn, and upstream of fish and salt)[346], and Eberbach (with freedom from toll also for 'fruit and vegetables, butter, oil, iron, leather')[347]. A 'navigator' was named (in 1241) amongst the *conversi* of Eberbach[348]. In northern Italy there is early note of boats of Morimondo Milano (1184) sailing on the rivers Po and Ticino[349]. In Flanders the boats of the Dunes sailed on canals taking wool to the drapers[350]. In France, Bonport (1190) had ships plying up the Seine as far as and beyond Conflans, and then perhaps to Paris[351]. A *conversus* with a wine-laden boat of Ourscamp (1306) sailed on the Oise under the bridge of Compiègne[352]. In England river traffic, on presumably relatively small boats, included that of Beaulieu[353], Hailes and Medmenham on the Thames, Dieulacres on the Dee[354] and Rievaulx on the Ouse[355]. A long-boat found in the old river bed of the Trent may have belonged to Hulton[356]. In the Lake District, Furness had a boat carrying timber on Lake Windermere[357]. In France, Hautecombe's boats could enter its 'Water Grange' by Lake Bourget[358]. In south-west Wales, Whitland had a half-share in the ferry boat of Llanstephan[359].

Shipping needed sheltered havens for beach landings, or harbours and wharfs – depending on vessel type and draught. In Ireland, St Mary's, Dublin, had the advantage of possessing coastal lands which allowed it to control four small ports, including Carrickbrennan (Monkstown now) and Blowick (Bullock today): in addition it had a quay in Dublin where Broadstone Street Station now stands[360]. Dunbrody, at the head of a calm ria inlet, had the indicative Latin official name of *Portus S. Mariae*[361]. In

Portugal Alcobaça had three harbours: one, Nazaré, was completely besanded by 1532[362]. In Spain Oia's ships harboured in the adjacent sheltered bay off the Ria de Vigo[363]. In England Meaux owned the port of Hull on the Humber: a major port by 1198, it was sold to Edward I in 1293[364]. Robertsbridge had a house in Rye, Sussex, with a quay attached[365]. In south-west Scotland the boats of Dundrennan moored at Abbey Burnfoot, 1½ miles (2·5 km) distant on the Solway Firth[366]. (This haven was later to be used, in 1568, by Mary, Queen of Scots[367].) The vessels of New Abbey (Sweeetheart) used the deep channel of the Abbey Pow, about 0·5 miles (0·8 km) away, where it enters the Nith estuary[368]. In Wales traces of a landing-stage at Strata Florida's reputed Cardigan Bay port at Aberarth remained a century or so ago[369]. Still to be seen (in Belgium) is the overgrown harbour of St Bernard-opt-Scheldt (at Hemiksem): the military now occupy the former monastery.

In France two abbeys (Fontmorigny[370] and La Bénissons-Dieu[371]) owned the river ports on the Loire of Laubray and of Randans (and later Briennon) respectively: both were quite close to their parent monastery. To oversee its interests in Laubray, for others shared and paid for its use[372], the abbey (in 1276) placed a former abbot, Nicholas, there as its representative on the spot[373]. In England an early deed gave Roche a landing site for loading and unloading its vessels at a point between North and South Stather on the river Trent: near its mouth into the Humber[374], which the abbey's goods could reach by land or on the Idle river[375]. From there its boats might go coastwise south to Boston, across the Humber to Hull, or upstream to York – where it also had a landing-stage (on the Ouse) by the orchard of St Clement's nunnery[376]. A nineteenth century plan marks the 'Monks' Harbour' at the site of Louth Park in Lincolnshire[377]. A ship-loading platform may have fronted the river Aire at Kirkstall[378]. The coastwise transhipment of Margam's corn, from Whitecross Grange to the abbey, can be demonstrated from medieval deeds[379]. In the instance of Tintern's grange at Woolaston by the Severn Estuary, recent excavation has uncovered a mid-twelfth century stone and timber harbour[376] capable of taking sea-going vessels as well as river craft[380]. This facilitated shipment of produce both up the Wye to the abbey and across the Channel to Bristol for sale or export.

Notes

1. Waddell (1994) 33–34.
2. *DCK* 199–201.
3. France (1992) 318.
4. Steinwascher (1981) 108.
5. Tromp (1989) 31.
6. Snell (1967) 42.
7. Donkin (1978) 160.
8. Schich (1987) 57.
9. Williams (1984) II, 318.
10. D'Arbois (1858) 240.
11. *CDSL* I, 262; II, 17, 20, 29, 490, 520.
12. *Statuta* I, 24–25 (1134/LI); *cf.* Graves (1957) 11–12.
13. *Statuta* I, 187 (1195/34).
14. Waddell (1994) 30, *cf.* his comments at 1993 Fontfroide Conference.
15. *Statuta* I, 24–25 (1134/LI).
16. Waddell (1994) 33.
17. *Statuta* I, 24–25 (1134/LI).
18. Schich (1987) 58–59; *cf.* Roehl (1972) 108.
19. Lekai (1977a) 311.
20. Wiswe (1953) 129.
21. *CDF* 186 (No. 529).
22. *DHGE* XIX (1981) 1218.
23. *CDF* I, 296–97, 300 (No. 825).
24. *CDF* 38.
25. *CDAC* 101 (No. 108).
26. *OSBS* (1) 2–3 (No. 2, of 1142).
27. *RCC* II, 256–60; IV, 421.
28. France (1992) 318.
29. *CTD* 38–50.
30. *CAS* II, 154 (No. DLXVI).
31. Wiswe (1953) 129.
32. Deck (1974) 34, 140.
33. *CAF* 21.
34. Wiswe (1953) 129.
35. *RN* xv, 161–62.
36. *RHC* 42.
37. Steinwascher (1981) 108.
38. Schulz (1979) 31.
39. Steinwascher (1981) 111–11.
40. Sculze (1979) 33.
41. Scherg (1976) 161.
42. *UE* I, 81–82, 118–19, 154–55, 199–201.
43. *RD* I, 605 (Nos 3581, 3584).
44. *RD* I, 581 (No. 3419).

398   *The Cistercians in the Early Middle Ages*

45.   *CPR* 1277/202, 1291/426.
46.   *KD* I, 64–65.
47.   *KDM* II, 42.
48.   *KD* I, 166–67.
49.   *KD* I, 22–28.
50.   Williams (1984) I, 13.
51.   *Ibid.* II 317.
51a. *CMM* I, 421.
51b. *CABR* 692–94 (No. X).
52.   Cf. *C.P.R.* 1278/250.
53.   Carville (1981) 44.
54.   *RHC* 94–95 (Nos 265–267).
55.   *CPR* 1280/397.
56.   *CCR* 1246/494.
57.   *CPR* 1227/136; *cf.* Morton (1936) 229.
58.   *CPR* 1282/59.
59.   *CPR* 1276/185, 1278/265.
60.   Williams (1984) II, 312, 318.
61.   *CPR* 1222/32.
62.   Carville (1981) 51*n.*
63.   *C.P.R.* 1281/457.
64.   *C.P.R.* 1279/315.
65.   Williams (1984) II, 315–17.
66.   *DCK* 219–20.
67.   *CHS* 250.
68.   Johnsen (1977) 44, 74.
69.   Thompson (1920) 91.
70.   Silva (1981) 115.
71.   Dimier (1964) 189.
72.   *RCC* III, 243 (No. 826); IV, 62 (No. 1019), 427 (No. 1201).
73.   Berman (1978) 304–05.
74.   Berman (1979) 205*n.*
75.   *CDCDS* 280.
76.   *CS* II, 82–83.
77.   *RHC* 13.
78.   *RHC* 90–91 (Nos 258–259).
79.   *SBC* II, 26 (No. 29).
80.   *DCK* 193–97, 200–01.
81.   Donkin (1978) 160.
82.   Boyd (1943) 143, 157.
83.   Donkin (1978) 154.
84.   *Ibid.* 155.
85.   VCH, *Stafford* III (1970) 231.
86.   *AF* 202, 208. *cf.* Donkin (1978) 158.
87.   Davidson (1843) 123.
88.   Stalley (1987) 21.
89.   Lekai (1977a) 311.
90.   Donkin (1978) 158.
91.   VCH, *Essex* II (1907) 125.
92.   VCH, *Hampshire* II (1903) 147.
93.   Sparks (1978) 56.
94.   Donkin (1967) 198–200.
95.   *ABB* 84.
96.   *ABB* 12.
97.   *ABB* 84.
98.   *RHC* 95–96 (Nos 267a-c).
99.   Williams (1984) II, 317.
100. *CDCDS* 121 (No.   99).
101. Thompson (1920) 92.
102. *Ibid.* 91.
103. *Ibid.* 92.
104. *Ibid.* 92.
105. *KD* I, 23–24, 26–28.
106. Staat Archiv, Cologne. Kl. Lond. I, ff. 45v–46r.
107. *C.P.R.* 1300/550.
108. Waddell (1994) 33; *cf. Statuta* I, 13 (1134/1), *LCC* (1) 36.
109. Henocq (1970) 528, Péchenard (1883) 339.
110. *Statuta* I, 112 (1189/11); *LCC* (1) 131.
111. *Statuta* I, 88 (1180/13), *LCC* (2) 321.
112. Elm (1980) 224.
113. *Ibid.* 224.
114. *UKA* 6–7 (No. 3).
115. Lohrmann (1975) 176*n.*
116. Redoutey (1982) 730.
117. Donkin (1978) 167–68.
118. *CSBW* 73–74, 88–89.
119. Sparks (1978) 29.
120. Donkin (1978) 167–68.
121. *Catal. Ancient Deeds* III, 294 (B. 4106).
122. Dimier (1978a) 49.
123. Lohrmann (1975) 176*n.*
124. Williams (1984) II, 314.
125. Donkin (1959) 112.
126. Moyne (1857) 267–70.
127. *CB* 35 (No. 52).
128. Lekai (1971b) 314.
129. Mellifont Guide, 21.
130. Richard (1991) 149.
131. *CDAC* 170–71 (No. 211).
132. *LMT* 193–94 (No. 87); *RCC* II, 263.
133. *Statuta* I, 169 (1193/60).
134. *Statuta* I, 194 (1195/82).
135. RCC III, 53 (No. 588).
136. Dubois (1879) 298–99.
137. Anton (1986) 103.
138. *RBM* III, 135 (No. 335); *cf. LKZ* 14–15.
139. *UKG* 46–48 (No. XVIII).
140. Rösener (1974) 132.
141. *CRS* II, *passim.*
142. *CABR* 239–40.
143. *CDSL* I, 202–03.
144. *RCC* IV, 423 (No. 1175, of 1231).
145. Humphrey (1982) 28.
146. Čechura (1987) 98.
147. *OSBS* (1) IV (of 1303).
148. Grandmottet (1958) 6.
149. Donkin (1959) 113 (of 1336).
150. Williams (1984) II, 313.
151. Waller (1903) 355–56.
152. *CSA* 146, 149, 161.
153. Lancaster (1895) 39.
154. Donkin (1959) 113 (of 1299).
155. Durand (1983) 109.
156. Hardenberg (1935) 66–69.
157. *RCC* III, 51 (No. 571, of 1208); VI, 163 (No. 1825, of 1265).
158. *DHGE* VI (1934) 556 (of 1272).
159. Silva (1981), Map 3.
160. De Montgolfier (1986) 13–16.
161. Donkin (1978) 163, 168–69.
162. VCH, *Stafford* III (1970) 231.
163. *TC* II, 169 (of *c.* 1240).
164. Donkin (1959) 112.
165. Midmer (1979) 66.
166. Schich (1979a) 86, *cf.* Elm (1980) 225.
167. Schlegel (1980) 21 (by 1355).
168. *CSV* 360 (of 1161).
169. Roth (1986) 552.
170. Schich (1979a) 48 (of 1154).
171. *CS* II, 98–99.
172. *RHC* 90–91.

173. *Statuta* II, 212 (1239/47).
174. Van Nerom (1983) 48.
175. *DHGE* XXII (1988) 643.
176. *AF* 197–99.
177. Wiswe (1953) 126–27.
178. Lindenthaal (1979) 18.
179. *Statuta* I, 493 (1218/43).
180. *CDF* 63 (No. 185).
181. Deck (1974) 139.
182. McGuire (1982) 134.
183. Roth (1986) 531.
184. Williams (1984) II, 315.
185. Tribout (1972) 221.
186. Henocq (1970) 528.
187. Rösener (1974) 132.
188. Steinwascher (1981) 61.
189. Williams (1984) II, 315.
190. *Cf.* Donkin (1959) 109.
191. Krausen (1977) 117.
192. *Cf.* Chapter 18.
193. Cazes (1982) 231.
194. Graves (1957) 13.
195. Elm (1980) 225.
196. Donkin (1959) 109.
197. Mullin (1932) 47.
198. Steinwascher (1981) 32–33.
199. Schich (1979a), 86 (Map).
200. Cauvet (1875) 147.
201. Lindenthaal (1979) 19.
202. *CAF* 259.
203. *RHC* 12–16.
204. Tromp (1989) 31.
205. *UKO* 78.
206. *CHS* 250.
207. Campbell (1899) 120.
208. Berman (1979) 212.
209. Bedini (1964) 139.
210. *Ibid.* 165; Van Der Meer (1965) 295.
211. Steinwascher (1981) 23.
212. Elm (1980) 226.
213. *CC* (2) B. 42.
214. Cauvet (1875) 144.
215. VCH, *Lancaster* II (1908) 120–21.
216. VCH, *Essex* II (1907) 134.
217. Fort i Cogul (1972) 296 (No. 73).
218. *RCC* II, 264.
219. *CM* 97.
220. *Cf.* Chauvin (1983a) 36.
221. *CRD* 34.
222. Lindenthaal (1979) 18.
223. Cauvet (1875) 144–45.
224. Macqueron (1904) 53, Tribout (1972) 221.
225. Steinwascher (1981) 24.
226. *PCP* 354–55 (No. 358).
227. Steinwascher (1981) 18.
228. *TG* 168–74.
229. *CO* 23–24 (No. XXXV).
230. Donkin (1978) 168.
231. Elm (1982) 151.
232. *MUK* 164 (No. 151).
233. Dimier (1972b) 64–67, (1974a) 54–55.
234. *CO* 101 (No. CLII).
235. De Montgolfier (1986) 15.
236. Blary (1989) 309, 332, 335.
237. Macqueron (1904) 55.
238. Dimier (1974a) 55.
239. Schich (1979a) 55.
240. *CAF* 260–61.
241. *RCC* V, 72 (No. 1280).
242. *TG* 168–74.
243. Berman (1986) 123.
244. Giessler-Wirsig (1979) 106.
245. Winter (1868) II, 187.
246. *CSBW* 74 (of 1182).
247. Fort i Cogul (1975) 220 (No. 56, of 1257).
248. Donkin (1959) 112.
249. Schich (1979a) 50, 71.
250. Lindenthaal (1979) 18–19.
251. Chauvin (1983a) 36.
252. Mullin (1932) 46–47.
253. Hall (1896) 4.
254. Vaslin (1990) 70.
255. Grandmottet (1958) 9.
256. *RD* I, 867 (No. 5228).
257. Richard (1991) 152.
258. Chèvre (1973) 55.
258a. Moyne (1981) 269–70 (No. 8).
259. Cauvet (1875) 146.
260. *CDRB* V: 1, 388 (No. 255).
261. *RCCH* 121.
262. Macqueron (1904) 53.
263. *DHG* I, 769–70.
264. Post (1922) II, 212.
265. *RCH* 106.
266. *RCH* 144.
267. Richard (1991) 152.
268. Fort i Cogul (1975) 221–24.
269. Macqueron (1904) 53.
270. Higounet (1982) 699.
271. *LFZ* 266–68.
272. Steinwascher (1981) 40.
273. *RCC* III, 51 (No. 575), 375 (No. 931).
274. *UKSH* 159 (No. CLXIX).
275. *Statuta* II, 193 (1238/44).
276. Steinwascher (1981) 191.
277. *E.g:* Dubois (1879) 299, Theurot (1995) 43.
278. *Statuta* III, 218 (1282/4).
279. Gottschalk (1955) I, 168–70 (No. XLIX).
280. *DHGE* XIX (1981) 85.
281. *UKAR* 9 (No. 15).
282. *PU* II, 40; *UKN* 21.
283. *CRD* 34.
284. *UKSH* 253 (No. CCLXXIX), *cf.* 105 (No. XCVII, of 1242).
285. Rösener (1974) 136–37.
286. Steinwascher (1981) 165.
287. *CO* 166–67 (No. CCLXXV).
288. Kinder (1976) 165.
289. Mousnier (1983c) 240.
290. Henocq (1970) 258–59.
291. Lekai (1977a) 320.
292. Rösener (1983a) 151.
293. Elm (1982) 151.
294. Lekai (1977a) 320.
295. Steinwascher (1981) 71.
296. Schich (1979a) 71.
297. Williams (1984) II, 314.
298. *UKA* 697–704 (No. 913, of 1375).
299. Donkin (1959) 112; *cf. CS* II, 91–93 (Sawley).
300. *CDSL* I, 246–27; *cf.* Rösener (1974) 135.
301. *RHC* 16; *cf.* PRO, E 40/ B. 2684 (Quarr).
302. Cauvet (1875) 147.
303. *CAF* 260–61, *cf.* 89, 92.

304. *CMM* II, xix; *cf.* Earle (1906) 14. I am grateful to Dr M. Redknap for comments on ship size and harbouring.
305. Hockey (1976) 143.
306. Donkin (1976) 143.
307. *Cf.* VCH, *Hampshire* II (1903) 138.
308. *CACW* 219.
309. *C.P.R.* 1225/519.
310. *C.P.R.* 1225/505 (in time for Lent).
311. *C.P.R.* 1327/216.
312. *Cf. C.P.R.* 1225/519 (Coupar).
313. Donkin (1978) 143.
314. VCH, *Lancaster* II (1908) 118.
315. *C.P.R.* 1300/554.
316. *C.P.R.* 1294/60.
317. *RHC* 95 (No. 267a).
318. *RHC* 94.
319. *RHC* 94 (No. 265a).
320. Williams (1984) II, 316.
321. *Ibid.* 316.
322. Donkin (1978) 143.
323. *C.P.R.* 1268/192, 308.
324. *ABB* 170*n*.
325. *C.P.R.* 1258/624.
326. *C.P.R.* 1271/577.
327. *C.P.R.* 1327/216.
328. Hockey (1970) 133.
329. *C.P.R.* 1294/60.
330. *ABB* 37, 171.
331. France (1992) 121.
332. Johnsen (1977) 51.
333. France (1992) 365.
334. *MG* 41–42 (No. No. XXI, of 1273), 158 (No. XLVI, of 1342).
335. Rijksarchief Groningen, OA 2.
336. Rijksarchief Groningen, OA 5.
337. Rijksarchief Groningen, OA 6.
338. Deck (1974) 140.
339. *CDL* 188.
340. *C.C.R.* 1237/471.
341. *CDF* 493 (No. 1364).
342. *E.g: Statuta* I, 130 (1190/63); *OHZ* II, 64–65 (No. 461; of 1223–26).
343. Van Nerom (1983) 41.
344. *CHDM* I, 66–69, 515–16, 522–23.
345. *UKA* 19–20 (No. 13).
346. Schulz (1979) 36–38.
347. Staab (1987) 89.
348. *Ibid.* 87.
349. Occhipinti (1983) 544.
350. Dimier (1964) 185.
351. *CBP* 7–8 (Nos VIII–X), 11 (No. XIV).
352. *CO* 32–33.
353. Hockey (1976) 80.
354. Donkin (1978) 193.
355. McDonnell (1963) 121*n*.
356. Wise (1985) 54.
357. *AF* 203.
358. Dimier (1964) 180, (1973) 56.
359. Lewis (1927) 121 (info. of Eiluned Rees).
360. Carville (1972b) 41.
361. Van Der Meer (1965) 277.
362. Mascarenhas (1994) 155.
363. Tomé (1991) 94, 96.
364. Mullin (1932) 47.
365. Cooper (1856) 154.
366. Butler and Given-Wilson (1979) 206.
367. Richardson (1981) 5.
368. Richardson (1951) 7.
369. Williams (1889) 107–08.
370. *Cf. CAF* 117 (of 1215), 307 (of 1276).
371. Peyron (1982) 219–20.
372. *CAF* 257, 316, 346, 352, 356–65.
373. *CAF* 307.
374. Aveling (1876) 111.
375. Mullin (1932) 48.
376. Aveling (1876) 159–60.
377. *CPL* 57–61, and Map opp. xlii.
378. Pirie (1967) 32–33.
379. Williams (1984) II, 318.
380. Fulford (1992) 101–27

Chapter 20

THE NUNNERIES

Growth and Distribution

Almost concurrent with the rapid spread of the male abbeys was a parallel growth of nunneries which were, or liked to think they were, Cistercian. The origins of many of them are obscure – and as often there is no record of their formal incorporation into the Order – it is not always certain which nunneries were truly Cistercian and which were simply following the Cistercian way of life. The earliest convents founded were so with the backing of senior figures of the Order: Tart (in 1125) established by Abbot Stephen Harding of Cîteaux[1], and Belfays (in 1128) by Abbot Walter of Morimond[2]. They may in part have been a solution as to what to do with the wives and other female relations of married men wishing to enter the Order, although the womenfolk of St Bernard and his companions entered the convent of Jully (fd 1113) which remained Benedictine[3]. Other nunneries came into the Order with the incorporation (in 1147) of the congregations of Obazine (notably Coyroux) and Savigny (as Villers-Canivet)[4]. In those early decades there appears to have been little or no hostility towards the female element: St Bernard expressly advised some nunneries to adopt the Cistercian way of life[5]. Until the thirteenth century formal admission of nunneries to the Order was (so far as we can tell) not a general practice, and the nuns, though counselled and inspected by Cistercian abbots, were seen as 'imitators' of the Order rather than as 'members' of it[6]. The paucity (before the 1180s) of information regarding individual houses in the published statutes of the General Chapter, means that relatively little is known of the life and activities of Cistercian nuns for much of the twelfth century.

By the early-thirteenth century there was a flood of existing nunneries wishing to enter the Order, and many benefactors hoping to endow new ones. The reasons are not far to seek. In north-western Europe it was a time of spiritual fervour epitomised by the 'religious women's' movement[7], and numerous Cistercian nunneries had their origins in the beguinages – including Fontenelle, Gnadental and Magdenau[8]. Other nunneries might also genuinely wish to share in the outstanding spirituality the white monks then presented. Some convents may have had mixed motives, wanting to avail themselves of Cistercian privileges – such as exemption from the payment of tithes and from episcopal control[9]. Would-be founders had the same reasons as those setting up male monasteries: as perhaps to be assured of an obit after one's death (Bonlieu, 1219), or in thanksgiving for a petition granted and the fulfilment of a vow made (Valduc, 1232)[10]. The latter's founder (Duke Henry of Brabant), as maybe others, had perhaps in mind a home where his unattached girls might find an honourable position: both its first two abbesses were his daughters[11].

A number of houses incorporated owed their new status to papal pressure, whilst the ban on any further acceptance of nunneries by the Premonstratensians (in 1198), and hurdles in their path also at first raised by the Dominicans and the Franciscans, were other factors making the Cistercian Order a favourite attraction for nunneries at the time[12]. Whatever the motives, by the year 1200 there were perhaps already some 100 nunneries in France, and the first half of the thirteenth century saw the foundation or incorporation of 66 nunneries in Belgium and 150 in Germany[13] (33 of them in the diocese of Mainz alone)[14]. They even appeared in the Near East, de Vitry (writing about 1230) told how the nunneries of the Order 'were multiplying like stars in the sky', and also 'newly constructed, in Constantinople and Cyprus, in Antioch, Tripoli and Acre'[15]. (Three of the latter, those in Nicosia, Tripoli and Acre were, coincidentally or otherwise, all dedicated to St Mary Magdalene[16].) By and large the nunneries ranked as abbeys, only in England were they mostly termed priories[17].

The sudden influx of so many nunneries created practical problems for the male houses, whose abbots had not only in person (or by delegation) to visit annually convents placed under their wing, hear the nuns' confessions, and see that there were sufficient personnel (chaplains and *conversi*) to aid them, but were also expected to advise on their economic situation and append their seal to any major transactions the nuns might make. Whilst certain abbots (as Eberhard of Salem [1194–40][18] and Walter of Villers [1214–21][19]) were to the fore in co-founding new monasteries or encouraging existing convents to join the Order, the General Chapter repeatedly tried to stem the flow. (Even Abbot Walter resigned eight of his convents into the paternity of Cîteaux because of the potential ill effects for his own community of too many experienced monks being sent to minister to the nuns[20].)

Several of the injunctions of the Chapter were (as was so often the case) not absolute, but left a loop-hole so that new additions were not barred altogether. In 1225 it ruled that no new foundations were to be made or existing ones incorporated, *unless* suitable property and buildings could be assured. In 1228 the prohibition allowed of no qualification, *save* that if a convent wanted to follow Cistercian usages the Chapter would not stop it, but would decline any responsibility for visitation and spiritual oversight[21]. From 1244 new foundations and incorporations could be made only *if* the diocesan bishop issued a charter freeing the nuns from all episcopal jurisdiction[22]. In 1245 came the further provision that such a charter must have both the bishop's seal and that of his cathedral chapter attached[23]. Finally, Innocent IV (1251) issued a bull promising firmly that the papacy would not request any more incorporations. Only now did the numbers of would-be members slacken seriously, and by this time the Dominicans and Franciscans were more readily accepting women into the religious life. There was still a trickle of known requests for Cistercian membership by nunneries until late in the thirteenth century[24].

By the mid-fourteenth century there may have been in France about 150 Cistercian nunneries, in the Germanic lands over 300, in the Low Countries some 70, in Iberia about 80, in Italy 70 and in England about thirty[25]. The total number of convents in Europe thus counting themselves 'Cistercian' was in excess of seven hundred, and some would suggest a still higher figure. (On the map accompanying this chapter only those nunneries with a proven Cistercian track record are plotted.) In Ireland, where Stephen Lexington had ordered the removal of presumably Celtic nuns who were living too close to monks of the Order[26], there were only two nunneries which could perhaps definitely be termed Cistercian – Ballymore and Derry[27]. In Wales there were two permanent convents of the Order: Llanllŷr (under the oversight of the abbot of Strata Florida), and Llanllugan (cared for by the abbot of Strata Marccella). Both were late twelfth century foundations, and medieval poets referred to them as 'proud Llanllugan' and 'holy Llanllŷr', and to their inmates (with the colour of their habit in mind) as 'the chalk-white ones' of Llanllugan and the 'white maidens' of Llanllŷr[28].

In the first half of the thirteenth century a number of the convents becoming Cistercian were Benedictine foundations – over twenty in Germany alone, but there was also a little-charted reverse flow[29]. Well known Benedictine nunneries

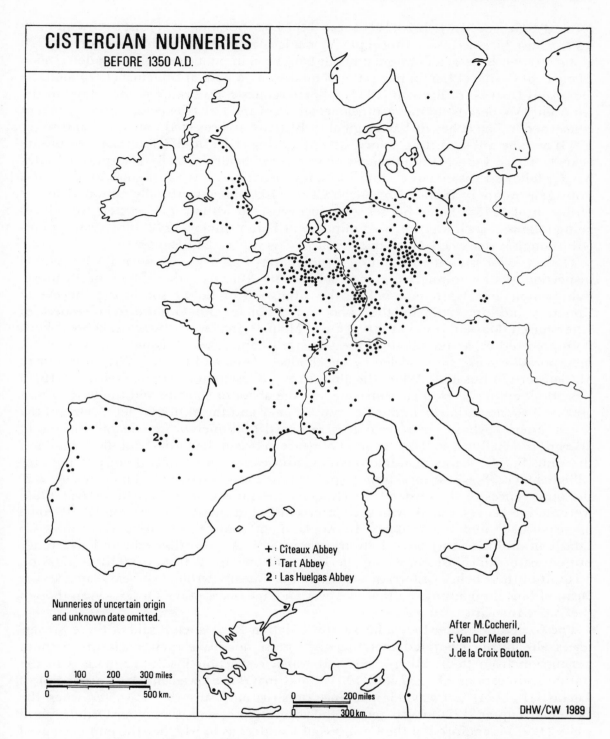

CISTERCIAN NUNNERIES
BEFORE 1350 A.D.

+ : Cîteaux Abbey
1 : Tart Abbey
2 : Las Huelgas Abbey

Nunneries of uncertain origin
and unknown date omitted.

After M. Cocheril,
F. Van Der Meer and
J. de la Croix Bouton.

0   100   200   300 miles

0   500 km.

0   200 miles

0   300 km.

DHW/CW 1989

incorporated included the double-monastery of Arouca in Portugal (1228)[30] and the ducal foundation of Trzebnica in Silesia (1218)[31]. In Portugal Queen Tarasia (about 1210) evicted the Benedictine monks of Lorvão in the diocese of Coimbra – despite the reservations of Innocent III – alleging their monastery to be at a low ebb. She replaced them with Cistercian nuns drawn from the Portugese nobility, and set over them her former nurse as abbess![32] Hermitages becoming Cistercian nunneries included Robertmont in Belgium (1180) and Tarrant Keynes in England (1228)[33].

One of the problems the Order faced in trying to limit the admission of nunneries was the status of would-be patrons – not least the pope – who could not easily be refused[34]. Gregory IX (1227–41) requested the incorporation of at least twelve nunneries[35], whilst his successor, Innocent IV, made a number of such demands in 1246 alone[36]. Other benefactors whom it might have been impolitic to slight included Queen Blanche of Castile (1236; in respect of Maubuisson), a king of Bohemia (1270) and the Duke and Duchess of Brabant (1244)[37]. Some requests were refused, including one by Innocent IV – because of the insufficient resources and lack of enclosure of the convent concerned[38]. The abbey of Val Virginal in Brittany was rejected four times and so (in 1253) became a Benedictine priory, despite having called itself 'Cistercian' for twenty years[39]. There were many instances of nunneries being formally incorporated after having followed Cistercian custom for many years: one was Saõ Benito de Castris, a Portugese nunnery founded by Alcobaça in 1169 but not officially admitted to the Order until 1275[40]. Some houses were incorporated without the proper procedures being followed: such was the Swiss nunnery of Fraubrunnen (1249) incorrectly admitted (though it remained so) by the abbots of Freinisberg and Hauterive[41].

The act of incorporation required a preliminary enquiry, with normally a personal inspection of the nunnery[42] as carried out (in 1236) by the abbots of Beaupré, Foucarmont and Mortemer, before the admission of Le Trésor in the diocese of Rouen[43], and (in 1267) by the abbots of Schönau and Otterberg in respect of Patershusen (Marienkron) in the diocese of Mainz[44]. If all was satisfactory these abbots, if empowered to act on behalf of the General Chapter, would issue formal letters of incorporation – like those sealed by the abbots of Osek and Pforta (1264) in favour of Marienstern in Lusatia[45]. When the almost-royal Silesian nunnery of Trebznica (1218) was admitted, it was by a charter issued by the abbot of Cîteaux and the four 'proto-abbots': 'By the authority of the General Chapter and the entire Order'[46]. One of the last nunneries whose incorporation is recorded ('Stunnemunster' in the diocese of Worms, in 1293) was so 'For the good of peace between the Order and the abbess and the nuns'[47]. The status of numerous monasteries remained uncertain: like perhaps Billigheim (1238) whose local bishop spoke of the nuns as having 'voluntarily received' the observances of the Order[48]. In Hungary the nuns of Poszony (Bratislava; 1235) were said to be 'associated' with the Cistercians[49], but those of Veszprém (1240) to be 'incorporated' into the Order[50]. In England, of some thirty nunneries, only two (Marham and Tarrant) were fully incorporated[51]. As for Stixwould and five other nunneries in Lincolnshire, whom the king had exempted from a tenth in 1268 on account of their being Cistercian – the abbot of Cîteaux wrote, two years later, to the Dean of Lincoln pointing out that they were not members of the Order – even though they wore the Cistercian habit[52].

The General Chapter took a far-reaching step in 1213 when it said of those monasteries already incorporated that the nuns must not leave their enclosure without permission from their father-abbot[53]. It was a restriction firmly maintained in the statute codifications of 1237 and 1257[54], and may have owed much to a precept of Lucius III (1184)[55]. It was the insistence on strict enclosure that was cited when the General Chapter (1220) ruled against the absorption of houses of other Orders[56], and when (1225) it enquired of the Countess of Flanders as to whether the endowment of a nunnery she wished to found would be sufficient – as the nuns would be unable to go out to beg[57]. Exceptions were made, though only with leave of the father-abbot if it were practicable to obtain it. An abbess might go out on business, but with an escort of two nuns; a sister-cellarer also – with an escort of one[58]. The rules of enclosure also forbade boys being educated[59], and secular ladies from staying overnight[60]. The nuns had to speak to all visitors through a 'strongly made' iron or timber barred grill. This provision was (from about 1237) mitigated, in that more open conversation could be held with 'good and honest persons', and (later on) with relatives[61].

Such strict enclosure had practical effects, for the nuns could no longer go out to work in the fields. There is evidence that previously – in the twelfth century – they did so: as at Montreuil-les-Dames (where Herman of Laon noted them as preparing and tilling the land just as did their male counterparts)[62], and (even later) as at La Ramée (whose field harvesters at Kerkom Grange included St Ida)[63]. In those convents with many nuns of noble blood the absence of hard manual work was perhaps not irksome, but it did mean that each convent became effectively a double-community (albeit men and women living quite separately), with a parallel household of clerks, chaplains and male *conversi* to attend not only to the nuns' spiritual needs but also to the necessary manual work and external business. There were in most houses a small number of female *conversae* (or 'sisters' as distinct from the 'nuns'), but they, too, were enclosed, and mostly employed in mundane household tasks and some gardening[64]. As the nuns themselves were (from 1213 at the latest) limited in what they could do (embroidery being common), it begs the question: Did the insistence on strict enclosure negate one of the very fundamentals of the Cistercian vocation: living by the labours of one's own hands?

Sites

The sites of nunneries newly founded were to be at least six 'leagues' away from a monastery of the Order, and ten or more 'leagues' distant from another Cistercian nunnery. It was because the convent of St Margaret was very close to the abbey of St Thomas by Venice, that there was a long-running dispute (1232–42) as to whether the nunnery should be transferred to another site or closed down altogether[65]. The proximity of the convents of La Paix Dieu and Val-Notre-Dame, in the diocese of Liége, also came to the attention of the General Chapter (1246)[66]. As for a male abbey, a site inspection was necessary before a foundation was made: the abbots of Beaupré and Vaucelles were sent to examine the location for a nunnery the Countess of Champagne (1221) wished to erect[67]. In England all Cistercian nunneries had a rural position, either in a village (like Marham) or more isolated (as Handale)[68]. In Ireland, Ballymore was but 300 feet (100 metres) from a motte and bailey of the founder, Walter de Lacy, and in clear sight of it – thus affording it protection by the garrison[69]. A grange of a male abbey might be converted into a Cistercian nunnery: as Fulda's Moppen Grange which became Schönau convent[70].

On the Continent many nunneries were sited in towns from their inception (perhaps because they were incorporated convents already there), or moved into towns later in their history. Town nunneries included Bergen (Nonneseter) in Norway[71], St Catherine's in Szczecin (by the river Oder) in Poland[72], St George's, Kelbra, in Thuringia[73] and St Clement's, Toledo (in Spain)[74]. The nunnery of Rulle moved (in 1243) from Haste to 'the gates of Osnabruck'[75]. Town houses were safer places in time of war. The duke of Brabant allowed Swybeeck nunnery (1235) to build the monastery of 'Little Bigard' in Brussels[76], the nuns of St Nicholas (1274) sought to keep some of their number in Vienna[77], and the convent of Clairmarais (1363) moved into Rheims[78]. A change of site might prove desirable for other reasons. The nuns of Suc-Ardu (*c.* 1200) in the Central Massif moved (on account of wolves) to Bellecombe – close to Yssingeaux[79]. The nuns of Vernaison, destroyed (in 1221) when the river Isère overflowed its banks, also found a new site[80]. The nuns of Toruń (1327) – living close by to the Hospital of the Holy Spirit in that city with many people coming and going – were offered a more peaceful site by the Grand Master of the Teutonic Knights[81]. Not all nunneries were well-endowed or well-peopled: where this was the case the abbots of Cîteaux and Clairvaux were permitted to unite two or more of the nunneries under their care and, if expedient, to transfer the new combined house to a more apt location[82]. At the close of the century (in 1294) any lesser nunnery could be united to another, if the respective father-abbots and founders agreed. The nuns seemingly had little say in the matter[83].

Churches

The majority of Cistercian convent churches were modest buildings, though there were exceptions like Las Huelgas and Trzebnica. Those in England and France mostly ranged in length from 23 metres (76 ft) to 42 metres (139 ft), averaging about 32 metres (110 ft). The width varied as to whether there were aisles or not. Based on the presence or absence of aisles and transepts, and the form of the chevet, some nine or ten types of nunnery church can be recognised in France including: cruciform – like Fabas and La Joie, only one transept – like Rosiers, two side aisles – such were Bellecombe and Spermalie, and no side aisle – as at Colonges and Fontes[84]. There were several unaisled churches in England – as at Ellerton and Gokewell, but Marham was cruciform[85]. In Germany, two aisleless churches of some length, with a polygonal chevet, were those of Mariaburghausen (50.5 metres/167 ft) and Sonnefeld (47.5 metres/165 ft)[86]. When the main altar at Oslavany in Bohemia was dedicated (in 1244) by the bishop of Prague, many relics were (as was usual) embedded in it[87]. Early simple churches might find later elaboration. In 1289 a 'votive chapel' was added to the church of Heiligengraben in Brandenburg, in reparation for the profanation of a sacred host at nearby Techow[88]. In 1309 at Wolin nunnery in Pomerania a chantry chapel was endowed: specific votive or requiem Masses were said there daily, save on Sundays[89]. By 1330 the convent church at Voisins (Loiret) was prolonged westwards by the addition of a chapel dedicated to St-Eloi[90]. At Mercoire (Lozère) a chapel for strangers was added to the right of the choir, but separated from it by a grille[91].

Little has been written regarding the other buildings of Cistercian convents. At Marham, the precinct wall existed until at least 1627, whilst excavation has demonstrated the sizes of the church (perhaps 194 x 30 ft/58 x 17 metres), refectory (72 x 50 ft/22 metres x 15 metres) and guest-house (141 x 36 ft/43 metres x 11 metres)[92]. Within the enclosure at Groeninghe (fd 1285), Princess Beatrice of Courtrai, its founder, had her own residence and chapel[93]. Stephen Lexington ordered the refectory bell at Mortain (1232) 'to be hung up high, according to the custom of the Order'[94]. In 1349 the new church and the dorter of Sonnefeld were both completed in stone[95]. The chapter-house of Tišnov retains its stone lectern, the cloister of Isenhagen has a series of fine medieval consoles, and in its church the nuns' stalls date from the mid-fourteenth century[95a]. The scriptorium at La Ramée was known for the quality of its work[96]. Gregory IX gave Cistercian nunneries the right to give burial to their benefactors[97], and Basedale (England) had a cemetery for the burial of 'nuns and sisters and our brethren who have taken our habit': the latter being their chaplains and *conversi* helpers[98].

The Male Community

The rule of strict enclosure meant that whilst both an abbess and her nun-cellarer could sometimes go out on essential matters, the day-to-day work and business of each Cistercian nunnery was in the hands of a band of its own *conversi*. The male household was headed by an official called variously its 'prior' or 'procurator' (the most common term, certainly after 1267)[99], or ' master' (as at Coldstream)[100], or 'guardian' (as at Basedale)[101] or ' keeper' or 'warden' (in some other English nunneries)[102] A priest,

Ascer, was in 1246 procurator for the nuns of Slangerup[103]. A *conversus* of Zwettl, Conrad, was in 1278 procurator of Maylan[104]. In the late thirteenth century archbishops of York sometimes appointed religious of other orders, or even secular clerics, to oversee the interests of the Yorkshire Cistercian nunneries[105]. Stephen Lexington (1230) assumed three resident monks in the nunneries of his congregation: one was to act as chaplain, another as vice-cellarer, and the third was to look after the gatehouse, granary and bakehouse. At meals one of them was to read from a book at the beginning and end of each repast. Monks staying in a nunnery did so in their own house, but had to rise – when the bell for vigils sounded from the nuns' church – and recite the hours in their oratory[106]. All clerks and *conversi* employed on a convent's business were to keep and render faithful accounts, with humility, to the prioress and council of the nunnery[107].

As the numbers of nunneries rapidly increased it became impracticable for male houses to send any *conversi* to assist the now-enclosed nuns. From the 1220s nunneries sought their own male live-in *conversi*, who made their profession kneeling before the abbess in chapter[108]. At first the attitude of the Order to these *conversi* was somewhat detached, but after successful petitions from Trebznica (1218)[109] and Argensolles (1224)[110], it was ruled by the General Chapter (1229) that any *conversi* from a convent visiting a male abbey – if they were 'in hair style, beard and habit' – as the monastic *conversi* of the Order, might be admitted to its *conversi* choir and refectory[111]. At their nunnery they lived separately, outside the nuns' enclosure. Alfonso VII (1203) gave 2,500 gold pieces for the building of the 'house of the *conversi*' at Las Huelgas[112]. The *conversi* performed the same range of duties as their counterparts in a male abbey, like baking, milling and caring for the stock[113]. They might prove difficult: the General Chapter ruled therefore (in 1254) that before serving a year's novitiate potential convent *conversi* were to spend six months in lay-clothes[114], and decreed (in 1281) that any nuns' *conversi* needing discipline were to be sent to a male abbey[115]. The tasks of the small number (usually) of female *conversae*[116] – termed 'sisters' rather than 'nuns' and, unlike them, wearing a white veil[117] – included domestic chores. At Eschenbach they worked in the kitchen, gardens, infirmary, pantry and gatehouse[118].

The immediate spiritual needs of the nuns, the daily Mass, was celebrated by resident 'clerks' or 'chaplains', (called 'canons' at Catesby in England)[119], who were recruited from the secular clergy and – after serving a year's novitiate in the nunnery – assumed a habit of cloak and scapular and made their profession before the abbess[120]. At first (1218) they made their vows before the church altar[121], but later (by 1257) kneeling in the chapter house and promising (like the *conversi*) 'good obedience until death'[122]. By their profession the chaplains did not become Cistercian monks, but had their own particular (and lowly) rank in the Order. Their secular background, or lack of good training, is reflected in the injunctions of the General Chapter (1220, 1258) reminding them that they must celebrate Mass in the Cistercian rite[123]. By 1288 chaplains might only be appointed with the approval of the father-abbot[124]. On visiting a male abbey they could worship in the church (perhaps in the retro-choir), and they were to be honourably catered for in accommodation separate from seculars[125]. One thirteenth century Cistercian chaplain, 'poor Martin', made a name for himself by translating the *Rule of St Benedict* and the *Usages* of the Order into French[126]. The chaplains did not normally hear the nuns' confessions[127]: this was done either by the father-abbot or experienced monks delegated by him[128]. Aulne, for example, provided confessors for the nuns of Herkenrode[129].The monks of Kołbacz (1283), going to hear the confessions of the nuns of Szczecin, journeyed 'by water or on horseback'[130]. Nuns were to make their confessions through the grille, save for the gravely ill and except to the Visitor – to whom it was possible to speak more openly in the chapter-house[131].

Visitation

Each officially recognised nunnery was subject to annual visitation by the abbot of the monastery under whose wing it had been placed. Much of his work might be undertaken by delegation: at monasteries such as Camp – with twenty-four dependent convents – this was the only practicable means of exercising regular oversight[132]. The abbot of Pforta (1219) found himself unable to visit Trebznica because of wars and long distance, so the nearby abbot of Lubiąż fulfilled the duty[133]. The nuns of Mègemont (in the Auvergne) said of the abbot of Montpeyroux (1282) that he was: 'Our father, on whom the abbess and the monastery depend spiritually'[134]. In fact, a Visitor also exercised a watchful eye over the temporal well-being of his nunneries, and no major transaction would be made without his approval. The seal of the abbot of Aulne ('our Visitor'), as well as that of the abbess, was appended to an agreement made by Val-St-Georges (1271)[135]. In the absence of its Visitor's seal (the abbot of Strata Florida) the seals of the abbots of Strata Marcella and of Valle Crucis (1284) were appended to Llanllŷr nunnery's receipt for war damage compensation[136].

The nuns' Visitors could have a difficult task as some convents had a tendency to want to go their own way: perhaps the nuns (often of noble blood) chafed at the restrictions placed upon them. This was certainly true (in 1243) when at three convents – 'Holy Cross' (in the diocese of Meissen)[137], Lieu Notre-Dame[138] and Moncey[139] – the Visitors were locked out. The reason for their discontent must have lain in the fact that in 1242 the male General Chapter, not content with having the previous year ordered that nuns who committed offences for which monks would be imprisoned should themselves be incarcerated[140], issued several more disciplinary statutes. These provided that nuns who would not live by the rules of the Order should be expelled[141], that in normal circumstances nuns were only to talk to visitors through the grille[142], that the number of nuns officially fixed was not to be exceeded[143], that nuns should use the name given them by the father-abbot at their blessing[144], and that enquiry should be made as to the lifestyle of their male chaplains and *conversi*[145]. These orders certainly upset the nuns of Parc-aux-Dames when, the next year (1243), their Visitor read the injunctions to them: they 'shouted, stamped and walked out of the chapter-house'[146]. It should not be thought that such behaviour was widespread, but from time to time other communities rebelled against lawful authority – including Colonges (1250)[147], Düsseren (1269)[148] and Bottenbroich (1294)[149]. Matters may not have been helped by the stipulation (1257) that abbesses, nuns and *conversae* should confess their faults 'on their hands and knees'[150]. Eventually the General Chapter (1320) found it necessary to refer to the 'many excesses and disobediences' of the Order's nuns, especially by breaking enclosure and going out[151].

Where charters of visitation survive something can be learnt of the failings of some nuns (and their male helpers) in their cloistered lives. The archbishops of York visited the Cistercian houses in their diocese, perhaps because they were not fully recognised by the Order. At Swine (in 1268) one heard that the chaplains and *conversi* had so misused the convent funds that the nuns were short of food, and (in 1290) certain rebellious nuns had to be transferred to another house. At Nun Appleton (in 1281) he had to remind the nuns that none should hold any private property[152]. The abbot of Silvanès visiting Nonenque (in 1303) urged the nuns to the better keeping of humility, obedience, silence and regular attendance at the daily chapter: he also gave instructions which helped the convent climb out of debt[153]. There could, very occasionally, be overbearing Visitors: as an abbot of Villelongue (1225) who at the convent of Garriga (in the Cevennes) excommunicated the nuns, took their keys and tore up their charters[154]. Despite the potential problems and the burden which oversight of nunneries could impose, there were several instances where the right of paternity to a particular convent was jealously guarded when challenged; even Cîteaux (1257) had to fight off a claim to the oversight of Port Royal from Vaux-de-Cernay[155], and Clairvaux (1235) from Aulne as regarding Aywières[156].

General Chapters

The usages prescribed for the nuns (1237) said that: 'Because the abbesses do not have a general chapter, faults are to be acknowledged to the Visitor'[157]. Two small groupings of Cistercian nuns did have their own chapter, but any statutes promulgated had to lie within the framework of the decisions of the male General Chapter at Cîteaux[158]. By the late twelfth century eighteen abbesses constituted the Chapter held each Michaelmas at Tart, under the joint presidency of the abbot of Cîteaux (or his delegate) and the abbess of Tart[159]. Tart's seniority stemmed from the fact that it was founded (about 1120) by St Stephen Harding[160]. The abbess had but limited authority in her 'congregation', and the statutes of her Chapter dealt with matters such as abstinence, absenteeism and dress[161]. In Spain the primacy of Las Huelgas owed much to its foundation by Alfonso VIII (1187)[162], to the papal bull (1188) which placed it 'under the protection of blessed Peter and mine own'[163], and to its having (like Tart) the abbot of Cîteaux as its Visitor[164]. The Chapter – held yearly at Las Huelgas at Martinmas[165] for the nunneries of Castile and León[166] – composed at first only eight abbesses[167], and some of them were not very willing to attend[168]. The abbess of Perales, for one, objected to oversight from Las Huelgas rather than from the mother house of Tulebras: she only came into line after a visit by the abbot of Cîteaux[169].

Recruitment

Many Cistercian nunneries, but not all, had an exclusive policy of admitting only girls of noble blood: this may have been partly to do with family ties, and less with class-consciousness than with the dowry postulants were expected to bring with them. One must question as to whether the restriction on entry to those of families of substance did not narrow the Holy Spirit's field of choice in guiding ladies to a religious vocation. Those convents where all the nuns were of noble birth included Las Huelgas (the abbess was often a princess)[170], as well as Gravenhorst[171] and Himmelkron[172] founded – in 1256 and 1280 respectively – for ladies of the upper class. Pope John XXII (1316–34) requested the admission of some noble girls at Dalheim[173]. The king of Bohemia (1278) petitioned the General Chapter that no nun of the founding family be forced to leave Trzebnica, even if elected an abbess elsewhere[174]. Bogislaw IV (1298) augmented the possessions of Wolin when his daughter, Jutte, became a nun there[175]. Entry dowries included an early grant to Coyroux (1187)[176], twenty-three known grants to Stixwould of temporal holdings as mills and tithes[177] and, from one nun at Gudhem alone, no less than three farms[178]. While such gifts may call into question the motives of some of the entrants, many vocations (especially in Belgium and other areas affected by the 'religious women' movement) were genuine calls from God. Of these Cistercian convents, Jacques de Vitry said: 'Virgins throng there, widows hasten there, and married women with their husbands' consent'[179].

The General Chapter (1219) ruled that Visitors were to fix the number of nuns convents could sustain, according to their resources[180]. The maximum numbers allowed might, therefore, fluctuate slightly from year to year. Stephen Lexington fixed at Moncey (1231) a total of 30 nuns, 6 *converses*, 4 priests and 2 male *conversi*[181]. He permitted sixty nuns at Port Royal (1233)[182] and fifty at Mortain (1231)[183]. The abbot of Arnsburg fixed the number of nuns at Patershausen (1327) also at fifty[184]. Large communities included Wechterswinkel (1231)[185] and Coyroux (1300)[186] – both long established houses and each having a hundred nuns. At Seligental (1288) were 88 nuns and *converses* as well as 20 male *conversi*[187]. Whilst Stephen Lexington enjoined twelve years old as the age at which girls could be received (with a view to later becoming nuns), and stipulated 18 years as the age when the novitiate might be entered[188], he did allow a minimum age of eight for entry at Saint-Antoine des Champs[189]. Young boys were not to be admitted[190]: there were later breaches of this rule at Esholt (1318) and Heynings (1347) in England[191]. Once professed, uniformity of habit was enjoined (1235): either 'cowl without cloak, or cloak without cowl'. A white habit was understood, but: 'Veils were always to be black, and scapulars were to be used in time of work'[192]. There had been undue diversity, as at Molèze (1232) where the nuns wore white veils and grew their hair long[193].

Notable Nunneries

Apart from Las Huelgas and Tart, there were several convents which were abbeys of status. One such was Saint Antoine-des-Champs (inc. 1206) sited outside the eastern gate of Paris. St Louis took it under his wing, giving it the title ' royal'[194], starting out from it on his journey to the Crusades and displaying here the Crown of Thorns upon his return[195]. In Bohemia, Queen Constance founded the nunnery of 'Porta coeli' close to Tišnov, backed by her two sons: she was buried there in 1240, the year after its consecration. An ornate portal was added later to the west front with an elaborate tympanum including a depiction of Christ looking down on the kneeling figures of Constance, and her son Margrave Přemysl (also interred there)[196]. On the Scottish Border lay the nunnery of Coldstream, named as Cistercian in a papal bull of 1259 but described about 1418 as not being Cistercian, because 'the nuns do not wear the Cistercian habit'. Were they Benedictines claiming to be Cistercian in order to gain the privileges of the Order?[197]. At any rate, when Edward I and his 8,000-strong army encamped at Coldstream in 1296 the nunnery provided the troops with food valued at £118: it received 700 sheep in recompense[198]. One unnamed Rhineland convent (1272) achieved notoriety when its nuns cut off the head of a noble lady who had died there, and refused to hand it over to her daughter[199]. Possibly the lady had a reputation for sanctity, and they wanted a relic!

In his visitation of his nunneries Stephen Lexington (1230s) had urged them only to receive as guests: 'The manifestly sick and truly poor'[200]. Some Cistercian nunneries in Flanders may indeed have originated in congregations of women who cared for the sick and poor, as the hospital of Sint-Gillis by Dendermunde. After its incorporation into the Order the community moved (in 1228) to a more apt location at Zwijveke[201]. A noted Cistercian hospital was that given in Ghent (1228) by the count and countess of Flanders to the nuns of Bijloke, with consent from the diocesan bishop and the abbot of Clairvaux. Its confirmatory charter makes it clear that the hospital was within the precincts of the nunnery[202]. Another convent (Marquette) had been founded with the duty of building a hospital within its precincts, but the countess of Flanders (in 1242) waived this requirement[203]. In Spain, Alfonso VIII named the abbess of Las Huelgas as administrator of the 'Hospital del Rey' not far distant, which he had founded to serve pilgrims (especially the sick and the poor) *en route* to Compostella. The Hospital was served by thirteen knights of Calatrava, of whom the abbess became the local 'commendador'[204]. In 1334 the dowager Queen Elizabeth of Bohemia endowed, at the nunnery of Maria Saal in Old Brno, a hospital for eight infirm seculars, eight priests and one deacon[205]. In Scotland, St Leonard's Hospital, Perth, was a Cistercian nunnery[206].

Notable Abbesses

A Cistercian nunnery had a parallel hierarchy of officials (as abbess, subprioress, cellarer, precentor) to their counterparts in a monastery. The General Chapter, from time to time, legislated regarding the position of abbess, and insisted that no one might be elected abbess until they were thirty years old (1251)[207]. Some abbesses had previously been too young and immature: a point emphasised by the countess of Flanders (1245) who successfully sought the Chapter's agreement that her daughter (Margaret of Constantinople) was not to be compelled to become an abbess before her thirtieth birthday[208]. Abbesses might carry their pastoral staff only in the procession at the profession of nuns, and even then the father-abbot had to be present to give his blessing[209]. The third abbess of Las Huelgas (1210), and possibly other Spanish abbesses, overstepped the mark when she blessed her own nuns, heard their confessions and preached in public[210]. Innocent III told her to desist, pointing out that Our Lord had not confided the keys of the kingdom of heaven to His Mother, even though more worthy than all the apostles[211].

Sensing perhaps a similar tendency of independence on the part of the abbess of Tart, abbot Guy of Cîteaux (1191–1202) reminded that nunnery that it was 'the peculiar daughter of Cîteaux'[212]. The abbess of Frauental (fd 1265) came to have the privilege of crowning the queen of Bohemia[213]. Not only were many nuns of noble blood, but there was for long (as noted above) a continuing attachment to the founding family. The first two abbesses of Valduc were daughters of its founder, Duke Henry of Lorraine and Brabant[214]. Four of the abbesses of Mollégès were nieces, several times removed, of its founder, and a similar nepotism existed at Notre-Dame-de-Sion. Members of the De Roquefort family often reached high office there: at least two rose to be abbess, and in 1287 they held the posts of prioress, subprioress, and precentor[215]. Can all elections of Cistercian abbesses have been entirely free and without constraint?

Visionaries and Mystics

It cannot be too strongly emphasised (as already done in this book), that so far as the statutes of the General Chapter were concerned, it was often only the bad news that hit the headlines. The known cases of (sometimes extreme) shortcomings in a handful of nunneries must not obscure the deep spirituality of the inmates of many Cistercian convents. One such was Margaret Rich, a sister of St Edmund Rich, and prioress of Catesby from 1245 to 1257. The chronicler Matthew Paris wrote of her as 'a woman of great holiness, through whose distinguished merits miracles have been made gloriously manifest'[216]. Most is known of the Cistercian mystics of Flanders and Belgium, sometimes from their own writings (like the autobiography of Beatrice of Nazareth; d. 1268)[217], or from biographies written by those who knew them well (as by abbot Philip of Clairvaux concerning Elizabeth of Spalbeek[218]. It must be remembered that it was not easy to be known as a mystic: it could be a cause of embarrassment and of persecution – sometimes within one's own convent[219].

Notable visionaries included St Lutgard of Aywières (d. 1246) who fasted rigorously, had visions of the Five Sacred Wounds and saw Our Lord pointing to His pierced side[220]. Poorly educated, she did not write a single line and was blind for the last ten years of her life[221]. Nor did Ida of Nivelles (d. 1231) leave any work of her own composition, but the gift of clairvoyance enabled her to tell others of their standing with God, and one Christmas Day at Mass she saw in the priest's uplifted hands not the host but the Infant Jesus[222]. Her mystical life was grounded in sublime experiences of the Blessed Trinity[223], and on her death-bed she uttered the words: 'The Holy Trinity is thundering to descend'[224]. Beatrice of Nazareth constantly dwelt on the Passion, and (about 1250) wrote her treatise on the *Seven Degrees of Love*[225]. Cistercian stigmatists of the period included Ida of Roosdaal[226] and Lukardis of Oberweimar[227], whilst the leper nun of La Cambre, Alice of Schaerbeek, was able to heal others simply by her touch[228]. In the later thirteenth century two mystics of the Benedictine but Cistercian-influenced Helfta convent, Gertrude and Mechtilde, were much influenced by the spirituality of St Bernard[229]. Further afield, Elizabeth, the first abbess of St Thomas an der Kyll (d. 1205), appeared after her death to the prioress discoursing on the life of the community: its confessor, the prior of Himmerod, subsequently wrote his work entitled 'Visions'[230]. In Italy, Saint Franca was buried at the Cistercian nunnery of Pittolo[231], whilst, in Silesia, St Hedwig found a retirement home at Trzebnica, her husband's foundation [232]. To Herkenrode in Belgium, pilgrims were attracted (from 1317) by a sacred Host miraculously bleeding[232a].

Economy

The rule of strict enclosure (from at latest 1213) meant that whilst the economy of the Cistercian nunneries in many respects resembled that of the male monasteries, there was a very important difference. The nuns themselves could no longer have much direct part in it, the manual labour and a great deal of the organisation fell on male shoulders. Otherwise, to outward appearances, much was alike. The nuns had the same need for charters: the convent of Val-Saint-Georges (near Namur) had its deeds of benefactions from the dukes of Brabant and the counts of Flanders and of Namur, and its confirmatory charters from the bishops of Cambria and Liège, as well as bulls of protection (including tithe exemption rights) from three popes[233]. Nuns might receive donations for spiritual services: Maria Saal in Old Brno was given one grant of 650 marks, partly in return for the right of burial[234]. In their manors their officials would exercise justice on their behalf (Chapter 14). Their granges might be well organised, like those of Tart: on four it practised mixed farming, at Beauvoir – arable – at Battalut – arable and viticulture, whilst Hautserre was near a vast forest where its herds might find pasture[235].

The nuns of Soleilmont had exclusive fishing rights (unsuccessfully challenged in litigation) in the adjacent lake[236]. The tenants of Rifreddo rendered rents in cash but also dues in kind – as of pork, grain, chestnuts, oats, eggs and wine, and performed labour services – including haymaking and the gathering of acorns and chestnuts[237]. At Nonenque, in 1303, the stock included 430 sheep, 103 pigs and 31 cows[238]. The thirteen Cistercian nunneries of Yorkshire contributed between them thirty-six sacks of wool to the export trade[239]. The nunnery of Mariental (Oslavany; fd 1228) built up its property rights throughout the thirteenth century, and came to hold the advowson of some ten churches, including St James in Brno[240]. In north-east Poland the convent of Żarnowiec was free of toll in Gdańsk, imported salt, fish and textiles, and sold what was surplus[241]. All this is not to say that every Cistercian nunnery was prosperous: some were financially constrained. Nonenque was very much in debt in 1303[242]. The Grand Master of the Teutonic Knights took pity (in 1345) on the poor nuns of Toruń, granting them a school and a church with its tithes[243].

Notes

1. Connor (1995) 40, Lekai (1977a) 347.
2. King (1954) 338.
3. Bouton (1995) 14–15, Carville (1995) 64.
4. Lekai (1977a) 348.
5. Degler-Spengler (1995) 87.
6. Boyd (1943) 81 (quoting *'Dialogue between a Cluniac and a Cistercian Monk'*).
7. Connor (1988) 188.
8. Bouton (1995) 88.
9. Nichols (1987)102.
10. Bouton (1995) 92.
11. Van Der Meer (1965) 300.
12. Degler-Spengler (1995) 99.
13. Bouton (1995) 84.
14. *Ibid.* 83.
15. Boyd (1943) 75 (quoting de Vitry's, *Libri Duo quorum Prior Orientalis*).
16. Hinnebusch (1972) 268.
17. Boyd (1943) 101*n*.
18. Kuhn-Refus (1995) 139.
19. De Moreau (1909) 55–56, 110–13.
20. De Ganck (1989) 227, De Moreau (1909) 55.
21. Degler-Spengler (1995) 100.
22. *Statuta* II, 275 (1244/7).
23. *Statuta* II, 291 (1245/6).
24. Degler-Spengler (1995) 101–07.
25. Bouton (1995) 84.
26. *SL* 163 (No. 45).
27. Gwynn and Hadcock (1970) 313, 316.
28. Williams (1975) 158, 165.
29. Bouton (1995) 83.
30. Durand (1983) 102.
31. David (1934) 217.
32. Boyd (1943) 85–86.
33. Bouton (1995) 63–64.
34. *LCC* (2) 349–50.
35. *Statuta* I, 85–234.
36. Bouton (1995) 75.
37. *Ibid.* 74, 79.
38. *Ibid.* 73.
39. Despy (1974) 68, (1975) 410.
40. Bouton (1995) 64.
41. *Ibid.* 76.
42. *Cf. LCC* (2) 350
43. *DHGE* XVII (1971) 1248.
44. *CDM* III, 747–50.
45. *AMO* 11.
46. *KDS* 226 (No. 213).
47. Bouton (1995) 82.
48. *CDM* II, 76–77.
49. *RCH* 32.
50. *Ibid.* 33.
51. Graves (1982) 333.
52. Graves (1979) 495–96.
53. *Statuta* I, 405 (1213/3).
54. *LCC* (2) 352.
55. Lekai (1977a) 350.
56. *Statuta* I, 517 (1220/4).
57. *Statuta* II, 40 (1225/24), *cf.* 64 (1227/45), 94 (1231/20).
58. *Statuta* I, 517 (1220/4); *LCC* (2) 352.
59. Bouton (1995) 68, *cf. LCC* (2) 351.
60. *LCC* (2) 351; *Statuta* II, 187 (1238/10).
61. *LCC* (2) 351.
62. Boyd (1943) 78–79.
63. Boudreau (1995) 329.
64. Mouret (1986) 303.
65. *Statuta* II, 110 (1232/52), 119–20 (1233/42), 138 (1234/51), 144 (1235/26), 213 (1239/52), 254 (1242/49).
66. *Statuta* II, 313 (1246/60).
67. Bouton (1995) 70.
68. Nichols (1982a) 151.
69. Carville (1995) 68.
70. Van Der Meer (1965) 297.
71. France (1992) 179, McGuire (1982) 3.
72. Coester (1984) 409–11; *cf.* (for site) Williams (1978) 243.
73. Holtmeyer (1906) 146 (town plan).
74. Borrero (1992) *passim.*
75. Van Der Meer (1965) 294.
76. *DNC* I, 420.
77. Bouton (1995) 79.
78. Van Der Meer (1965) 276.
79. Bouton (1995) 16.
80. *Ibid.* 16.
81. *UBC* 157–58.
82. *Statuta* II, 210 (1239/6).
83. *Statuta* III, 277 (1294/82).
84. Desmarchelier (1982) 79–119.
85. Nichols (1982a) 159, 165.
86. Coester (1984) 261.
87. *CDRB* IV: 1, 130 (No. 45).
88. Van Der Meer (1965) 282.
89. *PU* IV, 391–92.
90. Desmarchelier (1982) 83.
91. *Ibid.* 81.
92. Nichols (1978) 320–21.
93. Canivez (1926) 415–16.
94. *RSL* II, 241.
95. Coester (1984) 261.
95a. Appuhn (1981) 10 (illus.).
96. Bouton (1959) II, 239.
97. *CDVG* 57.
98. Burton (1979) 17.
99. *Cf. RSL* II, 254 (for prior in 1230).
100. Cowan and Easson (1976), 145.
101. Burton (1979) 35.
102. Nichols (1979) 28–29.
103. France (1992) 181.
104. *LFZ* 423–24.
105. Burton (1979) 35.
106. *RSL* II, 253.
107. *RSL* II, 241 (of 1232).
108. Bouton (1995) 70; Lekai (1977a) 353.
109. *KDS* 226 (No. 213); *cf. Statuta* I, 502 (1218/81).
110. *Statuta* II, 33–34 (1224/20).
111. *Statuta* II, 76 (1229/4).
112. *DMLH* I, 121 (No. 72).
113. Toepfer (1983) 176.
114. Mouret (1986) 288.
115. *Statuta* III, 210–11 (1281/26).
116. Mouret (1986) 301.
117. Nichols (1979) 33.
118. Mouret (1986) 303.
119. *VCH, Northampton* II (1906) 123.
120. Lackner (1981) 62; *cf. KDS* 226–27 (No. 213).

121. *KDS* 226–27 (No. 213).
122. *LCC* (2) 355.
123. Lackner (1981) 62.
124. *Statuta* III, 240 (1288/16); *cf.* III, 334 (1317/4).
125. *KDS* 226–27 (No. 213).
126. *DAC* (1978) 483.
127. *LCC* (2) 350; *Statuta* III, 334 (1317/4).
128. Lackner (1981) 62.
129. Vanden Bemden (1986) 190.
130. *PU* II, 507.
131. *LCC* (2) 350.
132. *DHGE* XI (1949) 619.
133. *KDS* 231 (No. 218).
134. Dodel-Brunello (1985) 159.
135. *CDVG* 190–91.
136. *LW* 89, 132–33.
137. *Statuta* II, 272 (1243/66).
138. *Statuta* II, 273 (1243/68).
139. *Statuta* II, 271 (1243/64).
140. *Statuta* II, 232 (1241/11).
141. *Statuta* II, 249 (1242/18).
142. *Statuta* II, 248–49 (1242/17).
143. *Statuta* II, 248 (1242/15).
144. *Statuta* II, 248 (1242/16).
145. *Statuta* II, 253 (1242/11).
146. Southern (1970) 317; *cf. Statuta* II, 271–73 (1243/67).
147. *Statuta* II, 357–58 (1250/55).
148. Dimier (1972a) 55–53.
149. *DHGE* XI (1949) 619.
150. *LCC* (2) 353.
151. *Statuta* III, 348 (1320/4).
152. Burton (1979) 30, 33–34.
153. *CDN* 184–88.
154. *Statuta* II, 39–40 (1225/23).
155. *LCC* (2) 349.
156. *Statuta* II, 146 (1235/32), 195 (1238/58).
157. *LCC* (2) 353.
158. Degler-Spengler (1995) 92.
159. Bouton (1995) 50, Connor (1995) 41–42.
160. Connor (1995) 40.
161. *Ibid.* 42–44.
162. Nichols (1987) 102–03.
163. Connor (1995) 30.
164. *Ibid.* 38, 40.
165. *DMLH* I, 85 (No. 47, of 1199).
166. *DMLH* I, 25–26 (No. 13, of 1187), 30–32 (No. 16, of 1187), 35–36 (No. 19, of 1188).
167. Connor (1995) 33; *cf. DMLH* I, 48 (No. 24, of 1189).
168. *DMLH* I, 53–54 (No. 29, of 1191).
169. *DMLH* I, 83–85 (Nos 44–48, of 1199).
170. Lekai (1977a) 349.
171. Van Der Meer (1965) 281.
172. *DHGE* XXIV (1993) 581.
173. *DHGE* XIV (1960) 26.
174. *Statuta* III, 182 (1278/47).
175. *PU* III, 355, 379; IV, 44–45.
176. Barrière (1989) 491 (No. 691).
177. Graves (1984) 218, 222, 227.
178. France (1992) 176.
179. Bouton (1995) 20–21.
180. Bouton (1986) 69.
181. *RSL* II, 239, *cf.* 244 (of 1233).
182. *RSL* II, 251.
183. *RSL* II, 234.
184. *CDM* III, 782–84.
185. Van Der Meer (1965) 302.
186. Barrière (1977) 108.
187. Weissenberger (1960) 2.
188. *RSL* II, 231, 241.
189. Lekai (1977a) 356.
190. *Statuta* I, 320 (1206/5).
191. Nichols (1979) 39.
192. *Statuta* II, 139 (1235/3); *LCC* (2) 352–53.
193. *Statuta* II, 104 (1232/23).
194. Willesme (1986) 135.
195. Berman (1995) 123–24.
196. Král (1987) 22–24.
197. Cowan (1976) 148.
198. *CRC* II, xiii-xiv.
199. *Statuta* III, 110 (1272/27).
200. Lekai (1977a) 356.
201. Veldeman (1965) 142–46.
202. *DNC* III, 88, 582–85.
203. *DNC* III, 405.
204. Connor (1988b) 322–23; *DHGE* XV (1963) 960.
205. *CDEM* VI, 344–49.
206. Carrick (1907) 31.
207. *Statuta* II, 361 (1251/6); *LCC* (2) 354 (of 1257 only).
208. *Statuta* II, 295(1245/30).
209. *Statuta* II, 248 (1242/16).
210. *DMLH* I, 168 (No. 104).
211. Dimier (1964) 29.
212. Boyd (1943) 84.
213. Van Der Meer (1965) 280.
214. *Ibid.* 300.
215. Aurell i Cardona (1986) 246, 249.
216. VCH, *Northampton* II (1906) 122.
217. Mikkers (1988) 776–76.
218. *Ibid.* 776.
219. Boudreau (1995) 328.
220. Shank (1995) 207.
221. Bussels (1995) 216–22.
222. Cawley (1995) 305–317.
223. Boudreau (1995) 336.
224. Cawley (1995) 314.
225. Sullivan (1995) 352, 354.
226. Wulf (1994) 98.
227. Mikkers (1988) 777.
228. Wulf (1944) 98.
229. Mikkers (1998) 777; *cf.* Caron (1995) 511, Schmitt (1995) 472.
230. Mikkers (1988) 775.
231. Tartara and Strola (1995) 283–303.
232. Wulf (1944) 100.
232a. Vanden Bemden (1986) 190.
233. *CDVG passim.*
234. *CDEM* VI, 2081–10.
235. Connor (1995) 46.
236. Daumont (1937) 74–75.
237. Boyd (1943) 152–53.
238. *CDN* 187.
239. Burton (1979) 14.
240. *CDEM* II, 207, 218, 233–34, 267–68, 279–80, 282–90, 372–73, 357–58; IV, 155–57, 159–61, 362; V, 130, 246, 248; VI, 109, 209–10.
241. Dąbrowski (1970) .
242. *CDN* 187.
243. *UBC* 211.

EPILOGUE

From small beginnings at Cîteaux in 1098 the Cistercian Order was to became a great force. The early 'simplicity' was in many ways lost, and some initial basic principles were later jettisoned. There was change but not of necessity decay. The transformation of the Order from a solitary humble monastery to a multitude of grand abbeys, was in some respects almost beyond its ability to control. By the year 1150 there were well-defined 'families' within the Order, by 1200 there were many great churches, by 1250 the ownership of tithes and vast landed estates was common, by 1300 there were (in many houses) hardly any *conversi* left, and by 1350 some abbots were appointed rather than elected, and (albeit on a limited scale) permission had been given for meat to be eaten. These changes were commented upon in their day. Alexander III (1169) said of the English Cistercians in particular: 'The entire way of life has undergone injury and change, (there is) a decline from established customs, a leaving behind of the original manner of life'[1]. At the close of the twelfth century a mystic (perhaps Hildegarde of Bingen) told the abbot of Cîteaux that what offended God most were the 'immense extent of the Order's estates, the variety of their buildings, and the mannered chant'[2].

Many of the criticisms that were made could be countered: to incorporate other congregations ought to have spiritually strengthened the Order, the large landed possessions – and economic success – were necessary to help fulfil the great burden of constant willing charity, the grandiose churches might be seen as befitting the majesty of God, and, not least, there was the constant worship of Almighty God in an especial way around the clock throughout Europe, and an austere and demanding form of spiritual life that reared many holy men and women. There had been in the twelfth century considerable change: it did not await later catastrophic events, as the Hundred Years War and the Black Death, it was an unavoidable concomitant of speedy growth and the bounty of many benefactors.

By the thirteenth century the Order had lost much of the esteem and popularity it enjoyed in St Bernard's day. The white monks suffered not only from a dislike of their growing privileges and from physical attacks on their properties, but also by the advent of the mendicant orders offering a different religious life-style[3]. By the time St Dominic (1221) and St Francis (1226) died, there was a haemorrhage of Cistercian monks from their Order to become Friars Minor or Preacher[4]. The numbers are unknown, and may not have been great, but the problem was serious enough to warrant the General Chapter (of 1242) sending the abbots of Beaubec and Vaux-de-Cernay to Paris to dissuade dissident white monks there from taking such a step[5]. The difficulty was in part solved by the Cistercians entering into pacts with the newer Orders (Chapter 2) mutually agreeing not normally to receive as a monk one of the other's religious.

Some would see the 'decline' or 'decay' of the Order as commencing in the mid-thirteenth century, and the General Chapter (1257) itself suggested that the 'world' was by then impinging too much on monastic life[6]. Others would sugggest a later date, and point out that the process (if decay it was) varied in time from one region of Europe to another: earliest perhaps in Burgundy (about 1250)[7], but some time after (perhaps around 1300) in Gascony and Poitou[8]. Much depends upon how 'decline' is enunciated. If it refers to the break-up of the landed estates – and perhaps to the diminution of *conversi* numbers – then these dates might hold good; but it has to be remembered that – certainly in central Europe and Iberia – many successful and profitable abbeys remained, whilst the large numbers of monks who died in the Black Death was itself a sign of continuing success. Yet other writers talk of a (so-called) 'Golden Age' for the Order, ending only (in 1342) with the death of the Cistercian pope Benedict XII[9].

In the early fourteenth century a number of monasteries encountered severe difficulties but – as it was only when such arose that abbeys might figure in official records – there is little way of telling whether many more houses might not have been in a completely satisfactory condition, both economically and spiritually. The General Chapter itself pointed to some of the problems: less than fervent observance of the *Rule* by monasteries in many regions (1312)[10], some monks, perhaps abbots, leading too grand a lifestyle (1331)[11], and, not least, a shortage of vocations (1337)[12] well before the Black Death. There were the widespread problems of bad weather, poor harvests and animal disease (from 1315 to 1317)[13]; there were difficulties (in England at any rate) from a peasantry fed up with its servile state[14]; there were monasteries (as on the Scottish Border[15] and in northern Italy[16]) which had greatly suffered from the effects of wars; there were many abbeys heavily in debt (Thame[17], Dunbrody[18], Sedlec[19], to name but a few); and there were abbey churches badly in need of restoration (as Croxden[20] and Ford[21]). There were isolated instances where a pope could speak of an abbey (as Benedict XII of Doberan) as 'a lair of sorcerers and a den of thieves'[22]. On the other hand there was in Germany and Bohemia a resurgence of mysticism which affected monasteries as well as nunneries, like Heilsbronn, Kaisheim, Waldsassen and Zbraslav[23]. In England ten indulgences granted in favour of pilgrims to Furness (mostly in 1336 to 1345) encouraged them to hear 'the preaching of the Word of God', and, especially, the sermons of a monk of Furness, Roger of Lancaster[24].

It is true that much land was being demised, and many granges were no longer worked directly, but this freed some houses (as the Dunes) from being dependent on a now near-rebellious *conversi*[25]. The General Chapter of 1344 received well over thirty major requests by monasteries wishing permission to sell, exchange, or lease (for more than fifteen years) lands sometimes called 'less useful' – but in fact not so – in order to gain its ready acquiescence[26]. At least the monasteries were seeking the Chapter's agreement, and thereby heeding the dictates of Benedict XII's Constitution for the Order nine years beforehand. Shortage of *conversi* certainly hastened the process of demising, and of establishing the *bastides* on what would otherwise have been little used monastic land[27]. It was in this period, during the reign of the preceding pope, John XXII (1316–34), that a number of monastic communities began to lose part of their freedom and independence of action by the appointment over them of a non-elected abbot, but rather one 'provided' by the Holy See[28]. At first such superiors were usually Cistercian monks, but in later centuries this system of commendatory abbots charged with protecting and administering their abbey, was to detract greatly from the Cistercian ideal. The papacy must have had mixed motives in initiating such a policy; for it received 800 *florins* from its appointee to Ebrach in 1328, and it, in effect, likewise sold the abbacy of Salem (in 1338) for no less than 1,650 *florins*[29].

It is somewhat surprising that Benedict XII (1334–42) continued this policy, for, as a former Cistercian abbot (of Fontfroide) himself, and – as he liked to say – one who had grown in the Order from adolescence[30], none knew better its traditions and the problems it faced. Indeed, in the first year of his pontificate, and after consulting the abbots of Cîteaux, Clairvaux, La Ferté and Morimond[31], he issued his prescriptions for the reform of the Order which were promulgated at the General Chapter of

September, 1335[32]. He praised the Order highly: he likened it to 'the morning star shining in the midst of the clouds'; hence the bull goes for name by its opening words, *Fulgens sicut stella matutina*. He commended the Order for combining the contemplative vocation of Mary with the good works of Martha[33]. Nonetheless he realised that many things needed reform, and he issued forty-two articles with that in mind: many of them already noted in the previous chapters of this book. It was not without significance that the bull was one of Benedict XII's earliest measures, later he issued like decrees for the Benedictines (1336) and the Augustinian Canons (1339)[34].

The several injunctions of Benedict XII's constitution ranged from the need for faithful accounting by bursars and other monastic officials to the care and custody of the common and the abbots' seals. They made provision for the avoidance of debt, and attempted to control the demising of lands. They laid down detailed regulations for the annual visitation of each abbey, they emphasised the need for attendance at the General Chapter, and they prescribed the correct colour of the Cistercian habit. They allowed meat to be eaten in the abbot's chamber and in the infirmary, but forbade monks to sleep in individual cells – only in a common dormitory[35]. An undue proportion (one-quarter) of the injunctions concerned the colleges of the Order[35a]. The bull was ordered to be read at General Chapter, and in each monastic chapter, once a year[36], but some abbots were slow to obtain a copy[37]. Unfortunately the constitution did not take the opportunity to reiterate the Cistercian custom of the unpressurised election of abbots by their respective communities. The only mention of newly-elected abbots was in regard to the oath they should take to defend the property of their monastery[38]. It may be that the pope felt this was already adequately covered by the constitution (in 1265) of Clement IV, or that such provision would run counter to the advantages to the Holy See of 'providing' abbots seemingly for financial gain. The bull of 1335 was a conservative and limited though well-intentioned reform measure, which most scholars believe had little effect[39]. In part this was due to resistance in some quarters of the Order and to a lack of follow-up by subsequent pontiffs. The almost immediate tragedies (especially in western Europe) of the Hundred Years' War and the Black Death set monastic minds on more pressing matters[40].

Not the least of the problems stemming from the Hundred Years' War (which commenced in 1337) was the inability for English abbots to attend the General Chapter[41]. The restrictions placed by the English Crown on foreign travel became more intense, and of course there were many difficulties to surmount *en route*. Between 1344 and 1365 English representatives only attended six Chapters[42]: this meant that Chapter decisions could not easily be transmitted, and that potential seeds of disunity within the Order were planted. As for the monasteries in France, whether in Gascony or Normany and Brittany, many knew destruction both of buildings and lands. The granges of Dalon were successively occupied by English and French forces[43], whilst armies passed and repassed by Cherlieu – it suffered greatly in 1336, 1339 and 1359[44]. The walls of La Charité (1336) were thrown down[45], the monks of Bégard abandoned their monastery for two years (1345–47)[46], Bonlieu (1358) was burnt and the community took refuge on a grange[47]. Duke John of Normandy (1347) rustled, for military food supplies, 400 of Bonneval's cattle[48]. The Battle of Crécy (1346) took place on the doorstep of Valloires[49]. These were but a few of the tribulations the French Cistercians had to suffer. No wonder the General Chapter (1348) spoke of 'the desolation and destruction of the times, due to the wars of kings and princes'[50]. Matters were no better, for other reasons, in Hungary, whose monasteries had perhaps never properly recovered from the Tartar invasions. A regional, though uncompleted visitation held by the abbot of Rein (in 1356–57) found only one abbey (Szepes) to be in good order, whilst Ercsi was uninhabited and lay in ruins[51].

Economic change, particularly for the monasteries of western Europe, was hastened by the Black Death, the plague which migrated northwards through much of the continent in 1348 and 1349. The chronicler of Croxden told how it was 'a great pestilence throughout the whole world'[52], the chronicler of Meaux saw the earth tremor there earlier in the year as a warning of what was to come[53], a contemporary record related how, at Tintern's valuable Norfolk manor of Acle, 'the brute beast raged hour by hour'[54]. Many monks and *conversi* died resulting in severe staffing problems. At Poblet 59 monks and 30 *conversi* perished[55], at Alcobaça – within two months – a total of 150 religious were no more[56]. Aduard lost 45 monks, 120 *conversi* and 29 'scholars', but it was still left with 99 monks, 200 *conversi* and 19 scholars[57]. The numbers at Morimond were reduced from 250 religious to 60, and three of its granges had to be used as infirmaries[58]. The General Chapter, to try to fill the depleted ranks, permitted a lowering (for two years) of the admission age for novices to fourteen. It also abandoned the need for a full year's probation – so long as the candidate knew the psalms by heart[59]. At Duiske, and no doubt elsewhere, the chanting of Nocturns had to be temporarily abandoned[60].

It was the loss of so many of their hired workers and tenants in the great plague, that saw the food supply of Villelongue diminished and the rents gained at La Garde-Dieu reduced[61]. Reviewing the effects of the Black Death seven years later, Sibton (1356) noted a severe fall in rent-income, a shortage of corn because of the lack of labourers (and consequent sterile lands), and many livestock lost due to the small number of available herdsmen[62]. Sibton (1354) sought additional income by demising Weybread Grange[63], and finally achieving the appropriation of Westleton church – with the tithes that brought[64]. Neath (1349) obtained the greater tithes of distant Exford in Somerset[65]. Other demises of lands can be traced for many monasteries (as Margam[66], Meaux[67] and Tamié[68]) in the years immediately following the plague. Good bargains were to be had: in one instance Meaux gained a ready cash payment of fifty marks, but the holding demised passed out of its hands for a century. Shortage of *conversi* saw Dore (1351) obliged to set up a joint-company with seculars to farm its several granges in Cantrefselyf[69]. Buckfast (1350) obtained the income of Brent Fair: its abbot had been one of the casualties of the plague[70]. It was the Black Death, perhaps more than any other factor, which saw the white monks of western Europe have to adopt the manorial system which their early institutes had rejected as unsuitable for their profession. It will remain a matter of debate as to how far, and when, the Cistercians knew 'decay 'or 'decadence', but the Order certainly presented by the mid-fourteenth century a very different aspect from its humble beginnings.

Notes

1. Fergusson (1984a) 20.
2. *Ibid.* 16.
3. Southern (1970) 269–70.
4. *Statuta* II, 24 (1223/12).
5. *Statuta* II, 253 (1242/42).
6. Buczek (1971) 108.
7. Chauvin (1983a) 44, Fossier (1983) 73.
8. Barrière (9183) 93.
9. Wulf (1944) 158.
10. *Statuta* III, 325 (1312/4).
11. *Statuta* III, 395 (1331/10).
12. *Statuta* III, 446 (1337/7).
13. Fossier (1983) 73.
14. See Chapter 14.
15. See Chapter 7.
16. Clair (1961) I, 129.
17. VCH, *Oxford* II (1907) 84.
18. *CPR* 1348/134.
19. Čechura (1987) 95.
20. VCH, *Stafford* (1970) 227.
21. *DHGE* XVII (1971) 1021. 22. *DHGE* XIV (1960) 533.
23. Lekai (1977a) 242.
24. PRO, DL 25/136, 285, 549–56.
25. Donnelly (1949) 58.
26. *Statuta* III, 485–98 (1344/30–36, 38–48, 53, 57–59, 63, 65–70, 72–75).
27. Chauvin (1983a) 40–41.
28. Telesca (1971) 164–65.
29. Lekai (1977a) 104.
30. *Statuta* III, 436 (1335/*bulla* 42).
31. *Statuta* III, 411 (1335/*bulla* 1).
32. For this bull, see: Mahn (1949) *passim*; McNulty (1943) *passim*.

33. *Statuta* III, 410 (1335/*bulla* 1).
34. McNulty (1943) 158n.
35. *Statuta* III, 411–28 (1335/*bulla* 2–30).
35a. *Statuta* III, 429–35 (1335/*bulla* 31–41).
36. McNulty (1943) 166.
37. Mahn (1949) 41.
38. *Statuta* III, 411–12 (1335/3).
39. *E.g:* King (1954) 52, 54; Zarnecki (1972) 70.
40. Desmond (1971) 156.
41. *Statuta* III, 485 (1344/27).
42. Hockey (1976) 108.
43. *DHGE* XIV (1960) 39.
44. *DHGE* XII (1953) 634.
45. *Ibid.* 417.
46. Denifle (1897) 50.
47. Delannoy (1911) 21.
48. Denifle (1897) 27.
49. Denifle (1897) 43.
50. *Statuta* III, 512 (1348/11).
51. Lekai (1976) 265.
52. *CC* (3) B. 59–60.
53. Earle (1906) 107–09.
54. Inscribed on a brass in Acle church.
55. Richards (1968) 102.
56. *DHGE* II (1914) 28.
57. *VGA* 17.
58. King (1954) 360.
59. Lekai (1977a) 101: not noted in Canivez's *Statuta.*
60. Carville (1979) 83–84.
61. Denifle (1897) 61n.
62. *SBC* IV, 87 (No. 1149).
63. *SBC* IV, 92 (No. 1156).
64. *SBC* IV, 87–89 (Nos 1149–50).
65. Williams (1984) I, 64.
66. *Ibid.* I, 64.
67. Snape (1968) 138.
68. Bernard (1967) 46.
69. Williams (1984) I, 64.
70. Stéphan (1970) 114–15

ABBREVIATIONS

Arch. Camb.	: *Archaeologia Cambrensis.*
BL	: British Library, London.
Cartae Glam.	: *Cartae de Glamorgan,* edit. G.T. Clark (1910-).
NLW	: National Library of Wales, Aberystwyth.
Mont. Collns.	: *Montgomeryshire Collections.*
PRO	: Public Record Office, Kew, Surrey.
RCAHM	: Royal Commission on Ancient and Historical Monuments.
SB (1)	: *Saint Bernard et Son Temps* (Assocn. Bourguignon des Soc. Savantes, Congrès de 1927; Dijon, 1928).
SB (2)	: *Mélanges St Bernard* (XXIV Congrès Assoc. Bourguignon Savantes, Dijon, 1953: Comm. d'Histoire de l'Ordre de Cîteaux; Paris, 1953).
VCH	: *Victoria County History of England.*

BIBLIOGRAPHY

PRIMARY SOURCES

ABB :   *Account Book of Beaulieu Abbey*, ed. S.F. Hockey (Camden Soc. 4th Ser. 16 : Royal Hist. Soc. 1975).

AC :   *Annales Colbazienses* in *MGH Scriptorum* XVIII-XIX, ed. G.H. Pertz (Hanover, 1866).

ACA: 'Extracts from the Annals of Crokesden Abbey', ed. F.F. Madden, in *Collectanea Topographica et Geneaologica* (London, 1835).

AD :   *Annales Dunemundensis* in *MGH, Scriptorum* XVIII, ed. G.H. Pertz (Hanover, 1866).

ADP :   *Alsatia Diplomatica* I-II, ed. J.D. Schoepflin (Mannheim, 1772–75).

AF :   *Annales Furnesienses*, ed. T.A. Beck (London, 1844).

AGM :   *Annales Grissowienses Maiores* in *MGH, Scriptorum* XVIII, ed. G.H. Pertz (Hanover, 1866).

AGN :   *Annales Gandenses*, ed. H. Johnstone (London, 1951).

AM :   *Annales Monastici*, I (1864), II (1865), ed. H.R. Luard (Rolls Ser. London).

AMA :   *Antiquitates Michaelsteinses et Amelunxbornenses*, ed. J.G. Leuckfeldt (Wolffenbüttel, 1710).

AMO :   *Analecta Monasterii Ossecensis*, ed. C. Schoettgen (Dresden, 1701).

ANC :   *Ancient Correspondence Concerning Wales*, ed. J. G. Edwards (Cardiff, 1935).

AO :   *Register of Adam of Orleton*, ed. A.T. Bannister (Hereford, 1907/8).

AS :   'Les Actes des Souverains dans les fonds de Fontmorigny', *Mémoires Soc. Antiq. du Centre* XLV, ed. A. Huchet (1931–33; publ. 1934).

AW :   *Antiquitates Walckenredenses*, ed. J.G. Leuckfeldt (Leipzig, 1705).

AZ :   *Annales Zwettl(enses)* in *MGH, Scriptorum* IX, ed. G.H. Pertz (Hanover, 1851).

BC :   *Bartholomaei de Cotton: Historia Anglicana*, ed. H. R. Luard (London, 1859).

BDB :   *Burchardus De Bellevaux : Apologia De Barbis*, ed. E.P. Goldschmidt (Cambridge, 1935).

BMS :   Seal No. as given in Birch (1887).

BT :   *Brut y Tywysogyon*, ed. T. Jones (Cardiff, 1955).

CA :   *Chronicon Alnense*, ed. B. de Give (Scourmont Abbey, Chimay: 1977–78).

CABR :   *Cartulaire de Bonneval*, ed. P-A. Verlaguet (Rodez, 1938).

CAC :   *Cartulaire de Cambron*, ed. J.J. de Smet (Coll. Chroniques Belges Inédites II : Brussels, 1869).

CACW :   *Calendar of Ancient Correspondence Concerning Wales*, ed. J.G. Edwards (Cardiff, 1935).

CADC :   *Cartario della Abbazia di Casanova*, ed. A. Tallone (Bibl. della Soc. Storica Subalpina XIV : Pinerolo, 1903).

CAF :   *Le Chartrier Ancien de Fontmorigny*, ed. A. Huchet (Bourges, 1936).

CAP :   *Calendar of Ancient Petitions relating to Wales*, ed. W. Rees (Cardiff, 1975).

CAS :   *Cartario della Abazia Di Staffarda*, ed. F. Gabotto and others (Bibl. della Soc. Storica Subalpina XI – XII; Pinerolo, 1900–02).

CB :   *Cartulaire de l'abbaye de Berdoues-près-Mirande* ed. Abbé Cazauran (The Hague, Nijhoff, 1905).

CBF :   *Coucher Book of Furness Abbey*, Vol. I, ed. J.C. Atkinson, Pt. 1 (Chetham Soc. N.S. 9; 1886), Pt. 2 (N.S. 14; 1888).

CBFA :   *Coucher Book of Furness Abbey,* Vol. II, ed. J. Brownbill., Pt. 1 (Chetham Soc., N.S. 74 1915) and Pt. 2 (N.S. 76 : 1916).

CBK :   *The Coucher Book of Kirkstall,* ed. W.T. Lancaster and W. Pailey Baildon (Publns. Thoresby Soc., 8; Leeds, 1904).

CBL :   *Cartularies of Balmerino and Lindores,* ed. W.B.D.D. Turnbull (Edinburgh, 1841).

CBN :   *Cartulaire de Bonnecombe,* ed. P-A. Verlaguet (Rodez, 1938).

CBP :   *Cartulaire de N-D. de Bon-Port,* ed. J. Andrieux (Évreux, 1862).

CBR :   *Codex Brandenburg,* ed. P. W. Gercken (Salzwedel, 1769).

CBW :   Coucher Book of Whalley, Pt. 1, ed. W.A. Hulton (Chetham Soc. X : 1847) and Pt. 2 (XI : 1847).

CC :   'Notes on the Chronicle of Croxden' in *Trans. N. Staffs. Field Club,* ed. M. Lawrence., (1) LXXXV : 1950–1; (2) LXXXVI : 1951–2; (3) LXXXVII : 1952–3; (4) LXXXVIII : 1953–4.

CCD :   *Compendium Chronologicum De Dunis,* ed. C. de Visch (Brussels, 1660).

CCR :   *Calendar of Close Rolls* (Rolls Ser., London).

CChR :   *Calendar of Charter Rolls* (Rolls Ser., London).

CChR var. :   *Calendar of Charter Rolls, various* (Rolls Ser., London).

CCO :   *Le cartulaire de Obazine,* ed. Barrière, B (Obazine, 1989).

CCS :   *Chartulary of Coldstream,* ed. C. Rogers (London, 1879).

CD :   'Chartulary of Dieulacres' in *Collns. Hist. Staffs.* ed. W.G. Wrottesley (Wm. Salt Arch. Soc. N.S. IX, 1906).

CDAA: *Chartes et Documents de l'Abbaye de Notre-Dame d'Aiguebelle,* I, ed. J. Font-Réaulx (Lyons, 1953).

CDAC :   *Chartes et Documents concernant l'Abbaye de Cîteaux,* ed. J. Marilier (Rome, 1961).

CDB :   *Codex dipl. Brandenburgensis* I-III, ed. A.F. Riedel (Berlin, 1838); X, Pt. 1, ed. A.F. Riedel (Berlin, 1956).

CDB(2) :   *Codex dipl. Brandenburgensis* I, ed. P.W. Gercken (Salzwedel, 1769).

CDC :   *Cartulaire de Chatelliers,* ed. L. Duval (Niort, 1872).

CDCDS :   *Codex dipl. Croatiae, Dalmatiae et Slavoniae* II and III, ed. T. Smičiklas (Zagreb, 1904–05).

CDCS :   'Consuetudines Domus Cisterciensis', ed. B. Griesser, *Analecta S.O. Cist.* III (1947).

CDEM :   *Codex dipl. et epist. Moraviae,* ed. A. Boczek (Brünn, 1836-).

CDF :   *Calendar of Documents preserved in France,* ed. J.H. Round (Rolls Ser., London, 1889).

CDH :   'Herrera : Coleccion Diplomatica', ed. S.L. Castillo, *Analecta Cist.* XXXVII (1985 : Pt. 1).

CDK :   'Charters of Duiske', ed. C.M. Butler and J.H. Bernard, *Proc. Royal Irish Acad.* XXXV (1918–20) Section C.

CDL :   'Duchy of Lancaster Charters', *36th Report of the Deputy Keeper of the Public Records,* Appendix 1 (London, 1875).

CDLD :   *Codice Diplomatico Laudense* II, ed. C. Vignate (Milan, 1883).

CDM :   *Codex dipl. Moguntiaca,* ed. W.F. de Gudenus (Leipzig, 1743–68).

CDN :   *Cronica de Dunis,* ed. A. de But (Bruges, 1864).

CDNM: *Chronico Dunamundense,* in: Schmidt, W., *Die Zistersienser im Baltikum und in Finland* (Suomen kirkohistoriallisen Seuran Vnosihirja, 29–30; Helsinki, 1941) – a rare work of which there is a copy in the Bodleian Library, Oxford).

CDNO :   *Cartulaire de l'Abbaye de Nonenque,* ed. C. Couderc and J-L. Rigal (Rodez, 1955).

CDNS :   *Codex Dunensis,* ed. J. Kervyn de Lettenhove (Brussels, 1875).

CDP :   *Cartulaire de l'Abbaye de Perseigne,* ed. J. Fleury (Mamers, 1880).

CDRB :   *Codex dipl. Regni Bohemiae,* ed. J. Friedrich and others (Prague, 1904–74).

CDS :   *Codex dipl. Saxoniae,* ed. O. Posse (Leipzig, 1898).

CDSL :   *Codex dipl. Salemitanus* I-III, ed. F.O.A. von Weech (Karlsruhe, 1883–95).

CDVG :   *Chartes et Documents du Val-Saint-Georges,* ed. É. Brouette (Achel Abbey, 1971).

CE :   *Codex Esromensis,* ed. O. Nielsen (Copenhagen, 1880–1).

CF :   *Cartulary of Flaxley,* ed. A.W. Crawley-Boevey (Exeter, 1887).

CFC :   'Chronicon Floridi Campi', ed. M. Schoengen, *Archief voor de Geschiedenis van het Aartsbisdom Utrecht* XXIX (1903).

CFN :   'Cronaca di Fossa-Nova', ed. S. Volpicella, *Cronisti e Scrittori Sincroni Napoletani* I (Naples, 1845).

CFR :   *Calendar of Fine Rolls* (Rolls Ser., London).

CG :   *Cartulaire de Gimont*, ed. Abbe Clergeac (Archives Historique de Gascogne, 2nd
            Ser. IX; Paris-Auch, 1905).
CH :   *Cartulary of Haughmond*, ed. Rees, U (Cardiff, 1985).
CHA :   *Cistercian History Abstracts* (Biennial Supplement to *Cîteaux*).
CHDM :   Caesarius of Heisterbach : Dialogue on Miracles, *ed. H. von E. Scott and C.C.
            Swinton Bland* (London, 1929).
CHS :   'Collections towards the History of Stanley', ed. W. de Gray Birch, *Wilts. Arch. and
            Nat. Hist. Magazine* XV (Dec. 1875).
CKA :   'Charters of Kirkstall Abbey', ed. F.R. Kitson and others, *Publns. Thoresby Soc.* IV
            (1895).
CL :   *Chartularium de Notre-Dame de Leoncello*, ed. C.U.J. Chevalier (Montélimar, 1869).
CM :   *The Chronicle of Melrose*, ed. J. Stevenson (Llanerch Press, 1991 reprint).
CM (2) :   'Chronicle of Melrose' in *Church Histories of England*, ed. J. Stevenson (London,
            1856).
CMA :   *Chronica Maiora*, ed. H. R. Luard (Rolls Ser., London; 1880).
CMH :   *Cartulario del Monasterio de Huerta*, ed. J.A.G. Lujan (Huerta, 1981).
CMM :   *Chronica de Melsa* I-III, ed. E.A. Bond (Rolls Ser., London, 1866–88).
CNM :   *Chartularium de Novo Monasterio*, ed. J.T. Fowler (Surtees Soc., LXVI, 1876; publ.
            1878).
CO :   *Cartulaire de Notre-Dame d'Ourscamp*, ed. A. Peigné-Delacourt (Mém. Soc. des Antiq.
            de Picardie, VI : Amiens, 1860).
CP :   *Chronicon Portense* I-II, ed. J. Bertuchius (*Pertuchius*; Leipzig, 1612).
CPL :   *Chronicle of Louth Park Abbey*, ed. E. Venables (Lincs. Rec. Soc. I, 1891).
CPR :   *Calendar of Patent Rolls* (Rolls Ser., London).
CR :   *Cartario di Rivalta Piemonte*, ed. G.B. Rosano (Bibl. della Soc. Storica Subalpina,
            LXVIII; Pinerolo, 1912).
CRA :   *XVI Charters of Roche Abbey*, ed. S.O. Addy (Sheffield, 1878).
CRC :   *Rental Book of Coupar Angus*, ed. C. Rogers (Grampian Club, 1880).
CRD :   *Chronicon Riddagshusense*, ed. G. Zimmermann (Brunswick, 1983).
CRS :   *Cartario dell'Abazia di Rivalta Scrivia*, ed. A. F. Trucco (Bibl. della Soc. Storica
            Subalpina, LIX-LX; Pinerolo, 1910–11).
CRSHR :   *Chronicles of the Reigns of Stephen, Henry II and Richard I*, ed. Howlett, R (Rolls Ser,
            London;1185; Kraus reprint, 1964).
CS :   *Chartulary of Salley* I and II, ed. J. McNulty (Yorkshire Archaeol. Rec. Ser.
            LXXXVII and XC, 1933 and 1934).
CSA :   *Cartulary of Shrewsbury Abbey*, ed. U. Rees (1975).
CSBW :   *Chartes de Saint-Benoît-en-Woëvre*, ed. J. Denaix (Verdun, 1959).
CSMD :   *Chartularies of St Mary's Abbey, Dublin*, ed. Gilbert, J.T (Rolls Ser; London, 1884).
CSMF :   *Cartulario de Santa Maria La Real de Fitero*, ed. M.A.Y. Lasa (Col. Doc. Ined. Para.
            La Hist. de Navarra, 1; Pamplona, 1900).
CSV :   *Cartulaire de Silvanès*, ed. P-A. Verlaguet (Rodez, 1910).
CTA :   *The Cottonian Annals*, ed. A.M. Freeman (Paris, 1929).
CTB :   *The Tax Book of the Cistercian Order*, ed. A.O. Johnsen and P. King
            (Universitetsforlaget, Oslo; 1979).
CTD :   *Chronique de Ter Doest*, ed. F. van de Putte and C. Carton (Bruges, 1845).
CV :   'Cartulari de Vallbona', ed. J.J.P. i Jover, in *Boletín de la Real Academia de Buenas
            Letras de Barcelona* XXXVII (1977–8).
CVL :   *Chronicon Valassense*, ed. F. Somménil (Rouen, 1868).
CW :   *Cartulary of Wardon*, ed. G.H. Fowler (Publns. Bedfordshire Hist. Rec. Soc. XIII,
            1931).
CWD :   *Ottonis Chronicon Waldsassense*, ed. Oefele, F.A., Rerum Boicarum Scriptores I
            (Augusta Vicindelicorum, 1763).
CWK :   *Chronicon Walkenredense*, ed. H. Eckstorm (Helmstedt, 1617).
CYM :   *The Charters of the Abbey of Ystrad Marchell*, ed. G.C.G. Thomas (Aberystwyth, 1997).
CZ :   *Continuatio Zwetlense*: MGH : *Scriptorum* IX, ed. G.H. Pertz (Hanover, 1851).

DAC :   *Dictionnaire des Auteurs Cisterciens*, ed. E. Brouette, A. Dimier and E. Manning
            (Abbaye N.D. et St. Remy, Rochefort, Belgium; 1975–).
DAM :   *Diplomatarium Arna-Magnaeaum* I, ed. G.J. Thorkelin (Copenhagen, 1786).
DCK :   'Documents relating to the Cistercian Monastery of Kingswood', ed. V.R. Perkins,
            Trans. Bristol and Gloucs. Arch. Soc. XXII (1899).

DD :   'Diplomatarium Doberanense', ed. E.J. de Westphalen, *Monumenta Inedita* III (Leipzig, 1743).
DHG :   *Diplomataria Historiae Germanicae* I – III, ed. C. Schoettgen (Altenburg, 1753–60).
DHS :   *Documents illustrative of the History of Scotland* II, ed. J. Stevenson (Glasgow, 1870).
DL :   'Duchy of Lancaster Charters', *36th Report of the Deputy Keeper of the Public Records*, Appendix 1 (London, 1875).
DMLH :   *Documentacion del Monasterio de Las Huelgas de Burgos* I and II, ed. J.M.L. Garrido (Burgos, 1985).
DNC :   *Diplomatum Nova Collectio*, ed. A. Miraeus (Brussels, 1734).
DR :   *Documenta Redivia*, ed. C. Besold (Tübingen, 1636).
DSMLR :   *Diplomatari del Monestir de Santa Maria De La Real de Mallorca* I : 1232–1360, ed. P. Mora and L. Andrinal (Palma, 1982).

EAY :   *Early Yorkshire Charters*, ed. C.T. Clay (Yorkshire Arch. Rec. Soc. Extra Ser. XI, 1963).
EOC :   Les *'Ecclesiastica Officia' Cisterciens du XIIème Siècle,* ed. D. Choisselet and P. Vernet (La Docum. Cist., 22; Oelenberg Abbey, Reiningue, 1989).

FH :   *Flores Historiarum* I-III, ed. H.R. Luard (Rolls Ser., London, 1890).
FHL :   *Fontes Historiae Latviae Medii Aevi* I, ed. A. Švābe (Riga, 1937).
FRB :   *Fontes Rerum Bohemicarum* II, IV and V, ed. J. Emler (Prague, 1874, 1884, 1893).

GCIK :   *Giraldi Cambrensis: Itinerarium Kambriae*, ed. J.F. Dimock. (Rolls Ser., London, 1868).

HVCP :   'Fragmente eines Heiligenkreuzer Visitations-chartenprotokolls', ed. H. Watzl, in *Cist. Chronik* N.S. 53, Pt. 4 (Dec. 1960).
HRA :   *Historia Rerum Anglicarum of William of Newburgh*, I., ed. Howlett, R. (Rolls Ser., London, 1884).

KAC :   *The Kirkstall Abbey Chronicles*, ed. J. Taylor (Publns. Thoresby Soc. XLII; Leeds, 1952).
KD :   *Kodeks Dyplomatycny Wielpolski*, ed. I. Zakrzewski (Poznan, 1877–86).
KDM :   *Kodeks Dyplomatyczny Małopolski* II, ed. Piekosiński (Kraków, 1886).
KDS :   *Kodeks Dyplomatyczny Śląska* I, ed. K. Maleczyński (Wrocław, 1955).
KKA :   'De Kroniek van het Klooster Aduard', ed. H. Brugmans, *Bijdragen en Mededeelingen* H.G. 23 (Utrecht, 1902).
KZ :   *Kalendarium Zwetlense* in *MGH: Scriptorum* IX, ed. G.H. Pertz (Hanover, 1851).

LCC(1) :   *La Codification Cistercienne de 1202*, ed. B. Lucet (Rome, 1964).
LCC(2) :   *Les Codifications Cisterciennes de 1237 et de 1257* ed. B. Lucet (Paris, 1977).
LECU :   *Liv-, Esth-, und Curländisches Urkundenbuch nebst Regesten* I, ed. Bunge, F.G. von. (Dorpat, 1853).
LFZ :   *Das 'Stiftungen-Buch' (Liber Fundationis) des Cistercienser- Klosters Zwettl*, ed. J. von Frast (Fontes Rerum Austriacarum, III; Vienna, 1851).
LKZ :   *Listy Kláštera Zbraslavského*, ed. F. Tadra (Historický Archiv, 23; Prague, 1904).
LJ :   *Le Livre Juratoire*, ed. G. Babinet (Montauban, 1888).
LM :   *Liber de Melrose*, ed. C. Innes (Bannantyne Club, 1837).
LMP :   *Les Monuments Primitifs*, ed. P. Guignard, (Dijon, 1928 edn.).
LMT :   'Letter Collections attributed to Master Transmundus', ed. S.J. Heathcote, *Analecta Cist.* XXI : 2 (1965).
LSB :   *The Letters of St Bernard of Clairvaux*, ed. B. Scott James (London, 1953).
LW :   *Littere Wallie*, ed. J. G. Edwards (Cardiff, 1940).

MA :   *Monasticon Anglicanum*, ed. W. Dugdale (London, 1846 edn).
MEB :   *Monumenta Eberacensis*, ed. F.X. Wegele, (Nördlingen, 1863).
MEX :   *Monasticon Exoniensis*, ed. G. Oliver (London, 1846).
MF :   *Memorials of Fountains*, ed. J.S. Walbran (Surtees Soc., XLII, 1863; LXVII, 1878), and J.T. Fowler (CXXX, 1918).
MG :   *Monumenta Groningana*, ed. R. Keuchenius Driessen (Groningen, 1822).
MGH :   *Monumenta Germaniae Historica* (Berlin).

MHP :   *Monumenta Historica Poloniae*, non-attrib. (Cracow, 1874–1927).
ML :   *Monumenta Lubiensa*, ed. W. Wattenbach (Breslau, 1861).
MPH :   *Monumenta Poloniae Historica*, ed. A. Bielowski (Cracow, 1864–93).
MPHA :   *Matthæi Parisiensis, Chronica Majora* V, ed. H.R. Luard (London, 1880).
MU :   *Mecklenburgische Urkunden* I-II, ed. G.C.F. Lisch (Schwerin, 1837–41).
MUK :   *Marienroder Urkundenbuch*, ed. C.L. Grotesend (Hanover, 1859-).

NG :   *Necrologia Germaniae* II: 1, ed. S. Herzberg-Fränkel, (Monumenta Germaniae Historica; (Berlin, 1904); IV, ed. W. Sturm, (1920).

OC :   *Originum Cisterciensium*, ed. L. Janauschek (Vienna, 1877).
OHZ :   *Oorkondenboek van Holland en Zeeland* I and II, ed. A.C.F. Koch (Gravenhage, 1970, and Maastricht, 1986).
OLSB :   *Obituarium Monasterii Loci Sancti Bernardi*, ed. B. van Doninck (Bornhem, 1901).
OM :   *Der Oculus Memorie* : Pt. 1, ed. H. Meyer zu Ermgassen (Wiesbaden, 1981).
OMA :   *Oorkondenboek der Witheerenabdij van S.-Michiels te Antwerpen*, ed. P.J. Goetschalckx (Eekeren-Donk, 1909).
OSBS(1) : *Oorkondenboek der Abdij van St-Bernardsaan de Schelde*, ed. E.H.P.J. Goetschalckx and B. van Doninck (Antwerp, 1926).
OSBS(2) : *Ibid.* continuation in *Bijdragen tot de Geschiedenis Hertogdom Brabant* (12th Yr; Jan. 1913).

PCP :   *La Premier Cartulaire de Pontigny*, ed. M. Garrigues, (Colln. de Documents Inédits sur l'Histoire de France; 14, 1981).
PD :   *The Pudsey Deeds*, ed. R.P. Littledale (Yorkshire Arch. Rec. Ser., LVI; 1916).
PM :   *Catalogue of the Penrice and Margam Charters*, ed. W. de Gray Birch (London, 1893–1905).
PU :   *Pommersches Urkundenbuch* I-II, ed. R. Klempin (Stettin, 1868–81).
PZKZ :   *Petra Žitavského Kronika Zbraslavská*, ed. J. Emlera (Fontes Rerum Bohemicarum, IV; Prague, 1884).

RBC :   'Regesta de Sant Bernat Calvo', ed. E. Fort i Cogul, *Studia Monastica* XI : 1 (1969).
RBS :   *Rerum Boicarum Scriptores*, ed. Oefele (Oefelius), A. F. (Augusta Vindelicorum , 1763).
RBM :   *Regesta Bohemiae et Moraviae*, ed. C.J. Erben (Prgue, 1859–90).
RC :   *Radulphi de Coggeshall : Chronicon Anglicanum*, ed. J. Stevenson (Rolls Ser., London, 1875).
RCA :   *Rental Book of Cupar-Angus* I and II , ed. C. Rogers (Grampian Club, 1880).
RCC :   'Recueil des Chartes et Bulles de Clairvaux', ed. A. Prevost, *Revue Mabillon* I-VI (1924–29).
RCCH :   *Recueil des Chartes de Cheminon*, ed. E. de Barthélemy (Paris, 1883).
RCH :   *Repertorium Historicum Ordinis Cisterciensis in Hungaria*, ed. F.L. Hervay (Rome-Budapest, 1984).
RCOC :   'Regula Conversorum ordinis Cisterciensis ex MS Alnensi', *Thesaurus Novus Anecdotorum* IV, ed. E. Martene and U. Durand (Paris, 1717).
RD :   *Regesta Dauphinois*, ed. U. Chevalier (Valence, 1912-).
RDM :   *Rouleaux des Morts*, ed. L. Delisle (Soc. de l'Hist. de France; Paris, 1866).
RDT :   *Regesta Diplomatica Thuringia* I-II, ed. O. Dobenecker (Jena, 1896–1900).
RFC :   *Rufford Charters*, ed. C.J. Holdsworth (Thoroton Rec. Soc., 29–30; 1972–74).
RH :   *Selected Rentals and Accounts of Medieval Hull*, ed. R. Horrox (Yorkshire Arch. Rec. Ser. CXLI, 1981; publ. 1983).
RHC :   'Register and Records of Holm Cultram', ed. F. Grainger and W.D. Collingwood, *Trans. Cumberland and Westm. Ant. Arch. Soc.*, Rec. Ser. VII (1929).
RN :   *Registrum Sancte Marie de Neubotle*, ed. C. Innes (Bannatyne Club, 1846).
RPR :   *Regesta Pontificum Romanorum* I-II, ed. A. Potthast (Berlin, 1874–5).
RSB :   *Households of God: The Rule of St Benedict*, ed. D. Parry (London, 1980).
RSL :   'Registrum Epistolarum Stephani de Lexington' I-II, ed. B. Griesser, *Analecta S.O. Cist.* 2 (1946) and 8 (1952).

SBC :   *Sibton Abbey Cartularies and Charters* I-IV, ed. P. Brown (Suffolk Record Soc. : Suffolk Charters* VII-X (1985–88).

SBE :   *Sibton Abbey Estates*, ed. A.H. Denney (Suffolk Rec. Soc. Publns. II, 1960).
SC :   *Sanctorum Conciliorum* XX, ed. G.D. Mansi (Florence, 1778).
SL :   *Stephen of Lexington : Letters from Ireland*, ed. B.W. O'Dwyer (Kalamazoo, 1982).
SLB :   *The Stoneleigh Ledger Book*, ed. R.H. Hilton (Publns. Dugdale Soc., XXIV, 1960).
SMD :   *Scriptores Minores Historicae Danicae Medii Aevi*, ed. Cl. Gertz (Copenhagen, 1917–20).
SRD :   *Scriptores Rerum Danicarum*, ed. J. Langebek (Copenhagen, 1776).
Statuta :   *Statuta Capit. Gen. Ord. Cist.* I – VII, ed. J. Canivez (Louvain, 1933–41).

TC :   *The Thame Cartulary* I-II, ed. H. Salter (Oxford Rec. Soc., XXV (1947) and XXVI (1948).
TG :   *Das Tennenbacher Güterbuch*, ed. M. Weber (Stuttgart, 1969).
TL :   *Das Todtenbuch des Lilienfeld*, ed. H.R. von Zeissberg (Fontes Rerum Austriacarum, XLI; Vienna, 1879).

UBC :   *Urkundenbuch des Bisthums Culm*, ed. C.P Woelky, (Danzig/Gdańsk, 1884).
UE :   *Urkundenbuch der Abtei Eberbach* I, ed. K. Rossel (Wiesgaden, 1862).
UGC :   'Unbekante Generalkapitelstatuten', ed. B. Griesser, *Cist. Chronik* N.S. 39/40 (July 1957).
UGDS :   *Urkundenbuch zur Geschichte der Deutschen in Siebenburgen* I, ed. F. Zimmermann and others (Sibiu : Hermannstadt, 1892).
UKA :   *Urkundenbuch der Abtei Altenberg* I, ed. Mosler, H (Bonn, 1912).
UKAR :   *Urkundenbuch des Klosters Arnsburg*, ed. L. Baur (Darmstadt, 1849/51).
UKB :   *Urkundenbuch der Abtei Bonnweg*, ed. N. van Werveke (Luxemburg, 1880).
UKG :   *Urkundenbuch des Cistercienserstiftes Goldenkron*, ed. M. Pangerl (Fontes Rerum Austriacarum, 37; Vienna, 1872).
UKH :   *Urkundenbuch zu Hohenfurt*, ed. M. Pangerl (Fontes Rerum Austriacarum, 23; Vienna, 1865).
UKN :   *Urkunden und Copiar des Klosters Neuenkamp*, ed. F. Fabricius (Stettin, 1891).
UKO :   *Urkundenbuch des Klosters Otterberg*, ed. M. Frey and F.X. Remling (Mainz, 1845).
UKP :   *Urkundenbuch des Klosters Pforte*, ed. E. Halbband Geschichtsquellen der Provinz Sachsen, 33; Halle, 1893).
UKS :   *Urkundenbuch des Klosters Scharnbeck*, ed. D. Brosius (Hildesheim, 1972).
UKSH :   *Urkunden des Cistercienser-Stiftes Heiligenkreuz*, ed. J.N. Weis (Fontes Rerum Austriacarum, XI : Pt. 1; Vienna, 1856).
UKW :   *Die Urkunden des Stiftes Walkenried*, ed. C.L. Grotefend (Hanover, 1852–55).
UKZ :   'Urkunden des Stiftes Zwettl', ed. J. von Frast, in *Archiv, fur Kunde osterreichischer Geschichts-Quellen* II (1849, Pt. 3).

VGA :   *Vitas ac Gesta Abbatum Adwerdensium*, ed. F. Koppius, (Groningen, 1850).
VKS :   'Auszüge aus den Visitationsakten des Klosters Stams', ed. B. Griesser, *Cist. Chronik* N.S. 62 (1955); also published in: Linder, P.K. ed. *Beiträge zur Wirtschafts und Kulturgeschichte des Zisterzienserstiftes Stams in Tirol* (Innsbruck, 1959).
VRL :   *The Ledger Book of Vale Royal Abbey*, ed. J. Brownbill, (Lancashire and Cheshire Record Soc., LVIII [1914]).

WAR :   *Welsh Assize Roll*, ed. J. Conway Davies (Cardiff, 1940).
WMG :   *Willelmi Malmiesbiriensis Monachi: De Gestis Regum Anglorum* II, ed. W. Stubbs (Rolls Ser., London, 1889).
WMG (2) :   *William of Malmesbury's Chronicle of the Kings of England*, ed. J.A Giles, (London, 1911).
WMR :   *List of Welsh Entries in the Memoranda Rolls*, ed. N. Fryde (Cardiff, 1974)

SECONDARY SOURCES

Affolter (1978) :   Affolter, E., *L'Abbaye de Clairefontaine* (Vesoul, 1978).
Albergo (1980) :   Albergo, V., *Eremo e Abbazia di San Galgano* (Pistoia, 1980).
Allendorff (1971) :   Allendorff, J., 'Kolbatz', *Cîteaux* XXII (1971 : 3–4).

Almeida Fernandes : (1973–76)
Almeida Fernandes, A. de, 'Acçâo dos Cistercienses de Tarouca *Revista Guimares* (I) LXXXIII (1973), (II) LXXXIV (1974), (III) LXXXV (1975), (IV) LXXXVI (1976).

Altermatt (1990) :
Altermatt, A., 'The Cistercian Patrimony', *Cistercian Studies* XXV (1990: 4).

Altisent (1970) :
Altisent, A., 'Dotació de Llits', *Studia Monastica* 12 (1970 :1).

Altisent (1972) :
Altisent, A., *Les Granges de Poblet* (Barcelona, 1972).

Altrichter (1979) :
Altrichter, H., *Die Zisterzienser in Mâhren* (Darmstadt, 1979).

Amon (1979) :
Amon, K. and others., *Stift Rein* (Rein Abbey, 1979).

Anderson (1978) :
Anderson, J.D., 'William of St Thierry', in Sommerfeldt (1978).

Andrea (1985) :
Andrea, A.J., 'Adam of Perseigne', *Cîteaux* XXXVI (1985 : 1–2).

Andrea (1987) :
Andrea, A.J., 'Conrad of Krosigk', *Anal. Cist.* XLIII (1987 :1).

Andrea and Motsiff (1972):
Andrea, A.J. and Motsiff, I., 'Pope Innocent III', *Byzantinoslavica* XXXIII (1972: 1).

Andrews and Boutwood (1984):
Andrews, D.D. and Boutwood, J., 'Coggeshall Barn', in *Essex Archaeology and History* 16 (1984–85).

Anselm (1943) :
Fr Anselm of Tamié, quoted in *Bull. Soc. Nat. des Antiq. de France* (1943–4).

Anstett (1987) :
Anstett, P.R., *Maulbronn Monastery* (Munich, 1987)

Antón (1923) :
Antón, F., *Monasterios de la Provincia de Valladolid* (Madrid, 1923).

Antón (1953) :
Antón, F., 'San Bernardo y Nuestra Arquitectura', *Cistercium* V, No. 30 (Nov. – Dec. 1953).

Anton (1986) :
Anton, I. A., *La Colonizacion Cisterciense en la Meseta del Duero* (Salamanca/Zamora, 1986).

Appuhn (1981) :
Appuhn, H., *Kloster Isenhagen* (Munich, 1981).

Aquilina (1991) :
Aquilina, L., Baptiste, P. and Deroin, J-P., 'Étude géologique', in Benoît and Cailleux (1991).

Arenas (1985) :
Arenas, J.F., *Les Monasterios de Santes Creus y Poblet* (Madrid, 1985).

Arens (1982) :
Arens, F., 'Die Türstürze und Tympana', Chauvin (1982a) III, Pt. 5.

Arnoux (1991) :
Arnoux, M., 'Le Cas Normandy', in Benoît and Cailleux (1991).

Arthaud (1947) :
Arthaud, B., *Hautecombe* (Grenoble, 1947).

Arvidsson (1986) :
Arvidsson, E., 'Cisterciensernas Kloster I Herrevad' , *Populär Arkeologi* 4 (Stockholm, 1986).

Ashmore (1962) :
Ashmore, O., *Whalley Abbey* (Whalley, 1962).

Astill (1989) :
Astill, G.G., 'Monastic research designs', in Gilchrist and Mytum (1989).

Astill (1993) :
Astill, G.G., *A Medieval Industrial Complex* (CBA Research Report 92; 1993).

Astill (1994) :
Astill, G.G., 'The Bordesley Abbey Granges Project', in Pressouyre 1994.

Aston (1988) :
Aston, M., *Medieval fish, fisheries and fishponds* (Oxford, 1988; BAR (British Series 182)

Aston (1993) :
Aston, M., *Monasteries* (Batsford, London; 1993).

Attwater (1965) :
Attwater, D., *The Penguin Dictionary of Saints* (Penguin, 1965).

Auberger (1986) :
Auberger, G.B., *L'Unanimité Cistercienne Primitive* (Cîteaux: Studia et Documenta III; Achel Abbey, 1986).

Aubert (1931) :
Aubert, M., *L'Abbaye des Vaux de Cernay* (Paris, 1931).

Aubert (1932) :
Aubert, M., *L'Abbaye de Noirlac* (Paris, 1932).

Aubert (1933) :
Aubert, M., 'L'Abbaye de l'Escaledieu', *Bull. Monumental* XCII (1933).

Aubert (1947) :
Aubert, M., *L'Architecture Cistercienne en France* (Paris, 1947).

Aubrun (1978) :
Aubert, M., 'Aubepierres', *Cîteaux* XXIX (1978 : 1–2).

Aurell i Cardona :
Aurell i Cardona, M., 'Les Cisterciennes en Provence rhodanienne', in Privat (1986).

Auvry (1897) :
Auvry, C., *Histoire de Savigny* II (Rouen, 1897).

Aveling (1876) :
Aveling, J.H., *Roche Abbey* (London, 1876).

Baigent (1882) :
Baigent, F.J., *Abbey and Church of Waverley* (London, 1882).

Baker (1975) :
Baker, D., 'Cistercian Chronicles in England', *Analecta Cist.* XXXI (1975 : 2).

Balleine (1962) :
Balleine, G.R., *The Bailiwick of Jersey* (London, 1962).

Bannister (1929) :
Bannister, A. T., 'Miraculous Happenings at Abbey Dore, *Trans. Woolhope Naturalists Field Club* (1929).

Bar (1985) :
Bar, J.R. and Świżek, K., *Błogosławiony Wincenty Kadłubek* (Warsaw, 1985).

Barakat (1975) :   Barakat, R.A., *Cistercian Sign Language* (Cist. St. Ser., 11; Kalamazoo, 1975).

Barber (1995):   Barber, M., *The new knighthood* (Cambridge, 1995).

Barea (1977) :   Barea, C.C., *El Cister Zaragozano* I-II (Saragossa, 1977).

Barley (1957) :   Barley, M.W., 'Cistercian Land Clearances', *Nottingham Medieval Studies* I (1957).

Barnes (1982) :   Barnes, G.D., *Kirkstall Abbey, 1141–1539* (Publns. Thoresby Soc., LVIII; Leeds, 1982).

Barrière (1977) :   Barrière, B., *L'Abbaye d'Obazine* (Tulle, 1977).

Barrière (1983) :   Barrière, B., 'L'économie du sud-ouest', in Higounet (1983).

Barrière (1986) :   Barrière, B., 'Les abbayes issues de l'érémitismé' in Privat (1986).

Barrière (1989) :   Barrière, B., *Le Cartulaire de l'Abbaye d'Obazine* (Publns. de l'Inst. d'Etudes du Massif Central, XXXIII; 1989).

Barrière (1990) :   Barrière, B., 'L'abbaye d'Obazine et ses granges', in Pressouyre (1990).

Barrière (1994) :   Barrière, B., 'Les patrimonies cisterciens en France' , in Fontfroide (1994).

Barron (1960) :   Barron, F., 'Les Eglises de Vaucelles', *Cîteaux* XI (1960).

Barry (und.) :   Barry, F., *L'Abbaye d'Aulne* (Montignies-le-Tilleul, und.).

Barton (1996) :   Barton, P.G., 'The Windmill of Strata Marcella', *Mont. Collns.* 84 (1996).

Batany (1964) :   Batany, J., 'Les moines blancs', in *Cîteaux* XV (1964 : 1).

Baugh and Cox :   Baugh, G.C. and Cox, D.C., *Monastic Shropshire* (Shrewsbury, 1982).
 (1982)

Bautier (1994) :   'Les "courts" de Prémontre', in Pressouyre (1994).

Baxter (1914) :   Baxter, W., 'Granges of Holm Cultram', *Trans. Cumberland and Westm. Antiq. and Arch. Soc.* XIV (1914).

Beaulah (1993) :   Beaulah, G.K.,'Thirteenth Century Square-Tile Mosaic Pavements', in Lillich (1993).

Beaumont (1921) :   Beaumont, G.F., 'The Remains of Coggeshall Abbey', *Trans. Essex Arch. Soc.* N.S. XV (1921).

Beaussart(1983) :   Beaussart, P. and Maliet, V., 'Les pavements de Fontenelle', *Revue de Nord* LXV (Jan.-Mar. 1983).

Bedini (1964) :   Bedini, B.G., *Breve prospetto delle Abazie Cisterciensi d'Italia* (Casamari Abbey, 1964).

Békefi (1896) :   Bedini, B.G., 'A czisztercziek Középkori Iskolázása Párisban', *Ertekezesek A Történelmi Tudományok Kórából* XVI (Budapest, 1896).

Bell (1984a) :   Bell, D.N., 'The Books of Meaux Abbey', *Analecta Cist.* XL (1984 : 1–2).

Bell (1984b) :   Bell, D.N., 'The works of Baldwin of Ford', *Cîteaux* XXXV (1984 : 3–4).

Bell (1987) :   Bell, D.N., 'Baldwin of Ford and the Sacrament of the Altar', in Sommerfeldt (1987).

Bell (1989) :   Bell, D.N., 'The English Cistercians and the Practice of Medicine', *Cîteaux* XL (1989:1–4.).

Bell (1992) :   Bell, D.N., *An Index of Authors and works in Cistercian Libraries in Great Britain'* I (Cist. St. Ser. 130; Kalamazoo, 1992), II (No. 132, 1994).

Bell (1993) :   Bell, D.N., ' Twelfth Century Divination', *Cîteaux* XLIV (1993: 1–4).

Bell (1994) :   Bell, D.N., 'Measurement of Cistercian Space', in Fontfroide (1994).

Bell (1995) :   Bell, D.N., 'The Book Collection of Fontfroide Abbey', *Cîteaux* XLVI: 1–2 (1995).

Bellero (1985) :   Bellero, M., 'I cistercensi e il paesaggio rurale', *Studi Storici* 26:2 (April–June, 1985).

Benoît and Cailleux   Benoît, P. and Cailleux, D., *Moines et Métallurgie* (Paris, 1991).
 (1991):

Benoît and others :   Benoît, P. and Guillot, Y. and Deschamp, C., 'Minerai et métallurgie à
 (1991):   Fontenay', in Benoît and Cailleux (1991).

Benoît and Sportes :   Benoît, P. and Sportes, N., 'Exploitation du fer', in Benoît and Cailleux
 (1991):   (1991).

Benouville (1889) :   Benouville, P. and Lauzun, P., 'L'Abbaye de Flaran', *Revue de Gascogne* XXX (1889).

Berckmans (1973) :   Berckmans, O. and others., *Le Domaine d'Orval* I (Liege, 1973).

Beresford (1967) :   Beresford, M., *New Towns of the Middle Ages* (London, 1967).

Berlière (1905) :	Berlière, U., 'Invasion de l'Abbaye des Dunes', *Annales de la Soc. d'Emulation de Bruges 55* (1905).
Berman (1978) :	Berman, C.H., 'Foundation and Early History of Silvanès', in Sommerfeldt (1978).
Berman (1979) :	Berman, C.H., 'Administrative Evidences for the Cistercian Grange', *Cîteaux* XXX (1979 : 2–4).
Berman (1981) :	Berman, C.H., 'Cistercian Development and Tithes', *Revue Benedictine* 91 (1981 : I-II).
Berman (1982) :	Berman, C.H., 'Land Acquisition by the Cistercians of Berdoues', *Speculum* 57 : 2 (April, 1982).
Berman (1983) :	Berman, C.H., 'Early Cistercian Expansion in Provence', in Elder (1983).
Berman (1986) :	Berman, C.H., *Medieval Agriculture, the Southern French Countryside, and the Early Cistercians* (Trans. American Philosophical Soc. 76, Pt. 5 ; 1986).
Berman (1990) :	Berman, C.H.,'Les Granges cisterciennes fortifées du Rouergue', *Les Cahiers de le Ligne Urbaine et Rurale* 109 (1990).
Berman (1992) :	Berman, C.H., 'Gifts, Counter-gifts, Donations, Sales', *Cîteaux* (1992).
Berman (1994) :	Berman, C.H., 'Cistercian Granges to Bastides', in Pressouyre (1994).
Berman (1995) :	Berman, C.H., 'Cistercian Nuns' in Elder (1995).
Bernard (1967) :	Bernard, F., *L'Abbaye de Tamié : Ses Granges* (Grenoble, 1967).
Bernier (1988) :	Bernier, J-Y., *L'Épau, une abbaye cistercienne* (Paris, 1988).
Bertuzzi (1972) :	Bertuzzi, G., 'Chiaravalle della Colomba', *Archiv. Storico Prov. Parmensi* XXVII (1972).
Bett (1931) :	Bett, H., *Joachim of Flora* (London, 1931).
Beuer (1957) :	Beuer, H.V., 'Evolution du Plan des Eglises Cisterciennes', *Cîteaux* VIII (1957 : 4).
Beuer-Szlechter (1970):	Beuer-Szlechter, H.V., 'L'art cistercien en Irland', *Cîteaux* XXI (1970 : 3–4).
Beverley Smith (1970):	Beverley Smith, L., 'The Middle March', *Bull. Board of Celtic Studies* XXIV:1 (1970).
Białoskórska (1962) :	Białoskórska, K., 'L'Abbaye Cistercienne de Wąchock', *Cahiers de Civilisation Médiévale* V (1962 : 3).
Białoskórska (1965) :	Białoskórska, K., 'Polish Cistercian Architecture and its Contacts with Italy', *Gesta* IV (Spring, 1965).
Bibolet (1986) :	Bibolet, F. and others, *L'Abbaye de Clairvaux* (Troyes, 1986).
Bigarne (1874) :	Bigarne, C., 'Abbaye de La Bussière', *Mém. Soc. d'Hist. d'Arch. et de Litt. de Beaune* I (1874).
Birch (1870) :	Birch, W. de Gray, 'On the date of foundation of the Cistercian abbeys of Great Britain', *Jnl. Brit. Archaeol. Assoc.* LXVI (1870).
Birch (1887) :	Birch, W. de Gray, *Catalogue of Seals in the British Museum* I–VI 1887–).
Birch (1897) :	Birch, W. de Gray, *Margam Abbey* (London, 1897).
Bird (1987) :	Bird, J. and D.G., *The Archaeology of Surrey to 1540* (Guildford: Surrey Arch. Soc. 1987).
Bishop (1936) :	Bishop, T.A.M., 'Monastic Granges in Yorkshire', *Engl. Hist. Review* LI (1936).
Blake (1901) :	Blake, M.J., 'Knockmoy Abbey', *Jnl. Galway Arch. and Hist. Soc.* I, Pt. ii (1901).
Blanco Trias (1953) :	Blanco Trias, P., 'Los Lijos de San Bernardo en Mallorca', *Cistercium* V: No. 25 (Jan.-Febr. 1953).
Blary (1989) :	Blary, F., *Le Domaine de Chaâlis, XIIe-XIVe* (Paris, 1989; Mém. de la Section d'Arch. et d'Hist. de l'Art, III).).
Blashill (1892) :	Blashill, T., 'Sutton in Holderness', *Jnl. Brit. Arch. Assoc.* XLVIII (1892).
Bligny (1960) :	Bligny, B., *L'Église et les Ordres Religieux* (Paris, 1960).
Böcek (1938) :	Böcek, B., *Podzemní Velehrad* (Velehrad, 1938).
Bogdan (1959) :	Bogdan, F., 'Egzempcia Polskich Cystersów', *Roczniki Humanistyczne* VIII : 2 (Lublin, 1959; publ. 1960).
Boháč (1996) :	Boháč, Z., 'Zisterzienserklöster in Der Lausitz', *Cîteaux* XLVII (1996).
Bolton (1990) :	Bolton, B., 'For the See of Simon Peter', in Loades (1990).
Bon (1969) :	Bon, A., *La Morée Franque* (Paris, 1969).
Bond (1989) :	Bond, C.J., 'Water management', in Gilchrist and Mytum (1989).

Bond (1994) :   Bond, C.J., 'Cistercian Mills in England and Wales', in Pressouyre (1994).

Bonnet-Laborderie   Bonnet-Laborderie, P. and P. and others., *Blé et Patrimonie: l'example*
(1985)   *cistercien* (Group d'Étude des Monuments et Oeuvres d'art du Beauvaisis; 1985; Bulletin No. 24, Special Number).

Bonport (1989) :   Bonport, *Abbaye de Bonport, 1189–1989* (Anon. MS).

Bony (1987) :   Bony, P., 'An Introduction to Cistercian Seals', in Lillich (1987).

Borkowska (1995) :   Borkowska, U., 'Dom Konwersów w Kołbaczu', in K. Kalita-Skiwirzyńska and M. Lewandowska (edit.) *Dziedzictwo Kulturowe Cystersówna Pomorzu* (Szczecin, 1995).

Borrero (1992) :   Borrero, M., *El Real Monasterio de San Clemente* (Seville, 1992).

Bouchard (1980) :   Bouchard, C.B., 'Changing Abbatial Tenure Patterns', *Revue Bénédictine* 90 (1980).

Boucsein (1986) :   Boucsein, H. and others, *800 Jahre Haina* (Kassel, 1986).

Boudreau (1995) :   Boudreau, C., 'With Desire I have Desired', in Nichols and Shank I (1995).

Bourgeois (1973) :   Bourgeois, G., 'Les Granges de Nonenque', *Cîteaux* XXIV (1973).

Bouton (1959) :   Bouton, J. de la Croix., *Histoire de l'Ordre de Cîteaux* (Westmalle Abbey, Belgium; I : 1959, II : 1964, III : 1968).

Bouton (1980) :   Bouton, J., 'Abbaye d'Aiguebelle', *Revue Dromoise* LXXXIII : No. 416 (June, 1980).

Bouton (1986) :   Bouton, J., *Les Moniales Cisterciennes* I (Aiguebelle Abbey, France; 1986).

Bouton (1995) :   Bouton, J., 'The Nuns of Cîteaux', in Nichols and Shank I (1995).

Boyd (1943) :   Boyd, C.E., *A Cistercian Nunnery in Medieval Italy* (Cambridge, Mass., 1943).

Brakspear (1908) :   Brakspear, H., 'Stanley Abbey', *Wiltshire Arch. and Nat. Hist. Mag.* XXXV (June, 1908).

Braun (1971) :   Braun, H., *English Abbeys* (London, 1971).

Bredero (1978) :   Bredero, A.H., 'The Canonisation of St Bernard', in Sommerfeldt (1978).

Breycha-Vauthier   Breycha-Vauthier, A.C., 'Deir Balamand', *Bulletin du Musee de Beyrouth*
(1967):   XX (1967).

Brisac (1982) :   Brisac, C., 'Grissailles', in Lillich (1982b).

Brouette (1978) :   Brouette, E., 'Torfin, Évêque de Hamar', *Cîteaux* XXIX (1978 : 1–2).

Brouwers (1983) :   Brouwers, J., 'Hocht', in *Cîteaux* XXXIV (1983 : 3–4).

Brouwers (1984) :   Brouwers, J., 'Le refuge de Val-Dieu', *Cîteaux* XXXV (1984 : 3–4).

Brown (1958) :   Brown, E.A.R., 'The Cistercians in the Latin Empire', *Traditio* XIV (1958).

Brown (1983) :   Brown, S., 'Medieval Buckfast Abbey', *Devon Archaeology* 1 (1983).

Bru (1982) :   Bru, Y., 'L'Abbaye de Saint-Sulpice', in Chauvin (1982a).

Brundage (1961) :   Brundage, J.A., *The Chronicle of Henry of Livonia* (1961).

Brundage (1971) :   Brundage, J.A., 'A Transformed Angel', in O'Callaghan (1971a).

Bruzelius (1981) :   Bruzelius, C.A., 'The Twelfth-Century Church at Ourscamp', *Speculum* 56 (1981 : 1).

Buczek (1971) :   Buczek, D.S., 'The French Cistercians and their Enemies', in O'Callaghan (1971a).

Buenago (1986) :   Buenago, I.M., 'De la Orden Cisterciense Zaragozanas', *Citeaux* XXXVIII (1986 : 1–2).

Buhot (1936) :   Buhot, J., 'L'Abbaye de Savigny', *Le Moyen Âge* XLVI (1936 : 1).

Burger (1986) :   Burger, E.K., *Enchiriodion super Apocalypsim Joachim De Fiore* (Toronto, 1986; Pontifical Institute of Medieval Studies; Studies and Texts, 78).

Burke (1982) :   Burke, M., 'Santa Maria de Ovila', in Lillich (1982b).

Burton (1979) :   Burton, J.E., *The Yorkshire Nunneries in the Twelfth and Thirteenth Centuries* (Univ. of York, 1979; Borthwick Papers, No. 56).

Burton (1989) :   Burton, J.E., *The Religious Orders in the East Riding of Yorkshire* (East Yorkshire Local Hist. Soc. 1989).

Bussels (1995) :   Bussels, A., 'Saint Lutgard's Mystical Spirituality', in Nichols and Shank I (1995).

Butler (1976) :   Butler, L.A.S.B., *Neath Abbey* (HMSO, 1976).

Butler (1978) :   Butler, L.A.S.B., *Rushen Abbey* (Interim Report, 1978).

Butler (1979) :   Butler, L.A.S.B., *Ibid.* (Interim Report, 1979).

Butler (1982) :   Butler, L.A.S.B., 'Recent Archaeological Work', in Lillich (1982b).

Butler (1988) :   Butler, L.A.S.B., 'Abbey of St Mary of Rushen', in *Jnl. Brit. Archaeol. Assoc.* CXLI (1988).

Butler (1989) :   Butler, L.A.S.B., 'The archaeology of rural monasteries', in Gilchrist and Mytum (1989).

Butler (1993) :   Butler, L.A.S.B., 'Cistercian Abbots' Tombs and Abbey Seals', in Lillich (1993).

Butler (1994) :   Butler, L.A.S.B., 'The Cistercian Landscape and the Isle of Man', in Fontfroide (1994).

Butler and Given-Wilson (1979):   Butler, L. and Given-Wilson, C., *Medieval Monasteries of Great Britain* (London, 1979).

Cabanes Pecourt (1982)   Cabanes Pecourt, M., 'Los Privilegios Reales de Veruela', in Chauvin (1982) II/4.

Cabau (1986) :   Cabau, P., 'Foulque, marchand et troubadour', in Privat (1986).

Cailleux (1991) :   Cailleux, D., 'Fer en Pays d'Othe', in Benoît and Chauvin (1991).

Cailleux (1991a) :   Cailleux, D., 'Enquête monumental', in Benoît and Chauvin (1991).

Calzolai (1976) :   Calzolai, C.C., *La Storia della Badia a Settimo* (Florence, 2nd edn, 1976).

Campbell (1899) :   Campbell, J., *Balmerino and its Abbey* (Edinburgh, 1899).

Campos de Sousa Real (1986):   Campos de Sousa Real, M.L., *Les fouilles de Salzedas'* (communication at the Conference on Archaeology of Cistercian Sites, Noirlac, 1986).

Canestrelli (1896) :   Canestrelli, A., *L'Abbazia di San Galgano* (Florence, 1896).

Canivez (1926) :   Canivez, J.M., *L'Ordre de Cîteaux en Belgique* (Scourmont Abbey, Chimay; 1926).

Canivez (1928) :   Canivez, J.M., 'Les Voyages de St Bernard en Belgique', in *SB* (1).

Caputo and Torre : (1972):   Caputo, P. and Torre, D., *L'Assistenza Ospedaliera e Farmaceutia nell'Abbazia di Casamari* (Casamari Abbey, 1972).

Carlson (1987) :   Carlson, D., 'The Practical Theology of St. Bernard', in Sommerfeldt (1987).

Caron (1995) :   Caron, A.M., 'Mechtild of Hackeborn', in Nichols and Shank II (1995).

Carrick (1907) :   Carrick, J.C., *Abbey of Newbottle* (Edinburgh, 1907).

Carsten (1941) :   Carsten, F.L., 'Slavs in NE Germany', *Econ. Hist. Review* XI : 1 (1941).

Carville (1971) :   Carville, G.C., 'Economic Activities of the Cistercians in Ireland', *Cîteaux* XXII (1971 : 3–4).

Carville (1972a) :   Carville, G.C., 'Beverages in Cistercian Monasteries', in *Cîteaux* XXIII (1972 : 3–4).

Carville (1972b) :   Carville, G.C., 'Urban Property of the Cistercians in Medieval Ireland', *Studia Monastica* 14 (1972 : 1).

Carville (1973a) :   Carville, G.C., 'Cistercian Settlement of Ireland', *Studia Monastica* 15 (1973 : 1).

Carville (1973b) :   Carville, G.C., *The Heritage of Holy Cross* (Belfast, 1973).

Carville (1973c) :   Carville, G.C., 'Cistercian Mills', *Cîteaux* XXIV (1973 : 3–4).

Carville (1979) :   Carville, G.C., *Norman Splendour* (Belfast, 1979).

Carville (1981) :   Carville, G.C., 'The Cistercians and the Irish Sea Link', *Cîteaux* XXXII (1981).

Carville (1982a) :   Carville, G.C., 'Cistercian Abbeys in Medieval Ireland', in Chauvin (1982a) III/5.

Carville (1982b) :   Carville, G.C., *Occupation of Celtic Sites in Medieval Ireland* (Cist. Studies Ser., 56; Kalamazoo, 1982).

Carville (1984) :   Carville, G.C., *Baltinglass* (West Wicklow Hist. Soc., 1984).

Carville (1995) :   Carville, G.C., 'Cistercian Nuns in Medieval Ireland', in Nichols and Shank I (1995).

Casey (1988) :   Casey, M., 'Solitude and Communion', *Cistercian Studies* XXIII (1988 : 4).

Cattana (1969) :   Cattana, V.M., 'A proposito di Monasterio Cistercensi in Italia', *Cîteaux* XX (1969 : 4).

Cauvet (1875) :   Cauvet, E., *Fontfroide* (Montpellier, 1875).

Cawley (1995) :   Cawley, M., 'Ida of Nivelles', in Nichols and Shank I (1995).

Cazes (1982) :   Cazes, D., 'L'Abbaye de Grandselve', in Chauvin (1982a).

Čechura (1987) :   Čechura, J., 'Wirtschaftsmodell der Zisterzienserkloster in Böhmen', in Strzelczyk (1987).

Čechura (1996) :   Čechura, J., 'Les Monastères Cisterciens en Bohême', *Cîteaux* XLVII (1996).

Chalvet (1888) :   Chalvet de Rochemonteix, A., *La Maison de Graule* (Paris, 1888).

Charvátová (1987) :   Charvátová, K., 'Manorial Farms of Cistercian Abbeys in Medieval Bohemia', in Strzelczyk (1987).

Charvátová (1987a) :   Charvátová, K., 'Le modèle économique cistercien', in *Cahiers de civilisation médiévale* XXX (1987).

Charvátová (1994) :   Charvátová, K., 'Development of Bohemian Possessions', in Fontfroide (1994).

Charvátová (1994a) :   Charvátová, K., 'Domaines cisterciens en France et en Bohême, *Cîteaux* XLV (1994:3–4).

Chase (1946) :   Chase, T.G., *The Story of Lithuania* (New York, 1946).

Chauvin (1973) :   Chauvin, B., 'Granges, I', *Cîteaux* XXIV (1973 : 1).

Chauvin (1976) :   Chauvin, B., 'La sidérurgie cistercienne', *Cîteaux* XXVII (1976 : 3–4).

Chauvin (1977) :   Chauvin, B., 'La Grange de Montorge', *Cîteaux* XXVIII (1977 : 4).

Chauvin (1982a) :   Chauvin, B., *Mélanges à la Mémoire du Père Anselme Dimier* (Pupillin, 1982–).

Chauvin (1982b) :   Chauvin, B., 'La Sidérurgie Cistercienne au Moyenne Age', in Chauvin (1982a) II/3.

Chauvin (1983a) :   Chauvin, B., 'L'économie dans Bourgogne' in Higounet (1983).

Chauvin (1983b) :   Chauvin, B., 'La terre de Glénon', in Janssen and Lohrmann (1983).

Chauvin (1989) :   Chauvin, B., 'Burchard de Balerne', *Cîteaux* XL: 1–4 (1989).

Chauvin (1991) :   Chauvin, B., 'Les archives cisterciennes' in Benoît and Cailleux (1991).

Chauvin (1995) :   Chauvin, B., 'Hildegarde de Bingen', *Cîteaux* XLVI (1995).

Chevalier (1906) :   Chevalier, J., 'N.-D. de Léoncel', in Mossant, C. (edit.)., *La vallee de la Gervanne* (Valence, 1906).

Chevallier (1855) :   Chevallier, P., 'L'Abbaye de la Boissière', *Revue de l'Anjou* 14 (1855).

Chèvre (1973) :   Chèvre, A., *Lucelle* (Bibl. Jurassienne, 1973).

Chłopocka (1953) :   Chłopocka, H., 'Opactwa Cystersów w Kolbaczu', *Poznanskie Towarzystwo przyjacíol Nauk* 17 (1953 : 2).

Clair (1961) :   Clair, R., 'Les filles d'Hautecombe', *Analecta S.O. Cist.* XVII (1961 : 3–4).

Clapham (1941) :   Clapham, J.H. and Power, E., *Cambridge Economic History of Europe* I (Cambridge, 1941).

Clark (1895) :   Clark, E.K., 'The Foundation of Kirkstall Abbey', *Publns. Thoresby Soc.* IV (Leeds, 1895).

Clark-Maxwell (1925) :   Clark-Maxwell, Preb., 'Some Letters of Confraternity', *Archaeologia* 75 (1925).

Clark-Maxwell (1929) :   Clark-Maxwell, Preb., 'Some Further Letters of Fraternity', *Archeologia* 79 (1929).

Clay (1928) :   Clay, C. T., 'Seals of the Religious Houses of Yorkshire', *Archaeologia* 78 (1928).

Clay (1929) :   Clay, C. T., 'Bradley, A Grange of Fountains', *Yorksh. Arch. Jnl.* XXIX (1929).

Clay (1952) :   Clay, C. T., 'Early Abbots of Yorkshire', *Ibid.* XXXVIII (1952 : 1).

Clementi (1971) :   Clementi, A., 'Sugli Insediamenti Medievali del Gran Sasso', *Archiv. Stor. Prov. Napolotanae*, 3rd Ser. IX (1971).

Cnotliwy (1987) :   Cnotliwy, E., 'Stan Dotychzasowych Badań Archeologicznych', in Strzelczyk (1987).

Cocheril (1959a) :   Cocheril, M., 'L'Ordre de Cîteaux au Portugal', *Studia Monastica* I (1959 : 1).

Cocheril (1959b) :   Cocheril, M., 'Recherches sur l'Ordre de Cîteaux au Portugal', *Bull. des Études Portugaises*, N.S. 22 (1959–60).

Cocheril (1961a) :   Cocheril, M., 'La Fondation de Moreruela', *Cîteaux* XII (1961 : 1).

Cocheril (1963) :   Cocheril, M., 'Les abbayes cisterciennes portugaises', *Bracara Augusta* XIV-XV (1963).

Cocheril (1964) :   Cocheril, M., 'Les Cisterciens dans la Péninsula Ibérique', *Anuario de Estudios Medievales* I (Barcelona, 1964).

Cocheril (1966) :   Cocheril, M., *Études sur le Monachisme en Espagne et au Portugal* (Lisbon, 1966).

Cocheril (1966b) :   Cocheril, M., 'Atlas de l'Ordre Cistercien', *Cîteaux* XVII (1966).
Cocheril (1982) :   Cocheril, M., 'Les Fondations Cisterciennes au Portugal', in Chauvin (1982a).
Coester (1984) :   Coester, E., *Die einschiffigen Cistercienserinnenkirchen West-und Suddeutschlands* (Mainz, 1984).
Coggeshall (und.) :   *Coggeshall Official Guide* (undated).
Collin (1978) :   Collin, H., 'Les débuts d'une fondation cistercienne', *Le Pays Lorrain* 59 (1978 : 3).
Colombet (1976) :   Colombet, A., 'Les Domains Ruraux de l'Abbaye de la Bussière', *Mem. Comm. Antiq. Dept. Côte-D'Or* XXX (1976–7).
Colvile (1850) :   Colvile, F.L., *Stoneleigh Abbey* (Warwick, 1850).
Colvin (1963) :   Colvin, H.M., *History of the King's Works* I (HMSO, London; 1963).
Comba (1978) :   Comba, R., 'Aspeti del Piemonte sud-occidentale', *Archéologia Médiévale* V (1978).
Comba (1983) :   Comba, R., 'Abbayes cisterciennes de l'Italia', in Higounet (1983).
Comba (1985) :   Comba, R., 'I cistercensi fra città e campagna', *Studi Storici* 26 : 2 April-June, 1985).
Compton (1892) :   Compton, C.H., 'Rievaulx Abbey', *Jnl. Brit. Arch. Assoc.* XLVIII (1892).
Conbhuí (1958) :   Conbhuí, C.S.Ó., *The Story of Mellifont* (Dublin, 1958).
Conbhuí (1959) :   Conbhuí, C.S.Ó., 'The Suppression', *Cîteaux* X (1959).
Conbhuí (1961) :   Conbhuí, C.S.Ó., 'Hore Abbey', *Cîteaux* XII (1961 : 4).
Conbhuí (1962) :   Conbhuí, C.S.Ó., 'Lands of St Mary's Abbey, Dublin', *Proc. Royal Irish Acad.* LXII, Sect. C., No. 3 (May, 1962).
Conbhuí (1963) :   Conbhuí, C.S.Ó., 'The Origins of Jerpoint Abbey', *Cîteaux* XIV (1963 : 4).
Conbhuí (1964) :   Conbhuí, C.S.Ó., 'Taxation of Irish Cistercian Houses', *Cîteaux* XV (1964 : 2).
Conbhuí (1980) :   Conbhuí, C.S.Ó., 'The Cistercian Abbot in Medieval Ireland', in Sommerfeldt (1980).
Conbhuí (1981) :   Conbhuí, C.S.Ó., 'Extent of Cistercian Lands in Medieval Ireland', in Elder (1981b).
Connor (1988) :   Connor, E., notes in *Cistercian Studies* XXIII (1988 : 1).
Connor (1988b) :   Connor, E., 'L'abbaye royale de Las Huelgas', *Coll. Cist.* 50 (1988 : 4).
Connor (1995) :   Connor, E., 'The Abbeys of Las Huelgas and Tart', in Nichols and Shank I (1995).
Constable (1953) :   Constable, G., 'The Second Crusade', *Traditio* IX (1953).
Constable (1964) :   Constable, G., *Monastic Tithes from their Origins to the Twelfth Century* (Cambridge, 1964).
Constable (1971) :   Constable, G., 'A Lost Sermon', in O'Callaghan (1971).
Constable (1987) :   Constable, G., 'The Idea of Inner Solitude', in Dubois, H., Hocquet, J-C., and Vauchez, A. (edit.)., *Horizons Marins Itinéraires Spirituels,* I: *Mentalités et Sociétés* (Sorbonne, Paris; 1987).
Conway Davies (1946) :   Conway Davies, J., *Episcopal Acts relating to Welsh Dioceses* I (1946).
Cook (1965) :   Cook, G.C., *Letters to Cromwell on the Suppression of the Monasteries* (London, 1965).
Coomans (1994) :   Coomans, T., 'Le patrimonie rural cistercien en Belgique', in Pressouyre (1994).
Cooper (1856) :   Cooper, G.M., 'Notices of the Abbey of Robertsbridge', *Sussex Arch. Collns.* 8 (1856).
Coppack (1986) :   Coppack, G., 'A Major Cistercian Precinct', *Jnl. Brit. Arch. Assoc.* CXXXIX (1986).
Coppack (1986a) :   Coppack, G., 'The Excavation of an Outer Court Building at Fountains Abbey', *Medieval Archaeology* 30 (1986).
Coppack (1990) :   Coppack, G., *Abbeys and Priories* (English Heritage, London; 1990).
Coppack (1993) :   Coppack, G., *Fountains Abbey* (English Heritage/Batsford; 1993).
Corbera (1986) :   Corbera, 'Les Ordres militaires', in Higounet (1986a).
Corbet (1991) :   Corbet, P., 'La Grange Claravalienne', in Leroux (1991).
Costello (1966) :   Costello, H., 'The Sermons of Guerric of Igny', *Cîteaux* IV (1966).
Cothren (1982) :   Cothren, M., 'Tile Pavements', in Lillich (1982b).
Cottam (1928) :   Cottam, A., 'Granges of Furness', *Trans. Hist. Soc. Lancs, and Cheshire* 80 (1928–9).

Cottineau (1935) :   Cottineau, L.H., *Répertoire Abbayes et Prieurés* I (Macon, 1935).
Cottje (1992) :   Cottje, R. (edit.)., *Die niederrheinischen Zisterzienser im späten Mittelalter* (Cologne, 1992).
Coulon (1912) :   Coulon, A., *Inventarie des Sceaux de la Bourgogne* (Paris, 1912).
Coulton (1960) :   Coulton, G.G., *Medieval Village, Manor and Monastery* (New York, 1960).
Coulton (1967) :   Coulton, G.G., *Life in the Middle Ages* (Cambridge, 1967).
Couriol (1980) :   Couriol, J-N., 'Le Cellier de Léoncel', *Revue Dromoise* LXXXIII : No. 416 (June, 1980).
Couriol (1986) :   Couriol, J-N., 'Chemins de Transhumance', *Revue Dromoise*, Special No: Cahiers de Léoncel, No. 1; *Les Moines et l'Elevage* (1986).
Courtney (1980) :   Courtney, P., 'Monastic Granges of Leicestershire', *Trans. Leics. Arch. and Hist. Soc.* LVI   (1980–1).
Courtney (1987) :   Courtney, L.T., 'The Hospital of Byloke Abbey', *Cîteaux* XXXVIII (1987 : 1–2).
Courtney (1989) :   Courtney, P., 'Excavations in the Outer Precinct of Tintern Abbey', *Medieval Archaeology* XXXIII (1989).
Courtois (1982) :   Courtois, R., 'L'Abbaye de Vauclair', in Chauvin (1982a) III/5.
Couvret (1969) :   Couvret, A.-M., 'Des Forges de Wassy', *Cahiers Haut-Marnais* 97 (1969 : 1).
Cowan (1976) :   Cowan, I.B. and Easson, D.E., *Medieval Religious Houses : Scotland* (London, 1976).
Cowley (1977) :   Cowley, F.G., *Monastic Order in South Wales* (Cardiff, 1977).
Crosnier Leconte   Crosnier Leconte, M-L., 'L'Architecture de l'Ordre de Chalais', in
  (1982):   Chauvin (1982a) III/5.
Cross (1957) :   Cross, F.L. (edit.)., *The Oxford Dictionary of the Christian Church* (O.U.P., London; 1957 edn.).
Crossley (1939) :   Crossley, F.H., *The English Abbey* (London, 2nd edn; 1939).
Cruden (1950) :   Cruden, S., 'Glenluce Abbey', *Trans. Dunfrieshire and Galloway Nat. Hist. and Antiq. Soc.* 3rd Ser. XXIX (1950–1).
Cruden (1951) :   Cruden, S., continuation in *Ibid.* XXX (1951–2).
Cruden (1960) :   Cruden, S., *Scottish Abbeys* (HMSO, 1960).
Cuissard (1885) :   Cuissard, C., 'L'Aumône', *Bull. Soc.Dunoise* IV (1885).
Cumming (1868) :   Cumming, J.G., 'Rushen Abbey', *Antiq. Manniae* (Manx Soc., XV; 1868).
Currie (1988) :   Currie, C.K., 'The Role of Fishponds in the Monastic Economy', in Aston (1988).
Cutts (1858) :   Cutts, E.L., 'The Remains of Coggeshall Abbey', *Trans. Essex Arch. Soc.* I (1858).

D'Alton (1838) :   D'Alton, J., *History of the County of Dublin* (Dublin, 1838).
D'Arbois (1857) :   D'Arbois de Jubainville, H., 'De la Nourriture des Cisterciens' *Bibl. de l'École des Chartes* IV (1857).
D'Arbois (1858) :   D'Arbois de Jubainville, H., *Études sur des Abbayes Cisterciennes* (Paris, 1858).
Dąbrowski (1970) :   Dąbrowski, K., *Rozwój Wielkiej Ziemskiej Klasztoru Cysterek w Żarnowcu* (Gdańsk, 1970).
Dalrymple (1899) :   Dalrymple, H.H., 'Five Great Churches of Galloway', *Arch. and Hist. Collns. Ayrshire and Galloway* X (1899).
Damme (1975) :   Damme, J.V., Review of Milis, L., 'Het site Ter Duinen', *Cîteaux* XXVI (1975 : 3).
Daniel (1950) :   Daniel, W., 'The Life of Ailred of Rievaulx', in: Powicke, F.M (ed.), *The Life of Ailred of Rievaulx by Walter Daniel* (London, 1950).
Darby (1940) :   Darby, H.C., *The Medieval Fenland* (Cambridge, 1940).
Da Silva Barros (1972): Da Silva Barros, C.V., *Monastery of Alcobaça* (Lisbon, 1972).
Daumont (1937) :   Daumont, O., *Soleilmont* (Courtrai, 1937).
Dautrey (1976) :   Dautrey, P., 'Croissance et adaptation', *Analecta Cist.* XXXII (1976 : 1–2).
Dautrey (1982) :   Dautrey, P., 'Simplicité', in Chauvin (1982a).
David (1934) :   David, P., *Les Sources de l'Histoire de Pologne* (Paris, 1934).
David-Roy (1973) :   David-Roy, M., 'Les Granges Monastiques', *Archéologia* 58 (1973).
Davidson (1843) :   Davidson, J., *Newenham Abbey* (London, 1843).
Davies (1984) :   Davies, M.T., 'Altenberg', in Lillich (1984).

De Bascher (1985) : De Bascher, J., 'Les fondations d'Isembaud', noted in *Cîteaux* XXXVI (1985 : 3–4).

De Brisay (1975) : De Brisay, K.W. and Evans, K.A. *Salt* (Colchester, 1975).

De Durainville (1856): De Durainville, L., *La Ville du Pont-de-l'Arche et l'Abbaye de Bonport* (Rouen, 1856).

De Ganck (1971) : De Ganck, R., 'Les pouvoirs de l'Abbé de Cîteaux', *Analecta Cist.* XXVII (1971:1).

De Ganck (1984) : De Ganck, R., 'Nuns in the Cistercian Order', *Cîteaux* XXXV (1984 : 3–4).

De Ganck (1989) : De Ganck, R., 'Visitation Cards', *Cîteaux*' XL: 1–4 (1989).

De Ganck (1995) : De Ganck, R., 'The Posthumous Legacy of Beatrice of Nazareth', *Cîteaux* XLV (1994: 1–2).

De Laplane (1863) : De Laplane, H., *L'Abbaye de Clairmarais* (Saint-Omer, 1863).

De Maillé (1930) : De Maillé, M., 'L'Église de Preuilly', *Bull. Monum.* LXXXIX (1930).

De Montesquiou(und.): De Montesquiou, A.-P., *Abbaye de Longpont* (Paris, undated).

De Montgolfier(1986) : De Montgolfier, B. (ed.), *Les Cisterciens à Paris* (Musée Carnavalet, Paris; 1986).

De Moreau (1909) : De Moreau, É., *L'Abbaye de Villers* (Receuil de travaux, Univ. of Louvain, 21; Brussels, 1909).

De Oyaga (1967) : De Oyaga, J.R., 'Un gran proyecto cisterciense', *Cistercium* XX : No. 109 (Jan.-Mar., 1967).

De Roucy (und.) : De Roucy, T., *'L'Abbaye N.-D. d'Ourscamp* (Paris, undated).

De Varabeke (1972) : De Varabeke, H.J., 'Abbots in Parliaments', *North Munster Antiq. Jnl.* XV (1972).

De Warren (1946) : De Warren, H. B., *La Bretagne Cistercienne* (Wandrille, 1946).

De Warren (1953) : De Warren, H. B., 'Tables chronologiques', in SB (2).

Deck (1964) : Deck, S., 'Les Salines de Bouteilles', *Annales de Normandie* 14 (1964 : 4).

Deck (1974) : Deck, S., 'Le Temporel de Beaubec'; Ibid. 24 (1974 : 2).

Defrance (1988) : Defrance, R. and others., *La Jardin Medieval* (Les Cahiers de l'Abbaye de Saint-Arnoult, No. 3; 1988).

Degler-Spengler(1995): Degler-Spengler, B., 'The Incorporation of Cistercian Nuns', in Nichols and Shank (1995).

Deladreue (1868) : Deladreue, L.-E., 'Abbaye de Froidmont', *Mém. Soc. Acad. Arch. Sciences et Arts du l'Oise* VII (1868).

Deladreue (1871) : Deladreue, L.-E., *Ibid.* VIII (1871).

Delesalle (1983) : Delesalle, D., 'A propos du clocher d'Obazine', *Cîteaux* XXXIV (1983 : 3–4).

Dendooven (1964) : Dendooven, L., *L'Abbaye der Ter Doest* (Bruges, 1964).

Dendooven (1972) : Dendooven, L., *Ibid.* (Bruges, 1972).

Denifle (1897) : Denifle, H., *La Désolation des Églises* (Paris, 1897–9).

Desmarchelier (1974) : Desmarchelier, M., 'L'Abbaye de Trizay', *Cîteaux* XXV (1974 : 1).

Desmarchelier (1982) : Desmarchelier, M., 'L'Architecture des Églises de Moniales Cisterciennes', in Chauvin (1982a).

Desmond (1971) : Desmond, L.A., 'The Statute of Carlisle', in O'Callaghan (1971).

Desmond (1974) : Desmond, L.A., 'The Statute *De viris religiosis*' *Cîteaux* XXV (1974 : 2).

Desmond (1975) : Desmond, L.A., 'Appropriation of Churches', *Analecta S.O. Cist.* XXXI (1975 : 2).

Despy (1974) : Despy, G., 'Les richesses de la terre', in Préaux, J. (edit.) *Problems d'Histoire du Christianisme* 5 (1974–5).

Despy (1975) : Despy, G., *Ibid. Revue de l'Université de Bruxelles* (1975 : 4).

Despy (1983) : Despy, G., '*Curtes* en Brabant', in Janssen and Lohrmann (1983).

Despy-Meyer (1964) : Despy-Meyer, A., 'Les débuts du Val-Saint-Bernard', *Bull. Comm. Royale d'Histoire* CXXX (1964 : 2).

Destombe (1969) : Destombe, M., 'Des Chartes de l'Abbaye du Gard', *Bull. trimestriel de la Soc. des Antiq. de Picardie* LIII (1969 : 3).

Detsicas (1981) : Detsicas, A. (ed.), *Collectanea Historica: Essays in Memory of Stuart Rigold* (Maidstone, 1981).

Devailly (1973) : Devailly, G., *Le Berry* (Paris, 1973).

Dickinson (1965) : Dickinson, J.C., *Furness Abbey* (HMSO, 1965).

Dickinson (1981) : Dickinson, J.C., *The Parish Church, Tilty, Essex* (1981).

Dimier (1952) :   Dimier, A., 'St Bernard et le recrûtement de Clairvaux', *Revue Mabillon*
                         XLII (Apl.- June, 1952).
Dimier (1954) :   Dimier, A., *St Louis et Cîteaux* (Paris, 1954).
Dimier (1957) :   Dimier, A., 'Les Fondations de Saint Bernard en Italie', *Analecta S.O.
                         Cist.* XIII (1957).
Dimier (1958) :   Dimier, A., 'Liste des monastères de la filiation de Morimond', *Anal.
                         S.O.C.* XIV (1958 : 1–2).
Dimier (1964) :   Dimier, A., *Les Moines Bâtisseurs* (Paris, 1964).
Dimier (1962) :   Dimier, A., *L'Art Cistercien* (La Pierre-qui-Vivre, Yonne; 1962).
Dimier (1965) :   Dimier, A., 'Une Abbaye Cistercienne', *Cîteaux* XVI (1965 : 3).
Dimier (1966) :   Dimier, A., 'The Cistercian Abbey of Vauclair', *Gesta* 5 (Jan. 1966).
Dimier (1969) :   Dimier, A., 'Saint Bernard et ses abbayes-filles', *Analecta Cist.* XXV
                         (1969).
Dimier (1972a) :   Dimier, A., 'Violences, Rixes et Homicides', *Revue des sciences religieuses*
                         46 (Strasbourg, 1972).
Dimier (1972b) :   Dimier, A., 'Pélerinage Cistercien à travers Paris', *Archéologia* 44 (Jan.-
                         Feb.) and 45 (Mar.-April, 1972).
Dimier (1973) :   Dimier, A., 'Granges, Celliers et Bâtiments d'Exploitation Cisterciens',
                         Archéologia 65 (Dec. 1973).
Dimier (1974a) :   Dimier, A., *Ibid.* 74 (Sept. 1974).
Dimier (1974b) :   Dimier, A., 'L'Architecture des moniales', *Cîteaux* XXV (1974 : 1).
Dimier (1974c) :   Dimier, A., 'L'Eglise de Clairvaux', *Cîteaux* XXV (1974 : 3).
Dimier (1975) :   Dimier, A., 'Henri de France', *Cîteaux* XXVI (1975 :1–2).
Dimier (1976) :   Dimier, A., 'Eberhard ou Evrard des Barres', *Cîteaux* XXVII (1976 :
                         1–2).
Dimier (1978a) :   Dimier, A., *St Peter de Tarentaise* (La Doc. Cist. 21; Rochefort Abbey,
                         Belgium; 1978).
Dimier (1982a) :   Dimier, A., 'Les Cisterciens et le Schisme d'Octavien' in Chauvin
                         (1982a).
Dimier (1982b) :   Dimier, A., 'Les Évêques Cisterciens' in Chauvin (1982a).
Dimier (1982c) :   Dimier, A., 'Les Préliminaires de la Bulle *"Parvus Fons"*' in Chauvin
                         (1982a).
Dimier (1982d) :   Dimier, A., 'Les captures de Saint Bernard aux Pays-Bas' in Chauvin
                         (1982a).
Dimier (1982e) :   Dimier, A., 'C'est en 1174 que Saint Bernard fut canonisé' in Chauvin
                         (1982a).
Dimier (1982f) :   Dimier, A., 'Saint Guérin' in Chauvin (1982a).
Dimier (1982h) :   Dimier, A., 'Infirmaries cisterciennes' in Chauvin (1982a).
Dimier (1982k) :   Dimier, A., 'La Salle des Morts D'Ourscamp' in Chauvin (1982a).
Dimier and Francey   Dimier, A., and Francey, M., 'La Grange de Montaon', *Bull. Monumental*
    (1973) :   131 (1973).
Dobosz (1991) :   Dobosz, J. and others, *Cystersi w średniowiecznej Polsce kultura i sztuka*
                         (Muzeum Początków Państwa Polskiego w Gnieżnie, 1991).
Dobosz (1995) :   Dobosz, J. and others, 'Les Fondations d'Abbayes Cisterciennes en
                         Petite Pologne', *Cîteaux* XLVI (1995: 3–4).
Dodel-Brunello (1985): Dodel-Brunello, A., 'Mègemont, abbaye cistercienne', *Cîteaux* XXXVII
                         (1985 : 3–4).
Dolan (1909) :   Dolan, G., 'Doberan', *Downside Review* XXVIII (N.S. IX : 1909).
Donkin (1959) :   Donkin, R.A., 'Urban Property', *Analecta S.O. Cist.* XV (1959).
Donkin (1964) :   Donkin, R.A., 'The English Cistercians and Assarting', *Analecta S.O. Cist.*
                         XX (1964).
Donkin (1965) :   Donkin, R.A., *Cîteaux* XVI: 2 (1965).
Donkin (1967) :   Donkin, R.A., 'Growth and Distribution of the Cistercian Order', *Studia
                         Monastica* 9 (1967).
Donkin (1978) :   Donkin, R.A., *The Cistercians* (Pontifical Inst., Toronto, 1978), which
                         incorporates the above, and other articles by Dr Donkin.
Donnelly (1949) :   Donnelly, J.S., *Decline of the Medieval Cistercian Laybrotherhood* (Fordham
                         U.P., New York, 1949).
Donnelly (1954) :   Donnelly, J.S., 'Changes in Grange Economy', *Traditio* X (1954).
Douët D'Arcq (1868) :   Douët D'Arcq, (Louis) M., *Collection des Sceaux de l'Empire* III (Paris,
                         1868).

Douglas (1927) :   Douglas, W., 'Culross Abbey', *Proc. Soc. Antiq. Scotl.* LX (1927).

Drury (1985) :   Drury, P.J., Note in *Antiq. Jnl.* LXV (1985 : 2).

Dubled (1959) :   Dubled, H., 'L'Économie Cistercienne en Alsace', *Rev. d'Hist. Eccles.* LIV (1959 : 4).

Dublois (1957) :   Dublois, A., 'Une Oblate aux Dunes', *Cîteaux* VIII (1957 : 1).

Dubois (1879) :   Dubois, Abbe., *Histoire de Morimond* (3rd edn., Dijon, 1879).

Dubord (1879) :   Dubord, R., 'The Bastide of Solomiac', *Revue de Gascogne* XX (1879).

Duby (1953) :   Duby. G., *Recueil des Pancartes de la Ferté-sur-Grosne* (Aix-en-Provence, 1953).

Duby (1968) :   Duby. G., *Rural Economy* (Univ. S. Carolina Press, 1968).

Duby (1965) :   Duby. G., and Mandrou, R., *A History of French Civilisation* (London, 1965).

Dugdale (1772) :   Dugdale, W., *History of Imbanking and Draining* (London; 2nd edn., 1772).

Dunin-Wąsowicz   Dunin-Wąsowicz, T. 'Projets missionaires cisterciens', *Harvard*
    (1988):   *Ukrainian Studies* XII-XIII (1988–89).

Dupont (1982) :   Dupont, S.M., 'Decorated Marks in Altzelle', in Chauvin (1982a) II/4.

Durand (1983) :   Durand, R., 'L'économie au Portugal',in Higounet (1983).

Durand (1984) :   Durand, G., 'L'Église de Sylvanès', *Archéologie du Midi Médiéval* 2 (1984).

Durliat (1980) :   Durliat, M., *Flaran* (Auch, *ca.* 1980).

Dustin (1973) :   Dustin, A.M., *Belgique : Abbayes et Béguinages* (Brussels, 1973).

Duval-Arnould (1968) : Duval-Arnould, L., 'Le vignoble de Longpont', *Le Moyen-Âge* LXXIV (1968).

Duvernay (1952) :   Duvernay, D.R., 'Cîteaux, Vallombreuse et Étienne Harding', *Analecta S.O. Cist.* VIII (1952 : 3–4).

Eames (1956) :   Eames, E.S. and Beaulah, G.K., 'Tile Mosaic Pavements', *Cîteaux* VII (1956 : 4).

Earle (1906) :   Earle, A., *Essays upon Meaux Abbey* (London, 1906).

Easson (1957) :   Easson, D.E., *Medieval Religious Houses : Scotland* (London, 1957).

Eckenrode (1973) :   Eckenrode, T.R., 'The English Cistercians and their Sheep', *Cîteaux* XXIV (1973 : 3–4).

Edenheim (1978) :   Edenheim, R. and Lidén, H., 'Julita kloster', *Antikvarist Arkiv* 62 (1978).

Edenheim (1982) :   Edenheim, R., and Rosell, I., *Varnhems klosterkyrka* (Stockholm, 1982).

Edwards (1964) :   Edwards, A.C., *Essex Monasteries* (Chelmsford, 1964).

Eeles (1905) :   Eeles, F. C. note in: Alcuin Club, 'Edwardian Inventories' , Appx. 1 (1905).

Ehresmann (1984) :   Ehresmann, D.L., 'The Doberan Altarpiece', *Cîteaux* XXXV (1984 : 1–2).

Einsingbach (1988) :   Einsingbach, W., *Eberbach Monastery* (Munich, 1988).

Elder (1978) :   Elder, E.R., 'William of St Thierry', in Sommerfeldt (1978).

Elder (1980) :   Elder, E.R. and Sommerfeldt, J.R. (ed.), *The Chimaera of His Age* (Cist. Studies Ser. 63; Kalamazoo, 1980).

Elder (1981a) :   Elder, E.R. (ed.), *Noble Piety and Reformed Monasticism* (Cist. Studies Ser. 65; Kalamazoo, 1981).

Elder (1981b) :   Elder, E.R. (ed.), *Cistercians in the Late Middle Ages* (Cist. Studies Ser. 64; Kalamazoo, 1981).

Elder (1983) :   Elder, E.R. (ed.), *Heaven on Earth* (Cist. St. Ser. 68; Kalamazoo, 1983).

Elder (1985) :   Elder, E.R., (ed.), *Goad and Nail* (Cist. Studies Ser., 84; Kalamazoo, 1985).

Elder (1995) :   Elder, E.R. (ed.), *The Joy of Learning and the Love of God* (Cistercian Studies Ser. 160; Kalamazoo, 1995).

Ellis (1986) :   Ellis, R.H., *Catalogue of Seals in the Public Record Office, Monastic Seals* I (1986).

Elm (1964) :   Elm, K., 'Zisterzienser und Wilhelmiten', *Cîteaux* XV (1964).

Elm (1980) :   Elm, K. and others, *Die Zisterzienser* (Bonn, 1980).

Elm (1982) :   Elm, K. and Joerissen, P., *Die Zisterzienser, ergänzungsband* (2nd Edn., Cologne, 1982).

Entz (1963) :   Entz, G., 'Le Chantier Cistercien de Kerc', *Acta Historiae Artium Academiae Scientarium Hungaricae* 9 (Budapest, 1963).

Entz (1968) :   Entz, G., 'Die Baukunst Transsilvaniens', Ibid. 14 (Budapest, 1968).

Epperlein (1967) :   Epperlein, S., 'Gründungsmythos', *Jahrbuch für Wirtschaftsgesichte* III (Berlin, 1967).
Espinas (1923) :   Espinas, G., *La Draperie dans la Flandre* II (Paris, 1923).
Espinos (1982) :   Espinos, J.R.D., *Santa Maria de Palazuelos* (Valladolid, 1982).
Esquieu (1986) :   Esquieu, Y., *Thoronet Abbey* (La Guerche-de Bretagne, 1986).
Estow (1982) :   Estow, C., 'Economic Development of the Order of Calatrava', *Speculum* 57 (1982 : 2).
Evans (1958) :   Evans, A. L., *Margam Abbey* (Port Talbot, 1958).
Evans (1997) :   Evans, F., 'The Engineer Monks', in Shoesmith and Richardson (1997).
Eydoux (1958) :   Eydoux, H.-P. 'L'Église abbatiale de Morimond', *Analecta S.O. Cist.* XIV (1958 : 1–2).
Eyton (1868) :   Eyton, R.W., *Antiquities of Shropshire* VII (London, 1868).

Fachinger (1986) :   Fachinger, E., 'Les documents pontificaux', in Privat (1986).
Fawcett (1994):   Fawcett, R., *Scottish abbeys and priories* (Batsford, 1994).
Felten (1986) :   Felten, F.J., 'Arnaud Nouvel', in Privat (1986).
Fergusson (1979) :   Fergusson, P., 'Two Cistercian Engraved Designs', *Speculum* LIV (1979 : 1).
Fergusson (1983) :   Fergusson, P., 'The First Architecture of the Cistercians in England', *Jnl. Brit. Arch. Assoc.* CXXXVI (1983).
Fergusson (1984a) :   Fergusson, P., *Architecture of Solitude* (Princeton U.P., 1984).
Fergusson (1984b) :   Fergusson, P., 'Builders of Cistercian Monasteries', in Lillich (1984).
Fergusson (1986) :   Fergusson, P., 'Twelfth-Century Refectories', in Norton and Park (1986).
Ferling (1979) :   Ferling, F., 'Wasserwirtschaftliche Erschliessungsarbeiten der Cistercienser in Norddeutschland', *Cist. Chronik* (1979 : 4).
Figg (1854) :   Figg, W., 'On "The Lantern" ', in *Sussex Arch. Collns.* VII (1854).
Finucane (1977) :   Finucane, R.C., *Miracles and Pilgrims* (London, 1977).
Fischer (1974) :   Fischer, G., *Klosteret På Hoveydøya* (Oslo, 1974).
Fisher (1990) :   Fisher, D., 'Luminality', *Cist. Studies* XXV (1990: 3).
Fiske (1960) :   Fiske, A., 'St Bernard and Friendship', *Cîteaux* XI (1960).
Fitzgerald (1906) :   Fitzgerald, W., 'Baltinglass Abbey', *Jnl. Kildare Arch. Soc.* V (1906–8).
Fixot (1986) :   Fixot, M. and Pelletier, J-P., *'L'Abbaye de Silvacane'*, *Archéologie Médievale* 16 (1986).
Fletcher (1919) :   Fletcher, J.S., *The Cistercians in Yorkshire* (London, 1919).
Flink (1980) :   Flink, R., 'Anmerkungen zu einer Geschichte des Klosters Heisterbach', in Kraus (1980).
Forey (1987) :   Forey, A.J., 'Women and the Military Orders', *Studia Monastica* 29 (1987 : 1).
Fornari (1978) :   Fornari, F.F.B., *L'Architecttura Cistercense* (Casamari Abbey, Italy; 1978).
Fort i Cogul (1965) :   Fort i Cogul, E., 'L'eremitisme a la Catalunya nova', *Studia Monastica* 7 (1965 : 1).
Fort i Cogul (1969) :   Fort i Cogul, E., 'Regesta de Sant Bernat Calvo', *Studia Monastica* XI:1 (1969).
Fort i Cogul (1972) :   Fort i Cogul, E., *El Senyoriu de Santa Creus* (Barcelona, 1972).
Fort i Cogul (1975) :   Fort i Cogul, E., *Fra Bonanat, Abat de Santes Creus* (Vila-seco-Salou, 1975).
Fossier (1975) :   Fossier, R., 'La Place des Cisterciens dans l'Économie Picardie', in Hodkin, L.E. (edit.) *Aureavallis* (Liége, 1975).
Fossier (1983) :   Fossier, R., 'L' Économie Cistercienne dans Nord-Ouest de l'Europe', in Higounet (1983).
Fossier (1991) :   Fossier, R., 'La Puissance Économique', in Leroux (1991).
Fotheringham (1890) :   Fotheringham, A.L., 'Introduction of Gothic Architecture into Italy', *American Jnl. of Archaeology* VI (1890).
Fraccaro (1958) :   Fraccaro de Longhi, L., *L'Architetture della Chiese Cistercensi Italiane* (Milan, 1958).
France (1964) :   France, C.A.J., 'Danish Cistercian Abbots', *Analecta S.O. Cist.* XX (1964: 3–4).
France (1988) :   France, C.A.J., 'St. Bernard, Archbishop Eskil, and the Danish Cistercians, *Cîteaux* XXXIX (1988 : 3–4).

France (1992) :   France, C.A.J., *The Cistercians in Scandinavia* (Cist. Studies Ser.131; Kalamazoo, 1992).

France (1993) :   France, C.A.J., 'The Northernmost Cistercian Abbey in Europe', *Cist. Studies* 28: 3–4 (1993).

France (1994) :   France, C.A.J., 'The Scandinavian Experience', in Pressouyre (1994).

France (1998) :   France, C.A.J., 'The Cellarer's Domain – Evidence from Denmark', *Studies in Cistercian Art and Architecture*, 5; ed. M.P. Lillich (in press).

Friedl (1965) :   Friedl, A., *Iluminovane Rukopisy Vysebrodske* (Prague, 1965).

Fry (1986) :   Fry, P.S., *Rievaulx Abbey* (English Heritage, 1986).

Fulford (1992) :   Fulford, M.G. and others., 'The Medieval Quay at Woolaston Grange', *Trans. Bristol and Gloucs. Arch. Assoc.* 110 (1992).

Fumagalli (1792) :   Fumagalli, A., *Delle Antichita Longobardico-Milanesi* (Milan, 1792).

Fuxhoffer (1869) :   Fuxhoffer, D., *Monasteriologiae Regni Hungariae* II (Vienna, 1869).

Fyfe Smith (1948) :   Fyfe Smith, R., and Johnson, N.M., 'Quarry to Abbey', *Proc. Soc. Antiq. Scotl.* LXXXIII (1948–9; publ. 1951).

Gallagher (1976) :   Gallagher, P.F., 'Conditions of Land Tenure', in Sommerfeldt (1976).

Gallagher (1982) :   Gallagher, P.F., 'Mortemer', in Lillich (1982b).

Galpin (1928) :   Galpin, F.W., 'The Abbey Church and Claustral Buildings of Tilty', *Trans. Essex Arch. Soc.* N.S. XVIII (1928).

Gardelles (1983) :   Gardelles, J., 'L'Abbaye de Faise', *Bull. Monum.* 141 (1983 : 1).

Gardner (1955) :   Gardner, J.S., 'Coggeshall Abbey', *Jnl. Brit. Arch. Assoc.* 3rd Ser., XVIII (1955).

Garner (1973) :   Garner, H.N., *Øm Kloster Museum* (Århus, 1973).

Gasquet (1908) :   Gasquet, F.A., *Greater Abbeys of England* (London, 1908).

Gentili (1978) :   Gentili, O., *L'Abbazia di Fiastra* (Rome, 1978).

Gérard (1957) :   Gérard, P., 'Origines du Collĕge Saint-Bernard', *Annales du Midi* 69 (1957).

Gerbet (1986) :   Gerbet, M-C., 'Les Ordres militaires dans l'Espagne', in Higounet (1986a).

Gerevich (1977) :   Gerevich, L., 'Pilis Abbey', in *Acta Archaeologica* XXIX (Budapest, 1977).

Gerevich (1982) :   Gerevich, L., 'Les Fouilles de Pilis', in Chauvin (1982a).

Gergelyffy (1959) :   Gergelyffy, A., 'L'Église de Bélapátfalva', *Acta Hist. Artium Acad. Scient. Hungaricae* 6 (Budapest, 1959).

Gervers (1992) :   Gervers, M., *The Second Crusade and the Cistercians* (New York, 1992).

Giessler-Wirsig (1979) : Giessler-Wirsig, E., 'Die Beziehungen zur Stadt Koln', *Zisterzienser Studien* IV (Berlin, 1979).

Gilbanks (1899) :   Gilbanks, G.E., *Records of Holm Cultram* (London, 1899).

Gilchrist and Mytum :   Gilchrist, R., and Mytum, H., *The Archaeology of Rural Monasteries* (1989):   (B.A.R. British Ser., 203; 1989).

Gilyard-Beer (1960) :   Gilyard-Beer, R., *Cleeve Abbey* (HMSO, 1960; 2nd edn. 1990).

Gilyard-Beer (1970) :   Gilyard-Beer, R., *Abbeys* (HMSO, 2nd edn. 1976).

Gilyard-Beer (1981) :   Gilyard-Beer, R., 'Boxley Abbey and the *Pulpitum Collationis*', in Detsicas (1981).

Gilyard-Beer (1986) :   Gilyard-Beer, R. and Coppack, G., 'Excavations at Fountains Abbey', in *Archaeologia* 108 (1986).

Gilyard-Beer (1987) :   Gilyard-Beer, R., 'The Graves of the Abbots of Fountains', *Yorkshire Archaeol. Jnl.* 59 (1987).

Gimpel (1977) :   Gimpel, J., *The Medieval Machine* (London, 1977).

Girardot (1970) :   Girardot, A., 'Forges monastiques', in *Rev. d'Hist. des Mines er de la Metallurgie* I (1970 : 1).

Glidden (1987) :   Glidden, A., 'Aelred the Historian', in Sommerfeldt (1987).

Gloede (1965) :   Gloede, G., *Das Doberan Münster* (Berlin, 1965).

Gand (1990):   Glorieux-de-Gand, T., *Manuscripts cisterciens de la Bibliothèque royale* (Brussels, 1990).

Goblet (1927) :   Goblet, F., *Histoire des Bois de Belgique* I (Paris-Brussels, 1927).

Goff (1980) :   Goff, H. le., *Bégard* (Kelenn, 1980).

Golding (1990) :   Golding, B., 'Hermit Monks and Women', in Loades (1990).

González (1964) :   González, H., 'Un Famoso Monasterio Cisteriense', *Cistercium* XVI : No. 92 (May–June, 1964).

Gosso (1940) :   Gosso, F., 'Vita economica della Abbazie Piemontesi', *Analecta Gregoriana* XXII (1940).
Gottschalk (1955) :   Gottschalk, M.K.E., *Historische Geografie van Westelijk Zeeuws-Vlaanderen* I (Assen, 1955).
Goutagny (1963) :   Goutagny, E., 'Carracedo', *Cîteaux* XIV (1963).
Goutagny (1964) :   Goutagny, E., 'Chassagne', *Cîteaux* XV (1964 : 3).
Goutagny (1965) :   Goutagny, E., 'Saint-Sulpice-en-Bugey', in *Cîteaux* XVI (1965 : 1).
Grand (1950) :   Grand, R., *L'Agriculture au Moyen Âge* (Paris, 1950).
Grandmottet (1958) : Grandmottet, O., 'Aspects du Temporel d'Auberive', *Les Cahiers Haut-Marnais* 52 (1958 : 1).
Graves (1957) :   Graves, C.V., 'Economic Activities of the Cistercians', *Analecta S.O. Cist.* XII (1957).
Graves (1979) :   Graves, C.V., 'English Cistercian Nunneries', *Speculum* LIV (1979 : 3).
Graves (1982) :   Graves, C.V., 'Organisation of an English Cistercian Nunnery', *Cîteaux* XXXIII 1982 : 3–4).
Graves (1984) :   Graves, C.V., 'Stixwould in the Market Place', in Nichols (1984).
Greatrex (1994) :   Greatrex, J., 'Medieval Converts from Judaism', *Monmouthshire Antiq.* X (1994).
Grebenc (1973) :   Grebenc, J.M., *Gospodarska ustanoviter Stične* (Samostan Stična, 1973).
Grégoire (1969) :   Grégoire, C., 'Prouilly', *Bull. des Sociétés d'Hist. et d'Arch. de la Meuse* 6 (1969).
Grégoire (1985) :   Grégoire, C., 'Aux origins de Clairlieu', noted in *Cîteaux* XXXVI (1985: 3–4).
Grégoire (1992) :   Grégoire, C., 'Everard, Evêque de Norwich', *Cîteaux* XLIII (1992: 1–4).
Grégoire (1991) :   Grégoire, P-C., 'Moines d'Orval dans la Siderurgie', in Benoît and Cailleux (1991).
Gresley (1854) :   Gresley, J.M., *Abbey of Stoneley-in-Arden* (Ashby, 1854).
Grèzes-Ruelff (1977) : Grèzes-Ruelff, F., 'Fontfroide et son Domaine', *Annales du Midi* 89 (1977).
Griesser (1949) :   Griesser, B., 'Eine Ungedruckte', *Analecta S.O. Cist.* V (1949).
Grillon (1963) :   Grillon, L., 'Le Prieuré des Touches', *Annales de Midi* 75 (1963).
Grolleau (1932) :   Grolleau, C. and Chastel, G., *La Trappe* (Paris, 1932).
Grüger (1977) :   Grüger, H., 'Das Patronsrecht', in *Cîteaux* XXVIII (1977 : 1–2).
Grüger (1978a) :   Grüger, H., *Heinrichau* (Cologne : Vienna; 1978).
Grüger (1978b) :   Grüger, H., 'Das Volkstum der Bevolkerung', *Zeitschrift für Ostforschung* 27 (1978 : 2).
Grüger (1982) :   Grüger, H., 'Schlesisches Klosterbuch', in *Jahrbuch der Schlesisches F-W Universitat* XXIII (1982).
Grüger (1984) :   Grüger, H., 'Fountain Houses', in Lillich (1984).
Grüger (1987) :   Grüger, H., 'Beobachtung der Statuten von Cîteaux', in Strzelczyk (1987).
Grüger (1996) :   Grüger, H., 'Der Zisterzienserorden in Schlesien', *Cîteaux* XLVII (1996).
Guerin (1966) :   Guerin, M.P., 'Atlas Cisterciense' *Cistercium* XVIII : No. 101 (Jan.-Mar. 1966).
Guidoni (1978) :   Guidoni, E., 'Cistercensi e città nuove', in Romanini A.M. (ed.)., *I Cistercensi e il Lazio* (Rome, 1978).
Gumowski (1966) :   Gumowski, M., *Handbuch der Polnischen Siegelkunde* 1966).
Gutton (1974) :   Gutton, F., 'L'ordre de Montesa', *Cîteaux* XXV (1974:2).
Gutton (1980) :   Gutton, F., 'La chevalrie militaire en Espagne', *Cîteaux* XXXI (1980).
Gwynn (1970) :   Gwynn, A. and Hadcock, R.N., *Medieval Religious Houses:Ireland* (London, 1970).
Gwynn (1992) :   Gwynn, A., *The Irish Church in the eleventh and twelfth centuries* (Dublin, 1992).

Haas (1966) :   Haas, T., 'Waldbesitz der Abtei Ebrach', *Cîteaux* XVII (1966 : 3).
Hahn (1957) :   Hahn, H., *Die Frühe Kirchenbaukunst der Zistercienser* (Berlin, 1957).
Halkin (1970) :   Halkin, L.-E., *Orval, Neuf Siècles d'Histoire* (Liége, 1970).
Hall (1896) :   Hall, J., 'The Book of the Abbot of Combermere', *Lancs, and Chesh. Rec. Soc.* XXX (1896), Misc. 2.

Hall (1899) :   Hall, F., *Bidrag till Kännedomen om Cistercienserorden i Sverige* (Gefle, 1899).

Hallam (1954) :   Hallam, H.E., *The New Lands of Elloe* (Leicester Univ., 1954).

Hallam (1986) :   Hallam, H.E., 'Wildmore Fen' in: Skelton, R.A. and Harvey, D.A. *Local Maps and Plans from Medieval England* (Oxford, 1986).

Hallberg (1965) :   Hallberg, S., 'Rune Norberg och Oloph Odenius Ambetsigill i det Medeltida Sverige', *Kyrkohistorisk årsskrift* 65 (1965).

Hamilton (1976) :   Hamilton, B., 'The Cistercians and the Crusade States', in Pennington (1976).

Hamilton (1979) :   Hamilton, B., *Monastic Reform* (London, 1979).

Hamlin (1983) :   Hamlin, A., 'Collation Seats', *Medieval Archaeology* XXVII (1983).

Hand (1919) :   Hand, C.R., 'Stanlawe Grange', *Trans. Hist. Soc. Lancs. and Chesh.* LXXI (N.S. XXXV; 1919).

Harbison (1970) :   Harbison, P., *Guide to the National Monuments of Ireland* (Dublin, 1970).

Hardenberg (1935) : Hardenberg, H., 'Het kloostergoed Heisterbach bij Dordrecht', *Bijdragen voor de gesch. van het bisdom Haarlem* 53 (1935 : 1).

Harper (1930) :   Harper, C.G., *Abbeys of Old Romance* (London, 1930).

Harper-Bill (1980) : Harper-Bill, C., 'Cistercian Visitation', *Bull. Inst. Hist. Research* LIII (1980).

Harrison (1986) :   Harrison, S.A., 'The Stonework of Byland Abbey', *The Ryedale Historian* 13 (1986).

Harrison (1997) :   Harrison, S.A. and Thurlby, M., 'An Architectural History', in Shoesmith and Richardson (1997).

Harrison (1998):   Harrison, J., 'The troubled foundation of Grace Dieu Abbey', *Monmouthshire Antiquary* XIV (1998).

Hart (1977) :   Hart, P., 'Seventh Conference of Cistercian Studies', *Cistercian Studies* XII (1977 : 2).

Hartwell Jones (1912) : (Hartwell) Jones, G., 'Celtic Britain and the Pilgrim Movement', *Y Cymmrodor* XXIIII (1912).

Hays (1963) :   Hays, R., *History of the Abbey of Aberconwy* (Cardiff, 1963).

Heath (1828) :   Heath, C., *Descriptive Account of Tintern Abbey* (11th edn., Monmouth, 1828).

Heath (1911) :   Heath, S., *Ford Abbey* (London, 1911).

Heiligenkreuz (1983) : *Heiligenkreuz* (Casa Editrice Bonechi, Florence, 1983).

Heins (1905) :   Heins, A., 'Les granges monumentales', *Maatschappij van Gesch. en Oudheidkunde*, Bull. 13 (1905).

Hennig (1950) :   Hennig, J., 'Medieval Ireland in Cistercian Records', *Irish Eccl. Record*, 5th Ser., LXXVIII (March, 1950).

Henocq (1970) :   Henocq, J-P., 'Valloires', *Bull. de la Soc. Émul. d'Abbeville* XXII (1970).

Hermano Juan (1960) : Hermano Juan, M., 'Orígenes de Mélon', *Cistercium* XII : No. 67 (Jan.-Febr. 1960).

Hermans (1968) :   Hermans, V., 'Le Procureur Général', *Analecta Cist.* XXIV (1968 : 1).

Heslop (1986) :   Heslop, T. A., 'Cistercians Seals', in Norton and Park (1986).

Heutger (1971) :   Heutger, N., *Loccum* (Hildesheim, 1971).

Heutger (1985) :   Heutger, N., 'Cistercian Architectural Remains', in Elder (1985).

Hiegel (1981) :   Hiegel, C., 'Le sel en Lorraine', *Annales de l'Est* 5th Ser. Yr. 33 (1981: 1).

Higounet (1948) :   Higounet, C., 'Bastides et Frontières', *Le Moyen Âge* LIV (1948).

Higounet (1950) :   Higounet, C., 'Cistercians et Bastides'; *Ibid.* LVI (4th Ser. V; 1950).

Higounet (1982) :   Higounet, C., 'La Maison de Grandselve à Bordeaux', in Chauvin (1982a).

Higounet (1983a) :   Higounet, C., (edit.) *L'Économie Cistercienne* (Auch, 1983).

Higounet (1983b) :   Higounet, C., 'Les Granges Cisterciennes', *Ibid.*

Higounet (1986) :   Higounet, C., 'Nouvelles réflexions sur les bastides', in Privat (1986).

Higounet (1986a) :   Higounet, C., (ed.) *Les Ordres Militaires* (Auch, 1986).

Hill (1865) :   Hill, G.M., 'Croxden Abbey', *Jnl. Brit. Arch. Assoc.* XXI (1865).

Hill (1961) :   Hill, M.C., *The King's Messengers* (London, 1961).

Hill (1968) :   Hill, B.D., *English Cistercian Monasteries and their Patrons* (Univ. of Illinois Press, 1968).

Hill (1971) :   Hill, B.D., 'Archbishop Thomas Becket', in *Analecta Cist.* XXVII (1971 : 1).

Hillgarth (1959) :   Hillgarth, J. N., 'Una Biblioteca Cisterciense Medieval', *Analecta Sacra Tarraconensia* 32 (1959).

Hilling (1992) :   Hilling, J.B., *Cilgerran Castle, St Dogmael's Abbey, etc.* (Cadw, Cardiff; 1992).
Hinnebusch (1972) :   Hinnebusch, J.F., *Historia Occidentalis de Jacques* de Vitry (Fribourg, 1972).
Hirst & Wright (1989):   Hirst, S. and Wright, S., 'Bordesley Abbey Church', in Gilchrist and Mytum (1989).
Hlaváčková (1996) :   Hlaváčková, J.H., 'A Thirteenth-Century Antiphonary', *Cîteaux* XLVII (1996).
Hoberg (1949) :   Hoberg, H., 'Taxae pro Communibus Servitiis', *Studi e Testi*, 144 (Vatican, 1949).
Hockey (1970) :   Hockey, S.F., *Quarr Abbey and its Lands* (Leicester U.P., 1970).
Hockey (1976) :   Hockey, S.F., *Beaulieu : King John's Abbey* (Pioneer Publns, 1976).
Hodges (1982) :   Hodges, R. and others., 'Roystone Grange', *Derbysh. Arch. Jnl.* CII (1982).
Hoffmann (1994) :   Hoffmann, R., 'Medieval Cistercian Fisheries', in Pressouyre (1994).
Hogg (1972) :   Hogg, G., *Priories and Abbeys of England* (Newton Abbot, 1972).
Hogg (1980) :   Hogg, J., *La Cartuja de Benifaçà* (Analecta Cartusiana, 41:Pt.7; Salzburg, 1980).
Holdsworth (1962) :   Holdsworth, C. J., 'Eleven Visions of Stratford Langthorne', *Cîteaux* XIII (1962).
Holdsworth (1980) :   Holdsworth, C. J., 'A Cistercian Monastery', *History Today* 30, No. 8 (Aug. 1980).
Holdsworth (1986) :   Holdsworth, C. J., 'Early Legislation on Art and Architecture', in Norton and Park (1986).
Holdsworth (1990) :   Holdsworth, C. J., 'Saint Bernard: What Kind of Saint?', in Loades (1990).'
Holdsworth (1994) :   Holdsworth, C. J., 'Barns at Cistercian Granges', in Pressouyre (1994).
Holdsworth (1994a) :   Holdsworth, C. J., 'The early writings of Bernard of Clairvaux', *Cîteaux* XLV (1994:1–2).
Holman (1986) :   Holman, J., 'Stephen of Sawley', *Cistercian Studies* XXI (1986 : 2).
Holman (1988) :   Holman, J., 'Baldwin of Ford', *Ibid.* XXIII (1988:4).
Holtmeyer (1906) :   Holtmeyer, A., *Cistercienskirchen Thüringens* (Jena, 1906).
Honeyman (1929) :   Honeyman, H.L. and others, 'Tile Pavements at Newminster', *Arch. Aeliana* VII (1929).
Hoppe (1914) :   Hoppe, W., *Kloster Zinna* (Leipzig, 1914).
Hørby (1962) :   Hørby, A.K., 'Skolen og Akademiet', *Academia Sorana* (Copenhagen, 1962).
Horn (1965) :   Horn, W. and Born, E., *Barns of Beaulieu* (Los Angeles, 1965).
Hugo (1855) :   Hugo, T., 'On the Charters of Cleeve Abbey', *Proc. Somersetshire Arch. and Nat. Hist. Soc.* VI (1855).
Hugoniot (1985) :   Hugoniot, J-Y., 'L'Abbaye de Noirlac', *Actes du Colloque Internat. Glyptographie de Cambrai, 1984* (publ. 1985).
Hugues (1863) :   Hugues, Fr, *Annales d'Aiguebelle* I (Valence, 1863).
Hümpfner (1927) :   Hümpfner, T., *Les fils de S. Bernard en Hongrie* (Budapest, 1927).
Humphrey (1982) :   Humphrey, W., *Garendon Abbey* (Loughborough, *ca.* 1982).
Hurt (1934) :   Hurt, R., *Děginy Cisterciáckého Klástera Na Velehradě* I (Olmütz, Mahren, 1934).

Isaac (1984) :   Isaac, M-T., *Les Livres Manuscrits de l'Abbaye des Dunes* (Aubel, 1984).

Jack (1972) :   Jack, R.I., *Medieval Wales* (London, 1972).
Jacob (1970) :   Jacob, A., Villers Abbey (Royal Belgian Touring Club, 1970).
James (1957) :   James, B. S., *Saint Bernard of Clairvaux* (London, 1957).
Jansen (1983) :   Jansen, V., 'Royal Patronage', *Cîteaux* XXXIV (1983 : 3–4).
Jansen (1984) :   Jansen, V., 'Beaulieu', in Lillich (1984).
Jansen (1987) :   Jansen, V., 'The Architecture of Cistercian Monasteries', *Cîteaux* XXXVIII (1987: 2–2).
Janssen (1983) :   Janssen, W. and Lohrmann, D., *Villa-Curtis-Grangia* (Munich, 1983).
Jaritz (1978) :   Jaritz, G., 'Konventualen der Zisterze Rein', *Cîteaux* XXIX (1978 : 1–2).
Jaritz (1985) :   Jaritz, G., 'The Standard of Living in Monasteries', in Elder (1985).
Jarossay (1891) :   Jarossay, E., 'Fontaine-Jean', *Annal. Soc. Hist. et Arch. de Gatinais* IX (1891: 4).

Jarry (1864) :⠀⠀⠀⠀⠀⠀Jarry, L., *L'Abbaye de la Cour-Dieu* (Orléans, 1864).
Jażdżewski (1987) :⠀⠀⠀Jażdżewski, K.K., 'Problem średniowiecznej szkoły', in Strzelcyk (1987).
Jażdżewski (1992) :⠀⠀⠀Jażdżewski, K.K., *Lubiąż* (Wrocław, 1992).
Ječný (1987) :⠀⠀⠀⠀⠀⠀Ječný, H. and Tryml, M., 'Klosterkirche in Zbraslav', in Strzelcyk (1987).

Jobin (1980) :⠀⠀⠀⠀⠀⠀Jobin, I., 'Abbaye de Valcroissant', *Revue Dromoise* LXXXIII : No. 416 (June, 1980).

Johnsen (1967) :⠀⠀⠀⠀⠀Johnsen, A.O., *Background of the Norwegian Church Province* (Universitetsforlaget, Oslo; 1967).

Johnsen (1977) :⠀⠀⠀⠀⠀Johnsen, A.O., *De Norske Cistercienserklostre* (*Ibid.* 1977).
Jones (1891) :⠀⠀⠀⠀⠀⠀Jones, M.C. and Williams, S.W., 'Excavations on the Site of Strata Marcella', *Mont. Collns.* XXV (1891).

Jones (1947) :⠀⠀⠀⠀⠀⠀Jones, T., *Gerallt Gymro* (Cardiff, 1947).
Jones (1981) :⠀⠀⠀⠀⠀⠀Jones, D. R. L., 'Margam in the post-dissolution era', *Trans. Port Talbot Hist. Soc.* III: 2 (1981).

Jones (1989) :⠀⠀⠀⠀⠀⠀Jones, A.K.G., 'The survival of fish remains', in Gilchrist and Mytum (1989).

Josephine (1976) :⠀⠀⠀Josephine, Sr, 'Centenaire de Bonneval', *Cîteaux* XXVII (1976 : 4–4).

Kaczmarek (1987) :⠀⠀⠀Kaczmarek, M., 'W Trosce o Najslabszych', in Strzelczyk (1987).
Kaczmarek(1993) :⠀⠀⠀Kaczmarek, K., 'Polish Cistercian Monks in the Middle Ages', *Cîteaux* XLIV (1993: 3–4).

Karłowska-Kamzowa⠀⠀Karłowska-Kamzowa, A., 'Znaczenie Iluminatorstwa Cysterskiego', in
⠀(1987):⠀⠀⠀⠀⠀⠀⠀⠀⠀Strzelczyk (1987).

Kaul (1949) :⠀⠀⠀⠀⠀⠀Kaul, B., 'De Kalendario Cisterciensi', *Analecta S.O. Cist.* V (1949).
Keenan (1969) :⠀⠀⠀⠀⠀Keenan, D., review of *Comhcheilg na Maïnistreach Moire* in *Cîteaux* XX (1969 : 1).

Keenan (1976) :⠀⠀⠀⠀⠀Keenan, J.M., 'The Cistercian Pilgrimage to Jerusalem', in Sommerfeldt (1976).

Kelecom (1975) :⠀⠀⠀⠀Kelecom, J., 'Les Biens d'Orval', in Halkin (1975).
Kelly (1926a) :⠀⠀⠀⠀⠀Kelly, P.V., 'A Bridge of Monastic Date', in *Trans. Cumb. and Westm. Antiq. and Arch. Soc.* N.S. XXVI (1926).

Kelly (1926b) :⠀⠀⠀⠀⠀Kelly, P.V., 'Finds at Furness Abbey', *Ibid.*
Kemp (1984) :⠀⠀⠀⠀⠀⠀Kemp, R., 'A fishkeeper's store at Byland Abbey', *Ryedale Historian* 12 (1984).

Kempf (1976) :⠀⠀⠀⠀⠀Kempf, J-P., L'Abbaye de Cherlieu (Salsa, Vesoul; 1976).
Ker (1984) :⠀⠀⠀⠀⠀⠀⠀Ker, N., 'An early twelfth-century manuscript', *Analecta Cist.* XL (1884 :1–2).

Kienzle (1985) :⠀⠀⠀⠀⠀Kienzle, B.M., 'Hélinand of Froidmont', in Elder (1985).
Kienzle (1989) :⠀⠀⠀⠀⠀Kienzle, B.M., 'Pons of Leras', *Cîteaux* XL (1989: 1–4).
Kinder (1976) :⠀⠀⠀⠀⠀Kinder, T.N., 'Blanche of Castile and the Cistercians', *Cîteaux* XXVII (1976 : 3).

Kinder (1980) :⠀⠀⠀⠀⠀Kinder, T.N., 'The Origins of Pontigny', *Cîteaux* XXXI (1980).
Kinder (1982) :⠀⠀⠀⠀⠀Kinder, T.N., 'Aspects of Cistercian Art', *Cîteaux* XXXIII (1982 : 3–4).
Kinder (1983) :⠀⠀⠀⠀⠀Kinder, T.N., 'Construction at Pontigny', *Cîteaux* XXXIV (1983 : 3–4).
Kinder (1984) :⠀⠀⠀⠀⠀Kinder, T.N., 'Abbey of Cercamp', *Cîteaux* XXXV (1984 : 1–2).
Kinder (1992) :⠀⠀⠀⠀⠀Kinder, T.N., 'Toward dating Construction of Pontigny', *Jnl. Brit. Arch. Assoc.* CXLV (1992).

Kinder (1993) :⠀⠀⠀⠀⠀Kinder, T.N., 'Medieval Tiles and Bricks at Pontigny', in Lillich (1993).
King (1954) :⠀⠀⠀⠀⠀⠀King, A.A., *Cîteaux and her Elder Daughters* (London, 1954).
King (1956) :⠀⠀⠀⠀⠀⠀King, P., 'Coupar Angus', *Innes Review* 27 (1956).
King (1965) :⠀⠀⠀⠀⠀⠀King, A.A., *Eucharistic Reservation* (London, 1965).
King (1973) :⠀⠀⠀⠀⠀⠀King, P., 'Financial History of Cîteaux', *Jnl. Eccles. Hist.* XXIV (1973 : 2).

King (1985) :⠀⠀⠀⠀⠀⠀King, P., *The Finances of the Cistercian Order* (Cist. St. Ser. 85; Kalamazoo, 1985).

King (1995) :⠀⠀⠀⠀⠀⠀King, D. A., 'Cistercian Numerical Notation', *Cîteaux* XLVI (1995: 3–4).

Kinvig (1950) :⠀⠀⠀⠀⠀Kinvig, R. H. *A History of the Isle of Man* (Univ. Press of Liverpool, 1950).
Kitson (1895) :⠀⠀⠀⠀⠀Kitson, F.R. and others, 'Charters of Kirkstall Abbey', *Publns. Thoresby Soc.* IV (1895).

Kłoczowski (1970) :   Kłoczowski, J., 'Les Cisterciens en Pologne', Cîteaux XXI (1970 : 2).
Kluit (1780) :   Kluit, A., *Historica critica* III (Middelburg, 1780).
Knight (1850) :   Knight, H. Hey., *Specimens of Inlaid Tiles from Neath Abbey* (Neath, 1850).
Knowles (1963a) :   Knowles, (M). D., *Monastic Order in England* (2nd. edn.; Cambridge, 1963).

Knowles (1963b) :   Knowles, (M). D., *Great Historical Enterprises* (London, 1963).
Knowles (1963c) :   Knowles, (M). D., *Saints and Scholars* (Cambridge, 1963).
Knowles (1969) :   Knowles, (M). D., *Christian Monasticism* (London, 1969).
Knowles (1979) :   Knowles, (M). D., *The Religious Orders in England* (1st paperback edn, Cambridge, 1979).

Köfler (1978)   Köfler, W., *Die Zisterzienserstiftes Stams* (Öster-Reichische Urbare, I : 5; Innsbruck, 1978).

Kohler (1994):   Kohler, M., *Die Bauten und die Ausstattung des ehemaligen Zisterzienserklosters Herrenalb* (Heidelberg, 1994).

Kornerup (1879) :   Kornerup, J.K.J., 'Minder om Cistercienserklostreti Esrom', *Aarbøger for Nordisk* Oldkyndighed Og Historie (1879).

Kornerup (1881) :   Kornerup, J.K.J., *Ibid. (1881)*.
Kottje (1992) :   Kottje, R. (ed.), *Die niederrheinischen Zisterzienser im späten Mittelalter* (Cologne: Bonn, 1992).

Kozłowska-Budkowa :   Kozłowska-Budkowa, Z. and Szczur, S., 'Dzieje Opactwa Cystersów w
    (1983)   Koprzywnicy', *Nasza* Przeszło 60 (1983).

Kozłowski (1972) :   Kozłowski, R., *Rozwój Uposażenia Klasztoru Cysterskiego w Byszewie* (Warsaw : Poznan; 1972).

Král (1987) :   Král, A.B., *Podhorácké muzeum a areál Porta Coeli* (Brno, 1987).
Krason (1950):   Krason, J., *Uposazenie Klastory Cystersów w Obrze.* (Travaux Comm. Hist. Poznan Society of Friends of Science, XVII, Pt. 1: 1950).

Kraus (1980) :   Kraus, G. (ed.), *Zisterzienser und Heisterbach* (Bonn, 1980).
Krausen (1977) :   Krausen, E., *Die Zisterzienserabtei Raitenhaslach* (Germania Sacra, N.S. 11; Berlin – New York, 1977).

Krausen (1966) :   Krausen, E. and Zakar, P., note in *Analecta Cist.* XXII (1966).
Kuhn-Refus (1995) :   Kuhn-Refus, M., 'Cistercian Nuns in Germany', in Nichols and Shank (1995).

Kuhne (und.) :   Kuhne, W., Hardehusen (Paderborn, undated).
Kunkel (1911) :   Kunkel, A., 'Stiftungsbriefe für Dargun', *Archiv. für Urkundenforschung* III (1911).

Kürbis (1987) :   Kürbis, B., 'Cystersi w kulturze polskiego średniowiecza', in Strzelczyk (1987).

Kuthan (1982) :   Kuthan, J., *Die Mittelalterliche Baukunst der Zisterzienser in Böhmen und Mähren* (Munich : Berlin, 1982).

Kutzner (1969) :   Kutzner, M., *Cysterska Architektura na Śląsku* (Univ. Mik. Kopernika, Toruń; 1969).

Kutzner (1995) :   Kutzner, M., 'Architektur in Schlesien', *Cîteaux* XLVI (1995).

Lacaze (1993) :   Lacaze, M., 'Les granges de Gimont', *Annales du Midi* CV (1993).
Lackner (1971) :   Lackner, B.K., 'The Liturgy of Early Cîteaux', in O'Callaghan (1971a).
Lackner (1972) :   Lackner, B.K., *The Eleventh-Century Background of Cîteaux* (Cist. Studies Ser., 8; Washington, 1972).

Lackner (1976) :   Lackner, B.K., 'Monastic Life according to St Bernard', in Sommerfeldt (1976).

Lackner (1978a) :   Lackner, B.K., 'Early Cistercian Life', in Sommerfeldt (1978).
Lackner (1978b) :   Lackner, B.K.,'Friends and Critics of Early Cîteaux', *Analecta Cist.* XXXIV (1978 : 1–2).

Lackner (1981) :   Lackner, B.K., 'Early Cîteaux and the Care of Souls', in Elder (1981).
Lacorte (1995) :   Lacorte, D.M., 'Pope Innocent IV's Rôle in the College of St Bernard in Paris', *Cîteaux* XLVI (1995: 3–4).

Laeman (1898) :   Laeman, J., 'Les autels de Villers', *Anal. Hist. Eccl. Belgique* 27 (1898).
Lancaster (1895) :   Lancaster, W.T., 'Possessions of Kirkstall Abbey in Leeds', *Publns. Thoresby Soc.* IV (1895).

Lancaster (1984) :   Lancaster, T. W., *Hulton Abbey* (Stoke-on-Trent, 1984).
Laurent (1928) :   Laurent, J., 'Les Noms des Monastères Cisterciens', in *SB* (1).

Lawrence (1960) :   Lawrence, C.H., 'Stephen of Lexington', *Jnl. Eccl. Hist.* XI (1960 : 2).
Lawrence (1984) :   Lawrence, C.H., *Medieval Monasticism* (London, 1984).
Le Blévec (1987) :   Le Blévec, D., 'Maladie et soins du corps', in: Dubois, H. and others, *Horizons Marins Itinéraires Spirituels*, I: *Mentalités et Sociétés* (Sorbonne, Paris; 1987).

Le Goff (1980) :   Le Goff, H., *Begard* (Guiparas, Finistère; 1980).
Le Hardy (1897) :   Le Hardy, M.G., 'D'Aunay-sur-Odon', *Bull. Soc. des Antiq. de Normandie* XIX (1897).

Le Moyne (1899) :   Le Moyne de la Borderie, A., *Histoire de Bretagne* (Rennes, 1899).
Le Waitte (1673) :   Le Waitte, A., *Historia Camberanensis* (Paris, 1673).
Lebecq (1972) :   Lebecq, S., 'Les Cisterciens de Vaucelles', *Revue du Nord* 54 (No. 215; Oct. – Dec. 1972).

Lebecq (1983) :   Lebecq, S., 'Vignes et vins de Vaucelles', in Higounet (1983).
Leblanc (1949) :   Leblanc, G., 'Abbayes Cisterciennes du Sud-Ouest', in: *France Méridionale*: Mélanges offert à Daniel Faucher (Toulouse, 1949).

Leclercq (1949) :   Leclercq, J., 'Manuscrits Cisterciens d'Italie d'Espagne', *Analecta S.O. Cist.* V (1949), VII (1951), X (1954).
Leclercq (1954) :   Leclercq, J., 'Épîtres d'Alexandre III', *Revue Benedictine* LXIV (1954).
Leclercq (1961) :   Leclercq, J., 'Monachisme et Peregrination', *Studia Monastica* 3 (1961).
Leclercq (1970) :   Leclercq, J., 'Violence and the Devotion to St Benedict', *Downside Review* 88 (No. 293; Oct. 1970).

Leclercq (1976) :   Leclercq, J., 'St Bernard's Attitude towards War', in Sommerfeldt (1976).

Leclercq (1976b) :   Leclercq, J., *Bernard of Clairvaux* (Cist. Studies Ser. 16., Kalamazoo, 1976).

Leclercq (1977) :   Leclercq, J., 'St Bernard and the Formative Community', *Tjurunga* 14 (1977).

Leclercq (1978) :   Leclercq, J., *The Love of Learning and the Desire for God* (London, 1978).
Leclercq (1988) :   Leclercq, J., 'Conventual Chapter and Council', *Cistercian Studies* XXIII (1988 : 1).

Leclercq (1990) :   Leclercq, J., 'The Joy of Dying', *Cist. Studies* XXV (1990: 3).
Lefèvre (1983) :   Lefèvre, S., 'Les granges de Jouy', *Bull. de la Soc. Hist. et Arch. de Provins* 137 (1983).

Lekai (1969) :   Lekai, L., 'Dès Colléges Cisterciens', *Analecta Cist.* XXV (1969 : 2).
Lekai (1971a) :   Lekai, L., 'The College of St Bernard in Toulouse', *Ibid.* XXVII (1971 : 1).

Lekai (1971b) :   Lekai, L., 'The "College of Boulbonne"', *Cîteaux* XXII (1971 : 4–4).
Lekai (1976) :   Lekai, L., 'Medieval Cistercians and Hungary', *Analecta Cist.* XXXII (1976 : 1–2).

Lekai (1977a) :   Lekai, L., *The Cistercians* (Kent State U.P., 1977).
Lekai (1977b) :   Lekai, L., 'Germans and the Medieval Cistercian Abbeys in Poland', *Cîteaux* XXVIII (1977 : 3).

Lekai (1978) :   Lekai, L., 'Ideals and Reality', in Sommerfeldt (1978).
Lenglet (1978) :   Lenglet, O., 'Géraud de Sales', *Cîteaux* XXIX (1978 : 1–2).
Lepage (1855) :   Lepage, H., 'Clairlieu', *Bull. Soc. d'Arch. Lorraine* V (1855).
Leroux (1990) :   Leroux, J-F., 'Les granges et celliers de Clairvaux', in Pressouyre (1990).
Leroy (1972) :   Leroy, A. and Wimet, P.-A., 'La Grange de la Longueroye', *Bull. Comm. Dept. Mon. Hist. du Pas-De-Calais* IX (1972 : 2).

Lescher (1988) :   Lescher, B., 'Laybrothers', *Cistercian Studies* XXIII (1988 : 1).
Lesher (1984) :   Lesher, M.K., 'St Bernard and the Republic of Florence', *Cîteaux* XXXV (1984 : 3- 4).

Letellier (1993) :   Letellier, D., *Pigeonniers de France* (Privat, Toulouse; 1993).
Levárdy (1982) :   Levardy, F., *Magyar Templomok Művészete* (Budapest, 1982).
Lewis (1927) :   Lewis, E.A., 'The castle and lordship of Llanstephan', *West Wales Historical Records* 12 (1927).

Lewis (1976) :   Lewis, J. M. and Williams, D. H., *White Monks in Wales* (National Museum, Cardiff; 1976).

Lewis (1976a) :   Lewis, J.M., *Medieval Paving Tiles* (National Museum, Cardiff; 1976).
Leyrer (1988) :   Leyrer, in Römer (1988).
Leyser (1984) :   Leyser, H., *Hermits and the New Monasticism* (London, 1984).
Lhwyd (1910) :   Lhwyd, E., 'Parochialia', *Arch. Camb.* 1909–11.

Lillich (1982a) :   Lillich, M.P., 'Medieval Monastic Plumbing', in Chauvin (1982a) III/5.
Lillich (1982b) :   Lillich, M.P. (ed.), *Studies in Cistercian Art and Architecture* I (Cist. Studies Ser., 66; Kalamazoo, 1982).
Lillich (1984) :   Lillich, M.P., *Ibid.* II (Cist. St. Ser. 69, 1984).
Lillich (1987) :   Lillich, M.P., *Ibid.* III (Cist. St. Ser. 89, 1987).
Lillich (1993) :   Lillich, M.P., *Ibid.* IV (Cist. St., Ser. 134; 1993).
Lillich (1993a) :   Lillich, M.P., 'Cistercian Windows', in Swietek (1993).
Lillich (1998) :   Lillich, M.P., *Studies in Cistercian Art and Architecture* V (1998).
Lindenthaal (1979) :   Lindenthaal, B.L., 'Die Stadhofe der Kloster Doberan und Dargun in Mecklenburg', *Cist. Chronik* (1979 : 1).
Lindley (1954) :   Lindley, E.S., 'Kingswood Abbey', *Trans. Bristol and Gloucestershire Arch. Soc.* LXXIII (1954).
Lindley (1955) :   Lindley, E.S., continuation in *Ibid.* LXXIV (1955).
Lingenberg (1982) :   Lingenberg, H., *Die Anfänge des Klosters Oliva* (Kieler Historische Studien, 30; Stuttgart, 1982).
Linnard (1982) :   Linnard, W., *Welsh Woods and Forests* (Cardiff, 1982).
Lipkin (1980) :   Lipkin, J., 'Cistercians in the Hierarchy', in Elder (1980).
Little (1893) :   Little, A.G., 'Cistercian Students at Oxford', *Engl. Hist. Rev.* VIII (1893).
Little (1976) :   Little, B., Portrait of Somerset (London, 1976).
Loades (1990) :   Loades, J. (ed.), *Monastic Studies* I (Headstart History, Bangor; 1990).
Loades (1991). :   Loades, J., *Ibid.* II (1991).
Locatelli (1975) :   Locatelli, R., 'L'Implantation Cistercienne en Bourgogne', *Cahiers d'Histoire* 20 (1975).
Locatelli (1994) :   Locatelli, R., 'Rappel des principes fondateurs', in Pressouyre (1994).
Lohrmann (1975) :   Lohrmann, D., 'Grange de Troussures-Sainte-Eusoye', *Cîteaux* XXVI (1975 : 3).
Lohrmann (1980) :   Lohrmann, D., 'Grand Domaine en Beauvaisis', *Francia* 8 (1980).
Lohrmann (1983a) :   Lohrmann, D., 'La tuilerie cistercienne de Commelles', in Higounet (1983).
Lohrmann (1983b) :   Lohrmann, D., 'Repartition et Creation de Nouveau Domaines Monastiques', in Janssen and Lohrmann (1983).
Longhi (1958) :   Longhi, L. Fraccaro de., *L'Architettura delle Chiese Cistercensi Italiane* (Milan, 1958).
Lopez (1987) :   Lopez, A.C. (ed.), *El Cister* (Saragossa, 1987).
Lorenzen (1949) :   Lorenzen, V., *De Danske Klostres Bygnings Histoire* XI (Copenhagen, 1949).
Luddy (1937) :   Luddy, A.J., *Life and Teaching of St Bernard* (Dublin, 1937).
Luipold (1994) :   Luipold – Comments at 1993 Fontfroide Conference.
Łużyniecka (1995) :   Łużyniecka,E., *Architektura Średniowiecznych Klasztorów Cysterkich Filiacji Lubiąskiej (Wrocław, 1995).*
Lynch (1973) :   Lynch, J.H., 'Underage Novices', *Cîteaux* XXIV (1973 : 43–4).

Maas (1944) :   Maas, W., *Les Moines-Défricheurs* (Moulins, 1944).
Machilek (1973) :   Machilek, F., 'Die Zisterzienser in Böhmen und Mähren', *Archiv für Kirchengeschichte von B-M-Schlesien* III (1973).
Macqueron (1904) :   Macqueron, H., 'Abbeville : Établissements monastiques', *La Picardie Historique* III, Pt. 1 (1906–6).
Madden (1963) :   Madden, J.E., 'English Cistercians in the Thirteenth Century', *Catholic Hist. Rev.* XLIX (Washington; 1963 : 3).
Mahn (1945) :   Mahn, J.B., *L'Ordre Cistercien et son Gouverment* (Paris, 1945).
Manneville (1979) :   Manneville, P., 'Les colombiers', in Dubuc, A. (ed.), *Les Abbayes de Normandie* (Rouen, 1979).
Marilier (1982) :   Marilier, J., 'Sigillographie des Abbés de Cîteaux', in Chauvin (1982a) II/3.
Mariotti (1927) :   Mariotti, G., 'L'Abbazia di Fontevivo', *Archiv. Stor. Prov. Parmensi* XXVII (1927).
Marks (1986) :   Marks, R. 'Cistercian Window Glass', in Norton and Park (1986).
Marriotte (1963) :   Mariotte, J.Y., 'Le Comté de Bourgogne sous les Hohenstaufen', *Ann. Litt. Univ. Besancon* LVI (1963).

Martin (1893) : Martin, G., 'Les Cisterciens et l'Agriculture', *Mém. de la Soc. Sciences, Nat. et Arch. de la Creuse,* 2nd Ser. III (1893).

Martin (1982) : Martin, B.-J., *Histoire des Moines de Tamié* (Saint-Étienne, 1982).

Martinez (1982) : Martinez, C. de la C. and Navarro, E.T., *Monasterio Cisterciense de Santa Maria de Huerta* (Huerta, 1982).

Martinez (1984) : Martinez, J.V., 'La Fundacion del Veruela', *Cistercium* XXXVI : No. 167 (July- Dec. 1984).

Mary (1977) : Mary, Sr Margaret, 'Commitment by Vow', *Cistercian Studies* XII (1977: 1).

Mascarenhas (1994) : Mascarenhas, J.M. de and others, 'Les cas d'Alcobaça', in Pressouyre (1994).

Matarasso (1993) : Matarasso, P., *The Cistercian World* (Penguin Classics; London, 1993).

Matei (1974) : Matei, H.C. and others., *Chronological History of Romania* (Bucharest, 1974).

Mauri (1985) : Mauri, L.C., 'La Grangia di Valera', *Studi Storici* 26, Pt. 2 (Apl.- Jun. 1985).

McCaffery (1978) : McCaffery, H., 'Isaac of Stella', in Sommerfeldt (1978).

McCorkell (1985) : McCorkell, E., 'Herald of the Holy Spirit', *Cistercian Studies* XX (1985: 4).

McCrank (1973) : McCrank, L.J., 'The Frontier of the Spanish Reconquest', *Analecta Cist.* XXIX (1973 : 1–2).

McCrank (1975) : McCrank, L.J., 'The Cistercians of Poblet as Landlords', *Cîteaux* XXVI (1975 : 4).

McCrank (1976) : McCrank, L.J., 'The Economic Administration of Poblet', in Sommerfeldt (1976).

McDonnell (1963) : McDonnell, J. (ed.), *A History of Helmsley, Rievaulx and District* (York, 1963).

McDonnell (1965) : McDonnell, J., and Everest, R.M., 'The Waterworks of of Byland Abbey', *Ryedale Historian* I (1965).

McGinn (1973) : McGinn, B., 'Isaac of Stella', in *Analecta Cist.* XXIX (1973 : 1–2).

McGinn (1985) : McGinn, B. *The Calabrian Abbot* (New York, 1985).

McGrath (1987) : McGrath, M., 'Irish Medieval Wall Painting', *Jnl. Royal Soc. of Antiquaries of Ireland* 117 (1987).

McGuire (1973) : McGuire, B.P., 'Property and Politics at Esrom Abbey', *Medieval Scandinavia* 6 (1973).

McGuire (1974) : McGuire, B.P., 'Patrons, Privileges, and Property', *Kirkehistoriske Samlinger,* 7th Ser. (1974).

McGuire (1976a) : McGuire, B.P., *Conflict and Continuity at Øm Abbey* (Copenhagen, 1976).

McGuire (1976b) : McGuire, B.P., 'Man and the Devil', *Cahiers de l'Institut du Moyen-Age Grec et Latin* 16 (Copenhagen, 1976).

McGuire (1982) : McGuire, B.P., *The Cistercians in Denmark* (Cist. Studies Ser., 35; Kalamazoo, 1982).

McGuire (1983a) : McGuire, B.P., 'A Lost Clairvaux Exemplum Found', *Analecta Cist.* XXXIX (1983 : 1).

McGuire (1983b) : McGuire, B.P., 'Monastic and Episcopal Biography', *Ibid.* XXXIX (1983 : 2).

McGuire (1985a) : McGuire, B.P., 'Was Bernard a Friend', in Elder (1985).

McGuire (1985b) : McGuire, B.P., 'Why Scandinavia'; *Ibid.*

McGuire (1995) : McGuire, B.P., 'Who founded the Order of Cîteaux?', in Elder (1995).

McGuire (1995a) : McGuire, B.P., 'Gerson and Bernard', *Cîteaux* XLVI (1995: 2-2).

McIntire (1943) : Mc Intire, W.T., 'Furness Abbey and the Isle of Man', *Trans. Cumb. and Westm. Antiq. and Arch. Soc.* N.S. XLIII (1943).

McLean (1981) : Mc Lean,T., *Medieval English Gardens* (Collins, 1981).

McNulty (1943) : Mc Nulty, J., 'Constitutions for the Cistercian Order', *Trans. Lancs. and Chesh. Antiq. Soc.* LVII (1943–4).

Meekings (1979) : Meekings, C.A.F., and Hunnisett, R.F., 'Early Years of Netley Abbey', *Jnl. Eccl. Hist.* 30, Pt. 1 (Jan. 1979).

Melczer (1982) : Melczer, E. and Soldwedal, E., 'Monastic Goals', in Lillich (1982b).

Mellifont (1980) : *Mellifont Abbey and its Environs* (anon., Mellifont, 1980).

Ménabrea (1843) : Ménabrea, L., 'L'Abbaye d'Aulps', *Mém. Soc. Acad. de Savoie* XI (1843).

Menapace (1971) :   Menapace, L., 'Arte ed Impegno Agrario', *Economia e Storia* XVIII
                       (1971 : 2).
Merton (1965) :   Merton, L., 'For a renewal of eremitism', *Collectanea Cist.* 27 (1965 :
                       2).
Merton (1988) :   Merton T. (al. L.)., 'St Aelred of Rievaulx', *Cistercian Studies* XXIII
                       (1988 : 1).
Meslé (1980) :   Meslé, E. and Jenn, J.-M., *'L'Abbaye de Noirlac'*, (Paris, 1980).
Meyerus (1561) :   Meyerus, J., *Commentarii Flandricarum* (Antwerp, 1561).
Michel (1923) :   Michel, E., *Abbayes de Belgique* (Brussels, 1923).
Midmer (1979) :   Midmer, R., *English Medieval Monasteries* (London, 1979).
Mikkers (1956) :   Mikkers, E., 'Een Onuitgegeven Van Thomas Van Beverely, Monik van
                       Froidmont', *Cîteaux* VII: 4 (1956).
Mikkers (1963) :   Mikkers, E., 'Eremitical Life', *Cîteaux* XIV (1963).
Mikkers (1978a) :   Mikkers, E., *Grandpré* (La Doc. Cist., 23; Rochefort Abbey, Belgium;
                       1978).
Mikkers (1988) :   Mikkers, E., 'La Spiritualité Cistercienne', *Dictionnaire de Spiritualité*, ed.
                       M. Villers, XIII (Paris, 1988).
Millard (1994) :   Millard, B (ed.), *The Book of Saints* (London, 1994 edn).
Millet (1899) :   Millet, G., *Le Monastere de Daphni* (Paris, 1899).
Mitchell (1959) :   Mitchell, C.M. and others, 'Kirkstall Abbey Excavations', *Publns.*
                       Thoresby Soc. XLVIII (No. 170 : 1959; publ. Leeds, 1961).
Mitkowski (1949) :   Mitkowski, J., Początki Klastoru Cystersów w Sulejowie (Poznan, 1949).
Mohr (1977) :   Mohr, L., *Greifswald-Eldena* (Museum der Stadt, Greifswald; 1979–9).
Mohs (1978) :   Mohs, M., 'Brave Old World', *Time* (Aug. 21, 1978).
Monterde Albiac(1978):Monterde Albiac, C., *Del Monasterio de Fitero* (Saragossa, 1978).
Moore (1968) :   Moore, P.D., in *Nature* 217 (1968).
Moore and Chater   Moore, P.D. and Chater, E.H., in *Jnl. of Ecology* 57 (1969).
     (1969) :
Moore (1974) :   Moore, R.I., 'St Bernard's Mission to the Languedoc', *Bull. Inst. Hist.*
                       Research XLVII (1974).
Moorhouse (1989) :   Moorhouse, S., 'Monastic estates', in Gilchrist and Mytum (1989).
Moorhouse and   Moorhouse, S., and Wrathmell, S., *Kirkstall Abbey, Volume I – The*
     Wrathmell (1987): *1956–64 Excavations: A Reassessment* (Leeds, 1987).
Moorhouse and   Moorhouse, S., and Wrathmell, *Kirkstall Abbey* I (*Yorkshire Archaeology*, I;
     Wrathmell (1988): 1988).
Morant (1995) :   Morant, R. W., *The Monastic Gatehouse* (The Book Guild, Lewes; 1995).
Morgades (1946) :   Morgades, B., *Gula de Poblet* (1946).
Morgan (1929) :   Morgan, J.L., *Economic Administration of Coupar Abbey* (Glasgow Univ.
                       thesis, 1929).
Morgan (1971) :   Morgan, F.C., *Abbey Dore* (Leominster, 1971).
Morkill (1891) :   Morkill, J.W., 'The Manor and the Park of Roundhall', *Publns. Thoresby*
                       Soc. II (Leeds, 1891).
Morkramer (1983) :   Morkramer, M., 'Mittelalterliche Fliesen in Kloster Arnsburg', *Cist.*
                       Chronik N.S. 159 (90th Yr : 1983 : 1).
Morton (1936) :   Morton, A.S., 'Glenluce Abbey', *Trans. Dunfrieshire and Galloway Nat.*
                       Hist. and Antiq. Soc. 3rd Ser., XXI (1936–8).
Mott (1973) :   Mott, R.A., 'Kirkstall forge', *Publns. Thoresby Soc.* LIII (Leeds, 1973).
Mouret (1986) :   Mouret, D. and Bouton, J. de la C., 'Convers et converses' in Privat
                       1986.
Mousnier (1982) :   Mousnier, M., *L'Abbaye de Grandselve* (Thesis doct. Le Mirail Univ.,
                       Toulouse; June, 1982).
Mousnier (1983a) :   Mousnier, M., 'Les Granges of Grandselve', *Annales du Midi* XCV (No.
                       161; 1983).
Mousnier (1983b) :   Mousnier, M., 'L'Abbaye de Grandselve' I, *Cîteaux* XXXIV (1983 : 1–2).
Mousnier (1983c) :   Mousnier, M., *Ibid.* II, in XXXIV (1983 : 3–4).
Mousnier (1986) :   Mousnier, M., 'Grandselve et la Société de Sons Temps', in Privat
                       (1986).
Moyne (1857) :   Moyne, K., *L'Abbaye de Sénanque* (Avignon, 1857).
Moyne (1981) :   Moyne, K., *Ibid.* (Lafitte Reprint; Marseille, 1981).
Muheim (1985) :   Muheim, E., *Sénanque Abbey* (Rennes, 1985).

Muheim (1987) :   Muheim, E., *Cistercian Architecture : Sénanque Abbey* (La Bernerie-en-Retz, 1987).
Muir (1982) :   Muir, R., *The Lost Villages of Britain* (London, 1982).
Müller (1918) :   Müller, F., *Kloster Buckow* (Stettin/Szczecin, 1918).
Mullin (1932) :   Mullin, F.A., *A History of the Cistercians in Yorkshire* (Washington, 1932).
Mulon (1972) :   Mulon, M., 'Le vignoble de l'abbaye de Preuilly', *Bull. Soc. Hist. et d'Arch. Provins* 126 (1972).
Munknon (1981) :   Munknon, B. K., 'L'êglise de Villers-la-Ville', *Bull. de la Comm. des Monuments et des sites X (Brussels, 1981)*.
Musset (1951) :   Musset, L., *Les Peuples Scandinaves* (Paris, 1951).
Musset (1979) :   Musset, L., and Aubreton, R., Abbaye N.-D. de Mortemer (Rouen, 1979).
Musso and Miguet (1990) :   Musso, J-M. and Miguet, M., 'Le bâtiment des convers de l'abbaye de Clairvaux', in Pressouyre (1990).
Muzzi (1990) :   Muzzi, A. and others., *Sigilli nel Museo Nazionale del Bargello*, I (Bargello, 1990).

Navarro (1974) :   Navarro, A. G., *Catálogo de Sellos* II – III (Madrid, 1974).
Neaverson (1949) :   Neaverson, E., notes in *Arch. Camb.* (1949).
Negri (1981) :   Negri, D., *Abbazie Cistercensi in Italia* (Pistoia, 1981).
Nelson (1986) :   Nelson, L., 'Quelques Documents', *Cîteaux* XXXVII (1986 : 1–2).
Newbolt (1957) :   Newbolt, M.R., *The Cistercians in Britain* (Wantage, 1957).
Nichols (1978) :   Nichols, J.A., 'An English Cistercian Nunnery', in Sommerfeldt (1978).
Nichols (1979) :   Nichols, J.A., 'Internal Organisation of English Cistercian Nunneries', *Cîteaux* XXX (1979 : 1).
Nichols (1982a) :   Nichols, J.A., 'Medieval English Cistercian Nunneries', in Chauvin (1982a) III/5.
Nichols (1987) :   Nichols, J.A., 'Early History of the Cistercian Nuns', *Cîteaux* XXXVIII (1987 : 1–2).
Nichols and Shank (1984) :   Nichols, J.A. and Shank, L.T., *Distant Echoes* (Cist. St. Ser. 71; Kalamazoo, 1984).
Nichols and Shank (1995) :   Nichols, J.A. and Shank, L.T., *Hidden Springs* I and II (Cist. Studies Ser. 113:1–2; Kalamazoo, 1995).
Niedermaier (1973) :   Niedermaier, H., 'Klostertranslation', *Cîteaux* XXIV (1973 : 1).
Nijhoff (1830) :   Nijhoff, I.A., *Gedenkwaardigheden uit de geschiedinis van Gelderland* (Arnhem, 1830).
Niwiński (1930)   Niwiński, M., *Opactwo Cystersów w Wąchocku* (Cracow, 1930).
Noel (1975) :   Noel, R., 'Orval et l'Économie Cistercienne', in Halkin (1975).
Norton and Park (1986) :   Norton, C. and Park, D., *Cistercian Art and Architecture in the British Isles* (Cambridge, 1986).
Nuttgens (1967) :   Nuttgens, P., 'Excavations at Garendon', *Cîteaux* XVIII (1967 : 3).

Obert-Piketty (1986) :   Obert-Piketty, C., 'Benoît XII et les Collèges Cisterciens du Languedoc', in Privat (1986).
O'Brien (1965) :   O'Brien, R., 'The *Stimulus Peccatoris* of William of Rymyngton', *Cîteaux* IV (1965).
O'Callaghan (1959) :   O'Callaghan, J.F., 'The Affiliation of the Order of Calatrava', *Analecta S.O. Cist.* XV (1959).
O'Callaghan (1960) :   O'Callaghan, J.F., Continued in *Ibid*. XVI (1960).
O'Callaghan (1961) :   O'Callaghan, J.F., 'The Earliest *Difiniciones*" of the Order of Calatrava, *Traditio* XVII
O'Callaghan (1962) :   O'Callaghan, J.F., 'The Foundation of the Order of Alcántara', *Catholic Hist. Rev.* XLVII (1962 : 4).
O'Callaghan (1969) :   O'Callaghan, J.F., 'Hermandades', *Speculum* XLIV (1969).
O'Callaghan (1971a) :   O'Callaghan, J.F. (ed.) *Studies in Medieval Cistercian History* I (Cist. Studies Ser. 13; Shannon, 1971).
O'Callaghan (1971b) :   O'Callaghan, J.F., 'The Order of Calatrava and the Archbishops of Toledo', *Ibid*.
Occhipinti (1983) :   Occhipinti, E., 'Morimondo in Lombardia', *Nuova Rivista Storica* LXXVII (1983).

Occhipinti (1985) :   Occhipinti, E., 'Fortuna e crisi di un patrimonio monastico', *Studi Storici* 26, Pt. 2 (Apl.–Jun. 1985).

O'Donnell (1987) :   O'Donnell, J.F., 'The Crypt of Mellifont Abbey', *Cîteaux* XXXVIII (1987: 1–2).

O'Dwyer (1964) :   O'Dwyer, B.W., 'The Problem of Reform in Irish Cistercian Monasteries', *Jnl. Eccl. Hist.* 8 (1965).

O'Dwyer (1967) :   O'Dwyer, B.W., 'The Native Irish and the Cistercians', *Ibid.* 4 (No. 4; Dec. 1967).

O'Dwyer (1975) :   O'Dwyer, B.W., 'Crisis in the Cistercian Monasteries in Ireland', *Analecta Cist.* XXXI (1975 : 2).

O'Dwyer (1976) :   O'Dwyer, B.W., Continued in *Ibid.* XXXII (1976 : 1–2).

Oexle and Maurer (1987) :   Oexele, J. and Maurer, H., 'Der Salmannsweiller Hof', *Schriften des Vereins für Geschichte des Bodensees und seiner Umgebung* CVI (1987).

Ogilvie-Forbes (1932) :   Ogilvie-Forbes, D., 'The Rivers of Rievaulx', *Ampleforth Jnl.* XXXVII (Pt. 2; Spring, 1932).

Orme (1973) :   Orme, N., *English Schools in the Middle Ages* (London, 1973).

Ortved (1933) :   Ortved, E., *Cistercieorden i Norden* II (Copenhagen, 1933).

Ostojić (1965) :   Ostojić, I., *Benediktinci u Hrvatskoj* III (Split, 1965).

O'Sullivan (1939) :   O'Sullivan, D., 'Abbey of Tracton', *Jnl. Cork Hist. and Arch. Soc.* N.S. XLIV (1939 : 1).

O'Sullivan (1945) :   O'Sullivan, D., 'Abbey of Middleton', in *Ibid.* N.S. L (1945 : 2).

O'Sullivan (1946) :   O'Sullivan, D., 'Abbey of Fermoy', in *Ibid.* N.S. LI (1946).

O'Sullivan (1947) :   O'Sullivan, J.F., *Cistercian Settlements in Wales and Monmouthshire* (Fordham U.P., New York, 1947).

Othon (1929) :   Othon, P., 'De l'Institution et des Us des Convers', in *SB* (1).

Owen (1904) :   Owen, H., *Gerald the Welshman* (1904).

Owen (1935) :   Owen, G.D., *Agricultural Conditions in West Wales* (Ph.D. thesis, Univ. of Wales, 1935).

Owen (1955a) :   Owen, D.E., *Kirkstall Abbey* (Leeds, 1955).

Owen (1955b) :   Owen, D.E. and others, *Kirkstall Abbey Excavations* (Publns. Thoresby Soc., XLIII: Leeds, 1955).

Owen (1971) :   Owen, D.M., *Church and Society in Medieval Lincolnshire* (Hist. of Lincs. 5; Lincoln, 1971).

Owen (1979) :   Owen, A.E.B., 'Louth Park Chronicle', *Cîteaux* XXX (1979 : 4–4).

Oyaga (1967) :   *See:* De Oyaga.

Pajzderski (1916) :   Pajzderski, N., 'Les abbayes cisterciennes en Pologne', *Bull. Monumental* XXIV (1916).

Palenzuela (1978) :   Palenzuela, V-A. A., *Monasterios Cistercienses en Castilla* (Univ. of Valladolid, 1978).

Panagopoulos (1979) :   Panagopoulos, B.K., *Cistercian and Mendicant Monasteries in Medieval Greece* (Chicago, 1979).

Pancotti (1927) :   Pancotti, V., 'Abbazia di Quartazzola', *Archiv. Stor. Province Parmensi* XXVII (1927).

Parisse (1981) :   Parisse, M., *La Lorraine Monastique* (Nancy, 1981).

Parisse (1994) :   Parisse, M., 'Morimond européenne', *Les Cahiers Haut-Marnais* Nos 199–99 (1994: 1–2).

Park (1986) :   Park, D.P.D., 'Cistercian Wall Painting', in Norton and Park (1986).

Parkes and Webster (1974)   Parkes, L.N. and Webster, P.V., 'Merthyr Geryn: A Grange of Tintern', *Arch.Camb.* CXXIII (1974).

Paulsell (1976) :   Paulsell, W.O., 'St Bernard on the Duties of a Christian Prince', in O'Callagahan (1971a).

Péchenard (1883) :   Péchenard, P.L., *L'Abbaye d'Igny* (Rheims, 1883).

Pegolotti (1936) :   Pegolotti, F.B., *La Pratica della Mercatura* (edit. A. Evans; Medieval Academy of America, 1936).

Perceval (1882) :   Perceval, C. S., 'The Classification of Seals', *Proc. Soc. Antiq.* 2nd Ser. IX (1882).

Perez-Embid (1994) :   *See:* Wamba (1994).

Peigné Delacourt (1876) :   Peigné-Delacourt, A., *Histoire de l'Abbaye d'Ourscamp* (Amiens, 1876).

Penco (1961) :   Penco, G., *Storia del Monachesimo in Italia* (Rome, 1961).

Pennington (1976) : Pennington, M.B., *One Yet Two* (Cist. St. Ser. 29; Kalamazoo, 1976).

Pérathan (1908) : Pérathan, C., 'L'Abbaye de Bonlieu', *Mém. Soc. Scien. Nat. et Arch. de la Creuse* XVI : 2 (1908).

Petersen (1886) : Petersen, H., *Sceaux de l'Eglise Danoise du Moyen Age* (Copenhagen, 1886).

Petrů (1972) : Petrů, J., *Velehrad* (Brno, 1972).

Peugniez (1994) : Peugniez, B., *Routier des Abbayes Cisterciennes de France* (Editions du Signe; Strasbourg, 1994).

Peyrafort and Bonnet (1984) : Peyrafort, M and Bonnet, M., 'Les manuscrits de Pontigny', *Cîteaux* XXXV (1984: 1–2).

Peyron (1982) : Peyron, P., 'Le Temporel des Abbayes Cisterciennes du Forez', *Cahiers d'Histoire* XXVII (1982 : 4–4).

Philippe (1991) : Philippe, M., 'Le Forge de Champagne', in Benoît and Cailleux (1991).

Picard (1882) : Picard, E., 'Les Forêts de Cîteaux', *Mém de la Soc. Éduenne*, N.S. XI (1882).

Pigeon (1976) : Pigeon, M., 'Où se situat l'Abbaye de Souleuvre?', *Cîteaux* XXVII (1976 : 4–4).

Pineault & Coomans (1994) : Pineault, J. and Coomans, T., 'Le "Soleil de Villers" ', *Cîteaux* XLV (1994: 2–2).

Pirenne (1929) : Pirenne, H., *Histoire de Belgique* I (Brussels, 1929).

Pirie (1967) : Pirie, E.J.E. and others, *Kirkstall Abbey Excavations* (Publns. Thoresby Soc., LI; Leeds, 1967).

Pittet (1934) : Pittet, R., 'L'Abbaye d'Hauterive', *Archiv. Soc. d'Hist. du Canton de Fribourg* XIII (1934).

Plaisance (1955) : Plaisance, G., 'Les Cisterciens et la Forêt', *Revue du Bois* X, Pts. 7/8 (Jul.-Aug. 1955).

Platt (1969) : Platt, C., *The Monastic Grange in Medieval England* (London, 1969).

Platt (1984) : Platt, C., *Abbeys and Priories of Medieval England* (London, 1984).

Pochin Mould (1976) : Pochin Mould, D., *The Monasteries of Ireland* (London, 1976).

Pojsl (1995) : Pojsl, M., 'Velehrad', *Cîteaux* XLVI (1995).

Poloni (1981) : Poloni, J., *Les Granges de Cîteaux* (M. Hist. thesis., Univ. of Dijon, 1981).

Pontus (1966) : Pontus, P., *Silvacane Abbey* (Mulhouse Dornach, 1966).

Post (1922) : Post, R., 'Aduard', *Archief voor de Gesched. van het Aartsbisdom Utrecht* 48–8 (1922–23).

Pouillon (1970) : Pouillon, F., *The Stones of Thoronet* (London, 1970).

Pratt (1982) : Pratt, D., *Dissolution of Valle Crucis Abbey* (1982).

Pressouyre (1994) : Pressouyre, L. (ed.)., *L'espace cistercien* (Paris, 1994).

Pressouyre & Kinder (1990): Pressouyre, L., and Kinder, T. N. (ed.), *Saint Bernard & le Monde Cistercien* (Paris, 1990).

Price (1952) : Price, G.V.P., *Valle Crucis Abbey* (Liverpool, 1952).

Pringle (1992) : Pringle, D., 'Cistercian houses in the Kingdom of Jerusalem', in Gervers (1992).

Privat (1986) : Privat, E. (ed.), *Les Cisterciens de Languedoc* (Cahiers de Fanjeaux, 21; Toulouse, 1986).

Pugh (1934) : Pugh, R.H., *Glimpses of West Gwent* (1934).

Quignon (1914) : Quignon, H., 'L'Hôtel de Chaâlis à Beauvais', *Bull. Hist. et philol. du Comité des travaux* 12 (1914).

Radford (1965) : Radford, C.A. Ralegh., *Cymmer Abbey* (HMSO, 1965 edn.).

Rahlves (1966) : Rahlves, F., *Cathedrals and Monasteries of Spain* (London, 1966).

Rahtz (1976) : Rahtz, P. and Hirst, S., *Bordesley Abbey* (Brit. Arch. Report 23; 1976).

Randall (1955) : Randall, H.J., *Bridgend* (1955).

Rappold (1979) : Rappold, P., *Stift Rein*, 1129–1979 (Rein, 1979).

Redoutey (1982) : Redoutey, J-P., 'L'Abbaye de Bellevaux', in Chauvin (1982a) II/4.

Reggiori (1970) : Reggiori, F., *L'Abbazia di Chiaravalle* (Milan, 1970).

Regné (1922) : Regné, J., 'L'Abbaye des Chambons', *Revue Mabillon* XII (1922).

Régnier (1913) : Régnier, E., 'Écharlis', *Bull. Soc. Scienc. Hist. et Nat. de l'Yonne* 67 (1913).

Reindel (1969) : Reindel, K., 'Ein Legendar dem Kloster Pomuc', in Albrecht, D. and others., *Festschrift für Max Spindler* (Munich, 1969).

Reissenberger (1894) : Reissenberger, L., *Die Kerzer Abtei* (Sibiu : Hermannstadt, 1894).

Renna (1978) : Renna, T.J., 'St Bernard and Abelard', *Cîteaux* XXIX (1978 : 1–2).

Renna (1980) :   Renna, T.J., 'Early Cistercian Attitudes to War', *Cîteaux* XXXI (1980).
Renna (1995) :   Renna, T.J., 'Aelred of Rievaulx and Isaiah', in Elder (1995).
Renna (1995a) :   Renna, T.J., 'Moses in Aelred of Rievaulx', *Cîteaux* XLVI (1995: 1–2).
Richard (1946) :   Richard, J., 'La Custodie de Scarborough', *Le Moyen Âge* LII (1946 : 1–2).
Richard (1969) :   Richard, Jean., 'L'Abbaye Cistercienne de Jubin', ·*Episihgouicvn* *Ezemnvn* II (1969–70).
Richard (1991) :   Richard, Jean., 'La Maison de Clairvaux', in Leroux (1991).
Richards (1968) :   Richards, I., *Abbeys of Europe* (Feltham, London; 1968).
Richardson (1928) :   Richardson, J.S., 'A Thirteenth-Century Tile Kiln', *Proc. Soc. Antiq. Scotl.* LXIII (1928–29).
Richardson (1951) :   Richardson, J.S., *Sweetheart Abbey* (HMSO, 1951).
Richardson (1977) :   Richardson, J.S., *Ibid.* (1977 edn.).
Richardson (1981) :   Richardson, J.S., *Dundrennan Abbey* (HMSO, 1981 edn).
Richardson (1981a) :   Richardson, J.S. and Wood, M., *Melrose Abbey* (HMSO, 1981).
Richardson (1994) :   Richardson, J.S., *Dundrennan Abbey* (Historic Scotland; revised edn. 1994).
Richter (1993) :   Richter, C., 'The Cistercian Stained Glass at Doberan,' in Lillich (1993).
Roblin (1937) :   Roblin, M., 'L'Habitat Rural de la Garonne', *Revue Géogr. des Pyrénées et du Sud-Ouest* VIII (1937).
Robinson (1992) :   Robinson, D.M. and Platt, C., *Strata Florida Abbey* (Cadw; Cardiff, 1992).
Robinson (1995) :   Robinson, D.M. and Platt, C., *Tintern Abbey* (Cadw, Cardiff; 3rd edn 1995).
Rocca (1936) :   Rocca, N., 'La gestione dei beni del Monastero di Chiaravalle', *Economie e Storia 3* (1936).
Roehl (1972) :   Roehl, R., 'Plan and Reality in a Medieval Monastic Economy', in Adelson, H.L. (ed.). *Studies in Medieval and Renaissance History* IX (Nebraska U.P., 1972).
Römer (1988) :   Römer, C., *Das Zisterzienserkloster Mariental* (Brunswick : Munich, 1988).
Rösener (1974) :   Rösener, W., 'Reichsabtei Salem', in *Vorträge und Forschungen* 13 (1974).
Rösener (1983a) :   Rösener, W., 'L'Économie de l'Allemagne Occidentale', in Higounet (1983).
Rosenman (1983) :   Rosenman, B., 'The Tomb Canopies of Santa Creus', *Cîteaux* XXXIV (1983 : 4–4).
Rossignol (1851) :   Rossignol, P., 'Sceaux de Cîteaux', *Recueil de la Soc. Sphragistique de Paris* I (1851).
Roth (1986) :   Roth, H.J., 'Zur Wirtschaftsgeschichte der Cistercienser', in Schneider (1986).
Rouse (1976) :   Rouse, R.H., 'Cistercian Aids to Study', in Sommerfeldt (1976).
Rudolph (1989) :   Rudolph, C., 'The Scholarship on Bernard of Clairvaux's *Apologia*', *Cîteaux* XL: 1–4 (1989).
Rumeau (1896) :   Rumeau, R., *Ville de Grenade* (Toulouse : Paris, 1896).
Russell (1944) :   Russell, J.C., 'Clerical Population of Medieval England', *Traditio* II (1944).
Ruwet (1966) :   Ruwet, J., *L'Abbaye du Val-Dieu* (Dison, 1966).
Rymar (1987) :   Rymar, E., 'Cystersi na Terytorium Nowej Marchii', in Strzelczyk (1987).

Sabersky (1987) :   Sabersky, D., 'The Style of Nicholas of Clairvaux's Letters', in Sommerfeldt (1987).
Sadler (1993) :   Sadler, D., 'The Retable of the Abbey of Fontenay', in Lillich (1993).
Samaran (1970) :   Samaran, C. and Higounet, C., 'Bonnefont', *Colln. de Docs. Inédits sur l'Hist. de France* X (Paris, 1970).
Sarrazin (1985) :   Sarrazin, J.L. 'Maitrise de l'Eau et Société en Marais Poitevin', *Annales de Bretagne et des Pays de l'Ouest* 92 (1985: 4).
Savare (1972) :   Savare, C., *L'Assistance aux malades* (Marseilles, 1972; thesis for doctorate in pharmacy).
Saward (1980) :   Saward, J., *Perfect Fools* (Oxford, 1980).
Sayers (1964a) :   Sayers, J., 'Judicial Activities of the General Chapter', *Jnl. Eccles. Hist.* XV, Pt. 1 (April 1964).
Sayers (1964b) :   Sayers, J., Continuation in *Ibid.* XV, Pt. 2 (Oct. 1964).
Schaab (1975) :   Schaab, M., 'Der Besitz der Südwestdeutshen Zisterzienserabteien', in *Historischer Atlas von Baden-Württemberg* (1975).

Scherg (1976) :   Scherg, L., *Die Zisterzienserabtei Bronnbach* (Mainfränkische Studien, 14; Würzburg, 1976).

Scheys (1982) :   Scheys, I.I., 'Maagdendaal', *Cîteaux* XXXIII (1982 : 1).

Schich (1979a) :   Schich, W., 'Die Stadthöfe der Zisterzienserkloster in Würzburg', *Zisterzienser-Studien* III (Berlin, 1979).

Schich (1979b) :   Schich, W., 'Wirtschaft der Zisterzienserkloster', *Ibid*. IV (1979).

Schich (1987) :   Schich, W., 'Einstieg der Zisterzienser in der Handel', in Strzelczyk (1987).

Schich (1992) :   Schich, W., 'Der Handel der rheinischen Zisterzienserklöster', in Kottje (1992).

Schiørrup (1986) :   Schiørrup – comments at 1986 Noirlac Conference.

Schittekat (1966) : Schittekat, P., *Trésors sous le Sable* (Brussels, 1966).

Schlegel (1980) :   Schlegel, G., *Das Zisterzienserkloster Dargun* (Studien zur Katholischen Bistums- und Klostergeschichte, 22; Leipzig, 1980).

Schlesinger (1975) : Schlesinger, W., 'Flemmingen und Kühren', Vorträge und Forschungen XVIII (1975).

Schmidt (und.) :   Schmidt, T., *Munster zu Heilsbronn*.

Schmitt (1995) :   Schmitt, M., 'Gertrude of Helfta', in Nichols and Shank (1995).

Schneider (1954) :   Schneider, A., *Die Cistercienserabtei Himmerod* (Speyer am Rhein 1954).

Schneider (1974) :   Schneider, A., *Die Cistercienser* (Cologne, 1st edn, 1974; 2nd edn 1977).

Schneider (1986) :   Schneider, A., *Die Cistercienser* (Cologne; 3rd edn, 1986).

Schneider (1975) :   Schneider, R., 'Garciones oder Pueri Abbatum', and 'Guter- und Gelddepositen', *Zisterzienser-Studien* I (Berlin, 1975).

Schneider (1992) :   Schneider, R., 'Rheinische Zisterzienser', in Kottje (1992).

Schonsgaard (1953) : Schonsgaard, A., 'L'Archevêque Eskil', in *SB* (2).

Schrader (1970) :   Schrader, F., 'Die Zisterzienserklöster in Diözesen Magdeburg und Halberstadt', *Cîteaux* XXI (1970 : 3–4).

Schreiner (1982) :   Schreiner, K., 'Zisterziensisches Mönchtum', in Elm (1982).

Schubert (1957) :   Schubert, H.R., *History of the British Iron and Steel Industry* (London, 1957).

Schultze (1930) :   Schultze, J., *Lehnin* (Bernburg, 1930).

Schulz (1979) :   Schulz, K., 'Fernhandel und Zollpolitik', *Zisterzienser-Studien* IV (1979).

Schulz (1982) :   Schulz, K., 'Die Rolle der Zisterzienser', in Elm (1982).

Schulze (1896) :   Schulze, E.O., 'Die Kolonisierung', *Fürstlich Jablonowski'sche Gesellschaft Preisschriften 33* (1896).

Sculze (1979) :   Sculze, H.K., 'Die Besiedlung der Mark Brandenburg', *Jahrbuch für die Geschichte Mittel-und Ostdeutschlands* 28 (1979).

Sebicht (1888) :   Sebicht, R., 'Die Cistercienser', *Zeitschrift Harz-Verein* XXI (1888).

Seibt (1974) :   Seibt, F., *Bohemia Sacra* (Düsseldorf, 1974).

Sellman (1955) :   Sellman, R.R., *The Crusades* (London, 1955).

Senior (1989) :   Senior, J.R., 'Stone Types', in Gilchrist and Mytum (1989).

Serra (1984) :   Serra, J.R. and Bignardi, M., 'Realvalle', in Lillich (1984).

Seward (1972) :   Seward, D., *The Monks of War* (London, 1972).

Seward (1974) :   Seward, D., *Monks and Wine* (London, 1979).

Shank (1995) :   Shank, L.T., 'Introduction', in Nicholas and Shank (1995).

Shelley (1926) :   Shelley, H. C., *Majorca* (London, 1926).

Sheppard (1997):   Sheppard, J. N., *The Buildwas books* (Oxford, 1997).

Sherwin (1927) :   Sherwin, C., 'Ford Abbey', *Trans. Devonshire Assoc.* LIX (1927).

Shoesmith
  and Richardson :   Shoesmith, R. and Richardson, R. (ed.), *A Definitive History of Dore Abbey* (1997) (Logaston Press, Herefordshire; 1997).

Silva (1981) :   Silva, E.P., *La Colonizacion Cisterciense en Galicia* (Univ. of Santiago de Compostela, 1981).

Sinor (1959) :   Sinor, D., *History of Hungary* (London, 1959).

Skelton (1843) :   Skelton, J., *Oxonia Antiqua Restaurata* (Oxford, 2nd. edn, 1843).

Smidt (1931) :   Smidt, C.M., *Cistercienser-Kirken i Løgum* (Copenhagen, 1931).

Snape (1968) :   Snape, R.H., *English Monastic Finances* (New York, 1926; reprinted, 1968).

Snell (1967) :   Snell, L.S., *Suppression of Religious Foundations of Devon and Cornwall* (Marazion, 1967).

Sommerfeldt (1971) : Sommerfeldt, J.R., 'Social Theory of St Bernard', in O'Callaghan (1971a),

Sommerfeldt (1976) :   Sommerfeldt, J.R. (ed.)., *Studies in Medieval Cistercian History* II (Cist. St. Ser. 24; Kalamazoo, 1976).
Sommerfeldt (1978) :   Sommerfeldt, J.R. (ed.)., *Cistercian Ideals and Reality* (I*bid*. 60; Kalamazoo, 1978).
Sommerfeldt (1980) :   Sommerfeldt, J.R., (ed.)., *Simplicity and Ordinariness* (*Ibid*. 61; 1980).
Sommerfeldt (1987) :   Sommerfeldt, J.R., (ed.)., *Erudition at God's Service* (*Ibid*. 98; 1987).
Sommerfeldt (1987a) :   Sommerfeldt, J.R., 'The Chimaera Revisited', *Cîteaux* XXXVIII (1987 : 1–2).
Sommer-Ramer(1982): Sommer-Ramer, C. and Braun, P., *Helvetia Sacra* III/3 (I) (1982).
Sonnet (1984) :   Sonnet, B., 'Le pont des Arvaux', *Mém. de la Comm. des antiquités du dépt. de la Côte-d'Or* 34 (1984–86).
Soriano (1979) :   Soriano, F.T., *Monasterios de Veruela, Rueda y Piedra* (Madrid, 1979).
Southern (1970) :   Southern, R.W., *Western Society and the Church in the Middle Ages* (Pelican Hist. of the Church, 2; 1970).
Sowell (1982) :   Sowell, J.E., 'Sacramenia', in Lillich (1982b).
Spahr (1953) :   Spahr, C., 'St Bernard et la Suisse', in *SB* (2)..
Spahr (1981) :   Spahr, K., 'Tennenbacher Güterbuch', *Cist. Chronik* N.S. 152 (88th Yr, 1981: 2).
Sparks (1978) :   Sparks, J.A., *In the Shadow of the Blackdowns* (Bradford-on-Avon, 1978).
Spence (1978) :   Spence, R., 'Gunther of Pairis', in Sommerfeldt (1978).
Speiss (1959) :   Speiss, K.H., 'Die Zisterzienserabteien zum Dortigen Berghau', *Analecta Cist.* XV (1959).
Spěváček (1996) :   Spěváček,J., 'The Cistercians in the Lands of Bohemia', *Cîteaux* XLVII (1996: 4–4).
Squire (1969) :   Squire, A., *Aelred of Rievaulx* (London, 1969).
St Clair Baddeley (1964) :   St Clair Baddeley, W., *Hailes Abbey* (National Trust, 1964).
St John Hope (1906) :   St John Hope, W.H. and Brakspear, H., 'Abbey of Beaulieu', *Arch. Jnl.* LXIII (1906).
Staab (1987) :   Staab, J. and others., *Eberbach im Rheingau* (Wiesbaden, 1987).
Stalley (1980) :   Stalley, R.A., 'Mellifont Abbey', *Proc. Royal Irish Acad.* 80, Sect. C. No. 14 (1980).
Stalley (1984) :   Stalley, R.A., 'Irish Gothic', in *The English in Medieval Ireland* (R.I.A., Dublin, 1984).
Stalley (1986) :   Stalley, R.A., 'Cistercian Churches of Ireland', in Parks and Norton (1986).
Stalley (1987) :   Stalley, R.A., *The Cistercian Monasteries of Ireland* (Yale U.P., 1987).
Steger (1984) :   Steger, M., 'Les Marques à La Chalade', *Cîteaux* XXXV (1984 : 1–2).
Steger (1985) :   Steger, M., 'Les Marques de Tacherons', *Ibid.* XXXVI (1985 : 1–2).
Stehlíková (1996) :   Stehlíková, D., 'Cistercian Seals in Bohemia and Moravia', *Cîteaux* XLVII (1996).
Steinwascher (1981) :   Steinwascher, G., *Die Zisterzienser-Stadthöfe in Köln* (Bergisch Gladbach, 1981).
Stéphan (1970) :   Stéphan, J., *Buckfast Abbey* (Bristol, 1970).
Sterum (1983) :   Sterum, N., 'Not on Rock', *Cîteaux* XXXIV (1983 : 3–4).
Stewart (1989) :   Stewart, F. J., 'Sweetheart Abbey', *Trans. Dumfriesshire and Galloway Nat. Hist. and Antiq. Soc. LXIV (1989).*
Stiegman (1987):   Stiegman, E., 'The Simplicity of the Cistercian Abbey Church', *Cîteaux* XXXVIII (1987 : 1–2).
Stones (1977) :   Stones, A., *Cistercian Thirteenth Century Book Decoration* (Univ. of Minnesota, 1977).
Storch (1958) :   Storch, W., *Klosterhof Siebenborn* (MS of 1958 at Abtei Himmerod).
Strzelczyk (1987):   Strzelczyk, J., *Historia I' Kultura Cystersów w Dawnej Polsce* (Poznan, 1987).
Stuart (1872) :   Stuart, J., *Records of Kinloss* (Edinburgh, 1872).
Sullivan (1989) :   Sullivan, L. M., 'Workers in Cistercian Legislation', *Cîteaux* XL (1989: 1–4).
Sullivan (1995) :   Sullivan, M.A., 'The *Vita Beatricis*', in Nichols and Shank (1995).
Sumption (1975) :   Sumption, J., *Pilgrimage* (London, 1975).
Sumption (1976) :   Sumption, J., *The Albigensian Crusade* (London, 1976).
Swartling (1967a) :   Swartling, I., *Nydala Abbey* (Stockholm Studies in History of Art, 11; 1967).

Swartling (1967b) :   Swartling, I., *Roma Abbey Church* (Antikvarist Archiv, 32; 1967).

Swartling (1969) :   Swartling, I., *Alvastra Abbey* (Stockholm Studies in History of Art, 17; 1969).

Swietek (1983) :   Swietek, F.R. and Deneen, T.M., 'The Episcopal Exemption of Savigny', *Church History* 52 (1983).

Swietek (1983a) :   Swietek, F.R., 'A Savigniac Miracle Story', *Cîteaux* XXXIV (1983: 3–4).

Swietek (1987) :   Swietek, F.R., 'King Henry II and Savigny', *Cîteaux* XXXVIII (1987 : 1–2).

Swietek (1993) :   Swietek, F.R., and Sommerfeldt, J.R., *Studiosorum Speculum* (Cist. Studies Ser. 141; Kalamazoo, 1993).

Sydow (1984) :   Sydow, J., *Die Zisterzienserabtei Bebenhausen* (Germania Sacra, N.S. 16 : Das Bistum Konstanz, 2; Berlin, 1984).

Szacherska (1968) :   Szacherska, S.M., *Rolaklasztorów duńskich w ekspansji Danii na Pomorzu Zachodnim u schylku XII wieka* (Wrocław, 1968).

Szacherska (1977) :   Szacherska, S.M., 'Political Role of the Danish Monasteries in Pomerania', *Medieval Scandinavia* 10 (1977).

Tadra (1904) :   Tadra, F., *Listy Klástera Zbraslavského* (Historický Archiv, 23; Prague, 1904).

Talbot (1939) :   Talbot, C.H., *Cistercian Abbeys of Scotland* (London, 1939)

Talbot (1951a) :   Talbot, C.H., 'The Testament of Gervase of Louth Park', *Analecta S.O. Cist.* VII (1951 : 1–2).

Talbot (1951b) :   Talbot, C.H., 'The *"De institutis inclusarum"* ', *Ibid.* (3–4).

Talbot (1954) :   Talbot, C.H., 'Notes on the Library of Pontigny', *Analecta S.O. Cist.* (1954).

Talbot (1954a) :   Talbot, C.H., 'Nicholas of St Alban's and St Bernard', *Revue Bénédictine* LXIV (1954).

Talbot (1958) :   Talbot, C.H., 'Beaulieu Account Book', *Cîteaux* IX (1958 : 3).

Talbot (1960) :   Talbot, C.H., 'Cîteaux and Scarborough', *Studia Monastica* II (1960 : 1).

Talbot (1963) :   Talbot, C.H., 'The English Cistercians and the Universities', *Los Monjes y los Etudios* (Poblet Abbey, 1963).

Tardieu (1986) :   Tardieu, J., 'Exploitation de la Forêt de Léoncel', *Revue Dromoise: Cahiers de Léoncel*, Sp. No. 2 (1986).

Tartara and Strola (1995) :   Tartara, L. and Strola, M., 'Saint Franca of Italy', in Nichols and Shank (1995).

Taupiac (1878) :   Taupiac, L., 'L'Abbaye de Belleperche', *Bull. de la Soc. Arch. de Tarn et Garonne* VI (1878).

Taylor (1899) :   Taylor, H., 'On Some Early Deeds', *Jnl. Chester and North Wales Arch. and Hist. Soc.* N.S. VI (1899).

Taylor-Vaisey (1976) :   Taylor-Vaisey, R., 'Cistercian Legislation', *Cîteaux* XXVII (1976 : 3).

Theurot (1995) :   Theurot, J., 'L'Abbaye de Cîteaux à Dole', *Cîteaux* XLVI: 1–2 (1995).

Thoen (1975) :   Thoen, H. and Milis, L., 'Het Site Ter Duinen', reviewed by Damme, J.V., *Cîteaux* XXVI (1975 : 3).

Thoma (1904) :   Thoma, W., *Die kolonisatriche Tätigkeit des Klosters Leubus* (Leipzig, 1904).

Thompson (1920) :   Thompson, J.W., 'The Cistercian Order and Colonisation', *American Jnl. of Theology* XXIV (1920).

Thompson (1928a) :   Thompson, J.W., *Feudal Germany* (Chicago, 1928).

Thompson (1928b) :   Thompson, A.H., 'A MS from Cîteaux', *Proc. Leeds Phil. and Lit. Soc.* (Lit. and Hist. Sect.) I, Pt. V (Jan. 1928).

Thompson (1931) :   Thompson, A.H. and others, 'The Cistercian Order in Ireland', *Arch. Jnl.* LXXXVIII (1931).

Thompson (1984) :   Thompson, S., 'Problems of the English Nunneries', in Nichols (1984).

Tinsley (1975) :   Tinsley, H.M., 'The Vegetation of Upper Nidderdale', in Phillips, A.D.M. and Turton, B.J., *Environment, man and economic changes* (London, 1975).

Thorpe (1978) :   Thorpe, L., *Gerald of Wales* (Penguin, 1978).

Tobin (1995) :   Tobin, S., *The Cistercians: Monks and Monasteries of Europe* (Herbert Press, 1995).

Toepfer (1983) :   Toepfer, M., *Die Konversen der Zisterzienser* (Berlin, 1983).

Tomasic (1972) :   Tomasic, T.M., 'William of Saint-Thierry', *Analecta S.O. Cist.* XXVIII (1972 : 1–2).

Tomé (1991) :   Tomé, A. M., *El monasterio cisterciense eu el origen los vinos españoles* (Madrid, 1991).

Tomkinson (1985) :   Tomkinson, J., 'History of Hulton Abbey', *Staffs. Archaeol. Studies* 2 (1985).

Tort (1974) :   Tort, J.S., *El Monasterio de Poblet* (Barcelona, 1974).

Tosti-Croce (1994) :   Tosti-Croce, M.R., 'Les granges en Italie central', in Pressouyre (1994).

Tower (und.) :   Tower, M., *Il Convento di Palazzola* (Rome, undated).

Traissac (1960) :   Traissac, E., 'Fontguilhem et Rivet', *Rev. Hist. de Bordeaux* N.S. 9 (1960 : 2–3).

Treuille (1978) :   Treuille, H., 'Les chemins dans les Landes', *Bull. de la Soc. de Borda* (1978).

Tribout (1966) :   Tribout de Morembert, H., 'L'Abbaye du Gard', *Cîteaux* XVII (1966 : 1–2).

Tribout (1972) :   Tribout de Morembert, H., 'Le maison du Petit-Gard', *Ibid.* XXIII (1972 : 2).

Tromp (1989) :   Tromp, C., *Groninger Kloosters* (Groninger Historische Reeks, 5; Assen/Maastricht, 1989).

Trout (1974) :   Trout, J.M., 'Alan of Lille', *Analecta Cist.* (1974 : 1).

Turner (1987) :   Turner, D.J., in Bird (1987).

Turner (1964) :   Turner, J. in *New Phytologist* 63 (1964).

Tuulse (1942) :   Tuulse, A., *Die Burgen in Estland und Lettland* (Ŏpetamd Eesti Seltsi Toimetused, XXXIII; Dorpat, 1942).

Tyburg (1964) :   Tyburg, W., 'San Bernardo', *Cistercium* XVI : No. 91 (Mar.-Apl. 1964).

Uitterdijk (1874) :   Uitterdijk, M.J.N., 'L'Abbaye d'Aduard', *Bull. Monumental* 5th Ser., Tom. 2, Vol. 40 (1874).

Urban (1975) :   Urban, W. L., *The Baltic Crusade* (Northern Illinois U.P., 1975).

Valter (1985) :   Valter, I., 'Cisterzi monostorok kutatása', *Studia Comitatensia* (Szentendre, 1985).

Valter (1994) :   Valter, I., 'Quelques établissements proto-industriels', in Pressouyre (1994).

Van Damme (1963) :   Van Damme, J-B., 'La Charte de Charité de Chalais', *Cîteaux* XIV (1963: 2).

Vanden Bemden   Vanden Bemden, Y. and Kerr, J., 'The Glass of Herkenrode Abbey',
(1986) :   *Archaeologia* 108 (1986).

Van Der Meer (1965) :   Van Der Meer, F., *Atlas de l'Ordre Cistercien* (Paris : Brussels, 1965).

Van Derveeghde   Van Derveeghde, D., 'La Houille du Val Saint-Lambert', *Le Moyen Âge*
(1946) :   LII (1946 : 2).

Van Derveeghde   Van Derveeghde, D., 'Le Domaine du Val Saint-Lambert', *Bibl. Faculté*
(1955) :   *Phil. et Lettres, Univ. de Liége* CXXX (1955).

Van Nerom (1983) :   Van Nerom, C., 'La donation d'Eastchurch', *Cîteaux* XXXIV (1983 : 1–2).

Van Nerom (1984a) :   Van Nerom, C., 'The grant of Eastchurch', *Arch. Cantiana* CI (1984).

Van Nerom (1984b) :   Van Nerom, C., 'Le Pavement des Dunes', *Cîteaux* XXXV (1984 : 3–4).

Van Nerom (1993) :   Van Nerom, C., 'Cistercian Tiles,' in Lillich (1993).

Vaslin (1990) :   Vaslin, M., 'Notre-Damede Fontmorigny', in Pressouyre (1990).

Veeder (1978) :   Veeder, M.H., 'Negation and Apocalypse', in Sommerfeldt (1978).

Veldeman (1965a) :   Veldeman, G., 'De Abdij van Zwijveke', *Cîteaux* XVI (1965 : 2).

Veldeman (1965b) :   Veldeman, G., continued in *Ibid.* XVI (1965 : 4).

Veldeman (1966) :   Veldeman, G., continued in *Ibid.* XVII (1966 : 3).

Verhulst (1972) :   Verhulst, A., 'La Laine indigene dans les Pays-Bas', *Revue Historique* 96 (1972).

Verna (1983) :   Verna, C., 'La Sidérurgie Cistercienne', in Higounet (1983).

Verna and Benoît   Verna, C. and Benoît, P., 'La Sidérurgie de Clairvaux', in Leroux
(1991) :   (1991).

Viard (1940) :   Viard, J., 'États des Abbayes Cisterciennes', *Rev. d'Hist. de l'Église de France* I (1940).

Vila-Grau (1993) :   Vila Grau, 'Cistercian Stained Glass at Santes Creus', in Lillich (1993).

Villers (1981) :   'L'Église de Villers-la-Ville', *Bull. de la Comm. Royale des Monum. et des Sites* N.S. X (Brussels, 1981).

Volk (1984) :   Volk, O., *Salzproduktion und Salzhandel Mittelalterlicher Zisterzienserklöster* (Vorträge und Forschungen, 30; 1984).

Vongrey and Hervay (1967):   Vongrey, F. and Hervay, F., 'Kritische Bemerkungen', *Analecta Cist.* XXIII (1967).

Všetečková (1996) :   Všetečková, Z., 'The Osek Lectionary', *Cîteaux* XLVII (1996).

Waddell (1976) :   Waddell, C., 'Peter Abelard's Letter 10', in Sommerfeldt (1976).

Waddell (1978a) :   Waddell, C., 'The Exordium Cistercii and the Summa Cartae Caritatis', in Sommerfeldt (1978).

Waddell (1978b) :   Waddell, C., 'Humility and the Sacraments of Faith', *Ibid.*

Waddell (1982) :   Waddell, C., 'Prelude to a Feast of Freedom', *Cîteaux* XXXIII (1982 : 3–4).

Waddell (1988) :   Waddell, C., 'The Place and Meaning of the Work of God', *Cist. Studies* XXIII (1988 : 1).

Waddell (1993) :   Waddell, C., 'A New Provisional Edition of the Statutes', in Swietek (1993).

Waddell (1994) :   Waddell, C., 'The Cistercian Institutes', in Pressouyre (1994).

Waddell (1995) :   Waddell, C., 'Ida of Léau', in Nichols and Shank (1995).

Waeber-Antiglio?:   Waeber-Antiglio, C., *Hauterive* (Fribourg, 1976).

Wagner (1976) :   Wagner, H., *Geschichte der Zisterzienserabtei Bildhausen* (Mainfränkische Studien, 15; Würzburg, 1976).

Wagner-Rieger (1956) :   Wagner-Rieger, R., *Die Italienische Baukunst Zu Beginn Der Gotik* I (1956), II (1957; Graz : Cologne).

Waites (1967) :   Waites, B., *Moorland and Vale-Land Farming in NE Yorkshire* (Borthwick Papers, 32; York, 1967).

Walford (1857) :   Walford, W. S. and Way, A., 'Examples of Medieval Seals', *Archaeol. Jnl.* XIV (1857).

Walker (1983) :   Walker, G., 'The Simplicity of our Order', *Tjurunga* 25 (1983).

Walker (1984) :   Walker, G., continued in *Ibid.* 27 (1984).

Waller (1903) :   Waller, W.C., 'Records of Tiltey Abbey', *Trans. Essex Arch. Soc.* N.S. VIII (1903).

Walsh (1982) :   Walsh, D.A., 'Bordesley', in Lillich (1982b).

Wamba (1986) :   Wamba, J.P.E., *El Cister en Castille y León* (Salamanca, 1986).

Wamba (1994) :   Wamba, J.P.E., 'La Péninsula ibérique', in Pressouyre (1994).

Ward (1971) :   Ward, P., *Touring Lebanon* (1971).

Wardrop (1987) :   Wardrop, J., *Fountains Abbey and its Benefactors* (Kalamazoo, 1987).

Wasowicz (1962) :   Wasowicz, T., 'O Roli Konwersów', in *Wieki Średnie Prace ofiarowane T. Manteufflowi* Warsaw, 1962).

Watson (1946) :   Watson, G.P.H., 'Glenluce Abbey', *Trans. Dumfriesshire and Galloway Nat. Hist. and Antiq. Soc. XXV (1946–7)*.

Watt (1972) :   Watt, J., *The Church in Medieval Ireland* (Dublin, 1972).

Watzl (1960) :   Watzl, H., 'Fragmente eines Heiligenkreuzzer Visitations-chartenprotokolls', *Cist. Chronik* N.S. 53, Pt. 4 (Dec. 1960).

Weale (1867) :   Weale, W.H.J., 'Abbaye de Ter Doest', *La Flandre* I (1867–8).

Weatherill (1954) :   Weatherill, J., 'Rievaulx Abbey', *Yorkshire Arch. Jnl.* XXXVIII (1954 : 3).

Weaver (1906) :   Weaver, F.W., 'Cleeve Abbey', *Proc. Somerset Arch. and Nat. Hist. Soc.* LII (1906 : 2).

Webber (1976) :   Webber, R., *The Devon and Somerset Blackdowns* (London, 1976).

Weissenberger (1960) : Weissenberger, P., 'Wirtschaftesgeschichtliche Nachrichten über einige bayrische Cist. – Frauenkloster', *Cist. Chronik* N.S. 51/2 (July, 1960).

Werland (1968) :   Werland, W., *Marienfelder Chronik* (Gemeinde Marienfeld, 1968).

Wetesko (1991) :   Wetesko, L., 'Cistercian monks in medieval Poland', in Dobosz (1991).

Whelan (und.) :   Whelan, K., *Tintern Abbey* (Saltmills, County Wexford; undated).

White (1938) :   White, L.T., *Latin Monasticism in Norman Sicily* (Medieval Acad. of America, Cambridge, Mass; Monograph 13, 1938).

White (1987) :   White, R. B., 'Excavations at Maenan Abbey', *Arch. Camb.* CXXXVI (1987).

Whitley (1920) :   Whitley, H.M., 'Sanctuary in Sussex', *Sussex Arch. Collns.* LXI (1920).

Whone (1987) :   Whone, H., *Fountains Abbey* (Settle, 1987).

Wiemer (1982) :   Wiemer, W., 'Die Geometrie des Ebracher Kirchenplans', *Kunst Chronik* XXXV (1982 : 1).

Wildhaber (1986) :   Wildhaber, B., 'Catalogue des Établissments Cisterciens', in Privat (1986).
Willems (1957) :   Willems, E., *Esquisse Histoire de l'Ordre de Cîteaux* (1957).
Willesme (1986) :   Willesme, J-P., 'Les Cisterciens à Paris', *Cîteaux* XXXVII (1986 : 1–2).
Williams (1889) :   Williams, S.W., *The Cistercian Abbey of Strata Florida* (London, 1889).
Williams (1890) :   Williams, S.W., 'The Abbey of Cwmhir', *Arch. Camb.* 1890.
Williams (1891) :   Williams, S.W., See: Jones (1891).
Williams (1935) :   Williams, W., *St Bernard of Clairvaux* (Manchester, 1935).
Williams (1965) :   Williams, B.C.J., 'Garendon Abbey', *Bull. Loughborough and Dist. Arch. Soc.* 8 (1965).
Williams (1966) :   Williams, D. H., 'Abbey Dore', *Monmouthshire Antiq.* II: 2 (1966).
Williams (1971) :   Williams, D. H., 'Fasti Cistercienses Cambrenses', *Bull. Board of Celtic Studies* XXIV : 2 (1971), with continuation in XXV: 2 (1973).
Williams (1974) :   Williams, D. H., 'Cistercian Settlement in the Lebanon', *Cîteaux* XXV (1974 : 1).
Williams (1975) :   Williams, D. H., 'Cistercian Nunneries in Medieval Wales', *Cîteaux* XXVI (1975 : 3).
Williams (1976) :   Williams, D. H., *White Monks in Gwent and the Border* (Pontypool, 1976).
Williams (1978) :   Williams, D. H., 'East of the Oder', *Cîteaux* XXIX (1978: 3–4).
Williams (1983) :   Williams, D. H., 'Corrodians and Residential Servants in Tudor Cistercian Monasteries', *Cîteaux* XXXIV (1983: 1–2).
Williams (1984) :   Williams, D. H., *The Welsh Cistercians* I and II (Caldey Island, 1984).
Williams (1984b) :   Williams, D. H., 'The Seal in Cistercian Usage', in: Chauvin (1982a) [II: 3; 1984].
Williams (1987) :   Williams, D. H., 'Seals of Cistercian Monasteries', *Arch. Camb.* CXXXVI (1987).
Williams (1990) :   Williams, D. H. (and Hudson, R), 'Gwent Seals : I', *Monmouthshire Antiq.* VI (1990).
Williams (1990a) :   Williams, D. H., *Atlas of Cistercian Lands in Wales* (Cardiff, 1990).
Williams (1991) :   Williams, D. H., 'Layfolk within Cistercian Precincts', in Loades (1991).
Williams (1992) :   Williams, D. H., 'The Life and Work of Stephen William Williams', *Mont. Collns.* 80 (1992).
Williams (1993) :   Williams, D. H., *Catalogue of Seals in the National Museum of Wales* I (Cardiff, 1993).
Williams (1997) :   Williams, D. H., 'The Abbey of Dore', in Shoesmith and Richardson (1995).
Williams-Jones (1957) : Williams-Jones, K., 'Llywelyn's Charter to Cymer Abbey', *Jnl. Merioneth Hist. and Rec. Soc.* III: 1 (1957).
Wilson (1986) :   Wilson, C., 'The Cistercians as "Missionaries of Gothic" ', in Norton and Park (1986).
Winkless (1990) :   Winkless, D., *Hailes Abbey* (Spredden Press, Northumberland; 1990).
Winter (1868) :   Winter, F., *Die Cistercienser des Nordöstlichen Deutschlands* (Gotha, 1868–71).
Wise (1985) :   Wise, P.J., 'Hulton Abbey', *Staffordshire Arch. Studies* 2 (1985).
Wiswe (1953) :   Wiswe, H., 'Grangien niedersächsischer Zisterzienserklöster', *Braunschweigisches Jahrbuch* 34 (1953).
Wollenberg (1984) :   Wollenberg, K., *Die Entwicklung der Eigenwirtschaft des Zisterzienserklösters Fürstenfeld* (Frankfurt-am-Main, 1984).
Wright (1905) :   Wright, T., *Historical Works of Giraldus Cambrensis* (1905).
Wright (1972) :   Wright, G.N., 'Order from a Wilderness', *Country Life* (Dec. 28, 1972).
Wulf (1944) :   Wulf, A., *Compendium of the History of the Cistercian Order* (Gethsemani Abbey, 1944).
Wullschleger (1986) :   Wullschleger, M., 'Les domaines de l'Abbaye du Léoncel', *Les Moines et la Forêt* (Cahiers de Léoncel, 2; Revue Dromoise, Sp. No. 1986).
Wullschleger (1991) :   Wullschleger, M. and others, *Léoncel* (Valence, 1991).
Wullschleger (1995) :   Wullschleger, M., 'Le Vercors', *Cîteaux* XLVI (1995).
Wyrwa (1984) :   Wyrwa, A.M., *Luckna-Secunda Filia Veteris-Montis* (Poznań, 1984).
Wyrwa (1989) :   Wyrwa, A.M., *Lekno: przewodnik po wykopaliskach* (Poznań, 1989).
Wyrwa (1992) :   Wyrwa, A.M., 'Cistercian monasteries in Wielkopolska', *Cîteaux* XLIII (1992).

Yañez Neira (1959) :   Yañez Neira, M.D.Y., 'Alfonso VII', *Cistercium* 11 : No. 61 (1959).

Yañez Neira (1970) :   Yañez Neira, M.D.Y., 'Influencia de la Orden Cisterciense', *Hidalguia* 18 : No. 101 (July-Aug. 1970).

Yañez Neira (1973) :   Yañez Neira, M.D.Y., 'Un español abad de Claraval', *Cistercium* 25 : No. 132 (1973).

Yañez Neira (1975a) :   Yañez Neira, M.D.Y., 'El monasterio de Herrera', *Ibid.* 27 : No. 137 (1975).

Yañez Neira (1975b) :   Yañez Neira, M.D.Y., 'San Clemente de Toledo', *Ibid.* 27 : No. 139 (1975).

Yañez Neira (1977) :   Yañez Neira, M.D.Y., 'El monasterio del Osera', *Ibid.* 29 : 148 (1977).

Yañez Neira (1982) :   Yañez Neira, M.D.Y., 'El monasterio del Benavente', *Cistercium* 34 : No. 161 (1982).

Yañez Neira (1989) :   Yañez Neira, M.D.Y., 'La Orden Concepcionista y el Cister', *Cîteaux* XL (1989: 1–4).

Yohe (1995) :   Yohe, K.T.P., 'Aelred's Guidelines', *Cîteaux* XLVI (1995: 3–4).

Zadnikar (1980) :   Zadnikar, M., 'Le batisseur bourguignon, Michael', *Cîteaux* XXXI (1980).

Zakin (1979) :   Zakin, H.J., *French Cistercian Grisaille Glass* (New York, 1979).

Zakin (1982) :   Zakin, H.J., 'Cistercian Glass', in Lillich (1982b).

Zakrzewski (1907) :   Zakrzewski, S., 'Analecta Cisterciensia', *Rozprawy Akademii Umiejętności wydział Historyczno-Filoficzny* Ser. II, Vol. XXIV (Kraków, 1907).

Załuska (1989) :   Załuska, Y., *L'enluminure et le Scriptorium de Cîteaux au XIIᵉ siècle* (Cîteaux, 1989).

Zanetti (1959) :   Zanetti, G., 'I Cistercensi in Sardegna', *Rendiconti del'Istituto Lombardo di accademia di scienze e lettere* 93 : 2 (Milan, 1959).

Zarnecki (1972) :   Zarnecki, G., *The Monastic Achievement* (London, 1972).

Index of Cistercian Abbeys

Key:
A: Austria
B: Belgium
C: Czech Republic
Cr: Croatia
Cy: Cyprus
D: Denmark
E: England
Es: Estonia

F: France
G: Germany
Gr: Greece
H: Hungary
Ho: Holland
I: Ireland
It: Italy
L: Lithuania

La: Latvia
Ln: Lebanon
Lu: Luxembourg
N: Norway
P: Poland
Pt: Portugal
R: Rumania
S: Scotland

Sb: Serbia
Sl: Slovak Republic
Slv: Slovenia
Sw: Sweden
Sy: 'Syria' (medieval)
Sz: Switzerland
T: Turkey
W: Wales

(The 'proto-abbeys' are indicated in **bold** type).

Abbeydorney (I) 180, 190 (n. 120).
Abbeylara (I) 58.
Abbeyleix (I) 177, 292.
Abbeyshrule (I) 179.
Aberconwy (W) 11, 38, 55, 73, 81, 92 (n. 206), 100, 110, 123–24, 127–28, 133, 143, 146, 148, 157, 180, 183, 216, 219, 279, 292, 301, 304, 317, 332–335, 347, 349, 360, 386–87, 396 (and see Maenan).
Ábrahám (H) 137, 175, 185.
Acey (F) 42, 220.
Acquafredda (It) 111, 176.
Acqualonga (It) 184.
Aduard (Ho) 22, 57, 97, 110, 118, 129, 131–132, 188, 196, 202–03, 214, 217, 226, 237 (n. 408), 242, 245, 250, 277, 321, 371, 385, 396, 417.
Águiar (Pt) 175, 214.
Águias (Pt) 76.
Aiguebelle (F) 37, 65, 72, 121, 132,147, 164, 172, 179, 185, 220, 240, 244, 285, 287, 307, 351–52, 372, 393.
Alafões (Pt) 16.
Alcobaça (Pt) 9–10, 16, 86, 97, 99, 102–03, 119, 121–22, 137, 146, 162, 175–76, 180, 208, 213–14, 240, 271, 296, 302, 306, 322. 334, 336, 360, 366, 373, 390, 397, 404, 417.
Alderspach (al. Aldersbach) (G) 108, 159, 376–77.
Altenberg (G) 9, 16, 53, 57, 62, 198, 214–216, 219–222, 278–79, 287, 310, 318, 335, 339, 341, 386, 389–96.
Altofonte (It) 178.
Altzelle (al. Altenzelle, G) 9, 100, 102, 126, 147, 166, 174, 266, 339, 367, 373.
Alvastra (Sw) 11, 21, 43, 59, 75, 85, 91 (n. 21), 108, 111, 127, 132, 173, 181, 195, 196, 226, 248, 374.

Amelunxborn (G) 53, 58, 87, 119, 165, 173, 218, 250, 252, 319, 360, 376–78, 391.
Arabona (It) 5, 18, 195, 218, 224.
Ardorel (F) 23, 287.
Armentera (Sp) 147.
Arnsburg (G) 97, 120, 122, 207–08, 228, 241, 251, 270, 376–77, 394.
Ås (Sw) 127, 369.
Assaroe (I) 133, 292.
Aubepierre (F) 61, 278, 296, 318, 331, 391.
Auberive (F) 37–39, 60, 259, 291, 341, 367, 376–77, 390, 393.
Aubignac (F) 175.
Aulne (B) 5, 39, 53, 65, 81–82, 85, 102, 173, 242, 287, 407–09.
Aulps (F) 2, 41, 88, 121, 226, 376–77.
Aunay (al. Aulnay, F) 22, 173, 214, 218, 242, 250, 259, 287, 386.

Balamand (al. Belmont, Ln) 19, 43, 144, 154, 177–78, 222.
Balerne (F) 14, 41, 80, 90, 278, 324, 340, 376–79.
Balmerino (S) 9, 75, 91 (n. 26), 117, 261, 317, 321, 338, 355, 366, 370–71, 392.
Baltinglass (I) 111, 226, 288, 361, 371, 376–77.
Barbeaux (F) 9, 37, 125, 132, 182.
Barbery (F) 62.
Barona (It) 148, 185.
Barzelle(F) 103, 145, 174.
Basingwerk (W) 43, 58, 130, 143, 156, 194, 220, 226, 231, 240, 245, 318, 321, 335, 347, 353, 357, 372–73, 376–77, 380, 388.
Baudeloo (B) 39, 60, 87–88, 277.
Baumgarten (F) 319.
Baumgartenberg (A) 64, 159, 106, 145, 376–77.
Beaubec (F) 20, 121, 146, 203,

220, 250, 276, 296, 307, 337, 339, 355, 369, 376–79, 386, 391, 396, 415.
Beaugerais (F) 148.
Beaulieu (E) 8, 10, 56, 73, 77, 83, 88–89, 101–02, 108, 111, 117–18, 120–21, 124–28, 131–32, 136, 148, 150, 154, 177–79, 181, 188, 195–209, 210 (n. 163), 215–16, 223–24, 229, 232, 245, 251, 267, 270–73, 282–292, 298–301, 305, 315–326, 331–339, 348, 352–53, 354–57, 360, 365–73, 376–77, 380, 387–88, 395–96.
Beaulieu-by-Nicosia (Cy) 19, 183.
Beaulieu-en-Bassigny (F) 132, 374.
Beaulieu-en-Rouergue (al. Belloc, F) 12, 216.
Beaupré (F, Meurthe-et-Moselle) 78, 374, 376–77.
Beaupré (F, Oise) 174, 404, ? 78, 217, 405.
Bebenhausen (G) 120, 203, 214, 241, 251, 265, 279, 324, 326, 393, 395.
Bective (I) 136, 174.
Bégard (F) 23, 64, 130, 417.
Bélakút (al. Pétervárad/ Petrovárad, Slavonia/Sb) 10, 59, 159, 376–77.
Bélapátfalva (H) 195, 215, 221.
Bellebranche (F) 369.
Belleperche (F) 73, 145, 183, 217.
Bellevaux (F) 14, 42, 53, 132, 152, 200, 299, 336, 375–77, 389.
Benifazá (Sp) 16.
Berdoues (F) 42, 54, 56, 79–82, 107, 132, 251, 260, 301, 308, 317, 323, 347, 389.
Biddlesden (E) 109, 186, 195, 282, 320, 390.
Bildhausen (G) 353.
Bindon (E) 12, 111, 126, 128, 144, 153, 182, 188, 195,

Index of Cistercian Nunneries

Index of Principal Persons

(ab: abbot, abp: archbishop, bl: *beatus,* bp: bishop, *conv: conversus,* kg: king, mk: monk, st: saint)

Index of Principal Places

Index of Principal Subjects

(Principal entries are indicated in **bold** type).

Gatehouse, with adjacent Chapel: Riddagshausen Abbey, Germany.

Monastery Church, Cîrţa Abbey, Rumania.

Precinct wall: Sweetheart (New) Abbey, Scotland

Conversi Lane: Byland Abbey, England.